HOCKEY REGISTER

S0-BGM-410

1986-87 EDITION

Editor/Hockey Register
LARRY WIGGE

Compiled by
FRANK POLNASZEK

Contributing Editors/Hockey Register
CRAIG CARTER
BARRY SIEGEL
DAVE SLOAN

President-Chief Executive Officer
RICHARD WATERS

Editor
TOM BARNIDGE

Director of Books and Periodicals
RON SMITH

Published by

The Sporting News

1212 North Lindbergh Boulevard
P.O. Box 56 — St. Louis, MO 63166

Copyright © 1986
The Sporting News Publishing Company

A Times Mirror
Company

ISBN 0-89204-230-3   ISSN 0090-2292

Table of Contents

Players included are those who played in at least one National Hockey League game in 1985-86 and selected invitees to training camps.

—————◆—————

ON THE COVER: Pittsburgh center Mario Lemieux blossomed during the 1985-86 season, finishing second in the National Hockey League with 141 points.

— Photograph by John Tremmel

EXPLANATIONS OF AWARDS

National Hockey League

HART MEMORIAL TROPHY (or Hart Trophy)—Most Valuable Player.
LADY BYNG MEMORIAL TROPHY (or Lady Byng Trophy)—Awarded to player exhibiting best type of sportsmanship and gentlemanly conduct combined with a high standard of playing ability.
CALDER MEMORIAL TROPHY (or Calder Trophy)—Rookie-of-the-Year.
WILLIAM JENNINGS TROPHY —Awarded to leading goaltender(s) based on goals against average. Must appear in minimum of 25 games to be eligible.
ART ROSS TROPHY—Leading scorer.
JAMES NORRIS MEMORIAL TROPHY—Outstanding defenseman.
CONN SMYTHE TROPHY—Most Valuable Player during Stanley Cup Playoffs.
BILL MASTERTON MEMORIAL TROPHY—Awarded to player who best exemplifies qualities of perseverance, sportsmanship and dedication to hockey.
LESTER PATRICK TROPHY—For outstanding service to hockey in the United States.
VEZINA MEMORIAL TROPHY (or Vezina Trophy)—Top goaltender.

American Hockey League

HARRY "HAP" HOLMES MEMORIAL TROPHY—Leading goaltender.
LES CUNNINGHAM AWARD (or Plaque)—Most Valuable Player.
DUDLEY "RED" GARRETT MEMORIAL TROPHY (or Award)—Rookie-of-the-Year.
EDDIE SHORE PLAQUE—Outstanding defenseman.
JOHN G. SOLLENBERGER TROPHY—Leading scorer (since 1955-56).
CARL LISCOMBE TROPHY—Leading scorer (prior to 1955-56).

Western Hockey League

FRED J. HUME AWARD—Most Gentlemanly Player.
LEADER CUP—Most Valuable Player.
HAL LAYCOE CUP—Outstanding defenseman.
GUYLE FIELDER CUP—Leading scorer.

International Hockey League

LEO P. LAMOUREUX MEMORIAL TROPHY—Leading scorer (since 1960-61).
GEORGE H. WILKENSON TROPHY—Leading scorer (1946-47 thru 1959-60).
GOVERNORS' TROPHY—Outstanding defenseman.
GARY LONGMAN MEMORIAL TROPHY—Rookie-of-the-Year.
JAMES NORRIS MEMORIAL TROPHY—Leading goaltender(s) based on goals against. (Formerly awarded to goaltender on first All-Star team.)
JAMES GATSCHENE MEMORIAL TROPHY—Most Valuable Player.

Other Leagues

BOB GASSOFF TROPHY—Central Hockey League's most improved defenseman (new in 1977-78).
TOMMY IVAN TROPHY—Most Valuable Player in Central Hockey League.
TERRY SAWCHUK AWARD—Leading goaltender in CHL.
EDDIE POWERS MEMORIAL TROPHY—Leading scorer in Jr. "A" OHA.
DAVE PINKNEY TROPHY—Leading goaltender in Jr. "A" OHA.
MAX KAMINSKY MEMORIAL TROPHY—Best defenseman in Jr. "A" OHA.
RED TILSON MEMORIAL TROPHY—Most Valuable Player in Jr. "A" OHA.

EXPLANATION OF ABBREVIATIONS

A—Assists.
AHL—American Hockey League.
AJHL—Alberta Junior Hockey League.
ASHL—Alberta Senior Hockey League.
Avg.—Goals against per game average.
BCHL—British Columbia Hockey League.
CAHL—Central Alberta Hockey League.
CCHA—Central Collegiate Hockey Association.
Cent. OHA—Central Ontario Hockey Association.
CHL—California Hockey League or Central Hockey League.
CMJHL—Canadian Major Junior Hockey League.
CPHL—Central Pro Hockey League.
EHL—Eastern Hockey League.
EPHL—Eastern Pro Hockey League.
G—Goals scored.
Games—Games played.
Goals—Goals against.
IHL—International Hockey League.
MJHL—Manitoba Junior Hockey League or Midwest Junior Hockey League.
NAHL—North American Hockey League.
NEHL—Northeastern Hockey League.
NHL—National Hockey League.
NOHA—Northern Ontario Hockey Association.
NSHL—North Shore (New Brunswick) Hockey League.
NYMJHA—New York Metropolitan Junior Hockey Association.
OHA—Ontario Hockey Association.
OMJHL—Ontario Major Junior Hockey League.
OPHL—Ontario Provincial Hockey League.
Pen.—Minutes in penalties.
PHL—Prairie Hockey League.
Pts.—Points.
QHL—Quebec Hockey League.
QJHL—Quebec Junior Hockey League.
SHL—Southern Hockey League.
SJHL—Saskatchewan Junior Hockey League.
SOJHL—Southern Ontario Junior Hockey League.
TBJHL—Thunder Bay Junior Hockey League.
USHL—United States Hockey League.
WCHA—Western Collegiate Hockey Association.
WCHL—Western Canada Hockey League (Juniors).
WCJHL—Western Canada Junior League.
WHA—World Hockey Association.
WHL—Western Hockey League.
WHL—Western Hockey League (Junior "A" League since 1978-79).
WIHL—Western International Hockey League.
WOJHL—Western Ontario Junior Hockey League.
*—Indicates either led or was tied for league lead.
    Footnotes (a) indicates player was member of first all-star team.
    Footnotes (b) indicates player was member of second all-star team.
Scoring totals (goals plus assists) do not always balance in certain leagues due to un-balanced schedules and scoring system.
Junior "A" Ontario Hockey Association also includes Metro League and OHA Major Junior.
Quebec Junior Hockey League also includes Montreal Metro League and OJHL Major.

FORWARDS AND DEFENSEMEN

(a)—First team all-star selection. (b)—Second team. * Denotes league leader.

ALLAN ACTON

Left Wing . . . 5'11" . . . 190 lbs. . . . Born, Unity, Sask., August 28, 1965 . . . Shoots left . . . Also plays Center.

Year	Team	League	Games	G.	A.	Pts.	Pen.
1981-82—Battleford Barons		SJHL	53	15	21	36	173
1982-83—Saskatoon Blades (c)		WHL	56	5	13	18	41
1983-84—Saskatoon Blades		WHL	14	3	3	6	19
1983-84—Regina Pats (d)		WHL	54	7	11	18	56
1984-85—Regina Pats		WHL	72	22	45	67	78
1985-86—Regina Pats		WHL	62	44	45	89	52

(c)—June, 1983—Drafted by Hartford Whalers in NHL entry draft. Thirteenth Whalers pick, 204th overall, 11th round.

(d)—June, 1984—Released by Hartford Whalers.

KEITH EDWARD ACTON

Center . . . 5'10" . . . 167 lbs. . . . Born, Newmarket, Ont., April 15, 1958 . . . Shoots left . . . (April 20, 1984)—Injured left wrist in playoff game at St. Louis.

Year	Team	League	Games	G.	A.	Pts.	Pen.
1974-75—Wexford Raiders		OPJHL	43	23	29	52	46
1975-76—Peterborough Petes		Jr."A"OHA	35	9	17	26	30
1976-77—Peterborough Petes		Jr."A"OHA	65	52	69	121	93
1977-78—Peterborough Petes (c)		Jr."A"OHA	68	42	86	128	52
1978-79—Nova Scotia Voyageurs		AHL	79	15	26	41	22
1979-80—Nova Scotia Voyageurs (b)		AHL	75	45	53	98	38
1979-80—Montreal Canadiens		NHL	2	0	1	1	0
1980-81—Montreal Canadiens		NHL	61	15	24	39	74
1981-82—Montreal Canadiens		NHL	78	36	52	88	88
1982-83—Montreal Canadiens		NHL	78	24	26	50	63
1983-84—Montreal Canadiens (d)		NHL	9	3	7	10	4
1983-84—Minnesota North Stars		NHL	62	17	38	55	60
1984-85—Minnesota North Stars		NHL	78	20	38	58	90
1985-86—Minnesota North Stars		NHL	79	26	32	58	100
NHL TOTALS			457	141	218	359	479

(c)—Drafted from Peterborough Petes by Montreal Canadiens in sixth round of 1978 amateur draft.

(d)—October, 1983—Traded with Mark Napier and third round 1984 draft pick (Kenneth Hodge) by Montreal Canadiens to Minnesota North Stars for Bobby Smith.

RUSSELL NORM ADAM

Center . . . 5'10" . . . 185 lbs. . . . Born, Windsor, Ont., May 5, 1961 . . . Shoots left . . . Also plays Left Wing . . . (December, 1985)—Broken wrist.

Year	Team	League	Games	G.	A.	Pts.	Pen.
1977-78—Windsor Spitfires		OMJHL	3	1	2	3	0
1978-79—Kitchener Rangers		OMJHL	63	20	17	37	37
1979-80—Kitchener Rangers (c)		OMJHL	54	37	34	71	143
1980-81—Kitchener Rangers		OHL	64	37	50	87	215
1981-82—New Brunswick Hawks		AHL	52	11	21	32	50
1982-83—Toronto Maple Leafs		NHL	8	1	2	3	11
1982-83—St. Catharines Saints		AHL	64	19	17	36	119
1983-84—St. Catharines Saints		AHL	70	32	24	56	76
1984-85—Fort Wayne Komets		IHL	60	28	46	74	56
1985-86—Fort Wayne Komets (d)		IHL	48	24	37	61	36
NHL TOTALS			8	1	2	3	11

(c)—June, 1980—Drafted as underage junior by Toronto Maple Leafs in 1980 NHL entry draft. Seventh Maple Leafs pick, 137th overall, seventh round.

(d)—Led IHL Playoffs with 13 assists.

GREG ADAMS

Center . . . 6'2" . . . 185 lbs. . . . Born, Nelson, B.C., August 1, 1963 . . . Shoots left.

Year	Team	League	Games	G.	A.	Pts.	Pen.
1980-81—Kelowna Wings		BCJHL	47	40	50	90	16
1981-82—Kelowna Wings		BCJHL	45	31	42	73	24
1982-83—Northern Arizona Univ.		NCAA	29	14	21	35	46
1983-84—Northern Arizona Univ. (c)		NCAA	47	40	50	90	16

Year	Team	League	Games	G.	A.	Pts.	Pen.
1984-85—Maine Mariners		AHL	41	15	20	35	12
1984-85—New Jersey Devils		NHL	36	12	9	21	14
1985-86—New Jersey Devils		NHL	78	35	43	78	30
NHL TOTALS			114	47	52	99	44

(c)—June, 1984—Signed by New Jersey Devils as a free agent.

GREGORY CHARLES ADAMS

Left Wing . . . 6'1" . . . 190 lbs. . . . Born, Duncan, B. C., May 31, 1960 . . . Shoots left.

Year	Team	League	Games	G.	A.	Pts.	Pen.
1977-78—Nanaimo		BCJHL	62	53	60	113	150
1978-79—Victoria Cougars		WHL	71	23	31	54	151
1979-80—Victoria Cougars (c)		WHL	71	62	48	110	212
1980-81—Philadelphia Flyers		NHL	6	3	0	3	8
1980-81—Maine Mariners		AHL	71	19	20	39	158
1981-82—Maine Mariners		AHL	45	16	21	37	241
1981-82—Philadelphia Flyers (d)		NHL	33	4	15	19	105
1982-83—Hartford Whalers		NHL	79	10	13	23	216
1983-84—Washington Capitals (e)		NHL	57	2	6	8	133
1984-85—Binghamton Whalers		AHL	28	9	16	25	58
1984-85—Washington Capitals		NHL	51	6	12	18	72
1985-86—Washington Capitals		NHL	78	18	38	56	152
NHL TOTALS			304	43	84	127	686

(c)—August, 1980—Signed by Philadelphia Flyers as a free agent.
(d)—August, 1982—Traded by Philadelphia Flyers with Ken Linseman and Flyers' No. 1 draft choice (David A. Jensen) in 1983 to Hartford Whalers for Mark Howe. Hartford and Philadelphia also swapped third-round choices in '83 draft.
(e)—October, 1983—Traded by Hartford Whalers to Washington Capitals for Torrie Robertson.

PAUL ADEY

Right Wing . . . 5'9" . . . 173 lbs. . . . Born, Montreal, Que., August 28, 1963 . . . Shoots right.

Year	Team	League	Games	G.	A.	Pts.	Pen.
1981-82—Hull Olympics		QMJHL	54	17	24	41	0
1982-83—Hull Olympics		QHL	70	58	104	162	14
1983-84—Shawinigan Cataracts		QHL	56	37	52	89	78
1983-84—Toledo Goaldiggers		IHL	2	0	0	0	0
1984-85—Fort Wayne Komets		IHL	81	30	31	61	135
1985-86—Fort Wayne Komets (c)		IHL	39	13	11	24	44
1985-86—Peoria Rivermen		IHL	14	8	7	15	7

(c)—February, 1986—Traded by Fort Wayne Komets to Peoria Rivermen for Rick Hendricks.

JIM AGNEW

Defense . . . 6'1" . . . 179 lbs. . . . Born, Deloraine, Man., March 21, 1966 . . . Shoots left.

Year	Team	League	Games	G.	A.	Pts.	Pen.
1982-83—Brandon Wheat Kings		WHL	14	1	1	2	9
1983-84—Brandon Wheat Kings (c)		WHL	71	6	17	23	107
1984-85—Brandon Wheat Kings		WHL	19	3	15	18	82
1984-85—Portland Winter Hawks		WHL	44	5	24	29	223
1985-86—Portland Winter Hawks (a)		WHL	70	6	30	36	386

(c)—June, 1984—Drafted as underage junior by Vancouver Canucks in NHL entry draft. Tenth Canucks pick, 157th overall, eighth round.

BRADLEY AITKEN

Left Wing and Center . . . 6'3" . . . 200 lbs. . . . Born, Scarborough, Ont., October 30, 1967 . . . Shoots left.

Year	Team	League	Games	G.	A.	Pts.	Pen.
1984-85—Peterborough Petes		OHL	63	18	26	44	36
1985-86—Peterborough Petes (c)		OHL	48	9	28	37	77
1985-86—Sault Ste. Marie Greyhounds (d)		OHL	20	8	19	27	11

(c)—February, 1986—Traded with future considerations by Peterborough Petes to Sault Ste. Marie Greyhounds for Graeme Bonar.
(d)—June, 1986—Drafted as underage junior by Pittsburgh Penguins in 1986 NHL entry draft. Third Penguins pick, 46th overall, third round.

ANDREW AKERVIK

Center . . . 6'3" . . . 190 lbs. . . . Born, Duluth, Minn., August 11, 1967 . . . Shoots right . . . (September, 1982)—Arthroscopic surgery to remove cartilage.

Year	Team	League	Games	G.	A.	Pts.	Pen.
1984-85—Eau Claire Memorial H.S. (c)	Wisc. H	22	21	23	44	....
1985-86—University of Wisconsin	WCHA	22	2	0	2	2

(c)—June, 1985—Drafted by Quebec Nordiques in NHL entry draft. Seventh Nordiques pick, 120th overall, sixth round.

CLIFF ALBRECHT

Defense . . . 6' . . . 185 lbs. . . . Born, Toronto, Ont., May 24, 1963 . . . Shoots right.

Year	Team	League	Games	G.	A.	Pts.	Pen.
1982-83—Princeton University (c)	ECAC	24	4	10	14	52
1983-84—Princeton University	ECAC	23	9	9	18	62
1984-85—Princeton University	ECAC	26	6	22	28	31
1985-86—Princeton University (a)	ECAC	30	15	26	41	42
1985-86—St. Catharines Saints	AHL	1	0	1	1	0

(c)—June, 1983—Drafted by Toronto Maple Leafs in NHL entry draft. Seventh Maple Leafs pick, 168th overall, ninth round.

JAMES ALDRED

Defense . . . 6'1" . . . 185 lbs. . . . Born, Toronto, Ont., April 28, 1963 . . . Shoots left.

Year	Team	League	Games	G.	A.	Pts.	Pen.
1979-80—Kingston Canadians	OMJHL	16	0	1	1	9
1980-81—Kingston Canadians (c)	OHL	67	20	28	48	140
1981-82—Kingston Canadians	OHL	10	2	4	6	18
1981-82—Sault Ste. Marie Greyhounds	OHL	43	16	15	31	179
1982-83—Sault Ste. Marie Greyhounds	OHL	63	22	22	44	176
1983-84—Rochester Americans	AHL	64	10	9	19	57
1984-85—Rochester Americans	AHL	2	0	0	0	0
1984-85—Flint Generals	IHL	28	5	3	8	10
1984-85—Toledo Goaldiggers	IHL	24	7	3	10	16
1985-86—Toledo Goaldiggers	IHL	51	9	17	26	110
1985-86—Rochester Americans	AHL	10	1	3	4	4

(c)—June, 1981—Drafted as underage junior by Buffalo Sabres in NHL entry draft. Third Sabres pick, 59th overall, third round.

KENNETH ALEXANDER

Defense . . . 6'2" . . . 185 lbs. . . . Born, Detroit, Mich., February 25, 1967 . . . Shoots right . . . (January, 1985)—Pulled tendons in shoulder.

Year	Team	League	Games	G.	A.	Pts.	Pen.
1983-84—Detroit Compuware	Mich. Midget	63	11	21	31	136
1984-85—Kitchener Rangers (c)	OHL	58	5	10	15	67
1985-86—Kitchener Rangers	OHL	62	12	31	43	80

(c)—June, 1985—Drafted as underage junior by Philadelphia Flyers in NHL entry draft. Seventh Flyers pick, 126th overall, sixth round.

TOM ALLEN

Defense . . . 6'2" . . . 180 lbs. . . . Born, London, Ont., May 3, 1966 . . . Shoots left.

Year	Team	League	Games	G.	A.	Pts.	Pen.
1982-83—London City Midgets	....	59	33	64	97	135
1983-84—Kingston Canadians	OHL	26	0	4	4	18
1983-84—Kingston Canadians (c)	OHL	50	1	7	8	30
1984-85—Kitchener Rangers	OHL	8	3	5	8	17
1984-85—Ottawa 67's	OHL	22	3	2	5	58
1985-86—London Knights	OHL	60	7	13	20	112

(c)—June, 1984—Drafted as underage junior by Philadelphia Flyers in NHL entry draft. Eighth Flyers pick, 142nd overall, seventh round.

DAVE BRYAN ALLISON

Defense and Right Wing . . . 6'1" . . . 198 lbs. . . . Born, Ft. Francis, Ontario, April 14, 1959 . . . Shoots right . . . Injured right shoulder in 1976-77 . . . Slipped vertabra in back in 1977-78 . . . Brother of Mike Allison.

Year	Team	League	Games	G.	A.	Pts.	Pen.
1976-77—Cornwall Royals	QMJHL	63	2	11	13	180
1977-78—Cornwall Royals	QMJHL	60	9	29	38	302
1978-79—Cornwall Royals	QMJHL	66	7	31	38	*407
1979-80—Nova Scotia Voyageurs	AHL	49	1	12	13	119
1980-81—Nova Scotia Voyageurs	AHL	70	5	12	17	298
1981-82—Nova Scotia Voyageurs (c)	AHL	78	8	25	33	332
1982-83—Nova Scotic Voyageurs	AHL	70	3	22	25	180

Year	Team	League	Games	G.	A.	Pts.	Pen.
1983-84—Montreal Canadiens		NHL	3	0	0	0	12
1983-84—Nova Scotia Voyageurs		AHL	53	2	18	20	155
1984-85—Sherbrooke Canadiens		AHL	4	0	1	1	19
1984-85—Nova Scotia Voyageurs		AHL	68	4	18	22	175
1985-86—Muskegon Lumberjacks		IHL	66	7	30	37	247
NHL TOTALS			3	0	0	0	12

(c)—Led AHL Playoffs with 84 penalty minutes.

MICHAEL EARNEST ALLISON

Center . . . 6' . . . 202 lbs. . . . Born, Ft. Francis, Ont., March 28, 1961 . . . Shoots right . . . Brother of Dave Allison . . . (January 13, 1981)—Strained ligaments in right knee . . . (October 25, 1981)—Bruised kneecap . . . (January 20, 1982)—Sprained medial collateral ligament in right knee vs. NY Islanders requiring surgery . . . (November 20, 1982) Strained ligaments in right knee at Toronto . . . (October, 1983)—Sprained left knee . . . (October, 1984)—Missed games with knee injury . . . (January, 1985)—Arthroscopic surgery to knee.

Year	Team	League	Games	G.	A.	Pts.	Pen.
1977-78—New Westminster Bruins		WCHL	5	0	1	1	2
1977-78—Kenora Thistles		MJHL	47	30	36	66	70
1978-79—Sudbury Wolves		OMJHL	59	24	32	56	41
1979-80—Sudbury Wolves (c)		OMJHL	67	24	71	95	74
1980-81—New York Rangers		NHL	75	26	38	64	83
1981-82—Springfield Indians		AHL	2	0	0	0	0
1981-82—New York Rangers		NHL	48	7	15	22	74
1982-83—Tulsa Oilers		CHL	6	2	2	4	2
1982-83—New York Rangers		NHL	39	11	9	20	37
1983-84—New York Rangers		NHL	45	8	12	20	64
1984-85—New York Rangers		NHL	31	9	15	24	17
1985-86—New Haven Nighthawks		AHL	9	6	6	12	4
1985-86—New York Rangers (d)		NHL	28	2	13	15	22
NHL TOTALS			266	63	102	165	297

(c)—June, 1980—Drafted as underage junior by New York Rangers in NHL entry draft. Second Rangers pick, 35th overall, second round.

(d)—August, 1986—Traded by New York Rangers to Toronto Maple Leafs for Walt Poddubny.

RAYMOND PETER ALLISON

Right Wing . . . 5'9" . . . 190 lbs. . . . Born, Cranbrook, B.C., March 4, 1959 . . . Shoots right . . . (February 17, 1983) Injured hip vs. Edmonton . . . (December 30, 1983)—Broke right ankle in game at N.Y. Rangers.

Year	Team	League	Games	G.	A.	Pts.	Pen.
1974-75—Brandon Wheat Kings		WCHL	2	0	0	0	0
1975-76—Brandon Travellers		MJHL	31	22	21	43	158
1975-76—Brandon Wheat Kings		WCHL	36	9	17	26	50
1976-77—Brandon Wheat Kings		WCHL	71	45	92	137	198
1977-78—Brandon Wheat Kings (b)		WCHL	71	74	86	160	254
1978-79—Brandon Wheat Kings (a-c)		WHL	62	60	93	153	191
1979-80—Hartford Whalers		NHL	64	16	12	28	13
1979-80—Springfield Indians		AHL	13	6	9	15	18
1980-81—Binghamton Whalers		AHL	74	31	39	70	81
1980-81—Hartford Whalers (d)		NHL	6	1	0	1	0
1981-82—Maine Mariners		AHL	26	15	13	28	75
1981-82—Philadelphia Flyers		NHL	51	17	37	54	104
1982-83—Philadelphia Flyers		NHL	67	21	30	51	57
1983-84—Philadelphia Flyers		NHL	37	8	13	21	47
1984-85—Hershey Bears		AHL	49	17	22	39	61
1984-85—Philadelphia Flyers		NHL	11	1	1	2	2
1985-86—Hershey Bears		AHL	77	32	46	78	131
NHL TOTALS			236	64	93	157	223

(c)—August, 1979—Drafted by Hartford Whalers in NHL entry draft. First Hartford pick, 18th overall, first round.

(d)—July, 1981—Traded with Fred Arthur, first and third round 1982 draft picks by the Hartford Whalers to Philadelphia Flyers for Rick MacLeish, Don Gillen, Blake Wesley, first, second and third round 1982 draft picks.

PAUL AMES

Defense . . . 6' . . . 165 lbs. . . . Born, Woburn, Mass., March 12, 1965 . . . Shoots right.

Year	Team	League	Games	G.	A.	Pts.	Pen.
1982-83—Billerica H.S. (c)		Mass.	16	9	26	35	....
1983-84—University of Lowell		ECAC	31	1	13	14	16

Year	Team	League	Games	G.	A.	Pts.	Pen.
1984-85—University of Lowell (b)		H. East	27	2	8	10	22
1985-86—University of Lowell		H. East	41	7	20	27	39

(c)—June, 1983—Drafted by Pittsburgh Penguins in NHL entry draft. Sixth Penguins pick, 123rd overall, seventh round.

JOHN ANDERSEN

Left Wing . . . 6' . . . 175 lbs. . . . Born, Toronto, Ont., January 18, 1968 . . . Shoots left . . . Also plays Center.

Year	Team	League	Games	G.	A.	Pts.	Pen.
1984-85—Toronto Marlboros		OHL	54	1	9	10	4
1985-86—Oshawa Generals (c)		OHL	60	13	11	24	15

(c)—June, 1986—Drafted as underage junior by New Jersey Devils in 1986 NHL entry draft. Eleventh Devils pick, 213th overall, 11th round.

DAVID ANDERSON

Right Wing . . . 6' . . . 190 lbs. . . . Born, Vancouver, B.C., July 30, 1962 . . . Shoots right.

Year	Team	League	Games	G.	A.	Pts.	Pen.
1981-82—Denver University		WCHA	43	10	10	20	42
1982-83—Denver University		WCHA	30	5	10	15	27
1983-84—Denver University		WCHA	38	23	27	50	75
1984-85—Denver University		WCHA	34	16	23	39	48
1985-86—Fort Wayne Komets (c)		IHL	79	33	41	74	156

(c)—August, 1986—Signed by New Jersey Devils as a free agent.

GLENN CHRIS ANDERSON

Right Wing . . . 5'11" . . . 175 lbs. . . . Born, Vancouver, B.C., October 2, 1960 . . . Shoots left . . . Played on Canadian Olympic Team in 1980 . . . (November, 1980)—Knee surgery to remove bone chips . . . (Spring, 1982)—Nose surgery to correct breathing problem caused during a December 1, 1981 altercation with Mark Hunter of Montreal . . . (December 13, 1985)—Given eight-game suspension by NHL for stick-swinging incident in game at Winnipeg . . . Also plays Left Wing.

Year	Team	League	Games	G.	A.	Pts.	Pen.
1977-78—New Westminster Bruins		WHL	1	0	1	1	2
1978-79—Seattle Breakers		WHL	2	0	1	1	0
1978-79—Denver University (c)		WCHA	40	26	29	55	58
1979-80—Canadian Olympic Team		Int'l	49	21	21	42	46
1979-80—Seattle Breakers		WHL	7	5	5	10	4
1980-81—Edmonton Oilers		NHL	58	30	23	53	24
1981-82—Edmonton Oilers		NHL	80	38	67	105	71
1982-83—Edmonton Oilers		NHL	72	48	56	104	70
1983-84—Edmonton Oilers		NHL	80	54	45	99	65
1984-85—Edmonton Oilers		NHL	80	42	39	81	69
1985-86—Edmonton Oilers		NHL	72	54	48	102	90
NHL TOTALS			442	266	278	544	389

(c)—August, 1979—Drafted by Edmonton Oilers in NHL entry draft. Third Oilers pick, 69th overall, fourth round.

JOHN MURRAY ANDERSON

Left Wing . . . 5'11" . . . 180 lbs. . . . Born, Toronto, Ont., March 28, 1957 . . . Shoots left . . . Missed part of 1975-76 season with shoulder separation . . . (December, 1981)—Elbow injury . . . (November, 1984)—Injured collarbone . . . (December 18, 1985)—Sprained back in game at Montreal . . . (January 20, 1986)—Injured shoulder vs. Montreal and missed one game.

Year	Team	League	Games	G.	A.	Pts.	Pen.
1973-74—Toronto Marlboros		Jr. "A" OHA	38	22	22	44	6
1974-75—Toronto Marlboros		Jr. "A" OHA	70	49	64	113	31
1975-76—Toronto Marlboros		Jr. "A" OHA	39	26	25	51	19
1976-77—Toronto Marlboros (a-c)		Jr. "A" OHA	64	57	62	119	42
1977-78—Dallas Black Hawks (b-d)		CHL	52	22	23	45	6
1977-78—Toronto Maple Leafs		NHL	17	1	2	3	2
1978-79—Toronto Maple Leafs		NHL	71	15	11	26	10
1979-80—Toronto Maple Leafs		NHL	74	25	28	53	22
1980-81—Toronto Maple Leafs		NHL	75	17	26	43	31
1981-82—Toronto Maple Leafs		NHL	69	31	26	57	306
1982-83—Toronto Maple Leafs		NHL	80	31	49	80	24
1983-84—Toronto Maple Leafs		NHL	73	37	31	68	22
1984-85—Toronto Maple Leafs (e)		NHL	75	32	31	63	27

Year	Team	League	Games	G.	A.	Pts.	Pen.
1985-86—Quebec Nordiques (f)		NHL	65	21	28	49	26
1985-86—Hartford Whalers		NHL	14	8	17	25	2
NHL TOTALS			613	218	249	467	196

(c)—Drafted from Toronto Marlboros by Toronto Maple Leafs in first round of 1977 amateur draft.
(d)—Led in goals (11) and points (19) during playoffs.
(e)—August, 1985—Traded by Toronto Maple Leafs to Quebec Nordiques for Brad Maxwell.
(f)—March, 1986—Traded by Quebec Nordiques to Hartford Whalers for Risto Siltanen.

MIKE ANDERSON

Center . . . 6'1" . . . 180 lbs. . . . Born, St. Paul, Minn., May 2, 1964 . . . Shoots left . . . Also plays Left Wing.

Year	Team	League	Games	G.	A.	Pts.	Pen.
1981-82—North St. Paul H.S. (c)		Minn. H.S.	24	19	31	50	18
1982-83—Univ. of Minnesota		WCHA	38	8	11	19	19
1983-84—Univ. of Minnesota		WCHA	23	1	7	8	4
1984-85—Univ. of Minnesota		WCHA	35	6	6	12	10
1985-86—Rochester Americans		AHL	25	3	1	4	2
1985-86—Buffalo Sabres (d)		NHL	33	1	9	10	4
NHL TOTALS			33	1	9	10	4

(c)—June, 1982—Drafted as underage player by Buffalo Sabres in NHL entry draft. Fourth Sabres pick, 26th overall, second round.
(d)—June, 1986—Released by Buffalo Sabres.

PERRY LYNN ANDERSON

Left Wing . . . 6' . . . 210 lbs. . . . Born, Barrie, Ont., October 14, 1961 . . . Shoots left . . . (March, 1984)—Broke bone in foot . . . (October 23, 1985)—Bruised right shoulder in game at N. Y. Rangers and missed five games . . . (December 17, 1985)—Bruised left knee vs. Philadelphia and missed five games . . . (January 13, 1986)—Strained abdominal muscle at Chicago and missed eight games.

Year	Team	League	Games	G.	A.	Pts.	Pen.
1978-79—Kingston Canadians		OMJHL	60	6	13	19	85
1979-80—Kingston Canadians (c)		OMJHL	63	17	16	33	52
1980-81—Kingston Canadians		OHL	38	9	13	22	118
1980-81—Brantford Alexanders		OHL	31	8	27	35	43
1981-82—Salt Lake Golden Eagles (b)		CHL	71	32	32	64	117
1981-82—St. Louis Blues		NHL	5	1	2	3	0
1982-83—Salt Lake Golden Eagles		CHL	57	23	19	42	140
1982-83—St. Louis Blues		NHL	18	5	2	7	14
1983-84—Montana Magic		CHL	8	7	3	10	34
1983-84—St. Louis Blues		NHL	50	7	5	12	195
1984-85—St. Louis Blues (d)		NHL	71	9	9	18	146
1985-86—New Jersey Devils		NHL	51	7	12	19	91
NHL TOTALS			195	29	30	59	446

(c)—June, 1980—Drafted by St. Louis Blues as an underage junior in NHL entry draft. Fifth Blues pick, 117th overall, sixth round.
(d)—August, 1985—Traded by St. Louis Blues to New Jersey Devils for Rick Meagher and 1986 12th round draft choice.

SHAWN ANDERSON

Defense . . . 6'1" . . . 190 lbs. . . . Born, Montreal, Que., February 7, 1968 . . . Shoots left . . . Also plays Left Wing.

Year	Team	League	Games	G.	A.	Pts.	Pen.
1984-85—Lac St. Louis Midget		Que.AAA Mid.	42	23	42	65	100
1985-86—University of Maine		H. East	16	5	8	13	22
1985-86—Team Canada (c)		Int'l	33	2	6	8	16

(c)—June, 1986—Drafted as underage player by Buffalo Sabres in 1986 NHL entry draft. First Sabres pick, fifth overall, first round.

WILL ANDERSON

Defense . . . 6' . . . 185 lbs. . . . Born, Kamloops, B.C., February 11, 1968 . . . Shoots left.

Year	Team	League	Games	G.	A.	Pts.	Pen.
1983-84—Williams Lake Mustangs		BCJHL	50	15	20	35	110
1984-85—Kamloops Blazers		WHL	52	3	16	19	82
1985-86—Kamloops Blazers		WHL	42	1	18	19	69
1985-86—Victoria Cougars (c)		WHL	29	4	18	22	44

(c)—June, 1986—Drafted as underage junior by N.Y. Islanders in 1986 NHL entry draft. Seventh Islanders pick, 138th overall, seventh round.

BO MIKAEL ANDERSSON
(Known by middle name)

Center . . . 5'9" . . . 183 lbs. . . . Born, Malmo, Sweden, May 10, 1966 . . . Shoots left.

Year	Team	League	Games	G.	A.	Pts.	Pen.
1983-84—Vastra Frolunda (c)		Sweden	12	0	2	2	6
1984-85—Vastra Frolunda		Sweden	32	16	11	27	....
1985-86—Rochester Americans		AHL	20	10	4	14	6
1985-86—Buffalo Sabres		NHL	33	1	9	10	4
NHL TOTALS			33	1	9	10	4

(c)—June, 1984—Drafted by Buffalo Sabres in NHL entry draft. Sabres first pick, 18th overall, first round.

PETER ANDERSSON

Defense . . . 6'2" . . . 195 lbs. . . . Born, Federalve, Sweden, March 2, 1962 . . . Shoots left . . . Played with Swedish National Junior team and Swedish National team . . . (September 25, 1983)—Injured knee in pre-season game vs. Pittsburgh and missed first three months of season.

Year	Team	League	Games	G.	A.	Pts.	Pen.
1979-80—Timra IF (c)		Sweden Jr.	....	...	....	....	....
1980-81—Timra IF		Sweden Jr.	....	...	....	....	....
1980-81—Bjorkloven IF Umea		Sweden	31	1	2	3	16
1981-82—Bjorkloven IF Umea		Sweden	33	7	7	14	36
1982-83—Bjorkloven IF Umea		Sweden	34	8	16	24	30
1983-84—Washington Capitals		NHL	42	3	7	10	20
1984-85—Washington Capitals		NHL	57	0	10	10	21
1984-85—Binghamton Whalers		AHL	13	2	3	5	6
1985-86—Washington Capitals (d)		NHL	61	6	16	22	36
1985-86—Quebec Nordiques		NHL	12	1	8	9	4
NHL TOTALS			172	10	41	51	81

(c)—June, 1980—Drafted by the Washington Capitals in NHL entry draft. Eighth Capitals pick, 173rd overall, ninth round.

(d)—March, 1986—Traded by Washington Capitals to Quebec Nordiques for third round 1986 draft pick (Shawn Simpson).

JIM ANDONOFF

Right Wing . . . 6'2" . . . 205 lbs. . . . Born, Grosse Point, Mich., August 7, 1965 . . . Shoots right.

Year	Team	League	Games	G.	A.	Pts.	Pen.
1981-82—Detroit Compuware		Midget	78	75	115	190	77
1982-83—Belleville Bulls (c)		OHL	69	17	24	41	36
1983-84—Belleville Bulls		OHL	68	7	24	31	55
1984-85—Belleville Bulls		OHL	64	10	52	62	82
1985-86—New Haven Nighthawks		AHL	38	5	7	12	25
1985-86—Salt Lake Golden Eagles		IHL	10	1	2	3	10
1985-86—Flint Spirit		IHL	39	9	12	21	17

(c)—June, 1983—Drafted by New York Rangers in NHL entry draft. Sixth Rangers pick, 93rd overall, fifth round.

DAVID ANDREYCHUK

Center . . . 6'4" . . . 198 lbs. . . . Born, Hamilton, Ont., September 29, 1963 . . . Shoots right . . . (March, 1983)—Sprained knee . . . Played with Team Canada in 1982-83 World Junior Championship . . . (March, 1985)—Fractured collarbone . . . (September, 1985)—Twisted knee in first day of Buffalo training camp.

Year	Team	League	Games	G.	A.	Pts.	Pen.
1980-81—Oshawa Generals		OHL	67	22	22	44	80
1981-82—Oshawa Generals (c)		OHL	67	58	43	101	71
1982-83—Oshawa Generals		OHL	14	8	24	32	6
1982-83—Buffalo Sabres		NHL	43	14	23	37	16
1983-84—Buffalo Sabres		NHL	78	38	42	80	42
1984-85—Buffalo Sabres		NHL	64	31	30	61	54
1985-86—Buffalo Sabres		NHL	80	36	51	87	61
NHL TOTALS			265	119	146	265	173

(c)—June, 1982—Drafted as underage junior by Buffalo Sabres in NHL entry draft. Third Sabres pick, 16th overall, first round.

JIM ARCHIBALD

Right Wing . . . 5'11" . . . 180 lbs. . . . Born, Craik, Sask., June 6, 1961 . . . Shoots right.

Year	Team	League	Games	G.	A.	Pts.	Pen.
1980-81—Moose Jaw Canucks (c)		SJHL	52	46	42	88	308
1981-82—Univ. of North Dakota		WCHA	41	10	16	26	96
1982-83—Univ. of North Dakota		WCHA	33	7	14	21	91
1983-84—Univ. of North Dakota		WCHA	44	21	15	36	156
1984-85—Univ. of North Dakota (a)		WCHA	41	37	24	61	197
1984-85—Springfield Indians		AHL	8	1	0	1	5
1984-85—Minnesota North Stars		NHL	4	1	2	3	11
1985-86—Springfield Indians		AHL	12	1	7	8	34
1985-86—Minnesota North Stars		NHL	11	0	0	0	32
NHL TOTALS			15	1	2	3	43

(c)—June, 1981—Drafted by Minnesota North Stars in 1981 NHL entry draft. Eleventh North Stars pick, 139th overall, seventh round.

HARRY ARMSTRONG

Defense . . . 6'2" . . . 195 lbs. . . . Born, Anchorage, Alaska, January 30, 1965 . . . Shoots right . . . (October 21, 1983)—Broke arm in CCHA game vs. Northern Michigan . . . Nephew of Boston Red Sox coach Rene Lachemann.

Year	Team	League	Games	G.	A.	Pts.	Pen.
1982-83—Dubuque (c)		USHL	63	1	6	7	34
1983-84—U. of Illinois-Chicago		CCHA	25	4	11	15	21
1984-85—U. of Illinois-Chicago		CCHA	38	6	21	27	40
1985-86—U. of Illinois-Chicago		CCHA	34	6	13	19	21

(c)—June, 1983—Drafted by Winnipeg Jets in NHL entry draft. Sixth Jets pick, 89th overall, fifth round.

IAN ARMSTRONG

Defense . . . 6'4" . . . 200 lbs. . . . Born, Peterborough, Ont., January 25, 1965 . . . Shoots right.

Year	Team	League	Games	G.	A.	Pts.	Pen.
1981-82—Lakefield Jr. C		OHA	35	8	25	33	46
1985-83—Peterborough Petes		OHL	63	1	6	7	29
1983-84—Peterborough Petes (c)		OHL	67	1	23	24	66
1984-85—Peterborough Petes (d)		OHL	66	13	21	34	63
1985-86—Hershey Bears		AHL	66	0	8	8	42

(c)—June, 1983—Drafted as underage junior by Boston Bruins in 1983 NHL entry draft. Seventh Bruins pick, 142nd overall, seventh round.

(d)—June, 1985—Released by Boston Bruins and signed by Philadelphia Flyers as a free agent.

TIM ARMY

Center . . . 6'1" . . . 180 lbs. . . . Born, Providence, R.I., April 26, 1963 . . . Shoots right.

Year	Team	League	Games	G.	A.	Pts.	Pen.
1980-81—East Providence H.S. (c)		RIHS	23	31	42	73	6
1981-82—Providence College		ECAC	32	10	15	25	4
1982-83—Providence College		ECAC	42	14	20	34	37
1983-84—Providence College		ECAC	34	20	26	46	40
1984-85—Providence College (a-d)		H. East	45	27	47	74	16
1985-86—Maine Mariners (e)		AHL	68	11	16	27	10

(c)—June, 1981—Drafted by Colorado Rockies in 1981 NHL entry draft. Ninth Rockies pick, 171st overall, ninth round.

(d)—Named to All-America Team (East).

(e)—June, 1986—Released by New Jersey Devils.

TROY ARNDT

Defense . . . 6' . . . 195 lbs. . . . Born, Regina, Sask., April 30, 1968 . . . Shoots left.

Year	Team	League	Games	G.	A.	Pts.	Pen.
1983-84—Weyburn Red Wings		WHL	56	3	8	11	63
1984-85—Portland Winter Hawks		WHL	65	5	14	19	172
1985-86—Portland Winter Hawks (c)		WHL	63	3	20	23	288

(c)—June, 1986—Drafted as underage junior by Buffalo Sabres in 1986 NHL entry draft. Twelfth Sabres pick, 215th overall, 11th round.

SCOTT ARNIEL

Left Wing . . . 6'1" . . . 170 lbs. . . . Born, Kingston, Ont., September 17, 1962 . . . Shoots left . . . Also plays Center.

Year	Team	League	Games	G.	A.	Pts.	Pen.
1979-80—Cornwall Royals		QMJHL	61	22	28	50	51
1980-81—Cornwall Royals (c)		QMJHL	68	52	71	123	102
1981-82—Cornwall Royals		OHL	24	18	26	44	43
1981-82—Winnipeg Jets		NHL	17	1	8	9	14
1982-83—Winnipeg Jets		NHL	75	13	5	18	46
1983-84—Winnipeg Jets		NHL	80	21	35	56	68
1984-85—Winnipeg Jets		NHL	79	22	22	44	81
1985-86—Winnipeg Jets (d)		NHL	80	18	25	43	40
NHL TOTALS			331	75	95	170	249

(c)—June, 1981—Drafted as underage junior by Winnipeg Jets in NHL entry draft. Second Jets pick, 22nd overall, second round.

(d)—June, 1986—Traded by Winnipeg Jets to Buffalo Sabres for Gilles Hamel.

CHAD ARTHUR

Left Wing . . . 5'11" . . . 195 lbs. . . . Born, Dekalb, Ill., February 18, 1967 . . . Shoots left . . . Also plays Defense.

Year	Team	League	Games	G.	A.	Pts.	Pen.
1984-85—Stratford Jr. B (c)		OHA	40	22	21	43	159
1985-86—Bowling Green University		CCHA	35	3	4	7	50

(c)—June, 1985—Drafted as underage junior by Montreal Canadiens in NHL entry draft. Thirteenth Canadiens pick, 205th overall, 10th round.

BRENT KENNETH ASHTON

Left Wing . . . 6'1" . . . 200 lbs. . . . Born, Saskatoon, Sask., May 18, 1960 . . . Shoots left . . . Missed part of 1979-80 season with knee ligament injury . . . (October, 1985)—Missed two weeks with injured hip in training camp . . . Also plays Center.

Year	Team	League	Games	G.	A.	Pts.	Pen.
1975-76—Saskatoon Blades		WCHL	11	3	4	7	11
1976-77—Saskatoon Blades		WCHL	54	26	25	51	84
1977-78—Saskatoon Blades		WCHL	46	38	28	66	47
1978-79—Saskatoon Blades (c)		WHL	62	64	55	119	80
1979-80—Vancouver Canucks		NHL	47	5	14	19	11
1980-81—Vancouver Canucks (d-e)		NHL	77	18	11	29	57
1981-82—Colorado Rockies		NHL	80	24	36	60	26
1982-83—New Jersey Devils		NHL	76	14	19	33	47
1983-84—Minnesota North Stars (f)		NHL	68	7	10	17	54
1984-85—Minnesota North Stars (g)		NHL	29	4	7	11	15
1984-85—Quebec Nordiques		NHL	49	27	24	51	38
1985-86—Quebec Nordiques		NHL	77	26	32	58	64
NHL TOTALS			503	125	153	278	312

(c)—August, 1979—Drafted by Vancouver Canucks as underage junior in NHL entry draft. Second Canucks pick, 26th overall, second round.

(d)—July, 1981—Traded with a fourth-round draft pick in 1982 by Vancouver to Winnipeg Jets as compensation for Canucks signing of Ivan Hlinka, a Czechoslovakian player drafted by Winnipeg in a special draft on May 28, 1981.

(e)—July, 1981—Traded with a third-round 1982 draft pick (Dave Kasper) by Winnipeg Jets to Colorado Rockies for Lucien DeBlois

(f)—October, 1983—Traded by New Jersey Devils to Minnesota North Stars for Dave Lewis.

(g)—December, 1984—Traded with Brad Maxwell by Minnesota North Stars to Quebec Nordiques for Tony McKegney and Bo Berglund.

ERIC AUBERTIN

Left Wing . . . 6' . . . 185 lbs. . . . Born, Laval, Que., December 17, 1967 . . . Shoots left.

Year	Team	League	Games	G.	A.	Pts.	Pen.
1984-85—Granby Bisons		QHL	67	24	26	50	26
1985-86—Granby Bisons (c)		QHL	68	37	47	84	61

(c)—June, 1986—Drafted as underage junior by Montreal Canadiens in 1986 NHL entry draft. Fifth Canadiens pick, 94th overall, fifth round.

PIERRE AUBRY

Center . . . 5'10" . . . 170 lbs. . . . Born, Cap-de-la-Madeleine, Que., April 15, 1960 . . . Shoots left . . . Also plays Left Wing . . . (January, 1985)—Injured shoulder in AHL game . . . (November, 1985)—Dislocated shoulder.

Year	Team	League	Games	G.	A.	Pts.	Pen.
1977-78—Quebec Remparts		QMJHL	32	18	19	37	19

Year	Team	League	Games	G.	A.	Pts.	Pen.
1977-78—Trois-Rivieres Draveurs	QMJHL	41	20	25	45	34
1978-79—Quebec Remparts	QMJHL	7	2	3	5	5
1978-79—Trois-Rivieres Draveurs	QMJHL	67	53	45	98	97
1979-80—Trois-Rivieres Draveurs	QMJHL	72	85	62	147	82
1980-81—Quebec Nordiques (c)	NHL	1	0	0	0	0
1980-81—Erie Blades (a)	EHL	71	*66	*68	*134	99
1980-81—Rochester Americans	AHL	1	0	0	0	0
1981-82—Fredericton Express	AHL	11	6	5	11	10
1981-82—Quebec Nordiques	NHL	62	10	13	23	27
1982-83—Quebec Nordiques	NHL	77	7	9	16	48
1983-84—Fredericton Express	AHL	12	4	5	9	4
1983-84—Quebec Nordiques (d)	NHL	23	1	1	2	17
1983-84—Detroit Red Wings	NHL	14	4	1	5	8
1984-85—Detroit Red Wings	NHL	25	2	2	4	33
1984-85—Adirondack Red Wings	AHL	29	13	10	23	74
1985-86—Adirondack Red Wings	AHL	66	28	31	59	124
NHL TOTALS		202	24	26	50	133

(c)—September, 1980—Signed by Quebec Nordiques as a free agent.
(d)—February, 1984—Sold by Quebec Nordiques to Detroit Red Wings.

BOB BABCOCK

Defense . . . 6'1" . . . 190 lbs. . . . Born, Agincourt, Ont., August 3, 1968 . . . Shoots left.

Year	Team	League	Games	G.	A.	Pts.	Pen.
1984-85—St. Michaels Midgets	OHA	40	8	30	38	140
1985-86—Sault Ste. Marie Greyhounds (c)	OHL	50	1	7	8	185

(c)—June, 1986—Drafted as underage junior by Washington Capitals in 1986 NHL entry draft. Eleventh Capitals pick, 208th overall, 10th round.

WARREN BABE

Left Wing . . . 6'2" . . . 190 lbs. . . . Born, Medicine Hat, Alta., September 7, 1968 . . . Shoots left.

Year	Team	League	Games	G.	A.	Pts.	Pen.
1984-85—Lethbridge Broncos	WHL	70	7	14	21	117
1985-86—Lethbridge Broncos (c)	WHL	63	33	24	57	125

(c)—June, 1986—Drafted as underage junior by Minnesota North Stars in 1986 NHL entry draft. First North Stars pick, 12th overall, first round.

DAVID MICHAEL BABYCH

Defense . . . 6'2" . . . 215 lbs. . . . Born, Edmonton, Alta., May 23, 1961 . . . Shoots left . . . Brother of Wayne Babych . . . First member of Winnipeg Jets to be voted to mid-season All-Star game (1983) starting team . . . (March, 1984)—Separated shoulder . . . (December, 1984)—Back spasms.

Year	Team	League	Games	G.	A.	Pts.	Pen.
1977-78—Portland Winter Hawks	WCHL	6	1	3	4	4
1977-78—Ft. Sask. Traders (a-c-d)	AJHL	56	31	69	100	37
1978-79—Portland Winter Hawks	WHL	67	20	59	79	63
1979-80—Portland Winter Hawks (a-e-f)	WHL	50	22	60	82	71
1980-81—Winnipeg Jets	NHL	69	6	38	44	90
1981-82—Winnipeg Jets	NHL	79	19	49	68	92
1982-83—Winnipeg Jets	NHL	79	13	61	74	56
1983-84—Winnipeg Jets	NHL	66	18	39	57	62
1984-85—Winnipeg Jets	NHL	78	13	49	62	78
1985-86—Winnipeg Jets (g)	NHL	19	4	12	16	14
1985-86—Hartford Whalers	NHL	62	10	43	53	36
NHL TOTALS		452	83	291	374	428

(c)—Named winner of AJHL Rookie of the Year Trophy.
(d)—Named winner of AJHL Top Defenseman Trophy.
(e)—Named winner of WHL Top Defenseman Trophy.
(f)—June, 1980—Drafted as underage junior by Winnipeg Jets in NHL entry draft. First Jets pick, second overall, first round.
(g)—November, 1985—Traded by Winnipeg Jets to Hartford Whalers for Ray Neufeld.

WAYNE JOSEPH BABYCH

Right Wing . . . 5'11" . . . 191 lbs. . . . Born, Edmonton, Alta., June 6, 1958 . . . Shoots right . . . Brother of Dave Babych . . . Missed part of 1978-79 season with a broken left ankle and parts of 1979-80 season with right shoulder and knee injuries . . . (September, 1981)— Missed first 12 games of season with training camp shoulder injury. Continued to aggravate injury and underwent shoulder manipulation in January, 1982 . . . (January 1, 1983)—

Suffered broken nose and cracked cheekbone in fight in game vs. Philadelphia . . . (January 14, 1986)—Bruised wrist vs. Winnipeg.

Year	Team	League	Games	G.	A.	Pts.	Pen.
1973-74—Edmonton Mets	AJHL	56	20	18	38	68
1973-74—Edmonton Oil Kings	WCHL	1	0	1	1	0
1974-75—Edmonton Oil Kings	WCHL	68	19	17	36	157
1975-76—Edmonton Oil Kings	WCHL	61	32	46	78	98
1976-77—Portland Winter Hawks (a)	WCHL	71	50	62	112	76
1977-78—Portland Winter Hawks (a-c)	WCHL	68	50	71	121	218
1978-79—St. Louis Blues	NHL	67	27	36	63	75
1979-80—St. Louis Blues	NHL	59	26	35	61	49
1980-81—St. Louis Blues	NHL	78	54	42	96	93
1981-82—St. Louis Blues	NHL	51	19	25	44	51
1982-83—St. Louis Blues	NHL	71	16	23	39	62
1983-84—St. Louis Blues	NHL	70	13	29	42	52
1984-85—Pittsburgh Penguins (d-e-f)	NHL	65	20	34	54	35
1985-86—Pittsburgh Penguins (g)	NHL	2	0	0	0	0
1985-86—Quebec Nordiques (h)	NHL	15	6	5	11	18
1985-86—Hartford Whalers	NHL	37	11	17	28	59
NHL TOTALS		515	192	246	438	494

(c)—Drafted from Portland Winter Hawks by St. Louis Blues in first round of 1978 amateur draft.
(d)—September, 1984—Conditionally traded by St. Louis Blues to Edmonton Oilers for future considerations.
(e)—October, 1984—Returned by Edmonton Oilers to St. Louis Blues to cancel the trade.
(f)—October, 1984—Selected by Pittsburgh Penguins in NHL waiver draft.
(g)—October, 1985—Traded by Pittsburgh Penguins to Quebec Nordiques for future considerations.
(h)—January, 1986—Traded by Quebec Nordiques to Hartford Whalers for Greg Malone.

JOEL BAILLARGEON

Left Wing . . . 6'1" . . . 205 lbs. . . . Born, Charlesbourg, Que., October 6, 1964 . . . Shoots left.

Year	Team	League	Games	G.	A.	Pts.	Pen.
1981-82—Trois-Rivieres Draveurs	QMJHL	26	1	3	4	47
1982-83—Trois-Rivieres	QHL	29	4	5	9	197
1982-83—Hull Olympics (c)	QHL	25	15	7	22	76
1983-84—Chicoutimi Sagueneens	QHL	60	48	35	83	184
1983-84—Sherbrooke Jets	AHL	8	0	0	0	26
1984-85—Granby Bisons	QHL	32	25	24	49	160
1985-86—Sherbrooke Canadiens	AHL	56	6	12	18	115

(c)—June, 1983—Drafted as underage junior by Winnipeg Jets in NHL entry draft. Seventh Jets pick, 109th overall, sixth round.

PETER GEORGE BAKOVIC

Right Wing . . . 6'1" . . . 190 lbs. . . . Born, Thunder Bay, Ont., January 31, 1965 . . . Shoots right.

Year	Team	League	Games	G.	A.	Pts.	Pen.
1982-83—Thunder Bay Jr. B	OHA	40	30	29	59	159
1983-84—Kitchener Rangers	OHL	28	2	6	8	87
1983-84—Windsor Spitfires	OHL	35	10	25	35	74
1984-85—Windsor Spitfires	OHL	58	26	48	74	*259
1985-86—Moncton Golden Flames (c)	AHL	80	18	36	54	349

(c)—October, 1985—Signed by Moncton Golden Flames as a free agent.

MIGUEL BALDRIS

Defense . . . 6' . . . 195 lbs. . . . Born, Montreal, Que., January 30, 1968 . . . Shoots left.

Year	Team	League	Games	G.	A.	Pts.	Pen.
1984-85—Richelieu Rivermen	Que. Midget	37	12	28	40	42
1985-86—Shawinigan Cataracts (c)	QHL	67	2	30	32	101

(c)—June, 1986—Drafted as underage junior by Buffalo Sabres in 1986 NHL entry draft. Seventh Sabres pick, 110th overall, sixth round.

MARK BAR

Defense . . . 6'3" . . . 197 lbs. . . . Born, Toronto, Ont., February 15, 1968 . . . Shoots left.

Year	Team	League	Games	G.	A.	Pts.	Pen.
1984-85—Toronto Nationals	OHA	42	10	23	33	78
1985-86—Peterborough Petes (c)	OHL	56	2	24	26	98

(c)—June, 1986—Drafted as underage junior by Philadelphia Flyers in 1986 NHL entry draft. Fourth Flyers pick, 83rd overall, fourth round.

MARIO BARBE

Defense . . . 6'1" . . . 195 lbs. . . . Born, Abitibi, Que., March 17, 1967 . . . Shoots left.

Year	Team	League	Games	G.	A.	Pts.	Pen.
1983-84—Bourassa AAA		Que.Midget	42	7	13	20	63
1984-85—Chicoutimi Sagueneens (c)		QHL	64	2	13	15	211
1985-86—Granby Bisons		QHL	70	5	25	30	261

(c)—June, 1985—Drafted as underage junior by Edmonton Oilers in NHL entry draft. Ninth Oilers pick, 209th overall, 10th round.

DON BARBER

Left Wing . . . 6'1" . . . 205 lbs. . . . Born, Victoria, B.C., December 2, 1964 . . . Shoots left.

Year	Team	League	Games	G.	A.	Pts.	Pen.
1982-83—Kelowna Buckaroos (c)		BCJHL	35	26	31	57	54
1983-84—St. Albert Saints		AJHL	53	42	38	80	74
1984-85—Bowling Green Univ.		CCHA	39	15	12	27	44
1985-86—Bowling Green Univ.		CCHA	35	21	22	43	64

(c)—June, 1983—Drafted as underage junior by Edmonton Oilers in NHL entry draft. Fifth Oilers pick, 120th overall, sixth round.

(d)—December, 1985—Traded with Marc Habscheid and Emanuel Viveiros by Edmonton Oilers to Minnesota North Stars for Gord Sherven and Don Biggs.

MURRAY BARON

Defense . . . 6'3" . . . 210 lbs. . . . Born, Prince George, B.C., June 1, 1967 . . . Shoots left.

Year	Team	League	Games	G.	A.	Pts.	Pen.
1984-85—Vernon Lakers		BCJHL	50	10	15	25	200
1985-86—Vernon Lakers (c)		BCJHL	46	12	32	44	....

(c)—June, 1986—Drafted as underage player by Philadelphia Flyers in 1986 NHL entry draft. Seventh Flyers pick, 167th overall, eighth round.

NORMAND BARON

Left Wing . . . 6' . . . 205 lbs. . . . Born, Verdun, Que., December 15, 1957 . . . Shoots left . . . Mr. Montreal and Mr. Quebec in 1981 bodybuilding competition . . . (January 7, 1986)—Injured shoulder at Quebec and missed five games.

Year	Team	League	Games	G.	A.	Pts.	Pen.
1983-84—Nova Scotia Voyageurs (c)		AHL	68	11	11	22	275
1983-84—Montreal Canadiens		NHL	4	0	0	0	12
1984-85—Sherbrooke Canadiens		AHL	39	5	5	10	98
1985-86—Peoria Rivermen		IHL	17	4	4	8	61
1985-86—St. Louis Blues (d)		NHL	23	2	0	2	39
1985-86—Flint Spirit (e)		IHL	11	1	7	8	43
NHL TOTALS			27	2	0	2	51

(c)—October, 1983—Signed by Montreal Canadiens as a free agent.

(d)—October, 1985—Sold by Montreal Canadiens to St. Louis Blues.

(e)—July, 1986—Released by St. Louis Blues.

DAVID BARR

Center . . . 6'1" . . . 185 lbs. . . . Born, Edmonton, Alta., November 30, 1960 . . . Shoots right . . . Also plays Right Wing . . . (March 19, 1986)—Sprained knee in game vs. Hartford.

Year	Team	League	Games	G.	A.	Pts.	Pen.
1977-78—Pincher Creek		AJHL	60	16	32	48	53
1978-79—Edmonton Oil Kings		WHL	72	16	19	35	61
1979-80—Lethbridge Broncos		WHL	60	16	38	54	47
1980-81—Lethbridge Broncos		WHL	72	26	62	88	106
1981-82—Erie Blades		AHL	76	18	48	66	29
1981-82—Boston Bruins (c)		NHL	2	0	0	0	0
1982-83—Baltimore Skipjacks		AHL	72	27	51	78	67
1982-83—Boston Bruins		NHL	10	1	1	2	7
1983-84—New York Rangers (d)		NHL	6	0	0	0	2
1983-84—Tulsa Oilers		CHL	50	28	37	65	24
1983-84—St. Louis Blues (e)		NHL	1	0	0	0	0
1984-85—St. Louis Blues		NHL	75	16	18	34	32
1985-86—St. Louis Blues		NHL	75	13	38	51	70
NHL TOTALS			169	30	57	87	111

(c)—September, 1981—Signed by Boston Bruins as a free agent.

(d)—October, 1983—Traded by Boston Bruins to New York Rangers for Dave Silk.

(e)—March, 1984—Traded with third-round 1984 draft pick (Alan Perry) and cash by New York Rangers to St. Louis Blues for Larry Patey and NHL rights to Bob Brooke.

JOHN DAVID BARRETT

Defense . . . 6'1" . . . 210 lbs. . . . Born, Ottawa, Ont., July 1, 1958 . . . Shoots left . . . (December 16, 1980)—Separated left shoulder vs. Edmonton . . . Brother of former NHLer Fred Barrett . . . (October 17, 1984)—Broke right hand in game vs. N.Y. Islanders . . . (January 13, 1986)—Injured groin in game at Toronto.

Year	Team	League	Games	G.	A.	Pts.	Pen.
1976-77	Windsor Spitfires	OMJHL	63	7	17	24	168
1977-78	Windsor Spitfires (c)	OMJHL	67	8	18	26	133
1978-79	Milwaukee Admirals	IHL	42	8	13	21	117
1978-79	Kalamazoo Wings	IHL	31	1	12	13	54
1979-80	Kalamazoo Wings	IHL	52	8	33	41	63
1979-80	Adirondack Red Wings	AHL	28	0	4	4	59
1980-81	Adirondack Red Wings	AHL	21	4	11	15	63
1980-81	Detroit Red Wings	NHL	56	3	10	13	60
1981-82	Detroit Red Wings	NHL	69	1	12	13	93
1982-83	Detroit Red Wings	NHL	79	4	10	14	74
1983-84	Detroit Red Wings	NHL	78	2	8	10	78
1984-85	Detroit Red Wings	NHL	71	6	19	25	117
1985-86	Detroit Red Wings (d)	NHL	65	2	12	14	125
1985-86	Washington Capitals	NHL	14	0	3	3	12
	NHL TOTALS		432	18	74	92	559

(c)—June, 1978—Drafted by Detroit Red Wings in NHL amateur draft. Tenth Red Wings pick, 129th overall, eighth round.

(d)—March, 1986—Traded with Greg Smith by Detroit Red Wings to Washington Capitals for Darren Veitch.

ROBIN BARTELL

Defense . . . 6' . . . 195 lbs. . . . Born, Drake, Sask., May 16, 1961 . . . Shoots left.

Year	Team	League	Games	G.	A.	Pts.	Pen.
1980-81	Prince Albert Raiders	SAJHL	86	22	63	85	....
1981-82	Prince Albert Raiders	SAJHL	83	17	73	90	....
1982-83	Univ. of Saskatchewan	CAHA	24	4	14	18	....
1983-84	Canadian Olympic Team	Oly.	....	...	....	....	....
1984-85	Switzerland	Switz.	....	...	....	....	....
1984-85	Moncton Golden Flames (c)	AHL	41	4	11	15	66
1985-86	Moncton Golden Flames	AHL	74	4	21	25	100
1985-86	Calgary Flames (d)	NHL	1	0	0	0	0
	NHL TOTALS		1	0	0	0	0

(c)—December, 1984—Signed by Moncton Golden Flames as a free agent.

(d)—July, 1986—Signed by Vancouver Canucks as a free agent.

DAVID BASEGGIO

Defense . . . 6'1" . . . 185 lbs. . . . Born, Niagara Falls, Ont., October 28, 1967 . . . Shoots left . . . Brother of Rob Basaggio (Teammate at Yale Univ.).

Year	Team	League	Games	G.	A.	Pts.	Pen.
1984-85	Niagara Falls Jr. B	OHA	39	16	45	61	88
1985-86	Yale University (c)	ECAC	30	7	17	24	54

(c)—June, 1986—Drafted by Buffalo Sabres in 1986 NHL entry draft. Fifth Sabres pick, 68th overall, fourth round.

BOB BASSEN

Center . . . 5'10" . . . 180 lbs. . . . Born, Calgary, Alta., May 6, 1965 . . . Shoots left . . . Son of Hank Bassen (Goalie with Chicago, Detroit and Pittsburgh in NHL in mid '60s) . . . (October 12, 1985)—Injured knee in game at Los Angeles.

Year	Team	League	Games	G.	A.	Pts.	Pen.
1982-83	Medicine Hat Tigers	WHL	4	3	2	5	0
1983-84	Medicine Hat Tigers	WHL	72	29	29	58	93
1984-85	Medicine Hat Tigers (a-c)	WHL	65	32	50	82	143
1985-86	New York Islanders	NHL	11	2	1	3	6
1985-86	Springfield Indians	AHL	54	13	21	34	111
	NHL TOTALS		11	2	1	3	6

(c)—June, 1985—Signed by New York Islanders as a free agent.

JOHN ROBERTSON (BOBBY) BATEMAN

Defense . . . 6'2" . . . 190 lbs. . . . Born, LaSalle, Que., February 24, 1968 . . . Shoots left.

Year	Team	League	Games	G.	A.	Pts.	Pen.
1984-85—Laurentide Pionniers		Que.AAA Mid.	39	5	12	17	56
1985-86—St. Lawrence College H.S. (c)		Que. H.S.	41	2	13	15	73

(c)—June, 1986—Drafted as underage player by Winnipeg Jets in 1986 NHL entry draft. Sixth Jets pick, 113th overall, sixth round.

KEN JAMES BAUMGARTNER

Defense . . . 6' . . . 200 lbs. . . . Born, Flin Flon, Manitoba, March 11, 1966 . . . Shoots left.

Year	Team	League	Games	G.	A.	Pts.	Pen.
1983-84—Prince Albert Raiders		WHL	57	1	6	7	203
1984-85—Prince Albert Raiders (c)		WHL	60	3	9	12	252
1985-86—Prince Albert Raiders (d)		WHL	70	4	23	27	277

(c)—June, 1985—Drafted as underage junior by Buffalo Sabres in 1985 NHL entry draft. Twelfth Sabres pick, 245th overall, 12th round.

(d)—January, 1986—Traded with Larry Playfair and Sean McKenna by Buffalo Sabres to Los Angeles Kings for Brian Engblom and Doug Smith.

PAUL GORDON BAXTER

Defense . . . 5'11" . . . 200 lbs. . . . Born, Winnipeg, Man., October 25, 1955 . . . Shoots right . . . Missed most of 1974-75 season with knee injury requiring surgery . . . (November, 1980)— Surgery for cut wrist tendons . . . (February, 1984)—Sprained right knee.

Year	Team	League	Games	G.	A.	Pts.	Pen.
1972-73—Winnipeg Monarchs		MJHL	44	9	22	31	*359
1973-74—Winnipeg Clubs (c)		WCHL	63	10	30	40	384
1974-75—Cape Codders		NAHL	2	1	0	1	11
1974-75—Cleveland Crusaders (d)		WHA	5	0	0	0	37
1975-76—Syracuse Blazers		NAHL	3	1	2	3	9
1975-76—Cleveland Crusaders		WHA	67	3	7	10	201
1976-77—Maine Nordiques		NAHL	6	1	4	5	52
1976-77—Quebec Nordiques		WHA	66	6	17	23	244
1977-78—Quebec Nordiques		WHA	76	6	29	35	240
1978-79—Quebec Nordiques (e)		WHA	76	10	36	46	240
1979-80—Quebec Nordiques (f)		NHL	61	7	13	20	145
1980-81—Pittsburgh Penguins		NHL	51	5	14	19	204
1981-82—Pittsburgh Penguins		NHL	76	9	34	43	*409
1982-83—Pittsburgh Penguins (g)		NHL	75	11	21	32	238
1983-84—Calgary Flames (h)		NHL	74	7	20	27	182
1984-85—Calgary Flames		NHL	70	5	14	19	126
1985-86—Calgary Flames		NHL	47	4	3	7	194
WHA TOTALS			290	25	89	114	962
NHL TOTALS			454	48	119	167	1498

(c)—Selected by Cleveland Crusaders in World Hockey Association amateur player draft, May, 1974.

(d)—Drafted from Cleveland Crusaders (WHA) by Pittsburgh Penguins in third round of 1975 amateur draft.

(e)—June, 1979—Selected by Pittsburgh Penguins in NHL reclaim draft, but remained with Quebec Nordiques as a priority selection for the expansion draft.

(f)—August, 1980—Signed by Pittsburgh Penguins as free agent with Quebec Nordiques receiving Kim Clackson as compensation.

(g)—August, 1983—Released by Pittsburgh Penguins.

(h)—September, 1983—Signed by Calgary Flames as a free agent.

TIM BEAN

Left Wing . . . 6'1" . . . 190 lbs. . . . Born, Sault Ste. Marie, Ont., March 9, 1967 . . . Shoots left.

Year	Team	League	Games	G.	A.	Pts.	Pen.
1982-83—North York Tier II		MTHL	45	9	11	20	57
1983-84—Belleville Bulls		OHL	63	12	13	25	131
1984-85—Belleville Bulls		OHL	31	10	11	21	60
1984-85—North Bay Centennials (c)		OHL	28	11	13	24	61
1985-86—North Bay Centennials		OHL	66	32	34	66	129

(c)—June, 1985—Drafted by Toronto Maple Leafs in 1985 NHL entry draft as an underage junior. Seventh Maple Leafs pick, 127th overall, seventh round.

DAN BEAUDETTE

Center . . . 6'3" . . . 200 lbs. . . . Born, St. Paul, Minn., February 18, 1968 . . . Shoots left.

Year	Team	League	Games	G.	A.	Pts.	Pen.
1985-86—St. Thomas Academy (c)		Minn. H.S.	23	21	15	36	18

(c)—June, 1986—Drafted by New York Islanders in 1986 NHL entry draft. Thirteenth Islanders pick, 227th overall, 11th round.

YVES BEAUDOIN

Defense . . . 5'11" . . . 180 lbs. . . . Born, Pointe Aux Trembles, Que., January 7, 1965 . . . Shoots right.

Year	Team	League	Games	G.	A.	Pts.	Pen.
1981-82—Hull Olympics		QMJHL	50	2	18	20	39
1982-83—Hull Olympics		QHL	6	1	2	3	9
1982-83—Shawinigan Cataracts (c)		QHL	56	11	23	34	51
1983-84—Shawinigan Cataracts		QHL	68	14	43	57	93
1984-85—Shawinigan Cataracts (a)		QHL	58	20	38	58	78
1985-86—Binghamton Whalers		AHL	48	5	12	17	36
1985-86—Washington Capitals		NHL	4	0	0	0	0
NHL TOTALS			4	0	0	0	0

(c)—June, 1983—Drafted as underage junior by Washington Capitals in NHL entry draft. Sixth Capitals pick, 195th overall, tenth round.

NICHOLAS BEAULIEU

Left Wing . . . 6'1" . . . 200 lbs. . . . Born, Rimouski, Que., August 19, 1968 . . . Shoots left.

Year	Team	League	Games	G.	A.	Pts.	Pen.
1984-85—Richelieu Rivermen		Que. Midget	42	4	18	22	68
1985-86—Drummondville Voltigeurs (c)		QHL	70	11	20	21	93

(c)—June, 1986—Drafted as underage junior by Edmonton Oilers in 1986 NHL entry draft. Eighth Oilers pick, 168th overall, eighth round.

BARRY DAVID BECK

Defense . . . 6'3" . . . 216 lbs. . . . Born, N. Vancouver, B.C., June 3, 1957 . . . Shoots left . . . Missed part of 1976-77 season with pneumonia . . . Set NHL record for goals by a rookie defenseman with 22 in 1977-78 . . . Missed part of 1978-79 season with knee injury . . . (October 3, 1980)—Broke middle finger on right hand in exhibition game vs. N.Y. Islanders at New Haven . . . (October, 1981)—Served three-game league suspension . . . (December, 1981)—Served six-game league suspension . . . Set New York Rangers record for penalty minutes in a single season in 1980-81 . . . (January, 1983)—Strained neck muscles . . . (February, 1984)—Sprained right wrist . . . (October 11, 1984)—Injured shoulder in opening game of season vs. Hartford . . . (March, 1985)—Reinjured shoulder . . . (October, 1985)—Bruised muscle in right shoulder in game at Minnesota and missed 43 games . . . (March 12, 1986)—Injured left shoulder in game vs. Calgary.

Year	Team	League	Games	G.	A.	Pts.	Pen.
1973-74—Langley		Jr. "A" BCHL	63	8	28	36	329
1973-74—Kamloops Chiefs		WCHL	1	0	0	0	0
1974-75—New Westminster Bruins		WCHL	58	9	33	42	162
1975-76—N. Westminster Bruins (a)		WCHL	68	19	80	99	325
1976-77—N. Westminster Bruins (a-c-d)		WCHL	61	16	46	62	167
1977-78—Colorado Rockies		NHL	75	22	38	60	89
1978-79—Colorado Rockies		NHL	63	14	28	42	91
1979-80—Colorado Rockies (e)		NHL	10	1	5	6	8
1979-80—New York Rangers		NHL	61	14	45	59	98
1980-81—New York Rangers		NHL	75	11	23	34	231
1981-82—New York Rangers		NHL	60	9	29	38	111
1982-83—New York Rangers		NHL	66	12	22	34	112
1983-84—New York Rangers		NHL	72	9	27	36	132
1984-85—New York Rangers		NHL	56	7	19	26	65
1985-86—New York Rangers		NHL	25	4	8	12	24
NHL TOTALS			563	103	244	347	961

(c)—Won Most Valuable Player and Outstanding Defenseman awards.
(d)—Drafted from New Westminster Bruins by Colorado Rockies in first round of 1977 amateur draft.
(e)—November, 1979—Traded by Colorado Rockies to New York Rangers for Mike McEwen, Lucien DeBlois, Pat Hickey, Dean Turner and future consideration (Bobby Crawford).

BRAD BECK

Defense . . . 5'11" . . . 185 lbs. . . . Born, Vancouver, B.C., February 10, 1964 . . . Shoots right.

Year	Team	League	Games	G.	A.	Pts.	Pen.
1980-81—Penticton Knights		BCJHL	....	10	24	34	....
1981-82—Penticton Knights (c)		BCJHL	52	13	32	45	116
1982-83—Michigan State Univ.		CCHA	42	5	15	20	40
1983-84—Michigan State Univ.		CCHA	42	2	7	9	67
1984-85—Michigan State Univ.		CCHA	42	5	18	23	60
1985-86—Michigan State Univ.		CCHA	41	3	15	18	40

(c)—June, 1982—Drafted as underage player by Chicago Black Hawks in NHL entry draft. Fifth Black Hawks pick, 91st overall, fifth round.

RUSS BECKER

Defense . . . 6'3" . . . 200 lbs. . . . Born, Iowa City, Iowa, December 20, 1965 . . . Shoots left.

Year	Team	League	Games	G.	A.	Pts.	Pen.
1983-84	Virginia H.S. (c)	Minn. H.S.	21	4	11	15	22
1984-85	Michigan Tech.	WCHA	15	2	1	3	14
1985-86	Michigan Tech.	WCHA	33	0	2	2	51

(c)—June, 1984—Drafted by New York Islanders in NHL entry draft. Twelfth Islanders pick, 228th overall, 11th round.

EDDY JOSEPH BEERS

Left Wing . . . 6'2" . . . 195 lbs. . . . Born, Merritt, B.C., October 12, 1959 . . . Shoots left . . . 1981-82 WCHA scoring leader with 49 points in 26 WCHA games (30g, 19a) . . . (March 16, 1983)—Concussion and twisted neck after collision with Bill Hajt in game at Buffalo . . . (February, 1984)—Sprained ankle . . . (October 11, 1985)—Fractured toe in game vs. Winnipeg and missed 10 games . . . (December 28, 1985)—Charley horse in game vs. Philadelphia and missed one game . . . (February 20, 1986)—Injured ribs in game at N.Y. Rangers and missed seven games.

Year	Team	League	Games	G.	A.	Pts.	Pen.
1978-79	University of Denver	WCHA	17	7	5	12	23
1979-80	University of Denver	WCHA	36	13	20	33	24
1980-81	University of Denver	WCHA	39	24	15	39	63
1981-82	University of Denver (a-c)	WCHA	42	50	34	84	59
1981-82	Calgary Flames	NHL	5	1	1	2	21
1982-83	Colorado Flames	CHL	29	12	17	29	52
1982-83	Calgary Flames	NHL	41	11	15	26	21
1983-84	Calgary Flames	NHL	73	36	39	75	88
1984-85	Calgary Flames	NHL	74	28	40	68	94
1985-86	Calgary Flames (d)	NHL	33	11	10	21	8
1985-86	St. Louis Blues	NHL	24	7	11	18	24
	NHL TOTALS		250	94	116	210	256

(c)—March, 1982—Signed by Calgary Flames as a free agent.

(d)—February, 1986—Traded by Calgary Flames with Gino Cavallini and Charles Bourgeois to St. Louis Blues for Terry Johnson, Joe Mullen and Rik Wilson.

ROGER BELANGER

Right Wing and Center . . . 6' . . . 192 lbs. . . . Born, St. Catharines, Ont., December 1, 1965 . . . Shoots right . . . (October 31, 1984)—Sprained knee in game at New Jersey and missed 11 games . . . (January, 1985)—Sprained knee.

Year	Team	League	Games	G.	A.	Pts.	Pen.
1981-82	London Midgets	Ont. Midget	25	20	21	41	..
1982-83	London Knights	OHL	68	17	14	31	53
1983-84	Kingston Canadians (c)	OHL	67	44	46	90	66
1984-85	Hamilton Steelhawks	OHL	3	3	3	6	0
1984-85	Pittsburgh Penguins	NHL	44	3	5	8	32
1985-86	Baltimore Skipjacks	AHL	69	17	21	38	61
	NHL TOTALS		44	3	5	8	32

(c)—June, 1984—Drafted by Pittsburgh Penguins in NHL entry draft. Third Penguins pick, 16th overall, first round.

BRUCE BELL

Defense . . . 5'11" . . . 195 lbs. . . . Born, Toronto, Ont., February 15, 1965 . . . Shoots left.

Year	Team	League	Games	G.	A.	Pts.	Pen.
1981-82	Sault Ste. Marie Greyhounds	OHL	67	11	18	29	63
1982-83	Sault Ste. Marie Greyhounds	OHL	5	0	2	2	2
1982-83	Windsor Spitfires (c)	OHL	61	10	35	45	39
1983-84	Brantford Alexanders	OHL	63	7	41	48	55
1984-85	Quebec Nordiques	NHL	75	6	31	37	44
1985-86	St. Louis Blues (d)	NHL	75	2	18	20	43
	NHL TOTALS		150	8	49	57	87

(c)—June, 1983—Drafted by Quebec Nordiques in NHL entry draft. Second Nordiques pick, 52nd overall, third round.

(d)—October, 1985—Traded by Quebec Nordiques to St. Louis Blues for Gilbert Delorme.

BRAD BELLAND

Center . . . 6'1" . . . 185 lbs. . . . Born, Windsor, Ont., January 4, 1967 . . . Shoots right.

Year	Team	League	Games	G.	A.	Pts.	Pen.
1983-84	Windsor Jr. B	OHA	43	26	25	51	63

Year	Team	League	Games	G.	A.	Pts.	Pen.
1984-85—Sudbury Wolves (c)		OHL	64	17	27	44	48
1985-86—Sudbury Wolves (d)		OHL	7	0	6	6	0
1985-86—Hamilton Steelhawks		OHL	52	20	20	40	40

(c)—June, 1985—Drafted by Chicago Black Hawks in NHL entry draft. Fifth Black Hawks pick, 95th overall, fifth round.

(d)—October, 1985—Traded by Sudbury Wolves to Hamilton Steelhawks for Mike Hudson and Keith Van Rooyen.

NEIL BELLAND

Defense . . . 5'11" . . . 175 lbs. . . . Born, Parry Sound, Ont., April 3, 1961 . . . Shoots left . . . (February, 1983)—Shoulder separation.

Year	Team	League	Games	G.	A.	Pts.	Pen.
1977-78—North Bay Trappers		OMJHL	49	25	35	60	24
1978-79—Kingston Canadians		OMJHL	64	8	41	49	14
1979-80—Kingston Canadians		OMJHL	54	7	44	51	44
1980-81—Kingston Canadians (c)		OHL	53	28	54	82	45
1981-82—Dallas Black Hawks		CHL	27	2	20	22	18
1981-82—Vancouver Canucks		NHL	28	3	6	9	16
1982-83—Vancouver Canucks		NHL	14	2	4	6	4
1982-83—Fredericton Express		AHL	46	4	17	21	12
1983-84—Vancouver Canucks		NHL	44	7	13	20	24
1983-84—Fredericton Express		AHL	17	3	15	18	2
1984-85—Vancouver Canucks		NHL	13	0	6	6	6
1984-85—Fredericton Express (b)		AHL	57	7	34	41	31
1985-86—Fredericton Express		AHL	36	6	18	24	10
1985-86—Vancouver Canucks		NHL	7	1	2	3	4
NHL TOTALS			106	13	31	44	54

(c)—October, 1980—Signed by Vancouver Canucks as a free agent.

BRIAN BELLEFEUILLE

Left Wing . . . 6'2" . . . 185 lbs. . . . Born, Natick, Mass., March 21, 1967 . . . Shoots left.

Year	Team	League	Games	G.	A.	Pts.	Pen.
1984-85—Framingham North H.S.		Mass.	20	35	26	61	..
1985-86—Canterbury H.S. (c)		Mass.	31	57	58	115	..

(c)—June, 1986—Drafted by Toronto Maple Leafs in 1986 NHL entry draft. Ninth Maple Leafs pick, 174th overall, ninth round.

BRIAN BELLOWS

Right Wing . . . 6' . . . 196 lbs. . . . Born, St. Catharines, Ont., September 1, 1964 . . . Shoots right . . . Also plays Center . . . (November, 1981)—Separated shoulder in game at Niagara Falls. Coached two games while recovering to become the youngest coach in OHL history (17) . . . (January, 1984)—Became youngest team captain in Minnesota North Stars history . . . (October, 1984)—Tendinitis in elbow.

Year	Team	League	Games	G.	A.	Pts.	Pen.
1980-81—Kitchener Rangers		OHL	66	49	67	116	23
1981-82—Kitchener Rangers (a-c)		OHL	47	45	52	97	23
1982-83—Minnesota North Stars		NHL	78	35	30	65	27
1983-84—Minnesota North Stars		NHL	78	41	42	83	66
1984-85—Minnesota North Stars		NHL	78	26	36	62	72
1985-86—Minnesota North Stars		NHL	77	31	48	79	46
NHL TOTALS			311	133	156	289	211

(c)—June, 1982—Drafted as underage junior by Minnesota North Stars in NHL entry draft. First North Stars pick, second overall, first round.

ERIC (RICK) BENNETT

Left Wing . . . 6'3" . . . 200 lbs. . . . Born, Springfield, Mass., July 24, 1967 . . . Shoots left.

Year	Team	League	Games	G.	A.	Pts.	Pen.
1985-86—Wilbraham Monson Acad. (c)		Mass. H.S.	20	30	39	69	25

(c)—June, 1986—Drafted by Minnesota North Stars in 1986 NHL entry draft. Fourth North Stars pick, 54th overall, third round.

BRIAN BENNING

Defense . . . 6' . . . 175 lbs. . . . Born, Edmonton, Alta., June 10, 1966 . . . Shoots left . . . Brother of Jim Benning . . . (December, 1983)—Cracked bone in his right wrist and missed 38 games . . . (December 28, 1984)—Broke right leg vs. Victoria.

Year	Team	League	Games	G.	A.	Pts.	Pen.
1983-84—Portland Winter Hawks (c)		WHL	38	6	41	47	108
1984-85—Kamloops Blazers		WHL	17	3	18	21	26
1984-85—St. Louis Blues		NHL	4	0	2	2	0
1985-86—Team Canada		Int'l	60	6	13	19	43
1985-86—St. Louis Blues (d)		NHL	..	..	..	..	..
NHL TOTALS			4	0	2	2	0

(c)—June, 1984—Drafted as underage junior by St. Louis Blues in NHL entry draft. First Blues pick, 26th overall, second round.

(d)—No regular season record. Played six playoff games.

JAMES BENNING

Defense . . . 6' . . . 183 lbs. . . . Born, Edmonton, Alta., April 29, 1963 . . . Shoots left . . . Brother of Brian Benning . . . (February 8, 1986)—Injured ligaments in right knee vs. St. Louis.

Year	Team	League	Games	G.	A.	Pts.	Pen.
1978-79—Ft. Saskatchewan Traders		AJHL	45	14	57	71	10
1979-80—Portland Winter Hawks		WHL	71	11	60	71	42
1980-81—Portland Winter Hawks (a-c-d)		WHL	72	28	*111	139	61
1981-82—Toronto Maple Leafs		NHL	74	7	24	31	46
1982-83—Toronto Maple Leafs		NHL	74	5	17	22	47
1983-84—Toronto Maple Leafs		NHL	79	12	39	51	66
1984-85—Toronto Maple Leafs		NHL	80	9	35	44	55
1985-86—Toronto Maple Leafs		NHL	52	4	21	25	71
NHL TOTALS			359	37	136	173	285

(c)—Winner of WHL Top Defenseman Trophy.

(d)—June, 1981—Drafted as underage junior by Toronto Maple Leafs in NHL entry draft. First Toronto pick, sixth overall, first round.

BRUNET BENOIT

Left Wing . . . 5'11" . . . 180 lbs. . . . Born, Montreal, Que., August 24, 1968 . . . Shoots left.

Year	Team	League	Games	G.	A.	Pts.	Pen.
1985-86—Hull Olympiques (c)		QHL	71	33	37	70	81

(c)—June, 1986—Drafted as underage junior by Montreal Canadiens in 1986 NHL entry draft. Second Canadiens pick, 27th overall, second round.

GUY BENOIT

Center . . . 5'10" . . . 190 lbs. . . . Born, Ste. Hyacinthe, Que., June 18, 1965 . . . Shoots left . . . (January, 1982)—Strained ligaments in left knee.

Year	Team	League	Games	G.	A.	Pts.	Pen.
1981-82—Richelieu AAA		Que. Midget	40	47	57	104	14
1982-83—Shawinigan Cataracts (c)		QHL	61	42	63	105	10
1983-84—Drummondville Voltigeurs		QHL	61	26	56	82	25
1984-85—Drummondville Voltigeurs		QHL	64	56	79	135	53
1985-86—New Haven Nighthawks		AHL	9	1	0	1	0
1985-86—Toledo Goaldiggers		IHL	55	40	46	86	8
1985-86—Muskegon Lumberjacks (d)		IHL	13	7	12	19	16

(c)—June, 1983—Drafted as underage junior by Los Angeles Kings in NHL entry draft. Second Kings pick, 67th overall, fourth round.

(d)—Won Garry F. Longman Memorial Trophy (Top IHL Rookie).

PAUL BERALDO

Right Wing . . . 6' . . . 180 lbs. . . . Born, Stoney Creek, Ont., October 5, 1967 . . . Shoots right.

Year	Team	League	Games	G.	A.	Pts.	Pen.
1984-85—Grimsby Jr.B.		OHA	25	9	4	13	24
1985-86—Sault Ste. Marie Greyhounds (c)		OHL	61	15	13	28	48

(c)—June, 1986—Drafted as underage junior by Boston Bruins in 1986 NHL entry draft. Sixth Bruins pick, 139th overall, seventh round.

PERRY BEREZAN

Center . . . 6'2" . . . 190 lbs. . . . Born, Edmonton, Alta., December 5, 1964 . . . Shoots right . . . (February, 1986)—Missed eight games with sinus problems . . . (March 19, 1986)—Broke ankle in game vs. Minnesota.

Year	Team	League	Games	G.	A.	Pts.	Pen.
1981-82—St. Albert Saints		AJHL	47	16	36	52	47
1982-83—St. Albert Saints (c)		AJHL	57	37	40	77	110
1983-84—Univ. of North Dakota		WCHA	44	28	24	52	29

Year	Team	League	Games	G.	A.	Pts.	Pen.
1984-85—Univ. of North Dakota		WCHA	42	23	35	58	32
1984-85—Calgary Flames		NHL	9	3	2	5	4
1985-86—Calgary Flames		NHL	55	12	21	33	39
NHL TOTALS			64	15	23	38	43

(c)—June, 1983—Drafted as underage junior by Calgary Flames in NHL entry draft. Third Flames pick, 55th overall, third round.

WILLIAM (BILL) BERG

Defense . . . 6' . . . 190 lbs. . . . Born, St. Catharines, Ont., October 21, 1967 . . . Shoots left . . . (March, 1985)—Broken ankle.

Year	Team	League	Games	G.	A.	Pts.	Pen.
1984-85—Grimsby Jr. B		OHA	42	10	22	32	153
1985-86—Toronto Marlboros (c)		OHL	64	3	35	38	143

(c)—June, 1986—Drafted as underage junior by New York Islanders in 1986 NHL entry draft. Third Islanders pick, 59th overall, third round.

TODD BERGEN

Center . . . 6'3" . . . 185 lbs. . . . Born, Prince Albert, Sask., July 11, 1963 . . . Shoots left.

Year	Team	League	Games	G.	A.	Pts.	Pen.
1981-82—Prince Albert Raiders (c)		SJHL	59	30	62	92	35
1982-83—Prince Albert Raiders		WHL	70	34	47	81	17
1983-84—Prince Albert Raiders		WHL	43	57	39	96	15
1983-84—Springfield Indians		AHL	1	0	0	0	0
1984-85—Hershey Bears		AHL	38	20	19	39	2
1984-85—Philadelphia Flyers		NHL	14	11	5	16	4
1985-86—Did not play (d-e)		....	..	..	..	..	..
NHL TOTALS			14	11	5	16	4

(c)—June, 1982—Drafted as underage player by Philadelphia Flyers in NHL entry draft. Fifth Flyers pick, 98th overall, fifth round.

(d)—September, 1985—Announced his retirement to pursue a career as a pro golfer. The Philadelphia Flyers suspended him for failure to report to training camp.

(e)—November, 1985—Traded by Philadelphia Flyers with Ed Hospodar to Minnesota North Stars for Dave Richter and Bo Berglund.

MIKE BERGER

Defense . . . 6'1" . . . 197 lbs. . . . Born, Edmonton, Alta., June 2, 1967 . . . Shoots right . . . (November, 1983)—Separated shoulder . . . (January, 1985)—Hyperextended left knee . . . (October, 1985)—Shoulder injury.

Year	Team	League	Games	G.	A.	Pts.	Pen.
1983-84—Lethbridge Broncos		WHL	41	2	9	11	60
1984-85—Lethbridge Broncos (c)		WHL	58	9	31	40	85
1985-86—Lethbridge Broncos		WHL	21	2	9	11	39
1985-86—Spokane Chiefs (b)		WHL	36	7	31	38	56

(c)—June, 1985—Drafted as underage junior by Minnesota North Stars in NHL entry draft. Second North Stars pick, 69th overall, fourth round.

JEAN-GUY BERGERON

Defense . . . 5'11" . . . 195 lbs. . . . Born, Montreal, Que., April 14, 1965 . . . Shoots right.

Year	Team	League	Games	G.	A.	Pts.	Pen.
1982-83—Shawinigan Cataracts (c)		QHL	66	1	16	17	59
1983-84—St. Jean Beavers		QHL	71	9	34	43	126
1984-85—St. Jean Beavers		QHL	66	17	57	74	71
1985-86—Drummondville Voltigeurs		QHL	61	12	52	64	40

(c)—June, 1983—Drafted as an underage junior by Montreal Canadiens in NHL entry draft. Fourteenth Canadiens pick, 238th overall, 12th round.

MARC BERGEVIN

Defense . . . 6' . . . 185 lbs. . . . Born, Montreal, Que., August 11, 1965 . . . Shoots left.

Year	Team	League	Games	G.	A.	Pts.	Pen.
1982-83—Chicoutimi Sagueneens (c)		QHL	64	3	27	30	113
1983-84—Chicoutimi Sagueneens		QHL	70	10	35	45	125
1983-84—Springfield Indians		AHL	7	0	1	1	2
1984-85—Chicago Black Hawks		NHL	60	0	6	6	54
1985-86—Chicago Black Hawks		NHL	71	7	7	14	60
NHL TOTALS			131	7	13	20	114

(c)—June, 1983—Drafted as underage junior by Chicago Black Hawks in NHL entry draft. Third Black Hawks pick, 59th overall, third round.

BOB BERGLOFF

Defense . . . 6'1" . . . 185 lbs. . . . Born, Dickinson, North Dakota, July 26, 1958 . . . Shoots right.

Year	Team	League	Games	G.	A.	Pts.	Pen.
1979-80	University of Minnesota (c)	WCHA	40	9	22	31	54
1980-81	University of Minnesota	WCHA	45	2	16	18	89
1981-82	Nashville South Stars	CHL	74	2	20	22	111
1981-82	Toledo Goaldiggers	IHL	3	1	1	2	11
1982-83	Birmingham South Stars	CHL	78	6	20	26	156
1982-83	Minnesota North Stars	NHL	2	0	0	0	5
1983-84	Salt Lake Golden Eagles	CHL	44	4	17	21	78
1984-85	Salt Lake Golden Eagles (d)	IHL	9	0	4	4	15
1985-86	New Haven Nighthawks (e)	AHL	7	0	1	1	7
	NHL TOTALS		2	0	0	0	5

(c)—June, 1978—Drafted by Minnesota North Stars in NHL amateur draft. Sixth North Stars pick, 87th overall, sixth round.

(d)—September, 1984—Released by Minnesota North Stars.

(e)—March, 1986—Signed by New Haven Nighthawks as a free agent.

BO BERGLUND

Right Wing . . . 5'10" . . . 175 lbs. . . . Born, Sjalevad, Sweden, April 6, 1955 . . . Shoots left . . . Member of 1980 Swedish Olympic Team (Bronze Medal).

Year	Team	League	Games	G.	A.	Pts.	Pen.
1976-77	MoDo AIK	Sweden	33	17	20	37	30
1977-78	—		..	..	..	..	..
1978-79	Djurgardens IF	Sweden	36	23	18	41	46
1979-80	Djurgardens IF	Sweden	36	21	16	37	50
1979-80	Olympics	Sweden	7	1	3	4	4
1980-81	Djurgardens IF	Sweden	31	13	9	22	64
1981-82	Djurgardens IF	Sweden	34	20	17	37	58
1982-83	Djurgardens IF (c)	Sweden	32	19	13	32	..
1983-84	Quebec Nordiques	NHL	75	16	27	43	20
1984-85	Quebec Nordiques (d)	NHL	12	4	1	5	6
1984-85	Minnesota North Stars	NHL	33	6	9	15	8
1984-85	Springfield Indians	AHL	3	1	2	3	0
1985-86	Minnesota North Stars (e)	NHL	3	2	0	2	2
1985-86	Philadelphia Flyers	NHL	7	0	2	2	4
1985-86	Hershey Bears	AHL	43	17	28	45	40
1985-86	Springfield Indians	AHL	3	0	1	1	2
	NHL TOTALS		130	28	39	67	40

(c)—June, 1983—Drafted by Quebec Nordiques in NHL entry draft. Eleventh Nordiques pick, 232nd overall, 12th round.

(d)—December, 1984—Traded with Tony McKegney by Quebec Nordiques to Minnesota North Stars for Brad Maxwell and Brent Ashton.

(e)—November, 1985—Traded with Dave Richter by Minnesota North Stars to Philadelphia Flyers for Todd Bergen and Ed Hospodar.

TIMOTHY BERGLUND

Center . . . 6'3" . . . 180 lbs. . . . Born, Crookston, Minn., January 11, 1965 . . . Shoots right.

Year	Team	League	Games	G.	A.	Pts.	Pen.
1982-83	Lincoln High School (c)	Minn. H.S.	20	26	22	48	....
1983-84	Univ. of Minnesota	WCHA	24	4	11	15	4
1984-85	Univ. of Minnesota	WCHA	46	7	12	19	16
1985-86	Univ. of Minnesota	WCHA	48	11	16	27	26

(c)—June, 1983—Drafted by Washington Capitals as underage junior in NHL entry draft. First Capitals pick, 75th overall, fourth round.

BRAD BERRY

Defense . . . 6'2" . . . 190 lbs. . . . Born, Barshaw, Alta., April 1, 1965 . . . Shoots left.

Year	Team	League	Games	G.	A.	Pts.	Pen.
1982-83	St. Albert Junior Saints (c)	AJHL	55	9	33	42	97
1983-84	Univ. of North Dakota	WCHA	32	2	7	9	8
1984-85	Univ. of North Dakota	WCHA	40	4	26	30	26
1985-86	Univ. of North Dakota	WCHA	40	6	29	35	26
1985-86	Winnipeg Jets	NHL	13	1	0	1	10
	NHL TOTALS		13	1	0	1	10

(c)—June, 1983—Drafted as underage junior by Winnipeg Jets in NHL entry draft. Third Jets pick, 29th overall, second round.

BRIAN BERTUZZI

Center . . . 5'11" . . . 175 lbs. . . . Born, Vancouver, B.C., January 24, 1966 . . . Shoots left.

Year	Team	League	Games	G.	A.	Pts.	Pen.
1983-84—Kamloops Junior Oilers (c)		WHL	69	29	21	50	99
1984-85—Kamloops Blazers		WHL	46	23	15	38	52
1985-86—New Westminster Bruins		WHL	47	24	24	48	58
1985-86—Kalamazoo Wings		IHL	4	2	0	2	2

(c)—June, 1984—Drafted as underage junior by Vancouver Canucks in NHL entry draft. Fifth Canucks pick, 73rd overall, fourth round.

JEFF BEUKEBOOM

Defense . . . 6'4" . . . 210 lbs. . . . Born, Ajax, Ont., March 28, 1965 . . . Shoots right . . . Brother of John Beukeboom and Brian Beukeboom. Nephew of Ed Kea (Atlanta/St. Louis, '73-'83) . . . First non-goalie to be drafted in first round not to have scored a goal in season prior to being drafted . . . (December, 1984)—Injured knee in World Junior Tournament in game vs. United States.

Year	Team	League	Games	G.	A.	Pts.	Pen.
1981-82—Newmarket		OPJHL	49	5	30	35	218
1982-83—Sault Ste. Marie Greyhounds (c)		OHL	70	0	25	25	143
1983-84—Sault Ste. Marie Greyhounds		OHL	61	6	30	36	178
1984-85—Sault Ste. Marie Greyhounds (a)		OHL	37	4	20	24	85
1985-86—Nova Scotia Oilers		AHL	77	9	20	29	175
1985-86—Edmonton Oilers (d)		NHL	....	...	....	....	....

(c)—June, 1983—Drafted as underage junior by Edmonton Oilers in NHL entry draft. First Oilers pick, 19th overall, first round.

(d)—No regular season record. Played one playoff game.

JOHN BEUKEBOOM

Right Wing and Defense . . . 6'2" . . . 195 lbs. . . . Born, Ajax, Ont., January 1, 1961 . . . Shoots left . . . (February, 1981)—Bruised knee . . . Brother of Jeff Beukeboom and Brian Beukeboom. Nephew of Ed Kea (Atlanta/St. Louis, '73-'83).

Year	Team	League	Games	G.	A.	Pts.	Pen.
1978-79—Peterborough Petes		OMJHL	65	3	15	18	132
1979-80—Peterborough Petes (c)		OMJHL	61	12	23	35	115
1980-81—Peterborough Petes		OHL	58	11	35	46	189
1981-82—Adirondack Red Wings		AHL	59	2	10	12	123
1982-83—Adirondack Red Wings		AHL	72	3	14	17	157
1983-84—Adirondack Red Wings		AHL	16	2	2	4	66
1983-84—Montana Magic		CHL	59	6	26	32	166
1984-85—Adirondack Red Wings		AHL	63	4	17	21	167
1985-86—Kalamazoo Wings		IHL	78	7	36	43	244

(c)—June, 1980—Drafted as underage junior by Detroit Red Wings in NHL entry draft. Sixth Red Wings pick, 151st overall, eighth round.

DON BIGGS

Center . . . 5'8" . . . 180 lbs. . . . Born, Mississauga, Ont., April 7, 1965 . . . Shoots right . . . (April, 1982)—Injured knee ligaments.

Year	Team	League	Games	G.	A.	Pts.	Pen.
1981-82—Mississauga Reds		MTHL	54	49	67	116	125
1982-83—Oshawa Generals (c)		OHL	70	22	53	75	145
1983-84—Oshawa Generals		OHL	58	31	60	91	149
1984-85—Oshawa Generals		OHL	60	48	69	117	105
1984-85—Springfield Indians		AHL	6	0	3	3	0
1984-85—Minnesota North Stars		NHL	1	0	0	0	0
1985-86—Springfield Indians (d)		AHL	28	15	16	31	46
1985-86—Nova Scotia Oilers		AHL	47	6	23	29	36
NHL TOTALS			1	0	0	0	0

(c)—June, 1983—Drafted as underage junior by Minnesota North Stars in NHL entry draft. Ninth North Stars pick, 156th overall, eighth round.

(d)—December, 1985—Traded with Gord Sherven by Minnesota North Stars to Edmonton Oilers for Marc Habscheid, Emanuel Viveiros and Don Barber.

CHRIS BIOTTI

Defense . . . 6'3" . . . 198 lbs. . . . Born, Waltham, Mass., April 22, 1967 . . . Shoots left . . . (August, 1985)—Injured shoulder during U.S. Sports festival.

Year	Team	League	Games	G.	A.	Pts.	Pen.
1983-84—Belmont Hill H.S.		Mass.H.S.	23	10	20	30	....

Year	Team	League	Games	G.	A.	Pts.	Pen.
1984-85—Belmont Hill H.S. (c)		Mass.H.S.	23	13	24	37	....
1985-86—Harvard University		ECAC	15	3	5	8	53

(c)—June, 1985—Drafted by Calgary Flames in 1985 NHL entry draft. First Flames pick, 17th overall, first round.

SCOT BIRNIE

Right Wing ... 6'1" ... 190 lbs. ... Born, Kingston, Ont., May 1, 1965 ... Shoots right.

Year	Team	League	Games	G.	A.	Pts.	Pen.
1981-82—Brockville Braves		OPJHL	46	10	22	32	145
1982-83—Cornwall Royals (c)		OHL	63	15	13	28	87
1983-84—Cornwall Royals		OHL	5	2	1	3	12
1983-84—North Bay Centennials		OHL	59	10	24	34	108
1984-85—North Bay Centennials		OHL	16	4	13	17	29
1984-85—Kingston Canadians		OHL	24	8	13	21	42
1984-85—Toledo Goaldiggers		IHL	12	2	1	3	48
1985-86—Toledo Goaldiggers (d)		IHL	45	11	19	30	65
1985-86—Flint Spirit		IHL	31	8	13	21	29

(c)—June, 1983—Drafted as underage junior by Chicago Black Hawks in NHL entry draft. Eighth Black Hawks pick, 139th overall, seventh round.

(d)—February, 1986—Claimed by Flint Spirit when placed on waivers by Toledo Goaldiggers.

MICHAEL BISHOP

Defense ... 6'2" ... 187 lbs. ... Born, Sarnia, Ont., June 15, 1966 ... Shoots left.

Year	Team	League	Games	G.	A.	Pts.	Pen.
1983-84—Mooretown Flags Jr.C		OHA	40	24	24	48	91
1984-85—Sarnia Bees Jr.B (c)		OHA	43	9	32	41	104
1985-86—Colgate University		ECAC	25	9	8	17	63

(c)—June, 1985—Drafted as underage junior by Montreal Canadiens in 1985 NHL entry draft. Fourteenth Canadiens pick, 226th overall, 11th round.

STEVEN GUY BISSON

Defense ... 6'1" ... 175 lbs. ... Born, Ottawa, Ont., May 24, 1968 ... Shoots left ... (September, 1985)—Broken thumb.

Year	Team	League	Games	G.	A.	Pts.	Pen.
1984-85—Ottawa Senators		OHA	49	1	15	16	96
1985-86—Sault Ste. Marie Greyhounds (c)		OHL	66	3	23	26	44

(c)—June, 1986—Drafted as an underage junior by Montreal Canadiens in 1986 NHL entry draft. Seventh Canadiens pick, 120th overall, sixth round.

JOHN BJORKMAN

Center ... 6'1" ... 180 lbs. ... Born, Dover, N.H., July 14, 1964 ... Shoots left.

Year	Team	League	Games	G.	A.	Pts.	Pen.
1982-83—Warroad H.S. (c)		Minn. H.S.	22	30	18	48	....
1983-84—Univ. of Michigan		CCHA	36	9	12	21	33
1984-85—Univ. of Michigan		CCHA	38	10	16	26	46
1985-86—Univ. of Michigan		CCHA	7	0	0	0	6

(c)—June, 1983—Drafted by New York Islanders in NHL entry draft. Thirteenth Islanders pick, 217th overall, 11th round.

SCOTT BJUGSTAD

Left Wing ... 6'1" ... 185 lbs. ... Born St. Paul, Minn., June 2, 1981 ... Shoots left ... 1979 graduate of Minnesota Irondale High School where he was All-Conference for three years and All-State as a senior ... Named prep All-America in Soccer ... Member of 1984 U.S. Olympic Team ... Also plays Center.

Year	Team	League	Games	G.	A.	Pts.	Pen.
1979-80—University of Minnesota		WCHA	18	2	2	4	2
1980-81—University of Minnesota (c)		WCHA	35	12	13	25	34
1981-82—University of Minnesota		WCHA	36	29	14	43	24
1982-83—University of Minnesota		WCHA	44	43	48	91	30
1983-84—U.S. National Team		Int'l	54	31	20	51	28
1983-84—U.S. Olympic Team		Int'l	6	3	2	5	6
1983-84—Minnesota North Stars		NHL	5	0	0	0	2
1983-84—Salt Lake Golden Eagles		CHL	15	10	8	18	6
1984-85—Minnesota North Stars		NHL	72	11	4	15	32
1984-85—Springfield Indians		AHL	5	2	3	5	6
1985-86—Minnesota North Stars		NHL	80	43	33	76	24
NHL TOTALS			157	54	37	91	58

(c)—June, 1981—Drafted by Minnesota North Stars in NHL entry draft. Thirteenth North Stars pick, 181st overall, ninth round.

MICHAEL WALTER BLAISDELL

Right Wing ... 6'1" ... 196 lbs. ... Born, Moose Jaw, Sask., January 18, 1960 ... Shoots right ... (November 6, 1985)—Pulled groin in game vs. Washington and missed two games.

Year	Team	League	Games	G.	A.	Pts.	Pen.
1977-78—Regina Pats		WCHL	6	5	5	10	2
1977-78—Regina Blues		SJHL	60	70	46	116	43
1978-79—University of Wisconsin		WCHA	20	7	1	8	15
1979-80—Regina Pats (b-c)		WHL	63	71	38	109	62
1980-81—Adirondack Red Wings		AHL	41	10	4	14	8
1980-81—Detroit Red Wings		NHL	32	3	6	9	10
1981-82—Detroit Red Wings		NHL	80	23	32	55	48
1982-83—Detroit Red Wings (d)		NHL	80	18	23	41	22
1983-84—Tulsa Oilers		CHL	32	10	8	18	23
1983-84—New York Rangers		NHL	36	5	6	11	31
1984-85—New Haven Nighthawks		AHL	64	21	23	44	41
1984-85—New York Rangers		NHL	12	1	0	1	11
1985-86—Pittsburgh Penguins (e)		NHL	66	15	14	29	36
NHL TOTALS			306	65	81	146	158

(c)—June, 1980—Drafted by Detroit Red Wings in NHL entry draft. First Red Wings pick, 11th overall, first round.

(d)—June, 1983—Traded with Mark Osborne and Willie Huber by Detroit Red Wings to New York Rangers for Ron Duguay, Eddie Johnstone and Eddie Mio.

(e)—October, 1985—Acquired by Pittsburgh Penguins in 1985 NHL waiver draft.

JEFF BLOEMBERG

Defense ... 6'1" ... 200 lbs. ... Born, Listowel, Ont., January 31, 1968 ... Shoots right.

Year	Team	League	Games	G.	A.	Pts.	Pen.
1984-85—Listowell Jr. B		OHA	31	7	14	21	73
1985-86—North Bay Centennials (c)		OHL	60	2	11	13	76

(c)—June, 1986—Drafted as underage junior by New York Rangers in 1986 NHL entry draft. Fifth Rangers pick, 93rd overall, fifth round.

TIMO BLOMQVIST

Defense ... 6' ... 198 lbs. ... Born, Helsinki, Finland, January 23, 1961 ... Shoots right ... (September, 1981)—Broken jaw during exhibition series in Finland ... (October, 1983)—Ankle injury.

Year	Team	League	Games	G.	A.	Pts.	Pen.
1978-79—Jokerit Helsinki		Finland	36	4	2	6	35
1979-80—Jokerit Helsinki		Finland	32	3	1	4	52
1980-81—Kiekkoreipas Lahti (c)		Finland	30	6	7	13	14
1981-82—Hershey Bears		AHL	13	0	8	8	13
1981-82—Washington Capitals		NHL	44	1	11	12	62
1982-83—Hershey Bears		AHL	8	2	7	9	16
1982-83—Washington Capitals		NHL	61	1	17	18	67
1983-84—Washington Capitals		NHL	65	1	19	20	84
1984-85—Washington Capitals		NHL	53	1	4	5	51
1985-86—Binghamton Whalers (d)		AHL	71	6	18	24	76
NHL TOTALS			223	4	51	55	264

(c)—June, 1980—Drafted by Washington Capitals in NHL entry draft. Fourth Capitals pick, 89th overall, fifth round.

(d)—July, 1986—Signed by New Jersey Devils as a free agent.

JOHN BLUM

Defense ... 6'3" ... 205 lbs. ... Born, Detroit, Mich., October 8, 1959 ... Shoots right.

Year	Team	League	Games	G.	A.	Pts.	Pen.
1980-81—University of Michigan		WCHA	....	8	32	40	....
1981-82—Wichita Wind (c)		CHL	79	8	33	41	247
1982-83—Moncton Alpines		AHL	76	10	30	40	219
1982-83—Edmonton Oilers		NHL	5	0	3	3	24
1983-84—Moncton Alpines		AHL	57	3	22	25	202
1983-84—Edmonton Oilers (d)		NHL	4	0	1	1	2
1983-84—Boston Bruins		NHL	12	1	1	2	30
1984-85—Boston Bruins		NHL	75	3	13	16	263
1985-86—Boston Bruins		NHL	61	1	7	8	80
1985-86—Moncton Golden Flames		AHL	12	1	5	6	37
NHL TOTALS			157	5	25	30	399

(c)—May, 1981—Signed by Edmonton Oilers as a free agent.

(d)—March, 1983—Traded by Edmonton Oilers to Boston Bruins for Larry Melnyk.

BRENT BOBYCK

Left Wing . . . 5'11" . . . 180 lbs. . . . Born, Regina, Sask., April 26, 1968 . . . Shoots left.

Year	Team	League	Games	G.	A.	Pts.	Pen.
1985-86—Notre Dame Hounds (c)		Sask.	25	13	27	40	12

(c)—June, 1986—Drafted by Montreal Canadiens in 1986 NHL entry draft. Fourth Canadiens pick, 78th overall, fourth round.

BOB BODAK

Left Wing . . . 6'2" . . . 190 lbs. . . . Born, Thunder Bay, Ont., May 28, 1961 . . . Shoots left.

Year	Team	League	Games	G.	A.	Pts.	Pen.
1983-84—Lakehead University		....	....	...	....	....	....
1984-85—Springfield Indians (c)		AHL	79	21	24	45	52
1985-86—Springfield Indians		AHL	4	0	0	0	4
1985-86—Moncton Golden Flames		AHL	58	27	15	42	114

(c)—September, 1984—Signed by Springfield Indians as a free agent.

DOUG BODGER

Defense . . . 6'2" . . . 200 lbs. . . . Born, Chemainus, B.C., June 18, 1966 . . . Shoots left . . . (February, 1985)—Missed four games with slight shoulder separation . . . (April, 1985)— Surgery to remove bone chip near big toe of left foot.

Year	Team	League	Games	G.	A.	Pts.	Pen.
1982-83—Kamloops Junior Oilers (b)		WHL	72	26	66	92	98
1983-84—Kamloops Junior Oilers (a-c)		WHL	70	21	77	98	90
1984-85—Pittsburgh Penguins		NHL	65	5	26	31	67
1985-86—Pittsburgh Penguins		NHL	79	4	33	37	63
NHL TOTALS			144	9	59	68	130

(c)—June, 1984—Drafted as underage junior by Pittsburgh Penguins in NHL entry draft. Second Penguins pick, ninth overall, first round.

DWAYNE BOETTGER

Defense . . . 6'1" . . . 190 lbs. . . . Born, Brampton, Ont., February 6, 1963 . . . Shoots left.

Year	Team	League	Games	G.	A.	Pts.	Pen.
1980-81—Markham Tier II		OPJHL	26	3	5	8	61
1981-82—Toronto Marlboros (c)		OHL	66	4	21	25	138
1982-83—Toronto Marlboros		OHL	68	3	15	18	120
1983-84—Moncton Alpines		AHL	75	1	18	19	160
1984-85—Nova Scotia Oilers		AHL	70	3	11	14	71
1985-86—Nova Scotia Oilers		AHL	64	2	15	17	103

(c)—June, 1982—Drafted as underage junior by Edmonton Oilers in NHL entry draft. Fifth Oilers pick, 104th overall, fifth round.

FRED BOIMISTRUCK

Defense . . . 5'11" . . . 190 lbs. . . . Born, Sudbury, Ont., January 14, 1962 . . . Shoots right.

Year	Team	League	Games	G.	A.	Pts.	Pen.
1979-80—Cornwall Royals (c)		QMJHL	70	12	34	46	99
1980-81—Cornwall Royals (a-d)		QMJHL	68	22	48	70	158
1981-82—Toronto Maple Leafs		NHL	57	2	11	13	32
1982-83—St. Catharines Saints		AHL	50	6	23	29	32
1982-83—Toronto Maple Leafs		NHL	26	2	3	5	13
1983-84—St. Catharines Saints		AHL	80	2	28	30	68
1984-85—Fort Wayne Komets (e)		IHL	2	0	1	1	5
1985-86—Flint Spirit		IHL	17	3	6	9	15
NHL TOTALS			83	4	14	18	45

(c)—June, 1980—Drafted as underage junior by Toronto Maple Leafs in NHL entry draft. Third Maple Leafs pick, 43rd overall, third round.
(d)—Winner of Emile "Butch" Bouchard Trophy (Top QMJHL Defenseman).
(e)—October, 1984—Released by Los Angeles Kings.

JEAN BOIS

Left Wing . . . 5'11" . . . 185 lbs. . . . Born, Sherbrooke, Que., May 2, 1967 . . . Shoots left.

Year	Team	League	Games	G.	A.	Pts.	Pen.
1983-84—Magog Cantonniers		Que.Midget	40	23	47	70	54
1984-85—Trois Rivieres Draveurs (c)		QHL	67	33	51	84	103
1985-86—Shawinigan Cataracts		QHL	69	31	64	95	111

(c)—June, 1985—Drafted as underage junior by Quebec Nordiques in 1985 NHL entry draft. 13th Nordiques pick, 246th overall, 12th round.

SERGE BOISVERT

Right Wing . . . 5'9" . . . 175 lbs. . . . Born, Drummondville, Que., June 1, 1959 . . . Shoots right . . . Also plays Center.

Year	Team	League	Games	G.	A.	Pts.	Pen.
1977-78—Sherbrooke Beavers		QMJHL	55	17	33	50	19
1978-79—Sherbrooke Beavers		QMJHL	72	50	72	122	45
1979-80—Sherbrooke Beavers		QMJHL	69	52	72	124	47
1979-80—New Brunswick Hawks (c)		AHL	..	..	..	..	..
1980-81—New Brunswick Hawks		AHL	60	19	27	46	31
1981-82—		...	...	..	...	...	..
1982-83—Toronto Maple Leafs (d)		NHL	17	0	2	2	4
1982-83—St. Catharines Saints		AHL	19	10	9	19	2
1982-83—Moncton Alpines		AHL	29	6	12	18	7
1983-84—Moncton Alpines		AHL	66	15	13	28	34
1984-85—Sherbrooke Canadiens (e)		AHL	63	38	41	79	8
1984-85—Montreal Canadiens		NHL	14	2	2	4	0
1985-86—Sherbrooke Canadiens (b)		AHL	69	40	48	88	18
1985-86—Montreal Canadiens		NHL	9	2	2	4	2
NHL TOTALS			40	4	6	10	6

(c)—No regular season record. Scored four goals in seven playoff games.
(d)—January, 1983—Traded by Toronto Maple Leafs to Edmonton Oilers for Reid Bailey.
(e)—September, 1984—Signed by Montreal Canadiens as a free agent.

SEAN BOLAND

Defense . . . 6'3" . . . 185 lbs. . . . Born, Toronto, Ont., February 18, 1968 . . . Shoots right.

Year	Team	League	Games	G.	A.	Pts.	Pen.
1984-85—Toronto Nationals		MTHL	60	17	24	41	90
1985-86—Toronto Marlboros (c)		OHL	52	2	10	12	85

(c)—June, 1986—Drafted as underage junior by Toronto Maple Leafs in 1986 NHL entry draft. Third Maple Leafs pick, 48th overall, third round.

MICHEL BOLDUC

Defense . . . 6'2" . . . 210 lbs. . . . Born, Ange-Gardien, Que., March 13, 1961 . . . Shoots left.

Year	Team	League	Games	G.	A.	Pts.	Pen.
1977-78—Hull Festivals		QMJHL	60	1	5	6	36
1978-79—Hull Olympics		QMJHL	6	0	1	1	5
1978-79—Chicoutimi Sagueneens		QMJHL	66	1	23	24	142
1979-80—Chicoutimi Sagueneens (c)		QMJHL	65	3	29	32	219
1980-81—Chicoutimi Sagueneens		QMJHL	67	11	35	46	244
1981-82—Quebec Nordiques		NHL	3	0	0	0	0
1981-82—Fredericton Express		AHL	69	4	9	13	130
1982-83—Fredericton Express		AHL	68	4	18	22	165
1982-83—Quebec Nordiques		NHL	7	0	0	0	6
1983-84—Fredericton Express		AHL	70	2	15	17	96
1984-85—Fredericton Express (d)		AHL	29	0	9	9	74
1984-85—Maine Mariners		AHL	31	1	7	8	86
1985-86—Maine Mariners		AHL	66	1	6	7	29
NHL TOTALS			10	0	0	0	6

(c)—June, 1980—Drafted as underage junior by Quebec Nordiques in NHL entry draft. Sixth Nordiques pick, 150th overall, eighth round.
(d)—January, 1985—Acquired by New Jersey Devils on waivers from Quebec Nordiques.

GRAEME BONAR

Right Wing . . . 6'3" . . . 205 lbs. . . . Born, Toronto, Ont., January 21, 1966 . . . Shoots right.

Year	Team	League	Games	G.	A.	Pts.	Pen.
1981-82—Henry Carr H.S.		MTJHL	35	27	24	51	32
1982-83—Windsor Spitfires		OHL	70	14	26	40	78

Year	Team	League	Games	G.	A.	Pts.	Pen.
1983-84—Windsor Spitfires		OHL	21	5	9	14	37
1983-84—Sault Ste. Marie Greyhounds (c)		OHL	44	10	30	40	43
1984-85—Sault Ste. Marie Greyhounds (a)		OHL	66	*66	71	137	93
1985-86—Sault Ste. Marie Greyhounds (d)		OHL	38	33	25	58	21
1985-86—Peterborough Petes (b)		OHL	18	20	15	35	20

(c)—June, 1984—Drafted as underage junior by Montreal Canadiens in NHL entry draft. Fifth Canadiens pick, 54th overall, third round.

(d)—February, 1986—Traded by Sault Ste. Marie Greyhounds to Peterborough Petes for Brad Aitken and future considerations.

JOHN BORRELL

Right Wing . . . 6'2" . . . 190 lbs. . . . Born, Shakopee, Minn., March 23, 1967 . . . Shoots right.

Year	Team	League	Games	G.	A.	Pts.	Pen.
1984-85—Burnsville H.S. (c)		Minn.H.S.	27	20	16	36	16
1985-86—University of Lowell		H. East	41	3	15	18	12

(c)—June, 1985—Drafted by Winnipeg Jets in 1985 NHL entry draft. Fifth Jets pick, 102nd overall, fifth round.

LUCIANO BORSATO

Center . . . 5'10" . . . 165 lbs. . . . Born, Richmond Hill, Ont., January 7, 1966 . . . Shoots right.

Year	Team	League	Games	G.	A.	Pts.	Pen.
1983-84—Bramalea Blues (c)		MTJHL	37	20	36	56	59
1984-85—Clarkson University		ECAC	33	15	17	32	37
1985-86—Clarkson University		ECAC	32	17	20	37	50

(c)—June, 1984—Drafted as underage junior by Winnipeg Jets in NHL entry draft. Seventh Jets pick, 135th overall, seventh round.

LAURIE JOSEPH BOSCHMAN

Center . . . 6' . . . 185 lbs. . . . Born, Major, Sask., June 4, 1960 . . . Shoots left . . . (December 7, 1980)—Finger tendon injury . . . (January, 1981)—Mononucleous . . . (December 7, 1983) —Dislocated shoulder in game at New Jersey.

Year	Team	League	Games	G.	A.	Pts.	Pen.
1976-77—Brandon		MJHL	47	17	40	57	139
1976-77—Brandon Wheat Kings		WCHL	3	0	1	1	0
1977-78—Brandon Wheat Kings		WCHL	72	42	57	99	227
1978-79—Brandon Wheat Kings (a-c)		WCHL	65	66	83	149	215
1979-80—Toronto Maple Leafs		NHL	80	16	32	48	78
1980-81—New Brunswick Hawks		AHL	4	4	1	5	47
1980-81—Toronto Maple Leafs		NHL	53	14	19	33	178
1981-82—Toronto Maple Leafs (d)		NHL	54	9	19	28	150
1981-82—Edmonton Oilers		NHL	11	2	3	5	37
1982-83—Edmonton Oilers (e)		NHL	62	8	12	20	183
1982-83—Winnipeg Jets		NHL	12	3	5	8	33
1983-84—Winnipeg Jets		NHL	61	28	46	74	234
1984-85—Winnipeg Jets		NHL	80	32	44	76	180
1985-86—Winnipeg Jets		NHL	77	27	42	69	241
NHL TOTALS			490	139	222	361	1314

(c)—August, 1979—Drafted by Toronto Maple Leafs in NHL entry draft. First Toronto pick, ninth overall, first round.

(d)—March, 1982—Traded by Toronto Maple Leafs to Edmonton Oilers for Walt Poddubny and Phil Drouillard.

(e)—March, 1983—Traded by Edmonton Oilers to Winnipeg Jets for Willy Lindstrom.

MICHEL (MIKE) BOSSY

Right Wing . . . 6' . . . 186 lbs. . . . Born, Montreal, Que., January 22, 1957 . . . Shoots right . . . Set NHL record for goals in season by a rookie (53 in 1977-78) . . . Set NHL record for fastest 100 goals (129 games) . . . Tied NHL record with goals in 10 straight games 1977-78 (Since broken by Charlie Simmer). . . Tied NHL record of Rocket Richard for fastest 50 goals (in 50 games) 1980-81 (Since broken by Wayne Gretzky) . . . Set record for most goals in regular season plus playoffs (85) 1980-81 (Since broken by Wayne Gretzky) . . . Set record for most points in a playoff year (35) 1981 (Since broken by Wayne Gretzky) . . . Set record for most hat tricks in one season (9) 1980-81 (Since broken by Wayne Gretzky) . . . Set NHL record for fastest 250 goals (315 games) (Since broken by Wayne Gretzky) . . . Set record for most goals (69) by a right wing 1978-79 (Since broken by Jari

Kurri) . . . Set record for most assists by a right wing (83) 1981-82 . . . Set record for most points by a right wing (147) 1981-82 . . . Injured left knee during 1983 playoffs . . . (October, 1983)—Pulled hip muscle . . . (January 28, 1984)—Sprained right knee in collision with Dwight Foster in game vs. Detroit . . . (September, 1984)—Injured right knee during training camp . . . (January 16, 1985)—Pulled muscle on left side in game at Edmonton . . . First NHL player to have eight consecutive 50-goal seasons . . . (1986 Playoffs)—Broke Maurice Richard's record for most playoff goals (82).

Year	Team	League	Games	G.	A.	Pts.	Pen.
1972-73—Laval National		QJHL	4	1	2	3	0
1973-74—Laval National		QJHL	68	70	48	118	45
1974-75—Laval National (a)		QJHL	67	*84	65	149	42
1975-76—Laval National (b)		QJHL	64	79	57	136	25
1976-77—Laval National (b-c-d)		QJHL	61	75	51	126	12
1977-78—New York Islanders (b-e)		NHL	73	53	38	91	6
1978-79—New York Islanders (b)		NHL	80	*69	57	126	25
1979-80—New York Islanders		NHL	75	51	41	92	12
1980-81—New York Islanders (a-f)		NHL	79	*68	51	119	32
1981-82—New York Islanders (a-g-h)		NHL	80	64	83	147	22
1982-83—New York Islanders (a-h-i)		NHL	79	60	58	118	20
1983-84—New York Islanders (a-i)		NHL	67	51	67	118	8
1984-85—New York Islanders (b)		NHL	76	58	59	117	38
1985-86—New York Islanders (a-i)		NHL	80	61	62	123	14
NHL TOTALS			689	535	516	1051	177

(c)—Most Gentlemanly Player Award winner.
(d)—Drafted from Laval National by New York Islanders in first round of 1977 amateur draft.
(e)—Won Calder Memorial Trophy and named THE SPORTING NEWS NHL Rookie of the Year.
(f)—Tied with Steve Payne (Minn.) for playoff lead in goals (17), tied Bryan Trottier (NYI) for playoff lead in assists (18) and led 1981 playoffs with 35 points.
(g)—Won Conn Smythe Trophy (Most Valuable Player in Stanley Cup Playoffs).
(h)—Led Stanley Cup Playoffs with 17 goals.
(i)—Won Lady Byng Trophy (Combination of Sportsmanship and Quality play).

MARK BOTELL

Defense . . . 6'4" . . . 220 lbs. . . . Born, Scarborough, Ont., August 27, 1961 . . . Shoots left.

Year	Team	League	Games	G.	A.	Pts.	Pen.
1978-79—Niagara Falls Flyers		OMJHL	55	2	8	10	122
1979-80—Niagara Falls Flyers		OMJHL	20	2	5	7	11
1979-80—Windsor Spitfires		OMJHL	2	0	0	0	2
1979-80—Brantford Alexanders (c)		OMJHL	15	2	3	5	24
1980-81—Brantford Alexanders		OHL	58	11	20	31	143
1980-81—Maine Mariners		AHL	2	0	1	1	0
1981-82—Maine Mariners		AHL	42	3	14	17	41
1981-82—Philadelphia Flyers		NHL	32	4	10	14	31
1982-83—Maine Mariners		AHL	30	1	4	5	26
1982-83—Toledo Goaldiggers		IHL	24	6	14	20	43
1983-84—Montana Magic		CHL	2	0	0	0	2
1983-84—Toledo Goaldiggers		IHL	78	16	27	43	164
1984-85—Peoria Rivermen		IHL	70	6	21	27	77
1985-86—St. Catharines Saints (d)		AHL	11	1	3	4	17
NHL TOTALS			32	4	10	14	31

(c)—June, 1980—Drafted as underage junior by Philadelphia Flyers in NHL entry draft. Eighth Flyers pick, 168th overall, eighth round.
(d)—March, 1986—Signed by St. Catharines Saints as a free agent.

TIM BOTHWELL

Defense . . . 6'3" . . . 195 lbs. . . . Born, Vancouver, B.C., May 6, 1955 . . . Shoots left . . . Missed part of 1974-75 season with broken ankle . . . Missed part of 1978-79 season with fractured cheekbone that required surgery . . . (October, 1981)—Badly strained stomach muscles . . . (March 1, 1983)—Cut tendons in left hand in game vs. Los Angeles . . . (January, 1984)—Injured ligament in right knee during CHL game . . . (October, 1985)—Missed seven games due to a parasitic infection caused by drinking tainted water . . . (March 17, 1986)—Missed four games with sprained right shoulder when checked in a team practice.

Year	Team	League	Games	G.	A.	Pts.	Pen.
1973-74—Burlington Mohawks		....	..	..	..	..	..
1974-75—Brown University JV		ECAC	9	6	9	15	14
1975-76—Brown University		ECAC	29	12	22	34	30
1976-77—Brown University (a)		ECAC	27	7	27	34	40
1977-78—Brown University (a-c)		ECAC	29	9	26	35	48
1978-79—New York Rangers		NHL	1	0	0	0	2
1978-79—New Haven Nighthawks		AHL	66	15	33	48	44

Year	Team	League	Games	G.	A.	Pts.	Pen.
1979-80—New Haven Nighthawks	AHL	22	6	7	13	25
1979-80—New York Rangers	NHL	45	4	6	10	20
1980-81—New Haven Nighthawks	AHL	73	10	53	63	98
1980-81—New York Rangers	NHL	3	0	1	1	0
1981-82—Springfield Indians	AHL	10	0	4	4	7
1981-82—New York Rangers (d)	NHL	13	0	3	3	10
1982-83—St. Louis Blues	NHL	61	4	11	15	34
1983-84—Montana Magic	CHL	4	0	3	3	0
1983-84—St. Louis Blues	NHL	62	2	13	15	65
1984-85—St. Louis Blues	NHL	79	4	22	26	62
1985-86—Hartford Whalers (e)	NHL	62	2	8	10	53
NHL TOTALS		326	16	64	80	246

(c)—Signed by New York Rangers, May, 1978.
(d)—October, 1982—Claimed by St. Louis Blues in NHL waiver draft.
(e)—October, 1985—Sold by St. Louis Blues to Hartford Whalers.

BRUCE ALLAN BOUDREAU

Center . . . 5'10" . . . 170 lbs. . . . Born, Toronto, Ont., January 9, 1955 . . . Shoots left . . . Set OMJHL record with 165 pts. in '74-75 (Broken in '75-76 by Mike Kaszycki's 170 pts.) . . . Set OMJHL record with 68 goals in '74-75 (Broken in '77-78 by Bobby Smith's 69) . . . (1983-84)—Assistant coach at St. Catharines . . . (February, 1986)—Broke hand in AHL game.

Year	Team	League	Games	G.	A.	Pts.	Pen.
1972-73—Toronto Marlboros	Jr."A"OHA	61	38	49	87	22
1973-74—Toronto Marlboros (b-c)	Jr."A"OHA	53	46	67	113	51
1974-75—Toronto Marlboros (d-e)	Jr."A"OHA	69	*68	97	*165	52
1975-76—Johnstown Jets	NAHL	34	25	35	60	14
1975-76—Minnesota Fighting Saints (f)	WHA	30	3	6	9	4
1976-77—Dallas Black Hawks	CHL	58	*37	34	71	40
1976-77—Toronto Maple Leafs	NHL	15	2	5	7	4
1977-78—Dallas Black Hawks	CHL	22	13	9	22	11
1977-78—Toronto Maple Leafs	NHL	40	11	18	29	12
1978-79—Toronto Maple Leafs	NHL	26	4	3	7	2
1978-79—New Brunswick Hawks	AHL	49	20	38	58	22
1979-80—Toronto Maple Leafs	NHL	2	0	0	0	2
1979-80—New Brunswick Hawks	AHL	75	36	54	90	47
1980-81—New Brunswick Hawks	AHL	40	17	41	58	22
1980-81—Toronto Maple Leafs	NHL	39	10	14	24	18
1981-82—Cincinnati Tigers (b)	AHL	65	42	61	103	42
1981-82—Toronto Maple Leafs	NHL	12	0	2	2	6
1982-83—St. Catharines Saints	AHL	80	50	72	122	65
1982-83—Toronto Maple Leafs (g)	NHL	..	..	..	..	..
1983-84—St. Catharines Saints	AHL	80	47	62	109	44
1984-85—Baltimore Skipjacks (h)	AHL	17	4	7	11	4
1985-86—Chicago Black Hawks (i)	NHL	7	1	0	1	2
1985-86—Nova Scotia Oilers	AHL	65	30	36	66	36
NHL TOTALS		141	28	42	70	46
WHA TOTALS		30	3	6	9	4

(c)—Selected by Minnesota Fighting Saints in World Hockey Association amateur player draft, May, 1974.
(d)—Won Eddie Powers Memorial Trophy (leading scorer).
(e)—Drafted from Toronto Marlboros by Toronto Maple Leafs in third round of 1975 amateur draft.
(f)—Signed by Toronto Maple Leafs, August, 1976.
(g)—Played four playoff games (1 goal), none in regular season.
(h)—March, 1985—Signed by Baltimore Skipjacks as a free agent after completing season in West Germany.
(i)—August, 1985—Released by Detroit Red Wings and signed by Chicago Black Hawks as a free agent.

MARTIN BOULIANE

Center . . . 5'10" . . . 175 lbs. . . . Born, Amqui, Que., April 9, 1965 . . . Shoots right.

Year	Team	League	Games	G.	A.	Pts.	Pen.
1981-82—Ste. Foy Midget	Que. Midget	44	48	45	93	14
1982-83—Granby Bisons (c)	QHL	70	39	64	103	10
1983-84—Granby Bisons	QHL	62	41	41	82	6
1984-85—Granby Bisons	QHL	67	52	82	134	11
1985-86—Team Canada	Int'l	67	16	23	39	28

(c)—June, 1983—Drafted as underage junior by Washington Capitals in 1983 NHL entry draft. Second Capitals pick, 95th overall, fifth round.

CHARLES BOURGEOIS

Defense . . . 6'4" . . . 205 lbs. . . . Born, Moncton, N.B., November 11, 1959 . . . Shoots right.

Year	Team	League	Games	G.	A.	Pts.	Pen.
1980-81	University of Moncton (a-c-d)	AUAA	24	8	23	31	..
1981-82	Oklahoma City Stars	CHL	13	2	2	4	17
1981-82	Calgary Flames	NHL	54	2	13	15	112
1982-83	Calgary Flames	NHL	15	2	3	5	21
1982-83	Colorado Flames	CHL	51	10	18	28	128
1983-84	Colorado Flames (a)	CHL	54	12	32	44	133
1983-84	Calgary Flames	NHL	17	1	3	4	35
1984-85	Calgary Flames	NHL	47	2	10	12	134
1985-86	Calgary Flames (e)	NHL	29	5	5	10	128
1985-86	St. Louis Blues	NHL	31	2	7	9	116
	NHL TOTALS		193	14	41	55	546

(c)—Named to All Canada Team (East).
(d)—April, 1981—Signed by Calgary Flames as free agent.
(e)—February, 1986—Traded with Gino Cavallini and Eddy Beers by Calgary Flames to St. Louis Blues for Joe Mullen, Terry Johnson and Rik Wilson.

GLEN ROBERT (BOB) BOURNE

Center and Left Wing . . . 6'3" . . . 195 lbs. . . . Born, Kindersley, Sask., June 21, 1954 . . . Shoots left . . . Signed a contract with Houston Astros at Covington, Va. Batted .257 . . . (October 17, 1981)—Pulled muscles in upper thigh . . . (October 8, 1983)—Scored first overtime goal in NHL since November 10, 1942 when Lynn Patrick scored in a N.Y. Rangers' 5-3 OT win vs. Chicago. Bourne's goal beat Washington Capitals, 7-6, at the Capital Centre at 2:01 of overtime . . . (November, 1984)—Took 21 stitches in head when hit by a shot during a team practice . . . (January 19, 1985)—Cut tendons in right hand during game at Los Angeles and required surgery . . . (September, 1985)—Injured ribs in training camp and missed first eight games . . . (November 30, 1985)—Injured mouth at Calgary and missed two games.

Year	Team	League	Games	G.	A.	Pts.	Pen.
1971-72	Saskatoon Blades	WCHL	63	28	32	60	36
1972-73	Saskatoon Blades	WCHL	66	40	53	93	74
1973-74	Saskatoon Blades (c-d)	WCHL	63	29	42	71	41
1974-75	New York Islanders	NHL	77	16	23	39	12
1975-76	Fort Worth Texans (b)	CHL	62	29	44	73	80
1975-76	New York Islanders	NHL	14	2	3	5	13
1976-77	New York Islanders	NHL	75	16	19	35	30
1977-78	New York Islanders	NHL	80	30	33	63	31
1978-79	New York Islanders	NHL	80	30	31	61	48
1979-80	New York Islanders	NHL	73	15	25	40	52
1980-81	New York Islanders	NHL	78	35	41	76	62
1981-82	New York Islanders	NHL	76	27	26	53	77
1982-83	New York Islanders	NHL	77	20	42	62	55
1983-84	New York Islanders	NHL	78	22	34	56	75
1984-85	New York Islanders	NHL	44	8	12	20	51
1985-86	New York Islanders	NHL	62	17	15	32	36
	NHL TOTALS		814	238	304	542	542

(c)—Drafted from Saskatoon Blades by Kansas City Scouts in third round of 1974 amateur draft.
(d)—NHL rights traded to New York Islanders by Kansas City Scouts for NHL rights to Larry Hornung and a player to be named later, September, 1974. (New York sent Bart Crashley to Kansas City to complete deal, September, 1974).

PHILLIPPE RICHARD BOURQUE

Defense . . . 6' . . . 180 lbs. . . . Born, Chelmsford, Mass., June 8, 1962 . . . Shoots left.

Year	Team	League	Games	G.	A.	Pts.	Pen.
1980-81	Kingston Canadians	OHL	47	4	4	8	46
1981-82	Kingston Canadians	OHL	67	11	40	51	111
1982-83	Baltimore Skipjacks	AHL	65	1	15	16	93
1983-84	Baltimore Skipjacks	AHL	58	5	17	22	96
1983-84	Pittsburgh Penguins	NHL	5	0	1	1	12
1984-85	Baltimore Skipjacks	AHL	79	6	15	21	164
1985-86	Pittsburgh Penguins	NHL	4	0	0	0	2
1985-86	Baltimore Skipjacks	AHL	74	8	18	26	226
	NHL TOTALS		9	0	1	1	14

RAYMOND JEAN BOURQUE

Defense . . . 5'11" . . . 197 lbs. . . . Born, Montreal, Que., December 28, 1960 . . . Shoots left . . . Set record for most points by a rookie defenseman 1979-80 (65 pts) (Broken by Larry Murphy of L.A. Kings in '80-81 with 76 pts.) . . . (November 11, 1980)—Broken jaw . . . Brother of Richard Bourque (203rd NHL '81 draft pick) . . . (October, 1981)—Injured left shoulder . . . (April 21, 1982)—Broke left wrist vs. Quebec in playoffs. During the summer he refractured the wrist and his left forearm . . . (October, 1982)—Broken bone over left eye when hit by puck during preseason game against Montreal.

Year	Team	League	Games	G.	A.	Pts.	Pen.
1976-77—Sorel Black Hawks		QMJHL	69	12	36	48	61
1977-78—Verdun Black Hawks (a)		QMJHL	72	22	57	79	90
1978-79—Verdun Black Hawks (a-c)		QMJHL	63	22	71	93	44
1979-80—Boston Bruins (a-d-e)		NHL	80	17	48	65	73
1980-81—Boston Bruins (b)		NHL	67	27	29	56	96
1981-82—Boston Bruins (a)		NHL	65	17	49	66	51
1982-83—Boston Bruins (b)		NHL	65	22	51	73	20
1983-84—Boston Bruins (a)		NHL	78	31	65	96	57
1984-85—Boston Bruins (a)		NHL	73	20	66	86	53
1985-86—Boston Bruins (b)		NHL	74	19	57	76	68
NHL TOTALS			502	153	365	518	418

(c)—August, 1979—Drafted by Boston Bruins in 1979 entry draft. First Bruins pick, eighth overall, first round.
(d)—Selected NHL Rookie of the Year in poll of players by THE SPORTING NEWS.
(e)—Won Calder Memorial Trophy (Top NHL Rookie).

PAUL ANDRE BOUTILIER

Defense . . . 5'11" . . . 188 lbs. . . . Born, Sydney, N.S., May 3, 1963 . . . Shoots left . . . (November, 1984)—Required 66 stitches to close cut when struck by a shot during a team practice.

Year	Team	League	Games	G.	A.	Pts.	Pen.
1980-81—Sherbrooke Beavers (c)		QMJHL	72	10	29	39	95
1981-82—Sherbrooke Beavers		QMJHL	57	20	60	80	62
1981-82—New York Islanders		NHL	1	0	0	0	0
1982-83—St. Jean Beavers (d)		QHL	22	5	14	19	30
1982-83—New York Islanders		NHL	29	4	5	9	24
1983-84—Indianapolis Checkers		CHL	50	6	17	23	56
1983-84—New York Islanders		NHL	28	0	11	11	36
1984-85—New York Islanders		NHL	78	12	23	35	90
1985-86—New York Islanders		NHL	77	4	30	34	100
NHL TOTALS			213	20	69	89	250

(c)—June, 1981—Drafted as underage junior by New York Islanders in 1981 NHL entry draft. Islanders first pick, 21st overall, first round.
(d)—January, 1983—QHL rights traded by St. Jean Beavers to Shawinigan Cataracts for Yves Lapointe.

RANDY KEITH JOSEPH BOYD

Defense . . . 5'11" . . . 192 lbs. . . . Born, Coniston, Ont., January 23, 1962 . . . Shoots left . . . (November 2, 1985)—Missed 14 games with injured ankle following collision with Alan Haworth vs. Washington.

Year	Team	League	Games	G.	A.	Pts.	Pen.
1979-80—Ottawa 67's (c)		OMJHL	65	3	21	24	148
1980-81—Ottawa 67's (a-d)		OHL	64	11	43	54	225
1981-82—Ottawa 67's		OHL	26	9	29	38	51
1981-82—Pittsburgh Penguins		NHL	23	0	2	2	49
1982-83—Baltimore Skipjacks		AHL	21	5	10	15	43
1982-83—Pittsburgh Penguins		NHL	56	4	14	18	71
1983-84—Pittsburgh Penguins		NHL	5	0	1	1	6
1983-84—Baltimore Skipjacks		AHL	20	6	13	19	69
1983-84—Chicago Black Hawks (e)		NHL	23	0	4	4	16
1983-84—Springfield Indians		AHL	27	2	11	13	48
1984-85—Milwaukee Admirals (a)		IHL	68	18	55	73	162
1984-85—Chicago Black Hawks		NHL	3	0	0	0	6
1985-86—New York Islanders (f)		NHL	55	2	12	14	79
NHL TOTALS			165	6	33	39	227

(c)—June, 1980—Drafted by Pittsburgh Penguins as underage junior in 1980 NHL entry draft. Second Penguins pick, 51st overall, third round.
(d)—Won Max Kaminsky Trophy (Top OHL Defenseman).
(e)—December, 1983—Traded by Pittsburgh Penguins to Chicago Black Hawks for Greg Fox.
(f)—October, 1985—Acquired by New York Islanders in 1985 NHL waiver draft.

STEVEN MICHAEL BOZEK

Left Wing . . . 5'11" . . . 170 lbs. . . . Born, Kelowna, B. C., November 26, 1960 . . . Shoots left . . . Set Los Angeles club record for most goals by a rookie in 1981-82 . . . (January 20, 1983)—Sprained left knee in game vs. Hartford . . . (October, 1984)—Torn ligament in baby finger of left hand in pre-season game . . . (January 19, 1986)—Strained both knees vs. New Jersey and missed two games . . . (March 12, 1986)—Injured knee vs. N. Y. Rangers.

Year	Team	League	Games	G.	A.	Pts.	Pen.
1978-79	Northern Michigan Univ.	CCHA	33	12	12	24	21
1979-80	Northern Michigan Univ. (a-c)	CCHA	41	42	47	89	32
1980-81	Northern Michigan Univ. (a-d)	CCHA	44	*35	*55	*90	46
1981-82	Los Angeles Kings	NHL	71	33	23	56	68
1982-83	Los Angeles Kings (e)	NHL	53	13	13	26	14
1983-84	Calgary Flames	NHL	46	10	10	20	16
1984-85	Calgary Flames	NHL	54	13	22	35	6
1985-86	Calgary Flames	NHL	64	21	22	43	24
	NHL TOTALS		288	90	90	180	128

(c)—June, 1980—Drafted by Los Angeles Kings in 1980 NHL entry draft. Fifth Kings pick, 52nd overall, third round.

(d)—Selected to All-America (West) team.

(e)—June, 1983—Traded by Los Angeles Kings to Calgary Flames for Kevin LaVallee and Carl Mokosak.

PHILLIPPE BOZON

Left Wing . . . 5'10" . . . 175 lbs. . . . Born, Chamonix, France, November 30, 1966 . . . Shoots left . . . Also plays Right Wing.

Year	Team	League	Games	G.	A.	Pts.	Pen.
1984-85	St. Jean Beavers (c)	QHL	67	32	50	82	82
1985-86	St. Jean Beavers (b)	QHL	65	59	52	111	72
1985-86	Peoria Rivermen (d)	IHL	..	..	..	..	..

(c)—October, 1985—Signed by St. Louis Blues as a free agent.

(d)—No regular season record. Played in five playoff games with one goal.

RICHARD BRACCIA

Left Wing . . . 6' . . . 195 lbs. . . . Born, Revere, Mass., September 5, 1967 . . . Shoots left.

Year	Team	League	Games	G.	A.	Pts.	Pen.
1984-85	Avon Old Farms (c)	Conn. H.S.	....	26	32	58	....
1985-86	Boston College	H. East	9	0	3	3	20

(c)—June, 1985—Drafted by Chicago Black Hawks in 1985 NHL entry draft. Twelfth Black Hawks pick, 242nd overall, 12th round.

BRIAN BRADLEY

Center . . . 5'9" . . . 165 lbs. . . . Born, Kitchener, Ont., January 21, 1965 . . . Shoots right.

Year	Team	League	Games	G.	A.	Pts.	Pen.
1981-82	London Knights	OHL	62	34	44	78	34
1982-83	London Knights (c)	OHL	67	37	82	119	37
1983-84	London Knights	OHL	49	40	60	100	24
1984-85	London Knights	OHL	32	27	49	76	22
1985-86	Calgary Flames	NHL	5	0	1	1	0
1985-86	Moncton Golden Flames	AHL	59	23	42	65	40
	NHL TOTALS		5	0	1	1	0

(c)—June, 1983—Drafted by Calgary Flames as underage junior in 1983 NHL entry draft. Second Flames pick, 51st overall, third round.

NEIL BRADY

Center . . . 6'2" . . . 180 lbs. . . . Born, Montreal, Que., April 12, 1968 . . . Shoots left.

Year	Team	League	Games	G.	A.	Pts.	Pen.
1984-85	Calgary Northstars (b)	Alta. Midget	37	25	50	75	75
1985-86	Medicine Hat Tigers (c-d)	WHL	72	21	60	81	104

(c)—WHL Rookie of the Year (East).

(d)—June, 1986—Drafted as underage junior by New Jersey Devils in 1986 NHL entry draft. First Devils pick, third overall, first round.

CHRIS BRANT

Left Wing . . . 6'1" . . . 190 lbs. . . . Born, Belleville, Ont., August 26, 1965 . . . Shoots left.

Year	Team	League	Games	G.	A.	Pts.	Pen.
1981-82—Belleville Jr. B		OHA	36	10	32	42	13
1982-83—Kingston Canadians		OHL	67	1	17	18	53
1983-84—Kingston Canadians		OHL	7	4	4	8	14
1983-84—Sault Ste. Marie Greyhounds		OHL	60	9	12	21	50
1984-85—Sault Ste. Marie Greyhounds (c)		OHL	52	16	33	49	110
1985-86—Binghamton Whalers		AHL	73	7	6	13	45
1985-86—Salt Lake Golden Eagles		IHL	5	2	1	3	4

(c)—June, 1985—Drafted by Hartford Whalers in 1985 NHL entry draft. Fifth Whalers pick, 131st overall, seventh round.

DAN BRENNAN

Left Wing . . . 6'3" . . . 210 lbs. . . . Born, Dawson Creek, B.C., October 1, 1962 . . . Shoots left.

Year	Team	League	Games	G.	A.	Pts.	Pen.
1980-81—Univ. of North Dakota (c)		WCHA	37	3	9	12	66
1981-82—Univ. of North Dakota		WCHA	42	10	17	27	78
1982-83—Univ. of North Dakota		WCHA	31	9	11	20	60
1983-84—Univ. of North Dakota		WCHA	45	28	37	65	36
1983-84—Los Angeles Kings		NHL	2	0	0	0	0
1984-85—New Haven Nighthawks		AHL	80	25	33	58	56
1985-86—New Haven Nighthawks		AHL	62	8	22	30	76
1985-86—Los Angeles Kings		NHL	6	0	1	1	9
NHL TOTALS			8	0	1	1	9

(c)—June, 1981—Drafted by Los Angeles Kings in 1981 NHL entry draft. Seventh Kings pick, 165th overall, eighth round.

RENE BRETON

Center . . . 5'11" . . . 190 lbs. . . . Born, Princeville, Que., January 10, 1964 . . . Shoots left.

Year	Team	League	Games	G.	A.	Pts.	Pen.
1980-81—Cantons L'est		Que. Midget 'AAA'	47	18	28	46	10
1981-82—Granby Bisons (c)		QMJHL	64	17	19	36	13
1982-83—Granby Bisons		QHL	59	38	48	86	21
1983-84—Granby Bisons		QHL	59	23	47	70	20
1984-85—Springfield Indians		AHL	4	0	0	0	0
1984-85—Indianapolis Checkers		IHL	13	0	4	4	6
1984-85—Erie Golden Blades		ACHL	33	29	24	53	10
1985-86—Flint Spirit		IHL	73	8	24	32	19

(c)—June, 1982—Drafted as underage junior by New York Islanders in 1982 NHL entry draft. Fifth Islanders pick, 105th overall, fifth round.

ANDY BRICKLEY

Left Wing . . . 5'11" . . . 185 lbs. . . . Born, Melrose, Mass., August 9, 1961 . . . Shoots left. . . . (December, 1983)—Strained ankle . . . (December, 1985)—Tendinitis in shoulder.

Year	Team	League	Games	G.	A.	Pts.	Pen.
1979-80—University of New Hampshire (c)		ECAC	27	15	17	32	8
1980-81—University of New Hampshire		ECAC	31	27	25	52	16
1981-82—University of New Hampshire (d)		ECAC	35	26	27	53	6
1982-83—Philadelphia Flyers		NHL	3	1	1	2	0
1982-83—Maine Mariners (b)		AHL	76	29	54	83	10
1983-84—Springfield Indians		AHL	7	1	5	6	2
1983-84—Pittsburgh Penguins (e)		NHL	50	18	20	38	9
1983-84—Baltimore Skipjacks		AHL	4	0	5	5	2
1984-85—Baltimore Skipjacks		AHL	31	13	14	27	8
1984-85—Pittsburgh Penguins		NHL	45	7	15	22	10
1985-86—Maine Mariners (f-g-h)		AHL	60	26	34	60	20
NHL TOTALS			98	26	36	62	19

(c)—June, 1980—Drafted by Philadelphia Flyers in 1980 NHL entry draft. Tenth Flyers pick, 210th overall, tenth round.

(d)—Named to All-American Team (East).

(e)—October, 1983—Traded with Ron Flockhart, Mark Taylor and first-round 1984 draft pick (Roger Belanger) by Philadelphia Flyers to Pittsburgh Penguins for Rich Sutter and second (Greg Smyth) and third round (David McLay) 1984 draft picks.

(f)—August, 1985—Released by Pittsburgh Penguins.

(g)—September, 1985—Attended Hartford Whalers training camp as an unsigned free agent. Released at the conclusion of camp and signed with Maine Mariners as a free agent.

(h)—June, 1986—Signed by New Jersey Devils as a free agent.

MELVIN JOHN BRIDGMAN

Center . . . 6' . . . 185 lbs. . . . Born, Trenton, Ont., April 28, 1955 . . . Shoots left . . . (September, 1985)—Also plays Left Wing.

Year	Team	League	Games	G.	A.	Pts.	Pen.
1971-72—Nanaimo Clippers		Jr."A" BCHL	....	...	....	....	....
1971-72—Victoria Cougars		WCHL	4	0	0	0	0
1972-73—Nanaimo Clippers		Jr."A" BCHL	49	37	50	87	13
1972-73—Victoria Cougars		WCHL	4	1	1	2	0
1973-74—Victoria Cougars		WCHL	62	26	39	65	149
1974-75—Victoria Cougars (a-c)		WCHL	66	66	91	*157	175
1975-76—Philadelphia Flyers		NHL	80	23	27	50	86
1976-77—Philadelphia Flyers		NHL	70	19	38	57	120
1977-78—Philadelphia Flyers		NHL	76	16	32	48	203
1978-79—Philadelphia Flyers		NHL	76	24	35	59	184
1979-80—Philadelphia Flyers		NHL	74	16	31	47	136
1980-81—Philadelphia Flyers		NHL	77	14	37	51	195
1981-82—Philadelphia Flyers (d)		NHL	9	7	5	12	47
1981-82—Calgary Flames		NHL	63	26	49	75	94
1982-83—Calgary Flames (e)		NHL	79	19	31	50	103
1983-84—New Jersey Devils		NHL	79	23	38	61	121
1984-85—New Jersey Devils		NHL	80	22	39	61	105
1985-86—New Jersey Devils		NHL	78	23	39	62	80
NHL TOTALS			841	232	401	633	1474

(c)—Drafted from Victoria Cougars by Philadelphia Flyers in first round of 1975 amateur draft (Flyers obtained draft choice from Washington Capitals for Bill Clement and Don McLean, June, 1975).

(d)—November, 1981—Traded by Philadelphia Flyers to Calgary Flames for Brad Marsh.

(e)—July, 1983—Traded by Calgary Flames with Phil Russell to New Jersey Devils for Steve Tambellini and Joel Quenneville.

GREG BRITZ

Right Wing . . . 6' . . . 190 lbs. . . . Born, Palos Verdes, Calif., March 1, 1961 . . . Shoots right.

Year	Team	League	Games	G.	A.	Pts.	Pen.
1979-80—Harvard University		ECAC	26	8	5	13	17
1980-81—Harvard University		ECAC	17	3	4	7	10
1981-82—Harvard University		ECAC	24	11	13	24	12
1982-83—Harvard University		ECAC	33	16	23	39	18
1983-84—St. Catharines Saints (c)		AHL	44	23	16	39	25
1983-84—Toronto Maple Leafs		NHL	6	0	0	0	2
1984-85—St. Catharines Saints		AHL	74	15	17	32	31
1984-85—Toronto Maple Leafs		NHL	1	0	0	0	2
1985-86—St. Catharines Saints		AHL	72	17	19	36	52
NHL TOTALS			7	0	0	0	4

(c)—October, 1983—Signed by Toronto Maple Leafs as a free agent.

STEPHANE BROCHU

Defense . . . 6'1" . . . 185 lbs. . . . Born, Sherbrooke, Que., August 15, 1967 . . . Shoots left . . . (December, 1983)—Separated shoulder.

Year	Team	League	Games	G.	A.	Pts.	Pen.
1983-84—Magog Cantonniers		Que. Midget	38	7	24	31	36
1984-85—Quebec Remparts (c)		QHL	59	2	16	18	56
1985-86—St. Jean Castors		QMJHL	63	14	27	41	121

(c)—June, 1985—Drafted as underage junior by New York Rangers in 1985 NHL entry draft. Ninth Rangers pick, 175th overall, ninth round.

LEE BRODEUR

Right Wing . . . 6'1" . . . 180 lbs. . . . Born, Grafton, N. Dak., February 14, 1966 . . . Shoots right . . . (December, 1985)—Left University of North Dakota and transferred to Western Michigan University.

Year	Team	League	Games	G.	A.	Pts.	Pen.
1983-84—Grafton H.S. (c)		No.Dak.H.S.	23	40	36	76	42
1984-85—Univ. North Dakota		WCHA	13	0	2	2	6
1985-86—Western Michigan Univ.		CCHA	20	1	4	5	22

(c)—June, 1984—Drafted by Montreal Canadiens in 1984 NHL entry draft. Sixth Canadiens pick, 65th overall, fourth round.

ROBERT W. BROOKE

Right Wing . . . 6'2" . . . 185 lbs. . . . Born, Melrose, Mass., December 18, 1960 . . . Shoots right

... Holds Yale career records for goals (42), assists (113) and points (155) ... Also plays Center and Defense ... Played shortstop on Yale baseball team ... Member of 1984 U.S. Olympic Team ... (October 11, 1984)—Separated shoulder in opening game of season vs. Hartford.

Year	Team	League	Games	G.	A.	Pts.	Pen.
1979-80	Yale University (c)	ECAC	24	7	22	29	38
1980-81	Yale University	ECAC	27	12	30	42	59
1981-82	Yale University	ECAC	25	12	30	42	60
1982-83	Yale University (a-d)	ECAC	27	11	31	42	50
1983-84	U.S. National Team	Int'l	54	7	18	25	75
1983-84	U.S. Olympic Team	Int'l	6	1	2	3	10
1983-84	New York Rangers (e)	NHL	9	1	2	3	4
1984-85	New York Rangers	NHL	72	7	9	16	79
1985-86	New York Rangers	NHL	79	24	20	44	111
	NHL TOTALS		160	32	31	63	194

(c)—June, 1980—Drafted by St. Louis Blues in 1980 NHL entry draft. Third Blues pick, 75th overall, fourth round.
(d)—Named to All-America Team (East).
(e)—March, 1984—Traded with Larry Patey by St. Louis Blues to New York Rangers for Dave Barr, a third round (Alan Perry) 1984 draft pick and cash.

DAN BROOKS

Defense ... 6'3" ... 205 lbs. ... Born, Minneapolis, Minn., April 26, 1967 ... Shoots left ... Son of Herb Brooks, former New York Rangers coach.

Year	Team	League	Games	G.	A.	Pts.	Pen.
1984-85	St. Thomas Academy (c)	Minn. H.S.	21	9	13	22	20
1985-86	St. Thomas Academy	Minn. H.S.	19	3	11	14	....

(c)—June, 1985—Drafted by St. Louis Blues in 1985 NHL entry draft. Fourth Blues pick, 100th overall, fifth round.

AARON BROTEN

Center ... 5'10" ... 168 lbs. ... Born, Roseau, Minn., November 14, 1960 ... Shoots left ... Brother of Neal Broten and Paul Broten ... Also plays Left Wing ... (February 15, 1986)—Sprained ankle vs. N.Y. Islanders ... (March 6, 1986)—Reinjured ankle vs. Detroit ... (March 19, 1986)—Reinjured ankle vs. Pittsburgh.

Year	Team	League	Games	G.	A.	Pts.	Pen.
1979-80	University of Minnesota (c-d)	WCHA	41	25	47	72	8
1980-81	University of Minnesota (b-e)	WCH	45	*47	*59	*106	24
1980-81	Colorado Rockies	NHL	2	0	0	0	0
1981-82	Ft. Worth Texans	CHL	19	15	21	36	11
1981-82	Colorado Rockies	NHL	58	15	24	39	6
1982-83	Wichita Wind	CHL	4	0	4	4	0
1982-83	New Jersey Devils	NHL	73	16	39	55	28
1983-84	New Jersey Devils	NHL	80	13	23	36	36
1984-85	New Jersey Devils	NHL	80	22	35	57	38
1985-86	New Jersey Devils	NHL	66	19	25	44	26
	NHL TOTALS		359	85	146	231	134

(c)—Named top WCHA Rookie.
(d)—June, 1980—Drafted by Colorado Rockies in 1980 NHL entry draft. Fifth Rockies pick, 106th overall, sixth round.
(e)—WCHA Scoring Leader.

NEAL LaMOY BROTEN

Center ... 5'9" ... 160 lbs. ... Born, Roseau, Minn., November 29, 1959 ... Shoots left ... Brother of Aaron Broten and Paul Broten ... Scored game winning goal to give University of Minnesota 1979 NCAA Championship over North Dakota ... Member of 1980 U.S. Olympic Gold Medal Team ... (December 26, 1981)—Ankle fracture ... Set NHL record for most points by American-born player (97), 1981-82 ... Set NHL record for most goals by an American-born player (38), 1981-82 (broken by Joe Mullen in 1983-84) ... Set NHL record for most assists by American-born player (59), 1981-82 ... (1985-86)—Became first American-born player to score 100 points in one season in NHL.

Year	Team	League	Games	G.	A.	Pts.	Pen.
1978-79	University of Minnesota (c-d)	WCHA	40	21	50	71	18
1979-80	U. S. Olympic Team	Int'l	62	27	31	58	22
1980-81	University of Minnesota (a-e-f-g)	WCHA	36	17	54	71	56
1980-81	Minnesota North Stars	NHL	3	2	0	2	12
1981-82	Minnesota North Stars	NHL	73	38	60	98	42
1982-83	Minnesota North Stars	NHL	79	32	45	77	43

Year	Team	League	Games	G.	A.	Pts.	Pen.
1983-84—Minnesota North Stars		NHL	76	28	61	89	43
1984-85—Minnesota North Stars		NHL	80	19	37	56	39
1985-86—Minnesota North Stars		NHL	80	29	76	105	47
NHL TOTALS			391	148	279	427	226

(c)—Named top WCHA Rookie player.
(d)—August, 1979—Drafted by Minnesota North Stars in 1979 NHL entry draft. Third North Stars pick, 42nd overall, second round.
(e)—Named to All-America Team (West).
(f)—Named to All-NCAA Tournament team.
(g)—First winner of Hobey Baker Memorial Trophy (Top U. S. College Hockey Player).

PAUL BROTEN

Center . . . 5'11" . . . 155 lbs. . . . Born, Roseau, Minn., October 27, 1965 . . . Shoots right . . . Brother of Aaron and Neal Broten.

Year	Team	League	Games	G.	A.	Pts.	Pen.
1983-84—Roseau H.S. (c)		Minn. H.S.	26	26	29	55	4
1984-85—Univ. of Minnesota		WCHA	44	8	8	16	26
1985-86—Univ. of Minnesota		WCHA	38	6	16	22	24

(c)—June, 1984—Drafted by New York Rangers in 1984 NHL entry draft. Third Rangers pick, 77th overall, fourth round.

ALLISTER BROWN

Defense . . . 6' . . . 185 lbs. . . . Born, Cornwall, Ont., November 12, 1965 . . . Shoots right.

Year	Team	League	Games	G.	A.	Pts.	Pen.
1983-84—Univ. of New Hampshire (c)		ECAC	36	1	7	8	12
1984-85—Univ. of New Hampshire		H. East	42	4	7	11	18
1985-86—Univ. of New Hampshire		H. East	36	2	5	7	28

(c)—June, 1984—Drafted by New York Islanders in 1984 NHL entry draft. Thirteenth Islanders pick, 249th overall, 12th round.

DAVID BROWN

Right Wing . . . 6'5" . . . 205 lbs. . . . Born, Saskatoon, Sask., October 12, 1962 . . . Shoots right . . . (March, 1985)—Bruised shoulder.

Year	Team	League	Games	G.	A.	Pts.	Pen.
1980-81—Spokane Flyers		WHL	9	2	2	4	21
1981-82—Saskatoon Blades (c)		WHL	62	11	33	44	344
1982-83—Maine Mariners (d)		AHL	71	8	6	14	*418
1982-83—Philadelphia Flyers		NHL	2	0	0	0	5
1983-84—Philadelphia Flyers		NHL	19	1	5	6	98
1983-84—Springfield Indians		AHL	59	17	14	31	150
1984-85—Philadelphia Flyers		NHL	57	3	6	9	165
1985-86—Philadelphia Flyers		NHL	76	10	7	17	277
NHL TOTALS			154	14	18	32	545

(c)—June, 1982—Drafted by Philadelphia Flyers in 1982 NHL entry draft. Seventh Flyers pick, 140th overall, seventh round.
(d)—Led AHL Playoffs with 107 penalty minutes.

DOUG BROWN

Right Wing . . . 5'11" . . . 190 lbs. . . . Born, Southborough, Mass., June 12, 1964 . . . Shoots right . . . Brother of Greg Brown.

Year	Team	League	Games	G.	A.	Pts.	Pen.
1982-83—Boston College		ECAC	22	9	8	17	0
1983-84—Boston College		ECAC	38	11	10	21	6
1984-85—Boston College		H. East	45	37	31	68	10
1985-86—Boston College (c)		H. East	38	16	40	56	16

(c)—August, 1986—Signed by New Jersey Devils as a free agent.

GREGORY BROWN

Defense . . . 6' . . . 185 lbs. . . . Born, Hartford, Conn., March 7, 1963 . . . Shoots right . . . Brother of Doug Brown.

Year	Team	League	Games	G.	A.	Pts.	Pen.
1984-85—St. Marks H.S.		Mass.	24	16	24	40	12
1985-86—St. Marks H.S. (c)		Mass.	19	22	28	50	30

(c)—June, 1986—Drafted by Buffalo Sabres in 1986 NHL entry draft. Second Sabres pick, 26th overall, second round.

JEFF BROWN

Defense . . . 6'1" . . . 185 lbs. . . . Born, Ottawa, Ont., April 30, 1966 . . . Shoots right.

Year	Team	League	Games	G.	A.	Pts.	Pen.
1981-82—Hawkesbury Tier II		Ont. Jr.	49	12	47	59	72
1982-83—Sudbury Wolves		OHL	65	9	37	46	39
1983-84—Sudbury Wolves (c)		OHL	68	17	60	77	39
1984-85—Sudbury Wolves		OHL	56	16	48	64	26
1985-86—Sudbury Wolves (a-d)		OHL	45	22	28	50	24
1985-86—Quebec Nordiques		NHL	8	3	2	5	6
1985-86—Fredericton Express (e)		AHL	....	...	....	....	....
NHL TOTALS			8	3	2	5	6

(c)—June, 1984—Drafted as underage junior by Quebec Nordiques in 1984 NHL entry draft. Second Nordiques pick, 36th overall, second round.
(d)—Shared Max Kaminsky Trophy (Top OHL Trophy) with Terry Carkner.
(e)—No regular season record. Played one playoff game.

KEITH JEFFREY BROWN

Defense . . . 6'1" . . . 192 lbs. . . . Born, Corner Brook, Nfld., May 6, 1960 . . . Shoots right . . . (December 23, 1981)—Torn ligaments in right knee . . . (January 26, 1983)—Separated right shoulder in game vs. Vancouver . . . (January, 1985)—Strained leg . . . (October, 1985)—Broken finger in three places in weight training accident and missed 10 games.

Year	Team	League	Games	G.	A.	Pts.	Pen.
1976-77—Ft. Saskatchewan Traders		AJHL	59	14	61	75	14
1976-77—Portland Winter Hawks		WCHL	2	0	0	0	0
1977-78—Portland Winter Hawks (b-c)		WCHL	72	11	53	64	51
1978-79—Portland Winter Hawks (a-d-e)		WHL	70	11	85	96	75
1979-80—Chicago Black Hawks		NHL	76	2	18	20	27
1980-81—Chicago Black Hawks		NHL	80	9	34	43	80
1981-82—Chicago Black Hawks		NHL	33	4	20	24	26
1982-83—Chicago Black Hawks		NHL	50	4	27	31	20
1983-84—Chicago Black Hawks		NHL	74	10	25	35	94
1984-85—Chicago Black Hawks		NHL	56	1	22	23	55
1985-86—Chicago Black Hawks		NHL	70	11	29	40	87
NHL TOTALS			439	41	175	216	389

(c)—Shared WCHL Top Rookie with John Ogrodnick.
(d)—Named outstanding WHL defenseman.
(e)—August, 1979—Drafted as underage junior by Chicago Black Hawks in 1979 NHL entry draft. First Black Hawks pick, seventh overall, first round.

ROBERT BROWN

Center . . . 6' . . . 180 lbs. . . . Born, Kingston, Ont., October 4, 1968 . . . Shoots left.

Year	Team	League	Games	G.	A.	Pts.	Pen.
1983-84—Kamloops Jr. Oilers		WHL	50	16	42	58	80
1984-85—Kamloops Blazers		WHL	60	29	50	79	95
1985-86—Kamloops Blazers (a-c-d)		WHL	69	58	*115	*173	171

(c)—Named WHL Most Valuable Player (West).
(d)—June, 1986—Drafted by Pittsburgh Penguins as underage junior in 1986 NHL entry draft. Fourth Penguins pick, 67th overall, fourth round.

JOHN J. (Jack) BROWNSCHIDLE, JR.

Defense . . . 6'2" . . . 195 lbs. . . . Born, Buffalo, N.Y., October 2, 1955 . . . Shoots left . . . Brother of Jeff Brownschidle.

Year	Team	League	Games	G.	A.	Pts.	Pen.
1972-73—Niagara Falls Flyers		SOJHL	32	9	19	28	20
1973-74—University of Notre Dame		WCHA	36	2	7	9	24
1973-74—U.S. National Team			18	2	3	5	....
1974-75—University of Notre Dame (c)		WCHA	38	4	12	16	24
1975-76—University of Notre Dame (d)		WCHA	38	12	24	36	24
1976-77—University of Notre Dame (d)		WCHA	38	13	35	48	30
1977-78—Salt Lake City Golden Eagles		CHL	25	4	12	16	0
1977-78—St. Louis Blues		NHL	40	2	15	17	23
1978-79—St. Louis Blues		NHL	64	10	24	34	14
1978-79—Salt Lake Golden Eagles		CHL	11	0	10	10	0
1979-80—St. Louis Blues		NHL	77	12	32	44	8
1980-81—St. Louis Blues		NHL	71	5	23	28	12
1981-82—St. Louis Blues		NHL	80	5	33	38	26

Year	Team	League	Games	G.	A.	Pts.	Pen.
1982-83—St. Louis Blues		NHL	72	1	22	23	30
1983-84—St. Louis Blues (e)		NHL	51	1	7	8	19
1983-84—Hartford Whalers		NHL	13	2	2	4	10
1984-85—Binghamton Whalers		AHL	56	4	17	21	8
1984-85—Hartford Whalers		NHL	17	1	4	5	5
1985-86—Hartford Whalers		NHL	9	0	0	0	4
1985-86—Binghamton Whalers (b)		AHL	58	5	26	31	18
NHL TOTALS			494	39	162	201	151

(c)—Drafted from University of Notre Dame by St. Louis Blues in sixth round of 1975 amateur draft.
(d)—Selected First Team (West) All America.
(e)—March, 1984—Claimed by Hartford Whalers on waivers from St. Louis Blues for the waiver price of $12,500.

JEFFREY BRUBAKER

Left Wing . . . 6'2" . . . 205 lbs. . . . Born, Hagerstown, Maryland, February 24, 1958 . . . Shoots left . . . Missed parts of 1979-80 season with dislocated shoulder and a sprained knee . . . (October, 1980)—Shoulder injury . . . (January, 1985)—Given 3-game suspension by NHL for stick-swinging incident . . . (December 29, 1985)—Sprained left ankle at Vancouver.

Year	Team	League	Games	G.	A.	Pts.	Pen.
1974-75—St. Paul Vulcans		MWJHL	57	13	14	27	130
1975-76—St. Paul Vulcans		MWJHL	47	6	34	40	152
1976-77—Michigan State University		WCHA	18	0	3	3	30
1976-77—Peterborough Petes		Jr."A" OHA	26	0	5	5	143
1977-78—Peterborough Petes (c-d)		Jr."A" OHA	68	20	24	44	307
1978-79—New England Whalers		WHA	12	0	0	0	19
1978-79—Rochester Americans		AHL	57	4	10	14	253
1979-80—Hartford Whalers		NHL	3	0	1	1	2
1979-80—Springfield Indians		AHL	50	12	13	25	165
1980-81—Binghamton Whalers		AHL	38	18	11	29	138
1980-81—Hartford Whalers		NHL	43	5	3	8	93
1981-82—Montreal Canadiens (e)		NHL	3	0	1	1	32
1981-82—Nova Scotia Voyageurs		AHL	60	28	12	40	256
1982-83—Nova Scotia Voyageurs		AHL	78	31	27	58	183
1983-84—Calgary Flames (f)		NHL	4	0	0	0	19
1983-84—Colorado Flames		CHL	57	16	19	35	218
1984-85—Toronto Maple Leafs (g)		NHL	68	8	4	12	209
1985-86—Nova Scotia Oilers		AHL	19	4	3	7	41
1985-86—Toronto Maple Leafs (h)		NHL	21	0	0	0	67
1985-86—Edmonton Oilers		NHL	4	1	0	1	12
WHA TOTALS			12	0	0	0	19
NHL TOTALS			146	14	9	23	434

(c)—Selected by New England Whalers in World Hockey Association amateur players' draft and signed by Whalers, June, 1978.
(d)—Drafted from Peterborough Petes by Boston Bruins in sixth round of 1978 amateur draft.
(e)—October, 1981—Selected by Montreal Canadiens in 1981 NHL waiver draft.
(f)—October, 1983—Selected by Calgary Flames in 1983 NHL waiver draft.
(g)—October, 1984—Selected by Toronto Maple Leafs in 1984 NHL waiver draft.
(h)—December, 1985—Acquired by Edmonton Oilers on waivers from Toronto Maple Leafs.

DAVE BRUCE

Right Wing . . . 5'11" . . . 170 lbs. . . . Born, Thunder Bay, Ont., October 7, 1964 . . . Shoots right . . . Also plays Center.

Year	Team	League	Games	G.	A.	Pts.	Pen.
1981-82—Thunder Bay Kings		Tier II	35	27	31	58	74
1982-83—Kitchener Rangers (c)		OHL	67	36	35	71	199
1983-84—Kitchener Rangers		OHL	62	52	40	92	203
1984-85—Fredericton Express		AHL	56	14	11	25	104
1985-86—Fredericton Express		AHL	66	25	16	41	151
1985-86—Vancouver Canucks		NHL	12	0	1	1	14
NHL TOTALS			12	0	1	1	14

(c)—June, 1983—Drafted as underage junior by Vancouver Canucks in 1983 NHL entry draft. Second Canucks pick, 30th overall, second round.

JAMES MURRAY BRUMWELL
(Known by middle name)

Defense . . . 6'1" . . . 190 lbs. . . . Born, Calgary, Alta., March 31, 1960 . . . Shoots left . . . (February, 1979)—Mononucleosis . . . (January, 1982)—Back injury.

Year	Team	League	Games	G.	A.	Pts.	Pen.
1977-78—Calgary Canucks		AJHL	59	4	40	44	79
1977-78—Calgary Wranglers		WCHL	1	0	0	0	2
1977-78—Saskatoon Blades		WCHL	1	0	2	2	0
1978-79—Billings Bighorns		WHL	61	11	32	43	62
1979-80—Billings Bighorns		WHL	67	18	54	72	50
1980-81—Minnesota North Stars (c)		NHL	1	0	0	0	0
1980-81—Oklahoma City Stars		CHL	79	12	43	55	79
1981-82—Nashville South Stars		CHL	55	4	21	25	66
1981-82—Minnesota North Stars (d)		NHL	21	0	3	3	18
1982-83—Wichita Wind		CHL	11	4	1	5	4
1982-83—New Jersey Devils		NHL	59	5	14	19	34
1983-84—Maine Mariners		AHL	34	4	25	29	16
1983-84—New Jersey Devils		NHL	42	7	13	20	14
1984-85—Maine Mariners		AHL	64	8	31	39	52
1985-86—New Jersey Devils		NHL	1	0	0	0	0
1985-86—Maine Mariners		AHL	66	9	28	37	35
NHL TOTALS			124	12	30	42	66

(c)—September, 1980—Signed by Minnesota North Stars as a free agent.
(d)—Claimed by New Jersey Devils in 1982 NHL waiver draft.

BOB BRYDEN

Left Wing . . . 6'3" . . . 205 lbs. . . . Born, Toronto, Ont., April 5, 1963 . . . Shoots left.

Year	Team	League	Games	G.	A.	Pts.	Pen.
1982-83—Henry Carr H.S. (c)		Toronto H.S.	32	28	39	67	65
1983-84—Western Michigan Univ.		CCHA	36	17	12	29	60
1984-85—Western Michigan Univ.		CCHA	39	18	19	37	59
1985-86—Western Michigan Univ.		CCHA	44	23	28	51	85
1985-86—Team Canada		Int'l	3	0	1	1	2

(c)—June, 1983—Drafted by Montreal Canadiens in 1983 NHL entry draft. Tenth Canadiens pick, 158th overall, eighth round.

PAUL BRYDGES

Center . . . 5'11" . . . 177 lbs. . . . Born, Guelph, Ont., June 21, 1965 . . . Shoots right.

Year	Team	League	Games	G.	A.	Pts.	Pen.
1983-84—Guelph Platers		OHL	68	27	23	50	37
1984-85—Guelph Platers		OHL	57	22	24	46	39
1985-86—Guelph Platers (c)		OHL	62	17	40	57	88

(c)—July, 1986—Signed by Buffalo Sabres as a free agent.

JIRI BUBLA

Defense . . . 5'11" . . . 197 lbs. . . . Born, Usti nad Labem, Czechoslovakia, January 27, 1950 . . . Shoots right . . . (November, 1981)—Broken ankle . . . (December, 1983)—Broken foot . . . (February 19, 1985)—Torn rib cartilage in game vs. New Jersey . . . (December 14, 1985)—Sprained knee vs. Calgary . . . (February 21, 1986)—Reinjured knee vs. Calgary and missed six games.

Year	Team	League	Games	G.	A.	Pts.	Pen.
1980-81—Sparta Praha (c)		Czech.	....	8	20	28	....
1981-82—Vancouver Canucks		NHL	23	1	1	2	16
1982-83—Vancouver Canucks		NHL	72	2	28	30	59
1983-84—Vancouver Canucks		NHL	62	6	33	39	43
1984-85—Vancouver Canucks		NHL	56	2	15	17	54
1985-86—Vancouver Canucks		NHL	43	6	24	30	30
NHL TOTALS			256	17	101	118	202

(c)—May, 1981—Drafted by Colorado Rockies in special draft of Czechoslovakian veterans. Colorado subsequently received a fourth-round draft choice and Brent Ashton from Vancouver via Winnipeg as compensation for Vancouver's signing of Bubla.

KELLY BUCHBERGER

Left Wing . . . 6'2" . . . 190 lbs. . . . Born, Langenburg, Sask., December 12, 1966 . . . Shoots left.

Year	Team	League	Games	G.	A.	Pts.	Pen.
1983-84—Melville Millionaires		SAJHL	60	14	11	25	139
1984-85—Moose Jaw Warriors (c)		WHL	51	12	17	29	114
1985-86—Moose Jaw Warriors		WHL	72	14	22	36	206

(c)—June, 1985—Drafted as underage junior by Edmonton Oilers in 1985 NHL entry draft. Eighth Oilers pick, 188th overall, ninth round.

RANDY BUCYK

Center . . . 6' . . . 190 lbs. . . . Born, Edmonton, Alta., November 9, 1962 . . . Shoots left . . .
Nephew of Johnny Bucyk (Hall of Famer and former Boston Bruin).

Year	Team	League	Games	G.	A.	Pts.	Pen.
1980-81—Northeastern Univ.		ECAC	26	9	7	16	18
1981-82—Northeastern Univ.		ECAC	33	19	17	36	10
1982-83—Northeastern Univ.		ECAC	28	16	20	36	16
1983-84—Northeastern Univ.		ECAC	29	16	13	29	11
1984-85—Sherbrooke Canadiens (c)		AHL	62	21	26	47	20
1985-86—Sherbrooke Canadiens		AHL	43	18	33	51	22
1985-86—Montreal Canadiens		NHL	17	4	2	6	8
NHL TOTALS			17	4	2	6	8

(c)—September, 1984—Signed by Montreal Canadiens as a free agent.

MICHAEL BRIAN BULLARD

Center . . . 5'10" . . . 183 lbs. . . . Born, Ottawa, Ont., March 10, 1961 . . . Shoots left . . .
(February 21, 1982)—Scored winning goal with 4:29 to play to stop N.Y. Islanders 15-game
win streak in 4-3 win at Pittsburgh . . . (October, 1982)—Missed first 20 games of the
season with mononucleosis . . . (1981-82)—Set Pittsburgh club record for goals in a
rookie season (36) . . . (December, 1984)—Chip fracture of left shoulder and missed 11
games . . . (January 31, 1985)—Arrested in Mount Lebanon, Pennsylvania when his car
struck two people . . . (December 2, 1985)—Suffered cracked ribs against N. Y. Rangers
and missed three games.

Year	Team	League	Games	G.	A.	Pts.	Pen.
1978-79—Brantford Alexanders		OMJHL	66	43	56	99	66
1979-80—Brantford Alexanders (b-c)		OMJHL	66	66	84	150	86
1980-81—Brantford Alexanders		OHL	42	47	60	107	55
1980-81—Pittsburgh Penguins		NHL	15	1	2	3	19
1981-82—Pittsburgh Penguins		NHL	75	36	27	63	91
1982-83—Pittsburgh Penguins		NHL	57	22	22	44	60
1983-84—Pittsburgh Penguins		NHL	76	51	41	92	57
1984-85—Pittsburgh Penguins		NHL	57	9	11	20	125
1985-86—Pittsburgh Penguins		NHL	77	41	42	83	69
NHL TOTALS			357	160	145	305	421

(c)—June, 1980—Drafted as underage junior by Pittsburgh Penguins in 1980 NHL entry draft. First
Penguins pick, ninth overall, first round.

GARY BURNS

Left Wing . . . 6'1" . . . 190 lbs. . . . Born, Cambridge, Mass., January 16, 1955 . . . Shoots left.

Year	Team	League	Games	G.	A.	Pts.	Pen.
1974-75—University of New Hampshire		ECAC	31	17	15	32	42
1975-76—University of New Hampshire		ECAC	....	6	12	18	....
1976-77—University of New Hampshire		ECAC	38	9	6	15	24
1977-78—University of New Hampshire		ECAC	29	9	19	28	55
1978-79—Rochester Americans		AHL	79	16	30	46	99
1979-80—Binghamton Dusters		AHL	79	30	29	59	105
1980-81—New Haven Nighthawks (c)		AHL	69	25	29	54	137
1980-81—New York Rangers		NHL	11	2	2	4	18
1981-82—Springfield Indians		AHL	78	27	39	66	71
1981-82—New York Rangers (d)		NHL	....	...	....	....	....
1982-83—Tulsa Oilers		CHL	80	21	33	54	61
1983-84—Tulsa Oilers		CHL	68	28	30	58	95
1984-85—Rochester Americans (e)		AHL	76	22	27	49	64
1985-86—Salt Lake Golden Eagles (f)		IHL	78	23	35	58	85
NHL TOTALS			11	2	2	4	18

(c)—September, 1980—Signed by New York Rangers as a free agent.
(d)—No regular-season record. Played four playoff games.
(e)—October, 1984—Signed by Buffalo Sabres as a free agent.
(f)—September, 1985—Signed by Salt Lake Golden Eagles as a free agent.

SHAWN BURR

Center . . . 6'1" . . . 180 lbs. . . . Born, Sarnia, Ont., July 1, 1966 . . . Shoots left.

Year	Team	League	Games	G.	A.	Pts.	Pen.
1982-83—Sarnia Midgets		OPHL	52	50	85	135	125
1983-84—Kitchener Rangers (c-d)		OHL	68	41	44	85	50
1984-85—Kitchener Rangers		OHL	48	24	42	66	50
1984-85—Detroit Red Wings		NHL	9	0	0	0	2

Year	Team	League	Games	G.	A.	Pts.	Pen.
1984-85—Adirondack Red Wings		AHL	4	0	0	0	2
1985-86—Kitchener Rangers (b)		OHL	59	60	67	127	83
1985-86—Adirondack Red Wings		AHL	3	2	2	4	2
1985-86—Detroit Red Wings		NHL	5	1	0	1	4
NHL TOTALS			14	1	0	1	6

(c)—June, 1984—Drafted as underage junior by Detroit Red Wings in 1984 NHL entry draft. First Red Wings pick, seventh overall, first round.

(d)—Won Emms Family Award (Top OHL Rookie).

RANDY BURRIDGE

Center . . . 5'9" . . . 170 lbs. . . . Born, Fort Erie, Ont., January 7, 1966 . . . Shoots left . . . (March 1, 1986)—Strained groin vs. New Jersey.

Year	Team	League	Games	G.	A.	Pts.	Pen.
1982-83—Fort Erie Jr.B		OHA	42	32	56	88	32
1983-84—Peterborough Petes		OHL	55	6	7	13	44
1984-85—Peterborough Petes (c)		OHL	66	49	57	106	88
1985-86—Peterborough Petes		OHL	17	15	11	26	23
1985-86—Boston Bruins		NHL	52	17	25	42	28
1985-86—Moncton Golden Flames (d)		AHL	..	..	..	..	..
NHL TOTALS			52	17	25	42	28

(c)—June, 1985—Drafted by Boston Bruins in 1985 NHL entry draft. Seventh Bruins pick, 157th overall, eighth round.

(d)—No regular season record. Played three playoff games.

ROD DALE BUSKAS

Defense . . . 6'2" . . . 195 lbs. . . . Born, Wetaskiwin, Alta., January 7, 1961 . . . Shoots right . . . (February, 1985)—Shoulder injury . . . (December 26, 1985)—Bruised ribs vs. Boston and missed five games.

Year	Team	League	Games	G.	A.	Pts.	Pen.
1978-79—Red Deer Rustlers		AJHL	37	13	22	35	63
1978-79—Billings Bighorns		WHL	1	0	0	0	0
1978-79—Medicine Hat Tigers		WHL	35	1	12	13	60
1979-80—Medicine Hat Tigers		WHL	72	7	40	47	284
1980-81—Medicine Hat Tigers (c)		WHL	72	14	46	60	164
1981-82—Erie Blades		AHL	69	1	18	19	78
1982-83—Muskegon Mohawks		IHL	1	0	0	0	9
1982-83—Baltimore Skipjacks		AHL	31	2	8	10	45
1982-83—Pittsburgh Penguins		NHL	41	2	2	4	102
1983-84—Baltimore Skipjacks		AHL	33	2	12	14	100
1983-84—Pittsburgh Penguins		NHL	47	2	4	6	60
1984-85—Pittsburgh Penguins		NHL	69	2	7	9	191
1985-86—Pittsburgh Penguins		NHL	72	2	7	9	159
NHL TOTALS			229	8	20	28	512

(c)—June, 1981—Drafted by Pittsburgh Penguins in 1981 NHL entry draft. Fifth Penguins pick, 112th overall, sixth round.

GARTH BUTCHER

Defense . . . 6' . . . 194 lbs. . . . Born, Regina, Sask., January 8, 1963 . . . Shoots right . . . (October, 1984)—Shoulder separation.

Year	Team	League	Games	G.	A.	Pts.	Pen.
1978-79—Regina Canadians		AMHL	22	4	22	26	72
1979-80—Regina Tier II		SJHL	51	15	31	46	236
1979-80—Regina Pats		WHL	13	0	4	4	20
1980-81—Regina Pats (a-c)		WHL	69	9	77	86	230
1981-82—Regina Pats (a)		WHL	65	24	68	92	318
1981-82—Vancouver Canucks		NHL	5	0	0	0	9
1982-83—Kamloops Junior Oilers		WHL	5	4	2	6	4
1982-83—Vancouver Canucks		NHL	55	1	13	14	104
1983-84—Fredericton Express		AHL	25	4	13	17	43
1983-84—Vancouver Canucks		NHL	28	2	0	2	34
1984-85—Vancouver Canucks		NHL	75	3	9	12	152
1985-86—Vancouver Canucks		NHL	70	4	7	11	188
NHL TOTALS			233	10	29	39	487

(c)—June, 1981—Drafted as underage junior by Vancouver Canucks in 1981 NHL entry draft. First Canucks pick, 10th overall, first round.

WILLIAM BUTLER

Left Wing . . . 6'2" . . . 195 lbs. . . . Born, West Hartford, Conn., March 3, 1967 . . . Shoots left.

Year	Team	League	Games	G.	A.	Pts.	Pen.
1985-86—Northwood Prep. (c)		Conn.	17	14	16	30	12

(c)—June, 1986—Drafted by St. Louis Blues in 1986 NHL entry draft. Twelfth Blues pick, 234th overall, 12th round.

LYNDON BYERS

Right Wing . . . 6'2" . . . 195 lbs. . . . Born, Nipawin, Sask., February 29, 1964 . . . Shoots right . . . (April, 1981)—Broken right wrist.

Year	Team	League	Games	G.	A.	Pts.	Pen.
1980-81—Notre Dame Hounds (b)		SCMHL	37	35	42	77	106
1981-82—Regina Pats (c-d)		WHL	57	18	25	43	169
1982-83—Regina Pats		WHL	70	32	38	70	153
1983-84—Regina Pats		WHL	58	32	57	89	154
1983-84—Boston Bruins		NHL	10	2	4	6	32
1984-85—Hershey Bears		AHL	27	4	6	10	55
1984-85—Boston Bruins		NHL	33	3	8	11	41
1985-86—Boston Bruins		NHL	5	0	2	2	9
1985-86—Moncton Golden Flames		AHL	14	2	4	6	26
1985-86—Milwaukee Admirals		IHL	8	0	2	2	22
NHL TOTALS			48	5	14	19	82

(c)—September, 1981—Traded by Saskatoon Blades to Regina Pats for Todd Strueby.

(d)—June, 1982—Drafted as underage junior by Boston Bruins in NHL entry draft. Third Bruins pick, 39th overall, second round.

SHAWN BYRAM

Left Wing . . . 6'2" . . . 190 lbs. . . . Born, Neepawa, Manitoba, September 12, 1968 . . . Shoots left . . . Also plays Center.

Year	Team	League	Games	G.	A.	Pts.	Pen.
1984-85—Regina Canadians		Sask. Midget	25	12	21	33	38
1985-86—Regina Pats (c)		WHL	46	7	6	13	45

(c)—June, 1986—Drafted as underage junior by New York Islanders in 1986 NHL entry draft. Fourth Islanders pick, 80th overall, fourth round.

GERALD BZDEL

Defense . . . 6' . . . 190 lbs. . . . Born, Wyryard, Sask., March 13, 1968 . . . Shoots right . . . (March, 1985)—Torn ligaments in left knee.

Year	Team	League	Games	G.	A.	Pts.	Pen.
1984-85—Regina Pats		WHL	20	0	4	4	6
1985-86—Regina Pats (c)		WHL	72	2	15	17	107

(c)—June, 1986—Drafted as underage junior by Quebec Nordiques in 1986 NHL entry draft. Fifth Nordiques pick, 102nd overall, fifth round.

KELLY CAIN

Center . . . 5'6" . . . 180 lbs. . . . Born, Toronto, Ont., April 19, 1968 . . . Shoots left.

Year	Team	League	Games	G.	A.	Pts.	Pen.
1984-85—London Knights		OHL	59	8	17	25	74
1985-86—London Knights (c)		OHL	62	46	51	97	87

(c)—June, 1986—Drafted as underage junior by Pittsburgh Penguins in 1986 NHL entry draft. Tenth Penguins pick, 193rd overall, 10th round.

GARY CALLAGHAN

Center . . . 5'11" . . . 176 lbs. . . . Born, Oshawa, Ont., August 12, 1967 . . . Shoots left . . . Also plays Left Wing . . . (January, 1985)—Strained medial collateral ligament in left knee.

Year	Team	League	Games	G.	A.	Pts.	Pen.
1983-84—Oshawa Parkway TV		OHA	57	76	56	132	54
1984-85—Belleville Bulls (c)		OHL	57	24	25	49	42
1985-86—Belleville Bulls		OHL	53	29	16	45	42

(c)—June, 1985—Drafted as underage junior by Hartford Whalers in NHL entry draft. Third Whalers pick, 68th overall, fourth round.

JOHN (JOCK) CALLANDER

Center . . . 6'1" . . . 170 lbs. . . . Born, Regina, Sask., April 23, 1961 . . . Shoots right . . . Brother of Drew Callander.

Year	Team	League	Games	G.	A.	Pts.	Pen.
1978-79—Regina Pats		WHL	19	3	2	5	0
1978-79—Regina Blues		SJHL	42	44	42	86	24
1979-80—Regina Pats		WHL	39	9	11	20	25
1980-81—Regina Pats		WHL	72	67	86	153	37
1981-82—Regina Pats (c-d)		WHL	71	79	111	*190	59
1982-83—Salt Lake Golden Eagles		CHL	68	20	27	47	26
1983-84—Montana Magic		CHL	72	27	32	59	69
1983-84—Toledo Goaldiggers		IHL	2	0	0	0	0
1984-85—Muskegon Lumberjacks		IHL	82	39	68	107	86
1985-86—Muskegon Lumberjacks (e)		IHL	82	39	72	111	121

(c)—Won Bob Brownridge Memorial Trophy (WHL scoring leader).
(d)—Led WHL playoffs with 26 assists.
(e)—Won Turner Cup Playoff MVP.

ANTHONY BERT (TONY) CAMAZZOLA

Defense . . . 6'2" . . . 205 lbs. . . . Born, Burnaby, B.C., September 11, 1962 . . . Shoots left . . . Brother of Jim Camazzola.

Year	Team	League	Games	G.	A.	Pts.	Pen.
1979-80—Brandon Wheat Kings (c)		WHL	7	0	2	2	21
1980-81—Brandon Wheat Kings		WHL	69	4	20	24	144
1981-82—Brandon Wheat Kings		WHL	64	6	23	29	210
1981-82—Washington Capitals		NHL	3	0	0	0	4
1982-83—Hershey Bears		AHL	52	3	8	11	106
1983-84—Hershey Bears		AHL	63	6	10	16	138
1984-85—Fort Wayne Komets		IHL	15	0	3	3	56
1984-85—Toledo Goaldiggers		IHL	28	2	8	10	84
1985-86—Fort Wayne Komets		IHL	54	5	7	12	144
NHL TOTALS			3	0	0	0	4

(c)—June, 1980—Drafted as underage junior by Washington Capitals in 1980 NHL entry draft. Ninth Capitals pick, 195th overall, 10th round.

JIM CAMAZZOLA

Left Wing . . . 5'11" . . . 190 lbs. . . . Born, Burnaby, B.C., January 5, 1964 . . . Shoots left . . . Brother of Tony Camazzola.

Year	Team	League	Games	G.	A.	Pts.	Pen.
1982-83—Kamloops Junior Oilers (c)		WHL	66	57	58	115	54
1983-84—Seattle Breakers		WHL	3	1	1	2	0
1983-84—Kamloops Junior Oilers		WHL	29	26	24	50	25
1983-84—Chicago Black Hawks		NHL	1	0	0	0	0
1984-85—New Westminster Bruins		WHL	25	19	29	48	25
1985-86—Saginaw Generals		IHL	42	16	22	38	10
1985-86—Nova Scotia Oilers		AHL	3	0	0	0	0
NHL TOTALS			1	0	0	0	0

(c)—June, 1982—Drafted as underage junior by Chicago Black Hawks in 1982 NHL entry draft. Tenth Black Hawks pick, 196th overall, 10th round.

BILLY CAMPBELL

Defense . . . 6' . . . 173 lbs. . . . Born, Montreal, Que., March 20, 1964 . . . Shoots right.

Year	Team	League	Games	G.	A.	Pts.	Pen.
1980-81—Montreal Juniors (c)		QMJHL	72	20	48	68	28
1981-82—Montreal Juniors (b-d)		QMJHL	64	21	41	62	30
1982-83—Verdun Juniors		QHL	67	35	64	99	34
1983-84—Verdun Juniors (e)		QHL	65	24	66	90	59
1984-85—Hershey Bears		AHL	80	6	43	49	34
1985-86—Hershey Bears		AHL	37	0	8	8	18
1985-86—Sherbrooke Canadiens (f)		AHL	22	1	6	7	25
1985-86—Kalamazoo Wings		IHL	1	0	0	0	0

(c)—First winner of Raymond Lagace Trophy (Top Rookie QMJHL Defenseman).
(d)—June, 1982—Drafted as underage junior by Philadelphia Flyers in 1982 NHL entry draft. Third Flyers pick, 47th overall, third round.
(e)—Won Emile "Butch" Bouchard Trophy (Top Defenseman).
(f)—January, 1986—Traded by Philadelphia Flyers to Montreal Canadiens for future considerations.

WADE CAMPBELL

Defense . . . 6'4" . . . 220 lbs. . . . Born, Peace River, Alta., February 1, 1961 . . . Shoots right.

Year	Team	League	Games	G.	A.	Pts.	Pen.
1980-81—University of Alberta		CWJAA	24	3	15	18	46
1981-82—University of Alberta (c)		CWJAA	24	6	12	18	....
1982-83—Sherbrooke Jets		AHL	18	4	2	6	23
1982-83—Winnipeg Jets		NHL	42	1	2	3	50
1983-84—Winnipeg Jets		NHL	79	7	14	21	147
1984-85—Winnipeg Jets		NHL	40	1	6	7	21
1984-85—Sherbrooke Canadiens		AHL	28	2	6	8	70
1985-86—Sherbrooke Canadiens		AHL	9	0	2	2	26
1985-86—Winnipeg Jets (d)		NHL	24	0	1	1	27
1985-86—Moncton Golden Flames		AHL	17	2	2	4	21
1985-86—Boston Bruins		NHL	8	0	0	0	15
NHL TOTALS			193	9	23	32	260

(c)—September, 1982—Signed by Winnipeg Jets as a free agent.
(d)—January, 1986—Traded by Winnipeg Jets to Boston Bruins for Bill Derlago.

DOMINIC CAMPEDELLI

Defense . . . 6'1" . . . 185 lbs. . . . Born, Cohasset, Me., April 3, 1964 . . . Shoots left.

Year	Team	League	Games	G.	A.	Pts.	Pen.
1982-83—Boston College (c)		ECAC	26	1	10	11	26
1983-84—Boston College		ECAC	37	10	19	29	24
1984-85—Boston College (d)		H. East	44	5	44	49	74
1985-86—Sherbrooke Canadiens		AHL	38	4	10	14	27
1985-86—Montreal Canadiens		NHL	2	0	0	0	0
NHL Totals			2	0	0	0	0

(c)—June, 1982—Drafted by Toronto Maple Leafs in 1982 NHL entry draft. Tenth Maple Leafs pick, 129th overall, seventh round.
(d)—September, 1985—Traded by Toronto Maple Leafs to Montreal Canadiens for third-round draft choice (Darryl Shannon) in 1986.

DAVID CAPUANO

Center . . . 6'2" . . . 190 lbs. . . . Born, Warwick, R.I., July 27, 1968 . . . Shoots left . . . Brother of Jack Capuano.

Year	Team	League	Games	G.	A.	Pts.	Pen.
1984-85—Mt. St. Charles H.S.		R.I.	....	41	38	79	....
1985-86—Mt. St. Charles H.S. (c)		R.I.	22	39	48	87	20

(c)—June, 1986—Drafted by Pittsburgh Penguins in 1986 NHL entry draft. Second Penguins pick, 25th overall, second round.

JACK CAPUANO

Defense . . . 6'2" . . . 210 lbs. . . . Born, Cranston, R.I., July 7, 1966 . . . Shoots left . . . Brother of Dave Capuano.

Year	Team	League	Games	G.	A.	Pts.	Pen.
1983-84—Kent Prep. (c)		Conn.	....	10	8	18	....
1984-85—University of Maine		H. East	....	...	....	....	....
1985-86—University of Maine		H. East	39	9	13	22	59

(c)—June, 1984—Drafted by Toronto Maple Leafs in 1984 NHL entry draft. Fourth Maple Leafs pick, 88th overall, fifth round.

GUY CARBONNEAU

Center . . . 5'10" . . . 165 lbs. . . . Born, Sept Iles, Que., March 18, 1960 . . . Shoots right.

Year	Team	League	Games	G.	A.	Pts.	Pen.
1976-77—Chicoutimi Sagueneens		QMJHL	59	9	20	29	8
1977-78—Chicoutimi Sagueneens		QMJHL	70	28	55	83	60
1978-79—Chicoutimi Sagueneens (c)		QMJHL	72	62	79	141	47
1979-80—Chicoutimi Sagueneens (b)		QMJHL	72	72	110	182	66
1979-80—Nova Scotia Voyageurs (d)		AHL	....	...	....	....	....
1980-81—Montreal Canadiens		NHL	2	0	1	1	0
1980-81—Nova Scotia Voyageurs		AHL	78	35	53	88	87
1981-82—Nova Scotia Voyageurs		AHL	77	27	67	94	124
1982-83—Montreal Canadiens		NHL	77	18	29	47	68
1983-84—Montreal Canadiens		NHL	78	24	30	54	75
1984-85—Montreal Canadiens		NHL	79	23	34	57	43
1985-86—Montreal Canadiens		NHL	80	20	36	56	57
NHL TOTALS			316	85	130	215	243

(c)—August, 1979—Drafted by Montreal Canadiens as underage junior in NHL entry draft. Fourth Canadiens pick, 44th overall, third round.
(d)—No regular season record. Played one playoff game.

TERRY CARKNER

Defense . . . 6'3" . . . 200 lbs. . . . Born, Smith Falls, Ont., March 7, 1966 . . . Shoots left.

Year	Team	League	Games	G.	A.	Pts.	Pen.
1982-83	Brockville Braves	COJHL	47	8	32	40	94
1983-84	Peterborough Petes (c)	OHL	66	4	21	25	91
1984-85	Peterborough Petes (b)	OHL	64	14	47	61	125
1985-86	Peterborough Petes (a-d)	OHL	54	12	32	44	106

    (c)—June, 1984—Drafted as underage junior by New York Rangers in NHL entry draft. First Rangers pick, 14th overall, first round.

    (d)—Shared Max Kaminsky Trophy (Top OHL Defenseman) with Jeff Brown.

TODD CARLILE

Defense . . . 5'11" . . . 185 lbs. . . . Born, St. Paul, Minn., January 22, 1964 . . . Shoots right . . . (June, 1980)—Partial separation of shoulder.

Year	Team	League	Games	G.	A.	Pts.	Pen.
1981-82	North St. Paul H.S. (c)	Minn. H.S.	22	8	18	26	32
1982-83	University of Michigan	CCHA	36	5	14	19	67
1983-84	University of Michigan	CCHA	33	11	20	31	70
1984-85	University of Michigan	CCHA	38	5	8	13	62
1985-86	University of Michigan	CCHA	38	6	20	26	84

    (c)—June, 1982—Drafted as underage player by Minnesota North Stars in NHL entry draft. Sixth North Stars pick, 122nd overall, sixth round.

KENT CARLSON

Left Wing and Defense . . . 6'3" . . . 200 lbs. . . . Born, Concord, N.H., January 11, 1962 . . . Shoots left . . . (January 8, 1985)—Broke right hand in game at N.Y. Islanders . . . (February, 1985)—Sprained shoulder during team practice . . . (February 18, 1986)—Missed eight games with back spasms.

Year	Team	League	Games	G.	A.	Pts.	Pen.
1981-82	St. Lawrence University (c)	ECAC	28	8	14	22	24
1982-83	St. Lawrence University	ECAC	36	10	23	33	56
1983-84	Montreal Canadiens	NHL	65	3	7	10	73
1984-85	Sherbrooke Canadiens	AHL	13	1	4	5	7
1984-85	Montreal Canadiens	NHL	18	1	1	2	33
1985-86	Sherbrooke Canadiens	AHL	35	11	15	26	79
1985-86	Montreal Canadiens (d)	NHL	2	0	0	0	0
1985-86	St. Louis Blues	NHL	26	2	3	5	42
	NHL TOTALS		111	6	11	17	148

    (c)—June, 1982—Drafted by Montreal Canadiens in NHL entry draft. Third Canadiens pick, 32nd overall, second round.

    (d)—January, 1986—Traded by Montreal Canadiens to St. Louis Blues for Graham Herring and a fifth round 1986 draft pick (Eric Aubertin).

STEVE CARLSON

Center . . . 6'3" . . . 180 lbs. . . . Born, Virginia, Minn., August 26, 1955 . . . Shoots left . . . Brother of Jack and Jeff Carlson . . . Missed part of 1975-76 season with broken right hand . . . (October, 1980)—Lower back problems . . . (December, 1982)—Separated shoulder . . . (December, 1985)—Back injury.

Year	Team	League	Games	G.	A.	Pts.	Pen.
1973-74	Marquette Rangers (a)	USHL	42	34	45	79	77
1974-75	Johnstown Jets	NAHL	70	30	58	88	84
1975-76	Johnstown Jets	NAHL	40	22	24	46	55
1975-76	Minnesota Fighting Saints (c-d)	WHA	10	0	1	1	23
1976-77	Minnesota Fighting Saints (e-f)	WHA	21	5	8	13	8
1976-77	New England Whalers	WHA	31	4	9	13	40
1977-78	Springfield Indians	AHL	37	21	15	36	46
1977-78	New England Whalers	WHA	38	6	7	13	11
1978-79	Edmonton Oilers (g-h)	WHA	73	18	22	40	50
1979-80	Los Angeles Kings	NHL	52	9	12	21	23
1980-81	Springfield Indians	AHL	32	10	14	24	44
1980-81	Houston Apollos	CHL	27	13	21	34	29
1981-82	Nashville South Stars (i)	CHL	59	23	39	62	63
1982-83	Birmingham South Stars	CHL	69	25	42	67	73
1983-84	Baltimore Skipjacks (j)	AHL	63	9	30	39	70
1984-85	Baltimore Skipjacks	AHL	76	18	29	47	69
1985-86	Baltimore Skipjacks	AHL	66	9	27	36	56
	WHA TOTALS		173	33	47	80	132
	NHL TOTALS		52	9	12	21	23

(c)—Signed by New England Whalers following demise of Minnesota Fighting Saints, March, 1976.
(d)—Drafted from New England Whalers by Cleveland Crusaders in intra-league draft, June, 1976. (Later rejoined Minnesota Fighting Saints.)
(e)—Sold to Edmonton Oilers by Minnesota Fighting Saints, January, 1977.
(f)—Traded to New England Whalers by Edmonton Oilers with Dave Dryden, Jack Carlson, Dave Keon and John McKenzie for Danny Arndt, WHA rights to Dave Debol and cash, January, 1977.
(g)—January, 1979—NHL rights traded by Detroit Red Wings to Los Angeles Kings for NHL rights to Steve Short.
(h)—June, 1979—Selected by Los Angeles Kings in NHL reclaim draft.
(i)—December, 1981—Signed by Minnesota North Stars as a free agent and assigned to Nashville South Stars.
(j)—August, 1983—Signed by Pittsburgh Penguins as a free agent.

ANDERS CARLSSON

Center . . . 5'11" . . . 185 lbs. . . . Born, Gavle, Sweden, November 25, 1960 . . . Shoots left.

Year	Team	League	Games	G.	A.	Pts.	Pen.
1985-86—Sodertalje (c)		Sweden	36	12	26	38	20

(c)—June, 1986—Drafted by New Jersey Devils in NHL entry draft. Fifth Devils pick, 66th overall, fourth round.

RANDY ROBERT CARLYLE

Defense . . . 5'10" . . . 198 lbs. . . . Born, Sudbury, Ont., April 19, 1956 . . . Shoots left. . . . Missed part of 1978-79 season with broken ankle . . . (October, 1982)—Injured back . . . (January, 1983)—Injured knee . . . (March, 1984)—Knee injury . . . (November 12, 1985)— Missed eight games with thigh injury . . . (December 7, 1985)—Missed four games after a calf contusion suffered vs. Los Angeles.

Year	Team	League	Games	G.	A.	Pts.	Pen.
1973-74—Sudbury Wolves		Jr."A" OHA	12	0	8	8	21
1974-75—Sudbury Wolves		Jr."A" OHA	67	17	47	64	118
1975-76—Sudbury Wolves (b-c)		Jr."A" OHA	60	15	64	79	126
1976-77—Dallas Black Hawks		CHL	26	2	7	9	63
1976-77—Toronto Maple Leafs		NHL	45	0	5	5	51
1977-78—Dallas Black Hawks		CHL	21	3	14	17	31
1977-78—Toronto Maple Leafs (d)		NHL	49	2	11	13	31
1978-79—Pittsburgh Penguins		NHL	70	13	34	47	78
1979-80—Pittsburgh Penguins		NHL	67	8	28	36	45
1980-81—Pittsburgh Penguins (a-e)		NHL	76	16	67	83	136
1981-82—Pittsburgh Penguins		NHL	73	11	64	75	131
1982-83—Pittsburgh Penguins		NHL	61	15	41	56	110
1983-84—Pittsburgh Penguins (f)		NHL	50	3	23	26	82
1983-84—Winnipeg Jets		NHL	5	0	3	3	2
1984-85—Winnipeg Jets		NHL	71	13	38	51	98
1985-86—Winnipeg Jets		NHL	68	16	33	49	93
NHL TOTALS			635	97	347	444	857

(c)—Drafted from Sudbury Wolves by Toronto Maple Leafs in second round of 1976 amateur draft.
(d)—Traded to Pittsburgh Penguins by Toronto Maple Leafs with George Ferguson for Dave Burrows, June, 1978.
(e)—Won James Norris Memorial Trophy (Top NHL Defenseman).
(f)—March, 1984—Traded by Pittsburgh Penguins to Winnipeg Jets for first round 1984 draft pick (Doug Bodger) and player to be named after the 1983-84 season (Moe Mantha).

TODD CARNELLEY

Defense . . . 5'11" . . . 190 lbs. . . . Born, Edmonton, Alta., September 18, 1966 . . . Shoots right . . . (December, 1984)—Tendinitis.

Year	Team	League	Games	G.	A.	Pts.	Pen.
1983-84—Kamloops Junior Oilers		WHL	70	7	23	30	66
1984-85—Kamloops Blazers (b-c)		WHL	56	18	29	47	69
1985-86—Kamloops Blazers		WHL	44	3	23	26	63

(c)—June, 1985—Drafted as underage junior by Edmonton Oilers in 1985 NHL entry draft. Second Oilers pick, 41st overall, second round.

ROBERT CARPENTER

Center . . . 6' . . . 190 lbs. . . . Born, Beverly, Mass., July 13, 1963 . . . Shoots left . . . First to play in NHL directly from U.S. high school hockey . . . (1984-85)—Set NHL record for goals in a season by an American-born player.

Year	Team	League	Games	G.	A.	Pts.	Pen.
1979-80—St. Johns Prep. H.S. (a)		Mass. H.S.	....	28	37	65	....
1980-81—St. Johns Prep. H.S. (a-c)		Mass. H.S.	....	14	24	38	....

Year	Team	League	Games	G.	A.	Pts.	Pen.
1981-82—Washington Capitals		NHL	80	32	35	67	69
1982-83—Washington Capitals		NHL	80	32	37	69	64
1983-84—Washington Capitals		NHL	80	28	40	68	51
1984-85—Washington Capitals		NHL	80	53	42	95	87
1985-86—Washington Capitals		NHL	80	27	29	56	105
NHL TOTALS			400	172	183	355	376

(c)—June, 1981—Drafted as underage junior by Washington Capitals in 1981 NHL entry draft. First Capitals pick, third overall, first round.

WILLIAM ALLAN (BILLY) CARROLL

Center . . . 5'10" . . . 191 lbs . . . Born, Toronto, Ont., January 19, 1959 . . . Shoots left . . . (1978-79)—Mononucleosis . . . (January 13, 1986)—Injured hip at Toronto . . . (January 19, 1986)—Fractured toe at Chicago and missed 14 games . . . (March, 1986)—Missed eight games with an ear infection.

Year	Team	League	Games	G.	A.	Pts.	Pen.
1976-77—London Knights		OMJHL	64	18	31	49	37
1977-78—London Knights		OMJHL	68	37	36	73	42
1978-79—London Knight (b-c)		OMJHL	63	35	50	85	38
1979-80—Indianapolis Checkers		CHL	49	9	17	26	19
1980-81—Indianapolis Racers		CHL	59	27	37	64	67
1980-81—New York Islanders		NHL	18	4	4	8	6
1981-82—New York Islanders		NHL	72	9	20	29	32
1982-83—New York Islanders		NHL	71	1	11	12	24
1983-84—New York Islanders		NHL	39	5	2	7	12
1984-85—Edmonton Oilers (d)		NHL	65	8	9	17	22
1985-86—Nova Scotia Oilers		AHL	26	7	18	25	15
1985-86—Edmonton Oilers (e)		NHL	5	0	2	2	0
1985-86—Detroit Red Wings		NHL	22	2	4	6	11
NHL TOTALS			292	29	52	81	107

(c)—August, 1979—Drafted by New York Islanders in 1979 NHL entry draft. Third Islanders pick, 38th overall, second round.

(d)—October, 1984—Selected by Edmonton Oilers in 1984 NHL waiver draft.

(e)—December, 1985—Traded by Edmonton Oilers to Detroit Red Wings for Bruce Eakin.

JAMES CARSON

Center . . . 6' . . . 185 lbs. . . . Born, Southfield, Mich., July 20, 1968 . . . Shoots right.

Year	Team	League	Games	G.	A.	Pts.	Pen.
1984-85—Verdun Juniors		QHL	68	44	72	116	16
1985-86—Verdun Juniors (b-c-d-e)		QHL	69	70	83	153	46

(c)—Won Frank Selke Trophy (Most Gentlemanly player).

(d)—Won Mike Bossy Trophy (Top Pro Prospect).

(e)—June, 1986—Drafted as underage junior by Los Angeles Kings in 1986 NHL entry draft. First Kings pick, second overall, first round.

LINDSAY WARREN CARSON

Center . . . 6'2" . . . 190 lbs. . . . Born, Oxbow, Sask., November 21, 1960 . . . Shoots left . . . Also plays Left Wing . . . (October 15, 1983)—Broke left arm when checked vs. N.Y. Islanders . . . (November 24, 1985)—Broke knuckle on left hand vs. Pittsburgh and missed 17 games.

Year	Team	League	Games	G.	A.	Pts.	Pen.
1977-78—Saskatoon Blades		WCHL	62	23	55	78	124
1978-79—Saskatoon Blades		WHL	37	21	29	50	55
1978-79—Billings Bighorns (c)		WHL	40	13	22	35	50
1979-80—Billings Bighorns		WHL	70	42	66	108	101
1980-81—Maine Mariners		AHL	79	11	25	36	84
1981-82—Maine Mariners		AHL	54	20	31	51	92
1981-82—Philadelphia Flyers		NHL	18	0	1	1	32
1982-83—Philadelphia Flyers		NHL	78	18	19	37	68
1983-84—Springfield Indians		AHL	5	2	4	6	5
1983-84—Philadelphia Flyers		NHL	16	1	3	4	10
1984-85—Philadelphia Flyers		NHL	77	20	19	39	123
1985-86—Philadelphia Flyers		NHL	50	9	12	21	84
NHL TOTALS			239	48	54	102	317

(c)—August, 1979—Drafted as underage junior by Philadelphia Flyers in 1979 NHL entry draft. Fourth Flyers pick, 56th overall, third round.

JOHN CARTER

Left Wing . . . 5'10" . . . 175 lbs. . . . Born, Winchester, Mass., May 3, 1963 . . . Shoots left . . . (February, 1986)—Sprained knee in ECAC game.

Year	Team	League	Games	G.	A.	Pts.	Pen.
1982-83—R.P.I.		ECAC	29	16	22	38	33
1983-84—R.P.I. (b)		ECAC	38	35	39	74	52
1984-85—R.P.I. (a-c)		ECAC	37	43	29	72	52
1985-86—R.P.I. (d)		ECAC	27	23	18	41	68
1985-86—Boston Bruins		NHL	3	0	0	0	0
NHL TOTALS			3	0	0	0	0

(c)—Named second-team All-American (East).
(d)—March, 1986—Signed by Boston Bruins as a free agent.

BRUCE CASSIDY

Defense . . . 5'11" . . . 175 lbs. . . . Born, Ottawa, Ont., May 20, 1965 . . . Shoots left . . . (Summer, 1984)—Injured knee and missed training camp.

Year	Team	League	Games	G.	A.	Pts.	Pen.
1981-82—Hawkesbury Hawks		COJHL	37	13	30	43	32
1982-83—Ottawa 67's (c-d)		OHL	70	25	86	111	33
1983-84—Ottawa 67's (b)		OHL	67	27	68	95	58
1983-84—Chicago Black Hawks		NHL	1	0	0	0	0
1984-85—Ottawa 67's		OHL	28	13	27	40	15
1985-86—Chicago Black Hawks		NHL	1	0	0	0	0
1985-86—Nova Scotia Oilers		AHL	4	0	0	0	0
NHL TOTALS			2	0	0	0	0

(c)—Won Emms Family Award (OHL Rookie-of-the-Year).
(d)—June, 1983—Drafted as underage junior by Chicago Black Hawks in NHL entry draft. First Black Hawks pick, 18th overall, first round.

RORY LOUIS CAVA

Defense . . . 6'5" . . . 220 lbs. . . . Born, Thunder Bay, Ont., February 12, 1960 . . . Shoots right.

Year	Team	League	Games	G.	A.	Pts.	Pen.
1977-78—Ottawa 67's		OMJHL	66	1	8	9	110
1978-79—Ottawa 67's		OMJHL	67	6	18	24	138
1979-80—Ottawa 67's		OMJHL	53	4	19	23	179
1980-81—Fort Wayne Komets (c)		IHL	69	2	20	22	139
1980-81—Dallas Black Hawks		CHL	1	0	0	0	4
1981-82—Dallas Black Hawks		CHL	66	4	27	31	184
1982-83—Carolina Thunderbirds (a-d)		ACHL	63	23	*60	83	151
1983-84—Adirondack Red Wings		AHL	75	2	19	21	160
1984-85—Carolina Thunderbirds		ACHL	54	20	56	76	83
1985-86—Indianapolis Checkers		IHL	12	0	3	3	9

(c)—September, 1980—Signed by Vancouver Canucks as a free agent.
(d)—Named ACHL MVP.

GINO CAVALLINI

Left Wing . . . 6'2" . . . 215 lbs. . . . Born, Toronto, Ont., November 24, 1962 . . . Shoots left.

Year	Team	League	Games	G.	A.	Pts.	Pen.
1981-82—Toronto St. Mikes		OJHL	37	27	56	83	..
1982-83—Bowling Green Univ.		CCHA	40	8	16	24	52
1983-84—Bowling Green Univ. (c)		CCHA	43	25	23	48	16
1984-85—Moncton Golden Flames		AHL	51	29	19	48	28
1984-85—Calgary Flames		NHL	27	6	10	16	14
1985-86—Moncton Golden Flames		AHL	4	3	2	5	7
1985-86—Calgary Flames (d)		NHL	27	7	7	14	26
1985-86—St. Louis Blues		NHL	30	6	5	11	36
NHL TOTALS			84	19	22	41	76

(c)—July, 1984—Signed by Calgary Flames as a free agent.
(d)—February, 1986—Traded with Eddy Beers and Charles Bourgeois by Calgary Flames to St. Louis Blues for Terry Johnson, Joe Mullen and Rik Wilson.

PAUL CAVALLINI

Defense . . . 6'2" . . . 202 lbs. . . . Born, Toronto, Ont., October 13, 1965 . . . Shoots left.

Year	Team	League	Games	G.	A.	Pts.	Pen.
1983-84—Henry Carr H.S. (c)		MTHL	54	20	41	61	190
1984-85—Providence College		H. East	45	5	14	19	64
1985-86—Team Canada		Int'l.	52	1	11	12	95
1985-86—Binghamton Whalers		AHL	15	3	4	7	20

(c)—June, 1984—Drafted as underage junior by Washington Capitals in NHL entry draft. Ninth Capitals pick, 205th overall, 10th round.

JOHN DAVID CHABOT

(Given Name: John Kahibaitche)

Center ... 6'1" ... 185 lbs. ... Born Summerside, P.E.I., May 18, 1962 ... Shoots left.

Year	Team	League	Games	G.	A.	Pts.	Pen.
1979-80—Hull Olympics (c)		QMJHL	68	26	57	83	28
1980-81—Hull Olympics		QMJHL	70	27	62	89	24
1980-81—Nova Scotia Voyageurs		AHL	1	0	0	0	0
1981-82—Sherbrooke Beavers (a-d-e)		QMJHL	62	34	*109	143	40
1982-83—Nova Scotia Voyageurs		AHL	76	16	73	89	19
1983-84—Montreal Canadiens		NHL	56	18	25	43	13
1984-85—Montreal Canadiens (f)		NHL	10	1	6	7	2
1984-85—Pittsburgh Penguins		NHL	67	8	45	53	12
1985-86—Pittsburgh Penguins		NHL	77	14	31	45	6
NHL TOTALS			210	41	107	148	33

(c)—June, 1980—Drafted as underage junior by Montreal Canadiens in 1980 NHL entry draft. Third Canadiens pick, 40th overall, second round.

(d)—September 1981—Traded by Hull Olympics to Sherbrooke Beavers for Tim Cranston and Rousell MacKenzie.

(e)—Won Michel Briere Trophy (regular season QMJHL MVP).

(f)—November, 1984—Traded by Montreal Canadiens to Pittsburgh Penguins for Ron Flockhart.

CRAIG CHANNELL

Defense ... 5'11" ... 195 lbs. ... Born, Moncton, N.B., April 24, 1962 ... Shoots left.

Year	Team	League	Games	G.	A.	Pts.	Pen.
1979-80—Seattle Breakers		WHL	70	3	21	24	191
1980-81—Seattle Breakers		WHL	71	9	66	75	181
1981-82—Seattle Breakers (c)		WHL	71	9	79	88	244
1982-83—Sherbrooke Jets		AHL	65	0	15	15	109
1983-84—Sherbrooke Jets		AHL	80	5	18	23	112
1984-85—Sherbrooke Canadiens		AHL	1	0	0	0	0
1984-85—Fort Wayne Komets		IHL	78	10	35	45	110
1985-86—Fort Wayne Komets		IHL	69	7	28	35	116

(c)—September, 1982—Signed by Winnipeg Jets as a free agent.

RENE CHAPDELAINE

Defense ... 6'1" ... 195 lbs. ... Born, Weyburn, Sask., September 27, 1966 ... Shoots right.

Year	Team	League	Games	G.	A.	Pts.	Pen.
1984-85—Weyburn		SJHL	61	3	17	20	..
1985-86—Lake Superior State (c)		CCHA	40	2	7	9	24

(c)—June, 1986—Drafted by Los Angeles Kings in 1986 NHL entry draft. Seventh Kings pick, 149th overall, eighth round.

BRIAN CHAPMAN

Defense ... 6' ... 185 lbs. ... Born, Brockville, Ont., February 10, 1968 ... Shoots left.

Year	Team	League	Games	G.	A.	Pts.	Pen.
1984-85—Brockville Braves		Jr.A. OPHL	50	11	32	43	145
1985-86—Belleville Bulls (c)		OHL	66	6	31	37	168

(c)—June, 1986—Drafted as underage junior by Hartford Whalers in 1986 NHL entry draft. Third Whalers pick, 74th overall, fourth round.

WALLY CHAPMAN

Center ... 6' ... 190 lbs. ... Born, Fort Leonard Wood, Mo., July 6, 1964 ... Shoots left.

Year	Team	League	Games	G.	A.	Pts.	Pen.
1981-82—Edina H.S. (c)		Minn. H.S.	26	27	11	38	14
1982-83—University of Minnesota		WCHA	20	3	6	9	18
1983-84—University of Minnesota		WCHA	30	10	6	16	20
1984-85—University of Minnesota		WCHA	47	25	13	38	22
1985-86—University of Minnesota		WCHA	47	29	29	58	35

(c)—June, 1982—Drafted by Minnesota North Stars as underage player in 1982 NHL entry draft. Second North Stars pick, 59th overall, third round.

JOSE CHARBONNEAU

Right Wing . . . 6' . . . 195 lbs. . . . Born, Ferme-Neuve, Que., November 2, 1966 . . . Shoots right . . . (November, 1984)—Separated right shoulder . . . (December, 1984)—Reinjured shoulder . . . (January, 1985)—Aggravated shoulder.

Year	Team	League	Games	G.	A.	Pts.	Pen.
1983-84—Drummondville Voltigeurs		QHL	65	31	59	90	110
1984-85—Drummondville Voltigeurs (c)		QHL	46	34	40	74	91
1985-86—Drummondville Voltigeurs		QHL	57	44	45	89	158

(c)—June, 1985—Drafted as underage junior by Montreal Canadiens in NHL entry draft. First Canadiens pick, 12th overall, first round.

TODD CHARLESWORTH

Defense . . . 6'1" . . . 185 lbs. . . . Born, Calgary, Alta., March 22, 1965 . . . Shoots left.

Year	Team	League	Games	G.	A.	Pts.	Pen.
1981-82—Gloucester Rangers		COJHL	50	13	24	37	67
1982-83—Oshawa Generals (c)		OHL	70	6	23	29	55
1983-84—Oshawa Generals		OHL	57	11	35	46	54
1983-84—Pittsburgh Penguins		NHL	10	0	0	0	8
1984-85—Pittsburgh Penguins		NHL	67	1	8	9	31
1985-86—Baltimore Skipjacks		AHL	19	1	3	4	10
1985-86—Muskegon Lumberjacks		IHL	51	9	27	36	78
1985-86—Pittsburgh Penguins		NHL	2	0	1	1	0
NHL TOTALS			79	1	9	10	39

(c)—June, 1983—Drafted as underage junior by Pittsburgh Penguins in NHL entry draft. Second Penguins pick, 22nd overall, second round.

LANDIS CHAULK

Left Wing . . . 6'1" . . . 200 lbs. . . . Born, Swift Current, Sask., May 17, 1966 . . . Shoots left.

Year	Team	League	Games	G.	A.	Pts.	Pen.
1983-84—Calgary Wranglers (c)		WHL	72	21	28	49	123
1984-85—Calgary Wranglers		WHL	65	25	40	65	174
1985-86—Spokane Chiefs (d)		WHL	22	6	6	12	40
1985-86—Lethbridge Broncos		WHL	22	2	4	6	39

(c)—June, 1984—Drafted as underage junior by Vancouver Canucks in 1984 NHL entry draft. Third Canucks pick, 55th overall, third round.

(d)—January, 1986—Traded with Ian Herbers and Mike Weigleitner by Spokane Chiefs to Lethbridge Broncos for Mike Berger.

CHRIS CHELIOS

Defense . . . 6'1" . . . 187 lbs. . . . Born, Chicago, Ill., January 25, 1962 . . . Shoots right. . . . Member of 1984 U.S. Olympic Team . . . (January, 1985)—Sprained right ankle . . . (April, 1985)—Injured left knee . . . Older brother of Steve Chelios (QHL player) . . . (December 19, 1985)—Sprained knee at Quebec . . . (January 20, 1986)—Reinjured knee at Quebec.

Year	Team	League	Games	G.	A.	Pts.	Pen.
1979-80—Moose Jaw Canucks		SJHL	53	12	31	43	118
1980-81—Moose Jaw Canucks (c)		SJHL	54	23	64	87	175
1981-82—University of Wisconsin		WCHA	43	6	43	49	50
1982-83—University of Wisconsin (b)		WCHA	45	16	32	48	62
1983-84—U.S. National Team		Int'l.	60	14	35	49	58
1983-84—U.S. Olympic Team		Int'l.	6	0	4	4	8
1983-84—Montreal Canadiens		NHL	12	0	2	2	12
1984-85—Montreal Canadiens		NHL	74	9	55	64	87
1985-86—Montreal Canadiens		NHL	41	8	26	34	67
NHL TOTALS			127	17	83	100	166

(c)—June, 1981—Drafted as underage junior by Montreal Canadiens in 1981 NHL entry draft. Fifth Canadiens pick, 40th overall, second round.

RICHARD CHERNOMAZ

Right Wing . . . 5'10" . . . 175 lbs. . . . Born, Selkirk, Man., September 1, 1963 . . . Shoots right . . . Missed parts of 1981-82 season with recurring pain caused by separated shoulder . . . (January, 1983)—Injured knee ligaments . . . (November 27, 1984)—Sprained left knee in game vs. Minnesota and needed arthroscopic surgery.

Year	Team	League	Games	G.	A.	Pts.	Pen.
1979-80—Saskatoon		SJHL	51	33	37	70	75
1979-80—Saskatoon Blades		WHL	25	9	10	19	33

Year	Team	League	Games	G.	A.	Pts.	Pen.
1980-81—Victoria Cougars (c)		WHL	72	49	64	113	92
1981-82—Victoria Cougars		WHL	49	36	62	98	69
1981-82—Colorado Rockies		NHL	2	0	0	0	0
1982-83—Victoria Cougars (a)		WHL	64	71	53	124	113
1983-84—Maine Mariners		AHL	69	17	29	46	39
1983-84—New Jersey Devils		NHL	7	2	1	3	2
1984-85—Maine Mariners		AHL	64	17	34	51	64
1984-85—New Jersey Devils		NHL	3	0	2	2	2
1985-86—Maine Mariners		AHL	78	21	28	49	82
NHL TOTALS			12	2	3	5	4

(c)—June, 1981—Drafted as underage junior by Colorado Rockies in 1981 NHL entry draft. Third Rockies pick, 26th overall, second round.

STEVE CHIASSON

Defense . . . 6'1" . . . 200 lbs. . . . Born, Barrie, Ont., April 14, 1967 . . . Shoots left . . . (October, 1985)—Hand injury.

Year	Team	League	Games	G.	A.	Pts.	Pen.
1982-83—Peterborough Midgets		OHA	40	25	35	60	120
1983-84—Guelph Platers		OHL	55	1	9	10	112
1984-85—Guelph Platers (c)		OHL	61	8	22	30	139
1985-86—Guelph Platers		OHL	54	12	29	41	126

(c)—June, 1985—Drafted as underage junior by Detroit Red Wings in 1985 NHL entry draft. Third Red Wings pick, 50th overall, third round.

COLIN CHIN

Center . . . 5'8" . . . 165 lbs. . . . Born, Fort Wayne, Ind., August 28, 1961 . . . Shoots left.

Year	Team	League	Games	G.	A.	Pts.	Pen.
1983-84—Univ. Illinois-Chicago		CCHA	35	11	25	36	14
1984-85—Univ. Illinois-Chicago (c)		CCHA	38	23	42	65	22
1985-86—Baltimore Skipjacks		AHL	78	17	28	45	38

(c)—October, 1985—Signed by Pittsburgh Penguins as a free agent.

PETER CHOMA

Right Wing . . . 6'1" . . . 215 lbs. . . . Born, St. Catharines, Ont., September 10, 1968 . . . Shoots right.

Year	Team	League	Games	G.	A.	Pts.	Pen.
1984-85—St. Catharines Midget		OHA	43	38	32	70	87
1985-86—Hamilton Steelhawks (c)		OHL	18	2	3	5	13
1985-86—Belleville Bulls (d)		OHL	46	9	11	20	25

(c)—November, 1985—Traded with Jason Lafreniere and Lawrence Hinch by Hamilton Steelhawks to Belleville Bulls for Sean Doyl, John Purves and Brian Hoard.

(d)—June, 1986—Drafted as underage junior by Washington Capitals in 1986 NHL entry draft. Eighth Capitals pick, 145th overall, seventh round.

THOMAS CHORSKE

Right Wing . . . 6'1" . . . 185 lbs. . . . Born, Minneapolis, Minn., September 18, 1966 . . . Shoots right.

Year	Team	League	Games	G.	A.	Pts.	Pen.
1984-85—Minn. Southwest H.S. (c)		Minn. H.S.	23	44	26	70	..
1985-86—University of Minnesota		WCHA	39	6	4	10	6

(c)—June, 1985—Drafted by Montreal Canadiens in 1985 NHL entry draft. Second Canadiens pick, 16th overall, first round.

GREGORY CHOULES

Left Wing . . . 5'9" . . . 170 lbs. . . . Born, Montreal, Que., May 1, 1966 . . . Shoots left . . . Brother of Ron Choules.

Year	Team	League	Games	G.	A.	Pts.	Pen.
1983-84—Granby Bisons		QHL	55	19	23	42	43
1984-85—Granby Bisons-Chic Sag (c-d)		QHL	65	21	28	49	126
1985-86—Chicoutimi Sagueneens		QHL	65	20	32	52	118

(c)—January, 1985—Traded with Stephane Richer by Granby Bisons to Chicoutimi Sagueneens for Stephane Roy, Marc Bureau, Lee Duhemee, Sylvain Demers and Rene Lecuyer.

(d)—June, 1985—Drafted as underage junior by Pittsburgh Penguins in 1985 NHL entry draft. Twelfth Penguins pick, 233rd overall, 12th round.

RON CHOULES

Left Wing . . . 6'1" . . . 205 lbs. . . . Born, Montreal, Que., July 11, 1963 . . . Shoots left . . . Brother of Greg Choules.

Year	Team	League	Games	G.	A.	Pts.	Pen.
1980-81	Hull Olympics	QMJHL	57	7	7	14	167
1981-82	Hull Olympics	QMJHL	47	10	14	24	140
1982-83	Hull Olympics	QHL	37	25	34	59	162
1982-83	Trois-Rivieres Draveurs(c-d)	QHL	31	28	26	54	127
1983-84	Quebec Remparts	QHL	37	24	31	55	145
1983-84	St. Catharines Saints	AHL	14	1	1	2	26
1984-85	Milwaukee Admirals	IHL	1	0	0	0	0
1984-85	Peoria Rivermen	IHL	5	2	1	3	38
1984-85	Kalamazoo Wings	IHL	3	0	0	0	6
1985-86	Peoria Rivermen	IHL	8	0	0	0	14

(c)—December, 1982—Traded with Michel Boucher and Alain Raymond by Hull Olympics to Trois-Rivieres Draveurs for Joel Baillargeon and Patrick Emond.
(d)—June, 1983—Drafted by Toronto Maple Leafs in 1983 NHL entry draft. Eleventh Maple Leafs pick, 228th overall, 12th round.

BLAINE CHREST

Center . . . 5'11" . . . 175 lbs. . . . Born, Gainsborough, Sask., January 10, 1966 . . . Shoots left.

Year	Team	League	Games	G.	A.	Pts.	Pen.
1982-83	Estevan Bruins	SJHL	45	19	28	47	30
1982-83	Brandon Wheat Kings	WHL	4	1	0	1	5
1983-84	Estevan	SJHL	66	50	53	103	12
1983-84	Portland Winter Hawks (c)	WHL	12	5	4	9	2
1984-85	Portland Winter Hawks	WHL	68	27	39	66	13
1985-86	Portland Winter Hawks	WHL	71	29	57	86	7

(c)—June, 1984—Drafted as underage junior by Vancouver Canucks in 1984 NHL entry draft. Eighth Canucks pick, 136th overall, seventh round.

MATHEW CHRISTENSEN

Center . . . 6'1" . . . 185 lbs. . . . Born, Aurora, Minn., June 6, 1964 . . . Shoots left . . . (February, 1986)—Suffered two strokes in a span of three days.

Year	Team	League	Games	G.	A.	Pts.	Pen.
1981-82	Aurora-Hoyt Lakes H.S. (c)	Minn. H.S.	23	26	37	63	8
1982-83	Univ. of Minnesota-Duluth	WCHA	45	6	16	22	10
1983-84	Univ. of Minnesota-Duluth	WCHA	42	24	39	63	16
1984-85	Univ. of Minnesota-Duluth (b)	WCHA	48	30	47	77	32
1985-86	Univ. of Minnesota-Duluth	WCHA	33	16	41	57	36

(c)—June, 1982—Drafted as underage player by St. Louis Blues in 1982 NHL entry draft. Sixth Blues pick, 176th overall, ninth round.

DAVE CHRISTIAN

Center . . . 5'11" . . . 170 lbs. . . . Born, Warroad, Minn., May 12, 1959 . . . Shoots right . . . Member of 1978 U.S. National Junior Team and 1980 U.S. Olympic Gold Medal Team . . . Son of Bill Christian ('60 & '64 Olympic Teams), Nephew of Roger Christian ('60 & '64 Olympic Teams) and nephew of Gordon Christian ('56 Olympic Team) . . . His Father (Bill) and Uncle (Roger) own the Christian Brothers Hockey Stick Company . . . Also plays Right Wing . . . Brother of Edward Christian (Winnipeg '80 draft pick) . . . (December, 1982)—Torn shoulder muscles and missed 25 games.

Year	Team	League	Games	G.	A.	Pts.	Pen.
1977-78	University of North Dakota	WCHA	38	8	16	24	14
1978-79	University of North Dakota (c)	WCHA	40	22	24	46	22
1979-80	U.S. Olympic Team	Int'l	*66	10	28	38	32
1979-80	Winnipeg Jets	NHL	15	8	10	18	2
1980-81	Winnipeg Jets	NHL	80	28	43	71	22
1981-82	Winnipeg Jets	NHL	80	25	51	76	28
1982-83	Winnipeg Jets (d)	NHL	55	18	26	44	23
1983-84	Washington Capitals	NHL	80	29	52	81	28
1984-85	Washington Capitals	NHL	80	26	43	69	14
1985-86	Washington Capitals	NHL	80	41	42	83	15
	NHL TOTALS		470	175	267	442	132

(c)—August, 1979—Drafted by Winnipeg Jets in 1979 NHL entry draft. Second Jets pick, 40th overall, second round.

(d)—June, 1983—Traded by Winnipeg Jets to Washington Capitals for first round draft pick in 1983 (Jets drafted Bob Dollas).

SHANE CHURLA

Right Wing . . . 6'1" . . . 200 lbs. . . . Born, Fernie, B.C., June 24, 1965 . . . Shoots right . . . (October, 1985)—Pulled stomach muscles.

Year	Team	League	Games	G.	A.	Pts.	Pen.
1983-84—Medicine Hat Tigers		WHL	48	3	7	10	115
1984-85—Medicine Hat Tigers (c)		WHL	70	14	20	34	*370
1985-86—Binghamton Whalers		AHL	52	4	10	14	306

(c)—June, 1985—Drafted by Hartford Whalers in 1985 NHL entry draft. Fourth Whalers pick, 110th overall, sixth round.

JEFF CHYCHRUN

Defense . . . 6'4" . . . 190 lbs. . . . Born, Lasalle, Que., May 3, 1966 . . . Shoots right.

Year	Team	League	Games	G.	A.	Pts.	Pen.
1983-84—Kingston Canadians (c)		OHL	83	1	13	14	137
1984-85—Kingston Canadians		OHL	58	4	10	14	206
1985-86—Kingston Canadians		OHL	61	4	21	25	127
1985-86—Kalamazoo Wings (d)		IHL	....	...	....	....	....
1985-86—Hershey Bears (e)		AHL	....	...	....	....	....

(c)—June, 1984—Drafted as underage junior by Philadelphia Flyers in 1984 NHL entry draft. Second Flyers pick, 37th overall, second round.

(d)—No regular season record. Played three playoff games.

(e)—No regular season record. Played four playoff games.

BARRY CHYZOWSKI

Center . . . 6' . . . 170 lbs. . . . Born, Edmonton, Alta., May 25, 1968 . . . Shoots right . . . Brother of Ron Chyzowski . . . (January 1986)—Separated shoulder.

Year	Team	League	Games	G.	A.	Pts.	Pen.
1984-85—Carnwood SSAC		Alta. Midget	36	32	39	71	10
1985-86—St. Albert Saints (a-c)		AJHL	45	34	34	68	33

(c)—June, 1986—Drafted by New York Rangers in 1986 NHL entry draft. Eighth Rangers pick, 156th overall, eighth round.

RON CHYZOWSKI

Center . . . 5'10" . . . 165 lbs. . . . Born, Edmonton, Alta., August 14, 1965 . . . Shoots right . . . Brother of Barry Chyzowski.

Year	Team	League	Games	G.	A.	Pts.	Pen.
1982-83—St. Albert Saints (c)		AJHL	59	34	43	77	38
1983-84—Northern Michigan University		CCHA	40	16	10	26	12
1984-85—Northern Michigan University		WCHA	40	15	18	33	6
1985-86—Northern Michigan University		WCHA	38	20	19	39	12

(c)—June, 1983—Drafted by Hartford Whalers in 1983 NHL entry draft. Sixth Whalers pick, 72nd overall, fourth round.

DINO CICCARELLI

Right Wing . . . 5'11" . . . 185 lbs. . . . Born, Sarnia, Ontario, February 8, 1960 . . . Shoots right . . . (Spring, 1978)—Fractured midshaft of right femur that required the insertion of 16 inch metal rod in leg . . . Set NHL Playoff record for most goals as a rookie (14) in 1981 . . . First Minnesota player to score 50 goals in a season. . . . (November, 1984)—Shoulder injury . . . (December, 1984)—Broken right wrist.

Year	Team	League	Games	G.	A.	Pts.	Pen.
1976-77—London Knights		OMJHL	66	39	43	82	45
1977-78—London Knights (b)		OMJHL	68	72	70	142	49
1978-79—London Knights (c)		OMJHL	30	8	11	19	25
1979-80—London Knights		OMJHL	62	50	53	103	72
1979-80—Oklahoma City Stars		CHL	6	3	2	5	0
1980-81—Oklahoma City Stars		CHL	48	32	25	57	45
1980-81—Minnesota North Stars		NHL	32	18	12	30	29
1981-82—Minnesota North Stars		NHL	76	55	51	106	138
1982-83—Minnesota North Stars		NHL	77	37	38	75	94

Year	Team	League	Games	G.	A.	Pts.	Pen.
1983-84—Minnesota North Stars		NHL	79	38	33	71	58
1984-85—Minnesota North Stars		NHL	51	15	17	32	41
1985-86—Minnesota North Stars		NHL	75	44	45	89	53
NHL TOTALS			390	207	196	403	413

(c)—September, 1979—Signed by Minnesota North Stars as free agent.

CHRIS CICHOCKI

Right Wing . . . 5'10" . . . 185 lbs. . . . Born, Detroit, Mich., September 17, 1963 . . . Shoots right . . . Member of 1983 U.S. Junior National Team . . . (January 7, 1986)—Injured mouth at Washington and missed three games.

Year	Team	League	Games	G.	A.	Pts.	Pen.
1982-83—Michigan Tech.		CCHA	36	12	10	22	10
1983-84—Michigan Tech.		CCHA	40	25	20	45	36
1984-85—Michigan Tech. (c)		WCHA	40	30	24	54	14
1985-86—Adirondack Red Wings		AHL	9	4	4	8	6
1985-86—Detroit Red Wings		NHL	59	10	11	21	21
NHL TOTALS			59	10	11	21	21

(c)—June, 1985—Signed by Detroit Red Wings as free agent.

TRENTON CIPRICK

Right Wing . . . 6'1" . . . 180 lbs. . . . Born, Russell, Manitoba, July 21, 1967 . . . Shoots right . . . (January, 1985)—Knee injury.

Year	Team	League	Games	G.	A.	Pts.	Pen.
1983-84—Russell Jr. Rams		Manitoba Midget	48	29	36	65	52
1984-85—Brandon Wheat Kings (c)		WHL	64	11	11	22	95
1985-86—Brandon Wheat Kings		WHL	52	13	19	32	82

(c)—June, 1985—Drafted as underage junior by Los Angeles Kings in 1985 NHL entry draft. Ninth Kings pick, 219th overall, 11th round.

JOE CIRELLA

Defense . . . 6'2" . . . 205 lbs. . . . Born, Hamilton, Ont., May 9, 1963 . . . Shoots right . . . Brother of Carmine Cirella . . . (December 17, 1984)—Hit by stick in game vs. Edmonton and needed 12 stitches . . . (November 26, 1985)—Injured left knee in game vs. Winnipeg.

Year	Team	League	Games	G.	A.	Pts.	Pen.
1979-80—Hamilton Major Midgets		....	21	5	26	31	....
1980-81—Oshawa Generals (c)		OHL	56	5	31	36	220
1981-82—Oshawa Generals		OHL	3	0	1	1	10
1981-82—Colorado Rockies		NHL	65	7	12	19	52
1982-83—Oshawa Generals (a)		OHL	56	13	55	68	110
1982-83—New Jersey Devils		NHL	2	0	1	1	4
1983-84—New Jersey Devils		NHL	79	11	33	44	137
1984-85—New Jersey Devils		NHL	66	6	18	24	143
1985-86—New Jersey Devils		NHL	66	6	23	29	147
NHL TOTALS			278	30	87	117	483

(c)—June, 1981—Drafted as underage junior by Colorado Rockies in 1981 NHL entry draft. First Rockies pick, fifth overall, first round.

MIKE CLARINGBULL

Defense . . . 6' . . . 185 lbs. . . . Born, St. Lawrence, Newfoundland, November 29, 1966 . . . Shoots right . . . (October, 1985)—Bruised shoulder.

Year	Team	League	Games	G.	A.	Pts.	Pen.
1983-84—Hobbema Hawks		AJHL	45	5	15	20	135
1984-85—Medicine Hat Tigers (c)		WHL	68	5	13	18	178
1985-86—Medicine Hat Tigers		WHL	69	2	15	17	123

(c)—June, 1985—Drafted as underage junior by Montreal Canadiens in 1985 NHL entry draft. Tenth Canadiens pick, 163rd overall, eighth round.

KERRY CLARK

Right Wing . . . 6'1" . . . 195 lbs. . . . Born, Kelvington, Sask., August 21, 1968 . . . Shoots right.

Year	Team	League	Games	G.	A.	Pts.	Pen.
1984-85—Regina Pats		WHL	36	1	1	2	66
1985-86—Regina Pats		WHL	23	4	4	8	58
1985-86—Saskatoon Blades (c)		WHL	39	5	8	13	104

(c)—June, 1986—Drafted as underage junior by New York Islanders in 1986 NHL entry draft. Twelfth Islanders pick, 206th overall, 10th round.

WENDEL CLARK

Left Wing . . . 5'11" . . . 190 lbs. . . . Born, Kelvington, Sask., October 25, 1966 . . . Shoots left . . (November, 1985) Virus . . . (November 26, 1986)—Missed 14 games with broken right foot in game at St. Louis . . . Also plays defense.

Year	Team	League	Games	G.	A.	Pts.	Pen.
1983-84—Saskatoon Blades		WHL	72	23	45	68	225
1984-85—Saskatoon Blades (a-c-d)		WHL	64	32	55	87	253
1985-86—Toronto Maple Leafs (e)		NHL	66	34	11	45	227
NHL TOTALS			66	34	11	45	227

(c)—Won WHL Top Defenseman Trophy.
(d)—June, 1985—Drafted as underage junior by Toronto Maple Leafs in 1985 NHL entry draft. First Maple Leafs pick, first overall, first round.
(e)—Named NHL Rookie of the Year in poll of players by THE SPORTING NEWS.

DOUG CLARKE

Defense . . . 6' . . . 190 lbs. . . . Born, Toronto, Ont., February 29, 1964 . . . Shoots left.

Year	Team	League	Games	G.	A.	Pts.	Pen.
1983-84—Colorado College (c)		WCHA	35	6	26	32	70
1984-85—Colorado College (b)		WCHA	37	12	36	48	77
1985-86—Team Canada		Int'l	72	7	7	14	38

(c)—June, 1984—Drafted by Vancouver Canucks in 1984 NHL entry draft. Twelfth Canucks pick, 219th overall, 11th round.

WILLIAM CLAVITER

Left Wing . . . 6'1" . . . 175 lbs. . . . Born, Virginia, Minn., March 24, 1965 . . . Shoots left.

Year	Team	League	Games	G.	A.	Pts.	Pen.
1982-83—Virginia H.S. (c)		Minn. H.S.	18	18	20	38	...
1983-84—Univ. of North Dakota		WCHA	18	2	5	7	4
1984-85—Univ. of North Dakota		WCHA	34	6	8	14	10
1985-86—Univ. of North Dakota		WCHA	35	4	10	14	34

(c)—June, 1983—Drafted by Calgary Flames in 1983 NHL entry draft. Sixth Flames pick, 77th overall, fourth round.

SEAN CLEMENT

Defense . . . 6'2" . . . 185 lbs. . . . Born, Winnipeg, Man., February 26, 1966 . . . Shoots left.

Year	Team	League	Games	G.	A.	Pts.	Pen.
1983-84—Brockville Braves (c)		COJHL	52	13	41	54	135
1984-85—Michigan State Univ.		CCHA	44	5	13	18	24
1985-86—Michigan State Univ.		CCHA	40	4	7	11	40

(c)—June, 1984—Drafted as underage junior by Winnipeg Jets in 1984 NHL entry draft. Third Jets pick, 72nd overall, fourth round.

KEVIN (CHET) CLEMENTS

Left Wing . . . 5'11" . . . 185 lbs. . . . Born, McLennan, Alta., February 2, 1967 . . . Shoots left.

Year	Team	League	Games	G.	A.	Pts.	Pen.
1983-84—Regina Pats		WHL	47	5	8	13	14
1984-85—Regina Pats (c)		WHL	70	31	16	47	40
1985-86—Regina Pats		WHL	71	26	32	58	70

(c)—June, 1985—Drafted as underage junior by Pittsburgh Penguins in 1985 NHL entry draft. Fifth Penguins pick, 107th overall, sixth round.

SHAUN CLOUSTON

Right Wing . . . 6' . . . 205 lbs. . . . Born, Viking, Alta., February 21, 1968 . . . Shoots left.

Year	Team	League	Games	G.	A.	Pts.	Pen.
1985-86—Univ. of Alberta (c)		CWUAA	25	10	9	19	59

(c)—June, 1986—Drafted by New York Rangers in 1986 NHL entry draft. Third Rangers pick, 53rd overall, third round.

REJEAN CLOUTIER

Defense . . . 6'1" . . . 185 lbs. . . . Born, Windsor, Que., February 15, 1960 . . . Shoots left . . . (September, 1984)—Broken hand during training camp.

Year	Team	League	Games	G.	A.	Pts.	Pen.
1977-78—Sherbrooke Beavers		QMJHL	23	8	11	19	59
1978-79—Sherbrooke Beavers		QMJHL	70	6	31	37	93
1979-80—Detroit Red Wings		NHL	3	0	1	1	0

Year	Team	League	Games	G.	A.	Pts.	Pen.
1979-80—Sherbrooke Beavers	QMJHL	65	11	57	68	163
1980-81—Adirondack Red Wings	AHL	76	7	30	37	193
1981-82—Adirondack Red Wings	AHL	64	11	27	38	140
1981-82—Detroit Red Wings	NHL	2	0	1	1	2
1982-83—Adirondack Red Wings (b)	AHL	80	13	44	57	137
1983-84—Adirondack Red Wings	AHL	77	9	30	39	218
1984-85—Adirondack Red Wings (c)	AHL	3	0	0	0	2
1984-85—Nova Scotia Oilers	AHL	72	8	19	27	152
1985-86—Saginaw Gears	IHL	2	0	0	0	4
1985-86—Sherbrooke Canadiens (d)	AHL	67	7	23	30	142
NHL TOTALS		5	0	2	2	2

(c)—October, 1984—Traded by Adirondack Red Wings to Nova Scotia Oilers for Todd Bidner.
(d)—August, 1985—Signed by Montreal Canadiens as a free agent.

GLEN MACLEOD COCHRANE

Defense . . . 6'3" . . . 205 lbs. . . . Born, Cranbrook, B. C., January 29, 1958 . . . Shoots left . . . (March, 1984)—Knee surgery . . . (October, 1984)—Missed first 42 games of season following surgery to repair kneecap . . . (September-October, 1985)—Missed first five games of the season due to pain in knee . . . (January 10, 1986)—Missed four games due to back spasms.

Year	Team	League	Games	G.	A.	Pts.	Pen.
1974-75—The Pass Red Devils	AJHL	16	1	4	5	61
1975-76—The Pass Red Devils	AJHL	60	17	42	59	210
1975-76—Calgary Centennials	WCHL	3	0	0	0	0
1976-77—Calgary Centennials	WCHL	35	1	5	6	105
1976-77—Victoria Cougars	WCHL	36	1	7	8	60
1977-78—Victoria Cougars (c)	WCHL	72	7	40	47	311
1978-79—Philadelphia Flyers	NHL	1	0	0	0	0
1978-79—Maine Mariners	AHL	76	1	22	23	320
1979-80—Maine Mariners	AHL	77	1	11	12	269
1980-81—Maine Mariners	AHL	38	4	13	17	201
1980-81—Philadelphia Flyers	NHL	31	1	8	9	219
1981-82—Philadelphia Flyers	NHL	63	6	12	18	329
1982-83—Philadelphia Flyers	NHL	77	2	22	24	237
1983-84—Philadelphia Flyers	NHL	67	7	16	23	225
1984-85—Philadelphia Flyers (d)	NHL	18	0	3	3	100
1984-85—Hershey Bears	AHL	9	0	8	8	35
1985-86—Vancouver Canucks	NHL	49	0	3	3	125
NHL TOTALS		306	16	64	80	1235

(c)—Drafted from Victoria Cougars by Philadelphia Flyers in third round of 1978 amateur draft.
(d)—March, 1985—Traded by Philadelphia Flyers to Vancouver Canucks for future third round draft pick.

PAUL DOUGLAS COFFEY

Defense . . . 6'1" . . . 185 lbs. . . . Born, Weston, Ont., June 1, 1961 . . . Shoots left . . . Became only third defenseman in NHL history to have a 100-point season (Potvin & Orr) with 126 points in 1983-84 . . . (May, 1985)—Set NHL record for most goals (12) assists (25) and points (37) in playoffs by a defenseman . . . (1985-86)—Set NHL record for most goals in one season by a defenseman, breaking Bobby Orr's mark of 46 goals in 1974-75.

Year	Team	League	Games	G.	A.	Pts.	Pen.
1977-78—Kingston Canadians	OHL	8	2	2	4	11
1977-78—North York Rangers	MTHL	50	14	33	47	64
1978-79—Sault Ste. Marie Greyhounds	OPJHL	68	17	72	89	99
1979-80—Sault Ste. Marie Grehhounds	OPJHL	23	10	21	31	63
1979-80—Kitchener Rangers (b-c)	OPJHL	52	19	52	71	130
1980-81—Edmonton Oilers	NHL	74	9	23	32	130
1981-82—Edmonton Oilers (b)	NHL	80	29	60	89	106
1982-83—Edmonton Oilers (b)	NHL	80	29	67	96	87
1983-84—Edmonton Oilers (b)	NHL	80	40	86	126	104
1984-85—Edmonton Oilers (a-d)	NHL	80	37	84	121	97
1985-86—Edmonton Oilers (a-d)	NHL	79	48	90	138	120
NHL TOTALS		473	192	410	602	644

(c)—June, 1980—Drafted by Edmonton Oilers in NHL entry draft. First Oilers pick, sixth overall, first round.
(d)—Won James Norris Memorial Trophy (Top NHL Defenseman).

DANTON COLE

Center . . . 5'10" . . . 180 lbs. . . . Born, Pontiac, Mich., January 10, 1967 . . . Shoots right . . . Also plays Right Wing.

Year	Team	League	Games	G.	A.	Pts.	Pen.
1984-85—Aurora Tigers (c)		OHA	41	51	44	95	91
1985-86—Michigan State Univ.		CCHA	43	11	10	21	22

(c)—June, 1985—Drafted by Winnipeg Jets in 1985 NHL entry draft. Sixth Jets pick, 123rd overall, sixth round.

PATRICK JOHN CONACHER

Center . . . 5'8" . . . 188 lbs. . . . Born, Edmonton, Alta., May 1, 1959 . . . Shoots left . . . (September 21, 1980)—Fractured left ankle in rookie scrimmage vs. Washington that required surgery . . . (November, 1982)—Injured shoulder . . . (December, 1984)—Severe groin injury.

Year	Team	League	Games	G.	A.	Pts.	Pen.
1977-78—Billings Bighorns		WCHL	72	31	44	75	105
1978-79—Billings Bighorns		WHL	39	25	37	62	50
1978-79—Saskatoon Blades (c)		WHL	33	15	32	47	37
1979-80—New York Rangers		NHL	17	0	5	5	4
1979-80—New Haven Nighthawks		AHL	53	11	14	25	43
1980-81—Did not play							
1981-82—Springfield Indians		AHL	77	23	22	45	38
1981-82—Springfield Indians		AHL	77	23	22	45	38
1982-83—Tulsa Oilers		CHL	63	29	28	57	44
1982-83—New York Rangers		NHL	5	0	1	1	4
1983-84—Moncton Alpines		AHL	28	7	16	23	30
1983-84—Edmonton Oilers		NHL	45	2	8	10	31
1984-85—Nova Scotia Oilers (d)		AHL	68	20	45	65	44
1985-86—New Jersey Devils		NHL	2	0	2	2	2
1985-86—Maine Mariners		AHL	69	15	30	45	83
NHL TOTALS			69	2	16	18	41

(c)—August, 1979—Drafted by New York Rangers in 1979 NHL entry draft. Third Rangers pick, 76th overall, fourth round.

(d)—August, 1985—Signed by New Jersey Devils as a free agent.

TODD COPELAND

Defense . . . 6'2" . . . 200 lbs. . . . Born, Ridgewood, N.J., May 18, 1968 . . . Shoots left . . . (February, 1986)—Knee injury.

Year	Team	League	Games	G.	A.	Pts.	Pen.
1984-85—Belmont Hill H.S.		Mass.	23	8	25	33	18
1985-86—Belmont Hill H.S. (c)		Mass.	19	4	19	23	19

(c)—June, 1986—Drafted by New Jersey Devils in 1986 NHL entry draft. Second Devils pick, 24th overall, second round.

BOB CORKUM

Right Wing . . . 6'2" . . . 200 lbs. . . . Born, Salisbury, Mass., December 18, 1967 . . . Shoots right.

Year	Team	League	Games	G.	A.	Pts.	Pen.
1984-85—Triton Regional H.S.		Mass.	18	35	36	71	....
1985-86—University of Maine (c)		H. East	39	7	16	23	53

(c)—June, 1986—Drafted by Buffalo Sabres in 1986 NHL entry draft. Third Sabres pick, 47th overall, third round.

JEFF CORNELIUS

Defense . . . 6'1" . . . 185 lbs. . . . Born, Kingston, Ont., February 28, 1966 . . . Shoots left.

Year	Team	League	Games	G.	A.	Pts.	Pen.
1982-83—Kingston Canadians		OHL	5	0	1	1	5
1983-84—Toronto Marlboros (c)		OHL	64	2	14	16	117
1984-85—Toronto Marlboros		OHL	24	1	5	6	74
1984-85—Kingston Canadians		OHL	29	1	4	5	49
1985-86—Kingston Canadians		OHL	59	2	17	19	143

(c)—June, 1984—Drafted as underage junior by Boston Bruins in 1984 NHL entry draft. Third Bruins pick, 61st overall, third round.

YVON CORRIVEAU

Left Wing . . . 6'1" . . . 195 lbs. . . . Born, Welland, Ont., February 8, 1967 . . . Shoots left . . . (March, 1985)—Shoulder injury.

Year	Team	League	Games	G.	A.	Pts.	Pen.
1983-84—Welland Cougars Jr.B		OHA	36	16	21	37	51
1984-85—Toronto Marlboros (c)		OHL	59	23	28	51	65
1985-86—Toronto Marlboros		OHL	59	54	36	90	75
1985-86—Washington Capitals		NHL	2	0	0	0	0
NHL TOTALS			2	0	0	0	0

(c)—June, 1985—Drafted as underage junior by Washington Capitals in NHL entry draft. First Capitals pick, 19th overall, first round.

SHAYNE CORSON

Center and Left Wing . . . 6' . . . 175 lbs. . . . Born, Barrie, Ont., August 13, 1966 . . . Shoots left . . . (1986)—Named to World Junior Hockey Championship All-Star team.

Year	Team	League	Games	G.	A.	Pts.	Pen.
1982-83—Barrie Flyers		COJHL	23	13	29	42	87
1983-84—Brantford Alexanders (c)		OHL	66	25	46	71	165
1984-85—Hamilton Steelhawks		OHL	54	27	63	90	154
1985-86—Hamilton Steelhawks		OHL	47	41	57	98	153
1985-86—Montreal Canadiens		NHL	3	0	0	0	2
NHL TOTALS			3	0	0	0	2

(c)—June, 1984—Drafted as underage junior by Montreal Canadiens in 1984 NHL entry draft. Second Canadiens pick, eighth overall, first round.

RICHARD COSTELLO

Center . . . 6' . . . 170 lbs. . . . Born, Natick, Mass., June, 27, 1963 . . . Shoots right . . . Member of 1984 U.S. Olympic Team.

Year	Team	League	Games	G.	A.	Pts.	Pen.
1979-80—Natick High School		Mass.H.S.	18	26	32	58	....
1980-81—Natick High School (a-c)		Mass.H.S.	....	30	36	66	....
1981-82—Providence College (d)		ECAC	32	11	16	27	39
1982-83—Providence College		ECAC	43	19	26	45	60
1983-84—U.S. National Team		Int'l.	38	7	19	26	31
1983-84—St. Catharines Saints		AHL	20	0	0	0	12
1983-84—Toronto Maple Leafs		NHL	10	2	1	3	2
1984-85—St. Catharines Saints		AHL	80	8	6	14	45
1985-86—Toronto Maple Leafs		NHL	2	0	1	1	0
1985-86—St. Catharines Saints		AHL	76	18	22	40	87
NHL TOTALS			12	2	2	4	2

(c)—June, 1981—Drafted as underage junior by Philadelphia Flyers in 1981 NHL entry draft. Second Flyers pick, 37th overall, second round.

(d)—January, 1982—NHL rights traded with second-round 1982 entry draft pick (Peter Ihnacak) by Philadelphia Flyers to Toronto Maple Leafs for Darryl Sittler and future considerations.

DARREN COTA

Right Wing . . . 5'11" . . . 195 lbs. . . . Born, McLellan, Alta., April 7, 1966 . . . Shoots right.

Year	Team	League	Games	G.	A.	Pts.	Pen.
1982-83—Kelowna Wings		WHL	49	5	13	18	141
1983-84—Kelowna Wings (c)		WHL	66	30	31	61	152
1984-85—Kelowna Wings (d)		WHL	34	26	20	46	75
1984-85—Medicine Hat Tigers		WHL	30	20	18	38	69
1985-86—Medicine Hat Tigers		WHL	59	34	37	71	258

(c)—June, 1984—Drafted as underage junior by Quebec Nordiques in 1984 NHL entry draft. Fifth Nordiques pick, 120th overall, sixth round.

(d)—January, 1985—Traded with Stu Wenaas by Kelowna Wings to Medicine Hat Tigers for Ron Viglasi and future considerations.

ALAIN COTE

Left Wing . . . 5'10" . . . 203 lbs. . . . Born, Matane, Que., May 3, 1957 . . . Shoots left . . . Brother-in-law of Luc Dufour.

Year	Team	League	Games	G.	A.	Pts.	Pen.
1974-75—Chicoutimi Sagueneens	QJHL	57	15	29	44	43
1975-76—Chicoutimi Sagueneens	QJHL	72	35	49	84	93
1976-77—Chicoutimi Sagueneens (c-d)	QJHL	56	42	45	87	86
1977-78—Hampton Gulls	AHL	36	15	17	32	38
1977-78—Quebec Nordiques	WHA	27	3	5	8	8
1978-79—Quebec Nordiques (e)	WHA	79	14	13	27	23
1979-80—Quebec Nordiques	NHL	41	5	11	16	13
1979-80—Syracuse Firebirds	AHL	6	0	5	5	9
1980-81—Rochester Americans	AHL	23	1	6	7	14
1980-81—Quebec Nordiques	NHL	51	8	18	26	64
1981-82—Quebec Nordiques	NHL	79	15	16	31	82
1982-83—Quebec Nordiques	NHL	79	12	28	40	45
1983-84—Quebec Nordiques	NHL	77	19	24	43	41
1984-85—Quebec Nordiques	NHL	80	13	22	35	31
1985-86—Quebec Nordiques	NHL	78	13	21	34	29
WHA TOTALS		106	17	18	35	31
NHL TOTALS		485	85	140	225	305

(c)—Drafted from Chicoutimi Sagueneens by Montreal Canadiens in third round of 1977 amateur draft.
(d)—Selected by Quebec Nordiques in World Hockey Association amateur players' draft, May, 1977.
(e)—June, 1979—Selected by Montreal Canadiens in NHL reclaim draft. Selected by Quebec Nordiques in NHL expansion draft.

ALAIN COTE

Defense . . . 6' . . . 200 lbs. . . . Born, Montmagny, Que., April 14, 1967 . . . Shoots right.

Year	Team	League	Games	G.	A.	Pts.	Pen.
1983-84—Quebec Remparts	QHL	60	3	17	20	40
1984-85—Quebec Remparts (c)	QHL	68	9	25	34	173
1985-86—Granby Bisons	QHL	22	4	12	16	48
1985-86—Moncton Golden Flames	AHL	3	0	0	0	0
1985-86—Boston Bruins	NHL	32	0	6	6	14
NHL TOTALS		32	0	6	6	14

(c)—June, 1985—Drafted as underage junior by Boston Bruins in NHL entry draft. First Bruins pick, 31st overall, second round.

RAYMOND COTE

Center . . . 5'11" . . . 165 lbs. . . . Born, Pincher Creek, Alberta, May 31, 1961 . . . Shoots right.

Year	Team	League	Games	G.	A.	Pts.	Pen.
1977-78—Pincher Creek Panthers	AJHL	59	13	34	47	12
1978-79—Calgary Chinooks	AJHL	53	17	30	47	35
1978-79—Calgary Wranglers	WHL	7	2	1	3	0
1979-80—Calgary Wranglers	WHL	72	33	34	67	43
1980-81—Calgary Wranglers	WHL	70	36	52	88	73
1981-82—Wichita Wind (c)	CHL	80	20	34	54	83
1982-83—Moncton Alpines	AHL	80	28	63	91	35
1982-83—Edmonton Oilers (d)	NHL	..	..	..	..	..
1983-84—Edmonton Oilers	NHL	13	0	0	0	2
1983-84—Moncton Alpines	AHL	66	26	36	62	99
1984-85—Edmonton Oilers	NHL	2	0	0	0	2
1984-85—Nova Scotia Oilers	AHL	79	36	43	79	63
1985-86—Schwenningen	W. Germany	15	12	9	21	....
1985-86—Nova Scotia Oilers (e)	AHL	20	7	3	10	17
1985-86—Team Canada	Int'l	8	1	3	4	6
NHL TOTALS		15	0	0	0	4

(c)—October, 1981—Signed by Edmonton Oilers as a free agent.
(d)—No regular season record. Played in 14 playoff games.
(e)—February, 1986—Signed by Nova Scotia Voyageurs as a free agent after playing in West Germany.

SYLVAIN COTE

Defense . . . 6' . . . 170 lbs. . . . Born, Quebec City, Que., January 19, 1966 . . . Shoots right . . . (1986)—Named to World Junior Championship All-Star Team.

Year	Team	League	Games	G.	A.	Pts.	Pen.
1982-83—Quebec Remparts	QHL	66	10	24	34	50
1983-84—Quebec Remparts (c)	QHL	66	15	50	65	89

Year	Team	League	Games	G.	A.	Pts.	Pen.
1984-85—Hartford Whalers		NHL	67	3	9	12	17
1985-86—Hartford Whalers		NHL	2	0	0	0	0
1985-86—Hull Olympiques (a-d-e)		QHL	26	10	33	43	14
NHL TOTALS			2	0	0	0	0

(c)—June, 1984—Drafted as underage junior by Hartford Whalers in 1984 NHL entry draft. First Whalers pick, 11th overall, first round.

(d)—Won Emile "Butch" Bouchard Trophy (Top Defenseman).

(e)—Shared Guy Lafleur Trophy (Playoff MVP) with Luc Robitaille.

TIM COULIS

Left Wing . . . 6' . . . 199 lbs. . . . Born, Kenora, Ont., February 24, 1958 . . . Shoots left . . . Missed entire 1978-79 season with a broken bone in left wrist . . . Also plays Right Wing . . . Suspended for all of 1982-83 season by Central Hockey League after slugging official during 1982 CHL playoffs . . . (March, 1985)—Strained stomach muscles . . . (September, 1985)—Missed 22 games following surgery to repair torn ankle ligaments injured during training camp.

Year	Team	League	Games	G.	A.	Pts.	Pen.
1975-76—Sault Ste. Marie Greyhounds		OMJHL	37	15	18	33	226
1976-77—Sault Ste. Marie Greyhounds (c)		OMJHL	27	13	20	33	114
1976-77—St. Catharines Fincups		OMJHL	28	10	22	32	136
1977-78—Hamilton Fincups (d)		OMJHL	46	27	25	52	203
1978-79—Did not play			..	..	..	..	....
1979-80—Hershey Bears		AHL	47	6	12	18	138
1979-80—Washington Capitals (e)		NHL	19	1	2	3	27
1980-81—Dallas Black Hawks		CHL	63	16	15	31	149
1981-82—Dallas Black Hawks (f)		CHL	68	20	32	52	209
1982-83—Did not play			..	..	..	..	....
1983-84—Minnesota North Stars (g)		NHL	2	0	0	0	4
1983-84—Salt Lake Golden Eagles		CHL	63	25	35	60	225
1984-85—Springfield Indians		AHL	52	13	17	30	86
1984-85—Minnesota North Stars		NHL	7	1	1	2	34
1985-86—Minnesota North Stars		NHL	19	2	2	4	73
1985-86—Springfield Indians		AHL	13	5	7	12	42
NHL TOTALS			47	4	5	9	138

(c)—January, 1977—Traded by Sault Ste. Marie Greyhounds to St. Catharines Fincups for Mark Locken.

(d)—June, 1978—Drafted by Washington Capitals in 1978 NHL amateur draft. Second Capitals pick, 18th overall, first round.

(e)—June, 1980—Traded with Robert Picard and second round (Bob McGill) 1980 draft pick by Washington Capitals to Toronto Maple Leafs for Mike Palmateer and third round (Torrie Robertson) 1980 draft pick.

(f)—October, 1981—Signed by Vancouver Canucks as a free agent.

(g)—July, 1983—Signed by Minnesota North Stars as a free agent.

NEAL COULTIER

Right Wing . . . 6'2" . . . 190 lbs. . . . Born, Toronto, Ont., January 2, 1963 . . . Shoots right . . . (December 6, 1985)—Sprained knee at Quebec.

Year	Team	League	Games	G.	A.	Pts.	Pen.
1979-80—Oakridge Midgets		...	60	35	30	65	150
1980-81—Toronto Marlboros (c)		OHL	18	4	3	7	22
1981-82—Toronto Marlboros		OHL	62	14	16	30	79
1982-83—Toronto Marlboros		OHL	59	13	37	50	60
1982-83—Indianapolis Checkers		CHL	3	0	1	1	0
1983-84—Toledo Goaldiggers		IHL	5	1	3	4	0
1983-84—Indianapolis Checkers		CHL	58	7	10	17	25
1984-85—Springfield Indians		AHL	2	1	0	1	0
1984-85—Indianapolis Checkers		IHL	82	31	26	57	95
1985-86—Springfield Indians		AHL	60	17	9	26	92
1985-86—New York Islanders		NHL	16	3	4	7	4
NHL TOTALS			16	3	4	7	4

(c)—June, 1981—Drafted as underage junior by New York Islanders in 1981 NHL entry draft. Fourth Islanders pick, 63rd overall, third round.

YVES COURTEAU

Right Wing . . . 5'11" . . . 183 lbs. . . . Born, Montreal, Que., April 25, 1964 . . . Shoots right.

Year	Team	League	Games	G.	A.	Pts.	Pen.
1980-81—Laval Voisins		QMJHL	70	24	39	63	80
1981-82—Laval Voisins (c)		QMJHL	64	30	38	68	15
1982-83—Laval Voisins (d)		QHL	68	44	78	122	52
1983-84—Laval Voisins		QHL	62	45	75	120	52
1984-85—Moncton Golden Flames		AHL	59	19	21	40	32
1984-85—Calgary Flames		NHL	14	1	4	5	4
1985-86—Moncton Golden Flames		AHL	70	26	22	48	19
1985-86—Calgary Flames		NHL	4	1	1	2	0
NHL TOTALS			18	2	5	7	4

(c)—June, 1982—Drafted as underage junior by Detroit Red Wings in 1982 NHL entry draft. Second Red Wings pick, 23rd overall, second round.

(d)—December, 1982—NHL rights traded by Detroit Red Wings to Calgary Flames for Bobby Francis.

GEOFF COURTNALL

Left Wing ... 6' ... 165 lbs. ... Born, Victoria, B.C., August 18, 1962 ... Shoots left.

Year	Team	League	Games	G.	A.	Pts.	Pen.
1980-81—Victoria Cougars		WHL	11	3	5	8	6
1981-82—Victoria Cougars		WHL	72	35	57	92	100
1983-84—Victoria Cougars		WHL	71	41	73	114	186
1983-84—Hershey Bears (c)		AHL	74	14	12	26	51
1983-84—Boston Bruins		NHL	5	0	0	0	0
1984-85—Hershey Bears		AHL	9	8	4	12	4
1984-85—Boston Bruins		NHL	64	12	16	28	82
1985-86—Moncton Golden Flames		AHL	12	8	8	16	6
1985-86—Boston Bruins		NHL	64	21	17	38	61
NHL TOTALS			133	33	33	66	143

(c)—September, 1983—Signed by Boston Bruins as a free agent.

RUSS COURTNALL

Center ... 5'10" ... 175 lbs. ... Born, Victoria, B.C., June 3, 1965 ... Shoots right ... Member of 1984 Canadian Olympic Team.

Year	Team	League	Games	G.	A.	Pts.	Pen.
1982-83—Victoria Cougars (c)		WHL	60	36	61	97	33
1983-84—Victoria Cougars		WHL	32	29	37	66	63
1983-84—Canadian Olympic Team		Int'l	16	4	7	11	10
1983-84—Toronto Maple Leafs		NHL	14	3	9	12	6
1984-85—Toronto Maple Leafs		NHL	69	12	10	22	44
1985-86—Toronto Maple Leafs		NHL	73	22	38	60	52
NHL TOTALS			156	37	57	94	102

(c)—June, 1983—Drafted by Toronto Maple Leafs as underage junior in NHL entry draft. First Maple Leafs pick, seventh overall, first round.

SYLVAIN COUTURIER

Center ... 6'1" ... 200 lbs. ... Born, Greenfield Park, Que., April 23, 1968 ... Shoots left ... Also plays Left Wing.

Year	Team	League	Games	G.	A.	Pts.	Pen.
1984-85—Richelieu Riverain Midget		Que.	42	41	70	111	62
1985-86—Laval Titans (c)		QHL	68	21	37	58	64

(c)—June, 1986—Drafted as underage junior by Los Angeles Kings in 1986 NHL entry draft. Third Kings pick, 65th overall, fourth round.

DAVID COWAN

Left Wing ... 5'10" ... 180 lbs. ... Born, Minneapolis, Minn., July 23, 1965 ... Shoots left.

Year	Team	League	Games	G.	A.	Pts.	Pen.
1982-83—Mpls. Washburn H.S. (c)		Minn. H.S.	23	35	30	65	....
1983-84—University of Minnesota-Duluth		WCHA	12	1	2	3	8
1984-85—University of Minnesota-Duluth		WCHA	46	12	27	39	26
1985-86—University of Minnesota-Duluth		WCHA	41	9	16	25	8

(c)—June, 1983—Drafted by Washington Capitals in 1983 NHL entry draft. Fifth Capitals pick, 175th overall, ninth round.

CRAIG COXE

Center ... 6'4" ... 185 lbs. ... Born, Chula Vista, Calif., January 21, 1964 ... Shoots left ... (October, 1985)—Broke hand in pre-season game with Calgary and missed 13 games.

Year	Team	League	Games	G.	A.	Pts.	Pen.
1980-81—Los Angeles Midgets		Calif.	..	..	..	..	..

Year Team	League	Games	G.	A.	Pts.	Pen.
1981-82—St. Albert Saints (c)	AJHL	51	17	48	65	212
1982-83—Belleville Bulls	OHL	64	14	27	41	102
1983-84—Belleville Bulls	OHL	45	17	28	45	90
1984-85—Vancouver Canucks (d)	NHL	9	0	0	0	49
1984-85—Fredericton Express	AHL	62	8	7	15	242
1985-86—Vancouver Canucks	NHL	57	3	5	8	176
NHL TOTALS		66	3	5	8	225

(c)—June, 1982—Drafted as underage junior by Detroit Red Wings in 1982 NHL entry draft. Fourth Red Wings pick, 66th overall, fourth round.

(d)—October, 1984—WHL rights traded by Portland Winter Hawks to Saskatoon Blades for future considerations.

VITO CRAMAROSSA

Right Wing . . . 6' . . . 195 lbs. . . . Born, Toronto, Ont., March 9, 1966 . . . Shoots right.

Year Team	League	Games	G.	A.	Pts.	Pen.
1982-83—Don Mills Midgets	COJHL	36	21	47	68	118
1983-84—Toronto Marlboros (c)	OHL	66	18	40	58	63
1984-85—Toronto Marlboros	OHL	63	27	37	64	63
1985-86—Toronto Marlboros	OHL	51	20	35	55	77
1985-86—Binghamton Whalers (d)	AHL	....	...	....	....	....

(c)—June, 1984—Drafted as underage junior by Washington Capitals in 1984 NHL entry draft. Fifth Capitals pick, 122nd overall, sixth round.

(d)—No regular season record. Played four playoff games.

MURRAY CRAVEN

Center . . . 6'2" . . . 175 lbs. . . . Born, Medicine Hat, Alta., July 20, 1964 . . . Shoots left . . . Also plays Left Wing . . . (January 15, 1983)—Injured left knee cartilage in game vs. Toronto.

Year Team	League	Games	G.	A.	Pts.	Pen.
1980-81—Medicine Hat Tigers	WHL	69	5	10	15	18
1981-82—Medicine Hat Tigers (c)	WHL	72	35	46	81	49
1982-83—Medicine Hat Tigers	WHL	28	17	29	46	35
1982-83—Detroit Red Wings	NHL	31	4	7	11	6
1983-84—Medicine Hat Tigers	WHL	48	38	56	94	53
1983-84—Detroit Red Wings	NHL	15	0	4	4	6
1984-85—Philadelphia Flyers (d)	NHL	80	26	35	61	30
1985-86—Philadelphia Flyers	NHL	78	21	33	54	34
NHL TOTALS		204	51	79	130	76

(c)—June, 1982—Drafted as underage junior by Detroit Red Wings in 1982 NHL entry draft. First Red Wings pick, 17th overall, first round.

(d)—October, 1984—Traded with Joe Paterson by Detroit Red Wings to Philadelphia Flyers for Darryl Sittler.

BOB CRAWFORD

Right Wing . . . 5'11" . . . 177 lbs. . . . Born, Belleville, Ont., April 6, 1959 . . . Shoots right . . . Brother of Peter and Marc Crawford . . . Son of Floyd Crawford (Member of Belleville MacFarlands, 1959 Canadian World Cup Winners) . . . (January 31, 1985)—Strained medial ligament in right knee in game at Los Angeles.

Year Team	League	Games	G.	A.	Pts.	Pen.
1976-77—Cornwall Royals	QMJHL	71	36	34	70	39
1977-78—Cornwall Royals	QMJHL	69	54	67	121	29
1978-79—Cornwall Royals (c)	QMJHL	65	62	70	132	45
1979-80—St. Louis Blues	NHL	8	1	0	1	2
1979-80—Salt Lake Golden Eagles	CHL	67	30	21	51	32
1980-81—Salt Lake Golden Eagles	CHL	79	35	26	61	27
1981-82—Salt Lake Golden Eagles (a)	CHL	74	54	45	99	43
1981-82—St. Louis Blues	NHL	3	0	1	1	0
1982-83—Salt Lake Golden Eagles	CHL	25	15	23	38	2
1982-83—St. Louis Blues	NHL	27	5	9	14	2
1983-84—Hartford Whalers (d)	NHL	80	36	25	61	32
1984-85—Hartford Whalers	NHL	45	14	14	28	8
1985-86—Hartford Whalers (e)	NHL	57	14	20	34	16
1985-86—New York Rangers	NHL	11	1	2	3	10
NHL TOTALS		231	71	71	142	70

(c)—August, 1979—Drafted by St. Louis Blues in 1979 NHL entry draft. Second Blues pick, 65th overall, fourth round.

(d)—October, 1983—Selected by Hartford Whalers in 1983 NHL waiver draft.

(e)—March, 1986—Traded by Hartford Whalers to New York Rangers for Mike McEwen.

LOUIS CRAWFORD

Left Wing . . . 5'11" . . . 175 lbs. . . . Born, Belleville, Ont., November 5, 1962 . . . Shoots left.

Year	Team	League	Games	G.	A.	Pts.	Pen.
1979-80—Belleville Jr. B		OHA	10	7	11	18	60
1980-81—Kitchener Rangers		OHL	53	2	7	9	134
1981-82—Kitchener Rangers		OHL	64	11	17	28	243
1982-83—Rochester Americans (c)		AHL	64	5	11	16	142
1983-84—Rochester Americans		AHL	76	7	6	13	234
1984-85—Rochester Americans		AHL	65	12	29	41	173
1985-86—Nova Scotia Oilers (d)		AHL	78	8	11	19	214

(c)—August, 1984—Signed by Buffalo Sabres as a free agent.
(d)—October, 1985—Signed by Nova Scotia Oilers as a free agent.

MARC JOSEPH JOHN CRAWFORD

Left Wing . . . 5'11" . . . 181 lbs. . . . Born, Belleville, Ont., February 13, 1961 . . . Shoots left . . . Son of Floyd Crawford (Member of Belleville MacFarlands, 1959 Canadian World Cup Winners) . . . Brother of Peter and Bob Crawford.

Year	Team	League	Games	G.	A.	Pts.	Pen.
1978-79—Cornwall Royals		QMJHL	70	28	41	69	206
1979-80—Cornwall Royals (c)		QMJHL	54	27	36	63	127
1980-81—Cornwall Royals		QMJHL	63	42	57	99	242
1981-82—Dallas Black Hawks		CHL	34	13	21	34	71
1981-82—Vancouver Canucks		NHL	40	4	8	12	29
1982-83—Fredericton Express		AHL	30	15	9	24	59
1982-83—Vancouver Canucks		NHL	41	4	5	9	28
1983-84—Vancouver Canucks		NHL	19	0	1	1	9
1983-84—Fredericton Express		AHL	56	9	22	31	96
1984-85—Fredericton Express		AHL	65	12	29	41	173
1984-85—Vancouver Canucks		NHL	1	0	0	0	4
1985-86—Fredericton Express		AHL	26	10	14	24	55
1985-86—Vancouver Canucks		NHL	54	11	14	25	92
NHL TOTALS			155	19	28	47	162

(c)—June, 1980—Drafted as underage junior by Vancouver Canucks in 1980 NHL entry draft. Third Canucks pick, 70th overall, fourth round.

WAYNE KENNETH CRAWFORD

Center and Right Wing . . . 5'11" . . . 180 lbs. . . . Born, Toronto, Ont., April 18, 1961 . . . Shoots left.

Year	Team	League	Games	G.	A.	Pts.	Pen.
1978-79—Niagara Falls Flyers		OMJHL	64	25	41	66	74
1979-80—Niagara Falls Flyers		OMJHL	2	0	0	0	0
1979-80—Toronto Marlboros (c)		OMJHL	64	48	66	114	18
1980-81—Toronto Marlboros		OHL	65	44	58	102	101
1981-82—Adirondack Red Wings		AHL	65	14	26	40	42
1982-83—Adirondack Red Wings		AHL	69	18	31	49	16
1983-84—Adirondack Red Wings		AHL	67	28	25	53	97
1984-85—Kalamazoo Wings		IHL	78	27	48	75	69
1985-86—Kalamazoo Wings		IHL	77	51	51	102	83

(c)—June, 1980—Drafted as underage junior by Detroit Red Wings in 1980 NHL entry draft. Fourth Red Wings pick, 109th overall, sixth round.

ADAM CREIGHTON

Center . . . 6'5" . . . 21) lbs. . . . Born, Burlington, Ont., June 2, 1965 . . . Shoots left . . . Son of Dave Creighton (NHL, '50s-'60s) . . . (May, 1984)—Named MVP of 1984 Memorial Cup.

Year	Team	League	Games	G.	A.	Pts.	Pen.
1981-82—Ottawa 67's		OHL	60	14	27	42	73
1982-83—Ottawa 67's (c)		OHL	68	44	46	90	88
1983-84—Ottawa 67's		OHL	56	42	49	91	79
1983-84—Buffalo Sabres		NHL	7	2	2	4	4
1984-85—Ottawa 67's		OHL	10	4	14	18	23
1984-85—Rochester Americans		AHL	6	5	3	8	2
1984-85—Buffalo Sabres		NHL	30	2	8	10	33
1985-86—Rochester Americans		AHL	32	17	21	38	27
1985-86—Buffalo Sabres		NHL	20	1	1	2	2
NHL TOTALS			57	5	11	16	39

(c)—June, 1983—Drafted as underage junior by Buffalo Sabres in 1983 NHL entry draft. Third Sabres pick, 11th overall, first round.

SHAWN CRONIN

Defense . . . 6'2" . . . 210 lbs. . . . Born, Flushing, Mich., August 20, 1963 . . . Shoots left.

Year	Team	League	Games	G.	A.	Pts.	Pen.
1982-83—U. of Illinois-Chicago		CCHA	36	1	5	6	52
1983-84—U. of Illinois-Chicago		CCHA	32	0	4	4	41
1984-85—U. of Illinois-Chicago		CCHA	31	2	6	8	52
1985-86—U. of Illinois-Chicago (c)		CCHA	38	3	8	11	70

(c)—March, 1986—Signed by Hartford Whalers as a free agent.

TOM CRONIN

Defense . . . 6' . . . 195 lbs. . . . Born, Melrose, Mass., September 9, 1960 . . . Shoots right.

Year	Team	League	Games	G.	A.	Pts.	Pen.
1982-83—Lowell University (c)		ECAC-II	26	3	13	16	37
1983-84—Binghamton Whalers		AHL	75	2	12	14	90
1984-85—Adirondack Red Wings (d)		AHL	56	7	17	24	72
1985-86—Rochester Americans (e-f)		AHL	14	0	2	2	9

(c)—September, 1983—Signed by Hartford Whalers as a free agent.
(d)—December, 1984—Signed by Adirondack Red Wings as a free agent.
(e)—July, 1985—Released by Adirondack Red Wings.
(f)—March, 1986—Signed by Rochester Americans as a free agent.

DOUG CROSSMAN

Defense . . . 6'2" . . . 190 lbs. . . . Born, Peterborough, Ont., June 30, 1960 . . . Shoots left . . . (February, 1983)—Injured thumb.

Year	Team	League	Games	G.	A.	Pts.	Pen.
1976-77—London Knights		OMJHL	1	0	0	0	0
1977-78—Ottawa 67's		OMJHL	65	4	17	21	17
1978-79—Ottawa 67's (c)		OMJHL	67	12	51	63	63
1979-80—Ottawa 67's (a)		OMJHL	66	20	96	116	48
1980-81—Chicago Black Hawks		NHL	9	0	2	2	2
1980-81—New Brunswick Hawks		AHL	70	13	43	56	90
1981-82—Chicago Black Hawks		NHL	70	12	28	40	24
1982-83—Chicago Black Hawks (d)		NHL	80	13	40	53	46
1983-84—Philadelphia Flyers		NHL	78	7	28	35	63
1984-85—Philadelphia Flyers		NHL	80	4	33	37	65
1985-86—Philadelphia Flyers		NHL	80	6	37	43	55
NHL TOTALS			397	42	168	210	255

(c)—August, 1979—Drafted by Chicago Black Hawks as underage junior in 1979 NHL entry draft. Sixth Black Hawks pick, 112th overall, sixth round.
(d)—June, 1983—Traded by Chicago Black Hawks with second-round draft pick (Scott Mellanby) in 1984 to Philadelphia Flyers for Behn Wilson.

JEFF CROSSMAN

Center . . . 6' . . . 200 lbs. . . . Born, Detroit, Mich., December 3, 1964 . . . Shoots left.

Year	Team	League	Games	G.	A.	Pts.	Pen.
1982-83—Western Michigan Univ.		CCHA	30	3	2	5	43
1983-84—Western Michigan Univ. (c)		CCHA	39	9	12	21	91
1984-85—Western Michigan Univ.		CCHA	35	5	12	17	87
1985-86—Western Michigan Univ.		CCHA	39	13	19	32	*154

(c)—June, 1984—Drafted by Los Angeles Kings in 1984 NHL entry draft. Tenth Kings pick. 191st overall. 10th round.

KEITH SCOTT CROWDER

Right Wing . . . 6' . . . 190 lbs. . . . Born, Windsor, Ont., January 6, 1959 . . . Shoots right . . . Also plays Center . . . Brother of former NHLer Bruce Crowder . . . (February, 1978)—Broken ankle . . . Set Bruins team record for most penalty minutes by a rookie (172) in 1980-81 . . . (December, 1983)—Sprained right knee and missed 16 games.

Year	Team	League	Games	G.	A.	Pts.	Pen.
1976-77—Peterborough Petes		Jr."A"OHA	58	13	19	32	99
1977-78—Peterborough Petes (c)		Jr."A"OHA	58	30	30	60	139
1978-79—Birmingham Bulls (d)		WHA	5	1	0	1	17
1978-79—Peterborough Petes (e)		OMJHL	43	25	41	66	76
1979-80—Binghamton Dusters		AHL	13	4	0	4	15
1979-80—Grand Rapids Owls		IHL	20	10	13	23	22
1980-81—Springfield Indians		AHL	26	12	18	30	34

Year	Team	League	Games	G.	A.	Pts.	Pen.
1980-81—Boston Bruins		NHL	47	13	12	25	172
1981-82—Boston Bruins		NHL	71	23	21	44	101
1982-83—Boston Bruins		NHL	74	35	39	74	105
1983-84—Boston Bruins		NHL	63	24	28	52	128
1984-85—Boston Bruins		NHL	79	32	38	70	142
1985-86—Boston Bruins		NHL	78	38	46	84	177
WHA TOTALS			5	1	0	1	17
NHL TOTALS			412	165	184	349	825

(c)—Signed by Birmingham Bulls (WHA) as underage player, July, 1978.

(d)—November, 1978—Returned to Peterborough to play final year of junior eligibility.

(e)—August, 1979—Drafted by Boston Bruins in entry draft. Fourth Boston pick, 57th overall, third round.

TROY CROWDER

Right Wing . . . 6'3" . . . 200 lbs. . . . Born, Sudbury, Ont., May 3, 1968 . . . Shoots right.

Year	Team	League	Games	G.	A.	Pts.	Pen.
1984-85—Walden Midgets		NOHA	28	20	21	41	63
1985-86—Hamilton Steelhawks (c)		OHL	55	4	4	8	178

(c)—June, 1986—Drafted as underage junior by New Jersey Devils in 1986 NHL entry draft. Sixth Devils pick, 108th overall, sixth round.

JIM CULHANE

Defense . . . 6' . . . 190 lbs. . . . Born, Haileybury, Ont., August 8, 1960 . . . Shoots left.

Year	Team	League	Games	G.	A.	Pts.	Pen.
1983-84—Western Michigan Univ. (c)		CCHA	42	1	14	15	88
1984-85—Western Michigan Univ.		CCHA	37	2	8	10	84
1985-86—Western Michigan Univ.		CCHA	40	1	21	22	61

(c)—June, 1984—Drafted by Hartford Whalers in 1984 NHL entry draft. Sixth Whalers pick, 214th overall, 11th round.

RANDY WILLIAM CUNNEYWORTH

Center and Left Wing . . . 6' . . . 180 lbs. . . . Born, Etobicoke, Ont., May 10, 1961 . . . Shoots left.

Year	Team	League	Games	G.	A.	Pts.	Pen.
1979-80—Ottawa 67's (c)		OMJHL	63	16	25	41	145
1980-81—Ottawa 67's		OHL	67	54	74	128	240
1980-81—Rochester Americans		AHL	1	0	1	1	2
1980-81—Buffalo Sabres		NHL	1	0	0	0	2
1981-82—Rochester Americans		AHL	57	12	15	27	86
1981-82—Buffalo Sabres		NHL	20	2	4	6	47
1982-83—Rochester Americans		AHL	78	23	33	56	111
1983-84—Rochester Americans		AHL	54	18	17	35	85
1984-85—Rochester Americans		AHL	72	30	38	68	148
1985-86—Pittsburgh Penguins (d)		NHL	75	15	30	45	74
NHL TOTALS			96	17	34	51	123

(c)—June, 1980—Drafted as underage junior by Buffalo Sabres in 1980 NHL entry draft. Ninth Sabres pick, 167th overall, eighth round.

(d)—October, 1985—After attending Pittsburgh's training camp as an unsigned free agent, his equalization rights were traded with Mike Moller by Buffalo Sabres to Pittsburgh Penguins for future considerations.

MARK CUPOLO

Left Wing . . . 6' . . . 180 lbs. . . . Born, Niagara Falls, Ont., November 17, 1965 . . . Shoots left.

Year	Team	League	Games	G.	A.	Pts.	Pen.
1982-83—Guelph Platers		OHL	8	0	0	0	7
1983-84—Guelph Platers (c)		OHL	60	28	13	41	61
1984-85—Guelph Platers (d)		OHL	30	13	11	24	33
1984-85—Peterborough Petes		OHL	17	5	3	8	18
1985-86—Peoria Rivermen		IHL	60	9	14	23	87

(c)—June, 1984—Drafted by St. Louis Blues in 1984 NHL entry draft. Thirteenth Blues pick, 217th overall, 11th round.

(d)—January, 1985—Traded by Guelph Platers to Peterborough Petes for Sandy Chisholm and future considerations.

BRIAN CURRAN

Defense . . . 6'4" . . . 200 lbs. . . . Born, Toronto, Ont., November 5, 1963 . . . Shoots left . . .

(November, 1981)—Appendectomy . . . (September, 1982)—Broken ankle . . . (November, 1984)—Charley Horse . . . (October 6, 1985)—Missed five games with fractured thumb . . . (February 1, 1986)—Broken leg at Montreal.

Year—Team	League	Games	G.	A.	Pts.	Pen.
1980-81—Portland Winter Hawks	WHL	51	2	16	18	132
1981-82—Portland Winter Hawks (c)	WHL	59	2	28	30	275
1982-83—Portland Winter Hawks	WHL	56	1	30	31	187
1983-84—Hershey Bears	AHL	23	0	2	2	94
1983-84—Boston Bruins	NHL	16	1	1	2	57
1984-85—Hershey Bears	AHL	4	0	0	0	19
1984-85—Boston Bruins	NHL	56	0	1	1	158
1985-86—Boston Bruins	NHL	43	2	5	7	192
NHL TOTALS		115	3	7	10	407

(c)—June, 1982—Drafted as underage junior by Boston Bruins in 1982 NHL entry draft. Second Bruins pick, 22nd overall, second round.

DAN CURRIE

Left Wing . . . 6'1" . . . 180 lbs. . . . Born, Burlington, Ont., March 15, 1968 . . . Shoots left.

Year—Team	League	Games	G.	A.	Pts.	Pen.
1984-85—Burlington Midgets	OHA	29	28	27	55	35
1985-86—Sault Ste. Marie Greyhounds (c)	OHL	66	21	22	43	37

(c)—June, 1986—Drafted as underage junior by Edmonton Oilers in 1986 NHL entry draft. Fourth Oilers pick, 84th overall, fourth round.

GLEN CURRIE

Center . . . 6'1" . . . 175 lbs. . . . Born, Lachine, Que., July 18, 1958 . . . Shoots left . . . Nephew of Jim Peters (NHL player in late '40s and early '50s) . . . (September, 1985)—Injured back during training camp.

Year—Team	League	Games	G.	A.	Pts.	Pen.
1975-76—Laval National	QJHL	72	15	54	69	20
1976-77—Laval National	QJHL	72	28	51	79	42
1977-78—Laval National (b-c)	QJHL	72	63	82	145	29
1978-79—Port Huron Flags	IHL	69	27	36	63	43
1979-80—Hershey Bears	AHL	45	17	26	43	16
1979-80—Washington Capitals	NHL	32	2	0	2	2
1980-81—Washington Capitals	NHL	40	5	13	18	16
1980-81—Hershey Bears	AHL	35	18	21	39	10
1981-82—Hershey Bears	AHL	31	12	12	24	6
1981-82—Washington Capitals	NHL	43	7	7	14	14
1982-83—Hershey Bears	AHL	12	5	11	16	6
1982-83—Washington Capitals	NHL	68	11	28	39	20
1983-84—Washington Capitals	NHL	80	12	24	36	20
1984-85—Binghamton Whalers	AHL	17	1	5	6	6
1984-85—Washington Capitals	NHL	44	1	5	6	19
1985-86—Los Angeles Kings (d)	NHL	12	1	2	3	9
1985-86—New Haven Nighthawks	AHL	8	0	4	4	2
NHL TOTALS		319	39	79	118	100

(c)—Drafted from Laval National by Washington Capitals in third round of 1978 amateur draft.
(d)—September, 1985—Traded by Washington Capitals to Los Angeles Kings for Daryl Evans.

TONY CURRIE

Right Wing . . . 5'11" . . . 166 lbs. . . . Born, Sidney, N. S., November 12, 1957 . . . Shoots right . . . (February, 1984)—Fractured toe.

Year—Team	League	Games	G.	A.	Pts.	Pen.
1973-74—Edmonton Mets	AJHL	29	20	16	36	35
1973-74—Edmonton Oil Kings	WCHL	22	0	1	1	2
1974-75—Spruce Grove Mets	AJHL	35	36	44	80	73
1974-75—Edmonton Oil Kings	WCHL	39	28	17	45	12
1975-76—Edmonton Oil Kings	WCHL	71	41	40	81	56
1976-77—Portland Winter Hawks (c)	WCHL	72	73	52	125	50
1977-78—S. L. City Golden Eagles (a)	CHL	53	33	17	50	17
1977-78—St. Louis Blues	NHL	22	4	5	9	4
1978-79—St. Louis Blues	NHL	36	4	15	19	0
1978-79—Salt Lake Golden Eagles	CHL	28	22	12	34	6
1979-80—Salt Lake Golden Eagles	CHL	33	24	23	47	17
1979-80—St. Louis Blues	NHL	40	19	14	33	4
1980-81—St. Louis Blues	NHL	61	23	32	55	38
1981-82—St. Louis Blues (d)	NHL	48	18	22	40	17

Year	Team	League	Games	G.	A.	Pts.	Pen.
1981-82—Vancouver Canucks		NHL	12	5	3	8	2
1982-83—Vancouver Canucks		NHL	8	1	1	2	0
1982-83—Fredericton Express (a)		AHL	68	47	48	95	16
1983-84—Fredericton Express		AHL	12	6	11	17	16
1983-84—Vancouver Canucks (e)		NHL	18	3	3	6	2
1983-84—Hartford Whalers		NHL	32	12	16	28	4
1984-85—Hartford Whalers (f)		NHL	13	3	8	11	2
1984-85—Nova Scotia Oilers (g)		AHL	53	16	31	47	8
1985-86—Fredericton Express		AHL	75	35	40	75	23
NHL TOTALS			290	92	119	211	73

(c)—Drafted from Portland Winter Hawks by St. Louis Blues in fourth round of 1977 amateur draft.
(d)—March, 1982—Traded with Rick Heinz, Jim Nill and a fourth-round 1982 draft pick (Shawn Kilroy) by St. Louis Blues to Vancouver Canucks for Glen Hanlon.
(e)—January, 1984—Released by Vancouver Canucks and signed by Hartford Whalers as a free agent.
(f)—December, 1984—Traded by Hartford Whalers to Edmonton Oilers for future considerations.
(g)—July, 1985—Signed by Quebec Nordiques as a free agent.

ANTHONY GLENN CURTALE

Defense . . . 6' . . . 190 lbs. . . . Born, Detroit, Mich., January 29, 1962 . . . Shoots left.

Year	Team	League	Games	G.	A.	Pts.	Pen.
1979-80—Brantford Alexanders (c)		OMJHL	59	10	35	45	227
1980-81—Brantford Alexanders		OHL	59	14	71	85	141
1980-81—Calgary Flames		NHL	2	0	0	0	0
1981-82—Brantford Alexanders		OHL	36	17	32	49	118
1981-82—Oklahoma City Stars (d)		CHL	..	..	..	..	....
1982-83—Colorado Flames		CHL	74	7	22	29	61
1983-84—Peoria Prancers		IHL	2	0	0	0	2
1983-84—Colorado Flames		CHL	54	3	20	23	80
1984-85—Peoria Rivermen		IHL	50	5	31	36	81
1985-86—Peoria Rivermen (b)		IHL	70	7	51	58	116
NHL TOTALS			2	0	0	0	0

(c)—June, 1980—Drafted by Calgary Flames as an underage junior in 1980 NHL entry draft. Second Flames pick, 31st overall, second round.
(d)—No regular-season record. Appeared in four playoff games.

JOEL CURTIS

Left Wing . . . 6'1" . . . 185 lbs. . . . Born, Montreal, Que., January 13, 1966 . . . Shoots left.

Year	Team	League	Games	G.	A.	Pts.	Pen.
1982-83—New Market Tier II		COJHL	48	15	18	33	47
1983-84—Oshawa Generals (c)		OHL	67	8	12	20	68
1984-85—Oshawa Generals		OHL	52	13	27	40	45
1985-86—Oshawa Generals		OHL	55	6	30	36	35

(c)—June, 1984—Drafted as underage junior by Edmonton Oilers in 1984 NHL entry draft. Ninth Oilers pick, 209th overall, 10th round.

DENIS CYR

Right Wing . . . 5'11" . . . 186 lbs. . . . Born, Verdun, Que., February 4, 1961 . . . Shoots left . . . (January, 1982)—Dislocated shoulder . . . (January 15, 1983)—Broke nose in game at Philadelphia.

Year	Team	League	Games	G.	A.	Pts.	Pen.
1977-78—Montreal Red White & Blue		QMJHL	72	46	55	101	25
1978-79—Montreal Juniors (b)		QMJHL	72	70	56	126	61
1979-80—Montreal Juniors (a-c)		QMJHL	70	70	76	146	61
1980-81—Calgary Flames		NHL	10	1	4	5	0
1980-81—Montreal Juniors		QMJHL	57	50	40	90	53
1981-82—Oklahoma City Stars		CHL	14	10	4	14	16
1981-82—Calgary Flames		NHL	45	12	10	22	13
1982-83—Calgary Flames (d)		NHL	11	1	1	2	0
1982-83—Chicago Black Hawks		NHL	41	7	8	15	2
1983-84—Springfield Indians		AHL	17	4	13	17	11
1983-84—Chicago Black Hawks (e-f)		NHL	46	12	13	25	19
1984-85—St. Louis Blues		NHL	9	5	3	8	0
1984-85—Peoria Rivermen (g-h)		IHL	62	26	51	77	28
1985-86—St. Louis Blues		NHL	31	3	4	7	2
1985-86—Peoria Rivermen (i)		IHL	34	15	26	41	15
NHL TOTALS			193	41	43	84	36

(c)—June, 1980—Drafted as underage junior by Calgary Flames in 1980 NHL entry draft. First Flames pick, 13th overall, first round.

(d)—November, 1982—Traded by Calgary Flames to Chicago Black Hawks for NHL rights to Carey Wilson.
(e)—June, 1984—Released by Chicago Black Hawks.
(f)—August, 1984—Signed by St. Louis Blues as a free agent.
(g)—Led IHL Playoffs with 18 goals and 32 points.
(h)—Won Turner Cup MVP (IHL Playoffs).
(i)—July, 1986—Released by St. Louis Blues.

PAUL CYR

Left Wing . . . 5'10" . . . 180 lbs. . . . Born, Port Alberni, B.C., October 31, 1963 . . . Shoots left . . . (December 16, 1982)—Injured thumb while playing for Team Canada at World Junior Championships . . . (March 6, 1984)—Broke knuckle in finger during game at Montreal . . . (December 13, 1985)—Pulled groin vs. Hartford.

Year	Team	League	Games	G.	A.	Pts.	Pen.
1979-80—Nanaimo		BCJHL	60	28	52	80	202
1980-81—Victoria Cougars		WHL	64	36	22	58	85
1981-82—Victoria Cougars (b-c)		WHL	58	52	56	108	167
1982-83—Victoria Cougars		WHL	20	21	22	43	61
1982-83—Buffalo Sabres		NHL	36	15	12	27	59
1983-84—Buffalo Sabres		NHL	71	16	27	43	52
1984-85—Buffalo Sabres		NHL	71	22	24	46	63
1985-86—Buffalo Sabres		NHL	71	20	31	51	120
NHL TOTALS			249	73	94	167	294

(c)—June, 1982—Drafted as underage junior by Buffalo Sabres in 1982 NHL entry draft. Second Sabres pick, ninth overall, first round.

DEAN DACHYSHYN

Left Wing . . . 6'1" . . . 195 lbs. . . . Born, West Bank, B.C., May 4, 1959 . . . Shoots left.

Year	Team	League	Games	G.	A.	Pts.	Pen.
1979-80—University of North Dakota		WCHA	40	12	8	20	88
1980-81—University of North Dakota		WCHA	35	8	13	21	91
1981-82—University of North Dakota		WCHA	30	6	13	19	82
1982-83—University of North Dakota		WCHA	20	5	1	6	28
1983-84—Moncton Alpines (c)		AHL	74	9	7	16	92
1984-85—Nova Scotia Oilers		AHL	74	10	10	20	143
1985-86—Nova Scotia Oilers		AHL	55	2	9	11	148

(c)—October, 1983—Signed by Edmonton Oilers as a free agent.

KJELL DAHLIN

Right Wing . . . 6' . . . 176 lbs. . . . Born, Timra, Sweden, February 2, 1963 . . . Shoots left.

Year	Team	League	Games	G.	A.	Pts.	Pen.
1984-85—Farjestad (c)		Sweden	35	21	26	47	..
1985-86—Montreal Canadiens		NHL	77	32	39	71	4
NHL TOTALS			77	32	39	71	4

(c)—June, 1981—Drafted by Montreal Canadiens in NHL entry draft. Seventh Canadiens pick, 82nd overall, fourth round.

CHRIS DAHLQUIST

Defense . . . 6'1" . . . 190 lbs. . . . Born, Fridley, Minn., December 14, 1962. . . . Shoots left.

Year	Team	League	Games	G.	A.	Pts.	Pen.
1981-82—Lake Superior State		CCHA	39	4	10	14	18
1982-83—Lake Superior State		CCHA	35	0	12	12	63
1983-84—Lake Superior State		CCHA	40	4	19	23	76
1984-85—Lake Superior State (c)		CCHA	44	4	15	19	112
1985-86—Baltimore Skipjacks		AHL	65	4	21	25	64
1985-86—Pittsburgh Penguins		NHL	5	1	2	3	2
NHL TOTALS			5	1	2	3	2

(c)—May, 1985—Signed by Pittsburgh Penguins as a free agent.

JEAN-JACQUES DAIGNEAULT

Defense . . . 5'11" . . . 180 lbs. . . . Born, Montreal, Que., October 12, 1965 . . . Shoots left . . . (March, 1984)—Knee surgery . . . (March 19, 1986)—Broke finger in game vs. Toronto.

Year	Team	League	Games	G.	A.	Pts.	Pen.
1981-82—Laval Voisins		QMJHL	64	4	25	29	41
1982-83—Longueuil Chevaliers (a)		QHL	70	26	58	84	58
1983-84—Canadian Olympic Team		Int'l	62	6	15	21	40

Year	Team	League	Games	G.	A.	Pts.	Pen.
1983-84—Longueuil Chevaliers (c)	QHL	10	2	11	13	6
1984-85—Vancouver Canucks	NHL	67	4	23	27	69
1985-86—Vancouver Canucks	NHL	64	5	23	28	45
NHL TOTALS		131	9	46	55	114

(c)—June, 1984—Drafted as underage junior by Vancouver Canucks in 1984 NHL entry draft. First Canucks pick, 10th overall, first round.

(e)—June, 1986—Traded by Vancouver Canucks with second-round draft choice (Kent Hawley) in 1986 and a fifth round choice in 1987 to Philadelphia Flyers for Rich Sutter, Dave Richter and third-round choice in 1986.

BRAD DALGARNO

Right Wing . . . 6'3" . . . 205 lbs. . . . Born, Vancouver, B.C., August 8, 1967 . . . Shoots right.

Year	Team	League	Games	G.	A.	Pts.	Pen.
1983-84—Markham Travelways	MTJHL	40	17	11	28	59
1984-85—Hamilton Steelhawks (c)	OHL	66	23	30	53	86
1985-86—Hamilton Steelhawks	OHL	54	22	43	65	79
1985-86—New York Islanders	NHL	2	1	0	1	0
NHL TOTALS		2	1	0	1	0

(c)—June, 1985—Drafted as underage junior by New York Islanders in 1985 NHL entry draft. First Islanders pick, sixth overall, first round.

MARTY DALLMAN

Center . . . 5'10" . . . 183 lbs. . . . Born, Niagara Falls, Ont., February 15, 1963 . . . Shoots right.

Year	Team	League	Games	G.	A.	Pts.	Pen.
1979-80—Niagara Falls Canucks	OPJHL	40	39	43	82	....
1980-81—R.P.I. (c)	ECAC	22	8	10	18	6
1981-82—R.P.I.	ECAC	28	22	18	40	27
1982-83—R.P.I.	ECAC	29	21	29	50	42
1983-84—R.P.I.	ECAC	38	30	24	54	32
1984-85—New Haven Nighthawks	AHL	78	18	39	57	26
1985-86—New Haven Nighthawks	AHL	69	23	33	56	92

(c)—June, 1981—Drafted as underage junior by Los Angeles Kings in 1981 NHL entry draft. Third Kings pick, 81st overall, fourth round.

ROD DALLMAN

Left Wing . . . 5'11" . . . 185 lbs. . . . Born, Quesnel, B.C., January 26, 1967 . . . Shoots left . . . (October, 1984)—Broken left ankle.

Year	Team	League	Games	G.	A.	Pts.	Pen.
1983-84—P. Albert Midget Raiders	BC-Midget	21	14	6	20	69
1984-85—Prince Albert Raiders (c)	WHL	40	8	11	19	133
1985-86—Prince Albert Raiders	WHL	59	20	21	41	198

(c)—June, 1985—Drafted as underage junior by New York Islanders in 1985 NHL entry draft. Eighth Islanders pick, 118th overall, eighth round.

VINCENT DAMPHOUSSE

Left Wing . . . 6'1" . . . 190 lbs. . . . Born, Montreal, Que., December 17, 1967 . . . Shoots left . . . Also plays Center.

Year	Team	League	Games	G.	A.	Pts.	Pen.
1983-84—Laval Voisins	QHL	66	29	36	65	25
1984-85—Laval Voisins	QHL	68	35	68	103	62
1985-86—Laval Titans (b-c)	QHL	69	45	110	155	70

(c)—June, 1986—Drafted as underage junior by Toronto Maple Leafs in 1986 NHL entry draft. First Maple Leafs pick, sixth overall, first round.

KENNETH DANEYKO

Defense . . . 6'1" . . . 195 lbs. . . . Born, Windsor, Ont., April 17, 1964 . . . Shoots left. . . . (November 2, 1983)—Broke right fibula in game at Hartford . . . (October, 1985)—Given one game suspension and fined $500 by the NHL for playing hockey in West Germany (Manheim) without NHL permission.

Year	Team	League	Games	G.	A.	Pts.	Pen.
1980-81—Spokane Flyers	WHL	62	6	13	19	140
1981-82—Spokane Flyers	WHL	26	1	11	12	147
1981-82—Seattle Breakers (c-d)	WHL	38	1	22	23	151
1982-83—Seattle Breakers	WHL	69	17	43	60	150
1983-84—Kamloops Junior Oilers	WHL	19	6	28	34	52
1983-84—New Jersey Devils	NHL	11	1	4	5	17

Year	Team	League	Games	G.	A.	Pts.	Pen.
1984-85—New Jersey Devils		NHL	1	0	0	0	10
1984-85—Maine Mariners		AHL	80	4	9	13	206
1985-86—Maine Mariners		AHL	21	3	2	5	75
1985-86—New Jersey Devils		NHL	44	0	10	10	100
NHL TOTALS			56	1	14	15	127

(c)—December, 1981—Drafted by Seattle Breakers in WHL Dispersal draft of players from Spokane Flyers.

(d)—June, 1982—Drafted as underage junior by New Jersey Devils in 1982 entry draft. Second Devils pick, 18th overall, first round.

JEFF DANIELS

Left Wing . . . 6' . . . 190 lbs. . . . Born, Oshawa, Ont., June 24, 1968 . . . Shoots left.

Year	Team	League	Games	G.	A.	Pts.	Pen.
1984-85—Oshawa Generals		OHL	59	7	11	18	16
1985-86—Oshawa Generals (c)		OHL	62	13	19	32	23

(c)—June, 1986—Drafted as underage junior by Pittsburgh Penguins in 1986 NHL entry draft. Sixth Penguins pick, 109th overall, sixth round.

DAN ARMAND DAOUST

Center . . . 5'11" . . . 160 lbs. . . . Born, Kirkland Lake, Ont., February 29, 1960 . . . Shoots left.

Year	Team	League	Games	G.	A.	Pts.	Pen.
1977-78—Cornwall Royals		QMJHL	68	24	44	68	74
1978-79—Cornwall Royals		QMJHL	72	42	55	97	85
1979-80—Cornwall Royals (c)		QMJHL	70	40	62	102	82
1980-81—Nova Scotia Voyageurs (a)		AHL	80	38	60	98	106
1981-82—Nova Scotia Voyageurs		AHL	61	25	40	65	75
1982-83—Montreal Canadiens (d)		NHL	4	0	1	1	4
1982-83—Toronto Maple Leafs		NHL	48	18	33	51	31
1983-84—Toronto Maple Leafs		NHL	78	18	56	74	88
1984-85—Toronto Maple Leafs		NHL	79	17	37	54	98
1985-86—Toronto Maple Leafs		NHL	80	7	13	20	88
NHL TOTALS			289	60	140	200	309

(c)—September, 1980—Signed by Montreal Canadiens as a free agent.

(d)—December, 1982—Traded by Montreal Canadiens with Gaston Gingras to Toronto Maple Leafs for future draft considerations.

MICHAEL DARK

Defense . . . 6'3" . . . 225 lbs. . . . Born, Sarnia, Ont., September 17, 1963 . . . Shoots right.

Year	Team	League	Games	G.	A.	Pts.	Pen.
1982-83—Rensselaer Poly. Inst. (c)		ECAC	29	3	16	19	54
1983-84—Rensselaer Poly. Inst.		ECAC	38	2	12	14	60
1984-85—Rensselaer Poly. Inst. (d)		ECAC	36	7	26	33	76
1985-86—Rensselaer Poly. Inst. (a-e)		ECAC	32	7	29	36	58

(c)—June, 1982—Drafted by Montreal Canadiens in NHL entry draft. Tenth Canadiens pick, 124th overall, sixth round.

(d)—June, 1985—NHL rights traded by Montreal Canadiens to St. Louis Blues along with Mark Hunter and future considerations for St. Louis' first-round draft choice (Jose Charboneau) and a switch of other choices.

(e)—Named to East All-America.

NEAL DAVEY

Defense . . . 6'2" . . . 205 lbs. . . . Born, Edmonton, Alta., December 29, 1965 . . . Shoots right.

Year	Team	League	Games	G.	A.	Pts.	Pen.
1983-84—Michigan State Univ. (c)		CCHA	33	1	5	6	50
1984-85—Prince Albert Raiders		WHL	54	6	28	34	20
1985-86—Maine Mariners		AHL	7	0	0	0	8
1985-86—Toledo Goaldiggers		IHL	49	5	8	13	35

(c)—June, 1984—Drafted by New Jersey Devils in 1984 NHL entry draft. Third Devils pick, 44th overall, third round.

LEE DAVIDSON

Center . . . 5'10" . . . 160 lbs. . . . Born, Winnipeg, Manitoba, June 30, 1968 . . . Shoots left.

Year	Team	League	Games	G.	A.	Pts.	Pen.
1985-86—Penticton Knights (c)		BCJHL	46	34	72	106	37

(c)—June, 1986—Drafted by Washington Capitals in 1986 NHL entry draft. Ninth Capitals pick, 166th overall, eighth round.

ROBERT SEAN DAVIDSON
(Known by middle name)

Right Wing . . . 5'11" . . . 180 lbs. . . . Born, Toronto, Ont., April 13, 1968 . . . Shoots right . . . (January, 1985)—Broken wrist.

Year	Team	League	Games	G.	A.	Pts.	Pen.
1984-85—Toronto Nationals		MTHL	60	58	55	113	80
1985-86—Toronto Marlboros (c)		OHL	65	18	34	52	23

(c)—June, 1986—Drafted by Toronto Maple Leafs as an underage junior in 1986 NHL entry draft. Tenth Maple Leafs pick, 195th overall, 10th round.

MALCOLM STERLING DAVIS

Right Wing . . . 5'11" . . . 180 lbs. . . . Born, Lockeport, Nova Scotia, October 10, 1956 . . . Shoots right . . . Attended University of Alberta . . . (February, 1986)—Injured left arm.

Year	Team	League	Games	G.	A.	Pts.	Pen.
1978-79—Kansas City Red Wings (a)		CHL	71	42	24	66	29
1978-79—Detroit Red Wings		NHL	6	0	0	0	0
1979-80—Adirondack Red Wings		AHL	79	34	31	65	45
1980-81—Detroit Red Wings		NHL	5	2	0	2	0
1980-81—Adirondack Red Wings		AHL	58	23	12	35	48
1981-82—Rochester Americans		AHL	75	32	33	65	14
1982-83—Rochester Americans		AHL	57	43	32	75	15
1982-83—Buffalo Sabres		NHL	24	8	12	20	0
1983-84—Buffalo Sabres (c)		NHL	11	2	1	3	4
1983-84—Rochester Americans (a-d)		AHL	71	*55	48	103	53
1984-85—Buffalo Sabres		NHL	47	17	9	26	26
1984-85—Rochester Americans		AHL	6	4	4	8	14
1985-86—Buffalo Sabres		NHL	7	2	0	2	4
1985-86—Rochester Americans		AHL	38	21	15	36	23
NHL TOTALS			100	31	22	53	34

(c)—October, 1981—Signed by Buffalo Sabres as a free agent.
(d)—Co-Winner of Les Cunningham Plaque (AHL MVP) with Garry Lariviere.

LUCIEN DeBLOIS

Right Wing . . . 5'11" . . . 200 lbs. . . . Born, Joliette, Que., June 21, 1957 . . . Shoots right . . . (November, 1980)—Groin pull . . . (November 6, 1984)—Pulled groin in game at Detroit . . . (January 2, 1985)—Pulled stomach muscles in game at Detroit . . . (October 16, 1985)—Sprained right knee in game vs. Buffalo and missed 16 games.

Year	Team	League	Games	G.	A.	Pts.	Pen.
1973-74—Sorel Black Hawks		QJHL	56	30	35	65	53
1974-75—Sorel Black Hawks		QJHL	72	46	53	99	62
1975-76—Sorel Black Hawks (a)		QJHL	70	56	55	111	112
1976-77—Sorel Black Hawks (a-c-d)		QJHL	72	56	78	134	131
1977-78—New York Rangers		NHL	71	22	8	30	27
1978-79—New York Rangers		NHL	62	11	17	28	26
1978-79—New Haven Nighthawks		AHL	7	4	6	10	6
1979-80—New York Rangers (e)		NHL	6	3	1	4	7
1979-80—Colorado Rockies		NHL	70	24	19	43	36
1980-81—Colorado Rockies (f)		NHL	74	26	16	42	78
1981-82—Winnipeg Jets		NHL	65	25	27	52	87
1982-83—Winnipeg Jets		NHL	79	27	27	54	69
1983-84—Winnipeg Jets (g)		NHL	80	34	45	79	50
1984-85—Montreal Canadiens		NHL	51	12	11	23	20
1985-86—Montreal Canadiens		NHL	61	14	17	31	48
NHL TOTALS			619	198	188	386	448

(c)—Won Most Valuable Player Award.
(d)—Drafted from Sorel Black Hawks by New York Rangers in first round of 1977 amateur draft.
(e)—November, 1979—Traded with Mike McEwen, Pat Hickey, Dean Turner and future considerations (Bobby Sheehan and Bobby Crawford) by New York Rangers to Colorado Rockies for Barry Beck.
(f)—July, 1981—Traded by Colorado Rockies to Winnipeg Jets for Brent Ashton and a third-round 1982 draft pick (Dave Kasper).
(g)—June, 1984—Traded by Winnipeg Jets to Montreal Canadiens for Perry Turnbull.

SHANNON DEEGAN

Center . . . 6'2" . . . 190 lbs. . . . Born, Montreal, Que., March 19, 1963 . . . Shoots left.

Year	Team	League	Games	G.	A.	Pts.	Pen.
1983-84—Univ. of Vermont (c)		ECAC	28	5	5	10	14
1984-85—Univ. of Vermont		ECAC	9	0	3	3	6
1985-86—Univ. of Vermont		ECAC	28	9	9	18	30

(c)—June, 1984—Drafted by Los Angeles Kings in 1984 NHL entry draft. Eighth Kings pick, 150th overall, eighth round.

DEAN DeFAZIO

Left Wing . . . 5'11" . . . 183 lbs. . . . Born, Ottawa, Ont., April 16, 1963 . . . Shoots left.

Year	Team	League	Games	G.	A.	Pts.	Pen.
1979-80—Ottawa Senators (c)		OPJHL	47	27	25	52	80
1980-81—Brantford Alexanders (d)		OHL	60	6	13	19	104
1981-82—Brantford Alexanders (e)		OHL	10	2	6	8	30
1981-82—Sudbury Wolves		OHL	50	21	32	53	81
1982-83—Oshawa Generals (f)		OHL	52	22	23	45	108
1983-84—Pittsburgh Penguins		NHL	22	0	2	2	28
1983-84—Baltimore Skipjacks		AHL	46	18	13	31	114
1984-85—Baltimore Skipjacks		AHL	78	10	17	27	88
1985-86—Baltimore Skipjacks		AHL	75	14	24	38	171
NHL TOTALS			22	0	2	2	28

(c)—June, 1980—Drafted by Brantford Alexanders in OHL player draft. First Brantford pick, fifth overall, first round.

(d)—June, 1981—Drafted as underage junior by Pittsburgh Penguins in 1981 NHL entry draft. Eighth Penguins pick, 175th overall, ninth round.

(e)—October, 1981—Traded with Tom DellaMaestra by Brantford Alexanders to Sudbury Wolves for Dan Zavarise and Gary Corbiere.

(f)—October, 1982—Traded by Sudbury Wolves to Oshawa Generals for Ali Butorac, Jim Uens and future considerations.

DALE DEGRAY

Defense . . . 5'10" . . . 190 lbs. . . . Born, Oshawa, Ont., September 3, 1963 . . . Shoots right.

Year	Team	League	Games	G.	A.	Pts.	Pen.
1979-80—Oshawa Legionaires		Metro Jr.B	42	14	14	28	34
1979-80—Oshawa Generals		OMJHL	1	0	0	0	2
1980-81—Oshawa Generals (c)		OHL	61	11	10	21	93
1981-82—Oshawa Generals		OHL	66	11	22	33	162
1982-83—Oshawa Generals		OHL	69	20	30	50	149
1983-84—Colorado Flames		CHL	67	16	14	30	67
1984-85—Moncton Golden Flames (b)		AHL	77	24	37	61	63
1985-86—Moncton Golden Flames		AHL	76	10	31	41	128
1985-86—Calgary Flames		NHL	1	0	0	0	0
NHL TOTALS			1	0	0	0	0

(c)—June, 1981—Drafted as underage junior by Calgary Flames in 1981 NHL entry draft. Seventh Flames pick, 162nd overall, eighth round.

JOHN DEL COL

Left Wing . . . 5'10" . . . 190 lbs. . . . Born, St. Catharines, Ont., May 1, 1965 . . . Shoots left.

Year	Team	League	Games	G.	A.	Pts.	Pen.
1982-83—Toronto Marlboros		OHL	5	2	0	2	0
1984-85—Toronto Marlboros (c)		OHL	67	22	24	46	94
1984-85—Toronto Marlboros		OHL	62	34	36	70	76
1985-86—Baltimore Skipjacks		AHL	26	1	2	3	16
1985-86—Muskegon Lumberjacks		IHL	5	0	0	0	0
1985-86—Toledo Goaldiggers		IHL	33	6	7	13	23

(c)—June, 1984—Drafted as underage junior by Pittsburgh Penguins in 1984 NHL entry draft. Seventh Penguins pick, 169th overall, ninth round.

GRANT DELCOURT

Right Wing . . . 5'11" . . . 180 lbs. . . . Born, Prince George, B.C., August 16, 1966 . . . Shoots right . . . Brother of Greg Delcourt (teammate at Spokane).

Year	Team	League	Games	G.	A.	Pts.	Pen.
1983-84—Kelowna Wings (c)		WHL	72	22	53	75	55
1984-85—Kelowna Wings		WHL	70	32	38	70	139
1985-86—Spokane Chiefs		WHL	67	39	51	90	154

(c)—June, 1984—Drafted as underage junior by Buffalo Sabres in 1984 NHL entry draft. Tenth Sabres pick, 226th overall, 11th round.

GILBERT DELORME

Defense . . . 5'11" . . . 205 lbs. . . . Born, Boucherville, Que., November 25, 1962 . . . Shoots right . . . (January 3, 1982)—Dislocated left shoulder in game at Buffalo . . . (November 19, 1985)—Injured throat in game vs. Edmonton and missed two games . . . (January 25, 1986)—Bruised knee vs. Buffalo and missed seven games.

Year	Team	League	Games	G.	A.	Pts.	Pen.
1978-79—Chicoutimi Sagueneens		QMJHL	72	13	47	60	53

Year	Team	League	Games	G.	A.	Pts.	Pen.
1979-80—Chicoutimi Sagueneens		QMJHL	71	25	86	111	68
1980-81—Chicoutimi Sagueneens (b-c)		QMJHL	70	27	79	106	77
1981-82—Montreal Canadiens		NHL	60	3	8	11	55
1982-83—Montreal Canadiens		NHL	78	12	21	33	89
1983-84—Montreal Canadiens (d)		NHL	27	2	7	9	8
1983-84—St. Louis Blues		NHL	44	0	5	5	41
1984-85—St. Louis Blues		NHL	74	2	12	14	53
1985-86—Quebec Nordiques (e)		NHL	65	2	18	20	55
NHL TOTALS			348	21	71	92	301

(c)—June, 1981—Drafted as underage junior by Montreal Canadiens in 1981 NHL entry draft. Second Canadiens pick, 18th overall, first round.

(d)—December, 1983—Traded with Doug Wickenheiser and Greg Paslawski by Montreal Canadiens to St. Louis Blues for Perry Turnbull.

(e)—October, 1985—Traded by St. Louis Blues to Quebec Nordiques for Bruce Bell.

ERIC DEMERS

Left Wing . . . 6'3" . . . 180 lbs. . . . Born, Montreal, Que., March 1, 1966 . . . Shoots left.

Year	Team	League	Games	G.	A.	Pts.	Pen.
1983-84—Shawinigan Cataracts (c)		QHL	65	5	13	18	153
1984-85—Shawinigan Cataracts		QHL	64	12	23	35	170
1985-86—Drummondville Voltigeurs (d)		QHL	55	13	10	23	243

(c)—June, 1984—Drafted as an underage junior by Montreal Canadiens in 1984 NHL entry draft. Eleventh Canadiens pick, 179th overall, ninth round.

(d)—October, 1985—Released by Shawinigan Cataracts and signed by Drummonville Voltigeurs as a free agent.

LARRY DePALMA

Left Wing . . . 6' . . . 180 lbs. . . . Born, Trenton, Mich., October 27, 1965 . . . Shoots left.

Year	Team	League	Games	G.	A.	Pts.	Pen.
1984-85—New Westminister Bruins		WHL	65	14	16	30	87
1985-86—Saskatoon Blades (b)		WHL	65	61	51	112	232
1985-86—Minnesota North Stars (c)		NHL	1	0	0	0	0
NHL TOTALS			1	0	0	0	0

(c)—March, 1986—Signed by Minnesota North Stars as a free agent.

WILLIAM ANTHONY DERLAGO

Center . . . 5'10" . . . 194 lbs. . . . Born, Birtle, Man., August 25, 1958 . . . Shoots left . . . Missed part of 1977-78 season with knee injury . . . Set WCHL record for goals in season with 96 in 1976-77 . . . Missed most of the 1978-79 season with severed knee ligaments that required surgery . . . (December, 1981)—Bruised ankle . . . (November 22, 1982)—Tore knee ligaments during team practice . . . (January, 1985)—Surgery for dislocated shoulder.

Year	Team	League	Games	G.	A.	Pts.	Pen.
1974-75—Brandon Travellers		MJHL	....	...	....	....	....
1974-75—Brandon Wheat Kings		WCHL	17	0	4	4	2
1975-76—Brandon Wheat Kings		WCHL	68	49	54	103	43
1976-77—Brandon Wheat Kings (a-c)		WCHL	72	*96	82	*178	63
1977-78—Brandon Wheat Kings (b)		WCHL	52	89	63	152	105
1978-79—Vancouver Canucks (d)		NHL	9	4	4	8	2
1978-79—Dallas Black Hawks		CHL	11	5	8	13	9
1979-80—Vancouver Canucks (e)		NHL	54	11	15	26	27
1979-80—Toronto Maple Leafs		NHL	23	5	12	17	13
1980-81—Toronto Maple Leafs		NHL	80	35	39	74	26
1981-82—Toronto Maple Leafs		NHL	75	34	50	84	42
1982-83—Toronto Maple Leafs		NHL	58	13	24	37	27
1983-84—Toronto Maple Leafs		NHL	79	40	20	60	50
1984-85—Toronto Maple Leafs		NHL	62	31	31	62	21
1985-86—Toronto Maple Leafs (f)		NHL	1	0	0	0	0
1985-86—Boston Bruins (g)		NHL	39	5	16	21	15
1985-86—Winnipeg Jets		NHL	27	5	5	10	6
NHL TOTALS			507	183	216	399	229

(c)—Led in goals (14), assists (16) and points (30) during playoffs.

(d)—Drafted from Brandon Wheat Kings by Vancouver Canucks in first round of 1978 amateur draft.

(e)—February, 1980—Traded with Rick Vaive by Vancouver Canucks to Toronto Maple Leafs for Jerry Butler and Dave Williams.

(f)—October, 1985—Traded by Toronto Maple Leafs to Boston Bruins for Tom Fergus.

(g)—January, 1986—Traded by Boston Bruins to Winnipeg Jets for Wade Campbell.

FRANCO DESANTIS

Defense . . . 6' . . . 190 lbs. . . . Born, Montreal, Que., September 5, 1966 . . . Shoots left.

Year	Team	League	Games	G.	A.	Pts.	Pen.
1983-84—Verdun Juniors (c)		QHL	69	9	26	35	76
1984-85—Verdun Juniors		QHL	56	3	20	23	85
1985-86—Verdun Juniors		QHL	66	9	22	31	94

(c)—June, 1984—Drafted as underage junior by New York Islanders in 1984 NHL entry draft. Ninth Islanders pick. 167th overall, eighth round.

JOHN DEVEREAUX

Center . . . 6' . . . 174 lbs. . . . Born, Scituate, Mass., June 8, 1965 . . . Shoots right.

Year	Team	League	Games	G.	A.	Pts.	Pen.
1983-84—Scituate H.S. (c)		Mass. H.S.	20	41	34	75	..
1984-85—Boston College		H. East	19	3	3	6	6
1985-86—Boston College		H. East	41	8	6	14	24

(c)—June, 1984—Drafted by Hartford Whalers in 1984 NHL entry draft. Fourth Whalers pick, 173rd overall, ninth round.

JOHN DeVOE

Right Wing . . . 6'2" . . . 190 lbs. . . . Born, Minneapolis, Minn., November 1, 1963 . . . Shoots right.

Year	Team	League	Games	G.	A.	Pts.	Pen.
1981-82—Edina H.S. (c)		Minn. H.S.	36	22	15	37	24
1982-83—University of Notre Dame		CCHA	34	7	8	15	52
1983-84—Providence College		ECAC	28	14	6	20	18
1984-85—Providence College		H. East	44	4	6	10	28
1985-86—Providence College		H. East	39	1	10	11	34

(c)—June, 1982—Drafted as underage player by Montreal Canadiens in 1982 NHL entry draft. Seventh Canadiens pick, 69th overall, fourth round.

GERALD DIDUCK

Defense . . . 6'2" . . . 195 lbs. . . . Born, Edmonton, Alta., April 6, 1965 . . . Shoots right.

Year	Team	League	Games	G.	A.	Pts.	Pen.
1981-82—Lethbridge Broncos		WHL	71	1	15	16	81
1982-83—Lethbridge Broncos (c)		WHL	67	8	16	24	151
1983-84—Lethbridge Broncos		WHL	65	10	24	34	133
1984-85—New York Islanders		NHL	65	2	8	10	80
1985-86—New York Islanders		NHL	10	1	2	3	2
1985-86—Springfield Indians		AHL	61	6	14	20	175
NHL TOTALS			75	3	10	13	82

(c)—June, 1983—Drafted as underage junior by New York Islanders in 1983 NHL entry draft. Second Islanders pick, 16th overall, first round.

DON ARMOND DIETRICH

Defense . . . 6'2" . . . 205 lbs. . . . Born, Deloraine, Man., April 5, 1961 . . . Shoots left.

Year	Team	League	Games	G.	A.	Pts.	Pen.
1978-79—Brandon Wheat Kings		WHL	69	6	37	43	29
1979-80—Brandon Wheat Kings (c)		WHL	63	15	45	60	56
1980-81—Brandon Wheat Kings		WHL	72	16	64	80	84
1981-82—New Brunswick Hawks		AHL	62	1	5	6	14
1982-83—Springfield Indians		AHL	76	6	26	32	26
1983-84—Springfield Indians		AHL	50	14	21	35	14
1983-84—Chicago Black Hawks (d)		NHL	17	0	5	5	0
1984-85—Maine Mariners		AHL	75	6	21	27	36
1985-86—Maine Mariners		AHL	68	9	11	20	33
1985-86—New Jersey Devils		NHL	11	0	2	2	10
NHL TOTALS			28	0	7	7	10

(c)—June, 1980—Drafted as underage junior by Chicago Black Hawks in 1980 NHL entry draft. Fourteenth Black Hawks pick, 183rd overall, ninth round.

(d)—June, 1984—Traded with Rich Preston and 2nd round 1985 draft pick (Eric Weinrich) by Chicago Black Hawks to New Jersey Devils for Bob MacMillan and fifth round 1985 draft pick (Rick Herbert).

RALPH DIFIORE

Defense . . . 6'1" . . . 180 lbs. . . . Born, Montreal, Que., April 20, 1966 . . . Shoots left.

Year	Team	League	Games	G.	A.	Pts.	Pen.
1983-84—Shawinigan Cataracts (c)		QHL	65	6	22	28	38
1984-85—Shawinigan Cataracts		QHL	55	4	30	34	38
1985-86—Trois Rivieres Draveurs		QHL	41	0	21	21	110

(c)—June, 1984—Drafted as underage junior by Chicago Black Hawks in 1984 entry draft. Ninth Black Hawks pick, 174th overall, ninth round.

GORDON DINEEN

Defense . . . 5'11" . . . 180 lbs. . . . Born, Toronto, Ont., September 21, 1962 . . . Shoots right . . . Brother of Shawn, Peter and Kevin Dineen and son of Bill Dineen (Detroit and Chicago, mid-1950s) . . . (January 15, 1985)—Bruised ribs in game vs. Vancouver.

Year	Team	League	Games	G.	A.	Pts.	Pen.
1979-80—St. Michaels Junior 'B'		....	42	15	35	50	103
1980-81—Sault Ste. Marie Greyhounds (c)		OHL	68	4	26	30	158
1981-82—Sault Ste. Marie Greyhounds		OHL	68	9	45	54	185
1982-83—Indianapolis Racers (a-d-e)		CHL	73	10	47	57	78
1982-83—New York Islanders		NHL	2	0	0	0	4
1983-84—Indianapolis Checkers		IHL	26	4	13	17	63
1983-84—New York Islanders		NHL	43	1	11	12	32
1984-85—Springfield Indians		AHL	25	1	8	9	46
1984-85—New York Islanders		NHL	48	1	12	13	89
1985-86—New York Islanders		NHL	57	1	8	9	81
1985-86—Springfield Indians		AHL	11	2	3	5	20
NHL TOTALS			150	3	31	34	206

(c)—June, 1981—Drafted as underage junior by New York Islanders in 1981 NHL entry draft. Second Islanders pick, 42nd overall, second round.

(d)—Won Bobby Orr Trophy (Most Valuable CHL Defenseman).

(e)—Won Bob Gassoff Award (Most Improved CHL Defenseman).

KEVIN DINEEN

Right Wing . . . 5'10" . . . 180 lbs. . . . Born, Toronto, Ont., October 28, 1963 . . . Shoots right . . . Brother of Shawn, Peter and Gordon Dineen and son of Bill Dineen (Detroit and Chicago, mid-1950s.) . . . Set University of Denver penalty-minute record (105) as a freshman . . . Member of 1984 Canadian Olympic Team . . . (October 24, 1985)—Sprained left shoulder at Philadephia and missed nine games . . . (January 12, 1986)—Broke knuckle at Chicago and missed seven games . . . (February 14, 1986)—Sprained knee at Winnipeg.

Year	Team	League	Games	G.	A.	Pts.	Pen.
1980-81—St. Michaels Jr. B		MTJHL	40	15	28	43	167
1981-82—University of Denver (c)		WCHA	38	12	22	34	105
1982-83—University of Denver		WCHA	36	16	13	29	108
1983-84—Canadian Olympic Team		Int'l.	..	..	..	..	..
1984-85—Binghamton Whalers		AHL	25	15	8	23	41
1984-85—Hartford Whalers		NHL	57	25	16	41	120
1985-86—Hartford Whalers		NHL	57	33	35	68	124
NHL TOTALS			114	58	51	109	244

(c)—June, 1982—Drafted as underage player by Hartford Whalers in 1982 NHL entry draft. Third Whalers pick, 56th overall, third round.

PETER DINEEN

Defense . . . 5'11" . . . 181 lbs. . . . Born, Kingston, Ont., November 19, 1960 . . . Shoots right . . . Brother of Shawn, Gordon and Kevin Dineen and son of Bill Dineen (Detroit and Chicago, mid-1950s) . . . (October, 1980)—Broken ankle.

Year	Team	League	Games	G.	A.	Pts.	Pen.
1977-78—Seattle Breakers		WCHL	2	0	0	0	0
1978-79—Kingston Canadians		OMJHL	60	7	14	21	70
1979-80—Kingston Canadians (c)		OMJHL	32	4	10	14	54
1980-81—Maine Mariners		AHL	41	6	7	13	100
1981-82—Maine Mariners		AHL	71	6	14	20	156
1982-83—Maine Mariners (d)		AHL	2	0	0	0	0
1982-83—Moncton Alpines		AHL	59	0	10	10	76
1983-84—Moncton Alpines		AHL	63	0	10	10	120
1983-84—Hershey Bears (e)		AHL	12	0	1	1	32
1984-85—Hershey Bears (f)		AHL	79	4	19	23	144
1985-86—Binghamton Whalers		AHL	11	0	1	1	35
1985-86—Moncton Golden Flames (g)		AHL	55	5	13	18	136

(c)—June, 1980—Drafted by Philadelphia Flyers in 1980 NHL entry draft. Ninth Flyers pick, 189th overall, ninth round.

(d)—October, 1982—Traded by Philadelphia Flyers to Edmonton Oilers for Bob Hoffmeyer.

(e)—September, 1984—Signed by Boston Bruins as a free agent.
(f)—August, 1985—Signed as free agent by Hartford Whalers.
(g)—July, 1986—Signed by Los Angeles Kings as a free agent.

MARCEL ELPHEGE DIONNE

Center . . . 5'8" . . . 185 lbs. . . . Born, Drummondville, Que., August 3, 1951 . . . Shoots right . . . Missed part of 1970-71 season with broken collarbone . . . Set NHL record for points in rookie season in 1971-72 (broken by Bryan Trottier in 1975-76) . . . Established record for shorthanded goals (10) in single season, 1974-75 (broken by Wayne Gretzky in 1983-84) . . . Missed part of 1977-78 season with shoulder separations . . . (January 7, 1981)—Collected 1,000th NHL point in 740th NHL game, the fastest by any player in history (record broken by Guy Lafleur, 720th game) . . . (January 11, 1984)—Sprained left ankle in game vs. Washington . . . (February 14, 1984)—Aggravated ankle injury in game at New Jersey.

Year	Team	League	Games	G.	A.	Pts.	Pen.
1967-68—Drummondville Rangers		QJHL	....	...	....	....	....
1968-69—St. Cath. Black Hawks		Jr."A"OHA	48	37	63	100	38
1969-70—St. Cath. B. Hawks (b-c)		Jr."A"OHA	54	*55	*77	*132	46
1970-71—St. Cath. B. Hawks (a-c-d)		Jr."A"OHA	46	62	81	*143	20
1971-72—Detroit Red Wings		NHL	78	28	49	77	14
1972-73—Detroit Red Wings		NHL	77	40	50	90	21
1973-74—Detroit Red Wings		NHL	74	24	54	78	10
1974-75—Detroit Red Wings (e-f)		NHL	80	47	74	121	14
1975-76—Los Angeles Kings		NHL	80	40	54	94	38
1976-77—Los Angeles Kings (a-f)		NHL	80	53	69	122	12
1977-78—Los Angeles Kings		NHL	70	36	43	79	37
1978-79—Los Angeles Kings (b)		NHL	80	59	71	130	30
1979-80—Los Angeles Kings (a-g-h)		NHL	80	53	84	*137	32
1980-81—Los Angeles Kings (b)		NHL	80	58	77	135	70
1981-82—Los Angeles Kings		NHL	78	50	67	117	50
1982-83—Los Angeles Kings		NHL	80	56	51	107	22
1983-84—Los Angeles Kings		NHL	66	39	53	92	28
1984-85—Los Angeles Kings		NHL	80	46	80	126	46
1985-86—Los Angeles Kings		NHL	80	36	58	94	42
NHL TOTALS			1163	665	934	1599	466

(c)—Won Eddie Powers Memorial Trophy (leading scorer award).
(d)—Drafted from St. Catharines Black Hawks by Detroit Red Wings in first round of 1971 amateur draft.
(e)—Signed by Los Angeles Kings as free agent after playing out option. Kings sent Terry Harper, Dan Maloney and second-round 1976 draft choice to Red Wings as compensation. L.A. received Bart Crashley from Detroit as part of deal, June, 1975.
(f)—Won Lady Byng Memorial Trophy.
(g)—Won Art Ross Trophy.
(h)—Selected NHL Player of the Year by THE SPORTING NEWS in poll of players.

ROBERT DIRK

Defense . . . 6'4" . . . 210 lbs. . . . Born, Regina, Sask., August 20, 1966 . . . Shoots left.

Year	Team	League	Games	G.	A.	Pts.	Pen.
1982-83—Regina Pats		WHL	1	0	0	0	0
1983-84—Regina Pats (c)		WHL	62	2	10	12	64
1984-85—Regina Pats		WHL	69	10	34	44	97
1985-86—Regina Pats (b)		WHL	72	19	60	79	140

(c)—June, 1984—Drafted as underage junior by St. Louis Blues in 1984 NHL entry draft. Fourth Blues pick, 53rd overall, third round.

BRIAN DOBBIN

Right Wing . . . 5'11" . . . 195 lbs. . . . Born, Petrolia, Ont., August 18, 1966 . . . Shoots right.

Year	Team	League	Games	G.	A.	Pts.	Pen.
1981-82—Mooretown Flags Jr. C		GLOHA	38	31	24	55	50
1982-83—Kingston Canadians		OHL	69	16	39	55	35
1983-84—London Knights (c)		OHL	70	30	40	70	70
1984-85—London Knights		OHL	53	42	57	99	63
1985-86—London Knights		OHL	59	38	55	93	113
1985-86—Hershey Bears		AHL	2	1	0	1	0

(c)—June, 1984—Drafted as underage junior by Philadelphia Flyers in 1984 NHL entry draft. Sixth Flyers pick, 100th overall, fifth round.

JIM HEROLD DOBSON

Right Wing and Center . . . 6'1" . . . 194 lbs. . . . Born, Winnipeg, Man., February 29, 1960 . . . Shoots right . . . (October, 1984)—Knee injury.

Year	Team	League	Games	G.	A.	Pts.	Pen.
1977-78—New Westminster Bruins		WCHL	12	4	2	6	121
1978-79—Portland Winter Hawks (c)		WHL	71	38	39	77	143
1979-80—Portland Winter Hawks (a)		WHL	72	66	68	134	181
1979-80—Minnesota North Stars		NHL	1	0	0	0	0
1980-81—Oklahoma City Stars		CHL	35	23	16	39	46
1980-81—Minnesota North Stars		NHL	1	0	0	0	0
1981-82—Nashville South Stars		CHL	29	19	13	32	29
1981-82—Minnesota North Stars (d)		NHL	6	0	0	0	4
1981-82—Colorado Rockies		NHL	3	0	0	0	2
1981-82—Fort Worth Texans		CHL	34	15	12	27	65
1982-83—Birmingham South Stars		CHL	80	36	37	73	100
1983-84—Quebec Nordiques		NHL	1	0	0	0	0
1983-84—Fredericton Express		AHL	75	33	44	77	74
1984-85—Fredericton Express (e)		AHL	21	8	10	18	52
1985-86—New Haven Nighthawks		AHL	29	5	6	11	12
NHL TOTALS			12	0	0	0	6

(c)—August, 1979—Drafted as underage junior by Minnesota North Stars in 1979 NHL entry draft. Fifth North Stars pick, 90th overall, fifth round.

(d)—December, 1981—Traded with Kevin Maxwell by Minnesota North Stars to Colorado Rockies for cash.

(e)—August, 1985—Signed by Philadelphia Flyers as a free agent.

BOBBY DOLLAS

Defense . . . 6'2" . . . 220 lbs. . . . Born, Montreal, Que., January 31, 1965 . . . Shoots left.

Year	Team	League	Games	G.	A.	Pts.	Pen.
1981-82—Lac St. Louis AAA		Que. Midget	44	9	31	40	138
1982-83—Laval Voisins (b-c-d)		QHL	63	16	45	61	144
1983-84—Laval Voisins		QHL	54	12	33	45	80
1983-84—Winnipeg Jets		NHL	1	0	0	0	0
1984-85—Winnipeg Jets		NHL	9	0	0	0	0
1984-85—Sherbrooke Canadiens		AHL	8	1	3	4	4
1985-86—Sherbrooke Canadiens		AHL	25	4	7	11	29
1985-86—Winnipeg Jets		NHL	46	0	5	5	66
NHL TOTALS			47	0	5	5	66

(c)—Won Raymond Lagace Trophy (Top rookie defenseman).

(d)—June, 1983—Drafted as underage junior by Winnipeg Jets in 1983 NHL entry draft. Second Jets pick, 14th overall, first round.

ANDREW DONAHUE

Center . . . 6'1" . . . 180 lbs. . . . Born, Boston, Mass., January 17, 1967 . . . Shoots right.

Year	Team	League	Games	G.	A.	Pts.	Pen.
1984-85—Belmont Hill H.S. (c)		Mass. H.S.	22	21	19	40	..
1985-86—Dartmouth College		ECAC	25	12	7	19	14

(c)—June, 1985—Drafted as underage junior by Toronto Maple Leafs in 1985 NHL entry draft. Eighth Maple Leafs pick, 148th overall, eighth round.

CLARK DONATELLI

Left Wing . . . 5'10" . . . 190 lbs. . . . Born, Providence, R.I., November 22, 1965 . . . Shoots left.

Year	Team	League	Games	G.	A.	Pts.	Pen.
1983-84—Stratford Collitons Jr. B (c)		MWOHA	38	41	49	90	46
1984-85—Boston University		H. East	40	17	18	35	46
1985-86—Boston University		H. East	43	28	34	62	30

(c)—June, 1984—Drafted by New York Rangers in 1984 NHL entry draft. Fourth Rangers pick, 98th overall, fifth round.

DAVID DONNELLY

Left Wing . . . 5'11" . . . 185 lbs. . . . Born, Edmonton, Alta., February 2, 1963 . . . Shoots left . . . Member of 1984 Canadian Olympic Team.

Year	Team	League	Games	G.	A.	Pts.	Pen.
1979-80—St. Albert Saints		AJHL	59	27	33	60	146
1980-81—St. Albert Saints (c)		AJHL	53	39	55	94	243
1981-82—University of North Dakota (d)		WCHA	38	10	15	25	38
1982-83—University of North Dakota		WCHA	34	18	16	34	106
1983-84—Canadian Olympic Team		Int'l	64	17	13	30	52
1983-84—Boston Bruins		NHL	16	3	4	7	2
1984-85—Boston Bruins		NHL	38	6	8	14	46

Year	Team	League	Games	G.	A.	Pts.	Pen.
1984-85—Hershey Bears		AHL	26	11	6	17	28
1985-86—Boston Bruins (e-f)		NHL	8	0	0	0	17
NHL TOTALS			62	9	12	21	65

(c)—June, 1981—Drafted as underage junior by Minnesota North Stars in 1981 NHL entry draft. Second North Stars pick, 27th overall, second round.

(d)—June, 1982—NHL rights traded by Minnesota North Stars along with Brad Palmer to Boston Bruins for future considerations (Boston passed over Brian Bellows in 1982 entry draft).

(e)—November, 1985—Assigned to Moncton of the AHL, refused to report and was suspended by Boston Bruins.

(f)—March, 1986—Traded by Boston Bruins to Detroit Red Wings for Dwight Foster.

GORDON DONNELLY

Defense . . . 6'2" . . . 202 lbs. . . . Born, Montreal, Que., April 5, 1962 . . . Shoots right.

Year	Team	League	Games	G.	A.	Pts.	Pen.
1978-79—Laval Nationals		QMJHL	71	1	14	15	79
1979-80—Laval Nationals		QMJHL	44	5	10	15	47
1979-80—Chicoutimi Sagueneens		QMJHL	24	1	5	6	64
1980-81—Sherbrooke Beavers (c)		QMJHL	67	15	23	38	252
1981-82—Sherbrooke Beavers (d)		QMJHL	60	8	41	49	250
1982-83—Salt Lake Golden Eagles (e)		CHL	67	3	12	15	222
1983-84—Fredericton Express		AHL	30	2	3	5	146
1983-84—Quebec Nordiques		NHL	38	0	5	5	60
1984-85—Fredericton Express		AHL	42	1	5	6	134
1984-85—Quebec Nordiques		NHL	22	0	0	0	33
1985-86—Fredericton Express		AHL	37	3	5	8	103
1985-86—Quebec Nordiques		NHL	36	2	2	4	85
NHL TOTALS			96	2	7	9	178

(c)—June, 1981—Drafted by St. Louis Blues in 1981 NHL entry draft. Third Blues pick, 62nd overall, third round.

(d)—Led QMJHL Playoffs with 106 penalty minutes.

(e)—August, 1983—Sent by St. Louis Blues along with Claude Julien to Quebec Nordiques as compensation for St. Louis signing coach Jacques Demers.

MIKE DONNELLY

Left Wing . . . 5'11" . . . 185 lbs. . . . Born, Livonia, Mich., October 10, 1963 . . . Shoots left.

Year	Team	League	Games	G.	A.	Pts.	Pen.
1982-83—Michigan State University		CCHA	24	7	13	20	8
1983-84—Michigan State University		CCHA	44	18	14	32	40
1984-85—Michigan State University		CCHA	44	26	21	47	48
1985-86—Michigan State Univeristy (c-d)		CCHA	44	59	38	97	65

(c)—Named to First-Team (West) All-America.

(d)—August, 1986—Signed by New York Rangers as a free agent.

ANDRE HECTOR DORE

Defense . . . 6'2" . . . 200 lbs. . . . Born, Montreal, Que., February 11, 1958 . . . Shoots right.

Year	Team	League	Games	G.	A.	Pts.	Pen.
1975-76—Hull Festivals		QJHL	59	4	11	15	67
1976-77—Hull Olympics		QJHL	72	9	42	51	178
1977-78—Hull Olympics		QJHL	15	3	9	12	22
1977-78—Trois-Rivieres Draveurs		QJHL	27	2	14	16	61
1977-78—Quebec Remparts (c)		QJHL	32	6	17	23	51
1978-79—New York Rangers		NHL	2	0	0	0	0
1978-79—New Haven Nighthawks		AHL	71	6	23	29	134
1979-80—New Haven Nighthawks		AHL	63	9	21	30	99
1979-80—New York Rangers		NHL	2	0	0	0	0
1980-81—New York Rangers		NHL	15	1	3	4	15
1980-81—New Haven Nighthawks		AHL	58	8	41	49	105
1981-82—Springfield Indians		AHL	23	3	8	11	20
1981-82—New York Rangers		NHL	56	4	16	20	64
1982-83—New York Rangers (d)		NHL	39	3	12	15	39
1982-83—St. Louis Blues		NHL	38	2	15	17	25
1983-84—St. Louis Blues (e)		NHL	55	3	12	15	58
1983-84—Quebec Nordiques		NHL	25	1	16	17	25
1984-85—New York Rangers (f)		NHL	25	0	7	7	35
1984-85—New Haven Nighthawks		AHL	39	3	22	25	48
1985-86—Hershey Bears (g)		AHL	65	10	18	28	124
NHL TOTALS			257	14	81	95	261

(c)—Drafted from Quebec Remparts by New York Rangers in fourth round of 1978 amateur draft.

(d)—January, 1983—Traded by New York Rangers to St. Louis Blues for Vaclav Nedomansky and Glen Hanlon.
(e)—February, 1984—Traded by St. Louis Blues to Quebec Nordiques for Dave Pichette.
(f)—October, 1984—Selected by New York Rangers in 1984 NHL waiver draft.
(g)—October, 1985—Assigned with Pierre Larouche by New York Rangers to Hershey Bears as compensation to the Philadelphia Flyers for the Rangers' signing of coach Ted Sator.

DAN DORION
Right Wing . . . 5'8" . . . 169 lbs. . . . Born, New York, N.Y., March 2, 1963 . . . Shoots right.

Year	Team	League	Games	G.	A.	Pts.	Pen.
1981-82—Austin Mavericks (c)		USHL	50	52	44	96	....
1982-83—U. of Western Michigan		CCHA	34	11	20	31	23
1983-84—U. of Western Michigan		CCHA	42	41	50	91	42
1984-85—U. of Western Michigan		CCHA	39	21	46	67	28
1985-86—U. of Western Michigan (d)		CCHA	42	42	62	104	48
1985-86—New Jersey Devils		NHL	3	1	1	2	0
NHL TOTALS			3	1	1	2	0

(c)—June, 1982—Drafted by New Jersey Devils in 1982 NHL entry draft. Thirteenth Devils pick, 232nd overall, 12th round.
(d)—Named first-team (West) All-America.

GREG DORNBACH
Center . . . 5'11" . . . 175 lbs. . . . Born, Huntington, W. Vir., November 1, 1966 . . . Shoots left.

Year	Team	League	Games	G.	A.	Pts.	Pen.
1984-85—Univ. of Miami (Ohio) (c)		CCHA	36	12	24	36	28
1985-86—Univ. of Miami (Ohio)		CCHA	35	13	18	31	42

(c)—June, 1985—Drafted by Hartford Whalers in 1985 NHL entry draft. Seventh Whalers pick, 173rd overall, ninth round.

PETER DOURIS
Center . . . 6' . . . 195 lbs. . . . Born, Toronto, Ont., February 19, 1966 . . . Shoots right.

Year	Team	League	Games	G.	A.	Pts.	Pen.
1983-84—Univ. of New Hampshire (c)		ECAC	38	19	15	34	14
1984-85—Univ. of New Hampshire		H. East	42	27	24	51	34
1985-86—Team Canada		Int'l	33	16	7	23	18
1985-86—Winnipeg Jets		NHL	11	0	0	0	0
NHL TOTALS			11	0	0	0	0

(c)—June, 1984—Drafted by Winnipeg Jets in 1984 NHL entry draft. First Jets pick, 30th overall, second round.

SHANE DOYLE
Defense . . . 6'2" . . . 195 lbs. . . . Born, Lindsay, Ont., April 26, 1967 . . . Shoots left . . . Brother of Rob Doyle (Colorado College).

Year	Team	League	Games	G.	A.	Pts.	Pen.
1983-84—Newmarket Flyers		OHA	37	6	15	21	337
1984-85—Belleville Bulls (c)		OHL	59	2	26	28	129
1985-86—Belleville Bulls (d)		OHL	13	1	5	6	41
1985-86—Hamilton Steelhawks (e)		OHL	10	0	7	7	24
1985-86—Cornwall Royals		OHL	32	3	16	19	139

(c)—June, 1985—Drafted as underage junior by Vancouver Canucks in 1985 NHL entry draft. Third Canucks pick, 46th overall, third round.
(d)—November, 1985—Traded with John Purves and Brian Hood by Belleville Bulls to Hamilton Steelhawks for Jason Lafreniere, Lawrence Hinch and Peter Choma.
(e)—January, 1986—Traded by Hamilton Steelhawks to Cornwall Royals for Brad Hyatt and Brent Thompson.

RON DREGER
Left Wing . . . 6' . . . 190 lbs. . . . Born, St. Boniface, Man., January 19, 1964 . . . Shoots left.

Year	Team	League	Games	G.	A.	Pts.	Pen.
1981-82—Saskatoon Blades (c)		WHL	59	18	15	33	41
1982-83—Saskatoon Blades		WHL	66	27	22	49	65
1983-84—Saskatoon Blades		WHL	71	29	37	66	56
1984-85—Saskatoon Blades		WHL	62	54	40	94	56
1985-86—Indianapolis Checkers		IHL	8	0	1	1	2

(c)—June, 1982—Drafted as underage junior by Toronto Maple Leafs in 1982 NHL entry draft. Eighth Maple Leafs pick, 108th overall, sixth round.

STEVE DRISCOLL

Left Wing . . . 5'9" . . . 175 lbs. . . . Born, Montreal, Que., June 7, 1964 . . . Shoots left.

Year	Team	League	Games	G.	A.	Pts.	Pen.
1980-81—Belleville Bulls		OPJHL	37	4	16	20	107
1981-82—Cornwall Royals (c)		OHL	65	24	50	74	28
1982-83—Cornwall Royals (b)		OHL	64	49	77	126	34
1983-84—Cornwall Royals		OHL	63	38	51	89	13
1983-84—Fredericton Express		AHL	2	0	0	0	0
1984-85—Fredericton Express		AHL	33	3	7	10	8
1984-85—St. Catharines Saints		AHL	18	4	3	7	4
1985-86—Kalamazoo Wings (d)		IHL	11	3	4	7	4
1985-86—Toledo Goaldiggers		IHL	68	26	28	54	8

(c)—June, 1982—Drafted as underage junior by Vancouver Canucks in 1982 NHL entry draft. Ninth Canucks pick, 221st overall, 11th round.

(d)—November, 1985—Traded by Kalamazoo Wings to Toledo Goaldiggers for Claude Noel.

BRUCE DRIVER

Defense . . . 6' . . . 174 lbs. . . . Born, Toronto, Ont., April 29, 1962 . . . Shoots left . . . Member of 1984 Canadian Olympic Team . . . (February, 1985)—Surgery to left knee . . . (April 2, 1985)—Reinjured knee when struck by stick in game at St. Louis . . . (March 9, 1986)—Bruised shoulder in game at Buffalo.

Year	Team	League	Games	G.	A.	Pts.	Pen.
1979-80—Royal York Royals		OPJHL	43	13	57	70	102
1980-81—University of Wisconsin (c)		WCHA	42	5	15	20	42
1981-82—University of Wisconsin (a-d)		WCHA	46	7	37	44	84
1982-83—University of Wisconsin (b)		WCHA	39	16	34	50	50
1983-84—Canadian Olympic Team		Int'l	61	11	17	28	44
1983-84—Maine Mariners		AHL	12	2	6	8	15
1983-84—New Jersey Devils		NHL	4	0	2	2	0
1984-85—New Jersey Devils		NHL	67	9	23	32	36
1985-86—Maine Mariners		AHL	15	4	7	11	16
1985-86—New Jersey Devils		NHL	40	3	15	18	32
NHL TOTALS			111	12	40	52	68

(c)—June, 1981—Drafted as underage junior by Colorado Rockies in 1981 NHL entry draft. Sixth Rockies pick, 108th overall, sixth round.

(d)—Named to All-America Team (West).

JOHN DRUCE

Right Wing . . . 6'1" . . . 190 lbs. . . . Born, Peterborough, Ont., February 23, 1966 . . . Shoots right . . . (October, 1983)—Broken collarbone . . . (December, 1984)—Partially torn ligaments in ankle . . . (October, 1985)—Torn thumb ligaments.

Year	Team	League	Games	G.	A.	Pts.	Pen.
1983-84—Peterborough Jr. B		OHA	40	15	18	33	69
1984-85—Peterborough Petes (c)		OHL	54	12	14	26	90
1985-86—Peterborough Petes		OHL	49	22	24	46	84

(c)—June, 1985—Drafted by Washington Capitals in 1985 NHL entry draft. Second Capitals pick, 40th overall, second round.

STAN DRULIA

Right Wing . . . 5'10" . . . 180 lbs. . . . Born, Elmira, N.Y., January 5, 1968 . . . Shoots right.

Year	Team	League	Games	G.	A.	Pts.	Pen.
1984-85—Belleville Bulls		OHL	63	24	31	55	33
1985-86—Belleville Bulls (c)		OHL	66	43	37	80	73

(c)—June, 1986—Drafted as underage junior by Pittsburgh Penguins in 1986 NHL entry draft. Eleventh Penguins pick, 214th overall, 11th round.

GAETAN DUCHESNE

Left Wing . . . 5'11" . . . 195 lbs. . . . Born, Quebec City, Que., July 11, 1962 . . . Shoots left . . . (December 30, 1981)—Bruised right ankle in game at Pittsburgh . . . (October 11, 1984)—Broke index finger of left hand on a shot in game at Philadelphia.

Year	Team	League	Games	G.	A.	Pts.	Pen.
1979-80—Quebec Remparts		QJHL	46	9	28	37	22
1980-81—Quebec Remparts (c)		QJHL	72	27	45	72	63
1981-82—Washington Capitals		NHL	74	9	14	23	46

Year	Team	League	Games	G.	A.	Pts.	Pen.
1982-83—Hershey Bears		AHL	1	1	0	1	0
1982-83—Washington Capitals		NHL	77	18	19	37	52
1983-84—Washington Capitals		NHL	79	17	19	36	29
1984-85—Washington Capitals		NHL	67	15	23	38	32
1985-86—Washington Capitals		NHL	80	11	28	39	39
NHL TOTALS			377	70	103	173	198

(c)—June, 1981—Drafted by Washington Capitals in 1981 NHL entry draft. Eighth Capitals pick, 152nd overall, eighth round.

TOBY DUCOLON

Left Wing . . . 6' . . . 195 lbs. . . . Born, St. Albans, Vt., June 18, 1966 . . . Shoots right.

Year	Team	League	Games	G.	A.	Pts.	Pen.
1983-84—Bellows Free Academy (c)		Ver. H.S.	22	38	26	64	36
1984-85—University of Vermont		ECAC	24	7	4	11	14
1985-86—University of Vermont		ECAC	30	10	6	16	48

(c)—June, 1984—Drafted by St. Louis Blues in 1984 NHL entry draft. Third Blues pick, 50th overall, third round.

LUC DUFOUR

Left Wing . . . 6' . . . 180 lbs. . . . Born, Chicoutimi, Que., February 13, 1963 . . . Shoots left . . . Brother-in-law of Alain Cote . . . (November, 1982)—Fractured finger on right hand.

Year	Team	League	Games	G.	A.	Pts.	Pen.
1980-81—Chicoutimi Sagueneens (c)		QMJHL	69	43	53	96	89
1981-82—Chicoutimi Sagueneens (a)		QMJHL	62	55	60	115	94
1982-83—Boston Bruins		NHL	73	14	11	25	107
1983-84—Boston Bruins		NHL	41	6	4	10	47
1983-84—Hershey Bears		AHL	37	9	19	28	51
1984-85—Hershey Bears (d)		AHL	6	1	1	2	10
1984-85—Fredericton Express		AHL	12	2	0	2	13
1984-85—Quebec Nordiques (e)		NHL	30	2	3	5	27
1984-85—St. Louis Blues		NHL	23	1	3	4	18
1985-86—Maine Mariners (f)		AHL	75	15	20	35	57
NHL TOTALS			167	23	21	44	199

(c)—June, 1981—Drafted as underage junior by Boston Bruins in 1981 NHL entry draft. Second Bruins pick, 35th overall, second round.
(d)—October, 1984—Traded with fourth round 1985 draft pick (Peter Massey) by Boston Bruins to Quebec Nordiques for Louis Sleigher.
(e)—February, 1985—Traded by Quebec Nordiques to St. Louis Blues for Alain Lemieux.
(f)—October, 1985—Signed by Maine Mariners as a free agent.

DONALD DUFRESNE

Defense . . . 6' . . . 187 lbs. . . . Born, Quebec City, Que., April 10, 1967 . . . Shoots left . . . (November, 1984)—Pneumonia.

Year	Team	League	Games	G.	A.	Pts.	Pen.
1983-84—Trois-Rivieres Draveurs		QHL	67	7	12	19	97
1984-85—Trois-Rivieres Draveurs (c)		QHL	65	5	30	35	112
1985-86—Trois-Rivieres Draveurs (b)		QHL	63	8	32	40	160

(c)—June, 1985—Drafted as underage junior by Montreal Canadiens in 1985 entry draft. Eighth Canadiens pick, 117th overall, sixth round.

KEN DUGGAN

Defense . . . 6'3" . . . 210 lbs. . . . Born, Toronto, Ont., February 21, 1963 . . . Shoots left.

Year	Team	League	Games	G.	A.	Pts.	Pen.
1985-86—University of Toronto (c)		CWUAA	44	12	32	44	106

(c)—July, 1986—Signed by New York Rangers as a free agent.

RON DUGUAY

Right Wing . . . 6'2" . . . 210 lbs. . . . Born, Sudbury, Ont., July 6, 1957 . . . Shoots right . . . Missed part of 1977-78 season with strained groin . . . (October 30, 1980)—Lacerated tendons in right leg . . . (January, 1982)—Separated left shoulder . . . (February, 1983)—Pulled stomach muscle.

Year	Team	League	Games	G.	A.	Pts.	Pen.
1973-74—Sudbury Wolves		Jr."A"OHA	59	20	20	40	73
1974-75—Sudbury Wolves		Jr."A"OHA	64	26	52	78	43
1975-76—Sudbury Wolves		Jr."A"OHA	61	42	92	134	101
1976-77—Sudbury Wolves (c)		Jr."A"OHA	61	43	66	109	109

Year	Team	League	Games	G.	A.	Pts.	Pen.
1977-78—New York Rangers		NHL	71	20	20	40	43
1978-79—New York Rangers		NHL	79	27	36	63	35
1979-80—New York Rangers		NHL	73	28	22	50	37
1980-81—New York Rangers		NHL	50	17	21	38	83
1981-82—New York Rangers		NHL	72	40	36	76	82
1982-83—New York Rangers (d)		NHL	72	19	25	44	58
1983-84—Detroit Red Wings		NHL	80	33	47	80	34
1984-85—Detroit Red Wings		NHL	80	38	51	89	51
1985-86—Detroit Red Wings (e)		NHL	67	19	29	48	26
1985-86—Pittsburgh Penguins		NHL	13	6	7	13	6
NHL TOTALS			657	247	294	541	455

(c)—Drafted from Sudbury Wolves by New York Rangers in first round of 1977 amateur draft.

(d)—June, 1983—Traded with Eddie Johnstone and Ed Mio by New York Rangers to Detroit Red Wings for Mark Osborne, Mike Blaisdell and Willie Huber.

(e)—March, 1986—Traded by Detroit Red Wings to Pittsburgh Penguins for Doug Shedden.

CLAUDE DUMAS

Center . . . 6' . . . 161 lbs. . . . Born, Thetford Mines, Que., January 10, 1967 . . . (February, 1985)—Sprained ankle.

Year	Team	League	Games	G.	A.	Pts.	Pen.
1983-84—Magog Cantoniers		Que. Midget	42	22	45	67	44
1984-85—Granby Bisons (c)		QHL	62	19	37	56	34
1985-86—Granby Bisons		QHL	64	31	58	89	78
1985-86—Binghamton Whalers		AHL	7	2	2	4	0

(c)—June, 1985—Drafted as underage junior by Washington Capitals in 1985 NHL entry draft. Sixth Capitals pick, 103rd overall, fifth round.

DALE DUNBAR

Defense . . . 6'1" . . . 200 lbs. . . . Born, Winthrop, Mass., October 14, 1961 . . . Shoots left . . . (September 22, 1985)—Concussion when struck by a deflected puck in pre-season game and missed three weeks.

Year	Team	League	Games	G.	A.	Pts.	Pen.
1981-82—Boston University		ECAC	6	0	0	0	0
1982-83—Boston University		ECAC	21	1	7	8	32
1983-84—Boston University		ECAC	34	0	15	15	49
1984-85—Boston University (c)		H. East	39	2	19	21	62
1985-86—Vancouver Canucks		NHL	1	0	0	0	2
1985-86—Fredericton Express		AHL	32	2	10	12	26
NHL TOTALS			1	0	0	0	2

(c)—May, 1985—Signed by Vancouver Canucks as a free agent.

CRAIG DUNCANSON

Left Wing . . . 6' . . . 190 lbs. . . . Born, Sudbury, Ont., March 17, 1967 . . . Shoots left . . . (September, 1984)—Torn knee ligaments.

Year	Team	League	Games	G.	A.	Pts.	Pen.
1982-83—St. Michaels Jr. B		OHA	32	14	19	33	68
1983-84—Sudbury Wolves		OHL	62	38	38	76	178
1984-85—Sudbury Wolves (c)		OHL	53	35	28	63	129
1985-86—Sudbury Wolves		OHL	21	12	17	29	55
1985-86—Cornwall Royals		OHL	40	31	50	81	135
1985-86—Los Angeles Kings		NHL	2	0	1	1	0
1985-86—New Haven Nighthawks (d)		AHL	..	..	..	..	..
NHL TOTALS			2	0	1	1	0

(c)—June, 1985—Drafted as underage junior by Los Angeles Kings in 1985 NHL entry draft. First Kings pick, ninth overall, first round.

(d)—No regular season record. Played two playoff games.

ROCKY DUNDAS

Right Wing . . . 6' . . . 195 lbs. . . . Born, Edmonton, Alta., January 30, 1967 . . . Shoots right . . . Brother of R.J. Dundas . . . Son of Ron Dundas (former CFL player).

Year	Team	League	Games	G.	A.	Pts.	Pen.
1983-84—Kelowna Wings		WHL	72	15	24	39	57
1984-85—Kelowna Wings (c)		WHL	71	32	44	76	117
1985-86—Spokane Chiefs		WHL	71	31	70	101	160

(c)—June, 1985—Drafted as underage junior by Montreal Canadiens in 1985 NHL entry draft. Fourth Canadiens pick, 47th overall, third round.

RICHARD DUNN

Defense . . . 6' . . . 192 lbs. . . . Born, Canton, Mass., May 12, 1957 . . . Shoots left . . . (December, 1981)—Shoulder injury.

Year	Team	League	Games	G.	A.	Pts.	Pen.
1975-76—Kingston Canadians		Jr."A"OHA	61	7	18	25	62
1976-77—Windsor Spitfires (c)		Jr."A"OHA	65	5	21	26	98
1977-78—Hershey Bears		AHL	54	7	22	29	17
1977-78—Buffalo Sabres		NHL	25	0	3	3	16
1978-79—Buffalo Sabres		NHL	24	0	3	3	14
1978-79—Hershey Bears		AHL	34	5	18	23	10
1979-80—Buffalo Sabres		NHL	80	7	31	38	61
1980-81—Buffalo Sabres		NHL	79	7	42	49	34
1981-82—Buffalo Sabres (d)		NHL	72	7	19	26	73
1982-83—Calgary Flames (e)		NHL	80	3	11	14	47
1983-84—Hartford Whalers		NHL	63	5	20	25	30
1984-85—Hartford Whalers		NHL	13	1	4	5	2
1984-85—Binghamton Whalers (a-f-g)		AHL	64	9	39	48	43
1985-86—Buffalo Sabres		NHL	29	4	5	9	25
1985-86—Rochester Americans		AHL	34	6	17	23	12
NHL TOTALS			465	34	138	172	300

(c)—September, 1977—Signed by Buffalo Sabres as free agent.
(d)—June, 1982—Traded by Buffalo Sabres with goaltender Don Edwards and a second-round choice in 1982 NHL entry draft to Calgary Flames for Calgary's first and second round draft choices in 1982 and their second round pick in 1983 plus the option to switch first-round picks in '83.
(e)—July, 1983—Traded by Calgary Flames with Joel Quenneville to Hartford Whalers for Mickey Volcan.
(f)—Won Eddie Shore Plaque (Top AHL defenseman).
(g)—August, 1985—Signed by Buffalo Sabres as a free agent.

CHRISTIAN DuPERRON

Defense . . . 6'1" . . . 185 lbs. . . . Born, Montreal, Que., January 29, 1965 . . . Shoots right . . . Also plays Right Wing.

Year	Team	League	Games	G.	A.	Pts.	Pen.
1982-83—Bourassa AAA		Que. Midget	31	4	2	6	63
1982-83—Chicoutimi Sagueneens (c)		QHL	60	1	5	6	20
1983-84—Chicoutimi Sagueneens (d)		QHL	62	3	13	16	115
1984-85—Chicoutimi Sagueneens		QHL	65	3	20	23	198
1985-86—Chicoutimi Sagueneens		QHL	70	0	26	26	149

(c)—June, 1983—Drafted as underage junior by Hartford Whalers in 1983 NHL entry draft. Ninth Whalers pick, 143rd overall, eighth round.
(d)—June, 1984—Released by Hartford Whalers.

JEROME DUPONT

Defense . . . 6'3" . . . 190 lbs. . . . Born, Ottawa, Ont., February 21, 1962 . . . Shoots left.

Year	Team	League	Games	G.	A.	Pts.	Pen.
1978-79—Toronto Marlboros		OMJHL	68	5	21	26	49
1979-80—Toronto Marlboros (c)		OMJHL	67	7	37	44	88
1980-81—Toronto Marlboros		OHL	67	6	38	44	116
1981-82—Toronto Marlboros		OHL	7	0	8	8	18
1981-82—Chicago Black Hawks		NHL	34	0	4	4	51
1982-83—Chicago Black Hawks		NHL	1	0	0	0	0
1982-83—Springfield Indians		AHL	78	12	22	34	114
1983-84—Springfield Indians		AHL	12	2	3	5	65
1983-84—Chicago Black Hawks		NHL	36	2	2	4	116
1984-85—Chicago Black Hawks		NHL	55	3	10	13	105
1985-86—Chicago Black Hawks		NHL	75	2	13	15	173
NHL TOTALS			201	7	29	36	445

(c)—June, 1980—Drafted as underage junior by Chicago Black Hawks in 1980 NHL entry draft. Second Black Hawks pick, 15th overall, first round.

BRIAN DURAND

Center . . . 6'2" . . . 190 lbs. . . . Born, Duluth, Minn., August 5, 1965 . . . Shoots right.

Year	Team	League	Games	G.	A.	Pts.	Pen.
1982-83—Cloquet H.S. (c)		Minn. H.S.	23	34	33	67	....
1983-84—University of Minnesota/Duluth		WCHA	24	2	5	7	4
1984-85—University of Minnesota/Duluth		WCHA	25	1	1	2	2
1985-86—University of Minnesota/Duluth		WCHA	11	1	0	1	6

(c)—June, 1983—Drafted by Minnesota North Stars in 1983 NHL entry draft. Fifth North Stars pick, 76th overall, fourth round.

HAROLD DUVALL

Left Wing . . . 5'11" . . . 185 lbs. . . . Born, Ogdenburg, N.Y., April 21, 1964 . . . Shoots left.

Year	Team	League	Games	G.	A.	Pts.	Pen.
1982-83	Belmont Hills H.S. (c)	Mass. H.S.	20	25	18	43	....
1983-84	Colgate University	ECAC	26	1	9	10	37
1984-85	Colgate University	ECAC	27	8	15	23	46
1985-86	Colgate University	ECAC	26	8	7	15	24

(c)—June, 1983—Drafted by Philadelphia Flyers in 1983 NHL entry draft. Eleventh Flyers pick, 241st overall, 12th round.

STEVE DYKSTRA

Defense . . . 6'2" . . . 190 lbs. . . . Born, Edmonton, Alta., February 3, 1962 . . . Shoots left . . . (February 19, 1986)—Injured shoulder at Hartford.

Year	Team	League	Games	G.	A.	Pts.	Pen.
1981-82	Seattle Flyers	WHL	57	8	26	34	139
1982-83	Rochester Americans (c)	AHL	70	2	16	18	100
1983-84	Rochester Americans	AHL	64	3	19	22	141
1984-85	Rochester Americans	AHL	51	9	23	32	113
1984-85	Flint Generals	IHL	15	1	7	8	36
1985-86	Buffalo Sabres	NHL	65	4	21	25	108
	NHL TOTALS		65	4	21	25	108

(c)—October, 1982—Signed by Buffalo Sabres as a free agent.

JOHN DZIKOWSKI

Left Wing . . . 6'3" . . . 190 lbs. . . . Born, Portage La Prairie, Man., January 28, 1966 . . . Shoots left.

Year	Team	League	Games	G.	A.	Pts.	Pen.
1983-84	Brandon Wheat Kings (c)	WHL	47	12	11	23	99
1984-85	Brandon Wheat Kings	WHL	59	38	35	73	58
1985-86	Brandon Wheat Kings (d)	WHL	44	35	20	55	72
1985-86	Seattle Thunderbirds	WHL	25	18	15	33	38

(c)—June, 1984—Drafted as underage junior by Philadelphia Flyers in 1984 entry draft. Seventh Flyers pick, 121st overall, sixth round.

(d)—February, 1986—Traded by Brandon Wheat Kings to Seattle Thunderbirds for Brian McFarlane and Kirk Phare.

MICHAEL EAGLES

Center . . . 5'10" . . . 180 lbs. . . . Born, Susex, N.B., March 7, 1963 . . . Shoots left . . . (October, 1984)—Broken hand . . . (February 21, 1986)—Injured ribs at Minnesota.

Year	Team	League	Games	G.	A.	Pts.	Pen.
1979-80	Melville	SJHL	55	46	30	76	77
1980-81	Kitchener Rangers (c)	OHL	56	11	27	38	64
1981-82	Kitchener Rangers	OHL	62	26	40	66	148
1982-83	Kitchener Rangers	OHL	58	26	36	62	133
1982-83	Quebec Nordiques	NHL	2	0	0	0	2
1983-84	Fredericton Express	AHL	68	13	29	42	85
1984-85	Fredericton Express	AHL	36	4	20	24	80
1985-86	Quebec Nordiques	NHL	73	11	12	23	49
	NHL TOTALS		75	11	12	23	51

(c)—June, 1981—Drafted as underage junior by Quebec Nordiques in 1981 NHL entry draft. Fifth Nordiques pick, 116th overall, sixth round.

BRUCE EAKIN

Center . . . 5'11" . . . 185 lbs. . . . Born, Winnipeg, Man., September 28, 1962 . . . Shoots left . . . Set WHL record for regular season assists (125), 1981-82.

Year	Team	League	Games	G.	A.	Pts.	Pen.
1979-80	St. James Canadians	MJHL	48	42	62	104	76
1980-81	Saskatoon Blades (c)	WHL	52	18	46	64	54
1981-82	Saskatoon Blades (a)	WHL	66	42	*125	167	120
1981-82	Calgary Flames	NHL	1	0	0	0	0
1981-82	Oklahoma City Stars	CHL	1	0	3	3	0
1982-83	Colorado Flames	CHL	73	24	46	70	45
1983-84	Colorado Flames (b)	CHL	67	33	69	102	18
1983-84	Calgary Flames	NHL	7	2	1	3	4
1984-85	Calgary Flames	NHL	1	0	0	0	0
1984-85	Moncton Golden Flames	AHL	78	35	48	83	60
1985-86	Detroit Red Wings (d)	NHL	4	0	1	1	0

Year	Team	League	Games	G.	A.	Pts.	Pen.
1985-86—Adirondack Red Wings (e)		AHL	25	8	10	18	23
1985-86—Nova Scotia Oilers		AHL	14	6	12	18	12
NHL TOTALS			13	2	2	4	4

(c)—June, 1981—Drafted by Calgary Flames in 1981 NHL entry draft. Ninth Flames pick, 204th overall, 10th round.

(d)—August, 1985—Signed by Detroit Red Wings as a free agent.

(e)—December, 1985—Traded by Detroit Red Wings to Edmonton Oilers for Billy Carroll.

DALLAS EAKINS

Defense . . . 6'1" . . . 180 lbs. . . . Born, Dade City, Fla., January 20, 1967 . . . Shoots left.

Year	Team	League	Games	G.	A.	Pts.	Pen.
1983-84—Peterborough Midgets		OHA	29	7	20	27	67
1984-85—Peterborough Petes (c)		OHL	48	0	8	8	96
1985-86—Peterborough Petes		OHL	60	6	16	22	134

(c)—June, 1985—Drafted as underage junior by Washington Capitals in 1985 NHL entry draft. Eleventh Capitals pick, 208th overall, 10th round.

JEFF EATOUGH

Right Wing . . . 5'9" . . . 168 lbs. . . . Born, Cornwall, Ont., June 2, 1963 . . . Shoots right.

Year	Team	League	Games	G.	A.	Pts.	Pen.
1979-80—Niagara Falls Flyers		OHL	6	0	1	1	4
1980-81—Cornwall Royals (c)		QMJHL	68	30	42	72	142
1981-82—Cornwall Royals		OHL	66	53	37	90	180
1981-82—Buffalo Sabres		NHL	1	0	0	0	0
1982-83—Cornwall Royals (d)		OHL	9	5	3	8	18
1982-83—North Bay Centennials		OHL	50	25	24	49	73
1983-84—Rochester Americans		AHL	24	1	5	6	5
1983-84—Flint Generals		IHL	5	4	1	5	6
1984-85—Flint Generals		IHL	4	0	1	1	0
1984-85—Pinebridge Bucks (e)		ACHL	12	4	8	12	31
1984-85—Mohawk Valley Stars		ACHL	42	27	33	60	37
1985-86—Flint Spirit		IHL	4	1	0	1	2
1985-86—Mohawk Valley Comets		ACHL	27	18	19	37	43
NHL TOTALS			1	0	0	0	0

(c)—June, 1981—Drafted as underage junior by Buffalo Sabres in 1981 NHL entry draft. Fifth Sabres pick, 80th overall, fourth round.

(d)—October, 1982—Traded by Cornwall Royals to North Bay Centennials for Tom Thornbury.

(e)—December, 1984—Traded by Pinebridge Bucks to Mohawk Valley Stars for Bill Grum.

MICHAEL GORDON EAVES

Center . . . 5'10" . . . 180 lbs. . . . Born, Denver, Colo., June 10, 1956 . . . Shoots right . . . Holds school records for points in season and career . . . (October, 1980)—Knee injury . . . (February 12, 1981)—Hip injury . . . (February 23, 1981)—Suffered concussion, one of three concussions of the season . . . Brother of Murray Eaves . . . (October, 1981)—Back Spasms . . . (December 26, 1981)—Injured ribs . . . (January, 1984)—Broken foot . . . (October, 1984)—Bruised shoulder . . . (September 21, 1985)—Suffered concussion at Quebec. It marked Eaves 10th concussion in the last six years. In October he announced his retirement.

Year	Team	League	Games	G.	A.	Pts.	Pen.
1973-74—Nepean Raiders	Cent. "A" Jr. OHA		....	54	48	*102	....
1974-75—University of Wisconsin		WCHA	38	17	37	54	12
1975-76—University of Wisconsin (c)		WCHA	34	18	25	43	22
1975-76—U. S. National Team			....	...	....	....	....
1976-77—University of Wisconsin (b-d)		WCHA	45	28	53	81	18
1977-78—University of Wisconsin (a-d)		WCHA	43	31	58	89	16
1978-79—Minnesota North Stars		NHL	3	0	0	0	0
1978-79—Oklahoma City Stars (b-e)		CHL	68	26	61	87	21
1979-80—Oklahoma City Stars		CHL	12	9	8	17	2
1979-80—Minnesota North Stars		NHL	56	18	28	46	11
1980-81—Minnesota North Stars		NHL	48	10	24	34	18
1981-82—Minnesota North Stars		NHL	25	11	10	21	0
1982-83—Minnesota North Stars (f)		NHL	75	16	16	32	21
1983-84—Calgary Flames		NHL	61	14	36	50	20
1984-85—Calgary Flames		NHL	56	14	29	43	10
1985-86—Calgary Flames (g-h)		NHL	....	...	....	....	....
NHL TOTALS			324	83	143	226	80

(c)—Drafted from University of Wisconsin by St. Louis Blues in seventh round of 1976 amateur draft.

(d)—Named to first-team (Western) All-America.

(e)—Won Ken McKenzie Trophy (CHL top rookie).
(f)—June, 1983—Traded by Minnesota North Stars with Keith Hanson to Calgary Flames for Steve Christoff and a second round pick in the 1983 NHL entry draft (Frantisek Musil).
(g)—October, 1985—Announced retirement.
(h)—No regular season record. Played eight playoff games.

MURRAY EAVES

Center . . . 5'10" . . . 185 lbs. . . . Born, Calgary, Alta., May 10, 1960 . . . Shoots right . . . Brother of Mike Eaves . . . (September, 1984)—Sprained ankle in training camp.

Year	Team	League	Games	G.	A.	Pts.	Pen.
1977-78—Windsor Spitfires		OMJHL	3	0	0	0	0
1978-79—University of Michigan		WCHA	23	12	22	34	14
1979-80—University of Michigan (a-c)		WCHA	33	36	49	85	34
1980-81—Winnipeg Jets		NHL	12	1	2	3	5
1980-81—Tulsa Oilers		CHL	59	24	34	58	59
1981-82—Tulsa Oilers		CHL	68	30	49	79	33
1981-82—Winnipeg Jets		NHL	2	0	0	0	0
1982-83—Winnipeg Jets		NHL	26	2	7	9	2
1982-83—Sherbrooke Jets		AHL	40	25	34	59	16
1983-84—Winnipeg Jets		NHL	2	0	0	0	0
1983-84—Sherbrooke Jets (a)		AHL	78	47	68	115	40
1984-85—Winnipeg Jets		NHL	3	0	3	3	0
1984-85—Sherbrooke Jets		AHL	47	26	42	68	28
1985-86—Sherbrooke Canadiens		AHL	68	22	51	73	26
1985-86—Winnipeg Jets (d)		NHL	4	1	0	1	0
NHL TOTALS			49	4	12	16	7

(c)—June, 1980—Drafted by Winnipeg Jets in 1980 NHL entry draft. Third Jets pick, 44th overall, third round.
(d)—July, 1986—Traded by Winnipeg Jets to Edmonton Oilers for future considerations.

PER-ERIK (Pelle) EKLUND

Center . . . 5'10" . . . 170 lbs. . . . Born, Stockholm, Sweden, March 22, 1963 . . . Shoots left . . . (October, 1985)—Named Sweden's Athlete of the Year for 1984. He was the second leading scorer in the elite league.

Year	Team	League	Games	G.	A.	Pts.	Pen.
1983-84—Stockholm AIK (c)		Sweden	35	9	18	27	24
1984-85—Stockholm AIK		Sweden	35	16	33	49	10
1985-86—Philadelphia Flyers		NHL	70	15	51	66	12
NHL TOTALS			70	15	51	66	12

(c)—June, 1983—Drafted by Philadelphia Flyers in 1983 NHL entry draft. Seventh Flyers pick, 161st overall, eighth round.

DAVE ELLETT

Defense . . . 6'1" . . . 200 lbs. . . . Born, Cleveland, O., March 30, 1964 . . . Shoots left . . . Son of Dave Ellett Sr., who played for Cleveland Barons in AHL.

Year	Team	League	Games	G.	A.	Pts.	Pen.
1981-82—Ottawa Senators		CJOHL	50	9	35	44	..
1982-83—Bowling Green Univ. (c)		CCHA	40	4	13	17	34
1983-84—Bowling Green Univ.		CCHA	43	15	39	54	9
1984-85—Winnipeg Jets		NHL	80	11	27	38	85
1985-86—Winnipeg Jets		NHL	80	15	31	46	96
NHL TOTALS			160	26	58	84	181

(c)—June, 1982—Drafted as underage player by Winnipeg Jets in NHL entry draft. Third Jets pick, 75th overall, fourth round.

PAT ELYNUIK

Right Wing . . . 6' . . . 185 lbs. . . . Born, Foam Lake, Sask., October 30, 1967 . . . Shoots right.

Year	Team	League	Games	G.	A.	Pts.	Pen.
1983-84—Prince Albert Midget Raiders		SAHA	26	33	30	63	54
1984-85—Prince Albert Raiders		WHL	70	23	20	43	54
1985-86—Prince Albert Raiders (a-c)		WHL	68	53	53	106	62

(c)—June 1986—Drafted as underage junior by Winnipeg Jets in 1986 NHL entry draft. First Jets pick, eighth overall, first round.

NELSON EMERSON

Center . . . 5'11" . . . 165 lbs. . . . Born, Hamilton, Ont., August 17, 1967 . . . Shoots right.

Year	Team	League	Games	G.	A.	Pts.	Pen.
1984-85—Stratford Cullitans Jr.B (c)		OHA	40	23	38	61	70
1985-86—Stratford Cullitans Jr.B		OHA	39	54	58	112	91

(c)—June, 1985—Drafted by St. Louis Blues in 1985 NHL entry draft. Second Blues pick, 44th overall, third round.

CRAIG T. ENDEAN

Right Wing . . . 6' . . . 170 lbs. . . . Born, Kamloops, B.C., April 13, 1968 . . . Shoots left . . . Also plays Center and Left Wing.

Year	Team	League	Games	G.	A.	Pts.	Pen.
1983-84—Seattle Breakers		WHL	67	16	6	22	14
1984-85—Seattle Breakers		WHL	69	37	60	97	28
1985-86—Seattle Thunderbirds (c)		WHL	70	58	70	128	34

(c)—June, 1986—Drafted as underage junior by Winnipeg Jets in 1986 NHL entry draft. Fifth Jets pick, 92nd overall, fifth round.

BRIAN PAUL ENGBLOM

Defense . . . 6'2" . . . 200 lbs. . . . Born Winnipeg, Man., January 27, 1955 . . . Shoots left . . . (March, 1983)—Eye injury.

Year	Team	League	Games	G.	A.	Pts.	Pen.
1973-74—University of Wisconsin	WCHA	36	10	21	31	54
1974-75—University of Wisconsin (c-d)	WCHA	38	13	23	36	58
1975-76—Nova Scotia Voyageurs	AHL	73	4	34	38	79
1976-77—Nova Scotia Voyageurs (a-e)	AHL	80	8	42	50	89
1976-77—Montreal Canadiens (f)	NHL	....	...	....	....	....
1977-78—Nova Scotia Voyageurs	AHL	7	1	5	6	4
1977-78—Montreal Canadiens	NHL	28	1	2	3	23
1978-79—Montreal Canadiens	NHL	62	3	11	14	60
1979-80—Montreal Canadiens	NHL	70	3	20	23	43
1980-81—Montreal Canadiens	NHL	80	3	25	28	96
1981-82—Montreal Canadiens (b-g)	NHL	76	4	29	33	76
1982-83—Washington Capitals	NHL	68	11	28	39	20
1983-84—Washington Capitals (h)	NHL	6	0	1	1	8
1983-84—Los Angeles Kings	NHL	74	2	27	29	59
1984-85—Los Angeles Kings	NHL	79	4	19	23	70
1985-86—Los Angeles Kings (i)	NHL	49	3	13	16	61
1985-86—Buffalo Sabres	NHL	30	1	4	5	16
NHL TOTALS		622	35	179	214	532

(c)—Drafted from University of Wisconsin by Montreal Canadiens in second round of 1975 amateur draft.

(d)—Named to All-American team (West).

(e)—Won Eddie Shore Plaque (outstanding defenseman in AHL).

(f)—No league record. Played two playoff games.

(g)—September, 1982—Traded by Montreal Canadiens with Rod Langway, Doug Jarvis and Craig Laughlin to Washington Capitals for Ryan Walter and Rick Green.

(h)—October, 1983—Traded with Ken Houston by Washington Capitals to Los Angeles Kings for Larry Murphy.

(i)—January, 1986—Traded with Doug Smith by Los Angeles Kings to Buffalo Sabres for Larry Playfair, Sean McKenna and Ken Baumgartner.

JOHN ENGLISH

Defense . . . 6'2" . . . 185 lbs. . . . Born, Toronto, Ont., May 3, 1966 . . . Shoots right.

Year	Team	League	Games	G.	A.	Pts.	Pen.
1982-83—St. Michaels Jr.	..	34	2	10	12	92
1983-84—Sault Ste. Marie Greyhounds (c)	OHL	64	6	11	17	144
1984-85—Sault Ste. Marie Greyhounds	OHL	15	0	3	3	61
1984-85—Hamilton Steelhawks	OHL	41	2	22	24	105
1985-86—Hamilton Steelhawks (d)	OHL	12	2	10	12	57
1985-86—Ottawa 67's	OHL	43	8	28	36	120

(c)—June, 1984—Drafted as underage junior by Los Angeles Kings in 1984 NHL entry draft. Third Kings pick, 48th overall, third round.

(d)—November, 1985—Traded by Hamilton Steelhawks to Ottawa 67's for a sixth round pick in 1986 OHL priority draft.

JIM ENNIS

Defense . . . 6' . . . 200 lbs. . . . Born, Edmonton, Alta., July 10, 1967 . . . Shoots left.

Year	Team	League	Games	G.	A.	Pts.	Pen.
1985-86—Boston University (c)		H. East	40	1	4	5	22

(c)—June, 1986—Drafted by Edmonton Oilers in 1986 NHL entry draft. Sixth Oilers pick, 126th overall, sixth round.

BRYAN (BUTSY) ERICKSON

Right Wing . . . 5'9" . . . 170 lbs. . . . Born, Roseau, Minn., March 7, 1960 . . . Shoots right . . . (January, 1983)—Fractured wrist . . . (October, 1984)—Broken thumb.

Year	Team	League	Games	G.	A.	Pts.	Pen.
1979-80—University of Minnesota		WCHA	23	10	15	25	14
1980-81—University of Minnesota		WCHA	44	39	47	86	30
1981-82—University of Minnesota (b)		WCHA	35	25	20	45	20
1982-83—University of Minnesota (a-c)		WCHA	42	35	47	82	30
1982-83—Hershey Bears		AHL	1	0	1	1	0
1983-84—Hershey Bears		AHL	31	16	12	28	11
1983-84—Washington Capitals		NHL	45	12	17	29	16
1984-85—Binghamton Whalers		AHL	13	6	11	17	8
1984-85—Washington Capitals		NHL	57	15	13	28	23
1985-86—Binghamton Whalers (d)		AHL	7	5	3	8	2
1985-86—New Haven Nighthawks		AHL	14	8	3	11	11
1985-86—Los Angeles Kings		NHL	55	20	23	43	36
NHL TOTALS			157	47	53	100	75

(c)—April, 1983—Signed by Washington Capitals as a free agent.
(d)—October, 1985—Traded by Washington Capitals to Los Angeles Kings for Bruce Shoebottom.

THOMAS ERIKSSON

Defense . . . 6'2" . . . 182 lbs. . . . Born, Stockholm, Sweden, October 16, 1959 . . . Shoots left . . . Member of Swedish Nationals in 1979 and 1980 and Swedish Olympic Team in 1980 . . . (February 12, 1986)—Injured left knee at Buffalo.

Year	Team	League	Games	G.	A.	Pts.	Pen.
1975-76—Norsborgs IF (jr.)		Stockholm	....	...	....	....	....
1976-77—			....	...	....	....	....
1977-78—Djurgardens IF		Swed. Elite	25	6	4	10	30
1978-79—Djurgardens IF (c)		Swed. Elite	35	6	13	19	70
1979-80—Djurgardens IF		Swed. Elite	36	12	11	23	63
1979-80—Swedish Olympic Team		Int'l	7	2	0	2	10
1980-81—Maine Mariners		AHL	54	11	20	31	75
1980-81—Philadelphia Flyers		NHL	24	1	10	11	14
1981-82—Philadelphia Flyers		NHL	1	0	0	0	4
1981-82—Djurgardens IF		Swed. Elite	27	7	5	12	48
1982-83—Djurgardens IF		Swed. Elite	32	12	9	21	51
1983-84—Philadelphia Flyers		NHL	68	11	33	44	37
1984-85—Philadelphia Flyers		NHL	72	10	29	39	36
1985-86—Philadelphia Flyers		NHL	43	0	4	4	16
NHL TOTALS			208	22	76	98	107

(c)—August, 1979—Drafted by Philadelphia Flyers in 1979 NHL entry draft. Sixth Flyers pick, 98th overall, fifth round.

JAN ERIXON

Right Wing . . . 6' . . . 190 lbs. . . . Born, Skelleftea, Sweden, July 8, 1962 . . . Shoots left . . . (February, 1985)—Bruised foot . . . (December 8, 1985)—Bruised leg vs. Philadelphia . . . (January 12, 1986)—Fractured tibia vs. St. Louis.

Year	Team	League	Games	G.	A.	Pts.	Pen.
1979-80—Skelleftea AIK		Sweden	32	9	3	12	22
1980-81—Skelleftea AIK (c)		Sweden	32	6	6	12	4
1981-82—Skelleftea AIK		Sweden	30	7	7	14	26
1982-83—Skelleftea AIK		Sweden	36	10	18	28	..
1983-84—New York Rangers		NHL	75	5	25	30	16
1984-85—New York Rangers		NHL	66	7	22	29	33
1985-86—New York Rangers		NHL	31	2	17	19	4
NHL TOTALS			172	14	64	78	53

(c)—June, 1981—Drafted by New York Rangers in 1981 NHL entry draft. Second Rangers pick, 30th overall, second round.

BOB ERREY

Left Wing . . . 5'10" . . . 185 lbs. . . . Born, Montreal, Que., September 21, 1964 . . . Shoots left.

Year	Team	League	Games	G.	A.	Pts.	Pen.
1981-82—Peterborough Petes		OHL	68	29	31	60	39
1982-83—Peterborough Petes (a-c)		OHL	67	53	47	100	74
1983-84—Pittsburgh Penguins		NHL	65	9	13	22	29
1984-85—Baltimore Skipjacks		AHL	59	17	24	41	14
1984-85—Pittsburgh Penguins		NHL	16	0	2	2	7
1985-86—Baltimore Skipjacks		AHL	18	8	7	15	28
1985-86—Pittsburgh Penguins		NHL	37	11	6	17	8
NHL TOTALS			118	20	21	41	44

(c)—June, 1983—Drafted as underage junior by Pittsburgh Penguins in 1983 NHL entry draft. Penguins first pick, 15th overall, first round.

DAVID ESPE

Defense . . . 6' . . . 185 lbs. . . . Born, St. Paul, Minn., November 3, 1966 . . . Shoots left.

Year	Team	League	Games	G.	A.	Pts.	Pen.
1984-85—White Bear Lake H.S. (c)		Minn. H.S.	21	11	16	27	30
1985-86—Univ. of Minnesota		WCHA	27	0	6	6	18

(c)—June, 1985—Drafted by Quebec Nordiques in 1985 NHL entry draft. Fifth Nordiques pick, 78th overall, fourth round.

DARYL THOMAS EVANS

Left Wing . . . 5'9" . . . 180 lbs. . . . Born, Toronto, Ont., January 12, 1961 . . . Shoots left . . . (1981-82)—Broken wrist while playing for New Haven Nighthawks.

Year	Team	League	Games	G.	A.	Pts.	Pen.
1977-78—Senaca Nats		OHA Jr. B	40	25	35	60	50
1978-79—Niagara Falls Flyers		OMJHL	65	38	26	64	110
1979-80—Niagara Falls Flyers (c)		OMJHL	63	43	52	95	47
1980-81—Niagara Falls Flyers (d)		OHL	5	3	4	7	11
1980-81—Brantford Alexanders (a)		OHL	58	58	54	112	50
1980-81—Saginaw Gears		IHL	3	3	2	5	0
1981-82—New Haven Nighthawks		AHL	41	14	14	28	10
1981-82—Los Angeles Kings		NHL	14	2	6	8	2
1982-83—Los Angeles Kings		NHL	80	18	22	40	21
1983-84—New Haven Nighthawks (b)		AHL	69	51	35	86	14
1983-84—Los Angeles Kings		NHL	4	0	1	1	0
1984-85—Los Angeles Kings		NHL	7	1	0	1	2
1984-85—New Haven Nighthawks		AHL	59	22	24	46	12
1985-86—Washington Capitals (e)		NHL	6	0	1	1	0
1985-86—Binghamton Whalers		AHL	69	40	52	92	50
NHL TOTALS			111	21	30	51	25

(c)—June, 1980—Drafted as underage junior by Los Angeles Kings in 1980 NHL entry draft. Eleventh Kings pick, 178th overall, ninth round.

(d)—October, 1980—Traded by Niagara Falls Flyers to Brantford Alexanders for Venci Sebek.

(e)—September, 1985—Traded by Los Angeles Kings to Washington Capitals for Glen Currie.

DOUG EVANS

Center . . . 5'9" . . . 178 lbs. . . . Born, Peterborough, Ont., June 2, 1963 . . . Shoots left.

Year	Team	League	Games	G.	A.	Pts.	Pen.
1980-81—Peterborough Petes		OHL	51	9	24	33	139
1981-82—Peterborough Petes		OHL	56	17	49	66	176
1982-83—Peterborough Petes		OHL	65	31	55	86	165
1983-84—Peterborough Petes		OHL	61	45	79	124	98
1984-85—Peoria Prancers (c)		IHL	81	36	61	97	189
1985-86—St. Louis Blues		NHL	13	1	0	1	2
1985-86—Peoria Rivermen (a)		IHL	69	46	51	97	179
NHL TOTALS			13	1	0	1	2

(c)—June, 1985—Signed by St. Louis Blues as a free agent.

SHAWN EVANS

Defense . . . 6'3" . . . 195 lbs. . . . Born, Kingston, Ont., September 7, 1965 . . . Shoots left . . . Cousin of Dennis Kearns (Vancouver, 1970s).

Year	Team	League	Games	G.	A.	Pts.	Pen.
1981-82—Kitchener Rangers MW Jr. B		OHA	21	9	13	22	55
1982-83—Peterborough Petes (c)		OHL	58	7	41	48	116
1983-84—Peterborough Petes (b)		OHL	67	21	88	109	116
1984-85—Peterborough Petes		OHL	66	16	83	99	78

Year	Team	League	Games	G.	A.	Pts.	Pen.
1985-86—Peoria Rivermen	IHL	55	8	26	34	36
1985-86—St. Louis Blues (d)	NHL	7	0	0	0	2
NHL TOTALS		7	0	0	0	2

(c)—June, 1983—Drafted by New Jersey Devils as underage junior in 1983 NHL entry draft. Second Devils pick, 24th overall, second round.

(d)—September, 1985—Traded with a fifth round 1986 draft pick (Mike Wolak) by New Jersey Devils to St. Louis Blues for Mark Johnson.

DEAN EVASON

Center . . . 5'10" . . . 175 lbs. . . . Born, Flin Flon, Man., August 22, 1964 . . . Shoots left . . . Brother of Dan Evason (1984-85 assistant coach of Brandon Wheat Kings).

Year	Team	League	Games	G.	A.	Pts.	Pen.
1980-81—Spokane Flyers	WHL	3	1	1	2	0
1981-82—Kamloops Junior Oilers (c-d)	WHL	70	29	69	98	112
1982-83—Kamloops Junior Oilers	WHL	70	71	93	164	102
1983-84—Kamloops Junior Oilers (a-e)	WHL	57	49	88	137	89
1983-84—Washington Capitals	NHL	2	0	0	0	2
1984-85—Binghamton Whalers	AHL	65	27	49	76	38
1984-85—Washington Capitals (f)	NHL	15	3	4	7	2
1984-85—Hartford Whalers	NHL	2	0	0	0	0
1985-86—Binghamton Whalers	AHL	26	9	17	26	29
1985-86—Hartford Whalers	NHL	55	20	28	48	65
NHL TOTALS		74	23	32	55	69

(c)—December, 1981—Drafted by Kamloops Junior Oilers in WHL disperal draft of players of Spokane Flyers.

(d)—June, 1982—Drafted as underage junior by Washington Capitals in 1982 NHL entry draft. Third Capitals pick, 89th overall, fifth round.

(e)—Shared WHL playoff scoring with Taylor Hall, each had 21 goals.

(f)—March, 1985—Traded with Peter Sidorkiewicz by Washington Capitals to Hartford Whalers for David A. Jensen.

GREG EVTUSHEVSKI

Right Wing . . . 5'10" . . . 185 lbs. . . . Born, St. Paul, Alta., May 4, 1965 . . . Shoots right.

Year	Team	League	Games	G.	A.	Pts.	Pen.
1982-83—Kamloops Junior Oilers (c)	WHL	70	32	49	81	245
1983-84—Kamloops Junior Oilers	WHL	64	27	43	70	176
1984-85—Kamloops Blazers (a)	WHL	71	47	93	140	167
1985-86—Kamloops Blazers	WHL	34	29	47	76	100
1985-86—Maine Mariners	AHL	21	3	4	7	60

(c)—June, 1983—Drafted as underage junior by New Jersey Devils in 1983 NHL entry draft. Fifth Devils pick, 125th overall, seventh round.

TODD EWEN

Right Wing . . . 6'2" . . . 185 lbs. . . . Born, Saskatoon, Sask., March 26, 1966 . . . Shoots right.

Year	Team	League	Games	G.	A.	Pts.	Pen.
1982-83—Vernon Lakers	BCJHL	42	20	23	53	195
1982-83—Kamloops Junior Oilers	WHL	3	0	0	0	2
1983-84—New Westminster Bruins (c)	WHL	68	11	13	24	176
1984-85—New Westminster Bruins	WHL	56	11	20	31	304
1985-86—New Westminster Bruins	WHL	60	28	24	52	289
1985-86—Maine Mariners (d)	AHL	....	...	...	....	....

(c)—June, 1984—Drafted as underage junior by Edmonton Oilers in 1984 NHL entry draft. Eighth Oilers pick, 168th overall, eighth round.

(d)—No regular season record. Played three playoff games.

DAVID ALLAN FARRISH

Defense . . . 6'1" . . . 195 lbs. . . . Born, Wingham, Ont., August 1, 1956 . . . Shoots left . . . Sprained ankle (March, 1980) . . . (November 1980)—Groin injury . . . (November, 1983)—Neck injury.

Year	Team	League	Games	G.	A.	Pts.	Pen.
1973-74—Sudbury Wolves	Jr."A" OHA	58	11	20	31	205
1974-75—Sudbury Wolves	Jr."A" OHA	60	20	44	64	258
1975-76—Sudbury Wolves (a-c)	Jr."A" OHA	66	27	48	75	155
1976-77—New York Rangers	NHL	80	2	17	19	102
1977-78—New Haven Nighthawks	AHL	10	0	3	3	4
1977-78—New York Rangers	NHL	66	3	5	8	62
1978-79—New York Rangers (d)	NHL	71	1	19	20	61

Year	Team	League	Games	G.	A.	Pts.	Pen.
1979-80—Syracuse Firebirds		AHL	14	4	10	14	17
1979-80—Quebec Nordiques (e)		NHL	4	0	0	0	0
1979-80—New Brunswick Hawks		AHL	20	3	1	4	22
1979-80—Toronto Maple Leafs		NHL	20	1	8	9	30
1980-81—Toronto Maple Leafs		NHL	74	2	18	20	90
1981-82—New Brunswick Hawks (a-f)		AHL	67	13	24	37	80
1982-83—St. Catharines Saints		AHL	14	2	12	14	18
1982-83—Toronto Maple Leafs		NHL	56	4	24	28	38
1983-84—St. Catharines Saints		AHL	4	0	2	2	6
1983-84—Toronto Maple Leafs		NHL	59	4	19	23	57
1984-85—St. Catharines Saints (g)		AHL	68	4	12	16	56
1985-86—Hershey Bears		AHL	74	5	17	22	78
NHL TOTALS			430	17	110	127	440

(c)—Drafted from Sudbury Wolves by New York Rangers in second round of 1976 amateur draft.
(d)—June, 1979—Selected by Quebec Nordiques in NHL expansion draft.
(e)—December, 1979—Traded by Quebec Nordiques to Toronto Maple Leafs for Reg Thomas.
(f)—Winner of Eddie Shore Plaque (Outstanding AHL Defenseman).
(g)—August, 1985—Signed by Philadelphia Flyers as a free agent.

GLEN FEATHERSTONE

Defense . . . 6'4" . . . 209 lbs. . . . Born, Toronto, Ont., July 8, 1968 . . . Shoots left . . . Father (Roy Featherstone) player professional soccer in Ireland.

Year	Team	League	Games	G.	A.	Pts.	Pen.
1984-85—Toronto National Midget		MTHL	45	7	24	31	94
1985-86—Windsor Spitfires (c)		OHL	49	0	6	6	135

(c)—June, 1986—Drafted as underage junior by St. Louis Blues in 1986 NHL entry draft. Fourth Blues' pick, 73rd overall, fourth round.

BERNARD ALLAN FEDERKO

Center . . . 6' . . . 185 lbs. . . . Born, Foam Lake, Sask., May 12, 1956 . . . Shoots left . . . Brother of Ken Federko (Salt Lake—CHL 1980-82) . . . Missed final games of 1978-79 season with broken right wrist . . . (December 29, 1981)—Tore rib cartilage in game vs. Hartford . . . (November 20, 1984)—Bruised left ankle in game at Vancouver . . . (January, 1985)— Bruised lung and ribs.

Year	Team	League	Games	G.	A.	Pts.	Pen.
1973-74—Saskatoon Blades		WCHL	68	22	28	50	19
1974-75—Saskatoon Blades (c)		WCHL	66	39	68	107	30
1975-76—Saskatoon Blades (a-d-e-f)		WCHL	72	72	*115	*187	108
1976-77—Kansas City Blues (b-g)		CHL	42	30	39	69	41
1976-77—St. Louis Blues		NHL	31	14	9	23	15
1977-78—St. Louis Blues		NHL	72	17	24	41	27
1978-79—St. Louis Blues		NHL	74	31	64	95	14
1979-80—St. Louis Blues		NHL	79	38	56	94	24
1980-81—St. Louis Blues		NHL	78	31	73	104	47
1981-82—St. Louis Blues		NHL	74	30	62	92	70
1982-83—St. Louis Blues		NHL	75	24	60	84	24
1983-84—St. Louis Blues		NHL	79	41	66	107	43
1984-85—St. Louis Blues		NHL	76	30	73	103	27
1985-86—St. Louis Blues		NHL	80	34	68	102	34
NHL TOTALS			718	290	555	845	325

(c)—Led in goals (15) during playoffs.
(d)—Named Most Valuable Player in WCHL.
(e)—Drated from Saskatoon Blades by St. Louis Blues in first round of 1976 amateur draft.
(f)—Led in assists (27) and points (45) during playoffs.
(g)—CHL Rookie-of-the-Year.

BRENT FEDYK

Right Wing . . . 6' . . . 180 lbs. . . . Born, Yorkton, Sask., March 8, 1967 . . . Shoots right . . . (Septmeber, 1985)—Strained hip in Detroit training camp and missed three weeks of WHL season.

Year	Team	League	Games	G.	A.	Pts.	Pen.
1982-83—Regina Pats		WHL	1	0	0	0	0
1983-84—Regina Pats		WHL	63	15	28	43	30
1984-85—Regina Pats (c)		WHL	66	35	35	70	48
1985-86—Regina Pats (b)		WHL	50	43	34	77	47

(c)—June, 1985—Drafted as underage junior by Detroit Red Wings in 1985 NHL entry draft. First Red Wings pick, eighth overall, first round.

TONY FELTRIN

Defense . . . 6'1" . . . 185 lbs. . . . Born, Ladysmith, B. C., December 6, 1961 . . . Shoots left . . . (October 18, 1980)—Injured ligaments in right knee.

Year	Team	League	Games	G.	A.	Pts.	Pen.
1977-78—Nanaimo		BCJHL	63	2	13	15	65
1978-79—Victoria Cougars		WHL	47	2	11	13	119
1979-80—Victoria Cougars (c)		WHL	71	6	25	31	138
1980-81—Victoria Cougars		WHL	43	4	25	29	81
1980-81—Pittsburgh Penguins		NHL	2	0	0	0	0
1981-82—Erie Blades		AHL	72	4	15	19	117
1981-82—Pittsburgh Penguins		NHL	4	0	0	0	4
1982-83—Baltimore Skipjacks		AHL	31	2	3	5	34
1982-83—Pittsburgh Penguins		NHL	32	3	3	6	40
1983-84—Baltimore Skipjacks		AHL	4	0	0	0	2
1983-84—Salt Lake Golden Eagles		CHL	65	8	22	30	94
1984-85—Salt Lake Golden Eagles		IHL	81	8	19	27	125
1985-86—New York Rangers (d)		NHL	10	0	0	0	21
1985-86—New Haven Nighthawks		AHL	22	0	2	2	38
NHL TOTALS			48	3	3	6	65

(c)—June, 1980—Drafted by Pittsburgh Penguins as underage junior in 1980 NHL entry draft. Third Penguins pick, 72nd overall, fourth round.
(d)—October, 1985—Signed by New York Rangers as a free agent.

PAUL FENTON

Center . . . 5'11" . . . 180 lbs. . . . Born, Springfield, Mass., December 22, 1959 . . . Shoots left.

Year	Team	League	Games	G.	A.	Pts.	Pen.
1979-80—Boston University		ECAC	28	12	21	33	18
1980-81—Boston University		ECAC	7	4	4	8	0
1981-82—Boston University		ECAC	28	20	13	33	28
1982-83—Peoria Prancers (b-c)		IHL	82	60	51	111	53
1982-83—Colorado Flames		CHL	1	0	1	1	0
1983-84—Binghamton Whalers (d)		AHL	78	41	24	65	67
1984-85—Binghamton Whalers		AHL	45	26	21	47	18
1984-85—Hartford Whalers		NHL	33	7	5	12	10
1985-86—Hartford Whalers		NHL	1	0	0	0	0
1985-86—Binghamton Whalers (a-e)		AHL	75	53	35	88	87
NHL TOTALS			34	7	5	12	10

(c)—Won Ken McKenzie Trophy (Top U.S. born IHL Rookie)
(d)—October, 1983—Signed by Hartford Whalers as a free agent.
(e)—July, 1986—Released by Hartford Whalers.

DAVE ALAN FENYVES

Defense . . . 5'10" . . . 188 lbs. . . . Born, Dunnville, Ont., April 29, 1960 . . . Shoots left . . . (October, 1977)—Separated shoulder . . . (December 26, 1985)—Missed five games with a concussion vs. N.Y. Rangers.

Year	Team	League	Games	G.	A.	Pts.	Pen.
1977-78—Peterborough Petes		OMJHL	59	3	12	15	36
1978-79—Peterborough Petes		OMJHL	66	2	23	25	122
1979-80—Peterborough Petes (c)		OMJHL	66	9	36	45	92
1980-81—Rochester Americans		AHL	77	6	16	22	146
1981-82—Rochester Americans		AHL	73	3	14	17	68
1982-83—Rochester Americans		AHL	51	2	19	21	45
1982-83—Buffalo Sabres		NHL	24	0	8	8	14
1983-84—Buffalo Sabres		NHL	10	0	4	4	9
1983-84—Rochester Americans		AHL	70	3	16	19	55
1984-85—Rochester Americans		AHL	9	0	3	3	8
1984-85—Buffalo Sabres		NHL	60	1	8	9	27
1985-86—Buffalo Sabres		NHL	47	0	7	7	37
NHL TOTALS			141	1	27	28	87

(c)—October, 1979—Signed by Buffalo Sabres as a free agent.

TOM JOSEPH FERGUS

Center . . . 6' . . . 176 lbs. . . . Born, Chicago, Ill., June 16, 1962 . . . Shoots left . . . (January 20, 1982)—Tore ligaments in left knee in game at Pittsburgh . . . (February, 1984)—Damaged knee ligaments.

Year	Team	League	Games	G.	A.	Pts.	Pen.
1979-80—Peterborough Petes (c)		OMJHL	63	8	6	14	14

Year	Team	League	Games	G.	A.	Pts.	Pen.
1980-81—Peterborough Petes		OMJHL	63	43	45	88	33
1981-82—Boston Bruins		NHL	61	15	24	39	12
1982-83—Boston Bruins		NHL	80	28	35	63	39
1983-84—Boston Bruins		NHL	69	25	36	61	12
1984-85—Boston Bruins		NHL	79	30	43	73	75
1985-86—Toronto Maple Leafs (d)		NHL	78	31	42	73	64
NHL TOTALS			367	129	180	309	202

(c)—June, 1980—Drafted as underage junior by Boston Bruins in 1980 NHL entry draft. Second Bruins pick, 60th overall, third round.

(d)—September, 1985—Traded by Boston Bruins to Toronto Maple Leafs for Bill Derlago.

IAN FERGUSON

Defense . . . 6'2" . . . 175 lbs. . . . Born, Winnipeg, Man., June 24, 1966 . . . Shoots left.

Year	Team	League	Games	G.	A.	Pts.	Pen.
1983-84—Oshawa Generals (c)		OHL	65	2	7	9	30
1984-85—Oshawa Generals		OHL	65	6	19	25	78
1985-86—Oshawa Generals		OHL	48	6	10	16	43

(c)—June, 1984—Drafted as underage junior by New Jersey Devils in 1984 NHL entry draft. Seventh Devils pick, 128th overall, seventh round.

MARK FERNER

Defense . . . 6' . . . 170 lbs. . . . Born, Regina, Sask., September 5, 1965 . . . Shoots left . . . (March, 1986)—Broken foot.

Year	Team	League	Games	G.	A.	Pts.	Pen.
1982-83—Kamloops Junior Oilers (c)		WHL	69	6	15	21	81
1983-84—Kamloops Junior Oilers		WHL	72	9	30	39	162
1984-85—Kamloops Blazers (a)		WHL	69	15	39	54	91
1985-86—Rochester Americans		AHL	63	3	14	17	87

(c)—June, 1983—Drafted as underage junior by Buffalo Sabres in 1983 NHL entry draft. Twelfth Sabres pick, 194th overall, 10th round.

RAY FERRARO

Center . . . 5'10" . . . 180 lbs. . . . Born, Trail, B.C., August 23, 1964 . . . Shoots left . . . (1983-84) Set WHL record for most goals in a season (108), most power-play goals (43) and most three-goal games (15) . . . (December 7, 1985)—Separated shoulder vs. Boston and missed four games.

Year	Team	League	Games	G.	A.	Pts.	Pen.
1981-82—Penticton (c)		BCJHL	48	65	70	135	50
1982-83—Portland Winter Hawks		WHL	50	41	49	90	39
1983-84—Brandon Wheat Kings (a-d-e-f)		WHL	72	*108	84	*192	84
1984-85—Binghamton Whalers		AHL	37	20	13	33	29
1984-85—Hartford Whalers		NHL	44	11	17	28	40
1985-86—Hartford Whalers		NHL	76	30	47	77	57
NHL TOTALS			120	41	64	105	97

(c)—June, 1982—Drafted as underage junior by Hartford Whalers in 1982 NHL entry draft. Fifth Whalers pick, 88th overall, fifth round.

(d)—Named WHL's Most Valuable Player.

(e)—Won Bob Brownridge Memorial Trophy (Top WHL Scorer).

(f)—WHL's Molson Player of the Year.

BRIAN P. FERREIRA

Right Wing . . . 6' . . . 180 lbs. . . . Born, Falmouth, Mass., February 1, 1968 . . . Shoots right . . . Also plays Center.

Year	Team	League	Games	G.	A.	Pts.	Pen.
1984-85—Falmouth H.S.		Mass.	24	31	32	63	....
1985-86—Falmouth H.S. (c)		Mass.	22	37	43	80	12

(c)—June, 1986—Drafted by Boston Bruins in 1986 NHL entry draft. Seventh Bruins pick, 160th overall, eighth round.

STEVEN FINN

Defense . . . 6' . . . 190 lbs. . . . Born, Laval, Que., August 20, 1966 . . . Shoots left.

Year	Team	League	Games	G.	A.	Pts.	Pen.
1982-83—Laval Voisins		QHL	69	7	30	37	108
1983-84—Laval Voisins (c)		QHL	68	7	39	46	159
1984-85—Laval Voisins		QHL	61	20	33	53	169
1984-85—Fredericton Express		AHL	4	0	0	0	14

Year	Team	League	Games	G.	A.	Pts.	Pen.
1985-86—Laval Titans		QHL	29	4	15	19	111
1985-86—Quebec Nordiques		NHL	17	0	1	1	28
NHL TOTALS			17	0	1	1	28

(c)—June, 1984—Drafted as underage junior by Quebec Nordiques in 1984 NHL entry draft. Third Nordiques pick, 57th overall, third round.

BRUCE FISHBACK

Center . . . 6'1" . . . 185 lbs. . . . Born, White Bear Lake, Minn., January 19, 1965 . . . Shoots right.

Year	Team	League	Games	G.	A.	Pts.	Pen.
1982-83—St. Paul Mariner H.S. (c)		Minn. H.S.	23	12	16	28	...
1983-84—Univ. of Minnesota-Duluth		WCHA	13	2	2	4	4
1984-85—Univ. of Minnesota-Duluth		WCHA	30	2	1	3	8
1985-86—Univ. of Minnesota-Duluth		WCHA	37	2	3	5	4

(c)—June, 1983—Drafted by Los Angeles Kings in 1983 NHL entry draft. Ninth Kings pick, 167th overall, ninth round.

THOMAS FITZGERALD

Center . . . 6'1" . . . 190 lbs. . . . Born, Melrose, Mass., August 28, 1968 . . . Shoots right . . . Also plays Right Wing.

Year	Team	League	Games	G.	A.	Pts.	Pen.
1984-85—Austin Prep.		Mass.	18	20	21	41	....
1985-86—Austin Prep. (c)		Mass.	24	35	38	73	....

(c)—June, 1986—Drafted by New York Islanders in 1986 NHL entry draft. First Islanders pick, 17th overall, first round.

ROSS FITZPATRICK

Left Wing . . . 6'1" . . . 190 lbs. . . . Born, Penticton, B.C., October 7, 1960 . . . Shoots left . . . (December, 1982)—Broke hand in game vs. Hershey (AHL) . . . (January 19, 1985)—Surgery for shoulder separation suffered in AHL game vs. Sherbrooke.

Year	Team	League	Games	G.	A.	Pts.	Pen.
1979-80—Univ. of Western Mich. (c)		CCHA	34	26	33	59	22
1980-81—Univ. of Western Mich. (a)		CCHA	36	28	43	71	22
1981-82—Univ. of Western Mich.		CCHA	33	30	28	58	34
1982-83—Maine Mariners		AHL	66	29	28	57	32
1982-83—Philadelphia Flyers		NHL	1	0	0	0	0
1983-84—Springfield Indians		AHL	45	33	30	63	28
1983-84—Philadelphia Flyers		NHL	12	4	2	6	0
1984-85—Hershey Bears		AHL	35	26	15	41	8
1984-85—Philadelphia Flyers		NHL	5	1	0	1	0
1985-86—Philadelphia Flyers		NHL	2	0	0	0	0
1985-86—Hershey Bears (b)		AHL	77	50	47	97	28
NHL TOTALS			20	5	2	7	0

(c)—June, 1980—Drafted by Philadelphia Flyers in 1980 NHL entry draft. Seventh Flyers pick, 147th overall, seventh round.

PAUL FITZSIMMONS

Defense . . . 6'2" . . . 200 lbs. . . . Born, Wethersfield, Ct. August 25, 1963 . . . Shoots right.

Year	Team	League	Games	G.	A.	Pts.	Pen.
1982-83—Northeastern Univ. (c)		ECAC	27	1	2	3	24
1983-84—Northeastern University		ECAC	24	2	3	5	56
1984-85—Northeastern University		H. East	33	0	1	1	74
1985-86—Northeastern University (b)		H. East	38	3	18	21	44

(c)—June, 1983—Drafted by Boston Bruins in 1983 NHL entry draft. Tenth Bruins pick, 202nd overall, 10th round.

JEFFREY FLAHERTY

Center . . . 6'3" . . . 210 lbs. . . . Born, Boston, Mass., July 16, 1968 . . . Shoots right . . . Also plays Right Wing.

Year	Team	League	Games	G.	A.	Pts.	Pen.
1984-85—Weymouth North H.S.		Mass.	....	19	18	37	....
1985-86—Weymouth North H.S. (c)		Mass.	19	27	23	50	12

(c)—June, 1986—Drafted by Boston Bruins in 1986 NHL entry draft. Eighth Bruins pick, 181st overall, ninth round.

MIKE FLANAGAN

Defense . . . 6'4" . . . 210 lbs. . . . Born, Boston, Mass., April 27, 1965 . . . Shoots left.

Year	Team	League	Games	G.	A.	Pts.	Pen.
1982-83—Acton-Boxboro H.S. (c)	Mass. H.S.	23	17	31	48	...
1983-84—Providence College	ECAC	19	1	0	1	2
1984-85—Providence College	H. East	25	0	1	1	12
1985-86—Providence College	H. East	33	0	4	4	45

(c)—June, 1983—Drafted by Edmonton Oilers in 1983 NHL entry draft. Third Oilers pick, 60th overall, third round.

TIM FLANAGAN

Right Wing . . . 6' . . . 185 lbs. . . . Born, Red Deer, Alta., March 6, 1967 . . . Shoots right.

Year	Team	League	Games	G.	A.	Pts.	Pen.
1984-85—Michigan Tech. (c)	WCHA	27	5	5	10	34
1985-86—Michigan Tech	WCHA	20	2	3	5	36
1985-86—Medicine Hat Tigers	WHL	2	0	1	1	0

(c)—June, 1985—Drafted by Los Angeles Kings in 1985 NHL entry draft. Sixth Kings pick, 135th overall, seventh round.

PATRICK FLATLEY

Right Wing . . . 6'3" . . . 200 lbs. . . . Born, Toronto, Ont., October 3, 1963 . . . Shoots right . . . Member of 1984 Canadian Olympic hockey team . . . (April, 1985)—Broke bone in left hand during playoff series with Washington . . . (November 16, 1985)—Injured shoulder in game vs. Edmonton and missed three games.

Year	Team	League	Games	G.	A.	Pts.	Pen.
1980-81—Henry Carr H.S.	Ont. Tier II	42	30	61	91	122
1981-82—University of Wisconsin (c)	WCHA	33	17	20	37	65
1982-83—University of Wisconsin (a-d)	WCHA	43	25	44	69	76
1983-84—Canadian Olympic Team	Int'l	57	33	17	50	136
1983-84—New York Islanders	NHL	16	2	7	9	6
1984-85—New York Islanders	NHL	78	20	31	51	106
1985-86—New York Islanders	NHL	73	18	34	52	66
NHL TOTALS		167	40	72	112	178

(c)—June, 1982—Drafted as underage player by New York Islanders in 1982 NHL entry draft. First Islanders pick, 21st overall, first round.

(d)—Named to All-America Team (West).

JOHN PATRICK FLESCH

Left Wing . . . 6'2" . . . 195 lbs. . . . Born, Sudbury, Ont., July 15, 1953 . . . Shoots left . . . Played defense prior to 1972-73 . . . Missed part of 1974-75 season with torn knee ligaments.

Year	Team	League	Games	G.	A.	Pts.	Pen.
1971-72—Sudbury Wolves	Jr. "A" NOHA	....	17	24	41	182
1972-73—Lake Superior St. College (c)	CCHA	29	28	32	60	108
1973-74—Omaha Knights (d)	CHL	69	27	27	54	98
1974-75—Minnesota North Stars	NHL	57	8	15	23	47
1975-76—New Haven Nighthawks	AHL	31	11	10	21	95
1975-76—Minnesota North Stars	NHL	33	3	2	5	47
1976-77—Columbus Owls	IHL	74	34	39	73	210
1977-78—Grand Rapids Owls	IHL	43	11	19	30	106
1977-78—Pittsburgh Penguins	NHL	29	7	5	12	19
1978-79—Grand Rapids Owls	IHL	67	26	56	82	149
1979-80—Colorado Rockies (e)	NHL	5	0	1	1	4
1979-80—Grand Rapid Owls	IHL	76	39	54	93	66
1980-81—Milwaukee Admirals	IHL	70	27	44	71	70
1981-82—Milwaukee Admirals (a)	IHL	82	39	54	93	45
1982-83—Milwaukee Admirals	IHL	51	24	31	55	56
1983-84—Milwaukee Admirals	IHL	81	43	44	87	27
1984-85—Kalamazoo Wings (f)	IHL	82	38	40	78	72
1985-86—Kalamazoo Wings (g)	IHL	48	15	15	30	33
NHL TOTALS		124	18	23	41	117

(c)—Drafted from Lake Superior State College by Atlanta Flames in fifth round of 1973 amateur draft.

(d)—May, 1974—Traded to Minnesota North Stars by Atlanta Flames with Don Martineau for Buster Harvey and Jerry Byers.

(e)—January, 1980—Acquired from Pittsburgh Penguins by Colorado Rockies.

(f)—October, 1984—Loaned with Dale Yakiwchuk by Milwaukee Admirals to Kalamazoo Wings.

(g)—October, 1985—Traded by Milwaukee Admirals to Kalamazoo Wings for Kevin Schamehorn.

STEVEN FLETCHER

Defense . . . 6'2" . . . 180 lbs. . . . Born, Montreal, Que., March 31, 1962 . . . Shoots left.

Year	Team	League	Games	G.	A.	Pts.	Pen.
1979-80—Hull Olympics (c)		QMJHL	61	2	14	16	183
1980-81—Hull Olympics		QMJHL	66	4	13	17	231
1981-82—Hull Olympics		QMJHL	60	4	20	24	230
1982-83—Fort Wayne Komets		IHL	34	1	9	10	115
1982-83—Sherbrooke Jets		AHL	36	0	1	1	119
1983-84—Sherbrooke Jets		AHL	77	3	7	10	208
1984-85—Sherbrooke Canadiens		AHL	50	2	4	6	192
1985-86—Sherbrooke Canadiens		AHL	64	2	12	14	293

(c)—June, 1980—Drafted as underage junior by Calgary Flames in 1980 NHL entry draft. Eleventh Flames pick, 202nd overall, 10th round.

RON FLOCKHART

Center and Left Wing . . . 5'11" . . . 185 lbs. . . . Born, Smithers, B.C., October 10, 1960 . . . Shoots left . . . Brother of Rob Flockhart . . . (January, 1984)—Missed games due to atopic dermitis (body rash) . . . (January 17, 1985)—Separated left shoulder in game at N.Y. Islanders and missed 17 games.

Year	Team	League	Games	G.	A.	Pts.	Pen.
1978-79—Revelstoke		BCJHL	61	47	41	88	54
1979-80—Regina Pats		WHL	65	54	76	130	63
1980-81—Philadelphia Flyers (c)		NHL	14	3	7	10	11
1980-81—Maine Mariners		AHL	59	33	33	66	76
1981-82—Philadelphia Flyers		NHL	72	33	39	72	44
1982-83—Philadelphia Flyers		NHL	73	29	31	60	49
1983-84—Philadelphia Flyers (d)		NHL	8	0	3	3	4
1983-84—Pittsburgh Penguins		NHL	68	27	18	45	40
1984-85—Pittsburgh Penguins (e)		NHL	12	0	5	5	4
1984-85—Montreal Canadiens (f)		NHL	42	10	12	22	14
1985-86—St. Louis Blues		NHL	79	22	45	67	26
NHL TOTALS			368	124	160	284	192

(c)—September, 1980—Signed by Philadelphia Flyers as a free agent.
(d)—October, 1983—Traded with Mark Taylor, Andy Brickley and first (Roger Belanger) and third (traded to Vancouver) round 1984 draft picks by Philadelphia Flyers to Pittsburgh Penguins for Rich Sutter and second (Greg Smyth) and third (David McLay) round 1984 draft picks.
(e)—November, 1984—Traded by Pittsburgh Penguins to Montreal Canadiens for John Chabot.
(f)—August, 1985—Traded by Montreal Canadiens to St. Louis Blues for Perry Ganchar.

PERRY FLORIO

Defense . . . 6' . . . 190 lbs. . . . Born, Glen Cove, N.Y., July 15, 1967 . . . Shoots left . . . Brother of Patty Florio (Former member of Ice Capades) . . . Missed parts of 1984-85 season with a broken wrist and mononucleosis.

Year	Team	League	Games	G.	A.	Pts.	Pen.
1983-84—Kent Prep.		Conn. H.S.	24	11	24	35	....
1984-85—Kent Prep. (c)		Conn. H.S.	13	3	12	15	....
1985-86—Providence College		H. East	39	4	5	9	90

(c)—June, 1985—Drafted by Los Angeles Kings in 1985 NHL entry draft. Fourth Kings pick, 72nd overall, fourth round.

LARRY FLOYD

Center . . . 5'8" . . . 180 lbs. . . . Born, Peterborough, Ont., May 1, 1961 . . . Shoots left.

Year	Team	League	Games	G.	A.	Pts.	Pen.
1979-80—Peterborough Petes		OMJHL	66	21	37	58	54
1980-81—Peterborough Petes		OHL	44	26	37	63	43
1981-82—Peterborough Petes		OHL	39	32	37	69	26
1981-82—Rochester Americans		AHL	1	0	2	2	0
1982-83—New Jersey Devils (c)		NHL	5	1	0	1	2
1982-83—Wichita Wind (d)		CHL	75	40	43	83	16
1983-84—New Jersey Devils		NHL	7	1	3	4	7
1983-84—Maine Mariners		AHL	69	37	49	86	40
1984-85—Maine Mariners		AHL	72	30	51	81	24
1985-86—Maine Mariners		AHL	80	29	58	87	25
NHL TOTALS			12	2	3	5	9

(c)—September, 1982—Signed by New Jersey Devils as a free agent.
(d)—Won Ken McKenzie Trophy (Top CHL Rookie).

LEE JOSEPH FOGOLIN

Defense . . . 6' . . . 200 lbs. . . . Born, Chicago, Ill., February 7, 1955 . . . Shoots right . . . Son of former NHL Defenseman Lee Fogolin . . . Missed part of 1974-75 season with injury to left eye and part for surgery for removal of bone chips from wrist . . . (December, 1982)—Hospitalized with severe case of influenza.

Year	Team	League	Games	G.	A.	Pts.	Pen.
1972-73	Oshawa Generals (c)	Jr. "A" OHA	55	5	21	26	132
1973-74	Oshawa Generals (d)	Jr. "A" OHA	47	7	19	26	108
1974-75	Buffalo Sabres	NHL	50	2	2	4	59
1975-76	Hershey Bears	AHL	20	1	8	9	61
1975-76	Buffalo Sabres	NHL	58	0	9	9	64
1976-77	Buffalo Sabres	NHL	71	3	15	18	100
1977-78	Buffalo Sabres	NHL	76	0	23	23	98
1978-79	Buffalo Sabres (e)	NHL	74	3	19	22	103
1979-80	Edmonton Oilers	NHL	80	5	10	15	104
1980-81	Edmonton Oilers	NHL	80	13	17	30	139
1981-82	Edmonton Oilers	NHL	80	4	25	29	154
1982-83	Edmonton Oilers	NHL	72	0	18	18	92
1983-84	Edmonton Oilers	NHL	80	5	16	21	125
1984-85	Edmonton Oilers	NHL	79	4	14	18	126
1985-86	Edmonton Oilers	NHL	80	4	22	26	129
	NHL TOTALS		880	43	190	233	1291

(c)—Traded to Oshawa Generals by Hamilton Red Wings for Dennis Higgins, Doug Ferguson and Oshawa's No. 1 draft choice in 1973 midget draft.
(d)—Drafted from Oshawa Generals by Buffalo Sabres in first round of 1974 amateur draft.
(e)—June, 1979—Selected by Edmonton Oilers in NHL expansion draft.

MIKE ANTHONY FOLIGNO

Right Wing . . . 6'2" . . . 190 lbs. . . . Born, Sudbury, Ont., January 29, 1959 . . . Shoots right . . . (December 27, 1980)—Set Detroit record for most penalty minutes in one game (37 vs. Philadelphia) . . . (October 31, 1982)—Injured tailbone in game vs. Montreal . . . (February 12, 1983)—Injured shoulder in game at Calgary.

Year	Team	League	Games	G.	A.	Pts.	Pen.
1975-76	Sudbury Wolves	OMJHL	57	22	14	36	45
1976-77	Sudbury Wolves	OMJHL	66	31	44	75	62
1977-78	Sudbury Wolves	OMJHL	67	47	39	86	112
1978-79	Sudbury Wolves (a-c-d-e-f)	OMJHL	68	65	85	*150	98
1979-80	Detroit Red Wings	NHL	80	36	35	71	109
1980-81	Detroit Red Wings	NHL	80	28	35	63	210
1981-82	Detroit Red Wings (g)	NHL	26	13	13	26	28
1981-82	Buffalo Sabres	NHL	56	20	31	51	149
1982-83	Buffalo Sabres	NHL	66	22	25	47	135
1983-84	Buffalo Sabres	NHL	70	32	31	63	151
1984-85	Buffalo Sabres	NHL	77	27	29	56	154
1985-86	Buffalo Sabres	NHL	79	41	39	80	168
	NHL TOTALS		534	219	238	457	1104

(c)—Won Red Tilson Memorial Trophy (OMJHL-MVP).
(d)—Won Eddie Powers Memorial Trophy (OMJHL leading scorer).
(e)—Won Jim Mahon Memorial Trophy (OMJHL top scoring right wing).
(f)—August, 1979—Drafted by Detroit Red Wings in 1979 NHL entry draft. First Red Wings pick, third overall, first round.
(g)—December, 1981—Traded with Dale McCourt, Brent Peterson and future considerations by Detroit Red Wings to Buffalo Sabres for Bob Sauve, Jim Schoenfeld and Derek Smith.

DWIGHT ALEXANDER FOSTER

Center . . . 5'11" . . . 190 lbs. . . . Born, Toronto, Ont., April 2, 1957 . . . Shoots right . . . Missed most of 1977-78 season with torn cartilage in left knee requiring surgery . . . Arthroscopic surgery to right knee (October 20, 1979) . . . (October 10, 1981)—Separated shoulder vs. N.Y. Islanders . . . (October 27, 1982)—Tore ligaments in right ankle during CHL game with Wichita . . . (March, 1984)—Shoulder injury . . . (January, 1985)—Arthroscopic surgery to fractured left kneecap . . . (January 5, 1986)—Injured knee at Toronto and missed 12 games.

Year	Team	League	Games	G.	A.	Pts.	Pen.
1973-74	Kitchener Rangers	Jr. "A" OHA	67	23	32	55	61
1974-75	Kitchener Rangers	Jr. "A" OHA	70	39	51	90	88
1975-76	Kitchener Rangers	Jr. "A" OHA	61	36	58	94	110
1976-77	Kitchener Rangers (c-d)	Jr. "A" OHA	64	60	*83	*143	88
1977-78	Rochester Americans	AHL	3	0	3	3	2

Year	Team	League	Games	G.	A.	Pts.	Pen.
1977-78—Boston Bruins		NHL	14	2	1	3	6
1978-79—Boston Bruins		NHL	44	11	13	24	14
1978-79—Rochester Americans		AHL	22	11	18	29	8
1979-80—Binghamton Dusters		AHL	7	1	3	4	2
1979-80—Boston Bruins		NHL	57	10	28	38	42
1980-81—Boston Bruins (e)		NHL	77	24	28	52	62
1981-82—Colorado Rockies (f)		NHL	70	12	19	31	41
1982-83—Wichita Wind		CHL	2	0	1	1	2
1982-83—New Jersey Devils (g)		NHL	4	0	0	0	2
1982-83—Detroit Red Wings		NHL	58	17	22	39	58
1983-84—Detroit Red Wings		NHL	52	9	12	21	50
1984-85—Detroit Red Wings		NHL	50	16	16	32	56
1985-86—Detroit Red Wings (h)		NHL	55	6	12	18	48
1985-86—Boston Bruins		NHL	13	0	0	0	4
NHL TOTALS			494	107	151	258	483

(c)—Won Eddie Powers Memorial Trophy (leading scorer).
(d)—Drafted from Kitchener Rangers by Boston Bruins in first round of 1977 amateur draft.
(e)—July, 1981—Traded by Boston Bruins to Colorado Rockies for Rockies second round 1982 draft pick. Boston also had the option of switching places with Colorado in the first round of the 1982 NHL Entry Draft.
(f)—June, 1982—Boston exercised option of changing places with Colorado (then New Jersey) and drafted Gord Kluzak in the first round, and Brian Curran in the second. New Jersey drafted Ken Danneyko in the first round.
(g)—October, 1982—Sold by New Jersey Devils to Detroit Red Wings for $1.00.
(h)—March, 1986—Traded by Detroit Red Wings to Boston Bruins for Dave Donnelly.

NICHOLAS EVLAMPIOS FOTIU

Left Wing . . . 6'2" . . . 200 lbs. . . . Born, Staten Island, N.Y., May 25, 1952 . . . Shoots left . . . Missed entire 1972-73 season with knee injury and part of 1975-76 season with severed tendons in right hand . . . (March, 1981)—Given 8-game suspension by NHL for going into stands at Detroit during a 7-3 loss on February 19, 1981 . . . (January 31, 1982)—Slight shoulder separation in game vs. Los Angeles Kings . . . First New York City-born player to play with N.Y. Rangers . . . (November, 1983)—Bruised left instep . . . (January, 1984)—Bruised ribs . . . (March 20, 1984)—Confrontation with fan at Madison Square Garden cost $500 and three-game suspension.

Year	Team	League	Games	G.	A.	Pts.	Pen.
1971-72—New Hyde Park Arrows		N.Y. MJHA	32	6	17	23	135
1972-73—Did not play							
1973-74—Cape Cod Cubs (c)		NAHL	72	12	24	36	*371
1974-75—Cape Codders		NAHL	5	2	1	3	13
1974-75—New England Whalers		WHA	61	2	2	4	144
1975-76—Cape Codders		NAHL	6	2	1	3	15
1975-76—New England Whalers (d)		WHA	49	3	2	5	94
1976-77—New York Rangers		NHL	70	4	8	12	174
1977-78—New Haven Nighthawks		AHL	5	1	1	2	9
1977-78—New York Rangers		NHL	59	2	7	9	105
1978-79—New York Rangers (e)		NHL	71	3	5	8	190
1979-80—Hartford Whalers		NHL	74	10	8	18	107
1980-81—Hartford Whalers (f)		NHL	42	4	3	7	79
1980-81—New York Rangers		NHL	27	5	6	11	91
1981-82—New York Rangers		NHL	70	8	10	18	151
1982-83—New York Rangers		NHL	72	8	13	21	90
1983-84—New York Rangers		NHL	40	7	6	13	115
1984-85—New York Rangers		NHL	46	4	7	11	54
1985-86—New Haven Nighthawks		AHL	9	4	2	6	21
1985-86—Calgary Flames (g)		NHL	9	0	1	1	21
WHA TOTALS			110	6	15	21	279
NHL TOTALS			580	55	74	129	1177

(c)—Tied for lead in penalty minutes (80) during playoffs.
(d)—Signed by New York Rangers, June, 1976.
(e)—June, 1979—Selected by Hartford Whalers in NHL expansion draft.
(f)—January, 1981—Traded by Hartford Whalers to New York Rangers for New York's fifth-round draft pick in 1981 (Bill McGuire).
(g)—March, 1986—Traded by New York Rangers to Calgary Flames for a sixth round 1987 draft pick.

JAMES CHARLES FOX

Right Wing . . . 5'8" . . . 183 lbs. . . . Born, Coniston, Ont., May 18, 1960 . . . Shoots right . . . (November 6, 1985)—Injured disc in a game at Los Angeles and missed 24 games . . . (January 29, 1986)—Bruised hip in game vs. Minnesota.

Year	Team	League	Games	G.	A.	Pts.	Pen.
1975-76—North Bay Trappers		OPJHL	44	30	45	75	16
1976-77—North Bay Trappers (c)		OPJHL	38	44	64	*108	4
1977-78—Ottawa 67's		OMJHL	59	44	83	127	12
1978-79—Ottawa 67's		OMJHL	53	37	66	103	4
1979-80—Ottawa 67's (d-e-f-g)		OMJHL	52	65	*101	*166	30
1980-81—Los Angeles Kings		NHL	71	18	25	43	8
1981-82—Los Angeles Kings		NHL	77	30	38	68	23
1982-83—Los Angeles Kings		NHL	77	28	40	68	8
1983-84—Los Angeles Kings		NHL	80	30	42	72	26
1984-85—Los Angeles Kings		NHL	79	30	53	83	10
1985-86—Los Angeles Kings		NHL	39	14	17	31	2
NHL TOTALS			423	150	215	365	77

(c)—Led OPJHL Playoffs in points (38) and assists (25) in 19 games, and was co-leader (with teammate Jim Omiciolli) in goals (13).
(d)—Won Eddie Powers Memorial Trophy (OMJHL Leading Scorer).
(e)—Won Albert (Red) Tilson Memorial Trophy (OMJHL—MVP).
(f)—Won Jim Mahon Memorial Trophy (Top Scoring OMJHL Right Wing).
(g)—June, 1980—Drafted by Los Angeles Kings in 1980 NHL entry draft. Second Kings pick, 10th overall, first round.

LOU FRANCESCHETTI

Left Wing . . . 6' . . . 190 lbs. . . . Born, Toronto, Ont., March 28, 1958 . . . Shoots left.

Year	Team	League	Games	G.	A.	Pts.	Pen.
1975-76—St. Catharines Black Hawks		OMJHL	1	0	0	0	0
1976-77—Niagara Falls Flyers		OMJHL	61	23	30	53	80
1977-78—Niagara Falls Flyers (c)		OMJHL	62	40	50	90	46
1978-79—Saginaw Gears		IHL	2	1	1	2	0
1978-79—Port Huron Flags		IHL	76	45	58	103	131
1979-80—Port Huron Flags		IHL	15	3	8	11	31
1979-80—Hershey Bears		AHL	65	27	29	56	58
1980-81—Hershey Bears		AHL	79	32	36	68	173
1981-82—Washington Capitals		NHL	30	2	10	12	23
1981-82—Hershey Bears		AHL	50	22	33	55	89
1982-83—Hershey Bears		AHL	80	31	44	75	176
1983-84—Washington Capitals		NHL	2	0	0	0	0
1983-84—Hershey Bears		AHL	73	26	34	60	130
1984-85—Binghamton Whalers		AHL	52	29	43	72	75
1984-85—Washington Capitals		NHL	22	4	7	11	45
1985-86—Washington Capitals		NHL	76	7	14	21	131
NHL TOTALS			130	13	31	44	199

(c)—June, 1978—Drafted by Washington Capitals in the 1978 NHL amateur draft. Seventh Capitals pick, 71st overall, fifth round.

BOBBY FRANCIS

Center . . . 5'9" . . . 175 lbs. . . . Born, North Battleford, Sask., December 5, 1958 . . . Shoots right . . . Son of Emile Francis (Hartford Whalers President and G.M.) . . . (January, 1981)—Injured knee . . . (November, 1984)—Surgery for separated shoulder.

Year	Team	League	Games	G.	A.	Pts.	Pen.
1978-79—University of New Hampshire		ECAC	35	20	46	66	44
1979-80—University of New Hampshire		ECAC	28	19	23	42	30
1980-81—Muskegon Mohawks (c)		IHL	27	16	17	33	33
1980-81—Birmingham Bulls		CHL	18	6	21	27	20
1981-82—Oklahoma City Stars (a-d-e-f)		CHL	80	48	66	*114	76
1982-83—Adirondack Red Wings		AHL	17	3	8	11	0
1982-83—Detroit Red Wings (g)		NHL	14	2	0	2	0
1982-83—Colorado Flames		CHL	26	20	16	36	24
1983-84—Colorado Flames		CHL	68	32	50	82	53
1984-85—Salt Lake Golden Eagles (h)		IHL	53	24	16	40	36
1985-86—Salt Lake Golden Eagles		IHL	82	32	44	76	163
NHL TOTALS			14	2	0	2	0

(c)—October, 1980—Signed by Calgary Flames as a free agent.
(d)—Winner of Phil Esposito Trophy (Leading CHL scorer).
(e)—Winner of Tom Ivan Trophy (CHL MVP).
(f)—Winner of Ken McKenzie Trophy (Top CHL Rookie).
(g)—November, 1982—Traded by Calgary Flames to Detroit Red Wings for Yves Courteau.
(h)—July, 1985—Named player/assistant coach of Salt Lake Golden Eagles.

RONALD FRANCIS

Center ... 6'1" ... 170 lbs. ... Born, Sault Ste. Marie, Ont. ... Shoots left ... Cousin of Mike Liut ... (January 27, 1982)—Out of lineup for three weeks with eye injury ... (November 30, 1983)—Strained ligaments in right knee vs. Vancouver ... (January 18, 1986)—Broke left ankle in game at Quebec and missed 27 games.

Year	Team	League	Games	G.	A.	Pts.	Pen.
1979-80—Sault Ste. Marie Legion		OMHL	45	57	92	149	....
1980-81—Sault Ste. Marie Greyhounds (c)		OHL	64	26	43	69	33
1981-82—Sault Ste. Marie Greyhounds		OHL	25	18	30	48	46
1981-82—Hartford Whalers		NHL	59	25	43	68	51
1982-83—Hartford Whalers		NHL	79	31	59	90	60
1983-84—Hartford Whalers		NHL	72	23	60	83	45
1984-85—Hartford Whalers		NHL	80	24	57	81	66
1985-86—Hartford Whalers		NHL	53	24	53	77	24
NHL TOTALS			343	127	272	399	246

(c)—June, 1981—Drafted as underage junior by Hartford Whalers in 1981 NHL entry draft. First Whalers pick, fourth overall, first round.

CURT FRASER

Left Wing ... 6' ... 190 lbs. ... Born, Cincinnati, Ohio, January 12, 1958 ... Shoots left ... (November, 1983)—Torn knee ligaments ... (January 13, 1985)—Multiple fractures to face when struck by goalie stick of Billy Smith in game vs. N.Y. Islanders. Smith was given a six-game suspension by NHL for the incident ... (December 14, 1985)—Sprained shoulder at Montreal and missed 19 games.

Year	Team	League	Games	G.	A.	Pts.	Pen.
1973-74—Kelowna Buckaroos		Jr."A"BCHL	52	32	32	64	85
1974-75—Victoria Cougars		WCHL	68	17	32	49	105
1975-76—Victoria Cougars		WCHL	71	43	64	107	167
1976-77—Victoria Cougars		WCHL	60	34	41	75	82
1977-78—Victoria Cougars (c)		WCHL	66	48	44	92	256
1978-79—Vancouver Canucks		NHL	78	16	19	35	116
1979-80—Vancouver Canucks		NHL	78	17	25	42	143
1980-81—Vancouver Canucks		NHL	77	25	24	49	118
1981-82—Vancouver Canucks		NHL	79	28	39	67	175
1982-83—Vancouver Canucks (d)		NHL	36	6	7	13	99
1982-83—Chicago Black Hawks		NHL	38	6	13	19	77
1983-84—Chicago Black Hawks		NHL	29	5	12	17	26
1984-85—Chicago Black Hawks		NHL	73	25	25	50	109
1985-86—Chicago Black Hawks		NHL	61	29	39	68	84
NHL TOTALS			549	157	203	360	947

(c)—Drafted from Victoria Cougars by Vancouver Canucks in second round of 1978 amateur draft.
(d)—January, 1983—Traded by Vancouver Canucks to Chicago Black Hawks for Tony Tanti.

WILLIAM DANNY FRAWLEY
(Known by middle name.)

Right Wing ... 6' ... 165 lbs. ... Born, Sturgeon Falls, Ont., June 2, 1962 ... Shoots right.

Year	Team	League	Games	G.	A.	Pts.	Pen.
1979-80—Sudbury Wolves (c)		OHL	63	21	26	47	67
1980-81—Cornwall Royals		QMJHL	28	10	14	24	76
1981-82—Cornwall Royals		OHL	64	27	50	77	239
1982-83—Springfield Indians		AHL	80	30	27	57	107
1983-84—Chicago Black Hawks		NHL	3	0	0	0	0
1983-84—Springfield Indians		AHL	69	22	34	56	137
1984-85—Milwaukee Admirals		IHL	26	11	12	23	125
1984-85—Chicago Black Hawks		NHL	30	4	3	7	64
1985-86—Pittsburgh Penguins (d)		NHL	69	10	11	21	174
NHL TOTALS			102	14	14	28	238

(c)—June, 1980—Drafted as underage junior by Chicago Black Hawks in 1980 NHL entry draft. Fifteenth Black Hawks pick, 204th overall, 10th round.
(d)—October, 1985—Acquired by Pittsburgh Penguins in 1985 NHL waiver draft.

TIM FRIDAY

Defense ... 6' ... 190 lbs. ... Born, Burbank, Calif., March 5, 1961 ... Shoots right ... (October 14, 1985)—Strained left knee ligaments in game at Buffalo and missed four games ... (November 2, 1985)—Reinjured knee ligaments in game at St. Louis and missed six games ... (December 3, 1985)—Injured shoulder vs. Philadelphia and missed six games.

Year	Team	League	Games	G.	A.	Pts.	Pen.
1981-82—R.P.I.		ECAC	25	1	12	13	10
1982-83—R.P.I.		ECAC	28	3	16	19	10
1983-84—R.P.I.		ECAC	32	4	14	18	22
1984-85—R.P.I. (c)		ECAC	36	5	29	34	26
1985-86—Adirondack Red Wings		AHL	43	2	31	33	23
1985-86—Detroit Wings		NHL	23	0	3	3	6
NHL TOTALS			23	0	3	3	6

(c)—June, 1985—Signed by Detroit Red Wings as a free agent.

MIROSLAV OPAVA FRYCER

Right Wing . . . 6' . . . 200 lbs. . . . Born, Ostrava, Czech., September 27, 1959 . . . Shoots left . . . (December 26, 1982)—Strained stomach muscles during team practice . . . Member of Czechoslovakian National team in 1979, 1980 and 1981 . . . (January, 1984)—Knee injury . . . (February 25, 1984)—Injured shoulder at Edmonton . . . (March 8, 1984)—Torn knee ligaments during game vs. New Jersey . . . (March, 1985)—Broken bone in foot . . . (September, 1985)—Injured shoulder in training camp . . . (January 13, 1986)—Injured groin vs. Detroit . . . (January 22, 1986)—Bruised knee vs. N.Y. Rangers.

Year	Team	League	Games	G.	A.	Pts.	Pen.
1977-78—VZKG Ostrava		Czech. Jr.	....	...	....	....	....
1978-79—Tj Vitkovice (b)		Czech.	44	22	12	34	....
1979-80—Tj Vitkovice		Czech.	44	31	15	46	....
1980-81—Tj Vitkovice		Czech.	34	33	24	57	....
1981-82—Fredericton Express (c)		AHL	11	9	5	14	16
1981-82—Quebec Nordiques		NHL	49	20	17	37	47
1981-82—Toronto Maple Leafs (d)		NHL	10	4	6	10	31
1982-83—Toronto Maple Leafs		NHL	67	25	30	55	90
1983-84—Toronto Maple Leafs		NHL	47	10	16	26	55
1984-85—Toronto Maple Leafs		NHL	65	25	30	55	55
1985-86—Toronto Maple Leafs		NHL	73	32	43	75	74
NHL TOTALS			311	116	142	258	352

(c)—April, 1980—Signed by Quebec Nordiques as a free agent.

(d)—March, 1982—Traded with seventh round 1982 draft pick (Toronto drafted Jeff Triano) by Quebec Nordiques to Toronto Maple Leafs for Wilf Paiement.

JOSEPH (JODY) GAGE

Right Wing . . . 5'11" . . . 182 lbs. . . . Born, Toronto, Ont., November 29, 1959 . . . Shoots right.

Year	Team	League	Games	G.	A.	Pts.	Pen.
1976-77—St. Catharines Black Hawks		OMJHL	47	13	20	33	2
1977-78—Hamilton Fincups		OMJHL	32	15	18	33	19
1977-78—Kitchener Rangers		OMJHL	36	17	27	44	21
1978-79—Kitchener Rangers (c)		OMJHL	59	46	43	89	40
1979-80—Adirondack Red Wings		AHL	63	25	21	46	15
1979-80—Kalamazoo Wings		IHL	14	17	12	29	0
1980-81—Detroit Red Wings		NHL	16	2	2	4	22
1980-81—Adirondack Red Wings		AHL	59	17	31	48	44
1981-82—Adirondack Red Wings		AHL	47	21	20	41	21
1981-82—Detroit Red Wings		NHL	31	9	10	19	2
1982-83—Adirondack Red Wings		AHL	65	23	30	53	33
1983-84—Detroit Red Wings		NHL	3	0	0	0	0
1983-84—Adirondack Red Wings		AHL	73	40	32	72	32
1984-85—Adirondack Red Wings		AHL	78	27	33	60	55
1985-86—Buffalo Sabres (d)		NHL	7	3	2	5	0
1985-86—Rochester Americans (a)		AHL	73	42	57	99	56
NHL TOTALS			57	14	14	28	24

(c)—August, 1979—Drafted by Detroit Red Wings in 1979 NHL Entry draft. Second Detroit pick, 46th overall, third round.

(d)—August, 1985—Signed by Buffalo Sabres as a free agent.

PAUL GAGNE

Left Wing . . . 5'10" . . . 178 lbs. . . . Born, Iroquois Falls, Ont., February 6, 1962 . . . Shoots left . . . (December 18, 1980)—Tore knee ligaments . . . (October, 1981)—Fractured cheekbone . . . (January 2, 1982)—Shoulder separation vs. Detroit . . . (February 15, 1986)—Injured back at N.Y. Islanders . . . (March 2, 1986)—Injured back in game vs. Winnipeg . . . (March 25, 1986)—Injured back in game vs. N.Y. Rangers.

Year	Team	League	Games	G.	A.	Pts.	Pen.
1978-79—Windsor Spitfires		OMJHL	67	24	18	42	64
1979-80—Windsor Spitfires (b-c)		OMJHL	65	48	53	101	67

Year	Team	League	Games	G.	A.	Pts.	Pen.
1980-81—Colorado Rockies		NHL	61	25	16	41	12
1981-82—Colorado Rockies		NHL	59	10	12	22	17
1982-83—Wichita Wind		CHL	16	1	9	10	9
1982-83—New Jersey Devils		NHL	53	14	15	29	13
1983-84—New Jersey Devils		NHL	66	14	18	32	33
1984-85—New Jersey Devils		NHL	79	24	19	43	28
1985-86—New Jersey Devils		NHL	47	19	19	38	14
NHL TOTALS			365	106	99	205	117

(c)—June, 1980—Drafted by Colorado Rockies in 1980 NHL entry draft as an underage junior. First Rockies pick, 19th overall, first round.

REMI GAGNE

Right Wing . . . 5'11" . . . 190 lbs. . . . Born, Gagnon, Que., January 24, 1962 . . . Shoots right.

Year	Team	League	Games	G.	A.	Pts.	Pen.
1978-79—Chicoutimi Sagueneens		QMJHL	72	15	15	30	120
1979-80—Chicoutimi Sagueneens (c)		QMJHL	70	24	40	64	191
1980-81—Chicoutimi Sagueneens (d)		QMJHL	72	23	58	81	2
1981-82—Trois-Rivieres Draveurs (e)		QMJHL	50	22	34	56	151
1982-83—Nova Scotia Voyageurs		AHL	7	1	1	2	9
1982-83—Flint Generals		IHL	66	30	36	66	159
1983-84—Nova Scotia Voyageurs		AHL	74	7	18	25	178
1984-85—Sherbrooke Canadiens		AHL	56	8	15	23	115
1985-86—Sherbrooke Canadiens		AHL	16	2	2	4	4

(c)—June, 1980—Drafted as underage junior by Montreal Canadiens in 1980 NHL entry draft. Seventh Canadiens pick, 103rd overall, fifth round.

(d)—November, 1980—Traded by Chicoutimi Sagueneens to Sorel Black Hawks for Andre Mercier. Mercier left Chicoutimi after arriving and Gagne was returned to Sagueneens.

(e)—August, 1981—Acquired by Trois-Rivieres Draveurs in QMJHL dispersal draft of players from defunct Sorel Black Hawks.

DAVE GAGNER

Center . . . 5'10" . . . 185 lbs. . . . Born, Chatham, Ont., December 11, 1964 . . . Shoots left . . . Member of 1984 Canadian Olympic Team . . . (February 5, 1986)—Fractured ankle at St. Louis.

Year	Team	League	Games	G.	A.	Pts.	Pen.
1981-82—Brantford Alexanders		OHL	68	30	46	76	31
1982-83—Brantford Alexanders (b-c)		OHL	70	55	66	121	57
1983-84—Canadian Olympic Team		Int'l	50	19	18	37	26
1983-84—Brantford Alexanders		OHL	12	7	13	20	4
1984-85—New Haven Nighthawks		AHL	38	13	20	33	23
1984-85—New York Rangers		NHL	38	6	6	12	16
1985-86—New York Rangers		NHL	32	4	6	10	19
1985-86—New Haven Nighthawks		AHL	16	10	11	21	11
NHL TOTALS			70	10	12	22	35

(c)—June, 1983—Drafted as underage junior by New York Rangers in 1983 NHL entry draft. First Rangers pick, 12th overall, first round.

ROBERT MICHAEL GAINEY

Left Wing . . . 6'2" . . . 195 lbs. . . . Born, Peterborough, Ont., December 13, 1953 . . . Shoots left . . . Missed part of 1977-78 season with shoulder separation.

Year	Team	League	Games	G.	A.	Pts.	Pen.
1970-71—Peterborough TPTs		Jr."A" OHA	4	0	0	0	0
1971-72—Peterborough TPTs		Jr."A" OHA	4	2	1	3	33
1972-73—Peterborough TPTs (c)		Jr."A" OHA	52	22	21	43	99
1973-74—Nova Scotia Voyageurs		AHL	6	2	5	7	4
1973-74—Montreal Canadiens		NHL	66	3	7	10	34
1974-75—Montreal Canadiens		NHL	80	17	20	37	49
1975-76—Montreal Canadiens		NHL	78	15	13	28	57
1976-77—Montreal Canadiens		NHL	80	14	19	33	41
1977-78—Montreal Canadiens (d)		NHL	66	15	16	31	57
1978-79—Montreal Canadiens (d-e)		NHL	79	20	18	38	44
1979-80—Montreal Canadiens (d)		NHL	64	14	19	33	32
1980-81—Montreal Canadiens (d)		NHL	78	23	24	47	36
1981-82—Montreal Canadiens		NHL	79	21	24	45	24
1982-83—Montreal Canadiens		NHL	80	12	18	30	43

Year	Team	League	Games	G.	A.	Pts.	Pen.
1983-84—Montreal Canadiens		NHL	77	17	22	39	41
1984-85—Montreal Canadiens		NHL	79	19	13	32	40
1985-86—Montreal Canadiens		NHL	80	20	23	43	20
NHL TOTALS			986	210	236	446	518

(c)—Drafted from Peterborough TPTs by Montreal Canadiens in first round of 1973 amateur draft.
(d)—Won Frank J. Selke Trophy (best defensive forward).
(e)—Won Conn Smythe Trophy (MVP-NHL Playoffs).

BERNARD GALLANT

Left Wing . . . 5'10" . . . 176 lbs. . . . Born, Montreal, Que., February 13, 1960 . . . Shoots left . . . Also plays Center and Right Wing.

Year	Team	League	Games	G.	A.	Pts.	Pen.
1978-79—Montreal Juniors		QMJHL	11	1	2	3	2
1978-79—Trois-Rivieres Draveurs		QMJHL	44	23	62	85	38
1979-80—Laval Voisins		QMJHL	17	4	8	12	25
1979-80—Sherbrooke Beavers		QMJHL	50	28	52	80	82
1980-81—Rochester Americans (c)		AHL	69	8	18	26	64
1981-82—Flint Generals		IHL	75	31	29	60	95
1982-83—Rochester Americans		AHL	3	0	0	0	0
1982-83—Flint Generals		IHL	80	27	54	81	19
1983-84—Flint Generals (a)		IHL	81	50	53	103	22
1984-85—Flint Generals		IHL	81	26	37	63	80
1985-86—Saginaw Gears		IHL	45	24	29	53	36

(c)—August, 1980—Signed by Buffalo Sabres as a free agent.

GERARD GALLANT

Left Wing . . . 5'11" . . . 164 lbs. . . . Born, Summerside, P.E.I., September 2, 1963 . . . Shoots left . . . Also plays Center . . . (December 11, 1985)—Broke jaw vs. Minnesota and missed 25 games.

Year	Team	League	Games	G.	A.	Pts.	Pen.
1979-80—Summerside		PEIHA	45	60	55	115	90
1980-81—Sherbrooke Beavers (c)		QMJHL	68	41	60	101	220
1981-82—Sherbrooke Beavers		QMJHL	58	34	58	92	260
1982-83—St. Jean Beavers		QHL	33	28	25	53	139
1982-83—Verdun Juniors		QHL	29	26	49	75	105
1983-84—Adirondack Red Wings		AHL	77	31	33	64	195
1984-85—Adirondack Red Wings		AHL	46	18	29	47	131
1984-85—Detroit Red Wings		NHL	32	6	12	18	66
1985-86—Detroit Red Wings		NHL	52	20	19	39	106
NHL TOTALS			84	26	31	57	172

(c)—June, 1981—Drafted as underage junior by Detroit Red Wings in 1981 NHL entry draft. Fourth Red Wings pick, 107th overall, sixth round.

GARRY GALLEY

Defense . . . 5'11" . . . 190 lbs. . . . Born, Ottawa, Ont., April 16, 1963 . . . Shoots left . . . (December 8, 1985)—Injured knee at Winnipeg.

Year	Team	League	Games	G.	A.	Pts.	Pen.
1981-82—Bowling Green Univ.		CCHA	42	3	36	39	48
1982-83—Bowling Green Univ. (a-c)		CCHA	40	17	29	46	40
1983-84—Bowling Green Univ.		CCHA	44	15	52	67	61
1984-85—Los Angeles Kings		NHL	78	8	30	38	82
1985-86—Los Angeles Kings		NHL	49	9	13	22	46
1985-86—New Haven Nighthawks		AHL	4	2	6	8	6
NHL TOTALS			127	17	43	60	128

(c)—June, 1983—Drafted by Los Angeles Kings in 1983 NHL entry draft. Fourth Kings pick, 100th overall, fifth round.

PERRY GANCHAR

Right Wing . . . 5'9" . . . 175 lbs. . . . Born, Saskatoon, Sask., October 28, 1963 . . . Shoots right.

Year	Team	League	Games	G.	A.	Pts.	Pen.
1977-78—Saskatoon Blades		WHL	4	2	0	2	2
1978-79—Saskatoon		SJHL	50	21	33	54	72
1978-79—Saskatoon Blades		WHL	14	5	3	8	15
1979-80—Saskatoon Blades		WHL	70	41	24	65	116

Year	Team	League	Games	G.	A.	Pts.	Pen.
1980-81—Saskatoon Blades		WHL	68	36	20	56	195
1981-82—Saskatoon Blades (c)		WHL	53	38	52	90	82
1982-83—Saskatoon Blades		WHL	68	68	48	116	105
1982-83—Salt Lake Golden Eagles (d)		CHL	..	..	..	..	..
1983-84—Montana Magic		CHL	59	23	22	45	77
1983-84—St. Louis Blues		NHL	1	0	0	0	0
1984-85—Peoria Rivermen (b)		IHL	63	41	29	70	114
1984-85—St. Louis Blues (e)		NHL	7	0	2	2	0
1985-86—Sherbrooke Canadiens		AHL	75	25	29	54	42
NHL TOTALS			8	0	2	2	0

(c)—June, 1982—Drafted as underage junior by St. Louis Blues in 1982 NHL entry draft. Third Blues pick, 113th overall, sixth round.

(d)—Appeared in one playoff game with one assist.

(e)—August, 1985—Traded by St. Louis Blues to Montreal Canadiens for Ron Flockhart.

DARREN GANI

Defense . . . 6' . . . 180 lbs. . . . Born, Perth, Australia, November 2, 1965 . . . Shoots left.

Year	Team	League	Games	G.	A.	Pts.	Pen.
1982-83—Belleville Bulls		OHL	63	1	21	22	22
1983-84—Belleville Bulls (c)		OHL	67	16	40	56	22
1984-85—Belleville Bulls		OHL	45	17	32	49	27
1985-86—Peterborough Petes		OHL	25	5	7	12	19

(c)—June, 1984—Drafted as underage junior by Edmonton Oilers in 1984 NHL entry draft. Eleventh Oilers pick, 250th overall, 12th round.

DAVID GANS

Center . . . 5'11" . . . 170 lbs. . . . Born, Brantford, Ont., June 6, 1964 . . . Shoots right.

Year	Team	League	Games	G.	A.	Pts.	Pen.
1980-81—Blue Haven Penguins		Brantford Jr. 'B'	36	46	45	91	146
1981-82—Oshawa Generals (c)		OHL	66	22	51	73	112
1982-83—Oshawa Generals (d)		OHL	64	41	64	105	90
1982-83—Los Angeles Kings		NHL	3	0	0	0	0
1983-84—Oshawa Generals		OHL	62	56	76	132	89
1984-85—Toledo Goaldiggers		IHL	81	52	53	105	65
1985-86—Los Angeles Kings		NHL	3	0	0	0	2
1985-86—Hershey Bears		AHL	56	24	32	56	88
1985-86—New Haven Nighthawks		AHL	17	11	12	23	14
NHL TOTALS			6	0	0	0	2

(c)—June, 1982—Drafted as underage junior by Los Angeles Kings in 1982 NHL entry draft. Second Kings pick, 64th overall, fourth round.

(d)—Led OHL Playoffs with 24 assists, and tied teammate John MacLean for playoff lead with 38 points.

PAUL MALONE GARDNER

Center . . . 5'11" . . . 193 lbs. . . . Born, Fort Erie, Ont., March 5, 1956 . . . Shoots left . . . Son of former NHL forward Cal Gardner and brother of Dave Gardner . . . Missed part of 1977-78 season with fractured vertebra . . . Missed part of 1978-79 season with knee surgery . . . (January 13, 1982)—Suffered broken jaw when punched by Jimmy Mann at Winnipeg . . . (December, 1983)—Broke both heels while falling off ladder in mishap at home . . . (April, 1985)—Pulled back muscle in AHL playoffs . . . In 1984-85, set AHL record for points in a season . . . Named coach of Newmarket Saints of AHL for 1986-87 season.

Year	Team	League	Games	G.	A.	Pts.	Pen.
1973-74—Toronto St. Michael's		Jr. 'B' OHA	....	...	....	....	....
1974-75—Oshawa Generals		Jr. "A" OHA	64	27	36	63	54
1975-76—Oshawa Generals (c)		Jr. "A" OHA	65	69	75	144	75
1976-77—Rhode Island Reds		AHL	14	10	4	14	12
1976-77—Colorado Rockies		NHL	60	30	29	59	25
1977-78—Colorado Rockies		NHL	46	30	22	52	29
1978-79—Colorado Rockies (d)		NHL	64	23	26	49	32
1978-79—Toronto Maple Leafs		NHL	11	7	2	9	0
1979-80—New Brunswick Hawks		AHL	20	11	16	27	14
1979-80—Toronto Maple Leafs		NHL	45	11	13	24	10
1980-81—Springfield Indians (e)		AHL	14	9	12	21	6
1980-81—Pittsburgh Penguins		NHL	62	34	40	74	59
1981-82—Pittsburgh Penguins		NHL	59	36	33	69	28
1982-83—Pittsburgh Penguins		NHL	70	28	27	55	12

Year	Team	League	Games	G.	A.	Pts.	Pen.
1983-84—Baltimore Skipjacks		AHL	54	32	49	81	14
1983-84—Pittsburgh Penguins (f)		NHL	16	0	5	5	6
1984-85—Binghamton Whalers (a-g-h-i)		AHL	64	*51	*79	*130	10
1984-85—Washington Capitals (j)		NHL	12	2	4	6	6
1985-86—Rochester Americans (a-g-h)		AHL	71	*61	51	*112	16
1985-86—Buffalo Sabres		NHL	2	0	0	0	0
NHL TOTALS			447	201	201	402	207

(c)—Drafted from Oshawa Generals by Kansas City Scouts in first round of 1976 amateur draft.

(d)—March, 1979—Traded by Colorado Rockies to Toronto Maple Leafs for Don Ashby and Trevor Johansen.

(e)—November, 1980—Traded by Toronto Maple Leafs with Dave Burrows to Pittsburgh Penguins for Paul Marshall and Kim Davis.

(f)—July, 1984—Signed by Washington Capitals as a free agent.

(g)—Won John B. Sollenberger Trophy (leading AHL scorer).

(h)—Won Les Cunningham Plaque (AHL MVP).

(i)—Won Fred Hunt Memorial Award (AHL Sportsmanship, determination and dedication).

(j)—August, 1985—Signed by Buffalo Sabres as a free agent.

WILLIAM SCOTT GARDNER

Center . . . 5'10" . . . 170 lbs. . . . Born, Toronto, Ont., March 19, 1960 . . . Shoots left . . . (February, 1985)—Pinched nerve in neck.

Year	Team	League	Games	G.	A.	Pts.	Pen.
1976-77—Peterborough Petes		OMJHL	1	0	0	0	0
1977-78—Peterborough Petes		OMJHL	65	23	32	55	10
1978-79—Peterborough Petes (c)		OMJHL	68	33	71	104	19
1979-80—Peterborough Petes		OMJHL	59	43	63	106	17
1980-81—New Brunswick Hawks		AHL	48	19	29	48	12
1980-81—Chicago Black Hawks		NHL	1	0	0	0	0
1981-82—Chicago Black Hawks		NHL	69	8	15	23	20
1982-83—Chicago Black Hawks		NHL	77	15	25	40	12
1983-84—Chicago Black Hawks		NHL	79	27	21	48	12
1984-85—Chicago Black Hawks		NHL	74	17	34	51	12
1985-86—Chicago Black Hawks (d)		NHL	46	3	10	13	6
1985-86—Hartford Whalers		NHL	18	1	8	9	4
NHL TOTALS			364	71	113	184	66

(c)—August, 1979—Drafted by Chicago Black Hawks as underage junior in entry draft. Third Chicago pick, 49th overall, third round.

(d)—February, 1986—Traded by Chicago Black Hawks to Hartford Whalers for future considerations.

DANIEL MIRL GARE

Right Wing . . . 5'10" . . . 176 lbs. . . . Born, Nelson, B. C., May 14, 1954 . . . Shoots right . . . Also plays Center . . . Son of Ernie Gare (Former hockey coach at B.C. Notre Dame University) . . . Set WCHL record by scoring goals in 13 consecutive games during 1973-74 season . . . Missed most of 1976-77 season with cracked vertebrae in back . . . (December, 1981)—Eye injury . . . (November, 1983)—Bruised sternum. Came back in December to play wearing a special flak-jacket . . . (December, 1984)—Given three-game NHL suspension . . . (November 8, 1985)—Injured groin vs. Toronto and missed four games . . . (January 18, 1986)—Sprained ankle vs. Calgary and missed seven games . . . Brother of Morrison Gare (1980 N.Y. Islanders draft pick).

Year	Team	League	Games	G.	A.	Pts.	Pen.
1971-72—Calgary Centennials		WCHL	56	10	17	27	15
1972-73—Calgary Centennials		WCHL	65	45	43	88	107
1973-74—Calgary Centennials (a-c)		WCHL	65	68	59	127	238
1974-75—Buffalo Sabres		NHL	78	31	31	62	75
1975-76—Buffalo Sabres		NHL	79	50	23	73	129
1976-77—Buffalo Sabres		NHL	35	11	15	26	73
1977-78—Buffalo Sabres		NHL	69	39	38	77	95
1978-79—Buffalo Sabres		NHL	71	27	40	67	90
1979-80—Buffalo Sabres		NHL	76	*56	33	89	90
1980-81—Buffalo Sabres		NHL	73	46	39	85	109
1981-82—Buffalo Sabres (d)		NHL	22	7	14	21	25
1981-82—Detroit Red Wings		NHL	36	13	9	22	74
1982-83—Detroit Red Wings		NHL	79	26	35	61	107
1983-84—Detroit Red Wings		NHL	63	13	13	26	147
1984-85—Detroit Red Wings		NHL	71	27	29	56	163
1985-86—Detroit Red Wings (e)		NHL	57	7	9	16	102
NHL TOTALS			809	353	328	681	1279

(c)—Drafted from Calgary Centennials by Buffalo Sabres in second round of 1974 amateur draft.

(d)—December, 1981—Traded with Bob Sauve, Jim Schoenfeld and Derek Smith by Buffalo Sabres to Detroit Red Wings for Dale McCourt, Mike Foligno, Brent Peterson and future considerations.
(e)—June, 1986—Released by Detroit Red Wings.

MICHAEL ALFRED GARTNER

Right Wing . . . 6' . . . 180 lbs. . . . Born, Ottawa, Ont., October 29, 1959 . . . Shoots right . . . (February, 1983)—Eye injury . . . (March, 1986)—Arthroscopic surgery to repair torn cartilage in left knee.

Year	Team	League	Games	G.	A.	Pts.	Pen.
1975-76—St. Cath. Black Hawks	Jr."A"OHA		3	1	3	4	0
1976-77—Niagara Falls Flyers	Jr."A"OHA		62	33	42	75	125
1977-78—Niagara Falls Flyers (a-c)	Jr."A"OHA		64	41	49	90	56
1978-79—Cincinnati Stingers (d)	WHA		78	27	25	52	123
1979-80—Washington Capitals	NHL		77	36	32	68	66
1980-81—Washington Capitals	NHL		80	48	46	94	100
1981-82—Washington Capitals	NHL		80	35	45	80	121
1982-83—Washington Capitals	NHL		73	38	38	76	54
1983-84—Washington Capitals	NHL		80	40	45	85	90
1984-85—Washington Capitals	NHL		80	50	52	102	71
1985-86—Washington Capitals	NHL		74	35	40	75	63
WHA TOTALS			78	27	25	52	123
NHL TOTALS			544	282	298	580	565

(c)—Signed by Cincinnati Stingers (WHA) as underage junior, August, 1978.
(d)—August, 1979—Drafted by Washington Capitals in 1979 entry draft. First Capitals pick, fourth overall, first round.

JAMES GASSEAU

Defense . . . 6'2" . . . 200 lbs. . . . Born, Carleton, Que., May 4, 1966 . . . Shoots right.

Year	Team	League	Games	G.	A.	Pts.	Pen.
1983-84—Drummondville Voltigeurs (c)	QHL		68	6	25	31	72
1984-85—Drummondville Voltigeurs	QHL		64	8	43	51	158
1985-86—Drummondville Voltigeurs (b)	QHL		46	20	31	51	155

(c)—June, 1984—Drafted as underage junior by Buffalo Sabres in 1984 NHL entry draft. Sixth Sabres pick, 123rd overall, sixth round.

STEVE GATZOS

Right Wing . . . 5'11" . . . 185 lbs. . . . Born, Toronto, Ont., June 22, 1961 . . . Shoots right . . . (December, 1982)—Ankle injury.

Year	Team	League	Games	G.	A.	Pts.	Pen.
1978-79—Sault Ste. Marie Greyhounds	OMJHL		36	3	9	12	21
1979-80—Sault Ste. Marie Greyhounds	OMJHL		64	36	38	74	64
1980-81—Sault Ste. Marie Greyhounds (c)	OHL		68	78	50	128	114
1981-82—Erie Blades	AHL		54	18	19	37	67
1981-82—Pittsburgh Penguins	NHL		16	6	8	14	14
1982-83—Pittsburgh Penguins	NHL		44	6	7	13	52
1982-83—Baltimore Skipjacks	AHL		12	5	4	9	22
1983-84—Baltimore Skipjacks	AHL		48	14	19	33	43
1983-84—Pittsburgh Penguins	NHL		23	3	3	6	15
1984-85—Muskegon Lumberjacks	IHL		24	18	10	28	24
1984-85—Baltimore Skipjacks	AHL		44	26	13	39	55
1984-85—Pittsburgh Penguins	NHL		6	0	2	2	2
1985-86—Baltimore Skipjacks (d)	AHL		53	25	8	33	34
NHL TOTALS			89	15	20	35	83

(c)—June, 1981—Drafted by Pittsburgh Penguins in 1981 NHL entry draft. First Penguins pick, 28th overall, second round.
(d)—June, 1986—Released by Pittsburgh Penguins.

JEAN-MARC GAULIN

Right Wing . . . 5'10" . . . 180 lbs. . . . Born, Balve, Germany, March 3, 1962 . . . Shoots right . . . (November, 1979)—Dislocated shoulder.

Year	Team	League	Games	G.	A.	Pts.	Pen.
1978-79—Sherbrooke Beavers	QMJHL		71	26	41	67	89
1979-80—Sherbrooke Beavers	QMJHL		16	6	15	21	14
1979-80—Sorel Black Hawks	QMJHL		43	15	25	40	105
1980-81—Sorel Black Hawks (b-c)	QMJHL		70	50	40	90	157
1981-82—Hull Olympics (d)	QMJHL		56	50	50	100	93
1982-83—Quebec Nordiques	NHL		1	0	0	0	0

Year	Team	League	Games	G.	A.	Pts.	Pen.
1982-83—Fredericton Express		AHL	67	11	17	28	58
1983-84—Fredericton Express		AHL	62	14	28	42	80
1983-84—Quebec Nordiques		NHL	2	0	0	0	0
1984-85—Fredericton Express		AHL	27	10	9	19	32
1984-85—Quebec Nordiques		NHL	22	3	3	6	8
1985-86—Quebec Nordiques		NHL	1	1	0	1	0
1985-86—Fredericton Express		AHL	58	16	26	42	66
NHL TOTALS			26	4	3	7	8

(c)—June, 1981—Drafted by Quebec Nordiques in 1981 NHL entry draft. Second Nordiques pick, 53rd overall, third round.

(d)—August, 1981—Acquired by Hull Olympics in QMJHL dispersal draft of players of defunct Sorel Black Hawks.

DALLAS GAUME

Center . . . 5'10" . . . 180 lbs. . . . Born, Innisfal, Alta., August 27, 1963 . . . Shoots left . . . Broke Bill Masterton record for career points at University of Denver.

Year	Team	League	Games	G.	A.	Pts.	Pen.
1982-83—University of Denver		WCHA	37	19	47	66	12
1983-84—University of Denver		WCHA	32	12	25	37	22
1984-85—University of Denver		WCHA	39	15	48	63	28
1985-86—University of Denver (a-c-d)		WCHA	47	32	*67	*99	18

(c)—Named WCHA MVP.

(d)—July, 1986—Signed by Hartford Whalers as a free agent.

ROBERT STEWART GAVIN
(Known By middle name.)

Left Wing . . . 6' . . . 180 lbs. . . . Born, Ottawa, Ont., March 15, 1960 . . . Shoots left . . . (October, 1981)—Shoulder separation . . . (December, 1981)—Reinjured shoulder . . . (October, 1982)—Sprained ankle.

Year	Team	League	Games	G.	A.	Pts.	Pen.
1976-77—Ottawa 67's		OMJHL	1	0	0	0	0
1977-78—Toronto Marlboros		OMJHL	67	16	24	40	19
1978-79—Toronto Marlboros		OMJHL	61	24	25	49	83
1979-80—Toronto Marlboros (c)		OMJHL	66	27	30	57	52
1980-81—Toronto Maple Leafs		NHL	14	1	2	3	13
1980-81—New Brunswick Hawks		AHL	46	7	12	19	42
1981-82—Toronto Maple Leafs		NHL	38	5	6	11	29
1982-83—St. Catharines Saints		OHL	6	2	4	6	17
1982-83—Toronto Maple Leafs		NHL	63	6	5	11	44
1983-84—Toronto Maple Leafs		NHL	80	10	22	32	90
1984-85—Toronto Maple Leafs		NHL	73	12	13	25	38
1985-86—Hartford Whalers (d)		NHL	76	26	29	55	51
NHL TOTALS			344	60	77	137	265

(c)—June, 1980—Drafted by Toronto Maple Leafs in 1980 NHL entry draft. Fourth Maple Leafs pick, 74th overall, fourth round.

(d)—October, 1985—Traded by Toronto Maple Leafs to Hartford Whalers for Chris Kotsopoulos.

ROBERT CHARLES GEALE

Center and Right Wing . . . 5'11" . . . 175 lbs. . . . Born, Edmonton, Alta., April 17, 1962 . . . Shoots right . . . Nephew of Roger Kozar (goalie) who played in minor leagues in mid 70's . . . Missed several games during 1980-81 season with recurring knee problems.

Year	Team	League	Games	G.	A.	Pts.	Pen.
1978-79—Sherwood Park Crusaders		AJHL	60	11	33	44	44
1979-80—Portland Winter Hawks (c)		WHL	72	17	29	46	32
1980-81—Portland Winter Hawks		WHL	54	30	32	62	54
1981-82—Portland Winter Hawks		WHL	72	31	54	85	89
1982-83—Baltimore Skipjacks		AHL	56	4	10	14	6
1983-84—Baltimore Skipjacks		AHL	74	17	23	40	50
1984-85—Baltimore Skipjacks		AHL	77	26	23	49	42
1984-85—Pittsburgh Penguins		NHL	1	0	0	0	2
1985-86—Baltimore Skipjacks		AHL	21	5	7	12	9
NHL TOTALS			1	0	0	0	2

(c)—June, 1980—Drafted as underage junior by Pittsburgh Penguins in 1980 NHL entry draft. Sixth Penguins pick, 156th overall, eighth round.

ERIC GERMAIN

Defense . . . 6'1" . . . 190 lbs. . . . Born, Quebec City, Que., June 26, 1966 . . . Shoots left.

Year	Team	League	Games	G.	A.	Pts.	Pen.
1983-84	St. Jean Beavers	QHL	57	2	15	17	60
1984-85	St. Jean Beavers	QHL	66	10	31	41	243
1985-86	St. Jean Castors (c)	QHL	66	5	38	43	183

(c)—June, 1986—Signed by Quebec Nordiques as a free agent.

DONALD SCOTT GIBSON

Defense . . . 6'1" . . . 210 lbs. . . . Born, Deloraine, Man., March 17, 1967 . . . Shoots right.

Year	Team	League	Games	G.	A.	Pts.	Pen.
1985-86	Winkler Flyers (c)	MJHL	34	24	29	53	210

(c)—June, 1986—Drafted by Vancouver Canucks in 1986 NHL entry draft. Second Canucks pick, 49th overall, third round.

LEE GIFFIN

Right Wing . . . 5'11" . . . 177 lbs. . . . Born, Chatham, Ont., April 1, 1967 . . . Shoots right.

Year	Team	League	Games	G.	A.	Pts.	Pen.
1982-83	Newmarket Flyers	OHA	47	10	21	31	123
1983-84	Oshawa Generals	OHL	70	23	27	50	88
1984-85	Oshawa Generals (c)	OHL	62	36	42	78	78
1985-86	Oshawa Generals	OHL	54	29	37	66	28

(c)—June, 1985—Drafted as underage junior by Pittsburgh Penguins in 1985 NHL entry draft. Second Penguins pick, 23rd overall, second round.

STEPHANE GIGUERE

Left Wing . . . 6' . . . 185 lbs. . . . Born, Montreal, Que., February 21, 1968 . . . Shoots left.

Year	Team	League	Games	G.	A.	Pts.	Pen.
1984-85	Laval Midget AAA	Que.	41	25	37	62	70
1985-86	St. Jean Castors (c)	QHL	71	13	20	33	110

(c)—June, 1986—Drafted as underage junior by Toronto Maple Leafs in 1986 NHL entry draft. Sixth Maple Leafs pick, 111th overall, sixth round.

GREG SCOTT GILBERT

Left Wing . . . 6' . . . 190 lbs. . . . Born, Mississauga, Ont., January 22, 1962 . . . Shoots left . . . (December, 1979)—Sprained ankle . . . (September, 1984)—Stretched ligaments in left ankle while jogging prior to training camp . . . (February 27, 1985)—Injured ligaments when checked into open door at players bench by Jamie Macoun in game at Calgary. He required major reconstructive surgery when the knee did not respond to therapy following arthroscopic surgery.

Year	Team	League	Games	G.	A.	Pts.	Pen.
1979-80	Toronto Marlboros (c)	OMJHL	68	10	11	21	35
1980-81	Toronto Marlboros	OHL	64	30	37	67	73
1981-82	Toronto Marlboros	OHL	65	41	67	108	119
1981-82	New York Islanders	NHL	1	1	0	1	0
1982-83	Indianapolis Checkers	CHL	24	11	16	27	23
1982-83	New York Islanders	NHL	45	8	11	19	30
1983-84	New York Islanders	NHL	79	31	35	66	59
1984-85	New York Islanders	NHL	58	13	25	38	36
1985-86	Springfield Indians	AHL	2	0	0	0	2
1985-86	New York Islanders	NHL	60	9	19	28	82
	NHL TOTALS		243	62	90	152	207

(c)—June, 1980—Drafted as underage junior by New York Islanders in 1980 NHL entry draft. Fifth Islanders pick, 80th overall, fourth round.

BRENT GILCHRIST

Center . . . 5'10" . . . 175 lbs. . . . Born, Moose Jaw, Sask., April 3, 1967 . . . Shoots left . . . (January, 1985)—Strained medial collateral ligament in game at Portland.

Year	Team	League	Games	G.	A.	Pts.	Pen.
1983-84	Kelowna Wings	WHL	69	16	11	27	16
1984-85	Kelowna Wings (c)	WHL	51	35	38	73	58
1985-86	Spokane Chiefs	WHL	52	45	45	90	57

(c)—June, 1985—Drafted as underage junior by Montreal Canadiens in 1985 NHL entry draft. Sixth Canadiens pick, 79th overall, sixth round.

CURT GILES

Defense . . . 5'8" . . . 180 lbs. . . . Born, The Pas, Manitoba, November 30, 1958 . . . Shoots left . . . Named to All-American College teams in 1978 and 1979 . . . (February, 1981)—Knee strain (right knee) . . . (January, 1984)—Knee injury . . . (January 25, 1986)—Sprained knee vs. Washington and missed three games . . . (March 24, 1986)—Left ring finger amputated due to a tumor that had grown into the bone. He returned for the playoffs.

Year	Team	League	Games	G.	A.	Pts.	Pen.
1975-76—Univ. of Minnesota-Duluth		WCHA	34	5	17	22	76
1976-77—Univ. of Minnesota-Duluth		WCHA	37	12	37	49	64
1977-78—Univ. of Minn.-Duluth (a-c)		WCHA	34	11	36	47	62
1978-79—Univ. of Minnesota-Duluth (a)		WCHA	30	3	38	41	38
1979-80—Oklahoma City Stars		CHL	42	4	24	28	35
1979-80—Minnesota North Stars		NHL	37	2	7	9	31
1980-81—Minnesota North Stars		NHL	67	5	22	27	56
1981-82—Minnesota North Stars		NHL	74	3	12	15	87
1982-83—Minnesota North Stars		NHL	76	2	21	23	70
1983-84—Minnesota North Stars		NHL	70	6	22	28	59
1984-85—Minnesota North Stars		NHL	77	5	25	30	49
1985-86—Minnesota North Stars		NHL	69	6	21	27	30
NHL TOTALS			470	29	130	159	382

(c)—June, 1978—Drafted by Minnesota North Stars in NHL amateur draft. Fourth North Stars pick, 54th overall, fourth round.

RANDY GILHEN

Left Wing . . . 5'11" . . . 195 lbs. . . . Born, Zweibrucken, West Germany, June 13, 1963 . . . Shoots left.

Year	Team	League	Games	G.	A.	Pts.	Pen.
1979-80—Saskatoon		SJHL	55	18	34	52	112
1979-80—Saskatoon Blades		WHL	9	2	2	4	20
1980-81—Saskatoon Blades		WHL	68	10	5	15	154
1981-82—Winnipeg Warriors (c)		WHL	61	41	37	78	87
1982-83—Winnipeg Warriors		WHL	71	57	44	101	84
1982-83—Hartford Whalers		NHL	2	0	1	1	0
1982-83—Binghamton Whalers (d)		AHL	..	..	..	..	..
1983-84—Binghamton Whalers		AHL	73	8	12	20	72
1984-85—Salt Lake Golden Eagles		IHL	57	20	20	40	28
1984-85—Binghamton Whalers (e)		AHL	18	3	3	6	9
1985-86—Fort Wayne Komets		IHL	82	44	40	84	48
NHL TOTALS			2	0	1	1	0

(c)—June, 1982—Drafted as underage junior by Hartford Whalers in 1982 NHL entry draft. Sixth Whalers pick, 109th overall, sixth round.

(d)—No regular season record. Played five playoff games.

(e)—August, 1985—Signed by Winnipeg Jets as a free agent.

TODD GILL

Defense . . . 6'1" . . . 175 lbs. . . . Born, Brockville, Ont., November 9, 1965 . . . Shoots left.

Year	Team	League	Games	G.	A.	Pts.	Pen.
1982-83—Windsor Spitfires		OHL	70	12	24	36	108
1983-84—Windsor Spitfires (c)		OHL	68	9	48	57	184
1984-85—Toronto Maple Leafs		NHL	10	1	0	1	13
1984-85—Windsor Spitfires		OHL	53	17	40	57	148
1985-86—St. Catharines Saints		AHL	58	8	25	33	90
1985-86—Toronto Maple Leafs		NHL	15	1	2	3	28
NHL TOTALS			25	2	2	4	41

(c)—June, 1984—Drafted as underage junior by Toronto Maple Leafs in 1984 NHL entry draft. Second Maple Leafs pick, 25th overall, second round.

CLARK GILLIES

Left Wing . . . 6'3" . . . 215 lbs. . . . Born, Moose Jaw, Sask., April 7, 1954 . . . Shoots left . . . Played three seasons of baseball with Houston Astros (NL) Covington, Virginia farm team . . . (April, 1983)—Arthroscopic surgery to left knee . . . Holds New York Islanders club record for goals by a left wing in a season (38) . . . (February, 1985)—Sprained ankle . . . (October 29, 1985)—Bruised shoulder vs. Boston and missed four games . . . (January 28, 1986)—Injured back vs. Toronto and missed eight games.

Year	Team	League	Games	G.	A.	Pts.	Pen.
1971-72—Regina Pats		WCHL	68	31	48	79	199
1972-73—Regina Pats		WCHL	68	40	52	92	192

Year	Team	League	Games	G.	A.	Pts.	Pen.
1973-74—Regina Pats (a-c)		WCHL	65	46	66	112	179
1974-75—New York Islanders		NHL	80	25	22	47	66
1975-76—New York Islanders		NHL	80	34	27	61	96
1976-77—New York Islanders		NHL	70	33	22	55	93
1977-78—New York Islanders (a)		NHL	80	35	50	85	76
1978-79—New York Islanders (a)		NHL	75	35	56	91	68
1979-80—New York Islanders		NHL	73	19	35	54	49
1980-81—New York Islanders		NHL	80	33	45	78	99
1981-82—New York Islanders		NHL	79	38	39	77	75
1982-83—New York Islanders		NHL	70	21	20	41	76
1983-84—New York Islanders		NHL	76	12	16	28	65
1984-85—New York Islanders		NHL	54	15	17	32	73
1985-86—New York Islanders		NHL	55	4	10	14	55
NHL TOTALS			872	304	359	663	891

(c)—Drafted from Regina Pats by New York Islanders in first round of 1974 amateur draft.

JERE ALAN GILLIS

Left Wing . . . 6'1" . . . 185 lbs. . . . Born, Bend, Ore., January 18, 1957 . . . Shoots left . . . (January, 1981)—Strained left knee.

Year	Team	League	Games	G.	A.	Pts.	Pen.
1973-74—Sherbrooke Beavers		QJHL	69	21	19	40	96
1974-75—Sherbrooke Beavers		QJHL	54	38	57	95	89
1975-76—Sherbrooke Beavers		QJHL	60	47	55	102	38
1976-77—Sherbrooke Beavers (a-c)		QJHL	72	55	85	140	80
1977-78—Vancouver Canucks		NHL	79	23	18	41	35
1978-79—Vancouver Canucks		NHL	78	13	12	25	33
1979-80—Vancouver Canucks		NHL	67	13	17	30	108
1980-81—Vancouver Canucks (d)		NHL	11	0	4	4	4
1980-81—New York Rangers		NHL	35	10	10	20	4
1981-82—New York Rangers (e)		NHL	26	3	9	12	16
1981-82—Quebec Nordiques		NHL	12	2	1	3	0
1981-82—Fredericton Express		AHL	28	2	17	19	10
1982-83—Buffalo Sabres		NHL	3	0	0	0	0
1982-83—Rochester Americans		AHL	53	18	24	42	69
1983-84—Vancouver Canucks (f)		NHL	37	9	13	22	7
1983-84—Fredericton Express		AHL	36	22	28	50	35
1984-85—Fredericton Express		AHL	7	2	1	3	2
1984-85—Vancouver Canucks		NHL	37	5	11	16	23
1985-86—Fredericton Express		AHL	29	4	14	18	21
NHL TOTALS			385	78	95	173	230

(c)—Drafted from Sherbrooke Beavers by Vancouver Canucks in first round of 1977 amateur draft.
(d)—November, 1980—Traded by Vancouver Canucks with Jeff Bandura to New York Rangers for Mario Marois and Jim Mayer.
(e)—December, 1981—Traded with Dean Talafous by New York Rangers to Quebec Nordiques for Robbie Ftorek and eighth-round 1982 draft pick (Brian Glynn). Talafous retired rather than report to Quebec and NHL awarded Pat Hickey to Nordiques as compensation in March, 1982.
(f)—August, 1983—Signed by Vancouver Canucks as a free agent.

PAUL C. GILLIS

Center . . . 6' . . . 195 lbs. . . . Born, Toronto, Ont., December 31, 1963 . . . Shoots left . . . Brother of Mike Gillis.

Year	Team	League	Games	G.	A.	Pts.	Pen.
1980-81—Niagara Falls Flyers		OHL	59	14	19	33	165
1981-82—Niagara Falls Flyers (c)		OHL	66	27	62	89	247
1982-83—North Bay Centennials		OHL	61	34	52	86	151
1982-83—Quebec Nordiques		NHL	7	0	2	2	2
1983-84—Fredericton Express		AHL	18	7	8	15	47
1983-84—Quebec Nordiques		NHL	57	8	9	17	59
1984-85—Quebec Nordiques		NHL	77	14	28	42	168
1985-86—Quebec Nordiques		NHL	80	19	24	43	203
NHL TOTALS			221	41	63	104	432

(c)—June, 1982—Drafted as underage junior by Quebec Nordiques in 1982 NHL entry draft. Second Nordiques pick, 34th overall, second round.

DOUGLAS GILMOUR

Center . . . 5'11" . . . 164 lbs. . . . Born, Kingston, Ont., June 25, 1963 . . . Shoots left . . . (October 7, 1985)—Sprained ankle in training camp and missed four regular season games.

Year	Team	League	Games	G.	A.	Pts.	Pen.
1980-81—Cornwall Royals		QMJHL	51	12	23	35	35
1981-82—Cornwall Royals (c)		OHL	67	46	73	119	42
1982-83—Cornwall Royals (a-d-e)		OHL	68	*70	*107	*177	62
1983-84—St. Louis Blues		NHL	80	25	28	53	57
1984-85—St. Louis Blues		NHL	78	21	36	57	49
1985-86—St. Louis Blues		NHL	74	25	28	53	41
NHL TOTALS			232	71	92	163	147

(c)—June, 1982—Drafted as underage junior by St. Louis Blues in 1982 NHL entry draft. Fourth Blues pick, 134th overall, seventh round.

(d)—Won Red Tilson Trophy (Outstanding OHL Player).

(e)—Won Eddie Powers Memorial Trophy (OHL Scoring Champion).

GASTON REGINALD GINGRAS

Defense . . . 6' . . . 191 lbs. . . . Born, Temiscaming, Que., February 13, 1959 . . . Shoots left . . . (October, 1980)—Severe Charley horse . . . (October, 1981)—Injured back . . . (September 18, 1982)—Injured back in preseason game vs. Buffalo . . . (February, 1983)—Back spasms.

Year	Team	League	Games	G.	A.	Pts.	Pen.
1974-75—North Bay Trappers		OPJHL	41	11	27	38	74
1975-76—Kitchener Rangers		Jr. "A" OHA	66	13	31	44	94
1976-77—Kitchener Rangers		Jr. "A" OHA	59	13	62	75	134
1977-78—Kitchener Rangers (c)		Jr. "A" OHA	32	13	24	37	31
1977-78—Hamilton Fincups (d)		Jr. "A" OHA	29	11	19	30	37
1978-79—Birmingham Bulls (e)		WHA	60	13	21	34	35
1979-80—Nova Scotia Voyageurs		AHL	30	11	27	38	17
1979-80—Montreal Canadiens		NHL	34	3	7	10	18
1980-81—Montreal Canadiens		NHL	55	5	16	21	22
1981-82—Montreal Canadiens		NHL	34	6	18	24	28
1982-83—Montreal Canadiens (f)		NHL	22	1	8	9	8
1982-83—Toronto Maple Leafs		NHL	45	10	18	28	10
1983-84—Toronto Maple Leafs		NHL	59	7	20	27	16
1984-85—Toronto Maple Leafs (g)		NHL	5	0	2	2	0
1984-85—St. Catharines Saints		AHL	36	7	12	19	13
1984-85—Sherbrooke Canadiens		AHL	21	3	14	17	6
1985-86—Sherbrooke Canadiens		AHL	42	11	20	31	14
1985-86—Montreal Canadiens		NHL	34	8	18	26	12
NHL TOTALS			288	40	107	147	114
WHA TOTALS			60	13	21	34	35

(c)—December, 1977—Traded to Hamilton Fincups by Kitchener Rangers for Jody Gage and future considerations.

(d)—Signed by Birmingham Bulls (WHA) as underage junior, July, 1978.

(e)—June, 1979—Drafted by Montreal Canadiens in entry draft. First Canadiens pick, 27th overall, second round.

(f)—December, 1982—Traded with Dan Daoust by Montreal Canadiens to Toronto Maple Leafs for future draft considerations.

(g)—February, 1985—Traded by Toronto Maple Leafs to Montreal Canadiens to complete earlier trade involving Larry Landon.

ERIN GINNELL

Center . . . 6'3" . . . 195 lbs. . . . Born, Flin Flon, Manitoba, September 9, 1968 . . . Shoots left . . . Son of Paddy Ginnell (Coach of New Westminster-WHL) . . . Brother of Kevin Ginnell (Drafted by Chicago in 1980) . . . (March, 1986)—Broken wrist.

Year	Team	League	Games	G.	A.	Pts.	Pen.
1984-85—Swift Current		SAJHL	61	36	39	75	90
1985-86—New Westminster Bruins		WHL	22	17	13	30	14
1985-86—Calgary Wranglers (c)		WHL	22	6	11	17	14

(c)—June, 1986—Drafted as underage junior by Washington Capitals in 1986 NHL entry draft. Fifth Capitals pick, 82nd overall, fourth round.

ROBERT GLASGOW

Right Wing . . . 6' . . . 205 lbs. . . . Born, Edmonton, Alta., April 22, 1968 . . . Shoots right.

Year	Team	League	Games	G.	A.	Pts.	Pen.
1984-85—Edmonton Anavets Midgets		Alta.	30	17	24	41	29
1985-86—Sherwood Park Crusaders (c-d)		AJHL	52	23	18	41	18

(c)—Named AJHL Rookie of the Year.

(d)—June, 1986—Drafted by Hartford Whalers in 1986 NHL entry draft. Eighth Whalers pick, 179th overall, ninth round.

BRIAN GLYNN

Defense . . . 6'4" . . . 224 lbs. . . . Born, Iserlohn, West Germany, November 23, 1967 . . . Shoots left.

Year	Team	League	Games	G.	A.	Pts.	Pen.
1984-85—Melville Millionaires		SAJHL	12	1	0	1	2
1985-86—Saskatoon Blades (c)		WHL	66	7	25	32	131

(c)—June, 1986—Drafted by Calgary Flames in 1986 NHL entry draft. Second Flames pick, 37th overall, second round.

DAVE GOERTZ

Defense . . . 5'11" . . . 205 lbs. . . . Born, Edmonton, Alta., March 28, 1965 . . . Shoots right.

Year	Team	League	Games	G.	A.	Pts.	Pen.
1981-82—Regina Pats		WHL	67	5	19	24	181
1982-83—Regina Pats (c)		WHL	69	4	22	26	132
1983-84—Prince Albert Raiders		WHL	60	13	47	60	111
1983-84—Baltimore Skipjacks		AHL	1	0	0	0	0
1984-85—Prince Albert Raiders		WHL	48	3	48	51	62
1984-85—Baltimore Skipjacks (d)		AHL	....	...	....	....	....
1985-86—Baltimore Skipjacks		AHL	74	1	15	16	76

(c)—June, 1983—Drafted as underage junior by Pittsburgh Penguins in 1983 NHL entry draft. Tenth Penguins pick, 223rd overall, 12th round.

(d)—Played two playoff games.

PATRICK GOFF

Defense . . . 6'1" . . . 185 lbs. . . . Born, St. Paul, Minn., June 29, 1964 . . . Shoots left . . . Brother of Michigan teammate Dan Goff.

Year	Team	League	Games	G.	A.	Pts.	Pen.
1980-81—Alexander Ramsey H.S.		Minn. H.S.	22	9	24	33	....
1981-82—Alexander Ramsey H.S. (c)		Minn. H.S.	23	5	20	25	....
1982-83—University of Michigan		CCHA	36	2	18	20	20
1983-84—University of Michigan		CCHA	37	4	17	21	38
1984-85—University of Michigan		CCHA	34	3	4	7	26
1985-86—University of Michigan		CCHA	38	2	12	14	30

(c)—June, 1982—Drafted as underage player by New York Islanders in 1982 NHL entry draft. Eleventh Islanders pick, 231st overall, 11th round.

JOHN GOODWIN

Center . . . 5'6" . . . 160 lbs. . . . Born, Toronto, Ont., September 25, 1961 . . . Shoots left . . . First OHL scoring leader since the NHL started drafting that wasn't drafted by an NHL club.

Year	Team	League	Games	G.	A.	Pts.	Pen.
1978-79—Sault Ste. Marie Greyhounds (c)		OMJHL	68	43	*86	129	20
1979-80—Sault Ste. Marie Greyhounds		OMJHL	65	34	60	94	14
1980-81—S.S. Marie Greyhounds (b-d-e-f)		OHL	68	56	*109	*165	42
1981-82—Nova Scotia Voyageurs		AHL	78	16	40	56	19
1982-83—Nova Scotia Voyageurs		AHL	80	35	49	84	24
1983-84—Nova Scotia Voyageurs (g)		AHL	35	12	21	33	11
1983-84—New Haven Nighthawks		AHL	44	12	41	53	35
1984-85—Peoria Rivermen (h)		IHL	82	31	64	95	45
1985-86—St. Catharines Saints (i)		AHL	78	21	35	56	37

(c)—Winner of Emms Family Trophy (OMJHL Top Rookie).

(d)—Winner of Eddie Powers Memorial Trophy (Leading OHL Scorer).

(e)—Winner of John Hanley Trophy (OHL Most Gentlemanly).

(f)—August, 1981—Signed by Montreal Canadiens as a free agent.

(g)—December, 1983—Traded by Montreal Canadiens to Los Angeles Kings for Dan Bonar.

(h)—October, 1984—Signed by Peoria Rivermen as a free agent.

(i)—October, 1985—Signed by St. Catharines Saints as a free agent.

GUY GOSSELIN

Defense . . . 5'10" . . . 185 lbs. . . . Born, Rochester, Minn., January 6, 1964 . . . Shoots left . . . Son of Gordon Gosselin, a member of 1952 Ft. Francis, Ontario Allen Cup Champions.

Year	Team	League	Games	G.	A.	Pts.	Pen.
1981-82—Rochester J. Marshall H.L. (c)		Minn.H.S.	22	14	15	29	48
1982-83—Univ. of Minn.-Duluth		WCHA	4	0	0	0	0
1983-84—Univ. of Minn.-Duluth		WCHA	37	3	3	6	26
1984-85—Univ. of Minn.-Duluth		WCHA	47	3	7	10	50
1985-86—Univ. of Minn.-Duluth		WCHA	39	2	16	18	53

(c)—June, 1982—Drafted as underage player by Winnipeg Jets in 1982 NHL entry draft. Sixth Jets pick, 159th overall, eighth round.

STEVE GOTAAS

Center . . . 5'9" . . . 170 lbs. . . . Born, Cumrose, Sask., May 10, 1967 . . . Shoots right . . . (May, 1984)—Shoulder surgery.

Year	Team	League	Games	G.	A.	Pts.	Pen.
1983-84—Prince Albert Raiders		WHL	65	10	22	32	47
1984-85—Prince Albert Raiders (c)		WHL	72	32	41	73	66
1985-86—Prince Albert Raiders		WHL	61	40	61	101	31

(c)—June, 1985—Drafted as underage junior by Pittsburgh Penguins in 1985 NHL entry draft. Fourth Penguins pick, 86th overall, fifth round.

ROBERT GOULD

Right Wing . . . 5'11" . . . 195 lbs. . . . Born, Petrolia, Ont., September 2, 1957 . . . Shoots right.

Year	Team	League	Games	G.	A.	Pts.	Pen.
1975-76—University of New Hampshire		ECAC	31	13	14	27	16
1976-77—University of New Hampshire (c)		ECAC	39	24	25	49	36
1977-78—University of New Hampshire		ECAC	30	23	34	57	40
1978-79—University of New Hampshire		ECAC	....	24	17	41	....
1978-79—Tulsa Oilers		CHL	5	2	0	2	4
1979-80—Atlanta Flames		NHL	1	0	0	0	0
1979-80—Birmingham Bulls		CHL	79	27	33	60	73
1980-81—Calgary Flames		NHL	3	0	0	0	0
1980-81—Birmingham Bulls		CHL	58	25	25	50	43
1980-81—Ft. Worth Texans		CHL	18	8	6	14	6
1981-82—Oklahoma City Stars		CHL	1	0	1	1	0
1981-82—Calgary Flames (d)		NHL	16	3	0	3	4
1981-82—Washington Capitals		NHL	60	18	13	31	69
1982-83—Washington Capitals		NHL	80	22	18	40	43
1983-84—Washington Capitals		NHL	78	21	19	40	74
1984-85—Washington Capitals		NHL	78	14	19	33	69
1985-86—Washington Capitals		NHL	79	19	19	38	26
NHL TOTALS			396	97	88	185	285

(c)—June, 1977—Drafted by Atlanta Flames in 1977 amateur draft. Sixth Flames pick, 118th overall, seventh round.

(d)—November, 1981—Traded with Randy Holt by Calgary Flames to Washington Capitals for Pat Ribble.

MICHEL GOULET

Left Wing . . . 6'1" . . . 195 lbs. . . . Born, Peribonqua, Que., April 21, 1960 . . . Shoots left . . . Set Nordiques NHL record for most goals in a season in 1982-83 (57) . . . (1983-84) Set NHL record for most points by left wing in a season (121) and tied record for assists by a left wing (65) set by John Bucyk of Boston in 1970-71 . . . (January 2, 1985)—Fractured thumb vs. Hartford Whalers . . . (September, 1985)—Left training camp to renegotiate contract. He was suspended by Quebec and did not return until after the regular season had started.

Year	Team	League	Games	G.	A.	Pts.	Pen.
1976-77—Quebec Remparts		QJHL	37	17	18	35	9
1977-78—Quebec Remparts (b-c)		QJHL	72	73	62	135	109
1978-79—Birmingham Bulls (d)		WHA	78	28	30	58	64
1979-80—Quebec Nordiques		NHL	77	22	32	54	48
1980-81—Quebec Nordiques		NHL	76	32	39	71	45
1981-82—Quebec Nordiques		NHL	80	42	42	84	48
1982-83—Quebec Nordiques (b)		NHL	80	57	48	105	51
1983-84—Quebec Nordiques (a)		NHL	75	56	65	121	76
1984-85—Quebec Nordiques		NHL	69	55	40	95	55
1985-86—Quebec Nordiques (a)		NHL	75	53	50	103	64
WHA TOTALS			78	28	30	58	64
NHL TOTALS			532	317	316	633	387

(c)—Signed by Birmingham Bulls (WHA) as underage player, July, 1978.

(d)—August, 1979—Drafted by Quebec Nordiques in 1979 NHL entry draft. First Nordiques pick, 20th overall, first round.

THOMAS KJELL GRADIN

Center . . . 5'11" . . . 180 lbs. . . . Born, Solleftea, Sweden, February 18, 1956 . . . Shoots left . . . Attended G.I.H. University (Sweden) . . . Brother of Peter Gradin . . . Was member of Swedish National Team . . . Missed part of 1977-78 season with broken hand . . . (October, 1985)—Headaches . . . (January 9, 1986)—Broke hand at Calgary and missed three games . . . (February 28, 1986)—Bruised shoulder vs. Philadelphia and missed three games.

Year	Team	League	Games	G.	A.	Pts.	Pen.
1974-75—AIK		Sweden	29	16	15	31	16
1975-76—AIK (c)		Sweden	35	16	23	39	23
1976-77—AIK		Sweden	35	16	12	28	14
1977-78—Tre Kronor (National Team)		Sweden	26	5	2	7	....
1977-78—AIK (d)		Sweden	36	22	14	36	22
1978-79—Vancouver Canucks		NHL	76	20	31	51	22
1979-80—Vancouver Canucks		NHL	80	30	45	75	22
1980-81—Vancouver Canucks		NHL	79	21	48	69	34
1981-82—Vancouver Canucks		NHL	76	37	49	86	32
1982-83—Vancouver Canucks		NHL	80	32	54	86	61
1983-84—Vancouver Canucks		NHL	75	21	57	78	32
1984-85—Vancouver Canucks (e)		NHL	76	22	42	64	43
1985-86—Vancouver Canucks (f)		NHL	71	14	27	41	34
NHL TOTALS			613	197	353	550	280

(c)—Drafted from Sweden by Chicago Black Hawks in third round of 1976 amateur draft.
(d)—NHL rights traded to Vancouver Canucks by Chicago Black Hawks for second-round 1980 draft pick (Steve Ludzik), June, 1978.
(e)—July, 1985—Named head coach of Swedish National Team when his NHL contract expires in 1987.
(f)—June, 1986—Signed by Boston Bruins as a free agent.

DIRK GRAHAM

Right Wing . . . 5'11" . . . 190 lbs. . . . Born, Regina, Sask., July 29, 1959 . . . Shoots right.

Year	Team	League	Games	G.	A.	Pts.	Pen.
1975-76—Regina Blues		SJHL	54	36	32	68	82
1975-76—Regina Pats		WCHL	2	0	0	0	0
1976-77—Regina Pats		WCHL	65	37	28	65	66
1977-78—Regina Pats		WCHL	72	49	61	110	87
1978-79—Regina Pats (b-c)		WHL	71	48	60	108	252
1979-80—Dallas Black Hawks		CHL	62	17	15	32	96
1980-81—Fort Wayne Komets		IHL	6	1	2	3	12
1980-81—Toledo Goaldiggers		IHL	61	40	45	85	88
1981-82—Toledo Goaldiggers		IHL	72	49	56	105	68
1982-83—Toledo Goaldiggers (a-d)		IHL	78	70	55	125	86
1983-84—Minnesota North Stars		NHL	6	1	1	2	0
1983-84—Salt Lake Golden Eagles (a)		CHL	57	37	57	94	72
1984-85—Springfield Indians		AHL	37	20	28	48	41
1984-85—Minnesota North Stars		NHL	36	12	11	23	23
1985-86—Minnesota North Stars		NHL	80	22	33	55	87
NHL TOTALS			122	35	45	80	110

(c)—August, 1979—Drafted by Vancouver Canucks in 1979 NHL entry draft. Fifth Canucks pick, 89th overall, fifth round.
(d)—Co-leader, with teammate Rick Hendricks, during IHL playoffs with 20 points.

ROBB GRAHAM

Right Wing . . . 6'3" . . . 205 lbs. . . . Born, Bellevue, Wash., April 7, 1968 . . . Shoots right.

Year	Team	League	Games	G.	A.	Pts.	Pen.
1984-85—Guelph Platers		OHL	62	3	4	7	28
1985-86—Guelph Platers (c)		OHL	62	10	18	28	78

(c)—June, 1986—Drafted as underage junior by New York Rangers in 1986 NHL entry draft. Seventh Rangers pick, 135th overall, seventh round.

DAVID GRANNIS

Right Wing . . . 6' . . . 190 lbs. . . . Born, St. Paul, Minn., January 18, 1966 . . . Shoots right.

Year	Team	League	Games	G.	A.	Pts.	Pen.
1983-84—South St. Paul H.S. (c)		Minn. H.S.	20	20	23	43	14
1984-85—University of Minnesota		WCHA	23	2	6	8	17
1985-86—University of Minnesota		WCHA	25	5	7	12	14

(c)—June, 1984—Drafted by Los Angeles Kings in 1984 NHL entry draft. Fifth Kings pick, 87th overall, fifth round.

DANNY GRATTON

Center and Left Wing . . . 6'1" . . . 185 lbs. . . . Born, Brantford, Ont., December 7, 1966 . . . Shoots left . . . Son of Ken Gratton (minor league player, 1967-1976).

Year	Team	League	Games	G.	A.	Pts.	Pen.
1981-82—Guelph Platers		OJHL	40	14	26	40	70
1982-83—Oshawa Generals		OHL	64	15	28	43	55

Year	Team	League	Games	G.	A.	Pts.	Pen.
1983-84—Oshawa Generals		OHL	65	40	34	74	55
1984-85—Oshawa Generals (c)		OHL	56	24	48	72	67
1985-86—Oshawa Generals		OHL	10	3	5	8	15
1985-86—Belleville Bulls (d)		OHL	20	12	14	26	11
1985-86—Ottawa 67's		OHL	25	18	18	36	19

(c)—June, 1985—Drafted as underage junior by Los Angeles Kings in 1985 NHL entry draft. Second Kings pick, 10th overall, first round.

(d)—February, 1986—Traded by Belleville Bulls to Ottawa 67's for Frank Dimuzio.

ADAM GRAVES

Center . . . 6' . . . 185 lbs. . . . Born, Toronto, Ont., April 12, 1968 . . . Shoots left . . . Also plays Left Wing . . . (February, 1986)—Bruised shoulder.

Year	Team	League	Games	G.	A.	Pts.	Pen.
1984-85—King City Jr. B.		OHL	25	23	33	56	29
1985-86—Windsor Spitfires (c)		OHL	62	27	37	64	35

(c)—June, 1986—Drafted as underage junior by Detroit Red Wings in 1986 NHL entry draft. Second Red Wings pick, 22nd overall, second round.

ALAN GLENN GRAVES

Left Wing . . . 6'1" . . . 182 lbs. . . . Born, Marseille, France, November 10, 1961 . . . Shoots left . . . Also plays Center and Right Wing.

Year	Team	League	Games	G.	A.	Pts.	Pen.
1978-79—Langley		BCJHL	6	0	0	0	4
1978-79—Kamloops Rockets		BCJHL	38	17	23	40	41
1978-79—Seattle Breakers		WHL	2	0	0	0	0
1979-80—Seattle Breakers (c)		WHL	70	41	20	61	68
1980-81—Seattle Breakers		WHL	69	47	43	90	98
1981-82—Saginaw Gears		IHL	55	14	11	25	89
1982-83—Saginaw Gears		IHL	32	7	9	16	76
1983-84—Milwaukee Admirals		IHL	3	0	0	0	2
1983-84—Peoria Prancers		IHL	28	6	4	10	75
1984-85—Milwaukee Admirals		IHL	31	3	7	10	78
1985-86—Milwaukee Admirals		IHL	63	25	21	46	105
1985-86—Salt Lake Golden Eagles		IHL	16	4	1	5	61

(c)—June, 1980—Drafted as underage junior by Los Angeles Kings in 1980 NHL entry draft. Sixth Kings pick, 94th overall, fifth round.

STEVE GRAVES

Left Wing and Center . . . 6' . . . 180 lbs. . . . Born, Kingston, Ont., April 7, 1964 . . . Shoots left . . . (February, 1986)—Torn groin muscle.

Year	Team	League	Games	G.	A.	Pts.	Pen.
1980-81—Ottawa Senators (c)		OPJHL	44	21	17	38	47
1981-82—Sault Ste. Marie Greyhounds (d)		OHL	66	12	15	27	49
1982-83—Sault Ste. Marie Greyhounds		OHL	60	21	20	41	48
1983-84—Sault Ste. Marie Greyhounds		OHL	67	41	48	89	47
1983-84—Edmonton Oilers		NHL	2	0	0	0	0
1984-85—Nova Scotia Oilers		AHL	80	17	15	32	20
1985-86—Nova Scotia Oilers		AHL	78	19	18	37	22
NHL TOTALS			2	0	0	0	0

(c)—May, 1981—Drafted by Sault Ste. Marie Greyhounds in OHL 1981 midget draft. First Greyhounds pick, 14th overall, first round.

(d)—June, 1982—Drafted as underage junior by Edmonton Oilers in 1982 NHL entry draft. Second Oilers pick, 41st overall, second round.

MARK GREEN

Center . . . 6'3" . . . 205 lbs. . . . Born, Massena, N.Y., December 12, 1967 . . . Shoots left . . . Also plays left wing.

Year	Team	League	Games	G.	A.	Pts.	Pen.
1985-86—New Hampton Prep. (c)		N.Y.	26	26	28	54	20

(c)—June, 1986—Drafted by Winnipeg Jets in 1986 NHL entry draft. Eighth Jets pick, 176th overall, ninth round.

RICHARD DOUGLAS (RICK) GREEN

Defense . . . 6'3" . . . 200 lbs. . . . Born, Belleville, Ont., February 20, 1956 . . . Shoots left . . . Missed part of 1976-77 season with broken right wrist . . . (November, 1980)—Broken hand . . . (December 14, 1981)—Separated shoulder in game at Montreal . . . (March, 1983)—Hip

injury . . . (October, 1983)—Broken right wrist . . . (February 21, 1984)—Broke rib in game at Buffalo . . . (September, 1985)—Injured ankle during training camp and missed the first eight games of the season . . . (December 31, 1985)—Broken thumb . . . (February 24, 1986)—Reinjured thumb at Edmonton.

Year	Team	League	Games	G.	A.	Pts.	Pen.
1972-73—London Knights		Jr."A"OHA	7	0	1	1	2
1973-74—London Knights		Jr."A"OHA	65	6	30	36	45
1974-75—London Knights		Jr."A"OHA	65	8	45	53	68
1975-76—London Knights (a-c-d)		Jr."A"OHA	61	13	47	60	69
1976-77—Washington Capitals		NHL	45	3	12	15	16
1977-78—Washington Capitals		NHL	60	5	14	19	67
1978-79—Washington Capitals		NHL	71	8	33	41	62
1979-80—Washington Capitals		NHL	71	4	20	24	52
1980-81—Washington Capitals		NHL	65	8	23	31	91
1981-82—Washington Capitals (e)		NHL	65	3	25	28	93
1982-83—Montreal Canadiens		NHL	66	2	24	26	58
1983-84—Montreal Canadiens		NHL	7	0	1	1	7
1984-85—Montreal Canadiens		NHL	77	1	18	19	30
1985-86—Montreal Canadiens		NHL	46	3	2	5	20
NHL TOTALS			573	37	172	209	496

(c)—Won Max Kaminsky Memorial Trophy (Outstanding Defenseman).
(d)—Drafted from London Knights by Washington Capitals in first round of 1976 amateur draft.
(e)—September, 1982—Traded by Washington Capitals with Ryan Walter to Montreal Canadiens for Rod Langway, Brian Engblom, Doug Jarvis and Craig Laughlin.

JEFF GREENLAW

Left Wing . . . 6'2" . . . 200 lbs. . . . Born, Toronto, Ont., February 28, 1968 . . . Shoots left.

Year	Team	League	Games	G.	A.	Pts.	Pen.
1984-85—St. Catharines Jr. B		OHA	33	21	29	50	141
1985-86—Team Canada (c)		Int'l.	57	3	16	19	81

(c)—June, 1986—Drafted by Washington Capitals in 1986 NHL entry draft. First Capitals pick, 19th overall, first round.

GLENN GREENOUGH

Right Wing . . . 5'11" . . . 195 lbs. . . . Born, Sudbury, Ont., July 20, 1966 . . . Shoots right.

Year	Team	League	Games	G.	A.	Pts.	Pen.
1982-83—Sudbury Wolves		OHL	60	10	9	19	9
1983-84—Sudbury Wolves (c)		OHL	67	26	43	69	33
1984-85—Sudbury Wolves		OHL	15	12	11	23	13
1985-86—Sudbury Wolves		OHL	64	30	41	71	34

(c)—June, 1984—Drafted as underage junior by Chicago Black Hawks in 1984 NHL entry draft. Eighth Black Hawks pick, 153rd overall, eighth round.

RANDY GREGG

Defense . . . 6'4" . . . 215 lbs. . . . Born, Edmonton, Alta., February 19, 1956 . . . Shoots left . . . Has a degree in medicine . . . Furthered medical studies while he played hockey in Japan . . . (December, 1984)—Bruised left shoulder . . . (January, 1985)—Sprained left knee . . . (October 28, 1985)—Separated ribs at Calgary and missed 16 games . . . Won Senator Joseph Sullivan Award as the top Canadian College player in 1979.

Year	Team	League	Games	G.	A.	Pts.	Pen.
1975-76—University of Alberta		CWUAA	20	3	14	17	27
1976-77—University of Alberta		CWUAA	24	9	17	26	34
1977-78—University of Alberta		CWUAA	24	7	23	30	37
1978-79—University of Alberta		CWUAA	24	5	16	21	47
1979-80—Canadian National Team		Int'l	56	7	17	24	36
1979-80—Canadian Olympic Team		Int'l	6	1	1	2	2
1980-81—Kokudo Bunnies (c)		Japan	35	12	18	30	30
1981-82—Kokudo Bunnies		Japan	36	12	20	32	25
1981-82—Edmonton Oilers (d)		NHL	....	...	....	....	....
1982-83—Edmonton Oilers		NHL	80	6	22	28	54
1983-84—Edmonton Oilers		NHL	80	13	27	40	56
1984-85—Edmonton Oilers		NHL	57	3	20	23	32
1985-86—Edmonton Oilers		NHL	64	2	26	28	47
NHL TOTALS			281	24	95	119	189

(c)—March, 1981—Signed by Edmonton Oilers as a free agent.
(d)—No regular-season record. Played in four playoff games.

BILL GREGOIRE

Defense . . . 6' . . . 175 lbs. . . . Born, Victoria, B.C., April 9, 1967 . . . Shoots left.

Year	Team	League	Games	G.	A.	Pts.	Pen.
1984-85	Victoria Cougars (c)	WHL	67	2	12	14	144
1985-86	Victoria Cougars	WHL	41	13	19	32	122

(c)—June, 1985—Drafted as underage junior by Calgary Flames in 1985 NHL entry draft. Thirteenth Flames pick, 248th overall, 12th round.

TONY GRENIER

Center . . . 5'10" . . . 175 lbs. . . . Born, St. Boniface, Manitoba, January 23, 1965 . . . Shoots left . . . Also plays Left Wing.

Year	Team	League	Games	G.	A.	Pts.	Pen.
1982-83	Winnipeg Warriors	WHL	69	9	12	21	21
1983-84	Winnipeg Warriors	WHL	60	42	31	73	28
1984-85	Prince Albert Raiders (b-c)	WHL	71	62	58	120	38
1985-86	Prince Albert Raiders	WHL	52	42	37	79	16

(c)—June, 1985—Drafted by New York Islanders in 1985 NHL entry draft. Fourteenth Islanders pick, 244th overall, 12th round.

RONALD JOHN GRESCHNER

Defense . . . 6'2" . . . 205 lbs. . . . Born, Goodsoil, Sask., December 22, 1954 . . . Shoots left . . . Set WCHL record for points by defenseman in season in 1973-74 (broken by Kevin McCarthy in 1975-76) . . . Missed part of 1978-79 season with shoulder separation . . . (November 18, 1981)—Pinched nerve in back during game vs. Philadelphia . . . (September, 1982)—Injured back in training camp, out until February, 1983 . . . (March, 1983)—Reinjured back . . . (November, 1984)—Shoulder separation that cost him 31 games at various points of the season . . . (May, 1985)—Surgery to resection the distal clavical of left shoulder . . . (April 15, 1986)—Fractured right hand in playoff game at Philadelphia . . . Also plays Center.

Year	Team	League	Games	G.	A.	Pts.	Pen.
1971-72	New Westminster Bruins	WCHL	44	1	9	10	126
1972-73	New Westminster Bruins	WCHL	68	22	47	69	169
1973-74	New Westminster Bruins (c)	WCHL	67	33	70	103	170
1974-75	Providence Reds	AHL	7	5	6	11	10
1974-75	New York Rangers	NHL	70	8	37	45	94
1975-76	New York Rangers	NHL	77	6	21	27	93
1976-77	New York Rangers	NHL	80	11	36	47	89
1977-78	New York Rangers	NHL	78	24	48	72	100
1978-79	New York Rangers	NHL	60	17	36	53	66
1979-80	New York Rangers	NHL	76	21	37	58	103
1980-81	New York Rangers	NHL	74	27	41	68	112
1981-82	New York Rangers	NHL	29	5	11	16	16
1982-83	New York Rangers	NHL	10	3	5	8	0
1983-84	New York Rangers	NHL	77	12	44	56	117
1984-85	New York Rangers	NHL	48	16	29	45	42
1985-86	New York Rangers	NHL	78	20	28	48	104
	NHL TOTALS		757	170	373	543	936

(c)—Drafted from New Westminster Bruins by New York Rangers in second round of 1974 amateur draft.

DOUG GRESCHUK

Defense . . . 6'2" . . . 195 lbs. . . . Born, Edmonton, Alta., August 21, 1967 . . . Shoots left.

Year	Team	League	Games	G.	A.	Pts.	Pen.
1984-85	St. Albert Saints (c)	AJHL	56	5	15	20	151
1985-86	St. Albert Saints	AJHL	44	6	25	31	100

(c)—June, 1985—Drafted by Pittsburgh Penguins in 1985 NHL entry draft. Eleventh Penguins pick, 212th overall, 11th round.

KEITH GRETZKY

Center . . . 5'9" . . . 155 lbs. . . . Born, Brantford, Ont., February 16, 1967 . . . Shoots left . . . Brother of Wayne Gretzky.

Year	Team	League	Games	G.	A.	Pts.	Pen.
1981-82	Brantford Midgets	OHL	78	70	74	144	10
1982-83	Brantford Alexanders	OHL	37	5	9	14	0
1983-84	Windsor Spitfires	OHL	70	15	38	53	8

Year	Team	League	Games	G.	A.	Pts.	Pen.
1984-85—Windsor Spitfires (c)		OHL	66	31	62	93	12
1985-86—Windsor Spitfires (d)		OHL	43	24	36	60	10
1985-86—Belleville Bulls		OHL	18	3	11	14	2

(c)—June, 1985—Drafted as underage junior by Buffalo Sabres in 1985 NHL entry draft. Third Sabres pick, 56th overall, third round.

(d)—February, 1986—Traded by Windsor Compuware Spitfires to Belleville Bulls for Ken Hulst and future considerations.

WAYNE GRETZKY

Center . . . 6' . . . 170 lbs. . . . Born, Brantford, Ont., January 26, 1961 . . . Shoots left . . . In 1979-80, his first NHL season, he became the youngest player in history to win an NHL trophy, to score 50 goals, to collect 100 points and the youngest to ever be named to the NHL All-Star team . . . Set new regular season NHL record for goals (92 in 1981-82), assists (135 in 1984-85) and points (212 in 1981-82) . . . Set new NHL records for goals (97 in 1981-82), assists (165 in 1984-85) and points (255 in 1984-85) regular season plus playoffs . . . Set new NHL playoff records for assists (30) and points (47) in 1984-85 . . . Tied single game record in playoffs for most assists in a period (3), and a game (5), in first game of 1981 playoffs (April 8, 1981) in a 6-3 win at Montreal despite not taking a single shot on goal . . . In 1981-82, also set NHL records for fastest (50) goals from the start of the year (39 games), fastest 500 career points (234 games), largest margin over second-place finisher in scoring race (65 points) and most 3-or-more goals in a season (10-later tied in 1983-84) . . . (December 27, 1981)—Became first hockey player to be named THE SPORTING NEWS MAN-OF-THE-YEAR . . . (March 19, 1982)—Youngest player to reach 500 NHL career points (21 years, 1 month, 21 days) . . . (February 8, 1983)—Set All-Star game record with four goals . . . Set NHL playoff record for most points in one game with 7 (vs. Calgary, April 17, 1983 and vs. Winnipeg, April 25, 1985) . . . (October 5, 1983-January 27, 1984)—Set NHL record by collecting points in 51 consecutive games (61g, 92a), the first 51 games of the season . . . (January 28, 1984)—Bruised right shoulder in game vs. Los Angeles and ended consecutive games played streak at 362, an Oilers club record . . . (June, 1984)—Surgery on left ankle to remove benign growth caused by lacing his skates too tight . . . Set NHL record for most shorthanded goals in a season (12 in 1983-84) . . . (November 26, 1983-January 4, 1984)—Set NHL record for collecting assists in 17 straight games . . . (December 19, 1984)—Collected his 1000th NHL point in fewer games than any player in history, 424 games (Previous fastest was 720 games by Guy Lafleur). He is also the youngest player to ever reach the plateau at 23 yrs., 10 mos., 23 days. The previous youngest was Lafleur at 29 yrs., 3 mos., 18 days . . . Set playoff record for most assists in a single series (14 vs. Chicago), 1985 . . . First player to have 100 point seasons in first seven years of NHL . . . Brother of Keith Gretzky . . . Named 1985 Canadian Athlete of the Year . . . Set new regular season NHL records for assists (163) and points (215) in 1985-86.

Year	Team	League	Games	G.	A.	Pts.	Pen.
1976-77—Peterborough Petes		OMJHL	3	0	3	3	0
1977-78—S. Ste. M. G'hounds (b-c)		OMJHL	64	70	112	182	14
1978-79—Indianapolis Racers (d)		WHA	8	3	3	6	0
1978-79—Edmonton Oilers (b-e-f-g)		WHA	72	43	61	104	19
1979-80—Edmonton Oilers (b-h-i)		NHL	79	51	*86	*137	21
1980-81—Edmonton Oilers (a-h-j-l)		NHL	80	55	*109	*164	28
1981-82—Edmonton Oilers (a-h-j-l-p)		NHL	80	*92	*120	*212	26
1982-83—Edmonton Oilers (a-h-k-l-p)		NHL	80	*71	*125	*196	59
1983-84—Edmonton Oilers (a-h-j-l-m-p)		NHL	74	*87	*118	*205	39
1984-85—Edmonton Oilers (a-h-j-l-n-o-p)		NHL	80	*73	*135	*208	52
1985-86—Edmonton Oilers (a-h-i-l)		NHL	80	52	*163	*215	46
NHL TOTALS			553	481	856	1337	271
WHA TOTALS			80	46	64	110	19

(c)—Signed to multi-year contract by Indianapolis Racers (WHA) as an underage junior, May, 1978.

(d)—November, 1978—Traded by Indianapolis to Edmonton with Peter Driscoll, Ed Mio for cash and future considerations.

(e)—Won WHA Rookie award.

(f)—Named WHA Rookie of the Year in poll of players by THE SPORTING NEWS.

(g)—Led in points (20) and tied for lead in goals (10) during playoffs.

(h)—Won Hart Memorial Trophy.

(i)—Won Lady Byng Memorial Trophy.

(j)—Won Art Ross Memorial Trophy (NHL Leading Scorer).

(k)—Led Stanley Cup Playoffs with 26 assists and 38 points.

(l)—Selected NHL Player of Year by The Sporting News in poll of players.

(m)—Led Stanley Cup Playoffs with 22 assists and 35 points.

(n)—Led Stanley Cup Playoffs with 30 assists and 47 points.

(o)—Won Conn Smythe Trophy (Stanley Cup Playoff MVP).

(p)—Won Lester Pearson Award (NHL Players MVP).

JARI GRONSTRAND

Defense ... 6'3" ... 197 lbs. ... Born, Tampere, Finland, November 14, 1962 ... Shoots left.

Year	Team	League	Games	G.	A.	Pts.	Pen.
1984-85—Tappara		Finland	33	9	6	15	..
1985-86—Tappara (c)		Finland	44	10	7	17	32

(c)—June, 1986—Drafted by Minnesota North Stars in 1986 NHL entry draft. Eighth North Stars pick, 96th overall, fifth round.

WAYNE GROULX

Center ... 5'9" ... 175 lbs. ... Born, Welland, Ont., February 2, 1965 ... Shoots right.

Year	Team	League	Games	G.	A.	Pts.	Pen.
1981-82—Sault Ste. Marie Greyhounds		OHL	66	25	41	66	66
1982-83—Sault Ste. Marie Greyhounds (c)		OHL	67	44	86	130	549
1983-84—Sault Ste. Marie Greyhounds (b-d)		OHL	70	59	78	137	48
1984-85—Sault Ste. Marie Greyhounds (a-e-f)		OHL	64	59	85	144	102
1984-85—Quebec Nordiques		NHL	1	0	0	0	0
1985-86—Muskegon Lumberjacks		IHL	55	22	27	49	56
1985-86—Fredericton Express		AHL	15	2	6	8	12
NHL TOTALS			1	0	0	0	0

(c)—June, 1983—Drafted as underage junior by Quebec Nordiques in 1983 NHL entry draft. Eighth Nordiques pick, 172nd overall, ninth round.
(d)—Shared OHL playoff lead with teammate Rick Tocchet with 36 points.
(e)—Led OHL playoffs with 18 goals and 36 points.
(f)—Won Red Tilson Trophy (Most outstanding OHL player).

SCOTT KENNETH GRUHL

Left Wing ... 5'11" ... 185 lbs. ... Born, Port Colborne, Ont., September 13, 1959 ... Shoots left ... Also plays Defense.

Year	Team	League	Games	G.	A.	Pts.	Pen.
1976-77—Northeastern University		ECAC	17	6	4	10	....
1977-78—Northeastern University		ECAC	28	21	38	59	46
1978-79—Sudbury Wolves		OMJHL	68	35	49	84	78
1979-80—Binghamton Dusters		AHL	4	1	0	1	6
1979-80—Saginaw Gears (b-c)		IHL	75	53	40	93	100
1980-81—Houston Apollos		CHL	4	0	0	0	0
1980-81—Saginaw Gears (d)		IHL	77	56	34	90	87
1981-82—New Haven Nighthawks		AHL	73	28	41	69	107
1981-82—Los Angeles Kings		NHL	7	2	1	3	2
1982-83—New Haven Nighthawks		AHL	68	25	38	63	114
1982-83—Los Angeles Kings		NHL	7	0	2	2	4
1983-84—Muskegon Mohawks (a)		IHL	56	40	56	96	49
1984-85—Muskegon Lumberjacks (a-e-f)		IHL	82	62	64	126	102
1985-86—Muskegon Lumberjacks		IHL	82	59	50	109	178
NHL TOTALS			14	2	3	5	6

(c)—September, 1980—Signed by Los Angeles Kings as free agent.
(d)—Led IHL playoff with 11 goals and 19 assists.
(e)—Won James Gatchene Memorial Trophy (IHL MVP).
(f)—Led IHL playoffs with 16 assists.

FRANCOIS GUAY

Center ... 6' ... 185 lbs. ... Born, Gatineau, Que., June 8, 1968 ... Shoots left.

Year	Team	League	Games	G.	A.	Pts.	Pen.
1984-85—Laval Voisins		QHL	66	13	18	31	21
1985-86—Laval Titans (c)		QHL	71	19	55	74	46

(c)—June, 1986—Drafted as underage junior by Buffalo Sabres in 1986 NHL entry draft. Ninth Sabres pick, 152nd overall, eighth round.

PAUL GUAY

Right Wing ... 6' ... 185 lbs. ... Born, Providence, R.I., September 2, 1963 ... Shoots right ... Member of 1984 U.S. Olympic Team.

Year	Team	League	Games	G.	A.	Pts.	Pen.
1979-80—Mt. St. Charles H.S.		R.I.H.S.	23	18	19	37	....
1980-81—Mt. St. Charles H.S. (c)		R.I.H.S.	23	28	38	66	....
1981-82—Providence College		ECAC	33	23	17	40	38
1982-83—Providence College (b)		ECAC	42	34	31	65	83
1983-84—U.S. National Team		Int'l	62	20	18	38	44
1983-84—U.S. Olympic Team		Int'l	6	1	0	1	8

Year	Team	League	Games	G.	A.	Pts.	Pen.
1983-84—Philadelphia Flyers (d)	NHL	14	2	6	8	14
1984-85—Hershey Bears	AHL	74	23	30	53	123
1984-85—Philadelphia Flyers	NHL	2	0	1	1	0
1985-86—Los Angeles Kings (e)	NHL	23	3	3	6	18
1985-86—New Haven Nighthawks	AHL	57	15	36	51	101
NHL TOTALS			39	5	10	15	32

(c)—June, 1981—Drafted as underage player by Minnesota North Stars in 1981 NHL entry draft. Tenth North Stars pick, 118th overall, sixth round.

(d)—February, 1984—Traded with third round 1985 draft pick by Minnesota North Stars to Philadelphia Flyers for Paul Holmgren.

(e)—October, 1985—Traded by Philadelphia Flyers to Los Angeles Kings for Steve Seguin.

DAVID GUDEN

Left Wing . . . 6'1" . . . 180 lbs. . . . Born, Brighton, Mass., April 26, 1968 . . . Shoots left . . . Also plays Center.

Year	Team	League	Games	G.	A.	Pts.	Pen.
1984-85—Roxbury Latin H.S.	Mass.	..	25	27	52	..
1985-86—Roxbury Latin H.S. (c)	Mass.	15	22	26	48	25

(c)—June, 1986—Drafted by Los Angeles Kings in 1986 NHL entry draft. Fourth Kings pick, 86th overall, fifth round.

STEPHANE GUERARD

Defense . . . 6'2" . . . 185 lbs. . . . Born, St. Elisabeth, Que., April 12, 1968 . . . Shoots left.

Year	Team	League	Games	G.	A.	Pts.	Pen.
1984-85—Laurentides Midget	Que.	36	6	12	18	140
1985-86—Shawinigan Cataracts (c-d)	QHL	59	4	16	20	167

(c)—Won Raymond Lagace Trophy (Top Rookie Defenseman or Goaltender).

(d)—June, 1986—Drafted as underage junior by Quebec Nordiques in 1986 NHL entry draft. Third Nordiques pick, 41st overall, second round.

VINCENT GUIDOTTI

Defense . . . 6' . . . 180 lbs. . . . Born, Sacramento, Calif., April 29, 1967 . . . Shoots left.

Year	Team	League	Games	G.	A.	Pts.	Pen.
1984-85—Noble Greenough H.S. (c)	Maine H.S.	25	14	24	38	32
1985-86—University of Maine	H. East	16	0	0	0	8

(c)—June, 1985—Drafted by St. Louis Blues in 1985 NHL entry draft. Ninth Blues pick, 201st overall, 10th round.

BENGT-AKE GUSTAFSSON

Left Wing . . . 6' . . . 185 lbs. . . . Born, Karlskoga, Sweden, March 23, 1958 . . . Shoots left . . . (November 12, 1980)—Cervical strain in back in game at Pittsburgh . . . (December 23, 1981)—Pulled tendons in right ankle in game vs. Boston . . . (March 17, 1984)—Partial tear of medial collateral ligament of left knee in game at New York Islanders . . . (February, 1985)—Pulled left hamstring . . . (April, 1986)—Broken leg.

Year	Team	League	Games	G.	A.	Pts.	Pen.
1977-78—Farjestads (c)	Sweden	32	15	10	25	10
1978-79—Farjestads	Sweden	32	13	11	24	10
1978-79—Edmonton Oilers (d-e)	WHA	....	...	....	....	....
1979-80—Washington Capitals	NHL	80	22	38	60	17
1980-81—Washington Capitals	NHL	72	21	34	55	26
1981-82—Washington Capitals	NHL	70	26	34	60	40
1982-83—Washington Capitals	NHL	67	22	42	64	16
1983-84—Washington Capitals	NHL	69	32	43	75	16
1984-85—Washington Capitals	NHL	51	14	29	43	8
1985-86—Washington Capitals (f)	NHL	70	23	52	75	26
NHL TOTALS			479	160	272	432	149

(c)—June, 1978—Drafted by Washington Capitals in NHL amateur draft. Seventh Washington pick, 55th overall, fourth round.

(d)—April, 1979—Signed by Edmonton Oilers. Played in two playoff games before being ruled ineligible by WHA office.

(e)—September, 1979—After being priority selection by Edmonton Oilers in NHL expansion draft in June, NHL President overturned case and ruled that Gustafsson was legally property of Washington Capitals because of rules governing expansion proceedings.

(f)—June, 1986—Signed to play with Bofors, a division II team in Sweden, for 1986-87.

KEVAN GUY

Defense . . . 6'2" . . . 190 lbs. . . . Born, Edmonton, Alta., July 16, 1965 . . . Shoots right.

Year	Team	League	Games	G.	A.	Pts.	Pen.
1982-83—Medicine Hat Tigers (c)		WHL	69	7	20	27	89
1983-84—Medicine Hat Tigers		WHL	72	15	42	57	117
1984-85—Medicine Hat Tigers		WHL	31	7	17	24	46
1985-86—Moncton Golden Flames		AHL	73	4	20	24	56

(c)—June, 1983—Drafted as underage junior by Calgary Flames in 1983 NHL entry draft. Fifth Flames pick, 71st overall, fourth round.

ARI EERIK HAANPAA

Right and Left Wing . . . 6'1" . . . 185 lbs. . . . Born, Nokia, Finland, November 28, 1965 . . . Shoots right . . . (1984-85)—Knee injury.

Year	Team	League	Games	G.	A.	Pts.	Pen.
1984-85—Ilves (c)		Finland	13	5	..	..	..
1985-86—Springfield Indians		AHL	20	3	1	4	13
1985-86—New York Islanders		NHL	18	0	7	7	20
NHL TOTALS			18	0	7	7	20

(c)—June, 1984—Drafted by New York Islanders in 1984 NHL entry draft. Fifth Islanders pick, 83rd overall, fourth round.

MARK HAARMANN

Defense . . . 6'3" . . . 195 lbs. . . . Born, Toronto, Ont., January 20, 1967 . . . Shoots left.

Year	Team	League	Games	G.	A.	Pts.	Pen.
1982-83—Toronto Young Nats		OHA Midget	40	9	27	36	50
1983-84—Oshawa Generals		OHL	70	6	9	15	68
1984-85—Oshawa Generals (c)		OHL	66	5	14	19	51
1985-86—Oshawa Generals (d)		OHL	20	1	4	5	22
1985-86—Sault Ste. Marie Greyhounds		OHL	36	6	16	22	37

(c)—June, 1985—Drafted as underage junior by Washington Capitals in 1985 NHL entry draft. Ninth Capitals pick, 166th overall, eighth round.

(d)—January, 1986—Traded by Oshawa Generals to Sault Ste. Marie Greyhounds for future draft considerations.

MARC JOSEPH HABSCHEID

Center . . . 6'2" . . . 180 lbs. . . . Born, Swift Current, Sask., March 1, 1963 . . . Shoots right . . . (November, 1982)—Head injury . . . (October, 1985)—Suspended by Edmonton Oilers for refusing to report to Nova Scotia Oilers (AHL).

Year	Team	League	Games	G.	A.	Pts.	Pen.
1980-81—Saskatoon Blades (c)		WHL	72	34	63	97	50
1981-82—Saskatoon Blades (b)		WHL	55	64	87	151	74
1981-82—Edmonton Oilers		NHL	7	1	3	4	2
1981-82—Wichita Wind (d)		CHL	..	..	..	..	..
1982-83—Kamloops Junior Oilers		WHL	6	7	16	23	8
1982-83—Edmonton Oilers		NHL	32	3	10	13	14
1983-84—Edmonton Oilers		NHL	9	1	0	1	6
1983-84—Moncton Alpines		AHL	71	19	37	56	32
1984-85—Edmonton Oilers		NHL	26	5	3	8	4
1984-85—Nova Scotia Oilers		AHL	48	29	29	58	65
1985-86—Minnesota North Stars (e)		NHL	6	2	3	5	0
1985-86—Springfield Indians		AHL	41	18	32	50	21
NHL TOTALS			80	12	19	31	26

(c)—June, 1981—Drafted as underage junior by Edmonton Oilers in 1981 NHL entry draft. Sixth Oilers pick, 113th overall, sixth round.

(d)—No regular season record. Played three playoff games.

(e)—December, 1985—Traded with Don Barber and Emanuel Viveiros by Edmonton Oilers to Minnesota North Stars for Gord Sherven and Don Biggs.

LEONARD HACHBORN

Center . . . 5'10" . . . 171 lbs. . . . Born, Brantford, Ont., September 9, 1961 . . . Shoots left . . . (December, 1982)—Knee injury . . . (December, 1984)—Separated left shoulder . . . (January 10, 1986)—Injured groin at Minnesota.

Year	Team	League	Games	G.	A.	Pts.	Pen.
1979-80—Hamilton Tier II		OPJHL	43	25	20	45	42
1980-81—Brantford Alexanders (c)		OHL	66	34	52	86	94
1981-82—Brantford Alexanders		OHL	55	43	50	93	141
1982-83—Maine Mariners		AHL	75	28	55	83	32
1983-84—Springfield Indians		AHL	28	18	42	60	15
1983-84—Philadelphia Flyers		NHL	38	11	21	32	4
1984-85—Hershey Bears		AHL	14	6	7	13	14
1984-85—Philadelphia Flyers		NHL	40	5	17	22	23
1985-86—Hershey Bears (d)		AHL	23	12	22	34	34
1985-86—New Haven Nighthawks		AHL	12	5	8	13	21
1985-86—Los Angeles Kings		NHL	24	4	1	5	2
NHL TOTALS			102	20	39	59	29

(c)—June, 1981—Drafted by Philadelphia Flyers in 1981 NHL entry draft. Twelfth Flyers pick, 184th overall, ninth round.

(d)—December, 1986—Sold by Philadelphia Flyers to Los Angeles Kings.

ALEC HAIDY

Right Wing . . . 6' . . . 175 lbs. . . . Born, Windsor, Ont., January 1, 1965 . . . Shoots right . . . (February, 1978)—Spinal fusion surgery . . . Son of Gordon Haidy (Detroit Red Wings, 1949-50 season).

Year	Team	League	Games	G.	A.	Pts.	Pen.
1981-82—Windsor Royals		OHA Jr. 'B'	30	8	16	24	201
1982-83—Sault Ste. Marie Greyhounds (c)		OHL	58	3	12	15	86
1983-84—Sault Ste. Marie Greyhounds		OHL	54	17	20	37	121
1984-85—Sault Ste. Marie Greyhounds		OHL	15	6	6	12	31
1984-85—Hamilton Steelhawks		OHL	48	20	16	36	66
1985-86—Hamilton Steelhawks		OHL	21	1	11	12	31
1985-86—Sudbury Wolves		OHL	25	9	10	19	48

(c)—June, 1983—Drafted as underage junior by Pittsburgh Penguins in 1983 NHL entry draft. Eighth Penguins pick, 183rd overall, 10th round.

RICHARD HAJDU

Left Wing . . . 6' . . . 175 lbs. . . . Born, Victoria, B.C., April 10, 1965 . . . Shoots left.

Year	Team	League	Games	G.	A.	Pts.	Pen.
1981-82—Kamloops Junior Oilers		WHL	64	19	21	40	50
1982-83—Kamloops Junior Oilers (c-d)		WHL	70	22	36	58	101
1983-84—Victoria Cougars		WHL	42	17	10	27	106
1984-85—Victoria Cougars		WHL	24	12	16	28	33
1984-85—Rochester Americans		AHL	2	0	2	2	0
1985-86—Buffalo Sabres		NHL	3	0	0	0	4
1985-86—Rochester Americans		AHL	54	10	27	37	95
NHL TOTALS			3	0	0	0	4

(c)—June, 1983—Drafted as underage junior by Buffalo Sabres in 1983 NHL entry draft. Fifth Sabres pick, 34th overall, second round.

(d)—July, 1983—Traded with Doug Kostynski by Kamloops Junior Oilers to Victoria Cougars for Ron Viglasi and Brian Bertuzzi.

WILLIAM ALBERT HAJT

Defense . . . 6'3" . . . 204 lbs. . . . Born, Radisson, Sask., November 18, 1951 . . . Shoots left . . . (November 8, 1980)—Broken bone in right foot . . . (February 8, 1985)—Separated shoulder in game at Calgary and required surgery . . . (December 9, 1985)—Missed 19 games with a groin injury.

Year	Team	League	Games	G.	A.	Pts.	Pen.
1967-68—Saskatoon Blades		WCJHL	60	4	10	14	35
1968-69—Saskatoon Blades		WCHL	60	3	18	21	54
1969-70—Saskatoon Blades		WCHL	60	10	21	31	40
1970-71—Saskatoon Blades (c)		WCHL	66	19	53	72	50
1971-72—Did not play			....	...	....	....	....
1972-73—Cincinnati Swords		AHL	69	4	31	35	40
1973-74—Cincinnati Swords		AHL	66	5	30	35	66
1973-74—Buffalo Sabres		NHL	6	0	2	2	0
1974-75—Buffalo Sabres		NHL	76	3	26	29	68
1975-76—Buffalo Sabres		NHL	80	6	21	27	48
1976-77—Buffalo Sabres		NHL	79	6	20	26	56
1977-78—Buffalo Sabres		NHL	76	4	18	22	30
1978-79—Buffalo Sabres		NHL	40	3	8	11	20

Year	Team	League	Games	G.	A.	Pts.	Pen.
1979-80—Buffalo Sabres		NHL	75	4	12	16	24
1980-81—Buffalo Sabres		NHL	68	2	19	21	42
1981-82—Buffalo Sabres		NHL	65	2	9	11	44
1982-83—Buffalo Sabres		NHL	72	3	12	15	26
1983-84—Buffalo Sabres (d)		NHL	79	3	24	27	32
1984-85—Buffalo Sabres		NHL	57	5	13	18	14
1985-86—Buffalo Sabres (e)		NHL	58	1	16	17	25
NHL TOTALS			821	42	200	242	429

(c)—Drafted from Saskatoon Blades by Buffalo Sabres in third round of 1971 amateur draft.
(d)—September/October, 1983—Announced intention to retire but changed his mind before the end of the Sabres' training camp.
(e)—June, 1986—Traded by Buffalo Sabres to Winnipeg Jets for Scott Arniel.

ANDERS HAKANSSON

Left Wing ... 6'2" ... 191 lbs. ... Born, Munkfors, Sweden, April 27, 1956 ... Shoots left ... (October, 1981)—Shoulder separation ... Member of Team Sweden in 1981 Canada Cup ... (June, 1985)—Surgery to repair torn cartilage in right knee.

Year	Team	League	Games	G.	A.	Pts.	Pen.
1979-80—Solna AIK		Sweden	36	9	11	20	12
1980-81—Solna AIK (c)		Sweden	22	5	11	16	18
1981-82—Minnesota North Stars		NHL	72	12	4	16	29
1982-83—Minnesota North Stars (d)		NHL	5	0	0	0	9
1982-83—Pittsburgh Penguins		NHL	62	9	12	21	26
1983-84—Los Angeles Kings (e)		NHL	80	15	17	32	41
1984-85—Los Angeles Kings		NHL	73	12	12	24	28
1985-86—Los Angeles Kings		NHL	38	4	1	5	8
NHL TOTALS			330	52	46	98	141

(c)—July, 1981—Signed by Minnesota North Stars as a free agent.
(d)—October, 1982—Traded by Minnesota North Stars with Ron Meighan and first-round draft pick in 1983 (Pittsburgh drafted Bob Errey) to Pittsburgh Penguins for George Ferguson and first-round draft pick in 1983 (Minnesota drafted Brian Lawton).
(e)—September, 1983—Traded by Pittsburgh Penguins to Los Angeles Kings for the NHL rights to Kevin Stevens.

BOB HALKIDIS

Defense ... 5'11" ... 195 lbs. ... Born, Toronto, Ont., March 5, 1966 ... Shoots left ... (September, 1982)—Broke ankle during training camp. In first game back, in November, he reinjured ankle and missed another two weeks ... (December 4, 1985)—Dislocated right shoulder at St. Louis and missed 15 games.

Year	Team	League	Games	G.	A.	Pts.	Pen.
1981-82—Toronto Young Nationals		MTMHL	40	9	27	36	54
1982-83—London Knights		OHL	37	3	12	15	52
1983-84—London Knights (c)		OHL	51	9	22	31	123
1984-85—London Knights (a-d)		OHL	62	14	50	64	154
1984-85—Buffalo Sabres (e)		NHL	..	..	..	..	..
1985-86—Buffalo Sabres		NHL	37	1	9	10	115
NHL TOTALS			37	1	9	10	115

(c)—June, 1984—Drafted as underage junior by Buffalo Sabres in 1984 NHL entry draft. Fourth Sabres pick, 81st overall, fourth round.
(d)—Won Max Kaminsky Trophy (Top OHL Defenseman).
(e)—Played four playoff games.

DEAN HALL

Center ... 6'2" ... 190 lbs. ... Born, Winnipeg, Manitoba, January 14, 1968 ... Shoots left.

Year	Team	League	Games	G.	A.	Pts.	Pen.
1985-86—St. James Jr. Canadians (c)		MJHL	47	31	49	80	94

(c)—June, 1986—Drafted by Boston Bruins in 1986 NHL entry draft. Third Bruins pick, 76th overall, fourth round.

TAYLOR HALL

Left Wing ... 5'11' ... 177 lbs. ... Born, Regina, Sask., February 20, 1964 ... Shoots left ... (October, 1984)—Damaged knee ligaments.

Year	Team	League	Games	G.	A.	Pts.	Pen.
1980-81—Regina Canadians		Midget	26	51	28	79	35
1981-82—Regina Pats (c)		WHL	48	14	15	29	43
1982-83—Regina Pats		WHL	72	37	57	94	78
1983-84—Regina Pats (a-d)		WHL	69	63	79	142	42

Year	Team	League	Games	G.	A.	Pts.	Pen.
1983-84—Vancouver Canucks		NHL	4	1	0	1	0
1984-85—Vancouver Canucks		NHL	7	1	4	5	19
1985-86—Fredericton Express		AHL	45	21	14	35	28
1985-86—Vancouver Canucks		NHL	19	5	5	10	6
NHL TOTALS			30	7	9	16	25

(c)—June, 1982—Drafted as underage junior by Vancouver Canucks in 1982 NHL entry draft. Fourth Canucks pick, 116th overall, sixth round.

(d)—Shared WHL playoff goal-scoring lead (21) with Dean Evason of Kamloops.

MATS HALLIN

Left Wing . . . 6'2" . . . 202 lbs. . . . Born, Eskilstuna, Sweden, March 19, 1958 . . . Shoots left . . . (October, 1981)—Shoulder injury . . . Also plays Right Wing.

Year	Team	League	Games	G.	A.	Pts.	Pen.
1980-81—Swedish Nationals (c)		Sweden	....	...	....	....	....
1980-81—Sodertalje SK (d)		Sweden	33	9	11	20	86
1981-82—Indianapolis Checkers		CHL	63	25	32	57	113
1982-83—Indianapolis Checkers		CHL	42	26	27	53	86
1982-83—New York Islanders		NHL	30	7	7	14	26
1983-84—New York Islanders		NHL	40	2	5	7	27
1984-85—New York Islanders		NHL	38	5	0	5	50
1985-86—Minnesota North Stars (e)		NHL	38	3	2	5	86
1985-86—Springfield Indians		AHL	2	1	1	2	0
NHL TOTALS			146	17	14	31	189

(c)—June, 1978—Drafted by Washington Capitals in 1978 NHL amateur draft. Tenth Capitals pick, 105th overall, seventh round.

(d)—June, 1981—Signed by New York Islanders as a free agent.

(e)—September, 1985—Traded by New York Islanders to Minnesota North Stars for seventh-round draft choice (Will Anderson) in 1986.

DOUGLAS ROBERT HALWARD

Defense . . . 6'1" . . . 198 lbs. . . . Born, Toronto, Ont., November 1, 1955 . . . Shoots left . . . Missed part of 1979-80 season with a bruised shoulder . . . (December, 1983)—Fractured ankle . . . (October 20, 1985)—Bruised hand at N.Y. Rangers.

Year	Team	League	Games	G.	A.	Pts.	Pen.
1973-74—Peterborough TPTs		Jr."A"OHA	69	1	15	16	103
1974-75—Peterborough TPTs (c)		Jr."A"OHA	68	11	52	63	97
1975-76—Rochester Americans		AHL	54	6	11	17	51
1975-76—Boston Bruins		NHL	22	1	5	6	6
1976-77—Rochester Americans		AHL	54	4	28	32	26
1976-77—Boston Bruins		NHL	18	2	2	4	6
1977-78—Rochester Americans		AHL	42	8	14	22	17
1977-78—Boston Bruins (d)		NHL	25	0	2	2	2
1978-79—Los Angeles Kings		NHL	27	1	5	6	13
1978-79—Springfield Indians		AHL	14	5	1	6	10
1979-80—Los Angeles Kings		NHL	63	11	45	56	52
1980-81—Los Angeles Kings (e)		NHL	51	4	15	19	96
1980-81—Vancouver Canucks		NHL	7	0	1	1	4
1981-82—Dallas Black Hawks		CHL	22	8	18	26	49
1981-82—Vancouver Canucks		NHL	37	4	13	17	40
1982-83—Vancouver Canucks		NHL	75	19	33	52	83
1983-84—Vancouver Canucks		NHL	54	7	16	23	35
1984-85—Vancouver Canucks		NHL	71	7	27	34	82
1985-86—Vancouver Canucks		NHL	70	8	25	33	111
NHL TOTALS			520	64	189	253	530

(c)—Drafted from Peterborough TPTs by Boston Bruins in first round of 1975 amateur draft.

(d)—September, 1978—Traded to Los Angeles Kings by Boston Bruins for future considerations.

(e)—March, 1981—Traded by Los Angeles Kings to Vancouver Canucks for future considerations. (Canucks sent goaltender Gary Bromley to Kings to complete deal, June, 1981.)

GILLES HAMEL

Left Wing . . . 6' . . . 183 lbs. . . . Born, Asbestos, Que., March 18, 1960 . . . Shoots left . . . (January, 1981)—Knee injury . . . Brother of Jean Hamel.

Year	Team	League	Games	G.	A.	Pts.	Pen.
1977-78—Laval National		QMJHL	72	44	37	81	68
1978-79—Laval National (b-c)		QMJHL	72	56	55	111	130
1979-80—Trois-Rivieres Draveurs		QMJHL	12	13	8	21	8
1979-80—Chicoutimi Sagueneens (a)		QMJHL	58	78	62	135	87
1979-80—Rochester Americans (d)		AHL	...	...	...	...	...

Year	Team	League	Games	G.	A.	Pts.	Pen.
1980-81—Rochester Americans	AHL	14	8	7	15	7
1980-81—Buffalo Sabres	NHL	51	10	9	19	53
1981-82—Rochester Americans	AHL	57	31	44	75	55
1981-82—Buffalo Sabres	NHL	16	2	7	9	2
1982-83—Buffalo Sabres	NHL	66	22	20	42	26
1983-84—Buffalo Sabres	NHL	75	21	23	44	37
1984-85—Buffalo Sabres	NHL	80	18	30	48	36
1985-86—Buffalo Sabres (e)	NHL	77	19	25	44	61
NHL TOTALS			365	92	114	206	215

(c)—August, 1979—Drafted by Buffalo Sabres as underage junior in entry draft. Fifth Sabres pick, 74th overall, fourth round.

(d)—No league record. Played one playoff game.

(e)—June, 1986—Traded by Buffalo Sabres to Winnipeg Jets for Scott Arniel.

BRADLEY HAMILTON

Defense . . . 6' . . . 175 lbs. . . . Born, Calgary, Alta., March 30, 1967 . . . Shoots left.

Year	Team	League	Games	G.	A.	Pts.	Pen.
1983-84—North York Rangers	OHA	42	4	25	29	126
1984-85—Aurora Tigers (c)	OHA	43	9	29	38	149
1985-86—Michigan State Univ.	CCHA	43	3	10	13	52

(c)—June, 1985—Drafted by Chicago Black Hawks in 1985 NHL entry draft. Tenth Black Hawks pick, 200th overall, 10th round.

KEN HAMMOND

Defense . . . 6'1" . . . 190 lbs. . . . Born, London, Ont., August 23, 1963 . . . Shoots left.

Year	Team	League	Games	G.	A.	Pts.	Pen.
1981-82—R.P.I.	ECAC	29	2	3	5	54
1982-83—R.P.I. (c)	ECAC	28	4	13	17	54
1983-84—R.P.I.	ECAC	34	5	11	16	72
1984-85—R.P.I (a-d)	ECAC	38	11	28	39	90
1984-85—Los Angeles Kings	NHL	3	1	0	1	0
1985-86—New Haven Nighthawks	AHL	67	4	12	16	96
1985-86—Los Angeles Kings	NHL	3	0	1	1	2
NHL TOTALS			6	1	1	2	2

(c)—June, 1983—Drafted by Los Angeles Kings in 1983 NHL entry draft. Eighth Kings pick, 147th overall, eighth round.

(d)—Named first team (East) All-America Team.

MARK HAMWAY

Right Wing . . . 5'11" . . . 169 lbs. . . . Born, Detroit, Mich., August 9, 1961 . . . Shoots right.

Year	Team	League	Games	G.	A.	Pts.	Pen.
1977-78—Adray Nationals Detroit	Midget	75	70	90	160	....
1978-79—Windsor Spitfires	OMJHL	66	27	42	69	29
1979-80—Michigan State University (c)	WCHA	38	16	28	44	28
1980-81—Michigan State University	WCHA	35	18	15	33	20
1981-82—Michigan State University	CCHA	41	34	31	65	37
1982-83—Michigan State University	CCHA	42	30	29	59	16
1983-84—Indianapolis Checkers	CHL	71	22	32	54	38
1984-85—New York Islanders	NHL	2	0	0	0	0
1984-85—Springfield Indians	AHL	75	29	34	63	29
1985-86—Springfield Indians	AHL	14	5	8	13	7
1985-86—New York Islanders	NHL	49	5	12	17	9
NHL TOTALS			51	5	12	17	9

(c)—June, 1980—Drafted as underage player by New York Islanders in 1980 NHL entry draft. Eighth Islanders pick, 143rd overall, seventh round.

RON HANDY

Left Wing . . . 5'11" . . . 165 lbs. . . . Born, Toronto, Ont., January 15, 1963 . . . Shoots left . . . (January, 1984)—Broken nose in CHL game.

Year	Team	League	Games	G.	A.	Pts.	Pen.
1979-80—Toronto Marlboro Midgets	Midget	39	48	60	108	....
1980-81—Sault Ste. Marie Greyhounds (c)	OHL	66	43	43	86	45
1981-82—Sault Ste. Marie	OHL	20	15	10	25	20
1981-82—Kingston Canadians	OHL	44	35	38	73	23
1982-83—Kingston Canadians	OHL	67	52	96	148	64

Year	Team	League	Games	G.	A.	Pts.	Pen.
1982-83—Indianapolis Checkers		CHL	9	2	7	9	0
1983-84—Indianapolis Checkers (b)		CHL	66	29	46	75	40
1984-85—New York Islanders		NHL	10	0	2	2	0
1984-85—Springfield Indians		AHL	69	29	35	64	38
1985-86—Springfield Indians		AHL	79	31	30	61	66
NHL TOTALS			10	0	2	2	0

(c)—June, 1981—Drafted as underage junior by New York Islanders in 1981 NHL entry draft. Third Islanders pick, 57th overall, third round.

TIMOTHY HANLEY

Center . . . 6' . . . 200 lbs. . . . Born, Greenfield, Mass., October 10, 1964 . . . Shoots right.

Year	Team	League	Games	G.	A.	Pts.	Pen.
1983-84—Deerfield Academy (c)		Mass. H.S.	22	18	25	43	..
1984-85—Univ. of New Hampshire		H. East	42	22	18	40	21
1985-86—Univ. of New Hampshire		H. East	29	9	13	22	22

(c)—June, 1984—Drafted by Los Angeles Kings in 1984 NHL entry draft. Seventh Kings pick, 129th overall, seventh round.

DAVE HANNAN

Center . . . 5'11" . . . 174 lbs. . . . Born, Sudbury, Ont., November 26, 1961 . . . Shoots left . . . Missed part of '80-81 season with a bruised shoulder.

Year	Team	League	Games	G.	A.	Pts.	Pen.
1977-78—Windsor Spitfires		OMJHL	68	14	16	30	43
1978-79—Sault Ste. Marie Greyhounds		OMJHL	26	7	8	15	13
1979-80—Sault Ste. Marie Greyhounds		OMJHL	28	11	10	21	31
1979-80—Brantford Alexanders		OMJHL	25	5	10	15	26
1980-81—Brantford Alexanders (c)		OHL	56	46	35	81	155
1981-82—Erie Blades		AHL	76	33	37	70	129
1981-82—Pittsburgh Penguins		NHL	1	0	0	0	0
1982-83—Baltimore Skipjacks		AHL	5	2	2	4	13
1982-83—Pittsburgh Penguins		NHL	74	11	22	33	127
1983-84—Baltimore Skipjacks		AHL	47	18	24	42	98
1983-84—Pittsburgh Penguins		NHL	24	2	3	5	33
1984-85—Baltimore Skipjacks		AHL	49	20	25	45	91
1984-85—Pittsburgh Penguins		NHL	30	6	7	13	43
1985-86—Pittsburgh Penguins		NHL	75	17	18	35	91
NHL TOTALS			204	36	50	86	294

(c)—June, 1981—Drafted by Pittsburgh Penguins in 1981 NHL entry draft. Ninth Penguins pick, 196th overall, 10th round.

MARK LEA HARDY

Defense . . . 5'11" . . . 190 lbs. . . . Born, Semaden, Switzerland, February 1, 1959 . . . Shoots left . . . Mother was a member of 1952 Olympic Figure Skating team from England . . . (October, 1985)—Missed 25 games due to surgery to sublexation tendon in left wrist injured in final pre-season game vs. Calgary.

Year	Team	League	Games	G.	A.	Pts.	Pen.
1975-76—Montreal Juniors		QMJHL	64	6	17	23	44
1976-77—Montreal Juniors		QMJHL	72	20	40	60	137
1977-78—Montreal Juniors (a-c)		QMJHL	72	25	57	82	150
1978-79—Montreal Juniors (d)		QMJHL	67	18	52	70	117
1979-80—Binghamton Dusters		AHL	56	3	13	16	32
1979-80—Los Angeles Kings		NHL	15	0	1	1	10
1980-81—Los Angeles Kings		NHL	77	5	20	25	77
1981-82—Los Angeles Kings		NHL	77	6	39	45	130
1982-83—Los Angeles Kings		NHL	74	5	34	39	101
1983-84—Los Angeles Kings		NHL	79	8	41	49	122
1984-85—Los Angeles Kings		NHL	78	14	39	53	97
1985-86—Los Angeles Kings		NHL	55	6	21	27	71
NHL TOTALS			455	44	195	239	608

(c)—Named top defenseman in QMJHL.
(d)—August, 1979—Drafted by Los Angeles Kings in 1979 entry draft. Third Kings pick, 30th overall, second round.

WARREN HARPER

Right Wing . . . 5'11" . . . 176 lbs. . . . Born, Prince Albert, Sask., May 10, 1963 . . . Shoots left.

Year	Team	League	Games	G.	A.	Pts.	Pen.
1979-80—Prince Albert AA	Midget	34	20	17	37	58
1980-81—Prince Albert Raiders (c)	SJHL	60	35	35	70	158
1981-82—Prince Albert Raiders	SJHL	39	23	29	52	108
1982-83—Prince Albert Raiders	WHL	41	17	15	32	38
1983-84—Rochester Americans	AHL	78	25	28	53	56
1984-85—Rochester Americans	AHL	78	29	34	63	43
1985-86—Rochester Americans	AHL	80	18	30	48	83

(c)—June, 1981—Drafted as underage junior by Buffalo Sabres in 1981 NHL entry draft. Twelfth Sabres pick, 206th overall, 10th round.

STEPHEN WILLIAM HARRISON

Defense . . . 5'11" . . . 190 lbs. . . . Born, Scarborough, Ont., April 25, 1958 . . . Shoots left . . . (October 25, 1980)—Knee surgery.

Year	Team	League	Games	G.	A.	Pts.	Pen.
1975-76—Toronto Marlboros	Jr."A"OHA	36	0	5	5	6
1976-77—Toronto Marlboros	Jr."A"OHA	49	6	13	19	59
1977-78—Toronto Marlboros (c)	Jr."A"OHA	68	16	42	58	70
1978-79—Salt Lake Golden Eagles	CHL	2	0	1	1	0
1978-79—Port Huron Flags (b)	IHL	80	20	56	76	98
1979-80—Salt Lake Golden Eagles	CHL	80	4	42	46	36
1980-81—Port Huron Flags	IHL	7	3	6	9	4
1980-81—Salt Lake Golden Eagles	CHL	39	9	28	37	50
1981-82—Salt Lake Golden Eagles	CHL	75	12	46	58	63
1982-83—Moncton Alpines	AHL	2	0	0	0	2
1982-83—Peoria Prancers (b)	IHL	72	14	55	69	76
1983-84—Peoria Prancers	IHL	82	11	40	51	52
1984-85—Toledo Goaldiggers (d)	IHL	49	9	18	27	39
1984-85—Salt Lake Golden Eagles	IHL	37	5	24	29	24
1985-86—Salt Lake Golden Eagles	IHL	77	17	53	70	48

(c)—Drafted from Toronto Marlboros by St. Louis Blues in third round of 1978 amateur draft.

(d)—February, 1985—Traded with Kevin Conway, Blake Stephan and Grant Rezansoff by Toledo Goaldiggers to Salt Lake Golden Eagles for Steve Martinson and Kurt Kleinendorst.

MIKE HARTMAN

Left Wing . . . 5'11" . . . 190 lbs. . . . Born, West Bloomfield, Mich., February 7, 1967 . . . Shoots left . . . Also plays Right Wing.

Year	Team	League	Games	G.	A.	Pts.	Pen.
1984-85—Belleville Bulls	OHL	49	13	12	25	119
1985-86—Belleville Bulls	OHL	4	2	1	3	5
1985-86—North Bay Centennials (c)	OHL	53	19	16	35	205

(c)—June, 1986—Drafted by Buffalo Sabres in 1986 NHL entry draft. Eighth Sabres pick, 131th overall, seventh round.

CRAIG HARTSBURG

Defense . . . 6'1" . . . 190 lbs. . . . Born, Stratford, Ont., June 29, 1959 . . . Shoots left . . . (September, 1977)—Torn ligaments in left knee . . . (September, 1980)—Separated shoulder . . . Member of Team Canada in 1981 Canada Cup . . . Son of Bill Hartsburg (WHL, 1960s) . . . (October 10, 1983)—Surgery to remove bone spur on knee, returned November 15 . . . (January 10, 1984)—Injured ligaments in left knee in game vs. Hartford and required arthoscopic surgery . . . Holds Minnesota club records for most assists (60) and points (77) in a season by a defenseman . . . (October, 1984)—Hip pointer in training camp . . . (December, 1984)—Fractured femur . . . (January 16, 1986)—Injured groin vs. St. Louis and missed four games.

Year	Team	League	Games	G.	A.	Pts.	Pen.
1975-76—S. Ste. Marie Greyhounds	Jr."A"OHA	64	9	19	28	65
1976-77—S. Ste. M. Greyhounds (b-c)	Jr."A"OHA	61	29	64	93	142
1977-78—S. Ste. M. Greyhounds (d)	Jr."A"OHA	36	15	42	57	101
1978-79—Birmingham Bulls (e)	WHA	77	9	40	49	73
1979-80—Minnesota North Stars	NHL	79	14	30	44	81
1980-81—Minnesota North Stars	NHL	74	13	30	43	124
1981-82—Minnesota North Stars	NHL	76	17	60	77	117
1982-83—Minnesota North Stars	NHL	78	12	50	62	109
1983-84—Minnesota North Stars	NHL	26	7	7	14	37
1984-85—Minnesota North Stars	NHL	32	7	11	18	54
1985-86—Minnesota North Stars	NHL	75	10	47	57	127
WHA TOTALS		77	9	40	49	73
NHL TOTALS		440	80	235	315	647

(c)—Won Max Kaminsky Memorial Trophy (outstanding defenseman).
(d)—July, 1978—Signed by Birmingham Bulls (WHA) as underage junior.
(e)—June, 1979—Drafted by Minnesota North Stars in 1979 NHL entry draft. First North Stars pick, sixth overall, first round.

DAVID HASS

Left Wing . . . 6'2" . . . 185 lbs. . . . Born, Toronto, Ont., July 23, 1968 . . . Shoots left.

Year	Team	League	Games	G.	A.	Pts.	Pen.
1984-85—Don Mills Flyers Midgets		MTHL	38	38	38	76	80
1985-86—London Knights (c)		OHL	62	4	13	17	91

(c)—June, 1986—Drafted as underage junior by Edmonton Oilers in 1986 NHL entry draft. Fifth Oilers pick, 105th overall, fifth round.

KEVIN HATCHER

Defense . . . 6'3" . . . 185 lbs. . . . Born, Detroit, Mich., September 9, 1966 . . . Shoots right.

Year	Team	League	Games	G.	A.	Pts.	Pen.
1982-83—Detroit Compuware		Mich. Midget	75	30	45	75	120
1983-84—North Bay Centennials (c)		OHL	67	10	39	49	61
1984-85—North Bay Centennials (b)		OHL	58	26	37	63	75
1984-85—Washington Capitals		NHL	2	1	0	1	0
1985-86—Washington Capitals		NHL	79	9	10	19	119
NHL TOTALS			81	10	10	20	119

(c)—June, 1984—Drafted as underage junior by Washington Capitals in 1984 NHL entry draft. First Capitals pick, 17th overall, first round.

DALE HAWERCHUK

Center . . . 5'11" . . . 170 lbs. . . . Born, Toronto, Ont., April 4, 1963 . . . Shoots left . . . Youngest player to have 100-point season (18 years, 351 days) . . . (March 7, 1984)—Set NHL record with five assists in a period during a 7-3 win at Los Angeles . . . (April 13, 1985)—Broken rib in playoff game when checked by Jamie Macoun at Calgary.

Year	Team	League	Games	G.	A.	Pts.	Pen.
1979-80—Cornwall Royals (c-d)		OMJHL	72	37	66	103	21
1980-81—Cornwall Royals (a-e-f-g-h-i)		OHL	72	*81	*102	*183	69
1981-82—Winnipeg Jets (j-k)		NHL	80	45	58	103	47
1982-83—Winnipeg Jets		NHL	79	40	51	91	31
1983-84—Winnipeg Jets		NHL	80	37	65	102	73
1984-85—Winnipeg Jets (b)		NHL	80	53	77	130	74
1985-86—Winnipeg Jets		NHL	80	46	59	105	44
NHL TOTALS			399	221	310	531	269

(c)—Winner of The Instructeurs Trophy (QMJHL Top Rookie).
(d)—Winner of Guy Lafleur Trophy (QMJHL Playoff MVP).
(e)—Winner of Jean Beliveau Trophy (QMJHL Leading Scorer).
(f)—Winner of Michel Briere Trophy (QMJHL MVP).
(g)—Winner of The Association of Journalists for Major Junior League Hockey Trophy (Best pro prospect). First year awarded.
(h)—Winner of CCM Trophy (Top Canadian Major Junior League Player).
(i)—Drafted as underage junior by Winnipeg Jets in 1981 NHL entry draft. First Jets pick, first overall, first round.
(j)—Named NHL Rookie of the Year by The Sporting News in poll of players.
(k)—Winner of Calder Memorial Trophy (NHL Rookie of the Year).

GREG HAWGOOD

Defense . . . 5'8" . . . 175 lbs. . . . Born, St. Albert, Alta., August 10, 1968 . . . Shoots left.

Year	Team	League	Games	G.	A.	Pts.	Pen.
1983-84—Kamloops Junior Oilers		WHL	49	10	23	33	39
1984-85—Kamloops Blazers		WHL	66	25	40	65	72
1985-86—Kamloops Blazers (a-c)		WHL	71	34	85	119	86

(c)—June, 1986—Drafted as underage junior by Boston Bruins in 1986 NHL entry draft. Ninth Bruins pick, 202nd overall, 10th round.

TODD HAWKINS

Right Wing . . . 5'11" . . . 190 lbs. . . . Born, Kingston, Ont., August 2, 1966 . . . Shoots right.

Year	Team	League	Games	G.	A.	Pts.	Pen.
1984-85—Belleville Bulls		OHL	58	7	16	23	117
1985-86—Belleville Bulls (c)		OHL	60	14	13	27	172

(c)—June, 1986—Drafted by Vancouver Canucks in 1986 NHL entry draft. Tenth Canucks pick, 217th overall, 11th round.

KENT HAWLEY

Center . . . 6'3" . . . 215 lbs. . . . Born, Kingston, Ont., February 20, 1968 . . . Shoots left.

Year	Team	League	Games	G.	A.	Pts.	Pen.
1984-85	Ottawa Senators	CJHL	54	19	37	56	119
1985-86	Ottawa 67's (c)	OHL	64	21	30	51	96

(c)—June, 1986—Drafted as underage junior by Philadelphia Flyers in 1986 NHL entry draft. Third Flyers pick, 28th overall, second round.

ALAN JOSEPH GORDON HAWORTH

Center . . . 5'10" . . . 188 lbs. . . . Born, Drummondville, Que., September 1, 1960 . . . Shoots right . . . (February 4, 1981)—Bruised shoulder . . . (March 11, 1986)—Fractured wrist vs. Pittsburgh.

Year	Team	League	Games	G.	A.	Pts.	Pen.
1977-78	Chicoutimi Sagueneens	QMJHL	59	17	33	50	40
1978-79	Sherbrooke Beavers (c)	QMJHL	70	50	70	120	63
1979-80	Sherbrooke Beavers	QMJHL	45	28	36	64	50
1980-81	Rochester Americans	AHL	21	14	18	32	19
1980-81	Buffalo Sabres	NHL	49	16	20	36	34
1981-82	Rochester Americans	AHL	14	5	12	17	10
1981-82	Buffalo Sabres (d)	NHL	57	21	18	39	30
1982-83	Washington Capitals	NHL	74	23	27	50	34
1983-84	Washington Capitals	NHL	75	24	31	55	52
1984-85	Washington Capitals	NHL	76	23	26	49	48
1985-86	Washington Capitals	NHL	71	34	39	73	72
	NHL TOTALS		402	141	161	302	270

(c)—August, 1979—Drafted by Buffalo Sabres as underage junior in 1979 entry draft. Sixth Sabres pick, 95th overall, fifth round.

(d)—June, 1982—Traded by Buffalo Sabres with third-round pick in 1982 entry draft to Washington Capitals for second and fourth-round choices in 1982.

NEIL HAWRYLIW

Right Wing . . . 5'11" . . . 185 lbs. . . . Born, Fielding, Sask., November 19, 1955 . . . Shoots left . . . (December, 1981)—Concussion . . . (October, 1982)—Knee injury.

Year	Team	League	Games	G.	A.	Pts.	Pen.
1972-73	Humboldt Broncos	SJHL	....	...	....	....	....
1973-74	Saskatoon Blades	WCHL	52	23	20	43	28
1974-75	Saskatoon Blades	WCHL	68	29	38	67	51
1975-76	Saskatoon Blades	WCHL	72	48	39	87	155
1976-77	Muskegon Mohawks	IHL	38	18	18	36	16
1977-78	Muskegon Mohawks	IHL	75	37	32	69	84
1978-79	Fort Worth Texans (c)	CHL	57	9	15	24	87
1978-79	Muskegon Mohawks	IHL	13	11	7	18	14
1979-80	Indianapolis Checkers	CHL	70	26	19	45	56
1980-81	Indianapolis Checkers (a)	CHL	80	37	42	79	61
1981-82	New York Islanders	NHL	1	0	0	0	0
1981-82	Indianapolis Checkers	CHL	58	20	14	34	89
1982-83	Wichita Wind	CHL	2	2	3	5	0
1982-83	Muskegon Mohawks	IHL	68	33	24	57	42
1983-84	Muskegon Mohawks	IHL	66	25	37	62	36
1984-85	Muskegon Lumberjacks	IHL	80	17	22	39	93
1985-86	Muskegon Lumberjacks	IHL	14	4	1	5	10
1985-86	Kalamazoo Wings	IHL	68	32	23	55	67
	NHL TOTALS		1	0	0	0	0

(c)—October, 1978—Signed as a free agent by New York Islanders.

BRIAN HAYTON

Defense . . . 6' . . . 197 lbs. . . . Born, Peterborough, Ont., January 22, 1968 . . . Shoots left . . . Also plays Left Wing.

Year	Team	League	Games	G.	A.	Pts.	Pen.
1984-85	Peterborough Jr. B	OHA	30	7	5	12	118
1985-86	Guelph Platers (c)	OHL	56	6	11	17	99

(c)—June, 1986—Drafted as underage junior by Los Angeles Kings in 1986 NHL entry draft. Eleventh Kings pick, 223rd overall, 12th round.

RANDY HEATH

Left Wing . . . 5'8" . . . 165 lbs. . . . Born, Vancouver, B.C., November 11, 1964 . . . Shoots left.

Year	Team	League	Games	G.	A.	Pts.	Pen.
1980-81—Vancouver Blue Hawks	BCJHL	50	35	35	70	30
1980-81—Portland Winter Hawks	WHL	2	1	0	1	0
1981-82—Portland Winter Hawks	WHL	65	52	47	99	65
1982-83—Portland Winter Hawks (a-c)	WHL	72	82	69	151	52
1983-84—Portland Winter Hawks (a)	WHL	60	44	46	90	107
1984-85—New Haven Nighthawks	AHL	60	23	26	49	29
1984-85—New York Rangers	NHL	12	2	3	5	15
1985-86—New York Rangers	NHL	1	0	1	1	0
1985-86—New Haven Nighthawks	AHL	77	36	38	74	53
NHL TOTALS		13	2	4	6	15

(c)—June, 1983—Drafted as underage junior by New York Rangers in 1983 NHL entry draft. Second Rangers pick, 33rd overall, second round.

KEVIN HEFFERNAN

Center . . . 6'1" . . . 185 lbs. . . . Born, Weymouth, Mass., January 18, 1966 . . . Shoots left.

Year	Team	League	Games	G.	A.	Pts.	Pen.
1983-84—Weymouth H.S. (c)	Mass. H.S.	24	22	35	57	..
1984-85—Northeastern Univ.	H. East	38	18	25	43	20
1985-86—Northeastern Univ.	H. East	35	8	21	29	12

(c)—June, 1984—Drafted by Boston Bruins in 1984 NHL entry draft. Ninth Bruins pick, 186th overall, ninth round.

ANTHONY J. HEJNA

Left Wing . . . 6' . . . 190 lbs. . . . Born, Buffalo, N.Y., January 8, 1968 . . . Shoots left.

Year	Team	League	Games	G.	A.	Pts.	Pen.
1984-85—Nichols H.S.	N.Y.	34	46	40	86	20
1985-86—Nichols H.S. (c)	N.Y.	33	51	27	78	26

(c)—June, 1986—Drafted by St. Louis Blues in 1986 NHL entry draft. Third Blues pick, 52nd overall, third round.

TIM HELMER

Center . . . 6'1" . . . 185 lbs. . . . Born, Woodstock, Ont., November 6, 1966 . . . Shoots right . . . Also plays Right Wing . . . (January, 1982)—Broken leg.

Year	Team	League	Games	G.	A.	Pts.	Pen.
1981-82—Ottawa Senators	CJHL	40	15	15	30	8
1982-83—North Bay Centennials	OHL	70	10	13	23	13
1983-84—North Bay Centennials	OHL	18	5	2	7	5
1983-84—Ottawa 67's	OHL	29	3	6	9	19
1984-85—Ottawa 67's (c)	OHL	61	28	28	56	52
1985-86—Ottawa 67's	OHL	28	13	12	25	25

(c)—June, 1985—Drafted as underage junior by Minnesota North Stars in 1985 NHL entry draft. Seventh North Stars pick, 174th overall, ninth round.

RAIMO HELMINEN

Center . . . 6' . . . 183 lbs. . . . Born, Tampere, Finland, March 11, 1964 . . . Shoots left . . . (October, 1985)—Hip injury.

Year	Team	League	Games	G.	A.	Pts.	Pen.
1983-84—Ilves (c)	Finland	37	17	13	30	14
1984-85—Ilves	Finland	36	21	36	57	20
1985-86—New York Rangers	NHL	66	10	30	40	10
NHL TOTALS		66	10	30	40	10

(c)—June, 1983—Drafted by New York Rangers in NHL entry draft. Second Rangers pick, 35th overall, second round.

ARCHIE HENDERSON

Right Wing . . . 6'6" . . . 216 lbs. . . . Born, Calgary, Alta., February 17, 1957 . . . Shoots right . . . Missed part of 1976-77 season with knee injury . . . (November, 1980)—Hand injury . . . (October 25, 1985)—Given six-game suspension by AHL for stick-swinging incident with Jim Archibald at Springfield. Henderson had received a match penalty . . . (December 7, 1985)—Given 12-game AHL suspension for crosschecking incident with Robin Bartel in Moncton.

Year	Team	League	Games	G.	A.	Pts.	Pen.
1974-75—Lethbridge Broncos	WCHL	65	3	10	13	177

Year	Team	League	Games	G.	A.	Pts.	Pen.
1975-76—Lethbridge Broncos (c)		WCHL	21	1	2	3	110
1975-76—Victoria Cougars		WCHL	31	8	7	15	205
1976-77—Victoria Cougars (d)		WCHL	47	14	10	24	208
1977-78—Port Huron Flags		IHL	71	16	16	32	419
1978-79—Hershey Bears		AHL	78	17	11	28	337
1979-80—Hershey Bears		AHL	8	0	2	2	37
1979-80—Fort Worth Texans (e)		CHL	49	8	9	17	199
1980-81—Washington Capitals		NHL	7	1	0	1	28
1980-81—Hershey Bears		AHL	60	3	5	8	251
1981-82—Minnesota North Stars (f)		NHL	1	0	0	0	0
1981-82—Nashville South Stars		CHL	77	12	23	35	*320
1982-83—Hartford Whalers (g)		NHL	15	2	1	3	64
1982-83—Binghamton Whalers (h)		AHL	50	8	9	17	172
1983-84—New Haven Nighthawks (i-j)		AHL	48	1	8	9	164
1984-85—Nova Scotia Oilers		AHL	72	5	7	12	271
1985-86—Maine Mariners (k)		AHL	57	4	6	10	72
NHL TOTALS			23	3	1	4	92

(c)—Traded to Victoria Cougars by Lethbridge Broncos for Rick Peter, December, 1975.
(d)—Drafted from Victoria Cougars by Washington Capitals in 10th round of 1977 amateur draft.
(e)—Led in penalty minutes (58) during playoffs.
(f)—September, 1981—Signed with Minnesota North Stars as a free agent after being released by Washington Capitals.
(g)—September, 1982—Signed by Hartford Whalers as a free agent.
(h)—March, 1983—Released by Hartford Whalers.
(i)—September, 1983—Signed by New Haven Nighthawks as a free agent.
(j)—February, 1984—Released by New Haven Nighthawks.
(k)—September, 1985—Signed by New Jersey Devils as a free agent.

RICK HENDRICKS

Defense . . . 6' . . . 195 lbs. . . . Born, Hardisty, Alta., May 15, 1957 . . . Shoots left.

Year	Team	League	Games	G.	A.	Pts.	Pen.
1975-76—Victoria Cougars		WCHL	39	2	10	12	66
1976-77—Victoria Cougars		WCHL	21	5	15	20	45
1976-77—Lethbridge Broncos		WCHL	55	12	32	44	161
1977-78—St. Albert		AJHL	50	13	22	35	92
1977-78—Lethbridge Broncos		WCHL	14	0	4	4	27
1978-79—Fort Wayne Komets		IHL	64	3	15	18	95
1978-79—Muskegon Mohawks		IHL	13	2	2	4	29
1979-80—Muskegon Mohawks		IHL	42	8	34	42	113
1979-80—Toledo Goaldiggers		IHL	37	8	20	28	20
1980-81—Toledo Goaldiggers		IHL	11	2	3	5	22
1980-81—Maine Mariners (c)		AHL	34	1	5	6	70
1981-82—Maine Mariners		AHL	74	3	17	20	145
1982-83—Toledo Goaldiggers (d)		IHL	81	10	44	54	108
1983-84—Salt Lake Golden Eagles		CHL	1	1	0	1	0
1983-84—Toledo Goaldiggers		IHL	80	13	42	55	154
1984-85—Peoria Rivermen (e)		IHL	67	7	27	34	171
1985-86—Peoria Rivermen (f)		IHL	37	5	16	21	44
1985-86—Fort Wayne Komets		IHL	26	3	18	21	39

(c)—January, 1981—Signed by Maine Mariners as a free agent.
(d)—Shared IHL playoff point lead (with teammate Dirk Graham) with 20 points.
(e)—Led IHL playoffs with 88 penalty minutes.
(f)—February, 1986—Traded by Peoria Rivermen to Fort Wayne Komets for Paul Adey.

DALE HENRY

Left Wing . . . 6' . . . 205 lbs. . . . Born, Prince Albert, Sask., September 24, 1964 . . . Shoots left.

Year	Team	League	Games	G.	A.	Pts.	Pen.
1981-82—Saskatoon Blades		WHL	32	5	4	9	50
1982-83—Saskatoon Blades (c)		WHL	63	21	19	40	213
1983-84—Saskatoon Blades		WHL	71	41	36	77	162
1984-85—Springfield Indians		AHL	67	11	20	31	133
1984-85—New York Islanders		NHL	16	2	1	3	19
1985-86—Springfield Indians		AHL	64	14	26	40	162
1985-86—New York Islanders		NHL	7	1	3	4	15
NHL TOTALS			23	3	4	7	34

(c)—June, 1983—Drafted as underage junior by New York Islanders in 1983 NHL entry draft. Tenth Islanders pick, 157th overall, eighth round.

ALAN HEPPLE

Defense . . . 5'10" . . . 200 lbs. . . . Born, Blaudon-on-Tyne, England, August 16, 1963 . . . Shoots right . . . Also plays Center . . . (October, 1980)—Eye injury.

Year	Team	League	Games	G.	A.	Pts.	Pen.
1980-81—Ottawa 67's		OHL	64	3	13	16	110
1981-82—Ottawa 67's (c)		OHL	66	6	22	28	160
1982-83—Ottawa 67's		OHL	64	10	26	36	168
1983-84—Maine Mariners		AHL	64	4	23	27	117
1983-84—New Jersey Devils		NHL	1	0	0	0	7
1984-85—Maine Mariners		AHL	80	7	17	24	125
1984-85—New Jersey Devils		NHL	1	0	0	0	0
1985-86—Maine Mariners		AHL	69	4	21	25	104
1985-86—New Jersey Devils		NHL	1	0	0	0	0
NHL TOTALS			3	0	0	0	7

(c)—June, 1982—Drafted as underage junior by New Jersey Devils in 1982 NHL entry draft. Ninth Devils pick, 169th overall, ninth round.

RICK HERBERT

Defense . . . 6'1" . . . 190 lbs. . . . Born, Toronto, Ont., July 10, 1967 . . . Shoots left.

Year	Team	League	Games	G.	A.	Pts.	Pen.
1982-83—Regina Pats		WHL	63	0	7	7	55
1983-84—Regina Pats		WHL	58	3	18	21	78
1984-85—Portland Winter Hawks (c)		WHL	70	7	39	46	192
1985-86—Portland Winter Hawks		WHL	42	2	19	21	60
1985-86—Spokane Chiefs		WHL	29	2	18	20	72

(c)—June, 1985—Drafted as underage junior by Chicago Black Hawks in 1985 NHL entry draft. Fourth Black Hawks pick, 87th overall, fifth round.

STEVE HERNIMAN

Defense . . . 6'4" . . . 200 lbs. . . . Born, Windsor, Ont., June 9, 1968 . . . Shoots left.

Year	Team	League	Games	G.	A.	Pts.	Pen.
1984-85—Kitchener Midgets		OHL	29	3	20	23	50
1984-85—Cornwall Royals (c)		OHL	55	3	12	15	128

(c)—June, 1986—Drafted as underage junior by Vancouver Canucks in 1986 NHL entry draft. Fifth Canucks pick, 112th overall, sixth round.

KEVIN HEROM

Left Wing . . . 6' . . . 195 lbs. . . . Born, Regina, Sask., July 6, 1967 . . . Shoots left.

Year	Team	League	Games	G.	A.	Pts.	Pen.
1983-84—Regina Pat Canadians		Sask. Midget	26	22	24	46	39
1984-85—Moose Jaw Warriors (c)		WHL	61	20	18	38	44
1985-86—Moose Jaw Warriors		WHL	66	22	18	40	103

(c)—June, 1985—Drafted as underage junior by New York Islanders in 1985 NHL entry draft. Fifth Islanders pick, 76th overall, fourth round.

YVES HEROUX

Right Wing . . . 5'11" . . . 185 lbs. . . . Born, Terrebonne, Que., April 27, 1965 . . . Shoots right . . . Brother of Alain Heroux . . . (December, 1981)—Foot infection.

Year	Team	League	Games	G.	A.	Pts.	Pen.
1981-82—Laurentides AAA		Que. Midget	48	53	53	106	84
1982-83—Chicoutimi Sagueneens (c)		QHL	70	41	40	81	44
1983-84—Chicoutimi Sagueneens		QHL	56	28	25	53	67
1983-84—Fredericton Express		AHL	4	0	0	0	0
1984-85—Chicoutimi Sagueneens		QHL	66	42	54	96	123
1985-86—Fredericton Express		AHL	31	12	10	22	42
1985-86—Muskegon Lumberjacks		IHL	42	14	8	22	41

(c)—June, 1983—Drafted as underage junior by Quebec Nordiques in 1983 NHL entry draft. First Nordiques pick, 32nd overall, second round.

GRAHAM HERRING

Defense . . . 6' . . . 170 lbs. . . . Born, Montreal, Que., October 27, 1965 . . . Shoots left . . . (September, 1984)—Injured knee, requiring surgery.

Year	Team	League	Games	G.	A.	Pts.	Pen.
1983-84—Longueuil Chevaliers (c)		QHL	68	9	44	53	101
1984-85—Shawinigan Cataracts		QHL	20	5	10	15	28
1985-86—Peoria Rivermen (d)		IHL	34	1	9	10	22
1985-86—Sherbrooke Canadiens		AHL	24	0	9	9	19

(c)—June, 1984—Drafted as underage junior by St. Louis Blues in 1984 NHL entry draft. Sixth Blues pick, 71st overall, fourth round.

(d)—January, 1986—Traded by St. Louis Blues with fifth-round draft choice (Eric Aubertin) in 1986 to Montreal Canadiens for Kent Carlson.

MEL HEWITT

Defense . . . 5'10" . . . 175 lbs. . . . Born, Saskatoon, Sask., November 15, 1958 . . . Shoots left.

Year	Team	League	Games	G.	A.	Pts.	Pen.
1975-76—Saskatoon		SJHL	41	1	5	6	241
1975-76—Saskatoon Blades		WCHL	13	0	1	1	43
1976-77—Saskatoon Blades		WCHL	69	8	18	26	373
1977-78—Saskatoon Blades		WCHL	13	3	8	11	96
1977-78—Calgary Wranglers (c)		WCHL	55	18	11	29	412
1978-79—Calgary		AJHL	16	11	5	16	113
1978-79—Saginaw Gears		IHL	2	1	2	3	10
1978-79—San Francisco Shamrocks		PHL	4	0	0	0	26
1979-80—Saginaw Gears (d)		IHL	70	28	26	54	*504
1980-81—New Brunswick Hawks		AHL	68	7	5	12	*304
1981-82—New Brunswick Hawks		AHL	66	11	10	21	119
1982-83—Maine Mariners		AHL	78	18	14	32	271
1983-84—Flint Generals		IHL	45	18	34	52	86
1983-84—Peoria Prancers		IHL	24	6	6	12	80
1984-85—Flint Generals		IHL	43	18	16	34	146
1985-86—Saginaw Generals		IHL	17	6	4	10	49
1985-86—Indianapolis Checkers		IHL	54	18	16	34	210

(c)—June, 1978—Drafted by Toronto Maple Leafs in 1978 NHL amateur draft. Fifth Maple Leafs pick, 92nd overall, sixth round.

(d)—Led IHL Playoffs with 82 penalty minutes.

GLENN HICKS

Left Wing . . . 5'10" . . . 177 lbs. . . . Born, Red Deer, Alta., August 28, 1958 . . . Shoots left . . . Brother of Doug Hicks.

Year	Team	League	Games	G.	A.	Pts.	Pen.
1975-76—Flin Flon Bombers		WCHL	71	16	19	35	103
1976-77—Flin Flon Bombers		WCHL	71	28	31	59	175
1977-78—Flin Flon Bombers (c-d)		WCHL	72	50	69	119	225
1978-79—Winnipeg Jets (e)		WHA	69	6	10	16	48
1979-80—Detroit Red Wings		NHL	50	1	2	3	43
1980-81—Adirondack Red Wings		AHL	19	10	6	16	56
1980-81—Detroit Red Wings		NHL	58	5	10	15	84
1981-82—Tulsa Oilers (f)		CHL	78	14	34	48	103
1982-83—Birmingham South Stars		CHL	80	13	26	39	40
1983-84—Salt Lake Golden Eagles		CHL	62	4	26	30	87
1984-85—Springfield Indians (g)		AHL	11	3	4	7	4
1985-86—Salt Lake Golden Eagles (h)		IHL	82	14	40	54	75
WHA TOTALS			69	6	10	16	48
NHL TOTALS			108	6	12	18	127

(c)—Drafted from Flin Flon Bombers by Detroit Red Wings in second round of 1978 amateur draft.

(d)—Selected by Winnipeg Jets in World Hockey Association amateur players draft. Signed by Winnipeg, July, 1978.

(e)—June, 1979—Selected by Detroit Red Wings in NHL reclaim draft.

(f)—September, 1981—Signed by Winnipeg Jets as a free agent.

(g)—March, 1985—Signed as free agent by Springfield Indians after a season in Europe.

(h)—October, 1985—Signed by Salt Lake Golden Eagles as a free agent.

ANDRE HIDI

Left Wing . . . 6'2" . . . 205 lbs. . . . Born, Toronto, Ont., June 5, 1960 . . . Shoots left.

Year	Team	League	Games	G.	A.	Pts.	Pen.
1983-84—University of Toronto		OUAA	49	45	63	108	89
1983-84—Washington Capitals (c)		NHL	1	0	0	0	0
1984-85—Binghamton Whalers		AHL	55	12	17	29	57
1984-85—Washington Capitals		NHL	6	2	1	3	9
1985-86—Binghamton Whalers (d)		AHL	66	19	24	43	104
NHL TOTALS			7	2	1	3	9

(c)—March, 1984—Signed by Washington Capitals as a free agent.

(d)—June, 1986—Released by Washington Capitals.

DANNY HIE

Center . . . 6' . . . 178 lbs. . . . Born, Mississauga, Ont., June 21, 1968 . . . Shoots left . . . Also plays Left Wing . . . (February, 1986)—Shoulder separation.

Year	Team	League	Games	G.	A.	Pts.	Pen.
1984-85—North York Jr. A		Tier II	37	12	12	24	100
1985-86—Ottawa 67's (c)		OHL	55	7	18	25	75

(c)—June, 1986—Drafted as underage junior by Toronto Maple Leafs in 1986 NHL entry draft. Seventh Maple Leafs pick, 132nd overall, seventh round.

ULLRICH HIEMER

Defense . . . 6'1" . . . 190 lbs. . . . Born, Fussen, West Germany, September 21, 1962 . . . Shoots left . . . (January, 1985)—Knee injury.

Year	Team	League	Games	G.	A.	Pts.	Pen.
1979-80—Fussen		W. Germany	44	6	10	16	....
1980-81—Fussen (c)		W. Germany	..	..	..	..	....
1981-82—Koln		W. Germany	36	19	27	46	....
1982-83—Koln		W. Germany	45	10	23	33	....
1983-84—Koln		W. Germany	50	23	23	46	....
1984-85—New Jersey Devils		NHL	53	5	24	29	70
1985-86—Maine Mariners		AHL	15	5	2	7	19
1985-86—New Jersey Devils		NHL	50	8	16	24	61
NHL TOTALS			103	13	40	53	131

(c)—June, 1981—Drafted by Colorado Rockies in the NHL entry draft. Third Rockies pick, 48th overall, third round.

TIM RAY HIGGINS

Right Wing . . . 6'1" . . . 185 lbs. . . . Born, Ottawa, Ont., February 7, 1958 . . . Shoots right . . . (January 16, 1983)—Broke index finger of right hand during a fight with Colin Campbell in game vs. Detroit . . . (February, 1983)—Strained knee ligaments . . . (October, 1985)—Missed two games with a stomach virus . . . (February 13, 1986)—Missed four games with infected foot blisters.

Year	Team	League	Games	G.	A.	Pts.	Pen.
1974-75—Ottawa 67's		Jr."A"OHA	22	1	3	4	6
1975-76—Ottawa 67's		Jr."A"OHA	59	15	10	25	59
1976-77—Ottawa 67's		Jr."A"OHA	66	36	52	88	82
1977-78—Ottawa 67's (c)		Jr."A"OHA	50	41	60	101	99
1978-79—Chicago Black Hawks		NHL	36	7	16	23	30
1978-79—New Brunswick Hawks		AHL	17	3	5	8	14
1979-80—Chicago Black Hawks		NHL	74	13	12	25	50
1980-81—Chicago Black Hawks		NHL	78	24	35	59	86
1981-82—Chicago Black Hawks		NHL	74	20	30	50	85
1982-83—Chicago Black Hawks		NHL	64	14	9	23	63
1983-84—Chicago Black Hawks (d)		NHL	32	1	4	5	21
1983-84—New Jersey Devils		NHL	37	18	10	28	27
1984-85—New Jersey Devils		NHL	71	19	29	48	30
1985-86—New Jersey Devils (e)		NHL	59	9	17	26	47
NHL TOTALS			525	125	162	287	439

(c)—Drafted from Ottawa 67's by Chicago Black Hawks in first round of 1978 amateur draft.
(d)—January, 1984—Traded by Chicago Black Hawks to New Jersey Devils for Jeff Larmer.
(e)—June, 1986—Traded by New Jersey Devils to Detroit Red Wings for Claude Loiselle.

ALAN DOUGLAS HILL

Left Wing and Center . . . 6' . . . 175 lbs. . . . Born, Nanaimo, B. C., April 22, 1955 . . . Shoots left . . . Set NHL record for most points in first NHL game with 2 goals, 3 assists, February 14, 1977 . . . (November 20, 1980)—Fractured hand.

Year	Team	League	Games	G.	A.	Pts.	Pen.
1973-74—Nanaimo		Jr."A"BCHL	64	29	41	70	60
1974-75—Victoria Cougars		WCHL	70	21	36	57	75
1975-76—Victoria Cougars (c)		WCHL	68	26	40	66	172
1976-77—Springfield Kings		AHL	63	13	28	41	125
1976-77—Philadelphia Flyers		NHL	9	2	4	6	27
1977-78—Maine Mariners (a)		AHL	80	32	59	91	118
1977-78—Philadelphia Flyers		NHL	3	0	0	0	2
1978-79—Philadelphia Flyers		NHL	31	5	11	16	28
1978-79—Maine Mariners		AHL	35	11	14	25	59
1979-80—Philadelphia Flyers		NHL	61	16	10	26	53

Year	Team	League	Games	G.	A.	Pts.	Pen.
1980-81	Philadelphia Flyers	NHL	57	10	15	25	45
1981-82	Philadelphia Flyers	NHL	41	6	13	19	58
1982-83	Moncton Alpines	AHL	78	22	22	44	78
1983-84	Maine Mariners (d)	AHL	51	8	16	24	51
1984-85	Hershey Bears	AHL	73	11	30	41	77
1985-86	Hershey Bears	AHL	80	17	40	57	129
	NHL TOTALS		202	39	53	92	213

(c)—September, 1976—Signed by Philadelphia Flyers as a free agent.
(d)—January, 1984—Signed by Maine Mariners as a free agent.

RANDY GEORGE HILLIER

Defense . . . 6'1" . . . 170 lbs. . . . Born, Toronto, Ont., March 30, 1960 . . . Shoots right . . . (April 19, 1982)—Injured knee in playoff series vs. Quebec . . . (December, 1982)—Injured left knee . . . (April 2, 1983)—Strained ligaments in right knee in game at Montreal . . . (December, 1984)—Surgery to remove bone chips from left shoulder, out 20 games . . . (March, 1985)—Broken finger . . . (November 30, 1985)—Tore knee ligaments vs. N. Y. Rangers.

Year	Team	League	Games	G.	A.	Pts.	Pen.
1977-78	Sudbury Wolves	OMJHL	60	1	14	15	67
1978-79	Sudbury Wolves	OMJHL	61	9	25	34	173
1979-80	Sudbury Wolves (c)	OMJHL	60	16	49	65	143
1980-81	Springfield Indians	AHL	64	3	17	20	105
1981-82	Erie Blades	AHL	35	6	13	19	52
1981-82	Boston Bruins	NHL	25	0	8	8	29
1982-83	Boston Bruins	NHL	70	0	10	10	99
1983-84	Boston Bruins	NHL	69	3	12	15	125
1984-85	Pittsburgh Penguins (d)	NHL	45	2	19	21	56
1985-86	Baltimore Skipjacks	AHL	8	0	5	5	14
1985-86	Pittsburgh Penguins	NHL	28	0	3	3	53
	NHL TOTALS		237	5	52	57	362

(c)—June, 1980—Drafted by Boston Bruins in 1980 NHL entry draft. Fourth Bruins pick, 102nd overall, fifth round.
(d)—October, 1984—Traded by Boston Bruins to Pittsburgh Penguins for 1985 fourth round draft pick.

TOM HIRSCH

Defense . . . 6'3" . . . 195 lbs. . . . Born, Minneapolis, Minn., January 27, 1963 . . . Shoots right . . . Member of 1984 U.S. Olympic team . . . (October, 1984)—Separated shoulder in pre-season game . . . (June, 1985)—Surgery to shoulder . . . (October, 1985)—Further surgery to shoulder.

Year	Team	League	Games	G.	A.	Pts.	Pen.
1980-81	Mpls. Patrick Henry H.S. (c)	Minn. H.S.	23	42	35	77	....
1981-82	University of Minnesota	WCHA	36	7	16	23	53
1982-83	University of Minnesota	WCHA	37	8	23	31	70
1983-84	U.S. National Team	Int'l	56	8	25	33	72
1983-84	U.S. Olympic Team	Int'l	6	1	2	3	10
1983-84	Minnesota North Stars	NHL	15	1	3	4	20
1984-85	Springfield Indians	AHL	19	4	5	9	2
1984-85	Minnesota North Stars	NHL	15	0	4	4	10
1985-86	Minnesota North Stars	NHL		Did not play			
	NHL TOTALS		30	1	7	8	30

(c)—June, 1981—Drafted by Minnesota North Stars in 1981 NHL entry draft. Fourth North Stars pick, 33rd overall, second round.

DOUG HOBSON

Defense . . . 6' . . . 185 lbs. . . . Born, Prince Albert, Sask., April 9, 1968 . . . Shoots left.

Year	Team	League	Games	G.	A.	Pts.	Pen.
1984-85	Prince Albert Raiders	WHL	59	7	12	19	73
1985-86	Prince Albert Raiders (c)	WHL	66	2	17	19	70

(c)—June, 1986—Drafted as underage junior by Pittsburgh Penguins in 1986 NHL entry draft. Seventh Penguins pick, 130th overall, seventh round.

KENNETH HODGE JR.

Center . . . 6'2" . . . 190 lbs. . . . Born, Windsor, Ontario, April 13, 1966 . . . Shoots left . . . Son of former NHL star Ken Hodge, who played for Chicago, Boston and New York Rangers in 1965 through 1978.

Year	Team	League	Games	G.	A.	Pts.	Pen.
1983-84—St. John's Prep. (c)		Mass. H.S.	22	25	38	63	..
1984-85—Boston College (d)		H. East	41	20	44	64	28
1985-86—Boston College		H. East	21	11	17	28	16

(c)—June, 1984—Drafted by Minnesota North Stars in 1984 NHL entry draft. Second North Stars pick, 46th overall, third round.

(d)—Named top Hockey East Freshman.

DAN HODGSON

Center . . . 5'11" . . . 173 lbs. . . . Born, Fort McMurray, Alta., August 29, 1965 . . . Shoots right . . . (October, 1985)—Broken nose and cheekbone.

Year	Team	League	Games	G.	A.	Pts.	Pen.
1982-83—Prince Albert Raiders (c-d)		WHL	72	56	74	130	66
1983-84—Prince Albert Raiders (b)		WHL	66	62	*119	181	65
1984-85—Prince Albert Raiders (a-e-f)		WHL	64	70	*112	182	86
1985-86—Toronto Maple Leafs		NHL	40	13	12	25	12
1985-86—St. Catharines Saints		AHL	22	13	16	29	15
NHL TOTALS			40	13	12	25	12

(c)—Won Stuart "Butch" Paul Memorial Trophy (Top WHL Rookie).

(d)—June, 1983—Drafted as underage junior by Toronto Maple Leafs in 1983 NHL entry draft. Fourth Maple Leafs pick, 83rd overall, fifth round.

(e)—Named WHL Molson Player of the Year.

(f)—Led WHL Playoffs with 26 assists and 36 points.

MICHAEL HOFFMAN

Left Wing . . . 5'11" . . . 179 lbs. . . . Born, Cambridge, Ont., February 26, 1963 . . . Shoots left . . . (March, 1980)—Shoulder dislocation.

Year	Team	League	Games	G.	A.	Pts.	Pen.
1979-80—Barrie		Midget	60	40	35	75	....
1980-81—Brantford Alexanders (c)		OHL	68	15	19	34	71
1981-82—Brantford Alexanders		OHL	66	34	47	81	169
1982-83—Brantford Alexanders		OHL	63	26	49	75	128
1982-83—Binghamton Whalers		AHL	1	0	0	0	0
1982-83—Hartford Whalers		NHL	2	0	1	1	0
1983-84—Binghamton Whalers		AHL	64	11	13	24	92
1984-85—Binghamton Whalers		AHL	76	19	26	45	95
1984-85—Hartford Whalers		NHL	1	0	0	0	0
1985-86—Binghamton Whalers		AHL	40	14	14	28	79
1985-86—Hartford Whalers		NHL	6	1	2	3	2
NHL TOTALS			9	1	3	4	2

(c)—June, 1981—Drafted as underage junior by Hartford Whalers in 1981 NHL entry draft. Third Whalers pick, 67th overall, fourth round.

ROBERT FRANK HOFFMEYER

Defense . . . 6' . . . 180 lbs. . . . Born, Dodsland, Sask., July 27, 1955 . . . Shoots left . . . Missed part of 1978-79 season with a broken jaw . . . (January 22, 1983)—Sprained wrist in game vs. N.Y. Islanders . . . (December 17, 1983)—Suspended for six games following stick swinging incident in game at Minnesota with Brian Bellows . . . (February, 1985)—Broken nose . . . (September, 1985)—Strained left knee in training camp.

Year	Team	League	Games	G.	A.	Pts.	Pen.
1972-73—Prince Albert Mintos		SJHL	..	..	..	..	..
1973-74—Saskatoon Blades		WCHL	62	2	10	12	198
1974-75—Saskatoon Blades (c)		WCHL	64	4	38	42	242
1975-76—Dallas Black Hawks		CHL	5	0	0	0	11
1975-76—Flint Generals		IHL	67	3	13	16	145
1976-77—Flint Generals		IHL	78	12	51	63	213
1977-78—Dallas Black Hawks		CHL	67	5	11	16	172
1977-78—Chicago Black Hawks		NHL	5	0	1	1	12
1978-79—Chicago Black Hawks		NHL	6	0	2	2	5
1978-79—New Brunswick Hawks		AHL	41	3	6	9	102
1979-80—New Brunswick Hawks		AHL	77	3	20	23	161
1980-81—Schwenningen		W. Germany	39	22	30	52	122
1980-81—Maine Mariners (d)		AHL	2	1	1	2	52
1981-82—Philadelphia Flyers		NHL	57	7	20	27	142
1981-82—Maine Mariners (e)		AHL	21	6	8	14	57
1982-83—Philadelphia Flyers (f)		NHL	35	2	11	13	40

Year	Team	League	Games	G.	A.	Pts.	Pen.
1982-83—Maine Mariners (g)		AHL	23	5	10	15	79
1983-84—Maine Mariners		AHL	14	3	1	4	27
1983-84—New Jersey Devils		NHL	58	4	12	16	61
1984-85—New Jersey Devils		NHL	37	1	6	7	65
1985-86—Maine Mariners (h-i)		AHL	8	0	0	0	6
NHL TOTALS			198	14	52	66	325

(c)—June, 1975—Drafted by Chicago Black Hawks in 1975 NHL amateur draft. Fifth Black Hawks pick, 79th overall, fifth round.

(d)—March, 1981—Signed by Philadelphia Flyers as a free agent.

(e)—Claimed by Edmonton Oilers in 1982 NHL waiver draft.

(f)—October, 1982—Traded by Edmonton Oilers to Philadelphia Flyers for Peter Dineen.

(g)—August, 1983—Signed by New Jersey Devils as a free agent.

(h)—October, 1985—Announced his retirement.

(i)—March, 1986—Reactivated by Maine Mariners.

JIM HOFFORD

Defense . . . 6' . . . 190 lbs. . . . Born, Sudbury, Ont., October 4, 1964 . . . Shoots right . . . (September, 1981)—Broken nose.

Year	Team	League	Games	G.	A.	Pts.	Pen.
1981-82—Windsor Spitfires		OHL	67	5	9	14	214
1982-83—Windsor Spitfires (c)		OHL	63	8	20	28	171
1983-84—Windsor Spitfires		OHL	1	0	0	0	2
1984-85—Rochester Americans		AHL	70	2	13	15	166
1985-86—Rochester Americans		AHL	40	2	7	9	148
1985-86—Buffalo Sabres		NHL	5	0	0	0	5
NHL TOTALS			5	0	0	0	5

(c)—June, 1983—Drafted as underage junior by Buffalo Sabres in 1983 NHL entry draft. Eighth Sabres pick, 114th overall, sixth round.

BENOIT HOGUE

Center . . . 5'11" . . . 170 lbs. . . . Born, Repentigny, Que., October 28, 1966 . . . Shoots left.

Year	Team	League	Games	G.	A.	Pts.	Pen.
1984-85—St. Jean Beavers		QHL	59	14	11	25	42
1984-85—St. Jean Beavers (c)		QHL	63	46	44	90	92
1985-86—St. Jean Beavers		QHL	65	54	54	108	115

(c)—June, 1985—Drafted as underage junior by Buffalo Sabres in 1985 NHL entry draft. Second Sabres pick, 35th overall, second round.

MARK HOLICK

Right Wing . . . 6'2" . . . 185 lbs. . . . Born, Saskatoon, Sask., September 5, 1968 . . . Shoots right . . . Also plays Center . . . (October, 1983)—Broken leg.

Year	Team	League	Games	G.	A.	Pts.	Pen.
1983-84—Penticton Midget Reps.		B.C. Midget	11	11	12	23	30
1984-85—Saskatoon Blades		WHL	68	3	6	9	60
1985-86—Saskatoon Blades (c)		WHL	60	6	11	17	137

(c)—June, 1986—Drafted as underage junior by Toronto Maple Leafs in 1986 NHL entry draft. Eleventh Maple Leafs pick, 216th overall, 11th round.

STEVE HOLLETT

Center . . . 6'1" . . . 168 lbs. . . . Born, St. John's, N.B., June 12, 1967 . . . Shoots left.

Year	Team	League	Games	G.	A.	Pts.	Pen.
1983-84—Niagara Falls Midget		OHA	30	46	54	100	95
1984-85—Sault Ste. Marie Greyhounds (c)		OHL	60	12	17	29	25
1985-86—Sault Ste. Marie Greyhounds		OHL	63	31	34	65	81
1985-86—Binghamton Whalers		AHL	8	0	0	0	2

(c)—June, 1985—Drafted as underage junior by Washington Capitals in 1985 NHL entry draft. Tenth Capitals pick, 187th overall, ninth round.

BRUCE HOLLOWAY

Defense . . . 6' . . . 200 lbs. . . . Born, Revelstoke, B.C., June 27, 1963 . . . Shoots left.

Year	Team	League	Games	G.	A.	Pts.	Pen.
1978-79—Revelstoke Bruins	BCJHL	61	4	14	18	52
1978-79—Billings Bighorns	WHL	9	0	1	1	0
1979-80—Melville	SJHL	9	3	2	5	10
1979-80—Billings Bighorns	WHL	49	1	9	10	6
1980-81—Regina Pats (c-d)	WHL	69	6	29	35	61
1981-82—Regina Pats	WHL	69	4	28	32	111
1982-83—Brandon Wheat Kings	WHL	7	0	5	5	8
1982-83—Kamloops Junior Oilers	WHL	51	16	53	69	82
1983-84—Fredericton Express	AHL	66	3	30	33	29
1984-85—Fredericton Express	AHL	31	2	4	6	16
1984-85—St. Catharines Saints	AHL	13	1	0	1	0
1984-85—Vancouver Canucks	NHL	2	0	0	0	0
1985-86—Kalamazoo Wings	IHL	38	7	11	18	45
1985-86—Peoria Rivermen	IHL	29	4	13	17	47
NHL TOTALS		2	0	0	0	0

(c)—October, 1980—Traded with Neil Girard and Wade Waters by Billings Bighorns to Regina Pats for Jim McGeough.

(d)—June, 1981—Drafted as underage junior by Vancouver Canucks in 1981 NHL entry draft. Sixth Canucks pick, 136th overall, seventh round.

DARIL HOLMES

Right Wing . . . 6'6" . . . 195 lbs. . . . Born, Cornwall, Ont., February 15, 1967 . . . Shoots right.

Year	Team	League	Games	G.	A.	Pts.	Pen.
1983-84—Nepean Midgets	OHA	56	31	26	57	74
1984-85—Kingston Canadians (c)	OHL	57	11	22	33	50
1985-86—Kingston Canadians	OHL	66	25	37	62	97

(c)—June, 1985—Drafted as underage junior by Philadelphia Flyers in 1985 NHL entry draft. Sixth Flyers pick, 105th overall, fifth round.

WARREN HOLMES

Center . . . 6'1" . . . 185 lbs. . . . Born, Beeton, Ont., February 18, 1957 . . . Shoots left . . . (November, 1980)—Sprained ankle.

Year	Team	League	Games	G.	A.	Pts.	Pen.
1974-75—Ottawa 67's	Jr."A"OHA	54	9	17	26	47
1975-76—Ottawa 67's	Jr."A"OHA	28	3	11	14	6
1976-77—Ottawa 67's (c)	Jr."A"OHA	36	18	29	47	31
1977-78—Saginaw Gears	IHL	78	48	33	81	51
1978-79—Springfield Indians	AHL	4	0	0	0	0
1978-79—Milwaukee Admirals	IHL	31	11	17	28	33
1978-79—Saginaw Gears (d)	IHL	38	11	18	29	30
1979-80—Saginaw Gears	IHL	72	37	55	92	62
1979-80—Binghamton Dusters	AHL	2	0	0	0	0
1980-81—Houston Apollos	CHL	25	7	7	14	18
1980-81—Saginaw Gears	IHL	40	21	26	47	27
1981-82—New Haven Nighthawks	AHL	73	28	28	56	29
1981-82—Los Angeles Kings	NHL	3	0	2	2	0
1982-83—New Haven Nighthawks	AHL	35	17	18	35	26
1982-83—Los Angeles Kings	NHL	39	8	16	24	7
1983-84—New Haven Nighthawks	AHL	76	26	35	61	25
1983-84—Los Angeles Kings	NHL	3	0	0	0	0
1984-85—Flint Generals	IHL	80	23	44	67	70
1985-86—Saginaw Generals	IHL	65	17	20	37	88
NHL TOTALS		45	8	18	26	7

(c)—Drafted from Ottawa 67's by Los Angeles Kings in fifth round of 1977 amateur draft.

(d)—December, 1978—Traded with Randy Rudnyk by Saginaw Gears to Milwaukee Admirals for first and second draft choices.

CRAIG HOMOLA

Center . . . 5'10" . . . 176 lbs. . . . Born, Eveleth, Minn., November 29, 1958 . . . Shoots left.

Year	Team	League	Games	G.	A.	Pts.	Pen.
1977-78—University of Vermont	ECAC	31	17	18	35	8
1978-79—University of Vermont	ECAC	30	24	31	55	39
1979-80—University of Vermont (a-c-d-e)	ECAC	34	28	*41	*69	18
1980-81—University of Vermont	ECAC	33	19	27	46	44
1980-81—Oklahoma City Stars	CHL	5	2	2	4	0
1981-82—Nashville South Stars (f)	CHL	76	19	35	54	47
1982-83—Birmingham South Stars	CHL	80	30	44	74	34
1983-84—Salt Lake Golden Eagles	CHL	68	29	27	56	37

Year	Team	League	Games	G.	A.	Pts.	Pen.
1984-85—Milwaukee Admirals		IHL	56	16	32	48	18
1985-86—Milwaukee Admirals		IHL	12	2	2	4	2

(c)—Named to All-America Team (East).
(d)—Named to First Team of All-New England Team.
(e)—Named ECAC Most Valuable Player.
(f)—September, 1981—Signed by Minnesota North Stars as a free agent.

TODD HOOEY

Right Wing . . . 6'1" . . . 180 lbs. . . . Born, Oshawa, Ont., June 23, 1963 . . . Shoots right . . . Nephew of Tom and Tim O'Connor (1958 World Champion Whitby Dunlops) . . . (October, 1984)—Knee injury.

Year	Team	League	Games	G.	A.	Pts.	Pen.
1979-80—Oshawa Reps		Midget	53	31	20	51	....
1980-81—Windsor Spitfires (c)		OHL	68	18	25	43	132
1981-82—Windsor Spitfires		OHL	68	39	62	101	158
1981-82—Oklahoma City Stars		CHL	4	1	1	2	0
1982-83—Windsor Spitfires (d)		OHL	4	0	1	1	6
1982-83—Oshawa Generals		OHL	62	31	34	65	64
1983-84—Colorado Flames		CHL	67	19	21	40	40
1984-85—Moncton Golden Flames		AHL	61	4	14	18	52
1985-86—Salt Lake Golden Eagles		IHL	80	15	23	38	95

(c)—June, 1981—Drafted as underage junior by Calgary Flames in 1981 NHL entry draft. Fifth Flames pick, 120th overall, sixth round.
(d)—October, 1982—Traded by Windsor Spitfires to Oshawa Generals for Ray Flaherty.

TIM HOOVER

Defense . . . 5'10" . . . 165 lbs. . . . Born, North Bay, Ont., January 9, 1965 . . . Shoots left . . . (March, 1986)—Broken foot.

Year	Team	League	Games	G.	A.	Pts.	Pen.
1982-83—Sault Ste. Marie Greyhounds (c)		OHL	60	6	21	27	53
1983-84—Sault Ste. Marie Greyhounds		OHL	70	8	34	42	50
1984-85—Sault Ste. Marie Greyhounds		OHL	49	6	28	34	29
1985-86—Rochester Americans		AHL	49	2	5	7	34

(c)—June, 1983—Drafted as underage junior by Buffalo Sabres in 1983 NHL entry draft. Eleventh Sabres pick, 174th overall, ninth round.

DEAN ROBERT HOPKINS

Right Wing . . . 6'1" . . . 205 lbs. . . . Born, Cobourg, Ont., June 6, 1959 . . . Shoots right . . . Played Center prior to 1978-79 . . . Missed 14 games during 1979-80 season with broken ankle . . . (December, 1981)—Dislocated elbow . . . Brother of Brent Hopkins . . . (March, 1986)—Broken jaw.

Year	Team	League	Games	G.	A.	Pts.	Pen.
1975-76—London Knights		OMJHL	53	4	14	18	50
1976-77—London Knights		OMJHL	63	19	26	45	67
1977-78—London Knights		OMJHL	67	19	34	53	70
1978-79—London Knights (c)		OMJHL	65	37	55	92	149
1979-80—Los Angeles Kings		NHL	60	8	6	14	39
1980-81—Los Angeles Kings		NHL	67	8	18	26	118
1981-82—Los Angeles Kings		NHL	41	2	13	15	102
1982-83—New Haven Nighthawks		AHL	20	9	8	17	58
1982-83—Los Angeles Kings		NHL	49	5	12	17	43
1983-84—New Haven Nighthawks		AHL	79	35	47	82	162
1984-85—New Haven Nighthawks (d)		AHL	20	7	10	17	38
1984-85—Nova Scotia Voyageurs		AHL	49	13	17	30	93
1985-86—Edmonton Oilers (e)		NHL	1	0	0	0	0
1985-86—Nova Scotia Voyageurs		AHL	60	23	32	55	131
NHL TOTALS			218	23	49	72	302

(c)—August, 1979—Drafted by Los Angeles Kings in 1979 entry draft. Second Kings pick, 29th overall, second round.
(d)—November, 1984—Traded with Mark Morrison by New Haven Nighthawks to Nova Scotia Oilers for Rob Tudor and Gerry Minor.
(e)—September, 1985—Signed by Edmonton Oilers as a free agent.

TONY HORACEK

Left Wing . . . 6'3" . . . 200 lbs. . . . Born, Vancouver, B.C., February 3, 1967 . . . Shoots left.

Year	Team	League	Games	G.	A.	Pts.	Pen.
1984-85—Kelowna Wings (c)		WHL	67	9	18	27	114
1985-86—Spokane Chiefs		WHL	64	19	28	47	129

(c)—June, 1985—Drafted as underage junior by Philadelphia Flyers in 1985 NHL entry draft. Eighth Flyers pick, 147th overall, seventh round.

PETER HORACHEK

Left Wing . . . 6'1" . . . 195 lbs. . . . Born, Stoney Creek, Ont., January 26, 1960 . . . Shoots left.

Year	Team	League	Games	G.	A.	Pts.	Pen.
1977-78—Oshawa Generals		OMJHL	66	22	26	48	163
1978-79—Oshawa Generals		OMJHL	67	15	35	50	32
1979-80—Oshawa Generals (c)		OHL	68	35	67	102	43
1979-80—Rochester Americans (d)		AHL	..	..	..	..	..
1980-81—Rochester Americans		AHL	63	20	26	46	61
1981-82—Rochester Americans		AHL	52	8	14	22	37
1982-83—Rochester Americans		AHL	1	0	0	0	0
1982-83—Flint Generals		IHL	51	27	28	55	23
1983-84—Flint Generals		IHL	82	34	52	86	34
1984-85—Flint Generals		IHL	77	38	30	68	30
1985-86—Saginaw Generals		IHL	79	21	32	53	16

(c)—November, 1979—Signed by Buffalo Sabres as a free agent.
(d)—No regular season record. Played in four playoff games.

STEVE HORNER

Right Wing . . . 6'1" . . . 195 lbs. . . . Born, Cowansville, Que., June 4, 1966 . . . Shoots right.

Year	Team	League	Games	G.	A.	Pts.	Pen.
1984-85—Henry Carr H.S. (c)		OHA	35	21	20	41	38
1985-86—Univ. of New Hampshire		H. East	30	3	5	8	14

(c)—June, 1985—Drafted by Los Angeles Kings in 1985 NHL entry draft. Eighth Kings pick, 177th overall, ninth round.

ED HOSPODAR

Defense and Right Wing . . . 6'2" . . . 210 lbs. . . . Born, Bowling Green, Ohio, February 9, 1959 . . . Shoots right . . . (September, 1977)—Surgery to remove cartilage from left knee . . . (September, 1978)—Injured ligaments in right knee . . . (October, 1980)—Bruised left ankle . . . (December 28, 1980)—Strained back . . . (December 30, 1981)—Suffered broken jaw and loss of several teeth in altercation with Clark Gillies of New York Islanders . . . (December, 1983)—Hamstring injury . . . (December 16, 1984)—Broke hand in game vs. Montreal . . . (October 13, 1985)—Missed four games with elbow infection . . . (January 21, 1986)—Strained back at Washington and missed five games . . . (February 10, 1986)—Strained knee at Montreal and missed seven games.

Year	Team	League	Games	G.	A.	Pts.	Pen.
1976-77—Ottawa 67's		OMJHL	51	3	19	22	140
1977-78—Ottawa 67's		OMJHL	62	7	26	33	172
1978-79—Ottawa 67's (b-c)		OMJHL	46	7	16	23	208
1979-80—New Haven Nighthawks		AHL	25	3	9	12	131
1979-80—New York Rangers		NHL	20	0	1	1	76
1980-81—New York Rangers (d)		NHL	61	5	14	19	214
1981-82—New York Rangers (e)		NHL	41	3	8	11	152
1982-83—Hartford Whalers		NHL	72	1	9	10	199
1983-84—Hartford Whalers (f)		NHL	59	0	9	9	163
1984-85—Philadelphia Flyers		NHL	50	3	4	7	130
1985-86—Philadelphia Flyers (g)		NHL	17	3	1	4	55
1985-86—Minnesota North Stars (h)		NHL	43	0	2	2	91
NHL TOTALS			363	15	48	63	1080

(c)—August, 1979—Drafted by New York Rangers in 1979 entry draft. Second Rangers pick, 34th overall, second round.
(d)—Led NHL playoffs with 93 penalty minutes.
(e)—October, 1982—Traded by New York Rangers to Hartford Whalers for Kent-Erik Andersson.
(f)—July, 1983—Released by Hartford Whalers and signed by Philadelphia Flyers as a free agent.
(g)—November, 1985—Traded with Todd Bergen by Philadelphia Flyers to Minnesota North Stars for Dave Richter and Bo Berglund.
(h)—June, 1986—Released by Minnesota North Stars and signed by Philadelphia Flyers as a free agent.

GREG HOTHAM

Defense . . . 5'11" . . . 183 lbs. . . . Born, London, Ont., March 7, 1956 . . . Shoots right . . . (November, 1982)—Injured knee . . . Missed parts of 1982-83 season with sprained knee, separated shoulder and injured back . . . (September, 1984)—Missed first 20 games of the season with mononucleosis.

Year	Team	League	Games	G.	A.	Pts.	Pen.
1973-74—Aurora Tigers		OPJHL	44	10	22	32	120
1974-75—Aurora Tigers		OPJHL	27	14	10	24	46
1974-75—Kingston Canadians		Jr."A"OHA	31	1	14	15	49
1975-76—Kingston Canadians (c)		Jr."A"OHA	49	10	32	42	76
1976-77—Saginaw Gears		IHL	69	4	33	37	100
1977-78—Saginaw Gears (b)		IHL	80	13	59	72	56
1977-78—Dallas Black Hawks (d)		CHL	....	...	...	...	....
1978-79—New Brunswick Hawks		AHL	76	9	27	36	88
1979-80—Toronto Maple Leafs		NHL	46	3	10	13	10
1979-80—New Brunswick Hawks		AHL	21	1	6	7	10
1980-81—Toronto Maple Leafs		NHL	11	1	1	2	11
1980-81—New Brunswick Hawks		AHL	68	8	48	56	80
1981-82—Cincinnati Tigers		CHL	46	10	33	43	94
1981-82—Toronto Maple Leafs (e)		NHL	3	0	0	0	0
1981-82—Pittsburgh Penguins		NHL	25	4	6	10	16
1982-83—Pittsburgh Penguins		NHL	58	2	30	32	39
1983-84—Pittsburgh Penguins		NHL	76	5	25	30	59
1984-85—Baltimore Skipjacks		AHL	44	4	27	31	43
1984-85—Pittsburgh Penguins		NHL	11	0	2	2	4
1985-86—Baltimore Skipjacks		AHL	78	2	26	28	94
NHL TOTALS			230	15	74	89	139

(c)—Drafted from Kingston Canadians by Toronto Maple Leafs in fifth round of 1976 amateur draft.
(d)—No league record. Played five playoff games.
(e)—January, 1982—Traded by Toronto Maple Leafs to Pittsburgh Penguins for future draft considerations.

PAUL HOUCK

Right Wing . . . 5'11" . . . 185 lbs. . . . . Born, North Vancouver, B.C., August 12, 1963 . . . Shoots right.

Year	Team	League	Games	G.	A.	Pts.	Pen.
1980-81—Kelowna Buckaroos (c)		BCJHL	....	...	....	....	....
1981-82—Univ. of Wisconsin		WCHA	43	9	16	25	38
1982-83—Univ. of Wisconsin		WCHA	47	38	33	71	56
1983-84—Univ. of Wisconsin		WCHA	37	20	20	40	29
1984-85—Univ. of Wisconsin (d)		WCHA	38	15	26	41	34
1984-85—Nova Scotia Oilers		AHL	10	1	0	1	0
1985-86—Minnesota North Stars		NHL	3	1	0	1	0
1985-86—Springfield Indians		AHL	61	15	17	32	27
NHL TOTALS			3	1	0	1	0

(c)—June, 1981—Drafted by Edmonton Oilers in 1981 NHL entry draft. Third Oilers pick, 71st overall, fourth round.
(d)—June, 1985—Traded by Edmonton Oilers to Minnesota North Stars for Gilles Meloche.

DOUG HOUDA

Defense . . . 6'2" . . . 195 lbs. . . . Born, Blairmore, Alta., June 3, 1966 . . . Shoots right.

Year	Team	League	Games	G.	A.	Pts.	Pen.
1981-82—Calgary Wranglers		WHL	3	0	0	0	0
1982-83—Calgary Wranglers		WHL	71	5	23	28	99
1983-84—Calgary Wranglers (c)		WHL	69	6	30	36	195
1984-85—Calgary Wranglers (b)		WHL	65	20	54	74	182
1984-85—Kalamazoo Wings (d)		IHL	....	...	....	....	....
1985-86—Calgary Wranglers		WHL	16	4	10	14	60
1985-86—Medicine Hat Tigers		WHL	35	9	23	32	80
1985-86—Detroit Red Wings		NHL	6	0	0	0	4
NHL TOTALS			6	0	0	0	4

(c)—June, 1984—Drafted as underage junior by Detroit Red Wings in 1984 NHL entry draft. Second Red Wings pick, 28th overall, second round.
(d)—Played seven playoff games.

MIKE L. HOUGH

Left Wing . . . 6'1" . . . 195 lbs. . . . Born, Montreal, Que., February 6, 1963 . . . Shoots left.

Year	Team	League	Games	G.	A.	Pts.	Pen.
1980-81—Dixie Beehives		OPJHL	24	15	20	35	84
1981-82—Kitchener Rangers (c)		OHL	58	14	34	48	172
1982-83—Kitchener Rangers		OHL	61	17	27	44	156
1983-84—Fredericton Express		AHL	69	11	16	27	142

Year	Team	League	Games	G.	A.	Pts.	Pen.
1984-85—Fredericton Express		AHL	76	21	27	48	49
1985-86—Fredericton Express		AHL	74	21	33	54	68

(c)—June, 1982—Drafted as underage junior by Quebec Nordiques in 1982 NHL entry draft. Seventh Nordiques pick, 181st overall, ninth round.

WILLIAM HOULDER

Defense . . . 6'2" . . . 192 lbs. . . . Born, Thunder Bay, Ont., March 11, 1967 . . . Shoots left.

Year	Team	League	Games	G.	A.	Pts.	Pen.
1983-84—Thunder Bay Beavers		TBAHA	23	4	18	22	37
1984-85—North Bay Centennials (c)		OHL	66	4	20	24	37
1985-86—North Bay Centennials		OHL	59	5	30	35	97

(c)—June, 1985—Drafted as underage junior by Washington Capitals in 1985 NHL entry draft. Fourth Capitals pick, 82nd overall, fourth round.

PHIL HOUSLEY

Defense . . . 5'11" . . . 170 lbs. . . . Born, St. Paul, Minn., March 9, 1964 . . . Shoots left . . . Member of Team U.S.A. at World Junior Championships, 1982 . . . Also plays Center . . . Member of Team U.S.A. at World Cup Tournament, 1982 . . . Set Buffalo record for most assists by a rookie (47) in 1982-83 . . . (January, 1984)—Bruised shoulder . . . (March 18, 1984)—Became youngest defenseman in NHL history to have 30-goal season (20 years, 9 days)—(Bobby Orr was 22 years, 2 days) . . . Set Buffalo record for points by a defenseman with 77 in 1983-84 . . . (October, 1984)—Given 3-game NHL suspension . . . Also plays Center.

Year	Team	League	Games	G.	A.	Pts.	Pen.
1980-81—St. Paul Volcans		USHL	6	7	7	14	6
1981-82—South St. Paul H.S. (c)		Minn. H.S.	22	31	34	65	18
1982-83—Buffalo Sabres		NHL	77	19	47	66	39
1983-84—Buffalo Sabres		NHL	75	31	46	77	33
1984-85—Buffalo Sabres		NHL	73	16	53	69	28
1985-86—Buffalo Sabres		NHL	79	15	47	62	54
NHL TOTALS			304	81	193	274	154

(c)—June, 1982—Drafted as underage player by Buffalo Sabres in 1982 NHL entry draft. First Sabres pick, sixth overall, first round.

TAREK HOWARD

Defense . . . 6'2" . . . 195 lbs. . . . Born, Tucson, Ariz., February 6, 1965 . . . Shoots left . . . (October, 1984)—Separated shoulder in season opener vs. Providence College.

Year	Team	League	Games	G.	A.	Pts.	Pen.
1981-82—Olds Grizzlys		AJHL	56	10	22	32	101
1982-83—Olds Grizzlys (b-c)		AJHL	54	18	34	52	229
1983-84—Olds Gruzzlys		AJHL	56	10	22	32	101
1983-84—Univ. of North Dakota		WCHA	24	0	1	1	14
1984-85—Univ. of North Dakota		WCHA	24	1	3	4	17
1985-86—Univ. of North Dakota		WCHA	32	2	11	13	28

(c)—June, 1983—Drafted by Chicago Black Hawks in 1983 NHL entry draft. Fourth Black Hawks pick, 79th overall, fourth round.

MARK STEVEN HOWE

Defense . . . 5'11" . . . 180 lbs. . . . Born, Detroit, Mich., May 28, 1955 . . . Shoots left . . . Brother of Marty Howe and son of Hall-of-Famer Gordie Howe . . . Was member of 1972 USA Olympic team . . . Missed most of 1971-72 season following corrective knee surgery and part of 1976-77 season with shoulder separation . . . Missed part of 1977-78 season with rib injury . . . (October 9, 1980)—First defenseman in NHL to score two shorthanded goals in one period in 8-6 loss at St. Louis . . . (December 27, 1980)—5-inch puncture wound to upper thigh . . . Set NHL record for most assists (56) and points (80) by an American born player in 1979-80 (Broken by Neal Broten in '81-82) . . . (February, 1984)—Injured shoulder . . . (January, 1985)—Bruised collarbone . . . Also plays Left Wing.

Year	Team	League	Games	G.	A.	Pts.	Pen.
1970-71—Detroit Jr. Wings (a-c)		SOJHL	44	37	*70	*107	....
1971-72—Detroit Jr. Wings		SOJHL	9	5	9	14	....
1971-72—USA Olympic Team		....	...	...	...	...	....
1972-73—Toronto Marlboros (d-e-f)		Jr."A"OHA	60	38	66	104	27
1973-74—Houston Aeros (b-g-h)		WHA	76	38	41	79	20
1974-75—Houston Aeros (i)		WHA	74	36	40	76	30
1975-76—Houston Aeros		WHA	72	39	37	76	38
1976-77—Houston Aeros (b-j)		WHA	57	23	52	75	46

Year	Team	League	Games	G.	A.	Pts.	Pen.
1977-78—New England Whalers		WHA	70	30	61	91	32
1978-79—New England Whalers (a-k)		WHA	77	42	65	107	32
1979-80—Hartford Whalers		NHL	74	24	56	80	20
1980-81—Hartford Whalers		NHL	63	19	46	65	54
1981-82—Hartford Whalers (l)		NHL	76	8	45	53	18
1982-83—Philadelphia Flyers (a)		NHL	76	20	47	67	18
1983-84—Philadelphia Flyers		NHL	71	19	34	53	44
1984-85—Philadelphia Flyers		NHL	73	18	39	57	31
1985-86—Philadelphia Flyers (a)		NHL	77	24	58	82	36
WHA TOTALS			426	208	296	504	198
NHL TOTALS			510	132	325	457	221

(c)—Won Most Valuable Player and Outstanding Forward Awards.
(d)—Traded to Toronto Marlboros by London Knights for Larry Goodenough and Dennis Maruk, August, 1972.
(e)—Led in points (26) during playoffs.
(f)—Signed by Houston Aeros (WHA), June, 1972.
(g)—Won WHA Rookie Award.
(h)—Drafted from Toronto Marlboros by Boston Bruins in second round of 1974 amateur draft.
(i)—Tied for lead in goals (10) and led in points (22) during playoffs.
(j)—Signed by New England Whalers as free agent, June, 1977.
(k)—June, 1979—Selected by Boston Bruins in NHL reclaim draft, but remained Hartford Whalers' property as a priority selection for the expansion draft.
(l)—August, 1982—Traded by Hartford Whalers to Philadelphia Flyers for Ken Linseman, Greg Adams and Philadelphia's first-round choice (David A. Jensen) in 1983 entry draft. Philadelphia and Hartford also agreed to exchange third-round choices in 1983.

BRUCE CRAIG HOWES

Defense . . . 6'2" . . . 201 lbs. . . . Born, New Westminster, B.C., July 4, 1960 . . . Shoots left.

Year	Team	League	Games	G.	A.	Pts.	Pen.
1976-77—Maple Ridge		BCJHL	67	5	28	33	248
1976-77—New Westminster Bruins		WCHL	4	0	0	0	2
1977-78—New Westminster Bruins		WCHL	34	2	5	7	78
1978-79—New Westminster Bruins		WHL	65	13	30	43	116
1979-80—New Westminster Bruins (c)		WHL	34	9	14	23	75
1980-81—Adirondack Red Wings		AHL	61	4	16	20	92
1981-82—Kalamazoo Wings		IHL	44	6	14	20	43
1981-82—Adirondack Red Wings		AHL	20	1	1	2	11
1982-83—Adirondack Red Wings		AHL	48	0	4	4	24
1982-83—Kalamazoo Wings		IHL	18	2	6	8	23
1983-84—Kalamazoo Wings		IHL	26	2	9	11	30
1984-85—Kalamazoo Wings		IHL	56	2	8	10	65
1985-86—Saginaw Generals		IHL	45	3	16	19	39

(c)—March, 1980—Signed by Detroit Red Wings.

DONALD SCOTT HOWSON
(Known by middle name.)

Center . . . 5'10" . . . 155 lbs. . . . Born, Toronto, Ont., April 9, 1960 . . . Shoots right . . . (January, 1983)—Injured wrist.

Year	Team	League	Games	G.	A.	Pts.	Pen.
1977-78—North York Rangers		OPJHL	55	27	31	58	30
1978-79—Kingston Canadians		OMJHL	63	27	47	74	45
1979-80—Kingston Canadians		OMJHL	68	38	50	88	52
1980-81—Kingston Canadians		OMJHL	66	57	83	140	53
1981-82—Indianapolis Checkers (c)		CHL	8	2	1	3	5
1981-82—Toledo Goaldiggers		IHL	71	55	65	120	14
1982-83—Indianapolis Checkers (d)		CHL	67	34	40	74	22
1983-84—Indianapolis Checkers		CHL	71	34	34	68	40
1984-85—Springfield Indians		AHL	57	20	40	60	31
1984-85—New York Islanders		NHL	8	4	1	5	2
1985-86—Springfield Indians		AHL	53	15	19	34	10
1985-86—New York Islanders		NHL	10	1	2	3	2
NHL TOTALS			18	5	3	8	4

(c)—September, 1981—Signed by New York Islanders as a free agent.
(d)—Led CHL playoffs with 12 goals.

ANTHONY HRKAC

Center . . . 5'11" . . . 165 lbs. . . . Born, Thunder Bay, Ont., July 7, 1966 . . . Shoots left . . . (January, 1985)—Suspended six games by coach for disciplinary reasons.

Year	Team	League	Games	G.	A.	Pts.	Pen.
1983-84—Orillia Travelways (c)		OJHL	42	*52	54	*106	20
1984-85—Univ. of North Dakota		WCHA	36	18	36	54	16
1985-86—Team Canada		Int'l.	62	19	30	49	36

(c)—June, 1984—Drafted as underage junior by St. Louis Blues in 1984 NHL entry draft. Second Blues pick, 32nd overall, second round.

STEVE HRYNEWICH

Center . . . 6'1" . . . 185 lbs. . . . Born, Kingsville, Ont., October 9, 1966 . . . Shoots left . . . Also plays Left Wing.

Year	Team	League	Games	G.	A.	Pts.	Pen.
1982-83—Stratford Jr. B		OHA	38	8	15	23	82
1983-84—Ottawa 67's		OHL	62	7	11	18	59
1984-85—Ottawa 67's (c)		OHL	47	18	14	32	43
1985-86—Ottawa 67's		OHL	59	18	19	37	65

(c)—June, 1985—Drafted as underage junior by Washington Capitals in 1985 NHL entry draft. Twelfth Capitals pick, 229th overall, 11th round.

TIM HRYNEWICH

Left Wing . . . 6' . . . 191 lbs. . . . Born, Leamington, Ont., October 2, 1963 . . . Shoots left.

Year	Team	League	Games	G.	A.	Pts.	Pen.
1980-81—Sudbury Wolves		OHL	65	25	17	42	104
1981-82—Sudbury Wolves (c)		OHL	64	29	41	70	144
1982-83—Sudbury Wolves		OHL	23	21	16	37	65
1982-83—Baltimore Skipjacks		AHL	9	2	1	3	6
1982-83—Pittsburgh Penguins		NHL	30	2	3	5	48
1983-84—Baltimore Skipjacks		AHL	52	13	17	30	65
1983-84—Pittsburgh Penguins		NHL	25	4	5	9	34
1984-85—Baltimore Skipjacks		AHL	21	4	3	7	31
1984-85—Muskegon Lumberjacks		IHL	30	10	13	23	42
1985-86—Muskegon Lumberjacks (d)		IHL	67	25	26	51	110
1985-86—Toledo Goaldiggers		IHL	13	8	13	21	25
NHL TOTALS			55	6	8	14	82

(c)—June, 1982—Drafted as underage junior by Pittsburgh Penguins in 1982 NHL entry draft. Second Penguins pick, 38th overall, second round.

(d)—September, 1985—NHL rights traded with Marty McSorley by Pittsburgh Penguins to Edmonton Oilers for Gilles Meloche.

WILHEILM HEINRICH (WILLIE) HUBER

Defense . . . 6'5" . . . 228 lbs. . . . Born, Strasskirchen, West Germany, January 15, 1958 . . . Shoots right . . . (March, 1982)—Fractured left cheekbone . . . (February 12, 1983)—Cracked rib during game vs. Winnipeg . . . (November, 1983)—Strained left thigh muscle . . . (January 2, 1984)—Tore ligaments in right knee during game at Washington and required arthoscopic surgery . . . (January, 1985)—Surgery for torn knee ligaments.

Year	Team	League	Games	G.	A.	Pts.	Pen.
1975-76—Hamilton Fincups		Jr. "A" OHA	58	2	8	10	64
1976-77—St. Catharines Fincups		Jr."A" OHA	36	10	24	34	111
1977-78—Hamilton Fincups (b-c)		Jr."A" OHA	61	12	45	57	168
1978-79—Detroit Red Wings		NHL	68	7	24	31	114
1978-79—Kansas City Red Wings		CHL	10	2	7	9	12
1979-80—Adirondack Red Wings		AHL	4	1	3	4	2
1979-80—Detroit Red Wings		NHL	76	17	23	40	164
1980-81—Detroit Red Wings		NHL	80	15	34	49	130
1981-82—Detroit Red Wings		NHL	74	15	30	45	98
1982-83—Detroit Red Wings (d)		NHL	74	14	29	43	106
1983-84—New York Rangers		NHL	42	9	14	23	60
1984-85—New York Rangers		NHL	49	3	11	14	55
1985-86—New York Rangers		NHL	70	7	8	15	85
NHL TOTALS			533	87	173	260	812

(c)—Drafted from Hamilton Fincups by Detroit Red Wings in first round of 1978 amateur draft.

(d)—July, 1983—Traded by Detroit Red Wings with Mark Osborne and Mike Blaisdell to New York Rangers for Ron Duguay, Eddie Mio and Ed Johnstone.

CHARLES WILLIAM HUDDY

Defense . . . 6' . . . 200 lbs. . . . Born, Oshawa, Ont., June 2, 1959 . . . Shoots left . . . (November 10, 1980)—Injured shoulder in game vs. N.Y. Islanders . . . (February, 1986)—Missed three games with back spasms . . . (April, 1986)—Broken finger.

Year	Team	League	Games	G.	A.	Pts.	Pen.
1977-78—Oshawa Generals		OMJHL	59	17	18	35	81
1978-79—Oshawa Generals		OMJHL	64	20	38	58	108
1979-80—Houston Apollos (c)		CHL	79	14	34	48	46
1980-81—Edmonton Oilers		NHL	12	2	5	7	6
1980-81—Wichita Wind		CHL	47	8	36	44	71
1981-82—Wichita Wind		CHL	32	7	19	26	51
1981-82—Edmonton Oilers		NHL	41	4	11	15	46
1982-83—Edmonton Oilers		NHL	76	20	37	57	58
1983-84—Edmonton Oilers		NHL	75	8	34	42	43
1984-85—Edmonton Oilers		NHL	80	7	44	51	46
1985-86—Edmonton Oilers		NHL	76	6	35	41	55
NHL TOTALS			360	47	166	213	254

(c)—September, 1979—Signed by Edmonton Oilers as a free agent.

MICHAEL HUDSON

Left Wing . . . 6'1" . . . 185 lbs. . . . Born, Guelph, Ont., February 6, 1967 . . . Shoots left . . . Also plays Center.

Year	Team	League	Games	G.	A.	Pts.	Pen.
1984-85—Hamilton Steelhawks		OHL	50	10	12	22	13
1985-86—Hamilton Steelhawks (c)		OHL	7	3	2	5	4
1985-86—Sudbury Wolves (d)		OHL	59	35	42	77	20

(c)—October, 1985—Traded with Keith Vanrooyen by Hamilton Steelhawks to Sudbury Wolves for Brad Belland.

(d)—June, 1986—Drafted as underage junior by Chicago Black Hawks in 1986 NHL entry draft. Sixth Black Hawks pick, 140th overall, seventh round.

TED HUESING

Defense . . . 6'1" . . . 185 lbs. . . . Born, Detroit, Mich., March 23, 1957 . . . Shoots right . . . (December, 1984)—Knee surgery . . . (November, 1985)—Arthrospcopic knee surgery.

Year	Team	League	Games	G.	A.	Pts.	Pen.
1982-83—Adirondack Red Wings (c)		AHL	16	2	3	5	2
1983-84—Adirondack Red Wings		AHL	74	7	31	38	35
1984-85—Adirondack Red Wings		AHL	61	5	15	20	18
1985-86—Adirondack Red Wings		AHL	57	0	8	8	26

(c)—March, 1983—Signed by Detroit Red Wings as a free agent.

KERRY HUFFMAN

Defense . . . 6'3" . . . 185 lbs. . . . Born, Peterborough, Ont., January 3, 1968 . . . Shoots left . . . Brother-in-law of Mike Posavad (St. Louis Blues).

Year	Team	League	Games	G.	A.	Pts.	Pen.
1984-85—Peterborough Jr. B		Metro Jr.B	24	2	5	7	53
1985-86—Guelph Platers (c)		OHL	56	3	24	27	35

(c)—June, 1986—Drafted as underage junior by Philadelphia Flyers in 1986 NHL entry draft. First Flyers pick, 20th overall, first round.

PAT HUGHES

Right Wing . . . 5'11" . . . 190 lbs. . . . Born, Calgary, Alta., March 25, 1955 . . . Shoots right . . . Attended University of Michigan . . . Had corrective surgery on right shoulder following 1974-75 season . . . Also plays Center . . . (November 14, 1981)—Strained knee ligaments in game at New York Islanders . . . (October, 1984)—Sprained knee in pre-season game . . . (January, 1985)—Sprained knee.

Year	Team	League	Games	G.	A.	Pts.	Pen.
1973-74—University of Michigan		WCHA	35	14	12	26	40
1974-75—University of Michigan (c)		WCHA	38	24	19	43	64
1975-76—University of Michigan		WCHA	35	16	18	34	70
1976-77—Nova Scotia Voyageurs		AHL	77	29	39	68	144
1977-78—Nova Scotia Voyageurs (d)		AHL	74	40	28	68	128
1977-78—Montreal Canadiens		NHL	3	0	0	0	2
1978-79—Montreal Canadiens (e)		NHL	41	9	8	17	22
1979-80—Pittsburgh Penguins		NHL	76	18	14	32	78
1980-81—Pittsburgh Penguins (f)		NHL	58	10	9	19	161
1980-81—Edmonton Oilers		NHL	2	0	0	0	0
1981-82—Edmonton Oilers		NHL	68	24	22	46	99
1982-83—Edmonton Oilers		NHL	80	25	20	45	85
1983-84—Edmonton Oilers		NHL	77	27	28	55	61
1984-85—Edmonton Oilers		NHL	73	12	13	25	85

Year	Team	League	Games	G.	A.	Pts.	Pen.
1985-86—Buffalo Sabres (g)		NHL	50	4	9	13	25
1985-86—Rochester Americans		AHL	10	3	3	6	7
NHL TOTALS			528	129	123	252	618

(c)—Drafted from University of Michigan by Montreal Canadiens in fifth round of 1975 amateur draft.
(d)—Led in assists (9) and points (14) during playoffs.
(e)—September, 1979—Traded with Bob Holland by Montreal Canadiens to Pittsburgh Penguins for Denis Herron and second round pick in 1982 entry draft.
(f)—March, 1981—Traded by Pittsburgh Penguins to Edmonton Oilers for Pat Price.
(g)—October, 1985—Traded by Edmonton Oilers to Pittsburgh Penguins for future considerations. Subsequently sent from Pittsburgh to Buffalo Sabres (Both deals part of Oilers maneuver in waiver draft).

BRETT HULL

Right Wing . . . 5'11" . . . 190 lbs. . . . Born, Belleville, Ont., August 9, 1964 . . . Shoots right . . . Brother of Blake Hull, son of Hall-of-Fame left wing Bobby Hull and nephew of Dennis Hull.

Year	Team	League	Games	G.	A.	Pts.	Pen.
1983-84—Penticton (c)		BCJHL	56	105	83	188	20
1984-85—Univ. of Minn.-Duluth (d)		WCHA	48	32	28	60	24
1985-86—Univ. of Minn.-Duluth (a)		WCHA	42	*52	32	84	46
1985-86—Calgary Flames (e)		NHL	....	...	....	....	....

(c)—June, 1984—Drafted by Calgary Flames in 1984 NHL entry draft. Sixth Flames pick, 117th overall, sixth round.
(d)—WCHA Freshman of the Year.
(e)—No regular season record. Played two playoff games.

KENT HULST

Center . . . 6'1" . . . 180 lbs. . . . Born, St. Thomas, Ont., April 8, 1968 . . . Shoots left.

Year	Team	League	Games	G.	A.	Pts.	Pen.
1984-85—St. Thomas Jr. B		OHA	47	21	25	46	29
1985-86—Belleville Bulls (c)		OHL	43	6	17	23	20
1985-86—Windsor Spitfires (d)		OHL	17	6	10	16	9

(c)—February, 1986—Traded with future considerations by Belleville Bulls to Windsor Compuware Spitfires for Keith Gretzky.
(d)—June, 1986—Drafted as underage junior by Toronto Maple Leafs in 1986 NHL entry draft. Fourth Maple Leafs pick, 69th overall, fourth round.

JEFF CURTIS HUNT
(Known by middle name.)

Defense . . . 6'1" . . . 175 lbs. . . . Born, North Battleford, Sask., January 28, 1967 . . . Shoots left.

Year	Team	League	Games	G.	A.	Pts.	Pen.
1984-85—Prince Albert Raiders (c)		WHL	64	2	13	15	61
1985-86—Prince Albert Raiders		WHL	72	5	29	34	108

(c)—June, 1985—Drafted as underage junior by Vancouver Canucks in 1985 NHL entry draft. Ninth Canucks pick, 172nd overall, ninth round.

DALE ROBERT HUNTER

Center . . . 5'9" . . . 189 lbs. . . . Born, Petrolia, Ont., July 31, 1960 . . . Shoots left . . . Brother of Dave and Mark Hunter . . . (March, 1984)—Given three-game suspension by NHL . . . (April 21, 1985)—Hand infection occurred during playoff game with Montreal.

Year	Team	League	Games	G.	A.	Pts.	Pen.
1977-78—Kitchener Rangers		Jr."A"OHA	68	22	42	64	115
1978-79—Sudbury Wolves (c)		Jr."A"OHA	59	42	68	110	188
1979-80—Sudbury Wolves		OMJHL	61	34	51	85	189
1980-81—Quebec Nordiques		NHL	80	19	44	63	226
1981-82—Quebec Nordiques		NHL	80	22	50	72	272
1982-83—Quebec Nordiques		NHL	80	17	46	63	206
1983-84—Quebec Nordiques		NHL	77	24	55	79	232
1984-85—Quebec Nordiques (d)		NHL	80	20	52	72	209
1985-86—Quebec Nordiques		NHL	80	28	43	71	265
NHL TOTALS			477	130	290	420	1410

(c)—August, 1979—Drafted as underage junior by Quebec Nordiques in entry draft. Second Nordiques pick, 41st overall, second round.
(d)—Led Stanley Cup playoffs with 97 penalty minutes.

DAVE HUNTER

Left Wing . . . 5'11" . . . 204 lbs. . . . Born, Petrolia, Ont., January 1, 1958 . . . Shoots left . . . Brother of Dale and Mark Hunter . . . (December, 1981)—Knee injury . . . (May, 1984)—Bruised spleen in playoff series with N.Y. Islanders . . . (September 26, 1985)—Sprained left knee ligaments and injured hamstring and missed the first seven games of the season . . . (December, 1985)—Sentenced to four months in jail for his third conviction of driving while impaired by alcohol and released on bail. He served the sentence at the conclusion of the season.

Year	Team	League	Games	G.	A.	Pts.	Pen.
1975-76—Sudbury Wolves		Jr."A"OHA	53	7	21	28	117
1976-77—Sudbury Wolves		Jr."A"OHA	62	30	56	86	140
1977-78—Sudbury Wolves (c-d)		Jr."A"OHA	68	44	44	88	156
1978-79—Dallas Black Hawks		CHL	6	3	4	7	6
1978-79—Edmonton Oilers (e)		WHA	72	7	25	32	134
1979-80—Edmonton Oilers		NHL	80	12	31	43	103
1980-81—Edmonton Oilers		NHL	78	12	16	28	98
1981-82—Edmonton Oilers		NHL	63	16	22	38	63
1982-83—Edmonton Oilers		NHL	80	13	18	31	120
1983-84—Edmonton Oilers		NHL	80	22	26	48	90
1984-85—Edmonton Oilers		NHL	80	17	19	36	122
1985-86—Edmonton Oilers		NHL	62	15	22	37	77
WHA TOTALS			72	7	25	32	134
NHL TOTALS			523	107	154	261	673

(c)—Drafted from Sudbury Wolves by Montreal Canadiens in first round of 1978 amateur draft.
(d)—June, 1978—Selected by Edmonton Oilers in World Hockey Association amateur players draft and signed.
(e)—Led in penalty minutes (42) during playoffs.

MARK HUNTER

Right Wing . . . 6'1" . . . 200 lbs. . . . Born, Petrolia, Ont., November 12, 1962 . . . Shoots right . . . Brother of Dale and Dave Hunter . . . (November 13, 1982)—Pulled tendon in right knee in game at Los Angeles . . . (November 29, 1982)—17-stitch cut under right arm in game vs. Winnipeg . . . (December 26, 1982)—Tore medial ligaments in right knee in collision with brother Dale in game vs. Quebec. Surgery was required, missed 42 games . . . (October, 1983)—Injured right knee that required surgery . . . (February 21, 1984)—Injured knee in game at Quebec . . . (February, 1985)—Recurring knee injury.

Year	Team	League	Games	G.	A.	Pts.	Pen.
1979-80—Brantford Alexanders		OMJHL	66	34	55	89	171
1980-81—Brantford Alexanders (c)		OHL	53	39	40	79	157
1981-82—Montreal Canadiens		NHL	71	18	11	29	143
1982-83—Montreal Canadiens		NHL	31	8	8	16	73
1983-84—Montreal Canadiens		NHL	22	6	4	10	42
1984-85—Montreal Canadiens (d)		NHL	72	21	12	33	123
1985-86—St. Louis Blues		NHL	78	44	30	74	171
NHL TOTALS			274	97	65	162	552

(c)—June, 1981—Drafted as underage junior by Montreal Canadiens in 1981 NHL entry draft. First Canadiens pick, seventh overall, first round.
(d)—June, 1985—Traded with NHL rights to Michael Dark and second-round (Herb Raglan), third (Nelson Emerson), fifth (Dan Brooks) and sixth (Rich Burchill) round 1985 draft picks by Montreal Canadiens to St. Louis Blues for first (Jose Charbonneau), second (Todd Richards), fourth (Martin Desjardins), fifth (Tom Sagissor) and sixth (Donald Dufresne) round 1985 draft picks.

TIM ROBERT HUNTER

Defense . . . 6'2" . . . 186 lbs. . . . Born, Calgary, Alta., September 10, 1960 . . . Shoots right . . . Also plays Right Wing.

Year	Team	League	Games	G.	A.	Pts.	Pen.
1977-78—Kamloops		BCJHL	51	9	28	37	266
1977-78—Seattle Breakers		WCHL	3	1	2	3	4
1978-79—Seattle Breakers (c)		WHL	70	8	41	49	300
1979-80—Seattle Breakers		WHL	72	14	53	67	311
1980-81—Birmingham Bulls		CHL	58	3	5	8	*236
1980-81—Nova Scotia Voyageurs		AHL	17	0	0	0	62
1981-82—Oklahoma City Stars		CHL	55	4	12	16	222
1981-82—Calgary Flames		NHL	2	0	0	0	9
1982-83—Calgary Flames		NHL	16	1	0	1	54
1982-83—Colorado Flames		CHL	46	5	12	17	225
1983-84—Calgary Flames		NHL	43	4	4	8	130

Year	Team	League	Games	G.	A.	Pts.	Pen.
1984-85—Calgary Flames		NHL	71	11	11	22	259
1985-86—Calgary Flames		NHL	66	8	7	15	291
NHL TOTALS			198	24	22	46	743

(c)—August, 1979—Drafted by Atlanta Flames in 1979 NHL entry draft. Fourth Flames pick, 54th overall, third round.

STEVE HURT

Right Wing . . . 6'3" . . . 185 lbs. . . . Born, St. Paul, Minn., March 28, 1966 . . . Shoots right.

Year	Team	League	Games	G.	A.	Pts.	Pen.
1983-84—Hill-Murray H.S. (c)		Minn. H.S.	26	20	16	36	10
1984-85—Lake Superior State		CCHA	40	6	4	10	18
1985-86—Lake Superior State		CCHA	12	1	1	2	4

(c)—June, 1984—Drafted by Pittsburgh Penguins in 1984 NHL entry draft. Eighth Penguins pick, 189th overall, tenth round.

JAMIE HUSGEN

Defense . . . 6'3" . . . 205 lbs. . . . Born, St. Louis, Mo., October 13, 1964 . . . Shoots right.

Year	Team	League	Games	G.	A.	Pts.	Pen.
1982-83—Des Moines Buccaneers (c)		MWJHL	45	8	25	33	157
1983-84—Univ. of Illinois/Chicago		CCHA	35	6	17	23	76
1984-85—Univ. of Illinois/Chicago		CCHA	37	3	7	10	44
1985-86—Univ. of Illinois/Chicago		CCHA	29	2	5	7	51

(c)—June, 1983—Drafted by Winnipeg Jets in 1983 NHL entry draft. Thirteenth Jets pick, 229th overall, 12th round.

JOHN HUTCHINGS

Defense . . . 6' . . . 185 lbs. . . . Born, Cobourg, Ont., August 17, 1964 . . . Shoots right . . . (July, 1980)—Broken leg when run over by a tractor, did not play during 1980-81 season.

Year	Team	League	Games	G.	A.	Pts.	Pen.
1981-82—Oshawa Generals (c)		OHL	59	5	38	43	64
1982-83—Oshawa Generals		OHL	67	16	33	49	102
1983-84—Oshawa Generals		OHL	65	20	60	80	113
1984-85—Oshawa Generals (d)		OHL	22	4	13	17	43
1984-85—Hamilton Steelhawks		OHL	29	12	21	33	47
1985-86—Binghamton Whalers		AHL	6	0	2	2	8
1985-86—Toledo Goaldiggers		IHL	13	1	6	7	19
1985-86—Fort Wayne Komets		IHL	56	1	25	26	79

(c)—June, 1982—Drafted by New Jersey Devils as underage junior in 1982 NHL entry draft. Eighth Devils pick, 148th overall, eighth round.

(d)—December, 1984—Traded with Steve Hedington and sixth round pick (Andy May) in 1985 OHL priority draft by Oshawa Generals to Hamilton Steelhawks for Gary McColgan and Brent Loney.

DWAINE HUTTON

Center . . . 5'11" . . . 175 lbs. . . . Born, Edmonton, Alta., April 18, 1965 . . . Shoots left . . . (January, 1985)—Broken kneecap.

Year	Team	League	Games	G.	A.	Pts.	Pen.
1982-83—Kelowna Wings (c)		WHL	65	21	47	68	17
1983-84—Regina Pats		WHL	14	2	2	4	2
1983-84—Saskatoon Blades		WHL	35	13	30	43	16
1984-85—Saskatoon Blades		WHL	8	3	5	8	6
1984-85—Kelowna Wings		WHL	37	32	35	67	28
1985-86—Spokane Chiefs		WHL	20	10	21	31	35
1985-86—Team Canada		Int'l	19	3	4	7	24

(c)—June, 1983—Drafted as underage junior by Washington Capitals in 1983 NHL entry draft. Third Capitals pick, 135th overall, seventh round.

GORD HYNES

Defense . . . 6'1" . . . 165 lbs. . . . Born, Montreal, Que., July 22, 1966 . . . Shoots left . . . (July, 1984)—Mononucleosis . . . (October, 1985)—Broken hand.

Year	Team	League	Games	G.	A.	Pts.	Pen.
1983-84—Medicine Hat Tigers		WHL	72	5	14	19	39
1984-85—Medicine Hat Tigers (c)		WHL	70	18	45	63	61
1985-86—Medicine Hat Tigers		WHL	58	22	39	61	45

(c)—June, 1985—Drafted as underage junior by Boston Bruins in 1985 NHL entry draft. Fifth Bruins pick, 115th overall, sixth round.

AL IAFRATE

Defense ... 6'3" ... 190 lbs. ... Born, Dearborn, Mich., March 21, 1966 ... Shoots left ... Member of 1984 U.S. Olympic Team ... (February, 1985)—Bruised knee ... (October 2, 1985)—Broken nose in fight and missed five games ... (January 29, 1986)—Strained neck vs. Washington and missed six games.

Year	Team	League	Games	G.	A.	Pts.	Pen.
1983-84—U.S. National Team		Int'l	55	4	17	21	26
1983-84—U.S. Olympic Team		Int'l	6	0	0	0	2
1983-84—Belleville Bulls (c)		OHL	10	2	4	6	2
1984-85—Toronto Maple Leafs		NHL	68	5	16	21	51
1985-86—Toronto Maple Leafs		NHL	65	8	25	33	40
NHL TOTALS			133	13	41	54	91

(c)—June, 1984—Drafted as underage junior by Toronto Maple Leafs in 1984 NHL entry draft. First Maple Leafs pick, fourth overall, first round.

MIROSLAV IHNACAK

Left Wing ... 6' ... 185 lbs. ... Born, Poprad, Czechoslovakia, February 19, 1962 ... Shoots left ... Brother of Peter Ihnacak.

Year	Team	League	Games	G.	A.	Pts.	Pen.
1985-86—St. Catharines Saints (c)		AHL	13	4	4	8	2
1985-86—Toronto Maple Leafs		NHL	21	2	4	6	27
NHL TOTALS			21	2	4	6	27

(c)—June, 1982—Drafted by Toronto Maple Leafs in 1982 NHL entry draft. Twelfth Maple Leafs pick, 171st overall, ninth round.

PETER IHNACAK

Center ... 6' ... 180 lbs. ... Born, Prague, Czech., May 5, 1957 ... Shoots right ... Set Toronto club rookie record with 66 points in 1982-83, and tied rookie record with 28 goals ... Brother of Miroslav Ihnacak ... (October 16, 1983)—Injured knee ligaments in game at New Jersey ... (February 29, 1984)—Injured shoulder in game vs. N.Y. Rangers, out for the season ... (October, 1984)—Knee injury ... (November 30, 1985)—Concussion vs. Buffalo and missed nine games ... (January, 1986)—Missed five games with a shoulder injury.

Year	Team	League	Games	G.	A.	Pts.	Pen.
1978-79—Dukla Jihlava		Czech.	44	22	12	34	....
1979-80—Sparta CKD Praha		Czech.	44	19	28	47	....
1980-81—Sparta CKD Praha		Czech.	44	23	22	45	....
1981-82—Sparta CKD Praha		Czech.	39	16	22	38	30
1982-83—Toronto Maple Leafs (c)		NHL	80	28	38	66	44
1983-84—Toronto Maple Leafs		NHL	47	10	13	23	24
1984-85—Toronto Maple Leafs		NHL	70	22	22	44	24
1985-86—Toronto Maple Leafs		NHL	63	18	27	45	16
NHL TOTALS			260	78	100	178	108

(c)—July, 1983—Signed by Toronto Maple Leafs as a free agent.

JAN INGMAN

Left Wing ... 6'2" ... 187 lbs. ... Born, Grumms, Sweden, November 25, 1961 ... Shoots left.

Year	Team	League	Games	G.	A.	Pts.	Pen.
1981-82—Farjestads (c)		Sweden	27	7	2	9	6
1982-83—Farjestads		Sweden	36	13	11	24	12
1983-84—Farjestads		Sweden	36	14	11	25	36
1984-85—Farjestads		Sweden	35	19	17	36	14
1985-86—Farjestads (d)		Sweden	33	19	13	32	20

(c)—June, 1981—Drafted by Montreal Canadiens in 1981 amateur draft. Third Canadiens pick, 19th overall, first round.

(d)—August, 1986—Traded by Montreal Canadiens with Steve Penney to Winnipeg Jets for Brian Hayward.

RANDY IRVING

Left Wing ... 6'1" ... 199 lbs. ... Born, Lake Cowichan, B. C., August 12, 1959 ... Shoots left.

Year	Team	League	Games	G.	A.	Pts.	Pen.
1976-77—Maple Ridge		BCJHL	67	47	36	83	244
1976-77—New Westminster Bruins		WCHL	2	1	0	1	0
1977-78—New Westminster Bruins		WCHL	72	31	42	73	160

Year	Team	League	Games	G.	A.	Pts.	Pen.
1978-79—Victoria Cougars		WHL	61	18	28	46	167
1979-80—Muskegon Mohawks		IHL	41	13	26	39	70
1979-80—Toledo Goaldiggers		IHL	28	7	21	28	20
1980-81—Toledo Goaldiggers		IHL	77	38	38	76	149
1981-82—Ft. Worth Texans		CHL	2	0	0	0	0
1981-82—Fort Wayne Komets		IHL	26	6	6	12	43
1982-83—Carolina Thunderbirds (b)		ACHL	63	8	46	54	139
1983-84—Carolina Thunderbirds (a)		ACHL	55	15	35	50	163
1984-85—Carolina Thunderbirds (a)		ACHL	63	10	50	60	98
1985-86—Rochester Americans		AHL	6	0	0	0	4
1985-86—Carolina Thunderbirds (b)		ACHL	54	9	33	42	111

KIM ISSEL

Right Wing . . . 6'3" . . . 185 lbs. Born, Regina, Sask., September 25, 1967 . . . Shoots left . . . Also plays Left Wing.

Year	Team	League	Games	G.	A.	Pts.	Pen.
1983-84—Prince Albert Raiders		WHL	31	9	9	18	24
1984-85—Prince Albert Raiders		WHL	44	8	15	23	43
1985-86—Prince Albert Raiders (b-c)		WHL	68	29	39	68	41

(c)—June, 1986—Drafted as underage junior by Edmonton Oilers in 1986 NHL entry draft. First Oilers pick, 21st overall, first round.

JEFF JABLONSKI

Left Wing . . . 6' . . . 175 lbs. . . . Born, Toledo, Ohio, June 20, 1967 . . . Shoots left . . . Brother of Pat Jablonski.

Year	Team	League	Games	G.	A.	Pts.	Pen.
1985-86—London Diamonds Jr. B (c)		OHA	42	28	32	60	47

(c)—June, 1986—Drafted by New York Islanders in 1986 NHL entry draft. Eleventh Islanders pick, 185th overall, ninth round.

DON CLINTON JACKSON

Defense . . . 6'3" . . . 210 lbs. . . . Born, Minneapolis, Minn., September 2, 1956 . . . Shoots left . . . Also plays Left Wing . . . (February, 1984)—Groin injury . . . (November 5, 1985)— Bruised knee at Vancouver and missed four games . . . (February 11, 1986)—Cracked cheekbone at Detroit and missed 10 games.

Year	Team	League	Games	G.	A.	Pts.	Pen.
1974-75—University of Notre Dame		WCHA	35	2	7	9	29
1975-76—University of Notre Dame (c)		WCHA	30	4	5	9	22
1976-77—University of Notre Dame		WCHA	38	2	9	11	52
1977-78—University of Notre Dame		WCHA	37	10	23	33	69
1977-78—Minnesota North Stars		NHL	2	0	0	0	2
1978-79—Minnesota North Stars		NHL	5	0	0	0	2
1978-79—Oklahoma City Stars		CHL	73	8	23	31	108
1979-80—Minnesota North Stars		NHL	10	0	4	4	18
1979-80—Oklahoma City Stars		CHL	33	5	9	14	54
1980-81—Oklahoma City Stars		CHL	59	5	33	38	67
1980-81—Minnesota North Stars (d)		NHL	10	0	3	3	19
1981-82—Edmonton Oilers		NHL	8	0	0	0	18
1981-82—Wichita Wind		CHL	71	7	37	44	116
1982-83—Edmonton Oilers		NHL	71	2	8	10	136
1982-83—Birmingham South Stars		CHL	4	1	4	5	8
1983-84—Edmonton Oilers		NHL	64	8	12	20	120
1984-85—Edmonton Oilers		NHL	78	3	17	20	141
1985-86—Edmonton Oilers		NHL	45	2	8	10	93
NHL TOTALS			293	15	52	67	549

(c)—Drafted from University of Notre Dame by Minnesota North Stars in third round of 1976 amateur draft.

(d)—September, 1981—Traded by Minnesota North Stars to Edmonton Oilers along with third-round draft choice in 1982 for Don Murdoch.

JAMES KENNETH JACKSON

Center . . . 5'8" . . . 190 lbs. . . . Born, Oshawa, Ont., February 1, 1960 . . . Shoots right . . . Also plays Right Wing and Defense . . . (January, 1981)—Groin injury.

Year	Team	League	Games	G.	A.	Pts.	Pen.
1976-77—Oshawa Generals		OMJHL	65	13	40	53	26
1977-78—Oshawa Generals		OMJHL	68	33	47	80	60
1978-79—Niagara Falls Flyers		OMJHL	64	26	39	65	73

Year	Team	League	Games	G.	A.	Pts.	Pen.
1979-80—Niagara Falls Flyers		OMJHL	66	29	57	86	55
1980-81—Richmond Rifles (b)		EHL	58	17	43	60	42
1981-82—Muskegon Mohawks (b)		IHL	82	24	51	75	72
1982-83—Colorado Flames		CHL	30	10	16	26	4
1982-83—Calgary Flames		NHL	48	8	12	20	7
1983-84—Calgary Flames		NHL	49	6	14	20	13
1983-84—Colorado Flames		CHL	25	5	27	32	4
1984-85—Moncton Golden Flames		AHL	24	2	5	7	6
1984-85—Calgary Flames		NHL	10	1	4	5	0
1985-86—Rochester Americans (c)		AHL	65	16	32	48	10
NHL TOTALS			107	15	30	45	20

(c)—November, 1985—Signed by Rochester Americans as a free agent.

JEFF JACKSON

Left Wing . . . 6'1" . . . 193 lbs. . . . Born, Chatham, Ont., April 24, 1965 . . . Shoots left . . . Also plays Center . . . (January, 1982)—Stretched knee ligaments.

Year	Team	League	Games	G.	A.	Pts.	Pen.
1981-82—Newmarket Flyers		OJHL	45	30	39	69	105
1982-83—Brantford Alexanders (c)		OHL	64	18	25	43	63
1983-84—Brantford Alexanders		OHL	58	27	42	69	78
1984-85—Hamilton Steelhawks		OHL	20	13	14	27	51
1984-85—Toronto Maple Leafs		NHL	17	0	1	1	24
1985-86—St. Catharines Saints		AHL	74	17	28	45	122
1985-86—Toronto Maple Leafs		NHL	5	1	2	3	2
NHL TOTALS			22	1	3	4	26

(c)—June, 1983—Drafted as underage junior by Toronto Maple Leafs in 1983 NHL entry draft. Second Maple Leafs pick, 28th overall, second round.

RISTO JALO

Center . . . 5'11" . . . 185 lbs. . . . Born, Humppila, Finland, July 18, 1962 . . . Shoots left . . . Missed most of 1985-86 season with eye problems.

Year	Team	League	Games	G.	A.	Pts.	Pen.
1980-81—Tampere Ilves		Finland	16	3	3	6	2
1981-82—Tampere Ilves (c)		Finland	34	17	20	37	8
1982-83—Tampere Ilves		Finland	....	....	....	....	....
1983-84—Tampere Ilves (d)		Finland	36	13	32	45	30
1984-85—Tampere Ilves		Finland	....	...	...	....	....
1985-86—Tampere Ilves		Finland	....	...	...	....	....
1985-86—Edmonton Oilers		NHL	3	0	3	3	0
NHL TOTALS			3	0	3	3	0

(c)—June, 1981—Drafted by Washington Capitals in 1981 NHL entry draft. Seventh Capitals pick, 131st overall, seventh round.

(d)—March, 1984—Traded by Washington Capitals to Edmonton Oilers for future considerations.

VALMORE JAMES

Left Wing . . . 6'2" . . . 205 lbs. . . . Born, Ocala, Fla., February 14, 1957 . . . Shoots left . . . First American-Born Black player to play in the NHL.

Year	Team	League	Games	G.	A.	Pts.	Pen.
1975-76—Quebec Remparts		QMJHL	72	14	19	33	83
1976-77—Quebec Remparts (c)		QMJHL	68	16	16	32	99
1979-80—Erie Blades		EHL	69	12	13	25	117
1980-81—Erie Blades (d)		EHL	70	3	18	21	179
1980-81—Rochester Americans		AHL	3	0	0	0	12
1981-82—Buffalo Sabres		NHL	7	0	0	0	16
1981-82—Rochester Americans		AHL	65	5	4	9	204
1982-83—Rochester Americans		AHL	68	3	4	7	88
1983-84—Rochester Americans		AHL	62	1	2	3	122
1984-85—Rochester Americans		AHL	55	1	4	5	70
1985-86—St. Catharines Saints (e)		AHL	80	0	3	3	162
NHL TOTALS			7	0	0	0	16

(c)—June, 1977—Drafted by Detroit Red Wings in 1977 NHL amateur draft. Fifteenth Red Wings pick, 184th overall, 16th round.

(d)—September, 1980—Signed by Buffalo Sabres as a free agent.

(e)—September, 1985—Signed by Toronto Maple Leafs as a free agent.

CRAIG JANNEY

Center . . . 6'1" . . . 180 lbs. . . . Born, Hartford, Conn., September 26, 1967 . . . Shoots left . . . (December, 1985)—Broken collarbone.

Year	Team	League	Games	G.	A.	Pts.	Pen.
1984-85—Deerfield Academy	Conn.	17	33	35	68	6
1985-86—Boston College (c)	H. East	34	13	14	27	8

(c)—June, 1986—Drafted by Boston Bruins in 1986 NHL entry draft. First Bruins pick, 13th overall, first round.

PAT JANOSTIN

Defense . . . 6' . . . 170 lbs. . . . Born, North Battleford, Sask., November 17, 1966 . . . Shoots right.

Year	Team	League	Games	G.	A.	Pts.	Pen.
1984-85—Notre Dame Hounds (c)	MWIHL	40	5	30	35	30
1985-86—Univ. Minnesota/Duluth	WCHA	26	1	2	3	4

(c)—June, 1985—Drafted by New York Rangers in 1985 NHL entry draft. Fourth Rangers pick, 70th overall, fourth round.

MARK JANSSENS

Center . . . 6'3" . . . 195 lbs. . . . Born, Surrey, B.C., May 19, 1968 . . . Shoots left . . . Also plays Left Wing.

Year	Team	League	Games	G.	A.	Pts.	Pen.
1983-84—Surrey Midgets	B.C.	48	40	58	98	64
1984-85—Regina Pats	WHL	70	8	22	30	51
1985-86—Regina Pats (c)	WHL	71	25	38	63	146

(c)—June, 1986—Drafted as underage junior by New York Rangers in 1986 NHL entry draft. Fourth Rangers pick, 72nd overall, fourth round.

DOUGLAS JARVIS

Center . . . 5'9" . . . 172 lbs. . . . Born, Brantford, Ont., March 24, 1955 . . . Shoots left . . . Cousin of Wes Jarvis.

Year	Team	League	Games	G.	A.	Pts.	Pen.
1971-72—Brantford Majors	SOJHL	11	2	10	12	0
1972-73—Peterborough TPTs	Jr."A" OHA	63	20	49	69	14
1973-74—Peterborough TPTs	Jr."A" OHA	70	31	53	84	27
1974-75—P'borough TPTs (b-c-d-e)	Jr."A" OHA	64	45	88	133	38
1975-76—Montreal Canadiens	NHL	80	5	30	35	16
1976-77—Montreal Canadiens	NHL	80	16	22	38	14
1977-78—Montreal Canadiens	NHL	80	11	28	39	23
1978-79—Montreal Canadiens	NHL	80	10	13	23	16
1979-80—Montreal Canadiens	NHL	80	13	11	24	28
1980-81—Montreal Canadiens	NHL	80	16	22	38	34
1981-82—Montreal Canadiens (f)	NHL	80	20	28	48	20
1982-83—Washington Capitals	NHL	80	8	22	30	10
1983-84—Washington Capitals (g)	NHL	80	13	29	42	12
1984-85—Washington Capitals	NHL	80	9	28	37	32
1985-86—Washington Capitals (h)	NHL	25	1	2	3	16
1985-86—Hartford Whalers	NHL	57	8	16	24	20
NHL TOTALS		882	130	251	381	241

(c)—Won William Hanley Trophy (most gentlemanly player).
(d)—Drafted from Peterborough TPTs by Toronto Maple Leafs in second round of 1975 amateur draft.
(e)—June, 1975—Traded to Montreal Canadiens by Toronto Maple Leafs for Greg Hubick.
(f)—September, 1982—Traded by Montreal Canadiens with Rod Langway, Brian Engblom and Craig Laughlin to Washington Capitals for Ryan Walter and Rick Green.
(g)—Won Frank Selke Trophy (Best Defensive Forward).
(h)—December, 1985—Traded by Washington Capitals to Hartford Whalers for Jorgen Pettersson.

WES JARVIS

Center . . . 5'11" . . . 190 lbs. . . . Born, Toronto, Ont., May 30, 1958 . . . Shoots left . . . Cousin of Doug Jarvis . . . (January, 1984)—Injured ligaments in left knee.

Year	Team	League	Games	G.	A.	Pts.	Pen.
1975-76—Sudbury Wolves	OMJHL	64	26	48	74	22
1976-77—Sudbury Wolves	OMJHL	65	36	60	96	24
1977-78—Sudbury Wolves	OMJHL	21	7	16	23	16
1977-78—Windsor Spitfires (c)	OMJHL	44	27	51	78	37
1978-79—Port Huron Flags (b-d)	IHL	73	44	65	109	39
1979-80—Hershey Bears	AHL	16	6	14	20	4
1979-80—Washington Capitals	NHL	63	11	15	26	8
1980-81—Washington Capitals	NHL	55	9	14	23	30
1980-81—Hershey Bears	AHL	24	15	25	40	39
1981-82—Hershey Bears	AHL	56	31	61	92	44

Year	Team	League	Games	G.	A.	Pts.	Pen.
1981-82—Washington Capitals (e)		NHL	26	1	12	13	18
1982-83—Birmingham South Stars (a-f)		CHL	75	40	*68	*108	36
1982-83—Minnesota North Stars (g)		NHL	3	0	0	0	2
1983-84—Los Angeles Kings		NHL	61	9	13	22	36
1984-85—Toronto Maple Leafs (h)		NHL	26	0	1	1	2
1984-85—St. Catharines Saints		AHL	52	29	44	73	22
1985-86—Toronto Maple Leafs		NHL	2	1	0	1	2
1985-86—St. Catharines Saints		AHL	74	36	60	96	38
NHL TOTALS			236	31	55	86	98

(c)—June, 1978—Drafted by Washington Capitals in 1978 amateur draft. Fifteenth Capitals pick, 213th overall, 14th round.

(d)—Won Garry F. Longman Memorial Trophy (IHL Top Rookie).

(e)—August, 1982—Traded with Rollie Boutin by Washington Capitals to Minnesota North Stars for Robbie Moore and future considerations.

(f)—Won Phil Esposito Trophy (CHL Scoring Leader).

(g)—August, 1983—Signed by Los Angeles Kings as a free agent.

(h)—September, 1984—Signed by Toronto Maple Leafs as a free agent.

GRANT JENNINGS

Defense . . . 6'3" . . . 190 lbs. . . . Born, Hudson Bay, Sask., May 5, 1965 . . . Shoots left . . . (1984-85)—Shoulder injury.

Year	Team	League	Games	G.	A.	Pts.	Pen.
1983-84—Saskatoon Blades		WHL	64	5	13	18	102
1984-85—Saskatoon Blades (c)		WHL	47	10	14	24	134
1985-86—Binghamton Whalers		AHL	51	0	4	4	109

(c)—June, 1985—Signed by Washington Capitals as a free agent.

CHRIS JENSEN

Center . . . 5'11" . . . 165 lbs. . . . Born, Fort St. John, B.C., October 28, 1963 . . . Shoots right . . . (October, 1985)—Injured knee.

Year	Team	League	Games	G.	A.	Pts.	Pen.
1980-81—Kelowna		BCJHL	53	51	45	96	120
1981-82—Kelowna (c)		BCJHL	48	46	46	92	212
1982-83—University of North Dakota		WCHA	13	3	3	6	28
1983-84—University of North Dakota		WCHA	44	24	25	49	100
1984-85—University of North Dakota		WCHA	40	25	27	52	80
1985-86—University of North Dakota		WCHA	34	25	40	65	53
1985-86—New York Rangers		NHL	9	1	3	4	0
NHL TOTALS			9	1	3	4	0

(c)—June, 1982—Drafted as underage player by New York Rangers in 1982 NHL entry draft. Fourth Rangers pick, 78th overall, fourth round.

DAVID A. JENSEN

Left Wing . . . 6' . . . 175 lbs. . . . Born, Newton, Mass., August 19, 1965 . . . Shoots left . . . Member of 1984 U.S. Olympic Team . . . (November, 1984)—Back injury . . . (September, 1985)—Missed 18 games while recovering from off-season knee surgery.

Year	Team	League	Games	G.	A.	Pts.	Pen.
1982-83—Lawrence Academy (c)		Mass. H.S.	25	41	48	89	....
1983-84—U.S. National Team		Int'l	61	22	56	78	6
1983-84—U.S. Olympic Team		Int'l	6	5	3	8	0
1984-85—Hartford Whalers (d)		NHL	13	0	4	4	6
1984-85—Binghamton Whalers		AHL	40	8	9	17	2
1985-86—Binghamton Whalers		AHL	41	17	14	31	4
1985-86—Washington Capitals		NHL	5	1	0	1	0
NHL TOTALS			18	1	4	5	6

(c)—June, 1983—Drafted by Hartford Whalers in 1983 NHL entry draft. Second Whalers pick, 20th overall, first round.

(d)—March, 1985—Traded by Hartford Whalers to Washington Capitals for Peter Sidorkiewicz and Dean Evason.

DAVE HENRY JENSEN

Defense . . . 6'1" . . . 190 lbs. . . . Born, Minneapolis, Minn., May 3, 1961 . . . Shoots left . . . Brother of Paul Jensen (played for '76 U.S. Olympic team) . . . Member of 1984 U.S. Olympic Team . . . (August, 1984)—Missed Team U.S.A. Training camp for the 1984 Canada Cup due to hepatitis.

Year	Team	League	Games	G.	A.	Pts.	Pen.
1979-80—University of Minnesota (c)	WCHA	26	0	4	4	26
1980-81—University of Minnesota	WCHA	35	0	13	13	64
1981-82—University of Minnesota	WCHA	32	3	13	16	68
1982-83—University of Minnesota	WCHA	38	5	24	29	48
1983-84—U.S. National Team	Int'l	47	3	15	18	38
1983-84—U.S. Olympic Team	Int'l	6	0	3	3	6
1983-84—Salt Lake Golden Eagles	CHL	13	0	7	7	6
1983-84—Minnesota North Stars	NHL	8	0	1	1	0
1984-85—Minnesota North Stars	NHL	5	0	1	1	4
1984-85—Springfield Indians	AHL	69	13	27	40	63
1985-86—Springfield Indians	AHL	40	4	18	22	31
1985-86—Minnesota North Stars	NHL	5	0	0	0	7
NHL TOTALS		18	0	2	2	11

(c)—June, 1980—Drafted as underage player by Minnesota North Stars in 1980 NHL entry draft. Fifth North Stars pick, 100th overall, fifth round.

PAUL JERRARD

Defense . . . 6'1" . . . 185 lbs. . . . Born, Winnipeg, Man., April 20, 1965 . . . Shoots right.

Year	Team	League	Games	G.	A.	Pts.	Pen.
1982-83—Notre Dame H.S. (c)	Man. Juv.	60	34	37	71	150
1983-84—Lake Superior State College	CCHA	40	8	18	26	48
1984-85—Lake Superior State College	CCHA	43	9	25	34	61
1985-86—Lake Superior State College	CCHA	40	13	11	24	34

(c)—June, 1983—Drafted by New York Rangers in 1983 NHL entry draft. Tenth Rangers pick, 173rd overall, ninth round.

JAMES JOHANNSON

Center . . . 6'1" . . . 175 lbs. . . . Born, Rochester, Minn., March 10, 1964 . . . Shoots right . . . Brother of John Johannson.

Year	Team	League	Games	G.	A.	Pts.	Pen.
1981-82—Rochester Mayo H.S. (c)	Minn. H.S.	27	28	32	60	20
1982-83—University of Wisconsin	WCHA	45	12	9	21	16
1983-84—University of Wisconsin	WCHA	35	17	21	38	52
1984-85—University of Wisconsin	WCHA	40	16	24	40	54
1985-86—University of Wisconsin	WCHA	30	18	13	31	44

(c)—June, 1982—Drafted as underage player by Hartford Whalers in 1982 NHL entry draft. Seventh Whalers pick, 130th overall, seventh round.

BRIAN JOHNSON

Defense . . . 5'10" . . . 180 lbs. . . . Born, Two Harbors, Minn., March 7, 1965 . . . Shoots left . . . Also plays Center.

Year	Team	League	Games	G.	A.	Pts.	Pen.
1982-83—Silver Bay H.S. (c)	Minn. H.S.	22	29	35	64	....
1983-84—Univ. of Minnesota-Duluth	WCHA	39	4	9	13	30
1984-85—Univ. of Minnesota-Duluth	WCHA	38	1	10	11	24
1985-86—Univ. of Minnesota-Duluth	WCHA	42	11	37	48	18

(c)—June, 1983—Drafted by Hartford Whalers in 1983 NHL entry draft. Seventh Whalers pick, 104th overall, sixth round.

JIM JOHNSON

Defense . . . 6' . . . 190 lbs. . . . Born, New Hope, Minn., August 9, 1962 . . . Shoots left.

Year	Team	League	Games	G.	A.	Pts.	Pen.
1981-82—Univ. of Minnesota-Duluth	WCHA	40	0	10	10	62
1982-83—Univ. of Minnesota-Duluth	WCHA	44	3	18	21	118
1983-84—Univ. of Minnesota-Duluth	WCHA	43	3	13	16	116
1984-85—Univ. of Minnesota-Duluth (c)	WCHA	47	7	29	36	49
1985-86—Pittsburgh Penguins	NHL	80	3	26	29	115
NHL TOTALS		80	3	26	29	115

(c)—June, 1985—Signed by Pittsburgh Penguins as a free agent.

MARK JOHNSON

Center . . . 5'9" . . . 160 lbs. . . . Born, Minneapolis, Minn., September 22, 1957 . . . Shoots left . . . Member of 1978 and 1979 U.S. National teams and 1980 U.S. Gold Medal Winning Hockey Team . . . Son of Bob Johnson (Coach of Calgary Flames) . . . (September,

1980)—Took 20 stitches near right eye in preseason game . . . (November, 1980)—Wrist injury . . . (February, 1985)—Rib injury.

Year	Team	League	Games	G.	A.	Pts.	Pen.
1976-77—University of Wisconsin (c-d)		WCHA	43	36	44	80	16
1977-78—University of Wisconsin (a-e)		WCHA	42	*48	38	86	24
1978-79—Univ. of Wisconsin (a-e-f)		WCHA	40	*41	49	*90	34
1979-80—U.S. Olympic Team		Int'l	60	*38	*54	*92	31
1979-80—Pittsburgh Penguins		NHL	17	3	5	8	4
1980-81—Pittsburgh Penguins		NHL	73	10	23	33	50
1981-82—Pittsburgh Penguins (g)		NHL	46	10	11	21	30
1981-82—Minnesota North Stars (h)		NHL	10	2	2	4	10
1982-83—Hartford Whalers		NHL	73	31	38	69	28
1983-84—Hartford Whalers		NHL	79	35	52	87	27
1984-85—Hartford Whalers (i)		NHL	49	19	28	47	21
1984-85—St. Louis Blues		NHL	17	4	6	10	2
1985-86—New Jersey Devils (j)		NHL	80	21	41	62	16
NHL TOTALS			444	135	206	341	188

(c)—June, 1977—Drafted by Pittsburgh Penguins in 1977 NHL amateur draft. Third Penguins pick, 66th overall, fourth round.
(d)—Named WCHA Outstanding Freshman.
(e)—Named to All-America Team (West).
(f)—Named WCHA MVP and NCAA Player of the Year.
(g)—March, 1982—Traded by Pittsburgh Penguins to Minnesota North Stars for second-round 1982 entry draft pick (Tim Hrynewich).
(h)—October, 1982—Traded by Minnesota North Stars with Kent-Erik Andersson to Hartford Whalers for 1984 fifth-round pick (Jordy Douglas) in NHL entry draft and future considerations (Jordy Douglas).
(i)—February, 1985—Traded with Greg Millen by Hartford Whalers to St. Louis Blues for Mike Liut and future considerations (Jorgen Pettersson).
(j)—September, 1985—Traded by St. Louis Blues to New Jersey Devils for Shawn Evans and a fifth round 1986 draft pick (Mike Wolak).

TERRANCE JOHNSON

Defense . . . 6'3" . . . 210 lbs. . . . Born, Calgary, Alta., November 28, 1958 . . . Shoots left.

Year	Team	League	Games	G.	A.	Pts.	Pen.
1975-76—Calgary		AJHL	55	3	13	16	100
1976-77—Calgary Canucks		AJHL	60	5	26	31	158
1977-78—Saskatoon Blades		WCHL	70	2	20	22	195
1978-79—University of Alberta		CWAA	24	1	5	6	100
1979-80—Quebec Nordiques (c)		NHL	3	0	0	0	2
1979-80—Syracuse Firebirds		AHL	74	0	13	13	163
1980-81—Quebec Nordiques		NHL	13	0	1	1	46
1980-81—Hershey Bears		AHL	63	1	7	8	207
1981-82—Fredericton Express		AHL	43	0	7	7	132
1981-82—Quebec Nordiques		NHL	6	0	1	1	5
1982-83—Fredericton Express		AHL	78	2	15	17	181
1982-83—Quebec Nordiques		NHL	3	0	0	0	2
1983-84—St. Louis Blues (d)		NHL	65	2	6	8	141
1984-85—St. Louis Blues		NHL	74	0	7	7	120
1985-86—St. Louis Blues (e)		NHL	49	0	4	4	87
1985-86—Calgary Flames		NHL	24	1	4	5	71
NHL TOTALS			237	3	23	26	474

(c)—September, 1979—Signed by Quebec Nordiques as a free agent.
(d)—October, 1983—Selected by St. Louis Blues in NHL waiver draft.
(e)—February, 1986—Traded with Joe Mullen and Rik Wilson by St. Louis Blues to Calgary Flames for Eddy Beers, Gino Cavallini and Charles Bourgeois.

GREG JOHNSTON

Right Wing . . . 6'1" . . . 195 lbs. . . . Born, Barrie, Ont., January 14, 1965 . . . Shoots right . . . Also plays Center . . . (September, 1982)—Broken ankle.

Year	Team	League	Games	G.	A.	Pts.	Pen.
1981-82—Barrie		OHA Midget	42	31	46	77	74
1982-83—Toronto Marlboros (c)		OHL	58	18	19	37	58
1983-84—Toronto Marlboros		OHL	57	38	35	73	67
1983-84—Boston Bruins		NHL	15	2	1	3	2
1984-85—Boston Bruins		NHL	6	0	0	0	0
1984-85—Hershey Bears		AHL	3	1	0	1	0
1984-85—Toronto Marlboros		OHL	42	22	28	50	55

Year	Team	League	Games	G.	A.	Pts.	Pen.
1985-86—Moncton Golden Flames		AHL	60	19	26	45	56
1985-86—Boston Bruins		NHL	20	0	2	2	0
NHL TOTALS			41	2	3	5	2

(c)—June, 1983—Drafted as underage junior by Boston Bruins in 1983 NHL entry draft. Second Bruins pick, 42nd overall, second round.

JOHN (JAY) JOHNSTON

Defense . . . 6' . . . 190 lbs. . . . Born, Hamilton, Ont., February 25, 1958 . . . Shoots left . . . Missed end of 1980-81 season with shoulder injury.

Year	Team	League	Games	G.	A.	Pts.	Pen.
1975-76—Hamilton		Jr. "B" OHA	36	1	25	26	70
1976-77—St. Catharines Fincups		Jr. "A" OHA	65	8	20	28	146
1977-78—Hamilton Fincups (c)		Jr. "A" OHA	48	2	12	14	163
1978-79—Port Huron Flags		IHL	75	5	19	24	409
1979-80—Hershey Bears		AHL	69	3	20	23	229
1980-81—Hershey Bears		AHL	61	1	11	12	187
1980-81—Washington Capitals		NHL	2	0	0	0	9
1981-82—Hershey Bears		AHL	67	4	9	13	228
1981-82—Washington Capitals		NHL	6	0	0	0	4
1982-83—Hershey Bears		AHL	76	3	13	16	148
1983-84—Hershey Bears		AHL	70	1	9	10	231
1984-85—Fort Wayne Komets		IHL	69	1	12	13	211
1985-86—Fort Wayne Komets		IHL	78	1	13	14	176
NHL TOTALS			8	0	0	0	13

(c)—Drafted from Hamilton Fincups by Washington Capitals in third round of 1978 amateur draft.

EDWARD LaVERN JOHNSTONE

Right Wing . . . 5'9" . . . 175 lbs. . . . Born, Brandon, Man., March 2, 1954 . . . Shoots right . . . (April 20, 1980)—Tore ligaments in left knee vs. St. Louis in playoffs . . . (February 4, 1982) Broken ring finger on right hand at Calgary . . . (February, 1983)—Missed 21 games with separated left shoulder . . . (November 25, 1983)—Suffered depressed right cheekbone in collision in game with Pittsburgh . . . (January, 1985)—Abdominal injuries.

Year	Team	League	Games	G.	A.	Pts.	Pen.
1970-71—Vernon Essos		Jr. "A" BCHL	....	45	49	94	79
1971-72—Medicine Hat Tigers		WCHL	27	14	15	29	46
1972-73—Medicine Hat Tigers		WCHL	68	58	44	102	70
1973-74—Medicine Hat Tigers (c-d)		WCHL	68	64	54	118	164
1974-75—Greensboro Generals		SHL	25	21	25	46	21
1974-75—Michigan Stags		WHA	23	4	4	8	43
1974-75—Providence Reds (e)		AHL	23	7	10	17	35
1975-76—Providence Reds		AHL	58	23	33	56	102
1975-76—New York Rangers		NHL	10	2	1	3	4
1976-77—New Haven Nighthawks (a)		AHL	80	40	58	98	79
1977-78—New Haven Nighthawks		AHL	17	10	12	22	20
1977-78—New York Rangers		NHL	53	13	13	26	44
1978-79—New York Rangers		NHL	30	5	3	8	27
1979-80—New York Rangers		NHL	78	14	21	35	60
1980-81—New York Rangers		NHL	80	30	38	68	100
1981-82—New York Rangers		NHL	68	30	28	58	57
1982-83—New York Rangers (f)		NHL	52	15	21	36	27
1983-84—Detroit Red Wings		NHL	46	12	11	23	54
1984-85—Adirondack Red Wings		AHL	69	27	28	55	70
1985-86—Detroit Red Wings		NHL	3	1	0	1	2
1985-86—Adirondack Red Wings		AHL	62	29	31	60	74
WHA TOTALS			23	4	4	8	43
NHL TOTALS			420	122	136	258	375

(c)—Drafted from Medicine Hat Tigers by New York Rangers in sixth round of 1974 amateur draft.
(d)—Drafted by Michigan Stags in World Hockey Association amateur player draft, May, 1974.
(e)—Signed by New York Rangers as free agent, February, 1975.
(f)—July, 1983—Traded by New York Rangers with Ron Duguay and Eddie Mio to Detroit Red Wings for Willie Huber, Mark Osborne and Mike Blaisdell.

GREGORY JAMES JOLY

Defense . . . 6'1" . . . 188 lbs. . . . Born, Calgary, Alta., May 30, 1954 . . . Shoots left . . . Missed part of 1974-75 season with knee injury and part of 1975-76 season with hairline ankle fracture . . . Had fractured left wrist during 1978 Stanley Cup playoffs . . . (January, 1983)— Injured knee in AHL game vs. Maine . . . (January, 1985)—Shoulder injury.

Year	Team	League	Games	G.	A.	Pts.	Pen.
1971-72—Regina Pats		WCHL	67	6	38	44	41
1972-73—Regina Pats (a)		WCHL	67	14	54	68	94
1973-74—Regina Pats (a-c)		WCHL	67	21	71	92	103
1974-75—Washington Capitals		NHL	44	1	7	8	44
1975-76—Richmond Robins		AHL	3	3	2	5	4
1975-76—Washington Capitals		NHL	54	8	17	25	28
1976-77—Springfield Indians (d)		AHL	22	0	8	8	16
1976-77—Detroit Red Wings		NHL	53	1	11	12	14
1977-78—Detroit Red Wings		NHL	79	7	20	27	73
1978-79—Detroit Red Wings		NHL	20	0	4	4	6
1979-80—Detroit Red Wings		NHL	59	3	10	13	45
1979-80—Adirondack Red Wings		AHL	8	3	3	6	10
1980-81—Adirondack Red Wings		AHL	62	3	34	37	158
1980-81—Detroit Red Wings		NHL	17	0	2	2	10
1981-82—Detroit Red Wings		NHL	37	1	5	6	30
1981-82—Adirondack Red Wings		AHL	36	3	22	25	59
1982-83—Adirondack Red Wings		AHL	71	8	40	48	118
1982-83—Detroit Red Wings		NHL	2	0	0	0	0
1983-84—Adirondack Red Wings (b)		AHL	78	10	33	43	133
1984-85—Adirondack Red Wing (a)		AHL	76	9	40	49	111
1985-86—Adirondack Red Wings		AHL	65	0	22	22	68
NHL TOTALS			365	21	76	97	250

(c)—Drafted from Regina Pats by Washington Capitals in first round of 1974 amateur draft.
(d)—Traded to Detroit Red Wings by Washington Capitals for Bryan Watson, December, 1976.

BRAD JONES

Center . . . 6' . . . 175 lbs. . . . Born, Sterling Heights, Mich., June 26, 1965 . . . Shoots left . . . (November, 1984)—Injured knee in game vs. Lake Superior State.

Year	Team	League	Games	G.	A.	Pts.	Pen.
1983-84—University of Michigan (c)		CCHA	37	8	26	34	32
1984-85—University of Michigan		CCHA	34	21	27	48	69
1985-86—University of Michigan (b)		CCHA	36	28	39	67	40

(c)—June, 1984—Drafted by Winnipeg Jets in 1984 NHL entry draft. Eighth Jets pick, 156th overall, eighth round.

TOMAS JONSSON

Defense . . . 5'10" . . . 176 lbs. . . . Born, Falun, Sweden, April 12, 1960 . . . Shoots left . . . (January 13, 1985)—Separated left shoulder in game at Chicago.

Year	Team	League	Games	G.	A.	Pts.	Pen.
1980-81—Ornskoldsvik Modo AIK (c)		Sweden	35	8	12	20	58
1981-82—New York Islanders		NHL	70	9	25	34	51
1982-83—New York Islanders		NHL	72	13	35	48	50
1983-84—New York Islanders		NHL	72	11	36	47	54
1984-85—New York Islanders		NHL	69	16	34	50	58
1985-86—New York Islanders		NHL	77	14	30	44	62
NHL TOTALS			360	63	160	223	275

(c)—August, 1979—Drafted by New York Islanders in 1979 NHL entry draft. Second Islanders pick, 25th overall, second round.

FRANK JOO

Defense . . . 6' . . . 180 lbs. . . . Born, Regina, Sask., January 19, 1966 . . . Shoots left.

Year	Team	League	Games	G.	A.	Pts.	Pen.
1982-83—Regina Pats		WHL	2	0	0	0	2
1983-84—Regina Pats (c)		WHL	50	2	7	9	90
1984-85—Regina Pats		WHL	68	1	9	10	125
1985-86—Regina Pats		WHL	22	1	8	9	39

(c)—June, 1984—Drafted as underage junior by Washington Capitals in 1984 NHL entry draft. Seventh Capitals pick. 164th overall, eighth round.

MARK JOORIS

Right Wing . . . 5'11" . . . 180 lbs. . . . Born, Burlington, Ont., February 3, 1964 . . . Shoots right.

Year	Team	League	Games	G.	A.	Pts.	Pen.
1982-83—Rensselaer Poly. Inst.		ECAC	28	17	26	43	8
1983-84—Rensselaer Poly. Inst.		ECAC	23	10	10	20	4
1984-85—Rensselaer Poly. Inst.		ECAC	35	23	37	60	22
1985-86—Rensselaer Poly. Inst.		ECAC	31	34	26	60	36

FABIAN JOSEPH

Center . . . 5'8" . . . 165 lbs. . . . Born, Sydney, N.S., December 5, 1965 . . . Shoots left.

Year	Team	League	Games	G.	A.	Pts.	Pen.
1982-83—Victoria Cougars		WHL	69	42	48	90	50
1983-84—Victoria Cougars (c)		WHL	72	52	75	127	27
1984-85—Toronto Marlboros		OHL	60	32	43	75	16
1985-86—Team Canada		Int'l	71	26	28	54	51

(c)—June, 1984—Drafted as underage junior by Toronto Maple Leafs in 1984 NHL entry draft. Fifth Maple Leafs pick, 109th overall, sixth round.

GARTH JOY

Defense . . . 5'11" . . . 180 lbs. . . . Born, Kirkland Lake, Ont., March 8, 1968 . . . Shoots left . . . (October, 1985)—Broken ankle . . . (November, 1985)—Broken foot.

Year	Team	League	Games	G.	A.	Pts.	Pen.
1984-85—Hamilton Steelhawks		OHL	58	4	23	27	36
1985-86—Hamilton Steelhawks (c)		OHL	50	6	31	37	64

(c)—June, 1986—Drafted as underage junior by Minnesota North Stars in 1986 NHL entry draft. Twelfth North Stars pick, 222nd overall, 11th round.

ROBERT JOYCE

Center . . . 6'1" . . . 180 lbs. . . . Born, St. Johns, N.B., July 11, 1966 . . . Shoots left . . . (October, 1985)—Tied a WCHA record with five goals in a game vs. Michigan Tech.

Year	Team	League	Games	G.	A.	Pts.	Pen.
1983-84—Wilcox Notre Dame H.S. (c)		Sask. HS	30	33	37	70	..
1984-85—Univ. of North Dakota		WCHA	41	18	16	34	10
1985-86—Univ. of North Dakota		WCHA	38	31	28	59	40

(c)—June, 1984—Drafted by Boston Bruins in 1984 NHL entry draft. Fourth Bruins pick, 82nd overall, fourth round.

CLAUDE JULIEN

Defense . . . 6' . . . 195 lbs. . . . Born, Orleans, Ont., November 11, 1958 . . . Shoots right . . . (February 1, 1986)—Broken nose at Quebec.

Year	Team	League	Games	G.	A.	Pts.	Pen.
1977-78—Newmarket Flyers		OPJHL	45	18	26	44	137
1977-78—Oshawa Generals		OMJHL	11	0	5	5	14
1978-79—		....	....	...	....	....	....
1979-80—Windsor Spitfires		OMJHL	68	14	37	51	148
1980-81—Windsor Spitfires		OHL	3	1	2	3	21
1980-81—Port Huron Flags		IHL	77	15	40	55	153
1981-82—Salt Lake Golden Eagles (c)		CHL	70	4	18	22	134
1982-83—Salt Lake Golden Eagles (b-d)		CHL	76	14	47	61	176
1983-84—Milwaukee Admirals		IHL	5	0	3	3	2
1983-84—Fredericton Express		AHL	57	7	22	29	58
1984-85—Fredericton Express		AHL	77	6	28	34	97
1984-85—Quebec Nordiques		NHL	1	0	0	0	0
1985-86—Quebec Nordiques		NHL	13	0	1	1	25
1985-86—Fredericton Express		AHL	49	3	18	21	74
NHL TOTALS			14	0	1	1	25

(c)—September, 1981—Signed by St. Louis Blues as a free agent.

(d)—August, 1983—Sent by St. Louis Blues along with Gordon Donnelly to Quebec Nordiques as compensation for St. Louis signing coach Jacques Demers.

TRENT KAESE

Right Wing . . . 6' . . . 205 lbs. . . . Born, Nanaimo, B.C., September 4, 1967 . . . Shoots right.

Year	Team	League	Games	G.	A.	Pts.	Pen.
1983-84—Lethbridge Broncos		WHL	64	6	6	12	33
1984-85—Lethbridge Broncos (c)		WHL	67	20	18	38	107
1985-86—Lethbridge Broncos		WHL	67	24	41	65	67

(c)—June, 1985—Drafted as underage junior by Buffalo Sabres in 1985 NHL entry draft. Eighth Sabres pick, 161st overall, eighth round.

NEVEN KARDUM

Center . . . 6'1" . . . 190 lbs. . . . Born, Toronto, Ont., March 30, 1967 . . . Shoots left.

Year	Team	League	Games	G.	A.	Pts.	Pen.
1984-85—Henry Carr H.S. (c)		OHA	39	19	32	51	33
1985-86—Providence College		H. East	12	1	0	1	0

(c)—June, 1985—Drafted by Winnipeg Jets in 1985 NHL entry draft. Ninth Jets pick, 186th overall, ninth round.

STEPHEN NEIL KASPER

Center . . . 5'8" . . . 159 lbs. . . . Born, Montreal, Que., September 28, 1961 . . . Shoots left . . . Brother of David Kasper (New Jersey, '82 draft pick) . . . (October 17, 1981)—Hip pointer in game at Los Angeles . . . (November 9, 1982)—Surgery to remove torn shoulder carti- lage . . . (December 7, 1982)—Surgery to left shoulder for a torn capsule . . . (April, 1983)—Concussion during playoff series vs. Buffalo . . . (November, 1983)—Separated left shoulder . . . (January 7, 1984)—Surgery to shoulder . . . (February, 1984)—Reinjured shoulder.

Year	Team	League	Games	G.	A.	Pts.	Pen.
1977-78	Verdun Black Hawks	QMJHL	63	26	45	71	16
1978-79	Verdun Black Hawks	QMJHL	67	37	67	104	53
1979-80	Sorel Black Hawks (c)	QMJHL	70	57	65	122	117
1980-81	Sorel Black Hawks	QMJHL	2	5	2	7	0
1980-81	Boston Bruins	NHL	76	21	35	56	94
1981-82	Boston Bruins (d)	NHL	73	20	31	51	72
1982-83	Boston Bruins	NHL	24	2	6	8	24
1983-84	Boston Bruins	NHL	27	3	11	14	19
1984-85	Boston Bruins	NHL	77	16	24	40	33
1985-86	Boston Bruins	NHL	80	17	23	40	73
	NHL TOTALS		355	79	130	209	315

(c)—June, 1980—Drafted by Boston Bruins in 1980 NHL entry draft. Third Bruins pick, 81st overall, fourth round.
(d)—Winner of Frank Selke Trophy (best defensive forward).

EDWARD KASTELIC

Right Wing . . . 6'3" . . . 203 lbs. . . . Born, Toronto, Ont., January 29, 1964 . . . Shoots right . . . Played Defense prior to 1981-82 season . . . (September 30, 1985)—Fractured left cheek- bone in pre-season game at Hartford . . . (January 20, 1986)—Suspended by Washington Capitals . . . (June, 1986)—Enrolled at York University and will be unavailable to play for Washington in 1986-87.

Year	Team	League	Games	G.	A.	Pts.	Pen.
1980-81	Mississauga Reps	Midget	51	4	10	14	....
1981-82	London Knights (c)	OHL	68	5	18	23	63
1982-83	London Knights	OHL	68	12	11	23	96
1983-84	London Knights	OHL	68	17	16	33	218
1984-85	Fort Wayne Komets	IHL	5	1	0	1	37
1984-85	Binghamton Whalers	AHL	4	0	0	0	7
1984-85	Moncton Golden Flames	AHL	62	5	11	16	187
1985-86	Washington Capitals	NHL	15	0	0	0	73
1985-86	Binghamton Whalers	AHL	23	7	9	16	76
	NHL TOTALS		15	0	0	0	73

(c)—June, 1982—Selected by Washington Capitals in 1982 NHL entry draft as an underage junior. Fourth Capitals pick, 110th overall, sixth round.

DANIEL KECZMER

Defense . . . 6'1" . . . 180 lbs. . . . Born, Mt. Clemens, Mich., May 25, 1968 . . . Shoots left.

Year	Team	League	Games	G.	A.	Pts.	Pen.
1985-86	Little Caesars Midget (c)	Mich.	65	6	48	54	116

(c)—June, 1986—Drafted by Minnesota North Stars in 1986 NHL entry draft. Eleventh North Stars pick, 201st overall, 10th round.

MICHAEL KELFER

Center . . . 5'10" . . . 180 lbs. . . . Born, Peabody, Mass., January 2, 1967 . . . Shoots right.

Year	Team	League	Games	G.	A.	Pts.	Pen.
1984-85	St. John's Prep. (c)	Mass. H.S.	25	33	48	81	....
1985-86	Boston University	H. East	39	13	14	27	40

(c)—June, 1985—Drafted by Minnesota North Stars in 1985 NHL entry draft. Fifth North Stars pick, 132nd overall, seventh round.

TONY KELLIN

Defense . . . 6'2" . . . 195 lbs. . . . Born, Grand Rapids, Minn., March 19, 1963 . . . Shoots right . . . Played quarterback for high school football team and named to All-State team.

Year	Team	League	Games	G.	A.	Pts.	Pen.
1980-81	Gr. Rapids High School (c)	Minn. HS	27	19	24	43	38
1981-82	Gr. Rapids High School	Minn. HS	20	22	18	40	30
1982-83	University of Minnesota	WCHA	38	8	6	14	38
1983-84	University of Minnesota	WCHA	38	12	21	33	66

Year	Team	League	Games	G.	A.	Pts.	Pen.
1984-85—University of Minnesota		WCHA	45	7	24	31	82
1985-86—University of Minnesota		WCHA	44	10	24	34	61

(c)—June, 1981—Drafted by Washington Capitals as underage player in 1981 NHL entry draft. Third Capitals pick, 68th overall, third round.

JOHN PAUL KELLY

Left Wing ... 6' ... 215 lbs. ... Born, Edmonton, Alta., November 15, 1959 ... Shoots left ... Unable to play in NHL until December 1, 1979 due to court ordered suspension from a Junior Hockey incident during the 1978-79 season ... (December, 1981)—Sprained ankle ... (December 14, 1982)—Fractured two bones in right foot when struck by puck during game at Washington.

Year	Team	League	Games	G.	A.	Pts.	Pen.
1975-76—Maple Ridge	BCJHL	64	34	35	69	68
1975-76—New Westminster Bruins	WCHL	2	0	0	0	2
1976-77—New Westminster Bruins	WCHL	68	35	24	59	62
1977-78—New Westminster Bruins	WCHL	70	26	30	56	124
1978-79—New Westminster Bruins (c)	WHL	70	25	22	47	207
1979-80—Los Angeles Kings	NHL	40	2	5	7	28
1980-81—Los Angeles Kings	NHL	19	3	6	9	8
1980-81—Houston Apollos	CHL	33	11	17	28	31
1980-81—Rochester Americans	AHL	16	5	10	15	32
1981-82—Los Angeles Kings	NHL	70	12	11	23	100
1982-83—Los Angeles Kings	NHL	65	16	15	31	52
1983-84—Los Angeles Kings	NHL	72	7	14	21	73
1984-85—Los Angeles Kings	NHL	73	8	10	18	55
1985-86—Los Angeles Kings (d)	NHL	61	6	9	15	50
NHL TOTALS		400	54	70	124	366

(c)—August, 1979—Drafted by Los Angeles Kings in 1979 entry draft. Fourth Kings pick, 50th overall, third round.

(d)—June, 1986—Released by Los Angeles Kings.

BRAD KEMPTHORNE

Center and Right Wing ... 6'2" ... 190 lbs. ... Born, Boisevain, Man., May 2, 1960 ... Shoots right.

Year	Team	League	Games	G.	A.	Pts.	Pen.
1977-78—Brandon Travellers	MJHL	38	22	52	74	68
1977-78—Brandon Wheat Kings	WCHL	24	5	5	10	2
1978-79—Brandon Wheat Kings (c)	WHL	56	22	31	53	89
1979-80—Medicine Hat Tigers	WHL	67	39	52	91	81
1980-81—Birmingham Bulls	CHL	44	10	25	35	65
1980-81—Rochester Americans	AHL	15	1	8	9	6
1980-81—Muskegon Mohawks	IHL	13	3	7	10	42
1981-82—Oklahoma City Stars	CHL	72	17	29	46	78
1982-83—Peoria Prancers	IHL	69	39	65	104	101
1983-84—Peoria Prancers	IHL	80	15	47	62	47
1984-85—Peoria Rivermen	IHL	70	13	45	58	60
1985-86—Peoria Rivermen	IHL	45	9	26	35	27

(c)—August, 1979—Drafted by Atlanta Flames as underage junior in 1979 NHL entry draft. Sixth Flames pick, 96th overall, fifth round.

EDWARD DEAN KENNEDY
(Known by middle name.)

Defense ... 6'2" ... 200 lbs. ... Born, Redvers, Sask., January 18, 1963 ... Shoots right ... (February 18, 1983)—Given four-game suspension by NHL after off-ice altercation with Ken Linseman at Edmonton (February 3) ... Missed part of 1981-82 season with a knee injury.

Year	Team	League	Games	G.	A.	Pts.	Pen.
1979-80—Weyburn Red Wings	SJHL	57	12	20	32	64
1979-80—Brandon Wheat Kings	WHL	1	0	0	0	0
1980-81—Brandon Wheat Kings (c)	WHL	71	3	29	32	157
1981-82—Brandon Wheat Kings	WHL	49	5	38	43	103
1982-83—Brandon Wheat Kings	WHL	14	2	15	17	22
1982-83—Los Angeles Kings	NHL	55	0	12	12	97
1982-83—Saskatoon Blades (d)	WHL	..	..	..	..	..
1983-84—New Haven Nighthawks	AHL	26	1	7	8	23
1983-84—Los Angeles Kings	NHL	37	1	5	6	50

Year	Team	League	Games	G.	A.	Pts.	Pen.
1984-85—New Haven Nighthawks		AHL	76	3	14	17	104
1985-86—Los Angeles Kings		NHL	78	2	10	12	132
NHL TOTALS			170	3	27	30	279

(c)—June, 1981—Drafted as underage junior by Los Angeles Kings in 1981 NHL entry draft. Second Kings pick, 39th overall, second round.

(d)—No regular season record. Played four playoff games.

ALAN KERR

Right Wing . . . 5'11" . . . 190 lbs. . . . Born, Hazelton, B.C., March 28, 1964 . . . Shoots right . . . Second cousin of former NHLer Reg Kerr.

Year	Team	League	Games	G.	A.	Pts.	Pen.
1981-82—Seattle Breakers (c)		WHL	68	15	18	33	1079
1982-83—Seattle Breakers		WHL	71	38	53	91	183
1983-84—Seattle Breakers (a)		WHL	66	46	66	112	141
1984-85—Springfield Indians		AHL	62	32	27	59	140
1984-85—New York Islanders		NHL	19	3	1	4	24
1985-86—Springfield Indians		AHL	71	35	36	71	127
1985-86—New York Islanders		NHL	7	0	1	1	16
NHL TOTALS			26	3	2	5	40

(c)—June, 1982—Drafted by New York Islanders as underage junior in 1982 NHL entry draft. Fourth Islanders pick, 84th overall, fourth round.

KEVIN KERR

Right Wing . . . 5'10" . . . 175 lbs. . . . Born, North Bay, Ont., September 18, 1967 . . . Shoots right.

Year	Team	League	Games	G.	A.	Pts.	Pen.
1984-85—Windsor Spitfires		OHL	57	5	16	21	189
1985-86—Windsor Spitfires (c)		OHL	59	21	51	72	*266

(c)—June, 1986—Drafted as underage junior by Buffalo Sabres in 1986 NHL entry draft. Fourth Sabres pick, 56th overall, third round.

TIM KERR

Right Wing and Center . . . 6'3" . . . 215 lbs. . . . Born, Windsor, Ont., January 5, 1960 . . . Shoots right . . . (November 1, 1980)—Injured shoulder . . . (October, 1981)—Injured knee cartilage . . . (September, 1982)—Hernia surgery . . . (November 10, 1982)—Stretched knee ligaments in game at Buffalo that required surgery . . . (March, 1983)—Cracked fibula of left leg . . . (March, 1985)—Strained knee ligaments . . . (April 13, 1985)—Set NHL playoff records for most goals (4) and power-play goals (3) in a single period in the 2nd period of a 6-5 win at N.Y. Rangers . . . (May 5, 1985)—Strained right knee in collision with teammate Todd Bergen in opening playoff game with Quebec . . . (September, 1985)—Hospitalized with aseptic meningitis, a viral infection of the brain lining . . . (1985-86)—Set NHL record for most power-play goals in one season with 34, breaking mark of 28 held jointly by Phil Esposito (1971-72) and Mike Bossy (1980-81).

Year	Team	League	Games	G.	A.	Pts.	Pen.
1976-77—Windsor Spitfires		OMJHL	9	2	4	6	7
1977-78—Kingston Canadians		OMJHL	67	14	25	39	33
1978-79—Kingston Canadians		OMJHL	57	17	25	42	27
1979-80—Kingston Canadians (c)		OMJHL	63	40	33	73	39
1979-80—Maine Mariners		AHL	7	2	4	6	2
1980-81—Philadelphia Flyers		NHL	68	22	23	45	84
1981-82—Philadelphia Flyers		NHL	61	21	30	51	138
1982-83—Philadelphia Flyers		NHL	24	11	8	19	6
1983-84—Philadelphia Flyers		NHL	79	54	39	93	29
1984-85—Philadelphia Flyers		NHL	74	54	44	98	57
1985-86—Philadelphia Flyers		NHL	76	58	26	84	79
NHL TOTALS			382	220	170	390	393

(c)—January, 1980—Signed by Philadelphia Flyers as a free agent.

MARTY KETOLA

Right Wing . . . 5'10" . . . 185 lbs. . . . Born, Clouquet, Minn., February 25, 1965 . . . Shoots right.

Year	Team	League	Games	G.	A.	Pts.	Pen.
1982-83—Clouquet H.S. (c)		Minn. H.S.	23	19	13	32	30
1983-84—Colorado College		WCHA	34	3	4	7	48
1984-85—Colorado College		WCHA	38	1	11	12	63
1985-86—Colorado College		WCHA	40	5	12	17	89

(c)—June, 1983—Drafted by Pittsburgh Penguins in 1983 NHL entry draft. Seventh Penguins pick, 163rd overall, ninth round.

DEREK KING

Left Wing . . . 6'1" . . . 210 lbs. . . . Born, Hamilton, Ont., February 11, 1967 . . . Shoots left . . . (September, 1985)—Sprained right knee in N.Y. Islanders training camp.

Year	Team	League	Games	G.	A.	Pts.	Pen.
1983-84—Hamilton Jr.A.		OHA	37	10	14	24	142
1984-85—Sault Ste. Marie Greyhounds (c-d)		OHL	63	35	38	73	106
1985-86—Sault Ste. Marie Greyhounds		OHL	25	12	17	29	33
1985-86—Oshawa Generals		OHL	19	8	13	21	15

(c)—Won Emms Family Award (OHL Top Rookie).
(d)—June, 1985—Drafted as underage junior by New York Islanders in 1985 NHL entry draft. Second Islanders pick, 13th overall, first round.

KRIS KING

Center . . . 5'10" . . . 185 lbs. . . . Born, Bracebridge, Ont., February 18, 1966 . . . Shoots left.

Year	Team	League	Games	G.	A.	Pts.	Pen.
1982-83—Gravenhurst		SOJHL	32	72	53	125	115
1983-84—Peterborough Petes (c)		OHL	62	13	18	31	168
1984-85—Peterborough Petes		OHL	61	18	35	53	222
1985-86—Peterborough Petes		OHL	58	19	40	59	254

(c)—June, 1984—Drafted as underage junior by Washington Capitals in 1984 NHL entry draft. Fourth Capitals pick, 80th overall, fourth round.

LOUIS KIRIAKOU

Defense . . . 5'11" . . . 174 lbs. . . . Born, Toronto, Ont., April 2, 1964 . . . Shoots left.

Year	Team	League	Games	G.	A.	Pts.	Pen.
1980-81—Toronto Young Nationals		MTHL	40	15	40	55	40
1981-82—Toronto Marlboros (c)		OHL	65	5	11	16	72
1982-83—Toronto Marlboros		OHL	67	6	38	44	100
1983-84—Toronto Marlboros		OHL	68	10	35	45	74
1984-85—Moncton Golden Flames		AHL	73	0	6	6	84
1985-86—Moncton Golden Flames		AHL	11	0	2	2	9

(c)—June, 1982—Drafted by Calgary Flames as underage junior in 1982 NHL entry draft. Sixth Flames pick, 93rd overall, fifth round.

MARK ROBERT KIRTON

Center . . . 5'10" . . . 170 lbs. . . . Born, Regina, Sask., February 3, 1958 . . . Shoots left . . . (March 7, 1981)—Separated left shoulder.

Year	Team	League	Games	G.	A.	Pts.	Pen.
1975-76—Peterborough Petes		Jr."A"OHA	65	22	38	60	10
1976-77—Peterborough Petes		Jr."A"OHA	48	18	24	42	41
1977-78—Peterborough Petes (c)		Jr."A"OHA	68	27	44	71	29
1978-79—New Brunswick Hawks		AHL	79	20	30	50	14
1979-80—Toronto Maple Leafs		NHL	2	1	0	1	2
1979-80—New Brunswick Hawks		AHL	61	19	42	61	33
1980-81—Toronto Maple Leafs (d)		NHL	11	0	0	0	0
1980-81—Detroit Red Wings		NHL	50	18	13	31	24
1981-82—Detroit Red Wings		NHL	74	14	28	42	62
1982-83—Adirondack Red Wings		AHL	20	6	10	16	12
1982-83—Detroit Red Wings (e)		NHL	10	1	1	2	6
1982-83—Vancouver Canucks		NHL	31	4	6	10	4
1982-83—Fredericton Express		AHL	3	2	0	2	2
1983-84—Vancouver Canucks		NHL	26	2	3	5	2
1983-84—Fredericton Express		AHL	35	8	10	18	8
1984-85—Fredericton Express		AHL	15	5	9	14	18
1984-85—Vancouver Canucks		NHL	62	17	5	22	21
1985-86—Fredericton Express		AHL	77	23	36	59	33
NHL TOTALS			266	57	56	113	121

(c)—Drafted from Peterborough Petes by Toronto Maple Leafs in third round 1978 amateur draft.
(d)—December, 1980—Traded by Toronto Maple Leafs to Detroit Red Wings for Jim Rutherford.
(e)—January, 1983—Traded by Detroit Red Wings to Vancouver Canucks for Ivan Boldirev.

KELLY KISIO

Center . . . 5'9" . . . 170 lbs. . . . Born, Wetaskwin, Alta., September 18, 1959 . . . Shoots right . . . Also plays Right Wing . . . (February, 1985)—Given 5-game suspension by NHL for stick-swinging incident.

Year	Team	League	Games	G.	A.	Pts.	Pen.
1976-77—Red Deer Rustlers		AJHL	60	53	48	101	101
1977-78—Red Deer Rustlers (a)		AJHL	58	74	68	142	66

Year	Team	League	Games	G.	A.	Pts.	Pen.
1978-79—Calgary Wranglers		WHL	70	60	61	121	73
1979-80—Calgary Wranglers		WHL	71	65	73	138	64
1980-81—Adirondack Red Wings		AHL	41	10	14	24	43
1980-81—Kalamazoo Wings (c)		IHL	31	27	16	43	48
1981-82—Dallas Black Hawks (d)		CHL	78	*62	39	101	59
1982-83—Davos HC		Switzerland	....	49	38	87	....
1982-83—Detroit Red Wings (e)		NHL	15	4	3	7	0
1983-84—Detroit Red Wings		NHL	70	23	37	60	34
1984-85—Detroit Red Wings		NHL	75	20	41	61	56
1985-86—Detroit Red Wings (f)		NHL	76	21	48	69	85
NHL TOTALS			236	68	129	197	175

(c)—February, 1981—Traded by Toledo Goaldiggers to Kalamazoo Wings for Jean Chouinard.
(d)—Led CHL Adams Cup Playoffs with 12 goals and 29 points and was co-leader (with Bruce Affleck) with 17 assists.
(e)—February, 1983—Signed by Detroit as a free agent at the conclusion of season in Switzerland.
(f)—July, 1986—Traded with Lane Lambert and Jim Leavins by New York Rangers to Detroit Red Wings for Glen Hanlon and third round 1987 and 1988 draft picks.

ED KISTER

Defense . . . 5'11" . . . 185 lbs. . . . Born, Becej, Czechoslovakia, January 7, 1966 . . . Shoots left.

Year	Team	League	Games	G.	A.	Pts.	Pen.
1982-83—Brantford		SOJHL	25	7	14	21	84
1983-84—London Knights (c)		OHL	60	2	15	17	30
1984-85—London Knights		OHL	27	2	5	7	12
1985-86—London Knights		OHL	39	2	18	20	44

(c)—June, 1984—Drafted as underage junior by Vancouver Canucks in 1984 NHL entry draft. Thirteenth Canucks pick, 239th overall, 12th round.

BILL KITCHEN

Defense . . . 6'1" . . . 195 lbs. . . . Born, Schomberg, Ont., October 2, 1960 . . . Shoots left . . . (February 26, 1983)—Injured knee in AHL game at Binghamton . . . Brother of Mike Kitchen . . . (February 23, 1985)—Lost four front teeth and suffered a broken jaw in team practice.

Year	Team	League	Games	G.	A.	Pts.	Pen.
1977-78—Ottawa 67's		OMJHL	67	5	6	11	54
1978-79—Ottawa 67's		OMJHL	55	3	16	19	188
1979-80—Ottawa 67's		OMJHL	63	7	19	26	195
1979-80—Nova Scotia Voyageurs (c)		AHL	....	...	....	....	....
1980-81—Nova Scotia Voyageurs		AHL	65	2	7	9	135
1981-82—Nova Scotia Voyageurs		AHL	71	3	17	20	135
1981-82—Montreal Canadiens		NHL	1	0	0	0	7
1982-83—Nova Scotia Voyageurs		AHL	53	3	11	14	71
1982-83—Montreal Canadiens		NHL	8	0	0	0	4
1983-84—Montreal Canadiens		NHL	3	0	0	0	2
1983-84—Nova Scotia Voyageurs		AHL	68	4	20	24	193
1984-85—St. Catharines Saints		AHL	31	3	7	10	52
1984-85—Toronto Maple Leafs		NHL	29	1	4	5	27
1985-86—St. Catharines Saints		AHL	72	7	32	39	109
NHL TOTALS			41	1	4	5	40

(c)—Played two playoff games.

ROBERT KIVELL

Defense . . . 6'1" . . . 205 lbs. . . . Born, North Bay, Ont., January 14, 1965 . . . Shoots left . . . (January, 1983)—Ruptured kidney.

Year	Team	League	Games	G.	A.	Pts.	Pen.
1982-83—Esquimalt Buccaneers		BCJHL	....	...	....	....	....
1982-83—Victoria Cougars (c)		WHL	26	6	7	13	83
1983-84—Victoria Cougars		WHL	52	16	33	49	145
1984-85—Victoria Cougars		WHL	71	38	62	100	185
1984-85—Moncton Golden Flames		AHL	5	1	1	2	8
1985-86—Moncton Golden Flames		AHL	41	7	3	10	85

(c)—June, 1983—Drafted as underage junior by Calgary Flames in 1983 NHL entry draft. Eleventh Flames pick, 171st overall, ninth round.

KURT KLEINENDORST

Center ... 6'2" ... 190 lbs. ... Born, Grand Rapids, Minn., December 31, 1960 ... Shoots left ... Brother of Scot Kleinendorst ... (December, 1985)—Broken thumb.

Year	Team	League	Games	G.	A.	Pts.	Pen.
1979-80—Providence College		ECAC	32	10	17	27	4
1980-81—Providence College (c)		ECAC	32	16	20	36	18
1981-82—Providence College		ECAC	..	..	..	..	..
1982-83—Providence College		ECAC	41	33	39	72	30
1983-84—U.S. National Team		Int'l	44	8	18	26	14
1983-84—Tulsa Oilers		CHL	24	4	9	13	10
1984-85—New Haven Nighthawks		AHL	3	0	0	0	0
1984-85—Salt Lake Golden Eagles (d)		IHL	44	21	21	42	10
1984-85—Toledo Goaldiggers		IHL	13	4	9	13	21
1985-86—Salt Lake Golden Eagles (e)		IHL	24	5	12	17	21
1985-86—Indianapolis Checkers		IHL	45	11	22	33	22

(c)—June, 1980—Drafted by New York Rangers in NHL entry draft. Third Rangers pick, 77th overall, fourth round.

(d)—February, 1985—Traded with Steve Martinson by Salt Lake Golden Eagles to Toledo Goaldiggers for Kevin Conway, Blake Stephan, Grant Rezansoff and Steve Harrison.

(e)—January, 1986—Traded by Salt Lake Golden Eagles to Indianapolis Checkers for Kelly Elcombe.

SCOT KLEINENDORST

Defense ... 6'3" ... 205 lbs. ... Born, Grand Rapids, Minn., January 16, 1960 ... Shoots left ... (September, 1982)—Preseason surgery for off-season knee injury ... Brother of Kurt Kleinendorst ... (February, 1984)—Suffered groin injury and out for the season ... (February, 1985)—Knee sprain ... (October 30, 1985)—Broken right foot vs. Quebec and missed 18 games ... (February 11, 1986)—Bruised ribs at St. Louis.

Year	Team	League	Games	G.	A.	Pts.	Pen.
1979-80—Providence College (b-c-d)		ECAC	30	1	12	13	38
1980-81—Providence College		ECAC	32	3	31	34	75
1981-82—Providence College (a)		ECAC	33	30	27	57	14
1981-82—Springfield Indians		AHL	5	0	4	4	11
1982-83—Tulsa Oilers		CHL	10	0	7	7	14
1982-83—New York Rangers		NHL	30	2	9	11	8
1983-84—Tulsa Oilers		CHL	24	4	9	13	10
1983-84—New York Rangers (e)		NHL	23	0	2	2	35
1984-85—Binghamton Whalers		AHL	30	3	7	10	42
1984-85—Hartford Whalers		NHL	35	1	8	9	69
1985-86—Hartford Whalers		NHL	41	2	7	9	62
NHL TOTALS			129	5	26	31	174

(c)—Named to All-New England Collegiate All-Star Team (Second team).

(d)—June, 1980—Drafted by New York Rangers in 1980 NHL entry draft. Fourth Rangers pick, 98th overall, fifth round.

(e)—February, 1984—Traded by New York Rangers to Hartford Whalers for Blaine Stoughton.

PETR KLIMA

Left Wing ... 6' ... 190 lbs. ... Born, Chaomutov, Czechoslovakia, December 23, 1964 ... Shoots right ... (January 18, 1986)—Injured hip vs. Calgary and missed five games.

Year	Team	League	Games	G.	A.	Pts.	Pen.
1982-83—Czechoslovakian Nationals (c)		Czech.	44	19	17	36	74
1983-84—Dukla Jihlava		Czech.	41	20	16	36	46
1983-84—Czechoslovakian Nationals		Czech.	7	6	5	11	....
1984-85—Dukla Jihlava		Czech.	35	23	22	45	....
1985-86—Detroit Red Wings		NHL	74	32	24	56	16
NHL TOTALS			74	32	24	56	16

(c)—June, 1983—Drafted by Detroit Red Wings in NHL entry draft. Fifth Red Wings pick, 88th overall, fifth round.

GORD KLUZAK

Defense ... 6'3" ... 214 lbs. ... Born, Climax, Sask., March 4, 1964 ... Shoots left ... (February 9, 1982)—Injured knee vs. Medicine Hat that required surgery ... (March 12, 1983)—Eye injured in game vs. Philadelphia ... (October 7, 1984)—Tore ligaments in left knee when he collided with Dave Lewis in final pre-season game with New Jersey Devils at Portland, Maine. Underwent major reconstructive surgery the following day and was lost for the season ... (January 29, 1986)—Injured shoulder at Washington and missed nine games.

Year	Team	League	Games	G.	A.	Pts.	Pen.
1980-81—Billings Bighorns		WHL	68	4	34	38	160

Year	Team	League	Games	G.	A.	Pts.	Pen.
1981-82—Billings Bighorns (b-c)		WHL	38	9	24	33	110
1982-83—Boston Bruins		NHL	70	1	6	7	105
1983-84—Boston Bruins		NHL	80	10	27	37	135
1984-85—Boston Bruins		NHL	....	...	....	....	....
1985-86—Boston Bruins		NHL	70	8	31	39	155
NHL TOTALS			220	19	64	83	395

(c)—June, 1982—Drafted as underage junior by Boston Bruins in 1982 NHL entry draft. First Bruins pick, first overall, first round.

JOE KOCUR

Right Wing ... 6' ... 204 lbs. ... Born, Calgary, Alta., December 21, 1964 ... Shoots right ... (December, 1981)—Stretched knee ligaments ... (January, 1985)—Took 20 stitches to back of right hand in fight with Jim Playfair in game with Nova Scotia Oilers ... (December 11, 1985)—Sprained thumb at Minnesota ... (March 26, 1986)—Strained ligaments in game at Chicago.

Year	Team	League	Games	G.	A.	Pts.	Pen.
1980-81—Yorkton Terriers		SJHL	48	6	9	15	307
1981-82—Yorkton Terriers		SJHL	47	20	21	41	199
1982-83—Saskatoon Blades (c)		WHL	62	23	17	40	289
1983-84—Saskatoon Blades		WHL	69	40	41	81	258
1984-85—Detroit Red Wings		NHL	17	1	0	1	64
1984-85—Adirondack Red Wings		AHL	47	12	7	19	171
1985-86—Adirondack Red Wings		AHL	9	6	2	8	34
1985-86—Detroit Red Wings		NHL	59	9	6	15	*377
NHL TOTALS			76	10	6	16	441

(c)—June, 1983—Drafted as underage junior by Detroit Red Wings in 1983 NHL entry draft. Sixth Red Wings pick, 88th overall, fifth round.

DEAN KOLSTAD

Defense ... 6'6" ... 200 lbs. ... Born, Edmonton, Alta., June 16, 1968 ... Shoots left.

Year	Team	League	Games	G.	A.	Pts.	Pen.
1984-85—New Westminster Bruins		WHL	13	0	0	0	16
1985-86—New Westminster Bruins		WHL	16	0	5	5	19
1985-86—Prince Albert Raiders (c)		WHL	54	2	15	17	80

(c)—June, 1986—Drafted as underage junior by Minnesota North Stars in 1986 NHL entry draft. Third North Stars pick, 33rd overall, second round.

STEPHEN MARK KONROYD

Defense ... 6'1" ... 195 lbs. ... Born, Scarborough, Ont., February 10, 1961 ... Shoots left ... (December, 1984)—Dislocated elbow ... (February, 1986)—Pulled chest muscle vs. Toronto.

Year	Team	League	Games	G.	A.	Pts.	Pen.
1978-79—Oshawa Generals		OMJHL	65	4	19	23	63
1979-80—Oshawa Generals (c-d)		OMJHL	62	11	23	34	133
1980-81—Calgary Flames		NHL	4	0	0	0	4
1980-81—Oshawa Generals (b)		OHL	59	19	49	68	232
1981-82—Oklahoma City Stars		CHL	14	2	3	5	15
1981-82—Calgary Flames		NHL	63	3	14	17	78
1982-83—Calgary Flames		NHL	79	4	13	17	73
1983-84—Calgary Flames		NHL	80	1	13	14	94
1984-85—Calgary Flames		NHL	64	3	23	26	73
1985-86—Calgary Flames (e)		NHL	59	7	20	27	64
1985-86—New York Islanders		NHL	14	0	5	5	16
NHL TOTALS			363	18	88	106	402

(c)—June, 1980—Drafted as underage junior by Calgary Flames in 1980 NHL entry draft. Fourth Flames pick, 39th overall, second round.

(d)—Named winner of Bobby Smith Award (OHL player who best combines high standards of play with academic excellence).

(e)—March, 1986—Traded by Calgary Flames with Richard Kromm to New York Islanders for John Tonelli.

CHRIS KONTOS

Center ... 6'1" ... 200 lbs. ... Born, Toronto, Ont., December 10, 1963 ... Shoots left ... Also plays Left Wing ... (November, 1983)—Suspended by New York Rangers when he refused to report to the Tulsa Oilers. He was reinstated in January, 1984.

Year	Team	League	Games	G.	A.	Pts.	Pen.
1979-80—North York Flames		OPJHL	42	39	55	94	37

Year	Team	League	Games	G.	A.	Pts.	Pen.
1980-81—Sudbury Wolves		OHL	56	17	27	44	36
1981-82—Sudbury Wolves (c)		OHL	12	6	6	12	18
1981-82—Toronto Marlboros (d)		OHL	59	36	56	92	68
1982-83—Toronto Marlboros		OHL	28	21	33	54	23
1982-83—New York Rangers		NHL	44	8	7	15	33
1983-84—New York Rangers		NHL	6	0	1	1	8
1983-84—Tulsa Oilers		CHL	21	5	13	18	8
1984-85—New Haven Nighthawks		AHL	48	19	24	43	30
1984-85—New York Rangers		NHL	28	4	8	12	24
1985-86—New Haven Nighthawks		AHL	21	8	15	23	12
NHL TOTALS			78	12	16	28	65

(c)—October, 1981—Traded by Sudbury Wolves to Toronto Marlboros for Keith Knight.
(d)—June, 1982—Drafted as underage junior by New York Rangers in 1982 NHL entry draft. First Rangers pick, 15th overall, first round.

BILL KOPECKY

Center . . . 5'11" . . . 170 lbs. . . . Born, Ipswich, Mass., January 11, 1966 . . . Shoots left.

Year	Team	League	Games	G.	A.	Pts.	Pen.
1983-84—Austin H.S. (c)		Minn. H.S.	21	31	36	67	..
1984-85—Boston College		H. East	29	6	10	16	18
1985-86—Rensselaer Poly. Inst.		ECAC	29	9	15	24	26

(c)—June, 1984—Drafted by Boston Bruins in 1984 NHL entry draft. Eleventh Bruins pick, 227th overall, 11th round.

JEFF KORCHINSKI

Defense . . . 6' . . . 190 lbs. . . . Born, Ottawa, Ont., May 13, 1966 . . . Shoots left.

Year	Team	League	Games	G.	A.	Pts.	Pen.
1983-84—Clarkson College (c)		ECAC	34	1	5	6	12
1984-85—Clarkson College		ECAC	33	0	11	11	20
1985-86—Clarkson College		ECAC	29	2	5	7	26

(c)—June, 1984—Drafted by Vancouver Canucks in 1984 NHL entry draft. Seventh Canucks pick. 115th overall, sixth round.

JOHN KORDIC

Right Wing . . . 6'1" . . . 190 lbs. . . . Born, Edmonton, Alta., March 22, 1965 . . . Shoots right . . . Uncle played pro soccer in Yugoslavia.

Year	Team	League	Games	G.	A.	Pts.	Pen.
1981-82—Edmonton K. of C. AA		Edm. Midget	48	23	41	64	178
1982-83—Portland Winter Hawks (c)		WHL	72	3	22	25	235
1983-84—Portland Winter Hawks		WHL	67	9	50	59	232
1984-85—Portland Winter Hawks		WHL	25	6	22	28	73
1984-85—Seattle Breakers (b)		WHL	46	17	36	53	154
1984-85—Sherbrooke Canadiens		AHL	4	0	0	0	4
1985-86—Sherbrooke Canadiens		AHL	68	3	14	17	238
1985-86—Montreal Canadiens		NHL	5	0	1	1	12
NHL TOTALS			5	0	1	1	12

(c)—June, 1983—Drafted as underage junior by Montreal Canadiens in 1983 NHL entry draft. Sixth Canadiens pick, 78th overall, fourth round.

JAMES A. KORN

Defense . . . 6'5" . . . 220 lbs. . . . Born, Hopkins, Minn., July 28, 1957 . . . Shoots left . . . Attended Providence College . . . (January 13, 1981)—Injured ligaments in right knee . . . (February 8, 1984)—Injured ribs in game vs. Boston . . . (November 5, 1984)—Dislocated shoulder when he collided with goal post in game at Minnesota . . . (January, 1985)—Given 3-game NHL suspension . . . (February 9, 1985)—Separated shoulder during fight with Chris Nilan at Montreal . . . Missed entire 1985-86 season with knee injury.

Year	Team	League	Games	G.	A.	Pts.	Pen.
1976-77—Providence College (c)		ECAC	29	6	9	15	73
1977-78—Providence College		ECAC	33	7	14	21	47
1978-79—Providence College		ECAC	27	5	19	24	72
1979-80—Adirondack Red Wings		AHL	14	2	7	9	40
1979-80—Detroit Red Wings		NHL	63	5	13	18	108
1980-81—Adirondack Red Wings		AHL	9	3	7	10	53
1980-81—Detroit Red Wings		NHL	63	5	15	20	246
1981-82—Detroit Red Wings (d)		NHL	59	1	7	8	104
1981-82—Toronto Maple Leafs		NHL	11	1	3	4	44
1982-83—Toronto Maple Leafs		NHL	80	8	21	29	238

Year	Team	League	Games	G.	A.	Pts.	Pen.
1983-84—Toronto Maple Leafs		NHL	65	12	14	26	257
1984-85—Toronto Maple Leafs		NHL	41	5	5	10	171
1985-86—Toronto Maple Leafs		NHL			Did not play		
NHL TOTALS			382	37	78	115	1168

(c)—June, 1977—Drafted by Detroit Red Wings in 1977 amateur draft. Fourth Detroit pick, 73rd overall, fifth round.

(d)—March, 1982—Traded by Detroit Red Wings to Toronto Maple Leafs for 1982 fourth-round pick (Craig Coxe) and a 1983 fifth-round pick in the NHL entry draft.

DAVID KOROL

Defense . . . 6' . . . 180 lbs. . . . Born, Winnipeg, Man., March 1, 1965 . . . Shoots left . . . (January, 1982)—Thumb surgery.

Year	Team	League	Games	G.	A.	Pts.	Pen.
1981-82—Winnipeg Warriors		WHL	64	4	22	26	55
1982-83—Winnipeg Warriors (c)		WHL	72	14	43	57	90
1983-84—Winnipeg Warriors		WHL	57	15	48	63	49
1983-84—Adirondack Red Wings		AHL	2	0	4	4	0
1984-85—Regina Pats		WHL	48	4	30	34	61
1985-86—Adirondack Red Wings		AHL	74	3	9	12	56

(c)—June, 1983—Drafted by Detroit Red Wings in 1983 NHL entry draft. Fourth Red Wings pick, 68th overall, fourth round.

ROGER KORTKO

Center . . . 5'11" . . . 175 lbs. . . . Born, Hafford, Sask., February 1, 1963 . . . Shoots left . . . (October, 1984 and January, 1985)—Sprained ankle . . . (November 1, 1985)—Missed five games with a virus infection . . . (March, 1986)—Damaged ligaments in left knee vs. St. Louis.

Year	Team	League	Games	G.	A.	Pts.	Pen.
1980-81—Humbolt Broncos		SJHL	60	43	82	125	52
1981-82—Saskatoon Blades (c)		WHL	65	33	51	84	82
1982-83—Saskatoon Blades		WHL	72	62	99	161	79
1983-84—Indianapolis Checkers		CHL	64	16	27	43	48
1984-85—Springfield Indians		AHL	30	8	30	38	6
1984-85—New York Islanders		NHL	27	2	9	11	9
1985-86—Springfield Indians		AHL	12	2	10	12	10
1985-86—New York Islanders		NHL	52	5	8	13	19
NHL TOTALS			79	7	17	24	28

(c)—June, 1982—Drafted as underage junior by New York Islanders in 1982 NHL entry draft. Sixth Islanders pick, 126th overall, sixth round.

DOUG KOSTYNSKI

Center . . . 6'1" . . . 170 lbs. . . . Born, Castlegar, B.C., February 23, 1963 . . . Shoots right.

Year	Team	League	Games	G.	A.	Pts.	Pen.
1979-80—New Westminster Bruins		WHL	11	1	4	5	12
1980-81—New Westminster Bruins		WHL	64	18	40	58	51
1981-82—Kamloops Jr. Oilers (c)		WHL	53	39	42	81	57
1982-83—Kamloops Jr. Oilers		WHL	75	57	59	116	55
1983-84—Hershey Bears		AHL	67	13	27	40	8
1983-84—Boston Bruins		NHL	9	3	1	4	2
1984-85—Boston Bruins		NHL	6	0	0	0	2
1984-85—Hershey Bears		AHL	55	17	27	44	26
1985-86—Moncton Golden Flames		AHL	72	18	36	54	24
NHL TOTALS			15	3	1	4	4

(c)—June, 1982—Drafted as underage junior by Boston Bruins in 1982 NHL entry draft. Ninth Bruins pick, 186th overall, ninth round.

CHRIS KOTSOPOULOS

Defense . . . 6'3" . . . 215 lbs. . . . Born, Toronto, Ont., November 27, 1958 . . . Shoots right . . . Brother of George Kotsopoulos . . . (October, 1980)—Broke right thumb during exhibition game . . . (January, 1981)—Infection in right arm . . . (January 24, 1981)—Hand infection developed after treatment for cut hand . . . (February, 1983)—Pulled stomach muscles . . . (January 24, 1984)—Strained ligaments in right knee in game at Montreal . . . (December 28, 1984)—Broke bone in left foot when hit by a Moe Mantha shot at Pittsburgh . . . (March 3, 1985)—Sprained left knee and ankle in game vs. Vancouver . . . (November 16, 1985)—Sprained ankle vs. Chicago and missed two games . . . (January 13, 1985)—Bruised shoulder vs. Detroit . . . (March 8, 1986)—Strained Achilles tendon vs. Chicago.

Year	Team	League	Games	G.	A.	Pts.	Pen.
1975-76—Windsor Spitfires		OMJHL	59	3	13	16	169
1978-79—Toledo Goaldiggers		IHL	64	6	22	28	153
1979-80—New Haven Nighthawks		AHL	75	7	27	34	149
1980-81—New York Rangers (c)		NHL	54	4	12	16	153
1981-82—Hartford Whalers		NHL	68	13	20	33	147
1982-83—Hartford Whalers		NHL	68	6	24	30	125
1983-84—Hartford Whalers		NHL	72	5	13	18	118
1984-85—Hartford Whalers		NHL	33	5	3	8	53
1985-86—Toronto Maple Leafs (d)		NHL	61	6	11	17	83
NHL TOTALS			356	39	83	122	679

(c)—October, 1981—Traded with Doug Sulliman and Gerry McDonald by New York Rangers to Hartford Whalers for Mike Rogers and a 10th-round 1982 draft pick (Simo Saarinen).

(d)—October, 1985—Traded by Hartford Whalers to Toronto Maple Leafs for Stewart Gavin.

JIM KOUDYS

Defense . . . 5'11" . . . 170 lbs. . . . Born, Grimsby, Ont., January 9, 1964 . . . Shoots left . . . Also plays Left Wing.

Year	Team	League	Games	G.	A.	Pts.	Pen.
1981-82—Sudbury Wolves (c)		OHL	68	10	29	39	25
1982-83—Sudbury Wolves		OHL	70	35	49	84	40
1983-84—Sudbury Wolves		OHL	70	46	45	91	34
1984-85—Springfield Indians		AHL	26	0	0	0	2
1984-85—Indianapolis Checkers		IHL	24	5	14	19	17
1985-86—Indianapolis Checkers		IHL	32	4	13	17	23
1985-86—Springfield Indians		AHL	40	3	10	13	32

(c)—June, 1982—Drafted by New York Islanders as underage junior in 1982 NHL entry draft. Twelfth Islanders pick, 252nd overall, 12th round.

SEAN KRAKIWSKY

Right Wing . . . 6' . . . 175 lbs. . . . Born, Calgary, Alta., December 29, 1967 . . . Shoots left.

Year	Team	League	Games	G.	A.	Pts.	Pen.
1985-86—Univ. of Minnesota/Duluth		WCHA	10	0	4	4	2
1985-86—Calgary Wranglers (c)		WHL	39	9	32	41	27

(c)—June, 1986—Drafted as underage junior by Los Angeles Kings in 1986 NHL entry draft. Sixth Kings pick, 128th overall, seventh round.

DALE KRENTZ

Left Wing . . . 5'11" . . . 185 lbs. . . . Born, Steinbach, Man., December 19, 1961 . . . Shoots left.

Year	Team	League	Games	G.	A.	Pts.	Pen.
1982-83—Michigan State Univ.		CCHA	42	11	24	35	50
1983-84—Michigan State Univ.		CCHA	44	12	20	32	34
1984-85—Michigan State Univ. (c)		CCHA	44	24	30	54	26
1985-86—Adirondack Red Wings		AHL	79	19	27	46	27

(c)—June, 1985—Signed by Detroit Red Wings as a free agent.

RICHARD KROMM

Left Wing . . . 5'11" . . . 180 lbs. . . . Born, Trail, B.C., March 29, 1964 . . . Shoots left . . . Son of Bobby Kromm (Member of World Champion 1961 Trail Smoke Eaters, and former WHA/NHL coach) . . . (October, 1981)—Broken ankle . . . Brother of David Kromm . . . Also plays Center . . . (February, 1985)—Pinched nerve.

Year	Team	League	Games	G.	A.	Pts.	Pen.
1980-81—Windsor Royals		Jr.'B'	39	22	31	53	40
1981-82—Portland Winter Hawks (c)		WHL	60	16	38	54	30
1982-83—Portland Winter Hawks		WHL	72	35	68	103	64
1983-84—Portland Winter Hawks		WHL	10	10	4	14	13
1983-84—Calgary Flames		NHL	53	11	12	23	27
1984-85—Calgary Flames		NHL	73	20	32	52	32
1985-86—Calgary Flames (d)		NHL	63	12	17	29	31
1985-86—New York Islanders		NHL	14	7	7	14	4
NHL TOTALS			203	50	68	118	94

(c)—June, 1982—Drafted as underage junior by Calgary Flames in 1982 NHL entry draft. Second Flames pick, 37th overall, second round.

(d)—March, 1986—Traded by Calgary Flames with Steve Konroyd to New York Islanders for John Tonelli.

MIKE KRUSHELNYSKI

Left Wing and Center . . . 6'2" . . . 200 lbs. . . . Born, Montreal, Que., April 27, 1960 . . . Shoots

left . . . Started the 1978-79 season at St. Louis University but left to return to junior hockey . . . (January, 1984)—Separated right shoulder . . . (December 10, 1985)—Sprained right knee at St. Louis and missed 17 games . . . (February 14, 1986)—Twisted knee vs. Quebec and missed nine games.

Year	Team	League	Games	G.	A.	Pts.	Pen.
1978-79—Montreal Juniors		QMJHL	46	15	29	44	42
1979-80—Montreal Juniors (c)		QMJHL	72	39	61	100	78
1980-81—Springfield Indians		AHL	80	25	38	53	47
1981-82—Erie Blades		AHL	62	31	52	83	44
1981-82—Boston Bruins		NHL	17	3	3	6	2
1982-83—Boston Bruins		NHL	79	23	42	65	43
1983-84—Boston Bruins (d)		NHL	66	25	20	45	55
1984-85—Edmonton Oilers		NHL	80	43	45	88	60
1985-86—Edmonton Oilers		NHL	54	16	24	40	22
NHL TOTALS			296	110	134	244	182

(c)—August, 1979—Drafted by Boston Bruins as an underage junior in 1979 NHL entry draft. Seventh Bruins pick, 120th overall, sixth round.

(d)—June, 1984—Traded by Boston Bruins to Edmonton Oilers for Ken Linseman.

MARK KUMPEL

Right Wing . . . 6' . . . 190 lbs. . . . Born, Wakefield, Mass., March 7, 1961 . . . Shoots right . . . Member of 1984 U.S. Olympic team . . . (October, 1980)—Suffered knee ligament damage in first game and missed remainder of season . . . (October 21, 1985)—Missed three games after breaking hand at Montreal . . . (February 16, 1986)—Separated shoulder at Calgary.

Year	Team	League	Games	G.	A.	Pts.	Pen.
1979-80—Lowell University (c)		ECAC	30	18	18	36	12
1980-81—Lowell University		ECAC	1	2	0	2	0
1981-82—Lowell University		ECAC	35	17	13	30	23
1982-83—Lowell University		ECAC	7	8	5	13	0
1982-83—U.S. National Team		Int'l	30	14	18	32	6
1983-84—U.S. National Team		Int'l	61	14	19	33	19
1983-84—U.S. Olympic Team		Int'l	6	1	0	1	2
1983-84—Fredericton Express		AHL	16	1	1	2	5
1984-85—Fredericton Express		AHL	18	9	6	15	17
1984-85—Quebec Nordiques		NHL	42	8	7	15	26
1985-86—Fredericton Express		AHL	7	4	2	6	4
1985-86—Quebec Nordiques		NHL	47	10	12	22	17
NHL TOTALS			89	18	19	37	43

(c)—June, 1980—Drafted by Quebec Nordiques in NHL entry draft. Fourth Nordiques pick, 108th overall, sixth round.

JARI KURRI

Right Wing . . . 6' . . . 183 lbs. . . . Born, Helsinki, Finland, May 18, 1960 . . . Shoots right . . . Played on Finnish Olympic Team in 1980 . . . (November 24, 1981)—Pulled groin during Oilers practice . . . First Finland-born player to have 100-point season in NHL . . . (January, 1984)—Missed 16 games with a pulled groin muscle . . . (May, 1985)—Set NHL playoff record for hat tricks (4) and goals (12) in a single series (vs. Chicago) . . . (May, 1985)—Tied NHL playoff record with 19 goals for a single playoff season . . . (November 17, 1986)—Injured eye in game at N.Y. Rangers and missed two games . . . (1985-86)—First European to lead NHL in goals in one season.

Year	Team	League	Games	G.	A.	Pts.	Pen.
1977-78—Jokerit		Fin. Elite	29	2	9	11	12
1978-79—Jokerit		Fin. Elite	33	16	14	30	12
1979-80—Jokerit (c)		Fin. Elite	33	23	16	39	22
1980-81—Edmonton Oilers		NHL	75	32	43	75	40
1981-82—Edmonton Oilers		NHL	71	32	54	86	32
1982-83—Edmonton Oilers		NHL	80	45	59	104	22
1983-84—Edmonton Oilers (b-d)		NHL	64	52	61	113	14
1984-85—Edmonton Oilers (a-e-f)		NHL	73	71	64	135	30
1985-86—Edmonton Oilers (b)		NHL	78	*68	63	131	22
NHL TOTALS			441	300	344	644	160

(c)—June, 1980—Drafted by Edmonton Oilers in NHL entry draft. Third Oilers pick, 69th overall, fourth round.

(d)—Led NHL Stanley Cup playoffs with 14 goals.

(e)—Led NHL Stanley Cup playoffs with 19 goals.

(f)—Won Lady Byng Memorial Trophy (Combination of Sportsmanship and Quality play).

TOM KURVERS

Defense . . . 6' . . . 190 lbs. . . . Born, Minneapolis, Minn., October 14, 1962 . . . Shoots left . . . Set UMD record with 149 career assists . . . (October 23, 1984)—Missed five games when Mario Marois' shot deflected off Chris Chelios' stick and struck Kurvers in the nose and above the right eye.

Year	Team	League	Games	G.	A.	Pts.	Pen.
1980-81—University of Minnesota/Duluth (c)		WCHA	39	6	24	30	48
1981-82—University of Minnesota/Duluth		WCHA	37	11	31	42	18
1982-83—University of Minnesota/Duluth		WCHA	45	8	36	44	42
1983-84—University of Minn/Duluth (a-d-e)		WCHA	43	18	58	76	46
1984-85—Montreal Canadiens		NHL	75	10	35	45	30
1985-86—Montreal Canadiens		NHL	62	7	23	30	36
NHL TOTALS			137	17	58	75	66

(c)—June, 1981—Drafted as underage player by Montreal Canadiens in 1981 NHL entry draft. Tenth Canadiens pick, 145th overall, seventh round.

(d)—Named to All-American Team (West).

(e)—Won Hobey Baker Award (Top NCAA Hockey Player).

MARK KURZAWSKI

Defense . . . 6'3" . . . 200 lbs. . . . Born, Chicago, Ill., February 25, 1968 . . . Shoots right.

Year	Team	League	Games	G.	A.	Pts.	Pen.
1984-85—Chicago Americans		Ill. Midget	63	23	37	60	88
1985-86—Windsor Spitfires (c)		OHL	66	11	26	37	66

(c)—June, 1986—Drafted by Chicago Black Hawks as an underage junior in 1986 NHL entry draft. Second Black Hawks pick, 35th overall, second round.

JIM KYTE

Defense . . . 6'5" . . . 200 lbs. . . . Born, Ottawa, Ont., March 21, 1964 . . . Shoots left . . . Wears hearing aids when he plays . . . (March, 1980)—Broken left wrist.

Year	Team	League	Games	G.	A.	Pts.	Pen.
1980-81—Hawksbury Hawks		Tier II	42	2	24	26	133
1981-82—Cornwall Royals (c)		OHL	52	4	13	17	148
1982-83—Cornwall Royals		OHL	65	6	30	36	195
1982-83—Winnipeg Jets		NHL	2	0	0	0	0
1983-84—Winnipeg Jets		NHL	58	1	2	3	55
1984-85—Winnipeg Jets		NHL	71	0	3	3	111
1985-86—Winnipeg Jets		NHL	71	1	3	4	126
NHL TOTALS			202	2	8	10	292

(c)—June, 1982—Drafted as underage junior by Winnipeg Jets in 1982 NHL entry draft. First Jets pick, 12th overall, first round.

JOHN LABATT

Center . . . 5'11" . . . 174 lbs. . . . Born, Minnetonka, Minn., August 16, 1965 . . . Shoots left.

Year	Team	League	Games	G.	A.	Pts.	Pen.
1982-83—Minnetonka H.S. (c)		Minn. H.S.	23	23	26	49	..
1983-84—University of Minnesota		WCHA	11	2	2	4	2
1984-85—University of Minnesota		WCHA	34	5	9	14	22
1985-86—University of Minnesota		WCHA	1	0	0	0	0

(c)—June, 1983—Drafted by Vancouver Canucks in 1983 NHL entry draft. Eighth Canucks pick, 150th overall, eighth round.

GARRY LACEY

Left Wing . . . 5'11" . . . 178 lbs. . . . Born, Sudbury, Ont., May 24, 1964 . . . Shoots left . . . Also plays Center.

Year	Team	League	Games	G.	A.	Pts.	Pen.
1980-81—Garson Midgets		OHA Midgets	28	38	34	72	....
1981-82—Toronto Marlboros (c)		OHL	65	17	28	45	140
1982-83—Toronto Marlboros		OHL	67	19	36	55	117
1983-84—Toronto Marlboros (a)		OHL	59	41	60	101	77
1984-85—Indianapolis Checkers		IHL	76	17	21	38	88
1985-86—Springfield Indians		AHL	52	12	11	23	41

(c)—June, 1982—Drafted as underage junior by New York Islanders in 1982 entry draft. Third Islanders pick, 63rd overall, third round.

KURT LACKTEN

Right Wing . . . 6' . . . 180 lbs. . . . Born, Kamsack, Sask., May 14, 1967 . . . Shoots right.

Year	Team	League	Games	G.	A.	Pts.	Pen.
1983-84—Notre Dame Hounds		SAHA	26	23	30	53	74
1984-85—Moose Jaw Warriors (c)		WHL	66	18	13	31	141
1985-86—Moose Jaw Warriors (d)		WHL	6	0	3	3	16
1985-86—Medicine Hat Tigers		WHL	27	2	5	7	51
1985-86—Calgary Wranglers		WHL	28	3	12	15	45

(c)—June, 1985—Drafted as underage junior by New York Islanders in 1985 NHL entry draft. Ninth Islanders pick, 139th, overall, seventh round.

(d)—November, 1985—Traded by Moose Jaw Warriors to Medicine Hat Tigers for Pat Beauchesne and Garth Lamb.

NORMAND LACOMBE

Right Wing . . . 5'11" . . . 205 lbs. . . . Born, Pierrefond, Que., October 18, 1964 . . . Shoots right . . . (February 21, 1986)—Fractured jaw vs. N.Y. Islanders.

Year	Team	League	Games	G.	A.	Pts.	Pen.
1981-82—Univ. New Hampshire		ECAC	35	18	16	34	38
1982-83—Univ. New Hampshire (b-c)		ECAC	35	18	25	43	48
1983-84—Rochester Americans		AHL	44	10	16	26	45
1984-85—Rochester Americans		AHL	33	13	16	29	33
1984-85—Buffalo Sabres		NHL	30	2	4	6	25
1985-86—Rochester Americans		AHL	32	10	13	23	56
1985-86—Buffalo Sabres		NHL	25	6	7	13	13
NHL TOTALS			55	8	11	19	38

(c)—June, 1983—Drafted by Buffalo Sabres in 1983 NHL entry draft. Second Sabres pick, 10th overall, first round.

RANDY LADOUCEUR

Defense . . . 6'2" . . . 220 lbs. . . . Born, Brockville, Ont., June 30, 1960 . . . Shoots left . . . (March, 1986)—Back spasms.

Year	Team	League	Games	G.	A.	Pts.	Pen.
1978-79—Brantford Alexanders		OMJHL	64	3	17	20	141
1979-80—Brantford Alexanders (c)		OMJHL	37	6	15	21	125
1980-81—Kalamazoo Wings		IHL	80	7	30	37	52
1981-82—Adirondack Red Wings		AHL	78	4	28	32	78
1982-83—Adirondack Red Wings		AHL	48	11	21	32	54
1982-83—Detroit Red Wings		NHL	27	0	4	4	16
1983-84—Adirondack Red Wings		AHL	11	3	5	8	12
1983-84—Detroit Red Wings		NHL	71	3	17	20	58
1984-85—Detroit Red Wings		NHL	80	3	27	30	108
1985-86—Detroit Red Wings		NHL	78	5	13	18	196
NHL TOTALS			256	11	61	72	378

(c)—November, 1979—Signed by Detroit Red Wings as a free agent.

PAT La FONTAINE

Center . . . 5'9" . . . 170 lbs. . . . Born, St. Louis, Mo., February 22, 1965 . . . Shoots right . . . Set Quebec Junior League records (1982-83) with points in 43 consecutive games (since broken by Mario Lemieux), and most goals (104), assists (130) and points (234) by a Quebec Junior League Rookie . . . Member of 1984 U.S. Olympic team . . . (August 16, 1984)—Damaged ligaments in left knee when checked by Team Canada's Scott Stevens in pre-Canada Cup game at Bloomington, Minn. . . . (January, 1985)—Mononucleosis . . . (January 25, 1986)—Separated right shoulder vs. Chicago.

Year	Team	League	Games	G.	A.	Pts.	Pen.
1981-82—Detroit Compuware		Mich. Midget	79	175	149	324	...
1982-83—Verdun Juniors (a-c-d-e-f-g)		QHL	70	*104	*130	*234	10
1983-84—U.S. National Team		Int'l	58	56	55	111	22
1983-84—U.S. Olympic Team		Int'l	6	5	5	10	0
1983-84—New York Islanders		NHL	15	13	6	19	6
1984-85—New York Islanders		NHL	67	19	35	54	32
1985-86—New York Islanders		NHL	65	30	23	53	43
NHL TOTALS			147	62	64	126	81

(c)—Won Frank Selke Trophy (Most Gentlemanly QHL player).

(d)—Won Des Instructeurs Trophy (Top QHL Rookie Forward).

(e)—Won Jean Beliveau Trophy (QHL Leading Scorer).

(f)—Won Guy Lafleur Trophy (QHL Playoff MVP).

(g)—June, 1983—Drafted as underage junior by New York Islanders in 1983 NHL entry draft. First Islanders pick, third overall, first round.

MARC LAFORGE

Defense . . . 6'2" . . . 200 lbs. . . . Born, Sudbury, Ont., January 3, 1968 . . . Shoots left.

Year	Team	League	Games	G.	A.	Pts.	Pen.
1984-85	Kingston Canadians	OHL	57	1	5	6	214
1985-86	Kingston Canadians (c)	OHL	60	1	13	14	248

(c)—June, 1986—Drafted as underage junior by Hartford Whalers in 1986 NHL entry draft. Second Whalers pick, 32nd overall, second round.

JASON LAFRENIERE

Center . . . 6' . . . 185 lbs. . . . Born, St. Catharines, Ont., December 6, 1966 . . . Shoots right . . . Son of Roger Lafreniere (Detroit 1962-63, and St. Louis 1972-73. He played several seasons in the old WHL, AHL and CPHL).

Year	Team	League	Games	G.	A.	Pts.	Pen.
1982-83	Orillia Travelways	OHA	48	17	40	57	9
1983-84	Brantford Alexanders	OHL	70	24	57	81	4
1984-85	Hamilton Steelhawks (c)	OHL	59	26	69	95	10
1985-86	Hamilton Steelhawks (d)	OHL	14	12	10	22	2
1985-86	Belleville Bulls (a-e)	OHL	48	37	73	110	2

(c)—June, 1985—Drafted as underage junior by Quebec Nordiques in 1985 NHL entry draft. Second Nordiques pick, 36th overall, second round.

(d)—November, 1985—Traded with Lawrence Hinch and Peter Choma by Hamilton Steelhawks to Belleville Bulls for Sean Doyl, John Purves and Brian Hoard.

(e)—Won William Hanley Trophy (Most gentlemanly OHL player).

TOM LAIDLAW

Defense . . . 6'2" . . . 215 lbs. . . . Born, Brampton, Ont., April 15, 1958 . . . Shoots left . . . (December, 1984)—Spleen surgery . . . (March 12, 1986)—Back spasms.

Year	Team	League	Games	G.	A.	Pts.	Pen.
1978-79	Northern Michigan Univ. (c)	CCHA	29	10	20	30	137
1979-80	Northern Michigan Univ. (a-d)	CCHA	39	8	30	38	83
1979-80	New Haven Nighthawks	AHL	1	0	0	0	0
1980-81	New York Rangers	NHL	80	6	23	29	100
1981-82	New York Rangers	NHL	79	3	18	21	104
1982-83	New York Rangers	NHL	80	0	10	10	75
1983-84	New York Rangers	NHL	79	3	15	18	62
1984-85	New York Rangers	NHL	61	1	11	12	52
1985-86	New York Rangers	NHL	68	6	12	18	103
	NHL TOTALS		447	19	89	108	496

(c)—June, 1978—Drafted by New York Rangers in 1978 NHL amateur draft. Seventh Rangers pick, 93rd overall, sixth round.

(d)—Named to All-NCAA-Tournament team.

BOB LAKSO

Left Wing . . . 6' . . . 180 lbs. . . . Born, Baltimore, Md., April 3, 1962 . . . Shoots left.

Year	Team	League	Games	G.	A.	Pts.	Pen.
1980-81	Univ. of Minnesota/Duluth (c)	WCHA	36	7	6	13	2
1981-82	Univ. of Minnesota/Duluth	WCHA	28	12	11	23	8
1982-83	Univ. of Minnesota/Duluth	WCHA	45	18	25	43	8
1983-84	Univ. of Minnesota/Duluth	WCHA	43	32	34	66	12
1984-85	Indianapolis Checkers	IHL	76	26	32	58	4
1984-85	Springfield Indians	AHL	8	2	1	3	0
1985-86	Indianapolis Checkers	IHL	58	41	35	76	4
1985-86	Springfield Indians	AHL	17	3	6	9	2

(c)—June, 1980—Drafted by Minnesota North Stars in NHL entry draft. Ninth North Stars pick, 184th overall, ninth round.

JOHN MICHAEL (MIKE) LALOR

Defense . . . 6' . . . 190 lbs. . . . Born, Fort Erie, Ont., March 8, 1963 . . . Shoots left.

Year	Team	League	Games	G.	A.	Pts.	Pen.
1981-82	Brantford Alexanders	OHL	64	3	13	16	114
1982-83	Brantford Alexanders	OHL	65	10	30	40	113
1983-84	Nova Scotia Voyageurs (c)	AHL	67	5	11	16	80
1984-85	Sherbrooke Canadiens	AHL	79	9	23	32	114
1985-86	Montreal Canadiens	NHL	62	3	5	8	56
	NHL TOTALS		62	3	5	8	56

(c)—September, 1983—Signed by Nova Scotia Voyageurs as a free agent.

MARK LAMB

Left Wing . . . 5'9" . . . 170 lbs. . . . Born, Swift Current, Sask., August 3, 1964 . . . Shoots left . . . (December, 1982)—Refused, with team captain Bob Rouse, to dress for a game after Nanaimo (WHL) released coach Les Calder. Both players asked to be traded . . . Also plays Center . . . Brother of Garth Lamb (Currently in WHL).

Year	Team	League	Games	G.	A.	Pts.	Pen.
1980-81	Billings Bighorns	WHL	24	1	8	9	12
1981-82	Billings Bighorns (c)	WHL	72	45	56	101	46
1982-83	Nanaimo Islanders (d)	WHL	30	14	37	51	16
1982-83	Medicine Hat Tigers	WHL	46	22	43	65	33
1983-84	Medicine Hat Tigers (a-e)	WHL	72	59	77	136	30
1984-85	Medicine Hat Tigers (f)	WHL	..	..	..	..	..
1984-85	Moncton Golden Flames	AHL	80	23	49	72	53
1985-86	Calgary Flames	NHL	1	0	0	0	0
1985-86	Moncton Golden Flames	AHL	79	26	50	76	51
	NHL TOTALS		1	0	0	0	0

(c)—June, 1982—Drafted as underage junior by Calgary Flames in 1982 NHL entry draft. Fifth Flames pick, 72nd overall, fourth round.

(d)—December, 1982—Traded by Nanaimo Islanders to Medicine Hat Tigers for Glen Kulka and Daryl Reaugh.

(e)—Won Frank Boucher Memorial Trophy (Most Gentlemanly WHL Player).

(f)—Played six playoff games, scoring three goals and two assists.

LANE LAMBERT

Right Wing . . . 6' . . . 175 lbs. . . . Born, Melfort, Sask., November 18, 1964 . . . Shoots right . . . (September, 1982)—Eye injured in game vs. Brandon . . . (March, 1985)—Surgery to left knee.

Year	Team	League	Games	G.	A.	Pts.	Pen.
1980-81	Swift Current Broncos	SJHL	55	43	54	97	63
1981-82	Saskatoon Blades	WHL	72	45	69	114	111
1982-83	Saskatoon Blades (b-c)	WHL	64	59	60	119	126
1983-84	Detroit Red Wings	NHL	73	20	15	35	115
1984-85	Detroit Red Wings	NHL	69	14	11	25	104
1985-86	Adirondack Red Wings	AHL	45	16	25	41	69
1985-86	Detroit Red Wings (d)	NHL	34	2	3	5	130
	NHL TOTALS		176	36	29	65	349

(c)—June, 1983—Drafted as underage junior by Detroit Red Wings in 1983 NHL entry draft. Second Red Wings pick, 25th overall, second round.

(d)—August, 1986—Traded by Detroit Red Wings with Kelly Kisio and Jim Leavins to New York Rangers for Glen Hanlon and Rangers' third-round draft choices in 1987 and '88.

HANK LAMMENS

Defense . . . 6'2" . . . 196 lbs. . . . Born, Brockville, Ont., February 21, 1966 . . . Shoots left . . . (November, 1984)—Broken wrist and separated shoulder.

Year	Team	League	Games	G.	A.	Pts.	Pen.
1983-84	Brockville Braves	OHA	46	7	11	18	106
1984-85	St. Lawrence Univ. (c)	ECAC	21	1	7	8	16
1985-86	St. Lawrence Univ.	ECAC	30	3	14	17	60

(c)—June, 1985—Drafted by New York Islanders in 1985 NHL entry draft. Tenth Islanders pick, 160th overall, 10th round.

MITCH LAMOUREUX

Center . . . 5'6" . . . 185 lbs. . . . Born, Ottawa, Ont., August 22, 1962 . . . Shoots left . . . Set AHL record for most goals by a rookie (57) in 1982-83, and most goals by an AHL player.

Year	Team	League	Games	G.	A.	Pts.	Pen.
1979-80	Oshawa Generals	OMJHL	67	28	48	76	63
1980-81	Oshawa Generals (c)	OMJHL	63	50	69	119	256
1981-82	Oshawa Generals	OHL	66	43	78	121	275
1982-83	Baltimore Skipjacks (b-d)	AHL	80	*57	50	107	107
1983-84	Baltimore Skipjacks	AHL	68	30	38	68	136
1983-84	Pittsburgh Penguins	NHL	8	1	1	2	6
1984-85	Pittsburgh Penguins	NHL	62	11	8	19	53
1984-85	Baltimore Skipjacks	AHL	18	10	14	24	34
1985-86	Baltimore Skipjacks	AHL	75	22	31	53	129
	NHL TOTALS		70	12	9	21	59

(c)—June, 1981—Drafted as underage junior by Pittsburgh Penguins in 1981 NHL entry draft. Sixth Penguins pick, 154th overall, eighth round.

(d)—Won Dudley (Red) Garrett Memorial Trophy (Top AHL Rookie).

CHRIS LANGEVIN

Left Wing . . . 6' . . . 190 lbs. . . . Born, Montreal, Que., November 27, 1959 . . . Shoots left . . . (October, 1985)—Needed 60 stitches to close a cut around his left eye when struck by a puck . . . (November 22, 1985)—Injured knee vs. Quebec.

Year	Team	League	Games	G.	A.	Pts.	Pen.
1977-78—Chicoutimi Sagueneens		QMJHL	67	8	20	28	183
1978-79—Chicoutimi Sagueneens		QMJHL	65	24	23	47	182
1979-80—Chicoutimi Sagueneens		QMJHL	46	22	30	52	97
1980-81—Saginaw Gears		IHL	75	35	48	83	179
1981-82—Rochester Americans (c)		AHL	33	3	5	8	150
1982-83—Rochester Americans		AHL	71	18	25	43	255
1983-84—Rochester Americans		AHL	41	11	14	25	133
1983-84—Buffalo Sabres		NHL	6	1	0	1	2
1984-85—Rochester Americans		AHL	63	19	21	40	212
1985-86—Buffalo Sabres		NHL	16	2	1	3	20
NHL TOTALS			22	3	1	4	22

(c)—September, 1981—Signed by Rochester Americans as a free agent.

DAVID LANGEVIN

Defense . . . 6'2" . . . 215 lbs. . . . Born, St. Paul, Minn., May 15, 1954 . . . Shoots left . . . (October 27, 1981)—Sprained right knee vs. Edmonton . . . (December, 1981)—Bruised tailbone . . . (November, 1982)—Recurring groin problems . . . (April, 1983)—Arthroscopic surgery to right knee following injury in first game of playoff series vs. New York Rangers . . . (January, 1984)—Cartilage injury to right knee requiring arthroscopic surgery, missed nine games . . . (April, 1984)—Separated shoulder in playoff series with Washington . . . (May, 1984)—Aggravated shoulder injury during playoff series with Montreal . . . (November, 1984)—Broken thumb.

Year	Team	League	Games	G.	A.	Pts.	Pen.
1972-73—University of Minn.-Duluth		WCHA	36	6	11	17	74
1973-74—Univ. of Minn.-Duluth (c-d)		WCHA	37	2	11	13	56
1974-75—University of Minn.-Duluth		WCHA	35	8	24	32	91
1975-76—University of Minn.-Duluth (b)		WCHA	34	19	26	45	82
1976-77—Edmonton Oilers		WHA	77	7	16	23	94
1977-78—Edmonton Oilers		WHA	62	6	22	28	90
1978-79—Edmonton Oilers (b-e)		WHA	77	6	21	27	76
1979-80—New York Islanders		NHL	76	3	13	16	109
1980-81—New York Islanders		NHL	75	1	16	17	122
1981-82—New York Islanders		NHL	73	1	20	21	82
1982-83—New York Islanders		NHL	73	4	17	21	64
1983-84—New York Islanders		NHL	69	3	16	19	53
1984-85—New York Islanders		NHL	56	0	13	13	35
1985-86—Minnesota North Stars (f)		NHL	80	0	8	8	58
WHA TOTALS			216	19	59	78	260
NHL TOTALS			502	12	103	115	523

(c)—Drafted from University of Minnesota-Duluth by New York Islanders in seventh round of 1974 amateur draft.
(d)—May, 1974—Selected by Edmonton Oilers in World Hockey Association amateur player draft.
(e)—June, 1979—Selected by New York Islanders in NHL reclaim draft.
(f)—October, 1985—Acquired by Minnesota North Stars in 1985 NHL waiver draft.

ROD CORRY LANGWAY

Defense . . . 6'3" . . . 215 lbs. . . . Born, Maag, Taiwan, May 3, 1957 . . . Shoots left . . . Attended University of New Hampshire and was member of football and hockey teams . . . Brother of Kim Langway . . . (January 5, 1982)—Bruised left foot in game vs. Boston . . . (February 9, 1982)—Injured left knee in NHL All-Star game. Examination in March discovered dried blood in the knee which had weakened the muscle in his left leg . . . (October 23, 1985)—Bruised right knee vs. Calgary and missed eight games.

Year	Team	League	Games	G.	A.	Pts.	Pen.
1975-76—University of New Hampshire		ECAC	..	..	..	..	....
1976-77—Univ. of New Hampshire (c-d)		ECAC	34	10	43	53	52
1977-78—Hampton Gulls		AHL	30	6	16	22	50
1977-78—Birmingham Bulls		WHA	52	3	18	21	52
1978-79—Montreal Canadiens (e)		NHL	45	3	4	7	30
1978-79—Nova Scotia Voyageurs		AHL	18	6	13	19	29
1979-80—Montreal Canadiens		NHL	77	7	29	36	81
1980-81—Montreal Canadiens		NHL	80	11	34	45	120
1981-82—Montreal Canadiens (f)		NHL	66	5	34	39	116
1982-83—Washington Capitals (a-g)		NHL	80	3	29	32	75
1983-84—Washington Capitals (a-g)		NHL	80	9	24	33	61

Year	Team	League	Games	G.	A.	Pts.	Pen.
1984-85—Washington Capitals (b)		NHL	79	4	22	26	54
1985-86—Washington Capitals		NHL	71	1	17	18	61
WHA TOTALS			52	3	18	21	53
NHL TOTALS			578	43	193	236	598

(c)—Drafted from University of New Hampshire by Montreal Canadiens in second round of 1977 amateur draft.

(d)—May, 1977—Selected by Birmingham Bulls in World Hockey Association amateur players' draft.

(e)—October, 1978—Signed by Montreal Canadiens as free agent.

(f)—September, 1982—Traded by Montreal Canadiens with Brian Engblom, Doug Jarvis and Craig Laughlin to Washington Capitals for Ryan Walter and Rick Green.

(g)—Won James Norris Memorial Trophy (Top NHL Defenseman).

MARC LANIEL

Defense . . . 6'1" . . . 185 lbs. . . . Born, Oshawa, Ont., January 16, 1968 . . . Shoots left.

Year	Team	League	Games	G.	A.	Pts.	Pen.
1984-85—Toronto Red Wings		MTHL	37	15	28	43	68
1985-86—Oshawa Generals (c)		OHL	66	9	25	34	27

(c)—June, 1986—Drafted as underage junior by New Jersey Devils in 1986 NHL entry draft. Fourth Devils pick, 62nd overall, third round.

JEAN-MARC LANTHIER

Right Wing . . . 6'2" . . . 198 lbs. . . . Born, Montreal, Que., March 27, 1963 . . . Shoots right.

Year	Team	League	Games	G.	A.	Pts.	Pen.
1979-80—Quebec Remparts		QMJHL	63	14	32	46	4
1980-81—Quebec Remparts (c)		QMJHL	37	13	32	45	18
1980-81—Sorel Black Hawks (d)		QMJHL	35	6	33	39	29
1981-82—Laval Voisins (e)		QMJHL	60	44	34	78	48
1982-83—Laval Voisins		QHL	69	39	71	110	54
1983-84—Fredericton Express		AHL	60	25	17	42	29
1983-84—Vancouver Canucks		NHL	11	2	1	3	2
1984-85—Fredericton Express		AHL	50	21	21	42	13
1984-85—Vancouver Canucks		NHL	27	6	4	10	13
1985-86—Fredericton Express		AHL	7	5	5	10	2
1985-86—Vancouver Canucks		NHL	62	7	10	17	12
NHL TOTALS			100	15	15	30	27

(c)—December, 1980—Traded by Quebec Remparts to Sorel Black Hawks for Andre Cote.

(d)—June, 1981—Drafted as underage junior by Vancouver Canucks in 1981 NHL entry draft. Second Canucks pick, 52nd overall, third round.

(e)—August, 1981—Acquired by Laval Voisins in QMJHL dispersal draft of players from defunct Sorel Black Hawks.

RICK ROMAN LANZ

Defense . . . 6'1" . . . 195 lbs. . . . Born, Karlouyvary, Czechoslovakia, September 16, 1961 . . . Shoots right . . . (January, 1982)—Surgery to repair torn knee ligaments . . . (December, 1984)—Dislocated disk in neck and missed 23 games.

Year	Team	League	Games	G.	A.	Pts.	Pen.
1977-78—Oshawa Generals		OMJHL	65	1	41	42	51
1978-79—Oshawa Generals		OMJHL	65	12	47	59	88
1979-80—Oshawa Generals (b-c)		OMJHL	52	18	38	56	51
1980-81—Vancouver Canucks		NHL	76	7	22	29	40
1981-82—Vancouver Canucks		NHL	39	3	11	14	48
1982-83—Vancouver Canucks		NHL	74	10	38	48	46
1983-84—Vancouver Canucks		NHL	79	18	39	57	45
1984-85—Vancouver Canucks		NHL	57	2	17	19	69
1985-86—Vancouver Canucks		NHL	75	15	38	53	73
NHL TOTALS			400	55	165	220	321

(c)—June, 1980—Drafted as underage junior in 1980 NHL entry draft by Vancouver Canucks. First Canucks pick, seventh overall, first round.

RICHARD PAUL (RICK) LaPOINTE

Defense . . . 6'2" . . . 200 lbs. . . . Born, Victoria, B.C., August 2, 1955 . . . Shoots left . . . Brother-in-law of Brad Maxwell.

Year	Team	League	Games	G.	A.	Pts.	Pen.
1971-72—Nanaimo Clippers		Jr."A" BCHL	..	..	..	..	....
1971-72—Victoria Cougars		WCHL	4	0	0	0	0

Year	Team	League	Games	G.	A.	Pts.	Pen.
1972-73	Victoria Cougars	WCHL	39	3	12	15	31
1973-74	Victoria Cougars	WCHL	66	8	18	26	207
1974-75	Victoria Cougars (a-c-d)	WCHL	67	19	51	70	177
1975-76	Detroit Red Wings	NHL	80	10	23	33	95
1976-77	Kansas City Blues	CHL	6	0	0	0	6
1976-77	Detroit Red Wings (e)	NHL	49	2	11	13	80
1976-77	Philadelphia Flyers	NHL	22	1	8	9	39
1977-78	Philadelphia Flyers	NHL	47	4	16	20	91
1978-79	Philadelphia Flyers (f)	NHL	77	3	18	21	53
1979-80	St. Louis Blues	NHL	80	6	19	25	87
1980-81	St. Louis Blues	NHL	80	8	25	33	124
1981-82	St. Louis Blues (g)	NHL	71	2	20	22	127
1982-83	Fredericton Express	AHL	31	4	14	18	50
1982-83	Quebec Nordiques	NHL	43	2	9	11	59
1983-84	Fredericton Express	AHL	54	8	22	30	79
1983-84	Quebec Nordiques	NHL	22	2	10	12	12
1984-85	Los Angeles Kings (h)	NHL	73	4	13	17	46
1985-86	Los Angeles Kings	NHL	20	0	4	4	18
	NHL TOTALS		664	44	176	220	831

(c)—Won WCHL Top Defenseman Award.
(d)—Drafted from Victoria Cougars by Detroit Red Wings in first round of 1975 amateur draft.
(e)—February, 1977—Traded to Philadelphia Flyers by Detroit Red Wings with Mike Korney for Terry Murray, Dave Kelly, Bob Ritchie and Steve Coates.
(f)—June, 1979—Traded with Blake Dunlop by Philadelphia Flyers to St. Louis Blues for Phil Myre.
(g)—August, 1982—Traded by St. Louis Blues to Quebec Nordiques for Pat Hickey.
(h)—September, 1984—Signed by Los Angeles Kings as a free agent.

GARRY JOSEPH LARIVIERE

Defense . . . 6' . . . 190 lbs. . . . Born, St. Catharines, Ont., December 6, 1954 . . . Shoots right . . . (December, 1981)—Knee injury . . . (October, 1984)—Named player/assistant coach of St. Catharines Saints.

Year	Team	League	Games	G.	A.	Pts.	Pen.
1972-73	St. Cath. Black Hawks	Jr."A" OHA	55	5	32	37	140
1973-74	St. C. Black Hawks (c-d-e)	Jr."A" OHA	60	3	35	38	153
1974-75	Tulsa Oilers (a)	CHL	76	15	38	53	168
1974-75	Phoenix Roadrunners (f)	WHA	4	0	1	1	28
1975-76	Phoenix Roadrunners	WHA	79	7	17	24	100
1976-77	Phoenix Roadrunners (g)	WHA	61	7	23	30	48
1976-77	Quebec Nordiques	WHA	15	0	3	3	8
1977-78	Quebec Nordiques	WHA	80	7	49	56	78
1978-79	Quebec Nordiques (h)	WHA	80	5	33	38	54
1979-80	Quebec Nordiques	NHL	75	2	19	21	56
1980-81	Quebec Nordiques (i)	NHL	52	3	13	16	50
1980-81	Edmonton Oilers	NHL	13	0	2	2	6
1981-82	Edmonton Oilers	NHL	62	1	21	22	41
1982-83	Edmonton Oilers	NHL	17	0	2	2	14
1983-84	St. Catharines Saints (a-j-k-l)	AHL	65	7	35	42	41
1984-85	St. Catharines Saints (m)	AHL	72	4	32	36	47
1985-86	St. Catharines Saints	AHL	52	0	9	9	10
	WHA TOTALS		319	26	126	152	316
	NHL TOTALS		219	6	57	63	167

(c)—Drafted from St. Catharines Black Hawks by Buffalo Sabres in fifth round of 1974 amateur draft.
(d)—May, 1974—Selected by Chicago Cougars in World Hockey Association amateur player draft.
(e)—September, 1974—Traded to Phoenix Roadrunners by Chicago Cougars for future considerations.
(f)—June, 1975—NHL rights transferred by Buffalo Sabres to New York Islanders to complete deal for Gerry Desjardins.
(g)—March, 1977—Sold to Quebec Nordiques by Phoenix Roadrunners.
(h)—June, 1979—Selected by New York Islanders in NHL reclaim draft, but remained with the Quebec Nordiques as a priority selection for the expansion draft.
(i)—March, 1981—Traded by Quebec Nordiques to Vancouver Canucks for Mario Marois. Vancouver then sent Lariviere and NHL rights to Ken Berry to Edmonton Oilers for Blair MacDonald and NHL rights to Lars Gunnar Petersson to complete a three-club deal.
(j)—November, 1983—Loaned by Edmonton Oilers to St. Catharines, after sitting out first month in contract dispute with Oilers.
(k)—Shared Les Cunningham Plaque (AHL-MVP) with Mal Davis (Rochester).
(l)—Won Eddie Shore Plaque (Top AHL Defenseman).
(m)—August, 1984—Traded with Ken Berry by Edmonton Oilers to New Jersey Devils for future considerations.

JEFF LARMER

Left Wing . . . 5'10" . . . 172 lbs. . . . Born, Peterborough, Ont., October 10, 1962 . . . Shoots left . . . Brother of Steve Larmer . . . Played in one game as a goalie in 1980-81 with Kitchener (No goals allowed in nine minutes) . . . (November, 1981)—Shoulder separation . . . Also plays Right Wing.

Year	Team	League	Games	G.	A.	Pts.	Pen.
1979-80—Kitchener Rangers		OMJHL	61	19	27	46	80
1980-81—Kitchener Rangers (c)		OHL	68	54	54	108	103
1981-82—Kitchener Canadians (b-d)		OHL	49	51	44	95	95
1981-82—Colorado Rockies		NHL	8	1	1	2	8
1982-83—Wichita Wind		CHL	10	6	5	11	2
1982-83—New Jersey Devils		NHL	65	21	24	45	21
1983-84—New Jersey Devils (e)		NHL	40	6	13	19	8
1983-84—Chicago Black Hawks		NHL	36	9	13	22	20
1984-85—Milwaukee Admirals		IHL	61	24	37	61	30
1984-85—Chicago Black Hawks		NHL	7	0	0	0	0
1985-86—Chicago Black Hawks		NHL	2	0	0	0	0
1985-86—Nova Scotia Oilers		AHL	77	20	44	64	46
NHL TOTALS			158	37	51	88	57

(c)—June, 1981—Drafted as underage junior by Colorado Rockies in 1981 NHL entry draft. Seventh Rockies pick, 129th overall, seventh round.

(d)—Led J. Ross Robertson Cup Playoffs (OHL) with 21 goals and 35 points.

(e)—January, 1984—Traded by New Jersey Devils to Chicago Black Hawks for Tim Higgins.

STEVE DONALD LARMER

Right Wing . . . 5'10" . . . 185 lbs. . . . Born, Peterborough, Ont., June 16, 1961 . . . Shoots left . . . Brother of Jeff Larmer . . . (1982-83)—Set Chicago club records for most goals by a right wing (43), most goals by a Chicago rookie (43) and most points by a Chicago rookie (90). He also tied club record for most assists by a Chicago rookie (47) set by Denis Savard in 1980-81.

Year	Team	League	Games	G.	A.	Pts.	Pen.
1977-78—Peterborough Petes		OMJHL	62	24	17	41	51
1978-79—Niagara Falls Flyers		OMJHL	66	37	47	84	108
1979-80—Niagara Falls Flyers (c)		OMJHL	67	45	69	114	71
1980-81—Niagara Falls Flyers (b)		OHL	61	55	78	133	73
1980-81—Chicago Black Hawks		NHL	4	0	1	1	0
1981-82—New Brunswick Hawks (b)		AHL	74	38	44	82	46
1981-82—Chicago Black Hawks		NHL	3	0	0	0	0
1982-83—Chicago Black Hawks (d-e)		NHL	80	43	47	90	28
1983-84—Chicago Black Hawks		NHL	80	35	40	75	34
1984-85—Chicago Black Hawks		NHL	80	46	40	86	16
1985-86—Chicago Black Hawks		NHL	80	31	45	76	47
NHL TOTALS			327	155	173	328	125

(c)—June, 1980—Drafted as underage junior in 1980 NHL entry draft by Chicago Black Hawks. Eleventh Black Hawks pick, 120th overall, sixth round.

(d)—Selected as NHL Rookie of the Year in vote of players conducted by The Sporting News.

(e)—Won Calder Memorial Trophy (Top NHL Rookie).

DENIS LAROCQUE

Defense . . . 6'1" . . . 200 lbs. . . . Born, Hawkesbury, Ont., October 5, 1967 . . . Shoots left.

Year	Team	League	Games	G.	A.	Pts.	Pen.
1982-83—Hawkesbury Hawks		CJHL	31	0	13	13	83
1983-84—Guelph Platers		OHL	65	1	5	6	74
1984-85—Guelph Platers		OHL	62	1	15	16	67
1985-86—Guelph Platers (c)		OHL	66	2	16	18	144

(c)—June, 1986—Drafted by Los Angeles Kings in 1986 NHL entry draft. Second Kings pick, 44th overall, third round.

GUY LAROSE

Center . . . 5'10" . . . 175 lbs. . . . Born, Hull, Que., July 31, 1967 . . . Shoots left . . . Son of Claude Larose (NHL 1960s and 70s, and currently assistant coach of Hartford Whalers) . . . (February 22, 1985)—Fractured third left metacarpal.

Year	Team	League	Games	G.	A.	Pts.	Pen.
1983-84—Ottawa Senators		COJL	54	37	66	103	66
1984-85—Guelph Platers (c)		OHL	58	30	30	60	639
1985-86—Guelph Platers		OHL	37	12	36	48	55
1985-86—Ottawa 67's		OHL	28	19	25	44	63

(c)—June, 1985—Drafted as underage junior by Buffalo Sabres in 1985 NHL entry draft. Eleventh Sabres pick, 224th overall, 11th round.

PIERRE LAROUCHE

Center . . . 5'11" . . . 175 lbs. . . . Born, Taschereau, Que., November 16, 1955 . . . Shoots right . . . Missed part of 1976-77 season with broken left thumb . . . Missed part of 1978-79 season with injury to left knee . . . Injured shoulder (March, 1980) . . . (November 1, 1980)—Broken left hand . . . (November 2, 1981)—Severe cut over eye at Quebec . . . (January 20, 1983)—Injured back during game at Los Angeles and missed remainder of season with recurring back spasms . . . Only player to have 50-goal seasons with two different NHL clubs . . . (March, 1985)—Injured wrist and bruised tailbone . . . (November, 1985)—Cut knee in AHL game . . . (March 11, 1986)—Broke right thumb at New Jersey.

Year	Team	League	Games	G.	A.	Pts.	Pen.
1972-73	Sorel Black Hawks	QJHL	63	52	62	114	44
1973-74	Sorel Black Hawks (b-c)	QJHL	67	94	*157	*251	53
1974-75	Pittsburgh Penguins (d)	NHL	79	31	37	68	52
1975-76	Pittsburgh Penguins	NHL	76	53	58	111	33
1976-77	Pittsburgh Penguins	NHL	65	29	34	63	14
1977-78	Pittsburgh Penguins (e)	NHL	20	6	5	11	0
1977-78	Montreal Canadiens	NHL	44	17	32	49	11
1978-79	Montreal Canadiens	NHL	36	9	13	22	4
1979-80	Montreal Canadiens	NHL	73	50	41	91	16
1980-81	Montreal Canadiens	NHL	61	25	28	53	28
1981-82	Montreal Canadiens (f)	NHL	22	9	12	21	0
1981-82	Hartford Whalers	NHL	45	25	25	50	12
1982-83	Hartford Whalers	NHL	38	18	22	40	8
1983-84	New York Rangers (g)	NHL	77	48	33	81	22
1984-85	New York Rangers	NHL	65	24	36	60	8
1985-86	Hershey Bears (h)	AHL	32	22	17	39	16
1985-86	New York Rangers	NHL	28	20	7	27	4
	NHL TOTALS		729	364	383	747	212

    (c)—Drafted from Sorel Black Hawks by Pittsburgh Penguins in first round of 1974 amateur draft.
    (d)—Named Prince of Wales Conference Rookie of the Year in poll of players by THE SPORTING NEWS.
    (e)—November, 1977—Traded to Montreal Canadiens by Pittsburgh Penguins for Peter Lee and Peter Mahovlich.
    (f)—December, 1981—Traded with first-round 1984 and third-round 1985 entry draft picks by Montreal Canadiens to Hartford Whalers for first-round 1984 and third-round 1985 entry draft picks.
    (g)—September, 1983—Signed by New York Rangers as a free agent.
    (h)—October, 1985—Assigned with Andre Dore to Hershey Bears by New York Rangers as compensation to Philadelphia Flyers for the Rangers' signing of coach Ted Sator.

REED DAVID LARSON

Defense . . . 6' . . . 195 lbs. . . . Born, Minneapolis, Minn., July 30, 1956 . . . Shoots right . . . (July, 1981)—Surgery to remove bone chips from right elbow . . . Holds NHL record for defensemen, scoring 20 goals in five straight seasons . . . Holds Detroit club record for most goals (27 in 1980-81), most assists (52 in 1982-83) and points (74 in 1982-83) by a defenseman in one season . . . (1983-84)—Passed Tommy Williams to become all-time U.S.-born NHL career leader in points (Williams had 430) and assists (Williams had 269) . . . (1984-85)—Passed Tommy Williams to become highest goal scoring U.S. born player ever (Williams had 161 goals) . . . Holds Detroit Red Wings career record for goals, assists and points by a defenseman.

Year	Team	League	Games	G.	A.	Pts.	Pen.
1974-75	University of Minnesota	WCHA	41	11	17	28	37
1975-76	University of Minnesota (a-c)	WCHA	42	13	29	42	94
1976-77	University of Minnesota	WCHA	21	10	15	25	30
1976-77	Detroit Red Wings	NHL	14	0	1	1	23
1977-78	Detroit Red Wings	NHL	75	19	41	60	95
1978-79	Detroit Red Wings	NHL	79	18	49	67	169
1979-80	Detroit Red Wings	NHL	80	22	44	66	101
1980-81	Detroit Red Wings	NHL	78	27	31	58	153
1981-82	Detroit Red Wings	NHL	80	21	39	60	112
1982-83	Detroit Red Wings	NHL	80	22	52	74	104
1983-84	Detroit Red Wings	NHL	78	23	39	62	122
1984-85	Detroit Red Wings	NHL	77	17	45	62	139
1985-86	Detroit Red Wings (d)	NHL	67	19	41	60	109
1985-86	Boston Bruins	NHL	13	3	4	7	8
	NHL TOTALS		721	191	386	577	1135

    (c)—Drafted from University of Minnesota by Detroit Red Wings in second round of 1976 amateur draft.
    (d)—March, 1986—Traded by Detroit Red Wings to Boston Bruins for Mike O'Connell.

MARTIN LATREILLE

Defense . . . 6'1" . . . 200 lbs. . . . Born, Montreal, Que., September 14, 1968 . . . Shoots left . . . (November, 1985)—Injured knee ligaments.

Year	Team	League	Games	G.	A.	Pts.	Pen.
1984-85—Montreal Concordia Midget		Que.	38	2	11	13	81
1985-86—Laval Titans (c)		QHL	65	1	11	12	48

(c)—June, 1986—Drafted as underage junior by Quebec Nordiques in 1986 NHL entry draft. Thirteenth Nordiques pick, 228th overall, 11th round.

DAVE LATTA

Left Wing ... 6' ... 185 lbs. ... Born, Thunder Bay, Ont., January 3, 1967 ... Shoots left ... Brother of Ken Latta ... (December, 1984)—Shoulder injury.

Year	Team	League	Games	G.	A.	Pts.	Pen.
1982-83—Orillia Travelways		OJHL	43	16	25	41	26
1983-84—Kitchener Rangers		OHL	66	17	26	43	54
1984-85—Kitchener Rangers (c)		OHL	52	38	27	65	26
1985-86—Kitchener Rangers		OHL	55	36	34	70	60
1985-86—Fredericton Express		AHL	3	1	0	1	0
1985-86—Quebec Nordiques		NHL	1	0	0	0	0
NHL TOTALS			1	0	0	0	0

(c)—June, 1985—Drafted as underage junior by Quebec Nordiques in 1985 NHL entry draft. First Nordiques pick, 15th overall, first round.

MICHAEL ARTHUR LAUEN

Right Wing ... 6'1" ... 185 lbs. ... Born, Marinette, Wis., February 9, 1961 ... Shoots right ... (September, 1985)—Failed pre-camp physical at Winnipeg due to lingering nerve problem in lower back.

Year	Team	League	Games	G.	A.	Pts.	Pen.
1979-80—Michigan Tech (c)		WCHA	28	22	18	40	40
1980-81—Michigan Tech		WCHA	44	24	20	44	14
1981-82—Michigan Tech		CCHA	30	13	15	28	28
1982-83—Michigan Tech		WCHA	38	12	17	29	18
1982-83—Sherbrooke Jets		AHL	5	0	3	3	0
1983-84—Sherbrooke Jets		AHL	61	23	29	52	13
1983-84—Winnipeg Jets		NHL	3	0	1	1	0
1984-85—Sherbrooke Canadiens		AHL	25	6	10	16	2
1985-86—Toledo Goaldiggers		IHL	27	4	10	14	16
NHL TOTALS			3	0	1	1	0

(c)—June, 1980—Drafted by Winnipeg Jets in 1980 NHL entry draft. Eighth Jets pick, 135th overall, seventh round.

BRAD LAUER

Right Wing ... 6' ... 195 lbs. ... Born, Humbolt, Sask., October 27, 1966 ... Shoots left.

Year	Team	League	Games	G.	A.	Pts.	Pen.
1983-84—Regina Pats		WHL	60	5	7	12	51
1984-85—Regina Pats (c)		WHL	72	33	46	79	57
1985-86—Regina Pats		WHL	57	36	38	74	69

(c)—June, 1985—Drafted as underage junior by New York Islanders in 1985 NHL entry draft. Third Islanders pick, 34th overall, second round.

CRAIG LAUGHLIN

Right Wing ... 5'11" ... 198 lbs. ... Born, Toronto, Ont., September 19, 1957 ... Shoots right ... (February 22, 1986)—Sprained ankle at Philadelphia.

Year	Team	League	Games	G.	A.	Pts.	Pen.
1976-77—Clarkson College (c)		ECAC	33	12	13	25	44
1977-78—Clarkson College		ECAC	30	17	31	48	56
1978-79—Clarkson College		ECAC	30	18	29	47	22
1979-80—Clarkson College		ECAC	34	18	30	48	38
1979-80—Nova Scotia Voyageurs		AHL	2	0	0	0	2
1980-81—Nova Scotia Voyageurs		AHL	46	32	29	61	15
1981-82—Nova Scotia Voyageurs		AHL	26	14	15	29	16
1981-82—Montreal Canadiens (d)		NHL	36	12	11	23	33
1982-83—Washington Capitals		NHL	75	17	27	44	41
1983-84—Washington Capitals		NHL	80	20	32	52	69
1984-85—Washington Capitals		NHL	78	16	34	50	38
1985-86—Washington Capitals		NHL	75	30	45	75	43
NHL TOTALS			344	95	149	244	224

(c)—June, 1977—Drafted by Montreal Canadiens in 1977 NHL amateur draft. Seventeenth Canadiens pick, 162nd overall, 10th round.

(d)—September, 1982—Traded by Montreal Canadiens with Rod Langway, Brian Engblom and Doug Jarvis to Washington Capitals for Ryan Walter and Rick Green.

KEVIN LaVALLEE

Left Wing . . . 5'8" . . . 180 lbs. . . . Born, Sudbury, Ont., September 16, 1961 . . . Shoots left . . . (December, 1982)—Separated shoulder . . . (January 25, 1985)—Surgery to remove torn medial collateral ligament in left knee. Out for the season.

Year	Team	League	Games	G.	A.	Pts.	Pen.
1978-79	Brantford Alexanders	OMJHL	66	27	23	50	30
1979-80	Brantford Alexanders (c)	OMJHL	65	65	70	135	50
1980-81	Calgary Flames	NHL	77	15	20	35	16
1981-82	Calgary Flames	NHL	75	32	29	61	30
1982-83	Colorado Flames	CHL	5	5	4	9	0
1982-83	Calgary Flames (d)	NHL	60	19	16	35	17
1983-84	New Haven Nighthawks	AHL	47	29	23	52	25
1983-84	Los Angeles Kings (e)	NHL	19	3	3	6	2
1984-85	St. Louis Blues	NHL	38	15	17	32	8
1985-86	St. Louis Blues (f)	NHL	64	18	20	38	8
	NHL TOTALS		333	102	105	207	81

(c)—June, 1980—Drafted as underage junior by Calgary Flames in 1980 NHL entry draft. Third Flames pick, 32nd overall, second round.

(d)—June, 1983—Traded by Calgary Flames with Carl Mokosak to Los Angeles Kings for Steve Bozek.

(e)—August, 1984—Released by Los Angeles Kings and signed by St. Louis Blues as a free agent.

(f)—August, 1986—Became free agent when St. Louis Blues bought out final year of contract.

MARK J. LaVARRE

Right Wing . . . 5'11" . . . 170 lbs. . . . Born, Evanston, Ill., February 21, 1965 . . . Shoots right . . . Also plays defense . . . (February, 1981)—Fractured two vertebras in back.

Year	Team	League	Games	G.	A.	Pts.	Pen.
1982-83	Stratford Cullitons (c)	MWJBHL	40	33	62	95	88
1983-84	North Bay Centennials	OHL	41	19	22	41	15
1984-85	Windsor Compuware Spitfires (d)	OHL	46	15	30	45	30
1985-86	Chicago Black Hawks	NHL	2	0	0	0	0
1985-86	Nova Scotia Oilers	AHL	62	15	19	34	32
	NHL TOTALS		2	0	0	0	0

(c)—June, 1983—Drafted as underage junior by Chicago Black Hawks in 1983 NHL entry draft. Seventh Black Hawks pick, 119th overall, sixth round.

(d)—October, 1984—Traded with Peter McGrath by North Bay Centennials to Windsor Compuware Spitfires for Jamie Jefferson, J.D. Urbanic and OHL rights to Rick Flamminio.

PAUL LAWLESS

Left Wing . . . 6' . . . 190 lbs. . . . Born, Scarborough, Ont., July 2, 1964 . . . Shoots left.

Year	Team	League	Games	G.	A.	Pts.	Pen.
1980-81	Wexford Midgets	MTHL	40	38	40	78	....
1981-82	Windsor Spitfires (c)	OHL	68	24	25	49	47
1982-83	Windsor Spitfires	OHL	33	15	20	35	25
1982-83	Hartford Whalers	NHL	47	6	9	15	4
1983-84	Hartford Whalers	NHL	6	0	3	3	0
1983-84	Windsor Spitfires (b)	OHL	55	31	49	80	26
1984-85	Binghamton Whalers	AHL	8	1	1	2	0
1984-85	Salt Lake Golden Eagles	IHL	72	49	48	97	14
1985-86	Hartford Whalers	NHL	64	17	21	38	20
	NHL TOTALS		117	23	33	56	24

(c)—June, 1982—Selected by Hartford Whalers in 1982 NHL entry draft. First Whalers pick, 14th overall, first round.

BRETT LAWRENCE

Right Wing . . . 6'2" . . . 180 lbs. . . . Born, Rochester, N.Y., November 4, 1968 . . . Shoots right . . . Brother-in-law of Clint Fehr (former AHL player with Rochester).

Year	Team	League	Games	G.	A.	Pts.	Pen.
1984-85	Rochester Jr. Americans	NEJBHL	57	49	43	92	62
1985-86	Rochester Jr. Americans (c)	NEJBHL	38	45	40	85	60

(c)—June, 1986—Drafted by Philadelphia Flyers in 1986 NHL entry draft. Tenth Flyers pick, 230th overall, 11th round.

BRIAN LAWTON

Center . . . 6' . . . 180 lbs. . . . Born, New Brunswick, N.J., June 29, 1965 . . . Shoots left . . . First American-born player to be a first overall draft choice in the NHL . . . (November, 1983)—Separated shoulder . . . (October, 1984)—Injured shoulder during training camp.

Year	Team	League	Games	G.	A.	Pts.	Pen.
1981-82—Mount St. Charles H.S.		R.I. H.S.	26	45	43	88	..
1982-83—Mount St. Charles H.S. (c)		R.I. H.S.	23	40	43	83	..
1982-83—U.S. National Team		Int'l	7	3	2	5	6
1983-84—Minnesota North Stars		NHL	58	10	21	31	33
1984-85—Springfield Indians		AHL	42	14	28	42	37
1984-85—Minnesota North Stars		NHL	40	5	6	11	24
1985-86—Minnesota North Stars		NHL	65	18	17	35	36
NHL TOTALS			163	33	44	77	93

(c)—June, 1983—Drafted by Minnesota North Stars in 1983 NHL entry draft. First North Stars pick, first overall, first round.

DEREK LAXDAL

Right Wing . . . 6'1" . . . 180 lbs. . . . Born, St. Boniface, Man., February 21, 1966 . . . Shoots right . . . (January, 1985)—Broken hand.

Year	Team	League	Games	G.	A.	Pts.	Pen.
1982-83—Portland Winter Hawks		WHL	39	4	9	13	27
1983-84—Brandon Wheat Kings (c)		WHL	70	23	20	43	86
1984-85—Brandon Wheat Kings		WHL	69	61	41	102	72
1984-85—St. Catharines Saints		AHL	5	3	2	5	2
1984-85—Toronto Maple Leafs		NHL	3	0	0	0	6
1985-86—Brandon Wheat Kings		WHL	42	34	35	69	62
1985-86—New Westminister Bruins		WHL	18	9	6	15	14
1985-86—St. Catharines Saints		AHL	7	0	1	1	15
NHL TOTALS			3	0	0	0	6

(c)—June, 1984—Drafted as an underage junior by Toronto Maple Leafs in 1984 NHL entry draft. Seventh Maple Leafs pick, 151st overall, eighth round.

STEPHEN LEACH

Right Wing . . . 5'11" . . . 180 lbs. . . . Born, Cambridge, Mass., January 16, 1966 . . . Shoots right.

Year	Team	League	Games	G.	A.	Pts.	Pen.
1983-84—Matignon H.S. (c)		Mass. H.S.	21	27	22	49	49
1984-85—Univ. of New Hampshire		H. East	41	12	25	37	53
1985-86—Univ. of New Hampshire		H. East	25	22	6	28	30
1985-86—Washington Capitals		NHL	11	1	1	2	2
NHL TOTALS			11	1	1	2	2

(c)—June, 1984—Drafted by Washington Capitals in 1984 NHL entry draft. Second Capitals pick, 34th overall, second round.

JAMES T. LEAVINS

Defense . . . 5'11" . . . 185 lbs. . . . Born, Dinsmore, Sask., July 28, 1960 . . . Shoots left.

Year	Team	League	Games	G.	A.	Pts.	Pen.
1980-81—Univ. of Denver		WCHA	40	8	18	26	18
1981-82—Univ. of Denver		WCHA	41	8	34	42	56
1982-83—Univ. of Denver		WCHA	33	16	24	40	20
1983-84—Univ. of Denver		WCHA	39	13	24	37	38
1983-84—Tulsa Oilers		CHL	1	0	0	0	0
1984-85—Fort Wayne Komets		IHL	76	5	50	55	57
1985-86—Adirondack Red Wings		AHL	36	4	21	25	19
1985-86—Detroit Red Wings (c-d)		NHL	37	2	11	13	26
NHL TOTALS			37	2	11	11	26

(c)—November, 1985—Signed by Detroit Red Wings as a free agent.

(d)—August, 1986—Traded by Detroit Red Wings with Kelly Kisio and Lane Lambert to New York Rangers for Glen Hanlon and Rangers' third-round draft choices in 1987 and '88.

JOHN LeBLANC

Left Wing . . . 6'l" . . . 190 lbs. . . . Born, Campellton, N.B., January 21, 1964 . . . Shoots left.

Year	Team	League	Games	G.	A.	Pts.	Pen.
1985-86—U. of New Brunswick (c-d)		CIAU	24	38	26	64	32

(c)—Named winner of the Senator Joseph A. Sullivan Trophy to the top Canadian college player.

(d)—April, 1986—Signed by Vancouver Canucks as a free agent.

GRANT LEDYARD

Defense . . . 6'2" . . . 190 lbs. . . . Born, Winnipeg, Man., November 19, 1961 . . . Shoots left . . . (October, 1984)—Hip injury.

Year	Team	League	Games	G.	A.	Pts.	Pen.
1979-80—Fort Garry Blues		MJHL	49	13	24	37	90
1980-81—Saskatoon Blades		WHL	71	9	28	37	148
1981-82—Fort Garry Blues (a-c)		MJHL	63	25	45	70	150
1982-83—Tulsa Oilers (d)		CHL	80	13	29	42	115
1983-84—Tulsa Oilers (e)		CHL	58	9	17	26	71
1984-85—New Haven Nighthawks		AHL	36	6	20	26	18
1984-85—New York Rangers		NHL	42	8	12	20	53
1985-86—New York Rangers (f)		NHL	27	2	9	11	20
1985-86—Los Angeles Kings		NHL	52	7	18	25	78
NHL TOTALS			121	17	39	56	151

(c)—Named Manitoba Junior Hockey League Most Valuable Player.
(d)—July, 1982—Signed by New York Rangers as a free agent.
(e)—Won Max McNab Trophy (CHL playoff MVP).
(f)—December, 1986—Traded by New York Rangers to Los Angeles Kings for Brian MacLellan and a 4th round 1987 draft pick. The Rangers also sent a second round 1986 (Neil Wilkinson) and a fourth round 1987 draft pick to Minnesota and the North Stars sent Roland Melanson to the Kings as part of the same deal.

EDWARD LEE

Right Wing and Center . . . 6'2" . . . 184 lbs. . . . Born, Rochester, N.Y., December 17, 1961 . . . Shoots right.

Year	Team	League	Games	G.	A.	Pts.	Pen.
1980-81—Princeton University (c)		ECAC	21	6	8	14	34
1981-82—Princeton University		ECAC	26	12	21	33	46
1982-83—Princeton University		ECAC	25	14	25	39	51
1982-83—U.S. National Team		Int'l	5	5	3	8	8
1983-84—Princeton University		ECAC	11	10	10	20	22
1983-84—Fredericton Express (d)		AHL	6	0	4	4	4
1984-85—Fredericton Express		AHL	21	11	7	18	45
1984-85—Quebec Nordiques		NHL	2	0	0	0	5
1985-86—Indianapolis Checkers		IHL	2	0	0	0	0
1985-86—Fredericton Express (e)		AHL	6	3	1	4	2
1985-86—Springfield Indians		AHL	24	3	4	7	26
NHL TOTALS			2	0	0	0	5

(c)—June, 1981—Drafted by Quebec Nordiques in 1981 NHL entry draft. Fourth Nordiques pick, 95th overall, fifth round.
(d)—February, 1984—Released by Fredericton Express.
(e)—November, 1985—Suspended by Quebec Nordiques for leaving Fredericton Express. He was later traded to Minnesota North Stars for a sixth round 1986 draft pick (Scott White).

GARY LEEMAN

Defense and Right Wing . . . 6' . . . 175 lbs. . . . Born, Toronto, Ont., February 19, 1964 . . . Shoots right . . . (January, 1984)—Broken finger . . . (March, 1984)—Broken wrist . . . (March, 1985)—Shoulder separation.

Year	Team	League	Games	G.	A.	Pts.	Pen.
1980-81—Notre Dame Midgets		SCMHL	24	15	23	38	28
1981-82—Regina Pats (c)		WHL	72	19	41	60	112
1982-83—Regina Pats (a-d)		WHL	63	24	62	86	88
1983-84—Toronto Maple Leafs		NHL	52	4	8	12	31
1984-85—St. Catharines Saints		AHL	7	2	2	4	11
1984-85—Toronto Maple Leafs		NHL	53	5	26	31	72
1985-86—St. Catharines Saints		AHL	25	15	13	28	6
1985-86—Toronto Maple Leafs		NHL	53	9	23	32	20
NHL TOTALS			158	18	57	75	123

(c)—June, 1982—Drafted by Toronto Maple Leafs as underage junior in 1982 NHL entry draft. Second Maple Leafs pick, 24th overall, second round.
(d)—Won WHL Top Defenseman Trophy.

BRIAN LEETCH

Defense . . . 5'11" . . . 170 lbs. . . . Born, Corpus Christi, Tex., March 3, 1968 . . . Shoots left.

Year	Team	League	Games	G.	A.	Pts.	Pen.
1984-85—Avon Old Farms H.S.		Conn.	26	30	46	76	15
1985-86—Avon Old Farms H.S. (c)		Conn.	28	40	44	84	18

(c)—June, 1986—Drafted by New York Rangers in 1986 NHL entry draft. First Rangers pick, ninth overall, first round.

TOMMY LEHMAN

Center . . . 6'1" . . . 185 lbs. . . . Born, Solna, Sweden, February 3, 1964 . . . Shoots left.

Year	Team	League	Games	G.	A.	Pts.	Pen.
1985-86	AIK Sweden (c)	Sweden	23	6	9	15	10

(c)—June, 1982—Drafted by Boston Bruins in 1982 NHL entry draft. Eleventh Bruins pick, 228th overall, eleventh round.

KEN LEITER

Defense . . . 6'1" . . . 195 lbs. . . . Born, Detroit, Mich., April 19, 1961 . . . Shoots left.

Year	Team	League	Games	G.	A.	Pts.	Pen.
1979-80	Michigan State Univ.	CCHA	38	0	10	10	96
1980-81	Michigan State Univ. (c)	CCHA	31	2	13	15	48
1981-82	Michigan State Univ.	CCHA	31	7	13	20	50
1982-83	Michigan State Univ.	CCHA	32	3	24	27	50
1983-84	Indianapolis Checkers	CHL	68	10	26	36	46
1984-85	Springfield Indians	AHL	39	3	12	15	12
1984-85	New York Islanders	NHL	5	0	2	2	2
1985-86	New York Islanders	NHL	9	1	1	2	6
1985-86	Springfield Indians	AHL	68	7	27	34	51
	NHL TOTALS		14	1	3	4	8

(c)—June, 1980—Drafted by New York Islanders in NHL entry draft. Sixth Islanders pick, 101st overall, fifth round.

MAURICE (MOE) LEMAY

Left Wing . . . 5'11" . . . 180 lbs. . . . Born, Saskatoon, Sask., February 18, 1962 . . . Shoots left . . . (March, 1983)—Hip injury . . . (April, 1983)—Injured knee during AHL playoffs . . . (January 10, 1986)—Injured hip at Hartford . . . (February 16, 1986)—Injured knee at Toronto.

Year	Team	League	Games	G.	A.	Pts.	Pen.
1979-80	Ottawa 67's	OMJHL	62	16	23	39	20
1980-81	Ottawa 67's (c)	OHL	63	32	45	77	102
1981-82	Ottawa 67's (a-d)	OHL	62	*68	70	138	48
1981-82	Vancouver Canucks	NHL	5	1	2	3	0
1982-83	Fredericton Express	AHL	26	7	8	15	6
1982-83	Vancouver Canucks	NHL	44	11	9	20	41
1983-84	Fredericton Express	AHL	23	9	7	16	32
1983-84	Vancouver Canucks	NHL	56	12	18	30	38
1984-85	Vancouver Canucks	NHL	56	0	0	0	4
1985-86	Vancouver Canucks	NHL	48	16	15	31	92
	NHL TOTALS		209	40	44	84	175

(c)—June, 1981—Drafted as an underage junior by Vancouver Canucks in 1981 NHL entry draft. Fourth Canucks pick, 105th overall, fifth round.

(d)—Led J. Ross Robertson Cup playoffs (OHL) with 19 assists.

ALAIN LEMIEUX

Center . . . 6' . . . 185 lbs. . . . Born, Montreal, Que., May 24, 1961 . . . Shoots left . . . Brother of Mario Lemieux . . . (September, 1985)—Separated shoulder at Quebec Nordiques training camp.

Year	Team	League	Games	G.	A.	Pts.	Pen.
1978-79	Chicoutimi Sagueneens	QMJHL	31	15	27	42	5
1978-79	Montreal Juniors	QMJHL	39	7	5	12	2
1979-80	Chicoutimi Sagueneens (c)	QMJHL	72	47	95	142	36
1980-81	Chicoutimi Sagueneens (d)	QMJHL	1	0	0	0	2
1980-81	Trois-Rivieres Draveurs (b-e)	QMJHL	69	68	98	166	62
1981-82	Salt Lake Golden Eagles	CHL	74	41	42	83	61
1981-82	St. Louis Blues	NHL	3	0	1	1	0
1982-83	Salt Lake Golden Eagles	CHL	29	20	24	44	35
1982-83	St. Louis Blues	NHL	42	9	25	34	18
1983-84	St. Louis Blues	NHL	17	4	5	9	6
1983-84	Montana Magic	CHL	38	28	41	69	36
1983-84	Springfield Indians	AHL	14	11	14	25	18
1984-85	Peoria Rivermen	IHL	2	1	0	1	0
1984-85	St. Louis Blues (f)	NHL	19	4	2	6	0
1984-85	Quebec Nordiques	NHL	30	11	11	22	12
1985-86	Quebec Nordiques	NHL	7	0	0	0	0
1985-86	Fredericton Express	AHL	64	29	46	75	54
	NHL TOTALS		118	28	44	72	36

     (d)—October, 1980—Traded by Chicoutimi Sagueneens to Trois-Rivieres Draveurs for Rene Labbe and Daniel Courcy.
     (e)—Winner of Guy Lafleur Trophy (QMJHL Playoff MVP).
     (f)—January, 1985—Traded by St. Louis Blues to Quebec Nordiques for Luc Dufour.

CLAUDE LEMIEUX

Right Wing . . . 6'1" . . . 215 lbs. . . . Born, Buckingham, Que., July 16, 1965 . . . Shoots right . . . Brother of Jocelyn Lemieux.

Year	Team	League	Games	G.	A.	Pts.	Pen.
1981-82—Richelieu Eclairevrs		Que. Midget	48	24	48	72	96
1982-83—Trois-Rivieres Draveurs (c)		QHL	62	28	38	66	187
1983-84—Verdun Juniors (b)		QHL	51	41	45	86	225
1983-84—Montreal Canadiens		NHL	8	1	1	2	12
1984-85—Verdun Juniors (a-d)		QHL	52	58	66	124	152
1984-85—Montreal Canadiens		NHL	1	0	1	1	7
1985-86—Sherbrooke Canadiens		AHL	58	21	32	53	145
1985-86—Montreal Canadiens		NHL	10	1	2	3	22
NHL TOTALS			19	2	4	6	41

     (c)—June, 1983—Drafted as underage junior by Montreal Canadiens in 1983 NHL entry draft. Second Canadiens pick, 26th overall, second round.
     (d)—Won Guy Lafleur Trophy (Playoff MVP).

JOCELYN LEMIEUX

Left Wing . . . 5'11" . . . 205 lbs. . . . Born, Mont Laurier, Que., November 18, 1967 . . . Shoots left . . . Brother of Claude Lemieux . . . Also plays Right Wing.

Year	Team	League	Games	G.	A.	Pts.	Pen.
1984-85—Laval Voisins		QHL	68	13	19	32	92
1985-86—Laval Titans (a-c)		QHL	71	57	68	125	131

     (c)—June, 1986—Drafted as underage junior by St. Louis Blues in 1986 NHL entry draft. First Blues pick, 10th overall, first round.

MARIO LEMIEUX

Center . . . 6'4" . . . 200 lbs. . . . Born, Montreal, Que., October 5, 1965 . . . Shoots right . . . Set single-season record in Quebec Junior League in 1983-84 for goals (133) and points (282) as well as a Quebec League record for most career assists (315) . . . Brother of Alain Lemieux . . . (September, 1984)—Sprained left knee in training camp. Fitted with a playing brace. . . . (December 2, 1984)—Resprained knee in collision with Darren Veitch in game at Washington . . . (November 24, 1985)—Missed one game with back injury at Philadelphia.

Year	Team	League	Games	G.	A.	Pts.	Pen.
1981-82—Laval Voisins		QMJHL	64	30	66	96	22
1982-83—Laval Voisins (b)		QHL	66	84	100	184	76
1983-84—Laval Voisins (a-c)		QHL	70	*133	*149	*282	92
1984-85—Pittsburgh Penguins (d-e)		NHL	73	43	57	100	54
1985-86—Pittsburgh Penguins (b-f)		NHL	79	48	93	141	43
NHL TOTALS			152	91	150	241	97

     (c)—June, 1984—Drafted as underage junior by Pittsburgh Penguins in 1984 NHL entry draft. First Penguins pick, first overall, first round.
     (d)—Won Calder Memorial Trophy (NHL Top Rookie).
     (e)—Named NHL Rookie of the Year in poll of players by The Sporting News.
     (f)—Won 1986 Lester B. Pearson Award as the NHL's outstanding player. Voting is done by the NHLPA.

TIM LENARDON

Center . . . 6'2" . . . 185 lbs. . . . Born, Trail, B.C., May 11, 1962 . . . Shoots left.

Year	Team	League	Games	G.	A.	Pts.	Pen.
1981-82—Trail		KIHL	40	48	61	138	....
1982-83—Trail		KIHL	38	86	86	172	....
1983-84—Univ. of Brandon		CWUAA	24	22	21	43	....
1984-85—Univ. of Brandon		CWUAA	24	21	39	60	....
1985-86—Univ. of Brandon (c-d)		CWUAA	26	26	40	66	33

     (c)—Named Canadian College Player of the Year.
     (d)—August, 1986—Signed by New Jersey Devils as a free agent.

RICHARD LESSARD

Defense . . . 6'2" . . . 200 lbs. . . . Born, Timmons, Ont., January 9, 1968 . . . Shoots left.

Year	Team	League	Games	G.	A.	Pts.	Pen.
1984-85—Ottawa 67's		OHL	60	2	13	15	128
1985-86—Ottawa 67's (c)		OHL	64	1	20	21	231

(c)—June, 1986—Drafted as an underage junior by Calgary Flames in 1986 NHL entry draft. Sixth Flames pick, 142nd overall, seventh round.

DANIEL LETENDRE

Right Wing . . . 6'1" . . . 200 lbs. . . . Born, Sorel, Que., January 21, 1965 . . . Shoots right.

Year	Team	League	Games	G.	A.	Pts.	Pen.
1981-82—Richelieu Eclairvers		Que. Midget	41	33	43	76	30
1982-83—Quebec Remparts (c)		QHL	61	28	25	53	22
1983-84—Quebec Remparts		QHL	67	25	41	66	35
1984-85—Trois Rivieres Draveurs		QHL	61	36	35	71	39
1984-85—Flint Generals		IHL	2	0	0	0	0
1985-86—Saginaw Generals		IHL	40	8	7	15	2

(c)—June, 1983—Drafted as underage junior by Montreal Canadiens in 1983 NHL entry draft. Fifth Canadiens pick, 45th overall, third round.

DONALD RICHARD LEVER

Center . . . 5'11" . . . 175 lbs. . . . Born, South Porcupine, Ont., November 14, 1952 . . . Shoots left . . . Missed part of 1977-78 season with fractured cheekbone . . . (January 13, 1981)—Strained ligaments in left knee . . . (March, 1981)—Torn rib cartilage . . . Also plays Left Wing . . . (February 19, 1986)—Torn rotator cuff at Hartford.

Year	Team	League	Games	G.	A.	Pts.	Pen.
1969-70—Niagara Falls Flyers		Jr."A"OHA	2	0	1	1	4
1970-71—Niagara Falls Flyers		Jr."A"OHA	59	35	36	71	112
1971-72—Niag. Falls Flyers (a-c-d-e)		Jr."A"OHA	63	61	65	126	69
1972-73—Vancouver Canucks		NHL	78	12	26	38	49
1973-74—Vancouver Canucks		NHL	78	23	25	48	28
1974-75—Vancouver Canucks		NHL	80	38	30	68	49
1975-76—Vancouver Canucks		NHL	80	25	40	65	93
1976-77—Vancouver Canucks		NHL	80	27	30	57	28
1977-78—Vancouver Canucks		NHL	75	17	32	49	58
1978-79—Vancouver Canucks		NHL	71	23	21	44	17
1979-80—Vancouver Caucks (f)		NHL	51	21	17	38	32
1979-80—Atlanta Flames		NHL	28	14	16	30	4
1980-81—Calgary Flames		NHL	62	26	31	57	56
1981-82—Calgary Flames (g)		NHL	23	8	11	19	6
1981-82—Colorado Rockies		NHL	59	22	28	50	20
1982-83—New Jersey Devils		NHL	79	23	30	53	68
1983-84—New Jersey Devils		NHL	70	14	19	33	44
1984-85—New Jersey Devils (h)		NHL	67	10	8	18	31
1985-86—Rochester Americans		AHL	29	6	11	17	16
1985-86—Buffalo Sabres		NHL	29	7	1	8	6
NHL TOTALS			1010	310	365	675	589

(c)—Won Red Tilson Memorial Trophy (MVP in Jr. "A" OHA).

(d)—Selected by Ottawa Nationals in World Hockey Association player selection draft, February, 1972.

(e)—Drafted from Niagara Falls Flyers by Vancouver Canucks in first round of 1972 amateur draft.

(f)—February, 1980—Traded with Brad Smith by Vancouver Canucks to Atlanta Flames for Ivan Boldirev and Darcy Rota.

(g)—December, 1981—Traded with Bob MacMillan by Calgary Flames to Colorado Rockies for Lanny McDonald and a fourth-round 1983 entry draft pick.

(h)—September, 1985—Traded by New Jersey Devils to Buffalo Sabres for future considerations.

CRAIG DEAN LEVIE

Defense . . . 5'10" . . . 198 lbs. . . . Born, Calgary, Alta., August 17, 1959 . . . Shoots right . . . Set new AHL record for points by a defenseman in one season with 82 in 1980-81 (previous record set in 1947-48 by Eddie Bush).

Year	Team	League	Games	G.	A.	Pts.	Pen.
1976-77—Pincher Creek Panthers		AJHL	27	8	10	18	32
1976-77—Calgary Wranglers		WCHL	2	0	1	1	0
1977-78—Flin Flon Bombers		WCHL	72	25	64	89	167
1978-79—Edmonton Oil Kings (b-c)		WHL	69	29	63	92	200
1979-80—Nova Scotia Voyageurs		AHL	72	6	21	27	74

Year	Team	League	Games	G.	A.	Pts.	Pen.
1980-81—Nova Scotia Voyageurs (a-d)	AHL	80	20	*62	82	162
1981-82—Tulsa Oilers	CHL	14	4	7	11	17
1981-82—Winnipeg Jets (e)	NHL	40	4	9	13	48
1982-83—Sherbrooke Jets	AHL	44	3	27	30	52
1982-83—Winnipeg Jets (f)	NHL	22	4	5	9	31
1983-84—Salt Lake Golden Eagles	CHL	37	8	20	28	101
1983-84—Minnesota North Stars	NHL	37	6	13	19	44
1984-85—St. Louis Blues (g)	NHL	61	6	23	29	33
1985-86—Springfield Indians	AHL	36	5	23	28	82
1985-86—Minnesota North Stars (h)	NHL	14	2	2	4	8
NHL TOTALS			174	22	52	74	164

(c)—August, 1979—Drafted by Montreal Canadiens in NHL entry draft. Third Montreal pick, 43rd overall, third round.

(d)—Winner of Eddie Shore Plaque (Top AHL Defenseman).

(e)—October, 1981—Acquired by Winnipeg Jets in 1981 NHL waiver draft.

(f)—August, 1983—Traded by Winnipeg Jets with Tom Hirsch to Minnesota North Stars for Tim Young.

(g)—October, 1984—Selected by St. Louis Blues in 1984 NHL waiver draft.

(h)—October, 1985—Acquired by Calgary Flames in 1985 NHL waiver draft. However, when the Flames tried to pass him through waivers after the draft so they could send him to Nova Scotia, he was claimed by the Minnesota North Stars.

DAVID RODNEY LEWIS

Defense . . . 6'3" . . . 205 lbs. . . . Born, Kindersley, Sask., July 3, 1953 . . . Shoots left . . . Missed last part of 1973-74 season with fractured right cheekbone . . . (January 14, 1981) —Broke right index finger at Hartford . . . (January 3, 1986)—Broke toe vs. Minnesota and missed four games.

Year	Team	League	Games	G.	A.	Pts.	Pen.
1971-72—Saskatoon Blades	WCHL	52	2	9	11	69
1972-73—Saskatoon Blades (c)	WCHL	67	10	35	45	89
1973-74—New York Islanders	NHL	66	2	15	17	58
1974-75—New York Islanders	NHL	78	5	14	19	98
1975-76—New York Islanders	NHL	73	0	19	19	54
1976-77—New York Islanders	NHL	79	4	24	28	44
1977-78—New York Islanders	NHL	77	3	11	14	58
1978-79—New York Islanders	NHL	79	5	18	23	43
1979-80—New York Islanders (d)	NHL	62	5	16	21	54
1979-80—Los Angeles Kings	NHL	11	1	1	2	12
1980-81—Los Angeles Kings	NHL	67	1	12	13	98
1981-82—Los Angeles Kings	NHL	64	1	13	14	75
1982-83—Los Angeles Kings	NHL	79	2	10	12	53
1983-84—New Jersey Devils (e-f)	NHL	66	2	5	7	63
1984-85—New Jersey Devils	NHL	74	3	9	12	78
1985-86—New Jersey Devils (g)	NHL	69	0	15	15	81
NHL TOTALS			944	34	182	216	869

(c)—Drafted from Saskatoon Blades by New York Islanders in third round of 1973 amateur draft.

(d)—March, 1980—Traded with Billy Harris by New York Islanders to Los Angeles Kings for Butch Goring.

(e)—October, 1983—Traded by Los Angeles Kings to Minnesota North Stars for Fred Barrett.

(f)—October, 1983—Traded by Minnesota North Stars to New Jersey Devils for Brent Ashton.

(g)—August, 1986—Signed by Detroit Red Wings as a free agent being released by New Jersey Devils on July 1.

DOUG LIDSTER

Defense . . . 6'1" . . . 195 lbs. . . . Born, Kamloops, B.C., October 18, 1960 . . . Shoots right . . . (1982-83)—Tied Colorado College record for most points by a defenseman in a season (56) . . . Member of 1984 Canadian Olympic Team . . . (January 3, 1986)—Injured knee vs. Winnipeg and missed two games.

Year	Team	League	Games	G.	A.	Pts.	Pen.
1979-80—Colorado College (c)	WCHA	39	18	25	43	52
1980-81—Colorado College	WCHA	36	10	30	40	54
1981-82—Colorado College (a)	WCHA	36	13	22	35	32
1982-83—Colorado College	WCHA	34	15	41	56	30
1983-84—Canadian Olympic Team	Int'l	59	6	20	26	28
1983-84—Vancouver Canucks	NHL	8	0	0	0	4
1984-85—Vancouver Canucks	NHL	78	6	24	30	55
1985-86—Vancouver Canucks	NHL	78	12	16	28	56
NHL TOTALS			164	18	40	58	115

(c)—June, 1980—Drafted by Vancouver Canucks in 1980 NHL entry draft. Sixth Canucks pick, 133rd overall, seventh round.

BO MORGAN (WILLY) LINDSTROM

Right Wing . . . 6' . . . 180 lbs. . . . Born, Grunns, Sweden, May 5, 1951 . . . Shoots left . . . (February, 1983)—Pulled hamstring . . . (January 25, 1986)—Bruised shoulder at Calgary and missed five games . . . (February 27, 1986)—Injured shoulder at N.Y. Rangers and missed two games.

Year	Team	League	Games	G.	A.	Pts.	Pen.
1974-75	Swedish National Team		....	...	....	....	....
1975-76	Winnipeg Jets	WHA	81	23	36	59	32
1976-77	Winnipeg Jets	WHA	79	44	36	80	37
1977-78	Winnipeg Jets	WHA	77	30	30	60	42
1978-79	Winnipeg Jets (c)	WHA	79	26	36	62	22
1979-80	Winnipeg Jets	NHL	79	23	26	49	20
1980-81	Winnipeg Jets	NHL	72	22	13	35	45
1981-82	Winnipeg Jets	NHL	74	32	27	59	33
1982-83	Winnipeg Jets (d)	NHL	63	20	25	45	8
1982-83	Edmonton Oilers	NHL	10	6	5	11	2
1983-84	Edmonton Oilers	NHL	73	22	16	38	38
1984-85	Edmonton Oilers	NHL	80	12	20	32	18
1985-86	Pittsburgh Penguins (e)	NHL	71	14	17	31	30
	WHA TOTALS		316	123	138	261	133
	NHL TOTALS		522	151	149	300	194

(c)—Tied for lead in goals (10) during playoffs.
(d)—March, 1983—Traded by Winnipeg Jets to Edmonton Oilers for Laurie Boschman.
(e)—October, 1985—Acquired by Pittsburgh Penguins in 1985 NHL waiver draft.

KEN LINSEMAN

Center . . . 5'11" . . . 175 lbs. . . . Born, Kingston, Ont., August 11, 1958 . . . Shoots left . . . (September, 1980)—Broke tibia bone in leg in preseason game vs. N. Y. Rangers . . . Brother of John, Ted and Steve Linseman . . . (February, 1983)—Suspended for four games for fight in stands at Vancouver . . . (November, 1984)—Shoulder injury . . . (November 21, 1985)—Broke right hand vs. N.Y. Islanders and missed 10 games . . . (December 28, 1985)—Injured hand at St. Louis and missed six games.

Year	Team	League	Games	G.	A.	Pts.	Pen.
1974-75	Kingston Canadians	Jr."A" OHA	59	19	28	47	70
1975-76	Kingston Canadians	Jr."A" OHA	65	61	51	112	92
1976-77	Kingston Canadians (b-c)	Jr"A" OHA	63	53	74	127	210
1977-78	Birmingham Bulls (d)	WHA	71	38	38	76	126
1978-79	Maine Mariners	AHL	38	17	23	40	106
1978-79	Philadelphia Flyers	NHL	30	5	20	25	23
1979-80	Philadelphia Flyers (e)	NHL	80	22	57	79	107
1980-81	Philadelphia Flyers	NHL	51	17	30	47	150
1981-82	Philadelphia Flyers (f)	NHL	79	24	68	92	275
1982-83	Edmonton Oilers	NHL	72	33	42	75	181
1983-84	Edmonton Oilers (g)	NHL	72	18	49	67	119
1984-85	Boston Bruins	NHL	74	25	49	74	126
1985-86	Boston Bruins	NHL	64	23	58	81	97
	WHA TOTALS		71	38	38	76	126
	NHL TOTALS		522	167	373	540	1078

(c)—June, 1977—Selected by Birmingham Bulls in World Hockey Association amateur player draft as underage junior.
(d)—Drafted from Birmingham Bulls by Philadelphia Flyers (with choice obtained from N. Y. Rangers) in first round of 1978 amateur draft.
(e)—Led in assists (18) during playoffs.
(f)—August, 1982—Traded with Greg Adams and first and third-round 1983 draft picks by Philadelphia Flyers to Hartford Whalers for Mark Howe and Whalers third-round '83 pick. Linseman was then traded with Don Nachbaur by Hartford Whalers to Edmonton Oilers for Risto Siltanen and Brent Loney.
(g)—June, 1984—Traded by Edmonton Oilers to Boston Bruins for Mike Krushelnyski.

LONNIE LOACH

Left Wing . . . 5'10" . . . 180 lbs. . . . Born, New Liskeard, Ont., April 14, 1968 . . . Shoots left.

Year	Team	League	Games	G.	A.	Pts.	Pen.
1984-85	St. Mary's Jr. B	OHA	44	26	36	62	113
1985-86	Guelph Platers (c-d)	OHL	65	41	42	83	63

(c)—Won Emms Family Award (OHL Rookie of the Year).
(d)—June, 1986—Drafted as underage junior by Chicago Black Hawks in 1986 NHL entry draft. Fourth Black Hawks pick, 98th overall, fifth round.

MARK LOFTHOUSE

Right Wing . . . 6'1" . . . 185 lbs. . . . Born, New Westminster, B.C., April 21, 1957 . . . Shoots right . . . (February, 1983)—Injured back.

Year	Team	League	Games	G.	A.	Pts.	Pen.
1973-74—Kelowna Buckaroos	Jr."A"BCHL	62	44	42	86	59
1974-75—New Westminster Bruins	WCHL	61	36	28	64	53
1975-76—New Westminster Bruins	WCHL	72	68	48	116	55
1976-77—New Westminster Bruins (b-c)	WCHL	70	54	58	112	59
1977-78—Hershey Bears	AHL	35	8	6	14	39
1977-78—Salt Lake City Golden Eagles	CHL	13	0	1	1	4
1977-78—Washington Capitals	NHL	18	2	1	3	8
1978-79—Washington Capitals	NHL	52	13	10	23	10
1978-79—Hershey Bears	AHL	16	7	7	14	6
1979-80—Hershey Bears	AHL	9	7	3	10	6
1979-80—Washington Capitals	NHL	68	15	18	33	20
1980-81—Washington Capitals	NHL	3	1	1	2	4
1980-81—Hershey Bears (a-d-e)	AHL	74	*48	55	*103	131
1981-82—Adirondack Red Wings	AHL	69	33	38	71	75
1981-82—Detroit Red Wings	NHL	12	3	4	7	13
1982-83—Adirondack Red Wings	AHL	39	27	18	45	20
1982-83—Detroit Red Wings (f)	NHL	28	8	4	12	18
1983-84—New Haven Nighthawks (b)	AHL	79	37	64	101	45
1984-85—New Haven Nighthawks	AHL	12	11	4	15	4
1985-86—New Haven Nighthawks	AHL	70	32	35	67	56
NHL TOTALS		181	42	38	80	73

(c)—Drafted from New Westminster Bruins by Washington Capitals in second round of 1977 amateur draft.
(d)—Winner of John B. Sollenberger Trophy (Leading Scorer of AHL).
(e)—August, 1981—Traded by Washington Capitals to Detroit Red Wings for Al Jensen.
(f)—August, 1983—Signed by Los Angeles Kings as a free agent.

CLAUDE LOISELLE

Center . . . 5'11" . . . 195 lbs. . . . Born, Ottawa, Ont., May 29, 1963 . . . Shoots left . . . (January 7, 1984)—Given six-game suspension by NHL for a stick-swinging incident with Paul Holmgren of Philadelphia . . . (December 17, 1985)—Injured knee at Minnesota and missed 11 games.

Year	Team	League	Games	G.	A.	Pts.	Pen.
1979-80—Gloucester Rangers	OPJHL	50	21	38	59	26
1980-81—Windsor Spitfires (c)	OHL	68	38	56	94	103
1981-82—Windsor Spitfires	OHL	68	36	73	109	192
1981-82—Detroit Red Wings	NHL	4	1	0	1	2
1982-83—Detroit Red Wings	NHL	18	2	0	2	15
1982-83—Windsor Spitfires	OHL	46	39	49	88	75
1982-83—Adirondack Red Wings	AHL	6	1	7	8	0
1983-84—Adirondack Red Wings	AHL	29	13	16	29	59
1983-84—Detroit Red Wings	NHL	28	4	6	10	32
1984-85—Adirondack Red Wings	AHL	47	22	29	51	24
1984-85—Detroit Red Wings	NHL	30	8	1	9	45
1985-86—Adirondack Red Wings	AHL	21	15	11	26	32
1985-86—Detroit Red Wings (d)	NHL	48	7	15	22	142
NHL TOTALS		128	22	22	44	236

(c)—June, 1981—Drafted as underage junior by Detroit Red Wings in 1981 NHL entry draft. First Red Wings pick, 23rd overall, second round.
(d)—June, 1986—Traded by Detroit Red Wings to New Jersey Devils for Tim Higgins.

BRENT LONEY

Left Wing . . . 6' . . . 170 lbs. . . . Born, Cornwall, Ont., May 25, 1964 . . . Shoots left . . . (January, 1983)—Involved in auto accident in Cornwall, Ontario. Suffered facial cuts when he went through windshield.

Year	Team	League	Games	G.	A.	Pts.	Pen.
1980-81—Ottawa Senators	CJHL	45	6	14	20	93
1981-82—Cornwall Royals (c-d)	OHL	65	13	12	25	57
1982-83—Cornwall Royals	OHL	47	11	24	35	69
1983-84—Cornwall Royals	OHL	62	24	38	62	56
1984-85—Hamilton Steelhawks (e)	OHL	13	11	8	19	19
1984-85—Oshawa Generals	OHL	32	13	16	29	21
1984-85—Salt Lake Golden Eagles	IHL	11	2	0	2	2
1984-85—Binghamton Whalers	AHL	4	0	0	0	0
1985-86—Hershey Bears	AHL	59	0	8	8	113

(c)—June, 1982—Drafted by Edmonton Oilers as underage junior in 1982 NHL entry draft. Third Oilers pick, 62nd overall, third round.
(d)—August, 1982—Traded with Risto Siltanen by Edmonton Oilers to Hartford Whalers for Don Nachbaur and Ken Linseman.
(e)—December, 1984—Traded with Gary McColgan by Hamilton Steelhawks to Oshawa Generals for Steve Hedington, John Hutchings and sixth round 1985 priority draft pick (Andy May).

TROY LONEY

Left Wing ... 6'3" ... 215 lbs. ... Born, Bow Island, Alta., September 21, 1963 ... Shoots left.

Year	Team	League	Games	G.	A.	Pts.	Pen.
1980-81—Lethbridge Broncos		WHL	71	18	13	31	100
1981-82—Lethbridge Broncos (c)		WHL	71	26	31	57	152
1982-83—Lethbridge Broncos		WHL	72	33	34	67	156
1983-84—Baltimore Skipjacks		AHL	63	18	13	31	147
1983-84—Pittsburgh Penguins		NHL	13	0	0	0	9
1984-85—Baltimore Skipjacks		AHL	15	4	2	6	25
1984-85—Pittsburgh Penguins		NHL	46	10	8	18	59
1985-86—Baltimore Skipjacks		AHL	33	12	11	23	84
1985-86—Pittsburgh Penguins		NHL	47	3	9	12	95
NHL TOTALS			106	13	17	30	163

(c)—June, 1982—Drafted as underage junior by Pittsburgh Penguins in 1982 NHL entry draft. Third Penguins pick, 52nd overall, third round.

HAKAN LOOB

Right Wing ... 5'9" ... 180 lbs. ... Born, Karlstad, Sweden, July 3, 1960 ... Shoots right ... Set Swedish records in 1982-83 for goals (42), assists (34) and points (76) in a season ... Brother of Peter Loob.

Year	Team	League	Games	G.	A.	Pts.	Pen.
1978-79—Karlskrona IK		Sweden Jr.	....	...	....	....	....
1979-80—Karlstad Farjestads BK (c)		Sweden	36	15	4	19	20
1980-81—Karlstad Farjestads BK (d-e)		Sweden	36	23	6	29	14
1981-82—Karlstad Farjestads BK		Sweden	36	26	15	41	28
1982-83—Karlstad Farjestads BK		Sweden	36	*42	*34	*76	18
1983-84—Calgary Flames		NHL	77	30	25	55	22
1984-85—Calgary Flames		NHL	78	37	35	72	14
1985-86—Calgary Flames		NHL	68	31	36	67	36
NHL TOTALS			223	98	96	194	72

(c)—June, 1980—Drafted by Calgary Flames in 1980 NHL entry draft. Tenth Flames pick, 181st overall, ninth round.
(d)—Shared Swedish National League playoffs goal scoring lead with teammate Jan Ingman (5 goals).
(e)—Shared Swedish National League playoff point lead with teammate Robin Eriksson (8 points).

ROBERT ROY LORIMER

Defense ... 6' ... 190 lbs. ... Born, Toronto, Ont., August 25, 1953 ... Shoots right ... Attended Michigan Tech ... Missed part of 1976-77 season with surgery for ruptured spleen and part with kidney injury ... (October, 1982)—Missed 16 games with stretched left knee ligaments ... (December, 1982)—Sprained wrist ... (February, 1985)—Pinched nerve in neck ... (January 14, 1986)—Bruised knee at Philadelphia ... (February 13, 1986)—Bruised shin vs. Montreal.

Year	Team	League	Games	G.	A.	Pts.	Pen.
1970-71—Aurora Tigers		OPJHL	....	...	....	....	....
1971-72—Michigan Tech		WCHA	32	1	7	8	63
1972-73—Michigan Tech (c)		WCHA	38	2	9	11	74
1973-74—Michigan Tech		WCHA	39	3	18	21	46
1974-75—Michigan Tech (b)		WCHA	38	10	21	31	68
1975-76—Fort Worth Texans		CHL	2	0	0	0	2
1975-76—Muskegon Mohawks		IHL	78	6	21	27	94
1976-77—Fort Worth Texans		CHL	28	4	6	10	38
1976-77—New York Islanders		NHL	1	0	1	1	0
1977-78—Fort Worth Texans		CHL	71	6	13	19	81
1977-78—New York Islanders		NHL	5	1	0	1	0
1978-79—New York Islanders		NHL	67	3	18	21	42
1979-80—New York Islanders		NHL	74	3	16	19	53
1980-81—New York Islanders		NHL	73	1	12	13	77
1981-82—Colorado Rockies (d)		NHL	79	5	15	20	68
1982-83—New Jersey Devils		NHL	66	3	10	13	42
1983-84—New Jersey Devils		NHL	72	2	10	12	62

Year	Team	League	Games	G.	A.	Pts.	Pen.
1984-85—New Jersey Devils		NHL	46	2	6	8	35
1985-86—New Jersey Devils		NHL	46	2	2	4	52
NHL TOTALS			529	22	90	112	431

(c)—Drafted by New York Islanders in ninth round of 1973 amateur draft.

(d)—October, 1981—Traded with Dave Cameron by New York Islanders to Colorado Rockies for first round 1983 entry draft pick (Pat LaFontaine).

KEVIN HUGH LOWE

Defense ... 6' ... 185 lbs. ... Born, Lachute, Que., April 15, 1959 ... Shoots left ... Cousin of Mike Lowe (St. Louis 1969 draft pick) ... (March 7, 1986)—Broke index finger vs. Pittsburgh and missed six games.

Year	Team	League	Games	G.	A.	Pts.	Pen.
1976-77—Quebec Remparts		QMJHL	69	3	19	22	39
1977-78—Quebec Remparts		QMJHL	64	13	52	65	86
1978-79—Quebec Remparts (b-c)		QMJHL	68	26	60	86	120
1979-80—Edmonton Oilers		NHL	64	2	19	21	70
1980-81—Edmonton Oilers		NHL	79	10	24	34	94
1981-82—Edmonton Oilers		NHL	80	9	31	40	63
1982-83—Edmonton Oilers		NHL	80	6	34	40	43
1983-84—Edmonton Oilers		NHL	80	4	42	46	59
1984-85—Edmonton Oilers		NHL	80	4	22	26	104
1985-86—Edmonton Oilers		NHL	74	2	16	18	90
NHL TOTALS			537	37	188	225	523

(c)—August, 1979—Drafted by Edmonton Oilers in 1979 entry draft. First Oilers pick, 21st overall, first round.

GLEN LOWES

Left Wing ... 6' ... 190 lbs. ... Born, Burlington, Ont., January 17, 1968 ... Shoots left.

Year	Team	League	Games	G.	A.	Pts.	Pen.
1984-85—Burlington Midgets		OMHA	41	22	39	61	168
1985-86—Toronto Marlboros (c)		OHL	64	8	14	22	134

(c)—June, 1986—Drafted as underage junior by Chicago Black Hawks in 1986 NHL entry draft. Ninth Black Hawks pick, 203rd overall, 10th round.

ED LOWNEY

Right Wing ... 5'11" ... 180 lbs. ... Born, Revere, Mass., June 10, 1965 ... Shoots right.

Year	Team	League	Games	G.	A.	Pts.	Pen.
1983-84—Boston University (c)		ECAC	40	21	12	33	26
1984-85—Boston University		H. East	42	18	21	39	10
1985-86—Boston University		H. East	43	18	20	38	14

(c)—June, 1984—Drafted by Vancouver Canucks in 1984 NHL entry draft. Eleventh Canucks pick, 198th overall, 10th round.

DAVE LOWRY

Left Wing ... 6'2" ... 175 lbs. ... Born, Sudbury, Ont., January 14, 1965 ... Shoots left ... (December, 1982)—Arthroscopic surgery on knee.

Year	Team	League	Games	G.	A.	Pts.	Pen.
1981-82—Nepean Midgets		Ont. Midget	60	50	64	114	46
1982-83—London Knights (c)		OHL	42	11	16	27	48
1983-84—London Knights		OHL	66	29	47	76	125
1984-85—London Knights (a)		OHL	61	60	60	120	94
1985-86—Vancouver Canucks		NHL	73	10	8	18	143
NHL TOTALS			73	10	8	18	143

(c)—June, 1983—Drafted as underage junior by Vancouver Canucks in 1983 NHL entry draft. Fourth Canucks pick, 110th overall, sixth round.

MIKE LUCKCRAFT

Defense ... 6'1" ... 186 lbs. ... Born, Jackson, Mich., November 28, 1966 ... Shoots right.

Year	Team	League	Games	G.	A.	Pts.	Pen.
1984-85—Burnsville H.S. (a-c)		Minn. H.S.	27	10	21	31	16
1985-86—University of Minnesota		WCHA	1	0	0	0	0

(c)—June, 1985—Drafted by Detroit Red Wings in 1985 NHL entry draft. Eighth Red Wings pick, 125th overall, eighth round.

JAN LUDVIG

Right Wing . . . 5'10" . . . 187 lbs. . . . Born, Liberec, Czechoslovakia, September 17, 1961 . . . Shoots right . . . (December, 1982)—Bruised ribs . . . (January, 1984)—Hip Injury . . . (December, 1985)—Injured left tibula . . . (January 21, 1986)—Missed two games with a bruised knee.

Year	Team	League	Games	G.	A.	Pts.	Pen.
1981-82—St. Albert Saints (c)		AJHL	4	2	4	6	20
1981-82—Kamloops Oilers		WHL	37	31	34	65	36
1982-83—Wichita Wind (d)		CHL	9	3	0	3	19
1982-83—New Jersey Devils		NHL	51	7	10	17	30
1983-84—New Jersey Devils		NHL	74	22	32	54	70
1984-85—New Jersey Devils		NHL	74	12	19	31	53
1985-86—New Jersey Devils		NHL	42	5	9	14	63
NHL TOTALS			241	46	70	116	216

(c)—October, 1981—Signed by Edmonton Oilers as a free agent.
(d)—November, 1982—Signed by New Jersey Devils as a free agent.

CRAIG LEE LUDWIG

Defense . . . 6'3" . . . 212 lbs. . . . Born, Rhinelander, Wis., March 15, 1961 . . . Shoots left . . . (October, 1984)—Fractured knuckle in left hand in pre-season game . . . (December 2, 1985)—Broke hand vs. Vancouver and missed nine games.

Year	Team	League	Games	G.	A.	Pts.	Pen.
1979-80—University of North Dakota (c)		WCHA	33	1	8	9	32
1980-81—University of North Dakota		WCHA	34	4	8	12	48
1981-82—University of North Dakota (b)		WCHA	47	5	26	31	70
1982-83—Montreal Canadiens		NHL	80	0	25	25	59
1983-84—Montreal Canadiens		NHL	72	4	13	17	45
1984-85—Montreal Canadiens		NHL	72	5	14	19	90
1985-86—Montreal Canadiens		NHL	69	2	4	6	63
NHL TOTALS			293	11	56	67	257

(c)—June, 1980—Drafted by Montreal Canadiens in 1980 NHL entry draft. Fifth Canadiens pick, 61st overall, third round.

STEVE LUDZIK

Center . . . 5'11" . . . 185 lbs. . . . Born, Toronto, Ont., April 3, 1961 . . . Shoots left . . . (October 19, 1985)—Broke left foot at Detroit . . . (December 29, 1985)—Injured foot vs. Boston and missed four games.

Year	Team	League	Games	G.	A.	Pts.	Pen.
1977-78—Markham Waxers		OPJHL	34	15	24	39	20
1978-79—Niagara Falls Flyers		OMJHL	68	32	65	97	138
1979-80—Niagara Falls Flyers (c)		OMJHL	67	43	76	119	102
1980-81—Niagara Falls Flyers		OHL	58	50	92	142	108
1981-82—Chicago Black Hawks		NHL	8	2	1	3	2
1981-82—New Brunswick Hawks		AHL	75	21	41	62	142
1982-83—Chicago Black Hawks		NHL	66	6	19	25	63
1983-84—Chicago Black Hawks		NHL	80	9	20	29	73
1984-85—Chicago Black Hawks		NHL	79	11	20	31	86
1985-86—Chicago Black Hawks		NHL	49	6	5	11	21
NHL TOTALS			282	34	65	99	245

(c)—June, 1980—Drafted as underage junior by Chicago Black Hawks in 1980 NHL entry draft. Third Black Hawks pick, 28th overall, second round.

MORRIS LUKOWICH

Left Wing . . . 5'8" . . . 165 lbs. . . . Born, Speers, Sask., June 1, 1956 . . . Shoots left . . . Cousin of Bernie Lukowich . . . Missed part of 1976-77 season with fractured left ankle . . . Also plays Right Wing and Center . . . (March, 1983)—Stretched knee ligaments when checked by teammate Tim Watters at a practice in Los Angeles . . . (September, 1984)—Orthroscopic knee surgery . . . (February, 1985)—Sprained ankle . . . (November 30, 1985)—Sprained arm vs. Chicago and missed four games.

Year	Team	League	Games	G.	A.	Pts.	Pen.
1973-74—Medicine Hat Tigers		WCHL	65	13	14	27	55
1974-75—Medicine Hat Tigers		WCHL	70	40	54	94	111
1975-76—Medicine Hat Tigers (a-c-d)		WCHL	72	65	77	142	195
1976-77—Houston Aeros		WHA	62	27	18	45	67
1977-78—Houston Aeros (e)		WHA	80	40	35	75	131
1978-79—Winnipeg Jets (b-f)		WHA	80	65	34	99	119
1979-80—Winnipeg Jets		NHL	78	35	39	74	77

Year	Team	League	Games	G.	A.	Pts.	Pen.
1980-81—Winnipeg Jets		NHL	80	33	34	67	90
1981-82—Winnipeg Jets		NHL	77	43	49	92	102
1982-83—Winnipeg Jets		NHL	69	22	21	43	67
1983-84—Winnipeg Jets		NHL	80	30	25	55	71
1984-85—Winnipeg Jets (g)		NHL	47	5	9	14	31
1984-85—Boston Bruins		NHL	22	5	8	13	21
1985-86—Boston Bruins (h)		NHL	14	1	4	5	10
1985-86—Los Angeles Kings		NHL	55	11	9	20	51
WHA TOTALS			222	132	87	219	317
NHL TOTALS			522	185	198	383	521

(c)—Drafted from Medicine Hat Tigers by Pittsburgh Penguins in third round of 1976 amateur draft.
(d)—Selected by Houston Aeros in World Hockey Association amateur player draft, May, 1976.
(e)—Sold to Winnipeg Jets with Houston Aeros' franchise, July, 1978.
(f)—June, 1979—Selected by Pittsburgh Penguins in NHL reclaim draft, but remained with the Jets as a priority selection for the expansion draft.
(g)—February, 1985—Traded by Winnipeg Jets to Boston Bruins for Jim Nill.
(h)—November, 1985—Claimed on waivers by Winnipeg Jets from Boston Bruins.

DAVID LUMLEY

Right Wing . . . 5'11" . . . 185 lbs. . . Born, Toronto, Ont., September 1, 1954 . . . Shoots right . . . Attended University of New Hampshire . . . Has also played Defense . . . (November 29, 1980)—Sprained shoulder . . . (December, 1983)—Injured knee ligaments.

Year	Team	League	Games	G.	A.	Pts.	Pen.
1973-74—Univ. of New Hampshire (c)		ECAC	31	12	19	31	38
1974-75—University of New Hampshire		ECAC	26	12	26	38	56
1975-76—University of New Hampshire		ECAC	30	9	32	41	55
1976-77—University of New Hampshire		ECAC	39	22	38	60	42
1977-78—Nova Scotia Voyageurs		AHL	58	22	21	43	58
1978-79—Montreal Canadiens		NHL	3	0	0	0	0
1978-79—Nova Scotia Voyageurs (b-d)		AHL	61	22	58	80	160
1979-80—Edmonton Oilers		NHL	80	20	38	58	138
1980-81—Edmonton Oilers		NHL	53	7	9	16	74
1981-82—Edmonton Oilers		NHL	66	32	42	74	96
1982-83—Edmonton Oilers		NHL	72	13	24	37	158
1983-84—Edmonton Oilers		NHL	56	6	15	21	68
1984-85—Hartford Whalers (e-f)		NHL	48	8	20	28	98
1984-85—Edmonton Oilers		NHL	12	1	3	4	13
1985-86—Edmonton Oilers		NHL	46	11	9	20	35
NHL TOTALS			436	98	160	258	680

(c)—Drafted from University of New Hampshire by Montreal Canadiens in 12th round of 1974 amateur draft.
(d)—June, 1979—Traded with Dan Newman by Montreal Canadiens to Edmonton Oilers for future considerations.
(e)—October, 1984—Selected by Hartford Whalers in 1984 NHL waiver draft.
(f)—February, 1985—Acquired by Edmonton Oilers on waivers from Hartford Whalers.

BENGT LUNDHOLM

Left Wing . . . 6' . . . 172 lbs. . . . Born, Falun, Sweden, August 4, 1955 . . . Shoots left . . . (February 2, 1983)—Injured right knee in game vs. Philadelphia, requiring surgery . . . Also plays Right Wing . . . (September, 1985)—Stretched knee ligaments in training camp.

Year	Team	League	Games	G.	A.	Pts.	Pen.
1977-78—Solna AIK		Sweden	54	23	25	48	36
1978-79—Solna AIK		Sweden	47	15	29	44	38
1979-80—Solna AIK		Sweden	51	21	36	57	48
1980-81—Solna AIK (c)		Sweden	39	11	15	26	48
1981-82—Winnipeg Jets		NHL	66	14	30	44	10
1982-83—Winnipeg Jets		NHL	58	14	28	42	16
1983-84—Winnipeg Jets		NHL	57	5	14	19	20
1984-85—Winnipeg Jets		NHL	78	12	18	30	20
1985-86—Winnipeg Jets (d)		NHL	16	3	5	8	16
NHL TOTALS			275	48	95	143	82

(c)—June, 1981—Signed by Winnipeg Jets as a free agent.
(c)—November, 1985—Announced he was returning to Sweden to play for Stockholm AIK.

DAVE LUNDMARK

Defense . . . 6' . . . 190 lbs. . . . Born, Minneapolis, Minn., February 14, 1965 . . . Shoots left.

Year	Team	League	Games	G.	A.	Pts.	Pen.
1982-83—Virginia H.S. (c)		Minn. H.S.	22	4	10	14	..

Year	Team	League	Games	G.	A.	Pts.	Pen.
1983-84—Kingston Canadians		OHL	65	2	9	11	66
1984-85—Kingston Canadians		OHL	12	1	2	3	44
1984-85—Sudbury Wolves		OHL	45	0	8	8	39
1984-85—New Haven Nighthawks		AHL	2	0	0	0	0
1985-86—Toledo Goaldiggers		IHL	12	0	1	1	7

(c)—June, 1983—Drafted by Los Angeles Kings in 1983 NHL entry draft. Fifth Kings pick, 107th overall, sixth round.

CHRISTOPHER LUONGO

Defense . . . 6' . . . 180 lbs. . . . Born, Detroit, Mich., March 17, 1967 . . . Shoots right.

Year	Team	League	Games	G.	A.	Pts.	Pen.
1984-85—St. Clair Shores Falcons (c)		NAJHL	41	2	25	27	....
1985-86—Michigan State Univ.		CCHA	38	1	5	6	29

(c)—June, 1985—Drafted by Detroit Red Wings in 1985 NHL entry draft. Fifth Red Wings pick, 92nd overall, fifth round.

GARY JOHN LUPUL

Center . . . 5'8" . . . 174 lbs. . . . Born, Powell River, B.C., April 4, 1959 . . . Shoots left . . . (August, 1977)—Torn ligaments in left knee . . . (August, 1978)—Injured ankle while working in a logging camp in B.C. . . . (November, 1983)—Broken knuckle . . . (February 26, 1985)—Strained both knees in game at Washington.

Year	Team	League	Games	G.	A.	Pts.	Pen.
1975-76—Victoria Cougars		WCHL	4	1	1	2	2
1976-77—Victoria Cougars		WCHL	71	38	63	101	116
1977-78—Victoria Cougars		WCHL	59	37	49	86	79
1978-79—Victoria Cougars		WHL	71	53	54	107	85
1979-80—Dallas Black Hawks (c)		CHL	26	9	15	24	4
1979-80—Vancouver Canucks		NHL	51	9	11	20	24
1980-81—Vancouver Canucks		NHL	7	0	2	2	2
1980-81—Dallas Black Hawks		CHL	53	25	32	57	27
1981-82—Dallas Black Hawks		CHL	31	22	17	39	76
1981-82—Vancouver Canucks		NHL	41	10	7	17	26
1982-83—Fredericton Express		AHL	35	16	26	42	48
1982-83—Vancouver Canucks		NHL	40	18	10	28	46
1983-84—Vancouver Canucks		NHL	69	17	27	44	51
1984-85—Vancouver Canucks		NHL	66	12	17	29	82
1985-86—Fredericton Express		AHL	43	13	22	35	76
1985-86—Vancouver Canucks		NHL	19	4	1	5	12
NHL TOTALS			293	70	75	145	243

(c)—September, 1979—Signed as free agent by Vancouver Canucks.

MARC LYONS

Defense . . . 6'1" . . . 190 lbs. . . . Born, Markham, Ont., January 8, 1967 . . . Shoots left.

Year	Team	League	Games	G.	A.	Pts.	Pen.
1984-85—Kingston Canadians		OHL	65	1	5	6	118
1985-86—Kingston Canadians (c)		OHL	58	4	11	15	78

(c)—June, 1986—Drafted as underage junior by Vancouver Canucks in 1986 NHL entry draft. Ninth Canucks pick, 196th overall, 10th round.

THOMAS JAMES LYSIAK

Center . . . 6'1" . . . 205 lbs. . . . Born, High Prairie, Alta., April 22, 1953 . . . Shoots left . . . Equalled WCHL record with 10 points in game (December 30, 1971 vs. Edmonton Oil Kings) . . . (February, 1981)—Recurring nerve condition in his back . . . (December 27, 1981)—Slight cartilage tear in right knee vs. St. Louis . . . (January 23, 1983)—Cracked bone in instep of right foot when hit by Dave Maloney shot during game vs. New York Rangers . . . (October 30, 1983)—Given a 20-game suspension by NHL for tripping linesman Ron Foyt in game vs. Hartford.

Year	Team	League	Games	G.	A.	Pts.	Pen.
1970-71—Medicine Hat Tigers		WCHL	60	14	16	30	112
1971-72—Medicine Hat Tigers (a)		WCHL	68	46	*97	*143	96
1972-73—Medicine Hat Tigers (a-c)		WCHL	67	58	*96	*154	104
1973-74—Atlanta Flames (d)		NHL	77	19	45	64	54
1974-75—Atlanta Flames		NHL	77	25	52	77	73
1975-76—Atlanta Flames		NHL	80	31	51	82	60
1976-77—Atlanta Flames		NHL	79	30	51	81	52
1977-78—Atlanta Flames		NHL	80	27	42	69	54
1978-79—Atlanta Flames (e)		NHL	52	23	35	58	36

Year	Team	League	Games	G.	A.	Pts.	Pen.
1978-79—Chicago Black Hawks		NHL	14	0	10	10	14
1979-80—Chicago Black Hawks		NHL	77	26	43	69	31
1980-81—Chicago Black Hawks		NHL	72	21	55	76	20
1981-82—Chicago Black Hawks		NHL	71	32	50	82	84
1982-83—Chicago Black Hawks		NHL	61	23	38	61	29
1983-84—Chicago Black Hawks		NHL	54	17	30	47	35
1984-85—Chicago Black Hawks		NHL	74	16	30	46	13
1985-86—Chicago Black Hawks		NHL	51	2	19	21	14
NHL TOTALS			919	292	551	843	560

(c)—Drafted from Medicine Hat Tigers by Atlanta Flames in first round of 1973 amateur draft.
(d)—Named Rookie-of-the-Year in NHL's West Division poll of players by THE SPORTING NEWS.
(e)—March, 1979—Traded with Harold Phillipoff, Pat Ribble, Greg Fox and Miles Zaharko to Chicago Black Hawks by Atlanta Flames for Ivan Boldirev, Phil Russell and Darcy Rota.

REGINALD ALAN (AL) MacADAM

Left Wing . . . 6' . . . 175 lbs. . . . Born, Charlottetown, P.E.I., March 16, 1952 . . . Shoots left . . . Missed part of 1973-74 season with fractured cheekbone . . . Also plays Right Wing . . . Missed part of 1978-79 season with ligament damage in right hand that required surgery . . . (March 14, 1981)—Broken cheekbone . . . (March, 1983)—Infected finger.

Year	Team	League	Games	G.	A.	Pts.	Pen.
1969-70—Charlottetown Islanders		MJHL	42	27	31	58	55
1970-71—Charlottetown Islanders (a)		MJHL	53	51	43	94	58
1971-72—Univ. of Prince Edward Island (a)			26	32	21	53	8
1971-72—Charlottetown Islanders (c-d)		MJHL	11	15	21	36	....
1972-73—Richmond Robins		AHL	68	19	32	51	42
1973-74—Richmond Robins		AHL	62	23	22	45	36
1973-74—Philadelphia Flyers (e)		NHL	5	0	0	0	0
1974-75—California Seals		NHL	80	18	25	43	55
1975-76—California Seals		NHL	80	32	31	63	49
1976-77—Cleveland Barons		NHL	80	22	41	63	68
1977-78—Cleveland Barons		NHL	80	16	32	48	42
1978-79—Minnesota North Stars		NHL	69	24	34	58	30
1979-80—Minnesota North Stars (f)		NHL	80	42	51	93	24
1980-81—Minnesota North Stars		NHL	78	21	39	60	94
1981-82—Minnesota North Stars		NHL	79	18	43	61	37
1982-83—Minnesota North Stars		NHL	73	11	22	33	60
1983-84—Minnesota North Stars (g)		NHL	80	22	13	35	23
1984-85—Vancouver Canucks		NHL	80	14	20	34	27
1985-86—Fredericton Express (h)		AHL	11	0	4	4	5
NHL TOTALS			864	240	351	591	509

(c)—No league record. Appeared in 11 playoff games and had 36 points.
(d)—Drafted from Charlottetown Islanders by Philadelphia Flyers in fourth round of 1972 amateur draft.
(e)—May, 1974—Traded to California Golden Seals by Philadelphia Flyers with Larry Wright and Flyers' first round draft choice in 1974 amateur draft (Ron Chipperfield) for Reg Leach.
(f)—Won Bill Masterton Memorial Trophy (Sportsmanship).
(g)—June, 1984—Traded by Minnesota North Stars to Vancouver Canucks for Harold Snepsts.
(h)—June, 1986—Announced retirement as a player and resigned his post as development coordinator for Vancouver Canucks to become hockey coach and assistant athletic director at St. Thomas University in Fredericton, N.B.

PAUL MacDERMID

Center . . . 6' . . . 188 lbs. . . . Born, Chesley, Ont., April 14, 1963 . . . Shoots right . . . (December, 1982)—Injured knee.

Year	Team	League	Games	G.	A.	Pts.	Pen.
1979-80—Port Elgin Bears		OHA Jr.'C'	30	23	20	43	87
1980-81—Windsor Spitfires (c)		OHL	68	15	17	32	106
1981-82—Windsor Spitfires		OHL	65	26	45	71	179
1981-82—Hartford Whalers		NHL	3	1	0	1	2
1982-83—Windsor Spitfires		OHL	42	35	45	80	90
1982-83—Hartford Whalers		NHL	7	0	0	0	2
1983-84—Hartford Whalers		NHL	3	0	1	1	0
1983-84—Binghamton Whalers		AHL	70	31	30	61	130
1984-85—Binghamton Whalers		AHL	48	9	31	40	87
1984-85—Hartford Whalers		NHL	31	4	7	11	299
1985-86—Hartford Whalers		NHL	74	13	10	23	160
NHL TOTALS			118	18	18	36	193

(c)—June, 1981—Drafted as underage junior in 1981 NHL entry draft by Hartford Whalers. Second Whalers pick, 61st overall, third round.

BRETT MacDONALD

Defense . . . 6' . . . 195 lbs. . . . Born, Bothwell, Ont., January 5, 1966 . . . Shoots left.

Year	Team	League	Games	G.	A.	Pts.	Pen.
1982-83	Dixie Beehives	MTJHL	44	5	18	23	28
1983-84	North Bay Centennials (c)	OHL	70	8	18	26	83
1984-85	North Bay Centennials	OHL	58	6	27	33	72
1985-86	North Bay Centennials	OHL	15	0	6	6	42
1985-86	Kitchener Rangers	OHL	53	10	27	37	52

(c)—June, 1984—Drafted as underage junior by Vancouver Canucks in NHL entry draft. Sixth Canucks pick, 94th overall, fifth round.

ALLAN MacINNIS

Defense . . . 6'1" . . . 183 lbs. . . . Born, Inverness, N.S., July 11, 1963 . . . Shoots right . . . (February, 1985)—Twisted knee . . . (March 23, 1986)—Lacerated hand at Winnipeg.

Year	Team	League	Games	G.	A.	Pts.	Pen.
1979-80	Regina Blues	SJHL	59	20	28	48	110
1980-81	Kitchener Rangers (c)	OHL	47	11	28	39	59
1981-82	Kitchener Rangers (a)	OHL	59	25	50	75	145
1981-82	Calgary Flames	NHL	2	0	0	0	0
1982-83	Kitchener Rangers (a-d)	OHL	51	38	46	84	67
1982-83	Calgary Flames	NHL	14	1	3	4	9
1983-84	Colorado Flames	CHL	19	5	14	19	22
1983-84	Calgary Flames	NHL	51	11	34	45	42
1984-85	Calgary Flames	NHL	67	14	52	66	75
1985-86	Calgary Flames (e)	NHL	77	11	57	68	76
	NHL TOTALS		211	37	146	183	202

(c)—June, 1981—Drafted as underage junior by Calgary Flames in 1981 NHL entry draft. First Flames pick, 15th overall, first round.
(d)—Won Max Kaminsky Trophy (Outstanding OHL Defenseman).
(e)—Led NHL playoffs with 15 assists.

JOSEPH MacINNIS

Center . . . 6' . . . 165 lbs. . . . Born, Cambridge, Mass., May 25, 1966 . . . Shoots left.

Year	Team	League	Games	G.	A.	Pts.	Pen.
1983-84	Watertown H.S. (c)	Mass. H.S.	18	28	18	46	....
1984-85	Northeastern University	H. East	33	4	3	7	20
1985-86	Northeastern University	H. East	20	4	3	7	10

(c)—June, 1984—Drafted by Toronto Maple Leafs in NHL entry draft. Sixth Maple Leafs pick, 130th overall, seventh round.

CRAIG MACK

Defense . . . 6'1" . . . 195 lbs. . . . Born, Grand Forks, N.D., March 27, 1965 . . . Shoots right.

Year	Team	League	Games	G.	A.	Pts.	Pen.
1982-83	E.Grand Forks H.S. (c)	Minn. H.S.	23	9	22	31	....
1983-84	University of Minnesota	WCHA	21	0	3	3	14
1984-85	University of Minnesota	WCHA	24	0	2	2	12
1985-86	University of Minnesota	WCHA	45	2	15	17	32

(c)—June, 1983—Drafted by Quebec Nordiques in 1983 NHL entry draft. Sixth Nordiques pick, 132nd overall, seventh round.

DAVID MACKEY

Left Wing . . . 6'3" . . . 190 lbs. . . . Born, New Westminster, B.C., July 24, 1966 . . . Shoots left.

Year	Team	League	Games	G.	A.	Pts.	Pen.
1981-82	Seafair	B.C. Midgets	60	48	62	110	99
1982-83	Victoria Cougars	WHL	69	16	16	32	53
1983-84	Victoria Cougars (c)	WHL	69	15	15	30	97
1984-85	Victoria Cougars	WHL	16	5	6	11	45
1984-85	Portland Winter Hawks	WHL	56	28	32	60	122
1985-86	Kamloops Blazers (d)	WHL	9	3	4	7	13
1985-86	Medicine Hat Tigers	WHL	60	25	32	57	167

(c)—June, 1984—Drafted as underage junior by Chicago Black Hawks in NHL entry draft. Twelfth Black Hawks pick, 224th overall, 11th round.
(d)—December, 1986—Traded with Rob Dimaio and Calvin Knibbs by Kamloops Blazers to Medicine Hat Tigers for Doug Pickel and Sean Pass.

DAVE MacLEAN

Right Wing . . . 6' . . . 200 lbs. . . . Born, Newmarket, Ont., January 12, 1965 . . . Shoots right . . . (June, 1982)—Shoulder surgery . . . (February, 1986)—Injured knee.

Year	Team	League	Games	G.	A.	Pts.	Pen.
1981-82—Oshawa Generals		OHL	54	6	8	14	38
1982-83—Oshawa Generals		OHL	11	8	6	14	6
1982-83—Belleville Bulls (c)		OHL	51	34	46	80	28
1983-84—Belleville Bulls		OHL	70	58	51	109	47
1984-85—Belleville Bulls (b-d-e-f)		OHL	63	64	*90	*154	41
1984-85—Binghamton Whalers (g)		AHL	....	...	....	....	....
1985-86—Binghamton Whalers		AHL	23	0	0	0	7
1985-86—Salt Lake Golden Eagles		IHL	41	9	14	23	14

(c)—June, 1983—Drafted as underage junior by Hartford Whalers in 1983 NHL entry draft. Fifth Whalers pick, 64th overall, fourth round.
(d)—Won Eddie Powers Memorial Trophy (OHL Scoring Leader).
(e)—Won Jim Mahon Memorial Trophy (Top scoring OHL Right Wing).
(f)—Molson/Cooper Player of the Year (CMJHL Player of the Year—OHL nominee).
(g)—No regular season record, played four playoff games.

JOHN MacLEAN

Right Wing . . . 6' . . . 195 lbs. . . . Born, Oshawa, Ont., November 20, 1964 . . . Shoots right . . . (November, 1984)—Bruised shoulder in game vs. N.Y. Rangers . . . (January 25, 1985)—Injured right knee in game at Edmonton . . . (January 31, 1985)—Reinjured knee and underwent arthroscopic surgery . . . (November 2, 1986)—Bruised ankle vs. N. Y. Rangers.

Year	Team	League	Games	G.	A.	Pts.	Pen.
1981-82—Oshawa Generals		OHL	67	17	22	39	197
1982-83—Oshawa Generals (c-d)		OHL	66	47	51	98	138
1983-84—New Jersey Devils		NHL	23	1	0	1	10
1983-84—Oshawa Generals		OHL	30	23	36	59	58
1984-85—New Jersey Devils		NHL	61	13	20	33	44
1985-86—New Jersey Devils		NHL	74	21	37	58	112
NHL TOTALS			158	35	57	92	166

(c)—Led OHL playoffs with 18 goals and shared OHL playoff point lead with teammate Dave Gans with 38 points.
(d)—June, 1983—Drafted as underage junior by New Jersey Devils in 1983 NHL entry draft. First Devils pick, sixth overall, first round.

PAUL MacLEAN

Right Wing . . . 6' . . . 205 lbs. . . . Born, Grostenquin, France, March 9, 1958 . . . Shoots right . . . Member of 1980 Canadian Olympic team . . . (October, 1985)—Jammed thumb.

Year	Team	League	Games	G.	A.	Pts.	Pen.
1977-78—Hull Festivals (c)		QMJHL	66	38	33	71	125
1978-79—Canadian National Team		Int'l	....	...	....	....	....
1979-80—Canadian National Team		Int'l	50	21	11	32	90
1979-80—Canadian Olympic Team		Olympics	6	2	3	5	6
1980-81—Salt Lake City		CHL	80	36	42	78	160
1980-81—St. Louis Blues (d)		NHL	1	0	0	0	0
1981-82—Winnipeg Jets		NHL	74	36	25	61	106
1982-83—Winnipeg Jets		NHL	80	32	44	76	121
1983-84—Winnipeg Jets		NHL	76	40	31	71	155
1984-85—Winnipeg Jets		NHL	79	41	60	101	119
1985-86—Winnipeg Jets		NHL	69	27	29	56	74
NHL TOTALS			379	176	189	365	575

(c)—June, 1978—Drafted by St. Louis Blues in 1978 NHL amateur draft. Sixth Blues pick, 109th overall, seventh round.
(d)—July, 1981—Traded by St. Louis Blues with Ed Staniowski and Bryan Maxwell to Winnipeg Jets for John Markell and Scott Campbell.

BRIAN MacLELLAN

Left Wing . . . 6'3" . . . 212 lbs. . . . Born, Guelph, Ont., October 27, 1958 . . . Shoots left.

Year	Team	League	Games	G.	A.	Pts.	Pen.
1978-79—Bowling Green University		CCHA	44	34	29	63	94
1979-80—Bowling Green University		CCHA	38	8	15	23	46
1980-81—Bowling Green University		CCHA	37	11	14	25	96
1981-82—Bowling Green University (c)		CCHA	41	11	21	32	109
1982-83—Los Angeles Kings		NHL	8	0	3	3	7
1982-83—New Haven Nighthawks		AHL	71	11	15	26	40
1983-84—New Haven Nighthawks		AHL	2	0	2	2	0

Year	Team	League	Games	G.	A.	Pts.	Pen.
1983-84—Los Angeles Kings		NHL	72	25	29	54	45
1984-85—Los Angeles Kings		NHL	80	31	54	85	53
1985-86—Los Angeles Kings (d)		NHL	27	5	8	13	19
1985-86—New York Rangers		NHL	51	11	21	32	47
NHL TOTALS			238	72	115	187	171

(c)—April, 1982—Signed by Los Angeles Kings as a free agent.

(d)—December, 1985—Traded with a fourth round 1987 draft pick by Los Angeles Kings to New York Rangers for Roland Melanson and Grant Ledyard. The Rangers had earlier traded a second round 1986 pick (Neil Wilkinson) and a fourth round 1987 draft pick to Minnesota for Melanson. Melanson was then traded with Ledyard to Los Angeles.

SCOTT MacLEOD

Center . . . 5'10" . . . 175 lbs. . . . Born, Vancouver, B.C., May 17, 1959 . . . Shoots left . . . Set record for most assists (75) and points (118) by a CHL rookie in 1983-84.

Year	Team	League	Games	G.	A.	Pts.	Pen.
1981-82—Jujyo Seishi		Japan	30	37	52	*89	..
1982-83—Jujyo Seishi		Japan	..	..	..	..	..
1983-84—Salt Lake Golden Eagles (a-c)		CHL	68	43	*75	*118	30
1984-85—Salt Lake Golden Eagles (a-d)		WHL	82	51	*88	*139	89
1985-86—Salt Lake Golden Eagles (a-d)		IHL	77	54	*80	*134	93

(c)—Won Phil Esposito Trophy (Top CHL Scorer).

(d)—Won Leo P. Lamoureux Memorial Trophy (IHL Scoring Title).

BILLIE MacMILLAN

Right Wing . . . 6'2" . . . 185 lbs. . . . Born, North Bay, Ont., April 3, 1967 . . . Shoots right.

Year	Team	League	Games	G.	A.	Pts.	Pen.
1983-84—North Bay Midgets		OHA	74	63	71	134	36
1984-85—Peterborough Petes (c)		OHL	61	12	22	34	10
1985-86—Peterborough Petes		OHL	56	16	31	47	67

(c)—June, 1985—Drafted as underage junior by New Jersey Devils in 1985 NHL entry draft. Sixth Devils pick, 108th overall, sixth round.

JAMIE MACOUN

Defense . . . 6'2" . . . 200 lbs. . . . Born, Newmarket, Ont., August 17, 1961 . . . Shoots left . . . (December 26, 1984)—Cheekbone fractured in altercation with Mark Messier in game vs. Edmonton. Messier was given a 10-game NHL suspension because of the incident.

Year	Team	League	Games	G.	A.	Pts.	Pen.
1980-81—Ohio State University		CCHA	38	9	20	29	83
1981-82—Ohio State University		CCHA	25	2	18	20	89
1982-83—Ohio State University (c)		CCHA	....	...	....	....	....
1982-83—Calgary Flames		NHL	22	1	4	5	25
1983-84—Calgary Flames		NHL	72	9	23	32	97
1984-85—Calgary Flames		NHL	70	9	30	39	67
1985-86—Calgary Flames		NHL	77	11	21	32	81
NHL TOTALS			241	30	78	108	270

(c)—January, 1983—Left Ohio State University to sign with Calgary Flames as a free agent.

DUNCAN MacPHERSON

Defense . . . 6'1" . . . 190 lbs. . . . Born, Saskatoon, Sask., February 3, 1966 . . . Shoots left . . . Missed almost half of the 1983-84 season with an ankle injury . . . (September, 1984)—Bruised left knee in N.Y. Islanders training camp.

Year	Team	League	Games	G.	A.	Pts.	Pen.
1982-83—Battleford Barons		SAJHL	59	6	11	17	215
1983-84—Saskatoon Blades (c)		WHL	45	0	14	14	74
1984-85—Saskatoon Blades		WHL	69	9	26	35	116
1985-86—Saskatoon Blades		WHL	70	10	54	64	147

(c)—June, 1984—Drafted as underage junior by New York Islanders in NHL entry draft. First Islanders pick, 20th overall, first round.

CRAIG MacTAVISH

Center . . . 6' . . . 185 lbs. . . . Born, London, Ont., August 15, 1958 . . . Shoots left . . . Also plays left wing . . . (January, 1984)—Involved in automobile accident in which Kim Lea Radley was killed. He was charged with vehicular homicide, driving while under the influence of alcohol and reckless driving. In May he pleaded guilty and was convicted by Essex, Mass., Superior court and sentenced to a year in prison.

Year	Team	League	Games	G.	A.	Pts.	Pen.
1977-78—University of Lowell (b-c-d)		ECAC	....	...	....	....	....
1978-79—University of Lowell (a-e)		ECAC-II	....	36	52	*88	....
1979-80—Binghamton Dusters		AHL	34	17	15	32	20
1979-80—Boston Bruins		NHL	46	11	17	28	8
1980-81—Boston Bruins		NHL	24	3	5	8	13
1980-81—Springfield Indians		AHL	53	19	24	43	89
1981-82—Erie Blades		AHL	72	23	32	55	37
1981-82—Boston Bruins		NHL	2	0	1	1	0
1982-83—Boston Bruins		NHL	75	10	20	30	18
1983-84—Boston Bruins		NHL	70	20	23	43	35
1984-85—Boston Bruins (f)		NHL	....	...	....	....	....
1985-86—Edmonton Oilers		NHL	74	23	24	47	70
NHL TOTALS			291	67	90	157	144

(c)—June, 1978—Drafted by Boston Bruins in amateur draft. Ninth Boston pick, 153rd overall, ninth round.
(d)—Named ECAC Division II Rookie of the year.
(e)—Named ECAC Division II Player of the Year.
(f)—February, 1984—Signed by Edmonton Oilers as a free agent.

MARC MAGNAN

Left Wing . . . 5'11" . . . 195 lbs. . . . Born, Beaumont, Alta., February 17, 1962 . . . Shoots left . . . Brother of Vince Magnan.

Year	Team	League	Games	G.	A.	Pts.	Pen.
1979-80—St. Albert Saints		AJHL	42	14	23	37	178
1979-80—Lethbridge Broncos		WHL	1	0	1	1	0
1980-81—Lethbridge Broncos (c)		WHL	66	16	30	46	284
1981-82—Lethbridge Broncos		WHL	64	33	38	71	406
1982-83—St. Catharines Saints		OHL	67	6	10	16	229
1982-83—Toronto Maple Leafs		NHL	4	0	1	1	5
1983-84—St. Catharines Saints		AHL	54	3	6	9	170
1983-84—Muskegon Mohawks		IHL	19	3	10	13	30
1984-85—Indianapolis Checkers		IHL	72	9	24	33	244
1985-86—Indianapolis Checkers		IHL	69	15	22	37	279
NHL TOTALS			4	0	1	1	5

(c)—June, 1981—Drafted as underage junior by Toronto Maple Leafs in 1981 NHL entry draft. Ninth Maple Leafs pick, 195th overall, 10th round.

KEVIN MAGUIRE

Right Wing . . . 6'2" . . . 200 lbs. . . . Born, Toronto, Ont., January 5, 1963 . . . Shoots right.

Year	Team	League	Games	G.	A.	Pts.	Pen.
1983-84—Orillia Travelways		OHA	....	35	42	77	....
1984-85—St. Catharines Saints (c)		AHL	76	10	15	25	112
1985-86—St. Catharines Saints		AHL	61	6	9	15	161

(c)—September, 1984—Signed by Toronto Maple Leafs as a free agent.

BRUCE MAJOR

Center . . . 6'3" . . . 180 lbs. . . . Born, Vernon, B.C., January 3, 1967 . . . Shoots left.

Year	Team	League	Games	G.	A.	Pts.	Pen.
1984-85—Richmond Sockeyes (c)		BCJHL	48	43	56	99	56
1985-86—University of Maine		H. East	38	14	14	28	39

(c)—June, 1985—Drafted by Quebec Nordiques in 1985 NHL entry draft. Sixth Nordiques pick, 99th overall, fifth round.

MIKKO MAKELA

Right Wing . . . 6'2" . . . 195 lbs. . . . Born, Tampere, Finland, February 28, 1965 . . . Shoots right . . . Also plays Center . . . (November 1, 1985)—Injured back at Washington and missed 15 games.

Year	Team	League	Games	G.	A.	Pts.	Pen.
1984-85—Ilves Tampere		Finland	35	17	11	28	....
1984-85—Ilves Tampere (a-c-d)		Finland	36	*34	25	59	24
1985-86—Springfield Indians		AHL	2	1	1	2	0
1985-86—New York Islanders		NHL	58	16	20	36	28
NHL TOTALS			58	16	20	36	28

(c)—June, 1983—Drafted by New York Islanders in 1983 NHL entry draft. Fifth Islanders pick, 65th overall, fourth round.
(d)—Won Most Gentlemanly Player Trophy.

JYRKI MAKI

Defense . . . 6' . . . 170 lbs. . . . Born, Helsinki, Finland, February 8, 1966 . . . Shoots left.

Year	Team	League	Games	G.	A.	Pts.	Pen.
1983-84—St. Paul Simley H.S. (c)		Minn. H.S.	22	9	24	33	8
1984-85—University of Lowell		H. East	33	0	5	5	12
1985-86—University of Lowell		H. East	26	1	2	3	9

(c)—June, 1984—Drafted by Quebec Nordiques in NHL entry draft. Seventh Nordiques pick, 162nd overall, eighth round.

DAVID MALEY

Center . . . 6'3" . . . 200 lbs. . . . Born, Beaver Dam, Wis., April 24, 1963 . . . Shoots left.

Year	Team	League	Games	G.	A.	Pts.	Pen.
1981-82—Edina H.S. (c)		Minn. H.S.	26	22	28	50	26
1982-83—University of Wisconsin		WCHA	47	17	23	40	24
1983-84—University of Wisconsin		WCHA	38	10	28	38	56
1984-85—University of Wisconsin		WCHA	35	19	9	28	86
1985-86—University of Wisconsin		WCHA	42	20	40	60	*135
1985-86—Montreal Canadiens		NHL	3	0	0	0	0
NHL TOTALS			3	0	0	0	0

(c)—June, 1982—Drafted by Montreal Canadiens as underage player in 1982 NHL entry draft. Fourth Canadiens pick, 33rd overall, second round.

WILLIAM GREGORY (GREG) MALONE

Center . . . 6' . . . 190 lbs. . . . Born, Chatham, N.B., March 8, 1956 . . . Shoots left . . . Missed parts of 1979-80 season with an infected instep and knee surgery to repair torn ligaments in right knee . . . Brother of Jim Malone . . . (October 11, 1980)—Strained ligaments in right knee . . . (October 19, 1985)—Broke nose vs. Montreal.

Year	Team	League	Games	G.	A.	Pts.	Pen.
1973-74—Oshawa Generals		Jr."A"OHA	62	11	45	56	63
1974-75—Oshawa Generals		Jr."A"OHA	68	37	41	78	86
1975-76—Oshawa Generals (c)		Jr."A"OHA	61	36	36	72	75
1976-77—Pittsburgh Penguins		NHL	66	18	19	37	43
1977-78—Pittsburgh Penguins		NHL	78	18	43	61	80
1978-79—Pittsburgh Penguins		NHL	80	35	30	65	52
1979-80—Pittsburgh Penguins		NHL	51	19	32	51	46
1980-81—Pittsburgh Penguins		NHL	62	21	29	50	68
1981-82—Pittsburgh Penguins		NHL	78	15	24	39	125
1982-83—Pittsburgh Penguins		NHL	80	17	44	61	82
1983-84—Hartford Whalers (d)		NHL	78	17	37	54	56
1984-85—Hartford Whalers		NHL	76	22	39	61	67
1985-86—Hartford Whalers (e)		NHL	22	6	7	13	24
1985-86—Quebec Nordiques		NHL	27	3	5	8	18
NHL TOTALS			698	191	309	500	661

(c)—Drafted from Oshawa Generals by Pittsburgh Penguins in second round of 1976 amateur draft.

(d)—October, 1983—Traded by Pittsburgh Penguins to Hartford Whalers for third round 1985 draft pick.

(e)—January, 1986—Traded by Hartford Whalers to Quebec Nordiques for Wayne Babych.

DONALD MICHAEL MALONEY

Left Wing . . . 6'1" . . . 190 lbs. . . . Born, Lindsay, Ont., September 5, 1958 . . . Shoots left . . . Brother of Dave Maloney . . . (October, 1980)—Mononucleosis . . . Set record for most points by a rookie in the playoffs (20) in 1979 (broken in 1981 by Dino Ciccarelli with 21) . . . (October 24, 1981)—Partial ligament tear in right knee in game at Toronto. He missed 25 games and returned to lineup December 23, 1981 . . . (November 28, 1983)—Broke ring finger of right hand in game with Vancouver . . . (October, 1984)—Pulled abdominal muscle injury . . . (November 18, 1984)—Broke leg and ankle in collision with Bruce Driver in game vs. New Jersey. He required surgery and a pin was inserted in his leg . . . (October 1, 1985)—Suspended by NHL for first three games of the season for a brawling incident in a pre-season game with Philadelphia . . . (November 20, 1985)—Injured knee vs. Toronto and missed nine games.

Year	Team	League	Games	G.	A.	Pts.	Pen.
1974-75—Kitchener Rangers		Jr."A"OHA	5	1	3	4	0
1975-76—Kitchener Rangers		Jr."A"OHA	61	27	41	68	132
1976-77—Kitchener Rangers		Jr."A"OHA	38	22	34	56	126
1977-78—Kitchener Rangers (c)		Jr."A"OHA	62	30	74	104	143
1978-79—New Haven Nighthawks		AHL	38	18	26	44	62
1978-79—New York Rangers (d)		NHL	28	9	17	26	39
1979-80—New York Rangers		NHL	79	25	48	73	97

Year	Team	League	Games	G.	A.	Pts.	Pen.
1980-81—New York Rangers		NHL	61	29	23	52	99
1981-82—New York Rangers		NHL	54	22	36	58	73
1982-83—New York Rangers		NHL	78	29	40	69	88
1983-84—New York Rangers		NHL	79	24	42	66	62
1984-85—New York Rangers		NHL	37	11	16	27	32
1985-86—New York Rangers		NHL	68	11	17	28	56
NHL TOTALS			484	160	239	399	546

(c)—Drafted from Kitchener Rangers by New York Rangers in second round of 1978 amateur draft.
(d)—Tied for lead in assists (13) during playoffs.

DAN MANDICH

Defense . . . 6'3" . . . 205 lbs. . . . Born, Brantford, Ont., June 12, 1960 . . . Shoots right . . . (February, 1983)—Injured ankle . . . (January 16, 1984)—Injured knee in game vs. Los Angeles and was lost for the remainder of the season and most of 1985-86.

Year	Team	League	Games	G.	A.	Pts.	Pen.
1978-79—Ohio State University		CCHA	38	7	18	25	126
1979-80—Ohio State University		CCHA	35	10	17	27	146
1980-81—Ohio State University		CCHA	39	20	26	46	188
1981-82—Ohio State University (c)		CCHA	33	14	26	40	157
1982-83—Birmingham South Stars		CHL	6	0	4	4	18
1982-83—Minnesota North Stars		NHL	67	3	4	7	169
1983-84—Minnesota North Stars		NHL	31	2	7	9	77
1983-84—Salt Lake Golden Eagles		CHL	3	2	2	4	13
1984-85—Minnesota North Stars		NHL	10	0	0	0	32
1985-86—Minnesota North Stars		NHL	3	0	0	0	25
1985-86—Springfield Indians		AHL	3	0	0	0	4
NHL TOTALS			111	5	11	16	303

(c)—August, 1982—Signed by Minnesota North Stars as a free agent.

JAMES EDWARD MANN

Right Wing . . . 6' . . . 202 lbs. . . . Born, Montreal, Que., April 17, 1959 . . . Shoots right . . . (March, 1980)—Served two-game suspension for his fourth game misconduct of 1979-80 season . . . (December 9, 1981)—Pushed NHL linesman Gord Broseker in game vs. Toronto. Mann was fined $500 and given a three-game suspension . . . (January 13, 1982)—Left Winnipeg bench and entered altercation on ice, breaking the jaw of Pittsburgh Penguin Paul Gardner in two places. Mann was given a 10-game suspension by NHL . . . He also was charged with assault by Province of Manitoba, found guilty and given a suspended sentence . . . (December, 1982)—Stretched knee ligaments . . . Set Winnipeg NHL club penalty-minute record in 1979-80 . . . (December, 1984)—Pulled abdominal muscles in AHL game . . . (November, 1985)—Missed seven games with the flu.

Year	Team	League	Games	G.	A.	Pts.	Pen.
1975-76—Laval National		QMJHL	65	8	9	17	107
1976-77—Sherbrooke Beavers		QMJHL	69	12	14	26	200
1977-78—Sherbrooke Beavers		QMJHL	67	27	54	81	277
1978-79—Sherbrooke Beavers (a-c)		QMJHL	65	35	47	82	260
1979-80—Winnipeg Jets		NHL	72	3	5	8	*287
1980-81—Tulsa Oilers		CHL	26	4	7	11	175
1980-81—Winnipeg Jets		NHL	37	3	3	6	105
1981-82—Winnipeg Jets		NHL	37	3	2	5	79
1982-83—Winnipeg Jets		NHL	40	0	1	1	73
1983-84—Sherbrooke Jets		AHL	20	6	3	9	94
1983-84—Winnipeg Jets (d)		NHL	16	0	1	1	54
1983-84—Quebec Nordiques		NHL	22	1	1	2	42
1984-85—Fredericton Express		AHL	13	4	4	8	97
1984-85—Quebec Nordiques		NHL	25	0	4	4	54
1985-86—Quebec Nordiques		NHL	35	0	3	3	148
NHL TOTALS			284	10	20	30	842

(c)—August, 1979—Drafted by Winnipeg Jets in NHL entry draft. First Winnipeg pick, 19th overall, first round.
(d)—January, 1984—Traded by Winnipeg Jets to Quebec Nordiques for future considerations.

RUSSELL MANN

Defense . . . 6'2" . . . 205 lbs. . . . Born, Metuen, Mass., July 8, 1967 . . . Shoots right . . . Also plays Right Wing.

Year	Team	League	Games	G.	A.	Pts.	Pen.
1984-85—Tewksbury H.S.		Mass	19	19	19	38	....
1985-86—St. Lawrence University (c)		ECAC	31	3	4	7	44

(c)—June, 1986—Drafted by Los Angeles Kings in 1986 NHL entry draft. Tenth Kings pick, 212th overall, 11th round.

MAURICE MANSI

Center ... 5'11" ... 172 lbs. ... Born, Montreal, Que., September 3, 1965 ... Shoots left ... Also plays Left Wing.

Year	Team	League	Games	G.	A.	Pts.	Pen.
1984-85—R.P.I (c)		ECAC	21	4	6	10	12
1985-86—R.P.I.		ECAC	31	16	21	37	35

(c)—June, 1985—Drafted by Montreal Canadiens in 1985 NHL entry draft. Twelfth Canadiens pick, 198th overall, tenth round.

DAVID MANSON

Defense ... 6'2" ... 192 lbs. ... Born, Prince Albert, Sask., January 27, 1967 ... Shoots left.

Year	Team	League	Games	G.	A.	Pts.	Pen.
1983-84—Prince Albert Raiders		WHL	70	2	7	9	233
1984-85—Prince Albert Raiders (c)		WHL	72	8	30	38	247
1985-86—Prince Albert Raiders (c)		WHL	70	14	34	48	177

(c)—June, 1985—Drafted as underage junior by Chicago Black Hawks in 1985 NHL entry draft. First Black Hawks pick, 11th overall, first round.

MAURICE (MOE) WILLIAM MANTHA

Defense ... 6'2" ... 197 lbs. ... Born, Lakewood, O., January 21, 1961 ... Shoots right ... Son of Maurice Mantha (AHL early 1960s) ... Missed 20 games during 1980-81 season with recurring back problems ... (October, 1981) ... Eye injury ... (October, 1982)—Surgery for injured shoulder ... (December 7, 1984)—Broke nose when hit by a puck in game at N.Y. Rangers ... (February, 1985)—Bruised spine ... (February 16, 1986)—Sprained knee at New Jersey.

Year	Team	League	Games	G.	A.	Pts.	Pen.
1978-79—Toronto Marlboros		OMJHL	68	10	38	48	57
1979-80—Toronto Marlboros (c)		OMJHL	58	8	38	46	86
1980-81—Winnipeg Jets		NHL	58	2	23	25	35
1981-82—Tulsa Oilers		CHL	33	8	15	23	56
1981-82—Winnipeg Jets		NHL	25	0	12	12	28
1982-83—Sherbrooke Jets		AHL	13	1	4	5	13
1982-83—Winnipeg Jets		NHL	21	2	7	9	6
1983-84—Sherbrooke Jets		AHL	7	1	1	2	10
1983-84—Winnipeg Jets (d)		NHL	72	16	38	54	67
1984-85—Pittsburgh Penguins		NHL	71	11	40	51	54
1985-86—Pittsburgh Penguins		NHL	78	15	52	67	102
NHL TOTALS			325	46	172	218	292

(c)—June, 1980—Drafted as underage junior by Winnipeg Jets in 1980 NHL entry draft. Second Jets pick, 23rd overall, second round.

(d)—May, 1984—Traded by Winnipeg Jets to Pittsburgh Penguins to complete March trade for Randy Carlyle.

HECTOR MARINI

Right Wing ... 6'1" ... 204 lbs. ... Born, Timmins, Ont., January 27, 1957 ... Shoots right ... (October 29, 1981)—Broke fifth metasarpic bone (little finger) in altercation with Jack McIlhargey at Hartford ... (October, 1984)—Injured knee in first game back from a pre-season injury ... (December, 1985)—Lost eye in an IHL game when struck by a puck to end his career.

Year	Team	League	Games	G.	A.	Pts.	Pen.
1974-75—Sudbury Wolves		Jr."A" OHA	69	12	19	31	70
1975-76—Sudbury Wolves		Jr."A" OHA	66	32	45	77	102
1976-77—Sudbury Wolves (c)		Jr."A" OHA	64	32	58	90	89
1977-78—Muskegon Mohawks		IHL	80	33	60	93	127
1977-78—Fort Worth Texans		CHL	2	0	0	0	4
1978-79—New York Islanders		NHL	1	0	0	0	2
1978-79—Fort Worth Texans		CHL	74	21	27	48	172
1979-80—Indianapolis Checkers		CHL	76	29	34	63	144
1980-81—New York Islanders		NHL	14	4	7	11	39
1980-81—Indianapolis Checkers		CHL	54	15	37	52	85
1981-82—New York Islanders (d)		NHL	30	4	9	13	53
1982-83—New Jersey Devils		NHL	77	17	28	45	105
1983-84—Maine Mariners		AHL	17	6	5	11	23
1983-84—New Jersey Devils		NHL	32	2	2	4	47
1984-85—Maine Mariners		AHL	30	1	5	6	67
1985-86—Maine Mariners		AHL	6	0	5	5	17
1985-86—Fort Wayne Komets		IHL	7	1	1	2	5
NHL TOTALS			154	27	46	73	246

(d)—October, 1982—Traded by New York Islanders to New Jersey Devils for option to switch fourth-round draft choices in 1983 NHL entry draft.

GORDON MARK

Defense . . . 6'3" . . . 210 lbs. . . . Born, Edmonton, Alta., September 10, 1964 . . . Shoots right . . . (December, 1984)—Knee injury.

Year	Team	League	Games	G.	A.	Pts.	Pen.
1982-83—Kamloops Junior Oilers (c)		WHL	71	12	20	32	135
1983-84—Kamloops Junior Oilers (b)		WHL	67	12	30	42	202
1984-85—Kamloops Blazers		WHL	32	11	23	34	68
1985-86—Maine Mariners		AHL	77	9	13	22	134

(c)—June, 1983—Drafted as underage junior by New Jersey Devils in 1983 NHL entry draft. Fourth Devils pick, 105th overall, sixth round.

NEVIN MARKWART

Left Wing . . . 5'11" . . . 175 lbs. . . . Born, Toronto, Ont., December 9, 1964 . . . Shoots left . . . (January, 1983)—Shoulder separation . . . (October, 1984)—Bruised hip . . . (December 28, 1985)—Hip-pointer at St. Louis and missed four games . . . (March 22, 1986)—Sprained right knee vs. N.Y. Islanders.

Year	Team	League	Games	G.	A.	Pts.	Pen.
1981-82—Regina Blues		SJHL	....	...	....	....	....
1981-82—Regina Pats		WHL	25	2	12	14	56
1982-83—Regina Pats (c)		WHL	43	27	39	66	91
1983-84—Boston Bruins		NHL	70	14	16	30	121
1984-85—Hershey Bears		AHL	38	13	18	31	79
1984-85—Boston Bruins		NHL	26	0	4	4	36
1985-86—Boston Bruins		NHL	65	7	15	22	207
NHL TOTALS			161	21	35	56	364

(c)—June, 1983—Drafted as underage junior by Boston Bruins in 1983 NHL entry draft. First Bruins pick, 21st overall, first round.

MARIO JOSEPH MAROIS

Defense . . . 5'11" . . . 170 lbs. . . . Born, Ancienne Lorette, Que., December 15, 1957 . . . Shoots right . . . Missed part of 1977-78 season with broken ankle . . . (March 27, 1982)— Broke right wrist in 4-2 loss at Montreal . . . (December 30, 1982)—Broke right leg in exhibition game vs. USSR National Team.

Year	Team	League	Games	G.	A.	Pts.	Pen.
1975-76—Quebec Remparts		QJHL	67	11	42	53	270
1976-77—Quebec Remparts (b-c)		QJHL	72	17	67	84	249
1977-78—New Haven Nighthawks		AHL	52	8	23	31	147
1977-78—New York Rangers		NHL	8	1	1	2	15
1978-79—New York Rangers		NHL	71	5	26	31	153
1979-80—New York Rangers		NHL	79	8	23	31	142
1980-81—New York Rangers (d)		NHL	8	1	2	3	46
1980-81—Vancouver Canucks (e)		NHL	50	4	12	16	115
1980-81—Quebec Nordiques		NHL	11	0	7	7	20
1981-82—Quebec Nordiques		NHL	71	11	32	43	161
1982-83—Quebec Nordiques		NHL	36	2	12	14	108
1983-84—Quebec Nordiques		NHL	80	13	36	49	151
1984-85—Quebec Nordiques		NHL	76	6	37	43	91
1985-86—Quebec Nordiques (f)		NHL	20	1	12	13	42
1985-86—Winnipeg Jets		NHL	56	4	28	32	110
NHL TOTALS			566	56	228	284	1154

(c)—Drafted from Quebec Remparts by New York Rangers in fourth round of 1977 amateur draft.

(d)—November, 1980—Traded by New York Rangers with Jim Mayer to Vancouver Canucks for Jere Gillis and Jeff Bandura.

(e)—March, 1981—Traded by Vancouver Canucks to Quebec Nordiques for Garry Lariviere in a three-way deal that saw Lariviere then go to Edmonton Oilers for Blair MacDonald.

(f)—November, 1985—Traded by Quebec Nordiques to Winnipeg Jets for Robert Picard.

CHARLES BRADLEY (BRAD) MARSH

Defense . . . 6'2" . . . 215 lbs. . . . Born, London, Ont., March 31, 1958 . . . Shoots left . . . Brother of Paul Marsh . . . Set NHL record by playing a total of 83 games in 1981-82 . . . (January 2, 1983)—Bruised knee tendon in game at Chicago . . . (March 24, 1983)—Broken fibula in game vs. Toronto.

Year	Team	League	Games	G.	A.	Pts.	Pen.
1974-75—London Knights		Jr."A"OHA	70	4	17	21	160

Year	Team	League	Games	G.	A.	Pts.	Pen.
1975-76	London Knights	Jr."A"OHA	61	3	26	29	184
1976-77	London Knights	Jr."A"OHA	63	7	33	40	121
1977-78	London Knights (a-c-d)	Jr."A"OHA	62	8	55	63	192
1978-79	Atlanta Flames	NHL	80	0	19	19	101
1979-80	Atlanta Flames	NHL	80	2	9	11	119
1980-81	Calgary Flames	NHL	80	1	12	13	87
1981-82	Calgary Flames (e)	NHL	17	0	1	1	10
1981-82	Philadelphia Flyers	NHL	66	2	22	24	106
1982-83	Philadelphia Flyers	NHL	68	2	11	13	52
1983-84	Philadelphia Flyers	NHL	77	3	14	17	83
1984-85	Philadelphia Flyers	NHL	77	2	18	20	91
1985-86	Philadelphia Flyers	NHL	79	0	13	13	123
	NHL TOTALS		624	12	119	131	772

(c)—Drafted from London Knights by Atlanta Flames in first round of 1978 amateur draft.

(d)—Shared Max Kaminsky Memorial Trophy (outstanding defenseman) with Rob Ramage.

(e)—November, 1981—Traded by Calgary Flames to Philadelphia Flyers for Mel Bridgman.

PAUL MARSHALL

Defense . . . 6'2" . . . 180 lbs. . . . Born, Quincy, Mass., October 22, 1966 . . . Shoots right.

Year	Team	League	Games	G.	A.	Pts.	Pen.
1984-85	Northwood Prep. (c)	Mass. H.S.	32	14	30	44	34
1985-86	Boston College	H. East	40	0	12	12	28

(c)—June, 1985—Drafted by Philadelphia Flyers in 1985 NHL entry draft. Fifth Flyers pick, 84th overall, fourth round.

STUART LEE MARSTON

Defense . . . 6'2" . . . 185 lbs. . . . Born, Cote St. Luc, Que., May 9, 1967 . . . Shoots left . . . (October, 1985)—Injured left wrist.

Year	Team	League	Games	G.	A.	Pts.	Pen.
1984-85	Longueuil Chevaliers (c)	QHL	62	4	16	20	84
1985-86	Laval Titans	QHL	32	7	18	25	63

(c)—June, 1985—Drafted as underage junior by Pittsburgh Penguins in 1985 NHL entry draft. Sixth Penguins pick, 114th overall, sixth round.

BRIAN MARTIN

Center . . . 6' . . . 180 lbs. . . . Born, St. Catharines, Ont., March 27, 1966 . . . Shoots left.

Year	Team	League	Games	G.	A.	Pts.	Pen.
1981-82	St. Catharines	Ont. Midget	40	28	35	63	16
1982-83	Guelph Platers	OHL	66	4	16	20	64
1983-84	Guelph Platers	OHL	19	3	9	12	7
1983-84	Belleville Bulls (c)	OHL	50	18	32	50	25
1984-85	Belleville Bulls (d)	OHL	2	0	1	1	6
1984-85	Windsor Spitfires	OHL	57	28	24	52	58
1985-86	Windsor Spitfires	OHL	60	42	41	83	115

(c)—June, 1984—Drafted as underage junior by Los Angeles Kings in NHL entry draft. 12th Kings pick, 232nd overall, 12th round.

(d)—October, 1984—Traded by Belleville Bulls to Windsor Compuware Spitfires for Pierre Dupuis.

GRANT MICHAEL MARTIN

Left Wing . . . 5'10" . . . 190 lbs. . . . Born, Smooth Rock Falls, Ont., March 13, 1962 . . . Shoots left.

Year	Team	League	Games	G.	A.	Pts.	Pen.
1979-80	Kitchener Rangers (c)	OMJHL	65	31	21	52	62
1980-81	Kitchener Rangers	OHL	66	41	57	98	77
1981-82	Kitchener Rangers	OHL	54	33	63	96	97
1982-83	Fredericton Express	AHL	80	19	27	46	73
1983-84	Fredericton Express	AHL	57	36	24	60	46
1983-84	Vancouver Canucks	NHL	12	0	2	2	6
1984-85	Vancouver Canucks	NHL	12	0	1	1	39
1984-85	Fredericton Express (d)	AHL	65	31	47	78	78
1985-86	Binghamton Whalers	AHL	54	27	49	76	97
1985-86	Washington Capitals	NHL	11	0	1	1	6
	NHL TOTALS		35	0	4	4	51

(c)—June, 1980—Drafted as underage junior by Vancouver Canucks in 1980 NHL entry draft. Ninth Canucks pick, 196th overall, 10th round.

(d)—August, 1985—Signed by Washington Capitals as a free agent.

TERRY GEORGE MARTIN

Left Wing . . . 5'11" . . . 175 lbs. . . . Born, Barrie, Ont., October 25, 1955 . . . Shoots left . . . (November, 1983)—Missed three weeks and lost 15 pounds after getting food poisoning from a roast beef sandwich at a New York City deli. He ended up in intensive care while teammates Gary Nylund and Greg Terrion also became ill, but not to the extent of Martin . . . (January, 1985)—Separated shoulder shortly after joining Minnesota.

Year	Team	League	Games	G.	A.	Pts.	Pen.
1972-73—London Knights		Jr. "A" OHA	59	17	22	39	25
1973-74—London Knights		Jr. "A" OHA	63	33	24	57	38
1974-75—London Knights (c)		Jr. "A" OHA	70	43	57	100	118
1975-76—Charlotte Checkers		SHL	25	12	10	22	30
1975-76—Hershey Bears		AHL	19	3	6	9	18
1975-76—Buffalo Sabres		NHL	1	0	0	0	0
1976-77—Hershey Bears		AHL	12	1	4	5	12
1976-77—Buffalo Sabres		NHL	62	11	12	23	8
1977-78—Hershey Bears		AHL	4	2	1	3	2
1977-78—Buffalo Sabres		NHL	21	3	2	5	9
1978-79—Buffalo Sabres (d)		NHL	64	6	8	14	33
1979-80—Syracuse Blazers		AHL	18	9	9	18	6
1979-80—Quebec Nordiques (e)		NHL	3	0	0	0	0
1979-80—New Brunswick Hawks		AHL	3	0	1	1	0
1979-80—Toronto Maple Leafs		NHL	37	6	15	21	2
1980-81—Toronto Maple Leafs		NHL	69	23	14	37	32
1981-82—Toronto Maple Leafs		NHL	72	25	24	49	39
1982-83—Toronto Maple Leafs		NHL	76	14	13	27	28
1983-84—Toronto Maple Leafs		NHL	63	15	10	25	51
1984-85—Nova Scotia Oilers		AHL	28	17	11	28	4
1984-85—Edmonton Oilers (f)		NHL	4	0	2	2	0
1984-85—Minnesota North Stars (g-h)		NHL	7	1	1	2	0
1985-86—Springfield Indians		AHL	72	19	22	41	17
NHL TOTALS			479	104	101	205	202

(c)—Drafted from London Knights by Buffalo Sabres in third round of 1975 amateur draft.

(d)—June, 1979—Selected by Quebec Nordiques in NHL expansion draft.

(e)—December, 1979—Traded with Dave Farrish by Quebec Nordiques to Toronto Maple Leafs for Reggie Thomas.

(f)—October, 1984—Claimed by Edmonton Oilers in 1984 NHL waiver draft as compensation for the Toronto selection of Jeff Brubaker (Clubs losing a player in the waiver draft have the option of taking the waiver price or a player off the drafting teams' unprotected list).

(g)—January, 1985—Traded with Gord Sherven by Edmonton Oilers to Minnesota North Stars for Mark Napier.

(h)—July, 1985—Signed by Toronto Maple Leafs as a free agent.

TOM MARTIN

Left Wing . . . 6'2" . . . 190 lbs. . . . Born, Kelowna, B.C., May 11, 1964 . . . Shoots left . . . Set University of Denver record for penalty minutes during his freshman year (1982-83).

Year	Team	League	Games	G.	A.	Pts.	Pen.
1981-82—Kelowna (c)		BCJHL	51	35	45	80	293
1982-83—University of Denver (d)		WCHA	37	8	18	26	128
1983-84—Victoria Cougars		WHL	60	30	45	75	261
1983-84—Sherbrooke Jets		AHL	5	0	0	0	16
1984-85—Sherbrooke Canadiens		AHL	58	4	15	19	212
1984-85—Winnipeg Jets		NHL	8	1	0	1	42
1985-86—Winnipeg Jets		NHL	5	0	0	0	0
1985-86—Sherbrooke Canadiens		AHL	69	11	18	29	227
NHL TOTALS			13	1	0	1	42

(c)—June, 1982—Drafted as underage player by Winnipeg Jets in 1982 NHL entry draft. Second Jets pick, 74th overall, fourth round.

(d)—January, 1983—WHL rights traded by Seattle Breakers with cash to Victoria Cougars for used team bus and player to be named later.

STEVE MARTINSON

Left Wing . . . 6'1" . . . 205 lbs. . . . Born, Minnetonka, Minn., June 21, 1957 . . . Shoots left . . . Set AHL single-season penalty minute record in 1985-86 . . . (May, 1986)—Disc operation.

Year	Team	League	Games	G.	A.	Pts.	Pen.
1981-82—Toledo Goaldiggers		IHL	35	12	18	30	128
1982-83—Birmingham Bulls (c)		CHL	43	4	5	9	184
1982-83—Toledo Goaldiggers		IHL	32	9	10	19	111
1983-84—Tulsa Oilers (d)		CHL	42	3	6	9	*240
1984-85—Salt Lake Golden Eagles		IHL	32	4	7	11	140

Year	Team	League	Games	G.	A.	Pts.	Pen.
1984-85—Toledo Goaldiggers (e)		IHL	22	0	3	3	160
1984-85—New Haven Nighthawks		AHL	4	0	0	0	17
1985-86—Hershey Bears (f)		AHL	69	3	6	9	*432

(c)—Led CHL playoffs with 80 penalty minutes.
(d)—Led CHL playoffs with 43 penalty minutes.
(e)—February, 1985—Traded with Kurt Kleinendorst by Salt Lake Golden Eagles to Toledo Goaldiggers for Kevin Conway, Blake Stephan, Grant Rezansoff and Steve Harrison.
(f)—September, 1985—Signed by Philadelphia Flyers as a free agent.

DENNIS JOHN MARUK

Center . . . 5'8" . . . 170 lbs. . . . Born, Toronto, Ont., November 17, 1955 . . . Shoots left . . . (October, 1979)—Torn ligaments in right knee, out for four months . . . Set NHL record for most shorthanded goals by a rookie (5) in 1975-76 . . . (December, 1984)—Sprained knee ligaments.

Year	Team	League	Games	G.	A.	Pts.	Pen.
1971-72—Toronto Marlboros		Jr. "A" OHA	8	2	1	3	4
1972-73—London Knights		Jr. "A" OHA	59	46	67	113	54
1973-74—London Knights		Jr. "A" OHA	69	47	65	112	61
1974-75—London Knights (c-d)		Jr. "A" OHA	65	66	79	145	53
1975-76—California Seals		NHL	80	30	32	62	44
1976-77—Cleveland Barons		NHL	80	28	50	78	68
1977-78—Cleveland Barons		NHL	76	36	35	71	50
1978-79—Minnesota North Stars (e)		NHL	2	0	0	0	0
1978-79—Washington Capitals		NHL	76	31	59	90	71
1979-80—Washington Capitals		NHL	27	10	17	27	8
1980-81—Washington Capitals		NHL	80	50	47	97	87
1981-82—Washington Capitals		NHL	80	60	76	136	128
1982-83—Washington Capitals (f)		NHL	80	31	50	81	71
1983-84—Minnesota North Stars		NHL	71	17	43	60	42
1984-85—Minnesota North Stars		NHL	71	19	41	60	56
1985-86—Minnesota North Stars		NHL	70	21	37	58	67
NHL TOTALS			793	333	487	820	692

(c)—Won Red Tilson Memorial Trophy (MVP).
(d)—Drafted from London Knights by California Seals in second round of 1975 amateur draft.
(e)—October, 1978—Traded by Minnesota North Stars to Washington Capitals for second of Washington's two picks in the first round, 10th overall, of the 1979 entry draft (Tom McCarthy).
(f)—July, 1983—Traded by Washington Capitals to Minnesota for second round draft pick in 1984 (Stephen Leach) and cash.

PETER MASSEY

Left Wing . . . 6'3" . . . 200 lbs. . . . Born, Lynn, Mass., June 16, 1966 . . . Shoots left.

Year	Team	League	Games	G.	A.	Pts.	Pen.
1984-85—New Hampton H.S. (c)		Mass. H.S.	26	25	13	38	....
1985-86—Northeastern University		H. East	36	4	0	4	22

(c)—June, 1985—Drafted by Quebec Nordiques in 1985 NHL entry draft. Fourth Nordiques pick, 65th overall, fourth round.

DWIGHT MATHIASEN

Right Wing . . . 6'2" . . . 190 lbs. . . . Born, New Westminster, B.C., December 5, 1963 . . . Shoots right.

Year	Team	League	Games	G.	A.	Pts.	Pen.
1983-84—University of Denver		WCHA	36	24	27	51	48
1984-85—University of Denver		WCHA	39	26	32	58	64
1985-86—University of Denver (b-c)		WCHA	48	40	49	89	48
1985-86—Pittsburgh Penguins		NHL	4	1	0	1	2
NHL TOTALS			4	1	0	1	2

(c)—March, 1986—Signed by Pittsburgh Penguins as a free agent.

BRAD ROBERT MAXWELL

Defense . . . 6'1" . . . 185 lbs. . . . Born, Brandon, Man., July 8, 1957 . . . Shoots right . . . Brother-in-law of Rick LaPointe . . . Missed part of 1979-80 season with stretched knee ligaments . . . (October 29, 1980)—Tore knee ligaments . . . (February, 1981)—Skate cut on foot developed blood poisoning . . . (November, 1981)—Slight concussion . . . (December, 1981)—Groin injury . . . (October, 1984)—Cracked rib in pre-season game . . . (October 13, 1985)—Pulled hamstring at Chicago and missed five games . . . (December 7, 1985)—Pulled hamstring vs. Montreal and missed 16 games . . . (January 10, 1986)—Pulled hamstring vs. Minnesota and missed five games.

Year	Team	League	Games	G.	A.	Pts.	Pen.
1973-74—Bellingham Blazers	Jr."A"BCHL	61	20	37	57	132
1974-75—New Westminster Bruins	WCHL	69	13	47	60	124
1975-76—New Westminster Bruins (b)	WCHL	72	19	80	99	239
1976-77—N. Westminster Bruins (b-c)	WCHL	70	21	58	79	205
1977-78—Minnesota North Stars	NHL	75	18	29	47	100
1978-79—Minnesota North Stars	NHL	70	9	28	37	145
1978-79—Oklahoma City Stars	CHL	2	0	1	1	21
1979-80—Minnesota North Stars	NHL	58	7	30	37	126
1980-81—Minnesota North Stars	NHL	27	3	13	16	98
1981-82—Minnesota North Stars	NHL	51	10	21	31	96
1982-83—Minnesota North Stars	NHL	77	11	28	39	157
1983-84—Minnesota North Stars	NHL	78	19	54	73	225
1984-85—Minnesota North Stars (d)	NHL	18	3	7	10	53
1984-85—Quebec Nordiques (e)	NHL	50	7	24	31	119
1985-86—Toronto Maple Leafs	NHL	52	8	18	26	108
NHL TOTALS		556	95	252	347	1227

(c)—Drafted from New Westminster Bruins by Minnesota North Stars in first round of 1977 amateur draft.
(d)—December, 1984—Traded with Brent Ashton by Minnesota North Stars to Quebec Nordiques for Tony McKegney and Bo Berglund.
(e)—August, 1985—Traded by Quebec Nordiques to Toronto Maple Leafs for John Anderson.

KEVIN MAXWELL

Center . . . 5'8" . . . 170 lbs. . . . Born, Edmonton, Alta., March 30, 1960 . . . Shoots right . . . (February, 1981)—Broke thumb . . . (October, 1981)—Back surgery . . . (December, 1981)—Groin injury.

Year	Team	League	Games	G.	A.	Pts.	Pen.
1978-79—Univ. of North Dakota (a-c-d)	WCHA	42	31	51	82	79
1979-80—Canadian National Team	Int'l	....	25	41	66	....
1979-80—Canadian Olympic Team	Olympic	6	0	5	5	4
1980-81—Oklahoma City Stars	CHL	31	8	13	21	38
1980-81—Minnesota North Stars	NHL	6	0	3	3	7
1981-82—Minnesota North Stars (e)	NHL	12	1	4	5	8
1981-82—Colorado Rockies	NHL	34	5	5	10	44
1982-83—Wichita Wind	CHL	68	24	41	65	47
1983-84—New Jersey Devils	NHL	14	0	3	3	2
1983-84—Maine Mariners	AHL	56	21	27	48	59
1984-85—Maine Mariners	AHL	52	25	21	46	70
1985-86—Maine Mariners	AHL	49	14	17	31	77
NHL TOTALS		66	6	15	21	61

(c)—Named to All-American Team (West).
(d)—August, 1979—Drafted as underage player in 1979 NHL entry draft by Minnesota North Stars. Fourth North Stars pick, 63rd overall, third round.
(e)—December, 1981—Traded with Jim Dobson by Minnesota North Stars to Colorado Rockies for cash.

DEREK MAYER

Defense . . . 6' . . . 190 lbs. . . . Born, Rossland, B.C., May 21, 1967 . . . Shoots right . . . (January, 1986)—Dislocated shoulder.

Year	Team	League	Games	G.	A.	Pts.	Pen.
1985-86—University of Denver (c)	WCHA	44	2	7	9	42

(c)—June, 1986—Drafted by Detroit Red Wings in 1986 NHL entry draft. Third Red Wings pick, 43rd overall, third round.

GARY McADAM

Right Wing . . . 5'11" . . . 180 lbs. . . . Born, Smith Falls, Ont., December 31, 1955 . . . Shoots left . . . Also plays Left Wing . . . Set AHL record in 1982-83 with 11 shorthanded goals.

Year	Team	League	Games	G.	A.	Pts.	Pen.
1972-73—Ottawa 67s	Jr."A"OHA	61	14	8	22	23
1973-74—		....	...	....	....	....
1974-75—St. Cath. Black Hawks (c)	Jr."A"OHA	65	24	53	77	111
1975-76—Hershey Bears	AHL	24	14	13	27	45
1975-76—Buffalo Sabres	NHL	31	1	2	3	2
1976-77—Buffalo Sabres	NHL	73	13	16	29	17
1977-78—Buffalo Sabres	NHL	79	19	22	41	44
1978-79—Buffalo Sabres (d)	NHL	40	6	5	11	13
1978-79—Pittsburgh Penguins	NHL	28	5	9	14	2
1979-80—Pittsburgh Penguins	NHL	78	19	22	41	63
1980-81—Pittsburgh Penguins (e)	NHL	34	3	9	12	30

Year	Team	League	Games	G.	A.	Pts.	Pen.
1980-81—Detroit Red Wings		NHL	40	5	14	19	27
1981-82—Dallas Black Hawks (f)		CHL	12	10	10	20	14
1981-82—Calgary Flames		NHL	46	12	15	27	18
1982-83—Buffalo Sabres		NHL	4	1	0	1	0
1982-83—Rochester Americans (g)		AHL	73	40	29	69	58
1983-84—Maine Mariners		AHL	10	3	4	7	18
1983-84—Washington Capitals (h)		NHL	24	1	5	6	12
1983-84—New Jersey Devils (i)		NHL	38	9	6	15	15
1984-85—Maine Mariners		AHL	70	32	20	52	39
1984-85—New Jersey Devils (j)		NHL	4	1	1	2	0
1985-86—St. Catharines Saints		AHL	27	15	18	33	16
1985-86—Toronto Maple Leafs		NHL	15	1	6	7	0
NHL TOTALS			534	96	132	228	243

(c)—Drafted from St. Catharines Black Hawks by Buffalo Sabres in third round of 1975 amateur draft.
(d)—February, 1979—Traded by Buffalo Sabres to Pittsburgh Penguins for Dave Schultz.
(e)—January, 1981—Traded by Pittsburgh Penguins to Detroit Red Wings for Errol Thompson.
(f)—November, 1981—Traded with fourth-round entry draft picks in 1982 (Dave Meszaros) and 1983 by Detroit Red Wings to Calgary Flames for Eric Vail.
(g)—August, 1983—Signed by New Jersey Devils as a free agent.
(h)—November, 1983—Acquired on waivers by Washington Capitals from New Jersey Devils.
(i)—January, 1984—Sold by Washington Capitals to New Jersey Devils.
(j)—August, 1985—Signed by Toronto Maple Leafs as a free agent.

ANDREW McBAIN

Right Wing . . . 6'1" . . . 190 lbs. . . . Born, Toronto, Ont., February 18, 1965 . . . Shoots right . . . (November, 1982)—Fractured cheekbone . . . (March, 1983)—Separated sterno clavicular joint . . . Also plays Center . . . (April 25, 1985)—Lost for the playoffs with mononucleosis . . . (September, 1985)—Switched to center . . . (December 8, 1985)—Injured knee vs. Los Angeles.

Year	Team	League	Games	G.	A.	Pts.	Pen.
1981-82—Niagara Falls Flyers		OHL	68	19	25	44	35
1982-83—North Bay Centennials (b-c)		OHL	67	33	87	120	61
1983-84—Winnipeg Jets		NHL	78	11	19	30	37
1984-85—Winnipeg Jets		NHL	77	7	15	22	45
1985-86—Winnipeg Jets		NHL	28	3	3	6	17
NHL TOTALS			183	21	37	58	99

(c)—June, 1983—Drafted as underage junior by Winnipeg Jets in 1983 NHL entry draft. First Jets pick, eighth overall, first round.

DAN McCARTHY

Center . . . 5'9" . . . 185 lbs. . . . Born, St. Mary's, Ont., April 7, 1958 . . . Shoots left.

Year	Team	League	Games	G.	A.	Pts.	Pen.
1975-76—Sudbury Wolves		OMJHL	65	17	30	47	23
1976-77—Sudbury Wolves		OMJHL	54	23	32	55	76
1977-78—Sudbury Wolves (c)		OMJHL	68	30	51	81	96
1977-78—Flint Generals		IHL	75	38	42	80	80
1979-80—New Haven Nighthawks		AHL	26	6	3	9	8
1979-80—Richmond Rifles		EHL	8	6	4	10	7
1980-81—New Haven Nighthawks		AHL	71	28	17	45	54
1980-81—New York Rangers		NHL	5	4	0	4	4
1981-82—Springfield Indians (d)		AHL	78	26	32	58	57
1982-83—Birmingham South Stars		CHL	76	30	35	65	67
1983-84—Baltimore Skipjacks (e)		AHL	27	8	11	19	8
1984-85—Baltimore Skipjacks (f)		AHL	32	3	11	14	19
1985-86—New Haven Nighthawks		AHL	33	7	9	16	46
NHL TOTALS			5	4	0	4	4

(c)—June, 1978—Drafted by New York Rangers in 1978 amateur draft. Sixteenth Rangers pick, 223rd overall, 15th round.
(d)—August, 1982—Traded by New York Rangers to Minnesota North Stars for Shawn Dineen.
(e)—January, 1984—Signed by Baltimore Skipjacks as a free agent.
(f)—February, 1985—Signed by Baltimore Skipjacks after playing in Europe.

KEVIN McCARTHY

Defense . . . 5'11" . . . 197 lbs. . . . Born, Winnipeg, Man., July 14, 1957 . . . Shoots right . . . Set WCHL record for points by Defenseman in 1975-76 (121) and broke own record in 1976-77 (127) and assists by Defenseman (105) in 1976-77 . . . Holds all-time WCHL record for career assists (276) . . . (December, 1979)—Bone chip lodged in hip muscles caused

disabling pain . . . (January, 1982)—Slight shoulder separation . . . (February, 1983)—Sprained wrist.

Year	Team	League	Games	G.	A.	Pts.	Pen.
1973-74—Winnipeg Clubs		WCHL	66	5	22	27	65
1974-75—Winnipeg Clubs		WCHL	66	20	61	81	102
1975-76—Winnipeg Clubs (a-c)		WCHL	72	33	88	121	160
1976-77—Winnipeg Monarchs (a-d)		WCHL	72	22	*105	127	110
1977-78—Philadelphia Flyers		NHL	62	2	15	17	32
1978-79—Philadelphia Flyers (e)		NHL	22	1	2	3	21
1978-79—Vancouver Canucks		NHL	1	0	0	0	0
1979-80—Vancouver Canucks		NHL	79	15	30	45	70
1980-81—Vancouver Canucks		NHL	80	16	37	53	85
1981-82—Vancouver Canucks		NHL	71	6	39	45	84
1982-83—Vancouver Canucks		NHL	74	12	28	40	88
1983-84—Vancouver Canucks (f)		NHL	47	2	14	16	61
1983-84—Pittsburgh Penguins		NHL	31	4	16	20	52
1984-85—Pittsburgh Penguins (g)		NHL	64	9	10	19	30
1985-86—Philadelphia Flyers		NHL	4	0	0	0	4
1985-86—Hershey Bears (a)		AHL	64	15	40	55	157
NHL TOTALS			535	67	191	258	527

(c)—Named Outstanding Defenseman in WCHL.

(d)—Drafted from Winnipeg Monarchs by Philadelphia Flyers in first round of 1977 amateur draft.

(e)—December, 1978—Traded with Drew Callander by Philadelphia Flyers to Vancouver Canucks for Dennis Ververgaert.

(f)—January, 1984—Traded by Vancouver Canucks to Pittsburgh Penguins for third round 1985 draft pick.

(g)—July, 1985—Signed by Philadelphia Flyers as a free agent.

TOM JOSEPH McCARTHY

Left Wing . . . 6'2" . . . 202 lbs. . . . Born, Toronto, Ont., July 31, 1960 . . . Shoots left . . . Rib injury (February, 1980) . . . (February, 1981)—Wrist surgery . . . (September 25, 1981)—Strained tendon in ankle during training camp . . . (November, 1981)—Tore calf muscle while conditioning from ankle injury . . . (April, 1984)—Injured back when a jeep overturned (he was a passenger). Ten days later he broke a bone in his back during playoff game with St. Louis when he collided with a goalpost . . . (October 18, 1984)—Torn tricep muscle in game vs. Edmonton . . . (December 21, 1984)—Sprained ankle . . . (February, 1985)—Vision problem . . . (September, 1985)—Moved to center and injured knee during training camp, missed the first five games of season . . . (November 23, 1985)—Bell's palsey . . . (December 14, 1985)—Injured shoulder vs. Toronto and missed 16 games . . . (March 5, 1986)—Broken thumb vs. Toronto.

Year	Team	League	Games	G.	A.	Pts.	Pen.
1976-77—Kingston Canadians		OMJHL	2	1	0	1	0
1976-77—North York Rangers		OPJHL	43	49	47	96	12
1977-78—Oshawa Generals		OMJHL	62	47	46	93	72
1978-79—Oshawa Generals (a-c)		OMJHL	63	69	75	144	98
1979-80—Minnesota North Stars		NHL	68	16	20	36	39
1980-81—Minnesota North Stars		NHL	62	23	25	48	62
1981-82—Minnesota North Stars		NHL	40	12	30	42	36
1982-83—Minnesota North Stars		NHL	80	28	48	76	59
1983-84—Minnesota North Stars		NHL	66	39	31	70	49
1984-85—Minnesota North Stars		NHL	44	16	21	37	36
1985-86—Minnesota North Stars (d)		NHL	25	12	12	24	12
NHL TOTALS			385	146	187	333	293

(c)—August, 1979—Drafted as underage player by Minnesota North Stars in 1979 entry draft. Second North Stars pick, 10th overall, first round.

(d)—May, 1986—Traded by Minnesota North Stars to Boston Bruins for third round 1986 draft pick (Rob Zettler) and second round pick in 1987.

KEVIN WILLIAM McCLELLAND

Center . . . 6' . . . 180 lbs. . . . Born, Oshawa, Ont., July 4, 1962 . . . Shoots right . . . (September 21, 1981)—Dislocated shoulder in preseason game . . . (January 24, 1983)—Dislocated shoulder in fight with Paul Higgins in game at Toronto. He required surgery on the shoulder and was lost for the season . . . (January, 1985)—Sprained left knee.

Year	Team	League	Games	G.	A.	Pts.	Pen.
1979-80—Niagara Falls Flyers (c)		OMJHL	67	14	14	28	71
1980-81—Niagara Falls Flyers (d)		OHL	68	36	72	108	184
1981-82—Niagara Falls Flyers		OHL	46	36	47	83	184
1981-82—Pittsburgh Penguins		NHL	10	1	4	5	4
1982-83—Pittsburgh Penguins		NHL	38	5	4	9	73
1983-84—Baltimore Skipjacks		AHL	3	1	1	2	0

Year	Team	League	Games	G.	A.	Pts.	Pen.
1983-84—Pittsburgh Penguins (e)	NHL	24	2	4	6	62
1983-84—Edmonton Oilers	NHL	52	8	20	28	127
1984-85—Edmonton Oilers	NHL	62	8	15	23	205
1985-86—Edmonton Oilers	NHL	79	11	25	36	266
NHL TOTALS		265	35	72	107	737

(c)—June, 1980—Drafted as underage junior by Hartford Whalers in 1980 NHL entry draft. Fourth Whalers pick, 71st overall, fourth round.

(d)—July, 1981—Acquired by Pittsburgh Penguins with Pat Boutette as compensation from Hartford Whalers for Hartford signing free agent Greg Millen. Decision required by NHL Arbitrator Judge Joseph Kane when Hartford and Pittsburgh were unable to agree on compensation.

(e)—December, 1983—Traded with sixth round 1984 draft pick (Emanuel Viveiros) by Pittsburgh Penguins to Edmonton Oilers for Tom Roulston.

GARY McCOLGAN

Left Wing . . . 6' . . . 192 lbs. . . . Born, Scarborough, Ont., March 27, 1966 . . . Shoots left . . . (October, 1986)—Separated shoulder.

Year	Team	League	Games	G.	A.	Pts.	Pen.
1982-83—Don Mills Midgets	MTMHL	40	32	27	59	28
1983-84—Oshawa Generals (c)	OHL	66	11	28	39	14
1984-85—Hamilton Steelhawks (d)	OHL	12	4	3	7	0
1984-85—Oshawa Generals	OHL	51	25	23	48	17
1985-86—Oshawa Generals	OHL	57	49	55	104	22

(c)—June, 1984—Drafted as underage junior by Minnesota North Stars in NHL entry draft. Sixth North Stars pick, 118th overall, sixth round.

(d)—December, 1984—Traded with Brent Loney by Hamilton Steelhawks to Oshawa Generals for Steve Hedington, John Hutchings and a sixth round pick in OHL 1985 priority draft (Andy May).

WILLIAM McCORMICK

Center . . . 6'1" . . . 185 lbs. . . . Born, Winchester, Mass., January 16, 1964 . . . Shoots left.

Year	Team	League	Games	G.	A.	Pts.	Pen.
1982-83—Westminster Heights H.S. (c)	Mass. H.S.	..	..	..	..	..
1983-84—University of Vermont	ECAC	22	0	1	1	10
1984-85—University of Vermont	ECAC	23	3	5	8	22
1985-86—University of Vermont	ECAC	30	8	7	15	36

(c)—June, 1983—Drafted by Philadelphia Flyers in 1983 NHL entry draft. Ninth Flyers pick, 201st overall, 10th round.

BILL McCREARY, JR.

Left Wing . . . 6' . . . 200 lbs. . . . Born, Springfield, Mass., April 15, 1960 . . . Shoots left . . . Son of Bill McCreary, Sr. and nephew of Keith McCreary . . . Also a nephew of Ron Attwell and a cousin of Bob Attwell.

Year	Team	League	Games	G.	A.	Pts.	Pen.
1978-79—Colgate University (c)	ECAC	24	19	25	44	70
1979-80—Colgate University	ECAC	12	7	13	20	44
1980-81—Toronto Maple Leafs	NHL	12	1	0	1	4
1980-81—New Brunswick Hawks	AHL	61	19	24	43	120
1981-82—Cincinnati Tigers	CHL	69	8	27	35	61
1982-83—Saginaw Gears	IHL	60	19	28	47	17
1982-83—Peoria Prancers	IHL	16	4	6	10	11
1982-83—St. Catharines Saints (d)	AHL	4	0	1	1	2
1983-84—Milwaukee Admirals	IHL	81	28	35	63	44
1984-85—Milwaukee Admirals	IHL	10	1	10	11	4
1985-86—Milwaukee Admirals	IHL	80	30	31	61	83
NHL TOTALS		12	1	0	1	4

(c)—August, 1979—Drafted by Toronto Maple Leafs in 1979 NHL entry draft. Fifth Maple Leafs pick, 114th overall, sixth round.

(d)—June, 1983—Released by Toronto Maple Leafs.

BYRON BRAD McCRIMMON
(Known by middle name.)

Defense . . . 5'11" . . . 193 lbs. . . . Born, Dodsland, Sask., March 29, 1959 . . . Shoots left . . . (February 2, 1985)—Broke bone in right hand during pre-game warmups and missed 13 games . . . (May 9, 1985)—Separated left shoulder, requiring surgery, during playoff game vs. Quebec when he was checked by Wilf Paiement.

Year	Team	League	Games	G.	A.	Pts.	Pen.
1976-77—Brandon Wheat Kings (b)	WCHL	72	18	66	84	96
1977-78—Brandon Wheat Kings (a-c)	WCHL	65	19	78	97	245

Year	Team	League	Games	G.	A.	Pts.	Pen.
1978-79	Brandon Wheat Kings (a-d)	WHL	66	24	74	98	139
1979-80	Boston Bruins	NHL	72	5	11	16	94
1980-81	Boston Bruins	NHL	78	11	18	29	148
1981-82	Boston Bruins (e)	NHL	78	1	8	9	83
1982-83	Philadelphia Flyers	NHL	79	4	21	25	61
1983-84	Philadelphia Flyers	NHL	71	0	24	24	76
1984-85	Philadelphia Flyers	NHL	66	8	25	33	81
1985-86	Philadelphia Flyers	NHL	80	13	42	55	85
	NHL TOTALS		524	42	149	191	628

(c)—Named outstanding defenseman in WCHL.
(d)—August, 1979—Drafted by Boston Bruins in 1979 entry draft. Second Boston pick, 15th overall, first round.
(e)—June, 1982—Traded by Boston Bruins to Philadelphia Flyers for Pete Peeters.

LANNY KING McDONALD

Right Wing . . . 6' . . . 185 lbs. . . . Born, Hanna, Alta., February 16, 1953 . . . Shoots right . . . Voted Colorado Athlete of the Year (1980) by state media . . . (February 18, 1984)—Fractured bone in right foot in game vs. Boston . . . (October, 1984)—Strained abdominal muscles in collision with Scott Stevens during pre-season game vs. Washington . . . (March, 1985)—Torn knee ligaments.

Year	Team	League	Games	G.	A.	Pts.	Pen.
1969-70	Lethbridge Sugar Kings	AJHL	34	2	9	11	19
1970-71	Lethbridge Sugar Kings (b)	AJHL	45	37	45	82	56
1970-71	Calgary Centennials	WCHL	6	0	2	2	6
1971-72	Medicine Hat Tigers	WCHL	68	50	64	114	54
1972-73	Medicine Hat Tigers (a-c)	WCHL	68	62	77	139	84
1973-74	Toronto Maple Leafs	NHL	70	14	16	30	43
1974-75	Toronto Maple Leafs	NHL	64	17	27	44	86
1975-76	Toronto Maple Leafs	NHL	75	37	56	93	70
1976-77	Toronto Maple Leafs (b)	NHL	80	46	44	90	77
1977-78	Toronto Maple Leafs	NHL	74	47	40	87	54
1978-79	Toronto Maple Leafs	NHL	79	43	42	85	32
1979-80	Toronto Maple Leafs (d)	NHL	35	15	15	30	10
1979-80	Colorado Rockies	NHL	46	25	20	45	43
1980-81	Colorado Rockies	NHL	80	35	46	81	56
1981-82	Colorado Rockies (e)	NHL	16	6	9	15	20
1981-82	Calgary Flames	NHL	55	34	33	67	37
1982-83	Calgary Flames (b-f)	NHL	80	66	32	98	90
1983-84	Calgary Flames	NHL	65	33	33	66	64
1984-85	Calgary Flames	NHL	43	19	18	37	36
1985-86	Calgary Flames	NHL	80	28	43	71	44
	NHL TOTALS		942	465	474	939	862

(c)—Drafted from Medicine Hat Tigers by Toronto Maple Leafs in first round of 1973 amateur draft.
(d)—December, 1979—Traded with Joel Quenneville by Toronto Maple Leafs to Colorado Rockies for Wilf Paiement and Pat Hickey.
(e)—December, 1981—Traded with fourth-round 1983 entry draft pick by Colorado Rockies to Calgary Flames for Bob MacMillan and Don Lever.
(f)—Won Bill Masterton Memorial Trophy (perseverance, sportsmanship and dedication).

JOE McDONNELL

Defense . . . 6'2" . . . 200 lbs. . . . Born, Kitchener, Ont., May 11, 1961 . . . Shoots right.

Year	Team	League	Games	G.	A.	Pts.	Pen.
1976-77	Kitchener Rangers	OMJHL	29	0	4	4	8
1977-78	Kitchener Rangers	OMJHL	55	0	4	4	14
1978-79	Kitchener Rangers	OMJHL	60	1	6	7	43
1979-80	Kitchener Rangers	OMJHL	62	6	21	27	81
1980-81	Kitchener Rangers	OMJHL	66	15	50	65	103
1981-82	Vancouver Canucks (c)	NHL	7	0	1	1	12
1981-82	Dallas Black Hawks	CHL	60	13	24	37	46
1982-83	Moncton Alpines	AHL	79	14	21	35	44
1983-84	Moncton Alpines (d)	AHL	78	12	33	45	44
1984-85	Baltimore Skipjacks (e)	AHL	41	7	27	34	22
1984-85	Pittsburgh Penguins	NHL	40	2	9	11	20
1985-86	Pittsburgh Penguins	NHL	3	0	0	0	0
1985-86	Baltimore Skipjacks	AHL	31	1	13	14	20
	NHL TOTALS		50	2	10	12	32

(c)—October, 1981—Signed by Vancouver Canucks as a free agent.
(d)—August, 1983—Signed by Edmonton Oilers as a free agent.
(e)—October, 1984—Signed by Pittsburgh Penguins as a free agent.

MICHAEL TODD McEWEN

Defense . . . 6'1" . . . 185 lbs. . . . Born, Hornepayne, Ont., August 10, 1956 . . . Shoots left . . . (November 2, 1981)—Broken nose in game vs. Calgary when struck by stick of Jim Peplinski . . . (February, 1983)—Sprained left ankle during team practice . . . (November, 1983)—Separated shoulder.

Year	Team	League	Games	G.	A.	Pts.	Pen.
1973-74	Toronto Marlboros	Jr. "A" OHA	68	5	32	37	81
1974-75	Toronto Marlboros	Jr. "A" OHA	68	18	63	81	52
1975-76	Toronto Marlboros (c)	Jr. "A" OHA	65	23	40	63	63
1976-77	New York Rangers	NHL	80	14	29	43	38
1977-78	New York Rangers	NHL	57	5	13	18	52
1978-79	New York Rangers	NHL	80	20	38	58	35
1979-80	New York Rangers (d)	NHL	9	1	7	8	8
1979-80	Colorado Rockies	NHL	67	11	40	51	33
1980-81	Colorado Rockies (e)	NHL	65	11	35	46	84
1980-81	New York Islanders	NHL	13	0	3	3	10
1981-82	New York Islanders	NHL	73	10	39	49	50
1982-83	New York Islanders	NHL	42	2	11	13	16
1983-84	New York Islanders (f)	NHL	15	0	2	2	6
1983-84	Los Angeles Kings	NHL	47	10	24	34	14
1983-84	New Haven Nighthawks (g)	AHL	9	3	7	10	26
1984-85	Binghamton Whalers	AHL	14	2	10	12	14
1984-85	Washington Capitals (h)	NHL	56	11	27	38	42
1985-86	Detroit Red Wings (i)	NHL	29	0	10	10	16
1985-86	New York Rangers (j)	NHL	16	2	5	7	8
1985-86	Hartford Whalers	NHL	10	3	2	5	6
1985-86	New Haven Nighthawks	AHL	2	0	3	3	2
NHL TOTALS			659	100	285	385	418

(c)—Drafted from Toronto Marlboros by New York Rangers in third round of 1976 amateur draft.
(d)—November, 1979—Traded with Lucien DeBlois, Pat Hickey, Dean Turner and future considerations (Bobby Sheehan and Bobby Crawford) by New York Rangers to Colorado Rockies for Barry Beck.
(e)—March, 1981—Traded by Colorado Rockies with Jari Kaarela to New York Islanders for Glenn Resch and Steve Tambellini.
(f)—November, 1983—Traded by New York Islanders to Los Angeles Kings for future considerations.
(g)—August, 1984—Signed by Washington Capitals as a free agent.
(h)—August, 1985—Signed by Detroit Red Wings as a free agent.
(i)—December, 1985—Traded by Detroit Red Wings to New York Rangers for Steve Richmond.
(j)—March, 1986—Traded by New York Rangers to Hartford Whalers for Bob Crawford.

DAN McFALL

Defense . . . 6' . . . 192 lbs. . . . Born, Kenmore, N.Y., April 8, 1963 . . . Shoots left.

Year	Team	League	Games	G.	A.	Pts.	Pen.
1981-82	Michigan State University (c)	CCHA	40	3	17	20	28
1982-83	Michigan State University	CCHA	36	12	14	26	22
1983-84	Michigan State University	CCHA	46	14	20	34	56
1984-85	Michigan State University (d)	CCHA	44	7	25	32	32
1984-85	Winnipeg Jets	NHL	2	0	0	0	0
1985-86	Winnipeg Jets	NHL	7	0	1	1	0
1985-86	Sherbrooke Canadiens	AHL	50	2	10	12	16
NHL TOTALS			9	0	1	1	0

(c)—June, 1981—Drafted by Winnipeg Jets in 1981 NHL entry draft. Eighth Jets pick, 148th overall, eighth round.
(d)—First-Team (West) All-America.

BRIAN McFARLANE

Right Wing . . . 5'11" . . . 180 lbs. . . . Born, Burnaby, B.C., September 7, 1967 . . . Shoots right . . . Nephew of Tom McVie (WHL player from 1957-1972 and coach of Washington, Winnipeg and New Jersey in the NHL.)

Year	Team	League	Games	G.	A.	Pts.	Pen.
1983-84	Seattle Breakers	WHL	65	6	10	16	12
1984-85	Seattle Breakers (c)	WHL	40	18	12	30	4
1985-86	Seattle Thunderbirds (d)	WHL	35	9	7	16	20
1985-86	Brandon Wheat Kings	WHL	19	4	5	9	4

(c)—June, 1985—Drafted as underage junior by Vancouver Canucks in 1985 NHL entry draft. Seventh Canucks pick, 130th overall, seventh round.
(d)—February, 1986—Traded with Kirk Phare by Seattle Thunderbirds to Brandon Wheat Kings for John Dzikowski.

JAMES McGEOUGH

Center . . . 5'8" . . . 161 lbs. . . . Born, Regina, Sask., April 13, 1963 . . . Shoots left . . . (November 6, 1985)—Bruised left knee vs. Washington.

Year	Team	League	Games	G.	A.	Pts.	Pen.
1979-80—Regina		SJHL	57	56	77	133	94
1979-80—Regina Pats		WHL	10	1	4	5	2
1980-81—Billings Bighorns (c-d)		WHL	71	50	44	94	141
1981-82—Billings Bighorns		WHL	71	*93	66	159	142
1981-82—Washington Capitals		NHL	4	0	0	0	0
1982-83—Nanaimo Islanders		WHL	72	76	56	132	126
1982-83—Hershey Bears		AHL	5	1	1	2	10
1983-84—Hershey Bears		AHL	79	40	36	76	108
1984-85—Binghamton Whalers		AHL	57	32	21	53	26
1984-85—Washington Capitals (e)		NHL	11	3	0	3	12
1984-85—Pittsburgh Penguins		NHL	14	0	4	4	4
1985-86—Baltimore Skipjacks		AHL	38	14	13	27	20
1985-86—Pittsburgh Penguins		NHL	17	3	2	5	8
NHL TOTALS			46	6	6	12	24

(c)—October, 1980—Traded by Regina Pats to Billings Bighorns for Neil Girard, Bruce Holloway and Wade Waters.
(d)—June, 1981—Drafted by Washington Capitals as underage junior in 1981 NHL entry draft. Tenth Capitals pick, 110th overall, sixth round.
(e)—March, 1985—Traded by Washington Captials to Pittsburgh Penguins for Mark Taylor.

ROBERT PAUL McGILL

Defense . . . 6' . . . 202 lbs. . . . Born, Edmonton, Alta., April 27, 1962 . . . Shoots right . . . (January, 1985)—Given 3-game NHL suspension . . . (January 4, 1986)—Separated shoulder vs. Los Angeles and missed three games . . . (March 1, 1986)—Suspended by NHL for seven games.

Year	Team	League	Games	G.	A.	Pts.	Pen.
1978-79—Abbotsford		BCJHL	46	3	20	23	242
1979-80—Victoria Cougars (c)		WHL	70	3	18	21	230
1980-81—Victoria Cougars		WHL	66	5	36	41	295
1981-82—Toronto Maple Leafs		NHL	68	1	10	11	263
1982-83—Toronto Maple Leafs		NHL	30	0	0	0	146
1982-83—St. Catharines Saints		AHL	32	2	5	7	95
1983-84—Toronto Maple Leafs		NHL	11	0	2	2	51
1983-84—St. Catharines Saints		AHL	55	1	15	16	217
1984-85—Toronto Maple Leafs		NHL	72	0	5	5	250
1985-86—Toronto Maple Leafs		NHL	61	1	4	5	141
NHL TOTALS			242	2	21	23	851

(c)—June, 1980—Drafted as underage junior by Toronto Maple Leafs in 1980 NHL entry draft. Second Maple Leafs pick, 26th overall, second round.

NORM McIVER

Defense . . . 5'11" . . . 180 lbs. . . . Born, Thunder Bay, Ont., September 1, 1964 . . . Shoots left.

Year	Team	League	Games	G.	A.	Pts.	Pen.
1982-83—U. of Minnesota-Duluth		WCHA	45	1	26	27	40
1983-84—U. of Minnesota-Duluth		WCHA	31	13	28	41	28
1984-85—U. of Minnesota-Duluth		WCHA	47	14	47	61	63
1985-86—U. of Minnesota-Duluth		WCHA	42	11	51	62	36

DARREN McKAY

Defense . . . 5'9" . . . 190 lbs. . . . Born, Lloydminster, Sask., February 10, 1962 . . . Shoots left.

Year	Team	League	Games	G.	A.	Pts.	Pen.
1977-78—Red Deer Rustlers		AJHL	59	2	11	13	50
1978-79—Red Deer Rustlers		AJHL	....	...	....	....	....
1978-79—Billings Bighorns		WHL	2	0	0	0	0
1979-80—Red Deer Rustlers		AJHL	....	...	....	....	....
1979-80—Billings Bighorns		WHL	14	6	2	8	23
1980-81—Billings Bighorns		WHL	68	10	29	39	183
1981-82—Billings Bighorns		WHL	70	12	64	76	176
1982-83—Binghamton Whalers (c)		AHL	65	4	32	36	113
1983-84—Binghamton Whalers		AHL	71	11	40	51	206
1984-85—Muskegon Mohawks		IHL	64	8	28	36	90
1985-86—Indianapolis Checkers		IHL	30	4	14	18	42
1985-86—Muskegon Lumberjacks		IHL	36	4	22	26	62

(c)—August, 1982—Signed by Hartford Whalers as a free agent.

RANDY McKAY

Right Wing . . . 6'1" . . . 170 lbs. . . . Born, Montreal, Que., January 25, 1967 . . . Shoots right.

Year	Team	League	Games	G.	A.	Pts.	Pen.
1983-84—Lac. St. Louis Midget		Que. Midget	38	18	28	46	62
1984-85—Michigan Tech. (c)		WCHA	25	4	5	9	32
1985-86—Michigan Tech.		WCHA	40	12	22	34	46

(c)—June, 1985—Drafted by Detroit Red Wings in 1985 NHL entry draft. Sixth Red Wings pick, 113th overall, sixth round.

GARNET McKECHNEY

Right Wing . . . 6'2" . . . 175 lbs. . . . Born, Swift Current, Sask., April 28, 1965 . . . Shoots right.

Year	Team	League	Games	G.	A.	Pts.	Pen.
1981-82—Thunder Bay Maroons		Ont. Midget	62	40	30	70	54
1982-83—Kitchener Rangers (c)		OHL	66	20	20	40	95
1983-84—Kitchener Rangers		OHL	68	31	45	76	107
1984-85—Kitchener Rangers (d)		OHL	40	12	25	37	52
1984-85—London Knights		OHL	23	10	9	19	23
1985-86—London Knights		OHL	27	16	14	30	50
1985-86—Milwaukee Admirals		IHL	15	0	2	2	11
1985-86—Indianapolis Checkers		IHL	3	0	1	1	2
1985-86—Saginaw Generals		IHL	8	2	2	4	2

(c)—June, 1983—Drafted as underage junior by New York Islanders in 1983 NHL entry draft. Third Islanders pick, 37th overall, second round.

(d)—January, 1985—Traded with Greg Puhalsky by Kitchener Rangers to London Knights for Brad Sparkes, third round 1985 OHL priority draft pick (Paul Porter) and future considerations.

ANTHONY SYIIYD (TONY) McKEGNEY

Left Wing . . . 6'1" . . . 195 lbs. . . . Born, Montreal, Que., February 15, 1958 . . . Shoots left . . . Brother of Mike (1974 Montreal draft pick) and Ian (Dallas-CHL) McKegney and adopted son of Lawrey McKegney . . . (February, 1985)—Separated shoulder that required surgery . . . (January 16, 1986)—Injured shoulder vs. St. Louis and missed seven games.

Year	Team	League	Games	G.	A.	Pts.	Pen.
1974-75—Kingston Canadians	Jr. "A" OHA		52	27	48	75	36
1975-76—Kingston Canadians	Jr. "A" OHA		65	24	56	80	20
1976-77—Kingston Canadians (a)	Jr. "A" OHA		66	58	77	135	30
1977-78—Kingston Canadians (b-c)	Jr. "A" OHA		55	43	49	92	19
1978-79—Buffalo Sabres		NHL	52	8	14	22	10
1978-79—Hershey Bears		AHL	24	21	18	39	4
1979-80—Buffalo Sabres		NHL	80	23	29	52	24
1980-81—Buffalo Sabres		NHL	80	37	32	69	24
1981-82—Buffalo Sabres		NHL	73	23	29	52	41
1982-83—Buffalo Sabres (d)		NHL	78	36	37	73	18
1983-84—Quebec Nordiques		NHL	75	24	27	51	23
1984-85—Quebec Nordiques (e)		NHL	30	12	9	21	12
1984-85—Minnesota North Stars		NHL	27	11	13	24	4
1985-86—Minnesota North Stars		NHL	70	15	25	40	48
NHL TOTALS			565	189	215	404	204

(c)—Drafted from Kingston Canadians by Buffalo Sabres in second round of 1978 amateur draft.

(d)—June, 1983—Traded by Buffalo Sabres with Andre Savard, Jean-Francois Sauve and Buffalo's third-round pick in 1983 (Iiro Jarvi) to Quebec Nordiques for Real Cloutier and Quebec's first-round draft choice in 1983 (Adam Creighton).

(e)—December, 1984—Traded with Bo Berglund by Quebec Nordiques to Minnesota North Stars for Brad Maxwell and Brent Ashton.

SEAN MICHAEL McKENNA

Right Wing . . . 6' . . . 186 lbs. . . . Born, Asbestos, Que., March 7, 1962 . . . Shoots right.

Year	Team	League	Games	G.	A.	Pts.	Pen.
1978-79—Montreal Juniors		QMJHL	66	9	14	23	14
1979-80—Sherbrooke Beavers (c)		QMJHL	59	20	19	39	24
1980-81—Sherbrooke Beavers (a)		QMJHL	71	57	47	104	122
1981-82—Sherbrooke Beavers (b-d-e)		QMJHL	59	57	33	90	29
1981-82—Buffalo Sabres		NHL	3	0	1	1	2
1982-83—Buffalo Sabres		NHL	46	10	14	24	4
1982-83—Rochester Americans (f)		AHL	26	16	10	26	14
1983-84—Buffalo Sabres		NHL	78	20	10	30	45
1984-85—Buffalo Sabres		NHL	65	20	16	36	41

Year	Team	League	Games	G.	A.	Pts.	Pen.
1985-86—Buffalo Sabres (g)		NHL	45	6	12	18	28
1985-86—Los Angeles Kings		NHL	30	4	0	4	7
NHL TOTALS			267	60	53	113	127

(c)—June, 1980—Drafted as underage junior by Buffalo Sabres in 1980 NHL entry draft. Third Sabres pick, 56th overall, third round.

(d)—Led QMJHL President Cup Playoffs with 26 goals.

(e)—Named MVP of 1982 Memorial Cup Tournament.

(f)—Led AHL playoffs with a record 14 goals.

(g)—January, 1986—Traded with Larry Playfair and Ken Baumgartner by Buffalo Sabres to Los Angeles Kings for Brian Engblom and Doug Smith.

JAMIE McKINLEY

Center . . . 6'1" . . . 165 lbs. . . . Born, Moncton, N.B., May 1, 1967 . . . Shoots right.

Year	Team	League	Games	G.	A.	Pts.	Pen.
1983-84—Fredericton Midgets		OHA	49	51	52	103	26
1984-85—Guelph Platers (c)		OHL	64	25	22	47	7
1985-86—Guelph Platers		OHL	66	23	30	53	48

(c)—June, 1985—Drafted as underage junior by New Jersey Devils in 1985 NHL entry draft. 11th Devils pick, 213th overall, Eleventh round.

BRIAN McKINNON

Center . . . 5'11" . . . 185 lbs. . . . Born, Toronto, Ont., October 4, 1964 . . . Shoots left.

Year	Team	League	Games	G.	A.	Pts.	Pen.
1981-82—Dixie Beehives		MTJHL	46	32	30	62	72
1982-83—Ottawa 67's		OHL	66	6	9	15	20
1983-84—Ottawa 67's (c)		OHL	58	31	27	58	27
1984-85—Rochester Americans		AHL	62	6	8	14	16
1985-86—Rochester Americans		AHL	51	4	7	11	14

(c)—June, 1984—Drafted as underage junior by Buffalo Sabres in NHL entry draft. Ninth Sabres pick, 106th overall, 10th round.

DAVID McLAY

Left Wing . . . 5'11" . . . 175 lbs. . . . Born, Chilliwak, B.C., May 13, 1966 . . . Shoots left.

Year	Team	League	Games	G.	A.	Pts.	Pen.
1983-84—Kelowna Wings (c)		WHL	71	34	34	68	112
1984-85—Kelowna Wings		WHL	17	9	10	19	44
1984-85—Portland Winter Hawks		WHL	53	23	26	49	176
1985-86—Portland Winter Hawks		WHL	80	37	49	86	219

(c)—June, 1984—Drafted as underage junior by Philadelphia Flyers in NHL entry draft. Third Flyers pick, 43rd overall, third round.

TODD McLELLAN

Center . . . 5'10" . . . 185 lbs. . . . Born, Melville, Sask., October 3, 1967 . . . Shoots left . . . (October, 1985)—Dislocated left shoulder.

Year	Team	League	Games	G.	A.	Pts.	Pen.
1982-83—Saskatoon Blazers Midgets		Sask.	25	6	9	15	6
1983-84—Saskatoon Blades		WHL	50	8	14	22	15
1984-85—Saskatoon Blades		WHL	41	15	35	50	33
1985-86—Saskatoon Blades (c)		WHL	27	9	10	19	13

(c)—June, 1986—Drafted by New York Islanders in 1986 NHL entry draft. Sixth Islanders pick, 104th overall, fifth round.

DAVID McLLWAIN

Right Wing . . . 6' . . . 190 lbs. . . . Born, Seaforth, Ont., January 9, 1967 . . . Shoots right.

Year	Team	League	Games	G.	A.	Pts.	Pen.
1984-85—Kitchener Rangers		OHL	61	13	21	34	29
1985-86—Kitchener Rangers (c)		OHL	13	7	7	14	12
1985-86—North Bay Centennials (d)		OHL	51	30	28	58	25

(c)—November, 1985—Traded with John Keller and Todd Stromback by Kitchener Rangers to North Bay Centennials for Ron Sanko, Peter Lisy, Richard Hawkins and Brett McDonald.

(d)—June, 1986—Drafted as underage junior by Pittsburgh Penguins in 1986 NHL entry draft. Ninth Penguins pick, 172nd overall, ninth round.

TOM McMURCHY

Right Wing . . . 5'10" . . . 170 lbs. . . . Born, New Westminster, B.C., December 2, 1963 . . . Shoots left . . . Also plays Center and Left Wing . . . Brother of Anthony McMurchy.

Year	Team	League	Games	G.	A.	Pts.	Pen.
1980-81	Medicine Hat Tigers (c)	WHL	14	5	0	5	46
1980-81	Brandon Wheat Kings	WHL	46	20	33	53	101
1981-82	Brandon Wheat Kings (d)	WHL	68	59	63	122	179
1982-83	Brandon Wheat Kings	WHL	42	43	38	81	48
1982-83	Springfield Indians	AHL	8	2	2	4	0
1983-84	Springfield Indians	AHL	43	16	14	30	54
1983-84	Chicago Black Hawks	NHL	27	3	1	4	42
1984-85	Milwaukee Admirals	IHL	69	30	26	56	61
1984-85	Chicago Blacks Hawks	NHL	15	1	2	3	13
1985-86	Chicago Black Hawks	NHL	4	0	0	0	2
1985-86	Nova Scotia Oilers (e)	AHL	49	26	21	47	73
1985-86	Moncton Golden Flames	AHL	16	7	3	10	27
	NHL TOTALS		46	4	3	7	57

(c)—November, 1980—Traded with Syd Cranston and future considerations by Medicine Hat Tigers to Brandon Wheat Kings for Mike Winther.

(d)—June, 1982—Drafted as underage junior by Chicago Black Hawks in 1982 NHL entry draft. Third Black Hawks pick, 49th overall, third round.

(e)—March, 1986—Traded by Chicago Black Hawks to Calgary Flames for Rik Wilson.

PETER MAXWELL McNAB

Center . . . 6'3" . . . 210 lbs. . . . Born, Vancouver, B.C., May 8, 1952 . . . Shoots left . . . Son of Max McNab, general manager of New Jersey Devils and former NHL forward . . . Brother of David McNab (Hartford Whalers scout) . . . Missed part of 1974-75 season with injured knee ligament . . . Given six-game suspension by NHL for fight in stands at New York Rangers on December 26, 1979 . . . Attended University of Denver on a baseball scholarship . . . (January, 1983)—Separated right shoulder . . . (February 24, 1984)—Tore ligaments in right thumb during game vs. Los Angeles and required surgery . . . (January 4, 1986)—Strained left knee at N. Y. Rangers and missed nine games.

Year	Team	League	Games	G.	A.	Pts.	Pen.
1970-71	University of Denver	WCHA	28	19	14	33	6
1971-72	University of Denver	WCHA	38	27	38	65	16
1972-73	University of Denver (c)	WCHA	28	23	29	52	12
1973-74	Cincinnati Swords	AHL	49	34	39	73	16
1973-74	Buffalo Sabres	NHL	22	3	6	9	2
1974-75	Buffalo Sabres	NHL	53	22	21	43	8
1975-76	Buffalo Sabres (d)	NHL	79	24	32	56	16
1976-77	Boston Bruins	NHL	80	38	48	86	11
1977-78	Boston Bruins	NHL	79	41	39	80	4
1978-79	Boston Bruins	NHL	76	35	45	80	10
1979-80	Boston Bruins	NHL	74	40	38	78	10
1980-81	Boston Bruins	NHL	80	37	46	83	24
1981-82	Boston Bruins	NHL	80	36	40	76	19
1982-83	Boston Bruins	NHL	74	22	52	74	23
1983-84	Boston Bruins (e)	NHL	52	14	16	30	10
1983-84	Vancouver Canucks	NHL	13	1	6	7	10
1984-85	Vancouver Canucks (f)	NHL	75	23	25	48	10
1985-86	New Jersey Devils	NHL	71	19	24	43	14
	NHL TOTALS		908	355	438	793	171

(c)—Drafted from University of Denver by Buffalo Sabres in sixth round of 1972 amateur draft.

(d)—NHL rights traded to Boston Bruins by Buffalo Sabres for NHL rights to Andre Savard, June, 1976.

(e)—February, 1984—Traded by Boston Bruins to Vancouver Canucks for Jim Nill.

(f)—August, 1985—Signed by New Jersey Devils as a free agent.

GEORGE McPHEE

Left Wing . . . 5'9" . . . 170 lbs. . . . Born, Guelph, Ont., July 2, 1958 . . . Shoots left . . . (January, 1983)—Back injury . . . (October, 1984)—Hip injury . . . (November 4, 1985)—Injured thumb in Pittsburgh and missed seven games.

Year	Team	League	Games	G.	A.	Pts.	Pen.
1977-78	Guelph Platers	OPJHL	48	53	57	110	150
1978-79	Bowling Green St. Univ.	CCHA	43	*40	48	*88	58
1979-80	Bowling Green St. Univ.	CCHA	34	21	24	45	51
1980-81	Bowling Green St. Univ. (b)	CCHA	36	25	29	54	68
1981-82	Bowling Green U. (a-c-d-e)	CCHA	40	28	52	80	57
1982-83	Tulsa Oilers (f)	CHL	61	17	43	60	145
1982-83	New York Rangers (g)	NHL	....	...	....	....	....

Year	Team	League	Games	G.	A.	Pts.	Pen.
1983-84—New York Rangers		NHL	9	1	1	2	11
1983-84—Tulsa Oilers		CHL	49	20	28	48	133
1984-85—New Haven Nighthawks		AHL	3	2	2	4	13
1984-85—New York Rangers		NHL	49	12	15	27	139
1985-86—New York Rangers		NHL	30	4	4	8	63
NHL TOTALS			88	17	20	37	213

(c)—CCHA Player of the Year.
(d)—Named to All-America Team (West).
(e)—Winner of Hobey Baker Award (Top NCAA hockey player).
(f)—May, 1983—Signed by New York Rangers as a free agent.
(g)—No regular-season record. Played in nine playoff games with three goals and three assists.

MICHAEL JOSEPH McPHEE

Left Wing . . . 6'2" . . . 200 lbs. . . . Born, Sydney, N.S., February 14, 1960 . . . Shoots left . . . (Sept., 1982)—Broke hand in training camp . . . (January 10, 1986)—Injured ankle at N. Y. Rangers and missed 10 games.

Year	Team	League	Games	G.	A.	Pts.	Pen.
1978-79—R.P.I.		ECAC	26	14	19	33	16
1979-80—R.P.I. (c)		ECAC	27	15	21	36	22
1980-81—R.P.I.		ECAC	29	28	18	46	22
1981-82—R.P.I.		ECAC	6	0	3	3	4
1982-83—Nova Scotia Voyageurs		AHL	42	10	15	25	29
1983-84—Nova Scotia Voyageurs		AHL	67	22	33	55	101
1983-84—Montreal Canadiens		NHL	14	5	2	7	41
1984-85—Montreal Canadiens		NHL	70	17	22	39	120
1985-86—Montreal Canadiens		NHL	70	19	21	40	69
NHL TOTALS			154	41	45	86	230

(c)—June, 1980—Drafted by Montreal Canadiens in 1980 NHL entry draft. Eighth Canadiens pick, 124th overall, sixth round.

BASIL PAUL McRAE

Left Wing . . . 6'2" . . . 200 lbs. . . . Born, Orillia, Ont., January 1, 1961 . . . Shoots left.

Year	Team	League	Games	G.	A.	Pts.	Pen.
1977-78—Seneca Nats		OHA Jr. "B"	36	21	38	59	80
1978-79—London Knights		OMJHL	66	13	28	41	79
1979-80—London Knights (c)		OMJHL	67	23	35	58	116
1980-81—London Knights		OHL	65	29	23	52	266
1981-82—Fredericton Express		AHL	47	11	15	26	175
1981-82—Quebec Nordiques		NHL	20	4	3	7	69
1982-83—Fredericton Express		AHL	53	22	19	41	146
1982-83—Quebec Nordiques		NHL	22	1	1	2	59
1983-84—Toronto Maple Leafs (d)		NHL	3	0	0	0	19
1983-84—St. Catharines Saints		AHL	78	14	25	39	187
1984-85—St. Catharines Saints		AHL	72	30	25	55	186
1984-85—Toronto Maple Leafs		NHL	1	0	0	0	0
1985-86—Detroit Red Wings (e)		NHL	4	0	0	0	5
1985-86—Adirondack Red Wings		AHL	69	22	30	52	259
NHL TOTALS			50	5	4	9	152

(c)—June, 1980—Drafted as underage junior by Quebec Nordiques in 1980 NHL entry draft. Third Nordiques pick, 87th overall, fifth round.
(d)—August, 1983—Traded by Quebec Nordiques to Toronto Maple Leafs for Richard Trumel.
(e)—August, 1985—Signed by Detroit Red Wings as a free agent.

BRIAN McREYNOLDS

Center . . . 6'1" . . . 180 lbs. . . . Born, Penetanguishene, Ont., January 5, 1965 . . . Shoots left.

Year	Team	League	Games	G.	A.	Pts.	Pen.
1984-85—Orillia Travelways (c)		OHA	48	40	54	94	....
1985-86—Michigan State Univ.		CCHA	45	14	24	38	78

(c)—June, 1985—Drafted by New York Rangers in 1985 NHL entry draft. Sixth Rangers pick, 112th overall, sixth round.

MARTY McSORLEY

Defense . . . 6'1" . . . 190 lbs. . . . Born, Hamilton, Ont., May 18, 1963 . . . Shoots right.

Year	Team	League	Games	G.	A.	Pts.	Pen.
1981-82—Belleville Bulls		OHL	58	6	13	19	234
1982-83—Belleville Bulls		OHL	70	10	41	51	183
1982-83—Baltimore Skipjacks (c)		AHL	2	0	0	0	22

Year	Team	League	Games	G.	A.	Pts.	Pen.
1983-84—Pittsburgh Penguins		NHL	72	2	7	9	224
1984-85—Baltimore Skipjacks		AHL	58	6	24	30	154
1984-85—Pittsburgh Penguins		NHL	15	0	0	0	15
1985-86—Edmonton Oilers (d)		NHL	59	11	12	23	265
1985-86—Nova Scotia Oilers		AHL	9	2	4	6	34
NHL TOTALS			146	13	19	32	504

(c)—April, 1983—Signed by Pittsburgh Penguins as a free agent.

(d)—August, 1985—Traded with Tim Hrynewich by Pittsburgh Penguins to Edmonton Oilers for Gilles Meloche.

NEIL ROBERT MEADMORE

Right Wing . . . 6'4" . . . 180 lbs. . . . Born, Winnipeg, Man., October 23, 1959 . . . Shoots right . . . Son of Ronald Meadmore, who played several seasons in CFL . . . Brother of Jim Meadmore . . . (November, 1983)—Knee surgery.

Year	Team	League	Games	G.	A.	Pts.	Pen.
1977-78—Flin Flon Bombers		WCHL	25	7	8	15	30
1977-78—New Westminster Bruins		WCHL	29	5	7	12	19
1978-79—New Westminster Bruins		WHL	71	30	36	66	128
1979-80—Kalamazoo Wings		IHL	79	23	37	60	160
1980-81—Kalamazoo Wings		IHL	82	31	41	78	179
1981-82—Adirondack Red Wings		AHL	52	13	11	24	106
1981-82—Kalamazoo Wings		IHL	24	18	11	29	51
1982-83—Kalamazoo Wings		IHL	26	10	7	17	97
1983-84—Kalamazoo Wings		IHL	82	39	48	87	267
1984-85—Kalamazoo Wings		IHL	45	10	23	33	167
1985-86—Kalamazoo Wings		IHL	37	12	17	29	118

RICK MEAGHER

Center . . . 5'8" . . . 175 lbs. . . . Born, Belleville, Ont., November 4, 1953 . . . Shoots left . . . Member of Boston University Hall of Fame . . . Named the Boston University Athlete of the Decade (1970-79) . . . Elected to ECAC All-Decade Team (1970-79) . . . Brother of Terry Meagher . . . (December, 1981)—Back and knee problems . . . (November, 1982)—Missed eight games with shoulder separation suffered in game at Montreal . . . (January, 1984)—Fractured rib . . . (October, 1984)—Cut right forearm when run over by a skate in pre-season game with Hartford Whalers . . . (January, 1985)—Bruised ribs.

Year	Team	League	Games	G.	A.	Pts.	Pen.
1973-74—Boston University		ECAC	30	19	21	40	26
1974-75—Boston University		ECAC	32	25	28	53	80
1975-76—Boston University		ECAC	28	12	25	37	22
1976-77—Boston University (a-c)		ECAC	34	34	46	80	42
1977-78—Nova Scotia Voyageurs		AHL	57	20	27	47	33
1978-79—Nova Scotia Voyageurs		AHL	79	35	46	81	57
1979-80—Nova Scotia Voyageurs		AHL	64	32	44	76	53
1979-80—Montreal Canadiens (d)		NHL	2	0	0	0	0
1980-81—Binghamton Whalers		AHL	50	23	35	58	54
1980-81—Hartford Whalers		NHL	27	7	10	17	19
1981-82—Hartford Whalers		NHL	65	24	19	43	51
1982-83—Hartford Whalers		NHL	4	0	0	0	0
1982-83—New Jersey Devils		NHL	57	15	14	29	11
1983-84—Maine Mariners		AHL	10	6	4	10	2
1983-84—New Jersey Devils		NHL	52	14	14	28	16
1984-85—New Jersey Devils (e)		NHL	71	11	20	31	22
1985-86—St. Louis Blues		NHL	79	11	19	30	28
NHL TOTALS			357	82	96	178	147

(c)—Named to first team (East) All-America.

(d)—June, 1980—Traded with third (Paul MacDermid) and fifth (Dan Bourbonnais) round picks in 1981 draft by Montreal Canadiens to Hartford Whalers for third (Dieter Hegen) and fifth (Steve Rooney) round Whalers picks in 1981 draft.

(e)—August, 1985—Traded with 1986 12th round draft choice (Bill Butler) by New Jersey Devils to St. Louis Blues for Perry Anderson.

ALLAN MEASURES

Defense . . . 5'11" . . . 165 lbs. . . . Born, Barrhead, Alta., May 8, 1965 . . . Shoots left.

Year	Team	League	Games	G.	A.	Pts.	Pen.
1981-82—Barrhead Midget		Alta. Midget	40	55	66	121	40
1982-83—Calgary Wranglers (c)		WHL	63	5	23	28	43
1983-84—Calgary Wranglers		WHL	69	17	36	53	96

Year	Team	League	Games	G.	A.	Pts.	Pen.
1984-85—Calgary Wranglers		WHL	42	16	27	43	28
1985-86—Calgary Wranglers		WHL	46	23	34	57	50

(c)—June, 1983—Drafted as underage junior by Vancouver Canucks in 1983 NHL entry draft. Ninth Canucks pick, 170th overall, ninth round.

ANSSI MELAMETSA

Left Wing . . . 6' . . . 195 lbs. . . . Born, Jyvaskyla, Finland, June 21, 1961 . . . Shoots left . . . Also plays Right Wing . . . Former captain of Finnish National team.

Year	Team	League	Games	G.	A.	Pts.	Pen.
1978-79—Peterborough Petes		OHL	64	9	21	30	27
1979-80—Jokerit		Finland	36	6	13	19	53
1980-81—Jokerit		Finland	36	14	22	36	46
1981-82—Helsinki IFK		Finland	28	16	12	28	30
1982-83—Helsinki IFK		Finland	....	...	....	....	....
1983-84—Helsinki IFK		Finland	....	...	....	....	....
1984-85—Helsinki IFK (c)		Finland	36	16	15	31	18
1985-86—Winnipeg Jets		NHL	27	0	3	3	2
1985-86—Sherbrooke Canadiens		AHL	14	7	5	12	6
NHL TOTALS			27	0	3	3	2

(c)—June, 1985—Drafted by Winnipeg Jets in 1985 NHL entry draft. Twelfth Jets pick, 249th overall, 12th round.

SCOTT MELLANBY

Right Wing . . . 6'1" . . . 195 lbs. . . . Born, Montreal, Que., June 11, 1966 . . . Shoots right.

Year	Team	League	Games	G.	A.	Pts.	Pen.
1983-84—Henry Carr H.S. (c)		MTJHL	39	37	37	74	97
1984-85—University of Wisconsin		WCHA	40	14	24	38	60
1985-86—University of Wisconsin		WCHA	32	21	23	44	89
1985-86—Philadelphia Flyers		NHL	2	0	0	0	0
NHL TOTALS			2	0	0	0	0

(c)—June, 1984—Drafted as underage junior by Philadelphia Flyers in NHL entry draft. First Flyers pick, 27th overall, second round.

LARRY JOSEPH MELNYK

Defense . . . 6' . . . 180 lbs. . . . Born, New Westminster, B.C., February 21, 1960 . . . Shoots left . . . (January 16, 1985)—Twisted knee in game vs. N.Y. Islanders . . . (December, 1985)—Separated shoulder.

Year	Team	League	Games	G.	A.	Pts.	Pen.
1977-78—Abbotsford		BCJHL	39	10	9	19	100
1977-78—New Westminster Bruins		WCHL	44	3	22	25	71
1978-79—New Westminster Bruins (c)		WHL	71	7	33	40	142
1979-80—New Westminster Bruins		WHL	67	13	38	51	236
1980-81—Boston Bruins		NHL	26	0	4	4	39
1980-81—Springfield Indians		AHL	47	1	10	11	109
1981-82—Erie Blades		AHL	10	0	3	3	36
1981-82—Boston Bruins		NHL	48	0	8	8	84
1982-83—Baltimore Skipjacks		AHL	72	2	24	26	215
1982-83—Boston Bruins		NHL	1	0	0	0	0
1983-84—Hershey Bears (d)		AHL	51	0	18	18	156
1983-84—Moncton Alpines		AHL	14	0	3	3	17
1983-84—Edmonton Oilers (e)		NHL	....	...	....	....	....
1984-85—Nova Scotia Voyageurs		AHL	37	2	10	12	97
1984-85—Edmonton Oilers		NHL	28	0	11	11	25
1985-86—Nova Scotia Oilers		AHL	19	2	8	10	72
1985-86—Edmonton Oilers (f)		NHL	6	2	3	5	11
1985-86—New York Rangers		NHL	46	1	8	9	65
NHL TOTALS			155	3	34	37	224

(c)—August, 1979—Drafted as underage junior by Boston Bruins in 1979 NHL entry draft. Fifth Bruins pick, 78th overall, fourth round.

(d)—March, 1983—Traded by Boston Bruins to Edmonton Oilers for John Blum.

(e)—Played in six NHL playoff games, one assist.

(f)—December, 1985—Traded with Todd Strueby by Edmonton Oilers to New York Rangers for Mike Rogers.

BARRY JAMES MELROSE

Defense . . . 6'1" . . . 201 lbs. . . . Born, Kelvington, Sask., July 15, 1956 . . . Shoots right . . . (March, 1986)—Injured knee in an AHL game.

Year	Team	League	Games	G.	A.	Pts.	Pen.
1973-74—Weyburn Red Wings		SJHL	50	2	19	21	162
1974-75—Kamloops Chiefs		WCHL	70	6	18	24	95
1975-76—Kamloops Chiefs (c-d)		WCHL	72	12	49	61	112
1976-77—Springfield Indians		AHL	23	0	3	3	17
1976-77—Cincinnati Stingers		WHA	29	1	4	5	8
1977-78—Cincinnati Stingers		WHA	69	2	9	11	113
1978-79—Cincinnati Stingers (e)		WHA	80	2	14	16	222
1979-80—Winnipeg Jets		NHL	74	4	6	10	124
1980-81—Winnipeg Jets (f)		NHL	18	1	1	2	40
1980-81—Toronto Maple Leafs		NHL	57	2	5	7	166
1981-82—Toronto Maple Leafs		NHL	64	1	5	6	186
1982-83—St. Catharines Saints		AHL	25	1	10	11	106
1982-83—Toronto Maple Leafs (g)		NHL	52	2	5	7	68
1983-84—Detroit Red Wings		NHL	21	0	1	1	74
1983-84—Adirondack Red Wings		AHL	16	2	1	3	37
1984-85—Adirondack Red Wings		AHL	72	3	13	16	226
1985-86—Adirondack Red Wings		AHL	57	4	4	8	204
1985-86—Detroit Red Wings		NHL	14	0	0	0	70
WHA TOTALS			178	5	27	32	343
NHL TOTALS			300	10	23	33	728

(c)—Drafted from Kamloops Chiefs by Montreal Canadiens in second round of 1976 amateur draft.

(d)—Selected by Cincinnati Stingers in WHA amateur player draft, June, 1976. Signed by Cincinnati, September, 1976.

(e)—June, 1979—Claimed by Quebec Nordiques in WHA dispersal draft. Selected by Montreal Canadiens in NHL reclaim draft. Chosen by Winnipeg Jets in NHL expansion draft.

(f)—November, 1980—Acquired by Toronto Maple Leafs on waivers from Winnipeg Jets.

(g)—July, 1983—Signed by Detroit Red Wings as a free agent.

GLENN MERKOSKY

Center ... 5'10" ... 175 lbs. ... Born, Edmonton, Alta., April 8, 1960 ... Shoots left.

Year	Team	League	Games	G.	A.	Pts.	Pen.
1977-78—Seattle Breakers		WCHL	6	4	3	7	2
1978-79—Michigan Tech		WCHA	38	14	29	43	22
1979-80—Calgary Wranglers		WHL	72	49	40	89	95
1980-81—Binghamton Whalers (c)		AHL	80	26	35	61	61
1981-82—Hartford Whalers		NHL	7	0	0	0	2
1981-82—Binghamton Whalers		AHL	72	29	40	69	83
1982-83—New Jersey Devils (d)		NHL	34	4	10	14	20
1982-83—Wichita Wind		CHL	45	26	23	49	15
1983-84—Maine Mariners		AHL	75	28	28	56	56
1983-84—New Jersey Devils		NHL	5	1	0	1	0
1984-85—Maine Mariners (b)		AHL	80	38	38	76	19
1985-86—Adirondack Red Wings		AHL	59	24	33	57	22
1985-86—Detroit Red Wings (e)		NHL	17	0	2	2	0
NHL TOTALS			63	5	12	17	22

(c)—August, 1980—Signed by Hartford Whalers as a free agent.

(d)—September, 1982—Signed by New Jersey Devils as a free agent.

(e)—August, 1985—Signed by Detroit Red Wings as a free agent.

MARK MESSIER

Center and Left Wing ... 6' ... 205 lbs. ... Born, Edmonton, Alta., January 18, 1961 ... Shoots left ... Son of Doug Messier (WHL), brother of Paul Messier and cousin of Mitch Messier ... (November 7, 1981)—Injured ankle in game at Chicago ... (March, 1983)—Chipped bone in wrist ... (January 18, 1984)—Given six-game suspension by NHL for hitting Vancouver's Thomas Gradin over the head with his stick ... Brother-in-law of John Blum ... (November, 1984)—Sprained knee ligaments ... (December 26, 1984)—Given 10-game NHL suspension for cracking cheekbone of Jamie Macoun in game at Calgary ... (September 6, 1985)—Charged with hit-and-run and careless driving. He was fined $250 for leaving the scene and $75 for careless driving ... (December 3, 1985)—Bruised left foot in game at Los Angeles and missed 17 games ... Cousin of Mitch Messier (Michigan State).

Year	Team	League	Games	G.	A.	Pts.	Pen.
1976-77—Spruce Grove Mets		AJHL	57	27	39	66	91
1977-78—St. Albert Saints		AJHL	....	....	....	....	....
1978-79—Indianapolis Racers (c)		WHA	5	0	0	0	0
1978-79—Cincinnati Stingers (d-e)		WHA	47	1	10	11	58
1979-80—Houston Apollos		CHL	4	0	3	3	4
1979-80—Edmonton Oilers		NHL	75	12	21	33	120
1980-81—Edmonton Oilers		NHL	72	23	40	63	102

Year	Team	League	Games	G.	A.	Pts.	Pen.
1981-82—Edmonton Oilers (a)		NHL	78	50	38	88	119
1982-83—Edmonton Oilers (a)		NHL	77	48	58	106	72
1983-84—Edmonton Oilers (b-f)		NHL	73	37	64	101	165
1984-85—Edmonton Oilers		NHL	55	23	31	54	57
1985-86—Edmonton Oilers		NHL	63	35	49	84	68
WHA TOTALS			52	1	10	11	58
NHL TOTALS			493	228	301	529	703

(c)—November, 1978—Given 5-game trial by Indianapolis Racers.
(d)—January, 1979—Signed by Cincinnati Stingers as free agent.
(e)—August, 1979—Drafted by Edmonton Oilers in NHL entry draft. Second Edmonton pick, 48th overall, third round.
(f)—Won Conn Smythe Trophy (NHL Playoff MVP).

MITCH MESSIER

Center . . . 6'2" . . . 185 lbs. . . . Born, Regina, Sask., August 21, 1965 . . . Shoots right . . . Cousin of Mark Messier.

Year	Team	League	Games	G.	A.	Pts.	Pen.
1981-82—Notre Dame H.S.		Sask. Midget	26	8	20	28	..
1982-83—Notre Dame H.S. (c)		Sask. Juvenile	60	108	73	181	160
1983-84—Michigan State University		CCHA	37	6	15	21	22
1984-85—Michigan State University		CCHA	42	12	21	33	46
1985-86—Michigan State University		CCHA	38	24	40	64	36

(c)—June, 1983—Drafted by Minnesota North Stars in 1983 NHL entry draft. Fourth North Stars pick, 56th overall, third round.

SCOTT METCALFE

Left Wing . . . 6' . . . 195 lbs. . . . Born, Toronto, Ont., January 6, 1967 . . . Shoots left.

Year	Team	League	Games	G.	A.	Pts.	Pen.
1982-83—Toronto Young Nats		OHA	39	22	43	65	74
1983-84—Kingston Canadians		OHL	68	25	49	74	154
1984-85—Kingston Canadians (c)		OHL	58	27	33	60	100
1985-86—Kingston Canadians		OHL	66	36	43	79	213

(c)—June, 1985—Drafted as underage junior by Edmonton Oilers in 1985 NHL entry draft. First Oilers pick, 20th overall, first round.

JOHN MEULENBROEKS

Defense . . . 6' . . . 181 lbs. . . . Born, Kingston, Ont., April 3, 1964 . . . Shoots left.

Year	Team	League	Games	G.	A.	Pts.	Pen.
1981-82—Brantford Alexanders (c)		OHL	58	4	4	8	45
1982-83—Brantford Alexanders		OHL	69	1	18	19	55
1983-84—Brantford Alexanders		OHL	68	7	25	32	39
1984-85—Hershey Bears		AHL	74	1	17	18	19
1985-86—Moncton Golden Flames		AHL	51	1	4	5	51

(c)—June, 1982—Drafted by Boston Bruins as underage junior in 1982 NHL entry draft. Seventh Bruins pick, 144th overall, seventh round.

JAYSON MEYER

Defense . . . 5'11" . . . 185 lbs. . . . Born, Regina, Sask., February 21, 1965 . . . Shoots left.

Year	Team	League	Games	G.	A.	Pts.	Pen.
1981-82—Regina Pats		WHL	59	3	20	23	106
1982-83—Regina Pats (c)		WHL	72	10	45	55	89
1983-84—Regina Pats		WHL	70	16	67	83	39
1984-85—New Westminster (d-e)		WHL	63	20	51	71	67
1985-86—Rochester Americans		AHL	76	7	28	35	74

(c)—June, 1983—Drafted as underage junior by Buffalo Sabres in 1983 NHL entry draft. Seventh Sabres pick, 94th overall, fifth round.
(d)—September, 1984—Traded with Larry Dyck and Dennis Holland by Regina Pats to Brandon Wheat Kings for Bryan Wells.
(e)—October, 1984—Traded with Lee Trimm by Brandon Wheat Kings to New Westminster Bruins for Pokey Reddick.

DAVID MICHAYLUK

Right Wing . . . 5'10" . . . 175 lbs. . . . Born, Wakaw, Sask., May 18, 1962 . . . Shoots left . . . Also plays Left Wing.

Year	Team	League	Games	G.	A.	Pts.	Pen.
1979-80—Prince Albert Saints		AJHL	60	46	67	113	49

Year	Team	League	Games	G.	A.	Pts.	Pen.
1980-81—Regina Pats (b-c-d)		WHL	72	62	71	133	39
1981-82—Regina Pats (b-e)		WHL	72	62	111	173	128
1981-82—Philadelphia Flyers		NHL	1	0	0	0	0
1982-83—Philadelphia Flyers		NHL	13	2	6	8	8
1982-83—Maine Mariners		AHL	69	32	40	72	16
1983-84—Springfield Indians		AHL	79	18	44	62	37
1984-85—Hershey Bears		AHL	3	0	2	2	2
1984-85—Kalamazoo Wings (b)		IHL	82	*66	33	99	49
1985-86—Nova Scotia Oilers		AHL	3	0	1	1	0
1985-86—Muskegon Lumberjacks		IHL	77	52	52	104	73
NHL TOTALS			14	2	6	8	8

(c)—Winner of Stewart "Butch" Paul Memorial Trophy (Top WHL Rookie).
(d)—June, 1981—Drafted as underage junior by Philadelphia Flyers in 1981 NHL entry draft. Fifth Flyers pick, 65th overall, fourth round.
(e)—Led WHL playoffs with 40 points.

PAT MICHELETTI

Right Wing ... 5'9" ... 170 lbs. ... Born, Hibbing, Minn., December 11, 1963 ... Shoots right ... Brother of former NHL defenseman Joe Micheletti.

Year	Team	League	Games	G.	A.	Pts.	Pen.
1982-83—University of Minnesota (c)		WCHA	31	14	19	33	74
1983-84—University of Minnesota		WCHA	39	26	34	60	62
1984-85—Universoty of Minnesota		WCHA	44	48	48	96	154
1985-86—University of Minnesota		WCHA	48	32	48	80	113
1985-86—Springfield Indians		AHL	2	1	0	1	0

(c)—June, 1982—Drafted by Minnesota North Stars in 1982 NHL entry draft. Ninth North Stars pick, 185th overall, ninth round.

MAX MIDDENDORF

Right Wing ... 6'4" ... 195 lbs. ... Born, Syracuse, N.Y., August 18, 1967 ... Shoots right.

Year	Team	League	Games	G.	A.	Pts.	Pen.
1983-84—New Jersey Rockets		N.J. Midget	58	94	74	168	....
1984-85—Sudbury Wolves (c)		OHL	63	16	28	44	106
1985-86—Sudbury Wolves		OHL	61	40	42	82	71

(c)—June, 1985—Drafted as underage junior by Quebec Nordiques in 1985 NHL entry draft. Third Nordiques pick, 57th overall, third round.

RICHARD DAVID (RICK) MIDDLETON

Right Wing ... 5'11" ... 170 lbs. ... Born, Toronto, Ont., December 4, 1953 ... Shoots right ... Missed parts of 1974-75 season with broken left leg and fractured cheek ... (March 11, 1982)—Scored hat trick in game vs. Winnipeg despite suffering sprained right shoulder ... (July, 1982)—Surgery to replace torn tendon in right shoulder ... (November 10, 1985)—Neck and shoulder spasms ... (February, 1986)—Hit in head by shot in practice. Suffered dizzy spells and missed remainder of season.

Year	Team	League	Games	G.	A.	Pts.	Pen.
1971-72—Oshawa Generals		Jr."A"OHA	53	36	34	70	24
1972-73—Oshawa Generals (b-c-d)		Jr."A"OHA	62	*67	70	137	14
1973-74—Providence Reds (a-e)		AHL	63	36	48	84	14
1974-75—New York Rangers		NHL	47	22	18	40	19
1975-76—New York Rangers (f)		NHL	77	24	26	50	14
1976-77—Boston Bruins		NHL	72	20	22	42	2
1977-78—Boston Bruins		NHL	79	25	35	60	14
1978-79—Boston Bruins		NHL	71	38	48	86	7
1979-80—Boston Bruins		NHL	80	40	52	92	24
1980-81—Boston Bruins		NHL	80	44	59	103	16
1981-82—Boston Bruins (b-g)		NHL	75	51	43	94	12
1982-83—Boston Bruins		NHL	80	49	47	96	8
1983-84—Boston Bruins		NHL	80	47	58	105	14
1984-85—Boston Bruins		NHL	80	30	46	76	6
1985-86—Boston Bruins		NHL	49	14	30	44	10
NHL TOTALS			870	404	484	888	140

(c)—Won Red Tilson Memorial Trophy (MVP).
(d)—Drafted from Oshawa Generals by New York Rangers in first round of 1973 amateur draft.
(e)—Won Dudley (Red) Garrett Memorial Trophy (leading rookie).
(f)—Traded to Boston Bruins by New York Rangers for Ken Hodge, May, 1976.
(g)—Winner of Lady Byng Memorial Trophy.

DAN MIELE

Right Wing . . . 6'2" . . . 190 lbs. . . . Born, LaSalle, Que., April 12, 1962 . . . Shoots right.

Year	Team	League	Games	G.	A.	Pts.	Pen.
1979-80—Providence College		ECAC	30	11	13	24	30
1980-81—Providence College		ECAC	28	16	13	29	20
1981-82—Hershey Bears (c)		AHL	67	7	11	18	25
1982-83—Hershey Bears		AHL	74	11	11	22	62
1983-84—Hershey Bears		AHL	65	23	17	40	18
1984-85—Fort Wayne Komets		IHL	34	7	14	21	21
1985-86—Indianapolis Checkers		IHL	55	5	11	16	68

(c)—June, 1980—Drafted as underage player by Washington Capitals in 1980 NHL entry draft. Second Capitals pick, 47th overall, third round.

MARIO MILANI

Right Wing . . . 6' . . . 176 lbs. . . . Born, Jonquiere, Que., January 9, 1968 . . . Shoots left.

Year	Team	League	Games	G.	A.	Pts.	Pen.
1984-85—Montreal Concordia Midget		Que.	41	21	32	53	63
1985-86—Verdun Junior Canadiens (c)		QHL	71	16	31	47	74

(c)—June, 1986—Drafted as underage junior by Montreal Canadiens in 1986 NHL entry draft. Sixth Canadiens pick, 99th overall, fifth round.

MICHAEL JAMES MILBURY

Defense . . . 6'1" . . . 195 lbs. . . . Born, Brighton, Mass., June 17, 1952 . . . Shoots left . . . Given six-game suspension by NHL for fight in stands at N.Y. Rangers, December 26, 1979 . . . Cousin of Dave Silk . . . Attended Colgate University on a football scholarship . . . (March 11, 1982)—Strained ligaments in right knee in game vs. Winnipeg . . . (March 29, 1983)— Broke right kneecap when hit by a Wally Weir shot in game at Quebec.

Year	Team	League	Games	G.	A.	Pts.	Pen.
1972-73—Colgate University			23	2	19	21	68
1973-74—Colgate University (c)			....	...	....	....	....
1974-75—Rochester Americans		AHL	71	2	15	17	246
1975-76—Rochester Americans		AHL	73	3	15	18	199
1975-76—Boston Bruins		NHL	3	0	0	0	9
1976-77—Boston Bruins (d)		NHL	77	6	18	24	166
1977-78—Boston Bruins		NHL	80	8	30	38	151
1978-79—Boston Bruins		NHL	74	1	34	35	149
1979-80—Boston Bruins		NHL	72	10	13	23	59
1980-81—Boston Bruins		NHL	77	0	18	18	222
1981-82—Boston Bruins		NHL	51	2	10	12	71
1982-83—Boston Bruins		NHL	78	9	15	24	216
1983-84—Boston Bruins		NHL	74	2	17	19	159
1984-85—Boston Bruins (e)		NHL	78	3	13	16	152
1985-86—Boston Bruins (f)		NHL	22	2	5	7	102
NHL TOTALS			686	43	173	216	1456

(c)—September, 1974—Signed by Boston Bruins as a free agent.
(d)—Led in penalty minutes (47) during playoffs.
(e)—May, 1985—Announced retirement as player to be assistant coach of the Boston Bruins.
(f)—February, 1986—Came out of retirement to play.

MIKE MILLAR

Right Wing . . . 5'10" . . . 170 lbs. . . . Born, St. Catharines, Ont., April 28, 1965 . . . Shoots left.

Year	Team	League	Games	G.	A.	Pts.	Pen.
1981-82—St. Catharines Midgets		Ont. Midget	30	32	32	64	24
1982-83—Brantford Alexanders		OHL	53	20	29	49	10
1983-84—Brantford Alexanders (c)		OHL	69	50	45	95	48
1984-85—Hamilton Steelhawks		OHL	63	*66	60	126	54
1985-86—Team Canada		Int'l.	69	50	38	88	74

(c)—June, 1984—Drafted as underage junior by Hartford Whalers in 1984 NHL entry draft. Second Whalers pick, 110th overall, sixth round.

COREY MILLEN

Center . . . 5'7" . . . 165 lbs. . . . Born, Cloquet, Minn., April 29, 1964 . . . Shoots right . . . (November, 1982)—Injured knee in WCHA game vs. Colorado College, requiring surgery . . . Member of 1984 U.S. Olympic team . . . (October, 1984)—Shoulder injury.

Year	Team	League	Games	G.	A.	Pts.	Pen.
1981-82—Cloquet H.S. (c)		Minn. H.S.	18	46	35	81	....
1982-83—University of Minnesota		WCHA	21	14	15	29	18

Year	Team	League	Games	G.	A.	Pts.	Pen.
1983-84—U.S. National Team		Int'l	45	15	11	26	10
1983-84—U.S. Olympic Team		Int'l	6	0	0	0	2
1984-85—University of Minnesota (b)		WCHA	38	28	36	64	60
1985-86—University of Minnesota (b)		WCHA	48	41	42	83	64

(c)—June, 1982—Drafted by New York Rangers in 1982 NHL entry draft as underage player. Third Rangers pick, 57th overall, third round.

JAY MILLER

Left Wing . . . 6'2" . . . 215 lbs. . . . Born, Wellesley, Mass., July 16, 1960 . . . Shoots left . . . (November, 1984)—Broken bone in right hand . . . Also plays Defense.

Year	Team	League	Games	G.	A.	Pts.	Pen.
1979-80—Univ. New Hampshire		ECAC	28	7	12	19	53
1981-82—Univ. New Hampshire		ECAC	10	4	8	12	14
1982-83—Univ. New Hampshire		ECAC	24	6	4	10	34
1983-84—Toledo Goaldiggers		IHL	2	0	0	0	4
1983-84—Mohawk Valley Comets		ACHL	48	15	36	51	167
1983-84—Maine Mariners		AHL	15	1	1	2	27
1984-85—Muskegon Mohawks		IHL	56	5	29	34	177
1985-86—Moncton Golden Flames		AHL	18	4	6	10	113
1985-86—Boston Bruins (c)		NHL	46	3	0	3	178
NHL TOTALS			46	3	0	3	178

(c)—September, 1985—Signed by Boston Bruins as a free agent.

KEITH MILLER

Left Wing . . . 6'2" . . . 212 lbs. . . . Born, Toronto, Ont., March 18, 1967 . . . Shoots left.

Year	Team	League	Games	G.	A.	Pts.	Pen.
1984-85—Guelph Platers		OHL	18	1	3	4	7
1984-85—Aurora Tigers Tier II		OJHL	24	7	11	18	31
1985-86—Guelph Platers (c)		OHL	61	32	17	49	30

(c)—June, 1986—Drafted by Quebec Nordiques in 1986 NHL entry draft. Tenth Nordiques pick, 165th overall, eighth round.

KELLY MILLER

Left Wing . . . 5'11" . . . 185 lbs. . . . Born, Lansing, Mich., March 3, 1963 . . . Shoots left . . . (September, 1985)—Injured ankle in training camp . . . (January 27, 1986)—Sprained knee at Quebec and missed five games.

Year	Team	League	Games	G.	A.	Pts.	Pen.
1981-82—Michigan State University (c)		CCHA	40	11	19	30	21
1982-83—Michigan State University		CCHA	36	16	19	35	12
1983-84—Michigan State University		CCHA	46	28	21	49	12
1984-85—Michigan State University (d)		CCHA	43	27	23	50	21
1984-85—New York Rangers		NHL	5	0	2	2	2
1985-86—New York Rangers		NHL	74	13	20	33	52
NHL TOTALS			79	13	22	35	54

(c)—June, 1982—Drafted by New York Rangers in NHL entry draft. Ninth Rangers pick, 183rd overall, ninth round.

(d)—First-Team (West) All-America.

CHRIS MILLS

Defense . . . 6'1" . . . 185 lbs. . . . Born, Scarborough, Ont., May 30, 1966 . . . Shoots left.

Year	Team	League	Games	G.	A.	Pts.	Pen.
1983-84—Bramalea Blues (c)		MTJHL	42	9	27	36	50
1984-85—Clarkson College		ECAC	29	0	1	1	22
1985-86—Clarkson College		ECAC	32	2	3	5	36

(c)—June, 1984—Drafted as underage junior by Winnipeg Jets in NHL entry draft. Second Jets pick, 68th overall, fourth round.

JOHN MINER

Defense . . . 5'10" . . . 170 lbs. . . . Born, Moose Jaw, Sask., August 28, 1965 . . . Shoots right . . . (September, 1982)—Eye injury.

Year	Team	League	Games	G.	A.	Pts.	Pen.
1981-82—Regina Pats		SJHL	..	..	..	..	..
1981-82—Regina Pats		WHL	10	0	1	1	11
1982-83—Regina Pats (c)		WHL	71	11	23	34	126
1983-84—Regina Pats (b)		WHL	70	27	42	69	132
1984-85—Regina Pats (a)		WHL	66	30	54	84	128

Year	Team	League	Games	G.	A.	Pts.	Pen.
1984-85—Nova Scotia Oilers (d)		AHL	....	...	....	....	....
1985-86—Nova Scotia Oilers		AHL	79	10	33	43	90

(c)—June, 1983—Drafted as underage junior by Edmonton Oilers in 1983 NHL entry draft. Tenth Oilers pick, 220th overall, 11th round.

(d)—Played three playoff games, scoring two goals and two assists.

GERALD (GERRY) MINOR

Center . . . 5'8" . . . 178 lbs. . . . Born, Regina, Sask., October 27, 1958 . . . Shoots left . . . Missed most of 1981-82 season due to skull fracture, broken ankle and torn knee ligaments . . . (February 19, 1983)—Strained ligaments in left knee during AHL game vs. Nova Scotia.

Year	Team	League	Games	G.	A.	Pts.	Pen.
1974-75—Regina Blues		SJHL	38	28	19	47	56
1974-75—Regina Pats		WCHL	16	2	6	8	6
1975-76—Regina Pats		WCHL	71	24	41	65	124
1976-77—Regina Pats		WCHL	48	22	32	54	122
1977-78—Regina Pats (c-d)		WCHL	66	54	75	129	238
1978-79—Fort Wayne Komets		IHL	42	18	28	46	67
1978-79—Dallas Black Hawks		CHL	37	14	25	39	76
2979-80—Dallas Black Hawks		CHL	73	31	52	83	162
1979-80—Vancouver Canucks		NHL	5	0	1	1	2
1980-81—Vancouver Canucks		NHL	74	10	14	24	108
1981-82—Vancouver Canucks		NHL	13	0	1	1	6
1981-82—Dallas Black Hawks		CHL	12	5	8	13	92
1982-83—Vancouver Canucks		NHL	39	1	5	6	57
1982-83—Fredericton Express		AHL	17	4	17	21	14
1983-84—Vancouver Canucks		NHL	9	0	0	0	0
1983-84—Fredericton Express		AHL	66	16	42	58	85
1984-85—Nova Scotia Oilers (e)		AHL	21	4	10	14	8
1984-85—New Haven Nighthawks (f)		AHL	52	11	29	40	65
1985-86—Indianapolis Checkers		IHL	72	28	46	74	108
NHL TOTALS			140	11	21	32	173

(c)—Led WCHL Playoffs in points (37).

(d)—June, 1978—Drafted by Vancouver Canucks in 1978 NHL amateur draft. Sixth Canucks pick, 90th overall, sixth round.

(e)—October, 1984—Signed by Nova Scotia Voyageurs as a free agent.

(f)—November, 1984—Traded with Rob Tudor by Nova Scotia Voyageurs to New Haven Nighthawks for Dean Hopkins and Mark Morrison.

CARL MOKOSAK

Left Wing . . . 6'1" . . . 181 lbs. . . . Born, Fort Saskatchewan, Alta., September 22, 1962 . . . Shoots left . . . Brother of John Mokosak.

Year	Team	League	Games	G.	A.	Pts.	Pen.
1978-79—Brandon		MJHL	44	12	11	23	146
1979-80—Brandon Wheat Kings		WHL	61	12	21	33	226
1980-81—Brandon Wheat Kings		WHL	70	20	40	60	118
1981-82—Brandon Wheat Kings (c)		WHL	69	46	61	107	363
1981-82—Oklahoma City Stars		CHL	2	1	1	2	2
1981-82—Calgary Flames		NHL	1	0	1	1	0
1982-83—Colorado Flames		CHL	28	10	12	22	106
1982-83—Calgary Flames (d)		NHL	41	7	6	13	87
1983-84—New Haven Nighthawks		AHL	80	18	21	39	206
1984-85—New Haven Nighthawks		AHL	11	6	6	12	26
1984-85—Los Angeles Kings (e)		NHL	30	4	8	12	43
1985-86—Philadelphia Flyers		NHL	1	0	0	0	5
1985-86—Hershey Bears (f)		AHL	79	30	42	72	312
NHL TOTALS			73	11	15	26	135

(c)—August, 1981—Signed by Calgary Flames as a free agent.

(d)—June, 1983—Traded by Calgary Flames with Kevin LaVallee to Los Angeles Kings for Steve Bozek.

(e)—June, 1985—Released by Los Angeles Kings and subsequently signed by Philadelphia Flyers as a free agent.

(f)—July, 1986—Signed by Pittsburgh Penguins as a free agent.

JOHN MOKOSAK

Defense . . . 5'11" . . . 185 lbs. . . . Born, Edmonton, Alta., September 7, 1963 . . . Shoots left . . . Brother of Carl Mokosak.

Year	Team	League	Games	G.	A.	Pts.	Pen.
1979-80—Fort Saskatchewan Traders		SJHL	58	5	13	18	57

Year	Team	League	Games	G.	A.	Pts.	Pen.
1980-81—Victoria Cougars (c)		WHL	71	2	18	20	59
1981-82—Victoria Cougars		WHL	69	6	45	51	102
1982-83—Victoria Cougars		WHL	70	10	33	43	102
1983-84—Binghamton Whalers		AHL	79	3	21	24	80
1984-85—Salt Lake Golden Eagles		CHL	22	1	10	11	41
1984-85—Binghamton Whalers		AHL	54	1	13	14	109
1985-86—Binghamton Whalers		AHL	64	0	9	9	196

(c)—June, 1981—Drafted as underage junior by Hartford Whalers in 1981 NHL entry draft. Sixth Whalers pick, 130th overall, seventh round.

MICHAEL JOHN MOLLER

Right Wing . . . 6' . . . 189 lbs. . . . Born, Calgary, Alta., June 16, 1962 . . . Shoots right . . . Brother of Randy Moller.

Year	Team	League	Games	G.	A.	Pts.	Pen.
1978-79—Red Deer Midgets		RDMHL	....	...	....	....	....
1979-80—Lethbridge Broncos (c)		WHL	72	30	41	71	55
1980-81—Lethbridge Broncos (a)		WHL	70	39	69	108	71
1980-81—Buffalo Sabres		NHL	5	2	2	4	0
1981-82—Lethbridge Broncos (a-d)		WHL	49	41	81	122	38
1981-82—Buffalo Sabres		NHL	9	0	0	0	0
1982-83—Rochester Americans		AHL	10	1	6	7	2
1982-83—Buffalo Sabres		NHL	49	6	12	18	14
1983-84—Buffalo Sabres		NHL	59	5	11	16	27
1984-85—Rochester Americans		AHL	73	19	46	65	27
1984-85—Buffalo Sabres		NHL	5	0	2	2	0
1985-86—Edmonton Oilers (e-f)		NHL	1	0	0	0	0
1985-86—Nova Scotia Oilers		AHL	62	16	15	31	24
NHL TOTALS			128	13	27	40	41

(c)—June, 1980—Drafted by Buffalo Sabres as underage junior in 1980 NHL entry draft. Second Sabres pick, 41st overall, second round.

(d)—Winner of Frank Bouchar Memorial Trophy (Most Gentlemanly WHL Player).

(e)—October, 1985—Traded with equalization rights of Randy Cunneyworth by Buffalo Sabres to Pittsburgh Penguins for future considerations.

(f)—October, 1985—Traded by Pittsburgh Penguins to Edmonton Oilers to complete earlier Gilles Meloche deal.

RANDY MOLLER

Defense . . . 6'2" . . . 205 lbs. . . . Born, Red Deer, Alta., August 23, 1963. . . Shoots right . . . (December, 1980)—Torn knee ligaments required surgery . . . Brother of Mike Moller.

Year	Team	League	Games	G.	A.	Pts.	Pen.
1979-80—Red Deer Rustlers		AJHL	56	3	34	37	253
1980-81—Lethbridge Broncos (c)		WHL	46	4	21	25	176
1981-82—Lethbridge Broncos (b)		WHL	60	20	55	75	249
1982-83—Quebec Nordiques		NHL	75	2	12	14	145
1983-84—Quebec Nordiques		NHL	74	4	14	18	147
1984-85—Quebec Nordiques		NHL	79	7	22	29	120
1985-86—Quebec Nordiques		NHL	69	5	18	23	141
NHL TOTALS			297	18	66	84	553

(c)—June, 1981—Drafted by Quebec Nordiques in 1981 NHL entry draft. First Nordiques pick, 11th overall, first round.

SERGIO MOMESSO

Left Wing . . . 6'3" . . . 205 lbs. . . . Born, Montreal, Que, September 4, 1965 . . . Shoots left . . . Also plays Center . . . (December 5, 1985)—Torn cruciate ligament in left knee. He required surgery and missed remainder of season.

Year	Team	League	Games	G.	A.	Pts.	Pen.
1982-83—Shawinigan Cataracts (c)		QHL	70	27	42	69	93
1983-84—Shawinigan Cataracts		QHL	68	42	88	130	235
1983-84—Montreal Canadiens		NHL	1	0	0	0	0
1984-85—Shawinigan Sagueneens (a)		QHL	64	56	90	146	216
1985-86—Montreal Canadiens		NHL	24	8	7	15	46
NHL TOTALS			25	8	7	15	46

(c)—June, 1983—Drafted as underage junior by Montreal Canadiens in 1983 NHL entry draft. Third Canadiens pick, 27th overall, second round.

CHARLIE MOORE

Left Wing . . . 6'1" . . . 218 lbs. . . . Born, Ottawa, Ont., April 26, 1967 . . . Shoots left . . . (October, 1985)—Broken hand.

Year	Team	League	Games	G.	A.	Pts.	Pen.
1984-85—Belleville Bulls		OHL	34	1	4	5	142
1985-86—Belleville Bulls (c)		OHL	47	4	4	8	100

(c)—June, 1986—Drafted as underage junior by Montreal Canadiens in 1986 NHL entry draft. Twelfth Canadiens pick, 225th overall, 11th round.

STEVE MOORE

Defense . . . 6'2" . . . 185 lbs. . . . Born, Toronto, Ont., January 21, 1967 . . . Shoots right.

Year	Team	League	Games	G.	A.	Pts.	Pen.
1983-84—London Diamonds Jr. B		OHA	46	6	21	27	43
1984-85—London Diamonds Jr. B (c)		OHA	46	12	26	38	112
1985-86—Rensselaer Poly. Inst.		ECAC	24	4	3	7	32

(c)—June, 1985—Drafted by Boston Bruins in 1985 NHL entry draft. Fourth Bruins pick, 94th overall, fifth round.

STEVE MORIA

Center . . . 6' . . . 175 lbs. . . . Born, Vancouver, B.C., February 3, 1961 . . . Shoots left . . . Set NCAA record for most points (109) in one season, breaking mark set by Dave Taylor of Clarkson in 1976-77 . . . (September, 1985)—Injured ankle in training camp.

Year	Team	League	Games	G.	A.	Pts.	Pen.
1982-83—U. of Alaska-Fairbanks		GWHC	26	29	46	75	....
1983-84—U. of Alaska-Fairbanks		GWHC	26	36	51	87	....
1984-85—U. of Alaska-Fairbanks (c-d)		GWHC	34	43	66	*109	....
1985-86—New Haven Nighthawks		AHL	74	19	37	56	29

(c)—Second Team All-American Forward (West).

(d)—August, 1985—Signed by New York Rangers as a free agent.

JON MORRIS

Center . . . 6' . . . 165 lbs. . . . Born, Lowell, Mass., May 6, 1966 . . . Shoots right.

Year	Team	League	Games	G.	A.	Pts.	Pen.
1983-84—Chelmsford H.S. (c)		Mass. H.S.	24	31	50	81	....
1984-85—University of Lowell		H. East	42	29	31	60	16
1985-86—University of Lowell		H. East	39	25	31	56	52

(c)—June, 1984—Drafted by New Jersey Devils in NHL entry draft. Fifth Devils pick, 86th overall, fifth round.

DOUG MORRISON

Right Wing and Center . . . 5'11" . . . 175 lbs. . . Born, Vancouver, B.C., February 1, 1960 . . . Shoots right . . . (February, 1981)—Knee injury . . . Brother of Mark Morrison . . . (December, 1982)—Broken hand . . . (December, 1984)—Concussions.

Year	Team	League	Games	G.	A.	Pts.	Pen.
1976-77—Lethbridge Broncos		WCHL	70	24	35	59	80
1977-78—Lethbridge Broncos		WCHL	66	25	45	70	116
1978-79—Lethbridge Broncos (c)		WHL	72	56	67	123	159
1979-80—Boston Bruins		NHL	1	0	0	0	0
1979-80—Lethbridge Broncos		WHL	68	58	59	117	188
1980-81—Boston Bruins		NHL	18	7	3	10	13
1980-81—Springfield Indians		AHL	42	19	30	49	28
1981-82—Erie Blades		AHL	75	23	35	58	31
1981-82—Boston Bruins		NHL	3	0	0	0	0
1982-83—Maine Mariners		AHL	61	38	29	67	44
1983-84—Hershey Bears		AHL	72	38	40	78	42
1984-85—Hershey Bears		AHL	65	28	25	53	25
1984-85—Boston Bruins		NHL	1	0	0	0	2
1985-86—Salt Lake Golden Eagles		IHL	80	27	34	61	30
NHL TOTALS			23	7	3	10	15

(c)—August, 1979—Drafted by Boston Bruins as underage junior in 1979 entry draft. Third Bruins pick, 36th overall, second round.

KEN MORROW

Defense . . . 6'4" . . . 210 lbs. . . . Born, Flint, Mich., October 17, 1956 . . . Shoots right . . . Member of 1980 U.S. Olympic Gold Medal Team . . . Member of 1979 Team U.S.A. . . . First ever All-American at Bowling Green University . . . First person in history to play for Gold Medal Olympic team and Stanley Cup Team in same season. . . . (October, 1983)—Water on the knee . . . (December, 1983)—Arthroscopic surgery on right knee . . . (May, 1983)—Missed one game in playoff series with Boston due to further arthroscopic surgery on right knee . . . (September, 1984)—Right knee swollen after first week of training camp . . .

(October, 1984)—Knee surgery . . . (October, 1985)—Injured shoulder . . . (December 1, 1985)—Injured back.

Year	Team	League	Games	G.	A.	Pts.	Pen.
1975-76—Bowling Green Univ. (a-c)		CCHA	31	4	15	19	34
1976-77—Bowling Green Univ. (b)		CCHA	39	7	22	29	22
1977-78—Bowling Green Univ. (a-d)		CCHA	39	8	18	26	26
1978-79—Bowling Green Univ. (a-e)		CCHA	45	15	37	52	22
1979-80—U.S. Olympic Team		Int'l	63	5	20	25	12
1979-80—New York Islanders		NHL	18	0	3	3	4
1980-81—New York Islanders		NHL	80	2	11	13	20
1981-82—New York Islanders		NHL	75	1	18	19	56
1982-83—New York Islanders		NHL	79	5	11	16	44
1983-84—New York Islanders		NHL	63	3	11	14	45
1984-85—New York Islanders		NHL	15	1	7	8	14
1985-86—New York Islanders		NHL	69	0	12	12	22
NHL TOTALS			399	12	73	85	205

(c)—May, 1976—Drafted by New York Islanders in 1976 NHL amateur draft. Fourth Islanders pick, 68th overall, fourth round.
(d)—All-American Team (West).
(e)—Named CCHA Player of the Year.

DEAN MORTON

Defense . . . 6'1" . . . 195 lbs. . . . Born, Peterborough, Ont., February 27, 1968 . . . Shoots right.

Year	Team	League	Games	G.	A.	Pts.	Pen.
1984-85—Peterborough Midgets		OHA	47	9	38	47	158
1985-86—Ottawa 67's (c)		OHL	16	3	1	4	32

(c)—June, 1986—Drafted as underage junior by Detroit Red Wings in 1986 NHL entry draft. Eighth Red Wings pick, 148th overall, eighth round.

DAVID MOYLAN

Defense . . . 6'1" . . . 195 lbs. . . . Born, Tillsonburg, Ont., August 13, 1967 . . . Shoots left . . . (November, 1983)—Separated shoulder.

Year	Team	League	Games	G.	A.	Pts.	Pen.
1983-84—St. Mary's Lincolns		OHA	46	7	13	20	143
1984-85—Sudbury Wolves (c)		OHL	66	1	15	16	108
1985-86—Sudbury Wolves		OHL	52	10	25	35	87

(c)—June, 1985—Drafted as underage junior by Buffalo Sabres in 1985 entry draft. Fourth Sabres pick, 77th overall, fourth round.

BRIAN MULLEN

Left Wing . . . 5'10" . . . 170 lbs. . . . Born, New York, N.Y., March 16, 1962 . . . Shoots left . . . Brother of Joe Mullen.

Year	Team	League	Games	G.	A.	Pts.	Pen.
1977-78—New York Westsiders		NYMJHL	33	21	36	57	38
1978-79—New York Westsiders		NYMJHL	....	...	....	....	....
1979-80—New York Westsiders		NYMJHL	....	...	....	....	....
1980-81—University of Wisconsin (c)		WCHA	38	11	13	24	28
1981-82—University of Wisconsin		WCHA	33	20	17	37	10
1982-83—Winnipeg Jets		NHL	80	24	26	50	14
1983-84—Winnipeg Jets		NHL	75	21	41	62	28
1984-85—Winnipeg Jets		NHL	69	32	39	71	32
1985-86—Winnipeg Jets		NHL	79	28	34	62	38
NHL TOTALS			303	105	140	245	112

(c)—June, 1980—Drafted by Winnipeg Jets in 1981 NHL entry draft. Seventh Jets pick, 128th overall, seventh round.

JOE MULLEN

Right Wing . . . 5'9" . . . 180 lbs. . . . Born, New York, N.Y., February 26, 1957 . . . Shoots right . . . Brother of Brian Mullen . . . First player to have 20-goal year in minors and majors in the same season (1981-82) . . . (October 18, 1982)—Leg injury in game at Minnesota . . . (January 29, 1983)—Tore ligaments in left knee during game vs. Los Angeles, requiring surgery. He was lost for remainder of season . . . Established record for goals in single season by U.S.-born player in 1983-84 (Broken by Bobby Carpenter).

Year	Team	League	Games	G.	A.	Pts.	Pen.
1971-72—New York 14th Precinct		NYMJHL	30	13	11	24	2
1972-73—New York Westsiders		NYMJHL	40	14	28	42	8
1973-74—New York Westsiders		NYMJHL	42	71	49	120	41

Year	Team	League	Games	G.	A.	Pts.	Pen.
1974-75—New York Westsiders (c)	NYMJHL	40	110	72	*182	20
1975-76—Boston College	ECAC	24	16	18	34	4
1976-77—Boston College	ECAC	28	28	26	54	8
1977-78—Boston College (a)	ECAC	34	34	34	68	12
1978-79—Boston College (a-d)	ECAC	25	32	24	56	8
1979-80—Salt Lake Golden Eagles (b-e-g)	CHL	75	40	32	72	21
1979-80—St. Louis Blues (f)	NHL	....	...	....	....	....
1980-81—Salt Lake Golden Eagles (a-h-i)	CHL	80	59	58	*117	8
1981-82—Salt Lake Golden Eagles	CHL	27	21	27	48	12
1981-82—St. Louis Blues	NHL	45	25	34	59	4
1982-83—St. Louis Blues	NHL	49	17	30	47	6
1983-84—St. Louis Blues	NHL	80	41	44	85	19
1984-85—St. Louis Blues	NHL	79	40	52	92	6
1985-86—St. Louis Blues (j)	NHL	48	28	24	52	10
1985-86—Calgary Flames (k)	NHL	29	16	22	38	11
NHL TOTALS		330	167	206	373	56

(c)—Named Most Valuable Player.
(d)—August, 1979—Signed as free agent by St. Louis Blues.
(e)—Co-leader with Red Laurence in goals (9) during CHL playoffs.
(f)—No regular season record. Played one playoff game.
(g)—Won Ken McKenzie Trophy (CHL Top Rookie).
(h)—Winner of Phil Esposito Trophy (Leading CHL Scorer).
(i)—Winner of Tommy Ivan Trophy (CHL MVP).
(j)—February, 1986—Traded with Terry Johnson and Rik Wilson by St. Louis Blues to Calgary Flames for Eddy Beers, Gino Cavallini and Charles Bourgeois.
(k)—Led NHL playoffs with 12 goals.

KIRK MULLER

Center . . . 5'11" . . . 185 lbs. . . . Born, Kingston, Ont., February 8, 1966 . . . Shoots left . . . Member of 1984 Canadian Olympic team . . . (January 13, 1986)—Strained knee . . . (April, 1986)—Fractured ribs at world championships in Soviet Union.

Year	Team	League	Games	G.	A.	Pts.	Pen.
1980-81—Kingston Canadians	OHL	2	0	0	0	0
1981-82—Kingston Canadians	OHL	67	12	39	51	27
1982-83—Guelph Platers (c)	OHL	66	52	60	112	41
1983-84—Canadian Olympic Team	Int'l	15	2	2	4	6
1983-84—Guelph Platers (d)	OHL	49	31	63	94	27
1984-85—New Jersey Devils	NHL	80	17	37	54	69
1985-86—New Jersey Devils	NHL	77	25	42	67	45
NHL TOTALS		157	42	79	121	114

(c)—Won William Hanley Trophy (OHL Most Gentlemanly).
(d)—June, 1984—Drafted as underage junior by New Jersey Devils in NHL entry draft. First Devils pick, second overall, first round.

DWIGHT MULLINS

Center . . . 5'11" . . . 190 lbs. . . . Born, Calgary, Alta., February 28, 1967 . . . Shoots right . . . Also plays Right Wing.

Year	Team	League	Games	G.	A.	Pts.	Pen.
1982-83—Lethbridge Broncos	WHL	66	5	2	7	71
1983-84—Lethbridge Broncos	WHL	70	20	23	43	101
1984-85—Lethbridge Broncos (c)	WHL	62	21	18	39	94
1985-86—Lethbridge Broncos	WHL	72	52	37	89	99

(c)—June, 1985—Drafted as underage junior by Minnesota North Stars in 1985 NHL entry draft. Third North Stars pick, 90th overall, fifth round.

MICHAEL MULLOWNEY

Defense . . . 6'1" . . . 190 lbs. . . . Born, Brighton, Mass., January 17, 1966 . . . Shoots left.

Year	Team	League	Games	G.	A.	Pts.	Pen.
1984-85—Deerfield Academy (c)	Mass. H.S.	17	17	30	47	18
1985-86—Boston College	H. East	26	0	2	2	20

(c)—June, 1985—Drafted by Minnesota North Stars in 1985 NHL entry draft. Fourth North Stars pick, 111th overall, sixth round.

CRAIG DOUGLAS MUNI

Defense . . . 6'2" . . . 201 lbs. . . . Born, Toronto, Ont., July 19, 1962 . . . Shoots left . . . (September, 1981)—Tore left knee ligaments while skating in Windsor, Ont., prior to the opening of Toronto training camp . . . (January, 1983)—Broken ankle in AHL game at Fredericton.

Year	Team	League	Games	G.	A.	Pts.	Pen.
1979-80—Kingston Canadians (c)		OMJHL	66	6	28	34	114
1980-81—Kingston Canadians		OHL	38	2	14	16	65
1980-81—Windsor Spitfires		OHL	25	5	11	16	41
1980-81—New Brunswick Hawks (d)		AHL	....	...	....	....	....
1981-82—Windsor Spitfires		OHL	49	5	32	37	92
1981-82—Cincinnati Tigers (e)		CHL	....	...	....	....	....
1982-83—Toronto Maple Leafs		NHL	2	0	1	1	0
1982-83—St. Catharines Saints		AHL	64	6	32	38	52
1983-84—St. Catharines Saints		AHL	64	4	16	20	79
1984-85—St. Catharines Saints		AHL	68	7	17	24	54
1984-85—Toronto Maple Leafs		NHL	8	0	0	0	0
1985-86—Toronto Maple Leafs		NHL	6	0	1	1	4
1985-86—St. Catharines Saints		AHL	73	3	34	37	91
NHL TOTALS			16	0	2	2	4

(c)—June, 1980—Drafted as underage junior by Toronto Maple Leafs in 1980 NHL entry draft. First Maple Leafs pick, 25th overall, second round.

(d)—No regular season appearance. Played two playoff games.

(e)—No regular season appearance. Played three playoff games.

ERIC A. MURANO

Center . . . 6' . . . 190 lbs. . . . Born, LaSalle, Que., May 4, 1967 . . . Shoots right.

Year	Team	League	Games	G.	A.	Pts.	Pen.
1985-86—Calgary Canucks (c)		AJHL	52	34	47	81	32

(c)—June, 1986—Drafted by Vancouver Canucks in 1986 NHL entry draft. Fourth Canucks pick, 91st overall, fifth round.

DONALD WALTER MURDOCH

Right Wing . . . 5'11" . . . 180 lbs. . . . Born, Cranbrook, B. C., October 25, 1956 . . . Shoots right . . . Brother of Robert Lovell Murdoch . . . Missed part of 1976-77 season with torn tendon in left ankle requiring surgery. Had second operation on ankle, May, 1977 . . . Missed part of 1977-78 season with slipped vertebrae and start of 1978-79 season under suspension imposed by NHL . . . Set CHL record with 17 goals in a playoff season in 1981 . . . (October, 1982)—Injured Achilles tendon . . . Set WCHL rookie point record with 141 points in 1974-75 (broken by Dale Derkatch) . . . (November, 1984)—Torn knee ligaments.

Year	Team	League	Games	G.	A.	Pts.	Pen.
1973-74—Vernon		Jr. "A" BCHL	45	50	32	82	69
1973-74—Kamloops Chiefs		WCHL	4	1	0	1	9
1974-75—Medicine Hat Tigers (a-c)		WCHL	70	*82	59	141	83
1975-76—Medicine Hat Tigers (a-d)		WCHL	70	*88	77	165	202
1976-77—New York Rangers		NHL	59	32	24	56	47
1977-78—New York Rangers		NHL	66	27	28	55	41
1978-79—New York Rangers		NHL	40	15	22	37	6
1979-80—New York Rangers (e)		NHL	56	23	19	42	16
1979-80—Edmonton Oilers		NHL	10	5	2	7	4
1980-81—Edmonton Oilers		NHL	40	10	9	19	18
1980-81—Wichita Wind (f-g)		CHL	22	15	10	25	48
1981-82—Adirondack Red Wings		AHL	24	11	13	24	24
1981-82—Detroit Red Wings		NHL	49	9	13	22	23
1982-83—Adirondack Red Wings (h)		AHL	35	10	12	22	19
1983-84—Adirondack Red Wings		AHL	59	26	20	46	19
1984-85—Muskegon Lumberjacks (i)		IHL	32	18	13	31	4
1985-86—Muskegon Lumberjacks (j)		IHL	12	4	4	8	0
1985-86—Indianapolis Checkers		IHL	11	4	3	7	4
1985-86—Toledo Goaldiggers		IHL	37	15	23	38	8
NHL TOTALS			320	121	117	238	155

(c)—WCHL Rookie-of-the-Year.

(d)—Drafted from Medicine Hat Tigers by New York Rangers in first round of 1976 amateur draft.

(e)—March, 1980—Traded by N.Y. Rangers to Edmonton Oilers for Cam Connor and a 1980 or 1981 third round draft choice.

(f)—Named Most Valuable Player of CHL playoffs.

(g)—September, 1981—Traded by Edmonton Oilers to Minnesota North Stars for Don Jackson and a 1982 third-round draft choice. Subsequently traded to Detroit Red Wings with Greg Smith, with North Stars acquiring option to switch first-round draft choices with Red Wings in 1982 which Minnesota used to draft Brian Bellows, Detroit selected Murray Craven.

(h)—December, 1983—Signed by Adirondack Red Wings as a free agent.

(i)—October, 1984—Signed by Muskegon Mohawks as a free agent.

(j)—Traded by Muskegon Lumberjacks to Indianapolis Checkers for Gord Paddock.

GARY MURPHY

Defense . . . 6'1" . . . 175 lbs. . . . Born, Winchester, Mass., March 23, 1967 . . . Shoots left.

Year	Team	League	Games	G.	A.	Pts.	Pen.
1983-84—Arlington Catholic H.S.		Mass. H.S.	....	9	18	27	....
1984-85—Arlington Catholic H.S. (c)		Mass. H.S.	20	7	26	33	40
1985-86—University of Lowell		H. East	27	0	9	9	32

(c)—June, 1985—Drafted by Quebec Nordiques in 1985 NHL entry draft. Twelfth Nordiques pick, 225th overall, 11th round.

GORDON MURPHY

Defense . . . 6'1" . . . 180 lbs. . . . Born, Willowdale, Ont., February 23, 1967 . . . Shoots right . . . (January, 1985)—Injured clavicle.

Year	Team	League	Games	G.	A.	Pts.	Pen.
1983-84—Don Mills Flyers		MTHL	65	24	42	66	130
1984-85—Oshawa Generals (c)		OHL	59	3	12	15	25
1985-86—Oshawa Generals		OHL	64	7	15	22	56

(c)—June, 1985—Drafted as underage junior by Philadelphia Flyers in 1985 NHL entry draft. Tenth Flyers pick, 189th overall, ninth round.

JOSEPH PATRICK MURPHY

Center . . . 6'1" . . . 185 lbs. . . . Born, London, Ont., October 16, 1967 . . . Shoots left . . . Also plays Left Wing.

Year	Team	League	Games	G.	A.	Pts.	Pen.
1984-85—Penticton Knights (c)		BCJHL	51	68	84	*152	92
1985-86—Michigan State Univ. (d-e)		CCHA	35	24	37	61	50
1985-86—Team Canada		Int'l	8	3	3	6	2

(c)—Named AJHL Rookie of the Year.
(d)—Named CCHA Rookie of the Year.
(e)—June, 1986—Drafted by Detroit Red Wings in 1986 NHL entry draft. First Red Wings pick, first overall, first round.

KELLY MURPHY

Defense . . . 6'1" . . . 175 lbs. . . . Born, Regina, Sask., April 24, 1966 . . . Shoots right.

Year	Team	League	Games	G.	A.	Pts.	Pen.
1983-84—Wilcox Notre Dame H.S.(c)		Sask.H.S.	40	15	45	60	..
1984-85—Michigan Tech.		WCHA	40	2	8	10	16
1985-86—Michigan Tech.		WCHA	40	0	11	11	20

(c)—June, 1984—Drafted by New York Islanders in NHL entry draft. Eighth Islanders pick, 146th overall, seventh round.

LAWRENCE THOMAS MURPHY

Defense . . . 6'1" . . . 210 lbs. . . . Born, Scarborough, Ont., March 8, 1961 . . . Shoots right . . . Set record for most points by NHL rookie defenseman in 1980-81 (76 points) . . . Holds Los Angeles Kings club record for most goals, assists and points by a defenseman in a career as well as L.A. records for assists and points by a rookie . . . (1981-82)—Set club record for most goals by a defenseman in a season (22) . . . (1980-81)—Set NHL record for most assists (60) and points (76) by a rookie defenseman . . . (October 29, 1985)—Injured foot.

Year	Team	League	Games	G.	A.	Pts.	Pen.
1978-79—Peterborough Petes		OMJHL	66	6	21	27	82
1979-80—Peterborough Petes (a-c-d)		OMJHL	68	21	68	89	88
1980-81—Los Angeles Kings		NHL	80	16	60	76	79
1981-82—Los Angeles Kings		NHL	79	22	44	66	95
1982-83—Los Angeles Kings		NHL	77	14	48	62	81
1983-84—Los Angeles Kings		NHL	6	0	3	3	0
1983-84—Washington Capitals (e)		NHL	72	13	33	46	50
1984-85—Washington Capitals		NHL	79	13	42	55	51
1985-86—Washington Capitals		NHL	78	21	44	65	50
NHL TOTALS			471	99	274	373	406

(c)—Won Max Kaminsky Memorial Trophy (Outstanding OMJHL Defenseman).
(d)—June, 1980—Drafted as underage junior by Los Angeles Kings in 1980 NHL entry draft. First Kings pick, 4th overall, first round. (L.A. obtained draft pick from Detroit Red Wings as part of the Dale McCourt/Andre St. Laurent trade of August, 1979).
(e)—October, 1983—Traded by Los Angeles Kings to Washington Capitals for Brian Engblom and Ken Houston.

MIKE MURRAY

Center ... 6' ... 183 lbs. ... Born, Kingston, Ont., April 29, 1966 ... Shoots left.

Year	Team	League	Games	G.	A.	Pts.	Pen.
1982-83—Sarnia		Ont. Midget	57	61	39	100	48
1983-84—London Knights (c)		OHL	70	8	24	32	14
1984-85—London Knights (d)		OHL	43	21	35	56	19
1984-85—Guelph Platers		OHL	23	10	9	19	8
1985-86—Guelph Platers (e)		OHL	56	27	38	65	19

(c)—June, 1984—Drafted as underage junior by New York Islanders in NHL entry draft. Sixth Islanders pick, 104th overall, fifth round.

(d)—January, 1985—Traded with Ron Coutts by Kitchener Rangers to Guelph Platers for Trevor Stienburg.

(e)—June, 1986—Traded by New York Islanders to Philadelphia Flyers for a fifth round 1986 draft pick (Todd McLellan).

ROBERT MURRAY

Center ... 6'1" ... 175 lbs. ... Born, Toronto, Ont., April 4, 1967 ... Shoots right.

Year	Team	League	Games	G.	A.	Pts.	Pen.
1983-85—Mississauga Reps		OHA	35	18	36	54	32
1984-85—Peterborough Petes (c)		OHL	63	12	9	21	155
1985-86—Peterborough Petes		OHL	52	14	18	32	125

(c)—June, 1985—Drafted as underage junior by Washington Capitals in 1985 NHL entry draft. Third Capitals pick, 61st overall, third round.

ROBERT FREDERICK MURRAY

Defense ... 5'9" ... 175 lbs. ... Born, Kingston, Ont., November 26, 1954 ... Shoots right ... (December 20, 1981)—Tore ligaments in left knee vs. Toronto and required surgery.

Year	Team	League	Games	G.	A.	Pts.	Pen.
1971-72—Cornwall Royals		QJHL	62	14	49	63	88
1972-73—Cornwall Royals		QJHL	32	9	26	35	34
1973-74—Cornwall Royals (c)		QJHL	63	23	76	99	88
1974-75—Dallas Black Hawks		CHL	75	14	43	57	130
1975-76—Chicago Black Hawks		NHL	64	1	2	3	44
1976-77—Chicago Black Hawks		NHL	77	10	11	21	71
1977-78—Chicago Black Hawks		NHL	70	14	17	31	41
1978-79—Chicago Black Hawks		NHL	79	19	32	51	38
1979-80—Chicago Black Hawks		NHL	74	16	34	50	60
1980-81—Chicago Black Hawks		NHL	77	13	47	60	93
1981-82—Chicago Black Hawks		NHL	45	8	22	30	48
1982-83—Chicago Black Hawks		NHL	79	7	32	39	73
1983-84—Chicago Black Hawks		NHL	78	11	37	48	78
1984-85—Chicago Black Hawks		NHL	80	5	38	43	56
1985-86—Chicago Black Hawks		NHL	80	9	29	38	75
NHL TOTALS			803	113	301	414	677

(c)—Drafted from Cornwall Royals by Chicago Black Hawks in third round of 1974 amateur draft.

TROY MURRAY

Center ... 6'1" ... 195 lbs. ... Born, Winnipeg, Man., July 31, 1962 ... Shoots right ... (November, 1983)—Knee ligament injury.

Year	Team	League	Games	G.	A.	Pts.	Pen.
1979-80—St. Albert Saints (c)		AJHL	60	53	47	100	101
1980-81—Univ. of North Dakota (b-d)		WCHA	38	33	45	78	28
1981-82—Univ. of North Dakota (b)		WCHA	42	22	29	51	62
1981-82—Chicago Black Hawks		NHL	1	0	0	0	0
1982-83—Chicago Black Hawks		NHL	54	8	8	16	27
1983-84—Chicago Black Hawks		NHL	61	15	15	30	45
1984-85—Chicago Black Hawks		NHL	80	26	40	66	82
1985-86—Chicago Black Hawks (e)		NHL	80	45	54	99	94
NHL TOTALS			276	94	117	211	248

(c)—June, 1980—Drafted by Chicago Black Hawks in 1980 NHL entry draft. Sixth Black Hawks pick, 57th overall, third round.

(d)—Named Outstanding Freshman in WCHA.

(e)—Won Frank Selke Trophy (Best defensive forward).

DANA MURZYN

Defense ... 6'3" ... 205 lbs. ... Born, Regina, Sask., December 9, 1966 ... Shoots left.

Year	Team	League	Games	G.	A.	Pts.	Pen.
1983-84—Calgary Wranglers		WHL	65	11	20	31	135
1984-85—Calgary Wranglers (a-c)		WHL	72	32	60	92	233
1985-86—Hartford Whalers (d)		NHL	78	3	23	26	125
NHL TOTALS			78	3	23	26	125

(c)—June, 1985—Drafted as underage junior by Hartford Whalers in 1985 NHL entry draft. First Whalers pick, fifth overall, first round.

FRANTISEK MUSIL

Defense . . . 6'3" . . . 205 lbs. . . . Born, Pardubice, Czechoslovakia, December 17, 1964 . . . Shoots left.

Year	Team	League	Games	G.	A.	Pts.	Pen.
1985-86—Dukla Jihlava (c)		Czech.	35	3	7	10	85

(c)—June, 1983—Drafted by Minnesota North Stars in 1983 NHL entry draft. Third North Stars pick, 38th overall, second round.

DONALD KENNETH NACHBAUR

Center . . . 6'2" . . . 200 lbs. . . . Born, Kitimat, B.C., January 30, 1959 . . . Shoots left . . . Also plays Left Wing . . . (October 20, 1984)—Injured forearm in game at Baltimore and spend remainder of season as assistant coach of Hershey Bears.

Year	Team	League	Games	G.	A.	Pts.	Pen.
1976-77—Merritt Luckies		......	54	22	27	49	31
1977-78—Billings Bighorns		WCHL	68	23	27	50	128
1978-79—Billings Bighorns (c)		WHL	69	44	52	96	175
1979-80—Springfield Indians		AHL	70	12	17	29	119
1980-81—Hartford Whalers		NHL	77	16	17	33	139
1981-82—Hartford Whalers (d)		NHL	77	5	21	26	117
1982-83—Edmonton Oilers		NHL	4	0	0	0	17
1982-83—Moncton Alpines		AHL	70	33	33	66	125
1983-84—New Haven Nighthawks (e)		AHL	70	33	32	65	194
1984-85—Hershey Bears		AHL	7	2	3	5	21
1985-86—Philadelphia Flyers (f)		NHL	5	1	1	2	7
1985-86—Hershey Bears		AHL	74	23	24	47	301
NHL TOTALS			163	22	39	61	280

(c)—August, 1979—Drafted by Hartford Whalers in entry draft. Third Hartford pick, 60th overall, third round.

(d)—August, 1982—Traded with Ken Linseman by Hartford Whalers to Edmonton Oilers for Risto Siltanen and Brent Loney.

(e)—October, 1983—Selected by Los Angeles Kings in NHL waiver draft.

(f)—July, 1985—Signed by Philadelphia Flyers as a free agent.

JAMIE NADJIWAN

Left Wing . . . 6'1" . . . 190 lbs. . . . Born, Sudbury, Ont., January 2, 1966 . . . Shoots left.

Year	Team	League	Games	G.	A.	Pts.	Pen.
1983-84—Nickel Center Native Sons		OHA	37	39	51	91	32
1984-85—Sudbury Wolves (c)		OHL	62	29	21	50	42
1985-86—Sudbury Wolves (d)		OHL	16	11	7	18	8
1985-86—Cornwall Royals (e)		OHL	9	2	7	9	2
1985-86—Hamilton Steelhawks		OHL	24	10	14	24	12

(c)—June, 1985—Drafted by Washington Capitals in 1985 NHL entry draft. Eighth Capitals pick, 145th overall, seventh round.

(d)—November, 1985—Traded with Neil Jones, Pat Malone and Dean Guitard by Sudbury Wolves to Cornwall Royals for fourth and 11th round picks in 1986 OHL priority draft.

(e)—January, 1986—Sold by Cornwall Royals to Hamilton Steelhawks.

MARTY NANNE

Right Wing . . . 6' . . . 180 lbs. . . . Born, Edina, Minn., July 21, 1967 . . . Shoots right . . . Son of Lou Nanne (Minnesota North Stars G.M.).

Year	Team	League	Games	G.	A.	Pts.	Pen.
1984-85—Edina H.S.		Minn.	17	10	7	17	..
1985-86—University of Minnesota (c)		WCHA	20	5	5	10	20

(c)—June, 1986—Drafted by Chicago Black Hawks in 1986 NHL entry draft. Seventh Black Hawks pick, 161st overall, eighth round.

MARK NAPIER

Right Wing . . . 5'10" . . . 182 lbs. . . . Born, Toronto, Ont., January 28, 1957 . . . Shoots left . . . Brother of Steve Napier, Cornell goalie in mid 1970's . . . (October 20, 1983)—Ankle tendon partially severed by skate of Dan Mandich in game at Minnesota.

Year	Team	League	Games	G.	A.	Pts.	Pen.
1972-73—Wexford Raiders		OPHL	44	41	27	68	201
1973-74—Toronto Marlboros		Jr."A"OHA	70	47	46	93	63
1974-75—Toronto Marlboros (a-c)		Jr."A"OHA	61	66	64	130	106
1975-76—Toronto Toros (d-e)		WHA	78	43	50	93	20
1976-77—Birmingham Bulls (f)		WHA	80	60	36	96	24
1977-78—Birmingham Bulls (g)		WHA	79	33	32	65	90
1978-79—Montreal Canadiens		NHL	54	11	20	31	11
1979-80—Montreal Canadiens		NHL	76	16	33	49	7
1980-81—Montreal Canadiens		NHL	79	35	36	71	24
1981-82—Montreal Canadiens		NHL	80	40	41	81	14
1982-83—Montreal Canadiens		NHL	73	40	27	67	6
1983-84—Montreal Canadiens (h)		NHL	5	3	2	5	0
1983-84—Minnesota North Stars		NHL	58	13	28	41	17
1984-85—Minnesota North Stars (i)		NHL	39	10	18	28	2
1984-85—Edmonton Oilers		NHL	33	9	26	35	19
1985-86—Edmonton Oilers		NHL	80	24	32	56	14
WHA TOTALS			237	136	118	254	134
NHL TOTALS			577	201	263	464	114

(c)—Signed by Toronto Toros (WHA), May, 1975.
(d)—Won WHA Rookie Award.
(e)—Named WHA Rookie of the Year in poll of players by THE SPORTING NEWS.
(f)—Drafted from Birmingham Bulls (WHA) by Montreal Canadiens in first round of 1977 amateur draft.
(g)—September, 1978—Signed by Montreal Canadiens.
(h)—October, 1983—Traded with Keith Acton and third-round 1984 draft pick (Kenneth Hodge) by Montreal Canadiens to Minnesota North Stars for Bobby Smith.
(i)—January, 1985—Traded by Minnesota North Stars to Edmonton Oilers for Terry Martin and Gord Sherven.

RICH NASHEIM

Right Wing . . . 5'11" . . . 185 lbs. . . . Born, Regina, Sask., January 15, 1963 . . . Shoots right.

Year	Team	League	Games	G.	A.	Pts.	Pen.
1985-86—University of Regina (c)		CWAUU	22	22	28	50	36

(c)—July, 1986—Signed by New York Rangers as a free agent.

MATS NASLUND

Left Wing . . . 5'7" . . . 158 lbs. . . . Born, Timra, Sweden, October 31, 1959 . . . Shoots left.

Year	Team	League	Games	G.	A.	Pts.	Pen.
1980-81—Brynas IF (c)		Sweden	....	17	25	42	....
1981-82—Brynas IF		Sweden	....	25	20	45	....
1982-83—Montreal Canadiens		NHL	74	26	45	71	10
1983-84—Montreal Canadiens		NHL	77	29	35	64	4
1984-85—Montreal Canadiens		NHL	80	42	37	79	14
1985-86—Montreal Canadiens		NHL	80	43	67	110	16
NHL TOTALS			311	140	184	324	44

(c)—August, 1979—Drafted by Montreal Canadiens in 1979 NHL entry draft. Second Canadiens pick, 37th overall, second round.

ERIC RIC NATTRESS
(Known by middle name.)

Defense . . . 6'2" . . . 208 lbs. . . . Born, Hamilton, Ont., May 25, 1962 . . . Shoots right . . . (August, 1983)—Fined $150 in Brantford, Ontario for possession of three grams of marijuana and one gram of hashish . . . (September, 1983)—Given 40-game suspension by NHL following his conviction in Ontario court . . . (March, 1984)—Fractured finger . . . (March 17, 1986)—Injured shoulder at Minnesota.

Year	Team	League	Games	G.	A.	Pts.	Pen.
1979-80—Brantford Alexanders (c)		OMJHL	65	3	21	24	94
1980-81—Brantford Alexanders		OHL	51	8	34	42	106
1981-82—Brantford Alexanders		OHL	59	11	50	61	126
1982-83—Nova Scotia Voyageurs		AHL	9	0	4	4	16
1982-83—Montreal Canadiens		NHL	40	1	3	4	19
1983-84—Montreal Canadiens		NHL	34	0	12	12	15
1984-85—Sherbrooke Canadiens		AHL	72	8	40	48	37
1984-85—Montreal Canadiens		NHL	5	0	1	1	2
1985-86—St. Louis Blues (d)		NHL	78	4	20	24	52
NHL TOTALS			157	5	36	41	88

(c)—June, 1980—Drafted as underage junior by Montreal Canadiens in 1980 NHL entry draft. Second Canadiens pick, 27th overall, second round.
(d)—September, 1985—Traded by Montreal Canadiens to St. Louis Blues to complete June deal for Mark Hunter.

DANIEL NAUD

Defense . . . 5'10" . . . 187 lbs. . . . Born, Trois-Rivieres, Que., February 20, 1962 . . . Shoots right . . . (November, 1980)—Fractured ankle.

Year	Team	League	Games	G.	A.	Pts.	Pen.
1979-80—Sorel Black Hawks (c)	OMJHL	72	17	53	70	30
1980-81—Sorel Black Hawks	QMJHL	62	17	32	49	28
1981-82—Granby Bisons (d)	QMJHL	29	8	21	29	26
1981-82—Hull Olympics	QMJHL	35	12	30	42	42
1982-83—Rochester Americans	AHL	71	6	52	58	34
1983-84—Rochester Americans	AHL	79	15	44	59	29
1984-85—Flint Generals	IHL	82	20	44	64	38
1985-86—Muskegon Lumberjacks (b)	IHL	80	13	52	65	34

(c)—June, 1980—Drafted by Buffalo Sabres as underage junior in 1980 NHL entry draft. Seventh Sabres pick, 125th overall, sixth round.

(d)—December, 1981—Traded by Granby Bisons to Hull Olympics for Sylvain Roy, Claude Labbe and Jocelyn Gauvreau.

JEAN-FRANCOIS NAULT

Center . . . 6'2" . . . 180 lbs. . . . Born, Montreal, Que., May 12, 1967 . . . Shoots left.

Year	Team	League	Games	G.	A.	Pts.	Pen.
1984-85—Levis Lauzon College	Que.	41	13	16	29	28
1985-86—Granby Bisons (c)	QHL	39	13	20	33	20

(c)—June, 1986—Drafted as underage junior by Quebec Nordiques in 1986 NHL entry draft. Ninth Nordiques pick, 144th overall, seventh round.

CAM NEELY

Right Wing . . . 6'1" . . . 185 lbs. . . . Born, Comox, B.C., June 6, 1965 . . . Shoots right . . . (October, 1984)—Dislocated kneecap.

Year	Team	League	Games	G.	A.	Pts.	Pen.
1981-82—Ridge Meadow	B.C. Midget	64	73	68	141	134
1982-83—Portland Winter Hawks (c)	WHL	72	56	64	120	130
1983-84—Portland Winter Hawks	WHL	19	8	18	26	29
1983-84—Vancouver Canucks	NHL	56	16	15	31	57
1984-85—Vancouver Canucks	NHL	72	21	18	39	137
1985-86—Vancouver Canucks (d)	NHL	73	14	20	34	126
NHL TOTALS		201	51	53	104	320

(c)—June, 1983—Drafted as underage junior by Vancouver Canucks in 1983 NHL entry draft. First Canucks' pick, ninth overall, first round.

(d)—June, 1986—Traded with first-round draft choice in 1987 by Vancouver Canucks to Boston Bruins for Barry Pederson.

MIKE NEILL

Defense . . . 6' . . . 195 lbs. . . . Born, Kenora, Ont., August 6, 1965 . . . Shoots left.

Year	Team	League	Games	G.	A.	Pts.	Pen.
1981-82—Kenora Thistles	MJHL	60	12	32	44	65
1982-83—Sault Ste. Marie Greyhounds (c)	OHL	65	4	13	17	115
1983-84—Sault Ste. Marie Greyhounds	OHL	20	2	6	8	42
1983-84—Windsor Spitfires	OHL	49	9	17	26	101
1984-85—Windsor Compuware Spitfires	OHL	62	3	17	20	143
1984-85—Springfield Indians	AHL	7	0	0	0	16
1984-85—Indianapolis Checkers (d)	IHL	....	...	....	....	....
1985-86—Indianapolis Checkers	IHL	71	2	11	13	117
1985-86—Springfield Indians	AHL	8	0	2	2	11

(c)—June, 1983—Drafted as underage junior by New York Islanders in 1983 NHL entry draft. Fourth Islanders' pick, 57th overall, third round.

(d)—Did not play in regular season. Played one playoff game.

BRIAN NELSON

Center . . . 5'11" . . . 170 lbs. . . . Born, Willmar, Minn., October 5, 1965 . . . Shoots left.

Year	Team	League	Games	G.	A.	Pts.	Pen.
1983-84—Willmar H.S. (c)	Minn. H.S.	20	42	44	86	30
1984-85—Univ. Minnesota/Duluth	WCHA	3	0	0	0	2
1985-86—Univ. Minnesota/Duluth	WCHA	14	1	2	3	2
1985-86—University of Minnesota	WCHA	23	1	7	8	14

(c)—June, 1984—Drafted by New York Rangers in NHL entry draft. Seventh Rangers pick, 161st overall, eighth round.

STEVE NEMETH

Center . . . 5'8" . . . 167 lbs. . . . Born, Calgary, Alta., February 11, 1967 . . . Shoots left . . . (November, 1984)—Dislocated left shoulder.

Year	Team	League	Games	G.	A.	Pts.	Pen.
1983-84	Lethbridge Broncos	WHL	68	22	20	42	33
1984-85	Lethbridge Broncos (c)	WHL	67	39	55	94	39
1985-86	Lethbridge Broncos	WHL	70	42	69	111	47

(c)—June, 1985—Drafted as underage junior by New York Rangers in 1985 NHL entry draft. Tenth Rangers pick, 196th overall, 10th round.

JIM NESICH

Right Wing and Center . . . 5'11" . . . 160 lbs. . . . Born, Dearborn, Mich., February 22, 1966 . . . Shoots right.

Year	Team	League	Games	G.	A.	Pts.	Pen.
1983-84	Verdun Juniors (c)	WHL	70	22	24	46	35
1984-85	Verdun Juniors	QHL	65	19	33	52	72
1985-86	Verdun Juniors	OHL	71	26	55	81	114
1985-86	Sherbrooke Canadiens	AHL	4	0	1	1	0

(c)—June, 1984—Drafted by Montreal Canadiens in NHL entry draft. Eighth Canadiens pick, 116th overall, sixth round.

RAY NEUFELD

Right Wing . . . 6'2" . . . 215 lbs. . . . Born, St. Boniface, Man., April 15, 1959 . . . Shoots right . . . (September, 1978)—Broken ribs . . . (January 7, 1985)—Injured shoulder when checked by Gary Leeman in game at Toronto.

Year	Team	League	Games	G.	A.	Pts.	Pen.
1976-77	Flin Flon Bombers	WCHL	68	13	19	32	63
1977-78	Flin Flon Bombers	WCHL	72	23	46	69	224
1978-79	Edmonton Oil Kings (c)	WCHL	57	54	48	102	138
1979-80	Springfield Indians	AHL	73	23	29	52	51
1979-80	Hartford Whalers	NHL	8	1	0	1	0
1980-81	Binghamton Whalers	AHL	25	7	7	14	43
1980-81	Hartford Whalers	NHL	52	5	10	15	44
1981-82	Binghamton Whalers (d)	AHL	61	28	31	59	81
1981-82	Hartford Whalers	NHL	19	4	3	7	4
1982-83	Hartford Whalers	NHL	80	26	31	57	86
1983-84	Hartford Whalers	NHL	80	27	42	69	97
1984-85	Hartford Whalers	NHL	76	27	35	62	129
1985-86	Hartford Whalers (e)	NHL	16	5	10	15	40
1985-86	Winnipeg Jets	NHL	60	20	28	48	62
	NHL TOTALS		391	115	159	274	462

(c)—August, 1979—Drafted by Hartford Whalers in 1979 entry draft. Fourth Whalers pick, 81st overall, fourth round.

(d)—Co-leader (with Florent Robidoux of New Brunswick) during AHL Calder Cup Playoffs with nine goals.

(e)—November, 1985—Traded by Hartford Whalers to Winnipeg Jets for Dave Babych.

JOHN NEWBERRY

Center . . . 6'1" . . . 185 lbs. . . . Born, Port Alberni, B.C., April 8, 1962 . . . Shoots left.

Year	Team	League	Games	G.	A.	Pts.	Pen.
1979-80	Nanaimo Clippers (c)	BCJHL	..	..	..	..	..
1980-81	University of Wisconsin (d)	WCHA	39	30	32	62	77
1981-82	University of Wisconsin (a-e)	WCHA	39	38	27	65	42
1982-83	Nova Scotia Voyageurs	AHL	71	29	29	58	43
1982-83	Montreal Canadiens (f)	NHL	...	...	...	...	...
1983-84	Montreal Canadiens	NHL	3	0	0	0	0
1983-84	Nova Scotia Voyageurs	AHL	78	25	37	62	116
1984-85	Sherbrooke Canadiens (g)	AHL	58	23	40	63	30
1984-85	Montreal Canadiens (h)	NHL	16	0	4	4	6
1985-86	Hartford Whalers	NHL	3	0	0	0	0
1985-86	Binghamton Whalers	AHL	21	6	11	17	38
1985-86	Moncton Golden Flames	AHL	44	10	24	34	31
	NHL TOTALS		22	0	4	4	6

(c)—June, 1980—Drafted as underage player by Montreal Canadiens in 1980 NHL entry draft. Fourth Canadiens pick, 45th overall, third round.

(d)—Named to NCAA Tournament All-Star team.

(e)—Named to All-America Team (West).

(f)—No regular season record. Played in two playoff games.

(g)—Led AHL playoffs with 20 points and shared AHL playoff assist lead with teammate Thomas Rundqvist with 14.

(h)—August, 1985—Signed as free agent by Hartford Whalers.

JIM NEWHOUSE

Left Wing . . . 5'10" . . . 180 lbs. . . . Born, Winchester, Mass., April 1, 1966 . . . Shoots left.

Year	Team	League	Games	G.	A.	Pts.	Pen.
1983-84—Matignon H.S. (c)		Mass. H.S.	22	18	30	48	..
1984-85—University of Lowell		H. East	37	6	7	13	16
1985-86—University of Lowell		H. East	39	20	13	33	32

(c)—June, 1984—Drafted by Boston Bruins in NHL entry draft. Twelfth Bruins pick, 248th overall, 12th round.

BERNIE IRVINE NICHOLLS

Center . . . 6' . . . 185 lbs. . . . Born, Haliburton, Ont., June 24, 1961 . . . Shoots right . . . (November 18, 1982)—Partial tear of medial colateral ligament in right knee in game vs. Detroit when hit by Willie Huber . . . (February, 1984)—Broken jaw, missed only two games but lost 13 pounds before the end of season with jaw wired shut.

Year	Team	League	Games	G.	A.	Pts.	Pen.
1978-79—Kingston Canadians		OMJHL	2	0	1	1	0
1979-80—Kingston Canadians (c)		OMJHL	68	36	43	79	85
1980-81—Kingston Canadians		OHL	65	63	89	152	109
1981-82—New Haven Nighthawks		AHL	55	41	30	71	31
1981-82—Los Angeles Kings		NHL	22	14	18	32	27
1982-83—Los Angeles Kings		NHL	71	28	22	50	124
1983-84—Los Angeles Kings		NHL	78	41	54	95	83
1984-85—Los Angeles Kings		NHL	80	46	54	100	76
1985-86—Los Angeles Kings		NHL	80	36	61	97	78
NHL TOTALS			331	165	209	374	388

(c)—June, 1980—Drafted by Los Angeles Kings as underage junior in 1980 NHL entry draft. Fourth Kings pick, 73rd overall, fourth round.

ROB NICHOLS

Left Wing . . . 5'11" . . . 172 lbs. . . . Born, Hamilton, Ontario, August 4, 1964 . . . Shoots left.

Year	Team	League	Games	G.	A.	Pts.	Pen.
1982-83—Kitchener Rangers (c)		OHL	54	17	26	43	208
1983-84—Kitchener Rangers		OHL	12	5	8	13	46
1983-84—North Bay Centennials		OHL	46	36	32	68	98
1984-85—North Bay Centennials		OHL	41	27	39	66	72
1984-85—Fredericton Express		AHL	1	0	0	0	2
1984-85—Kalamazoo Wings		IHL	8	2	1	3	0
1985-86—Kalamazoo Wings		IHL	73	38	41	79	406

(c)—June, 1983—Drafted as underage junior by Philadelphia Flyers in 1983 NHL entry draft. Eighth Flyers pick, 181st overall, ninth round.

TOM NICKOLAU

Center . . . 6'2" . . . 190 lbs. . . . Born, Scarborough, Ont., April 11, 1966 . . . Shoots left.

Year	Team	League	Games	G.	A.	Pts.	Pen.
1982-83—Wexford		Ont. Midget	40	25	35	60	67
1983-84—Guelph Platers (c)		OHL	61	5	13	18	98
1984-85—Guelph Platers		OHL	48	17	24	41	71
1985-86—Guelph Platers		OHL	39	6	26	32	81

(c)—June, 1984—Drafted as underage junior by Detroit Red Wings in NHL entry draft. Twelfth Red Wings pick, 236th overall, twelfth round.

JAMIE NICOLLS

Left Wing . . . 6'1" . . . 193 lbs. . . . Born, Vancouver, B.C., March 27, 1968 . . . Shoots left . . . Also plays Right Wing.

Year	Team	League	Games	G.	A.	Pts.	Pen.
1983-84—Portland Winter Hawks		WHL	44	7	12	19	14
1984-85—Portland Winter Hawks		WHL	70	12	24	36	56
1985-86—Portland Winter Hawks (c)		WHL	65	15	37	52	60

(c)—June, 1986—Drafted as underage junior by Edmonton Oilers in 1986 NHL entry draft. Second Oilers pick, 42nd overall, second round.

LEN NIELSEN

Center . . . 5'9" . . . 172 lbs. . . . Born, Moose Jaw, Sask., March 28, 1967 . . . Shoots left.

Year	Team	League	Games	G.	A.	Pts.	Pen.
1983-84—Regina Pats		WHL	57	9	15	24	20
1984-85—Regina Pats (c)		WHL	72	35	74	109	43
1985-86—Regina Pats		WHL	66	30	77	107	49
1985-86—Team Canada		Int'l	1	0	0	0	0

(c)—September, 1985—Invited to Winnipeg Jets training camp and signed as a free agent.

KRAIG NIENHUIS

Left Wing . . . 6'3" . . . 205 lbs. . . . Born, Sarnia, Ont., May 9, 1962 . . . Shoots left.

Year	Team	League	Games	G.	A.	Pts.	Pen.
1982-83—Rensselaer Poly. Inst.		ECAC	24	9	11	20	34
1983-84—Rensselaer Poly. Inst.		ECAC	35	10	12	22	26
1984-85—Rensselaer Poly. Inst. (c)		ECAC	36	11	10	21	55
1985-86—Boston Bruins		NHL	70	16	14	30	37
NHL TOTALS			70	16	14	30	37

(c)—June, 1985—Signed by Boston Bruins as a free agent.

JOE NIEUWENDYK

Center . . . 6'2" . . . 185 lbs. . . . Born, Oshawa, Ont., September 10, 1966 . . . Shoots left . . . Cousin of Jeff, John and Brian Beukeboom.

Year	Team	League	Games	G.	A.	Pts.	Pen.
1983-84—Pickering Panthers Jr. B.		MTJHL	38	30	28	58	35
1984-85—Cornell University (c-d)		ECAC	29	21	24	45	30
1985-86—Cornell University (a)		ECAC	29	26	28	54	67

(c)—Won Ivy-League Rookie of the Year Trophy.
(d)—June, 1985—Drafted by Calgary Flames in 1985 NHL entry draft. Second Flames pick, 27th overall, second round.

CHRIS NILAN

Right Wing . . . 6' . . . 200 lbs. . . . Born, Boston, Mass., February 9, 1958 . . . Shoots right . . . (November 21, 1981)—Threw puck at Paul Baxter of Pittsburgh while sitting in penalty box. Was given a three-game suspension by NHL . . . (January 22, 1985)—Became all-time Montreal Canadien career penalty minute leader (previous record held by Maurice Richard with 1285 minutes) . . . (October 13, 1985)—Given eight-game suspension by NHL for intentional injury of Rick Middleton in a game at Boston.

Year	Team	League	Games	G.	A.	Pts.	Pen.
1977-78—Northeastern University (c)		ECAC	....	...	....	....	....
1978-79—Northeastern University		ECAC	32	9	13	22	....
1979-80—Nova Scotia Voyageurs		AHL	49	15	10	25	*304
1979-80—Montreal Canadiens		NHL	15	0	2	2	50
1980-81—Montreal Canadiens		NHL	57	7	8	15	262
1981-82—Montreal Canadiens		NHL	49	7	4	11	204
1982-83—Montreal Canadiens		NHL	66	6	8	14	213
1983-84—Montreal Canadiens (d)		NHL	76	16	10	26	*338
1984-85—Montreal Canadiens		NHL	77	21	16	37	*358
1985-86—Montreal Canadiens (e)		NHL	72	19	15	34	274
NHL TOTALS			412	76	63	139	1699

(c)—June, 1978—Drafted by Montreal Canadiens in 1978 amateur draft. Twenty-first Canadiens pick, 231st overall, 19th round.
(d)—Led NHL playoffs with 81 penalty minutes.
(e)—Led NHL Playoffs with 141 penalty minutes.

JIM EDWARD NILL

Right Wing . . . 6' . . . 185 lbs. . . . Born, Hanna, Alta., April 11, 1958 . . . Shoots right . . . (March, 1983)—Concussion . . . (October 10, 1985)—Dislocated shoulder at Edmonton and missed 15 games.

Year	Team	League	Games	G.	A.	Pts.	Pen.
1974-75—Drumheller Falcons		AJHL	59	30	30	60	103
1975-76—Medicine Hat Tigers		WCHL	62	5	11	16	69
1976-77—Medicine Hat Tigers		WCHL	71	23	24	47	140
1977-78—Medicine Hat Tigers (c)		WCHL	72	47	46	93	252
1978-79—Canadian National Team			....	...	....	....	....
1979-80—Canadian National Team			51	14	21	35	58
1979-80—Canadian Olympic Team		Olympics	6	1	2	3	4
1980-81—Salt Lake Golden Eagles (b)		CHL	79	28	34	62	222
1981-82—St. Louis Blues (d)		NHL	61	9	12	21	127
1981-82—Vancouver Canucks		NHL	8	1	2	3	5
1982-83—Vancouver Canucks		NHL	65	7	15	22	136

Year	Team	League	Games	G.	A.	Pts.	Pen.
1983-84—Vancouver Canucks (e)		NHL	51	9	6	15	78
1983-84—Boston Bruins		NHL	27	3	2	5	81
1984-85—Boston Bruins (f)		NHL	49	1	9	10	62
1984-85—Winnipeg Jets		NHL	20	8	8	16	38
1985-86—Winnipeg Jets		NHL	61	6	8	14	75
NHL TOTALS			342	44	62	106	602

(c)—June, 1978—Drafted by St. Louis Blues in 1978 NHL amateur draft. Fourth Blues pick, 89th overall, sixth round.
(d)—March, 1982—Traded with Tony Currie and Rick Heinz by St. Louis Blues to Vancouver Canucks for Glen Hanlon and a fourth-round 1982 draft pick (Shawn Kilroy).
(e)—February, 1984—Traded by Vancouver Canucks to Boston Bruins for Peter McNab.
(f)—January, 1985—Traded by Boston Bruins to Winnipeg Jets for Morris Lukowich.

KENT NILSSON

Center . . . 6'1" . . . 185 lbs. . . . Born, Nynashamn, Sweden, August 31, 1956 . . . Shoots left . . . (November 1, 1981)—Tripped over stick of Mark Pavelich and crashed into boards dislocating his shoulder in game at N. Y. Rangers . . . (March, 1984)—Fractured left ankle in final week of season . . . (November 9, 1985)—Injured back vs. N. Y. Rangers, developed a viral infection and missed nine games . . . (January 7, 1986)—Separated shoulder at N. Y. Islanders and missed three games . . . (March 21, 1986)—Pulled groin at Edmonton.

Year	Team	League	Games	G.	A.	Pts.	Pen.
1975-76—Djurgardens (c)		Sweden	36	28	26	54	12
1976-77—AIK (d)		Sweden	36	30	19	49	18
1977-78—Winnipeg Jets (e)		WHA	80	42	65	107	8
1978-79—Winnipeg Jets (f-g)		WHA	78	39	68	107	8
1979-80—Atlanta Flames		NHL	80	40	53	93	10
1980-81—Calgary Flames		NHL	80	49	82	131	26
1981-82—Calgary Flames		NHL	41	26	29	55	8
1982-83—Calgary Flames		NHL	80	46	58	104	10
1983-84—Calgary Flames		NHL	67	31	49	80	22
1984-85—Calgary Flames (h)		NHL	77	37	62	99	14
1985-86—Minnesota North Stars		NHL	61	16	44	60	10
WHA TOTALS			158	81	133	214	16
NHL TOTALS			486	245	377	622	100

(c)—Drafted from Djurgardens, Sweden by Atlanta Flames in fourth round of 1976 amateur draft.
(d)—June, 1977—Signed by Winnipeg Jets (WHA).
(e)—Named WHA Rookie-of-the-Year and THE SPORTING NEWS WHA Rookie-of-the-Year.
(f)—Named WHA's Most Gentlemanly Player.
(g)—June, 1979—Selected by Atlanta Flames in NHL reclaim draft.
(h)—June, 1985—Traded with third round 1986 draft pick (Brad Turner) by Calgary Flames to Minnesota North Stars for second round 1985 draft pick (Joe Nieuwendyk) and second round pick in 1987.

JEFFREY NOBLE

Center . . . 5'10" . . . 170 lbs. . . . Born, Mount Forest, Ont., May 20, 1968 . . . Shoots left.

Year	Team	League	Games	G.	A.	Pts.	Pen.
1984-85—Kitchener Greenshirts Midgets		OHA	63	63	39	102	150
1985-86—Kitchener Rangers (c)		OHL	58	22	33	55	65

(c)—June, 1986—Drafted as underage junior by Vancouver Canucks in 1986 NHL entry draft. Seventh Canucks pick, 154th overall, eighth round.

THEODORE JOHN NOLAN

Left Wing . . . 6' . . . 185 lbs. . . . Born, Sault Ste. Marie, Ont., April 7, 1958 . . . Shoots left . . . (October, 1983)—Knee injury . . . (January 25, 1986)—Injured back at Calgary.

Year	Team	League	Games	G.	A.	Pts.	Pen.
1976-77—Sault Ste. Marie Greyhounds		OMJHL	60	8	16	24	109
1977-78—S. Ste. Marie Greyhounds (c)		OMJHL	66	14	30	44	106
1978-79—Kansas City Red Wings		CHL	73	12	38	50	66
1979-80—Adirondack Red Wings		AHL	75	16	24	40	106
1980-81—Adirondack Red Wings		AHL	76	22	28	50	86
1981-82—Adirondack Red Wings		AHL	39	12	18	30	81
1981-82—Detroit Red Wings		NHL	41	4	13	17	45
1982-83—Adirondack Red Wings		AHL	78	24	40	64	103
1983-84—Detroit Red Wings		NHL	19	1	2	3	26
1983-84—Adirondack Red Wings		AHL	31	10	16	26	76
1984-85—Rochester Americans		AHL	65	28	34	62	152
1985-86—Pittsburgh Penguins (d)		NHL	18	1	1	2	34
1985-86—Baltimore Skipjacks (e)		AHL	10	4	4	8	19
NHL TOTALS			78	6	16	22	105

(c)—June, 1978—Drafted by Detroit Red Wings in 1978 amateur draft. Seventh Red Wings pick, 78th overall, fifth round.
(d)—September, 1985—Traded by Buffalo Sabres to Pittsburgh Penguins for future considerations.
(e)—August, 1986—Signed by Buffalo Sabres as a free agent.

TODD NORMAN

Center . . . 6' . . . 170 lbs. . . . Born, St. Paul, Minn., February 26, 1966 . . . Shoots left . . . (January, 1986)—Lost for the season following major knee surgery.

Year	Team	League	Games	G.	A.	Pts.	Pen.
1983-84—Hill-Murray H.S. (c)	Minn. H.S.	24	35	32	67	..
1984-85—Univ. of North Dakota	WCHA	42	10	6	16	46
1985-86—Univ. of North Dakota	WCHA	19	4	1	5	32

(c)—June, 1984—Drafted by Edmonton Oilers in NHL entry draft. Third Oilers pick, 63rd overall, third round.

JEFF NORTON

Defense . . . 6'2" . . . 190 lbs. . . . Born, Cambridge, Mass., November 25, 1965 . . . Shoots left.

Year	Team	League	Games	G.	A.	Pts.	Pen.
1983-84—Cushing Academy (c)	Mass. H.S.	21	22	33	55	..
1984-85—University of Michigan	CCHA	37	8	16	24	103
1985-86—University of Michigan	CCHA	37	15	30	45	99

(c)—June, 1984—Drafted by New York Islanders in NHL entry draft. Third Islanders pick, 62nd overall, third round.

LEE CHARLES NORWOOD

Defense . . . 6' . . . 190 lbs. . . . Born, Oakland, Calif., February 2, 1960 . . . Shoots left.

Year	Team	League	Games	G.	A.	Pts.	Pen.
1977-78—Hull Olympiques	QMJHL	51	3	17	20	83
1978-79—Oshawa Generals (c)	OMJHL	61	23	38	61	171
1979-80—Oshawa Generals	OMJHL	60	13	39	52	143
1980-81—Hershey Bears	AHL	52	11	32	43	78
1980-81—Quebec Nordiques	NHL	11	1	1	2	9
1981-82—Fredericton Express	AHL	29	6	13	19	74
1981-82—Quebec Nordiques (d)	NHL	2	0	0	0	2
1981-82—Washington Capitals	NHL	26	7	10	17	115
1982-83—Washington Capitals	NHL	8	0	1	1	14
1982-83—Hershey Bears	AHL	67	12	36	48	90
1983-84—St. Catharines Saints	AHL	75	13	46	59	91
1984-85—Peoria Rivermen (a-e)	IHL	80	17	60	77	229
1985-86—St. Louis Blues (f)	NHL	71	5	24	29	134
NHL TOTALS		118	13	36	49	274

(c)—August, 1979—Drafted by Quebec Nordiques as underage junior in 1979 NHL entry draft. Third Nordiques pick, 62nd overall, third round.
(d)—January, 1982—Traded by Quebec Nordiques to Washington Capitals for Tim Tookey.
(e)—Won Governor's Trophy (Top IHL Defenseman).
(f)—August, 1986—Traded by St. Louis Blues to Detroit Red Wings for Larry Trader.

RICH NOVAK

Right Wing . . . 6'1" . . . 170 lbs. . . . Born, Squamish, B.C., February 19, 1966 . . . Shoots right.

Year	Team	League	Games	G.	A.	Pts.	Pen.
1983-84—Richmond (c)	BCJHL	40	20	29	49	60
1984-85—Michigan Tech.	WCHA	40	9	10	19	16
1985-86—Michigan Tech.	WCHA	38	9	20	29	20

(c)—June, 1984—Drafted as underage junior by Edmonton Oilers in NHL entry draft. Fourth Oilers pick, 84th overall, fourth round.

GARY NYLUND

Defense . . . 6'4" . . . 210 lbs. . . . Born, Surrey, B.C., October 28, 1963 . . . Shoots left . . . (September, 1982)—Injury to left knee in exhibition game, requiring surgery . . . (October, 1983)—Knee surgery . . . (November 5, 1984)—Concussion in game at Minnesota.

Year	Team	League	Games	G.	A.	Pts.	Pen.
1978-79—Delta	BCJHL	57	6	29	35	107
1978-79—Portland Winter Hawks	WHL	2	0	0	0	0
1979-80—Portland Winter Hawks	WHL	72	5	21	26	59
1980-81—Portland Winter Hawks (b)	WHL	70	6	40	46	186
1981-82—Portland Winter Hawks (a-c-d)	WHL	65	7	59	66	267
1982-83—Toronto Maple Leafs	NHL	16	0	3	3	16

Year	Team	League	Games	G.	A.	Pts.	Pen.
1983-84—Toronto Maple Leafs		NHL	47	2	14	16	103
1984-85—Toronto Maple Leafs		NHL	76	3	17	20	99
1985-86—Toronto Maple Leafs (e)		NHL	79	2	16	18	180
NHL TOTALS			218	7	50	57	398

(c)—Winner of WHL Top Defenseman Trophy.

(d)—June, 1982—Drafted as underage junior by Toronto Maple Leafs in 1982 NHL entry draft. First Maple Leafs pick, 3rd overall, first round.

(e)—August, 1986—Signed by Chicago Black Hawks as a free agent.

THORE ROBERT (BOB) NYSTROM

Right Wing . . . 6'1" . . . 195 lbs. . . . Born, Stockholm, Sweden, October 10, 1952 . . . Shoots right . . . (September, 1984)—Surgery to repair ligament damage to left wrist . . . (October, 1985)—Missed nine games with a back injury . . . (January 5, 1986)—Torn retina that required surgery.

Year	Team	League	Games	G.	A.	Pts.	Pen.
1969-70—Kamloops Rockets		Jr."A"BCHL	....	...	....	....	....
1970-71—Calgary Centennials		WCHL	66	15	16	31	153
1971-72—Calgary Centennials (c-d)		WCHL	64	27	25	52	178
1972-73—New Haven Nighthawks		AHL	60	12	10	22	114
1972-73—New York Islanders		NHL	11	1	1	2	10
1973-74—New York Islanders		NHL	77	21	20	41	118
1974-75—New York Islanders		NHL	76	27	28	55	122
1975-76—New York Islanders		NHL	80	23	25	48	106
1976-77—New York Islanders		NHL	80	29	27	56	91
1977-78—New York Islanders		NHL	80	30	29	59	94
1978-79—New York Islanders		NHL	78	19	20	39	113
1979-80—New York Islanders		NHL	67	21	18	39	94
1980-81—New York Islanders		NHL	79	14	30	44	145
1981-82—New York Islanders		NHL	74	22	25	47	103
1982-83—New York Islanders		NHL	74	10	20	30	98
1983-84—New York Islanders		NHL	74	15	29	44	80
1984-85—New York Islanders		NHL	36	2	5	7	58
1985-86—New York Islanders (e)		NHL	14	1	1	2	16
NHL TOTALS			900	235	278	513	1248

(c)—Selected by Miami Screaming Eagles in World Hockey Association player selection draft, February, 1972.

(d)—Drafted from Calgary Centennials by New York Islanders in third round of 1972 amateur draft.

(e)—August, 1986—Announced retirement to become assistant coach with New York Islanders.

ADAM OATES

Center . . . 5'11" . . . 190 lbs. . . . Born, Weston, Ont., August 27, 1962 . . . Shoots right . . . Holds All-time career record for assists at R.P.I. (150) . . . (1984-85)—Set R.P.I. record for assists and points in a single season . . . (March 3, 1986)—Strained knee vs. Minnesota and missed three games.

Year	Team	League	Games	G.	A.	Pts.	Pen.
1982-83—R.P.I.		ECAC	22	9	33	42	8
1983-84—R.P.I. (b)		ECAC	38	26	57	83	15
1984-85—R.P.I. (a-c-d)		ECAC	38	31	60	91	29
1985-86—Adirondack Red Wings		AHL	34	18	28	46	4
1985-86—Detroit Red Wings		NHL	38	9	11	20	10
NHL TOTALS			38	9	11	20	10

(c)—Named to All America Team (East).

(d)—June, 1985—Signed by Detroit Red Wings as a free agent.

DAVID O'BRIEN

Right Wing . . . 6'1" . . . 180 lbs. . . . Born, Brighton, Mass., September 13, 1966 . . . Shoots right.

Year	Team	League	Games	G.	A.	Pts.	Pen.
1984-85—Northeastern Univ.		H. East	30	8	7	15	6
1985-86—Northeastern Univ. (c)		H. East	39	23	16	39	18

(c)—June, 1986—Drafted by St. Louis Blues in 1986 NHL entry draft. Thirteenth Blues pick, 241st overall, 12th round.

JACK O'CALLAHAN

Defense . . . 6'1" . . . 185 lbs. . . . Born, Charlestown, Mass., July 24, 1957 . . . Shoots right . . . Member of Gold Medal Winning U.S. Olympic Hockey team . . . (December 28, 1983)—Given eight-game suspension by NHL for slashing Dave Maloney in game vs. N.Y. Rangers . . . (November, 1984)—Bruised shoulder.

Year	Team	League	Games	G.	A.	Pts.	Pen.
1975-76—Boston University		ECAC	....	...	....	....	....
1976-77—Boston University (c)		ECAC	31	1	23	24	90
1977-78—Boston University (a)		ECAC	31	8	47	55	61
1978-79—Boston University (a)		ECAC	29	6	16	22	72
1979-80—U.S. Olympic Team		Int'l.	55	7	30	37	*85
1980-81—New Brunswick Hawks		AHL	78	9	25	34	167
1981-82—New Brunswick Hawks		AHL	79	15	33	48	130
1982-83—Springfield Indians		AHL	35	2	24	26	25
1982-83—Chicago Black Hawks		NHL	39	0	11	11	46
1983-84—Chicago Black Hawks		NHL	70	4	13	17	67
1984-85—Chicago Black Hawks		NHL	66	6	8	14	105
1985-86—Chicago Black Hawks		NHL	80	4	19	23	116
NHL TOTALS			255	14	51	65	334

(c)—June, 1977—Drafted by Chicago Black Hawks in 1977 NHL amateur draft. Fifth Black Hawks pick, 96th overall, sixth round.

MICHAEL THOMAS O'CONNELL

Defense . . . 5'11" . . . 176 lbs. . . . Born, Chicago, Ill., November 25, 1955 . . . Shoots right . . . Son of former Cleveland Browns quarterback Tommy O'Connell . . . Brother of Tim O'Connell . . . Missed part of 1976-77 season with torn muscle in right shoulder . . . First member of the Black Hawks to be born in Chicago . . . (February 11, 1986)—Pulled rib muscles at Quebec and missed three games.

Year	Team	League	Games	G.	A.	Pts.	Pen.
1973-74—Kingston Canadiens		Jr."A"OHA	70	16	43	59	81
1974-75—King. Canadiens (a-c-d)		Jr."A"OHA	50	18	55	73	47
1975-76—Dallas Black Hawks (e)		CHL	70	6	37	43	50
1976-77—Dallas Black Hawks (a-f)		CHL	63	15	53	68	30
1977-78—Dallas Black Hawks (g)		CHL	62	6	45	51	75
1977-78—Chicago Black Hawks		NHL	6	1	1	2	2
1978-79—Chicago Black Hawks		NHL	48	4	22	26	20
1978-79—New Brunswick Hawks		AHL	35	5	20	25	21
1979-80—Chicago Black Hawks		NHL	78	8	22	30	52
1980-81—Chicago Black Hawks (h)		NHL	34	5	16	21	32
1980-81—Boston Bruins		NHL	48	10	22	32	42
1981-82—Boston Bruins		NHL	80	5	34	39	75
1982-83—Boston Bruins		NHL	80	14	39	53	42
1983-84—Boston Bruins		NHL	75	18	42	60	42
1984-85—Boston Bruins		NHL	78	15	40	55	64
1985-86—Boston Bruins (i)		NHL	63	8	21	29	47
1985-86—Detroit Red Wings		NHL	13	1	7	8	16
NHL TOTALS			603	89	266	355	434

(c)—Drafted from Kingston Canadiens by Chicago Black Hawks in third round of 1975 amateur draft.
(d)—Won Max Kaminsky Memorial Trophy (outstanding Defenseman).
(e)—Tied for lead in assists (5) during playoffs.
(f)—Won CHL Most Valuable Defenseman Award.
(g)—Tied for lead in assists (11) during playoffs.
(h)—December, 1980—Traded by Chicago Black Hawks to Boston Bruins for Al Secord.
(i)—March, 1986—Traded by Detroit Red Wings to Boston Bruins for Reed Larson.

MYLES O'CONNOR

Defense . . . 5'11" . . . 165 lbs. . . . Born, Calgary, Alta., April 2, 1967 . . . Shoots left.

Year	Team	League	Games	G.	A.	Pts.	Pen.
1984-85—Notre Dame Hounds (c)		MICHL	40	20	35	55	40
1985-86—University of Michigan		CCHA	37	6	19	25	73
1985-86—Team Canada		Int'l	8	0	0	0	0

(c)—June, 1985—Drafted by New Jersey Devils in 1985 NHL entry draft. Fourth Devils pick, 45th overall, third round.

LYLE ODELEIN

Defense . . . 6' . . . 180 lbs. . . . Born, Quill Lake, Sask., July 21, 1968 . . . Shoots right . . . Brother of Selmar Odelein.

Year	Team	League	Games	G.	A.	Pts.	Pen.
1984-85—Regina Pat Canadians		Sask. Midget	26	12	13	25	30
1985-86—Moose Jaw Warriors (c)		WHL	67	9	37	46	117

(c)—June, 1986—Drafted as underage junior by Montreal Canadiens in 1986 NHL entry draft. Eighth Canadiens pick, 141st overall, seventh round.

SELMAR ODELEIN

Defense . . . 6' . . . 195 lbs. . . . Born, Quill Lake, Sask., April 11, 1966 . . . Shoots right . . . Brother of Lyle Odelein.

Year	Team	League	Games	G.	A.	Pts.	Pen.
1982-83—Regina Canadians		Sask.Midget	70	30	84	114	38
1983-84—Regina Pats (c)		WHL	71	9	42	51	45
1984-85—Regina Pats		WHL	64	24	35	59	121
1985-86—Regina Pats		WHL	36	13	28	41	57
1985-86—Edmonton Oilers		NHL	4	0	0	0	0
NHL TOTALS			4	0	0	0	0

(c)—June, 1984—Drafted as underage junior by Edmonton Oilers in NHL entry draft. First Oilers pick, 21st overall, first round.

BILL O'DWYER

Center . . . 5'11" . . . 187 lbs. . . . Born, South Boston, Mass., January 25, 1960 . . . Shoots left . . . (October, 1985)—Injured jaw.

Year	Team	League	Games	G.	A.	Pts.	Pen.
1978-79—Boston College		ECAC	30	9	30	39	14
1979-80—Boston College (b-c-d)		ECAC	33	20	22	42	22
1980-81—Boston College (b)		ECAC	31	20	20	40	6
1981-82—Boston College (b)		ECAC	....	15	26	41	....
1982-83—New Haven Nighthawks		AHL	77	24	23	47	29
1983-84—Los Angeles Kings		NHL	5	0	0	0	0
1983-84—New Haven Nighthawks		AHL	58	15	42	57	39
1984-85—New Haven Nighthawks		AHL	46	19	24	43	27
1984-85—Los Angeles Kings (e)		NHL	13	1	0	1	15
1985-86—New Haven Nighthawks		AHL	41	10	15	25	41
NHL TOTALS			18	1	0	1	15

(c)—Named to second team All-New England Team (Division I).

(d)—June, 1980—Drafted by Los Angeles Kings in 1980 NHL entry draft. Ninth Kings pick, 157th overall, eighth round.

(e)—August, 1985—Signed by New York Rangers as a free agent.

JOHN ALEXANDER OGRODNICK

Left Wing . . . 6' . . . 190 lbs. . . . Born, Ottawa, Ont., June 20, 1959 . . . Shoots left . . . (February 26, 1984)—Fractured left wrist in game at Chicago . . . (January 21, 1986)—Missed three games with a sprained ankle.

Year	Team	League	Games	G.	A.	Pts.	Pen.
1976-77—Maple Ridge Bruins		BCJHL	67	54	56	110	63
1976-77—New Westminster Bruins		WCHL	14	2	4	6	0
1977-78—New Westminster Bruins (c)		WCHL	72	59	29	88	47
1978-79—New Westminster Bruins (d)		WHL	72	48	36	84	38
1979-80—Adirondack Red Wings		AHL	39	13	20	33	21
1979-80—Detroit Red Wings		NHL	41	8	24	32	8
1980-81—Detroit Red Wings		NHL	80	35	35	70	14
1981-82—Detroit Red Wings		NHL	80	28	26	54	28
1982-83—Detroit Red Wings		NHL	80	41	44	85	30
1983-84—Detroit Red Wings		NHL	64	42	36	78	14
1984-85—Detroit Red Wings (a)		NHL	79	55	50	105	30
1985-86—Detroit Red Wings		NHL	76	38	32	70	18
NHL TOTALS			500	247	247	494	142

(c)—Shared Rookie of Year award in WCHL with Keith Brown.

(d)—August, 1979—Drafted by Detroit Red Wings in 1979 entry draft. Fourth Red Wings pick, 66th overall, fourth round.

FREDERIK OLAUSSON

Defense . . . 6'2" . . . 200 lbs. . . . Born, Vaxsjo, Sweden, October 5, 1966 . . . Shoots left

Year	Team	League	Games	G.	A.	Pts.	Pen.
1983-84—Nybro		Sweden	28	8	14	22	32
1984-85—Farjestad (c)		Sweden	34	6	12	18	24
1985-86—Farjestad		Sweden	33	5	12	17	14

(c)—June, 1985—Drafted by Winnipeg Jets in NHL entry draft. Fourth Jets pick, 81st overall, fourth round.

ED OLCZYK

Right Wing . . . 6'1" . . . 195 lbs. . . . Born, Chicago, Ill., August 16, 1966 . . . Shoots left . . .

(September, 1984)—Hyperextended knee during training camp . . . (December 16, 1984)
—Broken bone in left foot when hit by shot of teammate (Doug Wilson) during 5-3 loss vs.
Minnesota . . . Also plays Center.

Year	Team	League	Games	G.	A.	Pts.	Pen.
1983-84—U.S. National Team		Int'l	56	19	40	59	36
1983-84—U.S. Olympic Team (c)		Int'l	6	2	7	9	0
1984-85—Chicago Black Hawks		NHL	70	20	30	50	67
1985-86—Chicago Black Hawks		NHL	79	29	50	79	47
NHL TOTALS			149	49	80	129	114

(c)—June, 1984—Drafted by Chicago Black Hawks in NHL entry draft. First Black Hawks pick, 3rd
overall, first round. (Black Hawks traded Rich Preston and Don Dietrich to New Jersey, who had the
2nd overall pick, not to draft Olczyk. Devils also sent Bob MacMillan to Chicago in the deal).

MICHAEL OLIVERIO

**Center . . . 5'10" . . . 180 lbs. . . . Born, Sault Ste. Marie, Ont., June 10, 1967 . . . Shoots left . . .
Also plays Left Wing.**

Year	Team	League	Games	G.	A.	Pts.	Pen.
1983-84—Sault Ste. Marie Leagion		Ont. Midget	45	72	78	150	8
1983-84—Sault Ste. Marie Greyhounds		OHL	66	17	24	41	6
1984-85—Sault Ste. Marie Greyhounds (c)		OHL	66	38	48	86	24
1985-86—Sault Ste. Marie Greyhounds		OHL	64	26	56	82	45

(c)—June, 1985—Drafted as underage junior by Quebec Nordiques in 1985 NHL entry draft. Eighth
Nordiques pick, 141st overall, seventh round.

JOHN OLLSON

Center . . . 5'9" . . . 170 lbs. . . . Born, Nepean, Ont., July 31, 1963 . . . Shoots left.

Year	Team	League	Games	G.	A.	Pts.	Pen.
1979-80—Nepean		Ont. Midget	24	24	21	45	..
1980-81—Ottawa 67's		OHL	31	6	6	12	12
1981-82—Ottawa 67's		OHL	67	36	42	78	49
1982-83—Ottawa 67's (c)		OHL	68	46	76	122	41
1982-83—Springfield Indians		AHL	75	29	43	72	51
1984-85—Milwaukee Admirals		IHL	55	17	24	41	23
1984-85—Indianapolis Checkers		IHL	17	9	11	20	6
1985-86—Saginaw Gears		IHL	13	6	6	12	9
1985-86—Nova Scotia Oilers		AHL	60	19	21	40	10

(c)—August, 1983—Signed by Chicago Black Hawks as a free agent.

DARRYL OLSEN

Defense . . . 6' . . . 180 lbs. . . . Born, Calgary, Alta., October 7, 1966 . . . Shoots left.

Year	Team	League	Games	G.	A.	Pts.	Pen.
1984-85—St. Albert Saints (c)		AJHL	57	19	48	67	77
1985-86—Univ. of Northern Michigan		WCHA	37	5	20	25	46

(c)—June, 1985—Drafted by Calgary Flames in 1985 NHL entry draft. Tenth Flames pick, 185th overall,
ninth round.

MARK OLSEN

Defense . . . 6'3" . . . 215 lbs. . . . Born, Irvine, Tex., September 6, 1966 . . . Shoots left.

Year	Team	League	Games	G.	A.	Pts.	Pen.
1985-86—Colorado College (c)		WCHA	39	2	4	6	48

(c)—June, 1986—Drafted by Calgary Flames in 1986 NHL entry draft. Seventh Flames pick, 163rd
overall, eighth round.

TOM O'REGAN

Center . . . 5'10" . . . 180 lbs. . . . Born, Cambridge, Mass., December 29, 1961 . . . Shoots left.

Year	Team	League	Games	G.	A.	Pts.	Pen.
1979-80—Boston University		ECAC	28	9	15	24	31
1980-81—Boston University		ECAC	20	10	10	20	41
1981-82—Boston University		ECAC	28	18	34	52	67
1982-83—Boston University		ECAC	27	15	17	32	43
1983-84—Pittsburgh Penguins (c)		NHL	51	4	10	14	8
1983-84—Baltimore Skipjacks		AHL	25	13	14	27	15
1984-85—Baltimore Skipjacks		AHL	62	28	28	56	62
1984-85—Pittsburgh Penguins		NHL	1	0	0	0	0
1985-86—Pittsburgh Penguins		NHL	9	1	2	3	2
1985-86—Baltimore Skipjacks		AHL	61	23	31	54	65
NHL TOTALS			61	5	12	17	10

(c)—September, 1983—Signed by Pittsburgh Penguins as a free agent.

GATES ORLANDO

Center . . . 5'8" . . . 175 lbs. . . . Born, LaSalle, Que., November 13, 1962 . . . Shoots right . . . (February, 1985)—Sprained right knee.

Year	Team	League	Games	G.	A.	Pts.	Pen.
1980-81—Providence College (c)		ECAC	31	24	32	56	45
1981-82—Providence College		ECAC	28	18	18	36	31
1982-83—Providence College		ECAC	40	30	39	69	32
1983-84—Providence College		ECAC	34	23	30	53	52
1983-84—Rochester Americans		AHL	11	8	7	15	2
1984-85—Rochester Americans		AHL	49	26	30	56	62
1984-85—Buffalo Sabres		NHL	11	3	6	9	6
1985-86—Rochester Americans		AHL	3	4	0	4	10
1985-86—Buffalo Sabres		NHL	61	13	12	25	29
NHL TOTALS			72	16	18	34	35

(c)—Drafted by Buffalo Sabres as underage player in 1981 NHL entry draft. Tenth Sabres pick, 164th overall, eighth round.

STEVE ORTH

Center . . . 5'8" . . . 150 lbs. . . . Born, St. Cloud, Minn., January 17, 1965 . . . Shoots left.

Year	Team	League	Games	G.	A.	Pts.	Pen.
1982-83—St. Cloud Tech. H.S. (c)		Minn. H.S.	22	27	38	65	...
1983-84—University of Minnesota		WCHA	8	4	4	8	2
1984-85—University of Minnesota		WCHA	38	7	14	21	8
1985-86—University of Minnesota		WCHA	38	6	7	13	4

(c)—June, 1983—Drafted by New York Rangers in 1983 NHL entry draft. Eighth Rangers pick, 133rd overall, seventh round.

MARK ANATOLE OSBORNE

Left Wing . . . 6'2" . . . 200 lbs. . . . Born, Toronto, Ont., August 13, 1961 . . . Shoots left . . . (October, 1984)—Hip Injury . . . (February 12, 1986)—Sprained ankle vs. Vancouver and missed 12 games.

Year	Team	League	Games	G.	A.	Pts.	Pen.
1978-79—Niagara Falls Flyers		OMJHL	62	17	25	42	53
1979-80—Niagara Falls Flyers (c)		OMJHL	52	10	33	43	104
1980-81—Niagara Falls Flyers		OHL	54	39	41	80	140
1980-81—Adirondack Red Wings (d)		AHL	....	....	....	....	....
1981-82—Detroit Red Wings		NHL	80	26	41	67	61
1982-83—Detroit Red Wings (e)		NHL	80	19	24	43	83
1983-84—New York Rangers		NHL	73	23	28	51	88
1984-85—New York Rangers		NHL	23	4	4	8	33
1985-86—New York Rangers		NHL	62	16	24	40	80
NHL TOTALS			318	88	121	209	345

(c)—June, 1980—Drafted as underage junior by Detroit Red Wings in 1980 NHL entry draft. Second Red Wings pick, 46th overall, third round.

(d)—No regular season appearance, 13 playoff games.

(e)—June, 1983—Traded by Detroit Red Wings with Willie Huber and Mike Blaisdell to New York Rangers for Ron Duguay, Eddie Mio and Ed Johnstone.

RANDY OSWALD

Defense . . . 6'3" . . . 185 lbs. . . . Born, Bowmanville, Ont., January 5, 1966 . . . Shoots left.

Year	Team	League	Games	G.	A.	Pts.	Pen.
1983-84—Michigan Tech. (c)		CCHA	41	0	2	2	44
1984-85—Michigan Tech.		WCHA	37	0	4	4	60
1985-86—Michigan Tech.		WCHA	30	4	9	13	58

(c)—June, 1984—Drafted by Boston Bruins in NHL entry draft. Sixth Bruins pick, 124th overall, sixth round.

JOEL OTTO

Center . . . 6'4" . . . 220 lbs. . . . Born, St. Cloud, Minn., October 29, 1961 . . . Shoots right.

Year	Team	League	Games	G.	A.	Pts.	Pen.
1980-81—Bemidji State Univ.		NCAA-II	23	5	11	16	10
1981-82—Bemidji State Univ.		NCAA-II	31	19	33	52	24
1982-83—Bemidji State Univ.		NCAA-II	37	33	28	61	68
1983-84—Bemidji State Univ. (c-d)		NCAA-II	31	32	43	75	32
1984-85—Moncton Golden Flames		AHL	56	27	36	63	89

Year	Team	League	Games	G.	A.	Pts.	Pen.
1984-85—Calgary Flames		NHL	17	4	8	12	20
1985-86—Calgary Flames		NHL	79	25	34	59	188
NHL TOTALS			96	29	42	71	208

(c)—Candidate for Hobey Baker Award.
(d)—September, 1984—Signed by Calgary Flames as a free agent.

GORDON PADDOCK

Defense . . . 6' . . . 180 lbs. . . . Born, Hamiota, Man., February 15, 1964 . . . Shoots right . . . Brother of John Paddock.

Year	Team	League	Games	G.	A.	Pts.	Pen.
1981-82—Saskatoon Jays		SJHL	59	8	21	29	232
1982-83—Saskatoon Blades		WHL	67	4	25	29	158
1983-84—Brandon Wheat Kings		WHL	72	14	37	51	151
1984-85—Indianapolis Checkers		IHL	65	10	21	31	92
1984-85—Springfield Indians		AHL	12	0	2	2	24
1985-86—Indianapolis Checkers (c)		IHL	11	1	1	2	11
1985-86—Muskegon Lumberjacks		IHL	47	1	20	21	87
1985-86—Springfield Indians		AHL	20	1	1	2	52

(c)—November, 1985—Traded by Indianapolis Checkers to Muskegon Lumberjacks for Don Murdoch.

JIM PAEK

Defense . . . 6' . . . 188 lbs. . . . Born, Weston, Ont., April 7, 1967 . . . Shoots left.

Year	Team	League	Games	G.	A.	Pts.	Pen.
1983-84—St. Michael's Midget		OHA	39	8	26	34	21
1984-85—Oshawa Generals (c)		OHL	54	2	13	15	57
1985-86—Oshawa Generals		OHL	64	5	21	26	122

(c)—June, 1985—Drafted as underage junior by Pittsburgh Penguins in 1985 NHL entry draft. Ninth Penguins pick, 170th overall, ninth round.

WILFRED (WILF) PAIEMENT JR.

Right Wing . . . 6'1" . . . 205 lbs. . . . Born, Earlton, Ont., October 16, 1955 . . . Shoots right . . . Brother of Rosaire Paiement . . . Missed final part of 1975-76 season with thigh injury . . . Suspended for 15 games by NHL for stick swinging incident in 1978-79 season . . . (October 12, 1980)—Credited with scoring NHL's 100,000th regular season goal in 4-2 win at Philadelphia into an empty net . . . (March 27, 1982)—Sprained right knee in game at Montreal . . . (September 26, 1985)—Tore knee ligaments in training camp and missed the first six games of season . . . (February 8, 1986)—Fractured left foot in first game with N.Y. Rangers at Boston and missed 19 games.

Year	Team	League	Games	G.	A.	Pts.	Pen.
1971-72—Niagara Falls Flyers		Jr."A" OHA	34	6	13	19	74
1972-73—St. Cath. Black Hawks (c)		Jr."A" OHA	61	18	27	45	173
1973-74—St. Cath. Black Hawks (a-d)		Jr."A" OHA	70	50	73	123	134
1974-75—Kansas City Scouts		NHL	78	26	13	39	101
1975-76—Kansas City Scouts		NHL	57	21	22	43	121
1976-77—Colorado Rockies		NHL	78	41	40	81	101
1977-78—Colorado Rockies		NHL	80	31	56	87	114
1978-79—Colorado Rockies		NHL	65	24	36	60	80
1979-80—Colorado Rockies (e)		NHL	34	10	16	26	41
1979-80—Toronto Maple Leafs		NHL	41	20	28	48	72
1980-81—Toronto Maple Leafs		NHL	77	40	57	97	145
1981-82—Toronto Maple Leafs (f)		NHL	69	18	40	58	203
1981-82—Quebec Nordiques		NHL	8	7	6	13	18
1982-83—Quebec Nordiques		NHL	80	26	38	64	170
1983-84—Quebec Nordiques		NHL	80	39	37	76	121
1984-85—Quebec Nordiques		NHL	68	23	28	51	165
1985-86—Quebec Nordiques (g)		NHL	44	7	12	19	145
1985-86—New York Rangers		NHL	8	1	6	7	13
NHL TOTALS			867	334	435	769	1610

(c)—Traded to St. Catharines Black Hawks by Sudbury Wolves for midget draft choice.
(d)—Drafted from St. Catharines Black Hawks by Kansas City Scouts in first round of 1974 amateur draft.
(e)—December, 1979—Traded with Pat Hickey by Colorado Rockies to Toronto Maple Leafs for Lanny McDonald and Joel Quenneville.
(f)—March, 1982—Traded by Toronto Maple Leafs to Quebec Nordiques for Miroslav Frycer and seventh-round 1982 entry draft pick (Jeff Triano).
(g)—February, 1986—Traded by Quebec Nordiques to N.Y. Rangers for Stephen Patrick.

ROBERT ROSS PALMER

Defense . . . 5'11" . . . 190 lbs. . . . Born, Sarnia, Ont., September 10, 1956 . . . Shoots right.

Year	Team	League	Games	G.	A.	Pts.	Pen.
1973-74—University of Michigan		WCHA	36	3	12	15	14
1974-75—University of Michigan		WCHA	40	5	15	20	26
1975-76—University of Michigan (c)		WCHA	42	5	16	21	58
1976-77—University of Michigan		WCHA	45	5	37	42	32
1977-78—Springfield Indians		AHL	19	1	7	8	18
1977-78—Los Angeles Kings		NHL	48	0	3	3	27
1978-79—Los Angeles Kings		NHL	78	4	41	45	26
1979-80—Los Angeles Kings		NHL	78	4	36	40	18
1980-81—Los Angeles Kings		NHL	13	0	4	4	13
1980-81—Houston Apollos		CHL	28	3	10	13	23
1980-81—Indianapolis Checkers		CHL	27	1	9	10	16
1981-82—Los Angeles Kings		NHL	5	0	2	2	0
1981-82—New Haven Nighthawks		AHL	41	2	23	25	22
1982-83—New Jersey Devils (d)		NHL	60	1	10	11	21
1983-84—Maine Mariners		AHL	33	5	10	15	10
1983-84—New Jersey Devils		NHL	38	0	5	5	10
1984-85—Maine Mariners		AHL	79	1	23	24	22
1985-86—Maine Mariners		AHL	73	2	10	12	18
NHL TOTALS			320	9	101	110	115

(c)—Drafted from University of Michigan by Los Angeles Kings in fifth round of 1976 amateur draft.
(d)—September, 1982—Signed by New Jersey Devils as a free agent.

SCOTT PALUCH

Defense . . . 6'3" . . . 185 lbs. . . . Born, Chicago, Ill., March 9, 1966 . . . Shoots left . . . Named to second all-star team at 1986 IIHF World Junior Championships as a member of Team USA.

Year	Team	League	Games	G.	A.	Pts.	Pen.
1983-84—Chicago Jets (c)		CJHL	50	44	46	90	42
1984-85—Bowling Green University		CCHA	42	11	25	36	64
1985-86—Bowling Green University		CCHA	34	10	11	21	44

(c)—June, 1984—Drafted by St. Louis Blues in NHL entry draft. Seventh Blues pick, 92nd overall, fifth round.

RYAN PARDOSKI

Left Wing . . . 6' . . . 165 lbs. . . . Born, Calgary, Alta., August 19, 1968 . . . Shoots left.

Year	Team	League	Games	G.	A.	Pts.	Pen.
1985-86—Calgary Canucks (c)		AJHL	50	16	27	43	61

(c)—June, 1986—Drafted by New Jersey Devils in 1986 NHL entry draft. Eighth Devils pick, 150th overall, eighth round.

RUSSELL L. PARENT

Defense . . . 5'9" . . . 180 lbs. . . . Born, Winnipeg, Manitoba, May 6, 1968 . . . Shoots left.

Year	Team	League	Games	G.	A.	Pts.	Pen.
1985-86—South Winnipeg Blues (c)		MJHL	47	16	65	81	106

(c)—June, 1986—Drafted by New York Rangers in 1986 NHL entry draft. Eleventh Rangers pick, 219th overall, 11th round.

JEFF PARKER

Right Wing . . . 6'3" . . . 198 lbs. . . . Born, St. Paul, Minn., September 7, 1964 . . . Shoots right . . . Brother of John Parker.

Year	Team	League	Games	G.	A.	Pts.	Pen.
1983-84—Michigan State University		CCHA	44	8	13	21	82
1984-85—Michigan State University		CCHA	42	10	12	22	85
1985-86—Michigan State University		CCHA	41	15	20	35	88

(c)—June, 1982—Drafted by Buffalo Sabres in 1982 NHL entry draft. Ninth Sabres pick, 111th overall, sixth round.

JOHN PARKER

Center . . . 6'1" . . . 180 lbs. . . . Born, St. Paul, Minn., March 5, 1968 . . . Shoots right . . . Brother of Jeff Parker (Michigan State).

Year	Team	League	Games	G.	A.	Pts.	Pen.
1984-85—White Bear Lake H.S.		Minn.	23	13	26	39	....
1985-86—White Bear Lake H.S. (c)		Minn.	24	12	13	25	....

(c)—June, 1986—Drafted by Calgary Flames in 1986 NHL entry draft. Fifth Flames pick, 121st overall, sixth round.

MALCOLM PARKS

Center ... 6 ... 185 lbs. ... Born, Edmonton, Alta., January 20, 1965 ... Shoots right ... Also plays Right Wing.

Year	Team	League	Games	G.	A.	Pts.	Pen.
1982-83	St. Albert Saints (c)	AJHL	54	59	57	116	185
1983-84	University of North Dakota	WCHA	33	11	10	21	42
1984-85	University of North Dakota	WCHA	39	4	7	11	41
1985-86	University of North Dakota	WCHA	39	6	14	20	38

(c)—June, 1983—Drafted by Minnesota North Stars in 1983 NHL entry draft. Second North Stars pick, 36th overall, second round.

DAVE PASIN

Right Wing ... 6'1" ... 195 lbs. ... Born, Edmonton, Alta., July 8, 1966 ... Shoots right ... (November 25, 1985)—Missed five games with sprained left knee.

Year	Team	League	Games	G.	A.	Pts.	Pen.
1982-83	Prince Albert Raiders	WHL	62	40	42	82	48
1983-84	Prince Albert Raiders (b-c)	WHL	71	68	54	122	68
1984-85	Prince Albert Raiders (b)	WHL	65	64	52	116	88
1985-86	Boston Bruins	NHL	71	18	19	37	50
	NHL TOTALS		71	18	19	37	50

(c)—June, 1984—Drafted as underage junior by Boston Bruins in 1984 NHL entry draft. First Bruins pick, 19th overall, first round.

GREGORY STEPHEN PASLAWSKI

Right Wing ... 5'11" ... 195 lbs. ... Born, Kindersley, Sask., August 25, 1961 ... Shoots right ... (February 20, 1986)—Injured knee at N.Y. Rangers.

Year	Team	League	Games	G.	A.	Pts.	Pen.
1980-81	Prince Albert Raiders	SJHL	59	55	60	115	106
1981-82	Nova Scotia Voyageurs (c)	AHL	43	15	11	26	31
1982-83	Nova Scotia Voyageurs	AHL	75	46	42	88	32
1983-84	Montreal Canadiens (d)	NHL	26	1	4	5	4
1983-84	St. Louis Blues	NHL	34	8	6	14	7
1984-85	St. Louis Blues	NHL	72	22	20	42	21
1985-86	St. Louis Blues	NHL	56	22	11	33	18
	NHL TOTALS		188	53	41	94	60

(c)—January, 1982—Signed by Montreal Canadiens as a free agent.
(d)—December, 1983—Traded with Doug Wickenheiser and Gilbert Delorme by Montreal Canadiens to St. Louis Blues for Perry Turnbull.

JOE ANDREW PATERSON

Left Wing and Center ... 6'1" ... 208 lbs. ... Born, Toronto, Ont., June 25, 1960 ... Shoots left ... (October, 1982)—Pulled groin muscle.

Year	Team	League	Games	G.	A.	Pts.	Pen.
1977-78	London Knights	OMJHL	68	17	16	33	100
1978-79	London Knights (c)	OMJHL	60	22	19	41	158
1979-80	London Knights	OMJHL	65	21	50	71	156
1979-80	Kalamazoo Wings	IHL	4	1	2	3	2
1980-81	Detroit Red Wings	NHL	38	2	5	7	53
1980-81	Adirondack Red Wings	AHL	39	9	16	25	68
1981-82	Adirondack Red Wings	AHL	74	22	28	50	132
1981-82	Detroit Red Wings	NHL	3	0	0	0	0
1982-83	Adirondack Red Wings	AHL	36	11	10	21	85
1982-83	Detroit Red Wings	NHL	33	2	1	3	14
1983-84	Detroit Red Wings	NHL	41	2	5	7	148
1983-84	Adirondack Red Wings (d)	AHL	20	10	15	25	43
1984-85	Hershey Bears	AHL	67	26	27	53	173
1984-85	Philadelphia Flyers	NHL	6	0	0	0	31
1985-86	Hershey Bears	AHL	20	5	10	15	68
1985-86	Philadelphia Flyers (e)	NHL	5	0	0	0	12
1985-86	Los Angeles Kings	NHL	47	9	18	27	153
	NHL TOTALS		173	15	29	44	411

(c)—August, 1979—Drafted by Detroit Red Wings as underage junior in 1979 NHL entry draft. Fifth Red Wings pick, 87th overall, fifth round.
(d)—October, 1984—Traded with Murray Craven by Detroit Red Wings to Philadelphia Flyers for Darryl Sittler.
(e)—December, 1985—Traded by Philadelphia Flyers to Los Angeles Kings for future considerations.

MARK PATERSON

Defense . . . 6' . . . 185 lbs. . . . Born, Ottawa, Ont., February 22, 1964 . . . Shoots left . . . (September, 1984)—Missed training camp and early part of season with mononucleosis.

Year	Team	League	Games	G.	A.	Pts.	Pen.
1980-81—Nepean Raiders		OPJHL	50	6	13	19	98
1981-82—Ottawa 67's (c)		OHL	64	4	14	18	66
1982-83—Ottawa 67's		OHL	57	7	14	21	140
1982-83—Hartford Whalers		NHL	2	0	0	0	0
1983-84—Ottawa 67's		OHL	45	8	16	24	114
1983-84—Hartford Whalers		NHL	9	2	0	2	4
1984-85—Binghamton Whalers		AHL	44	2	18	20	74
1984-85—Hartford Whalers		NHL	13	1	3	4	24
1985-86—Hartford Whalers		NHL	5	0	0	0	5
1985-86—Binghamton Whalers		AHL	67	2	16	18	121
NHL TOTALS			29	3	3	6	33

(c)—June, 1982—Drafted as underage junior by Hartford Whalers in 1982 NHL entry draft. Second Whalers pick, 35th overall, second round.

RICHARD DAVID (RICK) PATERSON

Center . . . 5'10" . . . 185 lbs. . . . Born, Kingston, Ont., February 10, 1958 . . . Shoots right . . . (January, 1981)—Chipped ankle bone . . . Also plays Right Wing.

Year	Team	League	Games	G.	A.	Pts.	Pen.
1974-75—Cornwall Royals		QJHL	68	18	20	38	50
1975-76—Cornwall Royals		QJHL	71	20	60	80	59
1976-77—Cornwall Royals		QJHL	72	31	63	94	90
1977-78—Cornwall Royals (c)		QJHL	71	58	80	138	105
1978-79—New Brunswick Hawks		AHL	74	21	19	40	30
1979-80—Chicago Black Hawks		NHL	11	0	2	2	0
1979-80—New Brunswick Hawks		AHL	55	22	30	52	18
1980-81—Chicago Black Hawks		NHL	49	8	2	10	18
1980-81—New Brunswick Hawks		CHL	21	7	8	15	6
1981-82—New Brunswick Hawks		AHL	30	8	16	24	45
1981-82—Chicago Black Hawks		NHL	48	4	7	11	8
1982-83—Chicago Black Hawks		NHL	79	14	9	23	14
1983-84—Chicago Black Hawks		NHL	72	7	6	13	41
1984-85—Chicago Black Hawks		NHL	79	7	12	19	25
1985-86—Chicago Black Hawks		NHL	70	9	3	12	24
NHL TOTALS			408	49	41	90	130

(c)—Drafted from Cornwall Royals by Chicago Black Hawks in third round of 1978 amateur draft.

JAMES PATRICK

Defense . . . 6'2" . . . 185 lbs. . . . Born, Winnipeg, Man., June 14, 1963 . . . Shoots right . . . Brother of Steve Patrick . . . Member of 1984 Canadian Olympic Team . . . (October, 1984)—Groin injury . . . (October 24, 1985)—Pinched nerve in neck and missed two games . . . (December 15, 1985)—Pinched nerve vs. Pittsburgh.

Year	Team	League	Games	G.	A.	Pts.	Pen.
1980-81—Prince Albert Raiders (a-c-d)		SJHL	59	21	61	82	162
1981-82—Univ. of North Dakota (b-e)		WCHA	42	5	24	29	26
1982-83—Univ. of North Dakota		WCHA	36	12	36	48	29
1983-84—Canadian Olympic Team		Int'l	63	7	24	31	52
1983-84—New York Rangers		NHL	12	1	7	8	2
1984-85—New York Rangers		NHL	75	8	28	36	71
1985-86—New York Rangers		NHL	75	14	29	43	88
NHL TOTALS			162	23	64	87	161

(c)—June, 1981—Drafted by New York Rangers as underage player in 1981 NHL entry draft. First Rangers pick, 9th overall, first round.

(d)—Named Chapstick Player-of-the-Year as top Tier II Canadian Junior Player.

(e)—Named WCHA Rookie-of-the-Year.

STEPHEN GARY PATRICK

Right Wing . . . 6'4" . . . 206 lbs. . . . Born, Winnipeg, Man., February 4, 1961 . . . Shoots right . . . (February 21, 1981)—Bruised right shoulder . . . Brother of James Patrick . . . (February, 1983)—Suspended by Buffalo Sabres for refusing to report to Rochester (AHL). Subsequently reinstated . . . (January, 1985)—Broken nose.

Year	Team	League	Games	G.	A.	Pts.	Pen.
1978-79—Brandon Wheat Kings		WHL	52	23	31	54	105
1979-80—Brandon Wheat Kings (c)		WHL	71	28	38	66	185
1980-81—Brandon Wheat Kings		WHL	34	29	30	59	56

Year	Team	League	Games	G.	A.	Pts.	Pen.
1980-81—Buffalo Sabres		NHL	30	1	7	8	25
1981-82—Rochester Americans		AHL	38	11	9	20	15
1981-82—Buffalo Sabres		NHL	41	8	8	16	64
1982-83—Buffalo Sabres		NHL	56	9	13	22	26
1983-84—Buffalo Sabres		NHL	11	1	4	5	6
1983-84—Rochester Americans		AHL	30	8	14	22	33
1984-85—Buffalo Sabres (d)		NHL	14	2	2	4	4
1984-85—New York Rangers		NHL	43	11	18	29	63
1985-86—New York Rangers (e)		NHL	28	4	3	7	37
1985-86—Quebec Nordiques		NHL	27	4	13	17	17
NHL TOTALS			250	40	68	108	242

(c)—June, 1980—Drafted by Buffalo Sabres as underage junior in 1980 NHL entry draft. First Sabres pick, 20th overall, first round.

(d)—December, 1984—Traded with Jim Wiemer by Buffalo Sabres to New York Rangers for Chris Renaud and Dave Maloney.

(e)—February, 1986—Traded by New York Rangers to Quebec Nordiques for Wilf Paiement.

COLIN PATTERSON

Right Wing . . . 6'2" . . . 195 lbs. . . . Born, Rexdale, Ont., May 11, 1960 . . . Shoots right . . . (March 14, 1984)—Shoulder injury . . . (January, 1985)—Torn knee ligaments.

Year	Team	League	Games	G.	A.	Pts.	Pen.
1980-81—Clarkson College		ECAC	34	20	31	51	8
1981-82—Clarkson College		ECAC	35	21	31	52	32
1982-83—Clarkson College (b)		ECAC	31	23	29	52	30
1982-83—Colorado Flames (c)		CHL	7	1	1	2	0
1983-84—Colorado Flames		CHL	6	2	3	5	9
1983-84—Calgary Flames		NHL	56	13	14	27	15
1984-85—Calgary Flames		NHL	57	22	21	43	5
1985-86—Calgary Flames		NHL	61	14	13	27	22
NHL TOTALS			174	49	48	97	42

(c)—March, 1983—Signed by Calgary Flames as a free agent.

MARK PAVELICH

Center . . . 5'8" . . . 170 lbs. . . . Born, Eveleth, Minn., February 28, 1958 . . . Shoots right . . . (1981-82)—Set N. Y. Ranger records for rookies for goals (33), assists (43) and total points (76) . . . (October 13, 1984)—Broke leg in game at Minnesota . . . (December 28, 1985)—Fractured finger at Minnesota and missed five games.

Year	Team	League	Games	G.	A.	Pts.	Pen.
1976-77—U. of Minnesota-Duluth		WCHA	37	12	7	19	8
1977-78—U. of Minnesota-Duluth		WCHA	36	14	30	44	44
1978-79—U. of Minnesota-Duluth (c)		WCHA	37	31	48	79	52
1979-80—U.S. National Team		.....	60	16	36	52	14
1979-80—U.S. National Team		Olympics	7	1	6	7	2
1980-81—HC Lugano		Switzerland	60	24	49	73	..
1981-82—New York Rangers (d)		NHL	79	33	43	76	67
1982-83—New York Rangers		NHL	78	37	38	75	52
1983-84—New York Rangers		NHL	77	29	53	82	96
1984-85—New York Rangers		NHL	48	14	31	45	29
1985-86—New York Rangers (e)		NHL	59	20	20	40	82
NHL TOTALS			341	133	185	318	326

(c)—Named to All-America Team (West).

(d)—June, 1981—Signed by New York Rangers as a free agent.

(e)—March, 1986—Announced retirement.

JAMES PETER PAVESE

Defense . . . 6'2" . . . 204 lbs. . . . Born, New York, N.Y., June 8, 1962 . . . Shoots left . . . (October, 1981)—Infected hand requiring hospitalization . . . (December 10, 1985)— Sprained ankle vs. Edmonton.

Year	Team	League	Games	G.	A.	Pts.	Pen.
1976-77—Suffolk Royals (c)		NYMJHL	32	6	31	37	32
1977-78—Suffolk Royals		NYMJHL	34	18	40	58	102
1978-79—Peterborough Petes		OMJHL	16	1	1	2	22
1979-80—Kitchener Rangers (d)		OMJHL	68	10	26	36	206
1980-81—Kitchener Rangers (e)		OHL	19	3	12	15	93
1980-81—Sault Ste. Marie Greyhounds		OHL	43	3	25	28	127
1981-82—Sault Ste. Marie Greyhounds		OHL	26	4	21	25	110
1981-82—Salt Lake Golden Eagles (f)		CHL	....	...	....	....	....
1981-82—St. Louis Blues		NHL	42	2	9	11	101

Year	Team	League	Games	G.	A.	Pts.	Pen.
1982-83—Salt Lake Golden Eagles		CHL	36	5	6	11	165
1982-83—St. Louis Blues		NHL	24	0	2	2	45
1983-84—Montana Magic		CHL	47	1	19	20	147
1983-84—St. Louis Blues		NHL	4	0	1	1	19
1984-85—St. Louis Blues		NHL	51	2	5	7	69
1985-86—St. Louis Blues		NHL	69	4	7	11	116
NHL TOTALS			190	8	24	32	350

(c)—Named co-winner of Most Valuable Defenseman award (Shared award with Tom Matthews)
(d)—June, 1980—Drafted as underage junior by St. Louis Blues in 1980 NHL entry draft. Second Blues pick, 54th overall, third round.
(e)—December, 1980—Traded by Kitchener Rangers with Rick Morrocco to Sault Ste. Marie Greyhounds for Scott Clements, Bob Hicks and Mario Michieli.
(f)—No regular-season record. Played one playoff game.

STEVEN JOHN PAYNE

Left Wing . . . 6'2" . . . 205 lbs. . . . Born, Toronto, Ont., August 16, 1958 . . . Shoots left . . . (April, 1985)—Cervical disc surgery and missed first 29 games of 1985-86 season . . . (February 8, 1986)—Injured knee at Philadelphia.

Year	Team	League	Games	G.	A.	Pts.	Pen.
1976-77—Ottawa 67's		Jr."A"OHA	61	21	26	47	22
1977-78—Ottawa 67's (c)		Jr."A"OHA	52	57	37	94	22
1978-79—Oklahoma City Stars		CHL	5	3	4	7	2
1978-79—Minnesota North Stars		NHL	70	23	17	40	29
1979-80—Minnesota North Stars		NHL	80	42	43	85	40
1980-81—Minnesota North Stars (d)		NHL	76	30	28	58	88
1981-82—Minnesota North Stars		NHL	74	33	44	77	11
1982-83—Minnesota North Stars		NHL	80	30	39	69	53
1983-84—Minnesota North Stars		NHL	78	28	31	59	49
1984-85—Minnesota North Stars		NHL	76	29	22	51	61
1985-86—Minnesota North Stars		NHL	22	8	4	12	8
NHL TOTALS			556	223	228	451	339

(c)—Drafted from Ottawa 67's by Minnesota North Stars in second round of 1978 amateur draft.
(d)—Tied with Mike Bossy for NHL playoff lead of 17 goals.

KENT PAYNTER

Defense . . . 6' . . . 186 lbs. . . . Born, Summerside, P.E.I., April 27, 1965 . . . Shoots left.

Year	Team	League	Games	G.	A.	Pts.	Pen.
1981-82—Western Capitals		P.E.I.JHL	35	7	23	30	66
1982-83—Kitchener Rangers (c)		OHL	65	4	11	15	97
1983-84—Kitchener Rangers		OHL	65	9	27	36	94
1984-85—Kitchener Rangers		OHL	58	7	28	35	93
1985-86—Nova Scotia Oilers		AHL	23	1	2	3	36
1985-86—Saginaw Generals		IHL	4	0	1	1	2

(c)—June, 1983—Drafted by Chicago Black Hawks as underage junior in 1983 NHL entry draft. Ninth Black Hawks pick, 159th overall, eighth round.

TED PEARSON

Left Wing . . . 5'10" . . . 175 lbs. . . . Born, Kitchener, Ont., January 9, 1962 . . . Shoots left . . . Son of Mel Pearson (Played pro hockey between 1957 and 1973 with QHL, AHL, WHL, EPHL, NHL, CPHL and WHA) . . . (October, 1984)—Shoulder injury.

Year	Team	League	Games	G.	A.	Pts.	Pen.
1980-81—University of Wisconsin		WCHA	36	6	9	15	59
1981-82—University of Wisconsin (c)		WCHA	41	15	23	38	85
1982-83—University of Wisconsin		WCHA	42	6	9	15	90
1983-84—University of Wisconsin		WCHA	35	13	20	33	60
1984-85—Moncton Golden Flames		AHL	65	9	17	26	70
1985-86—Salt Lake Golden Eagles		IHL	77	28	27	55	68

(c)—June, 1982—Drafted by Calgary Flames in 1982 NHL entry draft. Eleventh Flames pick, 177th overall, ninth round.

ALLEN PEDERSON

Defense . . . 6'3" . . . 180 lbs. . . . Born, Edmonton, Alta., January 13, 1965 . . . Shoots left.

Year	Team	League	Games	G.	A.	Pts.	Pen.
1982-83—Medicine Hat Tigers (c)		WHL	63	3	10	13	49
1983-84—Medicine Hat Tigers		WHL	44	0	11	11	47
1984-85—Medicine Hat Tigers		WHL	72	6	16	22	66
1985-86—Moncton Golden Flames		AHL	59	1	8	9	39

(c)—June, 1983—Drafted as underage junior by Boston Bruins in 1983 NHL entry draft. Fifth Bruins pick, 102nd overall, fifth round.

BARRY ALAN PEDERSON

Center . . . 5'11" . . . 171 lbs. . . . Born, Big River, Sask., March 13, 1961 . . . Shoots right . . . (1981-82)—Set Boston Bruin rookie records with 44 goals and 92 points . . . (1982-83)— Became youngest player to ever lead Boston in scoring . . . (October 2, 1984)—Broke knuckle on right hand during fight with Mario Marois in pre-season game at Quebec . . . (January, 1985)—Surgery to remove a benign fibrous tumor from rear shoulder muscle of right arm. Doctors had to cut away parts of the muscle when they removed the growth and he missed remainder of season . . . Cousin of Brian Skrudland.

Year	Team	League	Games	G.	A.	Pts.	Pen.
1977-78—Nanaimo		BCJHL	....	...	....	....	....
1977-78—Victoria Cougars		WCHL	3	1	4	5	2
1978-79—Victoria Cougars		WHL	72	31	53	84	41
1979-80—Victoria Cougars (b-c)		WHL	72	52	88	140	50
1980-81—Victoria Cougars (a)		WHL	55	65	82	147	65
1980-81—Boston Bruins		NHL	9	1	4	5	6
1981-82—Boston Bruins		NHL	80	44	48	92	53
1982-83—Boston Bruins		NHL	77	46	61	107	47
1983-84—Boston Bruins		NHL	80	39	77	116	64
1984-85—Boston Bruins		NHL	22	4	8	12	10
1985-86—Boston Bruins (d)		NHL	79	29	47	76	60
NHL TOTALS			347	163	245	408	240

(c)—June, 1980—Drafted as underage junior by Boston Bruins in 1980 NHL entry draft. First Bruins pick, 18th overall, first round.

(d)—June, 1986—Traded by Boston Bruins to Vancouver Canucks for Cam Neely and first round 1987 draft pick.

MARK PEDERSON

Left Wing . . . 6'1" . . . 195 lbs. . . . Born, Prelate, Sask., January 14, 1968 . . . Shoots left . . . (March, 1985)—Shoulder injury.

Year	Team	League	Games	G.	A.	Pts.	Pen.
1983-84—Cablevision Tigers		Alta. Midget	42	43	47	90	64
1984-85—Medicine Hat Tigers		WHL	71	42	40	82	63
1985-86—Medicine Hat Tigers (c)		WHL	72	46	60	106	46

(c)—June, 1986—Drafted as underage junior by Montreal Canadiens in 1986 NHL entry draft. First Canadiens pick, 15th overall, first round.

BLAINE PEERLESS

Defense . . . 6' . . . 195 lbs. . . . Born, Edmonton, Alta., October 13, 1961 . . . Shoots left.

Year	Team	League	Games	G.	A.	Pts.	Pen.
1980-81—Spokane Flyers		WHL	66	14	38	52	228
1981-82—Milwaukee Admirals		IHL	80	12	38	50	127
1982-83—Milwaukee Admirals		IHL	12	2	6	8	39
1982-83—Salt Lake Golden Eagles		CHL	45	1	8	9	38
1983-84—Montana Magic		CHL	73	6	18	24	80
1984-85—Toledo Goaldiggers		IHL	70	5	17	22	137
1985-86—Milwaukee Admirals		IHL	80	10	39	49	110

IN MEMORIAM
GEORGE DALE PELAWA

Right Wing . . . 6'3" . . . 230 lbs. . . . Born, St. Paul, Minn., February 22, 1968 . . . Shoots right . . . (August 30, 1986)—Killed in automobile accident in Bemidji, Minn.

Year	Team	League	Games	G.	A.	Pts.	Pen.
1984-85—Bemidji H.S.		Minn.	25	26	13	39	..
1985-86—Bemidji H.S. (c)		Minn.	26	29	26	55	..

(c)—June, 1986—Drafted by Calgary Flames in 1986 NHL entry draft. First Flames pick, 16th overall, first round.

STEVE PEPIN

Center . . . 5'10" . . . 170 lbs. . . . Born, Sherbrooke, Que., March 21, 1965 . . . Shoots left.

Year	Team	League	Games	G.	A.	Pts.	Pen.
1982-83—St. Jean Beavers (a-c)		QHL	69	51	61	112	83
1983-84—Drummondville Voltigeurs		QHL	64	54	58	112	173
1984-85—Drummondville Voltigeurs		QHL	65	56	61	117	158
1985-86—Drummondville Voltigeurs		QHL	52	47	56	103	110

(c)—June, 1983—Drafted as underage junior by Chicago Black Hawks in 1983 NHL entry draft. Twelfth Black Hawks pick, 219th overall, 11th round.

JIM DESMOND PEPLINSKI

Center . . . 6'2" . . . 201 lbs. . . . Born, Renfrew, Ont., October 24, 1960 . . . Shoots right.

Year	Team	League	Games	G.	A.	Pts.	Pen.
1977-78—Toronto Marlboros		OMJHL	66	13	28	41	44
1978-79—Toronto Marlboros (c)		OMJHL	66	23	32	55	60
1979-80—Toronto Marlboros		OMJHL	67	35	66	101	89
1980-81—Calgary Flames		NHL	80	13	25	38	108
1981-82—Calgary Flames		NHL	74	30	37	67	115
1982-83—Calgary Flames		NHL	80	15	26	41	134
1983-84—Calgary Flames		NHL	74	11	22	33	114
1984-85—Calgary Flames		NHL	80	16	29	45	111
1985-86—Calgary Flames		NHL	77	24	35	59	214
NHL TOTALS			465	109	174	283	796

(c)—August, 1979—Drafted by Atlanta Flames as underage junior in 1979 NHL entry draft. Fifth Flames pick, 75th overall, fourth round.

TERRY PERKINS

Right Wing . . . 6'1" . . . 190 lbs. . . . Born, Campbell River, B.C., June 21, 1966 . . . Shoots right.

Year	Team	League	Games	G.	A.	Pts.	Pen.
1983-84—Portland Winter Hawks (c)		WHL	68	35	30	65	75
1984-85—Portland Winter Hawks		WHL	63	33	38	71	81
1985-86—Portland Winter Hawks		WHL	6	5	4	9	9
1985-86—Spokane Chiefs (b)		WHL	60	66	42	108	65

(c)—June, 1984—Drafted as underage junior by Quebec Nordiques in NHL entry draft. Fourth Nordiques pick, 78th overall, fourth round.

FRED PERLINI

Center . . . 6'2" . . . 175 lbs. . . . Born, Sault Ste. Marie, Ont., April 12, 1962 . . . Shoots left.

Year	Team	League	Games	G.	A.	Pts.	Pen.
1979-80—Toronto Marlboros (c)		OMJHL	67	13	18	31	12
1980-81—Toronto Marlboros		OHL	55	37	29	66	48
1981-82—Toronto Marlboros		OHL	68	47	64	111	75
1981-82—Toronto Maple Leafs		NHL	7	2	3	5	0
1982-83—St. Catharines Saints		AHL	76	8	22	30	24
1983-84—Toronto Maple Leafs		NHL	1	0	0	0	0
1983-84—St. Catharines Saints		AHL	79	21	31	52	67
1984-85—St. Catharines Saints		AHL	77	21	28	49	26
1985-86—Baltimore Skipjacks		AHL	25	6	4	10	6
NHL TOTALS			8	2	3	5	0

(c)—June, 1980—Drafted as underage junior by Toronto Maple Leafs in 1980 NHL entry draft. Eighth Maple Leafs pick, 158th overall, eighth round.

GILBERT PERREAULT

Center . . . 5'11½" . . . 202 lbs. . . . Born, Victoriaville, Que., November 13, 1950 . . . Shoots left . . . Cousin of Bobby Perreault . . . Set NHL records for most goals and points in rookie season in 1970-71 (record for goals broken by Richard Martin and record for points broken by Marcel Dionne, both in 1971-72) . . . Missed part of 1973-74 season with fractured left ankle and part of 1974-75 season with strained left knee . . . (January 24, 1981)—Broken ribs . . . (September 7, 1981)—Broke right ankle in Canada Cup game vs. Sweden. Had pin inserted during surgery on September 8 . . . (March, 1984)—Back spasms . . . (December, 1984)—Broken knuckle . . . (December 21, 1985)—Bruised foot at Montreal and missed four games.

Year	Team	League	Games	G.	A.	Pts.	Pen.
1967-68—Montreal Jr. Canadiens		Jr."A"OHA	47	15	34	49	10
1968-69—Montreal Jr. Canadiens (a)		Jr."A"OHA	54	37	60	97	29
1969-70—Mont. Jr. Canadiens (a-c-d)		Jr."A"OHA	54	51	70	121	26

Year	Team	League	Games	G.	A.	Pts.	Pen.
1970-71—Buffalo Sabres (e-f)		NHL	78	38	34	72	19
1971-72—Buffalo Sabres		NHL	76	26	48	74	24
1972-73—Buffalo Sabres (g)		NHL	78	28	60	88	10
1973-74—Buffalo Sabres		NHL	55	18	33	51	10
1974-75—Buffalo Sabres		NHL	68	39	57	96	36
1975-76—Buffalo Sabres (b)		NHL	80	44	69	113	36
1976-77—Buffalo Sabres (b)		NHL	80	39	56	95	30
1977-78—Buffalo Sabres		NHL	79	41	48	89	20
1978-79—Buffalo Sabres		NHL	79	27	58	85	20
1979-80—Buffalo Sabres		NHL	80	40	66	106	57
1980-81—Buffalo Sabres		NHL	56	20	39	59	56
1981-82—Buffalo Sabres		NHL	62	31	42	73	40
1982-83—Buffalo Sabres		NHL	77	30	46	76	34
1983-84—Buffalo Sabres		NHL	73	31	59	90	32
1984-85—Buffalo Sabres		NHL	78	30	53	83	42
1985-86—Buffalo Sabres (h)		NHL	72	21	39	60	28
NHL TOTALS			1171	503	807	1310	494

(c)—Won Red Tilson Memorial Trophy (MVP).
(d)—Drafted from Montreal Jr. Canadiens by Buffalo Sabres in first round of 1970 amateur draft.
(e)—Won Calder Memorial Trophy.
(f)—Named Rookie of the Year in East Division of NHL by THE SPORTING NEWS.
(g)—Won Lady Byng Trophy.
(h)—June, 1986—Announced his retirement.

STEFAN PERSSON

Defense . . . 6'1" . . . 180 lbs. . . . Born, Umea, Sweden, December 22, 1954 . . . Shoots left . . . (April 20, 1981)—Broken jaw when hit by a shot during playoff game at Edmonton . . . (October 7, 1981)—Cracked two ribs in opening game of season at Los Angeles . . . (January, 1984)—Tonsillectomy . . . (February, 1984)—Knee injury . . . (April, 1984)—Separated shoulder during playoffs . . . (October, 1984)—Given five-game suspension . . . (January, 1985)—Broken foot.

Year	Team	League	Games	G.	A.	Pts.	Pen.
1976-77—Brynas		Sweden	31	7	13	20	70
1976-77—Swedish National Team (c)		Sweden	....	...	....	....	....
1977-78—New York Islanders		NHL	66	6	50	56	54
1978-79—New York Islanders		NHL	78	10	56	66	57
1979-80—New York Islanders		NHL	73	4	35	39	76
1980-81—New York Islanders		NHL	80	9	52	61	82
1981-82—New York Islanders		NHL	70	6	37	43	99
1982-83—New York Islanders		NHL	70	4	25	29	71
1983-84—New York Islanders		NHL	75	9	24	33	65
1984-85—New York Islanders		NHL	54	3	19	22	30
1985-86—New York Islanders (d)		NHL	56	1	19	20	40
NHL TOTALS			622	52	317	369	474

(c)—Signed by New York Islanders as free agent, September, 1977.
(d)—March, 1986—Traded by N.Y. Islanders to Winnipeg Jets for an eighth round 1986 draft pick. Persson refused to go to Winnipeg and announced his retirement instead to negate the trade.

MATTHEW PESKLEWIS

Left Wing . . . 6'2" . . . 185 lbs. . . . Born, Edmonton, Alta., May 21, 1968 . . . Shoots left.

Year	Team	League	Games	G.	A.	Pts.	Pen.
1984-85—St. Albert Midget Raiders		Alta.Midg	28	23	8	31	96
1985-86—St. Albert Saints (c)		WHL	51	13	26	39	259

(c)—June, 1986—Drafted as underage junior by Boston Bruins in 1986 NHL entry draft. Fourth Bruins pick, 97th overall, fifth round.

BRENT RONALD PETERSON

Center . . . 6'1" . . . 195 lbs. . . . Born, Calgary, Alta., February 15, 1958 . . . Shoots right . . . Missed most of 1978-79 season with broken leg . . . (October 15, 1980)—Fractured right cheekbone . . . (November 12, 1980)—Fractured left ankle . . . (February 10, 1983)—Dislocated shoulder in game at Los Angeles.

Year	Team	League	Games	G.	A.	Pts.	Pen.
1974-75—Edmonton Oil Kings		WCHL	66	17	26	43	44
1975-76—Edmonton Oil Kings		WCHL	70	22	39	61	57
1976-77—Portland Winter Hawks		WCHL	69	34	78	112	98
1977-78—Portland Winter Hawks (c)		WCHL	51	33	50	83	95
1978-79—Detroit Red Wings		NHL	5	0	0	0	0
1979-80—Adirondack Red Wings		AHL	52	9	22	31	61

Year	Team	League	Games	G.	A.	Pts.	Pen.
1979-80—Detroit Red Wings		NHL	18	1	2	3	2
1980-81—Detroit Red Wings		NHL	53	6	18	24	24
1980-81—Adirondack Red Wings		AHL	3	1	0	1	10
1981-82—Detroit Red Wings (d)		NHL	15	1	0	1	6
1981-82—Buffalo Sabres		NHL	46	9	5	14	43
1982-83—Buffalo Sabres		NHL	75	13	24	37	38
1983-84—Buffalo Sabres		NHL	70	9	12	21	52
1984-85—Buffalo Sabres		NHL	74	12	22	34	47
1985-86—Vancouver Canucks (e)		NHL	77	8	23	31	94
NHL TOTALS			433	59	106	165	306

(c)—Drafted from Portland Winter Hawks by Detroit Red Wings (with choice obtained from Toronto Maple Leafs) in first round of 1978 amateur draft.

(d)—December, 1981—Traded with Mike Foligno, Dale McCourt and future considerations by Detroit Red Wings to Buffalo Sabres for Danny Gare, Jim Schoenfeld, Derek Smith and Bob Sauve.

(e)—October, 1985—Acquired by Vancouver Canucks in 1985 NHL waiver draft.

MICHEL PETIT

Defense . . . 6'1" . . . 185 lbs. . . . Born, St. Malo, Que., February 12, 1964 . . . Shoots right . . . (March, 1984)—Separated shoulder.

Year	Team	League	Games	G.	A.	Pts.	Pen.
1980-81—St. Foy Midget AAA		QAAAMHL	48	10	45	55	84
1981-82—Sherbrooke Beavers (a-c-d-e)		QMJHL	63	10	39	49	106
1982-83—St. Jean Beavers (a)		QHL	62	19	67	86	196
1982-83—Vancouver Canucks		NHL	2	0	0	0	0
1983-84—Vancouver Canucks		NHL	44	6	9	15	53
1984-85—Vancouver Canucks		NHL	69	5	26	31	127
1985-86—Fredericton Express		AHL	25	0	13	13	79
1985-86—Vancouver Canucks		NHL	32	1	6	7	27
NHL TOTALS			147	12	41	53	207

(c)—Winner of Raymond Lagace Trophy (Top Rookie QMJHL Defenseman).

(d)—Winner of the Association of Journalist of Hockey Trophy (Top QMJHL Pro Prospect).

(e)—June, 1982—Drafted as underage junior by Vancouver Canucks in 1982 NHL entry draft. First Canucks pick, 11th overall, first round.

JORGEN PETTERSSON

Left Wing . . . 6'2" . . . 185 lbs. . . . Born, Gothenburg, Sweden, July 11, 1956 . . . Shoots left . . . (October, 1980)—Sprained ankle . . . (February, 1983)—Wrist injury . . . (January 24, 1986)—Bruised knee vs. N.Y. Islanders . . . (March 18, 1986)—Bruised knee vs. N.Y. Rangers.

Year	Team	League	Games	G.	A.	Pts.	Pen.
1974-75—Vastra Frolunda IF		Sweden	42	19	5	24	6
1975-76—Vastra Frolunda IF		Sweden	31	17	6	23	8
1976-77—Vastra Frolunda IF		Sweden	19	15	4	19	4
1977-78—Vastra Frolunda IF		Sweden	16	5	8	13	8
1978-79—Vastra Frolunda IF		Sweden	35	23	11	34	12
1979-70—Vastra Frolunda IF (c)		Sweden	32	21	19	40	....
1980-81—St. Louis Blues		NHL	62	37	36	73	24
1981-82—St. Louis Blues		NHL	77	38	31	69	28
1982-83—St. Louis Blues		NHL	74	35	38	73	4
1983-84—St. Louis Blues		NHL	77	28	34	62	29
1984-85—St. Louis Blues (d)		NHL	75	23	32	55	20
1985-86—Hartford Whalers (e)		NHL	23	5	5	10	2
1985-86—Washington Capitals		NHL	47	8	16	24	10
NHL TOTALS			435	174	192	366	117

(c)—May, 1980—Signed by St. Louis Blues as a free agent.

(d)—April, 1985—Traded by St. Louis Blues to Hartford Whalers to complete February, 1985 trade that saw Greg Millen and Mark Johnson go from the Whalers to St. Louis for Mike Liut and future considerations.

(e)—December, 1986—Traded by Hartford Whalers to Washington Capitals for Doug Jarvis.

LYLE PHAIR

Left Wing . . . 6'1" . . . 188 lbs. . . . Born, Pilot Mound, Man., March 8, 1961 . . . Shoots left.

Year	Team	League	Games	G.	A.	Pts.	Pen.
1981-82—Michigan State University		CCHA	42	24	19	43	49
1982-83—Michigan State University		CCHA	41	20	15	35	64
1983-84—Michigan State University		CCHA	45	15	16	31	58
1984-85—Michigan State University (c)		CCHA	43	23	27	50	84

Year	Team	League	Games	G.	A.	Pts.	Pen.
1985-86—Los Angeles Kings		NHL	15	0	1	1	2
1985-86—New Haven Nighthawks		AHL	35	9	9	18	15
NHL TOTALS			15	0	1	1	2

(c)—June, 1985—Signed by Los Angeles Kings as a free agent.

ROBERT RENE JOSEPH PICARD

Defense . . . 6'2" . . . 203 lbs. . . . Born, Montreal, Que., May 25, 1957 . . . Shoots left . . . Nephew of former NHL defenseman Noel Picard . . . (November 12, 1980)—Strained knee ligaments . . . (January, 1983)—Broken bone in foot . . . (September, 1985)—Concussion in training camp . . . (January 4, 1986)—Cut hand in game at Detroit . . . (February 25, 1986)—Broke ribs vs. Boston and missed five games.

Year	Team	League	Games	G.	A.	Pts.	Pen.
1973-74—Montreal Red, White and Blue		QJHL	70	7	46	53	296
1974-75—Montreal Red, White and Blue		QJHL	70	13	74	87	339
1975-76—Montreal Juniors (b)		QJHL	72	14	67	81	282
1976-77—Montreal Juniors (a-c-d)		QJHL	70	32	60	92	267
1977-78—Washington Capitals		NHL	75	10	27	37	101
1978-79—Washington Capitals		NHL	77	21	44	65	85
1979-80—Washington Capitals (e)		NHL	78	11	43	54	122
1980-81—Toronto Maple Leafs (f)		NHL	59	6	19	25	68
1980-81—Montreal Canadiens		NHL	8	2	2	4	6
1981-82—Montreal Canadiens		NHL	62	2	26	28	106
1982-83—Montreal Canadiens		NHL	64	7	31	38	60
1983-84—Montreal Canadiens (g)		NHL	7	0	2	2	0
1983-84—Winnipeg Jets		NHL	62	6	16	22	34
1984-85—Winnipeg Jets		NHL	78	12	22	34	107
1985-86—Winnipeg Jets (h)		NHL	20	2	5	7	17
1985-86—Quebec Nordiques		NHL	48	7	27	34	36
NHL TOTALS			638	86	264	350	742

(c)—Outstanding defenseman in QJHL.

(d)—Drafted from Montreal Juniors by Washington Capitals in first round of 1977 amateur draft.

(e)—June, 1980—Traded with Tim Coulis and second round draft choice in 1980 (Bob McGill) by Washington Capitals to Toronto Maple Leafs for Mike Palmateer and third round draft choice (Torrie Robertson).

(f)—March, 1981—Traded by Toronto Maple Leafs with a future eighth round draft pick to Montreal Canadiens for Michel Larocque.

(g)—November, 1983—Traded by Montreal Canadiens to Winnipeg Jets for third-round 1984 draft pick (Patrick Roy).

(h)—November, 1985—Traded by Winnipeg Jets to Quebec Nordiques for Mario Marois.

DAVE PICHETTE

Defense . . . 6'3" . . . 195 lbs. . . . Born, Grand Falls, N. B., February 4, 1960 . . . Shoots left . . . (January, 1983)—Back injury . . . (January 8, 1986)—Concussion at Chicago and missed eight games.

Year	Team	League	Games	G.	A.	Pts.	Pen.
1978-79—Quebec Remparts		QMJHL	57	10	16	26	134
1979-80—Quebec Remparts		QMJHL	56	8	19	27	129
1980-81—Quebec Nordiques (c)		NHL	46	4	16	20	62
1980-81—Hershey Bears		AHL	20	2	3	5	37
1981-82—Quebec Nordiques		NHL	67	7	30	37	152
1982-83—Fredericton Express		AHL	16	3	11	14	14
1982-83—Quebec Nordiques		NHL	53	3	21	24	49
1983-84—Fredericton Express		AHL	10	2	1	3	13
1983-84—Quebec Nordiques (d)		NHL	23	2	7	9	12
1983-84—St. Louis Blues		NHL	23	0	11	11	6
1984-85—New Jersey Devils (e)		NHL	71	17	40	57	41
1985-86—Maine Mariners		AHL	25	4	15	19	28
1985-86—New Jersey Devils		NHL	33	7	12	19	22
NHL TOTALS			316	40	137	177	344

(c)—September, 1980—Signed by Quebec Nordiques as a free agent.

(d)—February, 1984—Traded by Quebec Nordiques to St. Louis Blues for Andre Dore.

(e)—October, 1984—Drafted by New Jersey Devils in NHL waiver draft.

DOUG PICKELL

Left Wing . . . 6' . . . 185 lbs. . . . Born, London, Ont., May 7, 1968 . . . Shoots left.

Year	Team	League	Games	G.	A.	Pts.	Pen.
1983-84—Sherwood Park Midgets		WHL	40	31	33	64	84
1984-85—Medicine Hat Tigers		WHL	69	4	13	17	124

Year	Team	League	Games	G.	A.	Pts.	Pen.
1985-86—Medicine Hat Tigers (c)	WHL	8	2	4	6	11
1985-86—Kamloops Blazers (d)	WHL	62	25	16	41	101

(c)—December, 1985—Traded with Sean Pass by Medicine Hat Tigers to Kamloops Blazers for Rob Dimaio, Dave MacKey and Calvin Knibbs.

(d)—June, 1986—Drafted as underage junior by Calgary Flames in 1986 NHL entry draft. Ninth Flames pick, 205th overall, 10th round.

RANDY STEPHEN PIERCE

Right Wing . . . 6' . . . 190 lbs. . . . Born, Arnprior, Ont., November 23, 1957 . . . Shoots right . . . (December 2, 1980)—Suffered fractured nose and cheekbone, contusion and double vision of right eye and facial lacerations when hit by a puck. Surgery was required December 11 . . . (October, 1981)—Separated shoulder . . . (December, 1981)—Took 19 stitches when forehead and left eyelid were raked by a stick. . . . (January 3, 1986)—Injured shoulder in a fight with Dale Baldwin at Fort Wayne Komets. He required surgery and was lost for the season.

Year	Team	League	Games	G.	A.	Pts.	Pen.
1975-76—Sudbury Wolves	Jr. "A" OHA	56	21	44	65	72
1976-77—Sudbury Wolves (c)	Jr. "A" OHA	60	38	60	98	67
1977-78—Hampton Gulls	AHL	3	0	1	1	2
1977-78—Phoenix Roadrunners	CHL	12	3	1	4	11
1977-78—Colorado Rockies	NHL	35	9	10	19	15
1978-79—Philadelphia Firebirds	AHL	1	0	0	0	0
1978-79—Colorado Rockies	NHL	70	19	17	36	35
1979-80—Colorado Rockies	NHL	75	16	23	39	100
1980-81—Colorado Rockies	NHL	55	9	21	30	52
1981-82—Colorado Rockies	NHL	5	0	0	0	4
1981-82—Fort Worth Texans	CHL	15	6	6	12	19
1982-83—Wichita Wind	CHL	14	4	8	12	4
1982-83—New Jersey Devils (d)	NHL	3	0	0	0	0
1982-83—Binghamton Whalers	AHL	46	14	41	55	33
1983-84—Hartford Whalers	NHL	17	6	3	9	9
1983-84—Binghamton Whalers	AHL	46	21	24	45	41
1984-85—Hartford Whalers	NHL	17	3	2	5	8
1984-85—Binghamton Whalers	AHL	31	6	10	16	45
1985-86—Salt Lake Golden Eagles	IHL	20	5	5	10	25
NHL TOTALS		277	62	76	138	223

(c)—Drafted from Sudbury Wolves by Colorado Rockies in third round of 1977 amateur draft.

(d)—December, 1983—Signed by Binghamton Whalers as a free agent.

NEIL PILON

Defense . . . 6'4" . . . 185 lbs. . . . Born, Merritt, B.C., April 26, 1967 . . . Shoots right . . . (October, 1984)—Sprained wrist . . . (December, 1984)—Shoulder separation.

Year	Team	League	Games	G.	A.	Pts.	Pen.
1983-84—Williams Lake Mustangs	PCJHL	60	10	39	49	200
1984-85—Kamloops Blazers (c)	WHL	52	1	6	7	40
1985-86—Moose Jaw Warriors	WHL	59	2	18	20	112

(c)—June, 1985—Drafted as underage junior by New York Rangers in 1985 NHL entry draft. Seventh Rangers pick, 133rd overall, seventh round.

RICHARD PILON

Defense . . . 5'11" . . . 197 lbs. . . . Born, Saskatoon, Sask., April 30, 1968 . . . Shoots left.

Year	Team	League	Games	G.	A.	Pts.	Pen.
1984-85—Prince Albert Midget Raiders	Sask. Midg.	26	3	11	14	41
1985-86—Prince Albert Midget Raiders	Sask. Midg.	35	3	28	31	142
1985-86—Prince Albert Raiders (c)	WHL	6	0	0	0	0

(c)—June, 1986—Drafted as underage junior by New York Islanders in 1986 NHL entry draft. Ninth Islanders pick, 143rd overall, seventh round.

LANCE PITLICK

Defense . . . 6' . . . 185 lbs. . . . Born, Fridley, Minn., November 5, 1967 . . . Shoots right.

Year	Team	League	Games	G.	A.	Pts.	Pen.
1984-85—Cooper H.S.	Minn.	23	8	4	12	....
1985-86—Cooper H.S. (c)	Minn.	21	17	8	25	....

(c)—June, 1986—Drafted by Minnesota North Stars in 1986 NHL entry draft. Tenth North Stars pick, 180th overall, ninth round.

MICHAL PIVONKA

Center . . . 6'2" . . . 192 lbs. . . . Born, Kladno, Czechoslovakia, January 28, 1966 . . . Shoots left.

Year	Team	League	Games	G.	A.	Pts.	Pen.
1985-86—Dukla Jihlava (c)		Czech.	....	...	....	....	....

(c)—June, 1984—Drafted by Washington Capitals in 1984 NHL entry draft. Third Capitals pick, 59th overall, third round.

CAM PLANTE

Defense . . . 6' . . . 190 lbs. . . . Born, Brandon, Manitoba, March 12, 1964 . . . Shoots left . . . (1983-84)—Set WHL single season record for defensemen with 118 assists and 140 points . . . (September, 1984)—Shoulder separation.

Year	Team	League	Games	G.	A.	Pts.	Pen.
1980-81—Brandon Wheat Kings		WHL	70	3	14	17	17
1981-82—Brandon Wheat Kings		WHL	36	4	12	16	22
1982-83—Brandon Wheat Kings (c)		WHL	56	19	56	75	71
1983-84—Brandon Wheat Kings (a)		WHL	72	22	118	140	96
1984-85—St. Catharines Saints		AHL	54	5	31	36	42
1984-85—Toronto Maple Leafs		NHL	2	0	0	0	0
1985-86—St. Catharines Saints		AHL	49	6	15	21	28
NHL TOTALS			2	0	0	0	0

(c)—June, 1983—Drafted as underage junior by Toronto Maple Leafs in 1983 NHL entry draft. Fifth Maple Leafs' pick, 128th overall, seventh round.

JIM PLAYFAIR

Defense . . . 6'3" . . . 200 lbs. . . . Born, Vanderhoof, B.C., May 22, 1964 . . . Shoots left . . . Brother of Larry Playfair . . . (November, 1984)—Severe groin pull.

Year	Team	League	Games	G.	A.	Pts.	Pen.
1980-81—Fort Saskatchewan		AJHL	31	2	17	19	105
1981-82—Portland Winter Hawks (c)		WHL	70	4	13	17	121
1982-83—Portland Winter Hawks		WHL	63	8	27	35	218
1983-84—Portland Winter Hawks		WHL	16	5	6	11	38
1983-84—Calgary Wranglers		WHL	44	6	9	15	96
1983-84—Edmonton Oilers		NHL	2	1	1	2	2
1984-85—Nova Scotia Oilers		AHL	41	0	4	4	107
1985-86—Nova Scotia Oilers		AHL	73	2	12	14	160
NHL TOTALS			2	1	1	2	2

(c)—June, 1982—Drafted by Edmonton Oilers in 1982 NHL entry draft. First Oilers pick, 20th overall, first round.

LARRY WILLIAM PLAYFAIR

Defense . . . 6'4" . . . 215 lbs. . . . Born, Fort St. James, B. C., June 23, 1958 . . . Shoots left . . . (October 9, 1980)—Severely cut right hand kept him out of Sabres lineup for 10 days . . . Brother of Jim Playfair . . . (April, 1983)—Chipped bone in right elbow in playoff series vs. Boston . . . (January, 1986)—Injured shoulder . . . (March 1, 1986)—Injured left knee . . . (May, 1986)—Shoulder surgery.

Year	Team	League	Games	G.	A.	Pts.	Pen.
1975-76—Langley		Jr. "A" BCHL	72	10	20	30	162
1976-77—Portland Winter Hawks		WCHL	65	2	17	19	199
1977-78—Portland Winter Hawks (a-c)		WCHL	71	13	19	32	402
1978-79—Buffalo Sabres		NHL	26	0	3	3	60
1978-79—Hershey Bears		AHL	45	0	12	12	148
1979-80—Buffalo Sabres		NHL	79	2	10	12	145
1980-81—Buffalo Sabres		NHL	75	3	9	12	169
1981-82—Buffalo Sabres		NHL	77	6	10	16	258
1982-83—Buffalo Sabres		NHL	79	4	13	17	180
1983-84—Buffalo Sabres		NHL	76	5	11	16	209
1984-85—Buffalo Sabres		NHL	72	3	14	17	157
1985-86—Buffalo Sabres (d)		NHL	47	1	2	3	100
1985-86—Los Angeles Kings		NHL	14	0	1	1	26
NHL TOTALS			545	24	73	97	1304

(c)—Drafted from Portland Winter Hawks by Buffalo Sabres in first round of 1978 amateur draft.

(d)—January, 1986—Traded with Sean McKenna and Ken Baumgartner by Buffalo Sabres to Los Angeles Kings for Brian Engblom and Doug Smith.

WILLIAM (WILLI) PLETT

Right Wing . . . 6'3" . . . 205 lbs. . . . Born, Paraguay, South America, June 7, 1955 . . . Shoots

right . . . (October, 1982)—Suspended for seven games for swinging his stick at Detroit goalie Greg Stefan . . . (October 18, 1984)—Dislocated shoulder in fight with Don Jackson in game vs. Edmonton . . . (October 19, 1985)—Separated shoulder at Philadelphia and missed four weeks . . . (January 21, 1986)—Dislocated shoulder at Philadelphia and missed four games . . . (March 11, 1986)—Bruised shoulder vs. Edmonton and missed six games.

Year	Team	League	Games	G.	A.	Pts.	Pen.
1974-75—Niagara Falls Flyers	SOJHL	....	...	....	....	....	
1974-75—St. Cath. Black Hawks (c)	Jr. "A" OHA	22	6	8	14	63	
1975-76—Tulsa Oilers (d)	CHL	73	30	20	50	163	
1975-76—Atlanta Flames	NHL	4	0	0	0	2	
1976-77—Tulsa Oilers	CHL	14	8	4	12	68	
1976-77—Atlanta Flames (e)	NHL	64	33	23	56	123	
1977-78—Atlanta Flames	NHL	78	22	21	43	171	
1978-79—Atlanta Flames	NHL	74	23	20	43	213	
1979-80—Atlanta Flames	NHL	76	13	19	32	231	
1980-81—Calgary Flames	NHL	78	38	30	68	239	
1981-82—Calgary Flames (f)	NHL	78	21	36	57	288	
1982-83—Minnesota North Stars	NHL	71	25	14	39	170	
1983-84—Minnesota North Stars	NHL	73	15	23	38	316	
1984-85—Minnesota North Stars	NHL	47	14	14	28	157	
1985-86—Minnesota North Stars	NHL	59	10	7	17	231	
NHL TOTALS			702	214	207	421	2141

(c)—Drafted from St. Catharines Black Hawks by Atlanta Flames in fifth round of 1975 amateur draft.
(d)—Tied for lead in goals (5) during playoffs.
(e)—Won Calder Memorial Trophy and named THE SPORTING NEWS' NHL Rookie-of-the-Year.
(f)—June, 1982—Traded by Calgary Flames with a fourth-round draft choice in 1982 to Minnesota North Stars for Bill Nyrop, Steve Christoff and a second-round draft choice in 1982.

WALT MICHAEL PODDUBNY

Center . . . 6'1" . . . 203 lbs. . . . Born, Thunder Bay, Ont. February 14, 1960 . . . Shoots left . . . (October, 1982)—Injured leg . . . Shares Toronto goal scoring record for rookies (28) with Peter Ihnacak . . . (October, 1983)—Broken ankle . . . (February, 1985)—Broke thumb in AHL game . . . (September, 1985)—Infected foot during training camp.

Year	Team	League	Games	G.	A.	Pts.	Pen.
1978-79—Brandon Wheat Kings	WHL	20	11	11	22	12	
1979-80—Kitchener Rangers	OMJHL	19	3	9	12	35	
1979-80—Kingston Canadians (c)	OMJHL	43	30	17	47	36	
1980-81—Milwaukee Admirals	IHL	5	4	2	6	4	
1980-81—Wichita Wind	CHL	70	21	29	50	207	
1981-82—Edmonton Oilers (d)	NHL	4	0	0	0	0	
1981-82—Wichita Wind	CHL	60	35	46	81	79	
1981-82—Toronto Maple Leafs	NHL	11	3	4	7	8	
1982-83—Toronto Maple Leafs	NHL	72	28	31	59	71	
1983-84—Toronto Maple Leafs	NHL	38	11	14	25	48	
1984-85—St. Catharines Saints	AHL	8	5	7	12	10	
1984-85—Toronto Maple Leafs	NHL	32	5	15	20	26	
1985-86—St. Catharines Saints	AHL	37	28	27	55	52	
1985-86—Toronto Maple Leafs (e)	NHL	33	12	22	34	25	
NHL TOTALS			190	59	86	145	178

(c)—June, 1980—Drafted by Edmonton Oilers in 1980 NHL entry draft. Fourth Oilers pick, 90th overall, fifth round.
(d)—March, 1982—Traded with NHL rights to Phil Drouillard by Edmonton Oilers to Toronto Maple Leafs for Laurie Boschman.
(e)—August, 1986—Traded by Toronto Maple Leafs to New York Rangers for Mike Allison.

RAY PODLOSKI

Center . . . 6'2" . . . 210 lbs. . . . Born, Edmonton, Alta., January 5, 1966 . . . Shoots left.

Year	Team	League	Games	G.	A.	Pts.	Pen.
1982-83—Portland Winter Hawks	WHL	2	0	1	1	0	
1983-84—Portland Winter Hawks (c)	WHL	66	46	50	96	44	
1984-85—Portland Winter Hawks	WHL	67	63	75	138	41	
1985-86—Portland Winter Hawks	WHL	66	59	75	134	68	

(c)—June, 1984—Drafted by Boston Bruins as underage junior in NHL entry draft. Second Bruins pick, 40th overall, second round.

RUDY POESCHUK

Defense . . . 6'2" . . . 205 lbs. . . . Born, Terrace, B.C., September 19, 1966 . . . Shoots right . . . (December, 1984)—Knee injury.

Year	Team	League	Games	G.	A.	Pts.	Pen.
1983-84—Kamloops Jr. Oilers		WHL	47	3	9	12	93
1984-85—Kamloops Blazers (c)		WHL	34	6	7	13	100
1985-86—Kamloops Blazers		WHL	32	3	13	16	92

(c)—June, 1985—Drafted as underage junior by New York Rangers in 1985 NHL entry draft. Twelfth Rangers pick, 238th overall, 12th round.

GREGG POLAK

Center . . . 6'2" . . . 185 lbs. . . . Born, Providence, R.I., July 16, 1967 . . . Shoots left . . . Also plays Left Wing.

Year	Team	League	Games	G.	A.	Pts.	Pen.
1983-84—Lincoln, R.I.H.S.		R.I.H.S.	..	25	19	44	..
1984-85—Lincoln, R.I.H.S. (c)		R.I.H.S.	..	31	25	56	..
1985-86—Northeastern Univ.		H. East	4	1	1	2	6

(c)—June, 1985—Drafted by New Jersey Devils in 1985 NHL entry draft. Fifth Devils pick, 66th overall, fourth round.

DENNIS DANIEL POLONICH

Center and Right Wing . . . 5'6" . . . 166 lbs. . . . Born, Foam Lake, Sask., December 4, 1953 . . . Shoots right . . . Missed part of 1975-76 season with shoulder separation . . . (1978-79) Suffered severe facial injuries in stick-swinging incident with Wilf Paiement . . . (January, 1985)—Ankle injury.

Year	Team	League	Games	G.	A.	Pts.	Pen.
1971-72—Flin Flon Bombers		WCHL	65	9	21	30	200
1972-73—Flin Flon Bombers (c)		WCHL	68	26	48	74	222
1973-74—London Lions		England	67	17	43	60	57
1974-75—Virginia Wings		AHL	60	14	20	34	194
1974-75—Detroit Red Wings		NHL	4	0	0	0	0
1975-76—Kalamazoo Wings		IHL	5	1	8	9	32
1975-76—Detroit Red Wings		NHL	57	11	12	23	302
1976-77—Detroit Red Wings		NHL	79	18	28	46	274
1977-78—Detroit Red Wings		NHL	79	16	19	35	254
1978-79—Detroit Red Wings		NHL	62	10	12	22	208
1979-80—Detroit Red Wings		NHL	66	2	8	10	127
1980-81—Detroit Red Wings		NHL	32	2	2	4	77
1980-81—Adirondack Red Wings		AHL	40	16	13	29	99
1981-82—Adirondack Red Wings		AHL	80	30	26	56	202
1982-83—Detroit Red Wings		NHL	11	0	1	1	0
1982-83—Adirondack Red Wings		AHL	61	18	22	40	128
1983-84—Adirondack Red Wings		AHL	66	14	26	40	122
1984-85—Adirondack Red Wings		AHL	53	18	17	35	153
1985-86—Muskegon Lumberjacks (d)		IHL	78	32	36	68	222
NHL TOTALS			390	59	82	141	1242

(c)—Drafted from Flin Flon Bombers by Detroit Red Wings in eighth round of 1973 amateur draft.
(d)—September, 1985—Signed by Muskegon Lumberjacks as a free agent.

JIRI PONER

Right Wing . . . 6'2" . . . 175 lbs. . . . Born, Czechoslovakia, February 9, 1964 . . . Shoots left.

Year	Team	League	Games	G.	A.	Pts.	Pen.
1981-82—Czech. Nat. Jr. Team		Int'l	8	4	3	7	4
1982-83—...............			..	..	..	..	..
1983-84—Landshut Jr. (c)		West Germany	44	72	75	147	....
1984-85—Indianapolis Checkers		IHL	26	3	10	13	26
1984-85—Springfield Indians		AHL	27	2	4	6	17
1985-86—Indianapolis Checkers		IHL	3	0	0	0	2
1985-86—Muskegon Lumberjacks		IHL	70	17	43	60	118

(c)—June, 1984—Drafted by Minnesota North Stars in NHL entry draft. Fourth North Stars pick, 89th overall, fifth round.

PAUL POOLEY

Center . . . 6' . . . 175 lbs. . . . Born, Exeter, Ont., August 2, 1960 . . . Shoots left . . . Twin brother of Perry Pooley.

Year	Team	League	Games	G.	A.	Pts.	Pen.
1980-81—Ohio State University (c)		CCHA	38	28	31	59	41
1981-82—Ohio State University		CCHA	34	21	24	45	34
1982-83—Ohio State University		CCHA	36	33	36	69	50
1983-84—Ohio State University (d-e)		CCHA	41	32	64	96	40
1984-85—Sherbrooke Canadiens		AHL	57	18	17	35	16

Year	Team	League	Games	G.	A.	Pts.	Pen.
1984-85—Winnipeg Jets		NHL	12	0	2	2	0
1985-86—Winnipeg Jets		NHL	3	0	1	1	0
1985-86—Sherbrooke Canadiens		AHL	70	20	21	41	31
NHL TOTALS			15	0	3	3	0

(c)—Co-winner of CCHA Rookie-of-the-Year award (with Jeff Poeschl).
(d)—Named CCHA Player of the Year in 1983-84.
(e)—May, 1984—Signed by Winnipeg Jets as a free agent.

PERRY POOLEY

Right Wing . . . 6' . . . 175 lbs. . . . Born, Exeter, Ont., August 2, 1960 . . . Shoots right . . . Twin brother of Paul Pooley.

Year	Team	League	Games	G.	A.	Pts.	Pen.
1980-81—Ohio State University		CCHA	37	9	15	24	63
1981-82—Ohio State University		CCHA	34	8	8	16	24
1982-83—Ohio State University		CCHA	40	29	26	55	36
1983-84—Ohio State University (c)		CCHA	41	39	40	79	28
1984-85—Sherbrooke Canadiens		AHL	69	10	18	28	16
1985-86—Sherbrooke Canadiens		AHL	67	12	19	31	15

(c)—May, 1984—Signed by Winnipeg Jets as a free agent.

DON PORTER

Left Wing . . . 6'3" . . . 190 lbs. . . . Born, Geraldton, Ont., May 25, 1966 . . . Shoots left.

Year	Team	League	Games	G.	A.	Pts.	Pen.
1983-84—Michigan Tech. (c)		CCHA	31	4	4	8	8
1984-85—Michigan Tech.		WCHA	34	12	11	23	10
1985-86—Michigan Tech.		WCHA	40	17	10	27	28

(c)—June, 1984—Drafted as underage junior by St. Louis Blues in NHL entry draft. Tenth Blues pick, 148th overall, eighth round.

VICTOR POSA

Defense . . . 6'1" . . . 195 lbs. . . . Born, Bari, Italy, May 11, 1966 . . . Shoots left . . . Also plays Left Wing.

Year	Team	League	Games	G.	A.	Pts.	Pen.
1983-84—Henry Carr H.S.		OHA	25	16	21	37	139
1984-85—University of Wisconsin (c)		WCHA	33	1	5	6	47
1985-86—Toronto Marlboros		OHL	48	28	34	62	116
1985-86—Chicago Black Hawks		NHL	2	0	0	0	2
NHL TOTALS			2	0	0	0	2

(c)—June, 1985—Drafted by Chicago Black Hawks in 1985 NHL entry draft. Seventh Black Hawks pick, 137th overall, seventh round.

MIKE POSAVAD

Defense . . . 6' . . . 196 lbs. . . . Born, Brantford, Ont., January 3, 1964 . . . Shoots right . . . (December, 1980)—Broken nose . . . Brother-in-law of Kerry Huffman.

Year	Team	League	Games	G.	A.	Pts.	Pen.
1979-80—Brantford Jr. 'B'		OPJHL	43	11	22	33	18
1980-81—Peterborough Petes		OHL	58	3	12	15	55
1981-82—Peterborough Petes (b-c)		OHL	64	7	23	30	110
1982-83—Peterborough Petes		OHL	70	1	36	37	68
1982-83—Salt Lake Golden Eagles		CHL	1	0	0	0	0
1983-84—Peterborough Petes		OHL	63	3	25	28	78
1984-85—Peoria Rivermen		IHL	67	2	19	21	58
1985-86—St. Louis Blues		NHL	6	0	0	0	0
1985-86—Peoria Rivermen		IHL	72	1	17	18	75
NHL TOTALS			6	0	0	0	0

(c)—June, 1982—Drafted as underage junior by St. Louis Blues in 1982 NHL entry draft. First Blues pick, 50th overall, third round.

MICHAEL POSMA

Defense . . . 6'1" . . . 195 lbs. . . . Born, Utica, N.Y., December 16, 1967 . . . Shoots right.

Year	Team	League	Games	G.	A.	Pts.	Pen.
1984-85—Buffalo Junior Sabres		NAJHL	43	4	28	32	....
1985-86—Buffalo Junior Sabres (c)		NAJHL	40	16	47	63	62

(c)—June, 1986—Drafted by St. Louis Blues in 1986 NHL entry draft. Second Blues pick, 31st overall, second round.

DENIS CHARLES POTVIN

Defense . . . 6' . . . 204 lbs. . . . Born, Hull, Que., October 29, 1953 . . . Shoots left . . . Brother of Jean Potvin . . . Missed part of 1971-72 season with broken wrist . . . Set Jr. "A" OHA record for points by a defenseman in season (1972-73) . . . Set NHL record for goals in rookie season by defenseman with 17 in 1973-74 (broken by Barry Beck in 1977-78) . . . (October 14, 1978)—Set NHL defenseman record with three goals in one period in 10-7 loss at Toronto . . . Missed much of 1979-80 season after surgery to correct stretched ligaments in thumb . . . Set NHL record for most points by a defenseman (25) in the playoffs in 1981 (Broken by Paul Coffey in 1985 playoffs) . . . (May 21, 1981)—Pulled groin in final game of Stanley Cup Playoffs, aggravated injury during Canada Cup Tournament in August, 1981 and did not play until November 14, 1981 . . . Set NHL record for most career playoff assists with 101 (broke Jean Beliveau's record of 97 career playoff assists) . . . (November 21, 1985)—Missed four games with an ear infection . . . (February 5, 1986)—Injured ankle at Chicago and missed one game . . . (1985-86)—Became all-time NHL leader in goals and points by a defenseman, breaking records of Bobby Orr.

Year	Team	League	Games	G.	A.	Pts.	Pen.
1968-69—Ottawa 67's		Jr. "A" OHA	46	12	25	37	83
1969-70—Ottawa 67's		Jr. "A" OHA	42	13	18	31	97
1970-71—Ottawa 67's (a)		Jr. "A" OHA	57	20	58	78	200
1971-72—Ottawa 67's (a-c)		Jr. "A" OHA	48	15	45	60	188
1972-73—Ottawa 67's (a-c-d)		Jr. "A" OHA	61	35	88	123	232
1973-74—New York Islanders (e-f)		NHL	77	17	37	54	175
1974-75—New York Islanders (a)		NHL	79	21	55	76	105
1975-76—New York Islanders (a-g-h)		NHL	78	31	67	98	100
1976-77—New York Islanders (b)		NHL	80	25	55	80	103
1977-78—New York Islanders (a-g)		NHL	80	30	64	94	81
1978-79—New York Islanders (a-g)		NHL	73	31	70	101	58
1979-80—New York Islanders		NHL	31	8	33	41	44
1980-81—New York Islanders (a)		NHL	74	20	56	76	104
1981-82—New York Islanders		NHL	60	24	37	61	83
1982-83—New York Islanders		NHL	69	12	54	66	60
1983-84—New York Islanders		NHL	78	22	63	85	87
1984-85—New York Islanders		NHL	77	17	51	68	96
1985-86—New York Islanders		NHL	74	21	38	59	78
NHL TOTALS			930	279	680	959	1174

(c)—Won Max Kaminsky Memorial Trophy (Outstanding Defenseman).
(d)—Drafted from Ottawa 67's by New York Islanders in first round of 1973 amateur draft.
(e)—Won Calder Memorial Trophy.
(f)—Named NHL's East Division rookie of the year in poll of players by THE SPORTING NEWS.
(g)—Won James Norris Memorial Trophy (outstanding Defenseman).
(h)—Tied for lead in assists (14) during playoffs.

DANIEL POUDRIER

Defense . . . 6'2" . . . 175 lbs. . . . Born, Thetford Mines, Que., February 15, 1964 . . . Shoots left.

Year	Team	League	Games	G.	A.	Pts.	Pen.
1980-81—Magog AAA Midget		QAAAMHL	26	8	8	16	18
1981-82—Shawinigan Cataracts (c)		QMJHL	64	6	18	24	26
1982-83—Shawinigan Cataracts		QHL	67	6	28	34	31
1983-84—Drummondville Voltigeurs		QHL	64	7	28	35	15
1984-85—Fredericton Express		AHL	1	0	0	0	0
1984-85—Muskegon Lumberjacks		IHL	82	9	30	39	10
1985-86—Fredericton Express		AHL	65	5	26	31	9
1985-86—Quebec Nordiques		NHL	13	1	5	6	10
NHL TOTALS			13	1	5	6	10

(c)—June, 1982—Drafted as underage junior by Quebec Nordiques in 1982 NHL entry draft. Sixth Nordiques pick, 131st overall, seventh round.

DAVE POULIN

Center . . . 5'11" . . . 175 lbs. . . . Born, Mississauga, Ont., December 17, 1958 . . . Shoots left . . . (1983-84)—Set Philadelphia record for most points by a rookie . . . (February 13, 1986)—Missed one game with back spasms.

Year	Team	League	Games	G.	A.	Pts.	Pen.
1978-79—University of Notre Dame		WCHA	37	28	31	59	32
1979-80—University of Notre Dame		WCHA	24	19	24	43	46
1980-81—University of Notre Dame		WCHA	35	13	22	35	53
1981-82—University of Notre Dame		CCHA	39	29	30	59	44
1982-83—Rogle (c)		Sweden	33	35	18	53	..
1982-83—Maine Mariners		AHL	16	7	9	16	2

Year	Team	League	Games	G.	A.	Pts.	Pen.
1982-83—Philadelphia Flyers		NHL	2	2	0	2	2
1983-84—Philadelphia Flyers		NHL	73	31	45	76	47
1984-85—Philadelphia Flyers		NHL	73	30	44	74	59
1985-86—Philadelphia Flyers		NHL	79	27	42	69	49
NHL TOTALS			227	90	131	221	157

(c)—February, 1983—Signed by Philadelphia Flyers as free agent.

IAN POUND

Defense . . . 6'1" . . . 185 lbs. . . . Born, Brockville, Ont., January 22, 1967 . . . Shoots left.

Year	Team	League	Games	G.	A.	Pts.	Pen.
1983-84—Ottawa East Midget		OHA	36	10	17	27	64
1984-85—Kitchener Rangers (c)		OHL	57	1	9	10	60
1985-86—Kitchener Rangers		OHL	63	2	12	14	87

(c)—June, 1985—Drafted as underage junior by Chicago Black Hawks in 1985 NHL entry draft. Eleventh Black Hawks pick, 221st overall, 11th round.

GARTH PREMAK

Defense . . . 6'1" . . . 185 lbs. . . . Born, Ituna, Sask., March 15, 1968 . . . Shoots left . . . (November, 1984)—Broken hand.

Year	Team	League	Games	G.	A.	Pts.	Pen.
1984-85—Red Deer Rustlers		AJHL	46	8	30	38	56
1985-86—New Westminister Bruins (c)		WHL	72	10	18	28	55

(c)—June, 1986—Drafted as underage junior by Boston Bruins in 1986 NHL entry draft. Fifth Bruins pick, 118th overall, sixth round.

WAYNE PRESLEY

Right Wing . . . 5'11" . . . 175 lbs. . . . Born, Dearborn, Mich., March 23, 1965 . . . Shoots right.

Year	Team	League	Games	G.	A.	Pts.	Pen.
1981-82—Detroit Little Ceasars		Mich. Midget	61	38	56	94	146
1982-83—Kitchener Rangers (c)		OHL	70	39	48	87	99
1983-84—Kitchener Rangers (a-d)		OHL	70	63	76	139	156
1984-85—Kitchener Rangers (e)		OHL	31	25	21	46	77
1984-85—Sault Ste. Marie Greyhounds		OHL	11	5	9	14	14
1984-85—Chicago Black Hawks		NHL	3	0	1	1	0
1985-86—Nova Scotia Oilers		AHL	29	6	9	15	22
1985-86—Chicago Black Hawks		NHL	38	7	8	15	38
NHL TOTALS			41	7	9	16	38

(c)—June, 1983—Drafted as underage junior by Chicago Black Hawks in 1983 NHL entry draft. Second Black Hawks pick, 39th overall, second round.

(d)—Won Jim Mahon Memorial Trophy (Highest scoring OHL right wing).

(e)—January, 1985—Traded by Kitchener Rangers to Sault Ste. Marie Greyhounds for Shawn Tyers.

MIKE PRESTIDGE

Center . . . 6'3" . . . 203 lbs. . . . Born, Weston, Ont., August 14, 1959 . . . Shoots left.

Year	Team	League	Games	G.	A.	Pts.	Pen.
1978-79—Clarkson College		ECAC	31	16	24	40	2
1979-80—Clarkson College (a)		ECAC	34	28	30	58	24
1980-81—Clarkson College		ECAC	31	13	17	30	22
1981-82—Oklahoma City Stars (c)		CHL	53	20	19	39	6
1982-83—Colorado Flames		CHL	62	13	26	39	17
1983-84—Peoria Prancers		IHL	68	40	40	80	4
1984-85—Peoria Rivermen		IHL	82	42	48	90	27
1985-86—Peoria Rivermen		IHL	81	31	56	87	16

(c)—June, 1981—Signed by Calgary Flames as a free agent.

RICHARD JOHN (RICH) PRESTON

Left Wing . . . 5'11" . . . 185 lbs. . . . Born, Regina, Sask., May 22, 1952 . . . Shoots right . . . Attended Denver University . . . Son of Ken Preston, former general manager of Saskatchewan Roughriders football team . . . Also plays Right Wing . . . Missed final weeks of 1977-78 season and playoffs with fractured left ankle . . . (November 16, 1980)—Tore cartilage in left knee during a fight. Injury required surgery . . . (December 21, 1985)—Missed three games with lacerations suffered at Hartford.

Year	Team	League	Games	G.	A.	Pts.	Pen.
1969-70—Regina Pats		SJHL	....	15	15	30	4
1970-71—Denver University		WCHA	17	0	1	1	0

Year	Team	League	Games	G.	A.	Pts.	Pen.
1971-72—Denver University		WCHA	33	3	11	14	18
1972-73—Denver University		WCHA	39	23	25	48	24
1973-74—Denver University (c)		WCHA	38	20	25	45	36
1974-75—Houston Aeros		WHA	78	20	21	41	10
1975-76—Houston Aeros		WHA	77	22	33	55	33
1976-77—Houston Aeros		WHA	80	38	41	79	54
1977-78—Houston Aeros (d)		WHA	73	25	25	50	52
1978-79—Winnipeg Jets (e-f)		WHA	80	28	32	60	88
1979-80—Chicago Black Hawks		NHL	80	31	30	61	70
1980-81—Chicago Black Hawks		NHL	47	7	14	21	24
1981-82—Chicago Black Hawks		NHL	75	15	28	43	30
1982-83—Chicago Black Hawks		NHL	79	25	28	53	64
1983-84—Chicago Black Hawks (g)		NHL	75	10	18	28	50
1984-85—New Jersey Devils		NHL	75	12	15	27	26
1985-86—New Jersey Devils (h)		NHL	76	19	22	41	65
WHA TOTALS			388	133	152	285	237
NHL TOTALS			507	119	155	274	329

(c)—Signed by Houston Aeros (WHA), June, 1974.
(d)—Sold to Winnipeg Jets with Houston Aeros' franchise, July, 1978.
(e)—Named most valuable player of WHA playoffs.
(f)—May, 1979—Signed by Chicago Black Hawks as a free agent.
(g)—June, 1984—Traded with Don Dietrich by Chicago Black Hawks to New Jersey Devils for Bob MacMillan and past considerations (Devils did not draft Ed Olczyk).
(h)—July, 1986—Released by New Jersey Devils and signed by Chicago Black Hawks as a free agent.

SHAUN PATRICK (PAT) PRICE

Defense . . . 6'2" . . . 200 lbs. . . . Born, Nelson, B.C., March 24, 1955 . . . Shoots left . . . (January, 1983)—Headaches and nervous disorder . . . (November, 1984)—Separated shoulder . . . (January 2, 1986)—Sprained knee at Quebec and missed 11 games . . . (February 12, 1986)—Apendectomy and missed 13 games.

Year	Team	League	Games	G.	A.	Pts.	Pen.
1970-71—Saskatoon Blades		WCHL	66	2	16	18	56
1971-72—Saskatoon Blades		WCHL	66	10	48	58	85
1972-73—Saskatoon Blades		WCHL	67	12	56	68	134
1973-74—Saskatoon Blades (a-c-d)		WCHL	67	27	68	81	147
1974-75—Vancouver Blazers (e)		WHA	69	5	29	34	54
1975-76—Fort Worth Texans		CHL	72	6	44	50	119
1975-76—New York Islanders		NHL	4	0	2	2	2
1976-77—New York Islanders		NHL	71	3	22	25	25
1977-78—Rochester Americans		AHL	5	2	1	3	9
1977-78—New York Islanders		NHL	52	2	10	12	27
1978-79—New York Islanders (f)		NHL	55	3	11	14	50
1979-80—Edmonton Oilers		NHL	75	11	21	32	134
1980-81—Edmonton Oilers (g)		NHL	59	8	24	32	193
1980-81—Pittsburgh Penguins		NHL	13	0	10	10	33
1981-82—Pittsburgh Penguins		NHL	77	7	31	38	322
1982-83—Pittsburgh Penguins (h)		NHL	38	1	11	12	104
1982-83—Quebec Nordiques		NHL	14	1	2	3	28
1983-84—Quebec Nordiques		NHL	72	3	25	28	188
1984-85—Quebec Nordiques		NHL	68	1	26	27	118
1985-86—Quebec Nordiques		NHL	53	3	13	16	78
NHL TOTALS			651	43	208	251	1302
WHA TOTALS			69	5	29	34	54

(c)—Selected by Vancouver Blazers in WHA amateur player draft, May, 1974.
(d)—Named Outstanding Defenseman in WCHL.
(e)—Drafted from Saskatoon Blades by New York Islanders in first round of 1975 amateur draft.
(f)—June, 1979—Selected by Edmonton Oilers in NHL expansion draft.
(g)—March, 1981—Traded by Edmonton Oilers to Pittsburgh Penguins for Pat Hughes.
(h)—December, 1982—Released by Pittsburgh Penguins and subsequently claimed on waivers by Quebec Nordiques for $2,500.

KEN PRIESTLY

Center . . . 5'11" . . . 175 lbs. . . . Born, Vancouver, B.C., August 24, 1967 . . . Shoots left . . . (November, 1984)—Shoulder separation.

Year	Team	League	Games	G.	A.	Pts.	Pen.
1983-84—Victoria Cougars		WHL	55	10	18	28	31
1984-85—Victoria Cougars (c)		WHL	50	25	37	62	48
1985-86—Victoria Cougars (b)		WHL	72	73	72	145	45
1985-86—Rochester Americans		AHL	4	0	2	2	0

(c)—June, 1985—Drafted as underage junior by Buffalo Sabres in 1985 NHL entry draft. Fifth Sabres pick, 98th overall, fifth round.

ROBERT PROBERT

Left Wing . . . 6'3" . . . 205 lbs. . . . Born, Windsor, Ont., June 5, 1965 . . . Shoots left.

Year	Team	League	Games	G.	A.	Pts.	Pen.
1981-82—Windsor Club 240		Ont. Midget	55	60	40	100	40
1982-83—Brantford Alexanders (c)		OHL	51	12	16	28	133
1983-84—Brantford Alexanders		OHL	65	35	38	73	189
1984-85—Hamilton Steelhawks		OHL	4	0	1	1	21
1984-85—Sault Ste. Marie Greyhounds		OHL	44	20	52	72	172
1985-86—Adirondack Red Wings		AHL	32	12	15	27	152
1985-86—Detroit Red Wings		NHL	44	8	13	21	186
NHL TOTALS			44	8	13	21	186

(c)—June, 1983—Drafted as underage junior by Detroit Red Wings in 1983 NHL entry draft. Third Red Wings pick, 46th overall, third round.

BRIAN PROPP

Left Wing . . . 5'9" . . . 185 lbs. . . . Born, Lanigan, Sask., February 15, 1959 . . . Shoots left . . . All-time Western Hockey League scoring leader with 511 points . . . Brother of Ron Propp . . . (January, 1985)—Given four-game suspension . . . (March 4, 1986)—Injured eye vs. Buffalo and missed eight games.

Year	Team	League	Games	G.	A.	Pts.	Pen.
1975-76—Melville Millionaires		SJHL	57	76	92	168	36
1976-77—Brandon Wheat Kings (b-c-d)		WCHL	72	55	80	135	47
1977-78—Brandon Wheat Kings (a-e)		WCHL	70	70	*112	*182	200
1978-79—Brandon Wheat Kings (a-e-f)		WHL	71	*94	*100	*194	127
1979-80—Philadelphia Flyers		NHL	80	34	41	75	54
1980-81—Philadelphia Flyers		NHL	79	26	40	66	110
1981-82—Philadelphia Flyers		NHL	80	44	47	91	117
1982-83—Philadelphia Flyers		NHL	80	40	42	82	72
1983-84—Philadelphia Flyers		NHL	79	39	53	92	37
1984-85—Philadelphia Flyers		NHL	76	43	53	96	43
1985-86—Philadelphia Flyers		NHL	72	40	57	97	47
NHL TOTALS			546	266	333	599	480

(c)—Named WCHL Rookie of the Year.
(d)—Shared lead in goals (14) during playoffs.
(e)—WCHL leading scorer.
(f)—August, 1979—Drafted by Philadelphia Flyers in entry draft. First Flyers pick, 14th overall, first round.

CHRIS PRYOR

Defense . . . 5'11" . . . 210 lbs. . . . Born, St. Paul, Minn., January 31, 1961 . . . Shoots right.

Year	Team	League	Games	G.	A.	Pts.	Pen.
1979-80—Univ. of New Hampshire		ECAC	27	9	13	22	27
1980-81—Univ. of New Hampshire		ECAC	33	10	27	37	36
1981-82—Univ. of New Hampshire		ECAC	35	3	16	19	36
1982-83—Univ. of New Hampshire		ECAC	34	4	9	13	23
1983-84—Salt Lake Golden Eagles		CHL	72	7	21	28	215
1984-85—Springfield Indians		AHL	77	3	21	24	158
1984-85—Minnesota North Stars		NHL	4	0	0	0	16
1985-86—Springfield Indians		AHL	55	4	16	20	104
1985-86—Minnesota North Stars		NHL	7	0	1	1	0
NHL TOTALS			11	0	1	1	16

GREG PUHALSKI

Left Wing . . . 6' . . . 170 lbs. . . . Born, Thunder Bay, Ont., January 1, 1965 . . . Shoots left . . . Also plays Center.

Year	Team	League	Games	G.	A.	Pts.	Pen.
1981-82—Thunder Bay Maroons		Ont. Midgets	62	50	72	122	69
1982-83—Kitchener Rangers (c)		OHL	70	27	51	78	28
1983-84—Kitchener Rangers		OHL	44	30	69	99	55
1984-85—Kitchener Rangers (d)		OHL	28	17	29	46	42
1984-85—London Knights		OHL	23	8	29	37	17
1985-86—London Knights		OHL	58	38	63	101	59

(c)—June, 1983—Drafted as underage junior by Boston Bruins in NHL entry draft. Third Bruins pick, 62nd overall, third round.
(d)—January, 1985—Traded with Garnet McKechney by Kitchener Rangers to London Knights for Brad Sparkes, third round 1985 priority draft pick (Paul Porter) and future considerations.

PAUL PULIS

Right Wing . . . 6'5" . . . 200 lbs. . . . Born, Duluth, Minn., January 14, 1965 . . . Shoots right.

Year	Team	League	Games	G.	A.	Pts.	Pen.
1982-83	Hibbing H.S. (c)	Minn.H.S.	20	20	16	36	..
1983-84	University of Ill.-Chicago	CCHA	25	1	2	3	12
1984-85	University of Ill.-Chicago	CCHA	31	0	2	2	11
1985-86	University of Ill.-Chicago	CCHA	28	7	2	9	14

(c)—June, 1983—Drafted by Minnesota North Stars in NHL entry draft. Tenth North Stars pick, 176th overall, ninth round.

JOHN PURVES

Right Wing . . . 6'2" . . . 185 lbs. . . . Born, Toronto, Ont., February 12, 1968 . . . Shoots right.

Year	Team	League	Games	G.	A.	Pts.	Pen.
1984-85	Belleville Bulls	OHL	55	15	14	29	39
1984-85	Belleville Bulls	OHL	16	3	9	12	6
1984-85	Hamilton Steelhawks (c)	OHL	36	13	28	41	36

(c)—June, 1986—Drafted as underage junior by Washington Capitals in 1986 NHL entry draft. Sixth Capitals pick, 103rd overall, fifth round.

JEFF PYLE

Center . . . 6' . . . 175 lbs. . . . Born, Ft. Leonard Wood, Mo., October 7, 1958 . . . Shoots left.

Year	Team	League	Games	G.	A.	Pts.	Pen.
1978-79	Univ. of Northern Michigan	CCHA	34	15	27	42	4
1979-80	Univ. of Northern Michigan	CCHA	41	26	37	63	12
1980-81	Univ. of Northern Mich.(a-c-d)	CCHA	40	*35	53	88	20
1981-82	Saginaw Gears	IHL	4	2	3	5	0
1981-82	Mohawk Valley Stars	ACHL	29	16	34	50	16
1981-82	Binghamton Whalers	AHL	16	1	1	2	15
1982-83	Mohawk Valley Stars (a)	ACHL	59	53	48	101	44
1983-84	Flint Generals (e)	IHL	80	44	59	103	20
1984-85	Flint Generals	IHL	82	35	59	94	51
1985-86	Saginaw Generals	IHL	80	39	70	109	49

(c)—Named CCHA Most Valuable Player.

(d)—September, 1981—Signed by Hartford Whalers as a free agent.

(e)—Led IHL playoffs with seven goals and shared point lead (15) with Toledo's Kevin Conway and Jim Bissett and Flint's Lawrie Nisker.

JOEL NORMAN QUENNEVILLE

Defense . . . 6' . . . 187 lbs. . . . Born, Windsor, Ont., September 15, 1958 . . . Shoots left . . . (March, 1980)—Rib-cage injury . . . (March, 1980)—Surgery to repair torn ligaments in ring finger of left hand . . . (January 4, 1982)—Sprained ankle, twisted knee and suffered facial cuts when he crashed into boards during a Rockies practice . . . (December 16, 1985)—Pulled stomach muscle at Montreal and missed four games.

Year	Team	League	Games	G.	A.	Pts.	Pen.
1975-76	Windsor Spitfires	Jr."A"OHA	66	15	33	48	61
1976-77	Windsor Spitfires	Jr."A"OHA	65	19	59	78	169
1977-78	Windsor Spitfires (b-c)	Jr."A"OHA	66	27	76	103	114
1978-79	Toronto Maple Leafs	NHL	61	2	9	11	60
1978-79	New Brunswick Hawks	AHL	16	1	10	11	10
1979-80	Toronto Maple Leafs (d)	NHL	32	1	4	5	24
1979-80	Colorado Rockies	NHL	35	5	7	12	26
1980-81	Colorado Rockies	NHL	71	10	24	34	86
1981-82	Colorado Rockies	NHL	64	5	10	15	55
1982-83	New Jersey Devils (e-f)	NHL	74	5	12	17	46
1983-84	Hartford Whalers	NHL	80	5	8	13	95
1984-85	Hartford Whalers	NHL	79	6	16	22	96
1985-86	Hartford Whalers	NHL	71	5	20	25	83
	NHL TOTALS		567	44	110	154	571

(c)—Drafted from Windsor Spitfires by Toronto Maple Leafs in second round of 1978 amateur draft.

(d)—December, 1979—Traded with Lanny McDonald by Toronto Maple Leafs to Colorado Rockies for Wilf Paiement and Pat Hickey.

(e)—July, 1983—Traded by New Jersey Devils with Steve Tambellini to Calgary Flames for Mel Bridgman and Phil Russell.

(f)—August, 1983—Traded by Calgary Flames with Richie Dunn to Hartford Whalers for Mickey Volcan and third-round draft choice in 1984.

THOMAS QUINLAN

Right Wing ... 6'2" ... 185 lbs. ... Born, St. Paul, Minn., March 27, 1968 ... Shoots right ... Selected by Toronto Blue Jays in 27th round of June, 1986 baseball amateur draft.

Year	Team	League	Games	G.	A.	Pts.	Pen.
1984-85—Hill Murray H.S.		Minn.	28	21	29	50	....
1985-86—Hill Murray H.S. (c)		Minn.	26	24	29	53	....

(c)—June, 1986—Drafted by Calgary Flames in 1986 NHL entry draft. Third Flames pick, 79th overall, fourth round.

DAN QUINN

Center ... 5'11" ... 175 lbs. ... Born, Ottawa, Ont., June 1, 1965 ... Shoots left ... Son of Peter Quinn (former CFL player with Ottawa).

Year	Team	League	Games	G.	A.	Pts.	Pen.
1981-82—Belleville Bulls		OHL	67	19	32	51	41
1982-83—Belleville Bulls (c)		OHL	70	59	88	147	27
1983-84—Belleville Bulls		OHL	24	23	36	59	12
1983-84—Calgary Flames		NHL	54	19	33	52	20
1984-85—Calgary Flames		NHL	74	20	38	58	22
1985-86—Calgary Flames		NHL	78	30	42	72	44
NHL TOTALS			206	69	113	182	86

(c)—June, 1983—Drafted as underage junior by Calgary Flames in 1983 NHL entry draft. First Flames pick, 13th overall, first round.

DAVID QUINN

Defense ... 6' ... 205 lbs. ... Born, Cranston, R.I., July 30, 1966 ... Shoots left.

Year	Team	League	Games	G.	A.	Pts.	Pen.
1983-84—Kent Prep (c)		Conn.H.S.	24	12	20	32	..
1984-85—Boston University		H. East	30	3	11	14	26
1985-86—Boston University (a)		H. East	37	2	20	22	58

(c)—June, 1984—Drafted by Minnesota North Stars in NHL entry draft. First North Stars pick, 13th overall, first round.

DOUG QUINN

Defense ... 6'2" ... 177 lbs. ... Born, Red Deer, Alta., April 2, 1965 ... Shoots left.

Year	Team	League	Games	G.	A.	Pts.	Pen.
1982-83—Nanaimo Islanders (c)		WHL	55	3	14	17	81
1983-84—New Westminster Bruins		WHL	68	8	22	30	122
1984-85—New Westminster Bruins		WHL	41	7	12	19	82
1985-86—New Westminster Bruins (d)		WHL	10	1	5	6	31
1985-86—Lethbridge Broncos		WHL	58	7	27	34	63

(c)—June, 1982—Drafted as underage junior by Vancouver Canucks in 1983 NHL entry draft. Fifth Canucks pick, 90th overall, fifth round.

(d)—November, 1985—Traded by New Westminster Bruins to Lethbridge Broncos for Gary Ruff, Drago Adam and Tim Brantner.

JOSEPH D. QUINN

Right Wing ... 6'1" ... 185 lbs. ... Born, Calgary, Alta., February 19, 1967 ... Shoots right.

Year	Team	League	Games	G.	A.	Pts.	Pen.
1984-85—Abbotsford Flyers		BCJHL	31	7	29	36	52
1985-86—Calgary Canucks (c)		AJHL	29	17	24	41	20

(c)—June, 1986—Drafted by Hartford Whalers in 1986 NHL entry draft. Fifth Whalers pick, 116th overall, sixth round.

KEN QUINNEY

Right Wing ... 5'10" ... 195 lbs. ... Born, New Westminster, B.C., May 23, 1965 ... Shoots right ... (February, 1986)—Broken wrist.

Year	Team	League	Games	G.	A.	Pts.	Pen.
1981-82—Calgary Wranglers		WHL	63	11	17	28	55
1982-83—Calgary Wranglers		WHL	71	26	25	51	71
1983-84—Calgary Wranglers (c)		WHL	71	64	54	118	38
1984-85—Calgary Wranglers (a)		WHL	56	47	67	114	65
1985-86—Fredericton Express		AHL	61	11	26	37	34

(c)—June, 1984—Drafted as underage junior by Quebec Nordiques in NHL entry draft. Ninth Nordiques pick, 203rd overall, 10th round.

MARK RAEDEKE

Center . . . 5'11" . . . 190 lbs. . . . Born, Regina, Sask., January 7, 1963 . . . Shoots left.

Year	Team	League	Games	G.	A.	Pts.	Pen.
1985-86	University of Regina (c)	CWUAA	27	15	19	34	136

(c)—July, 1986—Signed by New York Rangers as a free agent.

HERB RAGLAN

Right Wing . . . 6' . . . 200 lbs. . . . Born, Peterborough, Ont., August 5, 1967 . . . Shoots right . . . Son of Clare Raglan (Detroit and Chicago in early '50s) . . . (December, 1985)—Severely sprained ankle.

Year	Team	League	Games	G.	A.	Pts.	Pen.
1983-84	Peterborough Midget	OHA	26	39	21	60	60
1984-85	Kingston Canadians (c)	OHL	58	20	22	42	166
1985-86	Kingston Canadians	OHL	28	10	9	19	88
1985-86	St. Louis Blues	NHL	7	0	0	0	5
	NHL TOTALS		7	0	0	0	5

(c)—June, 1985—Drafted as underage junior by St. Louis Blues in 1985 NHL entry draft. First Blues pick, 37th overall, second round.

GEORGE ROBERT (ROB) RAMAGE

Defense . . . 6'2" . . . 210 lbs. . . . Born, Byron, Ont., January 11, 1959 . . . Shoots right . . . (March 22, 1986)—Sprained knee vs. Montreal.

Year	Team	League	Games	G.	A.	Pts.	Pen.
1975-76	London Knights	Jr."A"OHA	65	12	31	43	113
1976-77	London Knights	Jr."A"OHA	65	15	58	73	177
1977-78	London Knights (a-c-d)	Jr."A"OHA	59	17	47	64	162
1978-79	Birmingham Bulls (a-e)	WHA	80	12	36	48	165
1979-80	Colorado Rockies	NHL	75	8	20	28	135
1980-81	Colorado Rockies	NHL	79	20	42	62	193
1981-82	Colorado Rockies (f)	NHL	80	13	29	42	201
1982-83	St. Louis Blues	NHL	78	16	35	51	193
1983-84	St. Louis Blues	NHL	80	15	45	60	121
1984-85	St. Louis Blues	NHL	80	7	31	38	178
1985-86	St. Louis Blues	NHL	77	10	56	66	171
	WHA TOTALS		80	12	36	48	165
	NHL TOTALS		549	89	258	347	1192

(c)—Signed by Birmingham Bulls (WHA) as underage junior, July, 1978.
(d)—Shared Max Kaminsky Memorial Trophy (outstanding defenseman) with Brad Marsh.
(e)—Drafted by Colorado Rockies in 1979 entry draft. First Colorado pick, first overall, first round.
(f)—June, 1982—Traded by Colorado Rockies to St. Louis Blues for St. Louis' first-round draft choices in 1982 (Rocky Trottier) and 1983 (John MacLean).

MICHAEL ALLEN RAMSEY

Defense . . . 6'2" . . . 185 lbs. . . . Born, Minneapolis, Minn., December 3, 1960 . . . Shoots left . . . Attended University of Minnesota . . . Member of 1980 gold-medal U.S. Olympic hockey team . . . (December 4, 1983)—Dislocated thumb in game vs. Montreal.

Year	Team	League	Games	G.	A.	Pts.	Pen.
1978-79	University of Minnesota (c)	WCHA	26	6	11	17	30
1979-80	U.S. Olympic Team	Int'l	63	11	24	35	63
1979-80	Buffalo Sabres	NHL	13	1	6	7	6
1980-81	Buffalo Sabres	NHL	72	3	14	17	56
1981-82	Buffalo Sabres	NHL	80	7	23	30	56
1982-83	Buffalo Sabres	NHL	77	8	30	38	55
1983-84	Buffalo Sabres	NHL	72	9	22	31	82
1984-85	Buffalo Sabres	NHL	79	8	22	30	102
1985-86	Buffalo Sabres	NHL	76	7	21	28	117
	NHL TOTALS		469	43	138	181	474

(c)—August, 1979—Drafted by Buffalo Sabres in entry draft. First Buffalo pick, 11th overall, first round.

JOE RANGER

Defense . . . 6'4" . . . 225 lbs. . . . Born, Sudbury, Ont., January 11, 1968 . . . Shoots left.

Year	Team	League	Games	G.	A.	Pts.	Pen.
1984-85	London Knights	OHL	37	1	3	4	38
1985-86	London Knights (c-d)	OHL	36	0	8	8	54

(c)—February, 1986—Left team.
(d)—June, 1986—Drafted as underage junior by New York Rangers in 1986 entry draft. Tenth Rangers pick, 198th overall, 10th round.

CRAIG REDMOND

Defense . . . 5'10" . . . 190 lbs. . . . Born, Dawson Creek, B.C., September 22, 1965 . . . Shoots left . . . Second cousin of Mickey and Dick Redmond (former NHL players through the 1970s).

Year	Team	League	Games	G.	A.	Pts.	Pen.
1980-81	Abbotsford Flyers	BCJHL	40	15	22	37	..
1981-82	Abbotsford Flyers	BCJHL	45	30	76	106	..
1982-83	University of Denver (c)	WCHA	34	18	36	54	44
1983-84	Canadian Olympic Team (d)	Int'l	55	10	11	21	38
1984-85	Los Angeles Kings	NHL	79	6	33	39	57
1985-86	Los Angeles Kings	NHL	73	6	18	24	57
	NHL TOTALS		152	12	51	63	114

(c)—Won WCHA Rookie of the Year Award.
(d)—June, 1984—Drafted by Los Angeles Kings in NHL entry draft. First Kings pick, sixth overall, first round.

MARK REEDS

Right Wing . . . 5'10" . . . 188 lbs. . . . Born, Burlington, Ont., January 24, 1960 . . . Shoots right . . . (November 19, 1983)—Cryotherapy to repair the margins of his retina.

Year	Team	League	Games	G.	A.	Pts.	Pen.
1976-77	Markham Waxers	OPJHL	24	17	23	40	62
1976-77	Toronto Marlboros	OMJHL	18	6	7	13	6
1977-78	Peterborough Petes	OMJHL	68	11	27	36	67
1978-79	Peterborough Petes (c)	OMJHL	66	25	25	50	91
1979-80	Peterborough Petes	OMJHL	54	34	45	79	51
1980-81	Salt Lake Golden Eagles	CHL	74	15	45	60	81
1981-82	Salt Lake Golden Eagles	CHL	59	22	24	46	55
1981-82	St. Louis Blues	NHL	9	1	3	4	0
1982-83	Salt Lake Golden Eagles	CHL	55	16	26	42	32
1982-83	St. Louis Blues	NHL	20	5	14	19	6
1983-84	St. Louis Blues	NHL	65	11	14	25	23
1984-85	St. Louis Blues	NHL	80	9	30	39	25
1985-86	St. Louis Blues	NHL	78	10	28	38	28
	NHL TOTALS		252	36	89	125	82

(c)—August, 1979—Drafted by St. Louis Blues as an underage junior in NHL entry draft. Third St. Louis pick, 86th overall, fifth round.

JOE JAMES REEKIE

Defense . . . 6'2" . . . 176 lbs. . . . Born, Victoria, B.C., February 22, 1965 . . . Shoots left.

Year	Team	League	Games	G.	A.	Pts.	Pen.
1981-82	Nepean Raiders	CJHL	16	2	5	7	4
1982-83	North Bay Centennials (c)	OHL	59	2	9	11	49
1983-84	North Bay Centennials	OHL	9	1	0	1	18
1983-84	Cornwall Royals (d)	OHL	53	6	27	33	166
1984-85	Cornwall Royals (e)	OHL	65	19	63	82	134
1985-86	Rochester Americans	AHL	77	3	25	28	178
1985-86	Buffalo Sabres	NHL	3	0	0	0	14
	NHL TOTALS		3	0	0	0	14

(c)—June, 1983—Drafted as underage junior by Hartford Whalers in 1983 NHL entry draft. Eighth Whalers pick, 124th overall, seventh round.
(d)—June, 1984—Released by Hartford Whalers.
(e)—June, 1985—Drafted by Buffalo Sabres in 1985 NHL entry draft. Sixth Sabres pick, 119th overall, sixth round.

DAVID REID

Left Wing . . . 6'1" . . . 205 lbs. . . . Born, Toronto, Ont., May 15, 1964 . . . Shoots left . . . (November 14, 1985)—Sprained ankle at Toronto and missed four games.

Year	Team	League	Games	G.	A.	Pts.	Pen.
1980-81	Mississauga Midgets	Ont. Midget	39	21	32	53	....
1981-82	Peterborough Petes (c)	OHL	68	10	32	42	41
1982-83	Peterborough Petes	OHL	70	23	34	57	33
1983-84	Peterborough Petes	OHL	60	33	64	97	12
1983-84	Boston Bruins	NHL	8	1	0	1	2
1984-85	Hershey Bears	AHL	43	10	14	24	6
1984-85	Boston Bruins	NHL	35	14	13	27	27
1985-86	Moncton Golden Flames	AHL	26	14	18	32	4
1985-86	Boston Bruins	NHL	37	10	10	20	10
	NHL TOTALS		80	25	23	48	39

(c)—June, 1982—Drafted by Boston Bruins as underage junior in 1982 NHL entry draft. Fourth Bruins pick, 60th overall, third round.

DAVE REIERSON

Defense . . . 5'11" . . . 172 lbs. . . . Born, Bashaw, Alta., August 30, 1964 . . . Shoots right.

Year	Team	League	Games	G.	A.	Pts.	Pen.
1980-81	Prince Albert Raiders	SAJHL	73	14	39	53	..
1981-82	Prince Albert Raiders (c)	SAJHL	87	23	76	99	..
1982-83	Michigan Tech.	CCHA	38	2	14	16	58
1983-84	Michigan Tech.	CCHA	38	4	15	19	63
1984-85	Michigan Tech.	WCHA	36	5	27	32	76
1985-86	Michigan Tech.	WCHA	39	7	16	23	51

(c)—June, 1982—Drafted as underage junior by Calgary Flames in 1982 NHL entry draft. First Flames pick, 29th overall, second round.

PAUL REIFENBERGER

Right Wing . . . 5'11" . . . 191 lbs. . . . Born, St. Paul, Minn., May 27, 1963 . . . Shoots right.

Year	Team	League	Games	G.	A.	Pts.	Pen.
1985-86	College of St. Thomas (c)	.....	22	29	31	60	40

(c)—July, 1986—Signed by New York Rangers as a free agent.

PAUL REINHART

Defense . . . 5'11" . . . 216 lbs. . . . Born, Kitchener, Ont., January 8, 1960 . . . Shoots left . . . (January 13, 1981)—Strained ligaments . . . (September, 1981)—Injured ligaments in right ankle during Canada Cup . . . Brother of Kevin Reinhart (Toronto '78 draft pick, 132nd overall) . . . Set Flames club records for goals (18 in '80-81), assists (58 in '82-83) and points (75 in '82-83) by a defenseman in one season . . . (November 24, 1983)—Injured back in game vs. Winnipeg . . . (April, 1984)—Reinjured back in playoff series with Edmonton . . . (December, 1984)—Recurring back problems.

Year	Team	League	Games	G.	A.	Pts.	Pen.
1975-76	Kitchener Rangers	OMJHL	53	6	33	39	42
1976-77	Kitchener Rangers	OMJHL	51	4	14	18	16
1977-78	Kitchener Rangers	OMJHL	47	17	28	45	15
1978-79	Kitchener Rangers (c)	OMJHL	66	51	78	129	57
1979-80	Atlanta Flames	NHL	79	9	38	47	31
1980-81	Calgary Flames	NHL	74	18	49	67	52
1981-82	Calgary Flames	NHL	62	13	48	61	17
1982-83	Calgary Flames	NHL	78	17	58	75	28
1983-84	Calgary Flames	NHL	27	6	15	21	10
1984-85	Calgary Flames	NHL	75	23	46	69	18
1985-86	Calgary Flames	NHL	32	8	25	33	15
	NHL TOTALS		427	94	279	373	171

(c)—August, 1979—Drafted by Atlanta Flames as underage junior in NHL entry draft. First Atlanta pick, 12th overall, first round.

BRUCE RENDALL

Left Wing . . . 6'1" . . . 180 lbs. . . . Born, Thunder Bay, Ont., April 8, 1967 . . . Shoots left.

Year	Team	League	Games	G.	A.	Pts.	Pen.
1984-85	Chatham Maroons (c)	OHA	46	32	33	65	62
1985-86	Michigan State Univ.	CCHA	45	14	18	32	68

(c)—June, 1985—Drafted by Philadelphia Flyers in 1985 NHL entry draft. Second Flyers pick, 42nd overall, second round.

ROBERT REYNOLDS

Center . . . 5'11" . . . 175 lbs. . . . Born, Flint, Mich., July 14, 1967 . . . Shoots left . . . Also plays Left Wing.

Year	Team	League	Games	G.	A.	Pts.	Pen.
1983-84	St. Clair Shores Falcons	GLJHL	60	25	34	59	....
1984-85	St. Clair Shores Falcons (c)	GLJHL	43	20	30	50	....
1985-86	Michigan State Univ.	CCHA	45	9	10	19	26

(c)—June, 1985—Drafted by Toronto Maple Leafs in 1985 NHL entry draft. Tenth Maple Leafs pick, 190th overall, tenth round.

GRANT REZANSOFF

Center . . . 5'11" . . . 181 lbs. . . . Born, Surrey, B.C., March 3, 1961 . . . Shoots right.

Year	Team	League	Games	G.	A.	Pts.	Pen.
1978-79	Delta	BCJHL	61	42	45	87	22
1979-80	Victoria Cougars	WHL	67	17	19	36	7
1980-81	Victoria Cougars (c)	WHL	72	40	57	97	27

Year	Team	League	Games	G.	A.	Pts.	Pen.
1981-82—Muskegon Mohawks		IHL	37	15	11	26	4
1981-82—Oklahoma City Stars		CHL	45	15	20	35	10
1982-83—Colorado Flames		CHL	22	4	3	7	16
1982-83—Peoria Prancers		IHL	49	23	42	65	23
1983-84—Peoria Prancers		IHL	82	36	46	82	11
1984-85—Toledo Goaldiggers		IHL	25	9	10	19	0
1984-85—Salt Lake Golden Eagles (d)		IHL	37	12	17	29	29
1985-86—Peoria Rivermen (e)		IHL	80	30	47	77	23

(c)—August, 1981—Signed by Calgary Flames as a free agent.

(d)—February, 1985—Traded with Kevin Conway, Blake Stephan and Steve Harrison by Toledo Goaldiggers to Salt Lake Golden Eagles for Steve Martinson and Kurt Kleinendorst.

(e)—September, 1985—Signed by Peoria Rivermen as a free agent.

PATRICK WAYNE RIBBLE

Defense . . . 6'3" . . . 225 lbs. . . . Born, Leamington, Ont., April 26, 1954 . . . Shoots left . . . (March, 1980)—Knee ligament injury . . . (February 3, 1981)—Shoulder and rib injuries . . . (November, 1982)—Broke foot.

Year	Team	League	Games	G.	A.	Pts.	Pen.
1972-73—Oshawa Generals		Jr."A"OHA	61	11	27	38	110
1973-74—Oshawa Generals (c)		Jr."A"OHA	70	8	16	24	134
1974-75—Omaha Knights		CHL	77	5	17	22	164
1975-76—Tulsa Oilers		CHL	73	3	22	25	98
1975-76—Atlanta Flames		NHL	3	0	0	0	0
1976-77—Tulsa Oilers (b)		CHL	51	9	20	29	140
1976-77—Atlanta Flames		NHL	23	2	2	4	31
1977-78—Atlanta Flames		NHL	80	5	12	17	68
1978-79—Atlanta Flames (d)		NHL	66	5	16	21	69
1978-79—Chicago Black Hawks		NHL	12	1	3	4	8
1979-80—Chicago Black Hawks (e)		NHL	23	1	2	3	14
1979-80—Toronto Maple Leafs (f)		NHL	13	0	2	2	8
1979-80—Washington Capitals		NHL	19	1	5	6	30
1980-81—Washington Capitals		NHL	67	3	15	18	103
1981-82—Washington Capitals (g)		NHL	12	1	2	3	14
1981-82—Calgary Flames		NHL	3	0	0	0	2
1981-82—Oklahoma City Stars		CHL	43	1	9	10	44
1982-83—Colorado Flames		CHL	10	1	4	5	8
1982-83—Calgary Flames		NHL	28	0	1	1	18
1983-84—Colorado Flames (b)		CHL	53	4	27	31	60
1984-85—Salt Lake Golden Eagles		IHL	54	4	23	27	50
1984-85—Indianapolis Checkers		IHL	24	10	14	24	18
1985-86—Indianapolis Checkers		IHL	52	6	21	27	45
NHL TOTALS			349	19	60	79	365

(c)—Drafted from Oshawa Generals by Atlanta Flames in fourth round of 1974 amateur draft.

(d)—March, 1979—Traded with Tom Lysiak, Harold Phillipoff, Greg Fox and Miles Zaharko to Chicago Blacks Hawks by Atlanta Flames for Ivan Boldirev, Phil Russell and Darcy Rota.

(e)—January, 1980—Traded by Chicago Black Hawks to Toronto Maple Leafs for Dave Hutchison.

(f)—February, 1980—Traded by Toronto Maple Leafs to Washington Capitals for future considerations (Mike Kaszycki sent to Washington to complete deal).

(g)—November, 1981—Traded with future considerations by Washington Capitals to Calgary Flames for Randy Holt and Bobby Gould.

TODD RICHARDS

Defense . . . 6' . . . 180 lbs. . . . Born, Robbinsdale, Minn., October 20, 1966 . . . Shoots right.

Year	Team	League	Games	G.	A.	Pts.	Pen.
1984-85—Armstrong H.S. (c)		Minn. H.S.	24	10	23	33	24
1985-86—Univ. of Minnesota		WCHA	38	6	23	29	38

(c)—June, 1985—Drafted by Montreal Canadiens in 1985 NHL entry draft. Third Canadiens pick, 33rd overall, second round.

STEPHANE RICHER

Center . . . 6' . . . 190 lbs. . . . Born, Buckingham, Que., June 7, 1966 . . . Shoots right . . . (November 18, 1985)—Sprained ankle vs. Boston and missed 13 games.

Year	Team	League	Games	G.	A.	Pts.	Pen.
1983-84—Granby Bisons (c)		QHL	67	39	37	76	58
1984-85—Granby Bisons/Chic. Sags. (b-d)		QHL	57	61	59	120	71
1984-85—Montreal Canadiens		NHL	1	0	0	0	0
1984-85—Sherbrooke Canadiens (e)		AHL	....	...	....	....	....
1985-86—Montreal Canadiens		NHL	65	21	16	37	50
NHL TOTALS			65	21	16	37	50

(c)—June, 1984—Drafted as underage junior by Montreal Canadiens in NHL entry draft. Third Canadiens pick, 29th overall, second round.

(d)—January, 1985—Traded with Greg Choules by Granby Bisons to Chicoutimi Sagueneens for Stephane Roy, Marc Bureau, Lee Duhemee, Sylvain Demers and Rene Lecuyer.

(e)—Did not play in regular season. Had six goals and three assists in nine playoff games.

STEVE RICHMOND

Defense . . . 6'1" . . . 205 lbs. . . . Born, Chicago, Ill., December 11, 1959 . . . Shoots left.

Year	Team	League	Games	G.	A.	Pts.	Pen.
1978-79—University of Michigan		WCHA	34	2	5	7	38
1979-80—University of Michigan		WCHA	38	10	19	29	26
1980-81—University of Michigan		WCHA	39	22	32	54	46
1981-82—University of Michigan (b-c)		CCHA	38	6	30	36	68
1982-83—Tulsa Oilers		CHL	78	5	13	18	187
1983-84—Tulsa Oilers		CHL	38	1	17	18	114
1983-84—New York Rangers		NHL	26	2	5	7	110
1984-85—New Haven Nighthawks		AHL	37	3	10	13	122
1984-85—New York Rangers		NHL	34	0	5	5	90
1985-86—New Haven Nighthawks		AHL	11	2	6	8	32
1985-86—New York Rangers (d)		NHL	17	0	2	2	63
1985-86—Adirondack Red Wings		AHL	20	1	7	8	23
1985-86—Detroit Red Wings (e)		NHL	29	1	2	3	82
NHL TOTALS			106	3	14	17	345

(c)—July, 1982—Signed by New York Rangers as a free agent.

(d)—December, 1985—Traded by New York Rangers to Detroit Red Wings for Mike McEwen.

(e)—August, 1986—Traded by Detroit Red Wings to New Jersey Devils for Sam St. Laurent.

DAVE RICHTER

Defense . . . 6'5" . . . 217 lbs. . . . Born, Winnipeg, Man., April 8, 1960 . . . Shoots right . . . (November, 1982)—Strained knee ligaments . . . (Summer, 1983)—Elbow surgery . . . (October, 1984)—Strained abdominal muscle during training camp . . . (February, 1985)—Shoulder injury . . . (September, 1985)—Missed first seven games of season due to a pulled groin from training camp . . . (January 17, 1986)—Sprained knee vs. N. Y. Islanders and missed six games.

Year	Team	League	Games	G.	A.	Pts.	Pen.
1979-80—University of Michigan		WCHA	34	0	4	4	54
1980-81—University of Michigan		WCHA	36	2	13	15	56
1981-82—University of Michigan		CCHA	36	9	12	21	78
1981-82—Nashville South Stars		CHL	2	0	1	1	0
1981-82—Minnesota North Stars (c)		NHL	3	0	0	0	11
1982-83—Minnesota North Stars		NHL	6	0	0	0	4
1982-83—Birmingham South Stars		CHL	69	6	17	23	211
1983-84—Salt Lake Golden Eagles		CHL	10	1	4	5	39
1983-84—Minnesota North Stars		NHL	42	2	3	5	132
1984-85—Springfield Indians		AHL	3	0	0	0	2
1984-85—Minnesota North Stars		NHL	55	2	8	10	221
1985-86—Minnesota North Stars (d)		NHL	14	0	3	3	29
1985-86—Philadelphia Flyers (e)		NHL	50	0	2	2	138
NHL TOTALS			170	4	16	20	535

(c)—June, 1982—Signed by Minnesota North Stars as a free agent.

(d)—November, 1985—Traded with Bo Berglund by Minnesota North Stars to Philadelphia Flyers for Todd Bergen and Ed Hospodar.

(e)—June, 1986—Traded by Philadelphia Flyers with Rich Sutter and a third-round draft choice in 1986 to Vancouver Canucks for J.J. Daigneault, a second-round draft choice (Kent Hawley) in 1986 and a fifth-round pick in 1987.

MIKE RIDLEY

Center . . . 6'1" . . . 200 lbs. . . . Born, Winnipeg, Man., July 8, 1963 . . . Shoots left.

Year	Team	League	Games	G.	A.	Pts.	Pen.
1983-84—University of Manitoba (c)		GPAC	46	39	41	80	..
1984-85—University of Manitoba		GPAC	30	29	38	67	..
1985-86—New York Rangers (d)		NHL	80	22	43	65	69
NHL TOTALS			80	22	43	65	69

(c)—Won Sen. Joseph Sullivan Award as the top Canadian College hockey player.

(d)—September, 1985—Signed by New York Rangers as a free agent.

DOUGLAS RISEBROUGH

Center . . . 5'11" . . . 170 lbs. . . . Born, Guelph, Ont., January 29, 1954 . . . Shoots left . . .

Missed final weeks of 1973-74 season with surgery for torn knee ligaments . . . Missed part of 1978-79 season with shoulder separation . . . (March, 1980)—dislocated shoulder . . . Missed parts of 1980-81 season due to arthritis flareup in injured left shoulder . . . Also plays Left Wing . . . (February 27, 1983)—Twisted right knee in game at Vancouver . . . (April 12, 1984)—Given six-game suspension by NHL for swinging his stick at Glenn Anderson of Edmonton during playoff game. Suspension was for the first six games of the 1984-85 season . . . (November, 1984)—Severe groin injury.

Year	Team	League	Games	G.	A.	Pts.	Pen.
1971-72—Guelph CMCs		SOJHL	56	19	33	52	127
1972-73—Guelph Biltmores		SOJHL	60	*47	*60	*107	229
1973-74—Kitchener Rangers (c)		Jr. "A" OHA	46	25	27	52	114
1974-75—Nova Scotia Voyageurs		AHL	7	5	4	9	55
1974-75—Montreal Canadiens		NHL	64	15	32	47	198
1975-76—Montreal Canadiens		NHL	80	16	28	44	180
1976-77—Montreal Canadiens		NHL	78	22	38	60	132
1977-78—Montreal Canadiens		NHL	72	18	23	41	97
1978-79—Montreal Canadiens		NHL	48	10	15	25	62
1979-80—Montreal Canadiens		NHL	44	8	10	18	81
1980-81—Montreal Canadiens		NHL	48	13	21	34	93
1981-82—Montreal Canadiens (d)		NHL	59	15	18	33	116
1982-83—Calgary Flames		NHL	71	21	37	58	138
1983-84—Calgary Flames		NHL	77	23	28	51	161
1984-85—Calgary Flames		NHL	15	7	5	12	49
1985-86—Calgary Flames		NHL	62	15	28	43	169
NHL TOTALS			718	183	283	466	1476

(c)—Drafted from Kitchener Rangers by Montreal Canadiens in first round of 1974 amateur draft.
(d)—September, 1982—Traded by Montreal Canadiens to Calgary Flames for switch of second-round draft choices in 1983 and option to switch third-round choices in 1984.

GARY DANIEL RISSLING

Left Wing . . . 5'11" . . . 180 lbs. . . . Born, Saskatoon, Sask., August 8, 1956 . . . Shoots left.

Year	Team	League	Games	G.	A.	Pts.	Pen.
1973-74—Edmonton Mets		AJHL	46	29	31	60	132
1974-75—Edmonton Oil Kings		WCHL	69	19	35	54	228
1975-76—Edmonton Oil Kings (c)		WCHL	18	5	9	14	25
1975-76—Calgary Centennials		WCHL	47	29	38	67	196
1976-77—Calgary Centennials		WCHL	68	40	49	89	317
1977-78—Port Huron Flags (d)		IHL	79	29	34	63	341
1978-79—Washington Capitals		NHL	26	3	3	6	127
1978-79—Hershey Bears		AHL	52	14	20	34	337
1979-80—Washington Capitals		NHL	11	0	1	1	49
1979-80—Hershey Bears (e)		AHL	46	16	24	40	279
1980-81—Hershey Bears		AHL	4	1	1	2	74
1980-81—Pittsburgh Penguins (f)		NHL	26	1	0	1	143
1980-81—Birmingham Bulls		CHL	19	5	7	12	161
1981-82—Pittsburgh Penguins		NHL	16	0	0	0	55
1981-82—Erie Blades		AHL	29	7	15	22	185
1982-83—Pittsburgh Penguins		NHL	40	5	4	9	128
1982-83—Baltimore Skipjacks		AHL	38	14	17	31	136
1983-84—Baltimore Skipjacks		AHL	30	12	13	25	47
1983-84—Pittsburgh Penguins		NHL	47	4	13	17	297
1984-85—Baltimore Skipjacks		AHL	22	9	17	26	60
1984-85—Pittsburgh Penguins		NHL	56	10	9	19	209
1985-86—Baltimore Skipjacks		AHL	76	19	34	53	340
NHL TOTALS			222	23	30	53	1008

(c)—Traded to Calgary Centennials by Edmonton Oil Kings for Dan Shearer and Doug Johnston.
(d)—December, 1978—Signed by Washington Capitals as free agent.
(e)—Led in penalty minutes (87) during AHL Playoffs.
(f)—January, 1980—Traded by Washington Capitals to Pittsburgh Penguins for fifth round 1981 draft pick (Peter Sidorkiewicz).

GARY ROBERTS

Left Wing . . . 6'1" . . . 190 lbs. . . . Born, North York, Ont., May 23, 1966 . . . Shoots left.

Year	Team	League	Games	G.	A.	Pts.	Pen.
1981-82—Whitby Midgets		Ont. Midgets	44	55	31	86	133
1982-83—Ottawa 67's		OHL	53	12	8	20	83
1983-84—Ottawa 67's (c-d)		OHL	48	27	30	57	144
1984-85—Ottawa 67's (b)		OHL	59	44	62	106	186
1984-85—Moncton Golden Flames		AHL	7	4	2	6	7

Year	Team	League	Games	G.	A.	Pts.	Pen.
1985-86—Ottawa 67's		OHL	24	26	25	51	83
1985-86—Guelph Platers (b)		OHL	23	18	15	33	65

(c)—Led OHL playoffs with 62 penalty minutes.
(d)—June, 1984—Drafted as underage junior by Calgary Flames in 1984 NHL entry draft. First Flames pick, 12th overall, first round.

GORDON ROBERTS

Defense . . . 6' . . . 195 lbs. . . . Born, Detroit, Mich., October 2, 1957 . . . Shoots left . . . Brother of former NHLers Dave and Doug Roberts . . . (April, 1984)—Bruised hip during playoff series with Edmonton . . . (November 13, 1985)—Injured foot at Hartford and missed four games.

Year	Team	League	Games	G.	A.	Pts.	Pen.
1973-74—Detroit Jr. Red Wings		SOJHL	70	25	55	80	340
1974-75—Victoria Cougars (c)		WCHL	53	19	45	64	145
1975-76—New England Whalers		WHA	77	3	19	22	102
1976-77—New England Whalers (d)		WHA	77	13	33	46	169
1977-78—New England Whalers		WHA	78	15	46	61	118
1978-79—New England Whalers		WHA	79	11	46	57	113
1979-80—Hartford Whalers		NHL	80	8	28	36	89
1980-81—Hartford Whalers (e)		NHL	27	2	11	13	81
1980-81—Minnesota North Stars		NHL	50	6	31	37	94
1981-82—Minnesota North Stars		NHL	79	4	30	34	119
1982-83—Minnesota North Stars		NHL	80	3	41	44	103
1983-84—Minnesota North Stars		NHL	77	8	45	53	132
1984-85—Minnesota North Stars		NHL	78	6	36	42	112
1985-86—Minnesota North Stars		NHL	76	2	21	23	101
WHA TOTALS			311	42	144	186	502
NHL TOTALS			547	39	243	282	831

(c)—September, 1975—Signed by New England Whalers (WHA).
(d)—Drafted from New England Whalers (WHA) by Montreal Canadiens in third round of 1977 amateur draft.
(e)—December, 1980—Traded by Hartford Whalers to Minnesota North Stars for Mike Fidler.

GEORDIE JAY ROBERTSON

Right Wing and Center . . . 6' . . . 163 lbs. . . . Born, Victoria, B.C., August 1, 1959 . . . Shoots right . . . (October, 1980)—Injured knee in training camp that required surgery . . . Brother of Torrie Robertson.

Year	Team	League	Games	G.	A.	Pts.	Pen.
1975-76—Nanaimo		BCJHL	....	...	....	....	....
1975-76—Victoria Cougars		WCHL	3	3	2	5	0
1976-77—Victoria Cougars		WCHL	72	39	44	83	107
1977-78—Victoria Cougars		WCHL	61	64	72	136	85
1978-79—Victoria Cougars		WHL	54	31	42	73	94
1979-80—Rochester Americans		AHL	55	26	26	52	66
1980-81—Rochester Americans		AHL	20	3	3	6	19
1981-82—Rochester Americans		AHL	46	14	15	29	45
1981-82—Flint Generals		IHL	11	6	14	20	19
1982-83—Buffalo Sabres		NHL	5	1	2	3	7
1982-83—Rochester Americans		AHL	72	46	73	119	83
1983-84—Rochester Americans		AHL	64	37	54	91	103
1984-85—Rochester Americans (c)		AHL	70	27	48	75	91
1985-86—Adirondack Red Wings		AHL	79	36	56	92	99
NHL TOTALS			5	1	2	3	7

(c)—August, 1985—Signed by Detroit Red Wings as a free agent.

TORRIE ANDREW ROBERTSON

Left Wing . . . 5'11" . . . 185 lbs. . . . Born, Victoria, B.C., August 2, 1961 . . . Shoots left . . . Brother of Geordie Robertson.

Year	Team	League	Games	G.	A.	Pts.	Pen.
1978-79—Victoria Cougars		WHL	69	18	23	41	141
1979-80—Victoria Cougars (c)		WHL	72	23	24	47	298
1980-81—Victoria Cougars (b)		WHL	59	45	66	111	274
1980-81—Washington Capitals		NHL	3	0	0	0	0
1981-82—Hershey Bears		AHL	21	5	3	8	60
1981-82—Washington Capitals		NHL	54	8	13	21	204
1982-83—Washington Capitals		NHL	5	2	0	2	4
1982-83—Hershey Bears		AHL	69	21	33	54	187
1983-84—Hartford Whalers (d)		NHL	66	7	14	21	198

Year	Team	League	Games	G.	A.	Pts.	Pen.
1984-85—Hartford Whalers		NHL	74	11	30	41	337
1985-86—Hartford Whalers		NHL	76	13	24	37	358
NHL TOTALS			278	41	81	122	1101

(c)—June, 1980—Drafted by Washington Capitals as underage junior in 1980 NHL entry draft. Third Capitals pick, 55th overall, third round.

(d)—October, 1983—Traded by Washington Capitals to Hartford Whalers for Greg Adams.

FLORENT ROBIDOUX

Center . . . 6'2" . . . 172 lbs. . . . Born, Cypress River, Man., May 5, 1960 . . . Shoots left.

Year	Team	League	Games	G.	A.	Pts.	Pen.
1977-78—New Westminster Bruins		WCHL	8	1	1	2	12
1978-79—Portland Winter Hawks		WHL	70	36	41	77	73
1979-80—Portland Winter Hawks		WHL	70	43	57	100	157
1980-81—Chicago Black Hawks (c)		NHL	39	6	2	8	75
1980-81—New Brunswick Hawks		AHL	35	12	11	23	110
1981-82—Chicago Black Hawks		NHL	4	1	2	3	0
1981-82—New Brunswick Hawks (d)		AHL	69	31	35	66	200
1982-83—Did not play			....	...	....	....	....
1983-84—Springfield Indians		AHL	68	26	22	48	123
1983-84—Chicago Black Hawks		NHL	9	0	0	0	0
1984-85—Milwaukee Admirals		IHL	76	29	35	64	184
1985-86—Hershey Bears (e)		AHL	47	6	3	9	81
NHL TOTALS			52	7	4	11	75

(c)—August, 1980—Signed by Chicago Black Hawks as free agent.

(d)—Co-Leader (with Ray Neufeld of Binghamton) in AHL Calder Cup playoffs with nine goals.

(e)—September, 1985—Signed by Philadelphia Flyers as a free agent.

LARRY CLARK ROBINSON

Defense . . . 6'3" . . . 210 lbs. . . . Born, Winchester, Ont., June 2, 1951 . . . Shoots left . . . Also plays Left Wing . . . Brother of Moe Robinson . . . Missed part of 1978-79 season with water on the knee . . . (March 6, 1980)—Right shoulder separation in game vs. Edmonton . . . (October, 1980)—Groin injury . . . (November 14, 1980)—Separated left shoulder . . . (January 8, 1981)—Broken nose . . . (October, 1982)—Sore left shoulder . . . (October, 1983)—Skin infection behind right knee . . . (March, 1985)—Hyperextended left elbow.

Year	Team	League	Games	G.	A.	Pts.	Pen.
1968-69—Brockville Braves		Cent. Jr. OHA	....	...	....	....	....
1969-70—Brockville Braves (a)		Cent. Jr. OHA	40	22	29	51	74
1970-71—Kitchener Rangers (c)		Jr. "A" OHA	61	12	39	51	65
1971-72—Nova Scotia Voyageurs		AHL	74	10	14	24	54
1972-73—Nova Scotia Voyageurs		AHL	38	6	33	39	33
1972-73—Montreal Canadiens		NHL	36	2	4	6	20
1973-74—Montreal Canadiens		NHL	78	6	20	26	66
1974-75—Montreal Canadiens		NHL	80	14	47	61	76
1975-76—Montreal Canadiens		NHL	80	10	30	40	59
1976-77—Montreal Canadiens (a-d)		NHL	77	19	66	85	45
1977-78—Montreal Canadiens (b-e-f)		NHL	80	13	52	65	39
1978-79—Montreal Canadiens (a)		NHL	67	16	45	61	33
1979-80—Montreal Canadiens (a-d)		NHL	72	14	61	75	39
1980-81—Montreal Canadiens (b)		NHL	65	12	38	50	37
1981-82—Montreal Canadiens		NHL	71	12	47	59	41
1982-83—Montreal Canadiens		NHL	71	14	49	63	33
1983-84—Montreal Canadiens		NHL	74	9	34	43	39
1984-85—Montreal Canadiens		NHL	76	14	33	47	44
1985-86—Montreal Canadiens (b)		NHL	78	19	63	82	39
NHL TOTALS			1005	174	589	763	610

(c)—Drafted from Kitchener Rangers by Montreal Canadiens in second round of 1971 amateur draft.

(d)—Won James Norris Memorial Trophy (Outstanding Defenseman).

(e)—Led in assists (17) and tied for lead in points (21) during playoffs.

(f)—Won Conn Smythe Trophy (MVP in Stanley Cup playoffs).

LUC ROBITAILLE

Left Wing . . . 6' . . . 180 lbs. . . . Born, Montreal, Que., February 17, 1966 . . . Shoots left.

Year	Team	League	Games	G.	A.	Pts.	Pen.
1983-84—Hull Olympiques (c)		QHL	70	32	53	85	48
1984-85—Hull Olympiques		QHL	64	55	94	148	115
1985-86—Hull Olympiques (a-d-e)		QHL	63	68	*123	*191	93

(c)—June, 1984—Drafted as underage junior by Los Angeles Kings in NHL entry draft. Ninth Kings pick, 171st overall, ninth round.
(d)—Named Canadian Major Junior Hockey League Player of the Year.
(e)—Shared Guy Lafleur Trophy (Playoff MVP) with Sylvain Cote.

NORMAND ROCHEFORT

Defense . . . 6'1" . . . 200 lbs. . . . Born, Trois-Rivieres, Que., January 28, 1961 . . . Shoots left . . . (November, 1980)—Neck injury . . . Missed parts of 1982-83 season with injured knee . . . Nephew of Leon Rochefort (NHL, 1961-1976) . . . (October 19, 1985)—Sprained ankle vs. Pittsburgh . . . (February 8, 1986)—Separated shoulder vs. Chicago.

Year	Team	League	Games	G.	A.	Pts.	Pen.
1977-78—Trois-Rivieres Draveurs		QMJHL	72	9	37	46	36
1978-79—Trois-Rivieres Draveurs		QMJHL	72	17	57	74	80
1979-80—Trois-Rivieres Draveurs		QMJHL	20	5	25	30	22
1979-80—Quebec Remparts (b-c)		QMJHL	52	8	39	47	68
1980-81—Quebec Remparts		QMJHL	9	2	6	8	14
1980-81—Quebec Nordiques		NHL	56	3	7	10	51
1981-82—Quebec Nordiques		NHL	72	4	14	18	115
1982-83—Quebec Nordiques		NHL	62	6	17	23	40
1983-84—Quebec Nordiques		NHL	75	2	22	24	47
1984-85—Quebec Nordiques		NHL	73	3	21	24	74
1985-86—Quebec Nordiques		NHL	26	5	4	9	30
NHL TOTALS			364	23	85	108	357

(c)—June, 1980—Drafted by Quebec Nordiques as underage junior in 1980 NHL entry draft. First Nordiques pick, 24th overall, second round.

MICHAEL ROGERS

Center . . . 5'9" . . . 170 lbs. . . . Born, Calgary, Alta., October 24, 1954 . . . Shoots left . . . (March, 1983)—Missed final seven games of season with back spasms . . . One of only three players to get 100 points in his first three NHL seasons (Wayne Gretzky and Peter Stastny being the others) . . . Cousin of Detroit Lions kicker Ed Murray.

Year	Team	League	Games	G.	A.	Pts.	Pen.
1971-72—Calgary Centennials		WCHL	66	27	30	57	19
1972-73—Calgary Centennials		WCHL	67	54	58	112	44
1973-74—Calgary Centennials (c-d)		WCHL	66	67	73	140	32
1974-75—Edmonton Oilers (e)		WHA	78	35	48	83	2
1975-76—Edmonton Oilers (f)		WHA	44	12	15	27	10
1975-76—New England Whalers		WHA	36	18	14	32	10
1976-77—New England Whalers		WHA	78	25	57	82	10
1977-78—New England Whalers		WHA	80	28	43	71	46
1978-79—New England Whalers		WHA	80	27	45	72	31
1979-80—Hartford Whalers		NHL	80	44	61	105	10
1980-81—Hartford Whalers		NHL	80	40	65	105	32
1981-82—New York Rangers (g)		NHL	80	38	65	103	43
1982-83—New York Rangers		NHL	71	29	47	76	28
1983-84—New York Rangers		NHL	78	23	38	61	45
1984-85—New York Rangers		NHL	78	26	38	64	24
1985-86—New Haven Nighthawks		AHL	20	9	15	24	28
1985-86—New York Rangers (h)		NHL	9	1	3	4	2
1985-86—Edmonton Oilers (i)		NHL	8	1	0	1	0
1985-86—Nova Scotia Oilers		AHL	33	15	28	43	14
WHA TOTALS			396	145	222	367	109
NHL TOTALS			484	202	317	519	184

(c)—Drafted from Calgary Centennials by Vancouver Canucks in fifth round of 1974 amateur draft.
(d)—May, 1974—Selected by Edmonton Oilers in World Hockey Association amateur player draft.
(e)—Won WHA Most Sportsmanlike Player Award.
(f)—January, 1976—Traded to New England Whalers by Edmonton Oilers with future considerations, for Wayne Carleton.
(g)—October, 1981—Traded with 10th-round 1982 entry draft pick (Simo Saarinen) by Hartford Whalers to New York Rangers for Chris Kotsopoulos, Doug Sulliman and Gerry McDonald.
(h)—December, 1985—Traded by New York Rangers to Edmonton Oilers for Todd Strueby and Larry Melnyk.
(i)—June, 1986—Announced he would be playing in Switzerland in 1986-87.

JEFF ROHLICEK

Left Wing . . . 5'11" . . . 165 lbs. . . . Born, Park Ridge, Ill., January 27, 1966 . . . Shoots left.

Year	Team	League	Games	G.	A.	Pts.	Pen.
1983-84—Portland Winter Hawks (b-c)		WHL	71	44	53	97	22
1984-85—Portland Winter Hawks		WHL	16	5	13	18	2

Year	Team	League	Games	G.	A.	Pts.	Pen.
1984-85—Kelowna Wings (b)		WHL	49	34	39	73	24
1985-86—Spokane Chiefs		WHL	57	50	52	102	39

(c)—June, 1984—Drafted as underage junior by Vancouver Canucks in NHL entry draft. Second Canucks pick, 31st overall, second round.

STEVE ROHLIK

Left Wing ... 6' ... 180 lbs. ... Born, St. Paul, Minn., May 15, 1968 ... Shoots left.

Year	Team	League	Games	G.	A.	Pts.	Pen.
1984-85—Hill Murray H.S.		Minn.	25	16	24	40	....
1985-86—Hill Murray H.S. (c)		Minn.	27	26	33	59	....

(c)—June, 1986—Drafted by Pittsburgh Penguins in 1986 NHL entry draft. Eighth Penguins pick, 151st overall, eighth round.

CLIFF RONNING

Center ... 5'8" ... 160 lbs. ... Born, Vancouver, B.C., October 1, 1965 ... Shoots left ... (1984-85)—Set WHL record with goals in 18 straight games ... (1984-85)—Set WHL single season record with 197 points.

Year	Team	League	Games	G.	A.	Pts.	Pen.
1982-83—New Westminster Royals		BCJHL	52	82	68	150	42
1983-84—New Westminster Bruins (b-c-d)		WHL	71	69	67	136	10
1984-85—New Westminster Bruins (a-e-f-g)		WHL	70	*89	108	*197	20
1985-86—Team Canada		Int'l	71	55	63	118	53
1985-86—St. Louis Blues (h)		NHL	....	...	....	....	....

(c)—Won Stewart Paul Memorial Trophy (Top WHL Rookie).
(d)—June, 1984—Drafted by St. Louis Blues as underage junior in NHL entry draft. Ninth Blues pick, 134th overall, seventh round.
(e)—Won Bob Brownridge Memorial Trophy (WHL Scoring Leader).
(f)—Won Frank Boucher Memorial Trophy (WHL Most Gentlemanly).
(g)—Won WHL MVP Trophy.
(h)—No regular season record. Played five playoff games, scoring one goal.

LARRY ROONEY

Defense ... 5'11" .. 165 lbs. ... Born, Boston, Mass., January 30, 1968 ... Shoots left.

Year	Team	League	Games	G.	A.	Pts.	Pen.
1984-85—Thayer H.S.		Mass.	15	15	20	35	....
1985-86—Thayer H.S. (c)		Mass.	24	20	35	55	....

(c)—June, 1986—Drafted by Buffalo Sabres in 1986 NHL entry draft. Sixth Sabres pick, 89th overall, fifth round.

STEVEN PAUL ROONEY

Left Wing ... 6'2" ... 195 lbs. ... Born, Canton, Mass., June 28, 1962 ... Shoots left ... (November 26, 1985)—Shoulder surgery.

Year	Team	League	Games	G.	A.	Pts.	Pen.
1981-82—Providence College (c)		ECAC	31	7	10	17	41
1982-83—Providence College		ECAC	42	10	20	30	31
1983-84—Providence College		ECAC	33	11	16	27	46
1984-85—Providence College		H. East	42	28	22	50	63
1984-85—Montreal Canadiens		NHL	3	1	0	1	7
1985-86—Montreal Canadiens		NHL	38	2	3	5	114
NHL TOTALS			41	3	3	6	121

(c)—June, 1981—Drafted by Montreal Canadiens in NHL entry draft. Eighth Canadiens pick, 88th overall, fifth round.

WILLIAM JOHN ROOT

Defense ... 6' ... 197 lbs. ... Born, Toronto, Ont., September 6, 1959 ... Shoots right ... (March, 1985)—Broken finger ... (October, 1985)—Broke foot when struck by a puck vs. Winnipeg.

Year	Team	League	Games	G.	A.	Pts.	Pen.
1976-77—Niagara Falls Flyers		OMJHL	66	3	19	22	114
1977-78—Niagara Falls Flyers		OMJHL	67	6	11	17	61
1978-79—Niagara Falls Flyers (c)		OMJHL	67	4	31	35	119
1979-80—Nova Scotia Voyageurs		AHL	55	4	15	19	57
1980-81—Nova Scotia Voyageurs		AHL	63	3	12	15	76
1981-82—Nova Scotia Voyageurs		AHL	77	6	25	31	105
1982-83—Montreal Canadiens		NHL	46	2	3	5	24
1982-83—Nova Scotia Voyageurs		AHL	24	0	7	7	29

Year	Team	League	Games	G.	A.	Pts.	Pen.
1983-84—Montreal Canadiens (d)		NHL	72	4	13	17	45
1984-85—St. Catharines Saints		AHL	28	5	9	14	10
1984-85—Toronto Maple Leafs		NHL	35	1	1	2	23
1985-86—Toronto Maple Leafs		NHL	27	0	1	1	29
1985-86—St. Catharines Saints		AHL	14	7	4	11	11
NHL TOTALS			180	7	18	25	121

(c)—October, 1979—Signed by Montreal Canadiens as a free agent.

(d)—August, 1984—Traded by Montreal Canadiens to Toronto Maple Leafs for future considerations.

JAY ROSE

Defense . . . 6' . . . 180 lbs. . . . Born, Newton, Mass., July 6, 1966 . . . Shoots right.

Year	Team	League	Games	G.	A.	Pts.	Pen.
1983-84—Boston New Prep. (c)		Mass. H.S.	30	3	26	29	..
1984-85—Clarkson Univ.		ECAC	15	1	4	5	18
1985-86—Clarkson Univ.		ECAC	32	1	7	8	40

(c)—June, 1984—Drafted by Detroit Red Wings in NHL entry draft. Tenth Red Wings pick, 195th overall, 10th round.

GUY ROULEAU

Center . . . 5'8" . . . 165 lbs. . . . Born, Beloeil, Que., February 16, 1965 . . . Shoots left.

Year	Team	League	Games	G.	A.	Pts.	Pen.
1982-83—Longueuil Chevaliers		QHL	68	25	31	56	23
1983-84—Longueuil Chevaliers		QHL	70	60	73	133	28
1984-85—Longueuil Chevaliers		QHL	60	*76	87	*163	68
1985-86—Hull Olympiques (a-c-d-e-f-g)		QHL	62	*92	99	*191	72

(c)—Attended St. Louis Blues training camp as an unsigned free agent.

(d)—October, 1985—Traded with Stephane Provost by Longueuil Chevaliers to Hull Olympiques for Michel Thibodeau, Mark Saumier and second and fifth round draft picks.

(e)—Won Michel Briere Trophy (Regular Season MVP).

(f)—Won Jean Beliveau Trophy (Leading Scorer).

(g)—May, 1986—Signed by Montreal Canadiens as a free agent.

TOM ROULSTON

Center . . . 6'1" . . . 195 lbs. . . . Born, Winnipeg, Man., November 20, 1957 . . . Shoots right . . . Set CHL record with nine hat tricks during 1980-81 season shattering old record of four set by Boom-Boom Caron in 1963-64.

Year	Team	League	Games	G.	A.	Pts.	Pen.
1975-76—Edmonton Oil Kings		WCHL	1	0	0	0	0
1975-76—Winnipeg Clubs		WCHL	60	18	17	35	56
1976-77—Winnipeg Monarchs (c)		WCHL	72	56	53	109	35
1977-78—Port Huron Flags (d)		IHL	49	27	36	63	24
1977-78—Salt Lake City Golden Eagles		CHL	21	2	1	3	2
1978-79—Dallas Black Hawks (e)		CHL	73	26	29	55	57
1979-80—Houston Apollos		CHL	72	29	41	70	46
1980-81—Wichita Wind (a-f)		CHL	69	*63	44	107	93
1980-81—Edmonton Oilers		NHL	11	1	1	2	2
1981-82—Wichita Wind		CHL	30	22	28	50	46
1981-82—Edmonton Oilers		NHL	35	11	3	14	22
1982-83—Edmonton Oilers		NHL	67	19	21	40	24
1983-84—Edmonton Oilers (g)		NHL	24	5	7	12	16
1983-84—Pittsburgh Penguins		NHL	53	11	17	28	8
1984-85—Baltimore Skipjacks		AHL	78	31	39	70	489
1985-86—Baltimore Skipjacks		AHL	73	38	49	87	38
1985-86—Pittsburgh Penguins		NHL	5	0	0	0	2
NHL TOTALS			195	47	49	96	74

(c)—Drafted from Winnipeg Monarchs by St. Louis Blues in third round of 1977 amateur draft.

(d)—Led in goals (17) during playoffs.

(e)—August, 1979—Traded with Risto Siltanen by St. Louis Blues to Edmonton Oilers for Joe Micheletti.

(f)—Led CHL Playoffs with 26 points.

(g)—December, 1983—Traded by Edmonton Oilers to Pittsburgh Penguins for Kevin McClelland and a middle-round future draft pick.

BOB ROUSE

Defense . . . 6'1" . . . 210 lbs. . . . Born, Surrey, B.C., June 18, 1964 . . . Shoots right . . . (January 2, 1986)—Injured thumb vs. Vancouver and missed two games.

Year	Team	League	Games	G.	A.	Pts.	Pen.
1980-81—Billings Bighorns		WHL	70	0	13	13	116

Year	Team	League	Games	G.	A.	Pts.	Pen.
1981-82—Billings Bighorns (c)	WHL	71	7	22	29	209
1982-83—Nanaimo Islanders	WHL	29	7	20	27	86
1982-83—Lethbridge Broncos	WHL	71	15	50	65	168
1983-84—Lethbridge Broncos (a-d)	WHL	71	18	42	60	101
1983-84—Minnesota North Stars	NHL	1	0	0	0	0
1984-85—Springfield Indians	AHL	8	0	3	3	6
1984-85—Minnesota North Stars	NHL	63	2	9	11	113
1985-86—Minnesota North Stars	NHL	75	1	14	15	151
NHL TOTALS		139	3	23	26	264

(c)—June, 1982—Drafted as underage junior by Minnesota North Stars in 1982 NHL entry draft. Third North Stars pick, 80th overall, fourth round.

(d)—Won WHL Top Defenseman Trophy.

JEAN-MARC ROUTHIER

Right Wing . . . 6'2" . . . 180 lbs. . . . Born, Quebec City, Que., February 2, 1968 . . . Shoots right.

Year	Team	League	Games	G.	A.	Pts.	Pen.
1984-85—Ste. Foy Midgets	Quebec	41	13	22	35	68
1985-86—Hull Olympiques (c)	QHL	71	18	16	34	111

(c)—June, 1986—Drafted as underage junior by Quebec Nordiques in 1986 NHL entry draft. Second Nordiques pick, 39th overall, second round.

MICHAEL ROWE

Defense . . . 6'1" . . . 208 lbs. . . . Born, Kingston, Ont., March 8, 1965 . . . Shoots left.

Year	Team	League	Games	G.	A.	Pts.	Pen.
1981-82—Toronto Marlboros	OHL	58	4	4	8	214
1982-83—Toronto Marlboros (c)	OHL	64	4	29	33	*262
1983-84—Toronto Marlboros	OHL	59	9	36	45	208
1984-85—Toronto Marlboros	OHL	66	17	34	51	202
1984-85—Pittsburgh Penguins	NHL	6	0	0	0	7
1984-85—Baltimore Skipjacks (d)	AHL	..	..	..	..	..
1985-86—Pittsburgh Penguins	NHL	3	0	0	0	4
1985-86—Baltimore Skipjacks	AHL	67	0	5	5	107
NHL TOTALS		9	0	0	0	11

(c)—June, 1983—Drafted as underage junior by Pittsburgh Penguins in 1983 NHL entry draft. Third Penguins pick, 58th overall, third round.

(d)—Played three playoff games.

DARCY ROY

Left Wing . . . 5'11" . . . 180 lbs. . . . Born, Haileybury, Ont., May 10, 1964 . . . Shoots left.

Year	Team	League	Games	G.	A.	Pts.	Pen.
1980-81—North York Rangers	MTHL	40	6	13	19	74
1981-82—Ottawa 67's (c)	OHL	65	22	20	42	79
1982-83—Ottawa 67's	OHL	70	28	40	68	151
1983-84—Ottawa 67's	OHL	70	21	41	62	98
1984-85—Toledo Goaldiggers	IHL	80	17	28	45	115
1984-85—New Haven Nighthawks	AHL	2	0	0	0	2
1985-86—Toledo Goaldiggers	IHL	3	0	0	0	4
1985-86—New Haven Nighthawks	AHL	38	1	10	11	43

(c)—June, 1982—Drafted by Los Angeles Kings as underage junior in 1982 NHL entry draft. Fifth Kings pick, 90th overall, fifth round.

STEPHANE ROY

Left Wing . . . 5'11" . . . 185 lbs. . . . Born, Ste. Foy, Que., June 29, 1967 . . . Shoots left . . . Also plays Center . . . Brother of Patrick Roy.

Year	Team	League	Games	G.	A.	Pts.	Pen.
1983-84—Chicoutimi Sagueneens	QHL	67	12	26	38	25
1984-85—Chicoutimi/Granby (c-d)	QHL	68	28	53	81	34
1985-86—Granby Bisons	QHL	61	33	52	85	68
1985-86—Team Canada	Int'l	10	0	1	1	4

(c)—January, 1985—Traded with Marc Bureau, Lee Duhemee, Sylvain Demers and Rene Lecuyer by Chicoutimi Sagueneens to Granby Bisons for Stephane Richer and Greg Choules.

(d)—June, 1985—Drafted as underage junior by Minnesota North Stars in 1985 NHL entry draft. First North Stars pick, 51st overall, third round.

BLAINE RUDE

Defense . . . 6'3" . . . 200 lbs. . . . Born, Devils Lake, North Dakota, October 21, 1967 . . . Shoots right.

Year	Team	League	Games	G.	A.	Pts.	Pen.
1984-85—Fergus Falls H.S.		Minn.	23	27	35	62	....
1985-86—Fergus Falls H.S. (c)		Minn.	23	10	35	45	....

(c)—June, 1986—Drafted by Philadelphia Flyers in 1986 NHL entry draft. Eighth Flyers pick, 188th overall, ninth round.

LINDY CAMERON RUFF

Defense . . . 6'2" . . . 190 lbs. . . . Born, Warburg, Alta., February 17, 1960 . . . Shoots left . . . (December, 1980)—Fractured ankle . . . Also plays left wing . . . Brother of Marty Ruff . . . (March, 1983)—Broken hand . . . (January 14, 1984)—Injured shoulder in game at Detroit . . . (October 26, 1984)—Separated shoulder in game at Detroit . . . (November 30, 1985)— Broke foot at Toronto and missed four games . . . (December 29, 1985)—Bruised knee vs. N. Y. Islanders and missed four games . . . (March 5, 1986)—Broke left clavicle at Hartford.

Year	Team	League	Games	G.	A.	Pts.	Pen.
1976-77—Taber Golden Suns		AJHL	60	13	33	46	112
1976-77—Lethbridge Broncos		WCHL	2	0	2	2	0
1977-78—Lethbridge Broncos		WCHL	66	9	24	33	219
1978-79—Lethbridge Broncos (c)		WHL	24	9	18	27	108
1979-80—Buffalo Sabres		NHL	63	5	14	19	38
1980-81—Buffalo Sabres		NHL	65	8	18	26	121
1981-82—Buffalo Sabres		NHL	79	16	32	48	194
1982-83—Buffalo Sabres		NHL	60	12	17	29	130
1983-84—Buffalo Sabres		NHL	58	14	31	45	101
1984-85—Buffalo Sabres		NHL	39	13	11	24	45
1985-86—Buffalo Sabres		NHL	54	20	12	32	158
NHL TOTALS			418	88	135	223	787

(c)—August, 1979—Drafted by Buffalo Sabres as underage junior in entry draft. Second Buffalo pick, 32nd overall, second round.

MARTY RUFF

Defense . . . 6'1" . . . 185 lbs. . . . Born, Warburg, Alta., May 19, 1963 . . . Shoots right . . . Brother of Lindy Ruff . . . Missed start of 1981-82 season with mononucleosis and part of season with knee injury . . . (November, 1982)—Shoulder injury.

Year	Team	League	Games	G.	A.	Pts.	Pen.
1980-81—Taber Golden Suns		AJHL	50	10	12	22	94
1980-81—Lethbridge Broncos (c)		WHL	71	9	37	46	222
1981-82—Lethbridge Broncos		WHL	46	7	28	35	188
1982-83—Lethbridge Broncos		WHL	53	7	23	30	128
1983-84—Montana Magic		CHL	1	0	0	0	2
1983-84—Toledo Goaldiggers		IHL	2	0	1	1	0
1983-84—Muskegon Mohawks		IHL	44	3	15	18	44
1983-84—Portland Winter Hawks		WHL	10	4	2	6	30
1984-85—Peoria Rivermen		IHL	5	0	1	1	0
1985-86—Peoria Rivermen		IHL	44	3	6	9	34

(c)—June, 1981—Drafted as underage junior by St. Louis Blues in NHL entry draft. First Blues pick, 20th overall, first round.

REIJO RUOTSALAINEN

Defense . . . 5'8" . . . 170 lbs. . . . Born, Kaakkuri, Finland, April 1, 1960 . . . Shoots right . . . (October 22, 1983)—Hip pointer injury in game at N.Y. Islanders.

Year	Team	League	Games	G.	A.	Pts.	Pen.
1977-78—Oulu Karpat		Finland	30	9	14	23	4
1978-79—Oulu Karpat		Finland	36	14	8	22	47
1979-80—Oulu Karpat (c)		Finland	30	15	13	28	31
1980-81—Oulu Karpat		Finland	36	28	23	51	28
1980-81—Finland Nationals		Finland	....	9	6	15	....
1981-82—New York Rangers		NHL	78	18	38	56	27
1982-83—New York Rangers		NHL	77	16	53	69	22
1983-84—New York Rangers		NHL	74	20	39	59	26
1984-85—New York Rangers		NHL	80	28	45	73	32
1985-86—New York Rangers		NHL	80	17	42	59	47
NHL TOTALS			389	99	217	316	154

(c)—June, 1980—Drafted by New York Rangers in NHL entry draft. Fifth Rangers pick, 119th overall, sixth round.

TERRY WALLACE RUSKOWSKI

Center . . . 5'10" . . . 178 lbs. . . . Born, Prince Albert, Sask., December 31, 1954 . . . Shoots left . . . Missed part of 1974-75 season with injured right hand and part of 1975-76 season with broken middle finger on right hand . . . (Summer, 1980)—Surgery to right knee . . . (March, 1981)—Viral infection . . . (December 9, 1981)—Ruptured ligaments in right thumb during fight with Timo Blomqvist of Washington . . . (December 31, 1985)—Sprained thumb at St. Louis . . . (March 26, 1986)—Sprained left knee vs. Edmonton.

Year	Team	League	Games	G.	A.	Pts.	Pen.
1971-72—Swift Current Broncos		WCHL	67	13	38	51	177
1972-73—Swift Current Broncos		WCHL	53	25	64	89	136
1973-74—Swift Current Broncos (c-d)		WCHL	68	40	93	133	243
1974-75—Houston Aeros		WHA	71	10	36	46	134
1975-76—Houston Aeros (e)		WHA	65	14	35	49	100
1976-77—Houston Aeros		WHA	80	24	60	84	146
1977-78—Houston Aeros (f)		WHA	78	15	57	72	170
1978-79—Winnipeg Jets (g-h)		WHA	75	20	66	86	211
1979-80—Chicago Black Hawks		NHL	74	15	55	70	252
1980-81—Chicago Black Hawks		NHL	72	8	51	59	225
1981-82—Chicago Black Hawks		NHL	60	7	30	37	120
1982-83—Chicago Black Hawks (i)		NHL	5	0	2	2	12
1982-83—Los Angeles Kings		NHL	71	14	30	44	127
1983-84—Los Angeles Kings		NHL	77	7	25	32	92
1984-85—Los Angeles Kings (j)		NHL	78	16	33	49	144
1985-86—Pittsburgh Penguins		NHL	73	26	37	63	162
WHA TOTALS			369	83	254	337	761
NHL TOTALS			510	93	263	356	1134

(c)—Drafted from Swift Current Broncos by Chicago Black Hawks in third round of 1974 amateur draft.
(d)—Selected by Houston Aeros in WHA amateur draft, May, 1974.
(e)—Led in assists (23) and penalty minutes (64) during playoffs.
(f)—Sold to Winnipeg Jets with Houston Aeros' franchise, July, 1978.
(g)—Led in assists (12) during playoffs.
(h)—June, 1979—Selected by Chicago Black Hawks in NHL reclaim draft.
(i)—October, 1982—Traded by Chicago Black Hawks to Los Angeles Kings for Larry Goodenough and future considerations.
(j)—July, 1985—Signed by Pittsburgh Penguins as a free agent.

PHILIP DOUGLAS RUSSELL

Defense . . . 6'2" . . . 200 lbs. . . . Born, Edmonton, Alta., July 21, 1952 . . . Shoots left . . . Missed part of 1977-78 season with injured ligaments in left knee . . . (September, 1981)—Injured knee during training camp . . . (December 2, 1985)—Bruised cheekbone . . . (February 1, 1986)—Bruised knee at Washington.

Year	Team	League	Games	G.	A.	Pts.	Pen.
1970-71—Edmonton Oil Kings		WCHL	34	4	16	20	113
1971-72—Edmonton Oil Kings (a-c)		WCHL	64	14	45	59	*331
1972-73—Chicago Black Hawks (d)		NHL	76	6	19	25	156
1973-74—Chicago Black Hawks		NHL	75	10	25	35	184
1974-75—Chicago Black Hawks		NHL	80	5	24	29	260
1975-76—Chicago Black Hawks		NHL	74	9	29	38	194
1976-77—Chicago Black Hawks		NHL	76	9	36	45	233
1977-78—Chicago Black Hawks		NHL	57	6	20	26	139
1978-79—Chicago Black Hawks (e)		NHL	66	8	23	31	122
1978-79—Atlanta Flames		NHL	13	1	6	7	28
1979-80—Atlanta Flames		NHL	80	5	31	36	115
1980-81—Calgary Flames		NHL	80	6	23	29	104
1981-82—Calgary Flames		NHL	71	4	25	29	110
1982-83—Calgary Flames (f)		NHL	78	13	18	31	112
1983-84—New Jersey Devils		NHL	76	9	22	31	96
1984-85—New Jersey Devils		NHL	66	4	16	20	110
1985-86—New Jersey Devils (g)		NHL	30	2	3	5	51
1985-86—Buffalo Sabres		NHL	12	2	3	5	12
NHL TOTALS			1010	99	323	422	2026

(c)—Drafted from Edmonton Oil Kings by Chicago Black Hawks in first round of 1972 amateur draft.
(d)—Led in penalty minutes (43) during playoffs.
(e)—March, 1979—Traded with Ivan Boldirev and Darcy Rota to Atlanta Flames by Chicago Black Hawks for Tom Lysiak, Harold Phillipoff, Pat Ribble, Greg Fox and Miles Zaharko.
(f)—July, 1983—Traded by Calgary Flames with Mel Bridgman to New Jersey Devils for Steve Tambellini and Joel Quenneville.
(g)—March, 1986—Traded by New Jersey Devils to Buffalo Sabres for 12th round draft pick (Doug Kirton).

TOM RYAN

Defense . . . 5'11" . . . 180 lbs. . . . Born, Boston, Mass., January 12, 1966 . . . Shoots right.

Year	Team	League	Games	G.	A.	Pts.	Pen.
1983-84—Newton North H.S. (c)	Mass.H.S.	..	..	..	..	..
1984-85—Boston University	H. East	34	6	8	14	14
1985-86—Boston University	H. East	42	2	8	10	22

(c)—June, 1984—Drafted by Pittsburgh Penguins in NHL entry draft. Sixth Penguins pick, 127th overall, seventh round.

SIMO SAARINEN

Defense . . . 5'10" . . . 170 lbs. . . . Born, Helsinki, Finland, February 10, 1963 . . . Shoots left . . . (November 11, 1984)—Tore ligaments in left knee.

Year	Team	League	Games	G.	A.	Pts.	Pen.
1980-81—IFK Helsinki	Finland	20	1	0	1	4
1981-82—IFK Helsinki (c)	Finland	36	5	10	15	20
1982-83—IFK Helsinki	Finland	36	9	6	15	24
1983-84—IFL Helsinki	Finland	36	7	7	14	32
1984-85—New York Rangers	NHL	8	0	0	0	8
1985-86—New Haven Nighthawks	AHL	13	3	4	7	11
NHL TOTALS		8	0	0	0	8

(c)—June, 1982—Drafted by New York Rangers in NHL entry draft. Tenth Rangers pick, 193rd overall, tenth round.

KEN SABOURIN

Defense . . . 6'4" . . . 200 lbs. . . . Born, Scarborough, Ont., April 28, 1966 . . . Shoots left.

Year	Team	League	Games	G.	A.	Pts.	Pen.
1981-82—Don Mills Midgets	MTHL	40	10	20	30	..
1982-83—Sault Ste. Marie Greyhounds	OHL	58	0	8	8	90
1983-84—Sault Ste. Marie Greyhounds (c)	OHL	63	7	13	20	157
1984-85—Sault Ste. Marie Greyhounds	OHL	63	5	19	24	139
1985-86—Sault Ste. Marie Greyhounds (d)	OHL	25	1	5	6	77
1985-86—Cornwall Royals	OHL	37	3	12	15	94
1985-86—Moncton Golden Flames	AHL	3	0	0	0	0

(c)—June, 1984—Drafted as underage junior by Washington Capitals in NHL entry draft. Second Capitals pick, 34th overall, second round.

(d)—March, 1986—Traded by Sault Ste. Marie Greyhounds to Cornwall Royals for Kent Trolley and a fifth round 1986 OHL priority draft pick.

TOM ST. JAMES

Left Wing . . . 5'11" . . . 175 lbs. . . . Born, Iroquois Falls, Ont., February 18, 1963 . . . Shoots left.

Year	Team	League	Games	G.	A.	Pts.	Pen.
1981-82—Sudbury Wolves	OHL	67	18	25	43	64
1982-83—Kitchener Rangers	OHL	64	32	48	80	35
1983-84—Rochester Americans (c)	AHL	31	6	7	13	8
1984-85—Flint Generals	IHL	80	40	38	78	54
1985-86—Saginaw Gears	IHL	53	16	34	50	36

(c)—March, 1984—Signed by Rochester Americans as a free agent.

ANDERS BORJE SALMING
(Known by middle name.)

Defense . . . 6'1" . . . 185 lbs. . . . Born, Kiruna, Sweden, April 17, 1951 . . . Shoots left . . . Missed part of 1974-75 season with cracked bone in heel and part of the 1978 playoffs with facial injuries . . . (January, 1980)—Surgery to clear sinus problem . . . (March, 1981)—Separated shoulder . . . (December 2, 1981)—Separated shoulder vs. Hartford . . . (December, 1982)—Suffered Charley horse and missed eight games . . . (January 17, 1983)—Cut by skate on knee in game at St. Louis . . . (March 12, 1984)—Broke kneecap in game vs. Winnipeg and out for the season . . . (October, 1984)—Eye infection . . . (January 19, 1985)—Injured sinus in game vs. Boston . . . (October 12, 1985)—Injured ribs vs. Quebec and missed one game . . . (November 8, 1985)—Injured back at Detroit and missed 38 games.

Year	Team	League	Games	G.	A.	Pts.	Pen.
1971-72—Swedish National Team		12	0	....	....	....
1972-73—Swedish National Team (c)		23	4	....	....	....
1973-74—Toronto Maple Leafs	NHL	76	5	34	39	48
1974-75—Toronto Maple Leafs (b)	NHL	60	12	25	37	34
1975-76—Toronto Maple Leafs (b-d)	NHL	78	16	41	57	70
1976-77—Toronto Maple Leafs (a-d)	NHL	76	12	66	78	46
1977-78—Toronto Maple Leafs (b)	NHL	80	16	60	76	70
1978-79—Toronto Maple Leafs (b-d)	NHL	78	17	56	73	76

Year	Team	League	Games	G.	A.	Pts.	Pen.
1979-80—Toronto Maple Leafs (b)		NHL	74	19	52	71	96
1980-81—Toronto Maple Leafs		NHL	72	5	61	66	154
1981-82—Toronto Maple Leafs		NHL	69	12	44	56	170
1982-83—Toronto Maple Leafs		NHL	69	7	38	45	104
1983-84—Toronto Maple Leafs		NHL	68	5	38	43	92
1984-85—Toronto Maple Leafs		NHL	73	6	33	39	76
1985-86—Toronto Maple Leafs		NHL	41	7	15	22	48
NHL TOTALS			914	139	563	702	1085

(c)—Selected most valuable player in Sweden.
(d)—Named winner of Viking Award (Top Swedish player in NHL/WHA as selected by poll of Swedish players).

STEVE SALVUCCI

Left Wing ... 5'10" ... 185 lbs.... Born, Brighton, Mass., September 23, 1959 ... Shoots left.

Year	Team	League	Games	G.	A.	Pts.	Pen.
1979-80—Saginaw Gears		IHL	2	1	1	2	0
1979-80—Johnstown Red Wings		EHL	22	9	10	19	39
1979-80—Hampton Aces		EHL	45	25	31	56	75
1980-81—Hampton Aces (b)		EHL	72	37	40	77	104
1981-82—Saginaw Gears		IHL	67	49	42	91	140
1982-83—Hershey Bears		AHL	73	8	6	14	68
1983-84—Fort Wayne Komets (c)		IHL	77	31	27	58	271
1984-85—Fort Wayne Komets		IHL	62	29	25	54	149
1985-86—Fort Wayne Komets		IHL	61	27	42	69	129

(c)—October, 1983—Signed by Fort Wayne Komets as a free agent.

GARY SAMPSON

Center ... 6' ... 190 lbs. ... Born, Atikokan, Ont., August 24, 1959 ... Shoots left ... Member of 1984 U.S. Olympic Team ... (December 27, 1984)—Ligament damage to left knee when checked by Pat Flatley in game at N.Y. Islanders ... (February 13, 1985)— Reinjured knee at Winnipeg.

Year	Team	League	Games	G.	A.	Pts.	Pen.
1978-79—Boston College		ECAC	30	10	18	28	4
1979-80—Boston College		ECAC	24	6	8	14	8
1980-81—Boston College		ECAC	31	8	16	24	8
1981-82—Boston College		ECAC	21	7	11	18	22
1982-83—U.S. National Team		Int'l	40	11	20	31	8
1983-84—U.S. National Team		Int'l	56	21	18	39	10
1983-84—U.S. Olympic Team		Int'l	6	1	3	4	2
1983-84—Washington Capitals (c)		NHL	15	1	1	2	6
1984-85—Binghamton Whalers		AHL	5	2	2	4	2
1984-85—Washington Capitals		NHL	46	10	15	25	13
1985-86—Washington Capitals		NHL	19	1	4	5	2
1985-86—Binghamton Whalers		AHL	49	9	21	30	16
NHL TOTALS			80	12	20	32	21

(c)—February, 1984—Signed by Washington Capitals as a free agent.

KJELL SAMUELSSON

Defense ... 6'6" ... 227 lbs.... Born, Tingsryd, Sweden, October 18, 1956 ... Shoots right.

Year	Team	League	Games	G.	A.	Pts.	Pen.
1983-84—Leksand (c)		Sweden	36	6	7	13	59
1984-85—Leksand		Sweden	35	9	5	14	34
1985-86—New York Rangers		NHL	9	0	0	0	10
1985-86—New Haven Nighthawks		AHL	56	6	21	27	87
NHL TOTALS			9	0	0	0	10

(c)—June, 1984—Drafted by New York Rangers in NHL entry draft. Fifth Rangers pick, 119th overall, sixth round.

ULF SAMUELSSON

Defense ... 6'1" ... 195 lbs. ... Born, Leksand, Sweden, March 26, 1964 ... Shoots left.

Year	Team	League	Games	G.	A.	Pts.	Pen.
1983-84—Leksands (c)		Sweden	36	5	10	15	53
1984-85—Binghamton Whalers		AHL	36	5	11	16	92
1984-85—Hartford Whalers		NHL	41	2	6	8	83
1985-86—Hartford Whalers		NHL	80	5	19	24	172
NHL TOTALS			121	7	25	32	255

(c)—June, 1982—Drafted by Hartford Whalers in NHL entry draft. Fourth Whalers pick, 67th overall, fourth round.

SCOTT SANDELIN

Defense . . . 6' . . . 190 lbs. . . . Born, Hibbing, Minn., August 8, 1964 . . . Shoots right . . . (October, 1984)—Stretched knee ligaments.

Year	Team	League	Games	G.	A.	Pts.	Pen.
1981-82—Hibbing High School (c)		Minn. H.S.	20	5	15	20	30
1982-83—Univ. of North Dakota		WCHA	30	1	6	7	10
1983-84—Univ. of North Dakota		WCHA	41	4	23	27	24
1984-85—Univ. of North Dakota		WCHA	38	4	17	21	30
1985-86—Univ. of North Dakota (a)		WCHA	40	7	31	38	38
1985-86—Sherbrooke Canadiens		AHL	6	0	2	2	2

(c)—June, 1982—Drafted as underage player by Montreal Canadiens in 1982 NHL entry draft. Fifth Canadiens pick, 40th overall, second round.

JAMES SANDLAK JR.

Right Wing . . . 6'3" . . . 205 lbs. . . . Born, Kitchener, Ont., December 12, 1966 . . . Shoots right . . . Named to All-Tournament team at 1986 World Junior Championships as well as being named top forward . . . (January, 1986)—Ruptured ligaments in right thumb.

Year	Team	League	Games	G.	A.	Pts.	Pen.
1982-83—Kitchener Rangers		OHA	38	26	25	51	100
1983-84—London Knights		OHL	68	23	18	41	143
1984-85—London Knights (c)		OHL	58	40	24	64	128
1985-86—London Knights		OHL	16	7	13	20	36
1985-86—Vancouver Canucks		NHL	23	1	3	4	10
NHL TOTALS			23	1	3	4	10

(c)—June, 1985—Drafted as underage junior by Vancouver Canucks in 1985 NHL entry draft. First Canucks pick, fourth overall, first round.

TOMAS SANDSTROM

Right Wing . . . 6'2" . . . 200 lbs. . . . Born, Fagersta, Sweden, September 4, 1964 . . . Shoots left . . . (October 23, 1985)—Bruised right shoulder vs. New Jersey and missed two games . . . (December 7, 1985)—Bruised tailbone at Philadelphia and missed three games . . . (February 24, 1986)—Concussion at Minnesota.

Year	Team	League	Games	G.	A.	Pts.	Pen.
1983-84—Brynas (c)		Sweden	....	20	10	30	....
1984-85—New York Rangers		NHL	74	29	30	59	51
1985-86—New York Rangers		NHL	73	25	29	54	109
NHL TOTALS			147	54	59	113	160

(c)—June, 1982—Drafted by New York Rangers in NHL entry draft. Second Rangers pick, 36th overall, second round.

EVERETT SANIPASS

Left Wing . . . 6'2" . . . 190 lbs. . . . Born, Big Cove, New Brunswick, February 13, 1968 . . . Shoots left . . . Micmac Indian descendant.

Year	Team	League	Games	G.	A.	Pts.	Pen.
1984-85—Verdun Junior Canadiens		QHL	38	8	11	19	84
1985-86—Verdun Junior Canadiens (c)		QHL	67	28	66	94	320

(c)—June, 1986—Drafted as underage junior by Chicago Black Hawks in 1986 NHL entry draft. First Black Hawks pick, 14th overall, first round.

DAVID SAUNDERS

Left Wing . . . 6'1" . . . 195 lbs. . . . Born, Ottawa, Ont., May 20, 1966 . . . Shoots left.

Year	Team	League	Games	G.	A.	Pts.	Pen.
1983-84—St. Lawrence Univ. (c)		CCHA	32	10	21	31	26
1984-85—St. Lawrence Univ.		ECAC	27	7	9	16	16
1985-86—St. Lawrence Univ.		ECAC	29	15	19	34	26

(c)—June, 1984—Drafted by Vancouver Canucks in NHL entry draft. Third Canucks pick, 52nd overall, third round.

JEAN FRANCOIS SAUVE

Center . . . 5'6" . . . 175 lbs. . . . Born, Ste. Genevieve, Que., January 23, 1960 . . . Shoots left . . . Brother of Bob Sauve . . . (December, 1980)—Knee injury.

Year	Team	League	Games	G.	A.	Pts.	Pen.
1977-78—Trois-Rivieres Draveurs		QMJHL	6	2	3	5	0
1978-79—Trois-Riveires Draveurs (b-c-d-e)		QMJHL	72	65	111	*176	31
1979-80—Trois-Rivieres Draveurs (a-c-d)		QMJHL	72	63	*124	*187	31
1980-81—Rochester Americans (b)		AHL	56	29	54	83	21

Year	Team	League	Games	G.	A.	Pts.	Pen.
1980-81—Buffalo Sabres		NHL	20	5	9	14	12
1981-82—Rochester Americans		AHL	7	5	8	13	4
1981-82—Buffalo Sabres		NHL	69	19	36	55	46
1982-83—Buffalo Sabres		NHL	9	0	4	4	9
1982-83—Rochester Americans (f-g)		AHL	73	30	69	99	10
1983-84—Fredericton Express		AHL	26	19	31	50	23
1983-84—Quebec Nordiques		NHL	39	10	17	27	2
1984-85—Quebec Nordiques		NHL	64	13	29	42	21
1985-86—Quebec Nordiques		NHL	75	16	40	56	20
NHL TOTALS			276	63	135	198	111

(c)—Won Frank Selke Trophy (QMJHL Most Gentlemanly Player).
(d)—Won Jean Beliveau Trophy (Leading QMJHL scorer).
(e)—Won Guy Lafleur Trophy (QMJHL playoff MVP).
(f)—June, 1983—Traded by Buffalo Sabres with Tony McKegney, Andre Savard and Buffalo's third-round draft choice in 1983 (Ilro Jarvi) to Quebec Nordiques for Real Cloutier and Quebec's first-round draft choice in 1983 (Adam Creighton).
(g)—Led AHL playoffs with 21 assists and 28 points.

DENIS SAVARD

Center . . . 5'9" . . . 157 lbs. . . . Born, Pointe Gatineau, Que., February 4, 1961 . . . Shoots right . . . Cousin of Jean Savard . . . Set Chicago rookie record with 75 points in 1980-81 (broken by Steve Larmer) . . . (October 15, 1980)—Strained knee vs. Vancouver . . . Set Chicago records for assists (87) and points (119) in one season in 1981-82 . . . Broke his own points record in 1982-83 . . . (January 7, 1984)—Broke nose in game at N.Y. Islanders . . . (October 13, 1984)—Injured ankle when he blocked a shot during game at N.Y. Islanders.

Year	Team	League	Games	G.	A.	Pts.	Pen.
1977-78—Montreal Juniors		QMJHL	72	37	79	116	22
1978-79—Montreal Juniors		QMJHL	70	46	*112	158	88
1979-80—Montreal Juniors (a-c-d)		QMJHL	72	63	118	181	93
1980-81—Chicago Black Hawks		NHL	76	28	47	75	47
1981-82—Chicago Black Hawks		NHL	80	32	87	119	82
1982-83—Chicago Black Hawks (b)		NHL	78	35	86	121	99
1983-84—Chicago Black Hawks		NHL	75	37	57	94	71
1984-85—Chicago Black Hawks		NHL	79	38	67	105	56
1985-86—Chicago Black Hawks		NHL	80	47	69	116	111
NHL TOTALS			468	217	413	630	466

(c)—Won Michel Briere Trophy (QMJHL MVP).
(d)—June, 1980—Drafted as underage junior by Chicago Black Hawks in 1980 NHL entry draft. First Black Hawks pick, third overall, first round.

PETER SAWKINS

Defense . . . 6'3" . . . 190 lbs. . . . Born, Skagen, Denmark, August 29, 1963 . . . Shoots right.

Year	Team	League	Games	G.	A.	Pts.	Pen.
1980-81—St. Paul Academy (c)		Minn. H.S.	23	6	27	33	0
1981-82—Yale University		ECAC	24	0	5	5	20
1982-83—Yale University		ECAC	26	2	8	10	10
1983-84—Yale University		ECAC	25	2	14	16	24
1984-85—Yale University (b)		ECAC	28	1	11	12	20
1984-85—New Haven Nighthawks		AHL	2	0	0	0	0
1985-86—Toledo Goaldiggers		IHL	25	4	8	12	25
1985-86—New Haven Nighthawks		AHL	7	1	2	3	14

(c)—June, 1981—Drafted as underage player by Los Angeles Kings in 1981 NHL entry draft. Sixth Kings pick, 144th overall, seventh round.

DARIN SCEVIOUR

Right Wing . . . 5'10" . . . 185 lbs. . . . Born, Lacombe, Alta., November 30, 1965 . . . Shoots right.

Year	Team	League	Games	G.	A.	Pts.	Pen.
1981-82—Red Deer		Alb. Midget	64	55	67	122	87
1982-83—Lethbridge Broncos		WHL	64	9	17	26	45
1983-84—Lethbridge Broncos (c)		WHL	71	37	28	65	28
1984-85—Lethbridge Broncos		WHL	67	36	36	72	37
1985-86—Nova Scotia Oilers		AHL	31	4	3	7	6
1985-86—Saginaw Generals		IHL	24	9	11	20	7

(c)—June, 1984—Drafted as underage junior by Chicago Black Hawks in NHL entry draft. Fifth Black Hawks pick, 101st overall, fifth round.

KEVIN DEAN SCHAMEHORN

Right Wing . . . 5'10" . . . 185 lbs. . . . Born, Calgary, Alta., July 28, 1956 . . . Shoots right.

Year	Team	League	Games	G.	A.	Pts.	Pen.
1973-74—Bellingham Blazers		Jr. "A" BCHL	58	17	8	25	293
1973-74—New Westminster Bruins		WCHL	2	1	1	2	7
1974-75—New Westminster Bruins		WCHL	37	14	6	20	175
1975-76—New Westminster Bruins (c)		WCHL	62	32	42	74	276
1976-77—Kalamazoo Wings		IHL	77	27	31	58	314
1976-77—Detroit Red Wings		NHL	3	0	0	0	9
1977-78—Kansas City Red Wings		CHL	36	5	3	8	113
1977-78—Kalamazoo Wings		IHL	39	18	14	32	144
1978-79—Kalamazoo Wings		IHL	80	45	57	102	245
1979-80—Detroit Red Wings		NHL	2	0	0	0	4
1979-80—Adirondack Red Wings (d)		AHL	60	10	13	23	145
1980-81—Los Angeles Kings		NHL	5	0	0	0	4
1980-81—Houston Apollos		CHL	26	7	9	16	43
1980-81—Rochester Americans		AHL	27	6	10	16	44
1981-82—Kalamazoo Wings		IHL	75	38	27	65	113
1982-83—Kalamazoo Wings		IHL	58	38	29	67	78
1983-84—Kalamazoo Wings		IHL	76	37	31	68	154
1984-85—Kalamazoo Wings		IHL	80	35	43	78	154
1985-86—Milwaukee Admirals (e)		IHL	82	47	34	81	101
NHL TOTALS			10	0	0	0	17

(c)—Drafted from New Westminster Bruins by Detroit Red Wings in fourth round of 1976 amateur draft.
(d)—September, 1980—Signed by Los Angeles Kings as a free agent.
(e)—October, 1985—Traded by Kalamazoo Wings to Milwaukee Admirals for John Flesch.

ANDREAS (ANDY) SCHLIEBENER

Defense . . . 6' . . . 190 lbs. . . . Born, Ottawa, Ont., August 16, 1962 . . . Shoots left.

Year	Team	League	Games	G.	A.	Pts.	Pen.
1979-80—Peterborough Petes (c)		OMJHL	68	8	20	28	47
1980-81—Peterborough Petes		OHL	68	9	48	57	144
1981-82—Peterborough Petes (d)		OHL	14	1	9	10	25
1981-82—Niagara Falls Flyers		OHL	27	6	26	32	33
1981-82—Dallas Black Hawks		CHL	8	2	2	4	4
1981-82—Vancouver Canucks		NHL	22	0	1	1	10
1982-83—Fredericton Express		AHL	76	4	15	19	20
1983-84—Fredericton Express		AHL	27	1	6	7	27
1983-84—Vancouver Canucks		NHL	51	2	10	12	48
1984-85—Fredericton Express		AHL	47	1	11	12	58
1984-85—Vancouver Canucks		NHL	11	0	0	0	16
1985-86—Fredericton Express		AHL	73	3	9	12	60
NHL TOTALS			84	2	11	13	74

(c)—June, 1980—Drafted by Vancouver Canucks as underage junior in 1980 NHL entry draft. Second Canucks pick, 49th overall, third round.
(d)—November, 1981—Traded with John Andrews by Peterborough Petes to London Knights for Venci Sebek and Scott McClellan.

ANTHONY SCHMALZBAUER

Defense . . . 6'2" . . . 215 lbs. . . . Born, New Brighton, Minn., April 23, 1968 . . . Shoots left.

Year	Team	League	Games	G.	A.	Pts.	Pen.
1984-85—Hill Murray H.S.		Minn.	16	1	11	12	..
1985-86—Hill Murray H.S. (c)		Minn.	28	5	11	16	..

(c)—June, 1986—Drafted by New York Islanders in 1986 NHL entry draft. Eighth Islanders pick, 122nd overall, sixth round.

NORM SCHMIDT

Defense . . . 5'11" . . . 190 lbs. . . . Born, Sault Ste. Marie, Ont., January 24, 1963 . . . Shoots right . . . (December, 1984)—Knee injury, missed remainder of season . . . (September, 1985)—Arthroscopic surgery to left knee and missed 13 games . . . (March 1, 1986)—Injured mouth vs. Hartford and missed one game.

Year	Team	League	Games	G.	A.	Pts.	Pen.
1979-80—Sault Ste. Marie Thunderbirds		OPJHL	18	8	16	24	....
1980-81—Oshawa Generals (c)		OMJHL	65	12	25	37	73
1981-82—Oshawa Generals		OHL	67	13	48	61	172
1982-83—Oshawa Generals (b)		OHL	61	21	49	70	114
1983-84—Pittsburgh Penguins		NHL	34	6	12	18	12

Year	Team	League	Games	G.	A.	Pts.	Pen.
1983-84—Baltimore Skipjacks		AHL	43	4	12	16	31
1984-85—Baltimore Skipjacks		AHL	33	0	22	22	31
1985-86—Pittsburgh Penguins		NHL	66	15	14	29	57
NHL TOTALS			100	21	26	47	69

(c)—June, 1981—Drafted as underage junior by Pittsburgh Penguins in 1981 NHL entry draft. Third Penguins pick, 70th overall, fourth round.

SCOTT SCHNEIDER

Center . . . 6'1" . . . 174 lbs. . . . Born, Rochester, Minn., May 18, 1965 . . . Shoots right.

Year	Team	League	Games	G.	A.	Pts.	Pen.
1983-84—Colorado College (c)		WCHA	35	19	14	33	24
1984-85—Colorado College		WCHA	33	16	13	29	60
1985-86—Colorado College		WCHA	40	16	22	38	32

(c)—June, 1984—Drafted by Winnipeg Jets in NHL entry draft. Fourth Jets pick, 93rd overall, fifth round.

DWIGHT SCHOFIELD

Defense . . . 6' . . . 187 lbs. . . . Born, Lynn, Mass., March 25, 1956 . . . Shoots left . . . Missed part of 1977-78 season following knee surgery.

Year	Team	League	Games	G.	A.	Pts.	Pen.
1974-75—London Knights		Jr."A" OHA	70	6	16	22	124
1975-76—London Knights (c)		Jr."A" OHA	59	14	29	43	121
1976-77—Kalamazoo Wings		IHL	73	20	41	61	180
1976-77—Detroit Red Wings		NHL	3	1	0	1	2
1977-78—Kansas City Red Wings		CHL	22	3	7	10	58
1977-78—Kalamazoo Wings		IHL	3	3	6	9	21
1978-79—Kansas City Red Wings		CHL	13	1	4	5	20
1978-79—Kalamazoo Wings		IHL	47	8	29	37	199
1978-79—Fort Wayne Komets		IHL	14	2	3	5	54
1979-80—Tulsa Oilers		CHL	1	0	0	0	0
1979-80—Dayton Gems		IHL	71	15	47	62	257
1980-81—Milwaukee Admirals		IHL	82	18	41	59	327
1981-82—Nova Scotia Voyageurs (d)		AHL	75	7	24	31	*335
1982-83—Montreal Canadiens		NHL	2	0	0	0	7
1982-83—Nova Scotia Voyageurs		AHL	73	10	21	31	248
1983-84—St. Louis Blues (e)		NHL	70	4	10	14	219
1984-85—St. Louis Blues		NHL	43	1	4	5	184
1985-86—Washington Capitals (f)		NHL	50	1	2	3	127
NHL TOTALS			168	7	16	23	539

(c)—Drafted from London Knights by Detroit Red Wings in fifth round of 1976 amateur draft.
(d)—September, 1981—Signed by Montreal Canadiens as a free agent.
(e)—October, 1983—Selected by St. Louis Blues in NHL waiver draft.
(f)—October, 1985—Acquired by Washington Capitals in 1985 NHL waiver draft.

KEVIN SCHRADER

Defense . . . 6'2" . . . 200 lbs. . . . Born, Wells, Minn., February 1, 1967 . . . Shoots right . . . (January, 1985)—Separated shoulder.

Year	Team	League	Games	G.	A.	Pts.	Pen.
1984-85—Burnsville H.S. (c)		Minn. H.S.	27	1	11	12	18
1985-86—Univ. of New Hampshire		H. East	32	1	0	1	22

(c)—June, 1985—Drafted by New Jersey Devils in 1985 NHL entry draft. Seventh Devils pick, 129th overall, seventh round.

WALLY SCHREIBER

Left Wing . . . 5'11" . . . 175 lbs. . . . Born, Edmonton, Alta., April 15, 1962 . . . Shoots right.

Year	Team	League	Games	G.	A.	Pts.	Pen.
1980-81—Fort Saskatchewan Traders		SJHL	55	39	41	80	105
1981-82—Regina Pats (c-d)		WHL	68	56	68	124	68
1982-83—Fort Wayne Komets		IHL	67	24	34	58	23
1983-84—Fort Wayne Komets (a-e)		IHL	82	47	66	*113	44
1984-85—Fort Wayne Komets (a)		IHL	81	51	58	109	45
1985-86—Fort Wayne Komets (b)		IHL	72	37	52	89	38
1985-86—Team Canada		Int'l	..	..	..	..	..

(c)—September, 1981—Traded by Portland Winter Hawks to Regina Pats for future considerations.
(d)—June, 1982—Drafted as underage junior by Washington Capitals in 1982 NHL entry draft. Fifth Capitals pick, 152nd overall, eighth round.
(e)—Won Leo P. Lamoureux Trophy (Leading IHL scorer).

RODNEY SCHUTT

Left Wing . . . 5'9" . . . 187 lbs. . . . Born, Bancroft, Ont., October 13, 1956 . . . Shoots left.

Year	Team	League	Games	G.	A.	Pts.	Pen.
1972-73	Pembroke Lumber Kings	CJHL	55	31	55	86	61
1973-74	Sudbury Wolves	Jr."A" OHA	67	15	41	56	47
1974-75	Sudbury Wolves (a)	Jr."A" OHA	69	43	61	104	66
1975-76	Sudbury Wolves (a-c)	Jr."A" OHA	63	72	63	135	42
1976-77	Nova Scotia Voyageurs (d-e)	AHL	80	33	51	84	56
1977-78	Nova Scotia Voyageurs	AHL	77	36	44	80	57
1977-78	Montreal Canadiens	NHL	2	0	0	0	0
1978-79	Pittsburgh Penguins (f)	NHL	74	24	21	45	33
1979-80	Pittsburgh Penguins	NHL	73	18	21	39	43
1980-81	Pittsburgh Penguins	NHL	80	25	35	60	55
1981-82	Erie Blades	AHL	35	12	15	27	40
1981-82	Pittsburgh Penguins	NHL	35	8	12	20	42
1982-83	Pittsburgh Penguins	NHL	5	0	0	0	0
1982-83	Baltimore Skipjacks	AHL	64	34	53	87	24
1983-84	Baltimore Skipjacks	AHL	36	15	19	34	48
1983-84	Pittsburgh Penguins	NHL	11	1	3	4	4
1984-85	Muskegon Lumberjacks	IHL	79	44	46	90	58
1985-86	Toronto Maple Leafs (g)	NHL	6	0	0	0	0
1985-86	St. Catharines Saints	AHL	70	21	28	49	44
	NHL TOTALS		286	76	92	168	177

(c)—Drafted from Sudbury Wolves by Montreal Canadiens in first round of 1976 amateur draft.
(d)—Won Dudley (Red) Garrett Memorial Trophy (Rookie-of-the-Year).
(e)—Tied for lead in goals (8) during playoffs.
(f)—October, 1978—Traded by Montreal Canadiens to Pittsburgh Penguins for a first-round draft choice in 1981 (Mark Hunter).
(g)—October, 1985—Signed by Toronto Maple Leafs as a free agent.

BARRY SCULLY

Right Wing . . . 5'10" . . . 200 lbs. . . . Born, Toronto, Ont., April 22, 1956 . . . Shoots right.

Year	Team	League	Games	G.	A.	Pts.	Pen.
1973-74	Kingston Canadians	Jr."A" OHA	69	15	27	42	87
1974-75	Kingston Canadians	Jr."A" OHA	67	23	34	57	74
1975-76	Kingston Canadians (c)	Jr."A" OHA	63	25	51	76	65
1976-77	Richmond Wildcats	SHL	38	18	26	44	51
1976-77	Johnstown Jets	NAHL	32	8	8	16	18
1976-77	New Haven Nighthawks	AHL	4	1	1	2	0
1977-78	Toledo Goaldiggers	IHL	75	42	38	80	76
1978-79	Toledo Goaldiggers (d)	IHL	18	9	6	15	8
1978-79	Fort Wayne Komets	IHL	61	33	24	57	24
1979-80	Fort Wayne Komets (b-e)	IHL	80	*61	47	108	22
1980-81	Fort Wayne Komets (a)	IHL	82	*69	39	108	40
1981-82	Fort Wayne Komets (b)	IHL	79	*60	40	100	40
1982-83	Fort Wayne Komets	IHL	76	57	44	101	22
1983-84	Fort Wayne Komets	IHL	18	8	7	15	8
1983-84	Muskegon Mohawks (f)	IHL	19	11	6	17	2
1983-84	Milwaukee Admirals (g)	IHL	4	2	1	3	0
1984-85	Toledo Goaldiggers	IHL	40	29	24	53	10
1985-86	Toledo Goaldiggers	IHL	23	9	9	18	10

(c)—Drafted from Kingston Canadians by New York Rangers in sixth round of 1976 amateur draft.
(d)—December, 1978—Traded by Toledo Goaldiggers to Fort Wayne Komets to complete deal made earlier to obtain IHL rights to Mike Dibble and Barry Marcheschuk.
(e)—Led IHL with 13 playoff goals.
(f)—January, 1984—Acquired on waivers from Fort Wayne Komets by Muskegon Mohawks.
(g)—March, 1984—Acquired on waivers from Muskegon Mohawks by Milwaukee Admirals.

GLEN SEABROOKE

Left Wing . . . 6'1" . . . 175 lbs. . . . Born, Peterborough, Ont., September 11, 1967 . . . Shoots left . . . Also plays Center . . . (July, 1983)—Broken collarbone . . . (February, 1985)—Groin Injury . . . (September, 1985)—Summer long injury, thought to be a pulled groin muscle, turned out to be a dislocated pelvis and he missed most of the 1985-86 season following surgery.

Year	Team	League	Games	G.	A.	Pts.	Pen.
1983-84	Peterborough Midget	OHA	29	36	31	67	31
1984-85	Peterborough Petes (c)	OHL	45	21	13	34	59
1985-86	Peterborough Petes	OHL	19	8	12	20	33

(c)—June, 1985—Drafted as underage junior by Philadelphia Flyers in 1985 NHL entry draft. First Flyers pick, 21st overall, first round.

VENCI SEBEK

Defense . . . 5'11" . . . 185 lbs. . . . Born, New York, N.Y., May 25, 1963 . . . Shoots right.

Year	Team	League	Games	G.	A.	Pts.	Pen.
1979-80—Brantford Alexanders		OHL	61	8	21	29	104
1980-81—Brantford Alexanders (c)		OHL	61	12	16	28	118
1981-82—Niagara Falls Flyers (d)		OHL	16	1	8	9	54
1981-82—Peterborough Petes		OHL	48	22	34	56	123
1981-82—Rochester Americans		AHL	3	0	0	0	2
1982-83—Peterborough Petes		OHL	60	13	44	57	88
1982-83—Rochester Americans (e)		AHL	..	..	..	..	..
1983-84—Rochester Americans		AHL	41	2	5	7	27
1984-85—Flint Generals		IHL	19	4	3	7	19
1984-85—Toledo Goaldiggers		IHL	37	8	14	22	34
1985-86—Toledo Goaldiggers		IHL	16	1	1	2	33

(c)—June, 1981—Drafted as underage junior by Buffalo Sabres in 1979 entry draft. Eleventh Sabres pick, 185th overall, ninth round.

(d)—October, 1980—Traded by Niagara Falls Flyers to Peterborough Petes for Daryl Evans.

(e)—No regular season record. Played in nine playoff games.

ALAN WILLIAM SECORD

Left Wing . . . 6'1" . . . 210 lbs. . . . Born, Sudbury, Ont., March 3, 1958 . . . Shoots left . . . (October, 1980)—Bruised right knee . . . (March, 1981)—Ankle injury . . . (April, 1981)—Suspended for one game in playoffs for abusive language to an official . . . (October, 1983)—Tore abdominal muscles . . . (December 12, 1984)—Pulled abductor muscles in thigh during a team practice.

Year	Team	League	Games	G.	A.	Pts.	Pen.
1974-75—Wexford Raiders		OPJHL	41	5	13	18	104
1975-76—Hamilton Fincups		Jr."A" OHA	63	9	13	22	117
1976-77—St. Catharines Fincups		Jr."A" OHA	57	32	34	66	343
1977-78—Hamilton Fincups (c)		Jr."A" OHA	59	28	22	50	185
1978-79—Rochester Americans		AHL	4	4	2	6	40
1978-79—Boston Bruins		NHL	71	16	7	23	125
1979-80—Boston Bruins		NHL	77	23	16	39	170
1980-81—Springfield Indians		AHL	8	3	5	8	21
1980-81—Boston Bruins (d)		NHL	18	0	3	3	42
1980-81—Chicago Black Hawks		NHL	41	13	9	22	145
1981-82—Chicago Black Hawks		NHL	80	44	31	75	303
1982-83—Chicago Black Hawks		NHL	80	54	32	86	180
1983-84—Chicago Black Hawks		NHL	14	4	4	8	77
1984-85—Chicago Black Hawks		NHL	51	15	11	26	193
1985-86—Chicago Black Hawks		NHL	80	40	36	76	201
NHL TOTALS			512	209	149	358	1436

(c)—Drafted from Hamilton Fincups by Boston Bruins in first round of 1978 amateur draft.

(d)—December, 1980—Traded by Boston Bruins to Chicago Black Hawks for Mike O'Connell.

STEVEN SEFTEL

Left Wing . . . 6'1" . . . 185 lbs. . . . Born, Kitchener, Ont., May 14, 1968 . . . Shoots left . . . (September, 1985)—Broken ankle.

Year	Team	League	Games	G.	A.	Pts.	Pen.
1984-85—Kitchener Greenshirts		OHA Midget	69	58	52	110	176
1985-86—Kingston Canadians (c)		OHL	42	11	16	27	53

(c)—June, 1986—Drafted as underage junior by Washington Capitals in 1986 NHL entry draft. Second Capitals pick, 40th overall, second round.

STEVE SEGUIN

Right Wing . . . 6'1" . . . 191 lbs. . . . Born, Cornwall, Ont., April 10, 1964 . . . Shoots left.

Year	Team	League	Games	G.	A.	Pts.	Pen.
1979-80—Cornwall Major Midgets		Ont. Midgets	55	61	48	109	....
1980-81—Kingston Canadians		OMJHL	49	8	8	16	18
1981-82—Kingston Canadians (c)		OHL	62	23	31	54	75
1982-83—Kingston Canadians		OHL	19	8	17	25	42
1982-83—Peterborough Petes		OHL	44	16	30	46	22
1983-84—Peterborough Petes		OHL	67	55	51	106	84
1984-85—New Haven Nighthawks		AHL	58	18	7	25	39
1984-85—Los Angeles Kings		NHL	5	0	0	0	9
1985-86—Hershey Bears		AHL	75	25	29	54	91
NHL TOTALS			5	0	0	0	9

(c)—June, 1982—Drafted as underage junior by Los Angeles Kings in 1982 NHL entry draft. Second Kings pick, 46th overall, third round.

RICHARD JAMES (RIC) SEILING

Right Wing . . . 6'1" . . . 180 lbs. . . . Born, Elmira, Ont., December 15, 1957 . . . Shoots right . . . Brother of Rod and Don Seiling . . . (January 30, 1982)—Injured eye when hit by stick in game vs. Calgary . . . (December 15, 1985)—Pulled groin vs. Quebec and missed eight games . . . (February 16, 1986)—Bruised knee at Edmonton and missed one game.

Year	Team	League	Games	G.	A.	Pts.	Pen.
1974-75	Hamilton Red Wings	Jr."A"OHA	68	33	30	63	74
1975-76	Hamilton Fincups	Jr."A"OHA	59	35	51	86	49
1976-77	St. Catharines Fincups (c)	Jr."A"OHA	62	49	61	110	103
1977-78	Buffalo Sabres	NHL	80	19	19	38	33
1978-79	Buffalo Sabres	NHL	78	20	22	42	56
1979-80	Buffalo Sabres	NHL	80	25	35	60	54
1980-81	Buffalo Sabres	NHL	74	30	27	57	80
1981-82	Buffalo Sabres	NHL	57	22	25	47	58
1982-83	Buffalo Sabres	NHL	75	19	22	41	41
1983-84	Buffalo Sabres	NHL	78	13	22	35	42
1984-85	Buffalo Sabres	NHL	73	16	15	31	86
1985-86	Buffalo Sabres	NHL	69	12	13	25	74
	NHL TOTALS		664	176	200	376	524

(c)—Drafted from St. Catharines Fincups by Buffalo Sabres in first round of 1977 amateur draft.

DAVID SEMENKO

Left Wing . . . 6'3" . . . 215 lbs. . . . Born, Winnipeg, Man., July 12, 1957 . . . Shoots left . . . (May 20, 1979)—Scored final WHA goal, sixth game of playoff series vs. Winnipeg Jets (Gary Smith in goal) . . . (January 4, 1984)—Sprained left knee in game vs. Minnesota.

Year	Team	League	Games	G.	A.	Pts.	Pen.
1974-75	Brandon Travellers	MJHL	42	11	17	28	55
1974-75	Brandon Wheat Kings	WCHL	12	2	1	3	12
1975-76	Brandon Wheat Kings	WCHL	72	8	5	13	194
1976-77	Brandon Wheat Kings (c-d)	WCHL	61	27	33	60	265
1977-78	Brandon Wheat Kings	WCHL	7	10	5	15	40
1977-78	Edmonton Oilers (e)	WHA	65	6	6	12	140
1978-79	Edmonton Oilers (f-g)	WHA	77	10	14	24	158
1979-80	Edmonton Oilers	NHL	67	6	7	13	135
1980-81	Edmonton Oilers	NHL	58	11	8	19	80
1980-81	Wichita Wind	CHL	14	1	2	3	40
1981-82	Edmonton Oilers	NHL	59	12	12	24	194
1982-83	Edmonton Oilers	NHL	75	12	15	27	141
1983-84	Edmonton Oilers	NHL	52	6	11	17	118
1984-85	Edmonton Oilers	NHL	69	6	12	18	172
1985-86	Edmonton Oilers	NHL	69	6	12	18	141
	WHA TOTALS		142	16	20	36	298
	NHL TOTALS		449	59	77	136	981

(c)—Drafted from Brandon Wheat Kings by Minnesota North Stars in second round of 1977 amateur draft.
(d)—June, 1977—Selected by Houston Aeros in World Hockey Association amateur players draft.
(e)—Signed by Edmonton Oilers (WHA), November, 1978.
(f)—June, 1979—Selected by Minnesota North Stars in NHL reclaim draft.
(g)—August, 1979—Traded by Minnesota North Stars to Edmonton Oilers for a draft choice.

GEORGE SERVINIS

Left Wing . . . 5'11" . . . 180 lbs. . . . Born, Toronto, Ont., April 29, 1962 . . . Shoots left.

Year	Team	League	Games	G.	A.	Pts.	Pen.
1980-81	Wexford Raiders	MTJBHL	40	35	45	80	....
1981-82	Aurora Tigers	OJHL	55	62	55	117	....
1982-83	R.P.I. (c)	ECAC	28	35	29	64	22
1983-84	Canadian National Team	Int'l	43	13	11	24	33
1983-84	R.P.I.	ECAC	12	5	13	18	14
1984-85	R.P.I. (d)	ECAC	35	34	25	59	44
1985-86	Springfield Indians	AHL	30	2	14	16	19

(c)—Named ECAC Top Rookie.
(d)—August, 1985—Signed by Minnesota North Stars as a free agent.

BRENT SEVERYN

Defense . . . 6'2" . . . 185 lbs. . . . Born, Vegreville, Alta., February 22, 1966 . . . Shoots left . . . (October, 1985)—Knee injury.

Year	Team	League	Games	G.	A.	Pts.	Pen.
1982-83	Vegreville Rangers	CAJHL	21	20	22	42	10

Year	Team	League	Games	G.	A.	Pts.	Pen.
1983-84—Seattle Breakers (c)		WHL	72	14	22	36	49
1984-85—Seattle Breakers		WHL	38	8	32	40	54
1984-85—Brandon Wheat Kings		WHL	26	7	16	23	57
1985-86—Seattle Thunderbirds		WHL	33	11	20	31	164
1985-86—Saskatoon Blades		WHL	9	1	4	5	38

(c)—June, 1984—Drafted as underage junior by Winnipeg Jets in NHL entry draft. Fifth Jets pick, 99th overall, fifth round.

DEAN SEXSMITH

Center . . . 6'1" . . . 180 lbs. . . . Born, Virden, Manitoba, May 13, 1968 . . . Shoots left.

Year	Team	League	Games	G.	A.	Pts.	Pen.
1983-84—Notre Dame Hounds		Sask. Midget	26	16	7	23	16
1984-85—Brandon Wheat Kings		WHL	47	8	8	16	31
1985-86—Brandon Wheat Kings (c)		WHL	65	13	23	36	34

(c)—June, 1986—Drafted as underage junior by New York Islanders in 1986 NHL entry draft. Fifth Islanders pick, 101st overall, fifth round.

JEFF SHARPLES

Defense . . . 6' . . . 190 lbs. . . . Born, Terrace, B.C., July 28, 1967 . . . Shoots left.

Year	Team	League	Games	G.	A.	Pts.	Pen.
1983-84—Kelowna Wings		WHL	72	9	24	33	51
1984-85—Kelowna Wings (b-c)		WHL	72	12	41	53	90
1985-86—Portland Winter Hawks		WHL	19	2	6	8	44
1985-86—Spokane Chiefs		WHL	3	0	0	0	4

(c)—June, 1985—Drafted as underage junior by Detroit Red Wings in 1985 NHL entry draft. Second Red Wings pick, 29th overall, second round.

SCOTT SHAUNESSY

Defense . . . 6'4" . . . 220 lbs. . . . Born, Newport, R.I., January 22, 1964 . . . Shoots left.

Year	Team	League	Games	G.	A.	Pts.	Pen.
1982-83—St. John's Prep. (c)		R.I. H.S.	23	7	32	39	....
1983-84—Boston University		ECAC	40	6	22	28	48
1984-85—Boston University (b)		H. East	42	7	15	22	87
1985-86—Boston University (a)		H. East	38	4	22	26	60

(c)—June, 1983—Drafted by Quebec Nordiques in 1983 NHL entry draft. Ninth Nordiques pick, 192nd overall, 10th round.

BRAD SHAW

Defense . . . 5'11" . . . 163 lbs. . . . Born, Cambridge, Ont., April 28, 1964 . . . Shoots right.

Year	Team	League	Games	G.	A.	Pts.	Pen.
1980-81—Kitchener Greenshirts		Ont. Midgets	62	14	58	72	14
1981-82—Ottawa 67's (c)		OHL	68	13	59	72	24
1982-83—Ottawa 67's		OHL	63	12	66	78	24
1983-84—Ottawa 67's (a-d-e-f)		OHL	68	11	71	82	75
1984-85—Salt Lake Golden Eagles		IHL	44	3	29	32	25
1984-85—Binghamton Whalers		AHL	24	1	10	11	4
1985-86—Hartford Whalers		NHL	8	0	2	2	4
1985-86—Binghamton Whalers		AHL	64	10	44	54	33
NHL TOTALS			8	0	2	2	4

(c)—June, 1982—Drafted as underage junior by Detroit Red Wings in 1982 NHL entry draft. Fifth Red Wings pick, 86th overall, fifth round.

(d)—Won Max Kaminsky Trophy (OHL's Top Defenseman).

(e)—Led OHL playoffs with 27 assists.

(f)—May, 1984—Traded by Detroit Red Wings to Hartford Whalers for eighth-round 1984 draft pick (Lars Karlsson).

BRIAN JAMES SHAW

Right Wing . . . 6' . . . 180 lbs. . . . Born, Edmonton, Alta., May 20, 1962 . . . Shoots right.

Year	Team	League	Games	G.	A.	Pts.	Pen.
1978-79—St. Albert Saints		AJHL	53	27	35	62	201
1978-79—Portland Winter Hawks		WHL	4	0	1	1	0
1979-80—Portland Winter Hawks (c)		WHL	68	20	25	45	161
1980-81—Portland Winter Hawks		WHL	72	53	65	118	176
1981-82—Portland Winter Hawks (d)		WHL	69	56	76	132	193
1982-83—Springfield Indians		AHL	79	15	17	32	62
1983-84—Springfield Indians		AHL	4	2	2	4	2
1983-84—Peoria Prancers		IHL	54	27	27	54	49

Year	Team	League	Games	G.	A.	Pts.	Pen.
1984-85—Peoria Rivermen		IHL	63	31	14	45	163
1985-86—Adirondack Red Wings		AHL	23	3	1	4	14
1985-86—Peoria Rivermen		IHL	54	41	23	64	139

(c)—June, 1980—Drafted by Chicago Black Hawks as underage junior in 1980 NHL entry draft. Ninth Black Hawks pick, 78th overall, fourth round.

(d)—Led WHL playoffs with 18 goals.

DAVE SHAW

Defense . . . 6'2" . . . 190 lbs. . . . Born, St. Thomas, Ont., May 25, 1964 . . . Shoots right . . . (December 18, 1985)—Sprained wrist at Montreal . . . (January 27, 1986)—Charley horse vs. N.Y. Rangers and missed two games.

Year	Team	League	Games	G.	A.	Pts.	Pen.
1980-81—Stratford Jr. B		OPJHL	41	12	19	31	30
1981-82—Kitchener Rangers (c)		OHL	68	6	25	31	99
1982-83—Kitchener Rangers		OHL	57	18	56	74	78
1982-83—Quebec Nordiques		NHL	2	0	0	0	0
1983-84—Kitchener Rangers (a)		OHL	58	14	34	48	73
1983-84—Quebec Nordiques		NHL	3	0	0	0	0
1984-85—Guelph Platers		OHL	2	0	0	0	0
1984-85—Fredericton Express		AHL	48	7	6	13	73
1984-85—Quebec Nordiques		NHL	14	0	0	0	11
1985-86—Quebec Nordiques		NHL	73	7	19	26	78
NHL TOTALS			92	7	19	26	89

(c)—June, 1982—Drafted as underage junior by Quebec Nordiques in 1982 NHL entry draft. First Nordiques pick, 13th overall, first round.

LARRY SHAW

Defense . . . 6' . . . 190 lbs. . . . Born, Guelph, Ont., February 10, 1967 . . . Shoots right.

Year	Team	League	Games	G.	A.	Pts.	Pen.
1981-82—Guelph Midgets		OHA	45	8	20	28	70
1982-83—Guelph Platers		OHL	67	0	13	13	107
1983-84—Peterborough Petes		OHL	64	1	11	12	64
1984-85—Peterborough Petes (c)		OHL	55	1	11	12	93
1985-86—Peterborough Petes		OHL	66	2	17	19	106

(c)—June, 1985—Drafted by Washington Capitals in 1985 NHL entry draft as an underage junior. Fifth Capitals pick, 83rd overall, fourth round.

DOUGLAS ARTHUR SHEDDEN

Right Wing . . . 6' . . . 184 lbs. . . . Born, Wallaceburg, Ont., April 29, 1961 . . . Shoots right . . . (October 25, 1981)—Suffered a broken finger and leg and ankle injuries during a team practice . . . Also plays Center . . . (March 24, 1986)—Kidney infection.

Year	Team	League	Games	G.	A.	Pts.	Pen.
1977-78—Hamilton Fincups		OMJHL	32	1	9	10	32
1977-78—Kitchener Rangers		OMJHL	18	5	7	12	14
1978-79—Kitchener Rangers		OMJHL	66	16	42	58	29
1979-80—Kitchener Rangers		OMJHL	16	10	16	26	26
1979-80—Sault Ste. Marie Greyhounds (c)		OMJHL	45	30	44	74	59
1980-81—Sault Ste. Marie Greyhounds		OHL	66	51	72	123	78
1981-82—Erie Blades		AHL	17	4	6	10	14
1981-82—Pittsburgh Penguins		NHL	38	10	15	25	12
1982-83—Pittsburgh Penguins		NHL	80	24	43	67	54
1983-84—Pittsburgh Penguins		NHL	67	22	35	57	20
1984-85—Pittsburgh Penguins		NHL	80	35	32	67	30
1985-86—Pittsburgh Penguins (d)		NHL	67	32	34	66	32
1985-86—Detroit Red Wings		NHL	11	2	3	5	4
NHL TOTALS			343	125	162	287	152

(c)—June, 1980—Drafted as underage junior by Pittsburgh Penguins in 1980 NHL entry draft. Fourth Penguins pick, 93rd overall, sixth round.

(d)—March, 1986—Traded by Pittsburgh Penguins to Detroit Red Wings for Ron Duguay.

NEIL SHEEHY

Defense . . . 6'2" . . . 210 lbs. . . . Born, Fort Francis, Ont., February 9, 1960 . . . Shoots right . . . Brother of Shawn and Tim Sheehy (hockey players) and nephew of Bronko Nagurski (football star for University of Minnesota and Hall-of-Famer with Chicago Bears).

Year	Team	League	Games	G.	A.	Pts.	Pen.
1979-80—Harvard University		ECAC	13	0	0	0	10
1980-81—Harvard University		ECAC	26	4	8	12	22

Year	Team	League	Games	G.	A.	Pts.	Pen.
1981-82—Harvard University		ECAC	30	7	11	18	46
1982-83—Harvard University		ECAC	34	5	13	18	48
1983-84—Colorado Flames (c)		CHL	74	5	18	23	151
1983-84—Calgary Flames		NHL	1	1	0	1	2
1984-85—Moncton Golden Flames		AHL	34	6	9	15	101
1984-85—Calgary Flames		NHL	31	3	4	7	109
1985-86—Moncton Golden Flames		AHL	4	1	1	2	21
1985-86—Calgary Flames		NHL	65	2	16	18	271
NHL TOTALS			97	6	20	26	382

(c)—August, 1983—Signed by Calgary Flames as a free agent.

RAY SHEPPARD

Right Wing . . . 5'11" . . . 175 lbs. . . . Born, Pembroke, Ont., May 27, 1966 . . . Shoots right.

Year	Team	League	Games	G.	A.	Pts.	Pen.
1982-83—Brockville		OPHL	48	27	36	63	81
1983-84—Cornwall Royals (c)		OHL	68	44	36	80	69
1984-85—Cornwall Royals		OHL	49	25	33	58	51
1985-86—Cornwall Royals (a-d-e-f)		OHL	63	*81	61	*142	25

(c)—June, 1984—Drafted as underage junior by Buffalo Sabres in NHL entry draft. Third Sabres pick, 60th overall, third round.
(d)—Won Eddie Powers Memorial Trophy (OHL Scoring Champion).
(e)—Won Jim Mahon Memorial Trophy (Top scoring OHL right winger).
(f)—Won Red Tilson Trophy (Outstanding OHL Player).

GORD SHERVEN

Right Wing . . . 6' . . . 185 lbs. . . . Born, Gravelbourg, Sask., August 21, 1963 . . . Shoots right.

Year	Team	League	Games	G.	A.	Pts.	Pen.
1980-81—Weyburn Red Wings (c)		SJHL	44	35	34	69	....
1981-82—University of North Dakota		WCHA	46	18	25	43	16
1982-83—University of North Dakota		WCHA	36	12	21	33	16
1983-84—Canadian National Team		Int'l	46	9	13	22	13
1983-84—University of North Dakota		WCHA	10	5	5	10	4
1983-84—Edmonton Oilers		NHL	2	1	0	1	0
1984-85—Nova Scotia Oilers		AHL	5	4	5	9	5
1984-85—Edmonton Oilers (d)		NHL	37	9	7	16	10
1984-85—Minnesota North Stars		NHL	32	2	12	14	8
1985-86—Springfield Indians		AHL	11	3	7	10	8
1985-86—Minnesota North Stars (e)		NHL	13	0	2	2	11
1985-86—Edmonton Oilers		NHL	5	1	1	2	4
1985-86—Nova Scotia Oilers		AHL	38	14	17	31	4
NHL TOTALS			89	13	22	35	33

(c)—June, 1981—Drafted by Edmonton Oilers in 1981 NHL entry draft. Ninth Oilers pick, 197th overall, 10th round.
(d)—January, 1985—Traded with Terry Martin by Edmonton Oilers to Minnesota North Stars for Mark Napier.
(e)—December, 1985—Traded with Don Biggs by Minnesota North Stars to Edmonton Oilers for Marc Habscheid, Emanuel Viveiros and Don Barber.

BRUCE SHOEBOTTOM

Defense . . . 6'2" . . . 200 lbs. . . . Born, Windsor, Ont., August 20, 1965 . . . Shoots left . . . (December, 1982)—Broken leg.

Year	Team	League	Games	G.	A.	Pts.	Pen.
1981-82—Peterborough Petes		OHL	51	0	4	4	67
1982-83—Peterborough Petes (c)		OHL	34	2	10	12	106
1983-84—Peterborough Petes		OHL	16	0	5	5	73
1984-85—Peterborough Petes		OHL	60	2	15	17	143
1985-86—New Haven Nighthawks (d)		AHL	6	2	0	2	12
1985-86—Binghamton Whalers		AHL	62	7	5	12	249

(c)—June, 1983—Drafted as underage junior by Los Angeles Kings in 1983 NHL entry draft. First Kings pick, 47th overall, third round.
(d)—October, 1985—Traded by Los Angeles Kings to Washington Capitals for Bryan Erickson.

TERRY SHOLD

Left Wing . . . 6'1" . . . 185 lbs. . . . Born, Grand Marais, Minn., July 29, 1966 . . . Shoots left.

Year	Team	League	Games	G.	A.	Pts.	Pen.
1984-85—Intl. Falls H.S. (c)		Minn. H.S.	23	29	30	59	6
1985-86—Univ. Minnesota/Duluth		WCHA	18	1	1	2	2

(c)—June, 1985—Drafted by New Jersey Devils in 1985 NHL entry draft. Tenth Devils pick, 192nd overall, tenth round.

RONALD SHUDRA

Defense . . . 6'1" . . . 180 lbs. . . . Born, Winnipeg, Manitoba, November 28, 1967 . . . Shoots left . . . Also plays Left Wing.

Year	Team	League	Games	G.	A.	Pts.	Pen.
1984-85	Red Deer Rustlers	AJHL	57	14	57	71	70
1985-86	Kamloops Blazers (b-c-d)	WHL	72	10	40	50	81

(c)—Co-winner of WHL Rookie-of-the-Year Trophy with Dave Waldie.
(d)—June, 1986—Drafted as underage junior by Edmonton Oilers in 1986 NHL entry draft. Third Oilers pick, 63rd overall, third round.

JOHN SHUMSKI, JR.

Center . . . 6'3" . . . 200 lbs. . . . Born, Stoneham, Mass., October 10, 1963 . . . Shoots right.

Year	Team	League	Games	G.	A.	Pts.	Pen.
1981-82	R.P.I. (c)	ECAC	25	5	11	16	16
1982-83	R.P.I.	ECAC	14	5	4	9	12
1983-84	South Shore Braves	NEJHL	..	..	..	..	..
1984-85	University of Lowell	H. East	41	22	31	53	66
1985-86	University of Lowell	H. East	16	1	6	7	10

(c)—June, 1982—Drafted as underage player by St. Louis Blues in 1982 NHL entry draft. Seventh Blues pick, 197th overall, 10th round.

DAVE SILK

Center . . . 5'11" . . . 190 lbs. . . . Born, Scituate, Mass., January 1, 1958 . . . Shoots right . . . Member of 1980 U.S. Olympic Gold Medal Winning Team . . . Cousin of Mike Milbury . . . Grandson of Hal Janvrin (Member of Boston Red Sox) . . . (January 24, 1981)—Bruised right knee . . . (January, 1982)—Bruised shoulder . . . (December, 1983)—Separated right shoulder . . . Also plays Right Wing . . . (February 27, 1984)—Sprained knee . . . (October 23, 1985)—Broke finger on right hand vs. Edmonton and missed six games . . . (December 13, 1985)—Suspended by NHL for six games following a stick-swinging incident with Edmonton's Glenn Anderson.

Year	Team	League	Games	G.	A.	Pts.	Pen.
1976-77	Boston University (c)	ECAC	34	35	30	65	50
1977-78	Boston University (d-e)	ECAC	28	27	31	58	57
1978-79	Boston University	ECAC	23	8	12	20	20
1979-80	U.S. Olympic Team	Int'l	56	12	36	48	32
1979-80	New York Rangers	NHL	2	0	0	0	0
1979-80	New Haven Nighthawks	AHL	11	1	9	10	0
1980-81	New York Rangers	NHL	59	14	12	26	58
1980-81	New Haven Nighthawks	AHL	12	0	4	4	34
1981-82	New York Rangers	NHL	64	15	20	35	39
1982-83	New York Rangers	NHL	16	1	1	2	15
1982-83	Binghamton Whalers	AHL	9	1	2	3	29
1982-83	Tulsa Oilers	CHL	40	28	29	57	67
1983-84	Boston Bruins (f)	NHL	35	13	17	30	64
1983-84	Hershey Bears	AHL	15	11	10	21	22
1984-85	Boston Bruins (g)	NHL	29	7	5	12	22
1984-85	Detroit Red Wings (h)	NHL	12	3	0	3	10
1985-86	Winnipeg Jets	NHL	32	2	4	6	63
1985-86	Sherbrooke Canadiens	AHL	18	5	14	19	18
	NHL TOTALS		249	55	59	114	271

(c)—Named ECAC top rookie.
(d)—Named to All-ECAC and All-New England Teams.
(e)—June, 1978—Draft by New York Rangers in 1978 NHL amateur draft. Third Rangers pick, 59th overall, fourth round.
(f)—October, 1983—Traded by New York Rangers to Boston Bruins for Dave Barr.
(g)—December, 1984—Claimed on waivers by Detroit Red Wings from Boston Bruins.
(h)—August, 1985—Signed by Winnipeg Jets as a free agent.

MICHAEL SILTALA

Right Wing . . . 5'10" . . . 173 lbs. . . . Born, Toronto, Ont., August 5, 1963 . . . Shoots right.

Year	Team	League	Games	G.	A.	Pts.	Pen.
1979-80	Sault Ste. Marie	Ont. Midget	57	78	83	161	....
1980-81	Kingston Canadians (c)	OMJHL	63	18	22	40	23
1981-82	Kingston Canadians	OHL	59	38	49	87	70
1981-82	Washington Capitals	NHL	3	1	0	1	2
1982-83	Kingston Canadians (a)	OHL	50	53	61	114	45
1982-83	Hershey Bears	AHL	9	0	3	3	2
1983-84	Hershey Bears	AHL	50	15	17	32	29

Year	Team	League	Games	G.	A.	Pts.	Pen.
1984-85—Binghamton Whalers (b)		AHL	75	42	36	78	53
1985-86—Binghamton Whalers (d)		AHL	50	25	22	47	36
NHL TOTALS			3	1	0	1	2

(c)—June, 1980—Drafted as underage junior by Washington Capitals in 1980 NHL entry draft. Fourth Capitals pick, 89th overall, fifth round.

(d)—August, 1986—Signed by New York Rangers as a free agent.

RISTO SILTANEN

Defense . . . 5'9" . . . 180 lbs. . . . Born, Manta, Finland, October 31, 1958 . . . Shoots right . . . (January 2, 1986)—Separated shoulder vs. Quebec and missed five games . . . (February 14, 1986)—Sprained knee vs. Winnipeg.

Year	Team	League	Games	G.	A.	Pts.	Pen.
1976-77—Ilves (a)		Finland	36	10	7	17	28
1977-78—Ilves		Finland	36	7	8	15	42
1978-79—Edmonton Oilers (c-d-e-f)		WHA	20	3	4	7	4
1979-80—Edmonton Oilers		NHL	64	6	29	35	26
1980-81—Edmonton Oilers		NHL	79	17	36	53	54
1981-82—Edmonton Oilers (g)		NHL	63	15	48	63	24
1982-83—Hartford Whalers		NHL	74	5	25	30	28
1983-84—Hartford Whalers		NHL	75	15	38	53	34
1984-85—Hartford Whalers		NHL	76	12	33	45	30
1985-86—Hartford Whalers (h)		NHL	52	8	22	30	30
1985-86—Quebec Nordiques		NHL	13	2	5	7	6
WHA TOTALS			20	3	4	7	4
NHL TOTALS			496	80	236	316	232

(c)—June, 1978—Drafted by St. Louis Blues in amateur draft. Thirteenth St. Louis pick, 173rd overall, 11th round.

(d)—March, 1979—Signed as a free agent by Edmonton Oilers.

(e)—June, 1979—Selected by St. Louis Blues in NHL reclaim draft.

(f)—August, 1979—Traded with Tom Roulston by St. Louis Blues to Edmonton Oilers for Joe Micheletti.

(g)—August, 1982—Traded with Brent Loney by Edmonton Oilers to Hartford Whalers for Ken Linseman and Don Nachbaur.

(h)—March, 1986—Traded by Hartford Whalers to Quebec Nordiques for John Anderson.

CHARLES ROBERT SIMMER

Left Wing . . . 6'3" . . . 210 lbs. . . . Born, Terrace Bay, Ont., March 20, 1954 . . . Shoots left . . . Also plays Center . . . Missed part of 1975-76 season with knee surgery . . . Scored goals in 13 straight games in 1979-80 to set modern NHL record . . . Missed 15 games in 1979-80 season with strained ligaments in knee . . . Only the second player in NHL history to not have a hat trick during a 50-goal season (Vic Hadfield was the first during 1971-72 season with N.Y. Rangers) . . . (March 2, 1981)—Broke right leg . . . (September, 1984)—Suspended by L.A. Kings for not reporting to training camp. He demanded to be traded . . . (October, 1984)—Reported to L.A. camp and suspended . . . (January, 1985)—Broken jaw . . . (November 10, 1985)—Torn medial collateral ligament of right knee vs. Minnesota and missed 19 games . . . (January 4, 1986)—Injured eye when struck by stick vs. Buffalo and missed six games.

Year	Team	League	Games	G.	A.	Pts.	Pen.
1971-72—Kenora Muskies		MJHL	45	14	31	45	77
1972-73—Kenora Muskies (a)		MJHL	48	43	*68	*111	57
1973-74—S Ste. Marie Greyh'ds (c)		Jr."A"OHA	70	45	54	99	137
1974-75—Salt Lake Golden Eagles		CHL	47	12	29	41	86
1974-75—California Seals		NHL	35	8	13	21	26
1975-76—Salt Lake Golden Eagles		CHL	42	23	16	39	96
1975-76—California Seals		NHL	21	1	1	2	22
1976-77—Salt Lake Golden Eagles (b)		CHL	51	32	30	62	37
1976-77—Cleveland Barons (d)		NHL	24	2	0	2	16
1977-78—Springfield Indians (b)		AHL	75	42	41	83	100
1977-78—Los Angeles Kings		NHL	3	0	0	0	2
1978-79—Springfield Indians		AHL	39	13	23	36	33
1978-79—Los Angeles Kings		NHL	38	21	27	48	16
1979-80—Los Angeles Kings (a)		NHL	64	*56	45	101	65
1980-81—Los Angeles Kings (a)		NHL	65	56	49	105	62
1981-82—Los Angeles Kings		NHL	50	15	24	39	42
1982-83—Los Angeles Kings		NHL	80	29	51	80	51
1983-84—Los Angeles Kings		NHL	79	44	48	92	78
1984-85—Los Angeles Kings (e)		NHL	5	1	0	1	4
1984-85—Boston Bruins		NHL	63	33	30	63	35
1985-86—Boston Bruins (f)		NHL	55	36	23	59	42
NHL TOTALS			582	302	311	613	461

(c)—Drafted from Sault Ste. Marie Greyhounds by California Golden Seals in third round of 1974 amateur draft.
(d)—August, 1977—Signed by Los Angeles Kings as free agent.
(e)—October, 1984—Traded by Los Angeles Kings to Boston Bruins for first round 1985 draft pick (Craig Duncanson).
(f)—Won Bill Masterton Memorial Trophy.

FRANK SIMONETTI

Defense . . . 6'1" . . . 190 lbs. . . . Born, Melrose, Mass., Sept. 11, 1962 . . . Shoots right . . . (Summer, 1985)—Mononucleosis . . . (November 12, 1985)—Surgery to left shoulder.

Year Team	League	Games	G.	A.	Pts.	Pen.
1983-84—Norwick University	ECAC-II	..	..	..	..	..
1984-85—Hershey Bears (c)	AHL	31	0	6	6	14
1984-85—Boston Bruins	NHL	43	1	5	6	26
1985-86—Boston Bruins	NHL	17	1	0	1	14
1985-86—Moncton Golden Flames	AHL	5	0	0	0	2
NHL TOTALS		60	2	5	7	40

(c)—September, 1984—Signed by Boston Bruins as a free agent.

CRAIG SIMPSON

Center . . . 6'2" . . . 185 lbs. . . . Born, London, Ont., February 15, 1967 . . . Shoot right . . . Brother of Dave Simpson . . . Son of Marion Simpson (Member of 1952 Canadian Women's Olympic Track Team).

Year Team	League	Games	G.	A.	Pts.	Pen.
1982-83—London Diamonds Jr. B.	OHA	..	48	63	*111	..
1983-84—Michigan State	CCHA	30	8	28	36	22
1984-85—Michigan State (a-c-d)	CCHA	42	31	53	84	33
1985-86—Pittsburgh Penguins	NHL	76	11	17	28	49
NHL TOTALS		76	11	17	28	49

(c)—First Team All-America (West).
(d)—June, 1985—Drafted by Pittsburgh Penguins in 1985 NHL entry draft. First Penguins pick, 2nd overall, first round.

DAVID STEWART SIMPSON

Center . . . 6' . . . 187 lbs. . . . Born, London, Ont., March 3, 1962 . . . Shoots left . . . Brother of Craig Simpson . . . Son of Marion Simpson (member of 1952 Canadian Olympic Track Team) . . . (November, 1982)—Strained tendon in left ankle.

Year Team	League	Games	G.	A.	Pts.	Pen.
1979-80—London Knights (c)	OHL	68	29	44	73	38
1980-81—London Knights	OHL	67	34	56	90	80
1981-82—London Knights (a-d-e-f)	OHL	68	67	88	*155	18
1981-82—Indianapolis Checkers	CHL	3	0	1	1	0
1982-83—Indianapolis Checkers	CHL	70	29	39	68	69
1983-84—Indianapolis Checkers	CHL	72	24	43	67	26
1984-85—Team Canada	Int'l	10	1	5	6	2
1985-86—Baltimore Skipjacks (g)	AHL	79	13	19	32	56

(c)—June, 1981—Drafted as underage junior by New York Islanders in 1980 NHL entry draft. Third Islanders pick, 59th overall, third round.
(d)—Winner of Red Tilson Trophy (Most outstanding OHL player).
(e)—Winner of William Hanley Trophy (Most Gentlemanly OHL player).
(f)—Winner of Eddie Powers Memorial Trophy (Leading OHL scorer).
(g)—September, 1985—Traded by New York Islanders to Pittsburgh Penguins for future considerations.

ILKKA SINISALO

Left Wing . . . 6'1" . . . 190 lbs. . . . Born, Valeskoski, Finland, July 10, 1958 . . . Shoots left . . . (September, 1982)—Broke collarbone . . . (December, 1984)—Missed 10 games with back spasms . . . (December 7, 1985)—Infected left ankle and missed three games.

Year Team	League	Games	G.	A.	Pts.	Pen.
1979-80—Helsinki IFK	Finland	35	16	9	25	16
1980-81—Helsinki IFK	Finland	36	27	17	44	14
1981-82—Philadelphia Flyers (c)	NHL	66	15	22	37	22
1982-83—Philadelphia Flyers	NHL	61	21	29	50	16
1983-84—Philadelphia Flyers	NHL	73	29	17	46	29
1984-85—Philadelphia Flyers	NHL	70	36	37	73	16
1985-86—Philadelphia Flyers	NHL	74	39	37	76	31
NHL TOTALS		344	140	142	282	114

(c)—February, 1981—Signed by Philadelphia Flyers as a free agent.

VILLE SIREN

Defense ... 6'2" ... 185 lbs. ... Born, Helsinki, Finland, November 2, 1964 ... Shoots left ... (October 16, 1985)—Fractured right ankle at Chicago and missed 19 games.

Year	Team	League	Games	G.	A.	Pts.	Pen.
1984-85—Ilves (c-d)		Finland	36	11	3	24	..
1985-86—Pittsburgh Penguins		NHL	60	4	8	12	32
	NHL TOTALS		60	4	8	12	32

   (c)—June, 1983—Drafted by Hartford Whalers in NHL entry draft. Third Whalers pick, 23rd overall, second round.

   (d)—November, 1984—Traded by Hartford Whalers to Pittsburgh Penguins for Pat Boutette.

RANDY SISKA

Center ... 6'2" ... 195 lbs. ... Born, Calgary, Alta., June 1, 1967 ... Shoots left ... Also plays Left Wing ... (March, 1984)—Fractured thumb that required surgery to insert two pins.

Year	Team	League	Games	G.	A.	Pts.	Pen.
1983-84—Victoria Cougars		WHL	57	3	4	7	4
1984-85—Victoria Cougars		WHL	11	4	0	4	4
1984-85—Medicine Hat Tigers (c)		WHL	56	16	12	28	35
1985-86—Medicine Hat Tigers		WHL	41	11	13	24	19

   (c)—June, 1985—Drafted as underage junior by Vancouver Canucks in 1985 NHL entry draft. Fourth Canucks pick, 67th overall, fourth round.

RANDALL SKARDA

Defense ... 6'1" ... 195 lbs. ... Born, St. Paul, Minn., May 5, 1968 ... Shoots right.

Year	Team	League	Games	G.	A.	Pts.	Pen.
1984-85—St. Thomas Academy		Minn.	23	14	42	56	....
1985-86—St. Thomas Academy (c)		Minn.	23	15	27	42	....

   (c)—June, 1986—Drafted by St. Louis Blues in 1986 NHL entry draft. Eighth Blues pick, 157th overall, eighth round.

PETRI SKRIKO

Right Wing ... 5'10" ... 172 lbs. ... Born, Laapeenranta, Finland, March 12, 1962 ... Shoots left ... (October, 1984)—Broken thumb.

Year	Team	League	Games	G.	A.	Pts.	Pen.
1980-81—Saipa		Finland	36	20	13	33	14
1981-82—Saipa		Finland	33	19	27	46	24
1982-83—Saipa		Finland	36	23	12	35	12
1983-84—Saipa (c)		Finland	32	25	26	51	13
1984-85—Vancouver Canucks		NHL	72	21	14	35	10
1985-86—Vancouver Canucks		NHL	80	38	40	78	34
	NHL TOTALS		152	59	54	113	44

   (c)—June, 1981—Drafted by Vancouver Canucks in NHL entry draft. Seventh Canucks pick, 157th overall, seventh round.

BRIAN SKRUDLAND

Center ... 6' ... 180 lbs. ... Born, Peace River, Alta, July 31, 1963 ... Shoots left ... Cousin of Barry Pederson.

Year	Team	League	Games	G.	A.	Pts.	Pen.
1980-81—Saskatoon Blades		WHL	66	15	27	42	97
1981-82—Saskatoon Blades		WHL	71	27	29	56	135
1982-83—Saskatoon Blades (c)		WHL	71	35	59	94	42
1983-84—Nova Scotia Voyageurs		AHL	56	13	12	25	55
1984-85—Sherbrooke Canadiens		AHL	70	22	28	50	109
1985-86—Montreal Canadiens		NHL	65	9	13	22	57
	NHL TOTALS		65	9	13	22	57

   (c)—August, 1983—Signed as free agent by Montreal Canadiens.

LOUIS SLEIGHER

Right Wing ... 5'11" ... 195 lbs. ... Born, Nouvelle, Que., October 23, 1958 ... Shoots right ... (February, 1981)—Back spasms ... (January 19, 1984)—Injured knee in game at Boston ... (January, 1985)—Damaged rib cartilage ... (October 16, 1985)—Pulled groin at Vancouver and missed 24 games ... (December 10, 1985)—Reinjured groin at Philadelphia and missed another 24 games.

Year	Team	League	Games	G.	A.	Pts.	Pen.
1976-77—Chicoutimi Sagueneens		QJHL	70	53	48	101	49
1977-78—Chicoutimi Sagueneens (c-d)		QJHL	71	65	54	119	125

Year	Team	League	Games	G.	A.	Pts.	Pen.
1978-79—Birmingham Bulls		WHA	62	26	12	38	46
1979-80—Quebec Nordiques		NHL	2	0	1	1	0
1979-80—Syracuse Blazers		AHL	58	28	15	43	37
1980-81—Erie Blades (b)		EHL	50	39	29	68	129
1981-82—Fredericton Express		AHL	59	32	34	66	37
1981-82—Quebec Nordiques		NHL	8	0	0	0	0
1982-83—Fredericton Express		AHL	12	8	2	10	9
1982-83—Quebec Nordiques		NHL	51	14	10	24	49
1983-84—Quebec Nordiques		NHL	44	15	19	34	32
1984-85—Quebec Nordiques (e)		NHL	6	1	2	3	0
1984-85—Boston Bruins		NHL	70	12	19	31	45
1985-86—Boston Bruins		NHL	13	4	2	6	20
WHA TOTALS			62	26	12	38	46
NHL TOTALS			194	46	53	99	146

(c)—Drafted from Chicoutimi Sagueneens by Montreal Canadiens in 21st round of 1978 amateur draft.
(d)—June, 1978—Selected by Birmingham Bulls in World Hockey Association amateur player draft.
(e)—October, 1984—Traded by Quebec Nordiques to Boston Bruins for Luc Dufour and fourth-round 1985 NHL entry draft pick (Peter Massey).

DOUG SMAIL

Left Wing . . . 5'10" . . . 175 lbs. . . . Born, Moose Jaw, Sask., September 2, 1957 . . . Shoots left . . . (January 10, 1981)—Suffered fractured jaw, also broke jaw in a November 1980 practice . . . (December 20, 1981)—Set NHL record for fastest goal at start of game (5 seconds) vs. St. Louis . . . (December, 1983)—Stretched knee ligaments . . . (October 25, 1985)—Pulled leg muscle vs. Washington and missed seven games.

Year	Team	League	Games	G.	A.	Pts.	Pen.
1977-78—Univ. of North Dakota		WCHA	38	22	28	50	52
1978-79—Univ. of North Dakota		WCHA	35	24	34	58	46
1979-80—Univ. of North Dakota (b-c-d)		WCHA	40	43	44	87	70
1980-81—Winnipeg Jets		NHL	30	10	8	18	45
1981-82—Winnipeg Jets		NHL	72	17	18	35	55
1982-83—Winnipeg Jets		NHL	80	15	29	44	32
1983-84—Winnipeg Jets		NHL	66	20	17	37	62
1984-85—Winnipeg Jets		NHL	80	31	35	66	45
1985-86—Winnipeg Jets		NHL	73	16	26	42	32
NHL TOTALS			401	109	133	242	271

(c)—Named to NCAA Tournament All-Star team and Tournament's Most Valuable Player.
(d)—May, 1980—Signed by Winnipeg Jets as free agent.

BRAD ALLAN SMITH

Right Wing . . . 6'1" . . . 195 lbs. . . . Born, Windsor, Ont., April 13, 1958 . . . Shoots right . . . (January 19, 1986)—Injured leg vs. Calgary.

Year	Team	League	Games	G.	A.	Pts.	Pen.
1975-76—Windsor Spitfires		OMJHL	4	4	2	6	4
1976-77—Windsor Spitfires		OMJHL	66	37	53	90	154
1977-78—Windsor Spitfires		OMJHL	20	18	16	34	39
1977-78—Sudbury Wolves (c)		OMJHL	46	21	21	42	183
1978-79—Vancouver Canucks		NHL	2	0	0	0	2
1978-79—Dallas Black Hawks		CHL	60	17	18	35	143
1979-80—Dallas Black Hawks		CHL	51	26	16	42	138
1979-80—Vancouver Canucks (d)		NHL	19	1	3	4	50
1979-80—Atlanta Flames		NHL	4	0	0	0	4
1980-81—Birmingham Bulls		CHL	10	5	6	11	13
1980-81—Calgary Flames (e)		NHL	45	7	4	11	65
1980-81—Detroit Red Wings		NHL	20	5	2	7	93
1981-82—Detroit Red Wings		NHL	33	2	0	2	80
1981-82—Adirondack Red Wings		AHL	34	10	5	15	126
1982-83—Detroit Red Wings		NHL	1	0	0	0	0
1982-83—Adirondack Red Wings		AHL	74	20	30	50	132
1983-84—Adirondack Red Wings		AHL	46	15	29	44	128
1983-84—Detroit Red Wings		NHL	8	2	1	3	36
1984-85—Detroit Red Wings		NHL	1	1	0	1	5
1984-85—Adirondack Red Wings (f)		AHL	75	33	39	72	89
1985-86—St. Catharines Saints		AHL	31	13	29	42	79
1985-86—Toronto Maple Leafs		NHL	42	5	17	22	84
NHL TOTALS			175	23	27	50	419

(c)—June, 1978—Drafted by Vancouver Canucks in 1978 NHL amateur draft. Fifth Canucks pick, 57th overall, fourth round.

(d)—February, 1980—Traded with Don Lever by Vancouver Canucks to Atlanta Flames for Ivan Boldirev and Darcy Rota.

(e)—February, 1981—Traded by Calgary Flames to Detroit Red Wings for future considerations. (Detroit sent Rick Vasko to Calgary in June to complete deal.)

(f)—August, 1985—Signed by Toronto Maple Leafs as a free agent.

DERRICK SMITH

Left Wing . . . 6'1" . . . 185 lbs. . . . Born, Scarborough, Ont., January 22, 1965 . . . Shoots left.

Year	Team	League	Games	G.	A.	Pts.	Pen.
1981-82—Wexford Midgets		Ont. Midgets	45	35	47	82	40
1982-83—Peterborough Petes (c)		OHL	70	16	19	35	47
1983-84—Peterborough Petes		OHL	70	30	36	66	31
1984-85—Philadelphia Flyers		NHL	77	17	22	39	31
1985-86—Philadelphia Flyers		NHL	69	6	6	12	57
NHL TOTALS			146	23	28	51	88

(c)—June, 1983—Drafted as underage junior by Philadelphia Flyers in 1983 NHL entry draft. Second Flyers pick, 44th overall, third round.

DOUG SMITH

Center . . . 6' . . . 185 lbs. . . . Born, Ottawa, Ont., May 17, 1963 . . . Shoots right . . . (October, 1980)—Knee injury . . . (October 27, 1982)—Broke left wrist and missed 34 games . . . Also plays Right Wing . . . (January 16, 1985)—Partially tore medial collateral ligament in right knee in game vs. Toronto.

Year	Team	League	Games	G.	A.	Pts.	Pen.
1979-80—Ottawa 67s		OJHL	64	23	34	57	45
1980-81—Ottawa 67s (c)		OHL	54	45	56	101	61
1981-82—Ottawa 67's		OHL	1	1	2	3	17
1981-82—Los Angeles Kings		NHL	80	16	14	30	64
1982-83—Los Angeles Kings		NHL	42	11	11	22	12
1983-84—Los Angeles Kings		NHL	72	16	20	36	28
1984-85—Los Angeles Kings		NHL	62	21	20	41	58
1985-86—Los Angeles Kings (d)		NHL	48	8	9	17	56
1985-86—Buffalo Sabres		NHL	30	10	11	21	73
NHL TOTALS			334	82	85	167	291

(c)—June, 1981—Drafted by Los Angeles Kings in NHL entry draft. First Kings pick, second overall, first round.

(d)—January, 1986—Traded with Brian Engblom by Los Angeles Kings to Buffalo Sabres for Larry Playfair, Sean McKenna and Ken Baumgartner.

GREGORY JAMES SMITH

Defense . . . 6' . . . 195 lbs. . . . Born, Ponoka, Alta., July 8, 1955 . . . Shoots left . . . Missed early part of 1979-80 season after knee surgery . . . (September, 1982)—Injured right knee during training camp and required arthroscopic surgery . . . (March, 1985)—Knee injury . . . (February 21, 1986)—Bruised ankle vs. Pittsburgh.

Year	Team	League	Games	G.	A.	Pts.	Pen.
1973-74—Colorado College		WCHA	31	7	13	20	80
1974-75—Colorado College (c)		WCHA	36	10	24	34	75
1975-76—Colorado College		WCHA	34	18	19	37	123
1975-76—Salt Lake Golden Eagles		CHL	5	0	2	2	2
1975-76—California Seals		NHL	1	0	1	1	2
1976-77—Cleveland Barons		NHL	74	9	17	26	65
1977-78—Cleveland Barons		NHL	80	7	30	37	92
1978-79—Minnesota North Stars		NHL	80	5	27	32	147
1979-80—Minnesota North Stars		NHL	55	5	13	18	103
1980-81—Minnesota North Stars (d)		NHL	74	5	21	26	126
1981-82—Detroit Red Wings		NHL	69	10	22	32	79
1982-83—Detroit Red Wings		NHL	73	4	26	30	79
1983-84—Detroit Red Wings		NHL	75	3	20	23	108
1984-85—Detroit Red Wings		NHL	73	2	18	20	117
1985-86—Detroit Red Wings (e)		NHL	62	5	19	24	84
1985-86—Washington Capitals		NHL	14	0	3	3	10
NHL TOTALS			730	55	217	272	1012

(c)—Drafted from Colorado College by California Seals in fourth round of 1975 amateur draft.

(d)—September, 1981—Traded by Minnesota North Stars with Don Murdoch to Detroit Red Wings giving North Stars option to switch first-round draft choices with Detroit in 1982 entry draft. Minnesota exercised option and drafted Brian Bellows. Detroit drafted Murray Craven.

(e)—March, 1986—Traded with John Barrett by Detroit Red Wings to Washington Capitals for Darren Veitch.

JIM SMITH

Defense . . . 6'1" . . . 215 lbs. . . . Born, Castlegar, B.C., January 18, 1964 . . . Shoots left.

Year	Team	League	Games	G.	A.	Pts.	Pen.
1982-83—Denver University		WCHA	36	10	18	28	10
1983-84—Denver University		WCHA	36	5	15	20	24
1984-85—Denver University		WCHA	37	7	18	25	40
1985-86—Denver University (c)		WCHA	47	10	40	50	37

(c)—July, 1986—Signed by Detroit Red Wings as a free agent.

RANDY SMITH

Center . . . 6'2" . . . 180 lbs. . . . Born, Saskatoon, Sask., July 15, 1965 . . . Shoots left.

Year	Team	League	Games	G.	A.	Pts.	Pen.
1982-83—Battleford Barons		SAJHL	64	25	20	45	141
1983-84—Saskatoon Blades		WHL	69	19	21	40	53
1984-85—Saskatoon Blades		WHL	25	6	16	22	9
1984-85—Calgary Wranglers		WHL	46	28	35	63	17
1985-86—Saskatoon Blades (b)		WHL	70	60	86	146	44
1985-86—Minnesota North Stars (c)		NHL	1	0	0	0	0
NHL TOTALS			1	0	0	0	0

(c)—March, 1986—Signed by Minnesota North Stars as a free agent.

ROBERT DAVID SMITH

Center . . . 6'4" . . . 210 lbs. . . . Born, N. Sydney, N.S., February 12, 1958 . . . Shoots left . . .
Missed part of 1979-80 season with fractured ankle . . . (December, 1984)—Broken Jaw.

Year	Team	League	Games	G.	A.	Pts.	Pen.
1975-76—Ottawa 67's		Jr."A"OHA	62	24	34	58	21
1976-77—Ottawa 67's (b)		Jr."A"OHA	64	*65	70	135	52
1977-78—Ottawa 67's (a-c-d)		Jr."A"OHA	61	69	*123	*192	44
1978-79—Minnesota North Stars (e-f)		NHL	80	30	44	74	39
1979-80—Minnesota North Stars		NHL	61	27	56	83	24
1980-81—Minnesota North Stars		NHL	78	29	64	93	73
1981-82—Minnesota North Stars		NHL	80	43	71	114	84
1982-83—Minnesota North Stars		NHL	77	24	53	77	81
1983-84—Minnesota North Stars (g)		NHL	10	3	6	9	9
1983-84—Montreal Canadiens		NHL	70	26	37	63	62
1984-85—Montreal Canadiens		NHL	65	16	40	56	59
1985-86—Montreal Canadiens		NHL	79	31	55	86	55
NHL TOTALS			600	229	426	655	486

(c)—Won Eddie Powers Memorial Trophy (leading scorer) and Albert "Red" Tilson Memorial Trophy (MVP).
(d)—Drafted from Ottawa 67's by Minnesota North Stars in first round of 1978 amateur draft.
(e)—Won Calder Memorial Trophy (NHL-Top Rookie).
(f)—Named THE SPORTING NEWS NHL Rookie of the Year in poll of players.
(g)—October, 1983—Traded by Minnesota North Stars to Montreal Canadiens for Mark Napier, Keith Acton and third-round draft pick (Kenneth Hodge).

SANDY SMITH

Center . . . 5'11" . . . 185 lbs. . . . Born, Brainerd, Minn., October 23, 1967 . . . Shoots right . . .
(September, 1985)—Torn knee ligaments.

Year	Team	League	Games	G.	A.	Pts.	Pen.
1984-85—Brainerd H.S.		Minn.	21	30	20	50	..
1985-86—Brainerd H.S. (c)		Minn.	17	28	22	50	..

(c)—June, 1986—Drafted by Pittsburgh Penguins in 1986 NHL entry draft. Fifth Penguins pick, 88th overall, fifth round.

STEVE SMITH

Defense . . . 6'2" . . . 190 lbs. . . . Born, Glasgow, Scotland, April 30, 1963 . . . Shoots left . . .
Also plays Right Wing . . . (November 1, 1985)—Strained right shoulder in fight vs. Buffalo
. . . (February, 1986)—Pulled stomach muscle.

Year	Team	League	Games	G.	A.	Pts.	Pen.
1980-81—London Knights (c)		OMJHL	62	4	12	16	141
1981-82—London Knights		OHL	58	10	36	46	207
1982-83—London Knights		OHL	50	6	35	41	133
1982-83—Moncton Alpines		AHL	2	0	0	0	0
1983-84—Moncton Alpines		AHL	64	1	8	9	176
1984-85—Nova Scotia Oilers		AHL	68	2	28	30	161
1984-85—Edmonton Oilers		NHL	2	0	0	0	2

Year	Team	League	Games	G.	A.	Pts.	Pen.
1985-86—Nova Scotia Oilers		AHL	4	0	2	2	11
1985-86—Edmonton Oilers		NHL	55	4	20	24	166
NHL TOTALS			57	4	20	24	168

(c)—June, 1981—Drafted as underage junior by Edmonton Oilers in 1981 NHL entry draft. Fifth Oilers pick, 111th overall, sixth round.

STEVE SMITH

Defense . . . 5'9" . . . 202 lbs. . . . Born, Trenton, Ont., April 4, 1963 . . . Shoots left.

Year	Team	League	Games	G.	A.	Pts.	Pen.
1979-80—Belleville Tier 2	OHL	41	8	25	33	105
1980-81—Sault Ste. Marie Greyhounds (b-c-d)	OHL	61	3	37	40	143
1981-82—Sault Ste. Marie Greyhounds (b)	OHL	50	7	20	27	179
1981-82—Philadelphia Flyers	NHL	8	0	1	1	0
1982-83—Sault Ste. Marie Greyhounds (b)	OHL	55	11	33	44	139
1983-84—Springfield Indians	AHL	70	4	25	29	77
1984-85—Philadelphia Flyers	NHL	2	0	0	0	7
1984-85—Hershey Bears	AHL	65	10	20	30	83
1985-86—Hershey Bears	AHL	49	1	11	12	96
1985-86—Philadelphia Flyers	NHL	2	0	0	0	2
NHL TOTALS		12	0	1	1	9

(c)—Won Max Kaminsky Award (outstanding OHL defenseman).
(d)—Drafted by Philadelphia Flyers in NHL entry draft. First Flyers pick, 16th overall, first round.

VERN SMITH

Defense . . . 6'1" . . . 190 lbs. . . . Born, Winnipeg, Man., May 30, 1964 . . . Shoots left.

Year	Team	League	Games	G.	A.	Pts.	Pen.
1981-82—Lethbridge Broncos (c)	WHL	72	5	38	43	73
1982-83—Lethbridge Broncos	WHL	30	2	10	12	54
1982-83—Nanaimo Islanders	WHL	42	6	21	27	62
1983-84—New Westminster Bruins	WHL	69	13	44	57	94
1984-85—Springfield Indians	AHL	76	6	20	26	115
1984-85—New York Islanders	NHL	1	0	0	0	0
1985-86—Springfield Indians	AHL	55	3	11	14	83
NHL TOTALS		1	0	0	0	0

(c)—June, 1982—Drafted as underage junior by New York Islanders in 1982 NHL entry draft. Second Islanders pick, 42nd overall, second round.

STAN SMYL

Right Wing . . . 5'8" . . . 200 lbs. . . . Born, Glendon, Alta., January 28, 1958 . . . Shoots right . . . Set Vancouver record for points in a season in 1982-83 (Broken by Patrick Sundstrom with 91 in '83-84) . . . Only player to ever play in four Memorial Cup Tournaments . . . (March 26, 1986)—Twisted knee vs. Quebec.

Year	Team	League	Games	G.	A.	Pts.	Pen.
1974-75—Bellingham Blazers	Jr. "A" BCHL	....	...	....	....	....
1974-75—New Westminster Bruins (c)	WCHL	....	...	....	....	....
1975-76—New Westminster Bruins	WCHL	72	32	42	74	169
1976-77—New Westminster Bruins	WCHL	72	35	31	66	200
1977-78—New Westminster Bruins (d)	WCHL	53	29	47	76	211
1978-79—Vancouver Canucks	NHL	62	14	24	38	89
1978-79—Dallas Black Hawks	CHL	3	1	1	2	9
1979-80—Vancouver Canucks	NHL	77	31	47	78	204
1980-81—Vancouver Canucks	NHL	80	25	38	63	171
1981-82—Vancouver Canucks	NHL	80	34	44	78	144
1982-83—Vancouver Canucks	NHL	74	38	50	88	114
1983-84—Vancouver Canucks	NHL	80	24	43	67	136
1984-85—Vancouver Canucks	NHL	80	27	37	64	100
1985-86—Vancouver Canucks	NHL	73	27	35	62	144
NHL TOTALS		606	220	318	538	1102

(c)—No league record. Played in three playoff games.
(d)—Drafted from New Westminster Bruins by Vancouver Canucks in third round of 1978 amateur draft.

GREG SMYTH

Defense . . . 6'3" . . . 195 lbs. . . . Born, Oakville, Ont., April 23, 1966 . . . Shoots right . . . (December, 1984)—Given 10-game OHL suspension for altercation with fans in Hamilton . . . (October, 1985)—Suspended by London Knights . . . (November 7, 1985)—Given eight-game suspension by OHL.

Year	Team	League	Games	G.	A.	Pts.	Pen.
1983-84—London Knights (c)		OHL	64	4	21	25	*252
1984-85—London Knights		OHL	47	7	16	23	188
1985-86—London Knights (b)		OHL	46	12	42	54	197
1985-86—Hershey Bears		AHL	2	0	1	1	5

(c)—June, 1984—Drafted as underage junior by Philadelphia Flyers in NHL entry draft. First Flyers pick, 22nd overall, second round.

HAROLD JOHN SNEPSTS

Defense . . . 6'3" . . . 215 lbs. . . . Born, Edmonton, Alta., October 24, 1954 . . . Shoots left . . . (October, 1981)—Knee injury . . . (November, 1982)—Fractured orbit bone of right eye . . . (January 12, 1983)—Five-game suspension for fight with Doug Risebrough outside Calgary lockerroom . . . Holds Vancouver club record for most career games (683) and penalty minutes (1351) . . . (October 12, 1985)—Strained left knee ligaments in Boston and missed 13 games . . . (November 16, 1985)—Injured knee at Minnesota and missed 19 games.

Year	Team	League	Games	G.	A.	Pts.	Pen.
1972-73—Edmonton Oil Kings		WCHL	68	2	24	26	155
1973-74—Edmonton Oil Kings (c)		WCHL	68	8	41	49	239
1974-75—Seattle Totems		CHL	19	1	6	7	58
1974-75—Vancouver Canucks		NHL	27	1	2	3	30
1975-76—Vancouver Canucks		NHL	78	3	15	18	125
1976-77—Vancouver Canucks		NHL	79	4	18	22	149
1977-78—Vancouver Canucks		NHL	75	4	16	20	118
1978-79—Vancouver Canucks		NHL	76	7	24	31	130
1979-80—Vancouver Canucks		NHL	79	3	20	23	202
1980-81—Vancouver Canucks		NHL	76	3	16	19	212
1981-82—Vancouver Canucks		NHL	68	3	14	17	153
1982-83—Vancouver Canucks		NHL	46	2	8	10	80
1983-84—Vancouver Canucks (d)		NHL	79	4	16	20	152
1984-85—Minnesota North Stars (e)		NHL	71	0	7	7	232
1985-86—Detroit Red Wings		NHL	35	0	6	6	75
NHL TOTALS			789	34	162	196	1658

(c)—Drafted from Edmonton Oil Kings by Vancouver Canucks in fourth round of 1974 amateur draft.

(d)—June, 1984—Traded by Vancouver Canucks to Minnesota North Stars for Al MacAdam.

(e)—August, 1985—Signed by Detroit Red Wings as a free agent.

KEN LAWRENCE SOLHEIM

Left Wing . . . 6'3" . . . 210 lbs. . . . Born, Hythe, Alta., March 27, 1961 . . . Shoots left.

Year	Team	League	Games	G.	A.	Pts.	Pen.
1977-78—St. Albert Saints		AJHL	60	26	16	42	31
1978-79—St. Albert Saints		AJHL	60	47	42	89	63
1979-80—Medicine Hat Tigers (b-c)		WHL	72	54	33	87	50
1980-81—Chicago Black Hawks (d)		NHL	5	2	0	2	0
1980-81—Medicine Hat Tigers (a)		WHL	64	*68	43	111	87
1980-81—Minnesota North Stars		NHL	5	2	1	3	0
1981-82—Nashville South Stars		CHL	44	23	18	41	40
1981-82—Minnesota North Stars		NHL	29	4	5	9	4
1982-83—Birmingham South Stars		CHL	22	14	3	17	4
1982-83—Minnesota North Stars (e)		NHL	25	2	4	6	4
1982-83—Detroit Red Wings		NHL	10	0	0	0	2
1983-84—Adirondack Red Wings		AHL	61	24	20	44	13
1984-85—Minnesota North Stars (f)		NHL	55	8	10	18	19
1984-85—Springfield Indians (g)		AHL	17	6	8	14	0
1985-86—Nova Scotia Oilers		AHL	71	19	27	46	45
1985-86—Edmonton Oilers		NHL	6	1	0	1	5
NHL TOTALS			135	19	20	39	34

(c)—June, 1980—Drafted by Chicago Black Hawks as underage junior in 1980 NHL entry draft. Fourth Black Hawks pick, 30th overall, second round.

(d)—December, 1980—Traded by Chicago Black Hawks with 1981 second-round draft pick (Tom Hirsch) to Minnesota North Stars for Glen Sharpley.

(e)—March, 1983—Traded by Minnesota North Stars to Detroit Red Wings for a player to be named.

(f)—September, 1984—Returned to Minnesota North Stars by Detroit Red Wings to cancel conditional trade of March, 1984.

(g)—September, 1985—Signed by Edmonton Oilers as a free agent.

ROY SOMMER

Left Wing . . . 5'11" . . . 180 lbs. . . . Born, Oakland, Calif., April 5, 1957 . . . Shoots left . . . (March, 1981)—Rib injury . . . Also plays Center . . . (February, 1986)—Dislocated shoulder.

Year	Team	League	Games	G.	A.	Pts.	Pen.
1974-75—Spruce Grove Mets		AJHL	85	20	21	41	200
1974-75—Edmonton Oil Kings		WCHL	1	0	0	0	5
1975-76—Calgary Centennials		WCHL	70	13	24	37	155
1976-77—Calgary Centennials (c)		WCHL	50	16	22	38	111
1977-78—Saginaw Gears		IHL	12	2	3	5	2
1977-78—Grand Rapids Owls		IHL	45	20	18	38	67
1978-79—Spokane Flyers		PHL	45	19	30	49	196
1979-80—Grand Rapids Owls		IHL	9	1	4	5	32
1979-80—Houston Apollos		CHL	69	24	31	55	246
1980-81—Edmonton Oilers		NHL	3	1	0	1	7
1980-81—Wichita Wind		CHL	57	13	22	35	212
1981-82—Wichita Wind		CHL	76	17	28	45	193
1982-83—Wichita Wind		CHL	73	22	39	61	130
1983-84—Maine Mariners		AHL	67	7	10	17	202
1984-85—Maine Mariners		AHL	80	12	13	25	175
1985-86—Muskegon Lumberjacks		IHL	27	5	8	13	109
1985-86—Indianapolis Checkers		IHL	37	9	10	19	118
NHL TOTALS			3	1	0	1	7

(c)—June, 1977—Drafted by Toronto Maple Leafs in 1977 NHL amateur draft. Seventh Maple Leafs pick, 101st overall, sixth round.

KENNETH W. SPANGLER

Defense . . . 5'11" . . . 190 lbs. . . . Born, Edmonton, Alta., May 2, 1967 . . . Shoots left.

Year	Team	League	Games	G.	A.	Pts.	Pen.
1983-84—Calgary Wranglers		WHL	71	1	12	13	119
1984-85—Calgary Wranglers (c)		WHL	71	5	30	35	251
1985-86—Calgary Wranglers (a)		WHL	66	19	36	55	237
1985-86—St. Catharines Saints		AHL	7	0	0	0	16

(c)—June, 1985—Drafted as underage junior by Toronto Maple Leafs in 1985 NHL entry draft. Second Maple Leafs pick, 22nd overall, second round.

TED SPEERS

Center . . . 5'11" . . . 190 lbs. . . . Born, Ann Arbor, Mich., January 21, 1961 . . . Shoots right.

Year	Team	League	Games	G.	A.	Pts.	Pen.
1979-80—University of Michigan		WCHA	30	13	16	29	16
1980-81—University of Michigan		WCHA	39	22	23	45	20
1981-82—University of Michigan		CCHA	38	23	16	39	46
1982-83—University of Michigan (a)		CCHA	36	18	41	59	40
1983-84—Adirondack Red Wings		AHL	79	15	25	40	27
1984-85—Adirondack Red Wings		AHL	80	22	31	53	40
1985-86—Detroit Red Wings		NHL	4	1	1	2	0
1985-86—Adirondack Red Wings		AHL	74	32	35	67	20
NHL TOTALS			4	1	1	2	0

JIM SPRENGER

Defense . . . 5'11" . . . 175 lbs. . . . Born, Cloquet, Minn., May 28, 1965 . . . Shoots right.

Year	Team	League	Games	G.	A.	Pts.	Pen.
1982-83—Cloquet H.S. (c)		Minn. H.S.	23	16	26	42	....
1983-84—Univ. of Minnesota/Duluth		WCHA	42	2	7	9	22
1984-85—Univ. of Minnesota/Duluth		WCHA	48	6	12	18	32
1985-86—Univ. of Minnesota/Duluth		WCHA	42	6	11	17	24

(c)—June, 1983—Drafted by New York Islanders in 1983 NHL entry draft. Ninth Islanders pick, 137th overall, seventh round.

GORD STAFFORD

Center . . . 5'10" . . . 180 lbs. . . . Born, Banff, Alta., October 10, 1960 . . . Shoots right.

Year	Team	League	Games	G.	A.	Pts.	Pen.
1977-78—Billings Bighorns		WCHL	59	11	22	33	54
1978-79—Billings Bighorns		WHL	72	37	66	103	70
1979-80—Billings Bighorns (c)		WHL	68	52	58	110	91
1980-81—Milwaukee Admirals		IHL	40	24	32	56	30
1980-81—Wichita Wind		CHL	27	5	3	8	34
1981-82—Wichita Wind		CHL	49	9	16	25	42
1982-83—Milwaukee Admirals		IHL	77	23	49	72	81
1983-84—Milwaukee Admirals		IHL	79	36	45	81	35
1984-85—Milwaukee Admirals		IHL	6	0	2	2	0
1985-86—Milwaukee Admirals		IHL	82	20	57	77	40

(c)—September, 1979—Signed by Edmonton Oilers as a free agent but returned to play junior hockey.

DARYL STANLEY

Defense . . . 6'2" . . . 200 lbs. . . . Born, Winnipeg, Man., December 2, 1962 . . . Shoots left . . . (January 21, 1985)—Dislocated neck vertebrae and bruised kidney in automobile accident and missed several games at start of 1985-86 season.

Year	Team	League	Games	G.	A.	Pts.	Pen.
1979-80	New Westminster Bruins	WHL	64	2	12	14	110
1980-81	New Westminster Bruins	WHL	66	7	27	34	127
1981-82	Saskatoon Blades (c-d)	WHL	65	7	25	32	175
1981-82	Maine Mariners (e)	AHL	....	....	....	....	....
1982-83	Toledo Goaldiggers	IHL	5	0	2	2	2
1982-83	Maine Mariners	AHL	44	2	5	7	95
1983-84	Springfield Indians	AHL	52	4	10	14	122
1983-84	Philadelphia Flyers	NHL	23	1	4	5	71
1984-85	Hershey Bears	AHL	24	0	7	7	13
1985-86	Philadelphia Flyers	NHL	33	0	2	2	69
1985-86	Hershey Flyers	AHL	27	0	4	4	88
	NHL TOTALS		56	1	6	7	140

(c)—October, 1981—Signed by Philadelphia Flyers as a free agent.
(d)—September, 1981—Traded by Kamloops Junior Oilers to Saskatoon Blades for Brian Propp and Mike Spencer.
(e)—Did not play in regular season. Played two playoff games.

PAUL STANTON

Defense . . . 6' . . . 175 lbs. . . . Born, Boston, Mass., June 22, 1967 . . . Shoots right.

Year	Team	League	Games	G.	A.	Pts.	Pen.
1983-84	Catholic Memorial H.S.	Mass.H.S.	....	15	20	35	....
1984-85	Catholic Memorial H.S. (c)	Mass.H.S.	20	16	21	37	17
1985-86	Univ. of Wisconsin	WCHA	36	4	6	10	16

(c)—June, 1985—Drafted by Pittsburgh Penguins in 1985 NHL entry draft. Eighth Penguins pick, 149th overall, eighth round.

MIKE STAPLETON

Center . . . 5'10" . . . 165 lbs. . . . Born, Sarnia, Ont., May 5, 1966 . . . Shoots right . . . Son of former Chicago defenseman Pat Stapleton.

Year	Team	League	Games	G.	A.	Pts.	Pen.
1982-83	Strathroy Braves	WOJBHL	40	39	38	77	99
1983-84	Cornwall Royals (c)	OHL	70	24	45	69	94
1984-85	Cornwall Royals	OHL	56	41	44	85	68
1985-86	Cornwall Royals	OHL	56	39	65	104	74

(c)—June, 1984—Drafted as underage junior by Chicago Black Hawks in NHL entry draft. Seventh Black Hawks pick, 132nd overall, seventh round.

JAY STARK

Defense . . . 6' . . . 190 lbs. . . . Born, Vernon, B.C., February 29, 1968 . . . Shoots right.

Year	Team	League	Games	G.	A.	Pts.	Pen.
1984-85	Kelowna Wings	WHL	4	0	0	0	0
1985-86	Portland Winter Hawks (c)	WHL	61	2	11	13	102
1985-86	Spokane Chiefs	WHL	8	0	2	2	13

(c)—June, 1986—Drafted as underage junior by Detroit Red Wings in 1986 NHL entry draft. Sixth Red Wings pick, 106th overall, sixth round.

ANTON STASTNY

Left Wing . . . 6' . . . 185 lbs. . . . Born, Bratislava, Czechoslovakia, August 5, 1959 . . . Shoots left . . . Brother of Peter, Marian and Bohuslav Stastny . . . (December, 1981)—Pulled knee ligaments . . . (November 9, 1985)—Missed two games with back spasms . . . (December 10, 1985)—Fractured toe at Buffalo and missed one game . . . (February 1, 1986)—Missed two games with broken ribs vs. Philadelphia.

Year	Team	League	Games	G.	A.	Pts.	Pen.
1977-78	Slovan Bratislava	Czech	44	19	17	36	....

Year	Team	League	Games	G.	A.	Pts.	Pen.
1977-78—Czechoslovakian Nat's.		Int'l.	6	1	1	2	....
1978-79—Slovan Bratislava (a-c)		Czech.	44	32	19	51	....
1978-79—Czechoslovakian Nat's.		Int'l.	20	9	6	15	....
1979-80—Slovan Bratislava		Czech.	40	30	30	60	....
1979-80—Czech. Olympic Team (d)		Olympics	6	4	4	8	2
1980-81—Quebec Nordiques		NHL	80	39	46	85	12
1981-82—Quebec Nordiques		NHL	68	26	46	72	16
1982-83—Quebec Nordiques		NHL	79	32	60	92	25
1983-84—Quebec Nordiques		NHL	69	25	37	62	14
1984-85—Quebec Nordiques		NHL	79	38	42	80	30
1985-86—Quebec Nordiques		NHL	74	31	43	74	19
NHL TOTALS			449	191	274	465	116

(c)—August, 1979—Drafted by Quebec Nordiques in 1979 NHL entry draft. Fourth Nordiques pick, 83rd overall, fourth round.

(d)—August, 1980—Signed by Quebec Nordiques.

MARIAN STASTNY

Right Wing . . . 5'10" . . . 192 lbs. . . . Born, Bratislava, Czechoslovakia, January 8, 1953 . . . Shoots left . . . Brother of Peter, Anton and Bohuslav Stastny . . . (February, 1983)—Surgery for shoulder separation . . . Has a law degree from Komensky University, Bratislava, Czechoslovakia . . . (November 6, 1985)—Injured groin vs. N.Y. Islanders and missed three games . . . (December 28, 1985)—Strained knee vs. Hartford and missed one game.

Year	Team	League	Games	G.	A.	Pts.	Pen.
1980-81—Slovan Bratislava		Czech.	....	...	....	....	....
1981-82—Quebec Nordiques (c)		NHL	74	35	54	89	27
1982-83—Quebec Nordiques		NHL	60	36	43	79	32
1983-84—Quebec Nordiques		NHL	68	20	32	52	26
1984-85—Quebec Nordiques (d-e)		NHL	50	7	14	21	4
1985-86—Toronto Maple Leafs		NHL	70	23	30	53	21
NHL TOTALS			322	121	173	294	110

(c)—August, 1980—Signed by Quebec Nordiques as a free agent.

(d)—August, 1985—Released by Quebec Nordiques.

(e)—August, 1985—Signed by Toronto Maple Leafs as a free agent.

PETER STASTNY

Center . . . 6'1" . . . 200 lbs. . . . Born, Bratislava, Czechoslovakia, September 18, 1956 . . . Shoots left . . . Brother of Anton, Marion and Bohuslav Stastny . . . (December 18, 1982)— Knee injury in game at Buffalo . . . One of only three players to break in NHL with three straight 100-point seasons (Wayne Gretzky and Mike Rogers being the others) . . . (1980-81)—Set NHL records for most assists and points by a rookie . . . One of only two players (Wayne Gretzky) to have 100-point seasons in their first six NHL seasons . . . (October, 1984)—Served five-game suspension . . . (May 2 and 5, 1985)—Scored overtime goals in consecutive playoff games to tie record by Mel Hill and Maurice Richard.

Year	Team	League	Games	G.	A.	Pts.	Pen.
1977-78—Slovan Bratislava (b)		Czech.	44	29	24	53	....
1977-78—Czechoslovakia Nat's.		Int'l.	16	5	2	7	....
1978-79—Slovan Bratislava (a)		Czech.	44	32	23	55	....
1978-79—Czechoslovakia Nat's.		Int'l.	18	12	9	21	....
1979-80—Slovan Bratislava		Czech.	40	28	30	58	....
1979-80—Czech. Olympic Team (c)		Olympics	6	7	7	14	6
1980-81—Quebec Nordiques (d-e)		NHL	77	39	70	109	37
1981-82—Quebec Nordiques		NHL	80	46	93	139	91
1982-83—Quebec Nordiques		NHL	75	47	77	124	78
1983-84—Quebec Nordiques		NHL	80	46	73	119	73
1984-85—Quebec Nordiques		NHL	75	32	68	100	95
1985-86—Quebec Nordiques		NHL	76	41	81	122	60
NHL TOTALS			463	251	462	613	434

(c)—August, 1980—Signed by Quebec Nordiques as a free agent.

(d)—Winner of Calder Trophy (NHL Rookie-of-the-Year).

(e)—Selected THE SPORTING NEWS NHL Rookie of the Year in a vote of the players.

RAY STASZAK

Right Wing . . . 6' . . . 200 lbs. . . . Born, Philadelphia, Pa., December 1, 1962 . . . Shoots right . . . Majored in physical education at U.I.C. . . . Worked in a Philadelphia steel mill, saving enough money to try out with Austin Mavericks in 1982 as a free agent . . . (November, 1985)—Suffered broken nose and concussion in AHL game vs. Maine.

Year	Team	League	Games	G.	A.	Pts.	Pen.
1982-83—Austin Mavericks		USHL	30	18	13	31	....

Year	Team	League	Games	G.	A.	Pts.	Pen.
1983-84—Univ. of Ill./Chicago		CCHA	31	15	17	32	42
1984-85—Univ. of Ill./Chicago (a-c-d)		CCHA	38	37	35	72	98
1985-86—Adirondack Red Wings		AHL	26	13	8	21	41
1985-86—Detroit Red Wings		NHL	4	0	1	1	7
NHL TOTALS			4	0	1	1	7

(c)—All-America second team forward (West).
(d)—July, 1985—Signed by Detroit Red Wings as a free agent.

THOMAS STEEN

Center . . . 5'10" . . . 195 lbs. . . . Born, Tocksmark, Sweden, June 8, 1960 . . . Shoots left . . . (September, 1981)—Lacerated elbow during Canada Cup as a member of Team Sweden . . . (October, 1981)—Injured knee in training camp.

Year	Team	League	Games	G.	A.	Pts.	Pen.
1978-79—Leksands IF		Sweden	25	13	4	17	35
1979-80—Leksands IF (c)		Sweden	18	7	7	14	14
1980-81—Farjestads BK (d)		Sweden	32	16	23	39	30
1981-82—Winnipeg Jets		NHL	73	15	29	44	42
1982-83—Winnipeg Jets		NHL	75	26	33	59	60
1983-84—Winnipeg Jets		NHL	78	20	45	65	69
1984-85—Winnipeg Jets		NHL	79	30	54	84	80
1985-86—Winnipeg Jets		NHL	78	17	47	64	76
NHL TOTALS			383	108	208	316	327

(c)—June, 1980—Drafted by Winnipeg Jets in 1980 NHL entry draft. Fifth Jets pick, 103rd overall, fifth round.
(d)—Named Player of the Year in Swedish National League.

STANLEY MICHAEL (BUD) STEFANSKI

Center . . . 5'10" . . . 170 lbs. . . . Born, South Porcupine, Ont., April 28, 1955 . . . Shoots left . . . Missed part of 1978-79 season with broken collarbone . . . (March, 1986)—Broken ankle.

Year	Team	League	Games	G.	A.	Pts.	Pen.
1973-74—Oshawa Generals		Jr."A" OHA	67	25	32	57	22
1974-75—Oshawa Generals (c)		Jr."A" OHA	61	18	48	66	35
1975-76—Port Huron Flags		IHL	71	26	30	56	59
1976-77—Port Huron Flags		IHL	77	49	54	103	61
1976-77—New Haven Nighthawks (d)		AHL	..	..	..	..	....
1977-78—New Haven Nighthawks		AHL	79	27	37	64	61
1977-78—New York Rangers		NHL	1	0	0	0	0
1978-79—New Haven Nighthawks		AHL	51	18	40	58	71
1979-80—Tulsa Oilers		CHL	71	19	44	63	61
1980-81—New Haven Nighthawks		AHL	20	9	18	27	46
1981-82—New Haven Nighthawks (e)		AHL	16	6	5	11	24
1982-83—Springfield Indians		AHL	80	30	40	70	65
1983-84—Maine Mariners (f-g-h)		AHL	57	26	23	49	47
1984-85—Maine Mariners		AHL	75	19	34	53	67
1985-86—Maine Mariners		AHL	68	32	39	71	70
NHL TOTALS			1	0	0	0	0

(c)—Drafted from Oshawa Generals by New York Rangers in ninth round of 1975 amateur draft.
(d)—No league record. Played two playoff games.
(e)—March, 1982—Signed by New Haven Nighthawks as a free agent.
(f)—January, 1983—Signed by Maine Mariners as a free agent.
(g)—Won Jack Butterfield Trophy (AHL Playoff MVP).
(h)—Led AHL playoffs with 12 goals (tied with Paul Gardner of Baltimore).

RONALD STERN

Right Wing . . . 6'1" . . . 195 lbs. . . . Born, Ste. Agatha Des Mont, Que., January 11, 1967 . . . Shoots right.

Year	Team	League	Games	G.	A.	Pts.	Pen.
1984-85—Longueuil Chevaliers		QHL	67	6	14	20	176
1985-86—Longueuil Chevaliers (c)		QHL	70	39	33	72	317

(c)—June, 1986—Drafted as underage junior by Vancouver Canucks in 1986 NHL entry draft. Third Canucks pick, 70th overall, fourth round.

JOHN STEVENS

Defense . . . 6'1" . . . 180 lbs. . . . Born, Completon, N.B., May 4, 1966 . . . Shoots left . . . (September, 1984)—Knee surgery.

Year	Team	League	Games	G.	A.	Pts.	Pen.
1982-83—Newmarket Flyers	OJHL	48	2	9	11	111
1983-84—Oshawa Generals (c)	OHL	70	1	10	11	71
1984-85—Oshawa Generals	OHL	45	2	10	12	61
1984-85—Hershey Bears	AHL	3	0	0	0	2
1985-86—Oshawa Generals (d)	OHL	65	1	7	8	146
1985-86—Kalamazoo Wings	IHL	6	0	1	1	8

(c)—June, 1984—Drafted as underage junior by Chicago Black Hawks in NHL entry draft. Second Black Hawks pick, 45th overall, third round.

KEVIN STEVENS

Center . . . 6'3" . . . 207 lbs. . . . Born, Brockton, Mass., April 15, 1965 . . . Shoots left . . . Also plays Left Wing.

Year	Team	League	Games	G.	A.	Pts.	Pen.
1982-83—Silver Lake H.S. (c)	Minn. H.S.	18	24	27	51	..
1983-84—Boston College (d)	ECAC	37	6	14	20	36
1984-85—Boston College	H. East	40	13	23	36	36
1985-86—Boston College	H. East	42	17	27	44	56

(c)—June, 1983—Drafted by Los Angeles Kings in 1983 NHL entry draft. Sixth Kings pick, 108th overall, sixth round.

(d)—September, 1983—Traded by Los Angeles Kings to Pittsburgh Penguins for Anders Hakansson.

MIKE STEVENS

Center . . . 5'11" . . . 195 lbs. . . . Born, Kitchener, Ont., December 30, 1965 . . . Shoots left . . . (October, 1984)—Arthroscopic knee surgery . . . Brother of Scott Stevens.

Year	Team	League	Games	G.	A.	Pts.	Pen.
1982-83—Kitchener Ranger B's	MWOJBHL	29	5	18	23	86
1983-84—Kitchener Rangers (c)	OHL	66	19	21	40	109
1984-85—Kitchener Rangers	OHL	37	17	18	35	121
1984-85—Vancouver Canucks	NHL	6	0	3	3	6
1985-86—Fredericton Express	AHL	79	12	19	31	208
NHL TOTALS		6	0	3	3	6

(c)—June, 1984—Drafted as underage junior by Vancouver Canucks in NHL entry draft. Fourth Canucks pick, 58th overall, third round.

SCOTT STEVENS

Defense . . . 6' . . . 197 lbs. . . . Born, Kitchener, Ont., April 1, 1964 . . . Shoots left . . . Brother of Mike Stevens . . . (November 6, 1985)—Bruised right knee at Pittsburgh and missed seven games.

Year	Team	League	Games	G.	A.	Pts.	Pen.
1980-81—Kitchener Jr. B.	OPJHL	39	7	33	40	82
1981-82—Kitchener Rangers (c)	OHL	68	6	36	42	158
1982-83—Washington Capitals	NHL	77	9	16	25	195
1983-84—Washington Capitals	NHL	78	13	32	45	201
1984-85—Washington Capitals	NHL	80	21	44	65	221
1985-86—Washington Capitals	NHL	73	15	38	53	165
NHL TOTALS		308	58	130	188	782

(c)—June, 1982—Drafted as underage junior by Washington Capitals in 1982 NHL entry draft. First Capitals pick, fifth overall, first round.

ALLAN STEWART

Left Wing . . . 5'11" . . . 173 lbs. . . . Born, Fort St. John, B.C., January 31, 1964 . . . Shoots left . . . (1983-84)—Set WHL record with 14 shorthanded goals.

Year	Team	League	Games	G.	A.	Pts.	Pen.
1981-82—Prince Albert Raiders	SJHL	46	9	25	34	53
1982-83—Prince Albert Raiders (c)	WHL	70	25	34	59	272
1983-84—Prince Albert Raiders	WHL	67	44	39	83	216
1984-85—Maine Mariners	AHL	75	8	11	19	241
1985-86—Maine Mariners	AHL	58	7	12	19	181
1985-86—New Jersey Devils	NHL	4	0	0	0	21
NHL TOTALS		4	0	0	0	21

(c)—June, 1983—Drafted as underage junior by New Jersey Devils in 1983 NHL entry draft. Ninth Devils pick, 205th overall, 11th round.

RYAN STEWART

Center . . . 6'1" . . . 175 lbs. . . . Born, Prince George, B.C., June 1, 1967 . . . Shoots right . . . Also plays Right Wing.

Year	Team	League	Games	G.	A.	Pts.	Pen.
1983-84	Kamloops Junior Oilers	WHL	69	31	38	69	88
1984-85	Kamloops Blazers (c)	WHL	54	33	37	70	92
1985-86	Winnipeg Jets	NHL	3	1	0	1	0
1985-86	Kamloops Blazers	WHL	10	7	11	18	27
1985-86	Prince Albert Raiders	WHL	52	45	33	78	55
	NHL TOTALS		3	1	0	1	0

(c)—June, 1985—Drafted as underage junior by Winnipeg Jets in 1985 NHL entry draft. First Jets pick, 18th overall, first round.

WILLIAM DONALD STEWART

Defense . . . 6'2" . . . 190 lbs. . . . Born, Toronto, Ont., October 6, 1957 . . . Shoots right . . . Missed part of 1978-79 season with back injury . . . (January, 1984)—Broken foot . . . (October, 1984)—Strained right shoulder.

Year	Team	League	Games	G.	A.	Pts.	Pen.
1973-74	Dixie Beehives	OPJHL	41	9	24	33	38
1974-75	Kitchener Rangers	Jr."A"OHA	55	6	15	21	70
1975-76	Kitchener Rangers (c)	Jr."A"OHA	4	1	3	4	4
1975-76	St. Cath. Black Hawks	Jr."A"OHA	48	9	31	40	57
1976-77	Niagara Falls Flyers (d)	Jr."A"OHA	59	18	37	55	202
1977-78	Hershey Bears	AHL	54	6	18	24	92
1977-78	Buffalo Sabres	NHL	13	2	0	2	15
1978-79	Buffalo Sabres	NHL	68	1	17	18	101
1979-80	Rochester Americans	AHL	63	12	28	40	189
1980-81	Rochester Americans (e)	AHL	6	1	6	7	12
1980-81	Salt Lake Golden Eagles	CHL	2	0	0	0	2
1980-81	St. Louis Blues	NHL	60	2	21	23	114
1981-82	St. Louis Blues	NHL	22	0	5	5	25
1981-82	Salt Lake Golden Eagles	CHL	40	2	12	14	93
1982-83	St. Louis Blues	NHL	7	0	0	0	8
1982-83	Salt Lake Golden Eagles	CHL	62	10	42	52	143
1983-84	Toronto Maple Leafs (f)	NHL	56	2	17	19	116
1984-85	St. Catharines Saints	AHL	12	2	5	7	11
1984-85	Toronto Maple Leafs (g)	NHL	27	0	2	2	32
1985-86	Springfield Indians	AHL	59	7	19	26	135
1985-86	Minnesota North Stars	NHL	8	0	2	2	13
	NHL TOTALS		261	7	64	71	424

(c)—Traded to St. Catharines Black Hawks by Kitchener Rangers with Ken Campbell and Marc Thiel for Joe Grant, December, 1975.

(d)—Drafted from Niagara Falls Flyers by Buffalo Sabres in fourth round of 1977 amateur draft.

(e)—October, 1980—Traded by Buffalo Sabres to St. Louis Blues for Bob Hess.

(f)—September, 1983—Signed by Toronto Maple Leafs as a free agent.

(g)—September, 1985—Signed by Minnesota North Stars as a free agent.

TREVOR STIENBURG

Right Wing . . . 6'1" . . . 180 lbs. . . . Born, Kingston, Ont., May 13, 1966 . . . Shoots right . . . (September, 1985)—Torn knee ligaments in Quebec training camp.

Year	Team	League	Games	G.	A.	Pts.	Pen.
1982-83	Brockville Braves	COJHL	47	39	30	69	182
1983-84	Guelph Platers (c)	OHL	65	33	18	51	104
1984-85	Guelph Platers (d)	OHL	18	7	12	19	38
1984-85	London Knights	OHL	22	9	11	20	45
1984-85	Fredericton Express (e)	AHL	....	....	....	....	....
1985-86	Quebec Nordiques	NHL	2	1	0	1	0
1985-86	London Knights	OHL	31	12	18	30	88
	NHL TOTALS		2	1	0	1	0

(c)—June, 1984—Drafted as underage junior by Quebec Nordiques in NHL entry draft. First Nordiques pick, 15th overall, first round.

(d)—January, 1985—Traded by Guelph Platers to London Knights for Mike Murray and Ron Coutts.

(e)—Played two playoff games (no points).

MICHAEL PATRICK STOTHERS

Defense . . . 6'4" . . . 210 lbs. . . . Born, Toronto, Ont., February 22, 1962 . . . Shoots left . . . (December, 1984)—Ankle injury.

Year	Team	League	Games	G.	A.	Pts.	Pen.
1979-80—Kingston Canadians (c)		OMJHL	66	4	23	27	137
1980-81—Kingston Canadians		OHL	65	4	22	26	237
1981-82—Kingston Canadians		OHL	61	1	20	21	203
1981-82—Maine Mariners		AHL	5	0	0	0	4
1982-83—Maine Mariners		AHL	80	2	16	18	139
1983-84—Maine Mariners		AHL	61	2	10	12	109
1984-85—Philadelphia Flyers		NHL	1	0	0	0	0
1984-85—Hershey Bears		AHL	59	8	18	26	142
1985-86—Hershey Bears		AHL	66	4	9	13	221
1985-86—Philadelphia Flyers		NHL	6	0	1	1	6
NHL TOTALS			7	0	1	1	6

(c)—June, 1980—Drafted as underage junior by Philadelphia Flyers in NHL entry draft. First Flyers pick, 21st overall, first round.

DOUGLAS STROMBACK

Right Wing . . . 6' . . . 175 lbs. . . . Born, Farmington, Mich., March 2, 1967 . . . Shoots right . . . Also plays Center.

Year	Team	League	Games	G.	A.	Pts.	Pen.
1983-84—Detroit Compuware		Mich. Midget	65	32	45	77	32
1984-85—Kitchener Rangers (c)		OHL	66	20	24	44	48
1985-86—Kitchener Rangers (d)		OHL	13	7	10	17	13
1985-86—North Bay Centennials		OHL	50	19	22	41	50

(c)—June, 1985—Drafted as underage junior by Washington Capitals in 1985 NHL entry draft. Seventh Capitals pick, 124th overall, sixth round.

(d)—November, 1985—Traded with John Keller and Dave McIlwain by Kitchener Rangers to North Bay Centennials for Ron Sanko, Peter Lisy, Richard Hawkins and Brett McDonald.

KEN STRONG

Left Wing . . . 5'11" . . . 175 lbs. . . . Born, Toronto, Ont., May 9, 1963 . . . Shoots left . . . (September, 1981)—Injured back . . . (January, 1983)—Pulled hamstring . . . (January, 1985)—Shoulder injury.

Year	Team	League	Games	G.	A.	Pts.	Pen.
1979-80—Streetsville Derbys		MTHL	35	47	51	98	116
1980-81—Peterborough Petes (c)		OMJHL	64	17	36	53	52
1981-82—Peterborough Petes (d)		OHL	42	21	22	43	69
1982-83—Peterborough Petes		OHL	57	41	48	89	80
1982-83—Toronto Maple Leafs		NHL	2	0	0	0	0
1983-84—Toronto Maple Leafs		NHL	2	0	2	2	2
1983-84—St. Catharines Saints		AHL	78	27	45	72	78
1984-85—St. Catharines Saints		AHL	45	15	19	34	41
1984-85—Toronto Maple Leafs		NHL	11	2	0	2	4
1985-86—St. Catharines Saints		AHL	33	16	25	41	14
NHL TOTALS			15	2	2	4	6

(c)—June, 1981—Drafted as underage junior by Philadelphia Flyers in 1981 NHL entry draft. Fourth Flyers pick, 58th overall, third round.

(d)—March, 1982—NHL rights were traded by Philadelphia Flyers to Toronto Maple Leafs to complete January trade for Darryl Sittler.

TODD STRUEBY

Left Wing . . . 6'1" . . . 186 lbs. . . . Born, Lannigan, Sask., June 15, 1963 . . . Shoots left . . . (October, 1985)—Left Edmonton Oilers' training camp.

Year	Team	League	Games	G.	A.	Pts.	Pen.
1979-80—Notre Dame Midgets		....	58	44	61	105	112
1980-81—Regina Pats (c)		WHL	71	18	27	45	99
1981-82—Saskatoon Blades (a-d)		WHL	61	60	58	118	160
1981-82—Edmonton Oilers		NHL	3	0	0	0	0
1982-83—Saskatoon Blades		WHL	65	40	70	110	119
1982-83—Edmonton Oilers		NHL	1	0	0	0	0
1983-84—Edmonton Oilers		NHL	1	0	1	1	2
1983-84—Moncton Alpines		AHL	72	17	25	42	38
1984-85—Nova Scotia Oilers		AHL	38	2	3	5	29
1984-85—Muskegon Lumberjacks		IHL	27	19	12	31	55
1985-86—Muskegon Lumberjacks (e)		IHL	58	25	40	65	191
NHL TOTALS			5	0	1	1	2

(c)—Drafted by Edmonton Oilers in NHL entry draft. Second Oilers pick, 29th overall, second round.

(d)—September, 1981—Traded by Regina Pats to Saskatoon Blades for Lyndon Byers.

(e)—December, 1985—Traded with Larry Melnyk by Edmonton Oilers to New York Rangers for Mike Rogers.

SIMON DOUGLAS SULLIMAN
(Known by middle name.)

Left Wing . . . 5'9" . . . 195 lbs. . . . Born, Glace Bay, Nova Scotia, August 29, 1959 . . . Shoots left . . . Missed part of 1979-80 season with injury to right knee . . . Also plays Right Wing . . . (November, 1983)—Groin pull . . . (December 14, 1985)—Bruised tailbone at Quebec.

Year	Team	League	Games	G.	A.	Pts.	Pen.
1976-77	Kitchener Rangers	OMJHL	65	30	41	71	123
1977-78	Kitchener Rangers	OMJHL	68	50	39	89	87
1978-79	Kitchener Rangers (c)	OMJHL	68	38	77	115	88
1979-80	New York Rangers	NHL	31	4	7	11	2
1979-80	New Haven Nighthawks	AHL	31	9	7	16	9
1980-81	New Haven Nighthawks	AHL	45	10	16	26	18
1980-81	New York Rangers	NHL	32	4	1	5	32
1981-82	Hartford Whalers (d)	NHL	77	29	40	69	39
1982-83	Hartford Whalers	NHL	77	22	19	41	14
1983-84	Hartford Whalers (e)	NHL	67	6	12	18	20
1984-85	New Jersey Devils	NHL	57	22	16	38	4
1985-86	New Jersey Devils	NHL	73	21	21	42	20
	NHL TOTALS		414	108	116	224	131

(c)—August, 1979—Drafted by New York Rangers in entry draft. First Rangers pick, 13th overall, first round.

(d)—October, 1981—Traded with Chris Kotsopoulos and Gerry McDonald by New York Rangers to Hartford Whalers for Mike Rogers and a 10th-round 1982 entry draft pick (Simo Saarinen).

(e)—July, 1984—Released by Hartford Whalers. Signed by New Jersey Devils as a free agent.

RAIMO SUMMANEN

Left Wing . . . 5'11" . . . 185 lbs. . . . Born, Jyvaskyla, Finland, March 2, 1962 . . . Shoots left . . . Member of 1984 Finland Olympic team.

Year	Team	League	Games	G.	A.	Pts.	Pen.
1981-82	Lahti Kiekkoreipas (c)	Finland	36	15	6	21	17
1981-82	Lahti Kiekkoreipas	Finland	....	...	....	....	....
1983-84	Tampere Ilves	Finland	36	28	19	47	26
1983-84	Finland Olympic Team	Int'l	4	4	7	11	2
1983-84	Edmonton Oilers	NHL	2	1	4	5	2
1984-85	Nova Scotia Oilers	AHL	66	20	33	53	2
1984-85	Edmonton Oilers	NHL	9	0	4	4	0
1985-86	Edmonton Oilers	NHL	73	19	18	37	16
	NHL TOTALS		84	20	26	46	18

(c)—June, 1982—Drafted by Edmonton Oilers in 1982 NHL entry draft. Sixth Oilers pick, 125th overall, sixth round.

PATRIK SUNDSTROM

Center . . . 6' . . . 195 lbs. . . . Born Skellefteaa, Sweden, December 14, 1961 . . . Shoots left . . . (November, 1982)—Shoulder separation . . . (1983-84)—Set Vancouver club records for most points in a season and most goals by a center . . . Twin brother of Peter Sundstrom . . . (September, 1985)—Broke left wrist in final game of Canada Cup Tournament.

Year	Team	League	Games	G.	A.	Pts.	Pen.
1979-80	Umea Bjorkloven IF (c)	Sweden	26	5	7	12	20
1980-81	Umea Bjorkloven IF	Sweden	36	10	18	28	30
1981-82	Umea Bjorkloven IF	Sweden	36	22	13	35	38
1982-83	Vancouver Canucks	NHL	74	23	23	46	30
1983-84	Vancouver Canucks (d)	NHL	78	38	53	91	37
1984-85	Vancouver Canucks	NHL	71	25	43	68	46
1985-86	Vancouver Canucks	NHL	79	18	48	66	28
	NHL TOTALS		302	104	167	271	141

(c)—June, 1980—Drafted by Vancouver Canucks in 1980 NHL entry draft. Eighth Canucks pick, 175th overall, ninth round.

(d)—Won Viking Award (Outstanding Swedish-born player in NHL as voted on by fellow Swedish-born NHL players).

PETER SUNDSTROM

Left Wing . . . 6' . . . 180 lbs. . . . Born, Skelleftea, Sweden, December 14, 1961 . . . Shoots left . . . Twin brother of Patrik Sundstrom.

Year	Team	League	Games	G.	A.	Pts.	Pen.
1979-80	Umea Bjorkloven IF	Sweden	8	0	0	0	2
1980-81	Umea Bjorkloven IF (c)	Sweden	29	7	2	9	8
1981-82	Umea Bjorkloven IF	Sweden	35	10	14	24	18

Year	Team	League	Games	G.	A.	Pts.	Pen.
1982-83—Umea Bjorkloven IF	Sweden	36	17	10	27	....
1983-84—New York Rangers	NHL	77	22	22	44	24
1984-85—New York Rangers	NHL	76	18	26	44	34
1985-86—New Haven Nighthawks	AHL	8	3	6	9	4
1985-86—New York Rangers	NHL	53	8	15	23	12
NHL TOTALS		206	48	63	111	70

(c)—June, 1981—Drafted by New York Rangers in NHL entry draft. Third Rangers pick, 50th overall, third round.

GARY SUTER

Defense . . . 6' . . . 190 lbs. . . . Born, Madison, Wis., June 24, 1964 . . . Shoots left.

Year	Team	League	Games	G.	A.	Pts.	Pen.
1983-84—Univ. of Wisconsin (c)	WCHA	35	4	18	22	68
1984-85—Univ. of Wisconsin	WCHA	39	12	39	51	110
1985-86—Calgary Flames (d)	NHL	80	18	50	68	141
NHL TOTALS		80	18	50	68	141

(c)—June, 1984—Drafted by Calgary Flames in NHL entry draft. Ninth Flames pick, 180th overall, ninth round.

(d)—Won Calder Memorial Trophy (Top NHL rookie).

BRENT BOLIN SUTTER

Center . . . 5'11" . . . 175 lbs. . . . Born, Viking, Alta., June 10, 1962 . . . Shoots right . . . Brother of Brian, Darryl, Ron, Gary, Rich and Duane Sutter . . . (January, 1984)—Missed 11 games with damaged tendon and infection in right hand . . . (March, 1985)—Separated shoulder . . . (October 19, 1985)—Bruised left shoulder vs. N.Y. Rangers and missed 12 games . . . (December 21, 1985)—Bruised shoulder vs. N.Y. Rangers and missed seven games.

Year	Team	League	Games	G.	A.	Pts.	Pen.
1977-78—Red Deer Rustlers	AJHL	60	12	18	30	33
1978-79—Red Deer Rustlers	AJHL	60	42	42	84	79
1979-80—Red Deer Rustlers (c)	AJHL	59	70	101	171	131
1980-81—New York Islanders	NHL	3	2	2	4	0
1980-81—Lethbridge Broncos	WHL	68	54	54	108	116
1981-82—Lethbridge Broncos	WHL	34	46	34	80	162
1981-82—New York Islanders	NHL	43	21	22	43	114
1982-83—New York Islanders	NHL	80	21	19	40	128
1983-84—New York Islanders	NHL	69	34	15	49	69
1984-85—New York Islanders	NHL	72	42	60	102	51
1985-86—New York Islanders	NHL	61	24	31	55	74
NHL TOTALS		328	144	149	293	436

(c)—June, 1980—Drafted by New York Islanders as underage junior in 1980 NHL entry draft. First Islanders pick, 17th overall, first round.

BRIAN SUTTER

Left Wing . . . 5'11" . . . 172 lbs. . . . Born, Viking, Alta., October 7, 1956 . . . Shoots left . . . Brother of Darryl, Brent, Ron, Rich, Gary and Duane Sutter . . . (November 3, 1983)—Hairline fracture of pelvis in game at Boston . . . Holds St. Louis record for most career games and power-play goals . . . (January 16, 1986)—Broke left shoulder . . . (March 8, 1986)—Reinjured shoulder vs. Vancouver. It was his first game back from previous injury.

Year	Team	League	Games	G.	A.	Pts.	Pen.
1972-73—Red Deer Rustlers	AJHL	51	27	40	67	54
1973-74—Red Deer Rustlers (a)	AJHL	59	42	*54	96	139
1974-75—Lethbridge Broncos	WCHL	53	34	47	81	134
1975-76—Lethbridge Broncos (c)	WCHL	72	36	56	92	233
1976-77—Kansas City Blues	CHL	38	15	23	38	47
1976-77—St. Louis Blues	NHL	35	4	10	14	82
1977-78—St. Louis Blues	NHL	78	9	13	22	123
1978-79—St. Louis Blues	NHL	77	41	39	80	165
1979-80—St. Louis Blues	NHL	71	23	35	58	156
1980-81—St. Louis Blues	NHL	78	35	34	69	232
1981-82—St. Louis Blues	NHL	74	39	36	75	239
1982-83—St. Louis Blues	NHL	79	46	30	76	254
1983-84—St. Louis Blues	NHL	76	32	51	83	162
1984-85—St. Louis Blues	NHL	77	37	37	74	121
1985-86—St. Louis Blues	NHL	44	19	23	42	87
NHL TOTALS		689	285	308	593	1621

(c)—Drafted from Lethbridge Broncos by St. Louis Blues in second round of 1976 amateur draft.

DARRYL SUTTER

Left Wing . . . 5'10" . . . 163 lbs. . . . Born, Viking, Alta., August 19, 1958 . . . Shoots left . . . Brother of Brian, Brent, Ron, Rich, Gary and Duane Sutter . . . Played most of 1978-79 season in Japan . . . (1980-81)—Set Chicago rookie record with 40 goals . . . (November 27, 1981)—Lacerated left elbow in game at Edmonton. It later developed an infection and required surgery . . . (November 7, 1982)—Broken nose when hit by high stick by Toronto's Paul Higgins . . . (November, 1983)—Broken ribs . . . (January 2, 1984)—Fractured left cheekbone and injured left eye when hit by slap shot in game at Minnesota . . . (September, 1984)—Arthroscopic surgery to right knee during first week of training camp . . . (October, 1984)—Bruised ribs . . . (December 26, 1984)—Broke left ankle when checked into boards at St. Louis . . . (November 13, 1985)—Separated right shoulder when checked by Randy Moller vs. Quebec. He required surgery and missed 30 games.

Year	Team	League	Games	G.	A.	Pts.	Pen.
1974-75	Red Deer Rustlers	AJHL	60	16	20	36	43
1975-76	Red Deer Rustlers	AJHL	60	43	93	136	82
1976-77	Red Deer Rustlers (a)	AJHL	56	55	*78	*133	131
1976-77	Lethbridge Broncos	WCHL	1	1	0	1	0
1977-78	Lethbridge Broncos (c)	WCHL	68	33	48	81	119
1978-79	New Brunswick Hawks	AHL	19	7	6	13	6
1978-79	Iwakura, Tomakomai (d)	Japan	20	28	13	41	....
1979-80	New Brunswick Hawks (e)	AHL	69	35	31	66	69
1979-80	Chicago Black Hawks	NHL	8	2	0	2	2
1980-81	Chicago Black Hawks	NHL	76	40	22	62	86
1981-82	Chicago Black Hawks	NHL	40	23	12	35	31
1982-83	Chicago Black Hawks	NHL	80	31	30	61	53
1983-84	Chicago Black Hawks	NHL	59	20	20	40	441
1984-85	Chicago Black Hawks	NHL	49	20	18	38	12
1985-86	Chicago Black Hawks	NHL	50	17	10	27	44
	NHL TOTALS		362	153	112	265	272

(c)—June, 1978—Drafted by the Chicago Black Hawks in 1978 NHL amateur draft. Eleventh Black Hawks pick, 179th overall, 11th round.
(d)—Named top rookie of Japan National League.
(e)—Named winner of Dudley (Red) Garrett Memorial Trophy (Top AHL Rookie).

DUANE CALVIN SUTTER

Right Wing . . . 6' . . . 181 lbs. . . . Born, Viking, Alta., March 16, 1960 . . . Shoots right . . . Brother of Brian, Brent, Ron, Rich, Gary and Darryl Sutter . . . (November 11, 1980)—Damaged ligaments in right knee. Injury required surgery . . . (April 2, 1981)—Two weeks after coming back from knee surgery he dislocated right shoulder . . . (November, 1983)—Strained ligaments in left knee in game vs. Quebec . . . (May, 1986)—Surgery to left shoulder.

Year	Team	League	Games	G.	A.	Pts.	Pen.
1976-77	Red Deer Rustlers	AJHL	60	9	26	35	76
1977-78	Red Deer Rustlers	AJHL	59	47	53	100	218
1977-78	Lethbridge Broncos	WCHL	5	1	5	6	19
1978-79	Lethbridge Broncos (c)	WHL	71	50	75	125	212
1979-80	Lethbridge Broncos	WHL	21	18	16	34	74
1979-80	New York Islanders	NHL	56	15	9	24	55
1980-81	New York Islanders	NHL	23	7	11	18	26
1981-82	New York Islanders	NHL	77	18	35	53	100
1982-83	New York Islanders	NHL	75	13	19	32	118
1983-84	New York Islanders	NHL	78	17	23	40	94
1984-85	New York Islanders	NHL	78	17	24	41	174
1985-86	New York Islanders	NHL	80	20	33	53	157
	NHL TOTALS		467	107	154	261	724

(c)—August, 1979—Drafted by New York Islanders as underage junior in entry draft. First Islanders pick, 17th overall, first round.

RICHARD SUTTER

Right Wing . . . 5'11" . . . 170 lbs. . . . Born, Viking, Alta., December 2, 1963 . . . Shoots right . . . Brother of Brian, Brent, Darryl, Duane, Gary and twin brother of Ron Sutter.

Year	Team	League	Games	G.	A.	Pts.	Pen.
1979-80	Red Deer Rustlers	AJHL	60	13	19	32	157
1980-81	Lethbridge Broncos	WHL	72	23	18	41	255
1981-82	Lethbridge Broncos (c)	WHL	57	38	31	69	263
1982-83	Lethbridge Broncos	WHL	64	37	30	67	200
1982-83	Pittsburgh Penguins	NHL	4	0	0	0	0
1983-84	Baltimore Skipjacks	AHL	2	0	1	1	0
1983-84	Pittsburgh Penguins (d)	NHL	5	0	0	0	0

Year	Team	League	Games	G.	A.	Pts.	Pen.
1983-84—Philadelphia Flyers		NHL	70	16	12	28	93
1984-85—Hershey Bears		AHL	13	3	7	10	14
1984-85—Philadelphia Flyers		NHL	56	6	10	16	89
1985-86—Philadelphia Flyers (e)		NHL	78	14	25	39	199
NHL TOTALS			213	36	47	83	381

(c)—June, 1982—Drafted as underage junior by Pittsburgh Penguins in 1982 NHL entry draft. First Penguins pick, 10th overall, first round.

(d)—October, 1983—Traded with second (Greg Smyth) and third (David McLay) round 1984 draft picks by Pittsburgh Penguins to Philadelphia Flyers for Ron Flockhart, Mark Taylor, Andy Brickley, first (Roger Belanger) and third-round 1984 draft picks.

(e)—June, 1986—Traded by Philadelphia Flyers with Dave Richter and a third-round draft choice in 1986 to Vancouver Canucks for J.J. Daigneault, a second-round draft choice (Kent Hawley) in 1986 and a fifth-round pick in 1987.

RONALD SUTTER

Center . . . 6' . . . 180 lbs. . . . Born, Viking, Alta., December 2, 1963 . . . Shoots right . . . Brother of Brian, Brent, Darryl, Duane, Gary and twin brother of Rich Sutter . . . (November 27, 1981)—Broke ankle in game against Medicine Hat . . . (March, 1985)—Bruised ribs . . . (September, 1985)—Pulled hip flexor muscle during training camp and missed the first three games of the season.

Year	Team	League	Games	G.	A.	Pts.	Pen.
1979-80—Red Deer Rustlers		AJHL	60	12	33	35	44
1980-81—Lethbridge Broncos		WHL	72	13	32	45	152
1981-82—Lethbridge Broncos (c)		WHL	59	38	54	92	207
1982-83—Lethbridge Broncos		WHL	58	35	48	83	98
1982-83—Philadelphia Flyers		NHL	10	1	1	2	9
1983-84—Philadelphia Flyers		NHL	79	19	32	51	101
1984-85—Philadelphia Flyers		NHL	73	16	29	45	94
1985-86—Philadelphia Flyers		NHL	75	18	41	59	159
NHL TOTALS			237	54	103	157	363

(c)—June, 1982—Drafted as underage junior by Philadelphia Flyers in 1982 NHL entry draft. First Flyers pick, fourth overall, first round.

JEFF SVEEN

Center . . . 5'11" . . . 175 lbs. . . . Born, Barrhead, Alta., February 5, 1967 . . . Shoots right . . . Also plays Right Wing.

Year	Team	League	Games	G.	A.	Pts.	Pen.
1984-85—Boston University (c)		H. East	42	14	10	24	10
1985-86—Boston University		H. East	35	15	8	23	18

(c)—June, 1985—Drafted by New York Islanders in 1985 NHL entry draft. Seventh Islanders pick, 97th overall, fifth round.

PETR SVOBODA

Defense . . . 6'1" . . . 160 lbs. . . . Born, Most, Czechoslovakia, February 14, 1966 . . . Shoots left . . . (January 20, 1986)—Injured shoulder at Quebec and missed three games.

Year	Team	League	Games	G.	A.	Pts.	Pen.
1983-84—Czechoslovakia Jr. (c)		Czech.	40	15	21	36	14
1984-85—Montreal Canadiens		NHL	73	4	27	31	65
1985-86—Montreal Canadiens		NHL	73	1	18	19	93
NHL TOTALS			146	5	45	50	158

(c)—June, 1984—Drafted by Montreal Canadiens in NHL entry draft. First Canadiens pick, fifth overall, first round.

BOB SWEENEY

Center . . . 6'3" . . . 200 lbs. . . . Born, Boxborough, Mass., January 25, 1964 . . . Shoots left . . . Brother of Timothy Sweeney.

Year	Team	League	Games	G.	A.	Pts.	Pen.
1982-83—Boston College (c)		ECAC	30	17	11	28	10
1983-84—Boston College		ECAC	23	14	7	21	10
1984-85—Boston College		H. East	44	32	32	64	43
1985-86—Boston College		H. East	41	15	24	39	52

(e)—June, 1982—Drafted by Boston Bruins in 1982 NHL entry draft. Sixth Bruins pick, 123rd overall, sixth round.

DON SWEENEY

Defense . . . 5'11" . . . 170 lbs. . . . Born, St. Stephen, N.B., August 17, 1966 . . . Shoots left.

Year	Team	League	Games	G.	A.	Pts.	Pen.
1983-84—St. Paul N.B. H.S. (c)		N.B.H.S.	22	33	26	59	....
1984-85—Harvard University		ECAC	29	3	7	10	30
1985-86—Harvard University		ECAC	31	4	5	9	29

(c)—June, 1984—Drafted by Boston Bruins in NHL entry draft. Eighth Bruins pick, 166th overall, eighth round.

TIMOTHY SWEENEY

Center . . . 5'11" . . . 180 lbs. . . . Born, Boston, Mass., April 12, 1967 . . . Shoots left . . . Brother of Bob Sweeney (Boston College All-America hockey player, 1984-85).

Year	Team	League	Games	G.	A.	Pts.	Pen.
1983-84—Weymouth North H.S.		Mass.H.S.	23	33	26	59	....
1984-85—Weymouth North H.S. (c)		Mass.H.S.	22	32	56	88	....
1985-86—Boston College		H. East	32	8	4	12	8

(c)—June, 1985—Drafted by Calgary Flames in 1985 NHL entry draft. Seventh Flames pick, 122nd overall, sixth round.

PHIL SYKES

Left Wing . . . 6' . . . 185 lbs. . . . Born, Dawson Creek, B.C., May 18, 1959 . . . Shoots left . . . (January 10, 1986)—Strained groin at Minnesota and missed four games.

Year	Team	League	Games	G.	A.	Pts.	Pen.
1978-79—North Dakota University		WCHA	41	9	5	14	16
1979-80—North Dakota University		WCHA	37	22	27	49	34
1980-81—North Dakota University		WCHA	38	28	34	62	22
1981-82—North Dakota University (c-d)		WCHA	45	39	24	63	20
1982-83—Los Angeles Kings		NHL	7	2	0	2	2
1982-83—New Haven Nighthawks		AHL	71	19	26	45	111
1983-84—New Haven Nighthawks		AHL	77	29	37	66	101
1983-84—Los Angeles Kings		NHL	3	0	0	0	2
1984-85—Los Angeles Kings		NHL	79	17	15	32	38
1985-86—Los Angeles Kings		NHL	76	20	24	44	97
NHL TOTALS			165	39	39	78	139

(c)—Named to Western All-America Team.

(d)—April, 1982—Signed by Los Angeles Kings as a free agent.

PETER TAGLIANETTI

Defense . . . 6'2" . . . 200 lbs. . . . Born, Framingham, Mass., August 15, 1963 . . . Shoots left . . . (October, 1985)—Dislocated shoulder in fight with Perry Turnbull during Winnipeg Jets' training camp . . . (February 20, 1986)—Dislocated shoulder . . . (March, 1986)—Surgery to correct recurring shoulder dislocations.

Year	Team	League	Games	G.	A.	Pts.	Pen.
1981-82—Providence College		ECAC	2	0	0	0	2
1982-83—Providence College (c)		ECAC	43	4	17	21	68
1983-84—Providence College		ECAC	30	4	25	29	68
1984-85—Providence College (a)		H. East	43	8	21	29	114
1984-85—Winnipeg Jets		NHL	1	0	0	0	0
1985-86—Sherbrooke Canadiens		AHL	24	1	8	9	75
1985-86—Winnipeg Jets		NHL	18	0	0	0	48
NHL TOTALS			19	0	0	0	48

(c)—June, 1983—Drafted by Winnipeg Jets in NHL entry draft. Fourth Jets pick, 43rd overall, third round.

TERRY TAIT

Center . . . 6'2" . . . 190 lbs. . . . Born, Thunder Bay, Ont., September 10, 1963 . . . Shoots left . . . Also plays Left Wing.

Year	Team	League	Games	G.	A.	Pts.	Pen.
1979-80—Kenora Tier II		MJHL	48	20	30	50	....
1980-81—Sault Ste. Marie Greyhounds (c)		OMJHL	54	6	10	16	90
1981-82—Sault Ste. Marie Greyhounds		OHL	60	18	17	35	96
1982-83—Sault Ste. Marie Greyhounds		OHL	65	29	47	76	59
1983-84—Salt Lake Golden Eagles		CHL	36	1	7	8	7
1983-84—Toledo Goaldiggers		IHL	5	0	0	0	2
1984-85—Springfield Indians		AHL	75	19	25	44	18
1985-86—Springfield Indians (d)		AHL	62	11	19	30	34

(c)—June, 1981—Drafted as underage junior in 1981 NHL entry draft. Seventh North Stars pick, 69th overall, fourth round.

(d)—August, 1986—Signed by New York Rangers as a free agent.

STEVE ANTHONY TAMBELLINI

Center . . . 6' . . . 190 lbs. . . . Born, Trail, B.C., May 14, 1958 . . . Shoots left . . . (December, 1982)—Shoulder separation . . . Son of Adolph Addie Tambellini (member of 1961 World Champion Trail Smoke Eaters) . . . (December, 1984)—Bruised elbow . . . (January 21, 1986)—Injured knee vs. New Jersey and missed 11 games . . . (March 15, 1986)—Broken thumb at Boston.

Year	Team	League	Games	G.	A.	Pts.	Pen.
1975-76—Lethbridge Broncos (c)		WCHL	72	38	59	97	42
1976-77—Lethbridge Broncos (d)		WCHL	55	42	42	84	23
1977-78—Lethbridge Broncos (e)		WCHL	66	75	80	155	32
1978-79—New York Islanders		NHL	1	0	0	0	0
1978-79—Fort Worth Texans		CH	73	25	27	52	32
1979-80—New York Islanders		NHL	45	5	8	13	4
1980-81—New York Islanders (f)		NHL	61	19	17	36	17
1980-81—Colorado Rockies		NHL	13	6	12	18	2
1981-82—Colorado Rockies		NHL	79	29	30	59	14
1982-83—New Jersey Devils (g)		NHL	73	25	18	43	14
1983-84—Calgary Flames		NHL	73	15	10	25	16
1984-85—Moncton Golden Flames		AHL	7	2	5	7	0
1984-85—Calgary Flames (h)		NHL	47	19	10	29	4
1985-86—Vancouver Canucks		NHL	48	15	15	30	12
NHL TOTALS			440	133	120	253	83

(c)—Won WCHL Rookie of the Year Award.
(d)—Won WCHL Most Gentlemanly Player Award.
(e)—Drafted from Lethbridge Broncos by New York Islanders in first round of 1978 amateur draft.
(f)—March, 1981—Traded by New York Islanders with Glenn Resch to Colorado Rockies for Mike McEwen and Jari Kaarela.
(g)—July, 1983—Traded by New Jersey Devils with Joel Quenneville to Calgary Flames for Mel Bridgman and Phil Russell.
(h)—August, 1985—Signed by Vancouver Canucks as a free agent.

TONY TANTI

Right Wing . . . 5'9" . . . 181 lbs. . . . Born, Toronto, Ont., September 7, 1963 . . . Shoots left . . . Broke Wayne Gretzky's record for most goals in rookie OHL season . . . (November, 1981)—Separated shoulder . . . (December, 1981)—Sore hip . . . (1983-84)—Set Vancouver club records for most goals (45) and most power-play goals (19) . . . (November, 1984)—Strained knee . . . Also plays Left Wing.

Year	Team	League	Games	G.	A.	Pts.	Pen.
1979-80—St. Michaels Jr. B		OHL	37	31	27	58	67
1980-81—Oshawa Generals (a-c-d)		OHL	67	81	69	150	197
1981-82—Oshawa Generals (b-e)		OHL	57	62	64	126	138
1981-82—Chicago Black Hawks		NHL	2	0	0	0	0
1982-83—Oshawa Generals		OHL	30	34	28	62	35
1982-83—Chicago Black Hawks (f)		NHL	1	1	0	1	0
1982-83—Vancouver Canucks		NHL	39	8	8	16	16
1983-84—Vancouver Canucks		NHL	79	45	41	86	50
1984-85—Vancouver Canucks		NHL	68	39	20	59	45
1985-86—Vancouver Canucks		NHL	77	39	33	72	85
NHL TOTALS			266	132	102	234	196

(c)—Won Hap Emms OHL Rookie Award.
(d)—June, 1981—Drafted by Chicago Black Hawks in NHL entry draft. First Black Hawks pick, 12th overall, first round.
(e)—Won Jim Mahon Memorial Trophy (Top scoring OHL right wing).
(f)—January, 1983—Traded by Chicago Black Hawks to Vancouver Canucks for Curt Fraser.

DARREN TAYLOR

Center . . . 6'1" . . . 170 lbs. . . . Born, Calgary, Alta., May 28, 1967 . . . Shoots left.

Year	Team	League	Games	G.	A.	Pts.	Pen.
1983-84—Calgary Spurs		AJHL	55	15	21	36	160
1984-85—Calgary Wranglers (c)		WHL	72	11	5	16	54
1985-86—Calgary Wranglers		WHL	41	9	11	20	83
1985-86—Seattle Thunderbirds		WHL	27	2	8	10	54

(c)—June, 1985—Drafted as underage junior by Vancouver Canucks in 1985 NHL entry draft. Twelfth Canucks pick, 235th overall, 12th round.

DAVID ANDREW TAYLOR

Right Wing . . . 6' . . . 185 lbs. . . . Born, Levack, Ont., December 4, 1955 . . . Shoots right . . . Set ECAC record and tied NCAA record with 108 points in 1976-77 . . . Missed parts of

1979-80 season with pulled back muscle and sprained left knee ... (November 5, 1980)—
Sprained shoulder ... (October 29, 1982)—Broke right wrist in collision with Kevin Lowe
at Edmonton, out 33 games ... (January, 1983)—Right knee injury ... (May 28, 1983)—Operation on right wrist he broke for second time in World Championships at West Germany
... Holds single season record for most goals, assists and points by a former college
player ... Holds Los Angeles club records for goals, assists and points by a right wing ...
(November 10, 1983)—Returned from broken wrist in game vs. St. Louis.

Year	Team	League	Games	G.	A.	Pts.	Pen.
1974-75—Clarkson College (c)		ECAC	....	20	34	54	....
1975-76—Clarkson College		ECAC	....	26	33	59	....
1976-77—Clarkson College (d-e)		ECAC	34	41	67	108	....
1976-77—Fort Worth Texans		CHL	7	2	4	6	6
1977-78—Los Angeles Kings		NHL	64	22	21	43	47
1978-79—Los Angeles Kings		NHL	78	43	48	91	124
1979-80—Los Angeles Kings		NHL	61	37	53	90	72
1980-81—Los Angeles Kings (b)		NHL	72	47	65	112	130
1981-82—Los Angeles Kings		NHL	78	39	67	106	130
1982-83—Los Angeles Kings		NHL	46	21	37	58	76
1983-84—Los Angeles Kings		NHL	63	20	49	69	91
1984-85—Los Angeles Kings		NHL	79	41	51	92	132
1985-86—Los Angeles Kings		NHL	76	33	38	71	110
NHL TOTALS			617	303	429	732	912

(c)—Drafted by Los Angeles Kings in 15th round of 1975 amateur draft.
(d)—Named ECAC Player of the Year.
(e)—Named to All-America team (East).

MARK TAYLOR

Center and Left Wing ... 5'11" ... 190 lbs. ... Born, Vancouver, B.C., January 26, 1958 ...
Shoots left ... Grandson of Cyclone Taylor ... (October, 1982)—Broke tibia in preseason
game ... (March 6, 1983)—Refractured same leg in game at Pittsburgh ... (December,
1983)—Strained knee.

Year	Team	League	Games	G.	A.	Pts.	Pen.
1976-77—Univ. of North Dakota		WCHA	31	16	19	35	20
1977-78—Univ. of North Dakota (c)		WCHA	37	18	22	40	28
1978-79—Univ. of North Dakota		WCHA	42	24	*59	83	28
1979-80—Univ. of North Dakota (d-e)		WCHA	40	33	*59	*92	30
1980-81—Maine Mariners (f)		AHL	79	19	50	69	56
1981-82—Maine Mariners		AHL	75	32	48	80	42
1981-82—Philadelphia Flyers		NHL	2	0	0	0	0
1982-83—Philadelphia Flyers		NHL	61	8	25	33	24
1983-84—Philadelphia Flyers (g)		NHL	1	0	0	0	0
1983-84—Pittsburgh Penguins		NHL	59	24	31	55	24
1984-85—Pittsburgh Penguins (h)		NHL	47	7	10	17	19
1984-85—Washington Capitals		NHL	9	1	1	2	2
1985-86—Washington Capitals		NHL	30	2	1	3	4
1985-86—Binghamton Whalers		AHL	43	19	38	57	27
NHL TOTALS			209	42	68	110	73

(c)—June, 1978—Drafted by Philadelphia Flyers in 1978 NHL amateur draft. Ninth Flyers pick, 100th
overall, sixth round.
(d)—Named to All-American (West) team.
(e)—Named WCHA's Most Valuable Player and NCAA Player of the Year (forerunner of Hobey Baker
Memorial Trophy).
(f)—Tied with Rick Vasko for AHL playoff lead of 21 points.
(g)—October, 1983—Traded with Ron Flockhart, Andy Brickley and first (Roger Belanger) and third
(traded to Vancouver) round 1984 draft picks by Philadelphia Flyers to Pittsburgh Penguins for Rich
Sutter and second (Greg Smyth) and third (David McLay) round 1984 draft picks.
(h)—March, 1985—Traded by Pittsburgh Penguins to Washington Capitals for Jim McGeough.

MEL SCOTT TAYLOR
(Known by middle name)

Defense ... 6' ... 185 lbs. ... Born, Toronto, Ont., March 23, 1968 ... Shoots right.

Year	Team	League	Games	G.	A.	Pts.	Pen.
1984-85—Markham Waxers		OJHL	43	1	13	14	247
1985-86—Kitchener Rangers (c)		OHL	59	4	13	17	211

(c)—June, 1986—Drafted as underage junior by Toronto Maple Leafs in 1986 NHL entry draft. Fifth
Maple Leafs pick, 90th overall, fifth round.

GREG TEBBUTT

Defense ... 6'2" ... 215 lbs. ... Born, North Vancouver, B.C., May 11, 1957 ... Shoots left ... (December, 1980)—Surgery to repair severe lacerations of tendons and muscles in left forearm.

Year	Team	League	Games	G.	A.	Pts.	Pen.
1975-76	Victoria Cougars	WCHL	51	3	4	7	217
1976-77	Victoria Cougars (c)	WCHL	29	7	12	19	98
1976-77	Regina Pats (d-e)	WCHL	40	8	17	25	138
1977-78	Flin Flon Bombers	WCHL	55	28	46	74	270
1978-79	Birmingham Bulls (f)	WHA	38	2	5	7	83
1978-79	Binghamton Dusters	AHL	33	8	9	17	50
1979-80	Quebec Nordiques	NHL	2	0	1	1	4
1979-80	Syracuse Firebirds	AHL	14	2	3	5	35
1979-80	Erie Blades (b-g)	EHL	48	20	53	75	138
1980-81	Erie Blades (h)	EHL	35	16	37	53	93
1981-82	Fort Wayne Komets (i)	IHL	49	13	34	47	148
1982-83	Baltimore Skipjacks (a-j)	AHL	80	28	56	84	140
1983-84	Baltimore Skipjacks	AHL	44	12	42	54	125
1983-84	Pittsburgh Penguins (k)	NHL	24	0	2	2	31
1984-85	Muskegon Lumberjacks (b)	IHL	73	23	55	78	220
1984-85	Baltimore Skipjacks	AHL	2	0	0	0	4
1985-86	Milwaukee Admirals	IHL	77	20	49	69	226
	WHA TOTALS		38	2	5	7	83
	NHL TOTALS		26	0	3	3	35

(c)—December, 1976—Traded to Regina Pats by Victoria Cougars with Hugh Ellis and Lorne Schmidt for Ron Trafford, Rick Odegard and Keith Hertz.

(d)—June, 1977—Selected by Birmingham Bulls in World Hockey Association amateur player draft.

(e)—Drafted from Regina Pats by Minnesota North Stars in eighth round of 1977 amateur draft.

(f)—June, 1979—Claimed by Quebec Nordiques in WHA dispersal draft. Selected by Minnesota North Stars in NHL reclaim draft.

(g)—Led EHL playoffs in goals (11) and points (23) and was co-leader with Daniel Poulin in assists (12).

(h)—Led EHL playoffs with 12 assists.

(i)—August, 1981—Released by Quebec Nordiques.

(j)—Won Eddie Shore Plaque (Outstanding AHL Defenseman).

(k)—June, 1983—Signed by Pittsburgh Penguins as a free agent.

MARK TEEVENS

Right Wing ... 6' ... 180 lbs. ... Born, Ottawa, Ont., June 17, 1966 ... Shoots left.

Year	Team	League	Games	G.	A.	Pts.	Pen.
1982-83	Ottawa Senators	COJHL	47	14	26	40	36
1983-84	Peterborough Petes (c)	OHL	70	27	37	64	70
1984-85	Peterborough Petes	OHL	65	43	*90	133	70
1985-86	Peterborough Petes	OHL	50	31	50	81	106

(c)—June, 1984—Drafted as underage junior by Pittsburgh Penguins in NHL entry draft. Fourth Penguins pick, 64th overall, fourth round.

GREG PATRICK TERRION

Center ... 6' ... 190 lbs. ... Born, Peterborough, Ont., May 2, 1960 ... Shoots left ... (December, 1981)—Separated shoulder ... (January 14, 1984)—Scored second penalty shot goal of the season. Only other NHL player to do that was Pat Egan, New York Americans, in 1941-42 ... (December 26, 1985)—Bruised knee at Detroit and missed four games.

Year	Team	League	Games	G.	A.	Pts.	Pen.
1977-78	Hamilton Fincups	OMJHL	64	11	30	41	43
1978-79	Brantford Alexanders	OMJHL	63	27	28	55	48
1979-80	Brantford Alexanders (c)	OMJHL	67	44	78	122	13
1980-81	Los Angeles Kings	NHL	73	12	25	37	99
1981-82	Los Angeles Kings	NHL	61	15	22	37	23
1982-83	New Haven Nighthawks (d)	AHL	4	0	1	1	7
1982-83	Toronto Maple Leafs	NHL	74	16	16	32	59
1983-84	Toronto Maple Leafs	NHL	79	15	24	39	36
1984-85	Toronto Maple Leafs	NHL	72	14	17	31	20
1985-86	Toronto Maple Leafs	NHL	76	10	22	32	31
	NHL TOTALS		435	82	126	208	268

(c)—June, 1980—Drafted by Los Angeles Kings in 1980 NHL entry draft. Second Kings pick, 33rd overall, second round.

(d)—October, 1982—Traded by Los Angeles Kings to Toronto Maple Leafs for future considerations.

TOM TERWILLIGER

Defense ... 6'2" ... 185 lbs. ... Born, Denver, Colo., September 1, 1965 ... Shoots right.

Year	Team	League	Games	G.	A.	Pts.	Pen.
1983-84—Edina H.S. (c)		Minn. H.S.	24	5	11	16	20
1984-85—Miami of Ohio Univ.		CCHA	29	2	3	5	18
1985-86—Miami of Ohio Univ.		CCHA	32	1	3	4	35

(c)—June, 1984—Drafted by Minnesota North Stars in NHL entry draft. Eleventh North Stars pick, 222nd overall, 11th round.

ROD THACKER

Defense . . . 6'2" . . . 200 lbs. . . . Born, Kitchener, Ont., July 16, 1968 . . . Shoots left . . . (December, 1984)—Torn knee ligaments . . . (December, 1985)—Fractured nose.

Year	Team	League	Games	G.	A.	Pts.	Pen.
1984-85—Kitchener Greenshirts Midgets		OHA	19	1	15	16	38
1985-86—Hamilton Steelhawks (c)		OHL	58	2	9	11	60

(c)—June, 1986—Drafted as underage junior by St. Louis Blues in 1986 NHL entry draft. Tenth Blues pick, 199th overall, 10th round.

CHRISTOPHER THAYER

Center . . . 6'2" . . . 180 lbs. . . . Born, Exeter, N.H., November 9, 1967 . . . Shoots right.

Year	Team	League	Games	G.	A.	Pts.	Pen.
1984-85—Exeter H.S.		New Hampshire	..	23	27	50	..
1985-86—Kent Prep. (c)		Conn.	25	7	10	17	..

(c)—June, 1986—Drafted by Chicago Black Hawks in 1986 NHL entry draft. Tenth Black Hawks pick, 224th overall, 11th round.

MATS THELIN

Defense . . . 5'10" . . . 185 lbs. . . . Born, Stockholm, Sweden, March 30, 1961 . . . Shoots left . . . (October 8, 1985)—Fractured right foot in team practice two days before start of season and missed 19 games . . . (February 11, 1986)—Injured knee at Chicago.

Year	Team	League	Games	G.	A.	Pts.	Pen.
1980-81—Solna AIK (c)		Sweden	9	0	0	0	4
1981-82—Solna AIK		Sweden	36	2	2	4	28
1981-82—Swedish National Team		Int'l	25	0	3	3	20
1982-83—Solna AIK		Sweden	....	...	....	....	....
1983-84—Solna AIK		Sweden	16	4	1	5	29
1984-85—Boston Bruins		NHL	73	5	13	18	78
1985-86—Boston Bruins		NHL	31	2	3	5	29
1985-86—Moncton Golden Flames		AHL	2	0	1	1	0
NHL TOTALS			104	7	16	23	107

(c)—June, 1981—Drafted by Boston Bruins in NHL entry draft. Sixth Bruins pick, 140th overall, seventh round.

MICHAEL THELVEN

Defense . . . 5'11" . . . 180 lbs. . . . Born, Stockholm, Sweden, January 7, 1961 . . . Shoots right . . . (January 13, 1986)—Facial surgery and missed five games . . . (February 6, 1986)—Injured groin vs. Buffalo . . . (February 18, 1986)—Dislocated shoulder at Calgary.

Year	Team	League	Games	G.	A.	Pts.	Pen.
1984-85—Djurgardens (c)		Sweden	..	8	13	21	..
1985-86—Boston Bruins		NHL	60	6	20	26	48
NHL TOTALS			60	6	20	26	48

(c)—June, 1980—Drafted by Boston Bruins in NHL entry draft. Eighth Bruins pick, 186th overall, ninth round.

STEVE THOMAS

Left Wing . . . 5'10" . . . 180 lbs. . . . Born, Markham, Ont., July 15, 1963 . . . Shoots left . . . (September, 1984)—Broke wrist on second day of training camp . . . Also plays Right Wing.

Year	Team	League	Games	G.	A.	Pts.	Pen.
1981-82—Markham Tier-II		OHA	48	68	57	125	113
1982-83—Toronto Marlboros		OHL	61	18	20	38	42
1983-84—Toronto Marlboros		OHL	70	51	54	105	77
1984-85—Toronto Maple Leafs (c)		NHL	18	1	1	2	2
1984-85—St. Catharines Saints (a-d)		AHL	64	42	48	90	56
1985-86—St. Catharines Saints		AHL	19	18	14	32	35
1985-86—Toronto Maple Leafs		NHL	65	20	37	57	36
NHL TOTALS			83	21	38	59	38

(c)—June, 1984—Signed by Toronto Maple Leafs as a free agent.
(d)—Won Dudley Red Garrett Memorial Trophy (Top AHL Rookie).

DAVE THOMLINSON

Left Wing . . . 6'1" . . . 185 lbs. . . . Born, Edmonton, Alta., October 22, 1966 . . . Shoots left . . . (November, 1983)—Separated shoulder . . . (November, 1984)—Separated shoulder.

Year	Team	League	Games	G.	A.	Pts.	Pen.
1983-84	Brandon Wheat Kings	WHL	41	17	12	29	62
1984-85	Brandon Wheat Kings (c)	WHL	26	13	14	27	70
1985-86	Brandon Wheat Kings	WHL	53	25	20	45	116

(c)—June, 1985—Drafted as underage junior by Toronto Maple Leafs in the 1985 NHL entry draft. Third Maple Leafs pick, 43rd overall, third round.

JIM THOMSON

Right Wing . . . 6'2" . . . 180 lbs. . . . Born, Edmonton, Alta., December 30, 1965 . . . Shoots right.

Year	Team	League	Games	G.	A.	Pts.	Pen.
1982-83	Markham Waxers	OJHL	35	6	7	13	81
1983-84	Toronto Marlboros (c)	OHL	60	10	18	28	68
1984-85	Toronto Marlboros	OHL	63	23	28	51	122
1984-85	Binghamton Whalers	AHL	4	0	0	0	2
1985-86	Binghamton Whalers	AHL	59	15	9	24	195

(c)—June, 1984—Drafted as underage junior by Washington Capitals in NHL entry draft. Eighth Capitals pick, 185th overall, ninth round.

TOM THORNBURY

Defense . . . 5'11" . . . 175 lbs. . . . Born, Lindsay, Ont., March 17, 1963 . . . Shoots right.

Year	Team	League	Games	G.	A.	Pts.	Pen.
1979-80	Aurora Tier II	OPJHL	44	19	30	49	84
1980-81	Niagara Falls Flyers (c)	OPJHL	60	15	22	37	138
1981-82	Niagara Falls Flyers	OHL	43	11	22	33	65
1982-83	North Bay Centennials	OHL	17	6	9	15	38
1982-83	Cornwall Royals	OHL	50	21	35	56	66
1983-84	Pittsburgh Penguins	NHL	14	1	8	9	16
1983-84	Baltimore Skipjacks (b)	AHL	65	17	46	63	64
1984-85	Baltimore Skipjacks (d)	AHL	22	4	12	16	21
1984-85	Fredericton Express	AHL	53	11	16	27	26
1985-86	Muskegon Lumberjacks	IHL	9	0	8	8	8
1985-86	Fredericton Express	AHL	24	0	15	15	30
1985-86	Moncton Golden Flames	AHL	40	6	12	18	38
	NHL TOTALS		14	1	8	9	16

(c)—June, 1981—Drafted as underage junior by Pittsburgh Penguins in 1981 NHL entry draft. Second Penguins pick, 49th overall, third round.

(d)—December, 1984—Traded by Pittsburgh Penguins to Quebec Nordiques for Brian Ford.

ESA TIKKANEN

Left Wing . . . 5'11" . . . 185 lbs. . . . Born, Jyvaskyla, Finland, March 2, 1962 . . . Shoots left . . . (December 10, 1985)—Broke foot at St. Louis.

Year	Team	League	Games	G.	A.	Pts.	Pen.
1984-85	IFK Helsinki (c)	Finland	....	21	33	54	....
1984-85	Edmonton Oilers (d)	NHL	....	...	....	....	....
1985-86	Nova Scotia Oilers	AHL	15	4	8	12	17
1985-86	Edmonton Oilers	NHL	35	7	6	13	28
	NHL TOTALS		35	7	6	13	28

(c)—August, 1983—Drafted by Edmonton Oilers in NHL entry draft. Fourth Oilers pick, 82nd overall, fourth round.

(d)—Played three playoff games (no points).

TOM TILLEY

Defense . . . 6' . . . 180 lbs. . . . Born, Trenton, Ont., March 28, 1965 . . . Shoots right.

Year	Team	League	Games	G.	A.	Pts.	Pen.
1983-84	Orillia Travelways (c)	OJHL	38	16	35	51	113
1984-85	Michigan State University	CCHA	37	1	5	6	58
1985-86	Michigan State University	CCHA	42	9	25	34	48

(c)—June, 1984—Drafted as underage junior by St. Louis Blues in NHL entry draft. Thirteenth Blues pick, 196th overall, 10th round.

DAVE TIPPETT

Center . . . 5'10" . . . 175 lbs. . . . Born, Moosomin, Sask., August 25, 1961 . . . Shoots left . . . Member of 1984 Canadian Olympic Team.

Year	Team	League	Games	G.	A.	Pts.	Pen.
1979-80—Prince Albert Raiders		SAJHL	85	72	95	177	..
1980-81—Prince Albert Raiders		SAJHL	84	62	93	155	..
1981-82—University of North Dakota		WCHA	43	13	28	41	24
1982-83—University of North Dakota		WCHA	36	15	31	46	44
1983-84—Canadian Olympic Team		Int'l	66	14	19	33	24
1983-84—Hartford Whalers (c)		NHL	17	4	2	6	2
1984-85—Hartford Whalers		NHL	80	7	12	19	12
1985-86—Hartford Whalers		NHL	80	14	20	34	18
NHL TOTALS			177	25	34	59	32

(c)—February, 1984—Signed by Hartford Whalers as a free agent.

RICK TOCCHET

Right Wing . . . 6' . . . 195 lbs. . . . Born, Scarborough, Ont., April 9, 1964 . . . Shoots right . . . (October 30, 1985)—Door of team bench slammed on his middle finger at Montreal and he missed four games . . . (November 23, 1985)—Bruised right knee at Philadelphia and missed seven games.

Year	Team	League	Games	G.	A.	Pts.	Pen.
1981-82—Sault Ste. Marie Greyhounds		OHL	59	7	15	22	184
1982-83—Sault Ste. Marie Greyhounds (c-d-e)		OHL	66	32	34	66	146
1983-84—Sault Ste. Marie Greyhounds (f)		OHL	64	44	64	108	209
1984-85—Philadelphia Flyers		NHL	75	14	25	39	181
1985-86—Philadelphia Flyers		NHL	69	14	21	35	284
NHL TOTALS			144	28	46	74	465

(c)—Led OHL playoffs with 67 penalty minutes.
(d)—June, 1983—Drafted as underage junior by Philadelphia Flyers in 1983 NHL entry draft. Fifth Flyers pick, 121st overall, sixth round.
(e)—Led OHL playoffs with 62 penalty minutes.
(f)—Led OHL playoffs witth 22 goals and co-leader (with teammate Wayne Groulx) with 36 points.

KEVIN TODD

Center . . . 5'11" . . . 180 lbs. . . . Born, Winnipeg, Manitoba, May 4, 1968 . . . Shoots left . . . (December, 1985)—Stretched knee ligaments.

Year	Team	League	Games	G.	A.	Pts.	Pen.
1984-85—Winnipeg Stars		Man. Midget	60	66	100	166	....
1985-86—Prince Albert Raiders (c)		WHL	55	14	25	39	19

(c)—June, 1986—Drafted as underage junior by New Jersey Devils in 1986 NHL entry draft. Seventh Devils pick, 129th overall, seventh round.

KIRK TOMLINSON

Center . . . 5'10" . . . 175 lbs. . . . Born, Toronto, Ont., March 2, 1968 . . . Shoots left.

Year	Team	League	Games	G.	A.	Pts.	Pen.
1984-85—New Westminster Bruins		WHL	66	9	14	23	48
1985-86—Hamilton Steelhawks (c)		OHL	58	28	23	51	230

(c)—June, 1986—Drafted as underage junior by Minnesota North Stars in 1986 NHL entry draft. Seventh North Stars pick, 75th overall, fourth round.

JOHN TONELLI

Left Wing and Center . . . 6'1" . . . 190 lbs. . . . Born, Hamilton, Ont., March 23, 1957 . . . Shoots left . . . Did not take part in 1975 playoffs after signing pro contract . . . Brother of Ray Tonelli . . . (February, 1981)—Shoulder injury . . . Set N.Y. Islanders club record for left wings with 93 points in 1981-82 . . . (December, 1983)—Knee injury . . . (Fall, 1985)—Sat out 22 days of the N. Y. Islanders' training camp in contract dispute.

Year	Team	League	Games	G.	A.	Pts.	Pen.
1973-74—Toronto Marlboros		Jr. "A" OHA	69	18	37	55	62
1974-75—Toronto Marlboros (a-c)		Jr. "A" OHA	70	49	86	135	85
1975-76—Houston Aeros		WHA	79	17	14	31	66
1976-77—Houston Aeros (d)		WHA	80	24	31	55	109
1977-78—Houston Aeros (e)		WHA	65	23	41	64	103
1978-79—New York Islanders		NHL	73	17	39	56	44
1979-80—New York Islanders		NHL	77	14	30	44	49
1980-81—New York Islanders		NHL	70	20	32	52	57
1981-82—New York Islanders (b)		NHL	80	35	58	93	57
1982-83—New York Islanders		NHL	76	31	40	71	55
1983-84—New York Islanders		NHL	73	27	40	67	66
1984-85—New York Islanders (b)		NHL	80	42	58	100	95

Year	Team	League	Games	G.	A.	Pts.	Pen.
1985-86—New York Islanders (f)		NHL	65	20	41	61	50
1985-86—Calgary Flames		NHL	9	3	4	7	10
WHA TOTALS			224	64	86	150	278
NHL TOTALS			603	209	342	551	483

(c)—Signed by Houston Aeros (WHA), March, 1975.
(d)—Drafted from Houston Aeros by New York Islanders in second round of 1977 amateur draft.
(e)—Signed to multi year contract by New York Islanders, July, 1978.
(f)—March, 1986—Traded by New York Islanders to Calgary Flames for Richard Kromm and Steve Konroyd.

TIMOTHY RAYMOND TOOKEY

Center . . . 5'11" . . . 180 lbs. . . . Born, Edmonton, Alta., August 29, 1960 . . . Shoots left . . . (December 30, 1981)—Sprained left ankle at Pittsburgh . . . (February, 1983)—Concussion . . . (April, 1983)—Injured shoulder during AHL playoffs.

Year	Team	League	Games	G.	A.	Pts.	Pen.
1977-78—Portland Winter Hawks		WCHL	72	16	15	31	55
1978-79—Portland Winter Hawks (c)		WHL	56	33	47	80	55
1979-80—Portland Winter Hawks		WHL	70	58	83	141	55
1980-81—Hershey Bears		AHL	47	20	38	58	129
1980-81—Washington Capitals		NHL	29	10	13	23	18
1981-82—Washington Capitals (d)		NHL	28	8	8	16	35
1981-82—Hershey Bears		AHL	14	4	9	13	10
1981-82—Fredericton Express		AHL	16	6	10	16	16
1982-83—Quebec Nordiques		NHL	12	1	6	7	4
1982-83—Fredericton Express		AHL	53	24	43	67	24
1983-84—Pittsburgh Penguins (e)		NHL	8	0	2	2	2
1983-84—Baltimore Skipjacks		AHL	58	16	28	44	25
1984-85—Baltimore Skipjacks (f)		AHL	74	25	43	68	74
1985-86—Hershey Bears (a-g-h)		AHL	69	35	*62	97	66
NHL TOTALS			77	19	29	48	59

(c)—August, 1979—Drafted by Washington Capitals as underage junior in 1979 NHL entry draft. Fourth Capitals pick, 88th overall, fifth round.
(d)—January, 1982—Traded by Washington Capitals to Quebec Nordiques for Lee Norwood.
(e)—August, 1983—Signed by Pittsburgh Penguins as a free agent.
(f)—August, 1985—Signed by Philadelphia Flyers as a free agent.
(g)—Led AHL Calder Cup Playoffs with 11 goals.
(h)—Won Jack Butterfield Trophy (AHL Playoff MVP).

SEAN TOOMEY

Center . . . 6'2" . . . 190 lbs. . . . Born, St. Paul, Minn., June 27, 1965 . . . Shoots left.

Year	Team	League	Games	G.	A.	Pts.	Pen.
1982-83—St. Paul Cretin H.S. (c)		Minn. H.S.	23	48	32	80	..
1983-84—Univ. of Minnesota-Duluth		WCHA	29	3	5	8	8
1984-85—Univ. of Minnesota-Duluth		WCHA	43	6	7	13	14
1985-86—Univ. of Minnesota-Duluth		WCHA	33	23	11	34	10

(c)—June, 1983—Drafted by Minnesota North Stars in 1983 NHL entry draft. Eighth North Stars pick, 136th overall, seventh round.

STEVE TORREL

Center . . . 6'3" . . . 195 lbs. . . . Born, Hibbing, Minn., May 27, 1967 . . . Shoots right.

Year	Team	League	Games	G.	A.	Pts.	Pen.
1985-86—Hibbing H.S. (c)		Minn.	26	7	30	37	30

(c)—June, 1986—Drafted by Hartford Whalers in 1986 NHL entry draft. Sixth Whalers pick, 137th overall, seventh round.

SCOTT TOTTLE

Right Wing . . . 5'11" . . . 175 lbs. . . . Born, Brantford, Ont., January 30, 1965 . . . Shoots right.

Year	Team	League	Games	G.	A.	Pts.	Pen.
1981-82—Hamilton Mountain A's		OJHL	49	15	25	40	16
1982-83—Peterborough Petes (c)		OHL	68	25	49	74	36
1983-84—Peterborough Petes		OHL	70	63	47	110	24
1984-85—Peterborough Petes (d)		OHL	64	55	71	126	19
1985-86—Fredericton Express		AHL	69	15	22	37	12

(c)—June, 1983—Drafted as underage junior by Vancouver Canucks in 1983 NHL entry draft. Third Canucks pick, 50th overall, third round.
(d)—Won Williams Hanley Trophy (Most Gentlemanly).

LARRY TRADER

Defense . . . 6'2" . . . 186 lbs. . . . Born, Barry's Bay, Ont., July 7, 1963 . . . Shoots left . . . (October, 1984)—Knee surgery.

Year	Team	League	Games	G.	A.	Pts.	Pen.
1979-80	Gloucester Tier II	OPJHL	50	13	20	33	70
1980-81	London Knights (c)	OPJHL	68	5	23	28	132
1981-82	London Knights	OHL	68	19	37	56	171
1982-83	Detroit Red Wings	NHL	15	0	2	2	6
1982-83	London Knights	OHL	39	16	28	44	67
1982-83	Adirondack Red Wings	AHL	6	2	2	4	4
1983-84	Adirondack Red Wings	AHL	80	13	28	41	89
1984-85	Adirondack Red Wings	AHL	6	0	4	4	0
1984-85	Detroit Red Wings	NHL	40	3	7	10	39
1985-86	Adirondack Red Wings (b-d)	AHL	64	10	46	56	77
	NHL TOTALS		55	3	9	12	45

(c)—June, 1981—Drafted as underage junior by Detroit Red Wings in 1981 NHL entry draft. Third Red Wings pick, 86th overall, fifth round.

(d)—August, 1986—Traded by Detroit Red Wings to St. Louis Blues for Lee Norwood.

DOUG TRAPP

Left Wing . . . 6' . . . 180 lbs. . . . Born, Balcarres, Sask., November 28, 1965 . . . Shoots left.

Year	Team	League	Games	G.	A.	Pts.	Pen.
1981-82	Regina	SJHL	43	25	28	53	102
1982-83	Regina Pats	WHL	71	23	28	51	123
1983-84	Regina Pats (b-c)	WHL	59	43	50	93	44
1984-85	Regina Pats	WHL	72	48	60	108	81
1985-86	Rochester Americans	AHL	75	21	42	63	86

(c)—June, 1984—Drafted as underage junior by Buffalo Sabres in NHL entry draft. Second Sabres pick, 39th overall, second round.

MARIO TREMBLAY

Right Wing . . . 6' . . . 185 lbs. . . . Born, Alma, Que., September 2, 1956 . . . Shoots right . . . (March 12, 1984)—Given three-game NHL suspension for being first off the bench during major altercation in game at Minnesota . . . (September 24, 1985)—Separated left shoulder in pre-season game at Sherbrooke and missed 16 games . . . (March 17, 1986)—Broke collarbone vs. Quebec.

Year	Team	League	Games	G.	A.	Pts.	Pen.
1972-73	Montreal Red, White and Blue	QJHL	56	43	37	80	155
1973-74	Mont. Red, White and Blue (c)	QJHL	47	49	51	100	154
1974-75	Nova Scotia Voyageurs	AHL	15	10	8	18	47
1974-75	Montreal Canadiens	NHL	63	21	18	39	108
1975-76	Montreal Canadiens	NHL	71	11	16	27	88
1976-77	Montreal Canadiens	NHL	74	18	28	46	61
1977-78	Montreal Canadiens	NHL	56	10	14	24	44
1978-79	Montreal Canadiens	NHL	76	30	29	59	74
1979-80	Montreal Canadiens	NHL	77	16	26	42	105
1980-81	Montreal Canadiens	NHL	77	25	38	63	123
1981-82	Montreal Canadiens	NHL	80	33	40	73	66
1982-83	Montreal Canadiens	NHL	80	30	37	67	87
1983-84	Montreal Canadiens	NHL	67	14	25	39	112
1984-85	Montreal Canadiens	NHL	75	31	35	66	120
1985-86	Montreal Canadiens	NHL	56	19	20	39	55
	NHL TOTALS		852	258	326	584	1043

(c)—Drafted from Montreal Red, White and Blue by Montreal Canadiens in first round of 1974 amateur draft.

BRYAN JOHN TROTTIER

Center . . . 5'10" . . . 205 lbs. . . . Born, Val Marie, Sask., July 17, 1956 . . . Shoots left . . . (1975-76)—Set NHL records for most assists and points in rookie season (broken by Peter Stastny, 1980-81) . . . Set Stanley Cup Playoff record with 29 points during 1980 playoffs (broken by Mike Bossy's 35 points in 1981) . . . Set NHL record for consecutive playoff games with points (25) covering more than one season . . . Set NHL record for consecutive playoff games with points one season (18) . . . Brother of Monty Trottier and Rocky Trottier . . . (April, 1983)—Sprained left knee during playoff series against New York Rangers . . . (January, 1984)—Injured left knee . . . (July, 1984)—Became U.S. citizen and played with Team USA in 1984 Canada Cup Tournament . . . (October, 1984)—Knee injury.

Year	Team	League	Games	G.	A.	Pts.	Pen.
1972-73—Swift Current Broncos		WCHL	67	16	29	45	10
1973-74—Swift Current Broncos (c)		WCHL	68	41	71	112	76
1974-75—Lethbridge Broncos (a)		WCHL	67	46	*98	144	103
1975-76—New York Islanders (d-e)		NHL	80	32	63	95	21
1976-77—New York Islanders		NHL	76	30	42	72	34
1977-78—New York Islanders (a)		NHL	77	46	*77	123	46
1978-79—New York Islanders (a-f-g-h)		NHL	76	47	*87	*134	50
1979-80—New York Islanders (i-j)		NHL	78	42	62	104	68
1980-81—New York Islanders (k)		NHL	73	31	72	103	74
1981-82—New York Islanders (b-l)		NHL	80	50	79	129	88
1982-83—New York Islanders		NHL	80	34	55	89	68
1983-84—New York Islanders (b)		NHL	68	40	71	111	59
1984-85—New York Islanders		NHL	68	28	31	59	47
1985-86—New York Islanders		NHL	78	37	59	96	72
NHL TOTALS			834	417	698	1115	627

(c)—Drafted from Swift Current Broncos by New York Islanders in second round of 1974 amateur draft.
(d)—Won Calder Memorial Trophy.
(e)—Selected NHL Rookie of the Year in poll of players by THE SPORTING NEWS.
(f)—Won Hart Memorial Trophy (NHL-MVP).
(g)—Won Art Ross Trophy (NHL-Top Scorer).
(h)—Named THE SPORTING NEWS NHL Player of the Year in poll of players.
(i)—Led NHL playoffs in points (29) and co-leader, with Bill Barber, in goals (12).
(j)—Won Conn Smythe Trophy (NHL Playoff MVP).
(k)—Tied for NHL playoff assist lead (18 assists) with teammate Mike Bossy.
(l)—Led NHL playoffs with 23 assists and 29 points.

MONTY TROTTIER

Center . . . 5'10" . . . 170 lbs. . . . Born, Val Marie, Sask., July 25, 1961 . . . Shoots left . . . Brother of Rocky and Bryan Trottier.

Year	Team	League	Games	G.	A.	Pts.	Pen.
1979-80—Billings Bighorns (c)		WHL	60	18	32	50	168
1980-81—Billings Bighorns		WHL	58	15	37	52	289
1981-82—Indianapolis Checkers		CHL	72	10	15	25	142
1982-83—Indianapolis Checkers		CHL	63	17	23	40	69
1983-84—Indianapolis Checkers		CHL	69	18	23	41	135
1984-85—Springfield Indians		AHL	60	6	12	18	40
1985-86—Indianapolis Checkers		IHL	81	27	38	65	106

(c)—June, 1980—Drafted by New York Islanders in NHL entry draft. Fourth Islanders pick, 68th overall, fourth round.

ROCKY TROTTIER

Center . . . 5'11" . . . 190 lbs. . . . Born, Climax, Sask., April 11, 1964 . . . Shoots right . . . Brother of Bryan and Monty Trottier . . . Missed most of 1981-82 season with knee injury . . . Also plays Right Wing.

Year	Team	League	Games	G.	A.	Pts.	Pen.
1980-81—Billings Bighorns		WHL	62	11	26	37	67
1981-82—Billings Bighorns (c)		WHL	28	13	21	34	36
1982-83—Nanaimo Islanders		WHL	34	13	22	35	12
1982-83—Medicine Hat Tigers		WHL	20	5	9	14	11
1982-83—Wichita Wind		CHL	2	0	1	1	0
1983-84—New Jersey Devils		NHL	5	1	1	2	0
1983-84—Medicine Hat Tigers		WHL	65	34	50	84	41
1984-85—Maine Mariners		AHL	34	17	16	33	4
1984-85—New Jersey Devils		NHL	33	5	3	8	2
1985-86—Maine Mariners		AHL	66	12	19	31	42
NHL TOTALS			38	6	4	10	2

(c)—June, 1982—Drafted as underage junior by New Jersey Devils in 1982 NHL entry draft. First Devils pick, eighth overall, first round.

STEVE TSUJIURA

Center . . . 5'5" . . . 155 lbs. . . . Born, Coaldale, Alta., February 28, 1962 . . . Shoots left . . . (February, 1985)—Strained knee ligaments.

Year	Team	League	Games	G.	A.	Pts.	Pen.
1977-78—Medicine Hat Tigers		WHL	17	5	8	13	0
1978-79—Medicine Hat Tigers		WHL	62	24	45	69	14
1979-80—Medicine Hat Tigers (c)		WHL	72	25	77	102	36
1980-81—Medicine Hat Tigers (b-c-d-e)		WHL	72	55	84	139	60
1981-82—Calgary Wranglers		WHL	37	26	53	79	33

Year	Team	League	Games	G.	A.	Pts.	Pen.
1981-82—University of Calgary		CWUAA	....	...	....	....	....
1982-83—Maine Mariners		AHL	78	15	51	66	46
1983-84—Springfield Indians (f)		AHL	78	24	56	80	27
1984-85—Maine Mariners		AHL	69	28	38	66	40
1985-86—Maine Mariners (g)		AHL	80	31	55	86	34

(c)—Won Frank Boucher Memorial Trophy (WHL Most Gentlemanly).
(d)—Won WHL Most Valuable Player Trophy.
(e)—June, 1981—Drafted by Philadelphia Flyers in NHL entry draft. Thirteenth Flyers pick, 205th overall, tenth round.
(f)—July, 1984—Signed by New Jersey Devils as a free agent.
(g)—Won Fred Hunt Memorial Award (Sportsmanship, Determination, Dedication).

JOHN TUCKER

Center . . . 6' . . . 185 lbs. . . . Born, Windsor, Ont., September 29, 1964 . . . Shoots right . . . (November 7, 1984)—Broke bone in foot in game at Minnesota . . . (March 7, 1986)— Bruised shoulder vs. Hartford and missed five games.

Year	Team	League	Games	G.	A.	Pts.	Pen.
1981-82—Kitchener Rangers		OHL	67	16	32	48	32
1982-83—Kitchener Rangers (c)		OHL	70	60	80	140	33
1983-84—Kitchener Rangers (a-d-e)		OHL	39	40	60	100	25
1983-84—Buffalo Sabres		NHL	21	12	4	16	4
1984-85—Buffalo Sabres		NHL	64	22	27	49	21
1985-86—Buffalo Sabres		NHL	75	31	34	65	39
NHL TOTALS			160	65	65	130	64

(c)—June, 1983—Drafted as underage junior by Buffalo Sabres in 1983 NHL entry draft. Fourth Sabres pick, 31st overall, second round.
(d)—Won Red Tilson Trophy (Most Outstanding OHL player).
(e)—OHL's Molson/Cooper Player of the Year Nominee.

ALLAN TUER

Defense . . . 6' . . . 175 lbs. . . . Born, North Battleford, Sask., July 19, 1963 . . . Shoots left.

Year	Team	League	Games	G.	A.	Pts.	Pen.
1980-81—Regina Pats (c)		WHL	31	0	7	7	58
1981-82—Regina Pats		WHL	63	2	18	20	*486
1982-83—Regina Pats		WHL	71	3	27	30	229
1983-84—New Haven Nighthawks		AHL	78	0	20	20	195
1984-85—New Haven Nighthawks		AHL	56	0	7	7	241
1985-86—New Haven Nighthawks		AHL	8	1	0	1	53
1985-86—Los Angeles Kings (d)		NHL	45	0	1	1	150
NHL TOTALS			45	0	1	1	150

(c)—June, 1980—Drafted as underage junior by Los Angeles Kings in NHL entry draft. Eighth Kings pick, 186th overall, ninth round.
(d)—August, 1986—Signed by Edmonton Oilers as a free agent.

STEVE TUITE

Defense . . . 6'1" . . . 205 lbs. . . . Born, Brockton, Mass., January 14, 1962 . . . Shoots right.

Year	Team	League	Games	G.	A.	Pts.	Pen.
1981-82—St. Lawrence University		ECAC	21	2	4	6	8
1982-83—St. Lawrence University		ECAC	36	2	11	13	12
1983-84—St. Lawrence University		ECAC	32	10	18	28	24
1984-85—St. Lawrence University (c)		ECAC	32	3	14	17	26
1985-86—Toledo Goaldiggers		IHL	47	5	31	36	36
1985-86—New Haven Nighthawks		AHL	14	0	2	2	6

(c)—July, 1985—Signed by Los Angeles Kings as a free agent.

ALFIE TURCOTTE

Center . . . 5'10" . . . 175 lbs. . . . Born, Gary, Ind., June 5, 1965 . . . Shoots left . . . Son of Real Turcotte (Coach and General Manager of Nanaimo Islanders of WHL).

Year	Team	League	Games	G.	A.	Pts.	Pen.
1981-82—Detroit Compuware		Mich. Midget	93	131	152	283	40
1982-83—Nanaimo Islanders		WHL	36	23	27	50	22
1982-83—Portland Winter Hawks (c)		WHL	39	26	51	77	26
1983-84—Portland Winter Hawks		WHL	32	22	41	63	39
1983-84—Montreal Canadiens		NHL	30	7	7	14	10
1984-85—Montreal Canadiens		NHL	53	8	16	24	35
1985-86—Sherbrooke Canadiens		AHL	75	29	36	65	60
1985-86—Montreal Canadiens (d)		NHL	2	0	0	0	2
NHL TOTALS			85	15	23	38	47

(c)—June, 1983—Drafted as underage junior by Montreal Canadiens in 1983 NHL entry draft. First Canadiens pick, 17th overall, first round.

(d)—July, 1986—Traded by Montreal Canadiens to Edmonton Oilers for future considerations.

DARREN TURCOTTE

Center . . . 6' . . . 170 lbs. . . . Born, Boston, Mass., March 2, 1968 . . . Shoots left.

Year	Team	League	Games	G.	A.	Pts.	Pen.
1984-85—North Bay Centennials		OHL	62	33	32	65	28
1985-86—North Bay Centennials (c)		OHL	62	35	37	72	35

(c)—June, 1986—Drafted as underage junior by New York Rangers in 1986 NHL entry draft. Sixth Rangers pick, 114th overall, sixth round.

SYLVAIN TURGEON

Left Wing . . . 6' . . . 190 lbs. . . . Born, Noranda, Que., January 17, 1965 . . . Shoots left . . . Also plays center . . . Set Hartford club record for goals and points by an NHL rookie in 1983-84 . . . (October, 1984)—Pulled abdominal muscles . . . Brother of Pierre Turgeon.

Year	Team	League	Games	G.	A.	Pts.	Pen.
1981-82—Hull Olympics (c)		QMJHL	57	33	40	73	78
1982-83—Hull Olympics (a-d-e)		QHL	67	54	109	163	103
1983-84—Hartford Whalers		NHL	76	40	32	72	55
1984-85—Hartford Whalers		NHL	64	31	31	62	67
1985-86—Hartford Whalers		NHL	76	45	34	79	88
NHL TOTALS			216	116	97	213	210

(c)—Won Des Instructeurs Trophy (Top Rookie QMJHL Forward).

(d)—Won The Association of Journalist of Hockey Trophy (Top QHL pro prospect).

(e)—June, 1983—Drafted as underage junior by Hartford Whalers in 1983 NHL entry draft. First Whalers pick, 2nd overall, first round.

PERRY TURNBULL

Left Wing . . . 6'2" . . . 200 lbs. . . . Born, Bentley, Alta., March 9, 1959 . . . Shoots left . . . Cousin of Randy Turnbull . . . (April, 1982)—Severed tendon just above right knee in playoff mishap when cut by teammate's skate . . . (October 21, 1984)—Strained knee ligaments when checked by Terry O'Reilly in game vs. Boston.

Year	Team	League	Games	G.	A.	Pts.	Pen.
1974-75—The Pass Red Devils		AJHL	69	6	4	10	134
1975-76—The Pass Red Devils		AJHL	45	27	23	50	140
1975-76—Calgary Centennials		WCHL	19	6	7	13	14
1976-77—Calgary Centennials (c)		WCHL	10	8	5	13	33
1976-77—Portland Winter Hawks		WCHL	58	23	30	53	249
1977-78—Portland Winter Hawks		WCHL	57	36	27	63	318
1978-79—Portland Winter Hawks (d-e)		WHL	70	75	43	118	191
1979-80—St. Louis Blues		NHL	80	16	19	35	124
1980-81—St. Louis Blues		NHL	75	34	22	56	209
1981-82—St. Louis Blues		NHL	79	33	26	59	161
1982-83—St. Louis Blues		NHL	79	32	15	47	172
1983-84—St. Louis Blues (f)		NHL	32	14	8	22	81
1983-84—Montreal Canadiens (g)		NHL	40	6	7	13	59
1984-85—Winnipeg Jets		NHL	66	22	21	43	130
1985-86—Winnipeg Jets		NHL	80	20	31	51	183
NHL TOTALS			531	177	149	326	1119

(c)—Traded to Portland Winter Hawks by Calgary Centennials for Doug Lecuyer and Dave Morrow, October, 1976.

(d)—Named Most Valuable Player of WHL.

(e)—August, 1979—Drafted by St. Louis Blues in 1979 entry draft. First Blues pick, second overall, first round.

(f)—December, 1983—Traded by St. Louis Blues to Montreal Canadiens for Gilbert Delorme, Greg Paslawski and Doug Wickenheiser.

(g)—June, 1984—Traded by Montreal Canadiens to Winnipeg Jets for Lucien DeBlois.

RANDY LAYNE TURNBULL

Defense . . . 6' . . . 186 lbs. . . . .Born, Bentley, Alta., February 7, 1962 . . . Shoots right . . . Cousin of Perry Turnbull.

Year	Team	League	Games	G.	A.	Pts.	Pen.
1977-78—Fort Saskatchewan Traders		AJHL	47	1	3	4	172
1978-79—Fort Saskatchewan Traders		AJHL	51	4	30	34	367
1978-79—Portland Winter Hawks		WHL	1	0	0	0	7
1979-80—Portland Winter Hawks (c)		WHL	72	4	25	29	355
1980-81—Portland Winter Hawks		WHL	56	1	31	32	295

Year	Team	League	Games	G.	A.	Pts.	Pen.
1981-82—Portland Winter Hawks		WHL	69	5	19	24	430
1981-82—Calgary Flames		NHL	1	0	0	0	2
1982-83—Colorado Flames		CHL	65	2	1	3	292
1983-84—New Haven Nighthawks		AHL	8	0	0	0	46
1983-84—Peoria Prancers		IHL	73	3	18	21	213
1984-85—Salt Lake Golden Eagles		IHL	81	10	14	24	282
1985-86—Salt Lake Golden Eagles		IHL	77	6	14	20	236
NHL TOTALS			1	0	0	0	2

(c)—June, 1980—Drafted by Calgary Flames as underage junior in 1980 NHL entry draft. Sixth Flames pick, 97th overall, fifth round.

BRAD TURNER

Defense . . . 6'2" . . . 200 lbs. . . . Born, Winnipeg, Manitoba, May 25, 1968 . . . Shoots right.

Year	Team	League	Games	G.	A.	Pts.	Pen.
1984-85—Darien H.S.		Conn.	24	32	34	66	....
1985-86—Calgary Canucks (c)		AJHL	52	14	21	35	109

(c)—June, 1986—Drafted by Minnesota North Stars in 1986 NHL entry draft. Sixth North Stars pick, 58th overall, third round.

BRIAN TUTT

Defense . . . 6'1" . . . 195 lbs. . . . Born, Swallwell, Alta., June 9, 1962 . . . Shoots left . . . (September, 1981)—Broke leg while attending Philadelphia Flyers training camp.

Year	Team	League	Games	G.	A.	Pts.	Pen.
1979-80—Calgary Canucks		AJHL	59	6	14	20	55
1979-80—Calgary Wranglers (c)		WHL	2	0	0	0	2
1980-81—Calgary Wranglers		WHL	72	10	41	51	111
1981-82—Calgary Wranglers		WHL	40	2	16	18	85
1982-83—Toledo Goaldiggers		IHL	42	7	13	20	56
1982-83—Maine Mariners		AHL	31	0	0	0	28
1983-84—Toledo Goaldiggers (b)		IHL	82	7	44	51	79
1983-84—Springfield Indians		AHL	1	0	0	0	2
1984-85—Hershey Bears		AHL	3	0	0	0	8
1984-85—Kalamazoo Wings (b)		IHL	80	8	45	53	62
1985-86—Kalamazoo Wings		IHL	82	11	39	50	129

(c)—June, 1980—Drafted as underage junior by Philadelphia Flyers in NHL entry draft. Sixth Flyers pick, 126th overall, sixth round.

STEVE TUTTLE

Right Wing . . . 6'1" . . . 180 lbs. . . . Born, Vancouver, B.C., January 5, 1966 . . . Shoots right.

Year	Team	League	Games	G.	A.	Pts.	Pen.
1983-84—Richmond (c)		BCJHL	46	46	34	80	22
1984-85—University of Wisconsin		WCHA	28	3	4	7	0
1985-86—University of Wisconsin		WCHA	32	2	10	12	2

(c)—June, 1984—Drafted by St. Louis Blues in NHL entry draft. Eighth Blues pick, 113th overall, sixth round.

SHAWN TYERS

Right Wing . . . 6'1" . . . 194 lbs. . . . Born, Toronto, Ont., January 14, 1967 . . . Shoots right . . . (September, 1984)—Broken nose . . . (October, 1984)—Broken wrist . . . Also plays Center.

Year	Team	League	Games	G.	A.	Pts.	Pen.
1983-84—North York Midget		OHA	60	41	65	106	227
1984-85—Hamilton Steelhawks		OHL	5	1	0	1	2
1984-85—Sault Ste. Marie Greyhounds (c)		OHL	30	7	12	19	7
1984-85—Kitchener Rangers (d)		OHL	22	5	14	19	17
1985-86—Kitchener Rangers		OHL	26	2	3	5	14

(c)—January, 1985—Traded by Sault Ste. Marie Greyhounds to Kitchener Rangers for Wayne Presley.

(d)—June, 1985—Drafted as underage junior by Edmonton Oilers in 1985 NHL entry draft. Sixth Oilers pick, 146th overall, seventh round.

JEFF URBAN

Left Wing . . . 6'2" . . . 185 lbs. . . . Born, Edina, Minn., March 23, 1967 . . . Shoots left.

Year	Team	League	Games	G.	A.	Pts.	Pen.
1984-85—Minnetonka H.S. (c)		Minn. H.S.	25	21	18	39	38
1985-86—Univ. of Michigan		CCHA	36	9	6	15	23

(c)—June, 1985—Drafted by St. Louis Blues in 1985 NHL entry draft. Eighth Blues pick, 180th overall, ninth round.

J. D. URBANIC

Left Wing . . . 6'1" . . . 165 lbs. . . . Born, St. Catharines, Ont., August 31, 1966 . . . Shoots left.

Year	Team	League	Games	G.	A.	Pts.	Pen.
1982-83—Aurora Tigers		OJHL	44	13	21	34	86
1983-84—Windsor Spitfires (c)		OHL	54	12	18	30	39
1984-85—Windsor Spitfires		OHL	57	15	15	30	64
1985-86—Windsor Spitfires		OHL	40	18	12	30	69

(c)—June, 1984—Drafted as underage junior by Boston Bruins in NHL entry draft. Tenth Bruins pick, 207th overall, 10th round.

RICK VAIVE

Right Wing . . . 6' . . . 180 lbs. . . . Born, Ottawa, Ont., May 14, 1959 . . . Shoots right . . . (February, 1981)—Slight groin pull . . . First Toronto Maple Leafs player to have a 50-goal season when he set a club record with 54 goals in 1981-82 . . . (February 25, 1984)—Injured ankle in loss at Edmonton . . . (December, 1984)—Knee injury . . . (November 27, 1985)—Injured hand at Pittsburgh and missed five games . . . (December 23, 1985)—Injured hand and missed 12 games.

Year	Team	League	Games	G.	A.	Pts.	Pen.
1976-77—Sherbrooke Beavers (c)		QJHL	68	51	59	110	91
1977-78—Sherbrooke Beavers (d)		QJHL	68	76	79	155	199
1978-79—Birmingham Bulls (e)		WHA	75	26	33	59	*248
1979-80—Vancouver Canucks (f)		NHL	47	13	8	21	111
1979-80—Toronto Maple Leafs		NHL	22	9	7	16	77
1980-81—Toronto Maple Leafs		NHL	75	33	29	62	229
1981-82—Toronto Maple Leafs		NHL	77	54	35	89	157
1982-83—Toronto Maple Leafs		NHL	78	51	28	79	105
1983-84—Toronto Maple Leafs		NHL	76	52	41	93	114
1984-85—Toronto Maple Leafs		NHL	72	35	33	68	112
1985-86—Toronto Maple Leafs		NHL	61	33	31	64	85
WHA TOTALS			75	26	33	59	248
NHL TOTALS			508	280	212	492	990

(c)—Won Rookie of the Year Award.
(d)—Signed by Birmingham Bulls (WHA) as underage junior, July, 1978.
(e)—Drafted by Vancouver Canucks in entry draft. First Vancouver pick, fifth overall, first round.
(f)—February, 1980—Traded with Bill Derlago by Vancouver Canucks to Toronto Maple Leafs for Dave Williams and Jerry Butler.

CARMINE VANI

Center . . . 6'1" . . . 180 lbs. . . . Born, Toronto, Ont., August 7, 1964 . . . Shoots left . . . Also plays Left Wing.

Year	Team	League	Games	G.	A.	Pts.	Pen.
1980-81—St. Michael Midgets		Ont. Midgets	33	29	35	64	....
1980-81—St. Michael Jr. B		OPJHL	13	2	2	4	20
1981-82—Kingston Canadians (c)		OHL	49	11	16	27	138
1982-83—Kingston Canadians		OHL	21	7	11	18	56
1982-83—North Bay Centennials		OHL	25	22	22	44	84
1983-84—North Bay Centennials		OHL	17	14	3	17	58
1983-84—Kitchener Rangers		OHL	24	15	8	23	75
1984-85—Kalamazoo Wings		IHL	5	0	0	0	21
1984-85—Adirondack Red Wings (d)		AHL	45	10	5	15	53
1985-86—Milwaukee Admirals		IHL	3	1	0	1	4
1985-86—Flint Spirits		IHL	58	27	26	53	100

(c)—June, 1982—Drafted as underage junior by Detroit Red Wings in 1982 NHL entry draft. Third Red Wings pick, 44th overall, third round.
(d)—July, 1985—Released by Detroit Red Wings.

ERNESTO VARGAS

Center . . . 6'2" . . . 205 lbs. . . . Born, St. Paul, Minn., January 3, 1964 . . . Shoots left . . . Also plays Left Wing.

Year	Team	League	Games	G.	A.	Pts.	Pen.
1981-82—Coon Rapids H.S. (c)		Minn. H.S.	24	28	28	56	22
1982-83—University of Wisconsin		WCHA	37	2	4	6	32
1983-84—University of Wisconsin		WCHA	36	5	15	20	32
1984-85—University of Wisconsin		WCHA	42	8	16	24	68
1985-86—University of Wisconsin		WCHA	41	20	23	43	67

(c)—June, 1982—Drafted as underage player by Montreal Canadiens in 1982 NHL entry draft. Ninth Canadiens pick, 117th overall, sixth round.

DENNIS VASKE

Defense ... 6'2" ... 210 lbs. ... Born, Rockford, Ill., October 11, 1967 ... Shoots left.

Year	Team	League	Games	G.	A.	Pts.	Pen.
1984-85	Armstrong H.S.	Minn.	22	5	18	23	..
1985-86	Armstrong H.S. (c)	Minn.	20	9	13	22	..

(c)—June, 1986—Drafted by New York Islanders in 1986 NHL entry draft. Second Islanders pick, 38th overall, second round.

DARREN WILLIAM VEITCH

Defense ... 5'11" ... 188 lbs. ... Born, Saskatoon, Sask., April 24, 1960 ... Shoots right ... (October 27, 1982)—Fractured collarbone in three places in game at Pittsburgh ... (February 19, 1983)—Broke collarbone again in game at Los Angeles ... (February 11, 1984)— Suffered broken ribs in game vs. Philadelphia ... (January, 1985)—Bruised ribs.

Year	Team	League	Games	G.	A.	Pts.	Pen.
1976-77	Regina Blues	SJHL	60	15	21	36	121
1976-77	Regina Pats	WCHL	1	0	0	0	0
1977-78	Regina Pats	WCHL	71	13	32	45	135
1978-79	Regina Pats	WHL	51	11	36	47	80
1979-80	Regina Pats (a-c)	WHL	71	29	*93	122	118
1980-81	Hershey Bears	AHL	26	6	22	28	12
1980-81	Washington Capitals	NHL	59	4	21	25	46
1981-82	Hershey Bears	AHL	10	5	10	15	16
1981-82	Washington Capitals	NHL	67	9	44	53	54
1982-83	Hershey Bears	AHL	5	0	1	1	2
1982-83	Washington Capitals	NHL	10	0	8	8	0
1983-84	Washington Capitals	NHL	46	6	18	24	17
1983-84	Hershey Bears	AHL	11	1	6	7	4
1984-85	Washington Capitals	NHL	75	3	18	21	37
1985-86	Washington Capitals (d)	NHL	62	3	9	12	27
1985-86	Detroit Red Wings	NHL	13	0	5	5	2
	NHL TOTALS		332	25	123	148	183

(c)—June, 1980—Drafted by Washington Capitals in 1980 NHL entry draft. First Capitals pick, fifth overall, first round.
(d)—March, 1986—Traded by Washington Capitals to Detroit Red Wings for John Barrett and Greg Smith.

RANDY VELISCHEK

Defense ... 6' ... 200 lbs. ... Born, Montreal, Que., February 10, 1962 ... Shoots left.

Year	Team	League	Games	G.	A.	Pts.	Pen.
1979-80	Providence College (c)	ECAC	31	5	5	10	20
1980-81	Providence College	ECAC	33	3	12	15	26
1981-82	Providence College (b)	ECAC	33	1	14	15	34
1982-83	Providence College (a-d-e)	ECAC	41	18	34	52	50
1982-83	Minnesota North Stars	NHL	3	0	0	0	2
1983-84	Salt Lake Golden Eagles	CHL	43	7	21	28	54
1983-84	Minnesota North Stars	NHL	33	2	2	4	10
1984-85	Springfield Indians	AHL	26	2	7	9	22
1984-85	Minnesota North Stars	NHL	52	4	9	13	26
1985-86	New Jersey Devils (f)	NHL	47	2	7	9	39
1985-86	Maine Mariners	AHL	21	0	4	4	4
	NHL TOTALS		135	8	18	26	77

(c)—June, 1980—Drafted by Minnesota North Stars as underage player in 1980 NHL entry draft. Third North Stars pick, 53rd overall, third round.
(d)—ECAC Player of the Year.
(e)—NCAA All-America Team (East).
(f)—Acquired by New Jersey Devils in 1985 NHL waiver draft.

MIKE VELLUCCI

Defense ... 6'1" ... 180 lbs. ... Born, Farmington, Mich., August 11, 1966 ... Shoots left ... (August, 1984)—Missed season with fractured vertebrae in automobile accident.

Year	Team	League	Games	G.	A.	Pts.	Pen.
1982-83	Detroit Compuware	Mich. Midget	70	23	20	43	98
1983-84	Belleville Bulls (c)	OHL	67	2	20	22	83
1984-85	Belleville Bulls	OHL	..	..	..	..	....
1985-86	Belleville Bulls	OHL	64	11	32	43	154

(c)—June, 1984—Drafted as underage junior by Hartford Whalers in NHL entry draft. Third Whalers pick, 131st overall, seventh round.

BRIAN VERBEEK

Center . . . 5'9" . . . 190 lbs. . . . Born, Wyoming, Ont., October 22, 1966 . . . Shoots left . . . Brother of Pat Verbeek.

Year	Team	League	Games	G.	A.	Pts.	Pen.
1982-83—Petrolia Jr. B		OHA	37	22	24	46	77
1983-84—Sudbury Wolves		OHL	69	24	38	62	50
1984-85—Sudbury Wolves		OHL	18	7	10	17	37
1984-85—Kingston Canadians		OHL	50	25	31	56	20
1985-86—Kingston Canadians (c)		OHL	62	50	40	90	132

(c)—June, 1986—Drafted by Hartford Whalers in 1986 NHL entry draft. Eleventh Whalers pick, 242nd overall, 12th round.

PAT VERBEEK

Center . . . 5'9" . . . 195 lbs. . . . Born, Sarnia, Ont., May 24, 1964 . . . Shoots right . . . (May 15, 1985)—Left thumb severed between knuckles in a corn planting machine on his farm near Forest, Ontario. Doctors reconnected the thumb surgically . . . Brother of Brian Verbeek.

Year	Team	League	Games	G.	A.	Pts.	Pen.
1980-81—Petrolia Jr. B.		OPJHL	42	44	44	88	155
1981-82—Sudbury Wolves (c-d)		OHL	66	37	51	88	180
1982-83—Sudbury Wolves		OHL	61	40	67	107	184
1982-83—New Jersey Devils		NHL	6	3	2	5	8
1983-84—New Jersey Devils		NHL	79	20	27	47	158
1984-85—New Jersey Devils		NHL	78	15	18	33	162
1985-86—New Jersey Devils		NHL	76	25	28	53	79
NHL TOTALS			239	63	75	138	407

(c)—Winner of Emms Family Award (OHL Rookie of the Year).
(d)—June, 1982—Drafted as underage junior by New Jersey Devils in 1982 NHL entry draft. Third Devils pick, 43rd overall, third round.

CLAUDE VERRET

Center . . . 5'10" . . . 164 lbs. . . . Born, Lachine, Que., April 20, 1963 . . . Shoots left.

Year	Team	League	Games	G.	A.	Pts.	Pen.
1980-81—Trois Rivieres Draveurs (c-d)		QMJHL	68	39	73	112	4
1981-82—Trois Rivieres Draveurs (a-c-e-f-g)		QMJHL	64	54	108	*162	14
1982-83—Trois Rivieres Draveurs		QHL	68	73	115	188	21
1983-84—Buffalo Sabres		NHL	11	2	5	7	2
1983-84—Rochester Americans (h)		AHL	65	39	51	90	4
1984-85—Rochester Americans (b)		AHL	76	40	53	93	12
1984-85—Buffalo Sabres		NHL	3	0	0	0	0
1985-86—Rochester Americans		AHL	52	19	32	51	14
NHL TOTALS			14	2	5	7	2

(c)—Winner of Frank Selke Trophy (QMJHL Most Gentlemanly Player).
(d)—Winner of the Instructeurs Trophy (QMJHL Top Rookie).
(e)—Winner of Jean Beliveau Trophy (QMJHL Leading Scorer).
(f)—Led QMJHL President Cup playoffs with 35 assists and 48 points.
(g)—June, 1982—Drafted as underage junior by Buffalo Sabres in 1982 NHL entry draft. Twelfth Sabres pick, 163rd overall, eighth round.
(h)—Won Dudley (Red) Garrett Memorial Trophy (Top AHL Rookie).

LEIGH VERSTRAETE

Right Wing . . . 5'11" . . . 183 lbs. . . . Born, Pincher Creek, Alta., January 6, 1962 . . . Shoots right.

Year	Team	League	Games	G.	A.	Pts.	Pen.
1981-82—Calgary Wranglers (c)		WHL	49	19	20	39	385
1982-83—Calgary Wranglers		WHL	4	0	1	1	11
1982-83—Toronto Maple Leafs		NHL	3	0	0	0	5
1982-83—St. Catharines Saints		AHL	61	5	3	8	221
1983-84—St. Catharines Saints		AHL	51	0	7	7	183
1983-84—Muskegon Mohawks		IHL	19	5	5	10	123
1984-85—Toronto Maple Leafs		NHL	2	0	0	0	0
1984-85—St. Catharines Saints		AHL	43	5	8	13	164
1985-86—St. Catharines Saints		AHL	75	8	12	20	300
NHL TOTALS			5	0	0	0	5

(c)—June, 1982—Drafted by Toronto Maple Leafs in 1982 NHL entry draft. Thirteenth Maple Leafs pick, 192nd overall, tenth round.

KEVIN VESCIO

Defense . . . 5'11" . . . 180 lbs. . . . Born, Fort William, Ont., March 15, 1965 . . . Shoots left.

Year	Team	League	Games	G.	A.	Pts.	Pen.
1981-82	Stratford Cullitons	MWJBHL	42	4	31	35	30
1982-83	North Bay Centennials (c)	OHL	70	5	30	35	33
1983-84	North Bay Centennials	OHL	67	2	26	28	75
1984-85	North Bay Centennials	OHL	57	1	16	17	37
1985-86	North Bay Centennials	OHL	51	12	38	50	70

(c)—June, 1983—Drafted as underage junior by New York Islanders in 1983 NHL entry draft. Eleventh Islanders pick, 177th overall, ninth round.

GREG VEY

Center . . . 6'1" . . . 190 lbs. . . . Born, Toronto, Ont., June 20, 1967 . . . Shoots left . . . Also plays either Wing.

Year	Team	League	Games	G.	A.	Pts.	Pen.
1983-84	Pickering Jr. B.	OHA	42	5	19	24	45
1984-85	Peterborough Petes (c)	OHL	61	11	15	26	25
1985-86	Peterborough Petes	OHL	61	14	20	34	49

(c)—June, 1985—Drafted as underage junior by Toronto Maple Leafs in 1985 NHL entry draft. Fourth Maple Leafs pick, 64th overall, fourth round.

RON VIGLASI

Defense . . . 5'11" . . . 180 lbs. . . . Born, Powell River, B.C., April 21, 1965 . . . Shoots right.

Year	Team	League	Games	G.	A.	Pts.	Pen.
1982-83	Victoria Cougars (c)	WHL	63	4	16	20	56
1983-84	Kamloops Junior Oilers	WHL	3	0	0	0	9
1984-85	Moose Jaw Warriors	WHL	22	0	10	10	6
1984-85	Medicine Hat Tigers (d)	WHL	15	0	4	4	12
1984-85	Kelowna Wings	WHL	38	8	14	22	42
1985-86	Victoria Cougars	WHL	27	9	15	24	14
1985-86	Spokane Chiefs	WHL	15	1	18	19	8

(c)—June, 1983—Drafted as underage junior by New York Islanders in 1983 NHL entry draft. Seventh Islanders pick, 97th overall, fifth round.

(d)—January, 1985—Traded with future consideratons by Medicine Hat Tigers to Kelowna Wings for Stu Wenaas and Darren Cota.

DANIEL VINCELETTE

Left Wing . . . 6'1" . . . 202 lbs. . . . Born, Verdun, Que., August 1, 1967 . . . Shoots left . . . (December, 1983)—Knee surgery.

Year	Team	League	Games	G.	A.	Pts.	Pen.
1983-84	Magog Cantonniers	Que. Midget	40	9	13	22	43
1984-85	Drummondville Voltigeurs (c)	QHL	64	11	24	35	124
1985-86	Drummondville Voltigeurs	QHL	70	37	47	84	234

(c)—June, 1985—Drafted as underage junior by Chicago Black Hawks in 1985 NHL entry draft. Third Black Hawks pick, 74th overall, fourth round.

KEN VINGE

Right Wing . . . 5'10" . . . 175 lbs. . . . Born, Edmonton, Alta., January 21, 1963 . . . Shoots right.

Year	Team	League	Games	G.	A.	Pts.	Pen.
1985-86	University of Calgary (c)	CWUAA	50	30	50	80	30

(c)—July, 1986—Signed by New York Rangers as a free agent.

HANNU VIRTA

Defense . . . 6' . . . 176 lbs. . . . Born, Turku, Finland, March 22, 1963 . . . Shoots left . . . (February 12, 1983)—Groin injury . . . (January, 1984)—Stretched knee ligaments . . . (January 27, 1986)—Injured knee at Montreal.

Year	Team	League	Games	G.	A.	Pts.	Pen.
1980-81	Turku TPS (c)	Finland	....	22	23	45	....
1981-82	Turku TPS	Finland	....	...	....	....	....
1981-82	Buffalo Sabres	NHL	3	0	1	1	4
1982-83	Buffalo Sabres	NHL	74	13	24	37	18
1983-84	Buffalo Sabres	NHL	70	6	30	36	12
1984-85	Buffalo Sabres	NHL	51	1	23	24	16
1985-86	Buffalo Sabres	NHL	47	5	23	28	16
	NHL TOTALS		245	25	101	126	66

(c)—June, 1981—Drafted as underage player by Buffalo Sabres in 1981 NHL entry draft. Second Sabres pick, 38th overall, second round.

EMANUEL VIVEIROS

Defense . . . 5'11" . . . 160 lbs. . . . Born, St. Albert, Alta., January 8, 1966 . . . Shoots left.

Year	Team	League	Games	G.	A.	Pts.	Pen.
1982-83	Prince Albert Raiders	WHL	59	6	26	32	55
1983-84	Prince Albert Raiders (b-c)	WHL	67	15	94	109	48
1984-85	Prince Albert Raiders (b)	WHL	68	17	71	88	94
1985-86	Prince Albert Raiders (a-d-e-f)	WHL	57	22	70	92	30
1985-86	Minnesota North Stars	NHL	4	0	1	1	0
	NHL TOTALS		4	0	1	1	0

(c)—June, 1984—Drafted as underage junior by Edmonton Oilers in NHL entry draft. Sixth Oilers pick, 106th overall, sixth round.
(d)—Named best WHL Defenseman (East).
(e)—Named WHL MVP (East).
(f)—December, 1985—Traded by Edmonton Oilers with Marc Habscheid and Don Barber to Minnesota North Stars for Gord Sherven and Don Biggs.

MICKEY VOLCAN

Defense . . . 6' . . . 190 lbs. . . . Born, Edmonton, Alta., March 3, 1962 . . . Shoots right . . . Son of Mike Volcan (Member of Edmonton Eskimos CFL team in 1950s).

Year	Team	League	Games	G.	A.	Pts.	Pen.
1977-78	St. Albert Saints	AJHL	60	28	40	68	106
1978-79	St. Albert Saints (c)	AJHL	50	20	47	67	109
1979-80	Univ. of North Dakota (d)	WCHA	33	2	14	16	38
1980-81	Binghamton Whalers	AHL	24	1	9	10	26
1980-81	Hartford Whalers	NHL	49	2	11	13	26
1981-82	Binghamton Whalers	AHL	33	4	13	17	47
1981-82	Hartford Whalers	NHL	26	1	5	6	29
1982-83	Hartford Whalers (e)	NHL	68	4	13	17	73
1983-84	Colorado Flames	CHL	30	8	9	17	20
1983-84	Calgary Flames	NHL	19	1	4	5	18
1984-85	Moncton Golden Flames	AHL	63	8	14	22	44
1985-86	Nova Scotia Oilers	AHL	66	12	36	48	114
	NHL TOTALS		162	8	33	41	146

(c)—Won W.G. (Bill) Scott Memorial Trophy (Best AJHL Defenseman).
(d)—June, 1980—Drafted by Hartford Whalers as underage player in 1980 NHL entry draft. Third Whalers pick, 50th overall, third round.
(e)—July, 1983—Traded by Hartford Whalers with third-round draft choice in 1984 to Calgary Flames for Richie Dunn and Joel Quenneville.

DUANE (DEWEY) WAHLIN

Right Wing . . . 5'11" . . . 165 lbs. . . . Born, St. Paul, Minn., June 3, 1965 . . . Shoots right.

Year	Team	League	Games	G.	A.	Pts.	Pen.
1983-84	St. Paul Johnson H.S. (c)	Minn. H.S.	29	55	36	91	30
1984-85	University of Maine	H. East	38	12	6	18	36
1985-86	University of Maine	H. East	12	0	3	3	14

(c)—June, 1984—Drafted by Minnesota North Stars in NHL entry draft. Ninth North Stars pick, 181st overall, ninth round.

BRADLEY WALCOT

Defense . . . 6' . . . 180 lbs. . . . Born, Calgary, Alta., March 22, 1965 . . . Shoots right . . . (January 19, 1982)—Injured back.

Year	Team	League	Games	G.	A.	Pts.	Pen.
1981-82	Toronto Midget Marlies	MTHL	37	29	70	99	38
1982-83	Kingston Canadians (c)	OHL	53	10	12	22	49
1983-84	Kingston Canadians	OHL	11	3	7	10	5
1983-84	Oshawa Generals	OHL	48	6	13	19	37
1984-85	Oshawa Generals	OHL	8	1	3	4	12
1984-85	Sudbury Wolves	OHL	49	10	25	35	35
1985-86	Flint Spirit	IHL	8	2	2	4	2
1985-86	Sudbury Wolves	OHL	64	5	28	33	34

(c)—June, 1983—Drafted as underage junior by Quebec Nordiques in 1983 NHL entry draft. Fifth Nordiques pick, 112th overall, sixth round.

DAVE EARL WALDIE

Left Wing . . . 6' . . . 180 lbs. . . . Born, Roseneath, Ont., April 8, 1965 . . . Shoots left.

Year	Team	League	Games	G.	A.	Pts.	Pen.
1982-83	Cornwall Royals	OHL	20	4	2	6	5

Year	Team	League	Games	G.	A.	Pts.	Pen.
1983-84—Cornwall Royals		OHL	50	16	22	38	21
1984-85—Cornwall Royals		OHL	66	35	56	91	29
1985-86—Portland Winter Hawks (a-c)		WHL	72	68	58	126	63

(c)—Co-winner of Rookie-of-the-Year Trophy (West) with Ron Shudra.

GORDON WALKER

Left Wing . . . 6' . . . 178 lbs. . . . Born, Castlegar, B.C., August 12, 1965 . . . Shoots left . . . Also plays center.

Year	Team	League	Games	G.	A.	Pts.	Pen.
1981-82—Drumheller Miners		AJHL	60	35	44	79	90
1982-83—Portland Winter Hawks (c)		WHL	66	24	30	54	95
1983-84—Portland Winter Hawks		WHL	58	28	41	69	65
1984-85—Kamloops Blazers (a-d-e)		WHL	66	67	67	134	76
1985-86—New Haven Nighthawks		AHL	46	11	28	39	66

(c)—June, 1983—Drafted as underage junior by New York Rangers in 1983 NHL entry draft. Fifth Rangers' pick, 53rd overall, third round.

(d)—September, 1984—Traded with Craig Benning by Portland Winter Hawks to Kamloops Blazers for Brad Werenka.

(e)—Led WHL Playoffs with 13 goals.

BRET WALTER

Center . . . 6'1" . . . 195 lbs. . . . Born, Calgary, Alta., April 28, 1968 . . . Shoots right . . . (October, 1985)—Injured shoulder.

Year	Team	League	Games	G.	A.	Pts.	Pen.
1984-85—Ft. Saskatchewan Manville Midgets		AMMHL	32	38	39	77	44
1985-86—University of Alberta (c)		CWUAA	18	3	11	14	6

(c)—June, 1986—Drafted by New York Rangers in 1986 NHL entry draft. Second Rangers pick, 51st overall, third round.

RYAN WILLIAM WALTER

Left Wing . . . 6' . . . 195 lbs. . . . Born, New Westminster, B. C., April 23, 1958 . . . Shoots left . . . Brother of George Walter . . . (November, 1983)—Injured groin muscle . . . (October 27, 1984)—Concussion and twisted knee when checked by Andy Brickley in game at Pittsburgh . . . (December 18, 1985)—Cut on left eyebrow vs. Quebec and missed three games . . . (March 8, 1986)—Back Spasms . . . (March, 1986)—Broke ankle and missed remainder of regular season and all of playoffs except for Stanley Cup finals.

Year	Team	League	Games	G.	A.	Pts.	Pen.
1973-74—Langley Lords		Jr."A"BCHL	....	...	....	....	....
1973-74—Kamloops Chiefs		WCHL	2	0	0	0	0
1974-75—Langley Lords		Jr."A"BCHL	....	...	....	....	....
1974-75—Kamloops Chiefs		WCHL	9	8	4	12	2
1975-76—Kamloops Chiefs		WCHL	72	35	49	84	96
1976-77—Kamloops Chiefs		WCHL	71	41	58	99	100
1977-78—Seattle Breakers (a-c)		WCHL	62	54	71	125	148
1978-79—Washington Capitals		NHL	69	28	28	56	70
1979-80—Washington Capitals		NHL	80	24	42	66	106
1980-81—Washington Capitals		NHL	80	24	45	69	150
1981-82—Washington Capitals (d)		NHL	78	38	49	87	142
1982-83—Montreal Canadiens		NHL	80	29	46	75	15
1983-84—Montreal Canadiens		NHL	73	20	29	49	83
1984-85—Montreal Canadiens		NHL	72	19	19	39	59
1985-86—Montreal Canadiens		NHL	69	15	34	49	45
NHL TOTALS			601	197	292	490	670

(c)—Drafted from Seattle Breakers by Washington Capitals in first round of 1978 amateur draft.

(d)—September, 1982—Traded by Washington Capitals with Rick Green to Montreal Canadiens for Rod Langway, Brian Engblom, Doug Jarvis and Craig Laughlin.

JAMIE WANSBROUGH

Right Wing . . . 5'11" . . . 176 lbs. . . . Born, Toronto, Ont., June 30, 1963 . . . Shoots right.

Year	Team	League	Games	G.	A.	Pts.	Pen.
1982-83—Bowling Green State U.		CCHA	40	23	17	40	22
1983-84—Bowling Green State U.		CCHA	40	34	16	50	18
1984-85—Bowling Green State U.		CCHA	42	37	33	70	28
1985-86—Bowling Green State U.		CCHA	42	33	44	77	28

TOM WARDEN

Defense . . . 6'2" . . . 190 lbs. . . . Born, Darbishire, England, January 12, 1966 . . . Shoots left.

Year	Team	League	Games	G.	A.	Pts.	Pen.
1983-84—Aurora Tigers		OJHL	2	0	0	0	0
1983-84—North Bay Centennials (c)		OHL	28	3	2	5	16
1984-85—North Bay Centennials		OHL	61	6	12	18	101
1985-86—North Bay Centennials		OHL	12	1	2	3	27

(c)—June, 1984—Drafted as underage junior by New York Islanders in NHL entry draft. Tenth Islanders pick, 187th overall, ninth round.

MICHAEL WARE

Right Wing . . . 6'5" . . . 200 lbs. . . . Born, York, Ont., March 22, 1967 . . . Shoots right . . . Also plays Defense . . . (October, 1985)—Broken collarbone.

Year	Team	League	Games	G.	A.	Pts.	Pen.
1983-84—Mississauga Reps		OHA	30	14	20	34	50
1984-85—Hamilton Steelhawks (c)		OHL	57	4	14	18	225
1985-86—Hamilton Steelhawks		OHL	44	8	11	19	155

(c)—June, 1985—Drafted as underage junior by Edmonton Oilers in 1985 NHL entry draft. Third Oilers pick, 62nd overall, third round.

WILLIAM (BILL) WATSON

Right Wing . . . 6' . . . 180 lbs. . . . Born, Pine Falls, Man., March 30, 1964 . . . Shoots right . . . (October 13, 1985)—Injured left shoulder.

Year	Team	League	Games	G.	A.	Pts.	Pen.
1980-81—Prince Albert Raiders		AJHL	54	30	39	69	27
1981-82—Prince Albert Raiders (c)		AJHL	47	43	41	84	37
1982-83—University of Minn./Duluth		WCHA	22	5	10	15	10
1983-84—University of Minn./Duluth		WCHA	40	35	51	86	12
1984-85—U of Minn./Duluth (a-d-e-f)		WCHA	46	49	60	109	48
1985-86—Chicago Black Hawks		NHL	52	8	16	24	2
NHL TOTALS			52	8	16	24	2

(c)—June, 1982—Drafted by Chicago Black Hawks in NHL entry draft. Fourth Black Hawks pick, 70th overall, fourth round.
(d)—WCHA MVP.
(e)—First team All-America forward (West).
(f)—Hobey Baker Award Winner (Top American College Hockey Player).

TIM WATTERS

Defense . . . 5'11" . . . 180 lbs. . . . Born, Kamloops, B.C., July 25, 1959 . . . Shoots left . . . Set record for assists and points by a defenseman at Michigan Tech in 1980-81 . . . (October, 1983)—Pulled hamstring . . . (December, 1984)—Broken wrist . . . (February, 1986)—Back spasms.

Year	Team	League	Games	G.	A.	Pts.	Pen.
1977-78—Michigan Tech		WCHA	37	1	15	16	47
1978-79—Michigan Tech (c)		WCHA	31	6	21	27	48
1979-80—Canadian Olympic Team		Int'l	56	8	21	29	43
1979-80—Canadian Olympic Team		Int'l	6	1	1	2	0
1980-81—Michigan Tech (a-d)		WCHA	43	12	38	50	36
1981-82—Tulsa Oilers		CHL	5	1	2	3	0
1981-82—Winnipeg Jets		NHL	69	2	22	24	97
1982-83—Winnipeg Jets		NHL	77	5	18	23	98
1983-84—Winnipeg Jets		NHL	74	3	20	23	169
1984-85—Winnipeg Jets		NHL	63	2	20	22	74
1985-86—Winnipeg Jets		NHL	56	6	8	14	95
NHL TOTALS			339	18	88	106	533

(c)—August, 1979—Drafted by Winnipeg Jets in NHL draft. Sixth Jets pick, 124th overall, sixth round.
(d)—Named to All-America Team (West).

ERIC WEINRICH

Defense . . . 6'1" . . . 190 lbs. . . . Born, Roanoke, Vir., December 19, 1966 . . . Shoots left . . . (December, 1984)—Dislocated shoulder.

Year	Team	League	Games	G.	A.	Pts.	Pen.
1983-84—North Yarmouth Acad.		Mass. H.S.	17	23	33	56	..
1984-85—North Yarmouth Acad. (c)		Mass. H.S.	20	6	21	27	..
1985-86—Univ. of Maine		H. East	34	0	15	15	26

(c)—June, 1985—Drafted by New Jersey Devils in 1985 NHL entry draft. Third Devils pick, 32nd overall, second round.

WALLY WEIR

Defense . . . 6'2" . . . 200 lbs. . . Born, Verdun, Que., June 3, 1954 . . . Shoots left . . . Missed most of 1977-78 season with injured left elbow requiring surgery . . . (October, 1984)— Dislocated shoulder in preseason game while playing for Quebec Nordiques . . . (October, 1984)—Given three-game NHL suspension for preseason game incident.

Year	Team	League	Games	G.	A.	Pts.	Pen.
1973-74—Longueil Rebels	Jr. "A" QHL	....	...	....	....	....	
1974-75—Did not play			....	...		....	....
1975-76—Beauce Jaros	NAHL	56	6	20	26	180
1976-77—Quebec Nordiques	WHA	69	3	17	20	197
1977-78—Quebec Nordiques	WHA	13	0	0	0	47
1978-79—Quebec Nordiques	WHA	68	2	7	9	166
1979-80—Quebec Nordiques	NHL	73	3	12	15	133
1980-81—Quebec Nordiques	NHL	54	6	8	14	77
1980-81—Rochester Americans	AHL	7	1	1	2	79
1981-82—Quebec Nordiques	NHL	62	3	5	8	173
1982-83—Quebec Nordiques	NHL	58	5	11	16	135
1983-84—Fredericton Express	AHL	44	6	17	23	45
1983-84—Quebec Nordiques	NHL	25	2	3	5	17
1984-85—Hartford Whalers (c)	NHL	34	2	3	5	56
1984-85—Pittsburgh Penguins (d)	NHL	14	0	3	3	34
1985-86—Baltimore Skipjacks	AHL	67	5	12	17	300
WHA TOTALS			150	5	24	29	410
NHL TOTALS			320	21	45	66	625

(c)—October, 1984—Selected by Hartford Whalers in the 1984 NHL waiver draft.
(d)—February, 1985—Claimed on waivers by Pittsburgh Penguins from Hartford Whalers.

TOM WEISS

Right Wing . . . 6'4" . . . 220 lbs. . . . Born, Englewood, Colo., January 31, 1962 . . . Shoots right.

Year	Team	League	Games	G.	A.	Pts.	Pen.
1983-84—Denver University	WCHA	38	12	7	19	34
1984-85—Denver University	WCHA	38	14	9	23	26
1985-86—Denver University (c)	WCHA	48	22	26	48	50

(c)—August, 1986—Signed by New York Islanders as a free agent.

GORDON JAY WELLS
(Known by middle name)

Defense . . . 6'1" . . . 205 lbs. . . . Born, Paris, Ont., May 18, 1959 . . . Shoots left . . . (October 16, 1981)—Broke right hand in team practice when hit by a puck . . . (December 14, 1982)—Tore medial collateral ligament in right knee in game at Washington . . . (December, 1983)—Sprained ankle.

Year	Team	League	Games	G.	A.	Pts.	Pen.
1976-77—Kingston Canadians	OMJHL	59	4	7	11	90
1977-78—Kingston Canadians	OMJHL	68	9	13	22	195
1978-79—Kingston Canadians (a-c)	OMJHL	48	6	21	27	100
1979-80—Los Angeles Kings	NHL	43	0	0	0	113
1979-80—Binghamton Dusters	AHL	28	0	6	6	48
1980-81—Los Angeles Kings	NHL	72	5	13	18	155
1981-82—Los Angeles Kings	NHL	60	1	8	9	145
1982-83—Los Angeles Kings	NHL	69	3	12	15	167
1983-84—Los Angeles Kings	NHL	69	3	18	21	141
1984-85—Los Angeles Kings	NHL	77	2	9	11	185
1985-86—Los Angeles Kings	NHL	79	11	31	42	226
NHL TOTALS			469	25	91	116	1132

(c)—August, 1979—Drafted by Los Angeles Kings in entry draft. First Los Angeles pick, 16th overall, first round.

JEFF WENAAS

Center . . . 5'11" . . . 185 lbs. . . . Born, Eastend, Sask., September 1, 1967 . . . Shoots left . . . Brother of Stu Wenaas (Pittsburgh 10th round 1982 draft pick).

Year	Team	League	Games	G.	A.	Pts.	Pen.
1983-84—Medicine Hat Midget Tigers	AHA	38	16	22	38	77
1984-85—Medicine Hat Tigers (c)	WHL	70	27	27	54	70
1985-86—Medicine Hat Tigers	WHL	65	20	26	46	57

(c)—June, 1985—Drafted as underage junior by Calgary Flames in 1985 NHL entry draft. Third Flames pick, 38th overall, second round.

BLAKE WESLEY

Defense . . . 6'3" . . . 210 lbs. . . . Born, Red Deer, Alta., July 10, 1959 . . . Shoots left.

Year	Team	League	Games	G.	A.	Pts.	Pen.
1974-75—Red Deer Rustlers		AJHL	3	1	0	1	4
1975-76—Red Deer Rustlers		AJHL	55	19	41	60	199
1976-77—Portland Winter Hawks		WCHL	63	8	25	33	111
1977-78—Portland Winter Hawks		WCHL	67	7	37	44	190
1978-79—Portland Winter Hawks (b-c)		WHL	69	10	42	52	292
1979-80—Philadelphia Flyers		NHL	2	0	1	1	2
1979-80—Maine Mariners		AHL	65	12	22	34	76
1980-81—Maine Mariners		AHL	24	6	10	16	20
1980-81—Philadelphia Flyers (d)		NHL	50	3	7	10	107
1981-82—Hartford Whalers		NHL	78	9	18	27	123
1982-83—Hartford Whalers (e)		NHL	22	0	1	1	46
1982-83—Quebec Nordiques		NHL	52	4	8	12	84
1983-84—Quebec Nordiques		NHL	46	2	8	10	75
1984-85—Fredericton Express		AHL	25	3	4	7	80
1984-85—Quebec Nordiques (f)		NHL	21	0	2	2	28
1985-86—Toronto Maple Leafs		NHL	27	0	1	1	21
1985-86—St. Catharines Saints		AHL	37	3	4	7	56
NHL TOTALS			298	18	46	64	486

(c)—August, 1979—Drafted by Philadelphia Flyers in entry draft. Second Philadelphia pick, 22nd overall, second round.

(d)—July, 1981—Traded by Philadelphia Flyers with Don Gillen, Rick MacLeish, first, second and third round picks in the 1982 NHL entry draft by Philadelphia Flyers to Hartford Whalers for Ray Allison, Fred Arthur and Whalers first and third round picks in 1982 draft.

(e)—December, 1982—Traded by Hartford Whalers to Quebec Nordiques for Pierre Lacroix.

(f)—August, 1985—Signed by Toronto Maple Leafs as a free agent.

SIMON WHEELDON

Center . . . 5'11" . . . 170 lbs. . . . Born, Vancouver, B.C., August 30, 1966 . . . Shoots left.

Year	Team	League	Games	G.	A.	Pts.	Pen.
1982-83—Kelowna Bucks		BCJHL	60	...	....	86	....
1983-84—Victoria Cougars (c)		WHL	56	14	24	38	43
1984-85—Victoria Cougars (b)		WHL	67	50	76	126	78
1984-85—Nova Scotia Oilers		AHL	4	0	1	1	0
1985-86—Victoria Cougars (b)		WHL	70	61	96	157	85

(c)—June, 1984—Drafted as underage junior by Edmonton Oilers in NHL entry draft. Eleventh Oilers pick, 229th overall, 11th round.

SHANE WHELAN

Center . . . 6'3" . . . 195 lbs. . . . Born, Kirkland Lake, Ont., February 15, 1967 . . . Shoots left.

Year	Team	League	Games	G.	A.	Pts.	Pen.
1983-84—Newmarket Tier II		OHA	12	1	4	5	4
1984-85—Oshawa Generals (c)		OHL	59	10	14	24	45
1985-86—Windsor Spitfires		OHL	64	9	29	38	69

(c)—June, 1985—Drafted as underage junior by Philadelphia Flyers in 1985 NHL entry draft. Fourth Flyers pick, 63rd overall, third round.

ROB WHISTLE

Defense . . . 6'2" . . . 195 lbs. . . . Born, Thunder Bay, Ont., April 30, 1961 . . . Shoots right.

Year	Team	League	Games	G.	A.	Pts.	Pen.
1984-85—Wilfred Laurier (c-d-e)		OUAA	....	...	....	....	....
1985-86—New York Rangers		NHL	32	4	2	6	10
1985-86—New Haven Nighthawks		AHL	20	1	4	5	5
NHL TOTALS			32	4	2	6	10

(c)—Member of All-Canadian Team.

(d)—Won Senator Joseph A. Sullivan Trophy (Top Canadian-College hockey player).

(e)—October, 1985—Signed by New York Rangers as a free agent.

GORD WHITAKER

Right Wing . . . 6'2" . . . 205 lbs. . . . Born, Edmonton, Alta., January 24, 1966 . . . Shoots right.

Year	Team	League	Games	G.	A.	Pts.	Pen.
1983-84—Colorado College (c)		WCHA	33	10	10	20	44
1984-85—Colorado College		WCHA	31	10	5	15	76
1985-85—Colorado College		WCHA	34	14	16	30	53

(c)—June, 1984—Drafted by Winnipeg Jets in NHL entry draft. Ninth Jets pick, 177th overall, ninth round.

GEORGE WHITE

Left Wing . . . 6' . . . 175 lbs. . . . Born, Arlington, Mass., February 17, 1961 . . . Shoots right . . . Also plays Center.

Year	Team	League	Games	G.	A.	Pts.	Pen.
1980-81—Univ. of New Hampshire (c)		ECAC	32	16	19	35	30
1981-82—Univ. of New Hampshire (d)		ECAC	31	10	15	25	45
1982-83—Univ. of New Hampshire		ECAC	34	15	11	26	21
1983-84—Peoria Prancers		IHL	7	2	0	2	7
1983-84—Colorado Flames		CHL	36	5	12	17	28
1984-85—Moncton Golden Flames		AHL	58	11	5	16	40
1985-86—Moncton Golden Flames		AHL	73	16	12	28	24

(c)—June, 1981—Drafted by Washington Capitals in 1981 NHL entry draft. Ninth Capitals pick, 173rd overall, ninth round.

(d)—June, 1982—Traded with Howard Walker, sixth round 1982 draft pick (Mats Kihlstrom), third round 1983 draft pick (Perry Berezan) and second round 1984 draft pick (Paul Ranheim) by Washington Capitals to Calgary Flames for Ken Houston and Pat Riggin.

DOUGLAS PETER WICKENHEISER

Center . . . 6' . . . 199 lbs. . . . Born, Regina, Sask., March 30, 1961 . . . Shoots left . . . Brother of Kurt Wickenheiser . . . (March 30, 1983)—Broke rib in game at Pittsburgh . . . (March 13, 1985)—Suffered complete tears of the entire medial complex and both cruciate ligaments in his left knee . . . (January 21, 1986)—Returned to St. Louis lineup after missing 56 games (12 in '84-85 and 44 in '85-86).

Year	Team	League	Games	G.	A.	Pts.	Pen.
1976-77—Regina Blues		SJHL	59	42	46	88	63
1977-78—Regina Pats		WCHL	68	37	51	88	49
1978-79—Regina Pats		WHL	68	32	62	94	141
1979-80—Regina Pats (a-c-d-e)		WHL	71	*89	81	*170	99
1980-81—Montreal Canadiens		NHL	41	7	8	15	20
1981-82—Montreal Canadiens		NHL	56	12	23	35	43
1982-83—Montreal Canadiens		NHL	78	25	30	55	49
1983-84—Montreal Canadiens (f)		NHL	27	5	5	10	6
1983-84—St. Louis Blues		NHL	46	7	21	28	19
1984-85—St. Louis Blues		NHL	68	23	20	43	36
1985-86—St. Louis Blues		NHL	36	8	11	19	16
NHL TOTALS			352	87	118	205	189

(c)—Won Bob Brownridge Memorial Trophy (WHL Leading Scorer).

(d)—Named WHL's Most Valuable Player.

(e)—June, 1980—Drafted as underage junior by Montreal Canadiens in 1980 NHL entry draft. First Canadiens pick, first overall, first round.

(f)—December, 1983—Traded by Montreal Canadiens with Gilbert Delorme and Greg Paslawski to St. Louis Blues for Perry Turnbull.

DOUG WIECK

Left Wing . . . 6' . . . 180 lbs. . . . Born, Rochester, Minn., March 12, 1965 . . . Shoots left.

Year	Team	League	Games	G.	A.	Pts.	Pen.
1983-84—Rochester Mayo H.S. (c)		Minn. H.S.	23	31	24	55	15
1984-85—Colorado College		WCHA	35	9	6	15	30
1985-86—Portland Winter Hawks		WHL	37	5	14	19	40

(c)—June, 1984—Drafted by New York Islanders in NHL entry draft. Fourth Islanders pick, 70th overall, fourth round.

JAMES DUNCAN WIEMER

Defense . . . 6'4" . . . 197 lbs. . . . Born, Sudbury, Ont., January 9, 1961 . . . Shoots left.

Year	Team	League	Games	G.	A.	Pts.	Pen.
1978-79—Peterborough Petes		OMJHL	63	15	12	27	50
1979-80—Peterborough Petes (c)		OMJHL	53	17	32	49	63
1980-81—Peterborough Petes		OHL	65	41	54	95	102
1981-82—Rochester Americans		AHL	74	19	26	45	57
1982-83—Rochester Americans		AHL	74	15	44	59	43
1982-83—Buffalo Sabres (d)		NHL	..	..	..	..	..
1983-84—Buffalo Sabres		NHL	64	5	15	20	48
1983-84—Rochester Americans		AHL	12	4	11	15	11
1984-85—Rochester Americans		AHL	13	1	9	10	24
1984-85—New Haven Nighthawks		AHL	33	9	27	36	39
1984-85—Buffalo Sabres (e)		NHL	10	3	2	5	4
1984-85—New York Rangers		NHL	22	4	3	7	30

Year	Team	League	Games	G.	A.	Pts.	Pen.
1985-86—New Haven Nighthawks (a-f)		AHL	73	24	49	73	108
1985-86—New York Rangers		NHL	7	3	0	3	2
NHL TOTALS			103	15	20	35	84

(c)—June, 1980—Drafted by Buffalo Sabres as underage junior in 1980 NHL entry draft. Fifth Sabres pick, 83rd overall, fourth round.

(d)—No regular-season appearance. Played one playoff game.

(e)—December, 1984—Traded with Steve Patrick by Buffalo Sabres to New York Rangers for Chris Renaud and Dave Maloney.

(f)—Won Eddie Shore Plaque (Top AHL Defenseman).

RICHARD WIEST

Center . . . 5'11" . . . 170 lbs. . . . Born, Lethbridge, Alta., June 22, 1967 . . . Shoots right.

Year	Team	League	Games	G.	A.	Pts.	Pen.
1983-84—Lethbridge Broncos		WHL	71	17	16	33	138
1984-85—Lethbridge Broncos (c)		WHL	65	18	19	37	305
1985-86—Lethbridge Broncos (d)		WHL	31	5	13	18	111
1985-86—Seattle Thunderbirds		WHL	2	0	0	0	2
1985-86—Calgary Wranglers		WHL	23	8	3	11	74

(c)—June, 1985—Drafted as underage junior by New York Islanders in 1985 NHL entry draft. Eleventh Islanders pick, 181st overall, ninth round.

(d)—January, 1986—Traded by Lethbridge Broncos to Seattle Thunderbirds for Mario Desjardins.

MARTIN WIITALA, JR.

Center . . . 6'2" . . . 175 lbs. . . . Born, Superior, Wis., February 24, 1964 . . . Shoots right.

Year	Team	League	Games	G.	A.	Pts.	Pen.
1981-82—Superior H.S. (c)		Wisc. H.S.	24	40	43	83	32
1982-83—Univ. of Wisconsin		WCHA	46	10	8	18	8
1983-84—Univ. of Wisconsin		WCHA	33	11	19	30	4
1984-85—Univ. of Wisconsin		WCHA	42	10	16	26	4
1985-86—Univ. of Wisconsin		WCHA	42	15	39	54	24

(c)—June, 1982—Drafted as underage player by Minnesota North Stars in 1982 NHL entry draft. Fifth North Stars pick, 101st overall, fifth round.

NEIL WILKINSON

Defense . . . 6'3" . . . 190 lbs. . . . Born, Selkirk, Manitoba, August 15, 1967 . . . Shoots right . . . (January, 1986)—Broken nose and concussion.

Year	Team	League	Games	G.	A.	Pts.	Pen.
1985-86—Selkirk Steelers (c)		MJHL	42	14	35	49	91

(c)—June, 1986—Drafted by Minnesota North Stars in 1986 NHL entry draft. Second North Stars pick, 30th overall, second round.

BRIAN WILKS

Center . . . 5'11" . . . 175 lbs. . . . Born, Toronto, Ont., February 22, 1966 . . . Shoots right.

Year	Team	League	Games	G.	A.	Pts.	Pen.
1981-82—Toronto Marlboro Midgets		MTMHL	36	40	48	88	22
1982-83—Kitchener Rangers		OHL	69	6	17	23	25
1983-84—Kitchener Rangers (c)		OHL	64	21	54	75	36
1984-85—Kitchener Rangers		OHL	58	30	63	93	52
1984-85—Los Angeles Kings		NHL	2	0	0	0	0
1985-86—Los Angeles Kings		NHL	43	4	8	12	25
NHL TOTALS			45	4	8	12	25

(c)—June, 1984—Drafted as underage junior by Los Angeles Kings in NHL entry draft. Second Kings pick, 24th overall, second round.

DAVID JAMES (TIGER) WILLIAMS

Left Wing . . . 5'11" . . . 180 lbs. . . . Born, Weyburn, Sask., February 3, 1954 . . . Shoots left . . . (October 10, 1980)—Fracture of lower lombar transverse in a goal-mouth crash in first game of 1980-81 season . . . (1982-83)—Missed 12 games due to various NHL suspensions . . . (October 30, 1983)—Given 8-game suspension by NHL for 'potentially dangerous' attempt to injure Paul Baxter in game at Calgary . . . All-time NHL penalty minute leader . . . Set career playoff record for most penalty minutes with 425 . . . (January 8, 1986)—Bruised shoulder at Pittsburgh and missed four games . . . (January 27, 1986)—Injured shoulder at Calgary and missed one game.

Year	Team	League	Games	G.	A.	Pts.	Pen.
1971-72—Swift Current Broncos		WCHL	68	12	22	34	278
1972-73—Swift Current Broncos		WCHL	68	44	58	102	266

Year	Team	League	Games	G.	A.	Pts.	Pen.
1973-74—Swift Current Broncos (c)		WCHL	68	52	56	108	310
1974-75—Oklahoma City Blazers		CHL	39	16	11	27	202
1974-75—Toronto Maple Leafs		NHL	42	10	19	29	187
1975-76—Toronto Maple Leafs		NHL	78	21	19	40	299
1976-77—Toronto Maple Leafs		NHL	77	18	25	43	*338
1977-78—Toronto Maple Leafs (d)		NHL	78	19	31	50	351
1978-79—Toronto Maple Leafs (e)		NHL	77	19	20	39	*298
1979-80—Toronto Maple Leafs (f)		NHL	55	22	18	40	197
1979-80—Vancouver Canucks		NHL	23	8	5	13	81
1980-81—Vancouver Canucks		NHL	77	35	27	62	*343
1981-82—Vancouver Canucks (g)		NHL	77	17	21	38	341
1982-83—Vancouver Canucks		NHL	68	8	13	21	265
1983-84—Vancouver Canucks (h)		NHL	67	15	16	31	294
1984-85—Adirondack Red Wings		AHL	8	5	2	7	4
1984-85—Detroit Red Wings (i)		NHL	55	3	8	11	158
1984-85—Los Angeles Kings		NHL	12	4	3	7	43
1985-86—Los Angeles Kings		NHL	72	20	29	49	320
NHL TOTALS			858	219	254	473	3515

(c)—Drafted from Swift Current Broncos by Toronto Maple Leafs in second round of 1974 amateur draft.

(d)—Led in penalty minutes (63) during playoffs.

(e)—Led in penalty minutes (48) during playoffs.

(f)—February, 1980—Traded with Jerry Butler by Toronto Maple Leafs to Vancouver Canucks for Rick Vaive and Bill Derlago.

(g)—Led NHL playoffs with 116 penalty minutes.

(h)—August, 1984—Traded by Vancouver Canucks to Detroit Red Wings for Rob McClanahan.

(i)—March, 1985—Traded by Detroit Red Wings to Los Angeles Kings for future considerations.

ROD WILLIAMS

Right Wing . . . 6'2" . . . 190 lbs. . . . Born, Lethbridge, Alta., February 14, 1967 . . . Shoots right.

Year	Team	League	Games	G.	A.	Pts.	Pen.
1984-85—Kelowna Wings (c)		WHL	71	15	26	41	56
1985-86—New Westminister Bruins (d)		WHL	1	0	0	0	0
1985-86—Brandon Wheat Kings (e)		WHL	37	8	18	26	55
1985-86—Victoria Cougars		WHL	29	7	6	13	88

(c)—June, 1985—Drafted as underage junior by Philadelphia Flyers in 1985 NHL entry draft. Eleventh Flyers pick, 231st overall, eleventh round.

(d)—October, 1985—Traded with future considerations by Spokane Chiefs to New Westminister Bruins for Marc Zeitlin.

(e)—November, 1985—Traded by New Westminister Bruins to Brandon Wheat Kings for Darwin McPherson and Perry Fafard.

SEAN WILLIAMS

Center . . . 6'2" . . . 180 lbs. . . . Born, Oshawa, Ont., January 28, 1968 . . . Shoots left.

Year	Team	League	Games	G.	A.	Pts.	Pen.
1984-85—Oshawa Generals		OHL	40	6	7	13	28
1985-86—Oshawa Generals (c)		OHL	55	15	23	38	23

(c)—June, 1986—Drafted as underage junior by Minnesota North Stars in 1986 NHL entry draft. Eleventh North Stars pick, 245th overall, 12th round.

KEVIN WILLISON

Defense . . . 5'11" . . . 172 lbs. . . . Born, Calgary, Alta., May 21, 1958 . . . Shoots left . . . (September, 1980)—Surgery for dislocated shoulder.

Year	Team	League	Games	G.	A.	Pts.	Pen.
1975-76—Merritt Luckies		Jr."A"BCHL	60	16	28	44	122
1976-77—Calgary Centennials		WCHL	55	11	32	43	161
1977-78—Billings Bighorns (c)		WCHL	68	21	42	63	151
1978-79—Port Huron Flags		IHL	55	12	35	47	116
1979-80—Salt Lake Golden Eagles		CHL	72	5	26	31	106
1980-81—Port Huron Flags		IHL	20	2	7	9	33
1980-81—Salt Lake Golden Eagles (d)		CHL	....	...	....	....	....
1981-82—Milwaukee Admirals		IHL	73	10	41	51	107
1982-83—Milwaukee Admirals		IHL	81	10	41	51	63
1983-84—Milwaukee Admirals (a-e)		IHL	82	21	52	73	73
1984-85—Muskegon Lumberjacks		IHL	60	6	20	26	39
1985-86—Milwaukee Admirals		IHL	77	9	29	38	57

(c)—Drafted from Billings Bighorns by St. Louis Blues in fifth round of 1978 amateur draft.
(d)—Appeared in three playoff games.
(e)—Co-winner of Governors Trophy (Top IHL Defenseman) with Jim Burton (Fort Wayne).

BEHN BEVAN WILSON

Defense . . . 6'3" . . . 207 lbs. . . . Born, Toronto, Ont., December 19, 1958 . . . Shoots left . . . (October, 1982)—Serious groin pull . . . (February 19, 1983)—Suspended for six games for high sticking New York Rangers goalie Glen Hanlon . . . (November, 1985)—Missed two games with a viral infection . . . (February 13, 1986)—Injured knee vs. Toronto.

Year	Team	League	Games	G.	A.	Pts.	Pen.
1975-76—Ottawa 67's		Jr."A"OHA	63	5	16	21	131
1976-77—Ottawa 67's (c)		Jr."A"OHA	31	8	29	37	115
1976-77—Windsor Spitfires		Jr."A"OHA	17	4	16	20	38
1976-77—Kalamazoo Wings		IHL	13	2	7	9	40
1977-78—Kingston Canadians (d)		Jr."A"OHA	52	18	58	76	186
1978-79—Philadelphia Flyers		NHL	80	13	36	49	197
1979-80—Philadelphia Flyers		NHL	61	9	25	34	212
1980-81—Philadelphia Flyers		NHL	77	16	47	63	237
1981-82—Philadelphia Flyers		NHL	59	13	23	36	135
1982-83—Philadelphia Flyers (e)		NHL	62	8	24	32	92
1983-84—Chicago Black Hawks		NHL	59	10	22	32	143
1984-85—Chicago Black Hawks		NHL	76	10	23	33	185
1985-86—Chicago Black Hawks		NHL	69	13	37	50	113
NHL TOTALS			543	92	237	329	1314

(c)—Traded to Windsor Spitfires by Ottawa 67's with John Wilson for Jim Fox, December, 1976.
(d)—Drafted from Kingston Canadians by Philadelphia Flyers (with choice obtained from Pittsburgh Penguins in trade for Tom Bladon, Orest Kindrachuk and Don Saleski) in first round of 1978 amateur draft.
(e)—June, 1983—Traded by Philadelphia Flyers to Chicago Black Hawks for Doug Crossman and a second-round draft choice in 1984 (Scott Mellanby).

CAREY WILSON

Center . . . 6'2" . . . 205 lbs. . . . Born, Winnipeg, Man., May 19, 1962 . . . Shoots right . . . Son of Dr. Gerry Wilson, former vice-president and team doctor of Winnipeg Jets (WHA) . . . (September 28, 1985)—Injured shoulder in pre-season game and missed the first three games of the regular season . . . (April 28, 1986)—Suffered ruptured spleen and missed remainder of playoffs.

Year	Team	League	Games	G.	A.	Pts.	Pen.
1978-79—Calgary Chinooks		AJHL	60	30	34	64	....
1979-80—Dartmouth College (c)		ECAC	31	16	22	38	20
1980-81—Dartmouth College		ECAC	21	9	13	22	52
1981-82—Helsinki IFK		Finland	39	15	17	32	58
1982-83—Helsinki IFK (d)		Finland	36	18	22	40	...
1983-84—Canadian Olympic Team		Int'l	59	21	24	45	34
1983-84—Calgary Flames		NHL	15	2	5	7	2
1984-85—Calgary Flames		NHL	74	24	48	72	27
1985-86—Calgary Flames		NHL	76	29	29	58	24
NHL TOTALS			165	55	82	137	53

(c)—June, 1980—Drafted by Chicago Black Hawks in NHL entry draft. Eighth Black Hawks pick, 67th overall, fourth round.
(d)—November, 1982—Traded by Chicago Black Hawks to Calgary Flames for Denis Cyr.

DOUGLAS WILSON

Defense . . . 6'1" . . . 187 lbs. . . . Born, Ottawa, Ont., July 5, 1957 . . . Shoots left . . . Missed part of 1976-77 season with knee surgery . . . Brother of Murray Wilson . . . Missed part of 1978-79 season with shoulder injury that required surgery . . . (November 25, 1981)—Broken jaw in game at Vancouver. Had his jaw wired shut, lost 25 pounds and has his vision restricted by special protective mask he had to wear . . . Set Chicago Black Hawks record for defensemen in 1981-82 with 39 goals and 85 points (Only Bobby Orr had ever scored more goals in one season as a defenseman in the NHL) . . . Set Chicago record of 54 assists by a defenseman in 1984-85 (broke own record of 51 set in 1982-83) . . . (November, 1983)—Ankle injury . . . Suffers from Hyperglycemia (High concentration of glucose in the blood) . . . (February 3, 1984)—Broke nose in game at Winnipeg . . . (March 4, 1984)—Played his first game without a facemask after recovering from broken nose. He was accidently hit by the stick of Walt Poddubny of Toronto and suffered a fractured skull. He was out for the rest of the season.

Year	Team	League	Games	G.	A.	Pts.	Pen.
1974-75—Ottawa 67's		Jr."A"OHA	55	29	58	87	75
1975-76—Ottawa 67's (b)		Jr."A"OHA	58	26	62	88	142

Year	Team	League	Games	G.	A.	Pts.	Pen.
1976-77—Ottawa 67's (a-c)	Jr."A"OHA		43	25	54	79	85
1977-78—Chicago Black Hawks	NHL		77	14	20	34	72
1978-79—Chicago Black Hawks	NHL		56	5	21	26	37
1979-80—Chicago Black Hawks	NHL		73	12	49	61	70
1980-81—Chicago Black Hawks	NHL		76	12	39	51	80
1981-82—Chicago Black Hawks (a-d)	NHL		76	39	46	85	54
1982-83—Chicago Black Hawks	NHL		74	18	51	69	58
1983-84—Chicago Black Hawks	NHL		66	13	45	58	64
1984-85—Chicago Black Hawks (b)	NHL		78	22	54	76	44
1985-86—Chicago Black Hawks	NHL		79	17	47	64	80
NHL TOTALS			655	152	372	524	559

(c)—Drafted from Ottawa 67's by Chicago Black Hawks in first round of 1977 amateur draft.
(d)—Won James Norris Memorial Trophy (Top NHL Defenseman).

MITCH WILSON

Right Wing . . . 5'8" . . . 185 lbs. . . . Born, Kelowna, B.C., February 15, 1962 . . . Shoots right.

Year	Team	League	Games	G.	A.	Pts.	Pen.
1980-81—Seattle Breakers	WHL		64	8	23	31	253
1981-82—Seattle Breakers	WHL		60	18	17	35	436
1982-83—Wichita Wind (c)	CHL		55	4	6	10	186
1983-84—Maine Mariners	AHL		71	6	8	14	*349
1984-85—Maine Mariners	AHL		51	6	3	9	220
1984-85—New Jersey Devils	NHL		9	0	2	2	21
1985-86—Maine Mariners	AHL		64	4	3	7	217
NHL TOTALS			9	0	2	2	21

(c)—October, 1982—Signed by New Jersey Devils as a free agent.

ROBERT WILSON

Defense . . . 6'3" . . . 195 lbs. . . . Born, Toronto, Ont., July 18, 1968 . . . Shoots left.

Year	Team	League	Games	G.	A.	Pts.	Pen.
1984-85—Mississauga Midget Reps.	OHA		61	11	35	46	106
1985-86—Sudbury Wolves (c)	OHL		61	1	5	6	93

(c)—June, 1986—Drafted as underage junior by Pittsburgh Penguins in 1986 NHL entry draft. Twelfth Penguins pick, 235th overall, 12th round.

RONALD LAWRENCE WILSON

Defense . . . 5'11" . . . 175 lbs. . . . Born, Windsor, Ont., May 28, 1955 . . . Shoots right . . . Son of former NHL forward Larry Wilson.

Year	Team	League	Games	G.	A.	Pts.	Pen.
1973-74—Providence College	ECAC		26	16	22	38	....
1974-75—Providence College (a-c-d)	ECAC		27	26	61	87	12
1974-75—U.S. National Team	Int'l		27	5	32	47	42
1975-76—Providence College (a-d)	ECAC		28	19	47	66	44
1976-77—Providence College	ECAC		30	17	42	59	62
1976-77—Dallas Black Hawks	CHL		4	1	0	1	2
1977-78—Dallas Black Hawks (a)	CHL		67	31	38	69	18
1977-78—Toronto Maple Leafs	NHL		13	2	1	3	0
1978-79—New Brunswick Hawks	AHL		31	11	20	31	13
1978-79—Toronto Maple Leafs	NHL		5	0	2	2	2
1979-80—New Brunswick Hawks	AHL		43	20	43	63	10
1980-81—Davos	Switz.		....	...	....	....	....
1981-82—Davos	Switz.		....	...	....	....	....
1982-83—Davos	Switz.		....	...	....	....	....
1983-84—Davos	Switz.		....	...	....	....	....
1984-85—Davos	Switz.		....	...	....	....	....
1984-85—Minnesota North Stars (e)	NHL		13	4	8	12	2
1985-86—Davos	Switz.		....	...	....	....	....
1985-86—Minnesota North Stars	NHL		11	1	3	4	8
NHL TOTALS			88	12	26	38	16

(c)—June, 1975—Drafted by Toronto Maple Leafs in 1975 amateur draft. Seventh Maple Leafs pick, 132nd overall, seventh round.
(d)—Named to first-team (East) All-America.
(e)—March, 1985—Loaned by Davos club to Minnesota North Stars for remainder of NHL season and playoffs. Teams had same agreement in 1985-86. North Stars sent Craig Levie to Davos club in May, 1986 to secure Wilson for 1986-87 season.

RONALD LEE WILSON

Left Wing . . . 5'9" . . . 170 lbs. . . . Born, Toronto, Ont., May 13, 1956 . . . Shoots left . . . Also plays Center.

Year	Team	League	Games	G.	A.	Pts.	Pen.
1974-75—Markham Waxers		OPJHL	43	26	28	54	24
1974-75—Toronto Marlboros		Jr."A"OHA	16	6	12	18	6
1975-76—St. Cath. Black Hawks (c)		Jr."A"OHA	64	37	62	99	44
1976-77—Nova Scotia Voyageurs		AHL	67	15	21	36	18
1977-78—Nova Scotia Voyageurs		AHL	59	15	25	40	17
1978-79—Nova Scotia Voyageurs (d)		AHL	77	33	42	75	91
1979-80—Winnipeg Jets		NHL	79	21	36	57	28
1980-81—Winnipeg Jets		NHL	77	18	33	51	55
1981-82—Tulsa Oilers		CHL	41	20	38	58	22
1981-82—Winnipeg Jets		NHL	39	3	13	16	49
1982-83—Sherbrooke Jets		AHL	65	30	55	85	71
1982-83—Winnipeg Jets		NHL	12	6	3	9	4
1983-84—Winnipeg Jets		NHL	51	3	12	15	12
1983-84—Sherbrooke Jets		AHL	22	10	30	40	16
1984-85—Winnipeg Jets		NHL	75	10	9	19	31
1985-86—Winnipeg Jets		NHL	54	6	7	13	16
1985-86—Sherbrooke Canadiens		AHL	10	9	8	17	9
NHL TOTALS			387	67	113	180	195

(c)—Drafted from St. Catharines Black Hawks by Montreal Canadiens in 15th round of 1976 amateur draft.

(d)—June, 1979—Sold by Montreal Canadiens to Winnipeg Jets.

WILLIAM RICHARD (RIK) WILSON

Defense . . . 6' . . . 195 lbs. . . . Born, Long Beach, Calif., June 17, 1962 . . . Shoots right . . . (October, 1982)—Sprained ankle . . . (December, 1984)—Bruised knee . . . (February, 1985)—Sprained ankle.

Year	Team	League	Games	G.	A.	Pts.	Pen.
1979-80—Kingston Canadians (c)		OMJHL	67	15	38	53	75
1980-81—Kingston Canadians (a)		OHL	68	30	70	100	108
1981-82—Kingston Canadians		OHL	16	9	10	19	38
1981-82—St. Louis Blues		NHL	48	3	18	21	24
1982-83—St. Louis Blues		NHL	56	3	11	14	50
1982-83—Salt Lake Golden Eagles		CHL	4	0	0	0	0
1983-84—Montana Magic		CHL	6	0	3	3	2
1983-84—St. Louis Blues		NHL	48	7	11	18	53
1984-85—St. Louis Blues		NHL	51	8	16	24	39
1985-86—Nova Scotia Oilers		AHL	13	4	5	9	11
1985-86—Moncton Golden Flames		AHL	8	3	3	6	2
1985-86—St. Louis Blues (d)		NHL	32	0	4	4	48
1985-86—Calgary Flames (e)		NHL	2	0	0	0	0
NHL TOTALS			237	21	60	81	214

(c)—June, 1980—Drafted by St. Louis Blues as underage junior in 1980 NHL entry draft. First Blues pick, 12th overall, first round.

(d)—February, 1986—Traded with Terry Johnson and Joe Mullen by St. Louis Blues to Calgary Flames for Gino Cavallini, Eddy Beers and Charles Bourgeois.

(e)—March, 1986—Traded by Calgary Flames to Chicago Black Hawks for Tom McMurchy.

MICHAEL LAWRENCE WOLAK

Center . . . 5'11" . . . 170 lbs. . . . Born, Utica, Mich., April 29, 1968 . . . Shoots left.

Year	Team	League	Games	G.	A.	Pts.	Pen.
1984-85—Detroit Compuware Midget		Mich.	75	85	95	180	80
1985-86—Kitchener Rangers (c)		OHL	62	24	44	68	48

(c)—June, 1986—Drafted as underage junior by St. Louis Blues in 1986 NHL entry draft. Fifth Blues pick, 87th overall, fifth round.

CRAIG WOLANIN

Defense . . . 6'3" . . . 190 lbs. . . . Born, Grosse Point, Mich., July 27, 1967 . . . Shoots left . . . (October 31, 1985)—Bruised left shoulder vs. Detroit . . . (February 1, 1986)—Broke ring finger on left hand at Washington . . . (February 19, 1986)—Surgery to finger.

Year	Team	League	Games	G.	A.	Pts.	Pen.
1983-84—Detroit Compuware		Mich. Midget	69	8	42	50	86

Year	Team	League	Games	G.	A.	Pts.	Pen.
1984-85—Kitchener Rangers (c)		OHL	60	5	16	21	95
1985-86—New Jersey Devils		NHL	44	2	16	18	74
NHL TOTALS			44	2	16	18	74

(c)—June, 1985—Drafted as underage junior by New Jersey Devils in 1985 NHL entry draft. First Devils pick, third overall, first round.

DAN WOOD

Right Wing . . . 5'11" . . . 190 lbs. . . . Born, Toronto, Ont., October 30, 1962 . . . Shoots right.

Year	Team	League	Games	G.	A.	Pts.	Pen.
1979-80—Kingston Canadians		OHL	66	7	19	26	89
1980-81—Kingston Canadians (c)		OHL	68	12	24	36	165
1981-82—Kingston Canadians		OHL	55	25	33	58	108
1981-82—Salt Lake Golden Eagles		CHL	8	0	1	1	11
1982-83—Salt Lake Golden Eagles		CHL	67	13	14	27	57
1983-84—Canadian Olympic Team		Int'l	41	5	4	9	38
1983-84—Montana Magic		CHL	14	2	7	9	14
1983-84—Springfield Indians (d)		AHL	13	5	8	13	4
1984-85—Fredericton Express		AHL	61	10	9	19	26
1985-86—Peoria Rivermen (e)		IHL	33	8	10	18	24

(c)—June, 1981—Drafted as underage junior by St. Louis Blues in 1981 NHL entry draft. Eighth Blues pick, 188th overall, ninth round.

(d)—August, 1984—Sold by St. Louis Blues to Quebec Nordiques.

(e)—March, 1986—Signed by Peoria Rivermen as a free agent.

RANDY WOOD

Right Wing . . . 6' . . . 190 lbs. . . . Born, Manchester, Mass., October 12, 1963 . . . Shoots left.

Year	Team	League	Games	G.	A.	Pts.	Pen.
1982-83—Yale University		ECAC	26	5	14	19	10
1983-84—Yale University		ECAC	18	7	7	14	10
1984-85—Yale University		ECAC	32	25	28	53	23
1985-86—Yale University		ECAC	31	25	30	55	26

DAN WOODLEY

Center . . . 5'11" . . . 190 lbs. . . . Born, Oklahoma City, Okla., December 29, 1967 . . . Shoots right . . . Also plays either Wing . . . (February 1985)—Torn cartilage in right knee.

Year	Team	League	Games	G.	A.	Pts.	Pen.
1983-84—Summerland Buckeroos		BCJHL	53	17	34	51	100
1984-85—Portland Winter Hawks		WHL	63	21	36	57	108
1985-86—Portland Winter Hawks (c)		WHL	62	45	47	92	100

(c)—June, 1986—Drafted as underage junior by Vancouver Canucks in NHL entry draft. First Canucks pick, seventh overall, first round.

KORY WRIGHT

Right Wing . . . 5'10" . . . 180 lbs. . . . Born, Anchorage, Alaska, June 10, 1965 . . . Shoots right.

Year	Team	League	Games	G.	A.	Pts.	Pen.
1982-83—Dubuque Juniors (c)		USHL	48	45	57	102	36
1983-84—Northern Michigan Univ.		CCHA	39	7	4	11	19
1984-85—Northern Michigan Univ.		WCHA	36	8	17	25	20
1985-86—Northern Michigan Univ.		WCHA	36	12	7	19	16

(c)—June, 1983—Drafted by Winnipeg Jets in 1983 NHL entry draft. Eleventh Jets pick, 189th overall, 10th round.

DALE ALEXANDER YAKIWCHUK

Left Wing . . . 6'4" . . . 200 lbs. . . . Born, Calgary, Alta., October 17, 1958 . . . Shoots left . . . Also plays Center.

Year	Team	League	Games	G.	A.	Pts.	Pen.
1975-76—Taber Golden Suns		AJHL	13	4	6	10	93
1975-76—Lethbridge Broncos		WCHL	43	3	14	17	146
1976-77—Portland Winter Hawks		WCHL	59	24	53	77	151
1977-78—Portland Winter Hawks (c-d)		WCHL	64	32	52	84	312
1978-79—Winnipeg Jets		WHA	4	0	0	0	0
1978-79—Philadelphia Firebirds		AHL	46	2	18	20	101
1978-79—Nova Scotia Voyageurs (e)		AHL	12	3	1	4	15
1979-80—Cincinnati Stingers		CHL	30	4	15	19	75
1979-80—Tulsa Oilers		CHL	37	3	9	12	76
1980-81—Richmond Rifles (f-g)		EHL	42	15	35	50	118

Year	Team	League	Games	G.	A.	Pts.	Pen.
1980-81—Baltimore Blades		EHL	18	11	14	25	73
1981-82—Milwaukee Admirals		IHL	72	18	57	75	249
1982-83—Milwaukee Admirals (a-h)		IHL	79	38	*100	*138	223
1983-84—Milwaukee Admirals		IHL	74	35	*69	104	67
1984-85—Kalamzoo Wings (i)		IHL	82	25	45	70	187
1985-86—Milwaukee Admirals		IHL	82	33	68	101	265
WHA TOTALS			4	0	0	0	0

(c)—Drafted from Portland Winter Hawks by Montreal Canadiens in second round of 1978 amateur draft.

(d)—Selected by Winnipeg Jets in World Hockey Association amateur player draft and signed by Winnipeg, July, 1978.

(e)—March, 1979—Sent to Nova Scotia Voyageurs as compensation for allowing Bill Prentice to be assigned to Philadelphia Firebirds.

(f)—October, 1980—Released by Winnipeg Jets.

(g)—February, 1981—Traded by Richmond Rifles with Jim Lockhurst and Gord Gejdos to Baltimore Clippers for Randy Ireland and Paul Pacific.

(h)—Won Leo P. Lamoureux Memorial Trophy (Top IHL Scorer).

(i)—October, 1984—Loaned with John Flesch by Milwaukee Admirals to Kalamazoo Wings for the 1984-85 season.

GARY YAREMCHUK

Center . . . 6' . . . 180 lbs. . . . Born, Edmonton, Alta., August 15, 1961 . . . Shoots left . . . Brother of Ken Yaremchuk . . . (October, 1982)—Bruised lung . . . (November, 1985)—Arthroscopic knee surgery.

Year	Team	League	Games	G.	A.	Pts.	Pen.
1979-80—Fort Saskatchewan		AJHL	27	27	44	71	61
1979-80—Portland Winter Hawks		WHL	41	21	34	55	23
1980-81—Portland Winter Hawks (c)		WHL	72	56	79	135	121
1981-82—Cincinnati Tigers		CHL	53	21	35	56	101
1981-82—Toronto Maple Leafs		NHL	18	0	3	3	10
1982-83—St. Catharines Saints		AHL	61	17	28	45	72
1982-83—Toronto Maple Leafs		NHL	3	0	0	0	2
1983-84—St. Catharines Saints		AHL	73	24	37	61	84
1983-84—Toronto Maple Leafs		NHL	1	0	0	0	0
1984-85—Toronto Maple Leafs		NHL	12	1	1	2	16
1984-85—St. Catharines Saints (d)		AHL	66	17	47	64	75
1985-86—Adirondack Red Wings		AHL	60	12	32	44	90
NHL TOTALS			34	1	4	5	28

(c)—Drafted by Toronto Maple Leafs in 1981 NHL entry draft. Second Maple Leafs pick, 24th overall, second round.

(d)—September, 1985—Signed by Detroit Red Wings as a free agent.

KEN YAREMCHUK

Center . . . 5'11" . . . 185 lbs. . . . Born, Edmonton, Alta., January 1, 1964 . . . Shoots right . . . Brother of Gary Yaremchuk . . . (January, 1984)—Serious groin injury, out two months . . . (November, 1984)—Bruised toe.

Year	Team	League	Games	G.	A.	Pts.	Pen.
1979-80—Fort Saskatchewan		AJHL	59	40	72	112	39
1980-81—Portland Winter Hawks		WHL	72	56	79	135	121
1981-82—Portland Winter Hawks (a-c)		WHL	72	58	99	157	181
1982-83—Portland Winter Hawks (b)		WHL	66	51	*109	160	76
1983-84—Chicago Black Hawks		NHL	47	6	7	13	19
1984-85—Milwaukee Admirals		IHL	7	4	6	10	9
1984-85—Chicago Black Hawks		NHL	63	10	16	26	16
1985-86—Chicago Black Hawks		NHL	78	14	20	34	43
NHL TOTALS			188	30	43	73	78

(c)—June, 1982—Drafted as underage junior by Chicago Black Hawks in 1982 NHL entry draft. First Black Hawks pick, 7th overall, first round.

TRENT YAWNEY

Defense . . . 6'3" . . . 185 lbs. . . . Born, Hudson Bay, Sask., September 29, 1965 . . . Shoots left.

Year	Team	League	Games	G.	A.	Pts.	Pen.
1981-82—Saskatoon Blades		WHL	6	1	0	1	0
1982-83—Saskatoon Blades		WHL	59	6	31	37	44
1983-84—Saskatoon Blades (c)		WHL	72	13	46	59	81
1984-85—Saskatoon Blades		WHL	72	16	51	67	158
1985-86—Team Canada		Int'l.	73	6	15	21	60

(c)—June, 1984—Drafted as underage junior by Chicago Black Hawks in NHL entry draft. Second Black Hawks pick, 45th overall, third round.

SCOTT YOUNG

Right Wing . . . 6' . . . 185 lbs. . . . Born, Clinton, Mass., October 1, 1967 . . . Shoots right.

Year	Team	League	Games	G.	A.	Pts.	Pen.
1984-85—St. Marks H.S.		Mass.	23	28	41	69	....
1985-86—Boston University (c)		H. East	38	16	13	29	31

(c)—June, 1986—Drafted by Hartford Whalers in 1986 NHL entry draft. First Whalers pick, 11th overall, first round.

WARREN HOWARD YOUNG

Left Wing . . . 6'3" . . . 195 lbs. . . . Born, Weston, Ont., January 11, 1956 . . . Shoots left.

Year	Team	League	Games	G.	A.	Pts.	Pen.
1974-75—Dixie Beehives		OPJHL	44	32	25	57	50
1975-76—Michigan Tech (c)		WCHA	42	16	15	31	48
1976-77—Michigan Tech		WCHA	37	19	26	45	86
1977-78—Michigan Tech		WCHA	32	14	16	30	54
1978-79—Michigan Tech		WCHA	26	11	7	18	45
1978-79—Oklahoma City Stars		CHL	4	0	1	1	2
1979-80—Oklahoma City Stars		CHL	13	4	8	12	9
1979-80—Baltimore Clippers (b)		EHL	65	*53	53	106	75
1980-81—Oklahoma City Stars		CHL	77	26	33	59	42
1981-82—Minnesota North Stars		NHL	1	0	0	0	0
1981-82—Nashville South Stars		CHL	60	31	28	59	154
1982-83—Minnesota North Stars		NHL	4	1	1	2	0
1982-83—Birmingham South Stars (b)		CHL	75	26	58	84	144
1983-84—Pittsburgh Penguins (d)		NHL	15	1	7	8	19
1983-84—Baltimore Skipjacks		AHL	59	25	38	63	142
1984-85—Pittsburgh Penguins (e)		NHL	80	40	32	72	174
1985-86—Detroit Red Wings		NHL	79	22	24	46	161
NHL TOTALS			179	64	64	128	354

(c)—May, 1976—Drafted by California Seals in NHL amateur draft. Fourth Seals pick, 59th overall, fourth round.

(d)—August, 1983—Signed by Pittsburgh Penguins as a free agent.

(e)—July, 1985—Signed by Detroit Red Wings as a free agent.

PAUL YSEBAERT

Center . . . 6'1" . . . 170 lbs. . . . Born, Sarnia, Ont., May 15, 1966 . . . Shoots left.

Year	Team	League	Games	G.	A.	Pts.	Pen.
1983-84—Petrolia Jets (c)		WOJBHL	33	35	42	77	20
1984-85—Bowling Green Univ.		CCHA	42	23	32	55	54
1985-86—Bowling Green Univ. (b)		CCHA	42	23	45	68	50

(c)—June, 1984—Drafted by New Jersey Devils in NHL entry draft. Fourth Devils pick, 74th overall, fourth round.

STEVE YZERMAN

Center . . . 5'11" . . . 175 lbs. . . . Born, Cranbrook, B.C., May 9, 1965 . . . Shoots right . . . (January 31, 1984)—Became youngest person to ever play in NHL All-Star Game . . . (January 31, 1986)—Broke collarbone vs. St. Louis.

Year	Team	League	Games	G.	A.	Pts.	Pen.
1981-82—Peterborough Petes		OHL	58	21	43	64	65
1982-83—Peterborough Petes (c)		OHL	56	42	49	91	33
1983-84—Detroit Red Wings (d)		NHL	80	39	48	87	33
1984-85—Detroit Red Wings		NHL	80	30	59	89	58
1985-86—Detroit Red Wings		NHL	51	14	28	42	16
NHL TOTALS			211	83	135	218	107

(c)—June, 1983—Drafted as underage junior by Detroit Red Wings in 1983 NHL entry draft. First Red Wings pick, 4th overall, first round.

(d)—Chosen NHL Rookie of the Year in poll of players by THE SPORTING NEWS.

ZARLEY ZALAPSKI

Defense . . . 6'1" . . . 195 lbs. . . . Born, Edmonton, Alta., April 22, 1968 . . . Shoots left.

Year	Team	League	Games	G.	A.	Pts.	Pen.
1984-85—Fort Saskatchewan Traders		AJHL	23	17	30	47	14
1985-86—Fort Saskatchewan Traders		AJHL	27	20	33	53	46
1985-86—Team Canada (c)		Int'l	32	2	4	6	10

(c)—June, 1986—Drafted by Pittsburgh Penguins in 1986 NHL entry draft. First Penguins pick, fourth overall, first round.

RICHARD ANDREW ZEMLAK

Center . . . 6'2" . . . 190 lbs. . . . Born, Wynard, Sask., March 3, 1963 . . . Shoots right.

Year	Team	League	Games	G.	A.	Pts.	Pen.
1979-80—Regina Pat Blues		SJHL	30	4	7	11	80
1980-81—Spokane Flyers (c)		WHL	72	19	19	38	132
1981-82—Spokane Flyers (d)		WHL	28	10	22	32	113
1981-82—Medicine Hat Tigers		WHL	41	11	20	31	70
1981-82—Salt Lake Golden Eagles		CHL	6	0	0	0	2
1982-83—Medicine Hat Tigers		WHL	51	20	17	37	119
1982-83—Nanaimo Islanders		WHL	18	2	8	10	50
1983-84—Montana Magic		CHL	14	2	2	4	17
1983-84—Toledo Goaldiggers (e)		IHL	45	8	19	27	101
1984-85—Fredericton Express		AHL	16	3	4	7	59
1984-85—Muskegon Lumberjacks		IHL	64	19	18	37	221
1985-86—Muskegon Lumberjacks		IHL	3	1	2	3	36
1985-86—Fredericton Express		AHL	58	6	5	11	305

(c)—June, 1981—Drafted as underage junior by St. Louis Blues in 1981 NHL entry draft. Ninth Blues pick, 209th overall, 10th round.

(d)—December, 1981—Selected by Medicine Hat Tigers in special WHL draft of players from defunct Spokane Flyers.

(e)—August, 1984—Sold by St. Louis Blues to Quebec Nordiques.

ROB ZETTLER

Defense . . . 6'2" . . . 180 lbs. . . . Born, Sept Illes, Que., March 8, 1968 . . . Shoots left.

Year	Team	League	Games	G.	A.	Pts.	Pen.
1984-85—Sault St. Marie Greyhounds		OHL	60	2	14	16	37
1985-86—Sault St. Marie Greyhounds (c)		OHL	57	5	23	28	92

(c)—June, 1986—Drafted as underage junior by Minnesota North Stars in 1986 NHL entry draft. Fifth North Stars pick, 55th overall, fifth round.

PETER ZEZEL

Center . . . 5'10" . . . 195 lbs. . . . Born, Toronto, Ont., April 22, 1965 . . . Shoots left . . . (November, 1984)—Broken hand.

Year	Team	League	Games	G.	A.	Pts.	Pen.
1981-82—Don Mills Flyers		MTHL	40	43	51	94	36
1982-83—Toronto Marlboros (c)		OHL	66	35	39	74	28
1983-84—Toronto Marlboros		OHL	68	47	86	133	31
1984-85—Philadelphia Flyers		NHL	65	15	46	61	26
1985-86—Philadelphia Flyers		NHL	79	17	37	54	76
NHL TOTALS			144	32	83	115	102

(c)—June, 1983—Drafted as underage junior by Philadelphia Flyers in 1983 NHL entry draft. First Flyers pick, 41st overall, second round.

RICK ZOMBO

Defense . . . 6'1" . . . 190 lbs. . . . Born, Des Plaines, Ill., May 8, 1963 . . . Shoots right . . . (December, 1984)—Injured knee.

Year	Team	League	Games	G.	A.	Pts.	Pen.
1980-81—Austin Mavericks (c)		USMWHL	....	...	....	....	....
1981-82—Univ. of North Dakota		WCHA	45	1	15	16	31
1982-83—Univ. of North Dakota		WCHA	33	5	11	16	41
1983-84—Univ. of North Dakota		WCHA	34	7	24	31	40
1984-85—Adirondack Red Wings		AHL	56	3	32	35	70
1984-85—Detroit Red Wings		NHL	1	0	0	0	0
1985-86—Adirondack Red Wings		AHL	69	7	34	41	94
1985-86—Detroit Red Wings		NHL	14	0	1	1	16
NHL TOTALS			15	0	1	1	16

(c)—June, 1981—Drafted by Detroit Red Wings in NHL entry draft. Sixth Red Wings pick, 149th overall, eighth round.

MIKE ZUKE

Center . . . 6' . . . 180 lbs. . . . Born, Sault Ste. Marie, Ont., April 16, 1954 . . . Shoots right . . . Missed part of 1977-78 season with partial separation of right shoulder . . . Missed start of 1978-79 season with shoulder separation . . . (Summer, 1983)—Shoulder surgery . . . (December, 1984)—Knee injury.

Year	Team	League	Games	G.	A.	Pts.	Pen.
1971-72—S. St. Marie Greyh'ds (a)		NOHA	48	45	40	*85	....
1972-73—Michigan Tech (d)		WCHA	38	23	30	53	20

Year	Team	League	Games	G.	A.	Pts.	Pen.
1973-74—Michigan Tech (c-e)		WCHA	40	28	47	75	38
1974-75—Michigan Tech		WCHA	42	35	43	78	20
1975-76—Michigan Tech (a-e-f)		WCHA	43	47	57	104	42
1976-77—Mohawk Valley Comets		NAHL	48	42	29	71	33
1976-77—Indianapolis Racers (g)		WHA	15	3	4	7	2
1977-78—Edmonton Oilers (h)		WHA	71	23	34	57	47
1978-79—Salt Lake Golden Eagles		CHL	29	9	13	22	4
1978-79—St. Louis Blues		NHL	34	9	17	26	18
1979-80—St. Louis Blues		NHL	69	22	42	64	30
1980-81—St. Louis Blues		NHL	74	24	44	68	57
1981-82—St. Louis Blues		NHL	76	13	40	53	41
1982-83—Salt Lake Golden Eagles		CHL	13	7	8	15	0
1982-83—St. Louis Blues		NHL	43	8	16	24	14
1983-84—Hartford Whalers (i)		NHL	75	6	23	29	36
1984-85—Hartford Whalers		NHL	67	4	12	16	12
1985-86—Hartford Whalers (j)		NHL	17	0	2	2	12
WHA TOTALS			86	26	38	64	49
NHL TOTALS			455	86	196	282	220

(c)—Drafted from Michigan Tech by St. Louis Blues in fifth round of 1974 amateur draft.
(d)—Named Freshman-of-the-Year in WCHA.
(e)—Selected first team All-America (West).
(f)—Selected Most Valuable Player in WCHA.
(g)—Traded to Edmonton Oilers by Indianapolis Racers with Blair MacDonald and Dave Inkpen for Barry Wilkins, Rusty Patenaude and Claude St. Sauveur, September, 1977.
(h)—Signed by St. Louis Blues, September, 1978.
(i)—October, 1983—Selected by Hartford Whalers in NHL waiver draft.
(j)—November, 1985—Announced retirement.

TARAS JOHN ZYTYNSKY

Defense . . . 6'1" . . . 191 lbs. . . . Born, Montreal, Que., May 30, 1962 . . . Shoots left . . . (December, 1980)—Torn knee ligaments . . . (April, 1983)—Injured ankle in AHL playoffs vs. Nova Scotia.

Year	Team	League	Games	G.	A.	Pts.	Pen.
1978-79—Montreal Juniors		QMJHL	59	4	12	16	25
1979-80—Montreal Juniors (c)		QMJHL	72	12	29	41	104
1980-81—Montreal Juniors		QMJHL	45	7	13	20	56
1981-82—Montreal Juniors (b)		QMJHL	64	18	39	57	82
1982-83—Maine Mariners		AHL	80	12	24	36	45
1983-84—Springfield Indians		AHL	70	1	17	18	55
1984-85—Peoria Rivermen		IHL	66	5	11	16	71
1985-86—Rochester Americans (d)		AHL	65	2	15	17	78

(c)—June, 1980—Drafted by Philadelphia Flyers as underage junior in 1980 NHL entry draft. Fourth Flyers pick, 84th overall, fourth round.
(d)—October, 1985—Signed by Rochester Americans as a free agent.

GOALTENDERS

MARTY ABRAMS

Goaltender . . . 5'11" . . . 203 lbs. . . . Born, Charlottetown, P.E.I., June 2, 1964 . . . Shoots right.

Year	Team	League	Games	Mins.	Goals	SO.	Avg.	A.	Pen.
1982-83—Pembroke Lumber Kings (c)		CJAHL	35	1689	176	...	6.25	..	....
1982-83—Toronto Marlboros		OHL	1	4	0	0	0.00	0	0
1983-84—Toronto Marlboros		OHL	20	1137	81	0	4.27	0	2
1984-85—Sault Ste. Marie Greyhounds (d)		OHL	39	1920	108	*2	3.38	0	8
1985-86—Ottawa 67's		OHL	4	202	16	0	4.75	0	0

(c)—June, 1983—Drafted by Washington Capitals in 1983 NHL entry draft. Fourth Capitals pick, 155th overall, eighth round.

(d)—Co-Winner (with teammate Scott Mosey) of Dave Pinkey Trophy (Lowest OHL GAA)

MURRAY BANNERMAN

Goaltender . . . 5'11" . . . 184 lbs. . . . Born, Fort Frances, Ont., April 27, 1957 . . . Shoots left . . . (June, 1985)—Fractured large bone of left index finger when he fell out of tree he was pruning in his backyard.

Year	Team	League	Games	Mins.	Goals	SO.	Avg.	A.	Pen.
1972-73—St. James Canadians (b)		MJHL	31	1788	104	*1	*3.49	1	6
1973-74—St. James Canadians		MJHL	17	930	69	0	4.45	1	16
1973-74—Winnipeg Clubs		WCHL	6	258	29	0	6.74	..	....
1974-75—Winnipeg Clubs		WCHL	28	1351	113	0	5.02	2	6
1975-76—Victoria Cougars		WCHL	44	2450	178	1	4.36	5	25
1976-77—Victoria Cougars (c)		WCHL	67	3893	262	2	4.04	3	24
1977-78—Fort Wayne Komets (a)		IHL	44	2435	133	1	3.28	6	10
1977-78—Vancouver Canucks (d)		NHL	1	20	0	0	0.00	0	0
1978-79—New Brunswick Hawks		AHL	47	2557	152	0	3.57	3	23
1979-80—New Brunswick Hawks (b)		AHL	61	3361	186	*3	3.32	3	25
1980-81—Chicago Black Hawks		NHL	15	865	62	0	4.30	0	0
1981-82—Chicago Black Hawks		NHL	29	1671	116	1	4.17	1	0
1982-83—Chicago Black Hawks		NHL	41	2460	127	4	3.10	1	2
1983-84—Chicago Black Hawks		NHL	56	3335	188	2	3.38	4	17
1984-85—Chicago Black Hawks		NHL	60	3371	215	0	3.83	1	8
1985-86—Chicago Black Hawks		NHL	48	2689	201	1	4.48	2	6
NHL TOTALS			250	14411	909	8	3.78	9	33

(c)—Drafted from Victoria Cougars by Vancouver Canucks in fourth round of 1977 amateur draft.

(d)—June, 1978—Sent to Chicago Black Hawks by Vancouver Canucks as the future consideration in a November, 1977 deal that saw Pit Martin go from Chicago to Vancouver. The Canucks had to choose between Bannerman and Glen Hanlon as future considerations.

THOMAS BARRASSO

Goaltender . . . 6'3" . . . 195 lbs. . . . Born, Boston, Mass., March 31, 1965 . . . Shoots right . . . Member of 1983 U.S. National Junior Team . . . Left 1984 U.S. Olympic team to sign with Buffalo Sabres . . . First U.S.-born player to win Calder Trophy (top NHL rookie) since Frank Brimsek (Boston goalie) in 1939 . . . First goaltender to win Calder Trophy since Ken Dryden in 1972 . . . (June, 1985)—Twisted knee during Molson Softball Tournament in Niagara Falls, Ont.

Year	Team	League	Games	Mins.	Goals	SO.	Avg.	A.	Pen.
1981-82—Acton Boxboro H.S.		Mass. H.S.	23	1035	32	7	1.86	..	....
1982-83—Acton Boxboro H.S. (c)		Mass. H.S.	23	1035	17	10	0.99	..	....
1983-84—Buffalo Sabres (a-d-e)		NHL	42	2475	117	2	2.84	2	20
1984-85—Rochester Americans		AHL	5	267	6	1	1.35	0	2
1984-85—Buffalo Sabres (b)		NHL	54	3248	144	5	2.66	6	41
1985-86—Buffalo Sabres		NHL	60	3561	214	2	3.61	4	28
NHL TOTALS			156	9284	475	9	3.07	12	89

(c)—June, 1983—Drafted by Buffalo Sabres in 1983 NHL entry draft. First Sabres pick, 5th overall, first round.

(d)—Won Calder Memorial Trophy (Top NHL Rookie).

(e)—Won Vezina Trophy (Outstanding NHL Goaltender).

DON BEAUPRE

Goaltender . . . 5'8" . . . 155 lbs. . . . Born, Kitchener, Ont., September 19, 1961 . . . Shoots left . . . (October, 1981)—Bruised ribs . . . (February, 1985)—Sprained knee.

Year	Team	League	Games	Mins.	Goals	SO.	Avg.	A.	Pen.
1978-79—Sudbury Wolves		OMJHL	54	3248	259	2	4.78	0	0
1979-80—Sudbury Wolves (a-c)		OMJHL	59	3447	248	0	4.32	4	18
1980-81—Minnesota North Stars		NHL	44	2585	138	0	3.20	1	20
1981-82—Nashville South Stars		CHL	5	299	25	0	5.02	0	4
1981-82—Minnesota North Stars		NHL	29	1634	101	0	3.71	0	19
1982-83—Birmingham South Stars		CHL	10	599	31	0	3.11	0	6
1982-83—Minnesota North Stars		NHL	36	2011	120	0	3.58	2	10
1983-84—Salt Lake Golden Eagles		CHL	7	419	30	0	4.30	0	0
1983-84—Minnesota North Stars		NHL	33	1791	123	0	4.12	0	17
1984-85—Minnesota North Stars		NHL	21	1770	109	1	3.69	0	4
1985-86—Minnesota North Stars		NHL	52	3073	182	1	3.55	0	34
NHL TOTALS			215	12864	773	2	3.61	3	104

(c)—June, 1980—Drafted by Minnesota North Stars as underage junior in 1980 NHL entry draft. Second North Stars pick, 37th overall, second round.

MARC BEHREND

Goaltender . . . 6'1" . . . 185 lbs. . . . Born, Madison, Wis., January 11, 1961 . . . Shoots left . . . Member of 1984 U.S. Olympic team.

Year	Team	League	Games	Mins.	Goals	SO.	Avg.	A.	Pen.
1979-80—Univ. of Wisconsin		WCHA	....	......	....	...	......	..	....
1980-81—Univ. of Wisconsin (c-d-e)		WCHA	16	913	50	0	3.29	..	....
1981-82—Univ. of Wisconsin		WCHA	25	1502	65	2	2.60	1	0
1982-83—Univ. of Wisconsin		WCHA	23	1315	49	2	2.24	1	4
1983-84—U.S. National Team		Int'l	33	1898	100	...	3.16	..	..
1983-84—U.S. Olympic Team		Int'l	4	200	11	0	3.30	0	0
1983-84—Winnipeg Jets		NHL	6	351	32	0	5.47	0	0
1984-85—Sherbrooke Canadiens		AHL	7	427	25	0	3.51	1	0
1984-85—Winnipeg Jets		NHL	24	1218	91	1	4.48	0	0
1985-86—Sherbrooke Canadiens		AHL	35	2028	132	1	3.91	1	6
1985-86—Winnipeg Jets		NHL	9	422	41	0	5.83	0	0
NHL TOTALS			39	1991	164	1	4.94	0	0

(c)—June, 1981—Drafted by Winnipeg Jets in NHL entry draft. Fifth Jets pick, 85th overall, fifth round.
(d)—Named to NCAA All-Tournament team.
(e)—Named NCAA Tournament MVP.

TIMOTHY JOHN BERNHARDT

Goaltender . . . 5'9" . . . 160 lbs. . . . Born, Sarnia, Ont., January 17, 1958 . . . Shoots left . . . (October, 1980)—Surgery to remove abscess at base of spine . . . (November 27, 1985)—Pulled muscle at Pittsburgh and missed four games.

Year	Team	League	Games	Mins.	Goals	SO.	Avg.	A.	Pen.
1975-76—Cornwall Royals		QJHL	51	2985	195	2	3.92	..	....
1976-77—Cornwall Royals (a-c)		QJHL	44	2497	151	0	*3.63	1	2
1977-78—Cornwall Royals (a-d)		QJHL	54	3165	179	2	3.39	..	....
1978-79—Tulsa Oilers		CHL	46	2705	191	0	4.24	1	4
1979-80—Birmingham Bulls		CHL	34	1933	122	1	3.79	0	0
1980-81—Birmingham Bulls		CHL	29	1598	106	1	3.98	1	0
1981-82—Oklahoma City Stars		CHL	10	526	45	0	5.13	0	0
1981-82—Rochester Americans		AHL	29	1586	95	0	3.59	2	0
1982-83—Calgary Flames		NHL	6	280	21	0	4.50	0	0
1982-83—Colorado Flames		CHL	34	1896	122	0	3.86	0	4
1983-84—St. Catharines Saints (b)		AHL	42	2501	154	0	3.69	0	0
1984-85—St. Catharines Saints (e)		AHL	14	801	55	0	4.12	0	2
1984-85—Toronto Maple Leafs		NHL	37	2182	136	0	3.74	2	4
1985-86—St. Catharines Saints		AHL	14	776	38	1	2.94	1	2
1985-86—Toronto Maple Leafs		NHL	23	1266	107	0	5.07	1	0
NHL TOTALS			66	3728	264	0	4.25	3	4

(c)—Won leading goalie award.
(d)—Drafted from Cornwall Royals by Atlanta Flames in third round of 1978 amateur draft.
(e)—September, 1984—Signed by Toronto Maple Leafs as a free agent.

DANIEL BERTHIAUME

Goaltender . . . 5'9" . . . 151 lbs. . . . Born, Longueuil, Que., January 26, 1966 . . . Shoots right.

Year	Team	League	Games	Mins.	Goals	SO.	Avg.	A.	Pen.
1983-84—Drummondville Voltigeurs		QHL	28	1562	131	0	5.03	1	0
1984-85—Drummondville/Chicoutimi (c-d)		QHL	59	3347	215	*2	*3.85	3	16
1985-86—Chicoutimi Sagueneens		QHL	*66	*3718	*286	1	4.62	2	12
1985-86—Winnipeg Jets (e)		NHL	....	......	....	...	......	..	....

(c)—October, 1984—Traded by Drummondville Voltigeurs to Chicoutimi Saguenees for Simon Masse.

(d)—June, 1985—Drafted as underage junior by Winnipeg Jets in 1985 NHL entry draft. Third Jets pick, 60th overall, third round.
(e)—No regular season record. Played one playoff game, allowing four goals.

ALLAN J. BESTER

Goaltender . . . 5'7" . . . 152 lbs. . . . Born, Hamilton, Ont., March 26, 1964 . . . Shoots right.

Year	Team	League	Games	Mins.	Goals	SO.	Avg.	A.	Pen.
1981-82	Brantford Alexanders	OHL	19	970	68	0	4.21	1	4
1982-83	Brantford Alexanders (a-c-d)	OHL	56	3210	188	0	3.51	0	16
1983-84	Brantford Alexanders	OHL	23	1271	71	1	3.35	1	4
1983-84	Toronto Maple Leafs	NHL	32	1848	134	0	4.35	0	6
1984-85	St. Catharines Saints	AHL	30	1669	133	0	4.78	0	2
1984-85	Toronto Maple Leafs	NHL	15	767	54	1	4.22	1	4
1985-86	St. Catharines Saints	AHL	50	2855	173	1	3.64	1	6
1985-86	Toronto Maple Leafs	NHL	1	20	2	0	6.00	0	0
	NHL TOTALS		48	2635	190	1	4.33	1	10

(c)—Led OHL playoffs with a 2.50 average and one shutout.
(d)—June, 1983—Drafted as underage junior by Toronto Maple Leafs in 1983 NHL entry draft. Third Maple Leafs pick, 48th overall, third round.

CRAIG BILLINGTON

Goaltender . . . 5'10" . . . 150 lbs. . . . Born, London, Ont., September 11, 1966 . . . Shoots left . . . (July, 1984)—Mononucleosis.

Year	Team	League	Games	Mins.	Goals	SO.	Avg.	A.	Pen.
1982-83	London Diamonds	WOJBHL	23	1338	76	0	3.39	..	..
1983-84	Belleville Bulls (c)	OHL	44	2335	162	1	4.16	2	7
1984-85	Belleville Bulls (a)	OHL	47	2544	180	1	4.25	0	2
1985-86	Belleville Bulls	OHL	3	180	11	0	3.67	0	0
1985-86	New Jersey Devils	NHL	18	902	77	0	5.12	1	0
	NHL TOTALS		18	902	77	0	5.12	1	0

(c)—June, 1984—Drafted as underage junior by New Jersey Devils in NHL entry draft. Second Devils pick, 23rd overall, second round.

MIKE BISHOP

Goaltender . . . 6' . . . 180 lbs. . . . Born, Kitchener, Ont., February 14, 1965 . . . Shoots left.

Year	Team	League	Games	Mins.	Goals	SO.	Avg.	A.	Pen.
1981-82	Elmira Jr. B	Ont. Jr. B	21	1090	149	0	8.20	..	..
1982-83	London Knights	OHL	27	1125	83	0	4.43	0	2
1983-84	London Knights (c)	OHL	37	1909	139	0	4.37	2	4
1984-85	Kitchener Rangers	OHL	52	2764	205	1	4.45	1	0
1985-86	Belleville Bulls (d)	OHL	34	1921	111	2	3.47	2	0

(c)—June, 1984—Drafted as underage junior by Boston Bruins in NHL entry draft. Fifth Bruins pick, 103rd overall, fifth round.
(d)—November, 1985—Traded by Kitchener Rangers to Belleville Bulls for future considerations.

GRANT BLAIR

Goaltender . . . 6' . . . 150 lbs. . . . Born, Stoney Creek, Ont., August 15, 1964 . . . Shoots left.

Year	Team	League	Games	Mins.	Goals	SO.	Avg.	A.	Pen.
1981-82	Guelph	Ont. Tier II	25	1506	82	1	3.27	..	..
1982-83	Harvard University (c)	ECAC	26	1575	72	..	2.74	0	0
1983-84	Harvard University (d)	ECAC	23	1391	71	..	3.06	1	8
1984-85	Harvard University (b)	ECAC	31	1785	86	1	2.89	0	26
1985-86	Harvard University	ECAC	31	1812	82	2	2.72	2	6

(c)—June, 1983—Drafted by Calgary Flames in 1983 NHL entry draft. Eighth Flames pick, 111th overall, sixth round.
(d)—Ivy League Player of the Year.

JOHN BLUE

Goaltender . . . 5'9" . . . 170 lbs. . . . Born, Huntington Beach, Calif., February 9, 1966 . . . Shoots left.

Year	Team	League	Games	Mins.	Goals	SO.	Avg.	A.	Pen.
1984-85	Univ. of Minnesota (b)	WCHA	34	1964	111	2	3.39	1	7
1985-86	Univ. of Minnesota (a-c)	WCHA	29	1588	80	3	3.02	1	4

(c)—June, 1986—Drafted by Winnipeg Jets in 1986 NHL entry draft. Ninth Jets pick, 197th overall, 10th round.

DANIEL HECTOR BOUCHARD

Goaltender . . . 6' . . . 191 lbs. . . . Born, Val D'Or, Que., December 12, 1950 . . . Shoots left . . . Brother of Guy Bouchard.

Year	Team	League	Games	Mins.	Goals	SO.	Avg.	A.	Pen.
1968-69—Sorel Black Hawks		QJHL	....	.....	.....	..	.....	..	....
1969-70—London Knights (c)		Jr."A"OHA	41	.....	159	2	3.89	0	55
1970-71—Hershey Bears		AHL	36	2029	106	1	3.13	0	8
1971-72—Oklahoma City Blazers		CHL	1	60	3	0	3.00	0	2
1971-72—Boston Braves (a-d-e)		AHL	50	2915	122	*4	2.51	2	54
1972-73—Atlanta Flames		NHL	34	1944	100	2	3.09	1	12
1973-74—Atlanta Flames		NHL	46	2660	123	5	2.77	0	10
1974-75—Atlanta Flames		NHL	40	2400	111	3	2.77	2	42
1975-76—Atlanta Flames		NHL	47	2671	113	2	2.54	1	10
1976-77—Atlanta Flames		NHL	42	2378	139	1	3.51	1	9
1977-78—Atlanta Flames		NHL	58	3340	153	2	2.75	3	6
1978-79—Atlanta Flames		NHL	64	3624	201	3	3.33	3	17
1979-80—Atlanta Flames		NHL	53	3076	163	2	3.18	1	34
1980-81—Calgary Flames (f)		NHL	14	760	51	0	4.03	4	6
1980-81—Quebec Nordiques		NHL	29	1740	92	2	3.17	0	4
1981-82—Quebec Nordiques		NHL	60	3572	230	1	3.86	3	36
1982-83—Quebec Nordiques		NHL	50	2947	197	1	4.01	4	8
1983-84—Quebec Nordiques		NHL	57	3373	180	1	3.20	3	19
1984-85—Quebec Nordiques		NHL	30	1798	103	0	3.44	2	2
1985-86—Winnipeg Jets (g)		NHL	32	1696	107	2	3.79	1	48
NHL TOTALS			656	37979	2063	27	3.26	29	263

(c)—Drafted from London Knights by Boston Bruins in second round of 1970 amateur draft.
(d)—Shared Harry "Hap" Holmes Memorial Trophy (leading goalie) with Ross Brooks.
(e)—June, 1972—Drafted from Boston Bruins by Atlanta Flames in expansion draft.
(f)—January, 1981—Traded by Calgary Flames to Quebec Nordiques for Jamie Hislop.
(g)—October, 1985—Traded by Quebec Nordiques to Winnipeg Jets for a seventh round draft pick in 1986 (Mark Vermette) and cash.

RICHARD BRODEUR

Goaltender . . . 5'7" . . . 185 lbs. . . . Born, Longueuil, Que., September 15, 1952 . . . Shoots left . . . Missed part of 1977-78 season with surgery on left knee . . . (February 15, 1981)—Injured left knee, resulting in surgery to remove bone spurs . . . (November, 1982)—Knee injury . . . (February 5, 1983)—Suffered 20-stitch cut and perforated eardrum when struck by shot of Toronto's Dan Daoust . . . Last player from the WHA's first season (1972-73) to still be playing in the NHL.

Year	Team	League	Games	Mins.	Goals	SO.	Avg.	A.	Pen.
1970-71—Cornwall Royals		QJHL	41	.....	191	0	4.66	..	....
1971-72—C'wall Royals (a-c-d-e)		QJHL	58	.....	170	*5	*2.93	..	....
1972-73—Quebec Nordiques		WHA	24	1288	102	0	4.75	0	4
1973-74—Maine Nordiques		NAHL	15	936	47	0	3.01	0	0
1973-74—Quebec Nordiques		WHA	30	1607	89	1	3.32	1	0
1974-75—Quebec Nordiques		WHA	51	2938	188	0	3.84	2	13
1975-76—Quebec Nordiques		WHA	69	3967	244	2	3.69	3	2
1976-77—Quebec Nordiques		WHA	53	2906	167	2	3.45	1	0
1977-78—Quebec Nordiques		WHA	36	1962	121	0	3.70	2	0
1978-79—Quebec Nordiques (b-f-g)		WHA	42	2433	126	*3	3.11	3	2
1979-80—Indianapolis Checkers (a-h-i)		CHL	46	2722	131	*4	2.89	0	12
1979-80—New York Islanders (j)		NHL	2	80	6	0	4.50	0	0
1980-81—Vancouver Canucks		NHL	52	3024	177	0	3.51	0	0
1981-82—Vancouver Canucks		NHL	52	3010	168	2	3.35	2	0
1982-83—Vancouver Canucks		NHL	58	3291	208	0	3.79	1	2
1983-84—Vancouver Canucks		NHL	36	2107	141	1	4.02	2	0
1984-85—Fredericton Express		AHL	4	249	13	0	3.13	0	0
1984-85—Vancouver Canucks		NHL	51	2930	228	0	4.67	1	4
1985-86—Vancouver Canucks		NHL	64	3541	240	2	4.07	2	16
WHA TOTALS			305	17101	1037	8	3.64	12	21
NHL TOTALS			315	17983	1168	5	3.90	8	22

(c)—Won leading goalie award.
(d)—February, 1972—Selected by Quebec Nordiques in World Hockey Association player selection draft.
(e)—Drafted from Cornwall Royals by New York Islanders in seventh round of 1972 amateur draft.
(f)—June, 1979—Selected by New York Islanders in NHL reclaim draft, but remained with Nordiques and was made a priority selection by Quebec for expansion draft.
(g)—August, 1979—Traded by Quebec Nordiques to New York Islanders for Goran Hogosta.
(h)—Led CHL Adams Playoff goaltenders with a 2.02 average and shared shutout lead (1) with Michel Plasse.

(j)—October, 1980—Traded with fifth round 1981 draft pick (Moe Lemay) by New York Islanders to Vancouver Canucks for fifth round 1981 draft pick (Jacques Sylvestri).

SCOTT BROWER

Goaltender . . . 6' . . . 185 lbs. . . . Born, Viking, Alta., September 26, 1964 . . . Shoots left.

Year	Team	League	Games	Mins.	Goals	SO.	Avg.	A.	Pen.
1983-84	Lloydminster (c)	SJHL	43	2566	173	2	4.04	..	....
1984-85	University of North Dakota	WCHA	31	1808	99	2	3.29	1	0
1985-86	University of North Dakota	WCHA	20	1096	67	1	3.67	0	0

(c)—June, 1984—Drafted by New York Rangers in NHL entry draft. Twelfth Rangers pick, 243rd overall, 12th round.

MARIO BRUNETTA

Goaltender . . . 6'3" . . . 180 lbs. . . . Born, St. Fidele, Que., January 25, 1967 . . . Shoots left.

Year	Team	League	Games	Mins.	Goals	SO.	Avg.	A.	Pen.
1983-84	Ste. Foy Midget	Que. Midget	39	2169	162	0	4.48	..	..
1984-85	Quebec Remparts (c)	QHL	45	2255	192	0	5.11	1	16
1985-86	Laval Titans	QHL	63	3383	279	0	4.95	3	34

(c)—June, 1985—Drafted as underage junior by Quebec Nordiques in 1985 NHL entry draft. Ninth Nordiques pick, 162nd overall, eighth round.

RICHARD BURCHILL

Goaltender . . . 6' . . . 180 lbs. . . . Born, Boston, Mass., January 3, 1967 . . . Shoots right.

Year	Team	League	Games	Mins.	Goals	SO.	Avg.	A.	Pen.
1983-84	Catholic Memorial H.S.	Mass. H.S.	20	..	..	1	2.50	..	..
1984-85	Catholic Memorial H.S. (c)	Mass. H.S.	22	990	37	0	2.25	..	..
1985-86	Univ. of New Hampshire	H. East	16	900	82	0	5.47	0	0

(c)—June, 1985—Drafted by St. Louis Blues in 1985 NHL entry draft. Fifth Blues pick, 121st overall, sixth round.

SEAN BURKE

Goaltender . . . 6'2" . . . 183 lbs. . . . Born, Windsor, Ont., January 29, 1967 . . . Shoots left.

Year	Team	League	Games	Mins.	Goals	SO.	Avg.	A.	Pen.
1983-84	St. Michael's H.S.	MTHL	25	1482	120	0	4.85	..	..
1984-85	Toronto Marlboros (c)	OHL	49	2987	211	0	4.24	2	6
1985-86	Toronto Marlboros	OHL	47	2840	*233	0	4.92	5	32
1985-86	Team Canada	Int'l	..	284	22	0	4.65	..	..

(c)—June, 1985—Drafted as underage junior by New Jersey Devils in 1985 NHL entry draft. Second Devils pick, 24th overall, second round.

FRANK CAPRICE

Goaltender . . . 5'9" . . . 160 lbs. . . . Born, Hamilton, Ont., May 2, 1962 . . . Shoots left . . . (December, 1985)—Injured knee.

Year	Team	League	Games	Mins.	Goals	SO.	Avg.	A.	Pen.
1979-80	London Knights	OHL	18	919	74	1	4.84	0	2
1980-81	London Knights (c)	OHL	42	2171	190	0	5.25	1	9
1981-82	London Knights	OHL	45	2614	196	0	4.50	3	6
1981-82	Dallas Black Hawks	CHL	3	178	19	0	6.40	0	0
1982-83	Vancouver Canucks	NHL	10	20	3	0	9.00	0	0
1982-83	Fredericton Express	AHL	14	819	50	0	3.67	3	0
1983-84	Vancouver Canucks	NHL	19	1099	62	1	3.38	0	2
1983-84	Fredericton Express	AHL	18	1089	49	2	2.70	0	2
1984-85	Vancouver Canucks	NHL	28	1523	122	0	4.81	2	0
1985-86	Fredericton Express	AHL	26	1526	109	0	4.29	0	4
1985-86	Vancouver Canucks	NHL	7	308	28	0	5.45	1	0
	NHL TOTALS		64	2950	215	1	4.37	3	2

(c)—June, 1981—Drafted as underage junior by Vancouver Canucks in NHL entry draft. Eighth Canucks pick, 178th overall, ninth round.

JON CASEY

Goaltender . . . 5'10" . . . 155 lbs. . . . Born, Grand Rapids, Minn., March 29, 1962 . . . Shoots left.

Year	Team	League	Games	Mins.	Goals	SO.	Avg.	A.	Pen.
1980-81	Univ. of North Dakota	WCHA	6	300	19	0	3.80	..	....
1981-82	Univ. of North Dakota	WCHA	18	1038	48	1	2.77	0	0

Year	Team	League	Games	Mins.	Goals	SO.	Avg.	A.	Pen.
1982-83—Univ. of North Dakota		WCHA	17	1021	42	0	2.47	1	4
1983-84—Univ. of North Dakota (c)		WCHA	37	2180	115	...	3.17	1	20
1983-84—Minnesota North Stars		NHL	2	84	6	0	4.29	0	0
1984-85—Baltimore Skipjacks (a-d)		AHL	46	2646	116	*4	*2.63	2	2
1985-86—Springfield Indians		AHL	9	464	30	0	3.88	0	6
1985-86—Minnesota North Stars		NHL	26	1402	91	0	3.89	0	6
NHL TOTALS			28	1486	97	0	3.92	0	6

(c)—March, 1984—Signed by Minnesota North Stars as a free agent.
(d)—Won Baz Bastien Award (AHL coaches pick as top Goaltender).

TIM CHEVELDAE

Goaltender . . . 5'11" . . . 175 lbs. . . . Born, Melville, Sask., February 15, 1968 . . . Shoots left.

Year	Team	League	Games	Mins.	Goals	SO.	Avg.	A.	Pen.
1984-85—Melville Millionaires		SAJHL	23	1167	98	0	5.04	..	
1985-86—Saskatoon Blades (c)		WHL	37	1862	143	0	4.61	3	0

(c)—June, 1986—Drafted as underage junior by Detroit Red Wings in 1986 NHL entry draft. Fourth Red Wings pick, 64th overall, fourth round.

ALAIN CHEVRIER

Goaltender . . . 5'8" . . . 170 lbs. . . . Born, Cornwall, Ont., April 23, 1961 . . . Shoots left.

Year	Team	League	Games	Mins.	Goals	SO.	Avg.	A.	Pen.
1980-81—Miami of Ohio Univ.		Ind.	16	778	44	0	4.01	..	..
1981-82—Miami of Ohio Univ.		CCHA	19	1053	73	..	4.16	..	..
1982-83—Miami of Ohio Univ.		CCHA	33	1894	125	..	3.96	1	..
1983-84—Miami of Ohio Univ.		CCHA	32	1509	123	..	4.89	1	0
1984-85—Fort Wayne Komets (c)		IHL	56	3219	194	0	3.62	1	8
1985-86—New Jersey Devils		NHL	37	1862	143	0	4.61	3	0
NHL TOTALS			37	1862	143	0	4.61	3	0

(c)—May, 1985—Signed by New Jersey Devils as a free agent.

CHRIS CLIFFORD

Goaltender . . . 5'9" . . . 140 lbs. . . . Born, Kingston, Ont., May 26, 1966 . . . Shoots left . . . First OHL Goalie to score a goal (1985-86).

Year	Team	League	Games	Mins.	Goals	SO.	Avg.	A.	Pen.
1982-83—Brockville Braves		COJHL	32	1746	126	1	4.33	..	....
1983-84—Kingston Canadians (c)		OHL	50	2808	229	2	4.89	3	6
1984-85—Kingston Canadians		OHL	52	2768	241	0	5.22	2	6
1984-85—Chicago Black Hawks		NHL	1	20	0	0	0.00	0	0
1985-86—Kingston Canadians		OHL	50	2988	178	1	3.57	7	16
NHL TOTALS			1	20	0	0	0.00	0	0

(c)—June, 1984—Drafted as underage junior by Chicago Black Hawks in NHL entry draft. Sixth Black Hawks pick, 111th overall, sixth round.

JACQUES CLOUTIER

Goaltender . . . 5'7" . . . 154 lbs. . . . Born, Noranda, Que., January 3, 1960 . . . Shoots left . . . (January, 1982)—Broken collarbone when hit by a slap shot in practice . . . (December, 1984)—Tore ligaments in knee and was lost for the season. He spent the year as an assistant coach with Rochester.

Year	Team	League	Games	Mins.	Goals	SO.	Avg.	A.	Pen.
1976-77—Trois-Riviere Draveurs		QMJHL	24	1109	93	0	5.03	0	0
1977-78—Trois-Riviere Draveurs		QMJHL	71	4134	240	*4	3.48	..	....
1978-79—Trois-Riviere Draveurs (a-c)		QMJHL	72	4168	218	*3	*3.14	..	....
1979-80—Trois-Riviere Draveurs		QMJHL	55	3222	231	*2	4.30	0	0
1980-81—Rochester Americans		AHL	61	3478	209	1	3.61	3	9
1981-82—Rochester Americans		AHL	23	1366	64	0	2.81	2	0
1981-82—Buffalo Sabres		NHL	7	311	13	0	2.51	0	0
1982-83—Buffalo Sabres		NHL	25	1390	81	0	3.50	0	0
1982-83—Rochester Americans		AHL	13	634	42	0	3.97	0	4
1983-84—Rochester Americans		AHL	*51	*2841	172	1	3.63	2	10
1984-85—Rochester Americans		AHL	14	803	36	0	2.69	0	6
1984-85—Buffalo Sabres		NHL	1	65	4	0	3.69	1	0
1985-86—Rochester Americans		AHL	14	835	38	1	2.73	0	4
1985-86—Buffalo Sabres		NHL	15	875	49	1	3.36	2	2
NHL TOTALS			48	2641	147	1	3.34	3	2

(c)—August, 1979—Drafted by Buffalo Sabres as underage junior in 1979 entry draft. Fourth Sabres pick, 55th overall, third round.

JEFF COOPER

Goaltender . . . 5'10" . . . 170 lbs. . . . Born, Nepean, Ont., June 12, 1962 . . . Shoots left.

Year	Team	League	Games	Mins.	Goals	SO.	Avg.	A.	Pen.
1981-82—Colgate University		ECAC	10	....	36	..	3.71	1	2
1982-83—Colgate University		ECAC	26	1486	100	..	4.03	..	..
1983-84—Colgate University		ECAC	32	1874	121	..	3.88	..	..
1984-85—Colgate University (c)		ECAC	31	1778	110	..	3.71	1	2
1985-86—Baltimore Skipjacks		AHL	23	1099	77	2	4.20	0	4

(c)—May, 1985—Signed by Pittsburgh Penguins as a free agent.

MIKE CRAIG

Goaltender . . . 5'7" . . . 155 lbs. . . . Born, Calgary, Alta., November 1, 1962 . . . Shoots right.

Year	Team	League	Games	Mins.	Goals	SO.	Avg.	A.	Pen.
1983-84—University of Alberta/Calgary		CWUAA	..	....	..	..	..	..	..
1984-85—Flint Generals		IHL	8	486	28	0	3.46	0	0
1984-85—Rochester Americans (c)		AHL	29	1431	88	0	3.69	0	6
1985-86—Rochester Americans		AHL	47	2573	183	0	4.27	2	4

(c)—September, 1984—Signed by Buffalo Sabres as a free agent.

DOUGLAS DADSWELL

Goaltender . . . 5'10" . . . 175 lbs. . . . Born, Scarborough, Ont., February 7, 1964 . . . Shoots left.

Year	Team	League	Games	Mins.	Goals	SO.	Avg.	A.	Pen.
1984-85—Cornell University		Ivy	28	1654	97	0	3.45	..	....
1985-86—Cornell University (c-d)		Ivy	30	1815	92	1	3.01	..	....

(c)—Named first-team (East) All-America.
(d)—August, 1986—Signed by Calgary Flames as a free agent.

MARC D'AMOUR

Goaltender . . . 5'10" . . . 167 lbs. . . . Born, Sudbury, Ont., April 29, 1961 . . . Shoots left . . . (December 17, 1985)—Pulled groin at Pittsburgh and missed five games . . . (January 28, 1986)—Pulled groin.

Year	Team	League	Games	Mins.	Goals	SO.	Avg.	A.	Pen.
1978-79—Sault Ste. Marie Greyhounds		OHL	30	1501	149	0	5.96	0	15
1979-80—Sault Ste. Marie Greyhounds		OHL	33	1429	117	0	4.91	2	31
1980-81—Sault Ste. Marie Greyhounds		OHL	16	653	38	0	3.49	0	0
1981-82—Sault Ste. Marie Greyhounds (a-c-d)		OHL	46	2384	130	1	*3.27	1	29
1982-83—Colorado Flames		CHL	42	2373	153	1	3.87	1	23
1983-84—Colorado Flames		CHL	36	1917	131	0	4.10	2	6
1984-85—Salt Lake Golden Eagles		IHL	12	694	33	0	2.85	0	4
1984-85—Moncton Golden Flames		AHL	37	2051	115	0	3.36	0	59
1985-86—Moncton Golden Flames		AHL	21	1129	72	0	3.83	0	10
1985-86—Calgary Flames		NHL	15	560	32	0	3.43	0	22
NHL TOTALS			15	560	32	0	3.43	0	22

(c)—Co-winner with teammate John Vanbiesbrouck, of Dave Pinkey Trophy (OHL Goaltending Trophy).
(d)—April, 1982—Signed by Calgary Flames as a free agent.

CLEON DASKALAKIS

Goaltender . . . 5'9" . . . 175 lbs. . . . Born, Boston, Mass., September 29, 1962 . . . Shoots left . . . (June, 1985)—Separated shoulder during Molson Softball Tournament in Niagara Falls, Ontario.

Year	Team	League	Games	Mins.	Goals	SO.	Avg.	A.	Pen.
1980-81—Boston University		ECAC	8	399	24	0	3.61	..	..
1981-82—Boston University		ECAC	20	1101	59	..	3.22	0	6
1982-83—Boston University (b)		ECAC	22	1278	69	1	3.24	1	4
1983-84—Boston University (c-d)		ECAC	35	1972	96	..	2.92	0	4
1984-85—Hershey Bears		AHL	30	1614	119	0	4.42	3	8
1984-85—Boston Bruins		NHL	8	289	24	0	4.98	0	0
1985-86—Moncton Golden Flames		AHL	41	2343	141	0	3.61	1	23
1985-86—Boston Bruins		NHL	2	120	10	0	5.00	0	0
NHL TOTALS			10	409	34	0	4.99	0	0

(c)—Won Walter Brown Award (Top U.S.-born player in New England colleges).
(d)—June, 1984—Signed by Boston Bruins as a free agent.

MICHEL DUFOUR

Goaltender . . . 5'6" . . . 160 lbs. . . . Born, Val d'Or, Que., August 31, 1962 . . . Shoots left.

Year	Team	League	Games	Mins.	Goals	SO.	Avg.	A.	Pen.
1979-80	Sorel Black Hawks	QMJHL	59	3178	306	0	5.78	2	6
1980-81	Sorel Black Hawks (b-c-d)	QMJHL	54	2703	164	0	*3.64	2	21
1981-82	Trois Rivieres Draveurs (e)	QMJHL	58	3316	238	*1	4.31	0	33
1982-83	Fredericton Express	AHL	1	60	5	0	5.00	0	0
1982-83	Milwaukee Admirals	IHL	4	244	16	0	3.93	0	0
1982-83	Kalamazoo Wings	IHL	23	1180	73	0	3.71	1	0
1983-84	Fredericton Express	AHL	6	365	19	0	3.12	0	2
1983-84	Milwaukee Admirals	IHL	21	1255	79	0	3.78	0	4
1984-85	Muskegon Lumberjacks	IHL	50	2937	174	1	3.55	3	16
1985-86	Muskegon Lumberjacks (b)	IHL	52	2935	151	0	3.09	1	12

(c)—Won Jacques Plante Trophy (Best Individual Goaltender).
(d)—August, 1980—Signed by Quebec Nordiques as underage junior.
(e)—Led QMJHL playoffs with two shutouts.

DONALD LAURIE EDWARDS

Goaltender . . . 5'9" . . . 160 lbs. . . . Born, Hamilton, Ont., September 28, 1955 . . . Shoots left . . . Nephew of former NHL goalie Roy Edwards . . . (December 4, 1982)—Fractured knee-cap in game vs. Edmonton.

Year	Team	League	Games	Mins.	Goals	SO.	Avg.	A.	Pen.
1973-74	Kitch. Rangers (a-c)	Jr. "A" OHA	35	2089	95	*3	*2.73	0	0
1974-75	Kitch. Rangers (a-d)	Jr. "A" OHA	55	.....	256	1	4.70	1	2
1975-76	Hershey Bears (b)	AHL	39	2253	128	3	3.41	3	10
1976-77	Hershey Bears	AHL	47	2797	136	*5	2.91	0	16
1976-77	Buffalo Sabres	NHL	25	1480	62	2	2.51	1	2
1977-78	Buffalo Sabres (b)	NHL	72	4209	185	5	2.64	3	12
1978-79	Buffalo Sabres	NHL	54	3160	159	2	3.02	2	8
1979-80	Buffalo Sabres (e)	NHL	49	2920	125	2	2.57	1	8
1980-81	Buffalo Sabres	NHL	45	2700	133	*3	2.96	2	0
1981-82	Buffalo Sabres (f)	NHL	62	3500	205	0	3.51	2	0
1982-83	Calgary Flames	NHL	39	2209	148	1	4.02	1	0
1983-84	Calgary Flames	NHL	41	2303	157	0	4.09	2	2
1984-85	Calgary Flames (g)	NHL	34	1691	115	1	4.08	0	4
1985-86	Toronto Maple Leafs	NHL	38	2009	160	0	4.78	0	4
	NHL TOTALS		459	26181	1449	16	3.32	14	42

(c)—Won Dave Pinkney Trophy (leading goalie).
(d)—Drafted from Kitchener Rangers by Buffalo Sabres in fifth round of 1975 amateur draft.
(e)—Shared Vezina Memorial Trophy with Bob Sauve (top NHL goaltender).
(f)—June, 1982—Traded by Buffalo Sabres with Richie Dunn and Buffalo's second-round pick in 1982 NHL entry draft to Calgary Flames for Calgary's first and second-round picks in 1982, second-round choice in 1983 and option to switch first-round picks in '83.
(g)—May, 1985—Traded by Calgary Flames to Toronto Maple Leafs for a fourth-round draft choice in 1987.

DARREN ELIOT

Goaltender . . . 6'1" . . . 175 lbs. . . . Born, Milton, Ont., November 26, 1961 . . . Shoots left . . . Member of 1984 Canadian Olympic team . . . Played every minute of every game on Cornell schedule in 1982-83 . . . (November 27, 1984)—Pulled hamstring in game vs. Winnipeg.

Year	Team	League	Games	Mins.	Goals	SO.	Avg.	A.	Pen.
1979-80	Cornell University (c)	ECAC	26	1362	94	0	4.14	..	..
1980-81	Cornell University	ECAC	18	912	52	1	3.42	..	..
1981-82	Cornell University	ECAC	7	338	25	0	4.44	0	2
1982-83	Cornell University (a-d)	ECAC	26	1606	100	1	3.66	0	4
1983-84	Canadian Olympic Team	Int'l	31	1676	111	0	3.97	..	..
1983-84	New Haven Nighthawks	AHL	7	365	30	0	4.93	0	0
1984-85	Los Angeles Kings	NHL	33	1882	137	0	4.37	0	0
1985-86	New Haven Nighthawks	AHL	3	180	19	0	6.33	0	2
1985-86	Los Angeles Kings	NHL	27	1481	121	0	4.90	1	4
	NHL TOTALS		60	3363	258	0	4.60	1	4

(c)—June, 1980—Drafted by Los Angeles Kings in NHL entry draft. Eighth Kings pick, 115th overall, sixth round.
(d)—Named to All-America Team (East).

BOB ESSENSA

Goaltender . . . 6' . . . 160 lbs. . . . Born, Toronto, Ont., January 14, 1965 . . . Shoots left . . . (February, 1985)—Severe lacerations to both hands and wrist from broken window.

Year	Team	League	Games	Mins.	Goals	SO.	Avg.	A.	Pen.
1981-82—Henry Carr H.S.		MJBHL	17	948	79	..	5.00	..	..
1982-83—Henry Carr H.S. (c)		MJBHL	31	1840	98	2	3.20	..	..
1983-84—Michigan State University		CCHA	17	947	44	...	2.79	2	0
1984-85—Michigan State University (a)		CCHA	18	1059	29	2	1.64	1	0
1985-86—Michigan State University (b-d)		CCHA	23	1333	74	0	3.33	1	2

(c)—June, 1983—Drafted by Winnipeg Jets in 1983 NHL entry draft. Fifth Jets pick, 69th overall, fourth round.

(d)—Member of CCHA All-Academic Team.

SEAN EVOY

Goaltender . . . 6'1" . . . 190 lbs. . . . Born, Sudbury, Ont., February 11, 1966 . . . Shoots left.

Year	Team	League	Games	Mins.	Goals	SO.	Avg.	A.	Pen.
1982-83—Don Mills Flyers		MTHL	25	1125	56	4	2.24	..	....
1983-84—Sudbury Wolves		OHL	34	1536	159	1	6.21	1	10
1984-85—Sudbury Wolves		OHL	49	2451	196	1	4.80	2	24
1985-86—Sudbury Wolves		OHL	21	1212	69	0	3.42	2	8
1985-86—Cornwall Royals (c)		OHL	27	1391	122	1	5.26	3	4

(c)—June, 1986—Drafted by Hartford Whalers in 1986 NHL entry draft. Ninth Whalers pick, 200th overall, 10th overall.

JAMES FALLE

Goaltender . . . 5'11" . . . 190 lbs. . . . Born, Montreal, Que., August 26, 1964 . . . Shoots left.

Year	Team	League	Games	Mins.	Goals	SO.	Avg.	A.	Pen.
1981-82—Gloucester Rangers		CJHL	31	1658	136	1	4.92	..	..
1982-83—Clarkson College (c)		ECAC	26	1394	75	..	3.23	0	6
1983-84—Clarkson College		ECAC	27	1494	77	...	3.09	0	12
1984-85—Clarkson College		ECAC	29	1668	81	0	2.91	0	22
1985-86—Clarkson College		ECAC	31	1881	101	0	3.22	1	4

(c)—June, 1983—Drafted by Hartford Whalers in 1983 NHL entry draft. Tenth Whalers pick, 144th overall, eighth round.

BRIAN FORD

Goaltender . . . 5'10" . . . 170 lbs. . . . Born, Edmonton, Alta., September 22, 1961 . . . Shoots left.

Year	Team	League	Games	Mins.	Goals	SO.	Avg.	A.	Pen.
1980-81—Billings Bighorns		WHL	44	2435	204	0	5.03	2	52
1981-82—Billings Bighorns		WHL	53	2791	256	0	5.50	0	0
1982-83—Fredericton Express (c-d)		AHL	27	1444	84	0	3.49	2	0
1982-83—Carolina Thunderbirds		ACHL	4	204	7	0	2.07	0	0
1983-84—Fredericton Express (a-e-f)		AHL	36	2142	105	2	*2.94	4	8
1983-84—Quebec Nordiques		NHL	3	123	13	0	6.34	0	0
1984-85—Pittsburgh Penguins (g)		NHL	8	457	48	0	6.30	0	0
1984-85—Baltimore Skipjacks		AHL	6	363	21	0	3.47	0	0
1984-85—Muskegon Lumberjacks		IHL	22	1321	59	1	2.68	3	4
1985-86—Baltimore Skipjacks		AHL	39	2230	136	1	3.66	1	8
1985-86—Muskegon Lumberjacks (h)		IHL	9	513	33	0	3.86	2	2
NHL TOTALS			11	580	61	0	6.31	0	0

(c)—August, 1982—Signed by Quebec Nordiques as a free agent.

(d)—Co-winner of Harry (Hap) Holmes Memorial Trophy (Top AHL Goaltenders) with teammate Ken Ellacott.

(e)—Won Harry (Hap) Holmes Memorial Trophy (Top AHL Goaltender).

(f)—Won Baz Bastien Trophy (Coaches pick as top AHL goalie; first time awarded).

(g)—December, 1984—Traded by Quebec Nordiques to Pittsburgh Penguins for Tom Thornbury.

(h)—Led IHL playoff goaltenders with 13 games, 793 minutes, 41 goals against and a 3.10 average.

NORM FOSTER

Goaltender . . . 5'9" . . . 175 lbs. . . . Born, Vancouver, B.C., February 10, 1965 . . . Shoots left.

Year	Team	League	Games	Mins.	Goals	SO.	Avg.	A.	Pen.
1981-82—Penticton Knights		BCJHL	21	1187	58	..	2.93	..	..
1982-83—Penticton Knights (c)		BCJHL	33	1999	156	0	4.68	..	..
1983-84—Michigan State University		CCHA	32	1814	83	...	2.75	0	2
1984-85—Michigan State University		CCHA	26	1531	67	1	2.63	1	0
1985-86—Michigan State University (d)		CCHA	24	1414	87	1	3.69	1	0

(c)—June, 1983—Drafted by Boston Bruins in 1983 NHL entry draft. Eleventh Bruins pick, 222nd overall, 11th round.

(d)—Named to NCAA All-Tournament team.

BOB FROESE

Goaltender . . . 5'11" . . . 178 lbs. . . . Born, St. Catharines, Ont., June 30, 1958 . . . Shoots left . . . (October, 1980)—Pulled hamstring . . . Set NHL record for most consecutive games without a loss from the start of an NHL career (13 games, 12-0-1) in 1982-83 . . . (December 8, 1984)—Strained left knee ligaments in game vs. N.Y. Rangers . . . (March 10, 1985) —Pulled groin in game vs. Pittsburgh . . . (November 13, 1985)—Pulled groin.

Year	Team	League	Games	Mins.	Goals	SO.	Avg.	A.	Pen.
1974-75—St. Cath. Black Hawks		OMJHL	15	871	71	0	4.89	0	2
1975-76—St. Cath. Black Hawks		OMJHL	39	1976	193	0	5.86	0	10
1976-77—Oshawa Generals		OMJHL	39	2063	161	*2	4.68	2	40
1977-78—Niagara Falls Flyers (c)		OMJHL	53	3128	246	0	4.72	1	39
1978-79—Saginaw Gears		IHL	21	1050	58	0	3.31	0	56
1978-79—Milwaukee Admirals		IHL	14	715	42	1	3.52	..	....
1979-80—Maine Mariners (d)		AHL	1	60	5	...	5.00	0	0
1979-80—Saginaw Gears		IHL	52	2827	178	0	3.78	7	45
1980-81—Saginaw Gears (e)		IHL	43	2298	114	3	2.98	2	22
1981-82—Maine Mariners		AHL	33	1900	104	2	3.28	0	2
1982-83—Maine Mariners		AHL	33	1966	110	2	3.36	1	11
1982-83—Philadelphia Flyers		NHL	24	1406	59	4	2.52	2	2
1983-84—Philadelphia Flyers		NHL	48	2863	150	2	3.14	2	10
1984-85—Hershey Bears		AHL	4	245	15	0	3.67	0	0
1984-85—Philadelphia Flyers		NHL	17	923	37	1	2.41	1	2
1985-86—Philadelphia Flyers (b-f)		NHL	51	2728	116	5	2.55	1	8
NHL TOTALS			140	7920	362	12	2.74	6	22

(c)—June, 1978—Drafted by St. Louis Blues in amateur draft. Eleventh St. Louis pick, 160th overall, 10th round.

(d)—September, 1979—Signed by Philadelphia Flyers as a free agent.

(e)—Led IHL playoffs in goals-against average (2.15) and shutouts (2).

(f)—Shared Bill Jennings Trophy with teammate Darren Jensen (team that allows the fewest goals).

GRANT FUHR

Goaltender . . . 5'10" . . . 181 lbs. . . . Born, Spruce Grove, Alta., September 28, 1962 . . . Shoots right . . . (December, 1981)—Partial separation of right shoulder . . . (December 13, 1983)—Strained left knee ligaments in game vs. Hartford and required surgery . . . (January 27, 1984)—Collected ninth assist of season to set NHL record for goaltenders. He ended the season with 14 . . . First black player to be on Stanley Cup-winning team . . . (February, 1985)—Separated shoulder . . . (November 3, 1985)—Bruised left shoulder vs. Toronto and missed 10 games.

Year	Team	League	Games	Mins.	Goals	SO.	Avg.	A.	Pen.
1979-80—Victoria Cougars (a-c)		WHL	43	2488	130	2	3.14	1	2
1980-81—Victoria Cougars (a-d-e)		WHL	59	*3448	160	*4	*2.78	2	6
1981-82—Edmonton Oilers (b)		NHL	48	2847	157	0	3.31	6	6
1982-83—Moncton Alpines		AHL	10	604	40	0	3.98	0	0
1982-83—Edmonton Oilers		NHL	32	1803	129	0	4.29	0	6
1983-84—Edmonton Oilers		NHL	45	2625	171	1	3.91	14	6
1984-85—Edmonton Oilers		NHL	46	2559	165	1	3.87	3	6
1985-86—Edmonton Oilers		NHL	40	2184	143	0	3.93	2	0
NHL TOTALS			211	12018	765	2	3.82	25	24

(c)—Won Stewart Paul Memorial Trophy (WHL Rookie of the Year).

(d)—Named outstanding goalie in WHL.

(e)—June, 1981—Drafted by Edmonton Oilers in NHL entry draft. First Oilers pick, eighth overall, first round.

FRANK FURLAN

Goaltender . . . 5'9" . . . 175 lbs. . . . Born, Nanaimo, B.C., March 8, 1968 . . . Shoots left.

Year	Team	League	Games	Mins.	Goals	SO.	Avg.	A.	Pen.
1985-86—Sherwood Park Crusaders (c)		AJHL	23	1290	91	0	4.23	0	12

(c)—June, 1986—Drafted by Winnipeg Jets in 1986 NHL entry draft. Seventh Jets pick, 155th overall, eighth round.

TROY GAMBLE

Goaltender . . . 5'11" . . . 180 lbs. . . . Born, Toronto, Ont., April 7, 1967 . . . Shoots left.

Year	Team	League	Games	Mins.	Goals	SO.	Avg.	A.	Pen.
1983-84—Hobbema Hawks		AJHL	22	1102	90	0	4.90	..	....

Year	Team	League	Games	Mins.	Goals	SO.	Avg.	A.	Pen.
1984-85—Medicine Hat Tigers (a-c-d)		WHL	37	2095	100	*3	*2.86	2	4
1985-86—Medicine Hat Tigers		WHL	45	2264	142	0	3.76	3	29

(c)—Won WHL Top Goaltender Trophy.

(d)—June, 1985—Drafted as underage junior by Vancouver Canucks in 1985 NHL entry draft. Second Canucks pick, 25th overall, second round.

DARRYL GILMOUR

Goaltender . . . 5'11" . . . 155 lbs. . . . Born, Winnipeg, Manitoba, February 13, 1967 . . . Shoots left.

Year	Team	League	Games	Mins.	Goals	SO.	Avg.	A.	Pen.
1983-84—St. James Canadiens		MJHL	15	900	45	...	3.00	..	....
1984-85—Moose Jaw Warriors (c)		WHL	58	3004	297	0	5.93	6	4
1985-86—Moose Jaw Warriors (a)		WHL	*62	*3482	*276	1	4.76	2	4

(c)—June, 1985—Drafted as underage junior by Philadelphia Flyers in 1985 NHL entry draft. Third Flyers pick, 48th overall, third round.

MARIO GOSSELIN

Goaltender . . . 5'8" . . . 160 lbs. . . . Born, Thetford Mines, Que., June 15, 1963 . . . Shoots left . . . Member of 1984 Canadian Olympic team . . . (February 25, 1984)—First NHL game was 5-0 shutout of St. Louis Blues . . . (March 8, 1984)—Injured knee in game vs. Pittsburgh, out for the season . . . (January 16, 1986)—Missed one game with the flu.

Year	Team	League	Games	Mins.	Goals	SO.	Avg.	A.	Pen.
1980-81—Shawinigan Cataracts		QMJHL	21	907	75	0	4.96	1	0
1981-82—Shawinigan Cataracts (b-c)		QMJHL	*60	*3404	230	0	4.50	3	10
1982-83—Shawinigan Cataracts (a-d)		QHL	46	2556	133	*3	*3.12	4	18
1983-84—Canadian Olympic Team		Int'l	36	2007	126	0	3.77	..	....
1983-84—Quebec Nordiques		NHL	3	148	3	1	1.22	0	2
1984-85—Quebec Nordiques		NHL	35	1960	109	1	3.34	0	2
1985-86—Fredericton Express		AHL	5	304	15	0	2.96	0	0
1985-86—Quebec Nordiques		NHL	31	1726	111	2	3.86	3	2
NHL TOTALS			69	3834	223	4	3.49	3	6

(c)—June, 1982—Drafted as underage junior by Quebec Nordiques in NHL entry draft. Third Nordiques pick, 55th overall, third round.

(d)—Won Jacques Plante Trophy (Top QHL Goalie).

MARK GOWANS

Goaltender . . . 6' . . . 160 lbs. . . . Born, Bay City, Mich., March 26, 1967 . . . Shoots left.

Year	Team	League	Games	Mins.	Goals	SO.	Avg.	A.	Pen.
1983-84—Detroit Compuware		Mich. Midget	30	1800	72	5	2.40	..	...
1984-85—Windsor Spitfires (c)		OHL	36	2112	162	0	4.60	2	0
1985-86—Oshawa Generals		OHL	25	1187	84	0	4.25	0	0

(c)—June, 1985—Drafted as underage junior by Detroit Red Wings in 1985 NHL entry draft. Fourth Red Wings pick, 71st overall, fourth round.

LUC GUENETTE

Goaltender . . . 5'9" . . . 160 lbs. . . . Born, St. Jerome, Que., July 22, 1964 . . . Shoots right.

Year	Team	League	Games	Mins.	Goals	SO.	Avg.	A.	Pen.
1981-82—Quebec Remparts		QMJHL	38	1809	202	0	6.70	0	4
1982-83—Quebec Remparts (b-c)		QHL	59	3285	299	0	5.46	1	14
1983-84—Quebec Remparts (b)		QHL	67	3729	314	0	5.05	3	6
1984-85—Muskegon Lumberjacks		IHL	13	674	48	1	4.27	0	4
1984-85—Fort Wayne Komets		IHL	2	94	10	0	6.38	0	0
1985-86—Fredericton Express		AHL	20	1021	76	0	4.47	0	2

(c)—June, 1983—Drafted as underage junior by Quebec Nordiques in 1983 NHL entry draft. Fourth Nordiques pick, 92nd overall, fifth round.

STEVE GUENETTE

Goaltender . . . 5'9" . . . 165 lbs. . . . Born, Montreal, Que., November 13, 1965 . . . Shoots left.

Year	Team	League	Games	Mins.	Goals	SO.	Avg.	A.	Pen.
1984-85—Guelph Platers		OHL	47	2593	200	1	4.63	1	2
1985-86—Guelph Platers (b-c)		OHL	50	2910	165	3	3.40	2	16

(c)—June, 1985—Signed by Pittsburgh Penguins as a free agent.

GLEN HANLON

Goaltender ... 6' ... 175 lbs. ... Born, Brandon, Man., February 20, 1957 ... Shoots right ... Missed part of 1977-78 season with torn ankle ligaments ... Missed part of 1979-80 season with shoulder injury ... (October 18, 1980)—Stretched knee ligaments ... (March, 1981) —Shoulder separation.

Year	Team	League	Games	Mins.	Goals	SO.	Avg.	A.	Pen.
1973-74—Brandon Travellers		MJHL	20	1059	64	*1	3.63	0	5
1974-75—Brandon Wheat Kings		WCHL	43	2498	176	0	4.22	1	6
1975-76—Brandon Wheat Kings (a)		WCHL	64	3523	234	4	3.99	2	35
1976-77—Brandon Wheat K. (a-c-d)		WCHL	65	3784	195	*4	*3.09	5	8
1977-78—Tulsa Oilers (a-e)		CHL	53	3123	160	*3	3.07	4	30
1977-78—Vancouver Canucks		NHL	4	200	9	0	2.70	0	2
1978-79—Vancouver Canucks		NHL	31	1821	94	3	3.10	1	30
1979-80—Vancouver Canucks		NHL	57	3341	193	0	3.47	1	43
1980-81—Dallas Black Hawks		CHL	4	239	8	1	2.01	1	0
1980-81—Vancouver Canucks		NHL	17	798	59	1	4.44	1	10
1981-82—Vancouver Canucks (f)		NHL	28	1610	106	1	3.95	0	22
1981-82—St. Louis Blues		NHL	2	76	8	0	6.32	0	0
1982-83—St. Louis Blues (g)		NHL	14	671	50	0	4.47	0	0
1982-83—New York Rangers		NHL	21	1173	67	0	3.43	0	2
1983-84—New York Rangers		NHL	50	2837	166	1	3.51	2	30
1984-85—New York Rangers		NHL	44	2510	175	0	4.18	0	4
1985-86—Adirondack Red Wings		AHL	10	605	33	0	3.27	0	2
1985-86—New Haven Nighthawks		AHL	5	279	22	0	4.73	1	4
1985-86—New York Rangers (h)		NHL	23	1170	65	0	3.33	1	4
NHL TOTALS			291	16207	992	6	3.67	6	147

(c)—Won WCHL Leading Goalie Award.
(d)—Drafted from Brandon Wheat Kings by Vancouver Canucks in third round of 1977 amateur draft.
(e)—Won CHL Rookie-of-the-Year Award.
(f)—March, 1982—Traded by Vancouver Canucks to St. Louis Blues for Tony Currie, Jim Nill, Rick Heinz and fourth-round 1982 entry draft pick (Shawn Kilroy).
(g)—January, 1983—Traded by St. Louis Blues with Vaclav Nedomansky to New York Rangers for Andre Dore and future considerations.
(h)—August, 1986—Traded by New York Rangers with third-round draft choices in 1987 and 1988 to Detroit Red Wings for Kelly Kisio, Lane Lambert and Jim Leavins.

RANDY HANSCH

Goaltender ... 5'10" ... 165 lbs. ... Born, Edmonton, Alta., February 8, 1966 ... Shoots right.

Year	Team	League	Games	Mins.	Goals	SO.	Avg.	A.	Pen.
1982-83—Victoria Cougars		WHL	6	229	23	0	6.03	0	0
1983-84—Victoria Cougars (c)		WHL	36	1894	144	0	4.56	0	4
1984-85—Victoria Cougars (a)		WHL	52	3021	260	0	5.16	2	0
1985-86—Victoria Cougars		WHL	26	1523	152	0	5.99	2	6
1985-86—Kamloops Blazers		WHL	5	298	20	0	4.03	0	6

(c)—June, 1984—Drafted as underage junior by Detroit Red Wings in NHL entry draft. Fifth Red Wings pick, 112th overall, sixth round.

BRIAN HAYWARD

Goaltender ... 5'10" ... 175 lbs. ... Born, Georgetown, Ont., June 25, 1960 ... Shoots left.

Year	Team	League	Games	Mins.	Goals	SO.	Avg.	A.	Pen.
1978-79—Cornell University		ECAC	25	1469	95	0	3.88	..	....
1979-80—Cornell University		ECAC	12	508	52	0	6.02	..	....
1980-81—Cornell University		ECAC	19	967	58	1	3.54	..	....
1981-82—Cornell University		ECAC	....	1320	68	0	3.09	..	....
1982-83—Sherbrooke Jets (c)		AHL	22	1208	89	1	4.42	0	0
1982-83—Winnipeg Jets		NHL	24	1440	89	1	3.71	1	0
1983-84—Sherbrooke Jets		AHL	15	781	69	0	5.30	1	2
1983-84—Winnipeg Jets		NHL	28	1530	124	0	4.86	1	2
1984-85—Winnipeg Jets		NHL	61	3436	220	0	3.84	4	10
1985-86—Sherbrooke Canadiens		AHL	3	185	5	0	1.62	1	0
1985-86—Winnipeg Jets (d)		NHL	52	2721	217	0	4.79	2	25
NHL TOTALS			165	9127	650	1	4.27	8	37

(c)—September, 1982—Signed by Winnipeg Jets as a free agent.
(d)—August, 1986—Traded by Winnipeg Jets to Montreal Canadiens for Steve Penney and Jan Ingman.

GLEN HEALY

Goaltender ... 5'10" ... 185 lbs. ... Born, Pickering, Ont., August 23, 1962 ... Shoots left.

Year	Team	League	Games	Mins.	Goals	SO.	Avg.	A.	Pen.
1981-82—Western Michigan Univ.		CCHA	27	1569	116	0	4.44	2	2
1982-83—Western Michigan Univ.		CCHA	30	1733	116	0	4.02	3	4
1983-84—Western Michigan Univ.		CCHA	38	2242	146	..	3.91	1	13
1984-85—Western Michigan Univ. (b-c-d)		CCHA	37	2172	118	..	3.26	2	8
1985-86—Toledo Goaldiggers		IHL	7	402	28	0	4.18	0	0
1985-86—New Haven Nighthawks		AHL	43	2410	160	0	3.98	2	18
1985-86—Los Angeles Kings		NHL	1	51	6	0	7.06	0	0
NHL TOTALS			1	51	6	0	7.06	0	0

    (c)—Second Team All-America Goaltender.
    (d)—June, 1985—Signed by Los Angeles Kings as a free agent.

RICK HEINZ

Goaltender . . . 5'10" . . . 165 lbs. . . . Born, Essex, Ont., May 30, 1955 . . . Shoots left . . . (January 26, 1985)—Tore medial collateral ligament of right knee in IHL game at Indianapolis.

Year	Team	League	Games	Mins.	Goals	SO.	Avg.	A.	Pen.
1973-74—Chatham Maroons		SOJHL	..	..	..	*4	*3.51	..	..
1974-75—Univ. of Minn.-Duluth		WCHA	18	1039	88	0	5.08	..	..
1975-76—Univ. of Minn.-Duluth		WCHA	34	2033	162	0	4.78	0	4
1976-77—Univ. of Minn.-Duluth		WCHA	..	....	..	..	..	..	..
1977-78—Univ. of Minn.-Duluth		WCHA	33	1961	157	0	4.80	..	..
1978-79—Salt Lake Golden Eagles		CHL	1	59	3	0	3.05	0	0
1978-79—Port Huron Flags		IHL	54	2800	157	*5	3.36	2	16
1979-80—Salt Lake Golden Eagles		CHL	39	2353	119	0	3.03	2	12
1980-81—Salt Lake Golden Eagles (c)		CHL	36	2210	128	3	3.48	1	26
1980-81—St. Louis Blues		NHL	4	220	8	0	2.18	1	0
1981-82—Salt Lake Golden Eagles		CHL	19	1167	71	0	3.65	4	4
1981-82—St. Louis Blues (d)		NHL	9	433	35	0	4.85	0	0
1981-82—Vancouver Canucks		NHL	3	180	9	1	3.00	0	0
1982-83—Salt Lake Golden Eagles		CHL	17	1031	58	1	3.38	0	4
1982-83—St. Louis Blues		NHL	9	335	24	1	4.30	0	2
1983-84—St. Louis Blues		NHL	22	1118	80	0	4.29	0	4
1984-85—St. Louis Blues		NHL	2	70	3	0	2.57	0	0
1984-85—Peoria Rivermen (a-e-f)		IHL	43	2443	129	2	*3.17	2	6
1985-86—Salt Lake Golden Eagles (g)		IHL	52	3000	185	1	3.70	3	12
1985-86—Binghamton Whalers		AHL	1	60	9	0	9.00	0	2
NHL TOTALS			49	2356	159	2	4.05	1	6

    (c)—Led CHL Playoffs with 2.72 average.
    (d)—March, 1982—Traded with Tony Currie, Jim Nill and fourth-round 1982 entry draft pick (Shawn
        Kilroy) by St. Louis Blues to Vancouver Canucks for Glen Hanlon. Returned to St. Louis, June, 1982.
    (e)—Won James Norris Memorial Trophy (Top IHL Goalie).
    (f)—Led IHL playoffs with one shutout.
    (g)—October, 1985—Signed by Hartford Whalers as a free agent.

ANDY HELMUTH

Goaltender . . . 5'10" . . . 170 lbs. . . . Born, Detroit, Mich., March 18, 1967 . . . Shoots left.

Year	Team	League	Games	Mins.	Goals	SO.	Avg.	A.	Pen.
1983-84—Detroit Little Caesar's		Mich. Midget	38	2466	119	4	3.14	..	....
1984-85—Ottawa 67's (c)		OHL	40	2102	189	0	5.39	3	8
1985-86—Ottawa 67's		OHL	20	1175	97	0	4.95	0	12
1985-86—Guelph Platers		OHL	12	620	39	0	3.77	0	8

    (c)—June, 1985—Drafted as underage junior by Chicago Black Hawks in 1985 NHL entry draft. Second
        Black Hawks pick, 53rd overall, third round.

DENIS HERRON

Goaltender . . . 5'11" . . . 165 lbs. . . . Born, Chambly, Que., June 18, 1952 . . . Shoots left . . . Missed part of 1979-80 season with a broken collarbone . . . (November 15, 1980)—Pulled muscle in upper back . . . (December 29, 1981)—Suffered concussion against New York Islanders . . . (November, 1982)—Concussion in game vs. New York Islanders . . . (January, 1983)—Severely bruised shoulder in practice . . . (December 15, 1983)—Broke finger when hit by Mats Naslund shot at Montreal . . . (January, 1984)—Pinched nerve in neck . . . (October 17, 1985)—Injured hand in team practice.

Year	Team	League	Games	Mins.	Goals	SO.	Avg.	A.	Pen.
1969-70—Three Rivers Dukes		QJHL	2	.....	10	0	6.25	..	....
1970-71—Three Rivers Dukes		QJHL	33	.....	136	0	4.12	..	....
1971-72—Three Riv. Dukes (b-c)		QJHL	40	.....	160	2	4.00	..	....
1972-73—Hershey Bears		AHL	21	1185	63	0	3.19	0	0
1972-73—Pittsburgh Penguins		NHL	18	967	55	2	3.41	1	0

Year Team	League	Games	Mins.	Goals	SO.	Avg.	A.	Pen.
1973-74—Hershey Bears	AHL	17	967	52	0	3.22	1	2
1973-74—S.L.C. Golden Eagles (d)	WHL	9	530	32	0	3.62	0	4
1973-74—Pittsburgh Penguins	NHL	5	260	18	0	4.15	0	0
1974-75—Hershey Bears	AHL	12	615	45	0	4.39	0	0
1974-75—Pittsburgh Penguins (e)	NHL	3	108	11	0	6.11	0	0
1974-75—Kansas City Scouts	NHL	22	1280	80	0	3.75	1	2
1975-76—Kansas City Scouts (f)	NHL	64	3620	243	0	4.03	0	16
1976-77—Pittsburgh Penguins	NHL	34	1920	94	1	2.94	1	4
1977-78—Pittsburgh Penguins	NHL	60	3534	210	0	3.57	1	6
1978-79—Pittsburgh Penguins (g)	NHL	56	3208	180	0	3.37	2	18
1979-80—Montreal Canadiens	NHL	34	1909	80	0	2.51	0	0
1980-81—Montreal Canadiens (h)	NHL	25	1147	67	1	3.50	2	0
1981-82—Montreal Canadiens (i-j)	NHL	27	1547	68	*3	*2.64	0	4
1982-83—Pittsburgh Penguins	NHL	31	1707	151	1	5.31	1	14
1983-84—Pittsburgh Penguins	NHL	38	2028	138	1	4.08	0	21
1984-85—Pittsburgh Penguins	NHL	42	2193	170	1	4.65	0	4
1985-86—Baltimore Skipjacks	AHL	27	1510	86	0	3.42	0	6
1985-86—Pittsburgh Penguins	NHL	3	180	14	0	4.67	0	0
NHL TOTALS		462	25608	1579	10	3.70	9	89

(c)—Drafted from Three Rivers Dukes by Pittsburgh Penguins in third round of 1972 amateur draft.

(d)—Loaned to Salt Lake City Golden Eagles by Pittsburgh Penguins, December, 1973.

(e)—Traded to Kansas City Scouts by Pittsburgh Penguins with Jean-Guy Lagace for Michel Plasse, January, 1975.

(f)—Signed by Pittsburgh Penguins as free agent, July, 1976. (Colorado Rockies received Simon Nolet, Colin Campbell and Michel Plasse as compensation).

(g)—September, 1979—Traded with second round pick in 1982 entry draft (Jocelyn Gauvreau) by Pittsburgh Penguins to Montreal Canadiens for Bob Holland and Pat Hughes.

(h)—Co-winner of Vezina Trophy (Top NHL Goaltenders) with teammates Richard Sevigny and Michel Larocque.

(i)—Co-winner of Bill Jennings Trophy (Lowest Team Goaltending Average) with teammate Rick Wamsley.

(j)—September, 1982—Traded by Montreal Canadiens to Pittsburgh Penguins for a third-round choice in the 1985 NHL entry draft.

RON HEXTALL

Goaltender ... 6'3" ... 170 lbs. ... Born, Winnipeg, Manitoba, May 3, 1964 ... Shoots left.

Year Team	League	Games	Mins.	Goals	SO.	Avg.	A.	Pen.
1980-81—Melville	SJHL	42	2127	254	0	7.17	..	....
1981-82—Brandon Wheat Kings (c)	WHL	30	1398	133	0	5.71	0	0
1982-83—Brandon Wheat Kings	WHL	44	2589	249	0	5.77	4	66
1983-84—Brandon Wheat Kings	WHL	46	2670	190	0	4.27	8	117
1984-85—Kalamazoo Wings	IHL	19	1103	80	0	4.35	2	18
1984-85—Hershey Bears	AHL	11	555	34	0	3.68	2	4
1985-86—Hershey Bears (a-d)	AHL	*53	*3061	*174	*5	3.41	2	54

(c)—June, 1982—Drafted as underage junior by Philadelphia Flyers in 1982 NHL entry draft. Sixth Flyers pick, 119th overall, sixth round.

(d)—Won Dudley (Red) Garrett Memorial Trophy (Top AHL Rookie).

MARK HOLDEN

Goaltender ... 5'10" ... 165 lbs. ... Born, Weymouth, Mass., June 12, 1957 ... Shoots left.

Year Team	League	Games	Mins.	Goals	SO.	Avg.	A.	Pen.
1976-77—Brown University (c)	ECAC	....	....	....	...	....	..	....
1977-78—Brown University	ECAC	10	590	33	0	3.36	..	....
1978-79—Brown University	ECAC	....	573	35	...	3.66	..	....
1979-80—Brown University (d)	ECAC	26	1508	93	0	3.70	..	....
1980-81—Nova Scotia Voyageurs	AHL	42	2223	127	2	3.43	1	4
1981-82—Montreal Canadiens	NHL	1	20	0	0	0.00	0	0
1981-82—Nova Scotia Voyageurs	AHL	44	2534	142	0	3.36	2	20
1982-83—Montreal Canadiens	NHL	2	87	6	0	4.14	0	0
1982-83—Nova Scotia Voyageurs	AHL	41	2369	160	0	4.05	6	4
1983-84—Montreal Canadiens	NHL	1	52	4	0	4.62	0	0
1983-84—Nova Scotia Voyageurs	AHL	47	2739	153	0	3.35	1	10
1984-85—Winnipeg Jets (e)	NHL	4	213	15	0	4.23	1	0
1984-85—Nova Scotia Oilers	AHL	22	1261	87	1	4.14	4	0
1985-86—Fort Wayne Komets	IHL	9	496	26	1	3.15	4	0
1985-86—Sherbrooke Canadiens	AHL	12	696	52	0	4.48	0	4
NHL TOTALS		8	372	25	0	4.03	1	0

(c)—June, 1977—Drafted by Montreal Canadiens in 1977 NHL amateur draft. Sixteenth Canadiens pick, 160th overall, 10th round.

(d)—Named to second team All-Ivy League All-Star Team.
(e)—October, 1984—Traded by Montreal Canadiens to Winnipeg Jets for Doug Soetaert.

ROBERT HOLLAND

Goaltender . . . 6'1" . . . 182 lbs. . . . Born, Montreal, Que., September 10, 1957 . . . Shoots left.

Year	Team	League	Games	Mins.	Goals	SO.	Avg.	A.	Pen.
1974-75—Longueuil Rebelles	Jr."A"QHL	36	2139	187	0	5.22	..	....
1975-76—Montreal Juniors	QJHL	37	1995	147	0	4.42	..	....
1976-77—Montreal Juniors (c)	QJHL	45	2314	184	0	4.77	1	4
1977-78—Nova Scotia Voyageurs (d)	AHL	38	2270	120	1	3.17	2	6
1978-79—Nova Scotia Voyageurs (e)	AHL	43	2377	154	*2	3.89	2	23
1979-80—Pittsburgh Penguins	NHL	34	1974	126	1	3.83	0	2
1980-81—Binghamton Whalers	AHL	7	354	28	0	4.75	0	0
1980-81—Indianapolis Checkers	CHL	15	845	41	1	2.91	0	4
1980-81—Pittsburgh Penguins (f)	NHL	10	539	45	0	5.01	0	0
1981-82—Toledo Goaldiggers	IHL	7	423	25	0	3.55	0	0
1981-82—Indianapolis Checkers (g)	CHL	30	1672	95	0	3.41	1	6
1982-83—Indianapolis Checkers (b-g)	CHL	37	2111	101	*4	*2.87	0	6
1983-84—Indianapolis Checkers	CHL	39	2149	131	0	3.66	1	10
1984-85—Indianapolis Checkers	IHL	57	3344	183	*4	3.28	1	14
1985-86—Indianapolis Checkers	IHL	41	2246	146	0	3.90	0	4
1985-86—Springfield Indians	AHL	8	479	23	0	2.88	0	0
NHL TOTALS		44	2513	171	1	4.08	0	2

(c)—Drafted from Montreal Juniors by Montreal Canadiens in fourth round of 1977 amateur draft.
(d)—Shared Harry "Hap" Holmes Memorial Trophy with Maurice Barrette.
(e)—September, 1979—Traded with Pat Hughes by Montreal Canadiens to Pittsburgh Penguins for Denis Herron and second-round pick in 1982 entry draft.
(f)—September, 1981—Signed by New York Islanders as a free agent.
(g)—Co-winner of Terry Sawchuk Trophy (Top CHL Goaltenders) with teammate Kelly Hrudey.

BILL HORN

Goaltender . . . 5'8" . . . 150 lbs. . . . Born, Regina, Sask., April 16, 1967 . . . Shoots right.

Year	Team	League	Games	Mins.	Goals	SO.	Avg.	A.	Pen.
1985-86—Western Michigan Univ. (c)	CCHA	30	1797	114	0	3.81	1	14

(c)—June, 1986—Drafted by Hartford Whalers in 1986 NHL entry draft. Fourth Whalers pick, 95th overall, fifth round.

JIMMY HRIVNAK

Goaltender . . . 6'1" . . . 180 lbs. . . . Born, Montreal, Que., May 28, 1968 . . . Shoots left.

Year	Team	League	Games	Mins.	Goals	SO.	Avg.	A.	Pen.
1984-85—Montreal Concordia Midgets	Que.	34	1822	182	0	5.99	..	....
1985-86—Merrimack College (c)	QMJHL	21	1230	75	...	3.66	..	....

(c)—June, 1986—Drafted by Washington Capitals in 1986 NHL entry draft. Fourth Capitals pick, 61st overall, third round.

KELLY HRUDEY

Goaltender . . . 5'10" . . . 183 lbs. . . . Born, Edmonton, Alta., January 13, 1961 . . . Shoots left.

Year	Team	League	Games	Mins.	Goals	SO.	Avg.	A.	Pen.
1978-79—Medicine Hat Tigers	WHL	57	3093	*318	0	6.17	2	43
1979-80—Medicine Hat Tigers (c)	WHL	57	3049	212	1	4.17	6	12
1980-81—Medicine Hat Tigers (b)	WHL	55	3023	200	*4	3.97	0	21
1980-81—Indianapolis Checkers (d)	CHL	....	......	....	...	......	..	....
1981-82—Indianapolis Checkers (a-e-f-g)	CHL	51	3033	149	1	*2.95	0	6
1982-83—Indianapolis Checkers (a-e-h-i)	CHL	47	2744	139	2	3.04	0	28
1983-84—Indianapolis Checkers	CHL	6	370	21	0	3.41	1	0
1983-84—New York Islanders	NHL	12	535	28	0	3.14	0	0
1984-85—New York Islanders	NHL	41	2334	141	2	3.62	1	17
1985-86—New York Islanders	NHL	45	2563	137	1	3.21	3	14
NHL TOTALS		98	5432	306	3	3.38	4	31

(c)—June, 1980—Drafted by New York Islanders as underage junior in 1980 NHL entry draft. Second Islanders pick, 38th overall, second round.
(d)—No regular season games. Two playoff appearances.
(e)—Co-winner of Terry Sawchuk Trophy (Top CHL Goaltenders) with teammate Robert Holland.
(f)—Winner of Max McNab Trophy (CHL Playoff MVP).
(g)—Led CHL Playoffs with 2.42 goals-against-average and one shutout.
(h)—Won Tommy Ivan Trophy (CHL MVP).
(i)—Led CHL playoffs with 2.64 average.

JOHN HYDUKE

Goaltender ... 5'10" ... 155 lbs. ... Born, Hibbing, Minn., June 23, 1967 ... Shoots left ... (November, 1984)—Arthroscopic knee surgery for torn cartilage.

Year	Team	League	Games	Mins.	Goals	SO.	Avg.	A.	Pen.
1984-85—Hibbing High School (c)		Minn. H.S.	15	645	29	3	1.93	..	..
1985-86—Univ. of Minnesota/Duluth		WCHA	24	1401	84	0	3.60	1	0

(c)—June, 1985—Drafted by Los Angeles Kings in 1985 NHL entry draft. Seventh Kings pick, 156th overall, eighth round.

PAT JABLONSKI

Goaltender ... 6' ... 170 lbs. ... Born, Toledo, O., June 20, 1967 ... Shoots right.

Year	Team	League	Games	Mins.	Goals	SO.	Avg.	A.	Pen.
1984-85—Detroit Compuware Jr. A. (c)		NASHL	29	1483	95	0	3.84	..	....
1985-86—Windsor Spitfires		OHL	29	1600	119	1	4.46	3	4

(c)—June, 1985—Drafted by St. Louis Blues in 1985 NHL entry draft. Sixth Blues pick, 138th overall, seventh round.

ROBERT JANECYK

Goaltender ... 6'1" ... 180 lbs. ... Born, Chicago, Ill., May 18, 1957 ... Shoots left ... Led IHL with a combined goals-against average of 3.43 in 1979-80 ... (February, 1983)—Strained knee ligaments.

Year	Team	League	Games	Mins.	Goals	SO.	Avg.	A.	Pen.
1979-80—Flint Generals (b-c)		IHL	2	119	5	0	2.53	0	2
1979-80—Fort Wayne Komets		IHL	40	2208	128	1	3.48	2	14
1980-81—New Brunswick Hawks (d)		AHL	34	1915	131	0	4.10	2	10
1981-82—New Brunswick Hawks (a-e-f)		AHL	53	3224	153	2	2.85	1	20
1982-83—Springfield Indians (a)		AHL	47	2754	167	*3	3.64	4	34
1983-84—Springfield Indians		AHL	30	1664	94	0	3.39	1	2
1983-84—Chicago Black Hawks (g)		NHL	8	412	28	0	4.08	0	2
1984-85—Los Angeles Kings		NHL	51	3002	183	2	3.66	2	27
1985-86—Los Angeles Kings		NHL	38	2083	162	0	4.67	2	11
NHL TOTALS			97	5497	373	2	4.07	4	40

(c)—December, 1979—Loaned to Flint Generals by Fort Wayne Komets.

(d)—June, 1980—Signed by Chicago Black Hawks as a free agent.

(e)—Co-winner of Harry (Hap) Holmes Memorial Trophy (Top AHL Goaltenders) with teammate Warren Skorodenski.

(f)—Led AHL Calder Cup Playoffs with 2.35 goals-against average and one shutout.

(g)—June, 1984—Traded with first (Craig Redmond), third (John English) and fourth (Thomas Glavine) round 1984 draft picks by Chicago Black Hawks to Los Angeles Kings for first (Ed Olczyk), third (Trent Yawney) and fourth round (Tommy Eriksson) 1984 draft picks.

ALLAN RAYMOND (AL) JENSEN

Goaltender ... 5'10" ... 180 lbs. ... Born, Hamilton, Ont., November 27, 1958 ... Shoots left ... Missed start of 1978-79 season with broken thumb ... (January, 1984)—Injured back while weightlifting ... (November, 1984)—Pulled thigh muscle ... (December, 1984)—Muscle spasms in back.

Year	Team	League	Games	Mins.	Goals	SO.	Avg.	A.	Pen.
1975-76—Hamilton Fincups		Jr."A"OHA	28	1451	97	0	3.97	1	7
1976-77—St. Cath. Fincups (b)		Jr."A"OHA	48	2727	168	*2	3.70	4	6
1977-78—Hamil. Fincups (a-c-d)		Jr."A"OHA	43	2582	146	*3	*3.35	1	6
1978-79—Kalamazoo Wings		IHL	47	2596	156	2	3.61	3	6
1979-80—Adirondack Red Wings		AHL	57	3406	199	2	3.51	0	10
1980-81—Adirondack Red Wings		AHL	60	3169	203	*3	3.84	2	10
1980-81—Detroit Red Wings (e)		NHL	1	60	7	0	7.00	0	0
1981-82—Washington Capitals		NHL	26	1274	81	0	3.81	2	6
1981-82—Hershey Bears		AHL	8	407	24	0	3.54	0	21
1982-83—Hershey Bears		AHL	6	316	14	1	2.66	0	0
1982-83—Washington Capitals		NHL	40	2358	135	1	3.44	0	0
1983-84—Hershey Bears		AHL	3	180	16	0	5.33	0	0
1983-84—Washington Capitals (f)		NHL	43	2414	117	*4	2.91	0	22
1984-85—Binghamton Whalers		AHL	3	180	9	0	3.00	0	2
1984-85—Washington Capitals		NHL	14	803	34	1	2.54	0	6
1985-86—Washington Capitals		NHL	44	2437	129	2	3.18	1	4
NHL TOTALS			168	9346	503	8	3.23	1	44

(c)—Shared Dave Pinkney Trophy (leading OMJHL goalies) with Rick Wamsley.

(d)—Drafted from Hamilton Fincups by Detroit Red Wings in second round of 1978 amateur draft.

(e)—August, 1981—Traded by Detroit Red Wings to Washington Capitals for Mark Lofthouse.

(f)—Co-winner of Bill Jennings Trophy (Top NHL goaltenders) with teammate Pat Riggin.

DARREN JENSEN

Goaltender . . . 5'9" . . . 165 lbs. . . . Born, Creston, B.C., May 27, 1960 . . . Shoots left.

Year	Team	League	Games	Mins.	Goals	SO.	Avg.	A.	Pen.
1979-80—Univ. of North Dakota (c)		WCHA	15	890	33	1	2.22	..	....
1980-81—Univ. of North Dakota		WCHA	25	1510	110	0	4.37	1	4
1981-82—Univ. of North Dakota (d)		WCHA	16	910	45	1	2.97	0	2
1982-83—Univ. of North Dakota		WCHA	16	905	45	0	2.98	1	0
1983-84—Fort Wayne Komets (a-e-f-g-h-i)		IHL	56	3325	162	*4	*2.92	2	6
1984-85—Hershey Bears		AHL	39	2263	150	1	3.98	1	0
1984-85—Philadelphia Flyers		NHL	1	60	7	0	7.00	0	0
1985-86—Hershey Bears		AHL	14	795	38	1	2.87	0	0
1985-86—Philadelphia Flyers (j)		NHL	29	1436	88	2	3.68	1	2
NHL TOTALS			30	1496	95	2	3.81	1	2

(c)—June, 1980—Drafted by Hartford Whalers in NHL entry draft. Fifth Whalers pick, 92nd overall, fifth round.

(d)—Named to NCAA All-Tournament team.

(e)—October, 1983—Released by Hartford Whalers and signed by Fort Wayne Komets as a free agent.

(f)—Won James Gatschene Memorial Trophy (IHL MVP).

(g)—Won Garry F. Longman Memorial Trophy (Top IHL Trophy).

(h)—Won James Norris Memorial Trophy (Top IHL Goaltender).

(i)—May, 1984—Signed by Philadelphia Flyers as a free agent.

(j)—Shared Bill Jennings Trophy with teammate Bob Froese (team that allows the fewest goals).

GARY JOHNSON

Goaltender . . . 5'10" . . . 170 lbs. . . . Born, Winnipeg, Manitoba, February 16, 1965 . . . Shoots left.

Year	Team	League	Games	Mins.	Goals	SO.	Avg.	A.	Pen.
1982-83—Winnipeg Warriors		WHL	29	1695	117	1	4.14	2	14
1983-84—Winnipeg Warriors		WHL	2	119	17	0	8.57	0	7
1983-84—Medicine Hat Tigers		WHL	35	1928	129	0	4.01	1	25
1984-85—Medicine Hat Tigers (b-c)		WHL	38	2092	114	2	3.27	1	47
1985-86—Brandon Wheat Kings		WHL	13	553	44	0	4.77	0	33

(c)—June, 1985—Signed by New York Islanders as a free agent.

DOUG KEANS

Goaltender . . . 5'7" . . . 174 lbs. . . . Born, Pembroke, Ont., January 7, 1958 . . . Shoots left . . . (March, 1981)—Injury to right ankle that required surgery to repair ligament damage . . . (February, 1983)—Torn hamstring muscle . . . (December 15, 1983)—Strained ligaments in left knee in game vs. Hartford Whalers and required surgery . . . (February 6, 1986)—Injured left hand vs. Buffalo and missed two games.

Year	Team	League	Games	Mins.	Goals	SO.	Avg.	A.	Pen.
1975-76—Oshawa Generals		OMJHL	1	29	4	0	8.28	0	0
1976-77—Oshawa Generals		OMJHL	48	2632	291	0	6.63	0	4
1977-78—Oshawa Generals (c)		OMJHL	42	2500	172	1	4.13	2	4
1978-79—Saginaw Gears		IHL	59	3207	217	0	4.06	1	11
1979-80—Saginaw Gears		IHL	22	1070	67	1	3.76	3	4
1979-80—Binghamton Dusters		AHL	8	488	31	0	3.81	3	4
1979-80—Los Angeles Kings		NHL	10	559	23	0	2.47	0	0
1980-81—Los Angeles Kings		NHL	9	454	37	0	4.89	0	7
1980-81—Houston Apollos		CHL	11	699	27	0	2.32	0	2
1980-81—Oklahoma City Stars		CHL	9	492	32	1	3.90	0	0
1981-82—New Haven Nighthawks		AHL	13	686	33	2	2.89	1	0
1981-82—Los Angeles Kings		NHL	31	1436	103	0	4.30	0	0
1982-83—Los Angeles Kings		NHL	6	304	24	0	4.73	1	0
1982-83—New Haven Nighthawks		AHL	30	1724	125	0	4.35	2	6
1983-84—Boston Bruins (d)		NHL	33	1779	92	2	3.10	0	2
1984-85—Boston Bruins		NHL	25	1497	82	1	3.29	0	6
1985-86—Boston Bruins		NHL	30	1757	107	1	3.65	1	12
NHL TOTALS			144	7786	468	4	3.61	2	27

(c)—June, 1978—Drafted by Los Angeles Kings in amateur draft. Second Los Angeles pick, 94th overall, sixth round.

(d)—June, 1983—Acquired on waivers from Los Angeles Kings by Boston Bruins.

JOHN KEMP

Goaltender . . . 6' . . . 185 lbs. . . . Born, Burlington, Ont., July 31, 1963 . . . Shoots left.

Year	Team	League	Games	Mins.	Goals	SO.	Avg.	A.	Pen.
1983-84—University of Toronto		CWUAA	29	...	..	0	2.95	...	....
1984-85—University of Toronto		CWUAA	22	....	...	3	2.69	...	....

Year	Team	League	Games	Mins.	Goals	SO.	Avg.	A.	Pen.
1985-86—Team Canada		Int'l	....	1368	96	0	4.21	..	....
1985-86—Hershey Bears (c)		AHL	8	440	40	0	5.45	0	0

(c)—February, 1986—Signed by Philadelphia Flyers as a free agent.

TERRY KLEISINGER

Goaltender ... 6' ... 190 lbs. ... Born, Nanaimo, B.C., October 22, 1960 ... Shoots left ... Missed entire 1984-85 with illness.

Year	Team	League	Games	Mins.	Goals	SO.	Avg.	A.	Pen.
1980-81—Univ. of Wisconsin		WCHA	21	1011	61	2	3.62	..	....
1981-82—Univ. of Wisconsin		WCHA	23	1337	59	4	2.65	1	20
1982-83—Univ. of Wisconsin		WCHA	19	1021	48	3	2.82	1	4
1983-84—Univ. of Wisconsin		WCHA	24	1406	96	...	4.10	0	16
1984-85—....									
1985-86—Flint Generals		IHL	4	200	25	0	7.50	0	19
1985-86—Toledo Goaldiggers		IHL	15	786	76	0	5.80	1	14
1985-86—New Haven Nighthawks		AHL	10	497	34	0	4.10	0	2
1985-86—New York Rangers (c)		NHL	4	191	14	0	4.40	0	2
NHL TOTALS			4	191	14	0	4.40	0	2

(c)—October, 1985—Signed by New York Rangers as a free agent.

RICK KNICKLE

Goaltender ... 5'10" ... 155 lbs. ... Born, Chatham, N.B., February 26, 1960 ... Shoots left ... (February, 1981)—Sprained thumb.

Year	Team	League	Games	Mins.	Goals	SO.	Avg.	A.	Pen.
1977-78—Brandon Wheat Kings		WCHL	49	2806	182	0	3.89	5	27
1978-79—Brandon Wheat Kings (a-c-d)		WHL	38	2240	118	0	*3.16	3	15
1979-80—Muskegon Mohawks		IHL	16	829	51	0	3.69	0	25
1980-81—Erie Blades (a-e)		EHL	43	2347	125	1	*3.20	0	12
1981-82—Rochester Americans		AHL	31	1753	108	1	3.70	1	0
1982-83—Flint Generals		IHL	27	1638	92	2	3.37	2	6
1982-83—Rochester Americans		AHL	4	143	11	0	4.64	0	0
1983-84—Flint Generals (b-f)		IHL	60	3518	203	3	3.46	6	16
1984-85—Sherbrooke Canadiens		AHL	14	780	53	0	4.08	0	6
1984-85—Flint Generals		IHL	36	2018	115	2	3.42	3	8
1985-86—Saginaw Gears		IHL	39	2235	135	2	3.62	0	6

(c)—Named top Goaltender in WHL.
(d)—August, 1979—Drafted by Buffalo Sabres as underage junior in entry draft. Seventh Buffalo pick, 116th overall, sixth round.
(e)—Led EHL playoffs with 1.88 goals-against average.
(f)—Led IHL playoffs with 3.00 average.

RICK KOSTI

Goaltender ... 5'10" ... 175 lbs. ... Born, Kincaid, Sask., September 13, 1963 ... Shoots left.

Year	Team	League	Games	Mins.	Goals	SO.	Avg.	A.	Pen.
1983-84—Univ. of Minnesota-Duluth		WCHA	38	2347	119	...	3.04	0	6
1984-85—Univ. of Minnesota-Duluth (c-d)		WCHA	45	2736	146	...	3.20	0	4
1985-86—Salt Lake Golden Eagles		IHL	25	1330	99	0	4.47	1	2
1985-86—Moncton Golden Flames		AHL	15	705	44	1	3.74	0	6

(c)—First-Team (West) All-America.
(d)—May, 1985—Signed by Calgary Flames as a free agent.

MARK LAFOREST

Goaltender ... 5'10" ... 175 lbs. ... Born, Welland, Ont., July 10, 1962 ... Shoots left.

Year	Team	League	Games	Mins.	Goals	SO.	Avg.	A.	Pen.
1981-82—Niagara Falls Flyers		OHL	24	1365	105	1	4.62	1	14
1982-83—North Bay Centennials		OHL	54	3140	195	0	3.73	4	20
1983-84—Adirondack Red Wings (c)		AHL	7	351	29	0	4.96	0	2
1983-84—Kalamazoo Wings		IHL	13	718	48	1	4.01	0	11
1984-85—Mohawk Valley Stars		ACHL	8	420	60	0	8.57	1	15
1984-85—Adirondack Red Wings		AHL	11	430	35	0	4.88	0	0
1985-86—Adirondack Red Wings		AHL	19	1142	57	0	2.29	1	14
1985-86—Detroit Red Wings		NHL	28	1383	114	1	4.95	0	23
NHL TOTALS			28	1383	114	1	4.95	0	23

(c)—September, 1983—Signed by Detroit Red Wings as a free agent.

ALLAN LAROCHELLE

Goaltender . . . 5'10" . . . 185 lbs. . . . Born, Ponteiz, Sask., October 27, 1964 . . . Shoots left.

Year	Team	League	Games	Mins.	Goals	SO.	Avg.	A.	Pen.
1981-82—Portland Winter Hawks		WHL	23	1245	94	0	4.53	0	0
1982-83—Saskatoon Blades (c)		WHL	41	2295	153	2	4.00	1	19
1983-84—Saskatoon Blades		WHL	56	3033	244	0	4.83	4	27
1984-85—Portland Winter Hawks		WHL	53	2785	268	0	5.77	2	13
1985-86—Milwaukee Admirals		IHL	8	455	34	0	4.48	0	0
1985-86—Moncton Golden Flames		AHL	6	216	17	0	4.72	0	0

(c)—June, 1983—Drafted as underage junior by Boston Bruins in 1983 NHL entry draft. Fourth Bruins pick, 82nd overall, fourth round.

REJEAN LEMELIN

Goaltender . . . 5'11" . . . 160 lbs. . . . Born, Sherbrooke, Que., November 19, 1954 . . . Shoots left . . . (February 8, 1981)—Broken thumb on right hand in pre-game warmups at Edmonton . . . (January, 1984)—Back injury.

Year	Team	League	Games	Mins.	Goals	SO.	Avg.	A.	Pen.
1972-73—Sherbrooke Beavers		QJHL	27	1117	146	0	5.21	2	4
1973-74—Sherbrooke Beavers (c)		QJHL	35	.....	158	0	4.60	1	2
1974-75—Philadelphia Firebirds		NAHL	43	2277	131	3	3.45	3	16
1975-76—Richmond Robins		AHL	7	402	30	0	4.48	0	0
1975-76—Philadelphia Firebirds		NAHL	29	1601	97	1	3.63	1	6
1976-77—Philadelphia Firebirds		NAHL	51	2763	170	1	3.61	2	0
1976-77—Springfield Indians		AHL	3	180	10	0	3.33	0	0
1977-78—Philadelphia Firebirds (a)		AHL	60	3585	177	4	2.96	1	22
1978-79—Atlanta Flames (d)		NHL	18	994	55	0	3.32	0	4
1978-79—Philadelphia Firebirds		AHL	13	780	36	0	2.77	1	12
1979-80—Birmingham Bulls		CHL	38	2188	137	0	3.76	2	14
1979-80—Atlanta Flames		NHL	3	150	15	0	6.00	0	0
1980-81—Birmingham Bulls		CHL	13	757	56	0	4.44	0	4
1980-81—Calgary Flames		NHL	29	1629	88	2	3.24	1	2
1981-82—Calgary Flames		NHL	34	1866	135	0	4.34	1	0
1982-83—Calgary Flames		NHL	39	2211	133	0	3.61	5	7
1983-84—Calgary Flames		NHL	51	2568	150	0	3.50	3	6
1984-85—Calgary Flames		NHL	56	3176	183	1	3.46	0	4
1985-86—Calgary Flames		NHL	60	3369	229	1	4.08	4	10
NHL TOTALS			290	15963	988	4	3.71	14	33

(c)—Drafted from Sherbrooke Beavers by Philadelphia Flyers in sixth round of 1974 amateur draft.
(d)—August, 1978—Signed by Atlanta Flames as free agent.

IN MEMORIAM
PER-ERIC (PELLE) LINDBERGH

Goaltender . . . 5'9" . . . 157 lbs. . . . Born, Stockholm, Sweden, May 24, 1959 . . . Shoots left . . . Has played for two Swedish National Teams ('79 & '80) and the 1980 Swedish Olympic Team that won the Bronze Medal (3rd place) in 1980 Olympics . . . (January, 1983)—Wrist injury in game vs. touring USSR team . . . (May, 1985)—Injured knee in playoffs . . . (November 12, 1985)—Killed in automobile accident in Somerdale, N.J.

Year	Team	League	Games	Mins.	Goals	SO.	Avg.	A.	Pen.
1978-79—Solna AIK (c)		Sweden	6	..	38	0	6.33	..	..
1979-80—Solna AIK		Sweden	32	..	..	1	3.41	..	..
1979-80—Swedish Olympic Team		Olympics	5	300	18	0	3.60	0	0
1980-81—Maine Mariners (a-d-e-f)		AHL	51	3035	165	1	3.26	5	2
1981-82—Maine Mariners		AHL	25	1505	83	0	3.31	0	2
1981-82—Philadelphia Flyers		NHL	8	480	35	0	4.38	0	0
1982-83—Philadelphia Flyers		NHL	40	2334	116	3	2.98	4	0
1983-84—Springfield Indians		AHL	4	240	12	0	3.00	0	0
1983-84—Philadelphia Flyers		NHL	36	1999	135	1	4.05	1	6
1984-85—Philadelphia Flyers (a-g)		NHL	65	3858	194	2	3.02	0	4
1985-86—Philadelphia Flyers		NHL	8	480	23	1	2.88	0	0
NHL TOTALS			157	9151	503	7	3.30	5	10

(c)—August, 1979—Drafted by Philadelphia Flyers in 1979 NHL entry draft. Third Flyers pick, 35th overall, second round.
(d)—Winner of Les Cunningham Plaque (AHL MVP).
(e)—Co-Winner of Harry (Hap) Holmes Memorial Trophy (Top AHL Goaltenders) with teammate Robbie Moore.
(f)—Winner of Dudley (Red) Garrett Memorial Trophy (Top AHL Rookie).
(g)—Won Vezina Trophy (Top NHL Goaltender).

MICHAEL LIUT

Goaltender . . . 6'2" . . . 195 lbs. . . . Born, Weston, Ont., January 7, 1956 . . . Shoots left . . . Attended Bowling Green State University . . . Missed part of 1977-78 season with torn cartilage in left knee . . . (February 10, 1981)—MVP of 1981 NHL All-Star game . . . (January 10, 1981)—Groin injury vs. Los Angeles . . . (March, 1984)—Strained knee ligaments.

Year	Team	League	Games	Mins.	Goals	SO.	Avg.	A.	Pen.
1973-74	Bowling Green State U.	CCHA	24	1272	88	0	4.00	0	4
1974-75	Bowling Green State U. (a)	CCHA	20	1174	78	0	3.99	0	10
1975-76	Bowling Green St. U.(b-c-d)	CCHA	21	1171	50	2	2.56	0	0
1976-77	Bowling Green St. U. (a-e-f)	CCHA	24	1346	61	2	2.72	2	4
1977-78	Cincinnati Stingers	WHA	27	1215	86	0	4.25	1	0
1978-79	Cincinnati Stingers (g)	WHA	54	3181	184	*3	3.47	2	9
1979-80	St. Louis Blues	NHL	64	3661	194	2	3.18	0	2
1980-81	St. Louis Blues (a)	NHL	61	3570	199	1	3.34	0	0
1981-82	St. Louis Blues	NHL	64	3691	250	2	4.06	2	2
1982-83	St. Louis Blues	NHL	68	3794	235	1	3.72	0	2
1983-84	St. Louis Blues	NHL	58	3425	197	3	3.45	4	0
1984-85	St. Louis Blues (h)	NHL	32	1869	119	1	3.82	1	4
1984-85	Hartford Whalers	NHL	12	731	37	1	3.04	0	2
1985-86	Hartford Whalers (i)	NHL	57	3282	197	2	3.60	2	0
	WHA TOTALS		81	4396	270	3	3.69	3	9
	NHL TOTALS		416	24023	1428	13	3.57	9	12

(c)—Drafted from Bowling Green State University by St. Louis Blues in fourth round of 1976 amateur draft.

(d)—Selected by New England Whalers in World Hockey Association amateur player draft, May, 1976.

(e)—WHA rights traded to Cincinnati Stingers by New England Whalers with second-round 1979 draft choice for Greg Carroll and Bryan Maxwell, May, 1977.

(f)—Named CCHA Player-of-the-Year.

(g)—June, 1979—Selected by St. Louis Blues in reclaim draft.

(h)—February, 1985—Traded with future considerations (Jorgen Pettersson) by St. Louis Blues to Hartford Whalers for Greg Millen and Mark Johnson.

(i)—Led Stanley Cup Playoffs with a 1.90 average. He was also one of four goalies to have a shutout.

SHAWN MacKENZIE

Goaltender . . . 5'10" . . . 175 lbs. . . . Born, Bedford, N.S., August 22, 1962 . . . Shoots right.

Year	Team	League	Games	Mins.	Goals	SO.	Avg.	A.	Pen.
1979-80	Windsor Spitfires (c)	OMJHL	41	1964	158	0	4.83	1	8
1980-81	Windsor Spitfires	OHL	*60	*3450	*282	1	4.78	0	8
1981-82	Windsor Spitfires	OHL	17	1001	77	0	4.62	0	6
1981-82	Oshawa Generals	OHL	32	1934	124	1	3.85	0	12
1982-83	New Jersey Devils	NHL	6	130	15	0	6.92	0	0
1982-83	Wichita Wind	CHL	36	2083	148	1	4.26	1	14
1983-84	Maine Mariners	AHL	34	1948	113	0	3.48	0	6
1984-85	Maine Mariners	AHL	24	1254	70	3	3.35	1	6
1985-86	Kalamazoo Wings (d)	IHL	6	362	27	0	4.48	0	4
1985-86	Hershey Bears	AHL	10	521	36	0	4.15	0	0
	NHL TOTALS		6	130	15	0	6.92	0	0

(c)—June, 1980—Drafted as underage junior by Colorado Rockies in 1980 NHL entry draft. Eighth Rockies pick, 169th overall, ninth round.

(d)—October, 1985—Released by New Jersey Devils.

CLINT MALARCHUK

Goaltender . . . 5'10" . . . 172 lbs. . . . Born, Grande, Alta., May 1, 1961 . . . Shoots left.

Year	Team	League	Games	Mins.	Goals	SO.	Avg.	A.	Pen.
1978-79	Portland Winter Hawks	WHL	2	120	4	0	2.00	..	....
1979-80	Portland Winter Hawks (c)	WHL	37	1948	147	0	4.53	2	10
1980-81	Portland Winter Hawks	WHL	38	2235	142	3	3.81	7	22
1981-82	Quebec Nordiques	NHL	2	120	14	0	7.00	0	0
1981-82	Fredericton Express	AHL	51	2962	*253	0	5.12	4	22
1982-83	Quebec Nordiques	NHL	15	900	71	0	4.73	0	0
1982-83	Fredericton Express	AHL	25	1506	78	1	*3.11	1	2
1983-84	Fredericton Express	AHL	11	663	40	0	3.62	1	5
1983-84	Quebec Nordiques	NHL	23	1215	80	0	3.95	1	9
1984-85	Fredericton Express	AHL	*56	*3347	*198	2	3.55	1	14
1985-86	Quebec Nordiques	NHL	46	2657	142	4	3.21	2	21
	NHL TOTALS		86	4892	307	4	3.77	3	30

(c)—October, 1980—Signed by Quebec Nordiques as a free agent.

BOB MASON

Goaltender . . . 6'1" . . . 180 lbs. . . . Born, International Falls, Minn., April 22, 1961 . . . Shoots right . . . Member of 1984 U.S. Olympic Team.

Year	Team	League	Games	Mins.	Goals	SO.	Avg.	A.	Pen.
1981-82—Univ. of Minnesota/Duluth		WCHA	26	1521	115	..	4.54	..	..
1982-83—Univ. of Minnesota/Duluth		WCHA	43	2594	151	..	3.49	1	4
1983-84—U.S. National Team		Int'l	33	1895	89	..	2.82	..	..
1983-84—U.S. Olympic Team		Int'l	3	160	10	0	3.75	0	0
1983-84—Washington Capitals (c)		NHL	2	120	3	0	1.50	0	0
1983-84—Hershey Bears		AHL	5	282	26	0	5.53	0	0
1984-85—Washington Capitals		NHL	12	661	31	1	2.81	1	0
1984-85—Binghamton Whalers		AHL	20	1052	58	1	3.31	1	0
1985-86—Binghamton Whalers		AHL	34	1940	126	0	3.90	3	6
1985-86—Washington Capitals		NHL	1	16	0	0	0.00	0	0
NHL TOTALS			15	797	34	1	2.56	1	0

(c)—February, 1984—Signed by Washington Capitals as a free agent.

DARRELL MAY

Goaltender . . . 6' . . . 190 lbs. . . . Born, Montreal, Que., March 6, 1962 . . . Shoots left.

Year	Team	League	Games	Mins.	Goals	SO.	Avg.	A.	Pen.
1979-80—Portland Winter Hawks		WHL	21	1113	64	0	3.45	0	2
1979-80—Portland Winter Hawks (c)		WHL	43	2416	143	1	3.55	2	16
1980-81—Portland Winter Hawks		WHL	36	2128	122	3	3.44	3	6
1981-82—Portland Winter Hawks		WHL	52	3097	226	0	4.38	0	0
1982-83—Fort Wayne Komets		IHL	46	2584	177	0	4.11	2	16
1983-84—Erie Golden Blades (b-d)		ACHL	43	2404	163	1	4.07	6	28
1984-85—Peoria Rivermen		IHL	19	1133	56	1	2.97	1	0
1985-87—Peoria Rivermen (a-e-f)		IHL	56	3321	179	1	3.23	0	20
1985-86—St. Louis Blues		NHL	3	184	13	0	4.24	1	2
NHL TOTALS			3	184	13	0	4.24	1	2

(c)—June, 1980—Drafted by Vancouver Canucks as underage junior in 1980 NHL entry draft. Fourth Canucks pick, 91st overall, fifth round.
(d)—Led ACHL playoffs with 2.08 average and one shutout.
(e)—September, 1985—Signed by St. Louis Blues as a free agent.
(f)—Won James Gatschene Memorial Trophy (IHL MVP).

KIRK McLEAN

Goaltender . . . 6' . . . 177 lbs. . . . Born, Willowdale, Ont., June 26, 1966 . . . Shoots left.

Year	Team	League	Games	Mins.	Goals	SO.	Avg.	A.	Pen.
1983-84—Oshawa Generals (c)		OHL	17	940	67	0	4.28	0	11
1984-85—Oshawa Generals		OHL	47	2581	143	1	*3.32	1	6
1985-86—Oshawa Generals		OHL	51	2830	169	1	3.58	0	8
1985-86—New Jersey Devils		NHL	2	111	11	0	5.95	0	0
NHL TOTALS			2	111	11	0	5.95	0	0

(c)—June, 1984—Drafted as underage junior by New Jersey Devils in NHL entry draft. Sixth Devils pick, 10th overall, sixth round.

ROLAND MELANSON

Goaltender . . . 5'10" . . . 178 lbs. . . . Born, Moncton, N.B., June 28, 1960 . . . Shoots left . . . Led OMJHL in games played by goaltenders in 1978-79 and co-leader in 1979-80 (with Bruce Dowie) . . . (November 19, 1985)—Pulled groin at Calgary. After missing 30 days with the injury he was traded to Los Angeles . . . (January 15, 1986)—Injured groin vs. N.Y. Rangers and missed 13 games.

Year	Team	League	Games	Mins.	Goals	SO.	Avg.	A.	Pen.
1977-78—Windsor Spitfires		OMJHL	44	2592	195	1	4.51	2	12
1978-79—Windsor Spitfires (b-c)		OMJHL	*62	*3461	254	1	4.40	7	16
1979-80—Windsor Spitfires		OMJHL	22	1099	90	0	4.91	0	8
1979-80—Oshawa Generals		OMJHL	38	2240	136	*3	3.64	2	14
1980-81—Indianapolis Checkers (a-d)		CHL	*52	*3056	131	2	*2.57	1	16
1980-81—New York Islanders		NHL	11	620	32	0	3.10	0	4
1981-82—New York Islanders		NHL	36	2115	114	0	3.23	0	14
1982-83—New York Islanders (e)		NHL	44	2460	109	1	2.66	3	22
1983-84—New York Islanders		NHL	37	2019	110	0	3.27	2	10
1984-85—New York Islanders (f)		NHL	8	425	35	0	4.94	0	0
1984-85—Minnesota North Stars		NHL	20	1142	78	0	4.10	0	9
1985-86—New Haven Nighthawks		AHL	3	179	13	0	4.36	0	0

Year	Team	League	Games	Mins.	Goals	SO.	Avg.	A.	Pen.
1985-86—Minnesota North Stars (g)		NHL	6	325	24	0	4.43	0	0
1985-86—Los Angeles Kings		NHL	22	1246	87	0	4.19	1	8
NHL TOTALS			184	10352	589	1	3.41	6	67

(c)—August, 1979—Drafted by New York Islanders as underage junior in 1979 NHL entry draft. Fourth Islanders pick, 59th overall, third round.

(d)—Winner of Ken McKenzie Trophy (CHL Top Rookie).

(e)—Shared William Jennings Trophy with Billy Smith for NHL's best team goaltending average.

(f)—November, 1984—Traded by New York Islanders to Minnesota North Stars for first round 1985 draft pick (Brad Dalgarno).

(g)—December, 1985—Traded by Minnesota North Stars to N.Y. Rangers for second round 1986 (Neil Wilkinson) and fourth round 1987 draft picks. He was then traded with Grant Ledyard by the Rangers to Los Angeles Kings for Brian MacLellan and a fourth round 1987 draft pick.

GILLES MELOCHE

Goaltender . . . 5'9" . . . 185 lbs. . . . Born, Montreal, Que., July 12, 1950 . . . Shoots left . . . Brother of Denis Meloche . . . Missed part of 1973-74 season with severed tendons in hand requiring surgery . . . Set NHL record for most assists by goalie in season with 6 in 1974-75 (Broken in 1980-81 by Mike Palmateer with eight) . . . (November 2, 1985)—Broke finger at Montreal and missed 10 games.

Year	Team	League	Games	Mins.	Goals	SO.	Avg.	A.	Pen.
1969-70—Verdun Maple Leafs (c)		QJHL	45	.....	221	1	4.95	..	....
1970-71—Flint Generals		IHL	33	1866	104	2	3.34	2	0
1970-71—Chicago Black Hawks (d)		NHL	2	120	6	0	3.00	0	0
1971-72—Calif. Golden Seals (e)		NHL	56	3121	173	4	3.32	2	6
1972-73—California Golden Seals		NHL	59	3473	235	1	4.06	2	4
1973-74—California Golden Seals		NHL	47	2800	198	1	4.24	1	2
1974-75—California Golden Seals		NHL	47	2771	186	1	4.03	*6	14
1975-76—California Golden Seals		NHL	41	2440	140	1	3.44	1	0
1976-77—Cleveland Barons		NHL	51	2961	171	2	3.47	3	18
1977-78—Cleveland Barons		NHL	54	3100	195	1	3.77	0	4
1978-79—Minnesota North Stars		NHL	53	3118	173	2	3.33	1	25
1979-80—Minnesota North Stars		NHL	54	3141	160	1	3.06	1	4
1980-81—Minnesota North Stars		NHL	38	2215	120	2	3.25	0	2
1981-82—Minnesota North Stars		NHL	51	3026	175	1	3.47	1	6
1982-83—Minnesota North Stars		NHL	47	2689	160	1	3.57	1	0
1983-84—Minnesota North Stars		NHL	52	2883	201	2	4.18	1	2
1984-85—Minnesota North Stars (f)		NHL	32	1817	115	0	3.80	0	2
1985-86—Pittsburgh Penguins (g)		NHL	34	1989	119	0	3.59	1	2
NHL TOTALS			718	41673	2527	20	3.64	21	91

(c)—Drafted from Verdun Maple Leafs by Chicago Black Hawks in fifth round of 1970 amateur draft.

(d)—Traded to California Golden Seals by Chicago Black Hawks with Paul Shmyr for Gerry Desjardins, October, 1971.

(e)—Named rookie-of-the-year in NHL's West Division by THE SPORTING NEWS.

(f)—May, 1985—Traded by Minnesota North Stars to Edmonton Oilers for NHL rights to Paul Houck.

(g)—September, 1985—Traded by Edmonton Oilers to Pittsburgh Penguins for Tim Hrynewich, Marty McSorley and future considerations (Mike Moller).

CORRADO MICALEF

Goaltender . . . 5'8" . . . 172 lbs. . . . Born, Montreal, Que., April 20, 1961 . . . Shoots right.

Year	Team	League	Games	Mins.	Goals	SO.	Avg.	A.	Pen.
1979-80—Sherbrooke Beavers (b-c)		QJHL	64	3598	252	1	*4.20	1	17
1980-81—Sherbrooke Beavers (a-d)		QJHL	64	3764	280	*2	4.46	8	26
1981-82—Adirondack Red Wings		AHL	1	10	0	0	0.00	1	0
1981-82—Kalamazoo Wings		IHL	20	1147	91	1	4.76	0	4
1981-82—Detroit Red Wings		NHL	18	809	63	0	4.67	0	0
1982-83—Adirondack Red Wings		AHL	11	660	37	0	3.36	0	2
1982-83—Detroit Red Wings		NHL	34	1756	106	2	3.62	1	18
1983-84—Adirondack Red Wings		AHL	29	1769	132	0	4.48	3	10
1983-84—Detroit Red Wings		NHL	14	808	52	0	3.86	1	2
1984-85—Adirondack Red Wings		AHL	1	60	2	0	2.00	1	0
1984-85—Detroit Red Wings		NHL	36	1856	136	0	4.40	3	6
1985-86—Kalamazoo Wings		IHL	7	398	29	0	4.37	0	2
1985-86—Adirondack Red Wings		AHL	25	1436	93	0	3.89	0	0
1985-86—Detroit Red Wings		NHL	11	565	52	0	5.52	0	8
NHL TOTALS			113	5794	409	2	4.24	5	34

(c)—Won Jacques Plante Trophy (best goals-against average in QJHL).

(d)—June, 1981—Drafted by Detroit Red Wings in NHL entry draft. Second Red Wings pick, 44th overall, third round.

LINDSAY MIDDLEBROOK

Goaltender ... 5'7" ... 170 lbs. ... Born, Collingwood, Ont., September 7, 1955 ... Shoots right.

Year	Team	League	Games	Mins.	Goals	SO.	Avg.	A.	Pen.
1973-74—St. Louis University		CCHA	2	41	6	0	8.82	0	2
1974-75—St. Louis University (a)		CCHA	24	1459	71	1	2.98	0	2
1975-76—St. Louis University		CCHA	30	1767	88	0	2.99	2	2
1976-77—St. Louis University		CCHA	18	1058	54	1	3.07	0	2
1977-78—New Haven Nighthawks		AHL	17	968	71	0	4.40	3	2
1977-78—Toledo Goaldiggers		IHL	16	949	45	*2	*2.85	1	0
1978-79—New Haven Nighthawks (a-c)		AHL	*54	*3221	*173	1	3.22	1	4
1979-80—Tulsa Oilers		CHL	37	2073	102	0	2.95	0	0
1979-80—Winnipeg Jets		NHL	10	580	40	0	4.14	0	0
1980-81—Tulsa Oilers (b)		CHL	36	2115	128	0	3.63	0	6
1980-81—Winnipeg Jets (d)		NHL	14	653	65	0	5.97	0	0
1981-82—Nashville South Stars		CHL	31	1868	93	*3	2.99	2	6
1981-82—Minnesota North Stars (e)		NHL	3	140	7	0	3.00	0	0
1982-83—New Jersey Devils		NHL	9	412	37	0	5.39	1	2
1982-83—Wichita Wind (f)		CHL	13	779	46	0	3.54	0	0
1982-83—Edmonton Oilers		NHL	1	60	3	0	3.00	0	0
1982-83—Moncton Alpines		AHL	11	669	42	0	3.77	0	2
1983-84—Montana Magic		CHL	36	2104	162	0	4.62	0	6
1984-85—Toledo Goaldiggers		IHL	50	2791	183	0	3.93	1	0
1985-86—Milwaukee Admirals (g)		IHL	56	3318	191	*3	3.45	3	6
NHL TOTALS			37	1845	152	0	4.94	1	2

(c)—June, 1979—Drafted by Winnipeg Jets in expansion draft.
(d)—June, 1981—Signed by Minnesota North Stars as a free agent.
(e)—July, 1982—Signed by New Jersey Devils as a free agent.
(f)—February, 1983—Traded by New Jersey Devils with Paul Miller to Edmonton Oilers for Ron Low.
(g)—September, 1985—Signed by Milwaukee Admirals as a free agent.

GREG MILLEN

Goaltender ... 5'9" ... 160 lbs. ... Born, Toronto, Ont., June 25, 1957 ... Shoots right ... (October, 1979)—Pulled hamstring muscle, out 18 games.

Year	Team	League	Games	Mins.	Goals	SO.	Avg.	A.	Pen.
1974-75—Peterborough TPT's		OMJHL	27	1584	90	2	*3.41	..	....
1975-76—Peterborough Petes		OMJHL	58	3282	233	0	4.26	0	6
1976-77—Peterborough Petes (c)		OMJHL	59	3457	244	0	4.23	2	14
1977-78—S. Ste. Marie Greyhounds		OMJHL	25	1469	105	1	4.29	2	4
1977-78—Kalamazoo Wings		IHL	3	180	14	0	4.67	0	0
1978-79—Pittsburgh Penguins		NHL	28	1532	86	2	3.37	0	0
1979-80—Pittsburgh Penguins		NHL	44	2586	157	2	3.64	3	14
1980-81—Pittsburgh Penguins (d)		NHL	63	3721	258	0	4.16	2	6
1981-82—Hartford Whalers		NHL	55	3201	229	0	4.29	5	2
1982-83—Hartford Whalers		NHL	60	3520	282	1	4.81	2	8
1983-84—Hartford Whalers		NHL	*60	*3583	*221	2	3.70	3	10
1984-85—Hartford Whalers (e)		NHL	44	2659	187	1	4.22	0	4
1984-85—St. Louis Blues		NHL	10	605	35	0	3.47	0	0
1985-86—St. Louis Blues		NHL	36	2168	129	1	3.57	1	8
NHL TOTALS			400	23575	1584	9	4.03	16	52

(c)—June, 1977—Drafted by Pittsburgh Penguins in 1977 NHL amateur draft. Fourth Penguins pick, 102nd overall, sixth round.
(d)—June, 1981—Signed by Hartford Whalers as a free agent. Pat Boutette and Kevin McLelland sent to Pittsburgh as compensation by NHL Arbitrator, Judge Joseph Kane, in July.
(e)—February, 1985—Traded with Mark Johnson by Hartford Whalers to St. Louis Blues for Mike Liut and future considerations (Jorgen Pettersson).

EDDIE MIO

Goaltender ... 5'10" ... 180 lbs. ... Born, Windsor, Ont., January 31, 1954 ... Shoots left ... (December 24, 1979)—Fractured cheekbone in team practice ... (January, 1981)—Bruised jaw in team practice ... (March, 1981)—Broken finger ... (February, 1983)—Hip muscle injury ... (November, 1983)—Bruised ribs ... (January 7, 1984)—Pulled hamstring in game vs. Philadelphia and missed 10 weeks ... (October 16, 1985)—Injured knee vs. Winnipeg ... (January 25, 1986)—Injured groin at Boston and missed two games.

Year	Team	League	Games	Mins.	Goals	SO.	Avg.	A.	Pen.
1971-72—Windsor Spitfires		SOJHL	....	......	...	...	......	..	....
1972-73—Colorado College		WCHA	22	......	119	0	5.41	2	2
1973-74—Colorado College (c-d)		WCHA	12	......	57	0	4.91	..	....
1974-75—Colorado College (b-e)		WCHA	21	......	83	0	3.95	1	2

Year	Team	League	Games	Mins.	Goals	SO.	Avg.	A.	Pen.
1975-76—Colorado College (a-e)	WCHA	34	.....	144	0	4.24	..	....
1976-77—Tidewater Sharks	SHL	19	1123	66	1	3.53	0	4
1976-77—Erie Blades	NAHL	17	771	42	0	3.27	0	2
1977-78—Hampton Gulls (f)	AHL	19	949	53	2	3.35	1	0
1977-78—Indianapolis Racers (g)	WHA	17	900	64	0	4.27	0	0
1978-79—Dallas Black Hawks	CHL	7	424	25	0	3.54	0	0
1978-79—Indianapolis Racers (h)	WHA	5	242	13	1	3.22	0	0
1978-79—Edmonton Oilers (i)	WHA	22	1068	71	1	3.99	1	2
1979-80—Edmonton Oilers	NHL	34	1711	120	1	4.21	1	4
1980-81—Edmonton Oilers	NHL	43	2393	155	0	3.89	5	6
1981-82—Wichita Wind (j)	CHL	11	657	46	0	4.20	1	0
1981-82—New York Rangers	NHL	25	1500	89	0	3.56	0	4
1982-83—New York Rangers (k)	NHL	41	2365	136	2	3.45	3	8
1983-84—Detroit Red Wings	NHL	24	1295	95	1	4.40	1	0
1983-84—Adirondack Red Wings	AHL	4	250	11	0	2.64	0	0
1984-85—Adirondack Red Wings	AHL	33	1871	117	2	3.75	2	16
1984-85—Detroit Red Wings	NHL	7	376	27	0	4.31	0	2
1985-86—Adirondack Red Wings	AHL	8	487	32	0	3.94	0	0
1985-86—Detroit Red Wings (l)	NHL	18	788	83	0	6.32	1	17
WHA TOTALS		44	2210	148	2	4.02	1	2
NHL TOTALS		192	10428	705	4	4.06	11	41

(c)—Drafted from Colorado College by Chicago Black Hawks in sixth round of 1974 amateur draft.

(d)—May, 1974—Selected by Vancouver Blazers in World Hockey Association amateur players draft.

(e)—Named to first team (Western) All-America.

(f)—February, 1978—Sold to Indianapolis Racers by Birmingham Bulls.

(g)—March, 1978—NHL rights traded to Minnesota North Stars by Chicago Black Hawks for Doug Hicks. (Chicago would receive third-round 1980 draft choice from Minnesota if Mio was signed by North Stars).

(h)—November, 1978—Sold with Wayne Gretzky and Peter Driscoll by Indianapolis Racers to Edmonton Oilers for cash and future consideration.

(i)—June, 1979—Selected by Minnesota North Stars in reclaim draft. Made a priority selection for expansion draft by Edmonton Oilers.

(j)—December, 1981—Traded by Edmonton Oilers to New York Rangers for Lance Nethery.

(k)—June, 1983—Traded by New York Rangers with Ron Duguay and Ed Johnstone to Detroit Red Wings for Willie Huber, Mark Osborne and Mike Blaisdell.

(l)—June, 1986—Released by Detroit Red Wings.

DONALD ANDREW (ANDY) MOOG

Goaltender . . . 5'8" . . . 165 lbs. . . . Born, Penticton, B.C., February 18, 1960 . . . Shoots left . . . (December, 1983)—While visiting a ward of sick children at a local hospital, he entered a quarantined area, caught a viral infection and lost six pounds . . . (March 1, 1985)—Injured ligaments in both knees in game vs. Los Angeles.

Year	Team	League	Games	Mins.	Goals	SO.	Avg.	A.	Pen.
1976-77—Kamloops Chiefs	WCHL	1	35	6	0	10.29	..	....
1977-78—Penticton	BCJHL	....	.....	....			..	....
1978-79—Billings Bighorns	WHL	26	1306	90	*3	4.13	0	6
1979-80—Billings Bighorns (b-c)	WHL	46	2435	149	1	3.67	1	17
1980-81—Wichita Wind	CHL	29	1602	89	0	3.33	0	4
1980-81—Edmonton Oilers	NHL	7	313	20	0	3.83	1	0
1981-82—Edmonton Oilers	NHL	8	399	32	0	4.81	1	2
1981-82—Wichita Wind (b)	CHL	40	2391	119	1	2.99	5	8
1982-83—Edmonton Oilers	NHL	50	2833	167	1	3.54	4	16
1983-84—Edmonton Oilers	NHL	38	2212	139	1	3.77	1	4
1984-85—Edmonton Oilers	NHL	39	2019	111	1	3.30	0	8
1985-86—Edmonton Oilers	NHL	47	2664	164	1	3.69	2	8
NHL TOTALS		189	10440	633	4	3.64	9	38

(c)—June, 1980—Drafted by Edmonton Oilers in 1980 NHL entry draft. Sixth Oilers pick, 132nd overall, seventh round.

PAUL PAGEAU

Goaltender . . . 5'9" . . . 160 lbs. . . . Born, Montreal, Que., October 1, 1959 . . . Shoots right . . . Member of Canadian 1980 Olympic Hockey Team.

Year	Team	League	Games	Mins.	Goals	SO.	Avg.	A.	Pen.
1976-77—Quebec Remparts	QMJHL	19	955	56	0	3.52	0	2
1977-78—Quebec Remparts	QMJHL	33	1656	138	0	5.00	..	....
1978-79—Quebec Remparts	QMJHL	7	345	28	0	4.87	0	0
1978-79—Shawinigan Cataracts	QMJHL	43	2352	199	0	5.08	1	5
1979-80—Shawinigan Cataracts (a-c)	QMJHL	43	2438	175	*2	4.31	0	0
1979-80—Canadian Olympic Team	(Oly.)	4	237	11	*1	2.78	0	0

Year	Team	League	Games	Mins.	Goals	SO.	Avg.	A.	Pen.
1980-81—Los Angeles Kings		NHL	1	60	8	0	8.00	0	0
1980-81—Houston Apollos		CHL	21	1282	64	0	3.00	0	0
1980-81—Oklahoma City Stars		CHL	11	590	32	0	3.25	0	2
1980-81—Saginaw Gears		IHL	1	60	4	0	4.00	0	0
1981-82—Saginaw Gears		IHL	29	1621	140	0	5.18	2	2
1982-83—Saginaw Gears		IHL	11	614	47	0	4.59	0	0
1982-83—New Haven Nighthawks		AHL	37	1939	123	2	3.81	1	2
1983-84—Sherbrooke Jets		AHL	45	2432	*205	0	5.06	1	0
1984-85—Sherbrooke Canadiens		AHL	20	1074	66	0	3.69	0	0
1984-85—Flint Generals		IHL	6	331	37	0	6.71	1	0
1985-86—Sherbrooke Canadiens (d)		AHL	31	1767	132	0	4.48	0	4
NHL TOTALS			1	60	8	0	8.00	0	0

(c)—May, 1980—Signed by Los Angeles Kings as free agent.
(d)—August, 1985—Signed by Sherbrooke Canadiens as a free agent.

DARREN PANG

Goaltender . . . 5'5" . . . 155 lbs. . . . Born, Medford, Ont., February 17, 1964 . . . Shoots left.

Year	Team	League	Games	Mins.	Goals	SO.	Avg.	A.	Pen.
1982-83—Belleville Bulls		OHL	12	570	44	0	4.63	1	0
1982-83—Ottawa 67's		OHL	47	2729	166	1	3.65	1	0
1983-84—Ottawa 67's		OHL	43	2313	117	2	3.03	2	8
1984-85—Milwaukee Admirals (c)		IHL	53	3129	226	0	4.33	1	16
1984-85—Chicago Black Hawks		NHL	1	60	4	0	4.00	0	0
1985-86—Saginaw Generals		IHL	44	2638	148	2	3.37	2	4
NHL TOTALS			1	60	4	0	4.00	0	0

(c)—September, 1984—Signed by Chicago Black Hawks as a free agent.

DAVID PARRO

Goaltender . . . 5'10" . . . 155 lbs. . . . Born, Saskatoon, Sask., April 30, 1957 . . . Shoots left . . . (February 5, 1981)—Dislocated shoulder.

Year	Team	League	Games	Mins.	Goals	SO.	Avg.	A.	Pen.
1973-74—Saskatoon Olympics		SJHL	29	.....	137	0	4.21	..	....
1974-75—Saskatoon Olympics		SJHL	35	.....	136	0	4.34	..	....
1974-75—Saskatoon Blades		WCHL	1	60	2	0	2.00	0	2
1975-76—Saskatoon Blades		WCHL	36	2100	119	1	3.40	0	6
1976-77—Saskatoon Blades (b-c)		WCHL	69	3956	246	1	3.73	1	10
1977-78—Rochester Americans		AHL	46	2694	164	2	3.65	2	0
1978-79—Grand Rapids Owls		IHL	7	419	25	0	3.58	0	4
1978-79—Rochester Americans (d)		AHL	36	2048	130	*2	3.81	1	10
1979-80—Hershey Bears		AHL	54	3159	172	0	3.27	2	20
1980-81—Hershey Bears		AHL	14	834	60	0	4.32	0	2
1980-81—Washington Capitals		NHL	18	811	49	1	3.63	1	2
1981-82—Washington Capitals		NHL	52	2492	206	1	4.20	1	4
1982-83—Washington Capitals		NHL	6	261	19	0	4.37	0	0
1982-83—Hershey Bears (b)		AHL	47	2714	175	1	3.87	1	10
1983-84—Washington Capitals		NHL	1	1	0	0	0.00	0	0
1983-84—Hershey Bears		AHL	42	2277	190	1	5.01	1	16
1984-85—Fort Wayne Komets		IHL	5	305	18	0	3.54	0	4
1984-85—Salt Lake Golden Eagles		IHL	28	1672	102	0	3.66	1	4
1985-86—Flint Spirit		IHL	46	2527	*235	0	5.58	1	8
NHL TOTALS			77	3565	274	2	4.61	2	6

(c)—Drafted from Saskatoon Blades by Boston Bruins in second round of 1977 amateur draft.
(d)—June, 1979—Drafted by Quebec Nordiques in expansion draft. Traded by Quebec Nordiques to Washington Capitals for Nelson Burton.

PETER PEETERS

Goaltender . . . 6' . . . 180 lbs. . . . Born, Edmonton, Alta., August 1, 1957 . . . Shoots left . . . (November 3, 1983)—Suffered concussion when his head struck crossbar during third period goalmouth pileup in game vs. St. Louis Blues . . . (September 17, 1984)—Sprained left ankle during Team Canada practice in Canada Cup Tournament . . . (January 28, 1986)—Pulled stomach muscle at Detroit.

Year	Team	League	Games	Mins.	Goals	SO.	Avg.	A.	Pen.
1975-76—Medicine Hat Tigers		WCHL	37	2074	147	0	4.25	2	29
1976-77—Medicine Hat Tigers (c)		WCHL	62	3423	232	1	4.07	2	30
1977-78—Maine Mariners		AHL	17	855	40	1	2.80	2	6
1977-78—Milwaukee Admirals		IHL	32	1698	93	1	3.29	4	14
1978-79—Philadelphia Flyers		NHL	5	280	16	0	3.43	0	6
1978-79—Maine Mariners (b-d)		AHL	35	2067	100	*2	*2.90	1	8

Year	Team	League	Games	Mins.	Goals	SO.	Avg.	A.	Pen.
1979-80—Philadelphia Flyers		NHL	40	2373	108	1	2.73	0	28
1980-81—Philadelphia Flyers		NHL	40	2333	115	2	2.96	1	8
1981-82—Philadelphia Flyers (e)		NHL	44	2591	160	0	3.71	1	19
1982-83—Boston Bruins (a-f)		NHL	62	*3611	142	*8	*2.36	2	33
1983-84—Boston Bruins		NHL	50	2868	151	0	3.16	0	36
1984-85—Boston Bruins		NHL	51	2975	172	1	3.47	0	20
1985-86—Boston Bruins (g)		NHL	8	485	31	0	3.84	2	4
1985-86—Washington Capitals		NHL	34	2021	113	1	3.35	0	8
NHL TOTALS			334	19537	1008	13	3.10	6	162

(c)—Drafted from Medicine Hat Tigers by Philadelphia Flyers in eighth round of 1977 amateur draft.
(d)—Shared Harry (Hap) Holmes Memorial Trophy (Top AHL goaltending) with Robbie Moore.
(e)—June, 1982—Traded by Philadelphia Flyers to Boston Bruins for Brad McCrimmon.
(f)—Won Vezina Trophy (Top Goaltender in NHL).
(g)—November, 1985—Traded by Boston Bruins to Washington Capitals for Pat Riggin.

STEVE PENNEY

Goaltender . . . 6'1" . . . 190 lbs. . . . Born, Ste. Foy, Que., February 2, 1961 . . . Shoots left . . . (February, 1985)—Out for two weeks due to being injured during a team practice . . . (December 28, 1985)—Bruised shoulder vs. New Jersey and missed three games . . . (March, 1986)—Sprained left knee which required surgery and was out remainder of regular season and playoffs.

Year	Team	League	Games	Mins.	Goals	SO.	Avg.	A.	Pen.
1978-79—Shawinigan Cataracts		QMJHL	36	1631	180	0	6.62	0	8
1979-80—Shawinigan Cataracts (c)		QMJHL	31	1682	143	0	5.10	0	31
1980-81—Shawinigan Cataracts		QMJHL	62	3456	244	0	4.24	6	45
1981-82—Flint Generals		IHL	36	2038	147	1	4.33	0	6
1981-82—Nova Scotia Voyageurs		AHL	6	308	22	0	4.29	1	0
1982-83—Flint Generals		IHL	48	2552	179	0	4.21	1	0
1983-84—Nova Scotia Voyageurs		AHL	27	1571	92	0	3.51	0	15
1983-84—Montreal Canadiens (d)		NHL	4	240	19	0	4.75	0	0
1984-85—Montreal Canadiens		NHL	54	3252	167	1	3.08	1	10
1985-86—Montreal Canadiens (e)		NHL	18	990	72	0	4.36	0	0
NHL TOTALS			76	4482	258	1	3.45	1	10

(c)—June, 1980—Drafted as underage junior by Montreal Canadiens in NHL entry draft. Tenth Canadiens pick, 166th overall, eighth round.
(d)—Led NHL playoffs with 2.20 average and three shutouts.
(e)—August, 1986—Traded by Montreal Canadiens with Jan Ingman to Winnipeg Jets for Brian Hayward.

ALAN PERRY

Goaltender . . . 5'8" . . . 155 lbs. . . . Born, Providence, R.I., August 30, 1966 . . . Shoots right.

Year	Team	League	Games	Mins.	Goals	SO.	Avg.	A.	Pen.
1983-84—Mt. St. Charles H.S. (c)		R.I.H.S.	20	900	28	1	1.87	..	..
1984-85—Windsor Spitfires		OHL	34	1905	135	1	4.25	3	4
1985-86—Windsor Spitfires		OHL	42	2424	131	*3	3.24	2	18

(c)—June, 1984—Drafted by St. Louis Blues in NHL entry draft. Fifth Blues pick, 56th overall, third round.

FRANK PIETRANGELO

Goaltender . . . 5'10" . . . 178 lbs. . . . Born, Niagara Falls, Ont., December 17, 1964 . . . Shoots left.

Year	Team	League	Games	Mins.	Goals	SO.	Avg.	A.	Pen.
1982-83—University of Minnesota (c)		WCHA	25	1348	80	1	3.56	0	4
1983-84—University of Minnesota		WCHA	20	1141	66	..	3.47	2	0
1984-85—University of Minnesota		WCHA	17	912	52	0	3.42	0	0
1985-86—University of Minnesota		WCHA	23	1284	76	0	3.55	1	0

(c)—June, 1983—Drafted by Pittsburgh Penguins in 1983 NHL entry draft. Fourth Penguins pick, 63rd overall, fourth round.

DARREN PUPPA

Goaltender . . . 6'3" . . . 195 lbs. . . . Born, Kirkland Lake, Ont., March 23, 1965 . . . Shoots right . . . (November 1, 1985—First NHL game was a 2-0 shutout at Edmonton . . . (February, 1986)—Injured knee in AHL game.

Year	Team	League	Games	Mins.	Goals	SO.	Avg.	A.	Pen.
1983-84—Rensselaer Poly. Inst. (c)		ECAC	32	1816	89	...	2.94	..	....
1984-85—Rensselaer Poly. Inst.		ECAC	32	1830	78	...	2.56	0	2

Year	Team	League	Games	Mins.	Goals	SO.	Avg.	A.	Pen.
1985-86—Buffalo Sabres		NHL	7	401	21	1	3.14	0	0
1985-86—Rochester Americans		AHL	20	1092	79	0	4.34	1	0
NHL TOTALS			7	401	21	1	3.14	0	0

(c)—June, 1983—Drafted by Buffalo Sabres in 1983 NHL entry draft. Sixth Sabres pick, 74th overall, fourth round.

CHRIS PUSEY

Goaltender . . . 6' . . . 180 lbs. . . . Born, Brantford, Ont., June 20, 1965 . . . Shoots left.

Year	Team	League	Games	Mins.	Goals	SO.	Avg.	A.	Pen.
1982-83—London Knights		OHL	1	60	7	0	7.00	0	2
1982-83—Brantford Alexanders (c)		OHL	20	991	85	0	5.15	0	6
1983-84—Brantford Alexanders (b)		OHL	50	2858	158	2	3.32	0	21
1984-85—Hamilton Steelhawks		OHL	49	2450	179	1	4.38	1	38
1985-86—Adirondack Red Wings		AHL	22	1171	76	1	3.89	1	8
1985-86—Detroit Red Wings		NHL	1	40	3	0	4.50	0	0
NHL TOTALS			1	40	3	0	4.50	0	0

(c)—June, 1983—Drafted as underage junior by Detroit Red Wings in 1983 NHL entry draft. Seventh Red Wings pick, 106th overall, sixth round.

BRUCE M. RACINE

Goaltender . . . 6'1" . . . 180 lbs. . . . Born, Cornwall, Ont., August 9, 1966 . . . Shoots left . . . Son of Maurice Racine (17 years in CFL).

Year	Team	League	Games	Mins.	Goals	SO.	Avg.	A.	Pen.
1984-85—Northeastern University (b-c)		H. East	26	1615	103	0	3.83	1	12
1985-86—Northeastern University		H. East	37	2212	171	0	4.64	3	0

(c)—June, 1985—Drafted by Pittsburgh Penguins in 1985 NHL entry draft. Third Penguins pick, 58th overall, third round.

BILL RANFORD

Goaltender . . . 5'11" . . . 165 lbs. . . . Born, Brandon, Manitoba, December 14, 1966 . . . Shoots left.

Year	Team	League	Games	Mins.	Goals	SO.	Avg.	A.	Pen.
1983-84—New Westminster Bruins		WHL	27	1450	130	0	5.38	2	0
1984-85—New Westminster Bruins (c)		WHL	38	2034	142	0	4.19	0	4
1985-86—New Westminster Bruins (b)		WHL	53	2791	225	1	4.84	1	23
1985-86—Boston Bruins		NHL	4	240	10	0	2.50	0	0
NHL TOTALS			4	240	10	0	2.50	0	0

(c)—June, 1985—Drafted as underage junior by Boston Bruins in 1985 NHL entry draft. Second Bruins pick, 52nd overall, third round.

ALAIN RAYMOND

Goaltender . . . 5'10" . . . 177 lbs. . . . Born, Rimouski, Que., June 24, 1965 . . . Shoots left.

Year	Team	League	Games	Mins.	Goals	SO.	Avg.	A.	Pen.
1981-82—Cantons de L'Est		Que. Midget	27	1505	128	...	5.10	..	....
1982-83—Hull Olympics		QHL	17	809	80	0	5.93	0	4
1982-83—Trois-Rivieres Draveurs (c)		QHL	22	1176	124	0	6.33	0	4
1983-84—Trois-Rivieres Draveurs (a)		QHL	53	2725	223	*2	4.91	0	6
1984-85—Trois-Rivieres Draveurs		QHL	58	3295	220	*2	4.01	3	2
1985-86—Team Canada		Int'l	..	2571	151	4	3.52	..	..

(c)—June, 1983—Drafted as underage junior by Washington Capitals in 1983 NHL entry draft. Seventh Capitals pick, 215th overall, 11th round.

DARYL REAUGH

Goaltender . . . 6'4" . . . 200 lbs. . . . Born, Prince George, B.C., February 13, 1965 . . . Shoots left.

Year	Team	League	Games	Mins.	Goals	SO.	Avg.	A.	Pen.
1983-84—Kamloops Junior Oilers (b-c-d)		WHL	55	2748	199	1	4.34	5	18
1984-85—Kamloops Blazers (a)		WHL	49	2749	170	2	3.71	3	19
1984-85—Edmonton Oilers		NHL	1	60	5	0	5.00	0	0
1985-86—Nova Scotia Oilers		AHL	38	2205	156	0	4.24	2	4
NHL TOTALS			1	60	5	0	5.00	0	0

(c)—Led WHL playoffs with 3.52 average.

(d)—June, 1984—Drafted as underage junior by Edmonton Oilers in NHL entry draft. Second Oilers pick, 42nd overall, second round.

JEFF REESE

Goaltender . . . 5'9" . . . 155 lbs. . . . Born, Brantford, Ont., March 24, 1966 . . . Shoots left.

Year	Team	League	Games	Mins.	Goals	SO.	Avg.	A.	Pen.
1982-83	Hamilton A's	OJHL	40	2380	176	0	4.43	..	....
1983-84	London Knights (c)	OHL	43	2308	173	0	4.50	1	4
1984-85	London Knights (d)	OHL	50	2878	186	1	3.88	1	4
1985-86	London Knights	OHL	*57	*3281	215	0	3.93	1	25

(c)—June, 1984—Drafted as underage junior by Toronto Maple Leafs in NHL entry draft. Third Maple Leafs pick, 67th overall, fourth round.

(d)—Led OHL playoffs with one shutout and a 2.73 average.

JOHN REID

Goaltender . . . 6'1" . . . 195 lbs. . . . Born, Windsor, Ont., February 18, 1967 . . . Shoots right.

Year	Team	League	Games	Mins.	Goals	SO.	Avg.	A.	Pen.
1983-84	Brantford Knights	OHA	30	1350	59	3	1.95	..	8
1984-85	Belleville Bulls (c)	OHL	31	1443	92	0	3.83	1	8
1985-86	Belleville Bulls	OHL	24	1309	100	0	4.58	0	5
1985-86	North Bay Centennials	OHL	23	1318	64	1	2.91	0	6

(c)—June, 1985—Drafted as underage junior by Chicago Black Hawks in 1985 NHL entry draft. Eighth Black Hawks pick, 158th overall, eighth round.

GLENN ALLAN (CHICO) RESCH

Goaltender . . . 5'9" . . . 165 lbs. . . . Born, Moose Jaw, Sask., July 10, 1948 . . . Shoots left . . . (October, 1980)—Partially torn ligaments in right knee . . . (November 15, 1981)—Pulled groin at Chicago . . . (March 11, 1982)—Partially torn ligaments in left knee.

Year	Team	League	Games	Mins.	Goals	SO.	Avg.	A.	Pen.
1968-69	U. of Minnesota-Duluth	WCHA	24	.....	117	0	4.90	..	....
1969-70	U. of Minnesota-Duluth	WCHA	25	.....	97	1	3.90	..	....
1970-71	U. of Minn.-Duluth (b)	WCHA	27	.....	114	0	4.23	..	....
1971-72	Muskegon Mohawks (a-c-d)	IHL	59	3482	180	*4	*3.09	0	12
1972-73	New Haven Nighthawks	AHL	43	2408	166	0	4.13	0	13
1973-74	Fort Worth Wings (a-e)	CHL	55	3300	175	2	3.18	4	2
1973-74	New York Islanders	NHL	2	120	6	0	3.00	0	0
1974-75	New York Islanders	NHL	25	1432	59	3	2.47	0	0
1975-76	New York Islanders (b)	NHL	44	2546	88	7	2.07	1	0
1976-77	New York Islanders	NHL	46	2711	103	4	2.28	1	0
1977-78	New York Islanders	NHL	45	2637	112	3	2.55	1	12
1978-79	New York Islanders (b)	NHL	43	2539	106	2	2.50	2	6
1979-80	New York Islanders	NHL	45	2606	132	3	3.04	3	4
1980-81	New York Islanders (f)	NHL	32	1817	93	*3	3.07	1	0
1980-81	Colorado Rockies	NHL	8	449	28	0	3.74	0	0
1981-82	Colorado Rockies (g)	NHL	61	3424	230	0	4.03	2	8
1982-83	New Jersey Devils	NHL	65	3650	242	0	3.98	3	6
1983-84	New Jersey Devils	NHL	51	2641	134	1	4.18	2	12
1984-85	New Jersey Devils	NHL	51	2884	200	0	4.16	0	6
1985-86	New Jersey Devils (h)	NHL	31	1769	126	0	4.27	0	14
1985-86	Philadelphia Flyers	NHL	5	187	10	0	3.21	0	0
	NHL TOTALS		554	31412	1669	26	3.19	16	68

(c)—Won James Norris Memorial Trophy (leading goalie in IHL) and Garry F. Longman Memorial Trophy (IHL rookie-of-the-year).

(d)—June, 1972—Sold to New York Islanders by Montreal Canadiens.

(e)—Won CHL Most Valuable Player Award.

(f)—March, 1981—Traded by New York Islanders with Steve Tambellini to Colorado Rockies for Mike McEwen and Jari Kaarela.

(g)—Won Bill Masterton Memorial Trophy (Perseverance, Sportsmanship and Dedication).

(h)—March, 1986—Traded by New Jersey Devils to Philadelphia Flyers for third round 1986 draft pick (Marc Laniel).

MIKE RICHTER

Goaltender . . . 5'11" . . . 170 lbs. . . . Born, Philadelphia, Pa., September 22, 1966 . . . Shoots left.

Year	Team	League	Games	Mins.	Goals	SO.	Avg.	A.	Pen.
1984-85	Northwood Prep. (c)	Mass. H.S.	24	..	52	2	2.27	..	..
1985-86	Univ. of Wisconsin (b-d)	WCHA	24	1394	92	1	3.96	0	0

(c)—June, 1985—Drafted by New York Rangers in 1985 NHL entry draft. Second Rangers pick, 28th overall, second round.

(d)—Named WCHA Freshman-of-the-Year.

PAT RIGGIN

Goaltender . . . 5'9" . . . 163 lbs. . . . Born, Kincardine, Ont., May 26, 1959 . . . Shoots right . . . Son of former Detroit goalie Dennis Riggin.

Year	Team	League	Games	Mins.	Goals	SO.	Avg.	A.	Pen.
1975-76—London Knights		Jr. "A" OHA	29	1385	86	0	3.68	1	0
1976-77—London Knights (a-c)		Jr. "A" OHA	48	2809	138	*2	*2.95	3	4
1977-78—London Knights (b-d)		Jr. "A" OHA	37	2266	140	0	3.65	0	2
1978-79—Birmingham Bulls (e)		WHA	46	2511	158	1	3.78	3	22
1979-80—Birmingham Bulls		CHL	12	746	32	0	2.57	0	2
1979-80—Atlanta Flames		NHL	25	1368	73	2	3.20	0	0
1980-81—Calgary Flames		NHL	42	2411	154	0	3.83	1	7
1981-82—Calgary Flames (f)		NHL	52	2934	207	2	4.23	5	4
1982-83—Washington Capitals		NHL	38	2161	121	0	3.36	0	4
1983-84—Hershey Bears		AHL	3	185	7	0	2.27	1	0
1983-84—Washington Capitals (g)		NHL	41	2299	102	*4	*2.66	0	4
1984-85—Washington Capitals		NHL	57	3388	168	2	2.98	1	2
1985-86—Washington Capitals (h)		NHL	7	369	23	0	3.74	0	2
1985-86—Boston Bruins		NHL	39	2272	127	1	3.35	0	4
WHA TOTALS			46	2511	158	1	3.78	3	22
NHL TOTALS			301	17202	975	11	3.40	7	27

(c)—Won Dave Pinkney Trophy (leading goalie).

(d)—July, 1978—Signed by Birmingham Bulls (WHA) as under-age junior.

(e)—August, 1979—Drafted by Atlanta Flames in entry draft. Third Atlanta pick, 33rd overall, second round.

(f)—June, 1982—Traded by Calgary Flames with Ken Houston to Washington Capitals for Howard Walker, NHL rights to George White plus sixth round 1982 draft pick (Mats Kihlstrom), 3rd round 1983 draft pick (Perry Berezan) and second round 1984 draft pick (Paul Ranheim).

(g)—Co-winner of Bill Jennings Memorial Trophy (Top NHL goaltenders) with teammate Al Jensen.

(h)—November, 1985—Traded by Washington Capitals to Boston Bruins for Pete Peeters.

ROBERTO ROMANO

Goaltender . . . 5'5" . . . 172 lbs. . . . Born, Montreal, Que., October 29, 1962 . . . Shoots left . . . (December 5, 1984)—Injured knee in game at St. Louis.

Year	Team	League	Games	Mins.	Goals	SO.	Avg.	A.	Pen.
1979-80—Quebec Remparts		QMJHL	52	2411	183	0	4.55	0	2
1980-81—Quebec Remparts		QMJHL	59	3174	233	0	4.40	1	0
1981-82—Quebec Remparts (c)		QMJHL	1	60	4	0	4.00	0	0
1981-82—Hull Olympics (a)		QMJHL	56	3090	194	*1	3.77	1	5
1982-83—Baltimore Skipjacks (d)		AHL	38	2164	146	0	4.05	2	6
1982-83—Pittsburgh Penguins		NHL	3	155	18	0	6.97	0	0
1983-84—Pittsburgh Penguins		NHL	18	1020	78	1	4.59	0	0
1983-84—Baltimore Skipjacks		AHL	31	1759	106	0	3.62	0	2
1984-85—Baltimore Skipjacks		AHL	12	719	44	0	3.67	0	0
1984-85—Pittsburgh Penguins		NHL	31	1629	120	1	4.42	0	2
1985-86—Pittsburgh Penguins		NHL	46	2684	159	2	3.55	1	4
NHL TOTALS			98	5488	375	4	4.10	1	6

(c)—September, 1981—Traded by Quebec Remparts to Hull Olympics for Dan Sanscartier, Alan Bremner and future considerations.

(d)—September, 1983—Signed by Pittsburgh Penguins as a free agent.

PATRICK ROY

Goaltender . . . 6' . . . 165 lbs. . . . Born, Quebec City, Que., October 5, 1965 . . . Shoots left.

Year	Team	League	Games	Mins.	Goals	SO.	Avg.	A.	Pen.
1982-83—Granby Bisons		QHL	54	2808	293	0	6.26	0	14
1983-84—Granby Bisons (c)		QHL	61	3585	265	0	4.44	6	15
1984-85—Granby Bisons		QHL	44	2463	228	0	5.55	2	74
1984-85—Montreal Canadiens		NHL	1	20	0	0	0.00	0	0
1984-85—Sherbrooke Canadiens (d)		AHL	1	60	4	0	4.00	0	0
1985-86—Montreal Canadiens (e)		NHL	47	2651	150	1	3.39	3	4
NHL TOTALS			48	2671	150	1	3.37	3	4

(c)—June, 1984—Drafted as underage junior by Montreal Canadiens in NHL entry draft. Fourth Canadiens pick, 51st overall, third round.

(d)—Led AHL playoffs with 2.89 average.

(e)—Won Conn Smythe Trophy (Playoff MVP) and was one of four goalies with one shutout.

RICK ST. CROIX

Goaltender . . . 5'11" . . . 170 lbs. . . . Born, Kenora, Ont., January 3, 1955 . . . Shoots left . . . (March, 1983)—Suffered cracked knuckle . . . (December, 1983)—Knee injury . . . (De-

cember, 1984)—Cut while reducing his Christmas tree to firewood . . . (January 9, 1985)—
Pulled hamstring in game vs. Boston . . . (February, 1985)—Aggravated hamstring pull.

Year	Team	League	Games	Mins.	Goals	SO.	Avg.	A.	Pen.
1970-71—Kenora Muskies		MJHL	23	1265	71	0	3.37	..	....
1971-72—Kenora Muskies		MJHL	43	2402	172	0	4.30	..	....
1971-72—Winnipeg Jets		WCHL	3	160	13	0	4.88	0	0
1972-73—Oshawa Gen. (b)		Jr."A"OHA	52	3176	247	0	4.67	1	2
1973-74—Oshawa Generals		Jr."A"OHA	33	1932	130	1	4.04	3	4
1974-75—Oshawa Gen. (c)		Jr."A"OHA	32	.....	131	1	4.00	0	0
1975-76—Flint Generals		IHL	42	2201	118	0	3.22	0	2
1976-77—Springfield Indians		AHL	1	60	3	0	3.00	0	0
1976-77—Flint Generals		IHL	53	2956	179	*3	3.63	4	12
1977-78—Maine Mariners		AHL	40	2266	116	2	3.07	2	6
1977-78—Philadelphia Flyers		NHL	7	395	20	0	3.04	0	0
1978-79—Philadelphia Flyers		NHL	2	117	6	0	3.08	0	0
1978-79—Philadelphia Firebirds		AHL	9	484	22	0	2.73	0	0
1978-79—Maine Mariners		AHL	22	1312	63	0	2.88	0	8
1979-80—Maine Mariners (a-d)		AHL	45	2669	133	1	*2.99	0	6
1979-80—Philadelphia Flyers		NHL	1	60	2	0	2.00	0	0
1980-81—Philadelphia Flyers		NHL	27	1567	65	2	2.49	1	0
1981-82—Philadelphia Flyers		NHL	29	1729	112	0	3.89	1	2
1982-83—Philadelphia Flyers (e)		NHL	16	940	54	0	3.45	0	0
1982-83—Toronto Maple Leafs		NHL	16	900	57	0	3.80	0	0
1983-84—Toronto Maple Leafs		NHL	20	939	80	0	5.11	0	0
1983-84—St. Catharines Saints		AHL	8	482	29	0	3.61	1	0
1984-85—St. Catharines Saints		AHL	18	1076	92	0	5.13	0	2
1984-85—Toronto Maple Leafs		NHL	11	628	54	0	5.16	0	0
1985-86—Fort Wayne Komets (b-f)		IHL	42	2474	132	2	3.20	3	6
NHL TOTALS			129	7375	450	2	3.66	2	2

(c)—Drafted from Oshawa Generals by Philadelphia Flyers in fourth round of 1975 amateur draft.
(d)—Shared Harry (Hap) Holmes Memorial Trophy (Top AHL Goaltenders) with teammate Robbie Moore.
(e)—January, 1983—Traded by Philadelphia Flyers to Toronto Maple Leafs for Michel Larocque.
(f)—Shared James Norris Memorial Trophy with teammate Pokey Reddick (Top IHL Goalies).

SAM ST. LAURENT

Goaltender . . . 5'10" . . . 190 lbs. . . . Born, Arvida, Que., February 16, 1959 . . . Shoots left.

Year	Team	League	Games	Mins.	Goals	SO.	Avg.	A.	Pen.
1975-76—Chicoutimi Sagueneens		QMJHL	17	889	81	0	5.47	..	....
1976-77—Chicoutimi Sagueneens		QMJHL	21	901	81	0	5.39	0	30
1977-78—Chicoutimi Sagueneens		QMJHL	60	3251	*351	0	6.46	..	....
1978-79—Chicoutimi Sagueneens		QMJHL	70	3806	290	0	4.57	1	0
1979-80—Toledo Goaldiggers (c)		IHL	38	2145	138	2	3.86	1	6
1979-80—Maine Mariners		AHL	4	201	15	0	4.48	0	0
1980-81—Maine Mariners		AHL	7	363	28	0	4.63	0	2
1980-81—Toledo Goaldiggers		IHL	30	1614	113	1	4.20	2	0
1981-82—Maine Mariners		AHL	25	1396	76	0	3.27	0	0
1981-82—Toledo Goaldiggers		IHL	4	248	11	0	2.66	0	0
1982-83—Toledo Goaldiggers		IHL	13	785	52	0	3.97	0	0
1982-83—Maine Mariners		AHL	30	1739	109	0	3.76	0	2
1983-84—Maine Mariners (d)		AHL	38	2158	145	0	4.03	0	0
1984-85—Maine Mariners (b)		AHL	55	3245	168	*4	3.11	1	8
1985-86—New Jersey Devils		NHL	4	188	13	1	4.15	0	0
1985-86—Maine Mariners (b-e-f-g)		AHL	50	2862	161	1	3.38	1	8
NHL TOTALS			4	188	13	1	4.15	0	0

(c)—September, 1979—Signed by Philadelphia Flyers as a free agent.
(d)—August, 1984—Traded by Philadelphia Flyers to New Jersey Devils for future considerations.
(e)—Shared Harry (Hap) Holmes Memorial Trophy with teammate Karl Friesen (Top AHL Goalies).
(f)—Won Baz Bastien Trophy (Coaches pick as top AHL goalie).
(g)—August, 1986—Traded by New Jersey Devils to Detroit Red Wings for Steve Richmond.

MIKE SANDS

Goaltender . . . 5'9" . . . 155 lbs. . . . Born, Mississauga, Ont., April 6, 1963 . . . Shoots left.

Year	Team	League	Games	Mins.	Goals	SO.	Avg.	A.	Pen.
1980-81—Sudbury Wolves (c)		OHL	50	2789	236	0	5.08	5	10
1981-82—Sudbury Wolves		OHL	53	2854	*265	1	5.57	6	25
1981-82—Nashville South Stars		CHL	7	380	26	0	4.11	0	0
1982-83—Sudbury Wolves		OHL	43	2320	204	1	5.28	0	24
1982-83—Birmingham South Stars		CHL	4	169	14	0	4.97	0	0
1983-84—Salt Lake Golden Eagles		CHL	23	1145	93	0	4.87	1	34

Year	Team	League	Games	Mins.	Goals	SO.	Avg.	A.	Pen.
1984-85—Springfield Indians		AHL	46	2589	140	2	3.24	2	48
1984-85—Minnesota North Stars		NHL	3	139	14	0	6.04	0	2
1985-86—Springfield Indians		AHL	27	1490	94	0	3.79	0	24
NHL TOTALS			3	139	14	0	6.04	0	2

(c)—June, 1981—Drafted as underage junior by Minnesota North Stars in 1981 NHL entry draft. Third North Stars pick, 31st overall, second round.

ROBERT SAUVE

Goaltender . . . 5'8" . . . 165 lbs. . . . Born, Ste. Genevieve, Que., June 17, 1955 . . . Shoots left . . . Brother of Jean-Francois Sauve . . . (December, 1984)—Sprained back . . . (November 2, 1985)—Pulled hamstring at Boston and missed eight games.

Year	Team	League	Games	Mins.	Goals	SO.	Avg.	A.	Pen.
1971-72—Verdun Maple Leafs		QJHL	33	.....	202	0	6.01	..	....
1972-73—Laval National		QJHL	35	1489	224	0	6.40	2	8
1973-74—Laval National (a)		QJHL	61	.....	341	0	5.65	5	8
1974-75—Laval National (c)		QJHL	57	3403	287	0	5.06	0	6
1975-76—Charlotte Checkers (d)		SHL	17	979	36	2	2.21	1	0
1975-76—Providence Reds (e)		AHL	14	848	44	0	3.11	0	0
1976-77—Rhode Island Reds		AHL	25	1346	94	0	4.14	0	2
1976-77—Hershey Bears		AHL	9	539	38	0	4.23	0	0
1976-77—Buffalo Sabres		NHL	4	184	11	0	3.59	0	0
1977-78—Hershey Bears		AHL	16	872	59	0	4.05	1	0
1977-78—Buffalo Sabres		NHL	11	480	20	0	2.50	1	0
1978-79—Buffalo Sabres		NHL	29	1610	100	0	3.73	0	2
1978-79—Hershey Bears		AHL	5	278	14	0	3.02	1	0
1979-80—Buffalo Sabres (f-g)		NHL	32	1880	74	4	*2.36	4	2
1980-81—Buffalo Sabres		NHL	35	2100	111	2	3.17	1	0
1981-82—Buffalo Sabres (h)		NHL	14	760	35	0	2.76	0	2
1981-82—Detroit Red Wings (i)		NHL	41	2365	165	0	4.19	0	0
1982-83—Buffalo Sabres		NHL	54	3110	179	1	3.45	1	8
1983-84—Buffalo Sabres		NHL	40	2375	138	0	3.49	0	2
1984-85—Buffalo Sabres (j)		NHL	27	1564	84	0	3.22	1	4
1985-86—Chicago Black Hawks (k)		NHL	38	2099	138	0	3.94	1	27
NHL TOTALS			325	18527	1055	7	3.42	9	47

(c)—Drafted from Laval National by Buffalo Sabres in first round of 1975 amateur draft.
(d)—Leading goalie during playoffs (1.43 average and 2 shutouts).
(e)—January, 1976—Loaned to Providence Reds by Buffalo Sabres.
(f)—Shared Vezina Memorial Trophy (Top NHL Goaltender) with teammate Don Edwards.
(g)—Led Stanley Cup Playoffs with 2.04 goals-against-average and two shutouts.
(h)—December, 1981—Traded by Buffalo Sabres to Detroit Red Wings for future considerations.
(i)—June, 1982—Signed by Buffalo Sabres as a free agent.
(j)—Co-Winner of Bill Jennings Trophy (Top NHL Goaltending) with teammate Tom Barrasso.
(k)—October, 1985—Traded by Buffalo Sabres to Chicago Black Hawks for third round 1986 draft pick (Kevin Kerr).

RON SCOTT

Goaltender . . . 5'8" . . . 155 lbs. . . . Born, Guelph, Ont., July 21, 1960 . . . Shoots left . . . (November, 1984)—Severe groin injury, out three weeks.

Year	Team	League	Games	Mins.	Goals	SO.	Avg.	A.	Pen.
1980-81—Michigan State Univ. (a)		WCHA	33	1899	123	0	3.89	1	4
1981-82—Michigan State Univ. (a-c)		CCHA	39	2298	109	2	2.85	2	2
1982-83—Michigan State Univ. (a-c-d)		CCHA	40	2273	100	...	2.64	5	10
1983-84—Tulsa Oilers		CHL	20	1717	109	0	3.81	0	2
1983-84—New York Rangers		NHL	9	485	29	0	3.59	0	0
1984-85—New Haven Nighthawks		AHL	37	2047	130	0	3.81	1	2
1985-86—New York Rangers		NHL	4	156	11	0	4.23	0	0
1985-86—New Haven Nighthawks		AHL	19	1069	66	1	3.70	2	7
NHL TOTALS			13	641	40	0	3.74	0	0

(c)—Named to All-American Team (West).
(d)—May, 1983—Signed by New York Rangers as a free agent.

RICHARD SEVIGNY

Goaltender . . . 5'8" . . . 172 lbs. . . . Born, Montreal, Que., April 11, 1957 . . . Shoots left . . . (January 7, 1982)—Broken left hand when hit by a shot in practice . . . (November 14, 1985)—Broke left hand at St. Louis and missed 19 games.

Year	Team	League	Games	Mins.	Goals	SO.	Avg.	A.	Pen.
1974-75—Granby Vics		Jr."A"QHL	50	2966	240	*2	4.85	..	....
1974-75—Sherbrooke Beavers		QJHL	2	62	4	,	3.87	0	0

Year	Team	League	Games	Mins.	Goals	SO.	Avg.	A.	Pen.
1975-76—Sherbrooke Beavers (b)		QJHL	55	3058	196	2	3.85	..	....
1976-77—Sherbrooke Beavers (c)		QJHL	65	3656	248	*2	4.07	4	33
1977-78—Kalamazoo Wings (b)		IHL	35	1897	95	1	3.01	2	27
1978-79—Springfield Indians		AHL	22	1302	77	0	3.55	0	29
1978-79—Nova Scotia Voyageurs		AHL	20	1169	57	1	2.93	0	6
1979-80—Nova Scotia Voyageurs		AHL	35	2104	114	*3	3.25	6	23
1979-80—Montreal Canadiens		NHL	11	632	31	0	2.94	0	4
1980-81—Montreal Canadiens (d)		NHL	33	1777	71	2	*2.40	0	30
1981-82—Montreal Canadiens		NHL	19	1027	53	0	3.10	0	10
1982-83—Montreal Canadiens		NHL	38	2130	122	1	3.44	1	8
1983-84—Montreal Canadiens (e)		NHL	40	2203	124	1	3.38	0	12
1984-85—Quebec Nordiques		NHL	20	1104	62	1	3.37	0	8
1985-86—Fredericton Express		AHL	6	362	21	0	3.48	0	7
1985-86—Quebec Nordiques		NHL	11	468	33	0	4.23	0	8
NHL TOTALS			172	9341	496	5	3.19	0	80

(c)—Drafted from Sherbrooke Beavers by Montreal Canadiens in seventh round of 1977 amateur draft.
(d)—Co-Winner of Vezina Trophy (Top NHL Goaltenders) with teammates Michel Larocque and Denis Herron.
(e)—July, 1984—Signed by Quebec Nordiques as a free agent.

PETER SIDORKIEWICZ

Goaltender . . . 5'9" . . . 165 lbs. . . . Born, Dabrown Bialostocka, Poland, June 29, 1963 . . . Shoots left.

Year	Team	League	Games	Mins.	Goals	SO.	Avg.	A.	Pen.
1980-81—Oshawa Generals (c)		OHL	7	308	24	0	4.68	0	0
1981-82—Oshawa Generals		OHL	29	1553	123	*2	4.75	1	6
1982-83—Oshawa Generals (d)		OHL	60	3536	213	0	3.61	4	2
1983-84—Oshawa Generals (e)		OHL	52	2966	205	1	4.15	4	16
1984-85—Fort Wayne Komets		IHL	10	590	43	0	4.37	0	0
1984-85—Binghamton Whalers (f)		AHL	45	2691	137	3	3.05	1	14
1985-86—Binghamton Whalers		AHL	49	2819	150	2	*3.19	0	7

(c)—June, 1981—Drafted as underage junior by Washington Capitals in NHL entry draft. Fifth Capitals pick, 91st overall, fifth round.
(d)—Co-winner of Dave Pinkney Trophy (Top OHL Goaltenders) with teammate Jeff Hogg.
(e)—Shared OHL playoff lead with one shutout with Darren Pang of Ottawa.
(f)—March, 1985—Traded with Dean Evason by Washington Capitals to Hartford Whalers for David A. Jensen.

WARREN SKORODENSKI

Goaltender . . . 6'1" . . . 180 lbs. . . . Born, Winnipeg, Man., March 22, 1960 . . . Shoots left . . . (November, 1983)—Suspended by AHL for throwing a stick into the crowd, then charging, pushing and verbally abusing referee Dave Lynch in an AHL game at Sherbrooke.

Year	Team	League	Games	Mins.	Goals	SO.	Avg.	A.	Pen.
1976-77—Kildonan		MJHL	22	1170	78	0	4.00	..	..
1977-78—Calgary Wranglers		WCHL	53	2460	213	1	5.20	1	48
1978-79—Calgary Wranglers (b-c)		WHL	*66	*3595	309	1	5.16	3	58
1979-80—Calgary Wranglers		WHL	66	3724	261	1	4.21	4	60
1980-81—New Brunswick Hawks		AHL	2	124	9	0	4.35	0	0
1980-81—Flint Generals		IHL	47	2602	189	2	4.36	1	64
1981-82—Chicago Black Hawks		NHL	1	60	5	0	5.00	0	0
1981-82—New Brunswick Hawks (d)		AHL	28	1644	70	*3	*2.55	0	2
1982-83—Springfield Indians		AHL	13	592	49	0	4.97	0	0
1982-83—Birmingham South Stars		CHL	25	1450	81	1	3.35	0	2
1983-84—Sherbrooke Jets		AHL	19	1048	88	0	5.04	0	12
1983-84—Springfield Indians		AHL	14	756	67	0	5.32	0	10
1984-85—Chicago Black Hawks		NHL	27	1396	75	2	3.22	0	2
1985-86—Nova Scotia Oilers		AHL	32	1716	109	0	3.81	0	10
1985-86—Chicago Black Hawks		NHL	1	60	6	0	6.00	0	0
NHL TOTALS			29	1516	86	2	3.40	0	2

(c)—August, 1979—Signed by Chicago Black Hawks as a free agent.
(d)—Co-winner of Harry (Hap) Holmes Memorial Trophy (Top AHL Goalie) with teammate Bob Janecyk.

WILLIAM JOHN SMITH

Goaltender . . . 5'10" . . . 185 lbs. . . . Born, Perth, Ont., December 12, 1950 . . . Shoots left . . . Brother of Gordon and Jack Smith . . . Holds NHL record for most playoff games by a goaltender, career (130) . . . Became first NHL goalie to score a goal Nov. 28, 1979 in a 7-4 loss at Denver vs. Colorado Rockies . . . (September, 1980)—Bell's palsy . . . (September 9, 1981)—Broken finger on left hand during Team Canada practice . . . Member of Long Island Sports Hall of Fame.

Year	Team	League	Games	Mins.	Goals	SO.	Avg.	A.	Pen.
1969-70—Cornwall Royals (c)		QJHL	55	.....	249	*1	4.52	..	....
1970-71—Springfield Kings (d)		AHL	49	2728	160	2	3.51	0	17
1971-72—Springfield Kings		AHL	28	1649	77	*4	2.80	1	38
1971-72—Los Angeles Kings (e)		NHL	5	300	23	0	4.60	0	5
1972-73—New York Islanders		NHL	37	2122	147	0	4.16	0	42
1973-74—New York Islanders		NHL	46	2615	134	0	3.07	0	11
1974-75—New York Islanders		NHL	58	3368	156	3	2.78	0	21
1975-76—New York Islanders		NHL	39	2254	98	3	2.61	1	10
1976-77—New York Islanders		NHL	36	2089	87	2	2.50	1	12
1977-78—New York Islanders		NHL	38	2154	95	2	2.65	0	35
1978-79—New York Islanders		NHL	40	2261	108	1	2.87	2	54
1979-80—New York Islanders		NHL	38	2114	104	2	2.95	0	39
1980-81—New York Islanders (f)		NHL	41	2363	129	2	3.28	0	33
1981-82—New York Islanders (a-g)		NHL	46	2685	133	0	2.97	1	24
1982-83—New York Islanders (h-i)		NHL	41	2340	112	1	2.87	0	41
1983-84—New York Islanders		NHL	42	2279	130	2	3.42	2	23
1984-85—New York Islanders		NHL	37	2090	133	0	3.82	0	25
1985-86—New York Islanders		NHL	41	2308	143	1	3.72	3	49
NHL TOTALS			585	33342	1732	19	3.12	10	424

(c)—Drafted from Cornwall Royals by Los Angeles Kings in fifth round of 1970 amateur draft.
(d)—Leading goalie (2.55 average and 1 shutout) during playoffs.
(e)—Drafted from Los Angeles Kings by New York Islanders in expansion draft, June, 1972.
(f)—Led NHL playoffs with a 2.54 goals-against average.
(g)—Winner of Vezina Trophy (Voted as outstanding NHL goaltender).
(h)—Winner of Conn Smythe Memorial Trophy (MVP in playoffs).
(i)—Shared William Jennings Trophy with Roland Melanson for NHL's best team goaltending average.

DOUGLAS HENRY SOETAERT

Goaltender . . . 6' . . . 185 lbs. . . . Born, Edmonton, Alta., April 21, 1955 . . . Shoots left . . . (February 17, 1986)—Sprained knees vs. Los Angeles.

Year	Team	League	Games	Mins.	Goals	SO.	Avg.	A.	Pen.
1970-71—Edmonton Movers		AJHL	3	180	21	0	7.00	0	0
1971-72—Edmonton Oil Kings		WCHL	37	1738	105	3	3.62	0	9
1972-73—Edmonton Oil Kings		WCHL	43	2111	129	1	3.67	2	18
1973-74—Edmonton Oil Kings		WCHL	39	2190	163	1	4.47	..	....
1974-75—Edmonton Oil Kings (c)		WCHL	65	3706	273	1	4.42	6	80
1975-76—Providence Reds		AHL	16	896	65	0	4.35	1	14
1975-76—New York Rangers		NHL	8	273	24	0	5.27	1	0
1976-77—New Haven Nighthawks		AHL	16	947	61	0	3.86	0	2
1976-77—New York Rangers		NHL	12	570	28	1	2.95	0	0
1977-78—New Haven Nighthawks		AHL	38	2252	141	0	3.75	6	20
1977-78—New York Rangers		NHL	6	360	20	0	3.33	0	0
1978-79—New York Rangers		NHL	17	900	57	0	3.80	0	4
1978-79—New Haven Nighthawks		AHL	3	180	11	1	3.67	0	2
1979-80—New Haven Nighthawks		AHL	32	1808	108	*3	3.58	1	16
1979-80—New York Rangers		NHL	8	435	33	0	4.55	0	0
1980-81—New Haven Nighthawks		AHL	12	668	35	2	3.14	0	2
1980-81—New York Rangers (d)		NHL	39	2320	152	0	3.93	0	2
1981-82—Winnipeg Jets		NHL	39	2157	155	2	4.31	2	14
1982-83—Winnipeg Jets		NHL	44	2533	174	0	4.12	1	10
1983-84—Winnipeg Jets		NHL	47	2536	182	0	4.31	3	14
1984-85—Montreal Canadiens (e)		NHL	28	1606	91	0	3.40	0	4
1985-86—Montreal Canadiens (f)		NHL	23	1215	54	3	2.67	0	6
NHL TOTALS			271	14905	970	6	3.90	7	54

(c)—Drafted from Edmonton Oil Kings by New York Rangers in second round of 1975 amateur draft.
(d)—October, 1981—Traded by New York Rangers to Winnipeg Jets for future considerations.
(e)—October, 1984—Traded by Winnipeg Jets to Montreal Canadiens for Mark Holden.
(f)—July, 1986—Signed by New York Rangers as a free agent.

GREG STEFAN

Goaltender . . . 6' . . . 178 lbs. . . . Born, Brantford, Ont., February 11, 1961 . . . Shoots left . . . (March, 1981)—Given six-game suspension by OHL for breaking his goalie stick over shoulder of Bart Wilson of Toronto Marlboros . . . (January, 1985)—Strained left shoulder . . . (April, 1985)—Suspended for first eight games of 1985-86 season for swinging his stick at Al Secord in playoff game vs. Chicago on April 13 . . . (December 14, 1985)—Suspended for six games for high-sticking incident vs. Pittsburgh . . . (January 7, 1986)—Injured back at Washington and missed 17 games . . . (March 20, 1986)—Dislocated thumb vs. St. Louis when he jammed it against the goalpost.

Year	Team	League	Games	Mins.	Goals	SO.	Avg.	A.	Pen.
1978-79—Oshawa Generals		OMJHL	33	1635	133	0	4.88	1	27
1979-80—Oshawa Generals		OMJHL	17	897	58	0	3.88	2	11
1980-81—Oshawa Generals (c)		OHL	46	2407	174	0	4.34	2	92
1981-82—Detroit Red Wings		NHL	2	120	10	0	5.00	0	0
1981-82—Adirondack Red Wings		AHL	29	1571	99	2	3.78	0	36
1982-83—Detroit Red Wings		NHL	35	1847	139	0	4.52	0	35
1983-84—Detroit Red Wings		NHL	50	2600	152	2	3.51	3	14
1984-85—Detroit Red Wings		NHL	46	2633	190	0	4.33	2	23
1985-86—Detroit Red Wings		NHL	37	2068	155	1	4.50	2	23
NHL TOTALS			170	9268	646	3	4.18	7	105

(c)—June, 1981—Drafted by Detroit Red Wings in 1981 NHL entry draft. Fifth Red Wings pick, 128th overall, seventh round.

KARI TAKKO

Goaltender . . . 6'2" . . . 182 lbs. . . . Born, Kaupunki, Finland, June 23, 1963 . . . Shoots left.

Year	Team	League	Games	Mins.	Goals	SO.	Avg.	A.	Pen.
1985-86—Springfield Indians		AHL	43	2386	161	1	4.05	0	6
1985-86—Minnesota North Stars (c)		NHL	1	60	3	0	3.00	0	0
NHL TOTALS			1	60	3	0	3.00	0	0

(c)—June, 1984—Drafted by Minnesota North Stars in 1984 NHL entry draft. Fifth North Stars pick, 97th overall, fifth round.

CHRISTOPHER ARNOLD TERRERI

Goaltender . . . 5'9" . . . 155 lbs. . . . Born, Warwick, R.I., November 15, 1964 . . . Shoots left.

Year	Team	League	Games	Mins.	Goals	SO.	Avg.	A.	Pen.
1982-83—Providence College (c)		ECAC	11	529	17	..	1.93	..	..
1983-84—Providence College		ECAC	10	391	20	..	3.07	0	2
1984-85—Providence College (d-e)		H. East	41	2515	131	..	3.12	0	10
1985-86—Providence College		H. East	27	1540	96	0	3.74	0	4

(c)—June, 1983—Drafted by New Jersey Devils in NHL entry draft. Third Devils pick, 87th overall, fifth round.

(d)—First-Team (East) All-America.

(e)—Hockey East MVP.

RON TUGNUTT

Goaltender . . . 5'11" . . . 150 lbs. . . . Born, Scarborough, Ont., October 22, 1967 . . . Shoots left.

Year	Team	League	Games	Mins.	Goals	SO.	Avg.	A.	Pen.
1984-85—Peterborough Petes (c)		OHL	18	938	59	0	3.77	1	4
1985-86—Peterborough Petes (d-e)		OHL	26	1543	74	1	2.88	0	4

(c)—Won F.W. Dinty Moore Trophy (Lowest average for a rookie goalie).

(d)—Shared Dave Pinkney Trophy with teammate Kay Whitmore (top OHL goalies).

(e)—June, 1986—Drafted as underage junior by Quebec Nordiques in 1986 NHL entry draft. Fourth Nordiques pick, 81st overall, fourth round.

JOHN VANBIESBROUCK

Goaltender . . . 5'9" . . . 165 lbs. . . . Born, Detroit, Mich., September 4, 1963 . . . Shoots left.

Year	Team	League	Games	Mins.	Goals	SO.	Avg.	A.	Pen.
1980-81—Sault Ste. Marie Greyhounds (c-d)		OHL	56	2941	203	0	4.14	2	10
1981-82—Sault Ste. Marie Greyhounds		OHL	31	1686	102	0	3.63	0	23
1981-82—New York Rangers		NHL	1	60	1	0	1.00	0	0
1982-83—Sault Ste. Marie Greyhounds		OHL	*62	3471	209	0	3.61	2	10
1983-84—New York Rangers		NHL	3	180	10	0	3.33	0	2
1983-84—Tulsa Oilers		CHL	37	2153	124	*3	3.46	0	6
1984-85—New York Rangers		NHL	42	2358	166	1	4.22	5	17
1985-86—New York Rangers (a-e)		NHL	61	3326	184	3	3.32	3	16
NHL TOTALS			107	5924	361	4	3.66	8	35

(c)—Winner of Dinty Moore Trophy (Lowest Individual OHA Goalie average in a rookie season).

(d)—June, 1981—Drafted by New York Rangers in 1981 NHL entry draft. Fifth Rangers pick, 72nd overall, fourth round.

(e)—Won Vezina Trophy (Top NHL Goaltender).

MIKE VERNON

Goaltender . . . 5'7" . . . 150 lbs. . . . Born, Calgary, Alta., February 24, 1963 . . . Shoots left . . . Set NHL record in 1986 playoffs for most minutes played (1229).

Year	Team	League	Games	Mins.	Goals	SO.	Avg.	A.	Pen.
1980-81—Calgary Wranglers (c)		WHL	59	3154	198	1	3.77	3	21
1981-82—Calgary Wranglers		WHL	42	2329	143	*3	*3.68	0	0
1982-83—Calgary Wranglers		WHL	50	2856	155	*3	*3.26	2	6
1982-83—Calgary Flames (a-d-e)		NHL	2	100	11	0	6.59	0	0
1983-84—Calgary Flames		NHL	1	11	4	0	21.82	0	0
1983-84—Colorado Flames (b)		CHL	*46	*2648	148	1	*3.35	3	4
1984-85—Moncton Golden Flames		AHL	41	2050	134	0	3.92	1	8
1985-86—Salt Lake Golden Eagles		IHL	10	601	34	1	3.39	2	2
1985-86—Moncton Golden Flames		AHL	6	374	21	0	3.37	0	0
1985-86—Calgary Flames (f)		NHL	18	921	52	1	3.39	1	4
NHL TOTALS			21	1032	67	1	3.90	1	4

(c)—June, 1981—Drafted by Calgary Flames in 1981 NHL entry draft. Second Flames pick, 56th overall, third round.
(d)—Named WHL MVP.
(e)—Won WHL goaltending trophy.
(f)—Led NHL playoffs in games played (21), minutes (1229) and goals allowed (60).

RICK WAMSLEY

Goaltender . . . 5'11" . . . 185 lbs. . . . Born, Simcoe, Ont., May 25, 1959 . . . Shoots left . . . (October 16, 1985)—Bruised right hand at Calgary and required surgery and missed nine games.

Year	Team	League	Games	Mins.	Goals	SO.	Avg.	A.	Pen.
1976-77—St. Catharines Fincups		OMJHL	12	647	36	0	3.34	0	0
1977-78—Hamilton Fincups (c)		OMJHL	25	1495	74	2	*2.97	1	12
1978-79—Brantford Alexanders (d)		OMJHL	24	1444	128	0	5.32	0	2
1979-80—Nova Scotia Voyageurs		AHL	40	2305	125	2	3.25	3	12
1980-81—Nova Scotia Voyageurs (e)		AHL	43	2372	155	0	3.92	5	10
1980-81—Montreal Canadiens		NHL	5	253	8	1	1.90	0	0
1981-82—Montreal Canadiens (f-g)		NHL	38	2206	101	2	2.75	2	4
1982-83—Montreal Canadiens		NHL	46	2583	151	0	3.51	1	4
1983-84—Montreal Canadiens (h)		NHL	42	2333	144	2	3.70	3	6
1984-85—St. Louis Blues		NHL	40	2319	126	0	3.26	1	0
1985-86—St. Louis Blues		NHL	42	2517	144	1	3.43	0	2
NHL TOTALS			213	12211	674	6	3.31	7	16

(c)—Shared Dave Pinkney Trophy (leading OMJHL goalies) with Al Jensen.
(d)—August, 1979—Drafted by Montreal Canadiens in entry draft. Fifth Canadiens pick, 58th overall, third round.
(e)—Led AHL playoffs with a 1.81 goals-against average.
(f)—Co-winner of Bill Jennings Trophy (Lowest team goaltending average) with teammate Denis Herron.
(g)—Led NHL playoffs with 2.20 goals-against average.
(h)—June, 1984—Traded with second round (Brian Benning) and third round (Robert Dirk) 1984 draft picks by Montreal Canadiens to St. Louis Blues for first round (Shayne Corson) and second round (Stephane Richer) 1984 draft picks.

STEVE WEEKS

Goaltender . . . 5'11" . . . 165 lbs. . . . Born, Scarborough, Ont., June 30, 1958 . . . Shoots left.

Year	Team	League	Games	Mins.	Goals	SO.	Avg.	A.	Pen.
1975-76—Toronto Marlboros		OMJHL	18	873	73	0	4.95	0	0
1976-77—Northern Michigan Univ.		CCHA	16	811	58	0	4.29	..	....
1977-78—Northern Michigan Univ. (c)		CCHA	19	1015	56	1	3.31	..	....
1978-79—Northern Michigan Univ.		CCHA	....	.....	...	...	.....	..	....
1979-80—N. Mich. U. (a-d-e)		CCHA	36	2133	105	0	*2.95	1	2
1980-81—New Haven Nighthawks		AHL	36	2065	142	1	4.13	0	4
1980-81—New York Rangers		NHL	1	60	2	0	2.00	0	0
1981-82—New York Rangers		NHL	49	2852	179	1	3.77	3	0
1982-83—Tulsa Oilers		CHL	19	1116	60	0	3.23	1	0
1982-83—New York Rangers		NHL	18	1040	68	0	3.92	2	0
1983-84—New York Rangers		NHL	26	1361	90	0	3.97	0	4
1983-84—Tulsa Oilers (f)		CHL	3	180	7	0	2.33	0	0
1984-85—Binghamton Whalers		AHL	5	303	13	0	2.57	0	0
1984-85—Hartford Whalers		NHL	24	1457	92	2	3.79	0	0
1985-86—Hartford Whalers		NHL	27	1544	99	1	3.85	1	9
NHL TOTALS			145	8314	530	4	3.82	6	13

(c)—June, 1978—Drafted by New York Rangers in 1978 NHL entry draft. Twelfth Rangers pick, 176th overall, 11th round.
(d)—Named as Most Valuable Player of the CCHA.
(e)—Named to NCAA Tournament All-Star team.
(f)—September, 1984—Traded by New York Rangers to Hartford Whalers for future considerations.

KAY WHITMORE

Goaltender ... 6' ... 170 lbs. ... Born, Sudbury, Ont., April 10, 1967 ... Shoots left.

Year	Team	League	Games	Mins.	Goals	SO.	Avg.	A.	Pen.
1982-83—Sudbury Major Midgets		OHA	43	2580	108	4	2.51	..	....
1983-84—Peterborough Petes		OHL	29	1471	110	0	4.49	2	2
1984-85—Peterborough Petes (c)		OHL	53	3077	172	*2	3.35	5	33
1985-86—Peterborough Petes (a-d)		OHL	41	2467	114	*3	*2.77	3	14

(c)—June, 1985—Drafted as underage junior by Hartford Whalers in 1985 NHL entry draft. Second Whalers pick, 26th overall, second round.

(d)—Shared Dave Pinkney Trophy with teammate Ron Tugnutt (Top OHL Goalies).

KEN WREGGET

Goaltender ... 6'1" ... 180 lbs. ... Born, Brandon, Man., March 25, 1964 ... Shoots left ... (December 26, 1985)—Injured knee at Hartford.

Year	Team	League	Games	Mins.	Goals	SO.	Avg.	A.	Pen.
1981-82—Lethbridge Broncos (c)		WHL	36	1713	118	1	4.13	0	0
1982-83—Lethbridge Broncos (d)		WHL	48	2696	157	1	3.49	1	18
1983-84—Lethbridge Broncos (a)		WHL	53	3052	161	0	*3.16	1	26
1983-84—Toronto Maple Leafs		NHL	3	165	14	0	5.09	0	0
1984-85—Toronto Maple Leafs		NHL	23	1278	103	0	4.84	1	10
1984-85—St. Catharines Saints		AHL	12	688	48	0	4.19	1	0
1985-86—St. Catharines Saints		AHL	18	1058	78	1	4.42	2	8
1985-86—Toronto Maple Leafs		NHL	30	1566	113	0	4.33	0	16
NHL TOTALS			56	3009	230	0	4.59	1	26

(c)—June, 1982—Drafted as underage junior by Toronto Maple Leafs in NHL entry draft. Fourth Maple Leafs pick, 45th overall, third round.

(d)—Led WHL playoffs with 3.02 average and one shutout.

WENDELL YOUNG

Goaltender ... 5'8" ... 185 lbs. ... Born, Halifax, N.S., August 1, 1963 ... Shoots left.

Year	Team	League	Games	Mins.	Goals	SO.	Avg.	A.	Pen.
1979-80—Cole Harbour		NSJHL	..	1446	94	0	3.90	..	..
1980-81—Kitchener Rangers (c)		OHL	42	2215	164	1	4.44	2	29
1981-82—Kitchener Rangers		OHL	*60	*3470	195	1	3.37	1	4
1982-83—Kitchener Rangers		OHL	61	*3611	231	1	3.84	7	22
1983-84—Salt Lake Golden Eagles		CHL	20	1094	80	0	4.39	1	2
1983-84—Fredericton Express		AHL	11	569	39	1	4.11	2	4
1983-84—Milwaukee Admirals		IHL	6	339	17	0	3.01	0	0
1984-85—Fredericton Express		AHL	22	1242	83	0	4.01	0	0
1985-86—Fredericton Express		AHL	24	1457	78	0	3.21	0	2
1985-86—Vancouver Canucks		NHL	22	1023	61	0	3.58	0	0
NHL TOTALS			22	1023	61	0	3.58	0	0

(c)—June, 1981—Drafted as underage junior by Vancouver Canucks in NHL entry draft. Third Canucks pick, 73rd overall, fourth round.

MIKE ZANIER

Goaltender ... 5'11" ... 183 lbs. ... Born, Trail, B.C., August 22, 1962 ... Shoots left.

Year	Team	League	Games	Mins.	Goals	SO.	Avg.	A.	Pen.
1979-80—New Westminster Bruins		WHL	1	20	3	0	9.00	..	..
1980-81—New Westminster Bruins		WHL	49	2494	275	0	6.62	1	44
1981-82—Spokane Flyers		WHL	9	476	55	0	6.93	0	0
1981-82—Medicine Hat Tigers		WHL	13	620	70	0	6.77	0	0
1981-82—Billings Bighorns		WHL	11	495	64	0	7.76	0	0
1981-82—Calgary Wranglers		WHL	11	526	28	1	3.19	0	0
1982-83—Trail Smoke Eaters (c)		WIHL	30	1734	116	0	4.01	..	..
1983-84—Moncton Alpines		AHL	31	1743	96	0	3.30	0	14
1984-85—Nova Scotia Oilers		AHL	44	2484	143	1	3.45	1	23
1984-85—Edmonton Oilers		NHL	3	185	12	0	3.89	0	0
1985-86—Indianapolis Checkers		IHL	47	2727	151	0	3.32	0	4
NHL TOTALS			3	185	12	0	3.89	0	0

(c)—August, 1983—Signed by Edmonton Oilers as a free agent.